THE

HISTORY

OF

NEW ENGLAND

FROM

1630 TO 1649

BY JOHN WINTHROP, ESQ.

Edited by James Savage

Volumes I and II

AYER COMPANY, PUBLISHERS, INC.
SALEM, NEW HAMPSHIRE 03079

Reprint Edition 1992
Ayer Company, Publishers, Inc.
Salem, New Hampshire 03079

Reprint Edition 1972 by Arno Press Inc.

Reprinted from a copy in
The Harvard University Library

LC# 70-141103
ISBN 0-405-03315-X

Manufactured in the United States of America

Drawn from the Original Picture by J. R. Penniman. J. Chorley sculp.

JOHN WINTHROP.

FIRST GOVERNOR OF MASSACHUSETTS.

THE

HISTORY

OF

NEW ENGLAND

FROM

1630 TO 1649.

BY JOHN WINTHROP, ESQ.

FIRST GOVERNOUR OF THE COLONY OF THE MASSACHUSETTS BAY.

FROM

HIS ORIGINAL MANUSCRIPTS.

WITH NOTES

TO ILLUSTRATE

THE CIVIL AND ECCLESIASTICAL CONCERNS, THE GEOGRAPHY, SETTLEMENT AND INSTITUTIONS OF THE COUNTRY, AND THE LIVES AND MANNERS OF THE PRINCIPAL PLANTERS.

BY JAMES SAVAGE,

MEMBER OF THE MASSACHUSETTS HISTORICAL SOCIETY.

VOL. I.

Sæpe audivi, Q. Maximum, P. Scipionem, præterea civitatis nostræ præclaros viros, solitos ita dicere, cum majorum imagines intuerentur, vehementissime sibi animum ad virtutem accendi. *Sallust. Bell. Jugurth.* c. *iv.*

Boston:

PRINTED BY PHELPS AND FARNHAM,

No. 5, Court Street.

1825.

PREFACE.

EARLY in the spring of 1816 was discovered, in the tower of the Old South Church in Boston, the third volume of the History of New England, in the original MS. of the author, John Winthrop, first governour of the Massachusetts Bay. When the precious book was presented to the Massachusetts Historical Society, at their next meeting, 25 April, the difficulty of transcribing it for the press seemed to appal several of the most competent members, whose engagement in more important duties afforded also a sufficient excuse for leaving such labour to be undertaken by any one, at any time, who could devote to it many weeks of leisure. The task appeared inviting to me. On the same evening the MS. was taken, and the study of its chirography was begun, the next day, by the aid of one of the former MSS. collated with the printed volume, usually called Winthrop's Journal. Of all the three MSS. and of the published Journal, a sufficient account may be seen in 2 Hist. Coll. IV. 200.

Before the collation of the former MS. with the volume printed in 1790 had proceeded through many pages, the discovery of numerous important errours seemed to make a new edition of the earlier part of the History very desirable; and when a transcript of the new-found volume was completed, my resolution was fixed, that it should not be printed without a perfect revision of the Journal. Notes, explanatory, in some instances, of the text, illustrating, in some degree, the biography of many persons named in it, and referring to better accounts of others than I could furnish, were thought necessary. Several hundred notes were prepared, and a careful collation of the whole printed volume, for the second time, with the original volumes of MS. was finished on 2 June, 1819. Being then required to visit a foreign country, all my preparations were suspended until I returned. Care, however, was taken to leave the corrected copy of the printed volume, with my copy of the third part, to be kept safely. Again called abroad in 1822, I so carefully disposed of my copy of the third volume, as to leave it in a forgotten place, which afforded me the gratification of making a new one, begun 8 December, 1823, and finished 30 March, 1824. This circumstance admonished me of the propriety of adopting early measures for guarding against farther accidents of that kind. Application was made, at the next session of the General Court of this commonwealth, by the Historical Society, for encouragement of the publication. In consequence of the liberal aid of the Legislature, the volume comes thus early before the publick.

To the account of the three MSS. above referred to, may be added, that the whole had been in possession of Hubbard, the reverend historian of Ipswich, who made the basis, and much the most valuable part of his work, out of Winthrop's materials, using them commonly without other labour than literal copying, and disposing them in a different order. See page 297 of this volume, for an estimate of the value of that work. Nor can I forgive the slight use of these invaluable documents, which is evinced by Mather, the unhappy author of Magnalia Christi Americana, who, in the hurry of composing that endless work, seems to have preferred useless quotations of worthless books, two or three centuries older, or popular and corrupt traditions, to the full matter and precise statement of facts, dates, principles and motives, furnished by authentick history. That he possessed these MSS. is plain enough from his citations of several passages in his Life of our author, book II. cap. 4. Perhaps he grudged the time, which must have been consumed by a devoted study of the volumes; for no other excuse can I imagine for his clumsy abbreviation of that excellent speech in § 9, that will appear in our next volume. From this mutilated transcript of Mather, we may presume, the authors of the Modern Universal History condensed and adorned, in vol. XXXIX. 291, 2, their report, as if delivered in St. Stephen's chapel, of "the following speech, which is equal to any thing of antiquity, whether we consider it as coming from a philosopher or a magistrate." It may be seen, also, in the valuable Summary History of New England by Hannah Adams, 79, 80. Agreeable as this commendation of the London compilers is, the original address from Winthrop's own pen is far superiour to their copy, and its simplicity is injured by their decorations. One would as soon exchange a portrait of full size from the life for an engraving in duodecimo, as receive the version of the oration in the Universal History for our author's report of his "little speech."

These venerable MSS. afterwards were in the hands of Prince, who used part of the first in compiling his Annals, II. Hutchinson, we know, did not enjoy the use of them.

Of the title of this work, it may be desirable for the reader to understand, that it is the exact language of the author. In the first volume of MS., indeed, it is not used, nor is any other designation given to the book. But Prince labels it "History of New England, by John Winthrop, governour of the Massachusetts," and both the other MS. volumes begin, in the writer's own hand, "A Continuation of the History of New England." Perhaps it would be more gratifying, could we determine, whether Winthrop designed by this term the colony of Massachusetts only, or all the country, before 1628 and since 1660, usually called New England. It is plain enough, that, in the early part of his work, his regards are confined to Massachusetts proper, exclusive of Maine, New Hampshire and Plimouth; nor is there, in later parts, so liberal a narrative of those colonies, or of Rhode Island and Connecticut, as we should be happy to receive from one so well acquainted with the history of all. Johnson certainly means, by New England, Massachusetts alone; and the omission of regular notices, by our author, of the annual elections, and, indeed, of all other incidents in each of the other colonies, except those incidents had close connexion with our colony, leaves it beyond question, that the name must have the same strict interpretation. Letters from private persons on the other side of the ocean were frequently addressed to John Winthrop, governour of New England. Sir William Berkley, the royal governour of Virginia, employs the same style; and the king and council usually designate *this* colony New England. Perhaps the great confederation of the four colonies in 1643, extended the name to them, or rather deprived Massachusetts of its improper appropriation. The next year the patent for Providence Plantations in New England was obtained, which name would certainly not have been allowed by their neighbours without authority of parliament.

My duty has called for a very scrupulous attention to the exact phraseology of the original MS. and the reader may confidently receive this text of Winthrop for a correct one, verified by collation of his autograph at three several periods in different years. The integrity of the text has, indeed, been as great an object of my labour, as the preparation of notes. Yet mistakes may have occurred; for, at different times, the same word has sometimes been variously read by me. The venerable authorities will remain in the archives of the Historical Society for my correction by any one, who doubts of the faithfulness of a single passage.

Perhaps some of my readers will be pleased with an explanation of the style, or supputation, of the year. Before 1752, the year was, by the legal method of computation, held to begin on 25 March, Lady Day, or Annunciation, so called from the notion entertained by the church, that the event recorded in the gospel of Luke, i. 26—38, occurred on that day. The general practice of England had, indeed, several years earlier, conformed to that of the rest of Christendom, in making the first of January new year's day; and the law, at last, followed the popular wisdom, as usual, in the correction. But, in our author's time, the custom coincided with the law. It is of more importance, however, to remark, that, in reckoning the months, March was called the first, February the twelfth, September, October, November and December, then having, consistent with their Latin etymology, the numerical rank, which is now lost. Yet it is still more important to be noticed, that a very dangerous diversity existed in styling the year by its old numeral until 25 March, or giving it the new designation from the beginning of that month. In the Appendix, A. 37, 38, 39, 40, our author dates the old year, and such course is generally followed through the History, though sometimes he varied. I have preferred uniformity with his general custom. In the Appendix, G., Davenport and Gov. Eaton use 1638, where Winthrop would have written 1637. Numerous errours from this source are observable in all the writers on our early history; and even the most careful sometimes fall into them. The accurate Hutchinson, I. 16, 17, mentions the purchase by our company from the Plimouth council, 19 March, 1627, and the charter from the king, confirming the same, 4 March, 1628, in which we might suppose he followed the old style. But the first election of officers, pursuant to the charter, on the last Wednesday in Easter term, he makes 13 May, 1628, by which we see his mistake. It was 1629.

An apology may be expected by the publick for my references to the edition of Morton's Memorial by Judge Davis, when that work is not published. It is easily made. The work had been several years nearly finished, when I began my labour in 1816; and the liberal editor,—liberal in every thing but withholding from the community the fruit of so many years acquisition,—allowed me freely to peruse his notes. His friends might reasonably expect, that the volume would be soon issued, of which nineteen-twentieths had so long been printed. My good fortune, however, permits the present publication to appear without the peril of a comparison with one, by which it must be so greatly overshadowed. If that long-desired work is to be postponed during the life of the editor, the community will gladly prolong their eager expectation.

For assistance received in the progress of my work, no other acknowledgments than will be seen in the notes is required by the living or the dead. But Hutchinson, Eliot, Bradford, Prince, Hazard, and other deceased writers,—Holmes, Davis, Allen, and other living ones,—are common property. The freedom used by me in correcting their errours will, I hope, entitle my humble notes to the same regard.

Hanc veniam petimusque damusque vicissim.

It would be thought only a childish affectation to give here the names of all, who lent their aid in rendering this book minutely accurate; yet, after all my obligation to them, it is expedient, for greater benefits than all their kindness bestowed, to refer to the free and unexhausted field, the soil of which is only partially turned up to the day, that lies for the cultivation of any, in our Colony, County, Town and Church Records, whence the information derived will be equally abundant and authentick. There is, however, one gentleman, to whom my readers will feel so much indebted, that to withhold his name would be greater affectation than to publish it. My friend, James Bowdoin, Esq. procured for me most of the articles in the Appendix, especially the family letters, received from his cousin, Francis B. Winthrop, Esq. of New Haven, which will, no doubt, be thought the most valuable appendage to the History of their great ancestor.

The title page, dedication and preface of the former edition are here added:

A

JOURNAL

OF THE

TRANSACTIONS AND OCCURRENCES IN THE SETTLEMENT OF MASSACHUSETTS AND THE OTHER NEW ENGLAND COLONIES, FROM THE YEAR 1630 TO 1644.

WRITTEN BY

JOHN WINTHROP, ESQ.

FIRST GOVERNOUR OF MASSACHUSETTS,

AND NOW FIRST PUBLISHED FROM A CORRECT COPY OF THE ORIGINAL MANUSCRIPT.

Utcumque erit, juvabit tamen, rerum gestarum memoriæ, ipsum consuluisse.

TIT. LIV. PREF.

HARTFORD:

PRINTED BY ELISHA BABCOCK.

M,DCC,XC.

TO

THE POSTERITY

OF

JOHN WINTHROP, ESQ.

THE FOUNDER OF THE MASSACHUSETTS COLONY,

AND, FOR MANY YEARS,

THE FATHER AND THE GOVERNOUR OF THAT INFANT SETTLEMENT,

The following Journal,

WRITTEN BY THEIR ILLUSTRIOUS ANCESTOR,

IS RESPECTFULLY INSCRIBED,

BY THEIR MOST OBEDIENT

HUMBLE SERVANT,

THE EDITOR.

HARTFORD, *July*, 1790.

B

THE EDITOR'S PREFACE.

THE following Journal was written by John Winthrop, Esq. first governour of Massachusetts. This distinguished gentleman was born at Groton in Suffolk, June 12, 1587. His grandfather was an eminent lawyer, in the reign of Henry VIII. and attached to the reformation. His father was of the same profession; and the governour himself was bred a lawyer, in which character he was eminent both for integrity and abilities. Indeed, he must have had the fairest reputation; for he was appointed a justice of peace at eighteen years of age.

When the design of settling a colony in New England was undertaken, Mr. Winthrop was chosen, with general consent, to conduct the enterprise. His estate, amounting to the value of six or seven hundred pounds sterling a year, he converted into money, and embarked for America, in the forty-third year of his age. He arrived at Salem, with the Massachusetts charter, June 12, 1630. He was many years governour of that infant colony, and conducted himself with such address and unshaken rectitude, as to render his character universally respectable among his cotemporaries, and his memory dear to posterity. He died March 26, 1649

Mr. Winthrop kept a Journal of every important occurrence, from his first embarking for America, in 1630, to the year 1644 This manuscript, as appears by some passages, was originally designed for publication; and it was formerly consulted by the first compilers of New England history, particularly by Hubbard, Mather and Prince. But it continued, unpublished and uncopied, in possession of the elder branch of the family, till the late revolution, when Gov. Trumbull of Connecticut procured it, and, with the assistance of his secretary, copied a considerable part of it. Soon after the governour's death, a gentleman, who has a taste for examining curious original papers, which respect his own country, came, by accident, to a knowledge of this manuscript; and, with consent of the governour's heirs, contracted for a copy, merely for his own improvement and amusement. On reading the work, he found it to contain many curious and interesting facts, relating to the settlement of Massachusetts and the other New England colonies, and highly descriptive of the character and views of the first inhabitants. This suggested to him the design of publishing the Journal *complete;* as any abridgment of it would tend to weaken its historical evidence, and put [it] in the power of captious criticks to impeach its authenticity. By consent of the descendants of Gov. Winthrop, proposals were issued for publishing a small number of copies; and the design is at length accomplished.

The copy here presented to the publick was made by John Porter, Esq. the secretary of the late Gov. Trumbull, whose declaration respecting its accuracy, is here annexed. It is an extract from his letter to the editor:

LEBANON, *January* 1*st*, 1788.

Dear Sir,

AGREEABLE to your request, I send you a copy of Gov. Winthrop's History. The transcribing has required more labour than I at first expected. I carefully examined the original, and, on comparing, found many errours in the first copy; which, upon further experience in reading the original, I have been able to correct; as also to fill up many blanks. This has caused me much study, and retarded the completion of the business for some time. You will observe some blanks in the present copy—some of them are so in the original; but, excepting the blanks, I believe this may be depended on as a genuine copy.

I am, dear Sir,
with sentiments of esteem,
your obedient humble servant,
JOHN PORTER.

The original is in the hand-writing common to that age, and is not read without difficulty. The first copy was made during Gov. Trumbull's life, and part of it by the governour himself. The last copy, here given to the world, was taken from the first, and, throughout the whole, compared with the original. The blanks are few, and, as the reader will observe, of no considerable consequence.

Many parts of the work are not interesting to modern readers; but even these are necessary to give future historians an accurate account of the first transactions of the settlers, and furnish posterity with a precise knowledge of the characters and manners of their forefathers.

Important institutions, and the general complexion of national government, often originate in the most trivial circumstances, or the minutest traits of character; and without a detail of the most trifling facts in the early history of New England, it will be impossible to understand the nature of their present religious and political establishments.

But, however unimportant particular passages in the following Journal may appear to the body of readers, the substance of the work is highly valuable; and, it is presumed, the historian, the philosopher, and the divine, will be gratified with a publication, which has long been a desideratum among the literati of the New World.

HARTFORD, *July*, 1790.

THE reader is desired to observe, that, at the head of the page, stands the name of the governour for the time being; that the references from the text to the notes are marked by Arabick numerals; that words doubtful in the original MSS. are printed in Italick characters, as on page 286; that words presumed to be deficient in the original are supplied by including them in brackets, as on page 19; that words in the original MSS. having a pen drawn through them are denoted by a star before and after, as on page 232; that some important omissions in the former edition are marked by a § before and after, as on page 148; that the difference in some particular places, between the correct reading of this edition and the erroneous ones of the former edition, is marked by giving the true word or words in the text between parallel lines before and after, and the word or words of the former edition between similar lines in the margin below, as on page 3.

In printing Indian names, I have followed the orthography of originals, however various at different times. Great literal correctness has been aimed at, and in general obtained in printing this volume. The reader may note the following errours, besides a few in punctuation, of less importance:

ERRATA.

Page 29, in note, last line but four, for *Ashby*, read *Ashley*.
—— 78, in note, last line but one, for *Thurlow*, read *Thurloe*.
—— 82, in note, last line but one, for *without*, read *with*.
—— 247, in note, last line but 10, and in note 2, on page 313, for *Thomson*, read *Tompson*.
—— 276, in note, last line but four, for *as*, read *at*.
—— 384, in text, line 33, for *Elizabeth*, read *Martha*.
—— 391, in text, line 11, for *Nath.* read *Math.*

Perhaps I should here notice, that the address of our governour and company on board the Arbella, printed for John Bellamie, London, 1630, has been found by me since writing the remark on page 5 of this volume. It is bound up with several other rare tracts in the Prince Collection, but, as it gives only the seven names, transcribed by Hubbard, its value is not so great as I imagined.

"AT ye Feast of St. Michael, Ano 1607, my Sister, ye Lady Mildmay, did give me a Stone Pot, tipped and covered wth a Silver Lydd."

THE above memorandum was taken out of my great great grandfather, Mr. Adam Winthrop, his notes, and given me, October 13th, 1707, by my cousin John Winthrop, relating to the Stone Pot, given him by his sister one hundred years ago; which Pot is now in my possession.

ADAM WINTHROP,

the son of Adam—the son of Adam—the son of John, governour of Massachusetts—the son of the abovesaid Adam, to whom the Pot was at first given.

BE it remembered, that the "Stone Pot, *tipped and covered with a Silver Lydd,*" descended to me upon the death of my father in 1779; and that it has, on this 29th day of September, 1807, (being the Feast of St. Michael,) been two hundred years in the family, and is now in my possession.

WILLIAM WINTHROP,

the son of John—the son of Adam—the son of Adam—the son of Adam—the son of John, (governour of Massachusetts,)—the son of Adam, to whom the Pot was at first given.

THE

HISTORY

OF

NEW ENGLAND.

ANNO DOMINI, 1630, MARCH 29, MONDAY.

Easter Monday.] **R**IDING at the Cowes, near the Isle of Wight, in the [1]Arbella, a ship of three hundred and fifty tons,

---

1 This name has been usually spelt Arabella, and thus Neal, Hutchinson, Trumbull, Dr. Holmes and Judge Davis, besides Eliot and Allen, in their Biographical Dictionaries, following chiefly Josselyn and Mather, have all written it. Yet these respectable writers could not have failed to adopt the right name, had they considered it worth attention. Other authorities, of even less value, though of earlier date, may have strengthened the mistake. Johnson, who probably was personally acquainted with the fact, in his "Wonder-working Providence," doubles the letter *r;* but surely the additional syllable gains little support from a book, whose innumerable inaccuracies of every sort can only be accounted for by the circumstance of its author living here while his work was printed at London. The grandson of Sir Ferdinando Gorges, in his "America painted to the Life," gives only a meagre abstract of Johnson, and therefore adds no evidence for the common orthography. But in the celebrated letter from these adventurers, dated on board *this* ship at Yarmouth 7 April, published in London, 1630, found in Hubbard, 126—128, and the first article in Hutchinson's Appendix, the true word may be seen. Hubbard is indeed of very little value usually in his narrative of events during the life of Winthrop, except for the closeness with which he copies his text. The unfailing accuracy of Prince led him beyond Hubbard to original private manuscripts and the Colony Records for the exact spelling. I testify that such is the original note of the meeting of the assistants, 23 March, on board *this* ship.

The principal vessels, which brought our fathers hither, are remembered by their descendants with no small degree of affection. The Mayflower had been a name of renown, without forming part of this fleet, because in her came the devoted planters of Plimouth, and she had also brought, in the year preceding this, some of Higginson's companions to Salem. Endicot and the first colonists of Massachusetts in 1628 demand our gratitude for the Abigail. But the circumstance of changing, "in honour of the Lady" Arbella, wife of Isaac Johnson, Esq. the original name of this *admiral* ship, which was the Eagle, makes us confident in the correctness of this name, while it pleases the imagination that would honour the vessel. In his epistle to the Countess of Lincoln,

whereof Capt. Peter [1]Milborne was master, being manned with fifty-two seamen and twenty-eight pieces of ordnance, (the wind coming to the N. and by W. the evening before,) in the morning there came aboard us Mr. [2]Cradock, the late governour, and the masters of his two ships, Capt. John Lowe, master of the Ambrose, and Mr. Nicholas Hurlston, master of the Jewel, and Mr. Thomas [3]Beecher, master of the Talbot, (which three ships rode then by us—the Charles, the Mayflower, the William and Francis, the Hopewell, the Whale, the Success and the Trial being still at [4]Hampton and not ready,) when, upon conference, it was agreed, that (in regard it was uncertain when the rest of the fleet would be ready) these four ships should consort together; the Arbella to be Admiral, the Talbot Vice-Admiral, the Am-

---

mother of this lady, Gov. Dudley uses the same letters with Winthrop, in whose MS. the word is more plainly written than almost any other, and we cannot suppose they could be mistaken in so simple a point about one of their most intimate friends. It was therefore only in compliance with popular opinion, that this errour found place in the former edition; and we may now hope that, in time to come, the correction will be always regarded.

1 By the company records it appears, the master owned one eighth of the ship.

2 Matthew Cradock, it is certain, never came to our country, though he maintained a small plantation for fishing at Mistick, in the present bounds of Malden, opposite to Winthrop's farm at Ten Hills. He was long honoured in our annual registers as first governour of the colony; yet, as he was in fact only the head of a commercial company in England, not ruler of the people, his services are adequately acknowledged without retaining his name in that most respectable list. To him is due the honour of the proposal, 28 July preceding the date of commencement of this History, for transferring the government from the company in London to the inhabitants here—a measure, of which the benefit was felt more and more every year till the independence of the United States, with which its connexion is apparent. This fact is by Prince, I. 189, verified from the records of that day. His death I refer to 1644, for in our county registry deeds are found of that year from his agent, and in the next year from the agent of his executors. A descendant, George Cradock, Esq. is mentioned by Douglas and Hutchinson as an inhabitant of Boston.

3 The same master, in the same ship, had the year before brought to Salem the venerable Higginson, the father and pattern of the New England clergy. His relation of the voyage, printed at London in a third edition, 1630, is preserved in Hutchinson's "Collection of Papers." Hubbard, 128, makes this name Belcher, but this is perhaps a misprint, for Higginson gives it like Winthrop, except that his first syllable has but one *e*. Thomas Beecher is among the early members of Boston church, being No. 112, and he was a representative from Charlestown in the first year, and often afterwards. He was by the General Court, in May, 1635, Col. Rec. I. 150, appointed "captain of the fort at Castle Island." Hubbard read our MS. as calling the master of the Jewel Harlston.

4 This port is usually called Southampton.

brose Rear-Admiral, and the Jewel a Captain; and accordingly articles of consortship were drawn between the said captains and masters; whereupon Mr. Cradock took leave of us, and our captain gave him a farewell with four or five shot.

About ten of the clock we weighed anchor and set sail, with the wind at N. and came to an anchor again over against Yarmouth, and the Talbot weighed likewise, and came and anchored by us. Here we met with a ship of Hampton, called the Plantation, newly come from Virginia. Our captain saluted her, and she us again; and the master, one Mr. [blank] [1]*Graves*, came on board our ship, and stayed with us about two or three hours, and in the mean time his ship came to an anchor by us.

Tuesday, 30.] In the morning, about ten of the clock, the wind being come to the W. with fair weather, we weighed and rode nearer Yarmouth. When we came before the town, the castle put forth a flag; our captain saluted them, and they answered us again. The Talbot, which rode farther off, saluted the castle also.

Here we saw, close by the shore of the Isle of Wight, a Dutch ship of one thousand tons, which, being bound to the East Indies, about two years since, in passing ||through the Needles,|| struck upon a rock, and being forced to run ashore to save her men, could never be weighed since, although she lies a great height above the water, and yet she hath some men aboard her.

Wednesday, 31.] The wind continued W. and S. W. with rain. Our captain and some of our company went to Yarmouth for supply of wood and other provisions; (our captain was still careful to fill our empty casks with water.)

Thursday, April 1.] The wind continued very strong at W. and by S. with much rain.

Friday, 2.] We kept a fast aboard our ship and the Talbot. The wind continued still very high at W. and S. and rainy. In the time of our fast, two of our landmen pierced a rundlet of strong water, and stole some of it, for which we laid them in bolts all the night, and the next morning the principal was openly whipped, and both kept with bread and water that day.

Saturday, 3.] The wind continued still at W. and with continual storms and rain.

Sunday, 4.] Fair, clear weather. In the morning the wind W. and by N. but in the afternoon S. S. W. This evening the

||thither the rudder||

---

1 I cannot satisfactorily make out this name from the MS. but am convinced the former edition was wrong, and note my uncertainty in the text.

Talbot weighed and went back to the Cowes, because her anchor would not hold here, the tide set with so strong a race.

Monday, 5.] The wind still W. and S. with fair weather. A maid of Sir Richard [1]Saltonstall fell down at the grating by the cook room, but the carpenter's man, who occasioned her fall unwittingly, caught hold of her with incredible nimbleness, and saved her; otherwise she had fallen into the hold.

Tuesday, 6.] Capt. Burleigh, captain of Yarmouth castle, a grave, comely gentleman, and of great age, came aboard us and stayed breakfast, and, offering us much courtesy, he departed, our captain giving him four shot out of the forecastle for his farewell. He was an old sea captain in Queen Elizabeth's time, and, being taken prisoner at sea, was kept prisoner in Spain three years. Himself and three of his sons were captains in [2]Roe's voyage.

The wind was now come about to N. E. with very fair weather.

In the afternoon Mr. Cradock came aboard us, and told us, that the Talbot, Jewel and Ambrose were fallen down into Stoke's Bay, intending to take their way by St. Helen's Point, and that they desired we would come back to them. Hereupon we came to council, and wrote unto them to take the first opportunity of the wind to fall down to us, and Mr. Cradock presently went back to them, our captain giving him three shot out of the steerage for a farewell.

Our captain called over our landmen, and tried them at their muskets, and such as were good shot among them were enrolled to serve in the ship, if occasion should be.

The lady Arbella and the gentlewomen, and Mr. [3]Johnson and some others went on shore to refresh themselves.

---

1 A copious collection of biographical memoirs of this gentleman and his descendants, of whom our country has justly been proud, may be seen in 2 Hist. Coll. IV. 154—168.

2 Sir Thomas Roe was named by the king to be of the council in the second charter of Virginia in May, 1609, and was in the same year sent by Prince Henry to explore the coast of Guiana. On the dangerous shores at the mouth of the Oronoco he laboured many months with great diligence, and ascended the Maragnon three hundred miles. After his return in 1611, he became a politician, was a member of parliament, and supported the rights of the people in 1614. After that year he was employed, first at the instance of the East India Company, in several embassies. Of these his own relation, after lying in manuscript more than a century, was given to the press; but, I believe, no account is extant of his voyage to America. He sat with John Selden for the University of Oxford in the Long Parliament, and died during the civil war. He was one of the forty, incorporated in 1620 as the Plimouth Council, whose names may be seen in Belknap's New Hampshire, I. 12, and Hubbard, 217.

3 Of this gentleman, who is usually regarded as the founder of Boston, an

[1]Wednesday, 7.] Fair weather, the wind easterly, in the morning a small gale, but in the afternoon it came about to the south. This afternoon our other consorts came up to us, and about ten or twelve Flemings, and all anchored by us, and the masters of the Jewel and of the Ambrose came aboard us, and our captain and they went on shore.

Towards night there came from the W. a Fleming, a small man of war, with a Brazil man which he had taken prize, and came to anchor by us.

Thursday, 8.] About six in the morning (the wind being E. and N. and fair weather) we weighed anchor and set sail, and before ten we gat through the Needles, having so little wind as we had much to do to stem the tide, so as the rest of our fleet (we being nine in all, whereof some were small ships, which were bound for Newfoundland) could not get out all then till the ebb. In the afternoon the wind came S. and W. and we were becalmed, so as being not able to get above three or four leagues from the Needles, our captain tacked about, and putting his fore-sheets aback stays, he stayed for the rest of the fleet, and as they came by us we spake to them, and about eight in the evening we let fall an anchor, intending to stop till the ebb. But before ten at night the wind came about to the N. a good gale; so we put up a light in the poop, and weighed and set sail, and by daylight, Friday, 9, we were come to Portland; but the other ships being not able to hold up with us, we were forced to spare our mainsail, and went on with a merry gale. In the ||morning|| we descried from the top eight sail astern of us, (whom Capt. Lowe told us he had seen at Dunnose in the evening.) We supposing they might be [2]Dunkirkers, our

||night||

---

interesting account may be found in Hutchinson, I. 22, to which neither myself nor the diligent historian of Boston, whose work is now in the press, have been able to make much addition. From the first volume of our Probate Records it may be seen, that he was the most liberal contributor to the company's funds. His early death prevented him from contributing much to the stability of the colony he so assiduously promoted at home, for I find no mention of him in our records, but at the Court 7 September, and again, 18 of same, acting with Winthrop in taking inquisition at Charlestown upon one of their company, who died after short illness.

1 On this day the admirable letter "to the rest of their brethren in and of the Church of England" was addressed by our adventurous pilgrims from Yarmouth, aboard the Arbella. It is most appropriately given by Hutchinson as the first article in the Appendix to his first volume. Only seven of the signers are named, which makes it very desirable to procure the 4to pamphlet, printed for John Bellamie, London, 1630, whence Hubbard, 126, derived it.

2 Dunkirk was then part of the Spanish Netherlands, and the war between England and Spain lasted till December following.

captain caused the gun room and gun deck to be cleared; all the hammocks were taken down, our ordnance loaded, and our powder chests and fireworks made ready, and our landmen quartered among the seamen, and twenty-five of them appointed for muskets, and every man written down for his quarter.

The wind continued N. [blank] with fair weather, and after noon it calmed, and we still saw those eight ships to stand towards us; having more wind than we, they came up apace, so as our captain and the masters of our consorts were more occasioned to think they might be Dunkirkers, (for we were told at Yarmouth, that there were ten sail of them waiting for us;) whereupon we all prepared to fight with them, and took down some cabins which were in the way of our ordnance, and out of every ship were thrown such bed matters as were subject to take fire, and we heaved out our long boats, and put up our waste cloths, and drew forth our men, and armed them with muskets and other weapons, and instruments for fireworks; and for an experiment our captain shot a ball of wild-fire fastened to an arrow out of a cross-bow, which burnt in the water a good time. The lady Arbella and the other women and children were removed into the lower deck, that they might be out of danger. All things being thus fitted, we went to prayer upon the upper deck. It was much to see how cheerful and comfortable all the company appeared; not a woman or child that shewed fear, though all did apprehend the danger to have been great, if things had proved as might well be expected, for there had been eight against four, and the least of the enemy's ships were reported to carry thirty brass pieces; but our trust was in the Lord of Hosts; and the courage of our captain, and his care and diligence, did much encourage us. It was now about one of the clock, and the fleet seemed to be within a league of us; therefore our captain, because he would shew he was not afraid of them, and that he might see the issue before night should overtake us, tacked about and stood to meet them, and when we came near we perceived them to be our friends—the Little Neptune, a ship of some twenty pieces of ordnance, and her two consorts, bound for the Straits; a ship of ||Flushing,|| and a Frenchman, and three other English ships bound for Canada and Newfoundland.[1] So when we

||Hampshire,||

---

1 Johnson, lib. I. c. 14, makes the number of these suspicious sail only four. But though he was, I presume, a passenger in the fleet with Winthrop, his story was probably committed to paper long after the events. Prince, I. 205—6, got into confusion between Johnson and Hubbard, and followed the carelessness of the latter, 129, who represents these ships as "the rest of the fleet," which, we know from Dudley, did not sail before May.

drew near, every ship (as they met) saluted each other, and the ||musketeers|| discharged their small shot; and so (God be praised) our fear and danger was turned into mirth and friendly entertainment. Our danger being thus over, we espied two boats on fishing in the channel; so every of our four ships manned out a skiff, and we bought of them great store of excellent fresh fish of divers sorts.

Saturday, 10.] The wind at E. and by N. a handsome gale with fair weather. By seven in the morning we were come over against Plimouth.

About noon the wind slacked, and we were come within sight of the Lizard, and towards night it grew very calm and a great fog, so as our ships made no way.

This afternoon Mr. Hurlston, the master of the Jewel, came aboard our ship, and our captain went in his skiff aboard the Ambrose and the Neptune, of which one Mr. Andrew Cole was master. There he was told, that the bark Warwick was taken by the Dunkirkers, for she came single out of the Downes about fourteen days since, intending to come to us to the Wight, but was never heard of since.[1] She was a pretty ship of about eighty tons and ten pieces of ordnance, and was set out by Sir Ferdinando [2]Gorges, Capt. Mason and others, §for discovery of the great lake in New England,§ so to have intercepted the trade of beaver. The master of her was one Mr. Weatherell, whose father was master of one of the cattle ships, which we left at Hampton.

This day two young men, falling at odds and fighting, contrary to the orders which we had published and set up in the ship, were adjudged to walk upon the deck till night with their hands bound behind them, which accordingly was executed; and another man, for using contemptuous speeches in our presence, was laid in bolts till he submitted himself and promised open confession of his offence.

I should have noted before, that the day we set sail from the Cowes, my son Henry Winthrop went on shore with one

||Mayflower and ours||

---

1 She was not taken, but had put into Plimouth, whence Ambrose Gibbens, a passenger in her, wrote 8 April to his employers, as Eyre in his letter next year acknowledges. Belknap, N. H. I. Appendix ii.

2 Of Gorges and Mason, whose names frequently occur in this History, no more perfect account can be expected, than is furnished by Dr. Belknap in the first volume of his admirable American Biography, though we must regret, that the information about Mason is very slight. The manner in which, in this work, Mason's death is related, sub an. 1636 and 1640, is much to be regretted.

of my servants to fetch an ox and ten wethers, which he had provided for our ship, and there went on shore with him Mr. [1]Pelham and one of his servants. They sent the cattle aboard, but returned not themselves. About three days after my servant and a servant of Mr. Pelham's came to us to Yarmouth, and told us they were all coming to us in a boat the day before, but the wind was so strong against them, as they were forced on shore in the night, and the two servants came to Yarmouth by land, and so came on ship-board, but my son and Mr. Pelham (we heard) went back to the Cowes and so to Hampton. We expected them three or four days after, but they came not to us, so we have left them behind, and suppose they will come after in Mr. [2]Goffe's ships. We were very sorry they had put themselves upon such inconvenience, when they were so well accommodated in our ship. This was not noted before, because we expected daily their return; and upon this occasion I must add here one observation, that we have many young gentlemen in our ship, who behave themselves well, and are conformable to all good orders.

About ten at night it cleared up with a fresh gale at N. and by W. so we stood on our course merrily.

Sunday, 11.] The wind at N. and by W. a very stiff gale.

About eight in the morning, being gotten past Scilly, and standing to the W. S. W. we met two small ships, which falling in among us, and the Admiral coming under our lee, we let him pass, but the Jewel and Ambrose, perceiving the other to be a Brazil man, and to take the wind of us, shot at them and made them stop and fall after us, and sent a skiff aboard them to know what they were. Our captain, fearing lest some mistake might arise, and lest they should take them for enemies which were friends, and so, through the unruliness of the mariners some wrong might be done them, caused his skiff to be heaved out, and sent Mr. [3]*Graves*, one of his mates and

---

[1] It may be concluded, from the letter of Herbert Pelham, Esq. to Gov. Winthrop, found in Hutch. Coll. 59, dated 23 February, 1635, that this gentleman was his brother. The list of persons, desiring to become freemen, in 1630, Prince, II. 4, has the name of Mr. William Pelham.

[2] Thomas Goffe, Esq. a merchant of London, had been an adventurer in the New Plimouth settlement, and was one of our original patentees, but never came to this country. He was in the charter named deputy governour of the company, and was at this time an assistant.

[3] One of this name had been mate of the Talbot in her voyage with Higginson. He was afterwards master of a vessel, perhaps, in several voyages, and, I think, settled in our country; but Prince, II. 4, makes him a rear-admiral.

our pilot, (a discreet man,) to see how things were, who returned soon after, and brought with him the master of one of the ships and Mr. Lowe and Mr. Hurlston. When they were come aboard us, they agreed to send for the captain, who came and showed his commission from the Prince of Orange. In conclusion he proved to be a Dutchman, and his a man of war of Flushing, and the other ship was a prize he had taken laden with sugar and tobacco; so we sent them aboard their ships again, and held on our course. In this time (which hindered us five or six ||leagues||) the Jewel and the Ambrose came foul of each other, so as we much feared the issue, but, through God's mercy, they came well off again, only the Jewel had her foresail torn, and one of her anchors broken. This occasion, and the sickness of our minister and people, put us all out of order this day, so as we could have no sermons.

Monday, 12.] The wind more large to the N. a stiff gale, with fair weather. In the afternoon less wind, and our people began to grow well again. Our children and others, that were sick, and lay groaning in the cabins, we fetched out, and having stretched a rope from the steerage to the mainmast, we made them stand, some of one side and some of the other, and sway it up and down till they were warm, and by this means they soon grew well and merry.

Tuesday, 13.] The night before it was calm, and the next day calm and close weather, so as we made little way, the wind with us being W.

Wednesday, 14.] The wind S. W. rainy weather, in the morning.

About nine in the forenoon the wind came about to N. N. W. a stiff gale; so we tacked about and steered our course W. S. W.

This day the ship heaved and set more than before, yet we had ||[2]but few|| sick, and of these such as came up upon the deck, and stirred themselves, were presently well again; therefore our captain set our children and ||[3]young|| men to some harmless exercises, which the seamen were very active in, and did our people much good, though they would sometimes play the wags with them. Towards night we were forced to take in some sail to stay for the Vice-Admiral, which was near a league astern of us.

[Large blank.]

Thursday, 15.] The wind still at N. N. W. fair weather, but less wind than the day and night before, so as our ship made but little way.

||days|| ||[2]still some|| ||[3]grown||

At noon our captain made observation by the cross-staff, and found we were in forty-seven degrees thirty-seven minutes north latitude.

All this forenoon our Vice-Admiral was much to leeward of us; so after dinner we bare up towards her, and having fetched her up and spoken with her, the wind being come to S. W. we tacked about and steered our course N. N. W. lying as near the wind as we could, and about four of the clock, with a stiff gale, we steered W. and by N. and at night the wind grew very strong, which put us on to the W. amain.

About ten at night the wind grew so high, and rain withal, that we were forced to take in our topsail, and having lowered our mainsail and foresail, the storm was so great as it split our foresail and tore it in pieces, and a knot of the sea washed our tub overboard, wherein our fish was a-watering. The storm still grew, and it was dark with clouds, (though otherwise moonlight,) so as (though it was the Jewel's turn to carry the light this night, yet) lest we should lose or go foul one of another, we hanged out a light upon our mizzen shrouds, and before midnight we lost sight of our Vice-Admiral.

Our captain, so soon as he had set the watch, at eight in the evening, called his men, and told them he feared we should have a storm, and therefore commanded them to be ready upon the deck, if occasion should be; and himself was up and down the decks all times of the night.

Friday, 16.] About four in the morning the wind slacked a little, yet it continued §a great storm§ still, and though in the afternoon it ||blew not|| much wind, yet the sea was so high as it tossed us more than before, and we carried no more but our mainsail, yet our ship steered well with it, which few such ships could have done.

About four in the afternoon, the wind still W. and by S. and rainy, we put on a new foresail and hoisted it up, and stood N. N. W. All this day our Rear-Admiral and the Jewel held up with us.

This night was very stormy.

All the time of the storm few of our people were sick, (||[2]except the women,|| who kept under hatches,) and there appeared no fear or dismayedness among them.

[Large blank.]

Saturday, 17.] The wind S. W. very stormy and boisterous. All this time we bore no more sail but our mainsail and foresail, and we steered our course W. and by N.

||cleared with|| ||[2]though no men||

This day our captain told me, that our landmen were very nasty and slovenly, and that the gun deck, where they lodged, was so beastly and noisome with their victuals and beastliness, as would much endanger the health of the ship. Hereupon, after prayer, we took order, and appointed four men to see to it, and to keep that room clean for three days, and then four others should succeed them, and so forth on.

The wind continued all this day at S. W. a stiff gale. In the afternoon it cleared up, but very hazy. Our captain, about four of the clock, sent one to the top to look for our Vice-Admiral, but he could not descry him, yet we saw a sail about two leagues to the leeward, which stood toward the N. E.

We were this evening (by our account) about ninety leagues from Scilly, W. and by S. At this place there came a swallow and lighted upon our ship.

Sunday, 18.] About two in the morning the wind N. W.; so we tacked about and steered our course S. W. We had still much wind, and the sea went very high, which tossed our ship continually.

After our evening sermon, about five of the clock, the wind came about to S. E. a good gale, but rainy; so we steered our course W. S. W. and the ship's way was about nine leagues a watch; (a watch is four hours.)

This day the captain sent to top again to discover our Vice-Admiral. We descried from thence to the eastward a sail, but we knew not what she was.

About seven of the clock the Jewel bare up so near as we could speak each to other, and after we bated some sail; so she went ahead of us, and soon after eight put forth her light.

Monday, 19.] In the morning the wind was come about to the N. W. a good gale and fair weather; so we held our course, but the ship made not so good way as when the wind was large.

This day, by observation and account, we found ourselves to be in forty-eight degrees north latitude, and two hundred and twenty leagues W. from the meridian of London.

Here I think good to note, that all this time since we came from the Wight, we had cold weather, so as we could well endure our warmest clothes. I wish therefore that all such as shall pass this way in the spring have care to provide warm clothing; for nothing breeds more trouble and danger of sickness, in this season, than cold.

In the afternoon the wind came to S. W. a stiff gale, with rain; so we steered westerly, till night; then the wind came about to N. W. and we tacked again and stood S. W.

Our Rear-Admiral being to leeward of us, we bare up to him. He told us all their people were in health, but one of their cows was dead.

Tuesday, 20.] The wind southerly, fair weather, and little wind. In the morning we stood S. and by E. in the afternoon W. and by N.

Wednesday, 21.] Thick, rainy weather; much wind at S. W. Our captain, over night, had invited his consorts to have dined with him this day, but it was such foul weather as they could not come aboard us.

Thursday, 22.] The wind still W. and by S. fair weather; then W. N. W.

This day at noon we found ourselves in forty-seven degrees and forty-eight minutes, and having a stiff gale, we steered S. W. about four leagues a watch, all this day and all the night following.

Friday, 23.] The wind still W. N. W. a small gale, with fair weather. Our captain put forth his ancient in the poop, and heaved out his skiff, and lowered his topsails, to give sign to his consorts, that they should come aboard us to dinner, for they were both a good way astern of us, and our Vice-Admiral was not yet seen of us since the storm, though we sent to the top every day to descry her.

About eleven of the clock, our captain sent his skiff and fetched aboard us the masters of the other two ships, and Mr. [1]Pynchon, and they dined with us in the round house, for the [2]lady and [3]gentlewomen dined in the great cabin.

---

1 William Pynchon, Esq. of whom frequent mention is made in this History, was named an assistant in the Massachusetts charter. Gov. Dudley relates, that his wife died here before the return of the ship they came in. Many papers in 2 Hist. Coll. VIII. 227 et seq. give honourable proof of his services. He settled first at Roxbury, but in a few years removed to Springfield, of which town he was the founder, and there lived till 1652, when, "having received some ill treatment" from the government, "on account of his religious principles, he, with Capt. Smith, his son-in-law, went to England, and with them went the minister of the town, the Rev. Mr. Moxon, never to return." See Breck's century sermon. I presume Pynchon had written a book above the spirit of that age; for our government, in a curious letter to the prince of fanaticks, Sir Henry Vane, give no clear idea of its doctrines. See 3 Hist. Coll. I. 35. His son, John, was of the council in 1665, and many of his descendants are in places of publick usefulness in Springfield and its neighbourhood and at Salem.

2 The lady was the wife of Johnson.

3 Mrs. Phillips, the minister's wife, the two daughters of Sir R. Saltonstall, and, probably, the wives of Coddington, Dudley, Bradstreet, Nowell, and others, are here intended, as the principal people, except Revell and Pynchon, seem to have been in the Arbella, which was chiefly owned by them.

This day and the night following we had little wind, so as the sea was very smooth, and the ship made little way.

Saturday, 24.] The wind still W. and by N. fair weather and calm all that day and night. Here we made observation again, and found we were in forty-five degrees twenty minutes, north latitude.

Sunday, 25.] The wind northerly, fair weather, but still calm. We stood W. and by S. and saw two ships ahead of us as far as we could descry.

In the afternoon the wind came W. and by S. but calm still. About five of the clock, the Rear-Admiral and the Jewel had fetched up the two ships, and by their saluting each other we perceived they were friends, (for they were so far to windward of us as we could only see the smoke of their pieces, but could not hear them.) About nine of the clock, they both fell back towards us again, and we steered N. N. W. Now the weather begins to be warm.

Monday, 26.] The wind still W. and by S. close weather, and scarce any wind.

The two ships, which we saw yesterday, were bound for Canada. Capt. [1]Kirk was aboard the Admiral. They bare up with us, and falling close under our lee, we saluted each other, and conferred together so long till his Vice-Admiral was becalmed by our sails, and we were foul one of another; but, there being little wind and the sea calm, we kept them asunder with oars, &c. till they heaved out their boat, and so towed their ship away.

They told us for certain, that the king of France had set out six of his own ships to recover the fort from them.

About one of the clock Capt. Lowe sent his skiff aboard us, (with a friendly token of his love to the governour,) to desire our captain to come aboard his ship, which he did, and there met the masters of the other ships and Capt. Kirk, and before night they all returned to their ships again, Capt. Lowe bestowing some shot upon them for their welcome.

The wind now blew a pretty gale, so as our ship made some way again, though it were out of our right course N. W. by N.

---

1 Probably a brother of Sir David Kirk, or Kertk, as Champlain, in his Voyage, and Charlevoix in his Histoire de la Nouvelle France, choose to spell the name. In the table of contents to the former, it is changed to Quer. Sir David, with his two brothers, Thomas and Lewis, had, the preceding year, taken Quebeck, an event then, and long after, thought of so little consequence, as not to be noticed in Hume's History of England. The name of Kirk will recur in the latter part of this History, when he was governour of Newfoundland, of which he had, in a charter of 1628, been one of the grantees.

Tuesday, 27.] The wind still westerly, a stiff gale, with close weather. We steered W. N. W. About noon some rain, and all the day very cold. We appointed Tuesdays and Wednesdays to catechise our people, and this day Mr. [1]Phillips began it.

Wednesday, 28.] All the night, and this day till noon, the wind very high at S. W. close weather, and some rain. Between eleven and twelve, in a shower, the wind came W. N. W. so we tacked about and stood S. W.

Thursday, 29.] Much wind all this night at W. and by N. and the sea went very high, so as the ship rolled very much, because we sailed but with one course; therefore, about twelve, our captain arose and caused the foretopsail to be hoisted, and then the ship went more steady. §He caused the quartermaster to look down into the hold to see if the cask lay fast and the.....§[2]

In the morning the wind continued with a stiff gale; rainy and cold all the day.

We had been now three weeks at sea, and were not come above three hundred leagues, being about one third part of

---

1 Of the Rev. George Phillips frequent mention will be found in the following pages, and an elaborate eulogy may be seen in the Magnalia. His wife died soon after arrival. In Gov. Bradford's Letter Book, the concluding part of which is preserved in 1 Hist. Coll. III. an epistle to him from Samuel Fuller, of 28 June of this year, only a few days after *our* colonists' arrival at Salem, discovers to us, that Phillips was of a straiter sect than most of the companions of Winthrop. "Here is come over," says he, "with these gentlemen, one Mr. Phillips, (a Suffolk man,) who hath told me in private, that if they will have him stand minister, by that calling, which he received from the prelates in England, he will leave them." This was not the spirit of the first settlers of Massachusetts, until they had lived some years in the wilderness; and I imagine Phillips was overcome, by the persuasion of his friends, to postpone the scruple he had communicated to the Plimouth colonist. Hubbard, 186, lets us a little into the cause of the change: "It is said, that Mr. Phillips was at the first more acquainted with the way of church discipline, since owned by Congregational churches; but being then without any to stand by him, (for wo to him that is alone,) he met with much opposition from some of the magistrates, till the time that Mr. Cotton came into the country, who, by his preaching and practice, did by degrees mould all their church administrations into the very same form, which Mr. Phillips laboured to introduce into the churches before." Yet his name is subscribed to the excellent letter, with Winthrop, Dudley, Johnson, Saltonstall, Fiennes and Coddington, dated on board the Arbella, wishing to be regarded "as those who esteem it our honour to call the church of England, from whence we rise, our dear mother."

The long list of men, distinguishing the name of Phillips in our country by their civil stations and munificent patronage of institutions of learning and benevolence, descend from this first pastor of Watertown.

2 This passage, being interlined, was extremely difficult to be made out, and part of it remains illegible, I think, by the aid of any eyes or glasses.

our way, viz. about forty-six north latitude, and near the meridian of the ||Terceras.||

This night Capt. Kirk carried the light as one of our consorts.

Friday, 30.] The wind at W. N. W. a strong gale, all the night and day, with showers now and then.

We made observation, and found we were in forty-four north latitude. At night the wind scanted towards the S. with rain; so we tacked about and stood N. W. and by N.

Saturday, May 1.] All the night much wind at S. S. W. and rain. In the morning the wind still strong, so as we could bear little sail, and so it continued a growing storm all the day, and towards night so much wind as we bore no more sail but so much as should keep the ship stiff. Then it grew a very great tempest §all the night,§ with fierce showers of rain intermixed and very cold.

Lord's day, 2.] The tempest continued all the day, with the wind W. and by N. and the sea raged and tossed us exceedingly; yet, through God's mercy, we were very comfortable, and few or none sick, but had opportunity to keep the Sabbath, and Mr. Phillips ||2preached|| twice that day. The Ambrose and Jewel were separated far from us the first night, but this day we saw them again, but Capt. Kirk's ships we saw not since.

Monday, 3.] In the night the wind abated, and by morning the sea was well assuaged, so as we bare our foresail again, and stood W. S. W.; but all the time of the tempest we could make no way, but were driven to the leeward, and the Ambrose struck all her sails but her mizzen, and lay a hull. She brake her main yard. This day we made observation, and found we were in forty-three and a half north latitude. We set two ||3fighters|| in the bolts, till night, with their hands bound behind them. A maid servant in the ship, being stomach sick, drank so much strong water, that she was senseless, and had near killed herself. We observed it a common fault in our ||4young|| people, that they gave themselves to drink hot waters very immoderately.

Tuesday, 4.] Much wind at S. W. close weather. In the morning we tacked about and stood N. W. and about ten in the morning W. N. W. but made little way in regard of the head sea.

Wednesday, 5.] The wind W. and by S. thick, foggy weather, and rainy; so we stood N. W. by W. At night the

||T——s.|| ||2prayed|| ||3sailors|| ||4grown||

Lord remembered us, and enlarged the wind to the N.; so we tacked about and stood our course W. and by S. with a merry gale in all our sails.

Thursday, 6.] The wind at N. a good gale, and fair weather. We made observation and found we were forty-three and a half north latitude; so we stood full west, and ran, in twenty-four hours, about thirty leagues.

||Four|| things I observed here. 1. That the declination of the pole star was much, even to the view, beneath that it is in England. 2. That the new moon, when it first appeared, was much smaller than at any time I had seen it in England. 3. That all the way we came, we saw fowls flying and swimming, when we had no land near by two hundred leagues. 4. That wheresoever the wind blew, we had still cold weather, and the sun did not give so much heat as in England.

Friday, 7.] The wind N. and by E. a small gale, very fair weather, and towards night a still calm. This day our captain and Mr. Lowe dined aboard the Jewel.

Saturday, 8.] All the night calm. In the morning the wind S. W. a handsome gale; so we tacked and stood N. W. and soon after, the wind growing more large, we stood W. N. W. with a good gale. About four of the clock we saw a whale, who lay just in our ship's way, (the bunch of his back about a yard above water.) He would not ||[2]shun us;|| so we passed within a stone's cast of him, as he lay spouting up water.

Lord's day, 9.] The wind still S. W. a good gale, but close weather and some rain; we held on our course W.N.W. About nine it cleared up, and towards night a great fog for an hour or two.

We were now in forty-four and a half north latitude, and a little west of ||[3]Corvos.||

Monday, 10.] The wind S. S. W. a good gale and fair weather; so we stood W. and by N. four or five leagues a watch, all this day. The wind increased, and was a great storm all the night. About midnight our Rear-Admiral put forth two lights, whereby we knew that some mischance had befallen her. We answered her with two lights again, and bare up to her, so near as we durst, (for the sea went very high, and she lay by the lee) ||and having hailed her, we thought she had sprung aleak; but she had broken some of her shrouds;[4]|| so we went a little ahead of her, and, bringing our foresail aback stays, we stayed for her, and,

||Some|| ||[2]swim up|| ||[3]Cowes||

||[4]but she had broken some of her shrouds. Having hailed her, we learnt she had sprung aleak||

about two hours after, she filled her sails, and we stood our course together, but our captain went not to rest till four of the clock, and some others of us slept but little that night.

Tuesday, 11.] The storm continued all this day, till three in the afternoon, and the sea went very high, so as our ship could make no way, being able to bear no more but our mainsail about midmast high. At three there fell a great storm of rain, ||which laid|| the wind, and the wind shifting into the W. we tacked and stood into the head sea, to avoid the rolling of our ship, and by that means we made no way, the sea beating us back as much as the wind put us forward.

We had still cold weather, and our people were so acquainted with ||[2]storms|| as they were not sick, nor troubled, though we were much tossed forty-eight hours together, viz. twenty-four during the storm, and as long the next night and day following, Wednesday, 12, when as we lay as it were a hull, for want of wind, and rolling continually in a high grown sea. This day was close and rainy.

Complaint was made to our captain of some injury that one of the under officers of the ship had done to one of our landmen. He called him and examined the cause, and commanded him to be tied up by the hands, and a weight to be hanged about his neck; but, at the intercession of the governour, (with some difficulty,) he remitted his punishment.

At night the wind blew at S. E. a handsome gale, with rain; so we put forth our sails and stood W. and by S.

Thursday, 13.] Toward morning the wind came to the south-westerly, with close weather and a strong gale, so as before noon we took in our topsails, (the Rear-Admiral having split her fore-topsail) and we stood west-southerly.

Friday, 14.] The wind W. S. W. thick, foggy weather, and in the afternoon rainy. We stood W. and by S. and after W. and by N. about five leagues a watch. We were in forty-four and a half. The sun set N. W. and by N. one third northerly. And towards night we stood W.

Saturday, 15.] The wind westerly all this day; fair weather. We tacked twice to small purpose.

Lord's day, 16.] As the 15 was.

Monday, 17.] The wind at S. a fine gale and fair weather. We stood W. and by S. We saw a great drift; so we heaved out our skiff, and it proved a fir log, which seemed to have been many years in the water, for it was all overgrown with barnacles and other trash. We sounded here and found no

||we layed to|| ||[2]showers||

ground at one hundred fathom and more. We saw two whales. About nine at night the wind grew very strong at S. W. and continued so, with much rain, till one of the clock; then it ceased raining, but the wind came to the W. with more violence. In this storm we were forced to take in all our sails, save our mainsail, and to lower that so much as we could.

Tuesday, 18.] In the morning the wind slacked, but we could stand no nearer our course than N. and we had much wind all this day. In the afternoon we tacked and stood S. by E. Towards night (our Rear-Admiral being near two leagues to leeward of us) we bare up, and drawing near her, we descried, ||some|| two leagues more to leeward, two ships, which we conceived were those two of Capt. Kirk's, which parted from us in the storm, May 2. We had still cold weather.

Wednesday, 19.] The wind S. S. W.; close and rainy; little wind. We tacked again and stood W.; but about noon the wind came full W. a very strong gale; so we tacked again and stood N. by E. and at night we took off our main bonnet, and took in all our sails, save our main-course and mizzen. We were now in forty-four degrees twelve minutes north, and by our account in the midway between the false bank and the main bank. All this night a great storm at W. by N.

Thursday, 20.] The storm continued all this day, the wind as it was, and rainy. In the forenoon we carried our fore-course and stood W. S. W. but in the afternoon we took it in, the wind increasing, and the sea grown very high; and lying with the helm a-weather, we made no way but as the ship drove. We had still cold weather.

[1]In the great cabin, at nine at night, &c. and the next day again, &c. The storm continued all this night.

Friday, 21.] The wind still N. W.; little wind, and close weather. We stood S. W. with all our sails, but made little way, and at night it was a still calm.

A servant of one of our company had bargained with a child to sell him a box worth 3*d.* for three biscuits a day all the voyage, and had received about forty, and had sold them and many more to some other servants. We caused his hands to be tied up to a bar, and hanged a basket with stones about his neck, and so he stood two hours.

Saturday, 22.] The wind S. S. W. much wind and rain.

||scarce||

---

1 In the margin of the MS. the word "fast" is written by the governour, and a later reader has put in a ☞ pointing at the paragraph. In this bad weather they were, probably, without food.

Our spritsail laid so deep in as it was split in pieces with a head sea at the instant as our captain was going forth of his cabin very early in the morning to give order to take it in. It was a great mercy of God, that it did split, for otherwise it had endangered the breaking of our bowsprit and topmasts at least, and then we had no other way but to have returned for England, except the wind had come east. About ten in the morning, in a very great fret of wind, it chopt suddenly into the W. as it had done divers times before, and so continued with a small gale and [we] stood N. and by W. About four in the afternoon there arose a sudden storm of wind and rain, so violent as we had not a greater. It continued thick and boisterous all the night.

About seven we descried a sail ahead of us, towards the N. and by E. which stood towards us. Our captain, supposing it might be our Vice-Admiral, hoisted up his mainsail, which before was struck down aboard, and came up to meet her. When we drew near her we put forth our [1]||ancient,|| and she ||[2]luffed|| up to get the wind of us; but when she saw she could not, she bare up, and hoisting up her foresail, stood away before the wind; yet we made all the signs we could, that we meant her no harm, but she would not ||[3]trust|| us. She was within shot of us, so as we perceived she was a small Frenchman, which we did suppose had been driven off the bank. When she was clear of us, she stood her course again, and we ours.

This day at twelve we made observation, and were about forty-three, but the storm put us far to the N. again. Still cold weather.

Lord's day, 23.] Much wind, still westerly, and very cold weather.

Monday, 24.] The wind N. W. by N. a handsome gale, and close weather and very cold. We stood S. W. About noon we had occasion to lie by the lee to straighten our mizzen shrouds, and the Rear-Admiral and Jewel, being both to windward of us, bare up and came under our lee, to inquire if any thing were amiss with us; so we heard the company was in health in the Jewel, but that two passengers were dead in the Ambrose, and one other §cow.§

||ensign|| ||[2]tuffled|| ||[3]hail||

---

[1] Some modern pen had been drawn through this word, that was originally as I have printed it, and the word given in the first edition was substituted. This unimportant alteration is noted, because it affords me an opportunity of assuring the reader that our MS. has not often been so corrupted.

Tuesday, 25.] The wind still N. W.; fair weather, but cold. We went on with a handsome gale, and at noon were in forty-three and a half; and the variation of the compass was a point and one sixth. All this day we stood W. S. W. about five or six leagues a watch, and towards night the wind enlarged, with a cold dash of snowy rain, and then we ran in a smooth sea about eight or nine leagues a watch, and stood due W.

Wednesday, 26.] The wind still N. W. a good gale and fair weather, but very cold still; yet we were about forty-three. At night we sounded, but found no ground.

Thursday, 27.] The wind N. W. a handsome gale; fair weather. About noon it came about to the S. W. and at night rain, with a stiff gale, and it continued to rain very hard till it was near midnight.

This day our skiff went aboard the Jewel for a hogshead of ||meal,|| which we borrowed, because we could not come by our own, and there came back in the skiff the master of the Jewel and Mr. ||[2]Revell;||[1] so our captain stayed them dinner, and sent for Capt. Lowe; and about two hours after dinner, they went aboard their own ships, our captain giving Mr. ||[3]Revell|| three shot, because he was one of the owners of our ship.

We understood now, that the two which died in the Ambrose were Mr. Cradock's servants, who were sick when they came to sea; and one of them should have been left at Cowes, if any house would have received him.

In the Jewel also one of the seamen died—a most profane fellow, and one who was very injurious to the passengers, though much against the will of the master.

At noon we tacked about and stood W. and by N. and so continued most part of that day and night following, and had much rain till midnight.

Friday, 28.] In the morning the wind veered to the W. yet we had a stiff gale, and steered N. W. and by N. It was so great a fog all this day, as we had lost sight of one of our

||water|| ||[2]Nowell|| ||[3]Nowell||

---

[1] I cannot dissemble the pleasure enjoyed by restoring the true name in this place, nor my surprise at finding the marginal substitute in the hand of the scrupulous Prince.

John Revell, Esq. was among those adventurers to New Plimouth, who, in 1626, assigned their interest to the colonists by an indenture, preserved by Bradford in 1 Hist. Coll. III. 47. He had been chosen one of our assistants in October preceding, and was one of those five undertakers to reside here for the management of the joint stock of the company, five others being in England. Yet he returned in the Lyon after a few weeks' visit, before the first meeting of the assistants. He was probably too rich to adventure life and fortune with us.

ships, and saw the other ||sometimes much|| to leeward. We had many ||[2]fierce|| showers of rain throughout this day.

At night the wind cleared up, and we saw both our consorts fair by us ; so that wind being very scant, we tacked and stood W. and by S. A [1]child was born in the Jewel about this time.

Saturday, 29.] The wind N. W. a stiff gale, and fair weather, but very cold; in the afternoon full N. and towards night N. and by E. ; so we stood W.

Lord's day, 30.] The wind N. by E. a handsome gale, but close, misty weather, and very cold ; so our ship made good way in a smooth sea, and our three ships kept close together. By our account we were in the same meridian with Isle Sable, and forty-two and a half.

Monday, 31.] Wind N. W. a small gale, close and cold weather. We sounded, but had no ground. About noon the wind came N. by E. a stiff, constant gale and fair weather, so as our ship's way was seven, eight, and sometimes twelve leagues a watch. This day, about five at night, we expected the eclipse, but there was not any, the sun being fair and clear from three till it set.

June 1, Tuesday.] The wind N. E. a small gale, with fair, clear weather ; in the afternoon full S. and towards night a good gale. We stood W. and by N. A woman in our ship fell in travail, and we sent and had a midwife out of the Jewel. She was so far ahead of us at this time, (though usually we could spare her some sail,) as we shot off a piece and lowered our topsails, and then she brailed her sails and stayed for us.

This evening we saw the new moon more than half an hour after sunset, being much smaller than it is at any time in England.

Wednesday, 2.] The wind S. S. W. a handsome gale ; very fair weather, but still cold ; in the evening a great fog. We stood W. and by N. and W. N. W.

Our captain, supposing us now to be near the N. coast, and knowing that to the S. there were dangerous shoals, fitted on a new mainsail, that was very strong, and double, and would not adventure with his old sails, as before, when he had sea-room enough.

Thursday, 3.] The wind S. by W. a good steady gale, and we stood W. and by N. The fog continued very thick, and

||some leagues|| ||2fine||

---

1 A note in the margin, "ergo fil. nullius," is an absurd conclusion of a stranger.

some rain withal. We sounded in the morning, and again at noon, and had no ground. We sounded again about two, afternoon, and had ground about eighty fathom, a fine grey sand; so we presently tacked and stood S. S. E. and shot off a piece of ordnance to give notice to our consorts, whom we saw not since last evening.

The fog continued all this night, and a steady gale at S. W.

Friday, 4.] About four in the morning we tacked again (the wind S. W.) and stood W. N. W. The fog continued all this day, so as we could not see a stone's cast from us; yet the sun shone very bright all the day. We sounded every two hours, but had no ground. At night we tacked again and stood S. [1]§In the great cabin, fast.§

Saturday, 5.] In the morning the wind came to N. E. a handsome gale, and the fog was dispersed; so we stood before the wind W. and by N. all the afternoon being rainy. At night we sounded, but had no ground. In the great cabin, thanksgiving.

It rained most part of this night, yet our captain kept abroad, and was forced to come in in the night to shift his clothes.

We sounded every half watch, but had no ground.

Lord's day, 6.] The wind N. E. and after N. a good gale, but still foggy at times, and cold. We stood W. N. W. both to make Cape Sable, if we might, and also because of the current, which, near the west shore, sets to the S. that we might be the more clear from the southern shoals, viz. of Cape Cod.

About two in the afternoon we sounded and had ground at about eighty fathom, and the mist then breaking up, we saw the shore to the N. about five or six leagues off, and were (as we supposed) to the S. W. of Cape Sable, and in forty-three and a quarter. Towards night it calmed and was foggy again, and the wind came S. and by E. We tacked and stood W. and by N. intending to make land at Aquamenticus, being to the N. of the Isles of Shoals.

Monday, 7.] The wind S. About four in the morning we sounded and had ground at thirty fathom, and was somewhat calm; so we put our ship a-stays, and took, in less than two hours, with a few hooks, sixty-seven codfish, most of them very great fish, some a yard and a half long, and a yard in compass.

---

[1] Comparing the close of this paragraph, perhaps, with that of the next following, some careless person had substituted *thanksgiving* for *fast*, and then struck out the whole sentence. The first edition was printed in conformity with this mutilation. As this was the sixty-eighth day passed on board ship, and the wind was adverse, the passengers might well keep a fast; and show their gratitude for the favourable gale the next day by thanksgiving.

This came very seasonably, for our salt fish was now spent, and we were taking care for victuals this day (being a fish day.)

After this we filled our sails, and stood W. N. W. with a small gale. *We hoisted out a great boat to keep our sounding the better.* The weather was now very cold. We sounded at eight, and had fifty fathom, and, being calm, we heaved out our hooks again, and took twenty-six cods; so we all feasted with fish this day. A woman was delivered of a child in our ship, still born. The woman had divers children before, but none lived, and she had some mischance now, which caused her to come near a month before her time, but she did very well. At one of the clock we had a fresh gale at N. W. and very fair weather all that afternoon, and warm, but the wind failed soon.

All the night the wind was W. and by S. a stiff gale, which made us stand to and again, with small advantage.

Tuesday, 8.] The wind still W. and by S. fair weather, but close and cold. We stood N. N. W. with a stiff gale, and, about three in the afternoon, we had sight of land to the N. W. about ten leagues, which we supposed was the Isles of Monhegan, but it proved Mount [1]Mansell. Then we tacked and stood W. S. W. We had now fair sun-shine weather, and so pleasant a ||sweet air|| as did much refresh us, and there came a smell off the shore like the smell of a garden.

There came a wild pigeon into our ship, and another small land bird.

Wednesday, 9.] In the morning the wind easterly, but grew presently calm. Now we had very fair weather, and warm. About noon the wind came to S. W.; so we stood W. N. W. with a handsome gale, and had the main land upon our starboard all that day, about eight or ten leagues off. It is very high land, lying in many hills very unequal. At night we saw many small islands, being low land, between us and the main, about five or six leagues off us; and about three leagues from us, towards the main, a small rock a little above water. At night we sounded and had soft oozy ground at

||scene here||

---

1 Now Mount Desert. I presume the name had been given in honour of Sir Robert Mansell, one of the patentees in the great patent for New England, usually called the Plimouth charter, of King James, 3 November, 1620, which, in the title page of his History of Connecticut, Trumbull incautiously says, had been "never before published in America," when it may be found in Haz. I. 103 et seq. See North Amer. Review, VIII. 117, where is found an examination of that work, ascribed to a gentleman thoroughly acquainted with the geography and history of this country.

sixty fathom; so, the wind being now ||scant|| at W. we tacked again and stood S. S. W. We were now in forty-three and a half.—This high land, which we saw, we judged to be at the W. cape of the great bay, which goeth towards Port Royal, called Mount Desert or Mount Mansell, and no island, but part of the main.[1] In the night the wind shifted oft.

Thursday, 10.] In the morning the wind S. and by W. till five. In the morning a thick fog; then it cleared up with fair weather, but somewhat close. After we had run some ten leagues W. and by S. we lost sight of the former land, but made other high land on our starboard, as far off as we could descry,[2] but we lost it again.

The wind continued all this day at S. a stiff steady gale, yet we bare all our sails, and stood W. S. W. About four in the afternoon we made land on our starboard bow, called the Three Turks' Heads, being a ridge of three hills upon the main, whereof the southmost is the greatest. It lies near Aquamenticus. We descried also another hill, more northward, which lies by Cape Porpus. We saw also, ahead of us, some four leagues from shore, a small [3]rock, not above a flight shot over, which hath a dangerous shoal to the E. and by S. of it, some two leagues in length. We kept our ||2luff|| and weathered it, and left it on our starboard about two miles off. Towards night we might see the trees in all places very plainly, and a small hill to the southward of the Turks' Heads. All the rest of the land to the S. was plain low land. Here we had a fine fresh smell from shore. Then, lest we should not get clear of the ledge of rocks, which lie under water from within a flight shot of the said rock, (called Boone Isle,) which we had now brought N. E. from us, towards Pascataquac, we tacked and stood S. E. with a stiff gale at S. by W.

Friday, 11.] The wind still S. W. close weather. We stood to and again all this day within sight of Cape Ann. The Isles of Shoals were now within two leagues of us, and we saw a ship lie there at anchor, and five or six shallops under sail up and down.

We took many mackerels, and met a shallop, which stood

||set|| ||2left||

---

1 But it is an island.

2 This was, undoubtedly, the White Hills, which the sun, at that season of the year, arrays in exquisite brilliance, frequently mistaken for that of clouds, as I have often observed.

3 "Called Boone Isle," is the governour's marginal note.

from Cape Ann towards the Isles of Shoals, which belonged to some English fishermen.[1]

Saturday, 12.] About four in the morning we were near our port. We shot off two pieces of ordnance, and sent our skiff to Mr. [2]Peirce his ship (which lay in the harbour, and had been there [blank] days before.) About an hour after, Mr. [3]Allerton came aboard us in a shallop as he was sailing to Pemaquid. As we stood towards the harbour, we saw another shallop coming to us; so we stood in to meet her, and passed through the narrow strait between Baker's Isle and Little Isle, and came to an anchor a little within the islands.

After Mr. Peirce came aboard us, and returned to fetch

---

1 Here is inserted, on a whole page of the original MS. a chart of the shore of Maine, Isles of Shoals, Boone Isle, Cape Ann, &c. with remarks on the appearance of the various landmarks on the several days, depth of water, bottom, bearings, distances, &c.

2 William Peirce deserves honourable mention among the early navigators between Old England and New. He made many voyages, of which the earliest known by me was in 1623, in the Ann, the sixth vessel, whose arrival in our bay, since the foundation of Plimouth, is mentioned. See Morton and Gov. Bradford in Prince, I. 114. 119. 121. 139. Edward Winslow, afterwards governour of Plimouth, and the celebrated commissioner of Cromwell in Admiral Penn's West India expedition, in that ship then returned with Peirce. He was, in 1629, in the Massachusetts Company's employment, master of the Mayflower, Haz. I. 278, and was now in the service of the Plimouth people, for whom, with Allerton, he had brought in the ship Lyon, this spring, from Bristol, many of their Leyden brethren. Hubbard unvaryingly, except on page 82, gives his name *Peirse*. So the Probate Record spells it, and so by himself, as I have seen, was it written. In another part of this volume his name will recur as the maker of the first American Almanack, viz. for 1639. He was killed at Providence, one of the Bahamas, in 1641, as will be seen in this History.

3 He was one of the principal men in Plimouth colony, of the memorable number of one hundred and one, who came in the first ship, and the first assistant chosen in that government. Dr. Eliot laments, that the later years of Allerton are not illustrated by publick services; but, we may presume, they would have been, had he, as our New England Biographer erroneously says, "spent the remainder of his days with the people of Plimouth." Notice of this gentleman will be found more than once in later portions of this work; and the reader, who would know of him all that diligent inquiry could redeem from oblivion, must consult the long-expected and invaluable edition of Morton's Memorial by Judge Davis. Hutchinson, whose accuracy of information may more generally be relied on than that of any other historian of any part of America, except original ones, I follow with some hesitation, when he tells us, he left this country for England to settle there, and adds, "his male posterity settled in Maryland. If they be extinct, Point Alderton, [in Boston harbour,] which took his name, will probably preserve it many ages." The latest notice of him I have found, is in the second volume of our County Registry of *Deeds*, p. 192, where is recorded a receipt by Isaac Allerton, senior, merchant, of New Haven, 29 November, 1653, for one hogshead and four barrels of mackerel from Evan Thomas, vintner, of Boston, to adventure for half profits. A letter, in my possession, of J. Davenport, 4 August, 1658, mentions *young* Allerton coming from the *Dutch* to New Haven.

Mr. [1]Endecott, who came to us about two of the clock, and with him Mr. [2]Skelton and Capt. [3]Levett. We that were of the assistants, and some other gentlemen, and some of the women, and our captain, returned with them to Nahumkeck, where we supped with a good venison pasty and good beer, and at night we returned to our ship, but some of the women stayed behind.

In the ||mean time most of our|| people went on shore upon

||morning the rest of the||

---

[1] This distinguished father of Massachusetts had, two years before, been sent to found the plantation, which was effected by the settlement of Salem, the oldest town in the colony. He had a commission from the company to act as governour, which was, of course, superseded by the arrival of Winthrop with the charter. With the history of his adopted country, that of Endecott is interwoven, till the time of his death, 15 March, 1665. He served four years as deputy governour, and sixteen years as governour, being at the head of administration a longer time than any other under the old patent, exceeded under the new charter by Shirley alone, and that only by one year. The farm, which he cultivated, remains in possession of an honourable descendant; and one pear tree, planted by the governour on it, is said still to repay his care.

[2] Samuel Skelton, pastor of Salem, came the year before in the same fleet with Higginson. The notices of his history are very brief; that of his death will be found in this volume, 2 August, 1634. His wife died 15 March, 1631, as we learn from Dudley, who says, "she was a godly and helpful woman; she lived desired, and died lamented, and well deserves to be honourably remembered."

[3] No satisfactory information has been obtained, by searching every quarter for some account of this gentleman, unless it may be he who died at sea about two years after this date, by which event some indiscreet letters fell into the hands of our adversaries, as will be seen in this work, 22 February, 1633. It might be conjectured, that we should identify him with Christopher Levett, *Esq.* named in 1623 by the council of New England, under the great charter, with Capt. Francis West and the governour of Plimouth for the time being, assistants to Robert Gorges, who had a commission to be general governour. But this is improbable; for those constituents were adversaries to our humble colony, and the representative would not have been at Salem on good terms with Endecott and Skelton; and that title seems hardly consistent with our text, being in those times very sparingly given, especially by Morton, the honest annalist of Plimouth, from whom all my information of that gentleman is derived. Nor do I more incline to the notion, that the person mentioned was Thomas Levet, who, with John Wheelwright, Augustine Story, Thomas Wite, and William Wentworth, is said to have purchased of four Indian sagamores, 17 May, 1629, a large tract of land in New Hampshire, by a very formal, though, it will be proved, a spurious deed, preserved in Belknap's New Hampshire, I. Appendix i. In that paper they are indeed called "all of the Massachusetts Bay in New England." The church of Exeter had in 1639, with Wheelwright, after his banishment from our colony, a member of that name, Haz. I. 463; but I imagine none of Wheelwright's followers had yet come to our country. From a long correspondence, in 1816 and 1817, with which the late Rev. Dr. Bentley of Salem favoured me, I obtained little more than his opinion that Winthrop here intended Lovett, one of Roger Conant's companions, ancestor of a numerous and respectable family in Beverly. But the arguments did not convince.

the land of Cape Ann, which lay very near us, and gathered store of fine strawberries.

An Indian came aboard us and lay there all night.

Lord's day, 13.] In the morning, the [1]sagamore of Agawam and one of his men came aboard our ship and stayed with us all day.

About two in the afternoon we descried the Jewel; so we manned out our skiff and wafted them in, and they went as near the harbour as the tide and wind would suffer.

Monday, 14.] In the morning early we weighed anchor, and the wind being against us, and the channel so narrow as we could not well turn in, we warped in our ship and came to an anchor in the inward harbour.

In the afternoon we went with most of our company on shore, and our captain gave us five pieces.

[Large blank.]

Thursday, 17.] We went to [2]Mattachusetts, to find out a place for our sitting down. We went up Mistick River about six miles.[3]

We lay at Mr. [4]Maverick's, and returned home on Satur-

---

1 Hubbard, 130, calls him Masconomo.

2 It would now seem strange to use this expression, 'From Salem we went to Massachusetts;' but the name, though sometimes more comprehensive, generally included only the country lying around the inner bay, usually called Boston harbour, from Nahant to Point Alderton.

3 We must presume the reckoning to be from Conant's, afterwards called Governour's, Island, on which now Fort Warren stands, or at least from Maverick's on Noddle's Island, because, being accustomed now to say, Mistick River empties into Charles River, or Boston harbour, at the easterly point of Charlestown, one would consider it little over three miles to the limit of boat navigation. The geography was then unknown or unsettled, and Mistick, at high tide, might as well appear the principal river, as Charles. Dudley speaks of Charlestown as "three leagues up Charles River," but he means undoubtedly to represent its mouth at the outer lighthouse.

4 Maverick was seated on Nottle's or Noddle's Island, and was a gentleman of good estate; but the time of his arrival in our country, I believe, has never been ascertained. As no assessment for the brief campaign against Merry Mount, 1628, is laid on him, perhaps he was not then here; yet I conclude from Johnson's language, lib. I. chap. xvii. he came in that year or the next. At a court 1 April, 1633, the first volume of our Colony Records, p. 96, informs us, "Noddle's Island is granted to Mr. Samuel Maverick, to enjoy to him and his heirs forever, yielding and paying yearly at the general court to the governour for the time being, either a fat wether, a fat hog, or £10 in money, and shall give leave to Boston and Charlestown to fetch wood continually, as their need requires, from the southern part of the said island." Winisemet Ferry, both to Charlestown and Boston, was also granted to him forever. Josselyn, who visited him 10 July, 1638, calls him, p. 12, "the only hospitable man in all the country, giving entertainment to all comers gratis;" but in the chronologi-

day. As we came [1]home, we came by Nataskott, and sent for Capt. Squib ashore—(he had brought the west-country people, viz. Mr. [2]Ludlow, Mr. [3]Rossiter, Mr. [4]Maverick, §&c. to the bay, who were set down at Mattapan,§)—and ended a [5]difference between him and the passengers; whereupon he

---

cal observations, p. 252, appended to his Voyages, he is strangely confounded, as the father of Samuel Maverick, Esq. the royal commissioner in 1664, with the Rev. John Maverick, minister of Dorchester. Samuel was not one of our church members, being, says Hutchinson, an Episcopalian. But so were all our fathers. Johnson, in the passage before referred to, designates him as "an enemy to the reformation in hand, being strong for the lordly prelatical power." This circumstance, perhaps, saved him from much trouble in the earlier years of his residence; but in the progress of this History he will be seen involved in difficulty with the party of Dr. Child, petitioners for enlargement of privileges. He died 10 March, 1664.

1 He means to Salem.

2 The name of Roger Ludlow often occurs in our early history. At the last general court of the company in England, he was chosen as assistant in the room of Samuel Sharp, who had the year before come over to Salem in the same ship with Skelton. He was one of the founders of Dorchester, whence, in about five years, he removed to Windsor, of which he may be called the father. In Connecticut he was deputy governour several times, but he seems to have been unquiet in his domicile, for in 1639 he removed from Windsor and founded Fairfield. In 1654 he removed in disgust to Virginia, where, perhaps, in his advanced years, he became stationary. Eliot has drawn his character with discrimination. From Hubbard, 165, we learn, that he was brother-in-law of Endecott, whom he rivalled in ardour of temperament.

3 Edward Rossiter, Esq. one of the assistants, Hutchinson informs us, was of a good family in the west of England, whence all the Dorchester people came. He was one of the principal encouragers of the settlement at that place, the first town in the ancient county of Suffolk, unless Quincy or Weymouth may dispute the honour. He died in a few months.

Of the Rev. John Maverick I learn nothing, before his coming to Dorchester, but that he had been a preacher about forty miles from Exeter in Old England, and after his arrival, so little, except what will be found in our History, during the few years of his life, that it may be unnecessary to prolong this note.

5 The cause of this difference, probably, is found in the landing of the passengers from the ship, in which they sailed 20 March, and arrived 30 May. Capt. Roger Clap, who was one of the sufferers, informs us in his brief memoirs, "when we came to Nantasket, Capt. Squeb, who was captain of that great ship of four hundred tons, would not bring us into Charles River, as he was bound to do, but put us ashore and our goods on Nantasket Point, and left us to shift for ourselves in a forlorn place in this wilderness;" and a little farther on, "Capt. Squeb turned ashore us and our goods, like a merciless man." Trumbull, in a note on I. p. 8, of his History of Connecticut, several of whose first settlers came in this vessel, says, the master "was afterwards obliged to pay damages for this conduct." He leaves us to conjecture his authority, which was perhaps a contemporaneous manuscript of some gentleman of greater age and distinction than Clap.

sent his boat to his ship, (the Mary and John,) and at our ||parting|| gave us five pieces. At our return we found the Ambrose in the harbour at Salem.

Thursday, July 1.] The Mayflower and the Whale arrived safe in Charlton harbour. Their passengers were all in health, but most of their cattle dead, (whereof a mare and horse of mine.) Some ||2stone|| horses came over in good plight.

Friday, 2.] The Talbot arrived there. She had lost fourteen passengers.

My son Henry [1]Winthrop was drowned at Salem.

Saturday, 3.] The Hopewell, and William and Francis arrived.

Monday, 5.] The Trial arrived at Charlton, and the Charles at Salem.

Tuesday, 6.] The Success arrived. She had [blank] goats and lost [blank] of them, and many of her passengers were near starved, &c.

Wednesday, 7.] The Lyon went back to Salem.[2]

Thursday, 8.] We kept a day of thanksgiving in all the plantations.

[Large blank.]

||firing|| ||2few||

---

[1] Delicacy permitted the author to say no more of this son, whose name in the original MS. is denoted only by the initials; but this brief sentence from Hubbard, 131, will be easily indulged: "A sprightly and hopeful young gentleman he was, who, though he escaped the danger of the main sea, yet was unhappily drowned in a small creek, not long after he came ashore, even the very next day, July the 2d, after his landing, to the no small grief of his friends, and the rest of the company." It will be recollected, that he, with Mr. Pelham, had accidentally lost his passage in the ship with his father, to find another in one of those remaining at Southampton. His father's touching notice of his untimely death will be found in the first letter to his wife from America, given in the Appendix A. From the language the conclusion is unavoidable, that the young man had been married before they came from England, leaving his wife with her mother-in-law; and from a previous letter, written 2 March after taking leave, she was, I presume, in an advanced state of pregnancy. The genealogy of the family mentions, that he married a Fones, probably his cousin, and left issue a daughter. He was the second son, and probably of the age of twenty-one or two years at his death.

[2] Whence she came *back*, is matter of conjecture, for in the text it has not been told, that she left Salem, after being first found by our author in that harbour on his arrival. I am induced to think, from a comparison of Prince, I. 201, 207, 241, contrary to his opinion of her landing Ashby at Penobscot in May, that she had gone there in June from Salem, being in the employment of the Plimouth people, probably, and not of ours. After this return our governour made a contract with the master to go to the nearest port in England for provisions.

Thursday, August 18.] Capt. Endecott and —— [1]Gibson were married by the governour and Mr. [2]Wilson.

Saturday, 20.] The French ship called the Gift came into the harbour at Charlton. She had been twelve weeks at sea, and lost one passenger and twelve goats; she delivered six.

Monday we kept a court.[3]

---

[1] In Prince, I. 178, is preserved a letter from Cradock in London to Endecott, of the year before, from which we learn, that Endecott brought a wife from England, of the time of whose death we are ignorant. Morton, the scandalous author of New English Canaan, insinuates, that she perished by the quackery of Fuller of Plimouth. Two seasons of disease had afflicted the colonists at Salem, and the highest seem, equally with the lowest, to have been exposed to its power. By the kindness of the late Rev. William Bentley, the diligent historian of Salem, I learn that the name of this second wife was Elizabeth, and, from our Probate Records, that she survived her husband.

[2] Of the Rev. John Wilson's biography abundant materials are furnished by this History and most other books about our early affairs, and most copiously by Mather, which are happily abbreviated by the amiable Eliot in his New England Dictionary, and Emerson in his History of the First Church. His will is in our Probate Records, VI. p. 1. Having been minister at Sudbury, he was well known to his neighbour, our author, before their undertaking this work of leaving their native country.

[3] Johnson says, this court was holden 23 August, on board the Arbella. As he adds, that Winthrop was then chosen governour, and Dudley deputy, which I agree with Prince in thinking improbable, since they had before been chosen in England, and our records have no trace of such election, it may also be doubted whether the assistants' meeting was held on shipboard. The record says, the court was at Charlton, and, we may imagine, the "great house" would have been the most convenient place. He is, however, right in his date, and the reader will remark, that, in noting events a few weeks before and after this time, the governour seems to fail of his usual diligence. It may be accounted for, either by his grief on account of his son's death, or anxiety from the extraordinary press of business in the circumstances of the new colony. The two preceding dates are erroneous. The 20th of August was Friday, not Saturday. Endecott's marriage, if it were on Thursday, was solemnized on the 19th, or if on the 18th it was Wednesday. The name of the month is indeed inserted, in the MS. not against the line in which the wedding is mentioned, but the next. But the dates before and after convince me, that August, and not July, is the date intended for Endecott's union; and I gather a slight confirmation of my judgment from the fact of his absence from this court.

The transactions of this *first* court are sufficiently interesting to excuse the extract from Prince, quoting the Colony Records: "Aug. 23. The first court of assistants held at Charlestown. Present Gov. Winthrop, Deputy Gov. Dudley, Sir Richard Saltonstall, Mr. Ludlow, Rossiter, Nowell, T. Sharp, Pynchon and Bradstreet; wherein the first thing propounded is, How the ministers shall be maintained, Mr. Wilson and Phillips only proposed; and ordered, that houses be built for them with convenient speed at the publick charge. Sir R. Saltonstall undertook to see it done at his plantation for Mr. Phillips; and the governour at the other plantation for Mr. Wilson; Mr. Phillips to have thirty pounds a year, beginning at the first of Sep-

Friday, 27.] We of the congregation kept a fast, and chose Mr. Wilson our [1]teacher, and Mr. [2]Nowell an [3]elder,

---

tember next; Mr. Wilson to have twenty pounds a year till his wife come over, beginning at 10 July last; all this at the common charge, those of Mattapan and Salem excepted. Ordered, that Morton of Mount Wollaston, be sent for presently; and that carpenters, joiners, bricklayers, sawyers and thatchers, take no more than two shillings a day, under pain of ten shillings to giver and taker."

Such was the first formal legislation of Massachusetts. But in March following, artificers were left at liberty to agree for their wages, Prince, II. 23, from Colony Records, though I am sorry to observe, that, two years after, the wisdom of experience was slighted, and the absurd policy of legal rates restored. For many years, this interference with the freedom of contracts was more or less severe, but the very means of enforcing it probably conduced to the abolition of the prejudice. It was left to the freemen of the several towns, from time to time, as occasion might require, to agree among themselves about the prices and rates of all workmen's labour and servants' wages; and to exceed those rates was made penal. In the adjustment, great diversity would soon arise in different places, to prevent which, it was provided, that if any town had cause of complaint against the freemen of any other town, for allowing greater wages than themselves, it should be in the power of the county court to adopt uniform regulations. During the war of our revolution, it is within the recollection of many, that, to counteract the inevitable embarrassment arising from the depreciation of the paper currency, arbitrary values were affixed to all commodities by an agreement, which was shown by experiment to be impracticable, after reason had in vain proved it unjust. See President Kirkland's Life of Fisher Ames, p. xi.

1 Between the offices of teacher and pastor there was, we know, some slight difference in the early times; for, on Cotton's arrival three years after, he was chosen teacher, Wilson having a year before been made pastor. Yet these terms, though at first distinct, soon became convertible, and not much can with certainty be known of the distinction. Eliot says—Biographical Dictionary, SKELTON,—"Mr. Skelton, being farther advanced in years, was constituted pastor of Salem church, Mr. Higginson teacher." That author, however, in his Essays on the Ecclesiastical History of Massachusetts, felt the same difficulty as I have; for he says, 1 Hist. Coll. VII. 271, "we, who make no such distinction of offices, think it strange, that there should have been such difference between pastor and teaching elders; for we suppose any man, who can feed the people with knowledge, is qualified for one office equally with another. But it appears from the ecclesiastical history of this country, that A VERY GREAT DISTINCTION was made in the early state of their settlement. They esteemed many to be excellent *teachers*, whom they would not endow with the pastoral care." This seems to me too strongly stated. Cotton was an older and a greater man than Wilson, yet the latter was pastor. Higginson cannot be postponed to Skelton, except for his years; and Maverick, the teacher of Dorchester, was older than Warham. Several instances in other towns of inferiority of the talents, if not character, of the pastor may be found, I think, in our early churches. Still the reason of Dr. Eliot's distinction may be supported by the rule of the clerical constitutions. See Trumbull, I. 282, 283, and the numerous authorities.

2 Increase Nowell, Esq. had been chosen an assistant in England, and was a person of high consideration in the colony, of which he was long secretary. He died, poor, 1 November, 1655. 3 Hist. Coll. I. 47.

3 This office of *ruling* elder was generally kept up hardly more than fifty years, though in a few churches it continued to the middle of the last century, much reduced, however, in importance, and hardly distinguishable

and Mr. Gager and Mr. [1]Aspinwall, deacons. We used imposition of hands, but with this protestation by all, that it was

---

from that of deacon. The title of elders is retained from the beginning as a name for ministers. Prince, I. 92, delineates from high authorities the difference between *teaching* and *ruling* elders, thus: "Pastors, or teaching elders, who have the power both of overseeing, teaching, administering the sacraments and ruling too, being chiefly to give themselves to studying, teaching and the spiritual care of the flock, are therefore to be maintained." "Mere ruling elders, who are to help the pastors in overseeing and ruling; that their offices be not temporary, as among the Dutch and French churches, but continual. And being also qualified in some degree to teach, they are to teach only occasionally, through necessity, or in their pastor's absence or illness; but being not to give themselves to study or teaching, they have no need of maintenance." In less than two years, it will be seen in this History, a question arose, whether the offices of magistrate and ruling elder might be filled at the same time by the same person. This may in our days appear quite unimportant, as the elder was not required to give himself to study or teaching, and was allowed no maintenance by the congregation. But in the primitive times it was so important, that our fathers of Boston took the advice of distant churches. Perhaps it was intended, by those who raised the inquiry, only to make Nowell lay down one of his titles. Happily he preferred to retain the station that demanded most service, and continued a magistrate.

The comparative disesteem, into which the office of ruling elder soon fell, was very pathetically lamented by many of the early planters in their later years. In a tract, by Joshua Scottow, 1691, under the whimsical title of "Old Men's Tears for their own Declensions, mixed with Fears of their and Posterities' further falling off from New England's primitive Constitution," this sad presage of portending judgments is thus treated: "It's not unknown, that some churches, in laying their foundation, did solemnly promise and covenant, before God, and one to another, that they would be furnished with two teaching and two ruling elders; but it's not attended to. It was not for want of maintenance; no, religion hath brought forth riches, but the daughter hath devoured the mother, as was said and observed of old."

"Where are the ruling elders, who as porters were wont to inspect our sanctuary gates, and to take a turn upon the walls? Is not the remembrance of such an officer almost lost and extinct, though the scripture and the platform of church discipline expressly declare for them, and set out their particular charge and work? It was an affecting question put forth by one of about fifty years old, born in the communion of our churches, concerning ruling elders, what these men were, who were formerly so called; professing, in time of their minority, there were such men to their remembrance, but since had forgotten what they were, and therefore desired resolution."

He proceeds to relate, that it is "questioned by some among us, whether such an officer be jure divino, or any rule for them in God's word, which occasions a reverend elder to take up the argument against such, and bewails the neglect of them in the churches, as a sad omen of their turning popular or prelatical, and if so, then to be regulated either by lord brethren or lord bishops. Is not this a great derogation from Christ's authority to say, that deacons may serve the churches' turn, who may officiate to do these elders' work? Is it not a preference of men's politicks before Christ's institutes? Did not the practice of men's prudentials prove the ruin of the churches and rise of Antichrist? That our colleges by God's blessing should afford materials for teaching elders, and that our churches should grow so barren, as not to bring forth, nor educate men qualified for the other, may seem to portend a threatening of Christ's departure from them, as to conjugal communion."

[1] Frequent notice of William Aspinwall will be found in this History.

only as a sign of election and confirmation, not of any intent that Mr. Wilson should renounce his ||ministry|| he received in England.

September 20.] Mr. [1]Gager died.

||money||

He had come over with his wife, I presume, in the fleet with Winthrop, and certainly was in high esteem with our people until the unhappy controversy about antinomianism, in which, being on the side of the majority of Boston church, he was too important to get off with impunity. With the other disfranchised or discontented members, he removed to Rhode Island, which they purchased 24 March, 1638, and was wise enough, after the heat subsided, to return. He was the first secretary of that colony. His official signature is found afterwards in our records, as notary publick, to protests of bills of exchange. I have seen a very curious tract, entitled, "A brief Description of the Fifth Monarchy, or Kingdom that shortly is to come into the World; the Monarch, Subjects, Officers and Laws thereof, and the surpassing Glory, Amplitude, Unity and Peace of that Kingdom, &c. And in the Conclusion there is added a Prognostick of the Time, when the Fifth Kingdom shall begin. By William Aspinwall. N. E." Its title page is garnished with several texts of scripture distorted in the usual style of that day. "London, printed by M. Simmons, and are to be sold by Livewell Chapman at the Crown in Popeshead Alley, 1653." It contains fourteen pages. After showing, "that there is such a thing to be expected in the world as a fifth monarchy," from Daniel's vision, fulfilled in part by the execution of Charles I., he anticipates a farther progress from the destruction of all other kings, though "they have a little prolonging in life granted after the death of Charles Stuart." He comforts himself with the confidence, that "the space will be short; it will be but for a season and time; and then will their lives go for it, as well as Charles; and then, these four monarchies being destroyed, the fifth kingdom or monarchy follows immediately." Proceeding through his inquiries of "the Sovereign, (Jesus Christ,) subjects, officers and laws of that kingdom," his fanatical vaticination favours us with "some hint of the time when the kingdom shall begin," which he had wit enough to delay so long, that the event might not probably injure the credit of the *living* soothsayer. "Know therefore, that the uttermost durance of Antichrist's dominion will be in the year 1673, as I have proved from scripture in a brief chronology, ready to be put forth." Cromwell, whose power was just then preparing to be established, knew well the dangerous tendency of such jargon, unless when used by himself; but though he applied the civil arm to many other dreamers of King Jesus, I believe he left the New England seer to the safety of oblivion or contempt. A more useful work, with a well-written preface by him, was two years after printed in London, by the same printer, for the same Chapman, with the ludicrous prænomen, "An Abstract of Laws and Government," &c. collected and digested by John Cotton of Boston in N. E. in his life time, presented to our General Court, "and now published after his death by William Aspinwall." This evidence of his talents is preserved in 1 Hist. Coll. V. 187. Our Registry of Births mentions, of his children, Edward, born 26 September, 1630, died 10 October following; Hannah, born 25 December, 1631; Elizabeth, (his wife's name,) born 30 September, 1633; Samuel, 30 September, 1635; Ethlan, 1 March, 1637; Dorcas, 14 February, 1640. But of him or his family we know nothing after some years. The respectable family bearing this name in our times is not descended from him, but Peter Aspinwall, from Lancashire, I think, in England, whose will is in our Register, lib. VIII. 67.

1 William Gager, whose election is mentioned in the former paragraph, Gov. Dudley calls "a right godly man, a skilful chyrurgeon." An al-

30.] About two in the morning, Mr. Isaac Johnson died; his wife, the lady Arbella, of the house of [1]Lincoln, being dead about one month before. He was a holy man, and wise, and died in sweet peace, leaving [2]some part of his substance to the colony.

The wolves killed six calves at Salem, and they killed one wolf.

Thomas [3]Morton adjudged to be imprisoned, till he were sent into England, and his house burnt down, for his many in-

---

lowance by the company, from the publick treasury, was made him, on account of his office, but this practice did not continue. He was reckoned of the governour's household; and his son John is remembered by our author in his will. See Appendix. This son was, probably, a youth, and went with the governour's son to New London, where, in September, 1659, he complained with others to the commissioners of the United Colonies against some Indian outrage. Haz. II. 412. The name is, perhaps, perpetuated by descendants in Connecticut; at least, in Trumbull, II. 532, a William Gager, of the second church of Lebanon, is among the ministers, 27 May, 1725.

1 Mather calls it "the best family of any nobleman then in England." Collins's Peerage informs us, that Thomas, third Earl of Lincoln, who was descended of a family that came in with William the Conqueror, had by one wife eight sons and nine daughters. Two sons and four daughters died young. One daughter, Frances, married John, son and heir of Sir Ferdinando Gorges; another, Susan, married John Humfrey; a third is the lady mentioned in the text. Dudley and Bradstreet, two other of our assistants, had lived many years in the family, so that a close relation to New England would be acknowledged by the brother of this lady, Theophilus, the fourth earl, who came to his title on the death of his father, 15 January, 1619. He was a warm patriot on the parliament's side in the civil war, but, after the captivity of the king, being inclined to moderation, was imprisoned and accused of treason by the usurping power of the army, which subverted, under Cromwell's direction, all the principles of the constitution. The earl was in reputation at the restoration, and bore a part in the solemnities of crowning Charles II., and his descendants, I believe, enjoy their hereditary honours with the augmented title of Duke of Newcastle.

2 Instead of *some*, was first written *a good.*

3 Notice of the court, at which this sentence passed, being the second, held 7 September, is omitted by the author. Prince, I. 248, gives, from the Colony Records, the proceedings at full length: "Ordered, that Thomas Morton of Mount Wollaston shall presently be set in the bilbowes, and after sent prisoner to England by the ship called the Gift, now returning thither; that all his goods shall be seized to defray the charge of his transportation, payment of his debts, and to give satisfaction to the Indians for a canoe he took unjustly from them; and that his house be burnt down to the ground in sight of the Indians, for their satisfaction for many wrongs he has done them."

This settlement at Mount Wollaston, called Merry Mount by Morton, had been begun in 1625, by Capt. Wollaston. In the Memorial of Nathaniel Morton, the pious secretary of Plimouth colony, a full history of its sufferings, perhaps an impartial one, may be found. The unhappy subject of this note had some years before been established at Weston's plantation at Wessaguscus. He informs us, in his book, that he arrived in June, 1622, of course, in the Charity. For this publication, called New English Canaan, by Thomas

juries offered to the Indians, and other misdemeanours. Capt. Brook, master of the Gift, refused to carry him.

[Large blank.]

Morton of Clifford's Inn, Gentleman, upon ten Years' Knowledge and Experiment of the Country, printed at Amsterdam by J. F. Stam, 1637, he undoubtedly repented, when again exposed to punishment here in 1644, as will be seen in the history of that time. This work is very rare, only one copy having ever been heard of by me, which is owned by his Excellency John Q. Adams. It is divided into three books; the first treating of the Indians; the second, of the natural history; the last, of the people planted there, their prosperity, what remarkable incidents have happened since, together with the tenets and practice of their church. This part, in thirty-one chapters, is written in an allegorical style, shadowing the principal characters under fictitious names, insomuch that it has to a great degree become hardly intelligible. Endecott suffers his vengeance under the appellation of Littleworth, and Winthrop is aptly called Joshua, and sirnamed Temperwell. Dedicating his work to the lords of the privy council, he says, "it is but a widow's mite, yet all that rapine and wrong hath left me to bring from thence." Laudatory verses are prefixed by Sir Chr. Gardiner and two others, and some of his own poetry is occasionally interspersed. In the 23 chapter of the third book, his own story of his sufferings is told, which we of this age may read without much injury to our forefathers' memory: "A court is called of purpose for mine host, he there convented, and must hear his doom, before he go. Nor will they admit him to capitulate, and know wherefore they are so violent to put such things in practice against a man they never saw before. Nor will they allow of it, though he decline their jurisdiction."

"There they all, with one assent, put him to silence, crying out, Hear the governour, Hear the governour, who gave this sentence against mine host at first sight," as above from the Records. He ascribes to the governour a reason, which the character of the age may induce us to believe was really uttered, "because the habitation of the wicked should no more appear in Israel."

He styles himself "of Clifford's Inn, Gent." but his namesake, the Memorialist, from whom all later authors have taken every thing to his discredit, calls him "a pettifogger at Furnival's Inn." No doubt he was a common disturber of the whole country, for the expenses of the expedition against him by Standish, in 1628, were assessed on eight different plantations, in several of which there was little religious sympathy with the worthies of Salem and Plimouth.

Thomas Morton is the first writer, who gave currency to a ludicrous report of a vicarious punishment, for which New England has been jeered at in former and later times. But justice to him requires me to add, that he mentions the fact only as a proposal, that was not agreed to, and thus overthrows the *possibility*, which Hubbard, 77, supposes, that justice "might be executed not on him that most deserved, but on him that could be best spared, or who was not like to live long, if he had been let alone."† Butler's Hudibras has admirably enlarged the ground-work, and decorated the edifice:

Our brethren of New England use
Choice malefactors to excuse,
And hang the guiltless in their stead,
Of whom the churches have less need.

---

† *He has indeed given the fact (which is put beyond doubt by the contemporary relation of Winslow) that the* guilty *man was hanged. See, Purchas's Pilg. lib. X. c.* 5, *Prince, I.* 131, *and* 1 *Hist. Coll. VIII.* 266.

Finch of Watertown had his wigwam burnt and all his goods.

[1]Billington executed at Plimouth for murdering one.

Mr. Phillips, the minister of Watertown, and others, had their [2]hay burnt.

The wolves killed some swine at Saugus.

---

* * * * * * * * * * * *
A precious brother having slain,
In time of peace, an Indian,
* * * * * * * * * * * *
The mighty †Tottipotimoy
Sent to our elders an envoy,
Complaining sorely of the breach
Of league, held forth by brother Patch.
* * * * * * * * *
For which he crav'd the saints to render
Into his hands, or hang the offender.
But they, maturely having weighed,
They had no more but him of the trade—
A man that served them in a double
Capacity, to preach and cobble—
Resolv'd to spare him ; yet to do
The Indian Hogan Mogan too
Impartial justice, in his stead did
Hang an old weaver that was bed-rid.

1 Of John Billington, and the circumstances of this case, it is remarkable, that no mention is made in Morton's New England Memorial, though written "with special reference to the first colony thereof, called Plimouth." Morton, the slanderer, alludes to the murder in a trifling manner. Something may be learned of it from Hubbard, 101, and Prince, II. 2, 3, extracting from Gov. Bradford's Register, a work unhappily lost. Hutchinson has perhaps digested all that can be known, in his Appendix, II. 413, in which he relates, that, on a doubt of their authority to inflict capital punishment, Winthrop's advice was sought and followed.

Billington had come over in the first ship, and was soon distinguished among that sober people ; for we find, Prince, I. 103, he was guilty of the *first offence* in the colony, being in March, 1621, "convented before the whole company for his contempt of the captain's lawful command with opprobrious speeches ; for which he is adjudged to have his neck and heels tied together." The family were four in number. John, his son, in the summer following, was five days lost in the woods, and preserved by the Indians. His son Francis had in January before discovered the lake, that from him has the name of Billington Sea. Gov. Bradford, writing to Cushman, June, 1625, says of the father, "Billington still rails against you, and threatens to arrest you, I know not wherefore ; he is a knave, and so will live and die." 1 Hist. Coll. III. 37. This is much nearer to prophecy than many sayings which have been so regarded.

2 Prince, II. 3, who had not then acquired so perfect a knowledge of the author's chirography, as his late experience furnished, in transcribing this passage, gave *houses*, instead of *hay*.

---

† *The poet may be excused for misappropriating the name of a sachem in Virginia.*

A cow died at Plimouth, and a goat at [1]Boston, with eating Indian corn.

October 23.] Mr. Rossiter, one of the assistants, died.

25.] Mr. [2]Colburn (who was chosen deacon by the congregation a week before) was invested by imposition of hands of the minister and elder.

The governour, upon consideration of the inconveniences which had grown in England by drinking one to another, restrained it at his own table, and wished others to do the like, so as it grew, by little and little, to disuse.[3]

29.] The Handmaid arrived at Plimouth, having been twelve weeks at sea, and spent all her masts, and of twenty-eight cows she lost ten. She had about sixty passengers, who came all well; John Grant, master.

Mr. Goffe wrote to me, that his shipping this year had utterly undone him.

She brought out twenty-eight heifers, but brought but seventeen alive.[4]

---

1 This is the first notice, in this work, of the name of the town, which had been given by the court of assistants, 7 September preceding, with those of Dorchester and Watertown. We may be confident, therefore, that the settlement had made good progress, though Gorges postpones it to the next spring.

2 William Colburn was a gentleman of great influence in Boston, and representative of the town in 1635, 6 and 7. The name is spelt with seven or eight variations, and his own signature, in a deed now before me, is Colbron, though the scrivener began, I, William Coleborne. He was long a ruling elder, after ceasing to be deacon, and died 1 August, 1662. His will is in our Probate office, lib. I. 400.

3 In the MS. volume of this work last found, I discovered a loose paper, containing reasons for a law against this custom, written, probably, by Winthrop, which appears sufficiently interesting, to inquirers into the customs of our fathers, to justify its insertion.

"(1.) Such a law as tends to the suppressing of a vain custom (quatenus it so doth) is a wholesome law. This law doth so,—ergo. The minor is proved thus: 1. Every empty and ineffectual representation of serious things is a way of vanity. But this custom is such: for it is intended to hold forth love and wishes of health, which are serious things, by drinking, which, neither in the nature nor use, it is able to effect; for it is looked at as a mere compliment, and is not taken as an argument of love, which ought to be unfeigned,—ergo. 2. To employ the creature out of its natural use, without warrant of authority, necessity or conveniency, is a way of vanity. But this custom doth so—ergo.

"(2.) Such a law as frees a man from frequent and needless temptations to dissemble love, &c. (quatenus it so doth) is a wholesome law. But this doth so—ergo."

On such arguments a law was passed, as may be seen, 10 mo. 1639, whose obligation is almost universally rejected, and probably unknown to more than reject it.

4 This is easily rendered consistent with loss of ten by supposing, that it

November 11.] The master came to Boston with Capt. [1]Standish and two gentlemen passengers, who came to plant here, but having no testimony, we would not receive them.

10.] [blank] Firmin of Watertown had his wigwam burnt. Divers had their hay-stacks burnt by burning the grass.

27.] Three of the governour's servants were from this day to the 1 of December abroad in his skiff among the islands, in bitter frost and snow, being kept from home by the N. W. wind, and without victuals. At length they gat to Mount [2]Wollaston, and left their boat there, and came home by land. Laus Deo.

December 6.] The governour and most of the assistants, and others, met at Roxbury, and there agreed to build a town fortified upon the neck between that and Boston, and a committee was appointed to consider of all things requisite, &c.

14.] The committee met at Roxbury, and upon further consideration, for reasons, it was concluded, that we could not have a town in the place aforesaid: 1. Because men would be forced to keep two families. 2. There was no running water; and if there were any springs, they would not suffice the town. 3. The most part of the people had built already, and would not be able to build again. So we agreed to meet at Watertown that day sen'night, and in the mean time other places should be viewed.

Capt. [3]Neal and three other gentlemen came hither to us.

---

became necessary to kill one for food, as the unusual length of the passage would induce them. I do not think the governour erased this sentence.

1 Miles Standish is treated by Dr. Belknap, in his American Biography, with such felicity, that it cannot be necessary for me to protract this note any further than to advise the reader, who desires more knowledge of him, to obtain Judge Davis's edition of Morton.

2 For some account of the first settlement in this place, which is the north-eastern promontory of Quincy, formerly of Braintree, see note on page 34.

3 Walter Neal, whose name will occur several times in the early parts of this History, had, in September preceding, as appears from the letter of Thomas Eyre, in Belknap's N. H. I. Appendix ii. promised to discover the lakes, in which the chief purpose of his employers probably was to secure a monopoly of the beaver trade. The vessel, as is before mentioned in the text, p. 7, had been fitted out in March, perhaps with Neal on board, to join, as was thought, the fleet, which brought Winthrop and his companions; but from her not joining, they feared she had been captured by the Dunkirkers. As the scheme of the adventurers would require secrecy and despatch, perhaps the report of their intention to join our fleet was only a pretence. She arrived late in May; for the letter of Eyre acknowledges "a good account of your times spent from the first of June." Neal left New England in August, 1633, as appears in this work and articles vi. vii. and viii. of the Ap-

He came in the bark Warwick this summer to Pascataqua, sent as governour there for Sir Ferdinando Gorges and others.

21.] We met again at Watertown, and there, upon view of a place a mile beneath the town, all agreed it a fit place for a [1]||fortified|| town, and we took time to consider further about it.

24.] Till this time there was (for the most part) fair, open weather, with gentle frosts in the night; but this day the wind came N. W. very strong, and some snow withal, but so cold as some had their fingers frozen, and in danger to be lost. Three of the governour's servants, coming in a shallop from Mistick, were driven by the wind upon [2]Noddle's Island, and forced to stay there all that night, without fire or food; yet, through God's mercy, they came safe to Boston next day, but the fingers of two of them were blistered with cold, and one swooned when he came to the fire.

26.] The rivers were frozen up, and they of Charlton could not come to the sermon at Boston till the afternoon at high water.

Many of our cows and goats were forced to be still ||[2]abroad|| for want of houses.

28.] Richard [3]Garrett, a shoemaker of Boston, and one of the congregation there, with one of his daughters, a young maid, and four others, went towards Plimouth in a shallop, against the advice of his friends; and about the Gurnett's Nose

||beautiful|| ||[2]aboard||

---

pendix above-mentioned; and nothing more is known of him, but the forgery of his name to a deed, as a witness, a little more than a year before the probable date of his first arrival.

1 Dr. Holmes, in his History of Cambridge, 1 Hist. Coll. VII. 6, and American Annals, I. 262. note 1, was led into errour by the former edition of this work. "A fit place for a *beautiful* town" it certainly was; but our fathers, at that time, were chiefly solicitous for the *security* of their dwellings. This note, however, is made, not so much to correct the mistake, as to express my high sense of the value of that writer's labours. His accuracy is wonderfully preserved through two large volumes, surpassing that of all other authors on American history, except Prince, the interruption of whose work is a misfortune that can never be compensated, because we can never retrieve the loss of his materials.

2 Prince, II. 29, giving the names of several admitted, in May following, freemen of the colony, among whom is William Noddle, adds in a note, "Perhaps Noddle's Island might derive its name from him."

3 The word is printed thus by me, although the governour's MS. rather looks like Garrard, because that was the true name of the sufferer. Prince makes the same correction, taking the story from our author. Hubbard, 138, has it Garn; but the *original* MS. of that author, who borrowed wholly from Winthrop, was, perhaps, more faithful in its representation. In the First Church Records, I find Garrett's name, as a member, No. 55, and he was, undoubtedly, one of the passengers in the fleet of 1630.

the wind overblew so much at N. W. as they were forced to come to a ||killock|| at twenty fathom, but their boat drave and shaked out the ||[2]stone,|| and they were put to sea, and the boat took in much water, which did freeze so hard as they could not free her; so they gave themselves for lost, and, commending themselves to God, they disposed themselves to die; but one of their company espying land near Cape Cod, they made shift to hoist up part of their sail, and, by God's special providence, were carried through the rocks to the shore, where some gat on land, but some had their legs frozen into the ice, so as they were forced to be cut out. Being come on shore they kindled a fire, but, having no hatchet, they could get little wood, and were forced to lie in the open air all night, being extremely cold. In the morning two of their company went towards Plimouth, (supposing it had been within seven or eight miles, whereas it was near fifty miles from them.) By the way they met with two Indian squaws, who, coming home, told their husbands that they had met two Englishmen. They thinking (as it was) that they had been shipwrecked, made after them, and brought them back to their wigwam, and entertained them kindly; and one of them went with them the next day to Plimouth, and the other went to find out their boat and the rest of their company, which were seven miles off, and having found them, he holp them what he could, and returned to his wigwam, and fetched a hatchet, and built them a wigwam and covered it, and gat them wood (for they were so weak and frozen, as they could not stir;) and Garrett died about two days after his landing; and the ground being so frozen as they could not dig his grave, the Indian hewed a hole about half a yard deep, with his hatchet, and having laid the corpse in it, he laid over it a great heap of wood to keep it from the wolves. By this time the governour of Plimouth had sent three men to them with provisions, who being come, and not able to launch their boat, (which with the strong N. W. wind was driven up to the high water mark,) the Indian returned to Plimouth and fetched three more; but before they came, they had launched their boat, and with a fair southerly wind were gotten to Plimouth, where another of their company died, his flesh being mortified with the frost; and the two who went towards Plimouth died also, one of them being not able to get thither, and the other had his feet so frozen as he died of it after. The girl escaped best, and one [1]Harwood, a godly man of the congrega-

||hillock|| ||[2]stern||

[1] Harwood was one of the earliest brethren of the church, being No. 27. From the Colony Records, I. 82, it may be learned, that our court of as-

tion of Boston, lay long under the surgeon's hands; and it was above six weeks before they could get the boat from Plimouth; and in their return they were much distressed; yet their boat was very well manned, the want whereof before was the cause of their loss.

January.] A house at Dorchester was burnt down.

February 11.] Mr. [1]Freeman's house at Watertown was burned down, but, being in the day time, his goods were saved.

5.] The ship Lyon, Mr. William Peirce master, arrived at Nantasket. She brought Mr. [2]Williams, (a godly ||minis-

---

sistants, 16 August following, ordered, "that the executors of Richard Garrett shall pay unto Henry Harwood the sum of twenty nobles, according to the proportion that the goods of the said Richard Garrett shall amount unto." This looks little like satisfaction of a debt, legally considered, and must, I think, be a provision, out of the estate of the dead, for the danger and suffering, into which the living man had been led by him. As such it may be considered an imitation of oriental jurisprudence.

1 Samuel Freeman, I am told, came from Devonshire, and was one of the chief planters at Watertown. His name is in the list of persons *desiring* to be made freemen, Prince, II. 4; but the record of his admission I find not till seven or eight years after. Tradition in the family informs of his return home. His elder son, Henry, it is said, died in 1672, on the paternal estate, and that branch of the family ceased with his grandchildren. Edmund Freeman, one of the earliest settlers at Sandwich, assistant of Plimouth colony in 1640 and following years, and John Freeman, one of the fathers of Eastham, assistant in that colony in 1660 and following years, are by tradition reported to have been brothers of this Watertown gentleman; but it is not known whether it were a son or grandson Edmund, who in 1646 married Rebecca, daughter of Gov. Prence, who had previously married his widowed mother. Part of the governour's estate at Eastham is still enjoyed by descendants of the Freeman race. This name is extremely common in the county of Barnstable, and has sent out its branches to other parts widely. My friend, the Rev. Dr. James Freeman, of this city, is great, great, great grandson of the first Samuel. Watertown Records show, "Samuel, the son of Samuel and Apphia Freeman, born 11 (3,) 1638."

2 The biography of Roger Williams deserves much more attention than it has ever received, but would lead me too far from my present undertaking, even were not the attempt to do full justice to his merit above my ability. In our common books he is said to have studied at the University of Oxford, and his life proves he had there learned more than in that day was commonly taught. Had Belknap lived to enlarge the number of volumes of his American Biography, his assiduity and judgment would have raised this pilgrim, whose name for some generations was oppressed with calumny, to a rank inferiour, non longo intervallo, only to the two Winthrops, Bradford and Penn. For the effect that bigotry and folly produced in Massachusetts, we refer to Hubbard, 208, who transcribed his facts from Morton, and to Mather, too long the chief authority in our ecclesiastical affairs, though justice was done nearly ninety years since by the reverend historian of Rhode Island. From the utter condemnation that most of our theologians of the first and second generation denounced against him, for vindicating the liberty of worshipping God according to the light of conscience, Williams was partially preserved by an inconsistency, to

ter,||[1]) with his wife, Mr. [2]Throgmorton, [blank] Perkins, [blank] ||[2]Ong,||[3] and others, with their wives and children, about twenty

||man|| ||[2]Augre||

which he was led in the latter years of his life by aversion to the Quakers; and this temporary change to intolerance gained him the title of "child of light," which the blameless policy and virtue of a long administration in the flourishing plantation of Providence had not deserved. The amiable historian of Salem, and the author of New England Biographical Dictionary, were, in our times, the first to confer due honour on his character. The examination *provoked* by the former does little injury to any but the writer of Remarks in 1 Hist. Coll. VII. introd. Deficiency in all former accounts of this great, *earliest* assertor of religious freedom, will, we may hope, soon be supplied by a gentleman, whose elegance and perspicuity of style are already known. Several quires of original letters of Williams have been seen by me, transcribed by or for the Rev. Mr. Greenwood of this city; and other materials are abundant. He lived to a good old age, and deserves peculiar honour from virtuous politicians for his conduct to the Indians, and from men of science for his researches into their language. In Benedict's General History of the Baptists, I. 473, it is said, that he received a liberal education under the patronage of the great Sir Edward Coke. The authority for this is the records of Williams's own church at Providence. I have examined that volume, and regret to say, that it was compiled within sixty years, probably by Gov. Hopkins. He is there said to have studied the law with the same oracle, but perhaps it was rather under his advice. The traditions in this case may be worth more than such traditions usually are. Williams certainly displays a knowledge of general principles of equity and jurisprudence beyond many practitioners of the science in that time, after all allowances for his rigid rejection of many harmless points, which will be disclosed in this History.

1 In the original MS. this word has been tampered with, perhaps by some zealot; yet it appears clearly enough to be Winthrop's usual abbreviation for that which is restored in the text, and Prince read it as I do.

2 John Throgmorton, from a note in Hutchinson, I. 371, it appears, was thought, by the fiery Hugh Peter, worthy of the same persecution that drove Williams to Providence. The original letter is preserved by our Historical Society. From Callender we learn, that he followed his spiritual guide, and by him he is mentioned in a letter of 1638, 3 Hist. Coll. I. 172. The name is perpetuated at Salem, as the Rev. Dr. Bentley informed me, by Throgmorton's Cove.

3 This word has perplexed me much. It was certainly given wrong in the former edition, for the first letter is a capital *O*. Presuming that the others were *n*, *y*, *e*, and that the governour wrote the word as frequently pronounced, I once inserted Olney, with much confidence in the substitution, as by Salem church Thomas Olney was excommunicated, Hutchinson, I. 371, for uniting in the errours with Williams. But it is actually written Onge, a name so unusual, that it was not adopted before I found, by Watertown Records, Frances Ong, widow, buried 12 (9,) 1638, and in our County Register, 1643, a mortgage to the children of the deceased, and in 1646 a deed from Simon Onge of that town.

Of Perkins, I am less able to speak with certainty, because the name is very common, but conclude he was not the man designed in an order of our assistants, 3 April, 1632, "that no person whatsoever shall shoot at fowl upon Pullen Point or Noddle's Island, but that the said places shall be preserved for John Perkins to take fowl with nets," Mass. Rec. I. 85; for he is

passengers, and about two hundred tons of goods. She set sail from Bristol, December 1. She had a very tempestuous passage, yet, through God's mercy, all her people came safe, except [1]Way his son, who fell from the spritsail yard in a tempest, and could not be recovered, though he kept in sight near a quarter of an hour. Her goods also came all in good condition.

8.] The governour went aboard the Lyon, riding by Long Island.

9.] The Lyon came to an anchor before Boston, where she rode very well, notwithstanding the great drift of ice.

10.] The frost brake up; and after that, though we had many ||snows|| and sharp frost, yet they continued not, neither were the waters frozen up as before. It hath been observed, ever since this bay was [2]planted by Englishmen, viz. seven years, that at this day the frost hath broken up every year.

||storms||

---

the same, whose sentence for drunkenness is given by Hutchinson, I. 385. But the gentleman mentioned in the text, probably, sat down, with Williams and his other fellow passengers, at Salem; to confirm which opinion, the reverend historian of that town assured me, that, from the earliest time, the name of Perkins has been found in possession of estates in that part of Salem since become Topsfield.

1 Way was, probably, of Dorchester, as, I presume, the name again occurring, 26 July next, refers to the same person, who was one of the principal men in that town.

2 This planting in Boston harbour deserves and will reward inquiry. In the autumn of 1622 Weymouth, under the aboriginal name of Wessaguscus, Wessaguscussett, Wessagussett, Wichaguscussett, or Wessagusquassett, had been planted by a small colony from England, sent by Thomas Weston; but the settlement was broken up the following year. See Winslow's Relation, 1 Hist. Coll. VIII. 248—271. A company under Capt. Robert Gorges, (son of Sir F.) together with the Rev. William Morell, reoccupied the same spot in a few months after. They, in November, 1623, lost all their goods and provisions at Plimouth by a fire, occasioned by the carelessness of the sailors celebrating, I presume, the anniversary of the gunpowder plot with less discretion than loyalty. From this and other misfortunes, the design was next year relinquished. See Bradford, in Prince, I. 141—144. Morell continued above a year in the country, and wrote a poetical, but not very particular account of the land and its productions, reprinted in English and Latin, 1 Hist. Coll. I. 125. Perhaps some stragglers remained on the soil. In 1625 Mount Wollaston was occupied by the captain of that name. This was in Quincy. Here was that disorderly band, among whom Morton, of whom see page 34, exhibited his talent for mischief. This settlement, I believe, was permanent, though the high authority of Gov. Dudley's Narrative, 1 Hist. Coll. VIII. 37, makes it vanish; and, if permanent, must be considered the oldest of Massachusetts colony, unless Weymouth should assert a claim of vitality through its state of suspended animation. Hubbard, 107, informs us, that, the same year, Nantasket was planted by Lyford, Oldham and Conant, persons discontented with the unseasonable rigour of their brethren of Plimouth. Not long,

The poorer sort of people (who lay long in tents, &c.) were much afflicted with the scurvy, and many died, especially at

---

however, did they remain there; at least Lyford and Conant went to Cape Ann, where some gentlemen of Dorchester, in Old England, attempted to establish a fishing station; but Conant soon removed thence to Salem, where Endecott, in 1628, found him. Hutchinson, I. 15, makes this last removal of Conant to be in the autumn of 1626, and adds, "I find mention made of planters at Winisimet about the same time, who probably removed there from some of the other plantations." From Hubbard, 105, we learn, that David Thomson, a Scotchman, who had been sent over in 1623 by Gorges, Mason and their associates, and had sat down at Piscataqua, "removed down into Massachusetts Bay within a year after." But I doubt, that Hubbard, who is not usually precise, except when he copies, has antedated this emigration of Thomson; for Gov. Bradford, in Prince, I. 161, mentions his abiding at Piscataqua in 1626. The business, however, in which he united, in the summer of that year, with the Plimouth colonists, seems to have been connected with an intention of seeking better quarters, which he found in an island of our harbour that has ever since borne his name. This island, with the neck of land (Squantum) on the neighbouring continent, Hubbard, from the Colony Records, says, "was confirmed to him and his heirs by the court of Massachusetts."

Of the exact time when Maverick first pitched his tent on Noddle's Island, or Thomas Walford at Charlestown, or William Blackstone at Boston, we shall, probably, remain forever uninformed. Walford was found in possession by the Spragues, who went from Salem soon after arriving there in 1628. That Blackstone had occupied our peninsula several years, and with no slight advantage, we may presume from the expenses assessed on the several plantations, from Plimouth northward, for the campaign against Morton at Merry Mount, in 1628; his proportion, though the least, being more than one third of that to be paid by the settlers at Salem, before the coming of Endecott. With him, too, was probably included the Winisimet people, if there were any, and Walford and Maverick, if they had dwellings. The apportionment of the charges, from Bradford, in 1 Hist. Coll. III. 63, is interesting:

Plimouth	£2.10	Natascot	£1.10
Naumkeak	1.10	Thomson	0.15
Pascataquack	2.10	Blackston	0.12
Jeffrey and Burslem	2.00	Edward Hilton	1.00
		Total	£12.7

It is not in my power to determine the residence of Jeffery and Burslem, but conjecture would fix it either at Cape Ann, or, more probably, Weymouth, from the latter town a Mr. Bursley being found a deputy so early as 1636.

Blackstone removed a few years after Winthrop's arrival, and seated himself about thirty-five miles to the southward, near the place which the famous Roger Williams soon rendered illustrious by the name of Providence, where a river, which flows into the harbour of that city, still bears the name of this pilgrim. See a memoir in 2 Hist. Coll. X. 170, which gives the time of his death 26 May, 1675, and contains all that the assiduous antiquary of Plimouth could rescue from the shades of forgetfulness. I am able to add only, that by our Colony Records he took the freeman's oath 18 May, 1631, being the first admission, and that in our Town Records it appears he "was married to Sarah Stephenson, widow, 4 July, 1659, by John Endecott, governour." He well improved his new estate, and the apples on his farm were long in high repute. 2 Hist. Coll. IX. 174.

Boston and [1]Charlestown; but when this ship came and ||brought store|| of juice of lemons, many recovered speedily. It hath been always observed here, that such as fell into discontent, and lingered after their former conditions in England, fell into the scurvy and died.

18.] Capt. [2]Welden, a hopeful young gentleman, and an experienced soldier, died at Charlestown of a consumption, and was buried at Boston with a military funeral.

Of the old planters, and such as came the year before, there

||brought us good stores||

An approximation to the time of Blackstone's coming to Boston is easily obtained. Lechford, who wrote in 1641, thus speaks of him: "One Mr. Blackstone, a minister, went from Boston, having lived there *nine* or *ten* years, because he would not join with the church; he lives near Mr. Williams, but is far from his opinions." Now, to ascertain when he withdrew from this spot first planted by him, is all that remains, and we may find reason, I believe, to reckon it the spring of 1635. That he was unjustly driven away, is an opinion not to be entertained for a moment. As all the right of soil, which the government at home could give, was by the charter given to our governour and company, we shall be convinced of the equity in their treatment, by reading their Records, I. 97. At a court, 1 April, 1633, "It is agreed, that Mr. Wm. Blackstone shall have fifty acres of ground set out for him near to his house in Boston to enjoy forever." All this right he sold next year to the other inhabitants, of whom none, now recollected, had so large a portion. See the depositions of Odlin, Walker, Hudson and Letherland about this purchase, 2 Hist. Coll. IV. 202. This evidence, taken after the tyrannical proceedings in chancery in 1683, against our charter, showed that all titles were in danger on our side of the ocean, states the price agreed to be six shillings for every householder in town, still reserving six acres for the grantor. The Town Records of that day, on the second *surviving* page, confirm the evidence: "10 November, 1634, at a general meeting upon publick notice, it was agreed that Edmund Quincy, Samuel Wilbore, William Balstone, Edward Hutchinson the elder, and William Cheeseborough the constable, shall make and assess all these rates, viz. a rate for £30 to Mr. Blackstone, a rate for cow's keeping, &c. &c." This sum was, undoubtedly, the consideration for his sale, and, taking from the depositions the proportion for each, would show the number of householders one hundred. I desire the reader to correct an errour in Shaw's Description of Boston, 308, where he has *Blackstone*, instead of Balstone, one of a committee in this month to divide the lands among the inhabitants. Blackstone probably removed the following spring. If so, and he had resided here as long as Lechford, who visited him at his new plantation, reports, he arrived at Boston in 1625 or 1626.

1 This is the first instance of thus spelling the name.

2 By Dudley, 1 Hist. Coll. VIII. 45, the loss of this gentleman is lamented in these terms: "Amongst others, who died about this time, was Mr. Robert Welden, who, in the time of his sickness, we had chosen to be captain of one hundred foot, but before he took possession of his place, he died, the *sixteenth* of February, and was buried as a soldier, with three vollies of shot." Our MS. is very plain in its date, and the discrepancy may be reconciled by referring it to the funeral honours, though Prince, II. 20, was not of this opinion. No. 91 of the members of Boston church is, "Elizabeth Welden, gone to Watertown," perhaps the widow of the captain.

were but two, (and those servants,) which had the scurvy in all the country. At Plimouth not any had it, ||no not|| of those, who came this year, whereof there were above sixty. Whereas, at their first planting ||[2]there,|| near the half of their people died of it.

A shallop of Mr. [1]Glover's was cast away upon the rocks about Nahant, but the men were saved.

Of those which went back in the ships this summer, for fear of death or famine, &c. many died by the way and after they were landed, and others fell very sick and low, &c.

The Ambrose, whereof Capt. Lowe was master, being new masted at Charlton, spent all her masts near Newfoundland, and had perished, if Mr. Peirce, in the Lyon, who was her consort, had not towed her home to Bristol. Of the other [2]ships which returned, three, viz. the Charles, the Success, and the Whale, were set upon by Dunkirkers, near Plimouth in England, and after long fight, having lost many men, and being much torn, (especially the Charles,) they gat into Plimouth.

The provision, which came to us this year, came at excessive rates, in regard of the dearness of corn in England, so as every bushel of wheat meal stood us in fourteen shillings, peas eleven shillings, &c. Tonnage was at £6.11.[3]

||nor out|| ||[2]time||

---

[1] John Glover was one of the chief men of Dorchester, and many times a deputy in the general court, from which station his services raised him to be an assistant. Johnson, lib. I. chap. xlv. calls him "a man strong for the truth, a plain, sincere, godly man, and of good abilities."

[2] A strange misapprehension by Hubbard, 140, who postpones to the following spring the voyage of these ships returning in the autumn, after bringing to this country the colony, with the relation of which our History begins, arose solely from his failing to observe, that the report of their disasters was brought hither by the Lyon, which, after towing one of them, the Ambrose, home, had left England, 1 December. His mistake would have been impossible, had he, as Prince, II. 19, combined the more perspicuous narrative of Dudley, on this subject, with that of Winthrop.

[3] We find this last sentence in the margin of the original MS. The extremity of want here, before the arrival of the Lyon, may be judged of from the anticipations announced by Winthrop in his letters. See Appendix. Mather says, probably from tradition, that the governour "was distributing the last handful of meal in the barrel unto a poor man distressed by the wolf at the door;" and the language of Capt. Clap, one of the sufferers, Prince II. 10, is much more satisfactory, because less figurative. Having been furnished with an original letter of the venerable John Rogers, of Dedham in Old England, father of *our* Nathaniel, addressed, probably, in November, 1630, to John Winthrop, jun. at Bristol, "or, in his absence, to Mr. Pelham of Buers," on this *foreseen* evil, I think it worth insertion:

22.] We held a day of thanksgiving for this ship's arrival, by order from the governour and council, directed to all the plantations.

"Good Mr. Winthrop,—I hope you have my letters with certain moneys that I sent to you to intreat you, of all love, to provide some little matter of butter and meal for such as I named, wherein I earnestly entreat your loving faithfulness and care to procure it and direct it to them, to Jeffery Ruggles, late of Sudbury, he is the chief. But this day I have received so lamentable a letter from one John Page, late of Dedham, that hath his wife and two children there, and he certifies me, that unless God stir up some friends to send him some provision, he is like to starve. Now I pity the man much, and have sent you twenty shillings, entreating you, for God's sake, to provide such a barrel of meal as this money will reach unto, and direct it over to John Page with this my letter enclosed. In which I pray God move your heart to be very careful, for it stands upon their lives; and it cuts me to the heart to hear that any of our neighbours should be like to famish. If we could possibly help to prevent it, I should be glad. So, ceasing to trouble you farther, I commend you and the weighty business you are about to the blessing of Almighty God, who speed it happily.

"I sent a letter to your father, which was directed to Mr. Harwood. I beseech you be a help to the safe sending of it.

Your worship's in the Lord,
JOHN ROGERS.

"Good Mr. Pelham,—If, in Mr. Winthrop's absence, this letter should come to your hand, I beseech you, good Sir, that you would be so good as fulfil the contents of it. I shall be much thankful unto you."

The Charlestown Records mention, that a fast had been appointed for the next day after this ship's coming, but this happy arrival caused the government to order a thanksgiving.

I have the original bill of Capt. Peirce for the governour's stores, as follows:

Provisions to be made at Bristol for the worshipful John Winthrop, Governour.

	£. s.d.
Wheat meal, 34 hhds. cont'g 8 bushels per hhd. at 8*s*. 6*d*. per bush.	115. 2.0
Peas, 15 hhds. cont'g 7 bushels, at 6*s*. per bushel	32. 2.0
Oatmeal, 4 hhds. cont'g 32 bushels, at 10*s*. per bushel	16. 0.0
Beef and pork, 4 hhds	24. 0.0
Cheese, 15 cwt. at 30*s*. per cwt. cask and all	22.10.0
Butter, 5 kinderkins, at 38*s*	9.10.0
Suet, 6 firkins	8. 0.0
Seed barley, 14 bushels	2.16.0
Seed rye, 1 hhd	1.10.0
Oakum, 1 cwt	0.12.0
For 20 (unknown) of cask, at 14*s*	7. 0.0
For haling, craneing and lightering, at 2*s*. 8*d*	2.13.4
For one half freight	40. 0.0
	280.11.4
More paid out to the apothecary for provision, for the cask	6. 6.4
Paid out for Samuel Sampson for his passage	3. 0.0
Paid him more for to bring him up to London	1.10.0
Paid more for him for physick and diet at Bristol	2.10.0
Paid for 300 trees	6. 0.0
	299.17.8

March 16.] About noon the chimney of Mr. [1]Sharp's house in Boston took [2]fire, (the splinters being not clayed at the top,) and taking the thatch burnt it down, and the wind being N. W. drove the fire to Mr. Colburn's house, being [blank] rods off, and burnt that down also, yet they saved most of their goods.

23.] [3]Chickatabot came with his sannops and squaws, and presented the governour with a ||hogshead|| of Indian corn.

||bushel||

---

1 Thomas Sharp, Esq. was an assistant chosen in England, and probably a passenger in the fleet with Winthrop; for he was present at the first court here, and the last in England on board the Arbella. He is the sixth member of Boston church. We conclude, that he made no preparations for rebuilding his house; for in a fortnight after this disaster he left America, and no account of his return is known. Nor was this the only misfortune that might induce him to go home: the death of his daughter, perhaps, had before fixed his resolution, if she deserved to be valued above, or even equally, with the wives of Johnson, Phillips, Coddington and Pynchon, as by Dudley, 1 Hist. Coll. VIII. 44: "Upon the third of January died the daughter of Mr. Sharp, a godly virgin, making a comfortable end, after a long sickness. The plantation here received not the like loss of any woman, since we came hither, and therefore she well deserves to be remembered in this place."

Another Sharp, Samuel, perhaps brother of Thomas, had been, in England, chosen an assistant, but was superseded before embarking, because the company then designed to consider themselves a corporation in London. They, however, desired Endecott to regard him as united in the commission with others, for his advisers. He accompanied Skelton in the George Bonadventure, and while on his passage, the deed of the Indian sachems to Wheelwright and others of the lower part of New Hampshire, to which his name as a witness is forged, purports to be executed. His friends, I presume, were restrained from choosing him an assistant again by that scruple, of the propriety of uniting in the same person the offices of ruling elder and magistrate, which compelled Nowell to forego the least honourable service. Elder Sharp died in 1658, as the historian of Salem writes, 1 Hist. Coll. VI. 243.

2 Gov. Dudley's account of this fire, 1 Hist. Coll. VIII. 46, seems worth transcribing, with the judicious comment: "The like accident of fire also befel Mr. Sharp and Mr. Colburn, upon the seventeenth of this March; both whose houses (which were as good and as well furnished as the most in the plantation) were in two hours space burned to the ground, together with much of their household stuff, apparel and other things; as also some goods of others, who sojourned with them in their houses; God so pleasing to exercise us with corrections of this kind, as he hath done with others. For the prevention whereof in our new town, intended this summer to be builded, we have ordered, that no man there shall build his chimney with *wood*, nor cover his house with thatch, which was readily assented unto; for that divers other houses have been burned since our arrival."

3 This sachem lived near the Neponset River, probably on the eastern side, as there Wood, in his map, 1634, places his wigwam, but his power, no doubt, reached several miles around. Dudley, who calls him Chickatalbot, says, he oppressed Weston's plantation, and intended to destroy it. Notice of his death will be found November, 1633. His son, Josiah, grandson, Jeremy, and great grandson, Charles Josiah, succeeded in the humble sovereignty. See the excellent History of Dorchester, 1 Hist. Coll. IX. 160, 161.

After they had all dined, and had each a small cup of sack and beer, and the men tobacco, he sent away all his men and women, (though the governour would have stayed them, in regard of the rain and thunder.) Himself and one squaw and one sannop stayed all night, and, being in English clothes, the governour set him at his own table, where he behaved himself as soberly, &c. as an Englishman. The next day after dinner he returned ||home,|| the governour giving him cheese and peas and a mug and some other small things.

26.] [1]John Sagamore and James his brother, with divers sannops, came to the governour to desire his letter for recovery of twenty beaver skins, which one Watts in England had *forced* him of. The governour entertained them kindly, and gave him his letter with directions to Mr. [2]Downing in England, &c.

The night before, alarm was given in divers of the plantations. It arose through the shooting off some pieces at Watertown, by occasion of a calf, which ||[2]Sir Richard Saltonstall|| had lost; and the soldiers were sent out with their pieces to ||[3]try|| the wilderness from thence till they might find it.

29.] Sir Richard Saltonstall and his two daughters, and one of his younger sons, (his two eldest sons remained still in the country,) came down to Boston, and stayed that night at the governour's, and the next morning, by seven of the clock, accompanied with Mr. Peirce and others in two shallops, they departed to go to the ship riding at Salem. The governour

||here|| ||[2]blank|| ||[3]search||

---

1 In assigning the residence of these Indians to the neighbourhood of Watertown, or between the Charles and Mistick Rivers, I rely on my slight information of them. A few days before, this sagamore with one of his subjects had made complaint of the burning of two of their wigwams, of which an account is given by Dudley; but Prince, II. 21, from the Colony Records, enlarges the information by the circumstance, that Sir R. Saltonstall was ordered to make satisfaction, which he did by seven yards of cloth, because the mischief had been occasioned by one of his servants.

2 Downing, whose Christian name was Emanuel, was of the Inner Temple, and related to Winthrop by marriage of his sister. Before coming over, he sent three of his children. In our Church Records, under November, 1633, I find, "Mary Downing, kinswoman to our brother John Winthrop, governour," admitted, No. 182. From several letters brought by her, I am satisfied, she was the daughter of this gentleman. He lived several years, in great esteem, at Salem, which he often represented in the general court, and was father of the celebrated Sir George Downing, ambassadour both of Cromwell and Charles II. in Holland, of whom mention will be found in the second volume of this History. A daughter of Emanuel was the second wife of the venerable Gov. Bradstreet, as Hutchinson, I. 23, says; but as the first died so late as 16 September, 1672, I presume the second gave no increase to the governour's family.

gave them three ||drakes||[1] at their setting sail, the wind being N. W. a stiff gale and full sea. Mr. Sharp went away at the same time in another shallop.

About ten of the clock, Mr. [2]Coddington and Mr. Wilson, and divers of the congregation, met at the governour's, and there Mr. Wilson, praying and exhorting the congregation to love, &c. commended to them the exercise of [3]prophecy in his absence, and designed those whom he thought most fit for it, viz. the governour, Mr. [4]Dudley, and Mr. Nowell the elder.

||ducks||

---

1 To mention, that discharges of artillery are intended by this phrase, would be unnecessary, had not the erroneous reading of the former edition permitted a careless reader to suppose, that birds were given for food on the voyage.

2 William Coddington, whose name is sometimes spelt Cottington, probably from the sound resembling that of Lord Cottington, then of the privy council, was a gentleman of great estate and influence in Boston, where, it is said by Callender, he built the first brick house. He was one of the earliest assistants, treasurer of the colony for some time, and is always mentioned with great esteem by our author, until the unhappy separation caused by the antinomian controversy. His name as a member of our church is not earlier than No. 92, and that of his wife, who died in the first season, is not found. On his return from England, in 1633, he brought another wife, Mary, who is among our church members No. 158. Besides what may be learned of him from these pages, the Biographical Dictionaries of Eliot and Allen, and still more the candid century discourse of the modest historian of Rhode Island, dedicated to his grandson, give ample attestation to the talents and integrity of Coddington, who was the father of that colony, and many years its governour.

3 After Wilson's departure, only the churches of Salem, Dorchester and Watertown were supplied with pastors. Since Dorchester had two ministers, Warham and Maverick, it may appear strange, that one of them was not spared for a season to the principal congregation in the colony, including the dwellers at Boston, Charlestown and Newtown; but perhaps their duties were so diverse, as pastor and teacher, that each was considered as necessary as either. The people of Roxbury had now, indeed, united themselves to Dorchester, as their church records show, Prince, II. 64, though in November before, we may be sure, from their assessment, Prince, II. 6, they had been part of Wilson's charge. This "exercise of prophecy," or office of preaching, was well entrusted, however, to the three eldest magistrates, though the instructions of Dudley and Nowell were probably rendered less serviceable by their severe tempers than the mild wisdom of Winthrop.

4 Of Thomas Dudley, little information should be expected in the narrow limits of this note. Much may be learned from Mather, though his miserable intermeddling in politicks, 1 Hist. Coll. 137, made the governour's son, probably, distrustful of his authority, and therefore the Magnalia contains this curious passage: "I had prepared and intended a more *particular* account of this gentleman; but not having any opportunity to commit it unto the *perusal* of any descended from him, (unto whom I am told it will be unacceptable for me to publish any thing of this kind, by *them* not perused,) I have laid it aside, and summed all up in this more *general account.*"

Then he desired the governour to commend himself and the rest to God by prayer; which being done, they accompanied him to the boat, and so they went over to Charlestown to go by [1]land

---

Being the first deputy governour in the colony, many years governour, and, when he filled neither of these offices, one of the assistants, his history must be embodied in that of his country; and the diligence of Eliot has gleaned almost all that the Records omitted. A hardness in publick, and rigidity in private life, are too observable in his character, and even an eagerness for pecuniary gain, which might not have been expected in a soldier and a statesman. Gov. Belcher wrote an epitaph for him:

Here lies Thomas Dudley, that trusty old stud,
A bargain's a bargain, and must be made good.

Dudley lost, in 1643, the wife he brought over, two of whose children are known, Samuel and Ann; but he married again the next year, and the celebrated Gov. Joseph was child of the second wife. Samuel married Mary, daughter of Gov. Winthrop, in 1633, I presume, as our First Church Records verify the baptisms of their children, Thomas, 9 March, 1634; John, 28 June, 1635; Samuel, 2 August, 1639. Why these children were baptized here, when the father was not a church member, though the mother was, must be referred to a liberality of practice much controverted in after times, and even to the present day. He was sometime at Salisbury, and deputy from that town 1641, settled at Exeter in 1650, where he was a preacher, and is called a person of good capacity and learning. Belknap's New Hampshire, I. 48, in note.

His daughter, Ann, married, at sixteen years of age, to Bradstreet, before our colonists left England, bore him eight children. She is the most distinguished of the early matrons of our land by her literary powers, of which proof is given in a volume of poems, the second edition of which, printed at Boston, 1678, by John Foster, in a very respectable 12mo of 255 pages, is now before me. It does credit to her education, and is a real curiosity, though no reader, free from partiality of friendship, might coincide in the commendation of the funeral elogy by John Norton:

Could Maro's muse but hear her lively strain,
He would condemn his works to fire again.
* * * * * *
Her breast was a brave palace, a *broad street*,
Where all heroick ample thoughts did meet,
Where nature such a tenement had ta'en,
That other souls, to hers, dwelt in a lane.

The grandson, Thomas, was graduated at Harvard College in 1651, fourteen years before his uncle Joseph, and died in 1655. His will comes but a few pages after that of his grandfather in our first volume of Records. Of so distinguished descendants as the sons of the second governour, Paul, chief justice of the province, and William, speaker of the representatives, it cannot be necessary to speak. Eliot has done better than any one else will ever attempt.

1 That is, to Salem. Dudley's letter went by this ship, in which were embarked Coddington and Wilson, as well as Sharp and Saltonstall with three of his children. The two first returned soon; the others came no more. So many persons of distinction went in this vessel, that the court's order, of 1 March preceding, for the transportation of some unquiet spirits, I

to the ship. This ship set sail from Salem April 1, and arrived at London (all safe) April 29.[1]

April.] The beginning of this month we had very much rain and warm weather. It is a general rule, that when the wind blows twelve hours in any part of the east, it brings rain or snow in great abundance.

4.] Wahginnacut, a sagamore upon the River Quonehtacut, which lies west of Naragancet, came to the governour at Boston, with John Sagamore, and Jack Straw, (an Indian, who had lived in England and had served Sir Walter *Raleigh*, and was now turned Indian again,) and divers of their sannops, and brought a letter to the governour from Mr. Endecott to this effect: That the said Wahginnacut was very desirous to have some Englishmen to come plant in his country, and offered to find them corn, and give them yearly eighty skins of beaver, and that the country was very fruitful, &c. and wished that there might be two men sent with him to see the country. The governour entertained them at dinner, but would send none with him. He discovered after, that the said sagamore is a very treacherous man, and at war with the Pekoath (a far greater sagamore.) His country is ||not above|| five days' journey from us by land.

12.] At a court holden at Boston, (upon information to the governour, that they of Salem had [2]called Mr. Williams to the office of a teacher,) a letter was written from the court to Mr. Endecott to this effect: That whereas Mr. Williams had refus-

||at about||

---

imagine, could not be thoroughly executed. Mr. Aleworth, Mr. Weaver, Mr. Plastow, Mr. Shuter, Cobbet, Wormewood, Sir Chr. Gardiner and Mr. Wright, "or so many of them as the ship can carry," were ordered to be sent to England "as persons unmeet to inhabit here." The knight, who caused so much uneasiness, and Plastow, are afterwards named in the Records as present, though Hutchinson hastily gave Gardiner passage in this ship.

1 This sentence is by the governour given in the margin.

2 In opposition to this extraordinary interference, as we should now think it, of the civil power in election of a church officer, Bentley informs us, the congregation of Salem received him, on this same day, as teacher. He succeeded Higginson, the time of whose death is mistaken by that author, 1 Hist. Coll. VI. 244. Certainly it was not 15 March, 1630, unless Dudley, 1 Hist. Coll. VIII. 40, Hubbard, 120, and the Memorialist of Plimouth, are in a strange errour. Hubbard's precise date, 6 August, is probable, as it differs little, if at all, from Dudley, and is consistent with Morton. See mention of his death in a letter of our author, 9 September, 1630, in Appendix. At what time the violence of opposition, by such as had no real interest in the transaction, caused Williams to separate from his affectionate people, does not clearly appear; but in this History it will appear, that he was driven out of the jurisdiction, and had found refuge at Plimouth, before 25 October, 1632.

ed to join with the ||congregation|| at Boston, because they would not make a publick declaration of their repentance for having communion with the churches of England, while they ||[2]lived|| there; and, besides, had declared his opinion, that the magistrate might not punish the breach of the Sabbath, nor any other offence, ||[3]as it|| was a breach of the first [1]table; therefore, they marvelled they would choose him without advising with the council; and withal desiring him, that they would forbear to proceed till they had conferred about it.[2]

13.] Chickatabot came to the governour, and desired to buy some English clothes for himself. The governour told him, that English sagamores did not use to truck; but he called his tailor and gave him order to make him a suit of clothes;

||churches|| ||[2]tarried|| ||[3]that||

---

[1] All, who are inclined to separate that connexion of secular concerns with the duties of religion, to which most governments, in all countries, have been too much disposed, will think this opinion of Roger Williams redounds to his praise. The laws of the first table, or the four commandments of the decalogue first in order, should be rather impressed by early education than by penal enactments of the legislature; and the experience of Rhode Island and other states of our Union is perhaps favourable to the sentiment of this earliest American reformer. By a restoration of the true reading in the text, the sentiment is made more distinct. Too much regulation was the errour of our fathers, who were perpetually arguing from analogies in the Levitical institutions, and encumbering themselves with the yoke of Jewish customs.

[2] From the Records of the Colony, I. 71, I introduce another sentence of this court: "Thomas Walford of Charlton is fined £10, and is enjoined, he and his wife, to depart out of the limits of this patent before the 20th day of October next, under pain of confiscation of his goods, for his contempt of authority and confronting officers, &c." This severity must be regretted; for he was the first Englishman at that place, being by the Spragues (who went thither, in 1628, from Endecott's company at Salem) found there a *smith;* but it is not told for whom he was labouring. Prince, I. 175, from the Records of the town. Walford was, however, a valuable man at Piscataqua, being one of two trustees or wardens for the church property. Conf. Hubbard, 220, and 1 Hist. Coll. X. 64. In a record of the court, only a month later than that in the text, I observe, that, being fined £2, "he paid it by killing a wolf." But our rulers distrusted him; for, 3 September, 1633, "it is ordered, that the goods of Thomas Walford shall be sequestered and remain in the hands of *Ancient* Gennison, to satisfy the debts he owes in the bay to several persons." John Walford, probably a son of this person, was by the king named, in 1692, one of the council to Gov. Allen. Belknap's N. H. I. 193. One Jane Walford, perhaps the wife of Thomas, was, in 1656, persecuted by her neighbours as a witch, and, ten or twelve years later, recovered damages against one for calling her by that odious name.

At the same court, in an action of battery by Thomas Dexter against Endecott, a jury was empanneled, and their names are given, whose verdict was £10 damages. For an account of this strange affair, see the very curious letter of the defendant, Hutchinson's Coll. 52, in which the meek ruler of Salem permits himself to say, "If it were lawful to try it at blows, and he a fit man for me to deal with, you should not hear me complain."

whereupon he gave the governour two large skins of coat beaver, and, after he and his men had dined, they departed, and said he would come again three days after for his suit.

14.] *We began a court of guard upon the neck between Roxbury and Boston, whereupon should be always resident an officer and six men.*

An order was made §last court,§ that no man should discharge a piece after sunset, except by occasion of alarm.

15.] Chickatabot came to the governour again, and he put him into a very good new suit from head to foot, and after he set meat before them; but he would not eat till the governour had given thanks, and after meat he desired him to do the like, and so departed.

21.] The house of John [1]Page of Watertown was burnt by carrying a few coals from one house to another: a coal fell by the way and kindled in the leaves.

One *Mr. Gardiner, (calling himself* Sir Christopher [2]Gar-

---

1 John Page is among the first freemen, admitted at the general court of all the company next month, when the number was 118, not 110, as Johnson, lib. I. c. 17, has it. He fell into another errour, in mistaking the *desire* to become freemen, expressed at the court in October preceding, for the *admission*. From Prince, II. 29, who makes only 116 take the oath of freemen, the reason of my differing is, that I count, in the original Record of the Colony, two more names, viz. Robert Coles and Thomas Dexter, which indeed were afterwards erased, but it is evident that they could not have been inserted by the secretary, unless justly entitled to the place. Besides, there is the *old* enumeration of the three columns of names, 44, 40 and 34, to make up my reckoning. We know, that Dexter was disfranchised some years after, and Coles probably was.

Of Page, I know only what is given in the fine letter of Rogers on p. 47; that he was of Dedham in Old England, and had, on coming over, a wife and two children; and, from the Colony Records, that, at the first general court, in October, 1630, held at Boston, he was made constable of Watertown; and, from the Watertown Records of Births, "Daniel, the son of John and Phebe Page, born 10 August, 1634."

2 I apprehend, that the original cause of dislike to Sir Chr. Gardiner by our colonists, or of his enmity to the company, must be forever left to uncertain conjecture. He arrived, probably, in 1630, but at which plantation, or in what vessel, our early writers leave us uninformed. "Some miscarriages, for which he should have answered," is the doubtful phrase, in which Morton assigns the reason of his flight from Massachusetts; and Hubbard, 149—153, who does some service by correcting the chronology of the Plimouth historian, has enlarged his slender narrative only by an humble sarcasm. The accusation mentioned in the text should have been supported by a warrant from England to arrest the culprit; but as no such legal cause of imprisonment is noted, and he seems to have escaped, on returning to England, any suspicion or even inquiry, we may safely conclude, that Gardiner's disaffection to the worship of our churches first rendered him obnoxious to the charge of popery, for which the evidence afterwards appeared sufficient. The letter of Winthrop to Bradford, 5 May, the day after the prisoner's arrival, preserved

diner, knight of the golden ||melice,||) being accused to have two wives in England, was sent for; but he had intelligence, and escaped, and travelled up and down among the Indians about a ||[2]month;|| but, by means of the governour of Plimouth, he was taken §by the Indians§ about [1]Namasket, and brought to Plimouth, and from thence he was brought, by Capt. [2]Underhill and his Lieut. [3]Dudley, May 4, to Boston.

16.] There was an alarm given to all our towns in the night, by occasion of a piece which was shot off, (but where could not be known,) and the Indians having sent us word the day before, that the Mohawks were coming down against them and us.

[4]17.] A general court at Boston. The former governour was chosen again, and all the freemen of the commons were sworn to this government. At noon, [5]Cheeseborough's house was burnt down, all the people being present.

||blank|| ||[2]week||

---

in Prince, II. 27, was composed in a temper, the mildness of which scarcely comports with the writer's belief of the misconduct imputed to the knight by the later historian.

1 This name belonged to part of the tract, now included in Middleborough; but the lines of Indian geography were probably not very precise, or are forgotten.

2 Of John Underhill, his errours, fanaticism and hypocrisy, sufficient notice will be found in subsequent pages, and in most of the early histories of our country; but all, I think, derived from this work. He was early a member of our Boston church, being No. 57, and one of the first deputies in the general court. After removal from Massachusetts to Piscataqua, where he staid not long, he was living in good repute at New Haven colony, as is proved by his election as a representative from Stamford in 1643, Trumbull, I. 124, and by Gov. Welles's letter, eleven years later, in Hutchinson's Coll. 253. In 1655 he dwelt on Long Island, as appears in Haz. I. 341.

3 This is thought to be that son of Gov. Dudley, who married Winthrop's daughter, mentioned in note on page 51. He died, probably, at Exeter, in 1683. New Hamp. Hist. Coll. II. 238. Mather does not rank him with the ministers.

4 Prince, II. 28, remarks the errour of this date. The court was held on 18th.

5 William Cheeseborough, or Cheesbrough, was one of the earliest members of Boston church, and in 1634 chosen constable of the town. He moved soon after to Mount Wollaston, where he lived several years, and had a considerable estate. His character is known, by being one of the two appointed for Boston, to unite with committees from other towns in advising the governour and council about raising a publick stock, as hereafter mentioned in this History, May, 1632. That measure, as Prince supposed, was, undoubtedly, the natural introduction of a house of representatives. In October, 1640, he was deputy for Braintree, and is, I presume,

27.] There came from Virginia into Salem a pinnace of eighteen tons, laden with corn and tobacco. She was bound to the north, and put in there by foul weather. She sold her corn at ten shillings the bushel.

June 14.] At a court, John Sagamore and Chickatabot being told at last court of some injuries that their men did to our cattle, and giving consent to make satisfaction, &c. now one of their men was complained of for shooting a pig, &c. for which Chickatabot was ordered to pay a small skin of beaver, which he presently paid.

At this court one Philip [1]Ratcliff, a servant of Mr. Cradock, being convict, ore tenus, of most foul, scandalous invectives against our churches and government, was censured to be whipped, lose his ears, and be banished the plantation, which was presently executed.

25.] There came a shallop from Pascataqua, which brought news of a small English ship come thither with provisions and some Frenchmen to make salt. By this boat, Capt. Neal,

---

the same person, whom Trumbull, I. 234, makes first planter of Stonington, coming thither from Rehoboth in 1649. He had some trouble in Connecticut about title to his lands, but soon prevailed; and among the principal people, enumerated soon after by the same author, are William, Elisha and Samuel Cheeseborough, the two latter being, probably, his sons. I find, however, William, witness to a deed of land in or near Rehoboth, so late as 1658; yet the distance in those days was thought so little of, that we may suppose he was on a short visit to old neighbours. Descendants are found in Connecticut.

1 A foreign hand has inserted in the text the Christian name of the culprit; but as it is true, we should not complain of the interpolation. In our Colonial Records, vol. I. 86, is found the sentence, as in the governour's text, with an addition of some importance—a fine of £40. The offence is there stated, with a little more precision, "for uttering malicious and scandalous speeches against the government, and *the church of Salem*, &c. as appeareth by a particular thereof proved upon oath." No trace of this evidence is known, and the &c. must go unexplained, though the proof would be quite curious, if we may trust the brother libeller, Morton, who represents Ratcliff, by the name of "Mr. Innocence Faircloth, by Mr. Mathias Charterparty sent over," as an injured man, whose chief offence was, asking payment of his debts in his sickness. The New English Canaan aggravates the cruelty of the judgment by the additional circumstances of boring and slitting his tongue, branding his face, and whipping in every plantation; but the adversary felt a momentary emotion of candour, when he wrote, that Sir Chr. Gardiner's interference with Gov. Winthrop prevented the execution of part of it.

Still I am compelled to regret the cruelty of the punishment, and am not surprised at the dissatisfaction it produced in England. A letter in my possession to J. Winthrop, jun. from his relative, Edward Howes, London, 3 April, 1632, says, "I have heard divers complaints against the severity of your government, especially Mr. Endecott's, and that he shall be sent for over, about cutting off the lunatick man's ears, and other grievances."

governour of Pascataqua, sent a packet of letters to the governour, directed to Sir Christopher Gardiner, which when the governour had opened, he found it came from Sir Ferdinando Gorges, (who claims a great part of the Bay of Massachusetts.) In the packet was one letter to Thomas Morton, (sent prisoner before into England upon the lord chief justice's warrant:) by both which letters it appeared, that he had some secret design to recover his pretended right, and that he reposed much trust in Sir Christopher Gardiner.

These letters we opened, because they were directed to one, who was our prisoner, and had declared himself an ill willer to our government.[1]

27.] There came to the governour Capt. [2]*Southcot* of Dorchester, and brought letters out of the White Angel, (which was lately arrived at Sauco.) She brought [blank] cows, goats and hogs, and many provisions, for the bay and for Plimouth. Mr. Allerton returned in this ship, and by him we heard, that the Friendship, which put out from Barnstable [blank] weeks before the Angel, was forced home again by extremity of foul weather, and so had given over her voyage. This ship, the Angel, set sail from [blank.]

July 4.] The governour built a bark at [3]Mistick, which was launched this day, and called the Blessing of the Bay.

---

[1] The task of justifying this breach of confidence, in opening the letters of Gorges, forwarded by his agent, might, to many politicians, appear easy; but I shall merely remark, that a little dislike of the proceeding is by the governour indicated, by giving this paragraph only in the margin, and, probably, at a later date. Perhaps, as in the case of Ratcliff, some other of the council is chargeable with the influence that moved the court.

[2] Southcot was one of the principal planters of Dorchester, 1 Hist. Coll. IX. 150; but this is all the information obtained of him, except, from Capt. Clap, we may infer, that the "worthy gentleman, Mr. William Southcot, about three miles from the city of Exeter," with whom he first went to live, is the same person. Prince, II. 32, from the Colony Records, shows, that, at a court, 26 July following, "Captain Southcot hath liberty to go for England, promising to return with all convenient speed." Thomas Southcot was one of the original patentees of Massachusetts, but he probably never came over.

[3] I imagine this was the author's residence, during the summer, for the first two or three years, and that Boston then became his constant home; though, from the disagreement between him and Dudley, related hereafter under date of 3 August, 1632, it seems, that he was prevented from sitting down at Newtown only by the affection borne by the people of Boston towards him. The court of assistants, 6 September, 1631, as by the Records, I. 82, is shown, "granted to Mr. Governour six hundred acres of land, to be set forth by metes and bounds, near his house at Mistick, to enjoy to him and his heirs forever." He called this farm Ten Hills—a name it has retained ever since. It is in the town of Charlestown, nearly opposite the entrance of Malden River into the Mistick, where they form a broad bay.

6.] A small ship of sixty tons arrived at Natascott, Mr. Graves master. She brought ten passengers from London. They came with a patent to Sagadahock, but, not liking the place, they came hither. Their ship drew ten feet, and went up to Watertown, but she ran on ground twice by the way. These were the company called the Husbandmen, and their ship called the Plough. Most of them proved familists and vanished away.[1]

13.] Canonicus' son, the great sachem of Naraganset, came to the governour's house with John Sagamore. After they had dined, he gave the governour a skin, and the governour requited him with a fair pewter pot, which he took very thankfully, and stayed all night.

14.] The ship called the Friendship, of Barnstable, arrived at Boston, after she had been at sea eleven weeks, and beaten back again by foul weather. She set sail from Barnstable again about the midst of May. She landed here eight heifers, and one calf, and five sheep.

21.] The governour and deputy, and Mr. Nowell, the elder of the congregation at Boston, went to Watertown to confer with Mr. Phillips, the pastor, and Mr. [2]Brown, the elder of the congregation there, about an [3]opinion, which they had pub-

---

1 This last sentence was, as might be supposed by the reader, and as the original proves, added after the lapse of some time. Gentlemen, who remained in England, I suppose, had fitted out the expedition; for, it appears by the Colony Records, I. 89, that, 5 June, 1632, the court "ordered, that the goods of the company of Husbandmen shall be inventoried by the beadle, and preserved here for the use and benefit of the said company."

2 Richard Brown is among those, who first applied for admission as freemen, and, by an order, 5 November, 1633, in Colony Records, I. 105, I find, is "allowed by the court to keep a ferry over Charles River against his house, and is to have two pence for every single person he so transports, and one penny a piece, if there be two or more." He seems to have been a person of consequence, and was the representative of Watertown in the first, second, fourth, ninth, and many following courts of deputies. But no information of him, more than our author's, is obtained, except in Hubbard, 187, who, after saying "he was discharged from his office," which certainly was a good thing, though meant as no honour, because it permitted him to come into civil service, adds, "He was a man of good understanding, and well versed in the discipline of the separation, having been a ruler in one of their churches in London, where he was known to be very violent and passionate in his proceedings." Still he commends him for "his faithfulness and care of Dr. Ames and Mr. Robert Parker, safely conveying them (being himself one that kept a wherry) aboard their vessel at Gravesend, when they were pursued by some that would willingly have shortened their journey."

3 Of this opinion, more will be found in future pages. To rigid Puritans it seemed, no doubt, very strange; for only the high church party entertained it; and all the unintelligible wonders of the Apocalypse were usually employed to prove the bishop of Rome to be Antichrist.

lished, that the churches of Rome were true churches. The matter was debated before many of both congregations, and, by the approbation of all the assembly, except three, was concluded an errour.

22.] The White Angel came into the bay. She landed here twenty-one heifers.

26.] A small bark of Salem, of about twelve tons, coming towards the bay, John [1]Elston and two of Mr. Cradock's fishermen being in her, and two tons of [2]stone, and three ||hogsheads|| of train oil, was overset in a gust, and, being buoyed up by the oil, she floated up and down ||forty-eight hours, and the three men sitting upon her, till Henry Way his|| boat, coming by, espied them and saved them.

29.] The Friendship set sail for the Christopher Islands, and ran on ground behind ||[3]Conant's||[3] Island.

30.] The White Angel fell down for Plimouth, but, the wind not serving, she came to an anchor by Long Island, and ran on ground a week after, near Gurnett's Nose.

Mr. Ludlow, in digging the foundation of his house at Dorchester, found two pieces of French money: one was coined in 1596. They were in several places, and above a foot within the firm ground.[4]

August 8.] The Tarentines, to the number of one hundred, came in three canoes, and in the night assaulted the wigwam of the sagamore of Agawam, by Merimack, and slew seven men, and wounded John Sagamore, and James, and some others,

||barrels|| ||[2]till then, when a|| ||[3]C——||

---

1 Of this man I know nothing. Prince reckons him one of Cradock's servants.

2 I am satisfied that Prince, II. 32, is mistaken in reading this word *stores*.

3 The island has been called Governour's Island, probably, ever since it was, by the court, in April following, demised to Gov. Winthrop; but the rent reserved, being part of the produce, was several times varied. The property remained in the family of the father of Massachusetts, until, within a few years, it has been obtained by the national government for the purpose of fortification.

4 Perhaps no reader will expect, that the occasion of these coins being lodged here should be satisfactorily ascertained; yet I may be pardoned for offering a conjecture, that they came from a French ship, wrecked at Cape Cod about fourteen years before, whose crew were soon murdered by the savages, except three or four, that were "kept and sent from one sachem to another to make sport with them." Two were redeemed by Dormer, about three years after their calamity, and one died among the Indians, having lived with them long enough to give them some instruction. See Morton's Memorial, sub an. 1620; and Prince, I. 45, relying for his narrative on Bradford and Purchas.

(whereof some died after,) and rifled a wigwam where Mr. Cradock's men kept to catch sturgeon, took away their nets and biscuit, &c.[1]

[Large blank.]

19.] The Plough returned to Charlestown, after she had been on her way to the Christopher Islands about three weeks, and was so broke she could not return home.

31.] The governour's bark, called the Blessing of the Bay, being of thirty tons, went to sea.

September 6.] The White Angel set sail from Marble Harbour.

About this time last year the company here set forth a pinnace to the parts about Cape Cod, to trade for corn, and it brought here above eighty bushels. This year again the Salem pinnace, being bound thither for corn, was, by contrary winds, put into Plimouth, where the governour, &c. fell out §with them,§ not only forbidding them to trade, but also telling them they would oppose them by force, even to the spending of their lives, &c.; whereupon they returned, and acquainting the governour of Massachusetts with it, he wrote to the governour of Plimouth this letter, here inserted, with their answer, which came about a month after.[2]

The wolves did much hurt to calves and swine between Charles River and Mistick.[3]

At the last court, a young [4]fellow was whipped for soliciting

---

1 Hubbard, 145, says, that the Agawam sachem "was the less pitied of the English," because they heard that he "had treacherously killed some of those Tarratine families." The invaders were from the east. Johnson, lib. I. chap. xxv. in his usual prolix manner, mentions the alarm among the English from this expedition, and the precautions of our fathers; but it is not a very probable story, or at least is much ornamented.

The number of canoes, thirty, in the former edition, appeared to me too large for the forces; and as the Arabic numeral in Winthrop's writing is commonly followed by a :, which easily deceives a common reader, and he had first written *two fishing shallops*, I have determined to reject the cypher, and adhere to my resolution, though both Hubbard, 145, and Prince II. 32, read our MS. 30. On a later page, October 2, 1633, our author observes, that the Indians of Long Island have canoes "so great as one will carry *eighty* men." Had the fierce natives of the eastern shore so small craft for their expedition as to want thirty to carry one hundred?

2 Since the days of the first generation of the statesmen of the two colonies, it may be presumed, these documents have never been seen; for no other notice of them is known. Perhaps each side desired afterwards to destroy them. The jealousy of the weaker power seems, in this instance, less reasonable than in some succeeding.

3 This sentence is in the margin.

4 The name of the offender is found in the first volume of our Colony

an Indian squaw to incontinency. Her husband and she complained of the ||wrong,|| and were present at the execution, and very well satisfied.

At the same court, one Henry [1]Linne was whipped and banished, for writing letters into England full of slander against our government and orders of our churches.

17.] Mr. [2]Shurd of [3]Pemaquid, sent home James Sagamore's wife, who had been taken away at the surprise at Agawam, and writ that the Indians demanded [blank] fathom of wampampeague and [blank] skins for her ||[2]ransom.||

27.] At a court, one Josias Plaistowe and two of his servants were censured for stealing corn from Chickatabot and his men, (who were present,) the master to restore two fold, and to be degraded from the title of a gentleman, and fined five pounds, and his men to be whipped.[4]

[Blank.]

||injury|| ||[2]remission||

Records, page 82, and, immediately after the sentence, is added by the court, "Upon this occasion it is propounded, whether adultery, either with English or Indian, shall not be punished with death. Referred to the next court to be considered of." At the next court of assistants, held 18 of next month, such an act was adopted, though it could not at first be enforced. It certainly indicates rather the rigorous purity than the wisdom of our early legislators.

1 Lynn, who was of Boston, had been sentenced, in September of the first year, to be whipped. Colony Records, I. 59. Dissatisfaction with this discipline, probably, led to his second offence, which, from the Records, I. 82, consisted only of writing into England "against the government and execution of justice here;" but it may naturally be imagined, that his letters contained some slander of the "orders of our churches," though not included in the judgment against him. His banishment was certainly remitted, though the Records do not mention it; for, in November, 1632, the court fined him "ten shillings, for absenting himself from training." Four years later I find, in our town proceedings, an order about the ranging of his fence.

2 Abraham Shurd, or Shurt, or Short, lived many years at the eastward; for Thomas Gorges, in a letter to Winthrop, Hutchinson's Coll. 114, 28 June, 1643, says, that he had information of the governour's writing to him by that person. From this fact, with the mention of him by our author in June and July, 1644, it is rendered certain, that he was a man of some consideration. In 1662, I have found his testimony, that he was agent of Aldworth and Elbridge at their establishment. He was, therefore, one of those who, under the grant of Sir F. Gorges, Haz. I. 315, had, for three years preceding, lived at this plantation, which was prosperous. Randolph, in his letter to Porey, Hutchinson's Coll. 563, represents one of the name, in June, 1688, as town clerk of Pémaquid, who perhaps was a son of the earliest settler.

3 The president (Sir F. Gorges) and council of New England, in a grant, 29 February, 1631, to Aldworth and Elbridge, Haz. I. 315, recite, that their people or servants had occupied the mouth of the river three years or more.

4 Copying exactly the sentence of the court, appears to me the best ex-

October 4.] The Blessing went on a voyage to the eastward.

11.] The governour, being at his farm house at Mistick, walked out after supper, and took a piece in his hand, supposing he might see a wolf, (for they came daily about the house, and killed swine and calves, &c.;) and, being about half a mile off, it grew suddenly dark, so as, in coming home, he mistook his path, and went till he came to a little house of Sagamore John, which stood empty. There he stayed, and having a piece of match in his pocket, (for he always carried about him match and a compass, and in ||summer time snake-weed,||) he made a good fire ||[2]near|| the house, and lay down upon some old mats, which he found there, and so spent the night, sometimes walking by the fire, sometimes singing psalms, and sometimes getting wood, but could not sleep. It was (through God's mercy) a ||[3]warm|| night; but a little before day it began to rain, and, having no cloak, he made shift by a long pole to climb up into the house. In the morning, there came thither an Indian squaw, but perceiving her before she had opened the door, he barred her out; yet she stayed there a great while essaying to get in, and at last she went away, and he returned safe home, his servants having been much perplexed for him, and having walked about, and shot off pieces, and hallooed in the night, but he heard them not.

22.] The governour received a letter from Capt. [1]Wiggin of Pascataquack, informing him of a murder committed the third of this month at Richman's Isle, by an Indian sagamore, called Squidrayset, and his company, upon one Walter Bagnall, called Great Watt, and one John P——, who kept with him. They,

||the former there spake need|| ||[2]and warmed|| ||[3]weary||

---

planation of this passage: "It is ordered, that Josias Plastowe shall (for stealing four baskets of corn from the Indians) return them eight baskets again, be fined £5, and hereafter to be called by the name of Josias, and not Mr. as formerly he used to be; and that William Buckland and Thomas Andrew shall be whipped for being accessary to the same offence." We must conclude, therefore, that our fathers thought the whipping of the servants a lighter punishment than the degradation of the master.

1 Thomas Wiggin was agent, or governour, of the upper plantation, as Neal was of the lower. He was a worthy man, without doubt; for the Puritan peers, Say and Brooke, employed him as their representative, and he gave evidence in favour of our people against Gorges and Mason. In 1650, after the union of New Hampshire with our colony, he became one of the assistants, Hutch. I. 150, and, two years later, was among the commissioners to receive the submission of the inhabitants of Maine. Probably descendants perpetuate his name.

having killed them, burnt the house over them, and carried away their guns and what else they liked. He persuaded the governour to send twenty men presently to take revenge; but the governour, advising with some of the council, thought best to sit still awhile, partly because he heard that Capt. Neal, &c. were gone after them, and partly because of the season, (it being then frost and snow,) and want of ||boats|| fit for that expedition. This Bagnall was sometimes servant to one in the bay, and these three years had dwelt alone in the said isle, and had gotten about £400 ||2most in goods.|| He was a wicked fellow, and had much wronged the Indians.

25.] The governour, with Capt. Underhill and others of the officers, went on foot to Sagus, and next day to Salem, where they were bountifully entertained by Capt. Endecott, &c. and, the 28th, they returned to Boston by the ||3ford|| at Sagus River, and so over at Mistick.

A plentiful crop.

30.] The governour, having erected a building of stone at Mistick, there came so violent a storm of rain, for twenty-four hours, from the N. E. and S. E. as (it being not finished, and laid with clay for want of lime) two sides of it were washed down to the ground; and much harm was done to other houses by that storm.

§Mr. Pynchon's boat, coming from Sagadahock, was cast away at Cape Ann, but the men and chief goods saved, and the boat recovered.§[1]

November 2.] The ship Lyon, William Peirce master, arrived at Natascot. There came in her the governour's [2]wife,

||boots|| ||2interest in government|| ||3fort||

1 Our author wrote this sentence in the margin; but Prince understood it to refer to the same storm, in which the governour's new building had received such injury.

2 In the latter part of this History, 1647, notice of this lady's death will be found. She was the governour's third wife, and the mother of all his children named in this work, except John, Henry, Mary, and Forth. In an Almanack of 1617, belonging to Adam Winthrop, Esq. father of the governour, against 17th September, is this note: "My son rid first to Maplested." At 12 January, he remarks, "This day J. W. the elder, is twenty-nine years old;" at 12 February, "This day J. W. the younger, is eleven years old; at 10 August, "This day I, A. W., am sixty-nine years old." He used the same little book for a register next year; for, in another part, I find it written, "that on Friday the 24th of April, 1618, my son's third wife came first to Groton. She was married to him the 29th day of the same month at Great Maplested, anno 1618." Her baptismal name was Margaret, and her admission at our church was, probably, on the first Sunday after arrival, the number being 111, next to John Eliot.

§his eldest son, and his [1]wife,§ and others of his children, and Mr. [2]Eliot, a minister, and other families, being in all about sixty persons, who all arrived in good health, having been ten weeks at sea, and lost none of their company but two children, whereof one was the governour's daughter Ann, about one year and half [3]old, who died about a week after they came to sea.

3.] The wind being contrary, the ship stayed at Long Island, but the governour's [4]son came on shore, and that night

---

1 Her name was Martha, admitted of our church, No. 130, her husband being 121. She was daughter of Henry Painter, I presume, married after Gov. Winthrop came over, bore no children, and died early at Agawam, before it obtained the name of Ipswich. In one of the letters in Appendix the governour mentions his *sister* Painter, and I have a letter of Mr. Painter to John Winthrop the younger, before leaving England, on this voyage with his mother, in which the writer speaks of his *sister*, whom his correspondent was to accompany, and of his *daughter* Winthrop. I am the more particular in this statement, because the family genealogy, by some substitution, probably of another branch, names the two wives of John, jun. neither Painter nor Peter.

2 This was the celebrated apostle of the Massachusetts Indians, whose fame has been too widely diffused in Europe and America to need any addition from the humble pen of the editor. He joined Boston church, No. 110, and our pages will show how soon he was removed to higher usefulness. Just praise is given him in 1 Hist. Coll. VIII. 5, by his amiable namesake of the last generation.

3 From the age of the daughter, thus mentioned, we conclude, that her father had never seen her. The situation of his wife in the spring of the preceding year, (see Appendix,) was the reason, probably, why she did not accompany him.

4 This distinguished gentleman, the governour, for many years, of Connecticut, whose name will frequently recur in our History, was the heir of all his father's talents, prudence and virtues, with a superiour share of human learning. His birth was on 12 February, 1605—6, his father having married, 16 April preceding, being then only seventeen years and three months old, Mary, daughter of John Forth, Esq. of Great Stanbridge, Essex. By that wife, as we learn from a letter to the eldest son, published by Mather, and which I consider the most valuable part of the Magnalia, our author had three sons and three daughters. The sons were John, Henry and Forth. Of the daughters, since the name of Mary alone is preserved, I presume the two others died in infancy. All the children of that union, except the subject of this note, he says, were deceased before the date of that letter, 1643.

Belknap has honoured the son in his American Biography, though we regret much the brevity of the memoir. He probably relied too far upon Mather, as we are sure he did in the life of the father. Mather, speaking of John, jun. with his customary carelessness, says, he was "not above twenty-three years of age" when chosen assistant, in 1632. Two sons, Fitz-John, born 14 March, 1638, and Wait-Still, born 27 February, 1641—2, and five daughters, survived him, and are remembered in his will in the Registry of Suffolk, lib. VI. fol. 156. He died in Boston, 5 April, 1676. He was a member of Boston church, and his wife, Martha, soon after coming. She died in a few years.

the governour went to the ship, and lay aboard all night; and the next morning, the wind coming fair, she came to an anchor before Boston.

---

and, the family memoirs say, was buried at Ipswich. All his children were born of the second wife, Elizabeth, the eldest, of the same name with her mother, 24 July, 1636. One of the wives, and, to me it seems probable, the second, was daughter of the famous Hugh Peter, though two tempers more unlike than the father-in-law and the son-in-law could hardly be found in such near connexion. Yet I cannot doubt the fact, though the family memoirs give a different name to either wife. In a letter of Roger Williams, 12 July, 1654, soon after returning from England, to John Winthrop of Connecticut, he says, "I had no letters for you, but yours were all well. I was at the lodgings of Major Winthrop and Mr. Peters, but I missed them. Your brother flourisheth in good esteem, and is eminent for maintaining the freedom of the conscience, as to matters of belief, religion and worship. Your father Peters preacheth the same doctrine, though not so zealously as some years since; yet cries out against New English rigidities and persecutions, their civil injuries and wrongs to himself, and their unchristian dealing with him in excommunicating his distracted wife. All this he told me in his lodgings at Whitehall, those lodgings which I was told were Canterbury's; but he himself told me that that library, wherein we were together, was Canterbury's, and given him by the parliament. His wife lives from him, not wholly, but much distracted. He tells me, he had but two hundred a year, and he allowed her four score per annum of it. Surely, Sir, the most holy Lord is most wise in all the trials he exerciseth his people with. He told me, that his affliction from his wife stirred him up to action abroad, and when success tempted him to pride, the bitterness in his bosom comforts was a cooler and a bridle to him." In letters in the Appendix, from our historian to his son, he speaks of *my brother* Peter, and *my sister* Peter; but this might only refer to Christian fellowship. But it is put beyond question by another letter of Williams to Winthrop of Connecticut, 6 February, 1659—60, giving premature rumour of Peter's death: "Sir, you were not long since the son of two noble fathers, Mr. John Winthrop and Mr. H. Peters. It is said, they are both extinguished. Surely, I did ever, from my soul, honour and love them, even when their judgments led them to afflict me."

Fitz-John, who was a captain in Col. Read's regiment at the restoration, in 1660, continued to reside in Connecticut, of which he was governour, by nine annual elections, from 1698 to his death. Thus father, son and grandson died in the highest office, to which the affections of the people could exalt them. Wait-Still, after living in Connecticut during the life of his father, with whom he was colleague commissioner of the United Colonies, in 1675, removed to Boston during the usurpation of the charter rights by Andros, to whom he and his brother, the governour, were made counsellors. Hutchinson, I. 317. In the spirit of that oppressor, we know, he did not sympathize; for, on the breaking out of the Boston revolution, he was made by the patriots commander of the militia. He was named of the council by the new charter of William and Mary; but why Increase Mather permitted his name of baptism, in that instrument, to be curtailed to Wait, I cannot divine, unless he thought the dissyllable, as one word, sounding Puritanick, might be unpleasant to courtly ears. But that middle name was derived from intermarriage of Adam, his great grandfather, with the family of Still, and this gentleman was not designated by a perverse simplicity, which characterized the age. He was afterwards chief justice of the superiour court of Massachusetts, and died 7 November, 1717. His wife was Mary, daughter of Hon. William Browne of Salem. The inven-

4.] The governour, his wife and [1]children, went on shore, with Mr. Peirce, in his ship's boat. The ship gave them six or seven pieces. At their landing, the captains, with their companies in arms, entertained them with a guard, and divers vollies of shot, and three drakes; and divers of the assistants and

---

tory of his estate, that was divided between his son John, of New London, born in Boston 26 August, 1681, and his daughter, Ann, wife of Thomas Lechmere, surveyor of the customs in Boston, brother of Lord Lechmere, returned January, 1717—18, found in lib. XX. fol. 91, of Suffolk Registry, appraises the property over £3000, of which the Elizabeth Islands and stock thereon made £2000. In the settlement of the estate, a controversy arose, from the decision of which, in Connecticut, for his sister, John appealed to the king in council, and obtained an ultimate decree in his favour, consistent with the laws of England, and overruling those of the colony. See an account in Trumbull's Connecticut, II. 54; but observe a strange mistake of the reverend author, who makes the parties children of the last governour of the family, who was their uncle. He was chosen into the Royal Society, of which his grandfather had been, from its beginning, a valued correspondent, and remained to his death in England. Eliot's Biographical Dictionary contains a valuable extract of the dedication to him of the 40th volume of their Transactions. The family have preserved many communications of Sir Robert Boyle, Sir Kenelm Digby, Oldenburgh, and other distinguished naturalists, to the first governour of Connecticut, and many of the second generation after, to this descendant. I have been favoured with a copy of the recommendation by Sir Hans Sloane and three other members, 10 January, 1733, in favour of the "grandson of the learned John Winthrop, Esq. who was one of the first members of this society, and who, in conjunction with others, did greatly contribute to the obtaining our charter, to whom the Royal Society, in its early days, was not only indebted for various ingenious communications, but their museum still contains many testimonies of his generosity, especially of things relating to the natural history of New England." He is the third of the name in Harvard College Catalogue, 1700, married a daughter of Gov. Jo. Dudley, and died 1 August, 1747. Of seven children, two were sons, John Still, born at New London, 15th January, 1720, and Basil. The latter died a bachelor. One daughter married Gov. Wanton of Rhode Island. John Still married, 4 September, 1750, Jane, only daughter of Francis Borland of Boston, by whom he had John, H. C., 1770, Jane, Francis B., Ann, William, Joseph, Mary, Thomas L., died at New London, 6 June, 1776. Francis B. died at New York, leaving four sons and three daughters. From the second of the sons, Francis B., I have derived most of the original papers, that illustrate the private affairs of the family. Ann married the late David Sears, Esq. of Boston; William is of New York; Joseph of Charleston, S.C.; and Thomas L., H. C., 1780, a distinguished gentleman of Boston. By a second wife, daughter of William Sheriff, a British officer, John Still had six children, of whom three survive, viz. Benjamin, of New York, married a daughter of Peter Stuyvesant, Esq. descendant of his ancestor's great antagonist; Robert, an admiral in the British navy; Elizabeth Bebor of Middletown, Conn.

1 Besides Henry, one son, probably Adam, came with his father. The other children, to come with John, jun. could only have been Mary, Forth, Stephen, Deane, Samuel and Ann; but Forth, I conjecture, had died in England some few months before their embarkation, and that the letter of Ursula Sherman, in the Appendix, relates to him; and the loss of Ann on the voyage has just been told in the text.

most of the people, of the near plantations, came to welcome them, and brought and sent, for divers days, great store of provisions, as fat hogs, kids, venison, poultry, geese, partridges, &c., so as the like joy and manifestation of love had never been seen in New England. It was a great marvel, that so much people and such store of provisions could be gathered together at so few hours' warning.

11.] We kept a day of thanksgiving at Boston.

17.] The [1]governour of Plimouth came to Boston, and lodged in the ship.

23.] Mr. Peirce went down to his ship, which lay at Nantascot. Divers went home with him into England by Virginia, as Sir Richard Saltonstall his eldest son and others; and they were six weeks in going to Virginia.

The congregation at Watertown (whereof Mr. George Phillips was pastor) had chosen one Richard Brown for their elder, before named, who, persisting in his opinion of the truth of the Romish church, and maintaining other errours withal, and being a man of a very violent spirit, the court wrote a letter to the congregation, directed to the pastor and brethren, to advise them to take into consideration, whether Mr. Brown were fit to be continued their elder or not; to which, after some weeks, they returned answer to this effect: That if we would take the pains to prove such things as were objected against him, they would ||endeavour|| to redress them.

December 8.] The said congregation being much divided about their elder, both parties repaired to the governour for assistance, &c.; whereupon he went to Watertown, with the deputy governour and Mr. Nowell, and the congregation being assembled, the governour told them, that being come to settle peace, &c. they might proceed in three distinct respects: 1. As the magistrates, (their assistance being desired.) 2. As members of a neighbouring congregation. 3. Upon the answer which we received of our letter, which did no way satisfy us.—But the pastor, Mr. Phillips, desired us to sit with them as members of a neighbouring congregation only, whereto the governour, &c. consented.

Then the one side, which had first complained, were ||2moved to open|| their grievances; which they did to this effect: That they could not communicate with their elder, being guilty of errours, both in judgment and conversation. After much de-

||undertake|| ||2noticed to exhibit||

1 William Bradford, whose character is sufficiently illustrated in Belknap's American Biography.

bate of these things, at length they were reconciled, and agreed to seek God in a day of humiliation, and so to have a solemn ||uniting;|| each party promising to reform what hath been amiss, &c.; and the pastor gave thanks to God, and the assembly brake up.[1]

January 27.] The governour, and some company with him, went up by Charles River about eight miles above Watertown, and named the first brook, on the north side of the river, (being a fair stream, and coming from a pond a mile from the river,) Beaver Brook, because the beavers had shorn down divers great trees there, and made divers dams across the brook. Thence they went to a great rock, upon which stood a high stone, cleft in sunder, that four men might go through, which they called Adam's Chair, because the youngest of their company was [2]Adam Winthrop. Thence they came to another brook, greater than the former, which they called Masters'

||writing||

---

1 The subject of this controversy is thus introduced by the ecclesiastical historian of Massachusetts in 1 Hist. Coll. IX. 21: "Very particular mention is made of an elder in the church at Watertown, much to his honour in an age of bigotry, though censured by worthy men, who were influenced by the spirit of the age."

2 He was probably the eldest son of the governour's third wife, and now between twelve and thirteen years of age, as I find his admission to the freemen's oath, 2 June, 1641. In the Suffolk Registry of Deeds, I. 25, is found an indenture, by which John Winthrop, Margaret his wife, and Adam their son, grant the island, called the Governour's Island, to Henry Dunster, president of Harvard College, and Capt. George Cooke, to the use of said Adam and Elizabeth Glover, and the heirs of their two bodies, remainder to the said Adam and his heirs, reserving to the governour and his wife one third of the apples, pears, grapes and plums yearly growing. This was made on consideration of a marriage contracted and intended between the said Adam and Elizabeth, and bears date 1 February, 1641—2. He died 24 August, 1652, and the inventory of his estate, taken 4 September, is entered in our Probate Records, II. 64. His son, of the same name, is the first of the family in the catalogue of Harvard College, 1668, was named of the council in the charter of William and Mary, and died August, 1700; and the grandson, of the same name, son of Adam, second in H. C., 1694, was of the council, and died 2 October, 1743. Administration of his estate is in our Probate Records, XXXVI. 221. His son, Adam, the fourth, born 12 Aug. 1706, H. C., 1724, married Mary, daughter of Hugh Hall, Esq. of Boston, was clerk of our judicial courts, died 12 December, 1744. His will is in our Probate Records, XXXVII. 194. John, brother of the last Adam, H. C., 1732, was a member of the Royal Society, and distinguished as a professor at the University. The Dictionaries of Eliot and Allen duly honour him. The professor had four sons at the University; John, 1765, lived in Boston, a merchant; Adam, 1767, was master of a vessel in Gov. Hancock's employment, and in the Downs was knocked overboard and lost; James, 1769, a man of much curious erudition; William, 1770, the only survivor. Of these, John alone was married, and had issue, John, H. C., 1796, and Adam, H. C., 1800.

Brook, because the eldest of their company was one John [1]Masters. Thence they came to another high pointed rock, having a fair ascent on the west side, which they called Mount Feake, from one Robert [2]Feake, who had married the governour's daughter-in-law. On the west side of Mount Feake, they went up a very high rock, from whence they might see all over ||Neipnett,|| and a very high hill due west, about forty miles off, and to the N. W. the high hills by Merrimack, above sixty miles off.[3]

February 7.] The governour, Mr. Nowell, Mr. Eliot, and others, went over Mistick River at Medford, and going N. and by E. among the rocks about two or three miles, they came to a very great pond, having in the midst an island of about one acre, and very thick with trees of pine and ||beech;|| and the pond had divers small rocks, standing up here and there in it, which they therefore called [4]Spot Pond. They went all about it upon the ice. From thence (towards the N. W. about half a mile,) they came to the top of a very high rock, beneath which, (towards the N.) lies a goodly plain, part open land, and part woody, from whence there is a fair prospect, but it being then close and rainy, they could see but a small distance. This place they called Cheese Rock, because, when they went

||Whipcutt|| ||birch||

---

1 Masters was at this time, I presume, an inhabitant of Watertown, though the preceding year he lived, perhaps, at Newtown, where he made a dock, paid for by contribution of the whole colony. See Prince, II. 30, 31, 60, and Dr. Holmes's History of Cambridge, in 1 Hist. Coll. VII. 8, 10. Cambridge Records say, he died 21 December, 1639, and his wife five days after. His will, dated 19 December, 1639, is one of the earliest in our Probate Registry, being vol. I. 11.

2 At a court, 4 September following, he was "chosen into the place of lieutenant to Capt. Patrick," and he represented Watertown in the first, second, third, fifth, sixth, seventh and eighth courts of deputies; but my information of him reaches no farther than that, following the fortunes of Patrick, he united with him in the purchase of Greenwich, Conn. Trumbull, I. 116. The same gentleman is meant, where Hazard, II. 214, has erroneously given *Fenner*, as I know from the original act of the commissioners, preserved in the archives of the Massachusetts Historical Society. Feake's relation to the governour would certainly have saved him from the *necessity* of this emigration, which can only be ascribed to regard for his commander, or friendship to the settlers of the infant colony. In a very accurate description of Waltham, in 2 Hist. Coll. III. 261, the scene of this early survey, we are informed, that the name of the mountain is perpetuated.

3 The very high hill is Wachusett, the only elevation in Massachusetts, that justly asserts the name of mountain, though several heights claim it. The Merrimack hills are, I think, the spurs of Monadnock, usually called the Peterborough Mountains.

4 Succeeding generations have reverenced the first nomination.

to eat somewhat, they had only cheese, (the governour's man forgetting, for haste, to put up some bread.)

14.] The governour and some other company went to view the country as far as Neponsett, and returned that night.

[Large blank.]

17.] The governour and assistants called before them, at Boston, divers of Watertown; the pastor and elder by letter, and the others by warrant. The occasion was, for that a warrant being sent to Watertown for levying of £8, part of a rate of £60, ordered for the fortifying of the new town, the pastor and elder, &c. assembled the people and delivered their opinions, that it was not safe to pay moneys after that sort, for fear of bringing themselves §and posterity§ into bondage. Being come before the governour and council, after much debate, they acknowledged their fault, confessing freely, that they were in an errour, and made a retractation and submission under their hands, and were enjoined to read it in the assembly the next Lord's day. The ground of their errour was, for that they took this government to be no other but as of a mayor and aldermen, who have not power to make laws or raise taxations without the people; but understanding that this government was rather in the nature of a parliament, and that no assistant could be chosen but by the freemen, who had power likewise to remove the assistants and put in others, and therefore at every general court (which was to be held once every year) they had free liberty to consider and propound any thing concerning the same, and to declare their grievances, without being subject to question, or, &c. they were fully satisfied; and so their submission was accepted, and their offence pardoned.[1]

---

1 In the objection of these gentlemen of Watertown, there was much force, for no power was by the charter granted to the governour and assistants to raise money by levy, assessment or taxation. Indeed, the same may be said of the right of making general orders or laws; for the directors of the company, or court of assistants, could only be executive. The company, or great body of the corporation, however, submitted at first to the mild and equal temporary usurpation of the officers, chosen by themselves, which was also justified by indisputable necessity. So simply patriarchal was the government, and so indifferent was the majority of the settlers to retain their full charter rights, that, at the first general court, or meeting of the whole company, held at Boston, 19 October after their arrival, "for the establishing of the government, it was propounded, if it were not the best course, that the freemen should have the power of choosing assistants, when there are to be chosen, and the assistants, from amongst themselves, to choose a governour and deputy governour, who, with the assistants, should have the power of making laws and choosing officers to execute the same. This was fully assented unto by the general vote of the people and erection of hands." Col. Rec. I. 62.

March 5.] The first court after winter. It was ordered, that the courts (which before were every three weeks) should now be held the first Tuesday in every month.[1]

Commissioners appointed to set out the bounds of the towns.

14.] The bark Warwick arrived at Natascott, having been at Pascataquack and at Salem to sell corn, which she brought

---

Such an extraordinary surrender of power proves, that no jealousy was excited by the former assumption, by the governour and assistants, of the legislative, in addition to the executive and judicial functions, with which the charter seems to invest them. From the circumstance of omission of any mention, by our author, of that general court, we may conclude, that the grant was not viewed as very important. The crudity of their political system is farther evidenced by the neglecting to notice in the Records the choice of assistants the next year after such enlargement of their authority, especially if we remember, that, besides the governour and deputy, only five of the council remained, though the charter required eighteen. The manner of the early elections also, which was by proposing the former tenant of office for the new year, and calling for a show of hands, rendered the continuance of the assistants almost certain. But though the secretary has left no trace of the exercise of their rights, at the general meeting of May, 1631, in the choice of assistants, the people appear to have made inquiry on the subject, since it is recorded, I. 72, after notice of the election of governour and deputy, as follows: "For explanation of an order made the last general court, holden the 19th October last, it was ordered now, with full consent of all the *commons* then present, that, once in every year, at least, a general court shall be holden, at which court it shall be lawful for the commons to propound any person or persons, whom they shall desire to be chosen assistants, and if it be doubtful, whether it be the greater part of the commons or not, it shall be put to the poll. The like course to be holden, when they, the said commons, shall see cause, for any defect or misbehaviour, to remove any one or more of the assistants."

The cause of uneasiness, the second year, was, we may presume, the small number that constituted the supreme council or parliament. We may be certain, at least, that no inequality in the proportion of burdens sharpened the opposition to the assessment in the text; for of the thirty pounds levied in July preceding, Boston and Watertown had each *five*, and each paid equally in the subsequent rate. It might, by modern conjecture, be supposed, that the Watertown people were less satisfied with the object of the present expenditure; but this would be erroneous, for the other plantations would derive as little protection as they from this palisado; yet Dudley and Bradstreet were the only members of the court, by which the rate was levied, who lived at Newtown. To the agitation of this subject, we may refer the origin of that committee of two from each town to advise with the court about raising publick moneys, "so as what they should agree upon should bind all," which will be found a few pages onward, under date of May of this year. This led to the representative body, having the full powers of all the freemen, except that of elections.

[1] An order of extraordinary character was passed at this court, "that no planter within the limits of this jurisdiction, returning for England, shall carry either money or beaver with him, without leave from the governour (for the time being) under pain of forfeiting the money or beaver so intended to be transported." No comment can increase our sense of the dangerous power thus given, nor display the folly of such inhibition.

from Virginia. At her coming into Natascott, with a S. E. wind, she was in great danger, by a sudden gust, to be cast away upon the rocks.

19.] She came to Winysemett.

Mr. Maverick, one of the ministers of Dorchester, in drying a little powder, (which took fire by the heat of the fire pan,) fired a small barrel of two or three pounds, yet did no other harm but singed his clothes. It was in the new meeting-house, which was thatched, and the thatch only blacked a little.

April 3.] At a court at Boston, the deputy, Mr. Dudley, went away before the court was ended, and then the secretary delivered the governour a letter from him, directed to the governour and assistants, wherein he declared a resignation of his deputyship and place of assistant; but it was not allowed.

At this court an act was made expressing the governour's power, &c. and the office of the secretary and treasurer, &c.[1]

9.] The bark Warwick, and Mr. Maverick's pinnace, went out towards Virginia.

12.] The governour received letters from Plimouth, signifying, that there had been a broil between their men at Sowamset and the Naraganset Indians, who set upon the English house there to have taken [2]Owsamequin, the sagamore of Packanocott, who was fled thither with all his people for refuge; and that Capt. Standish, being gone thither to relieve the three English, which were in the house, had sent home in all haste for more men and other provisions, upon intelligence that Canonicus, with a great army, was coming against them. Withal they writ to our governour for some powder to be sent with all possible speed, (for it seemed they were unfurnished.) Upon this the governour presently despatched away the messenger with so much powder as he could carry, viz. twenty-seven pounds.

16.] The messenger returned, and brought a letter from the governour, signifying, that the Indians were retired from Sowams to fight with the Pequins, which was probable, because John Sagamore and Chickatabott were gone with all their men, §viz. John Sagamore with thirty, and Chickatabott with [blank]§ to Canonicus, who had sent for them.

---

1 No mention of the resignation of Dudley is found in the Colony Records; and it is remarkable, that equal disregard of these acts about the governour, secretary and treasurer is evinced, though to us they appear very important. One *curious* occurrence is, however, preserved there: "Thomas Knower was set in the bilbows for threatening the court, that if he should be punished, he would have it tried in England, whether he was lawfully punished or not."

2 Formerly called Massassoiet, father of the celebrated Philip.

A wear was erected by Watertown men upon Charles River, three miles above the town, where they took great store of shads.

A Dutch ship brought from Virginia two thousand bushels of corn, which was sold at four shillings sixpence the bushel.

May 1.] The governour and [1]assistants met at Boston to consider of the deputy his deserting his place. The points discussed were two. The 1st, upon what grounds he did it: 2d, whether it were good or void. For the 1st, his main reason was for publick peace; because he must needs discharge his conscience in speaking freely; and he saw that bred disturbance, &c. For the 2d, it was maintained by all, that he could not leave his place, except by the same power which put him in; yet he would not be put from his contrary opinion, nor would be persuaded to continue till the general court, which was to be the 9th of this month.

Another question fell out with him, about some bargains he had made with some poor men, members of the same congregation, to whom he had sold seven bushels and an half of corn to receive ten for it after harvest, which the governour and some others held to be oppressing usury,[2] and within compass of the statute; but he persisted to maintain it to be lawful, and there arose hot words about it, he telling the governour, that, if he had thought he had sent for him to his house to give him such usage, he would not have come there; and that he never knew any man of understanding of other opinion; and that the governour thought otherwise of it, it was his weakness. The governour took notice of these speeches, and bare them with more patience than he had done, upon a like occasion, at another time. Upon this there arose another question, about his house. The governour having ||formerly|| told him, that he did not well to bestow such cost about wainscoting and adorning his house, in the beginning of a plantation, both in regard of the necessity of publick charges, and for example, &c. his answer now was, that it was for the warmth of his house, and the charge was little, being but clapboards nailed to the wall

||freely||

---

1 Undoubtedly this was a private meeting, for notice of it is not found in the Records.

2 Common sense vindicated her rights long since in Massachusetts, though she has not yet obtained a full triumph in all dealings between man and man. The proviso in our statute against usury, 1783, c. 55, directs, that "nothing in this act shall extend to the letting of cattle, or other usages of the like nature, in practice amongst farmers, &c. *as hath been heretofore accustomed.*"

in the form of wainscot. These and other speeches passed before dinner. After dinner, the governour told ||them,|| that he had heard, that the people intended, at the next general court, to desire, that the assistants might be chosen anew every year, and that the governour might be chosen by the whole court, and not by the assistants only. Upon this, Mr. [1]Ludlow grew into passion, and said, that then we should have no government, but there would be an interim, wherein every man might do what he pleased, &c. This was answered and cleared in the judgment of the rest of the assistants, but he continued stiff in his opinion, and protested he would then return back into England.

Another ||[2]business|| fell out, which was this. Mr. [2]Clark of Watertown had complained to the governour, that Capt. [3]Patrick, being removed out of their town to Newtown, did compel them to watch near Newtown, and desired the governour, that they might have the ordering within their own town. The governour answered him, that the ordering of the watch did properly belong to the constable; but in those towns where the captains dwelt, they had thought fit to leave it to them, and since Capt. Patrick was removed, the constable might take

||him|| ||[2]question||

---

1 This name standing here, as in the former edition, though the reader was informed, in the list of errata, *four* in number, at the end, that it should be Dudley,—I must give a short explanation. Our original MS. is plain enough; the copy, too, prepared for the press by the secretary of Connecticut, written in an uncommonly fair hand, now in the archives of our Historical Society, I testify, follows Winthrop. The former editor, as he himself assured me, never read the original; and we must conjecture, and only conjecture, why, in making this errour, he did not follow the copy. Ludlow's name had not, in this conference, been mentioned before, as Dudley's had. The editor, by his correction of the text, against the authority of original and copy, must have thought proper, while reading the proof of the page, to insert Dudley, because he was the *only* person likely to fall into a passion.

2 William Clark, whom I presume the author to mean, was among the first freemen admitted; and, the week after this inquiry, a Mr. Clark was by the court chosen constable of Watertown. Nothing more of him is known by me, except he were the person of that name, among others, sent with the governour's son, in March following, to plant Ipswich.

3 He came in the fleet, it is probable, with the governour, as a military leader and instructer; for, at the court of assistants, 23 September, 1630, we find, Prince, II. 1, that fifty pounds were assessed on the plantations for him and Underhill. I suppose their pay was raised, as the colony became more able to bear the expense. At a court, 4 March, 1633, thirty pounds were levied, as their half year's compensation. Col. Rec. I. 96. Patrick was admitted a freeman in May, 1631; but for any farther information of him, except about his removing to Connecticut, it is in my power to do no more than refer to the second volume of this History, in which his death is commemorated, near the close of 1643.

care of it; but advised him withal to acquaint the deputy with it, and at the court it should be ordered. Clark went right home and told the captain, that the governour had ordered, that the constable should set the watch, (which was false;) but the captain answered somewhat rashly, and like a soldier, which being certified to the governour by three witnesses, he sent a warrant to the constable to this effect, that whereas some difficulty was fallen out, &c. about the watch, &c. he should, according to his office, see due watch should be kept till the court had taken order in it. This much displeased the captain, who came to this meeting to have it redressed. The governour told the rest what he had done, and upon what ground; whereupon they refused to do any thing in it till the court.

While they were thus sitting together, an Indian brings a letter from Capt. Standish, then at Sowams, to this effect, that the Dutchmen (which lay for trading at Anygansett or Naragansett) had lately informed him, that many Pequins (who were professed enemies to the Anagansetts) had been there divers days, and advised us to be watchful, &c. giving other reasons, &c.

Thus the day was spent and no good done, which was the more uncomfortable to most of them, because they had commended this meeting to God in more earnest manner than ordinary at other meetings.

May 8.] A general court at Boston. Whereas it was (at our first coming) agreed, that the freemen should choose the assistants, and they the governour, the whole court agreed now, that the governour and assistants should all be new chosen every year by the general court, (the governour to be always chosen out of the assistants;) and accordingly the old governour, John Winthrop, was chosen; accordingly all the rest as before, and Mr. [1]Humfrey and Mr. Coddington also, because they were daily expected.

---

1 This distinguished planter deserves greater honour than he has received from the brief note of Hutchinson, which Eliot transcribed, but could not enlarge. Allen has forgotten to name him; but his importance in the colony will be observed from many passages of this History. He had been chosen deputy governour at a general court of our company in England, 20 October, 1629, though our annual registers, that used to record, in their list of gentlemen who had filled that office, the name of Goffe, who never came to our country, omitted that of Humfrey. He was also one of the original patentees of the colony of Connecticut. Haz. I. 318. An adventurous desire of planting new colonies consumed his estate; and all wish to end his life with us must have been destroyed by the shocking calamities in his family, of which notice will be found in these pages, under date of No-

The deputy governour, Thomas Dudley, Esq. having submitted the validity of his resignation to the vote of the court, it was adjudged a nullity, and he accepted of his place again, and the governour and he being reconciled the day before, all things were carried very lovingly amongst all, &c. and the people carried themselves with much silence and modesty.

John Winthrop, the governour's son, was chosen an assistant.

A proposition was made by the people, that every company of trained men might choose their own captain and officers; but the governour giving them reasons to the contrary, they were satisfied ||without|| it.

Every town chose two men to be at the next court, to advise with the governour and assistants about the raising of a publick stock, so as what they should agree upon should bind all, &c.[1]

This court was begun and ended with speeches for the, &c. as formerly.

||with||

---

vember, 1641. If any reader would excuse his natural indignation, felt on perusal of the narrative of Hubbard, 379, when obscurely commenting on these sufferings, which he almost calls a judgment for the offence of leaving our country, he may recollect, that the full relation of Winthrop was then lying before Hubbard, and then study the character of the afflicted father in his letter to our author, 4 September, 1646, in Hutchinson's Coll. 159. No praise of the subject of this note can be equivalent to that epistle.

Humfrey was brother-in-law of Isaac Johnson, having married Susan, sister of the lady Arbella. From his connexion with the Earl of Lincoln, I presume, that he was *not* the person, *honoured* by an order of the celebrated "High Court of Justice," 20 January, 1648—9, "that Sir Henry Mildmay be desired to deliver unto John Humphreys, Esq. the sword of state in his custody, which said sword, the said Mr. Humphreys is to bear before the lord president of this court." Perhaps he had no connexion with those proceedings, which, in a few days, terminated in the execution of his sovereign. I have been favoured with four letters from him to John Winthrop, the younger, of 18 August and 4 November, 1631, 21 June and 3 December, 1632; the first directed for him "at the Dolphin, Mr. Humfries' house, in Sandwich," when preparing to come over with his father's wife and his own, the other three to him here at Boston, all written before Humfrey left England. They are full of pious reflections and encouragement to the plantation; but give no assistance to merely historical inquirers.

[1] Prince, II. 60, gives, from the Colony Records, the names of the gentlemen that formed this embryo of a parliament:

1. Mr. Oldham and Mr. Masters, for Watertown.
2. Robert Coles and John Johnson, for Roxbury.
3. Mr. William Colbron and William Cheesbrough, for Boston.
4. Richard Wright and ————, for Sagus.
5. Mr. Lockwood and Mr. Spencer, for Newton.
6. Mr. Gibbons and Mr. Palmer, for Charlestown.
7. Mr. Conant and Peter Palfrey, for Salem.
8. William Felps and John Gallard, for Dorchester.

The governour, among other things, used this speech to the people, after he had taken his oath: That he had received gratuities from divers towns, which he received with much comfort and content; he had also received many kindnesses from particular persons, which he would not refuse, lest he should be accounted uncourteous, &c.; but he ||professed,|| that he received them with a trembling heart, in regard of God's rule, and the consciousness of his own ||[2]infirmity;|| and therefore desired them, that hereafter they would not take it ill, if he did refuse presents from particular persons, except they were from the assistants, or from some special friends; to which no answer was made; but he was told after, that many good people were much grieved at it, for that he never had any allowance towards the charge of his place.

24.] The fortification upon the Corn Hill at Boston was begun.

25.] Charlestown men came and wrought upon the fortification.

Roxbury the next, and Dorchester the next.

26.] The Whale arrived with Mr. Wilson, Mr. [1]Dummer, and about thirty passengers, all in health; and of seventy cows lost but two. She came from Hampton April 8th. Mr. Graves was master.

June 5.] The William and Francis, Mr. Thomas master, with about sixty passengers, whereof Mr. [2]Welde and old Mr.

||expressed|| ||[2]inconformity||

---

[1] Richard Dummer will be frequently mentioned in this History, and Hutchinson and Eliot have well preserved his reputation. It is less remarkable, that the former fell into an errour of three years in the date of this gentleman's arrival, than that the latter copied it, with Winthrop in his possession. The mistake of one letter of the name in the former edition, however, prevented Eliot, perhaps, from obtaining the fact from the text, though it had been correctly given by Prince. In this place, it may be proper to observe another errour in the New England Biography of Dummer. He was of Roxbury, not Boston, before his settlement at Newbury. In the antinomian controversy, he was of the heterodox, or weaker party, and of course punished for his opinions. With others of the same principles, he purchased Rhode Island; but soon after returned to Massachusetts; and even Johnson praises him. He was grandfather of the celebrated Jeremy Dummer; and from the selection of Newbury for his charity, I incline to think Lieut. Gov. William Dummer, founder of Dummer Academy, derived his descent from this gentleman.

[2] Of Thomas Welde, enough, it may seem, to an indifferent reader, will be found in the progress of this History, or in the Dictionaries of Eliot and Allen. But as he figures in one of the most important events of our colonial history, and himself furnished a Narrative of it, I shall not be restrained from honouring him further in these notes, at a more proper place. It may now only be necessary to suggest, connected with Eliot's compliment, that "we

[1]Batchelor (being aged 71) were, with their families, and many other honest men; also, the Charles of Barnstable, with near eighty cows and six mares, Mr. [2]Hatherly, the merchant, and about twenty passengers, all safe, and in health. They set sail, viz. the William and Francis from London, March the 9th, and the Charles from ||Barnstable,|| April 10th, and met near Cape Ann. Mr. [3]Winslow of Plimouth came in the William and Francis.

12.] The James, Mr. Grant master, arrived. Her passage was eight weeks from London. ||[2]She|| brought sixty-one heifers and lost forty, and brought twelve passengers.

13.] A day of thanksgiving in all the plantations, by publick

||Portsmouth|| ||[2]He||

---

may suppose him a very prudent and judicious man," the cautions of the same author, in the history of his celebrated namesake, before referred to. 1 Hist. Coll. VIII. 7 and 8. Welde had suffered in England from the follies of the bishops. See the interesting letters of Henry Jacie, in 3 Hist. Coll. I. 235. There was a brother of the clergyman, Joseph, at Roxbury; and, I believe, of both, certainly of Thomas, descendants are spread in the land.

1 This unfortunate gentleman, Stephen Batchelor, whose name does not occur in either of the Biographical Dictionaries, will often be noticed in the pages of this work, about the close of 1635, while he remained at Lynn, in November, 1641, when he was pastor at Hampton, and in July, 1644, when he was restrained from the exercise of his office at Exeter. Hubbard, 193, mentions Newbury, as another scene of his disquiet, which might be in the progress from Lynn to Hampton; and in Belknap's New Hampshire, I. 37 and 52, his name is introduced. An unfavourable opinion of Batchelor seems to have prevailed soon after his arrival; for, in our Colony Records, I. 93, I find, he was, at a court, 3 October, 1632, "required to forbear exercising his gifts as a pastor or teacher publickly in our patent, unless it be to those he brought with him, for his contempt of authority, and till some scandals be removed." But, at the court, 4 March following, he was relieved from this inhibition. Johnson, in the wretched verses, with which he usually closes his notice of the distinguished men of the colony, advises him, as if he were alive at the period, when his age of ninety must have disinclined him to regard the precept,

"Teach thyself with others thou hast need;
Thy flowing fame unto low ebb is brought."

2 It is not to be expected, that any thing can be added by me to the acquisitions of the distinguished antiquary, who honours Timothy Hatherly, "the principal founder and father of the town of Scituate," in his account of that place, 2 Hist. Coll. IV. 241.

3 To the life of Edward Winslow, governour of Plimouth, a great man in all circumstances, the elaborate work of Dr. Belknap has afforded sufficient care; but whatever, beyond the American Biographer, can be acquired by diligence and adorned by affection, must be expected from the new edition of Morton's Memorial. A very interesting letter from Winslow, at Barbados, March, 1654—5, on Cromwell's great expedition against the Spanish West Indies, in which he died, is contained in Thurlow's State Papers, published by Birch, III. 250.

authority, for the good success of the king of Sweden, and Protestants in Germany, against the emperour, &c., and for the safe arrival of all the ships, they having not lost one person, nor one sick among them.

§14.] The governour was invited to dinner aboard the Whale. The master fetched him in his boat, and gave him three pieces at his going off.§

The French came in a pinnace to Penobscot, and rifled a trucking house belonging to Plimouth, carrying thence three hundred weight of beaver and other goods.[1] *They took also one Dixy Bull and his shallop and goods.*

One Abraham ||Shurd|| of Pemaquid, and one Capt. [2]Wright, and others, coming to Pascataquack, being bound for this bay in a shallop with £200 worth of commodities, one of the seamen, going to light a pipe of tobacco, set fire on a barrel of powder, which tare the ||2boat|| in pieces. That man was never seen: the rest were all saved, but the goods lost.

The man, that was blown away with the powder in the boat at Pascataquack, was after found[3] with his hands and feet torn off. This fellow, being wished by another to forbear to take any tobacco, till they came to the shore, which was hard by, answered, that if the devil should carry him away quick, he would take one pipe. Some in the boat were so drunk and fast asleep, as they did not awake with the noise.

A shallop of one Henry Way of Dorchester, having been missing all the winter, it was found that the men in her, being five, were all killed treacherously by the eastern Indians.

Another shallop of his being sent out to seek out the other, was cast away at Aquamenticus, and two of the men drowned.[4] A fishing shallop at Isle of Shoals was overset. One

||Sheert|| ||2bark||

---

1 Ample account is given of this hostile, or felonious, transaction, by Gov. Bradford, preserved by Prince, II. 62.

2 I presume this to be the same person, who was one of two chosen for Sagus, about a publick stock, as mentioned in a note on page 76. Hubbard, 195, makes all the people in the boat belong to Pemaquid; but I give little credit to him, because it is evident, that he took all his information from Winthrop, in this place, and copied him so carelessly as to give the year 1633.

3 Mather introduced this accident, sixty-five years after, into a sermon, Magn. VI. with a ridiculous addition, of the body being found in *the woods long after*, torn in pieces.

4 My chief object, in this note, is to observe an errour in one of the most accurate and complete of all our topographical histories, that of Dorchester, by the Rev. Dr. T. M. Harris. In 1 Hist. Coll. IX. 152, after inserting the

Noddle, an honest man of Salem, ||carrying|| wood in a canoe, in the South River, was overturned and drowned.

July.] At a training at Watertown, a man of John ||²Oldham's,||[1] having a musket, which had been long charged with

||running|| ||²Alden's||

---

substance of the two preceding sentences, on the authority of Hubbard, 198, then existing only in MS., instead of Winthrop, from whom Hubbard took his story, with a trifling addition, which probably is a mistake, that *Way* with his company perished by the Indians,—these absurd remarks are added, from Hubbard, but ascribed to our author: "Thus ofttimes, he that is greedy of gain troubles his own house; and, instead of acquiring a little pelf of this world, loses his own life in the conclusion; which hath been observed as very remarkable on many, who have followed that course of life." Some gratitude might be due to Hubbard, perhaps, had he enlarged the facts, as well as the words, of the text; but as his work was written nearly fifty years after the occurrence of an event so comparatively unimportant, I am convinced, that he carelessly added the murder of Way, without any information, having intended nothing more than to transcribe, as usual with him, the contemporary narrative. From the silence of Winthrop on a particular, which would have been the principal incident of the tragedy, as reported at the time, and from the subsequent expedition of another shallop of *his*, that Way was *not* killed, would be a probable conclusion; but this is rendered certain by the MS. annals of Blake of Dorchester, who, under 1667, mentions his death at the mature age of eighty-four years.

1 Copious materials for the character of this person are found in Morton's Memorial, 74—82, condensed by Hubbard, 92—94, who suggests to our judgment some reasonable cautions in perusing the Plimouth secretary. The contemporary, Gov. Bradford, in Prince, I. 149, 153, 154, affords also some better information, which proves that Oldham was much disliked. But he was so far restored to the affections of the first colonists, after some years, as to be intrusted with their letters to England, in June, 1628, when Thomas Morton was sent home a prisoner. 1 Hist. Coll. III. 63. Oldham was, probably, very enterprising, and less disposed to overlook this world, in his regard for the next, than most of his early neighbours. His boldness and acquaintance with the natives, and perhaps disaffection to the rigid church discipline of the separatists at Plimouth, rendered him not unacceptable to our planters, though he desired to pursue a course independent of their territorial rights. See, in Hazard, I. 256, a most valuable letter from the governour and company to Endecott in 1629. This planter was certainly held in respect in this colony; for he was one of that assembly, mentioned in May preceding, page 76, and was chosen from Watertown, where dwelt many gentlemen, esteemed even by the authority of Plimouth. He had, perhaps, seated himself at Watertown, before the arrival of Winthrop, coming over after the fleet that brought Higginson, Skelton and Sharp; or he may have come in the great fleet of 1630; but we are confident he was not here in season to witness the Indian deed to Wheelwright. Trumbull, in two places, I. 34 and 72, erroneously called him of Dorchester, one of Warham's congregation. Oldham's favour with the Narragansetts, and murder by some of those of Block Island, which was a principal incitement in Massachusetts to the great Pequot war, will be found hereafter in this History.

In copying the relation of the accident mentioned in the text, Prince assumes the date of it to be Monday, 2 July, because, at a court on the 3d, the first order that passed, was, "that the captain and other officers take a special care to search all pieces brought into the field, for being charged with shot or pistol bullets, ||not|| knowing of it, gave fire, and shot three men, two into their bodies, and one into his hands;[1] but it was so far off, as the shot entered the skin and stayed there, and they all recovered.

The congregation at Boston wrote to the elders and brethren of the churches of Plimouth, Salem, &c. for their advice in three questions: 1. Whether one person might be a civil magistrate and a ruling elder at the same time? 2. If not, then ||2which|| should be ||3laid down?|| 3. Whether there might be divers pastors in the same church?—The 1st was agreed by all negatively; the 2d doubtfully; the 3d doubtful also.

[Large blank.]

The strife in Watertown congregation continued still; but at length they gave the separatists a day to come in, or ||4else|| to be proceeded against.

5.] At the day, all came in and submitted, except John Masters, who, though he were advised by divers ministers and others, that he had offended in turning his back upon the sacrament, and departing out of the assembly, &c. because ||5they|| had then admitted a member whom he judged unfit, &c.; yet he persisted. So the congregation (being loath to proceed against him) gave him a further day; 8, at which time, he continuing obstinate, they excommunicated him; but, about a fortnight after, he submitted himself, and was received in again.

[Blank.]

At Watertown there was (in the view of divers witnesses) a great combat between a mouse and a snake; and, after a long fight, the mouse prevailed and killed the snake. The ||6pastor|| of Boston, Mr. Wilson, a very sincere, holy man, hearing of it, gave this interpretation: That the snake was the devil; the mouse was a poor contemptible people, which God had brought hither, which should overcome Satan here, and dispossess him of his kingdom. Upon the same occasion, he told the governour, that, before he was resolved to come into this country, he dreamed he was here, and that he saw a church arise out of the earth, which grew up and became a marvellous goodly church.

||and|| ||2what|| ||3best done|| ||4all|| ||5he|| ||6minister||

---

bullets; and that no person whatever shall, at any time, charge any piece of service with bullets or shot, other than for defence of their houses, or at command from the captain, upon such penalty as the court shall think meet to inflict."

[1] Prince, II. 63, reads this word *head*. It does not look so to me.

After many ||imparlances|| and days of humiliation, by those of Boston and Roxbury, to seek the Lord for Mr. Welde his disposing, and the advice of those of Plimouth being taken, &c. at length he resolved to sit down with them of Roxbury.

[Large blank.]

August 3.] The deputy, Mr. Thomas Dudley, being still discontented with the governour, partly for that the governour had removed the frame of his house, which he had set up at Newtown, and partly for that he took too much authority upon him, (as he conceived,) renewed his complaints to Mr. Wilson and Mr. Welde, who acquainting the governour therewith, a meeting was agreed upon at Charlestown, where were present the governour and deputy, Mr. Nowell, Mr. Wilson, Mr. Welde, Mr. Maverick, and Mr. [1]Warham. The conference being begun with calling upon the Lord, the deputy began,—that howsoever he had some ||[2]particular|| grievances, &c.; yet, seeing he was advised by those present, and divers of the assistants, to be silent in them, he would let them pass, and so come first to complain of the breach of promise, both in the governour and others, in not building at Newtown. The governour answered, that he had performed the words of the promise; for he had a house up, and seven or eight servants abiding in it, by the day appointed: and for the removing of his house, he alleged, that, seeing that the rest of the assistants went not about to build, and that his neighbours of Boston had been discouraged from removing thither by Mr. Deputy himself, and thereupon had (under all their hands) petitioned him, that (according to the promise he made to them when they first sate down with him at Boston, viz. that he would not remove, except they went with him) he would not leave them;—this was the occasion that he removed his house. Upon these and other speeches to this purpose, the ministers went apart for one hour; then returning, they delivered their opinions, that the governour was in fault

||importunings|| ||[2]publick||

---

[1] John Warham receives little notice from Eliot and Allen, to which, after consulting their authorities, I presume nothing can be added. Fuller, in his letter to Bradford, June, 1630, 1 Hist. Coll. III. 74, mentions his colloquy on religion with the people of Dorchester, till *he was weary*. "Mr. Warham holds, that the visible church may consist of a mixed people—godly and openly ungodly; upon which point we had all our conference, to which, I trust, the Lord will give a blessing." This is sufficient, even though not reported, perhaps, with adequate precision, to satisfy us, that this gentleman's opinions were less strict than those of the Plimouth colonists. From Mather's 18th chapter of the 3d book of the Magnalia, devoted to Warham, it would not be easy to learn more of him, than that he preached without notes, went to Windsor, Conn. and was of a melancholy temperament.

for removing of his house so suddenly, without conferring with the deputy and the rest of the assistants; but if the deputy were the occasion of discouraging Boston men from removing, it would excuse the governour a ||tanto,|| but not a ||[2]toto||. The governour, professing himself willing to submit his own opinion to the judgment of so many wise and godly friends, acknowledged himself faulty.

After dinner, the deputy proceeded in his complaint, yet with this protestation, that what he should charge the governour with, was in love, and out of his care of the publick, and that the things which he should produce were but for his own satisfaction, and not by way of accusation. Then demanded he of him the ground and limits of his authority, whether by the patent or otherwise. The governour answered, that he was willing to stand to that which he propounded, and would challenge no greater authority than he might by the patent. The deputy replied, that then he had no more authority than every assistant, (except power to call courts, and ||[3]precedency,|| for honour and order.) The governour answered, he had more; for the patent, making him a governour, gave him whatsoever power belonged to a governour by common law or the statutes, and desired him to show wherein he had exceeded, &c.; and speaking this somewhat apprehensively, the deputy began to be in passion, and told the governour, that if he were so round, he would be round too. The governour bad him be round, if he would. So the deputy rose up in great fury and passion, and the governour grew very hot also, so as they both fell into bitterness; but, by mediation of the mediators, they were soon pacified. Then the deputy proceeded to particulars, as followeth:

1st. By what authority the governour removed the ordnance and erected a fort at Boston.—The governour answered, that the ordnance lying upon the beach in danger of spoiling, and having often complained of it in the court, and nothing done, with the help of divers of the assistants, they were mounted upon their carriages, and removed where they might be of some use: and for the fort, it had been agreed, above a year before, that it should be erected there: and all this was done without any penny charge to the publick.

2d. By what authority he lent twenty-eight pounds of powder to those of Plimouth.—Governour answered, it was of his own powder, and upon their urgent distress, their own powder proving naught, when they were to send to the ||[4]rescue|| of their men at Sowamsett.

||quanto|| ||[2]tanto|| ||[3]proceedings|| ||[4]rest||

3d. By what authority he had licensed Edward [1]Johnson to sit down at Merrimack.—Governour answered, that he had licensed him only to go forth on trading, (as he had done divers others,) as belonging to his place.

4th. By what authority he had given them of Watertown leave to erect a wear upon Charles River, and had disposed of lands to divers, &c.—Governour answered, the people of Watertown, falling very short of corn the last year, for want of fish,[2] did complain, &c., and desired leave to erect a wear; and upon this the governour told them, that he could not give them leave, but they must seek it of the court; but because it would be long before the courts began again, and, if they deferred till then, the season would be lost, he wished them to do it, and there was no doubt but, being for so general a good, the court would allow of it; and, for his part, he would employ all his power in the court, so as he should sink under it, if it were not allowed; and besides, those of Roxbury had erected a wear

---

1 This person I presume to be the same, of whom mention will recur in our second volume, September, 1643, as one of the leaders of the expedition against Gorton, for which station he seems to be designated by his severe bigotry. He probably came in the fleet with Winthrop, is enumerated with those desiring to be made freemen, 19 October, 1630, and admitted in May following. From the phrase, "at Merrimack," in the text, we must not imagine, that a permanent settlement was made by Johnson; for no such was made for some years, and his residence was Charlestown, probably in the upper part, which became Woburn in 1642. It is strange, that his name is omitted in Eliot's Dictionary, and that Allen has given but seven lines to the enthusiastick historian of "The Wonder-working Providence of Zion's Saviour in New England." This work, published in London, 1654, had become very scarce, and was republished in 2 Hist. Coll. II. III. IV. VII. and VIII., the editor of this History supervising the proof-sheets of that, and faithfully preserving the exact reading of the original, with *most* of its errours, in some instances furnishing a certain or conjectural correction in the margin. Johnson was one year speaker of the house of deputies, as will be seen in another part of this work, and his reputation was maintained by one, at least, of his sons, William, a sturdy supporter of the old charter. Robert, H. C., 1645, is also thought to be one, and to be alluded to by his father, lib. II. c. 19, as acting in the Summer Islands. A good account of this pilgrim is furnished by Rev. Mr. Chickering, formerly minister of Woburn, extracted into 2 Hist. Coll. II. 95—and a letter in the Columbian Centinel, 16 June, 1819, written by a descendant, John Farmer, Esq. one of the editors of the New Hampshire Historical Collections, and, with some improvement, taken into their volume now in the press, page 252. There are some interesting materials in the work of Johnson, that can be found in no other place; but the style is above or below criticism.

2 For manure. The husbandry, taught our fathers by the Indians, whose contented indolence permitted them to seek no better compost, with materials for which, especially marine grasses, the shores and woods abounded, lasted, I imagine, not much beyond their exclusive devotion to the cultivation of maize.

without any license from the court. And for lands, he had ||disposed of none,|| otherwise than the deputy and other of the assistants had done,—he had only given his consent, ||[2]but|| referred them to the court, &c. But the deputy had taken more upon him, in that, without order of court, he had empaled, at Newtown, above one thousand acres, and had assigned lands to some there.

5th. By what authority he had given license to Ratcliff and [1]Grey (being banished men) to stay within our limits.—Governour answered, he did it by that authority, which was granted him in court, viz. that, upon any sentence in criminal causes, the governour might, upon cause, stay the execution till the next court. Now the cause was, that, being in the winter, they must otherwise have perished.

6th. Why the fines were not levied.—Governour answered, it belonged to the secretary and not to him: he never refused to sign any that were brought to him; nay, he had called upon the secretary for it; yet he confessed, that it was his judgment, that it were not fit, in the infancy of a commonwealth, to be too strict in levying fines, though severe in other punishments.

§7th. That when a cause had been voted by the rest of the court, the governour would bring new reasons, and move them to alter the sentence:—which the governour justified, and all approved.§

The deputy having made an end, the governour desired the mediators to consider, whether he had exceeded his authority or not, and how little cause the deputy had to charge him with it; for if he had made some slips, in two or three years' government, he ought rather to have covered them, seeing he could not be charged that he had taken advantage of his au-

||not disposed any|| ||[2]and||

---

1 Of Ratcliff nothing need be added to the note on page 56. The other culprit was early obnoxious to censure. At the court, 28 September, 1630, he was "enjoined, under the penalty of £10, to attend on the court in person, this day three weeks, to answer divers things objected against him, and to remove himself out of the limits of this patent before the end of March next." Col. Rec. I. 59. His disregard of the latter part of this order was, perhaps, not the only cause of the severity of the sentence in October of the next year, "that Thomas Gray's house at Marble Harbour shall be pulled down, and that no Englishman shall hereafter give house-room to him, or entertain him, under such penalty as the court shall think meet to inflict." The delay, in executing this interdict, by the governour, was the honourable occasion of Dudley's accusation of him. But the sentence remained, probably, inoperative; for, so long after as the court, 5 June, 1638, I find the same fellow "censured to be severely whipped, and the former execution of banishment to be inflicted." Col. Rec. I. 225.

thority to oppress or wrong any man, or to benefit himself; but, for want of a publick stock, had disbursed all common charges out of his own estate; whereas the deputy would never lay out one penny, &c.; and, besides, he could shew that under his hand, that would convince him of a greater exceeding his authority, than all that the deputy could charge him with, viz. that whereas Binks and Johnson were bound in open court to appear at next court to account to, &c. he had, out of court, discharged them of their appearance. The deputy answered, that the party, to whom they were to account, came to him and confessed that he was satisfied, and that the parties were to go to Virginia; so he thought he might discharge them.

Though the governour might justly have refused to answer these seven articles, wherewith the deputy had charged him, both for that he had no knowledge of them before, (the meeting being only for the deputy his personal grievances,) and also for that the governour was not to give account of his actions to any but to the court; yet, out of his desire of the publick peace, and to clear his reputation with those to whom the deputy had accused him, he was willing to give him satisfaction, to the end, that he might free him of such jealousy as he had conceived, that the governour intended to make himself popular, that he might gain absolute power, and bring all the assistants under his subjection; which was very improbable, seeing the governour had propounded in court to have an order established for limiting the governour's authority, and had himself drawn articles for that end, which had been approved and established by the whole court; neither could he justly be charged to have transgressed any of them. So the meeting breaking up, without any other conclusion but the commending the success of it by prayer to the Lord, the governour brought the deputy onward of his way, and every man went to his own home. §See two pages after.§

5.] The sachem, who was joined with Canonicus the great sachem of Naragansett, called Mecumeh, after Miantonomoh, being at Boston, where [he] had lodged two nights with his squaw, and about twelve sanapps, being present at the sermon, three of his sanapps went, in the mean time, and brake into a neighbour's house, &c. Complaint being made thereof to the governour, after evening exercise, he told the sachem of it, and with some difficulty caused him to make one of his sanapps to beat them, and then sent them out of the town; but brought the sachem and the rest of [the] company to his house, and made much of them, (as he had done before,) which he seemed to be well pleased with; but that evening he departed.

At a court not long before, two of Chickatabott's men were convented and convicted for assaulting some English of Dorchester in their houses, &c. They were put in the bilboes, and Chickatabot required to beat them, which he did.

[Large blank.]

The congregation of Boston and Charlestown began the meeting-house at Boston, for which, and Mr. Wilson's house, they had made a voluntary contribution of about one hundred and twenty pounds.

[Blank.]

14.] Fair weather and small wind, and N. E. at Boston, and, at the same time, such a tempest of wind N. E. a little without the bay, as no boat could bear sail, and one had her mast borne by the board. So again, when there hath [been] a very tempest at N. W. or W. in the bay, there hath been a stark calm one league or two off shore.[1]

This summer was very wet and cold, (except now and then a hot day or two,) which caused great store of musketoes and rattle-snakes. The corn, in the dry, sandy grounds, was much better than other years, but in the ||fatter|| grounds much worse; and in Boston, &c. much shorn down close by the ground with worms.

The windmill was brought down to Boston, because, where it stood near ||[2]Newtown,|| it would not grind but with a westerly wind.

Mr. ||[3]Oldham|| had a small house near the wear at Watertown, made all of clapboards, burnt down by making a fire in it when it had no chimney.

This week they ||[4]had|| in barley and oats, at Sagus, above twenty acres good corn, and ||[5]sown|| with the plough.

Great store of eels and lobsters in the bay. Two or three boys have brought in a bushel of great eels at a time, and sixty great lobsters.

The [2]Braintree company, (which had begun to sit down at

||flatter|| ||[2]Watertown|| ||[3]Pelham|| ||[4]harvested|| ||[5]strove||

[1] This sentence, in different ink, was probably written some time after the preceding.

[2] Deriving their name from a village in England, near Chelmsford, where Mr. Hooker was the preacher. It was, like many others, perpetuated, by the affection of the settlers, in Massachusetts; but, on a division of the town, the part, first occupied, nearest the bay, in which Mount Wollaston is included, was called Quincy. See note on page 43.

Mount Wollaston,) by order of court, removed to Newtown. These were Mr. [1]Hooker's company.

The governour's wife was delivered of a son, who was baptized by the name of [2]William. The governour himself held the child to baptism, as others in the congregation did use. William signifies a common man, &c.

30.] Notice being given of ten sagamores and many Indians assembled at [3]Muddy River, the governour sent Capt. ||Underhill,|| with twenty musketeers, to discover, &c.; but at Roxbury they heard they were broke up.

September 4.] One [4]Hopkins, of Watertown, was convict for selling a piece and pistol, with powder and shot, to James Sagamore, for which he had sentence to be whipped and branded in the cheek. It was discovered by an Indian, one of James's men, upon promise of concealing him, (for otherwise he was sure to be killed.)

[Large blank.]

The ministers afterward, for an end of the difference between the governour and deputy, ordered, that the governour should procure them a minister at Newtown, and contribute somewhat towards his maintenance for a time; or, if he could not, by the spring, effect that, then to give the deputy, towards his charges in building there, twenty pounds. The governour accepted this order, and promised to perform it in one of the kinds. But the deputy, having received one part of the order,

1 His company came before their pastor. Of Hooker enough will be found in the Magnalia, in Holmes's History of Cambridge, 1 Hist. Coll. VII. 38, in Trumbull's Connecticut, I. 293, and in the biographical works of Eliot and Allen, to excuse the editor from any farther research. The high esteem, in which he was held, will often appear in the progress of this work. A line of pious, useful and honourable descendants have embalmed the memory of their ancestor; and, in a former age, his writings were valued with those of the very first class of New England divines.

2 Knowing nothing more of this son, I presume he died soon, as our Town Registry does not even enrol his birth. The church record is, " William, son of our brother John Winthrop, governour, baptized 26 of 6, 1632."

3 This place is now the village of Brookline, the most beautiful in New England; for a very minute account of which, see 2 Hist. Coll. II. 140.

4 Notice of this misdemeanour, in Colony Records, I. 93, concludes with a suggestion, proving the correct estimate by our ancestors of the dangers of such trade with the Indians, though melancholy experience showed the impracticability of prevention: " Hereupon it was propounded, if this offence should not be punished hereafter by death. Referred to the next court to be determined." Of the offender nothing more is discoverable, than that his given name was Richard.

returned the same to the governour, with this reason to Mr. Wilson, that he was so well persuaded of the governour's love to him, and did prize it so much, as if ||they|| had given him one hundred pounds instead of twenty pounds, he would not have taken it.

Notwithstanding the heat of contention, which had been between the governour and deputy, yet they ||[2]usually|| met about their affairs, and that without any appearance of any breach or discontent; and ever after kept peace and good correspondency together, in love and friendship.[1]

One [2]Jenkins, late an inhabitant of Dorchester, and now removed to Cape Porpus, went with an Indian up into [the] country with store of goods to truck, and, being asleep in a wigwam ||[3]of|| one of Passaconamy's men, was killed in the night by an Indian, dwelling near the Mohawks' country, who fled away with his goods, but was fetched back by Passaconamy. There was much suspicion, that the Indians had some plot against the English, both for that many Naragansett men, &c. gathered together, who, with those of these parts, pretended to make war upon the Neipnett men, and divers insolent speeches were used by some of them, and they did not frequent our houses as they were wont, and one of their pawawes told us, that there was a conspiracy to cut us off to get our victuals and other substance. Upon this there was a camp pitched at Boston in the night, to exercise the soldiers against need might be; and Capt. Underhill (to try how they would behave themselves) caused an alarm to be given upon the quarters, which discovered the weakness of our people, who, like men amazed, knew not how to behave themselves, so as the officers could not draw them into any order. All the rest of the plantations took the alarm and answered it; but it caused much fear and distraction among the common sort, so as some, which knew of it before, yet through fear had forgotten, and believed the Indians had been upon us. We doubled our guards, and kept watch each day and night.

14.] The rumour still increasing, the three next sagamores were sent for, who came presently to the governour.

||he|| ||[2]peaceably|| ||[3]with||

1 In a later hand the last clause appears; and it was, perhaps, introduced after the family union between the respective children.

2 Perhaps the settlement of that portion of the coast of Maine, which is now in the town of Arundel, would not be known to have been made so early, without this sentence of our text. Nothing more of Jenkins is known to me, than here inserted, of the manner of his death.

16, being the Lord's day.] In the evening Mr. Peirce, in the ship Lyon, arrived, and came to an anchor before Boston. He brought one hundred and twenty-three passengers, whereof fifty children, all in health; and ||lost|| not one person by the way, save his carpenter, who fell overboard as he was caulking a port. They had been twelve weeks aboard, and eight weeks from the Land's End. He had five days east wind and thick fog, so as he was forced to come, all that time, by the lead; and the first land he made was Cape Ann.

22.] The Barnstable ship went out at ||[2]Pullen|| Point to Marble Harbour.

27.] A day of thanksgiving at Boston for the good news of the prosperous success of the king of Sweden, &c., and for the safe arrival of the last ship and all the passengers, &c.

October 18.] Capt. [1]Camock, and one Mr. [2]Godfry, a

||left|| ||[2]Helen's||

---

1 Hubbard, 216, was therefore mistaken in saying, that Cammock came not "to New England till about the year 1633;" and as he, with Henry Josselyn, Belk. N. H. I. 21, was appointed attorney, in a deed of 3 November, 1631, to give possession to Sir F. Gorges and other grantees of the president and council of New England, I conclude, that he had either settled before at Piscataqua, or a little to the eastward, or was at that time projecting the expedition, which he made in the following spring. Sullivan, in his History of Maine, 128, says, that "the council of Plimouth, in the year 1629, granted to Thomas Cammock, five thousand acres in Black Point, now in Scarborough, which are held on the east side of that town, under the title of that grant, at this day. Cammock was the *nephew* of the Earl of Warwick, and came over in 1663, and died at Scarborough." Perhaps this was designed to show the first voyage, and, if so, the errour arose from inadvertently taking the date of John Josselyn's *second* voyage for the first, in 1638, in which this *gentleman*, page 10, informs us, that Cammock, whom he calls "a near kinsman of the earl," was his fellow passenger. But it is plain enough, from the text, that he was here long before.

2 Edward Godfrey was very honourably entrusted by Mason and his joint adventurers, as appears by a letter of 5 December, 1632, preserved in Belknap's N. H., I. Appendix iii. In the charter from Sir F. Gorges, for incorporation of Agamenticus, or Acomenticus, 10 April, 1641, in Haz. I. 472, he is named first of the aldermen. He became governour of the province of Maine in 1651; but was compelled, the following year, to submit, with the other inhabitants of that quarter of the country, to the government of Massachusetts, whose commissioners appointed him, with three others, to hold county courts. Haz. I. 564—577. Yet, in 1658, his hopes of independence seem to have revived; for, in Hutchinson's Coll. 314, we find a petition from York, Kittery, Wells, &c. to his highness, the lord protector, against his design; and from the document next in that collection, a letter from Leverett to the government of Massachusetts, it seems, that Godfrey was the most active or most powerful of the discontented. That petition of the *loyal* inhabitants was a strange libel on their country, representing the parts eastward, which are now found to be much the best, as "uninhabitable, sterile lands, swamps and rocky mountains, as not more than a few shreds are left by the sea shore fit for cohabitation." Any good or evil consequences at that time

merchant, came from Pascataquack in Captain Neal his pinnace, and brought sixteen hogsheads of corn to the mill. They went away November [blank.]

25.] The governour, with Mr. Wilson, pastor of Boston, and the two captains, &c. went aboard the Lyon, and from thence Mr. Peirce carried them in his shallop to Wessaguscus. The next morning Mr. Peirce returned to his ship, and the governour and his company went on foot to Plimouth, and came thither within the evening. The governour of Plimouth, Mr. William Bradford, (a very discreet and grave man,) with Mr. [1]Brewster, the elder, and some others, came forth and met them without the town, and conducted them to the governour's house, where they were very kindly entertained, and feasted every day at several houses. On the Lord's day there was a sacrament, which they did partake in; and, in the afternoon, Mr. Roger Williams (according to their custom) propounded a question, to which the pastor, Mr. [2]Smith, spake

---

were prevented by the decease of the great protector. But though the complaints were renewed after the restoration, (see Leverett's letter of 13 September, 1660, in Hutchinson's Coll. 322,) and thus afforded a pretext for the temporary separation directed by the royal commissioners some years after, I know not that any benefit was obtained by Godfrey. He is, perhaps, the gentleman referred to in the Narrative, Hutchinson's Coll. 423, " who refused to submit to the Massachusetts, and suffered great loss by them, showed the commissioners a warrant the Massachusetts made to have him brought to Boston, alive or dead, and now demands justice against them."

The errour of Prince, II. 70, who, transcribing this passage from our author, gives *Vesey* instead of Godfrey, must render cautious all decypherers of ancient proper names, in which I have often fallen, for a time, into as great mistakes.

1 It would be presumption, without hope, for me to attempt any memoir of Elder William Brewster, after the elaborate account in Belknap's American Biography, II. 252.

2 In the governour and company's letter to Endecott, 1629, is contained the earliest notice of the Rev. Ralph Smith, " his difference in judgment in some things from our ministers" being therein referred to as a caution against distraction in the Salem church. Haz. I. 260. His stay at that place, however, was very short; for we learn from Bradford, in Prince, I. 188, that he went to Nantasket, where he was found living " in a poor house, that would not keep him dry," and desired a better residence. Being carried to Plimouth, he became their minister for several years. In Morton, I discern his name only twice, and then with no epithets of reverence or circumstance of importance, except that of making, in 1638, complaint against Gorton; thus being the earliest of the numerous adversaries of the unhappy sectarian. But the History of Plimouth Church, 1 Hist. Coll. IV. 108, written, indeed, so lately as 1760, informs of his resignation of office in 1635, at the request of some of the flock, and partly of his own accord; and therefore I infer, that the controversy with Gorton arose not from his station. In that tract Smith is called " a man of low gifts and parts." How long he continued to reside,

briefly; then Mr. Williams prophesied; and after the governour of Plimouth spake to the question; after him the elder; then some two or three more of the congregation. Then the elder desired the governour of Massachusetts and Mr. Wilson to speak to it, which they did. When this was ended, the deacon, Mr. [1]Fuller, put the congregation in mind of their duty of contribution; whereupon the governour and all the rest went down to the deacon's seat, and put into the box, and then returned.

27.] The wind N. W., Mr. Peirce set sail for Virginia.

31, being Wednesday.] About five in the morning the governour and his company came out of Plimouth; the governour of Plimouth, with the pastor and elder, &c. accompanying them near half a mile out of town in the dark. The Lieut. [2]Holmes, with two others, and the governour's ||mare,||[3] came along with them to the great swamp, about ten miles. When they came to the great [4]river, they were carried over by one [5]Luddam, their guide, (as they had been when they came, the stream being very strong, and up to the crotch;) so the governour called that passage Luddam's Ford. Thence they came to a place called [6]Hue's Cross. The governour, being displeased

||man||

---

where he was so lightly esteemed, is not certainly known; but the latter part of this History, 1645, tells, that the people of Manchester, not then formed into a church body, had employed him to preach to them. Neither Eliot nor Allen have given him a place in their dictionaries.

1 Samuel Fuller was a gentleman high in esteem at Plimouth. He had been chosen to his office in Holland, with Gov. Carver, whom he accompanied in the first ship. He is duly honoured by Eliot, though his article should have been enlarged, from Morton's Memorial, with the date of his death, 1633.

2 After the perfect memoir of Holmes, by Judge Davis, in his edition of the New England Memorial, nothing should be expected here to extend the reader's acquaintance with him.

3 Winthrop had gone to Plimouth, on foot, from Wessaguscus, as his narrative just before showed. His friend, the governour of the elder colony, sent him back with his own horse. I have no doubt of the MS., though the former edition had *man*.

4 Now called North River—a stream rendered important by the great number of ships built upon its banks. See the copious account of Scituate, 2 Hist. Coll. IV. 227.

5 I have not learned any thing of this man, nor been able even to ascertain precisely where the fording place was.

6 Hue could hardly have been of much consequence in the governour's opinion, and we can scarcely justify his displeasure at the trifle. Anticipa-

at the name, in respect that such things might hereafter give the Papists occasion to say, that their religion was first planted in these parts, changed the name, and called it Hue's Folly. So they came, that evening, to [1]Wessaguscus, where they were bountifully entertained, as before, with store of turkeys, geese, ducks, &c., and the next day came safe to Boston.

About this time Mr. Dudley his house, at ||Newtown,|| was preserved from burning down, and all his family from being destroyed by gunpowder, by a marvellous deliverance;—the hearth of the hall chimney burning all night upon a principal §beam,§ and store of powder being near, and not discovered till they arose in the morning, and then it began to flame out.

Mr. John Eliot, a member of Boston congregation, and one whom the ||[2]congregation|| intended presently to call to the office of teacher, was called to be a teacher to the ||[3]church|| at Roxbury; and though Boston laboured all they could, both with the congregation of Roxbury and with Mr. Eliot himself, alleging their want of him, and the covenant between them, &c. yet he could not be diverted from accepting the call of Roxbury, November 5. So he was dismissed.

About a fortnight before this, those of Charlestown, who had formerly been joined to Boston congregation, now, in regard of the difficulty of passage in the winter, and having op-

||Watertown|| ||[2]company|| ||[3]company||

---

tion of so great an empire as grew in two hundred years from their planting, could not consist with the fear, that Papists might say their religion was first settled here. By the antiquary of Plimouth we are told of "Hewes' Cross Brook," and that John Hewes was one of the first settlers of Scituate. 2 Hist. Coll. IV. 303. The act of jurisdiction by Winthrop, in thus changing a name within the limits of another colony, was a slight usurpation.

[1] The settlements of this place are mentioned, in order of time, on page 43. In 1624, "some addition to the few inhabitants of Wessaguscus, from Weymouth in England," is given by Prince, I. 150; but his authority being only manuscript letters, written, perhaps, more than a hundred years later, and probably embodying idle traditions, I am not disposed to give much credit to them, especially as the contemporary, Gov. Bradford, remarks with emphasis, ib. 144, that the *second* plantation came to an end in the spring of that very year. Besides, the exquisite diligence of the Annalist found no opportunity even to name the spot again before the year 1628. p. 176. Then the ill conduct of Morton and his clan rendered necessary the interference of "the chief of the straggling plantations from Piscatoway, Naumkeak, Winisimet, Wesaguscusset, Natasco, and other places." This was the celebrated and efficient expedition of Standish. Prince's authority for this is the same chief of Plimouth, whose information is always most minute and satisfactory. Perhaps, in 1627, some settlers had reoccupied the vacant fields.

portunity of a pastor, one Mr. [1]James, who came over at this time, were dismissed from the congregation of Boston.[2]

---

[1] He remained at Charlestown little over three years, as, in the progress of this History, will be seen. Thence he removed to New Haven, where he resided some years, except while engaged on a mission, in 1642 and 3, to Virginia; and Eliot has erroneously related, that at New Haven he finished the remainder of his days. He was at Easthampton, on Long Island, in 1655. Haz. II. 341. Hubbard, 191, says, James "returned back to England, where he was accepted as a faithful minister of the gospel, and continued in that work till the year 1678, at Needham, in Suffolk, which was about the eighty-sixth year of his age, and may yet be living." I am the more diposed to value highly this original information of Hubbard, as it is of so very rare occurrence. Prince, II. 77, is still more full than the contemporary historian. But Calamy, there quoted, must be wrong in making him resign "the parochial church of Needham August 24, 1662;" for, by the accounts of the commissioners of the United Colonies, he seems to have been in their employment as a teacher of the Indians on Long Island, until 1665. Mather blunders in giving *two* of the name, one at Charlestown—as if he had continued in our neighbourhood—the other at Easthampton; but, with his habitual carelessness, he omits the name of baptism of both. Had he ascertained that, he might, perhaps, have inferred the identity of the person, and struck out No. 10 of his second classis. Allen omits the name of Thomas James.

[2] In the books of our divines, the order of time, in which the churches of Massachusetts were gathered, has often been noticed; but it will be found, that they have, in general, deferred too easily to the authority of Johnson's Wonder-working Providence. That writer did not, probably, mean to be precise on this point; or, if he did, is entitled to little regard. Holmes, in his History of Cambridge, 1 Hist. Coll. VII. 15, follows the general current; and, though he made a partial correction, 1 Hist. Coll. X. 314, he only increases the injustice on Johnson's authority. The six churches next after Salem, he assigns to 1631, when *not one* was gathered that year. Half were in 1630, and half in 1632. With reference to Boston, he made amends, indeed, in Annals, I. 267, by suggesting, what nobody can fail to acquiesce in, that our church *may* be considered as translated in its organized state from Charlestown; though his expressions, compared with those of page 262, where he enumerates only six, instead of seven, show his timidity. Still his injustice to Watertown remains unexpiated. The scrupulous attention of this most diligent annalist would have protected him from my humble animadversion, in a particular of so slight importance, did he not receive encouragement from companions of the highest character. Judge Davis, in the beautiful address on the anniversary of the Plimouth forefathers' landing, 22 December, 1813, with which the *first* volume of 2 Hist. Coll. appropriately commences, has, page ix, injuriously postponed Watertown to Roxbury and Lynn. In his note F. a severe observer will, indeed, find reason to presume, that the author's judgment would give Watertown priority over those churches, notwithstanding the rank of Johnson. The body of that note, however, is occupied with disputing the claim of Watertown to stand second only to Salem. Eliot, in his invaluable essays on our ecclesiastical history, 1 Hist. Coll. X. 26, obeys, against his own knowledge, the direction of Wonder-working Providence; and Harris's History of Dorchester betrays the right to the *second* honour for that church. The Century Sermon of the late Dr. Kendall, in a note on pages 20, 21, irresistibly draws me to his opinion, by which Watertown is determined to a rank equal with Boston. "July 30, 1630, at Watertown, forty men subscribed a church covenant." Now, there

The congregation of Watertown discharged their elder, Richard Brown, of his office, for his unfitness in regard of his

---

can be no evidence, that any others, but Salem and Dorchester, *preceded;* though the right of Wilson's (Boston) church to date from the *same* day is established by Judge Davis's argument from the contemporaneous narrative of Bradford, in Prince, I. 243. We cannot doubt the precedence of Dorchester, and its claim to be reckoned in June, 1630, because, when the first court of assistants, 23 August, provided "how the ministers shall be maintained," and made a common charge on the colony for Wilson's (Boston) and Phillips's (Watertown) salaries, Mattapan and Salem were *excepted.* This, from the Records of Massachusetts, Prince, I. 247, must satisfy every one, that the former was considered in a church state no less than the latter. Our Dorchester settlers had an embodied church, we know, when they left home in March, and undoubtedly had regular ordinances with their two ministers after arrival in Massachusetts, in June. Prince, I. 200. Whether Roxbury, or Lynn, which come in the third year, have records to show which may certainly claim priority, is unknown, probably, to themselves. Books cannot assist us in determining. See Prince, II. 64, 68, and Johnson, lib. I. c. 21, 22.

A strange obliquity of judgment has applied the facts in our text to sustain the precedency of Charlestown to Boston church. The pastor and the flock, rather than the place of their assembly, ought surely to entitle any society of worshippers to be thought the same, and not another. Even if exclusive regard be paid to place, the church of Charlestown loses more than it can gain; for, in September, 1630, the greater part of the congregation lived on this side of the river; and in that month, for the last time, the court of assistants met at Charlestown. *There* the body of the church remained, therefore, less than three months. The worship, afterwards, was always *here;* yet, for twenty-five months more, there was but one church of worshippers from both sides. The History always calls this congregation—a word, which, unless plainly used as a distinction from those in more intimate brotherhood, must always be understood by the reader as signers of the church covenant—the congregation of Boston. The dismission of Mr. James, and the thirty-two other brethren, little more than one fourth of the whole, is from Boston to Charlestown. We have every light on this subject, that Prince enjoyed, and are fully justified in forming a different conclusion from his, if his, which is doubtful, be adverse to this now expressed. If reference be made to custom or common law, the identity of a body corporate, like each of our churches, must be shown by its records. This evidence is, of course, in favour of Boston. In future days, I persuade myself, a contrary opinion will seem as strange, as the assertion in the Historical Sketch of Charlestown, 2 Hist. Coll. II. 164, that Winthrop and his company came in 1629.

To conclude this long note, I solicit indulgence for the following arrangement of the early churches of Massachusetts proper, which to me appears most probable:

I.	Salem, 1629, 6 August.	X.	Newbury, 1635.
II.	Dorchester, 1630, June.	XI.	Weymouth, 1635, July.
III.	Boston, } 1630, 30 July.	XII.	Hingham, 1635, September.
IV.	Watertown, } 1630, 30 July.	XIII.	Concord, 1636, 5 July.
V.	Roxbury, 1632, July.	XIV.	Dedham, 1638, 8 November.
VI.	Lynn, 1632.	XV.	Quincy, 1639, 17 Sept.
VII.	Charlestown, 1632, 2 Nov.	XVI.	Rowley, 1639, 3 December.
VIII.	Cambridge, 1633, 11 October.	XVII.	Salisbury.
IX.	Ipswich, 1634.	XVIII.	Sudbury, 1640, August.

passion and distemper in speech, having been oft admonished and declared his repentance for it.

21.] The governour received a letter from Capt. Neal, that ||Dixy|| [1]Bull and fifteen more of the English, who kept about the east, were turned pirates, and had taken divers boats, and rifled Pemaquid, &c.—23. Hereupon the governour called a council, and it was agreed to send his bark with twenty men, to join with those of Pascataquack, for the taking of the said pirates.

22.] A fast was held by the congregation of Boston, and Mr. Wilson (formerly their teacher) was chosen pastor, and [blank] [2]Oliver a ruling elder, and both were ordained by impo-

||D.||

XIX.	Gloucester, 1642.	XXV.	Reading, 1645, 5 Nov.
XX.	Woburn, 1642, 24 August.	XXVI.	Springfield, 1645.
XXI.	Hull, 1644, July.	XXVII.	Manchester.
XXII.	Wenham, 1644, 8 October.	XXVIII.	Malden.
XXIII.	Haverhill, } 1645, October.	XXIX.	Boston, 2d, 1650, 5 June.
XXIV.	Andover, } 1645, October.		

1 Of this miserable fellow, it cannot be expected, that any memoirs should remain. It seems probable, that the loss of his shallop and goods, *reported*, in June preceding, to be taken by the French, may have led him and his companions to this renunciation of the friendship of the rest of the settlements on the coast. They seem to have committed no outrages. Capt. Clap, in Prince, II. 91, gives the largest account of their operations, and concludes, " Bull got into England ; but God destroyed this wretched man."

2 Thomas Oliver, whose name occurs several times in the course of this History, was undoubtedly an estimable and useful man ; but little is known of him. Reverence for his eldership, probably, kept him from other services, either offered by his townsmen, or sought by his own ambition ; but he was several years one of the selectmen. He died in the latter part of 1657, I conclude, from finding his will proved, 27 January following, in our Registry, I. 300. His wife had, with himself, accompanied John Winthrop the younger, probably, as their numbers in our church are 132 and 133. She died in 1635. His son, John, H. C., 1645, is honourably mentioned in a later part of this work. His son, Peter, was father of Nathaniel, born 8 March, 1651, of whom the first newspaper printed in North America, the Boston Newsletter, 24 April, 1704, has this notice : " Mr. Nathaniel Oliver, a principal merchant of this place, died April 15, and was decently interred April 18, ætatis 53." The same son, one of the chief founders of Boston Third Church, was also father of the Hon. Daniel Oliver, who died 1732. Of him and the sons, Andrew, lieutenant governour, and Peter, chief justice, distinguished in the political history of the province of Massachusetts Bay, as well as others of the name, full biographies are given by Eliot. They are written with an honourable impartiality, for the want of which, in a son of the chief justice, to whom application was made by a son of the biographer, for leave to copy a small part of his transcript of Hubbard's History, liberal minds will make large estimate of the evils of rancorous remembrance incident to civil conflicts. See 2 Hist. Coll. III. 288. But the denial was of no detriment to any other than the possessor ; for every careful student of Hubbard would easily part with half that we have.

sition of hands, first by the teacher, and ||the|| two deacons, (in the name of the congregation,) upon the elder, and then by the elder and the deacons upon the pastor.

December 4.] At a meeting of all the assistants, it was agreed, in regard that the extremity of the ||2snow|| and frost had hindered the making ready of the bark, and that they had certain intelligence, that those of Pascataquack had sent out two pinnaces and two shallops, above a fortnight before, to defer any further expedition against the pirates till they heard what was done by those; and for that end it was agreed, to send presently a shallop to Pascataquack to learn ||3more,|| &c.

5.] Accordingly, the governour despatched away John [1]Gallopp with his shallop. The wind being very great at S. W., he could reach no farther than Cape Ann harbour that night; and the winds blowing northerly, he was kept there so long, that it was January the 2d before he returned.

By letters from Capt. Neal and Mr. [2]Hilton, &c. it was

||then|| ||2season|| ||3news||

1 Mention is often made of this person, who was a fisherman well acquainted with our harbour, in which an island perpetuates his name. He was admitted of the church 5 January, 1633—4. His will, Prob. Rec. I. 292, made 20 December, 1649, proved 9 February following, shows that he had less education than most of our early inhabitants, since it is signed with a cross. In it he gives forty shillings towards building the new meeting-house, which was that for the Second Church.

2 Edward Hilton and his brother William, with a few others, sent by Gorges and Mason, were the first planters of New Hampshire in 1623. See Hubbard, 214. The name of Edward, who was a gentleman of good judgment, is often found in our History; and in 1641, when Massachusetts usurped the jurisdiction of the colony of New Hampshire, he became a magistrate. William had visited New Plimouth, before settling on the Piscataqua, as appears by a letter from him, Haz. I. 120, extracted from "New England's Tryals," published, in 1622, by the celebrated John Smith. The note of Hazard, that the vessel, which carried this letter, left New England the beginning of April, 1621, is not given with his usual accuracy. The Mayflower, in which came the first company of one hundred and one, among whom was not Hilton, was the only vessel, Prince, I. 104, that could leave Plimouth in April, 1621. On recurring to the original authority of Hazard, Purchas's Pilgrims, lib. X. c. 3, page 1840 of vol. IV. compared with Prince, I. 114, I find the Fortune arrived again at Plimouth in November, 1621. William Hilton was, therefore, a passenger in her, with the venerable Cushman, and by her, in December of the same year, was his epistle returned. Descendants of one, or both, of these brothers, are found in New Hampshire, of whom one, Winthrop, a distinguished officer in the Indian and French wars, was killed by the savages near his own home, 23 June, 1710. Some genealogical account of the families may be seen in Alden's Collection of Epitaphs, II. 131. One, a grandchild of the above-named Winthrop, died in March, 1822, in possession of part of the unalienated estate of two centuries. Gov. Joseph Dudley calls the grandfather his dear *kinsman*, and it is agreeable to find the adoption by this family of a name of baptism from the father of Massachusetts. It is still borne by a gentleman of Newmarket.

certified, that they had sent out all the forces they could make against the pirates, viz. four pinnaces and shallops, and about forty men, who, coming to Pemaquid, were there wind-bound about three weeks.

It was further advertised, by some who came from Penobscott, that the pirates had lost one of their chief men by a musket shot from Pemaquid; and that there remained but fifteen, whereof four or five were detained against their wills; and that they had been at some English plantations, and taken nothing from them but what they paid for; and that they had given another pinnace in exchange for that of Mr. Maverick, and as much beaver and otter as it was worth more, &c.; and that they had made a law against excessive drinking; and that their order was, at such times as other ships use to have prayer, they would assemble upon the deck, and one sing a song, or speak a few senseless sentences, &c. They also sent a writing, directed to all the governours, signifying their intent not to do harm to any more of their countrymen, but to go to the southward, and to advise them not to send against them; for they were resolved to ||sink|| themselves rather than be taken: Signed underneath, Fortune le garde, and no ||²name|| to it.

January 1.] Mr. Edward Winslow chosen governour of Plimouth, Mr. Bradford having been governour about ten years, and now by importunity gat off.[1]

9.] Mr. Oliver, a right godly man, and elder of the church of Boston, having three or four of his sons, all very young, cutting down wood upon the ||³neck||, one of them, being about fifteen years old, had his brains beaten out with the fall of a tree, which he had felled. The good old father (having the news of it in as fearful a manner as might be, by another boy, his brother) called his wife (being also a very godly woman) and went to prayer, and bare it with much patience and honour.

17.] The governour, having intelligence from the east, that the French had bought the Scottish [2]plantation near Cape

||strike|| ||²more|| ||³rocks||

1 From Prince, II. 75, we learn, that the people of Plimouth this year enacted, "that whoever refuses the office of governour shall pay £20, unless he was chose two years going." A proportional penalty was laid on any refusing to be a counsellor. This severity has become unnecessary for such high offices, though it is found useful to provide similar fines for declining subordinate ones.

2 We presume this to mean the plantation, for which Sir William Alexander had patents from James I. and Charles I. 10 September, 1621, and 12 July, 1625, soon after ceded to the French. The settlement was at Port Royal.

Sable, and that the fort and all the ammunition were delivered to them, and that the cardinal, having the managing thereof, had sent some companies already, and preparation was made to send many more the next year, and divers priests and Jesuits among them,—called the assistants to Boston, and the ministers and captains, and some other chief men, to advise what was fit to be done for our safety, in regard the French were like to prove ill neighbours (being Papists;) at which meeting it was agreed, that a plantation and a fort should forthwith be begun at Natascott, partly to be ||some|| block in an enemy's way, (though it could not bar ||[2]his|| entrance,) and especially to prevent an enemy from taking that passage from us; and also, that the fort begun at Boston should be finished;—also, that a plantation should be begun at Agawam, (being the best place in the land for tillage and cattle,) least an enemy, finding it void, should possess and take it from us. The governour's son (being one of the assistants) was to undertake this, and to take no more out of the bay than twelve men; the rest to be supplied at the coming of the next ships.

A maid servant of Mr. Skelton of Salem, going towards Sagus, was lost seven days, and at length came home to Salem. All that time she was in the woods, having no kind of food, the snow being very deep, and as cold as at any time that winter. She was so frozen into the snow some mornings, as she was one hour before she could get up; yet she soon recovered and did well, through the Lord's wonderful providence.

[Large blank.]

About the beginning of this month of January the pinnaces, which went after the pirates, returned, the cold being so great as they could not pursue them; but, in their return, they hanged up at Richman's Isle an Indian, one Black Will, one of those who had there [1]murdered Walter Bagnall. Three of the pirates' company ran from them and came home.

[Large blank.]

February 21.] The governour and four of the assistants, with three of the ministers, and others, about twenty-six in all, went, in three boats, to view Natascott, the wind W., fair weather; but the wind arose at N. W. so strong, and extreme cold, that they were kept there two nights, being forced to lodge upon the ground, in an open cottage, upon a little old

||stone|| ||[2]their||

---

[1] That murder was mentioned under date of October, 1631, page 62, a year and a quarter before. The process mentioned in the text is more like revenge than justice. Richman's, or Richmond's Isle, is part of Scarborough.

straw, which they pulled from the thatch. Their victuals also grew short, so as they were forced to eat muscles,—yet they were very ||mean,||—and came all safe home the third day after, through the Lord's special providence. Upon view of the place, it was agreed by all, that to build a fort there would be of too great charge, and of little use; whereupon the planting of that place was deferred.[1]

22, or thereabouts.] The ship William, Mr. Trevore master, arrived at Plimouth with some passengers and goods for the Massachusetts Bay; but she came to set up a fishing at Scituate, and so to go to trade at Hudson's River.

By this ship we had intelligence from our friends in England, that Sir Ferdinando Gorges and Capt. Mason (upon the instigation of Sir Christopher Gardiner, Morton, and Ratcliff) had preferred a petition to the lords of the privy council against us, charging us with many false accusations; but, through the Lord's good providence, and the care of our friends in England, (especially Mr. §Emanuel§ Downing, who had married the governour's sister,) and the good testimony given on our behalf by one Capt. Wiggin, (who dwelt at Pascataquack,) and had been divers times among us,) their malicious practice took not effect. The principal matter they had against us was, the letters of some indiscreet persons among us, who had written against the church government §in England,§ &c. which had been intercepted by occasion of the death of Capt. Levett, who carried them, and died at sea.

26.] Two little girls of the governour's family were sitting under a great heap of logs, plucking of birds, and the wind driving the feathers into the house, the governour's wife caused them to remove away. They were no sooner gone, but the whole heap of logs fell down in the place, and had crushed them to death, if the Lord, in his special providence, had not delivered them.

March.] The governour's son, John Winthrop, went, with

||merry||

1 Readers accustomed to receive, with some hesitation, any information from Johnson, will compare the narrative in our text with his, lib. I. c. 28, or as it is reprinted in 2 Hist. Coll. III. 138, 9. A scrutiny of his representation discloses a mistake of the time, making it "the vernal of the year 1634;" of the place, "a small island, about two miles distant from Boston," that is, Castle Island, instead of Nantasket; and of the number, "some eight or ten persons of note." He wrote eighteen years after the event, and shows little precision in any thing but his creed; yet his book is one of the most curious that an inquirer into the manners and institutions of our fathers can peruse.

[1]twelve ||more,|| to begin a plantation at Agawam, after called Ipswich.

[Large blank.]

One John Edye, a godly man of Watertown congregation, fell distracted, and, getting out one evening, could not be found; but, eight days after, he came again of himself. He had kept his strength and colour, yet had eaten nothing (as must needs be conceived) all that time. He recovered his understanding again in good measure, and lived very orderly, but would, now and then, be a little distempered.[2]

[Blank.]

April 10.] Here arrived Mr. Hodges, one of Mr. Peirce his mates. He came from Virginia in a shallop, and brought news that Mr. Peirce's ship was cast away upon a shoal four miles from [3]Feake Isle, ten leagues to the N. of the mouth of Virginia Bay, November 2d, about ||[2]five|| in the morning, the wind S. W., through the negligence of one of his mates, who had the watch, and kept not his lead as he was ||[3]exhorted||. They had a shallop and their ship's boat aboard. All that went into the shallop came safe on shore, but the ship's boat was sunk by the ship's side, and [blank] men drowned in her, and ten of them were taken up alive into the shallop. There were in the ship twenty eight seamen and ten passengers. Of these were drowned seven seamen and five passengers, and all the goods were lost, except one hogshead of beaver; and most of the letters were saved, and some other small things, which were driven on shore the next day, when the ship was broken in

||men|| ||[2]one|| ||[3]appointed||

---

1 At the court, 1 April next, it was "ordered, that no person whatsoever shall go to plant or inhabit at Agawam, without leave from the court, except those that are already gone with Mr. John Winthrop, jun." Then follows in the Record, I. 96, the list of the others: "Mr. Clerke, Robert Coles, Thomas Howlett, John Biggs, John Gage, Thomas Hardy, William Perkins, Mr. Thorndike, William Sarjeant," as in Prince, II. 86. Of course, there were three more.

2 The last sentence appears to have been written, as the sense would induce us also to suppose, sometime later than the preceding. A blank had been left for the sufferer's Christian name, which is inserted in a different ink from the rest of the page. From Watertown Records, I find, "Pilgrim, daughter of John and Amie Eddie, born 25 August, 1634; John, son of J. and A. E., born 16 February, 1636—7, died soon; Benjamin, son of J. and A. E., buried 1639; Samuel, son of J. and A. E., born 30 September, 1640." Another daughter is also mentioned of a later date.

3 Probably this name was given as a compliment to the relative of Gov. Winthrop, and may not have been perpetuated. The island is undoubtedly on the ocean side of the eastern shore of Virginia. In the map of Maryland, in Ogilby's History of America, it is called Fetche's Island.

pieces. They were nine days in much distress, before they found any English. Plimouth men lost four hogsheads, [1]900 pounds of beaver, and 200 otter skins. The governour of Massachusetts lost, in beaver and fish, which he sent to Virginia, &c. near £100. Many others lost ||beaver,|| and Mr. Humfrey fish.[2]

[Large blank.]

May.] The William and Jane, Mr. Burdock master, arrived with thirty passengers and ten cows ||[2]or more.|| She came in six weeks from London.

[Blank.]

The Mary and Jane arrived, Mr. Rose master. She came from London in seven weeks, and brought one hundred and ninety-six passengers, (only two children died.) Mr. Coddington, one of the assistants, and his [3]wife, came in her. In her return she was cast away upon Isle Sable, but [blank] men were saved.

By these ships we understood, that Sir Christopher Gardiner, and Thomas Morton, and Philip Ratcliff, (who had been punished here for their misdemeanours,) had petitioned to the king and council against us, (being set on by Sir Ferdinando Gorges and Capt. Mason, who had begun a plantation at Pascataquack, and aimed at the general government of New England for their agent there, Capt. Neal.) The petition was of many sheets of paper, and contained many false accusations, (and among some truths misrepeated,) accusing us to intend rebellion, to have cast off our allegiance, and to be wholly separate from the church and laws of England; that our ministers and people did

||skins|| ||[2]one mare||

1 These figures, taken from the margin, were designed, as I think, to represent the quantity, not the value; the pounds avoirdupois, not, as the former editor had it, pounds sterling. Of this construction I felt confident before knowing the concurrence of Prince, II. 87. He inserts a characteristick letter from Capt. Peirce about the shipwreck.

2 She was bound to England, after stopping to trade at Virginia, probably to receive tobacco for her fish. The skins from Massachusetts were, of course, destined for London. I have seen several letters from friends in England to John Winthrop, jun. here, acknowledging receipt of epistles sent by this vessel, which, having been drenched in the sea, were hardly legible by his correspondents.

3 Her name was Mary, and she is the 158th member of Boston church. Coddington had lost the wife he brought in the first expedition, as appears by Dudley's letter, in the great mortality of the seasoning. He went to England early in 1631. Gov. Winthrop, in writing to his son, in a letter of that date, in the Appendix, desires him to favour Coddington's application to his *sister*, whom I presume to be the widow of Henry.

continually rail against the state, church and bishops there, &c. Upon which such of our company as were then in England, viz. Sir Richard Saltonstall, Mr. Humfrey, and Mr. Cradock, were called before a committee of the council, to whom they delivered in an answer in writing;[1] upon reading whereof, it pleased the Lord, our gracious God and Protector, so to work with the lords, and after with the king's majesty, when the whole matter was reported to him by Sir Thomas Jermin, one of the council, (but not of the committee, who yet had been present at the three days of hearing, and spake much in the commendation of the governour, both to the lords and after to his majesty,) that he said, he would have them severely punished, who did abuse ||his governour|| and the plantation; that the defendants were dismissed with a favourable order for their encouragement, being assured from some of the council, that his majesty did not intend to impose the ceremonies of the church of England upon us; for that it was considered, that it was the freedom from such things that made people come over to us; and it was credibly informed to the council, that this country would, in time, be very beneficial to England for masts, cordage, &c. if the Sound should be debarred.[2]

||this government||

---

1 A letter from Winthrop to his friend Bradford, giving a relation of this inquiry, and the order of the privy council thereon, is preserved in Prince, II. 89—91, which is worth perusal.

2 The fears, entertained by our friends in England, while this subject was before the council, will be fully exhibited by extracts from two letters in my possession to J. Winthrop the younger. Edward Howes writes, 18 March, 1632—3, "I am glad, and exceedingly rejoice at your prosperity, and the prosperity of the whole colony, and that it hath pleased God to show his power and mercy upon you all in a wonderful manner, beyond the expectation of the great ones of this land, in delivering you, not from a Spanish powder plot, nor an accounted invincible armada, but from a Spanish-like French infection, which was like to have tainted the halest and best men amongst you, yea all of you, as may appear by the writings and letters written with mine own hand, and sent to your father, my honoured friend. Sir, I am the more sensible hereof, in regard I was a daily and hourly auditor and spectator of all the passages, which hath caused me to take it into consideration, that your plantation hath need of some hearty and able friends to back you upon all occasions, which must remain here and have friends at court. I, though not so able as I could wish, (if God saw it good,) yet as hearty as the best, considering Mr. Humfrey's preparation for departure, and my master's desire and resolution to be with you, have betaken myself now, at last, to the study of the laws, and to that purpose have admitted myself as a student of Clifford's Inn. Not that I mean absolutely, or presently, to leave my master, but to enable myself to leave when he is gone, and to retire myself, in the vacation time, to my study, which shall ever tend, to the utmost of my poor ability, to the good and welfare of your plantation and state."

Francis Kirby writes, 26 March, 1633, "Your friends here, who are mem-

We sent forth a pinnace after the pirate Bull, but, after she had been forth two [1]months, she came home, having not found him. After, we heard he was gone to the French.

A Dutch pink arrived, which had been to the southward a trading.

June 2.] Capt. [2]Stone arrived with a small ship with cows and some salt. The governour of Plimouth sent Capt. Standish to prosecute against him for piracy. The cause ||was, being|| at the Dutch plantation, where a pinnace of Plimouth coming, and Capt. Stone and the Dutch governour having been drinking together, Capt. Stone, upon pretence that those of Plimouth had reproached them of Virginia, from whence he came, seized upon their pinnace, (with the governour's consent,) and offered to carry her away, but the Dutchmen ||[2]rescued|| her; and the next day the governour and Capt. Stone entreated the master of the pinnace (being one of the council of Plimouth) to pass it by, which he promised by a solemn instrument under his hand; yet, upon their earnest prosecution at court, we bound over Capt. Stone (with two sureties) to appear in the admiralty court in England, &c. But, after, those of Plimouth, being persuaded that it would turn to their reproach, and that it could be no piracy, with their consent, we withdrew the recognizance.

15.] Mr. Graves, in the ship [3]Elizabeth Bonadventure, from Yarmouth, arrived with ninety-five passengers, and thirty-four Dutch sheep, and two mares. They came from Yarmouth in six weeks; lost not one person, but above forty sheep.

19.] A day of thanksgiving was kept in all the congrega-

||was began|| ||[2]wrested||

---

bers of your plantation, have had much to do to answer the unjust complaints made to the king and council of your government there. I understand that you are an assistant, and so have a voice in the weighty affairs of that commonwealth. I know I shall not need to advise you, that the prayers for our king be not neglected in any of your publick meetings; and I desire that you differ no more from us in church government, than you shall find that we differ from the prescript rule of God's word, and further I meddle not." Our fathers and all their descendants may be content with so liberal a permission of difference on church government.

1 Prince, II. 91, gives this word *weeks*. The court, 2 July after, directed the treasurer to pay Lieut. Mason £10 for his services in this expedition; and the other charges amounted to £24.7.6, for which see the treasurer's account, in 2 Hist. Coll. VIII. 232, 3.

2 More will be found of this unhappy man in September and January following, and in November, 1634. A very bad report of him, under this latter year, is also given by Morton.

3 Here, at first, a blank had been left for the ship's name, which the governour afterwards inserted.

tions, for our delivery from the plots of our enemies, and for the safe arrival of our friends, &c.

July 2.] At a court it was agreed, that the governour, John Winthrop, should have, towards his charges this year, [1]£150, and the money, which he had disbursed in publick businesses, as officers' wages, &c., being between two and three hundred pounds, should be forthwith paid.

12.] Mr. Edward Winslow, governour of Plimouth, and Mr. Bradford, came into the bay, and went away the 18th. They came partly to confer about joining in a trade to Connecticut, for beaver and hemp. There was a motion to set up a trading house there, to prevent the Dutch, who were about to build one; but, in regard the place was not fit for plantation, there being three or four thousand warlike Indians, and the river not to be gone into but by small pinnaces, having a bar affording but six feet at high water, and for that no vessels can get in for seven months in the year, partly by reason of the ice, and then the violent stream, &c., we thought not fit to meddle with it.[2]

24.] A ship arrived from Weymouth, with about eighty passengers, and twelve kine, who sate down at Dorchester. They were twelve weeks coming, being forced into the Western Islands by a leak, where they stayed three weeks, and were very courteously used by the Portugals; but the extremity of the heat there, and the continual rain, brought sickness upon them, so as [blank] died.

---

1 The figures in the MS. are 130, or 150, the 3 being, I think, written upon the 5; but it is observable, that the Colony Record has it only £100. The treasurer's account of all the payments to Winthrop, as referred to in my note above, amounts to £328.10.

2 Under date of 4 April, 1631, the reader has seen the earliest mention of Connecticut arising in the History of Massachusetts. But, from Bradford's Register, in Prince, II. 94, we may be sure, that Plimouth had entertained views of establishing a plantation there, at an earlier season, and was willing to admit our colonists, her neighbours, to partake the advantage. On the first proposal from the Indian sachem, a sufficient cause for declining to send out a colony, to such a distance, would be found in our weakness; but I am constrained to remark, that the reasons, in the text above assigned, the strength of the current, shoalness of the water, continuance of the ice, and multitude of Indians, look to me more like pretexts, than real motives. Some disingenuousness, I fear, may be imputed to our council, in starting difficulties to deter our brethren of the humble community of Plimouth from extending their limits to so advantageous a situation; for we next season were careful to warn the Dutch against occupation of it, and the following year took possession ourselves. Honest Morton complains, that his people "deserved to have held it, and not by friends to have been thrust out, as, in a sort, they afterwards were;" and his complaint appears very natural, if not unanswerable.

Much sickness at Plimouth, and above [1]twenty died of pestilent fevers.

Mr. Graves returned, and carried a freight of fish from hence and Plimouth.

By him the governour and assistants sent an answer to the petition of Sir Christopher Gardiner, and withal a certificate from the old [2]planters concerning the carriage of affairs, &c.

August 6.] Two men servants to one Moodye, of Roxbury, returning in a boat from the windmill, struck upon the oyster bank. They went out to gather oysters, and, not making fast their boat, when the flood came, it floated away, and they were both drowned, although they might have waded out on either side; but it was an evident [3]judgment of God upon them, for they were wicked persons. One of them, a little before, being reproved for his lewdness, and put in mind of hell, answered, that if hell were ten times hotter, he had rather be there than he would serve his master, &c. The occasion was, because he had bound himself for divers years, and saw that, if he had been at liberty, he might have had greater wages, though otherwise his master used him very well.[4]

Mr. Graves returned. He carried between five and six thousand weight of beaver, and about thirty passengers. Capt. Walter Neal, of Pascataquack, and some eight of his company, went with him. He had been in the bay above ten days, and

---

1 For the number a blank was left, when the line was first written.

2 Of these *old* planters, we may conjecture the names to be, Blackstone, Jefferies, Maverick, Thomson; and perhaps Bursley, Conant and Oldham.

3 Too many instances of more extraordinary providential or fortuitous occurrences, perverted in their interpretation, will be observed in the progress of this History. It was the vice of the age, and indeed of most ages. The great historian of the civil war abounds in such judgments; but on the other side they are still more numerous.

4 With the incomplete transcript of this paragraph, and in the midst of a sentence, Prince's *third* pamphlet, II. 96, abruptly terminates. To omit here the expression of deepest regret for thus parting with such a companion, would be injurious to his memory. Yet deeper will be the regret of all inquirers after the minute circumstances of New England history, that such a patient and judicious student had not begun his Annals with the discovery by Columbus, rather than the creation of Moses. No other antiquary will ever enjoy advantages equal to his for an exact chronological series of our events; and when great opportunities are afforded, a dozen Hubbards, or a score of Mathers, may rise for one Prince. Civil convulsions, disregard of manuscripts, and the lapse of time, favourable to worms and damp, have each robbed us of many of his dearest treasures; but for those which himself made publick, all succeeding admirers of the days of old must unite with me in the oblation of highest regard,

"His saltem accumulem donis."

came not all that time to see the governour. Being persuaded by divers of his friends, his answer was, that he was not well entertained the first time he came hither, and, besides, he had some letters opened in the bay; ||ergo,|| except he were invited, he would not go see him. The 13th[1] day he wrote to the governour, to excuse his not coming to see him, upon the same reasons. The governour returned him answer, that his entertainment was such as time and place could afford, (being at their first coming, before they were housed, &c.) and retorted the discourtesy upon him, in that he would thrust himself, with such a company, (he had five or six gentlemen with him,) upon a stranger's entertainment, at such an unseasonable time, and having no need so to do; and for his letters, he protested his innocency, (as he might well, for the letters were opened before they came into the bay;) and so concluded courteously, yet with plain demonstration of his errour. And, indeed, if ||2the governour|| should have invited him, standing upon those terms, he had blemished his reputation.

There is mention made before of the answer, which was returned to Sir Christopher Gardiner his accusations, to which the governour and all the assistants subscribed, only the deputy refused. He made three exceptions: 1. For that we termed the bishops reverend bishops; which was only in repeating the ||3accuser's words.|| 2. For that we professed to believe all the articles of the ||4Christian|| faith, according to the scriptures and the common received tenets of the churches of England. This he refused, because we differed from them in matter of discipline, and about the meaning of Christ's descension into hell; ||5yet|| the faithful in England (whom we account the churches) expound it as we do, and not of a local descent, as some of the bishops do. 3. For that we gave the king the title of sacred majesty, which is the most proper title of princes, *being the Lord's anointed,*[2] and the word a mere civil word, never applied in scripture to any divine thing, but sanctus used always, (Mr. Knox called the ||6queen of Scotland|| by the same

||Government;|| ||2he courteously|| ||3accusations made|| ||4gospel|| ||5that|| ||6In. of S——||

[1] Of the month, not of his visit, I presume to be meant. William Wood, to whom we are obliged for New England's Prospect, printed at London, 1634, went undoubtedly with Graves; for he says, he sailed from Boston, 15th August, 1633.

[2] I am certain, from the difference of the ink, that the pen was drawn through this passage some time after it was written. If it were the governour's pen, his sentiments, but not his principles, were changed in a few years.

title.) Yet by no reasons could he be drawn to yield to these things, although they were allowed by divers of the ministers and the chief of Plimouth.

There was great scarcity of corn, by reason of the spoil our hogs had made at harvest, and the great quantity they had ||even|| in the winter, (there being no acorns;) yet people lived well with fish and the fruit of their gardens.[1]

Sept. 4.] The Griffin, a ship of three hundred tons, arrived, (having been eight weeks from the Downs.) §This ship was brought in by John Gallop a [2]new way by *Lovell's* Island, at low water, now called Griffin's Gap.§ She brought about two hundred passengers, having lost some four, §whereof one was drowned two days before, as he was casting forth a line to take mackerel.§ In this ship came Mr. [3]Cotton, Mr. Hooker and Mr. [4]Stone,

||eaten||

---

1 At the court, 5 November after, the adoption of two remarkable regulations was caused by this scarcity: 1. "That no man shall give his swine any corn, but such as, being viewed by two or three neighbours, shall be judged unfit for man's meat." 2. "Also, that every plantation shall agree how many swine every person may keep, winter and summer, about the plantation; this order to take place ten days hence."

2 The *new* way is not so clearly indicated, that I should dare to pilot the reader through it. On first reading this sentence, it seemed as if the passage must be our present ship channel, between Lovell's and George's with Gallop's Islands, and, of course, that Broad Sound was the former common way. But this would be wrong; for the governour has noticed, that, in July, 1643, when La Tour sailed from us with the ships hired here, they went out at Broad Sound, *where no ships of such burden had gone out before, or not more than one.* So I conclude, that our present ship channel is the same that was first used; and that Gallop brought the Griffin in between Lovell's Island and the Great Brewster from the northward. We are confident, that very great changes have occurred in the harbour; and, within the recollection of many, such violences are known, as may justify the conjecture, that the long shoal, to the south-west from the Great Brewster, was solid upland when the bay was first settled.

3 Nothing can be added to the abundant materials offered by this History, and all the contemporary books, which Mather, Hutchinson, Eliot, Allen and Emerson, have exhausted in their notices of "the great Cotton." The first author derived his name and part of his blood from this spiritual guide of Boston; and the last adorned, in his History of the First Church, all who had preceded himself in ministration at that altar.

4 Samuel Stone was, happily, in favour with the author of the Magnalia; and readers that dread to pursue an inquiry in such a work, will find ample account of him in Trumbull, Eliot's and Allen's Dictionaries, Holmes's History of Cambridge, 1 Hist. Coll. VII.; and in the Plimouth Memorialist, at the date of his death, 1663, an elegy in the worst style of that age. He performed good service with Mason, whom he accompanied as chaplain in the expedition against the Pequots, 1637. See 2 Hist. Coll. VIII. 134. A Body of Divinity, in a catechetical way, by him, in a 4to MS. of 540 pages, is in the library of our Historical Society.

ministers, and §Mr. [1]Peirce,§ Mr. [2]Haynes, (a gentleman of great estate,) Mr. ||Hoffe,||[3] and many other men of good estates. They gat out of England with much difficulty, all places being belaid to have taken Mr. Cotton and Mr. Hooker, who had been long sought for to have been brought into the high commission; but the master being bound to touch at the Wight, the ||[2]pursuivants|| attended there, and, in the mean time, the said ministers were taken in at the Downs. Mr. Hooker and Mr. Stone went presently to Newtown, where they were to be entertained, and Mr. Cotton stayed at Boston. ||[3]On Saturday||[4] evening, the congregation met in their ordinary ex-

||Goffe|| ||[2]pursuants|| ||[3]One Sunday||

---

[1] He was a gentleman of high repute in Boston, being one of the selectmen with Winthrop and Coddington the next year, and must not be confounded with the mariner, who had the same name of baptism. His freeman's oath, at the general court, 14 May, 1634, was taken at the same time with eighty others, of whom Hooker, Stone, Cotton, Thomas Mayhew and William Brenton are all, besides Peirce, that have the respectful title, Mr., prefixed to their names. Col. Rec. I. 112. Prince, enumerating the principal members of Boston church, II. 69, has mistaken him for the master of the Lyon, as I infer from finding in their Records but one of the name, and being satisfied, that he could not be honoured with such office in the civil line, unless in full communion with the brethren. His wife, Bridget, was admitted of our church 26 January after her husband. A second wife survived him, and had administration of his estate in December, 1669. See Prob. Rec. VII. 2, by which we find his estate much reduced, the inventory amounting only to £85.2, unless another person of the same name, but not the navigator mentioned in a note on page 25, be in that record intended; for administration of the estate of *one* William Peirce was granted, January, 1661, to his wife, Prob. Rec. IV. 66, and the inventory of it is £228.5. Several children survived, of whom the Prob. Rec. VII. 213, affords the names. It is not now easy to refer to each stock the numerous descendants in our country.

[2] There can be no need of saying more of this gentleman than will be found in a few pages of this History, in Trumbull, the Magnalia, and the biographies. He was fortunate in being governour of Massachusetts, and more fortunate in removing after his first year of office, thereby avoiding our bitter contentions, to become father of the new colony of Connecticut.

[3] Drs. Trumbull and Holmes were, by the errour of the former edition, led into mistake of this gentleman's name. Atherton Haugh, or Hough, pronounced as the text gives it, was of great influence in Boston, as this work, in its progress, will show. He was early chosen into the council, and afterwards a deputy from Boston in several general courts. I presume he came from Boston in Lincolnshire; for, in 1628, the mayor of that borough was of the same name. His descendants, in male and female lines, if we may judge from the perpetuation of the unusual name of baptism, continued long in Boston and its vicinity; and the derivation is probably not yet extinct. He died 11 September, 1650.

[4] In any other place, I know not that evidence of a regular religious assembly, on the evening before the first day of the week, can be found. The time was observed as holy in private families for many years; and writings in favour of the custom, nearly a century, are recollected, particularly in 1722, by Stoddard of

ercise, and Mr. Cotton, being desired to speak to the question, (which was of the church,) he showed, out of the Canticles, 6, that some churches were as queens, some as concubines, some as damsels, and some as doves,[1] &c. He was then (with his wife) propounded to be admitted a member. The Lord's day following, he exercised in the afternoon, and being to be admitted, he signified his desire and readiness to make his confession according to order, which he said might be sufficient in declaring his faith about baptism, (which he then desired for his child, born in their passage, and therefore named [2]Seaborn.) He gave two reasons why he did not baptize it at sea, (not for want of fresh water, for he held, sea water would have served:) 1, because they had no settled congregation there; 2, because a minister hath no power to give the seals but in his own congregation. He desired his wife might also be admitted a member, and gave a modest testimony of her, but withal requested, that she might not be put to make open confession, &c. which he said was against the apostle's rule, and not fit for women's modesty; but that the elders might examine her in private. So she was asked, if she did consent in the confession of faith made by her husband, and if she did desire to be admitted, &c.; whereto she answered affirmatively; and so both were admitted, and their child baptized, the father presenting it, (the

---

Northampton, one of the greatest divines of that age in our country. The practice still subsists, with greater or less punctuality, in Connecticut, where, on the evening of Sunday, it is said, many recur to their secular labours; and by the statute of Massachusetts, 1791, c. 58, certain regulations, "respecting the due observation of the Lord's day, shall be construed to extend to the time included between the midnight preceding and the sun setting of the same day."

1 Most of the early Protestants, and especially the Puritans, paid no less attention to the Song, than to the Wisdom of Solomon; and sometimes, by their extreme fondness for spiritualizing what needs great distortion to make it "profitable for doctrine, for reproof, for correction, for instruction in righteousness," seem to be ignorant of the strong doubts of its canonical authority. Piety is shocked, when prudence is thus slighted.

2 Of this son, whose name, in the catalogue of Harvard College, is found, Marigena, 1651, a brief note is found in Allen. I am less surprised at the omission of him by Eliot, whose account of the father is admirable for its propriety, than of his younger brother, John, H. C. 1657, who, after officiating several years as teacher of the Indians, and thirty years as pastor at Plimouth, removed to Charleston, S. C., and there gathered a Congregational church. We cannot here avoid the expression of regret, that, in Ramsay's "History of the Independent or Congregational Church in Charleston," so little is related of him; but the ample account of the Plimouth church, 1 Hist. Coll. IV. 122—128, affords all the information that might be desired. For his acquirements in the language of the aborigines, no man of New England, I presume, except Eliot and Williams, ranks higher.

child's baptism being, as he did then affirm, in another case, the father's ||incentive|| for the help of his faith, &c.)

The said 4th of September, came in also the ship called the Bird, (Mr. Yates master.) She brought [blank] passengers, having lost [blank;] and [blank] cows, §having lost [blank;]§ and four mares. She had been twelve weeks at sea, being, at her first coming out, driven northerly to fifty-three.

About ten days before this time, a bark was set forth to Connecticut and those parts, to trade.

John Oldham, and three with him, went over land to Connecticut, to trade. The sachem used them kindly, and gave them some beaver. They ||2brought of the hemp, which grows|| there in great abundance, and is much better than the English. He accounted it to be about one hundred and sixty miles.[1] He brought some black lead, whereof the Indians told him there was a whole rock. He lodged at Indian towns all the way.

12.] Capt. John Stone (of whom mention is made before) carried himself very dissolutely in drawing company to drink, &c. and being found upon the bed in the night with one Barcroft's wife, he was brought before the governour, &c. and though it appeared he was in drink, and no act to be proved, yet it was thought fit he should abide his trial, for which ||3end|| warrant was sent out to stay his pinnace, which was ready to set sail; whereupon he went to Mr. Ludlow, one of the assistants, and used ||4braving|| and threatening speeches against him, for which he raised some company and apprehended him, and brought him to the governour, who put him in irons, and kept a guard upon him till the court, (but his irons were taken off the same day.) At the court his indictment was framed for adultery, but found *ignoramus* by the great jury; but, for his other misdemeanours, he was fined £100, which yet was not levied of him; and ordered upon pain of death to come here no more, without license of the court; and the woman was bound to her good behaviour.[2]

||instruction|| ||2bought of him the hemp that grew|| ||3a|| ||4———||

---

1 The former editor, desirous of shortening the road to the capital, put this annotation on the text: "From Boston to Connecticut River, in a direct line, is not more than half that distance." Probably Oldham and his fellow travellers followed winding paths for the convenience of lodging all the way, as in modern times we are compelled to for some part.

2 Though the Colony Records, I. 103, in the account of Stone's offence, take not any notice of the supposed adultery, yet the whole severity of the sentence is found there. Hubbard, 156, borrows from them the vituperative language, going, in this instance, beyond our author, whom, almost uniformly, he follows

17.] The governour and council met at Boston, and called the ministers and elders of all the churches, to consider about Mr. Cotton his sitting down. He was desired to divers places, and those who came with him desired he might sit down where they might keep store of cattle; but it was agreed, by full consent, that the fittest place for him was Boston, and in that respect those of Boston might take farms in any part of the bay not belonging to other towns; and that (keeping a ||lecture)|| he should have some maintenance out of the treasury. But divers of the council, upon their second thoughts, did after refuse this contribution.[1]

October 2.] The bark Blessing, which was sent to the southward, returned. She had been at an island over against Connecticut, called Long Island, because it is near fifty leagues long, the east part about ten leagues from the main, but the west end not one mile. There they had store of the best wampampeak, both white and blue. The Indians there are a very treacherous people. They have many canoes so great as one will carry eighty men. They were also in the River of Connecticut, which is barred at the entrance, so as they could not find above one fathom water. They were also at the Dutch plantation upon Hudson's River, (called New Netherlands,) where they were very kindly entertained, and had some beaver and other things, for such commodities as they put off. They showed the governour (called Gwalter Van [2]Twilly) their

||lecturer||

---

with undeviating prudence. But the judgment mentions assaulting, as part of the misdemeanour, which both the historians overlook.

1 I think the refusal was proper. There was certainly no propriety in making the colony, after Boston was so much increased in wealth and numbers, contribute to the support of her minister, because he was the most able man on this side of the ocean.

The rate of £400, voted at the court, 1 October next, shows the relative importance of the towns. The proportions are, to Boston, Roxbury, Newtown, Watertown and Charlestown, £48 each; Dorchester, £80; Sagus, £36; Salem, £28; Medford, £12; Wenetsemit and Agawam, £8 each. The aggregate exceeds the amount of the levy by £12; but that does not appear so unexpected as the large tax on Dorchester. Some new comers of large estate had, I imagine, settled in that town.

2 Authentick history preserves little account of the administration of this gentleman. But a work of exquisite humour, in which fiction builds on the ground-work of truth, has fully amplified his renown; and the name of Diedrick Knickerbocker, his panegyrist, will forever remind posterity of "the unutterable ponderings of Walter the doubter." William Smith, History of New York, 4to, London, 1757, dates the arrival of the governour, whom he calls Wouter Van Twiller, in June, 1629. Hubbard, 323, with more than his usual negligence, calls *Kieft* first governour, when he had transcribed, 171, 2,

commission, which was to signify to them, that the king of England had granted the river and country of Connecticut to his own subjects; and therefore desired them to forbear to build there, &c. The Dutch governour wrote back to our governour, (his letter was very courteous and respectful, as it had been to a very honourable person,) whereby he signified, that the Lords the States had also granted the same parts to the West India Company, and therefore requested that ||we|| would forbear the same till the matter were decided between the king of England and the said lords.

The said bark did pass and repass over the shoals of Cape Cod, about three or four leagues from Nantucket Isle, where the breaches are very terrible, yet they had three fathom water all over.

[Large blank.]

The company of Plimouth sent a bark to Connecticut, at this time, to erect a trading house there. When they came, they found the Dutch had built there, and did forbid the Plimouth men to proceed; but they set up their house notwithstanding, about a mile above the Dutch.[1] This river runs so far northward, that it comes within a day's journey of a part of Merrimack called [blank,] and so runs thence N. W. so near the Great Lake, as [allows] the Indians to pass their canoes into it over land. From this lake, and the hideous swamps about it, come most of the beaver which is traded between Virginia and Canada, which runs forth of this lake; and Patomack River in Virginia comes likewise out of it, or very near, so as from this lake there comes yearly to the Dutch about ten thousand skins, which might easily be diverted by Merrimack, if a course of trade were settled above in that river.[2]

||he||

---

from Winthrop, this and the two following paragraphs, with hardly the change of a letter.

1 Smith, N. Y. 2, asserts the priority of the Dutch settlement, by erection of a fort in 1623; but there can hardly be a particle of doubt, that an errour of ten years must be allowed for, since the negotiations between the Dutch commissioner, De Razier, and the Plimouth colony, in 1627, are so totally silent on the subject of Connecticut, that it is impossible for us to believe they had then formed such an establishment. See 2 Hist. Coll. III. 51—57. See also the Dutch governour, Stuyvesant's, case stated by himself in Haz. II. 262, beginning with an allegation of purchase, by Jacobus Van Corlis, in 1633, and complaining of the expedition of Holmes from Plimouth in October following. See further a full account, by Gov. Bradford, of the origin of the controversy, Hutchinson's Mass. II. 416, 17. Trumbull, I. 21, says the Dutch fort was at Hartford; the Plimouth house at Windsor.

2 Here is an ignorance of geography, at which we might be surprised, were not similar instances, in the early times, very common. The Connecticut is,

10.] A fast was kept at Boston, and Mr. [1]Leverett, an ancient, sincere professor, of Mr. Cotton's congregation in England, was chosen a ruling elder, and Mr. [2]Firmin, a godly man, an apothecary of Sudbury in England, was chosen deacon, by imposition of hands; and Mr. Cotton was then chosen teacher of the congregation of Boston, and ordained by imposition of the hands §of the presbytery, in this manner: First, he was chosen by all the congregation testifying their consent by erection of hands.§ Then Mr. Wilson, the pastor, demanded of him, if he did ||accept|| of that call. He paused, and then spake to this effect: that howsoever he knew himself unworthy and unsufficient for that place; yet, having observed all the passages of God's providence, (which he ||[2]reckoned|| up in particular) in calling him to it, he could not but ||[3]accept|| it. Then the pastor and the two elders laid their hands upon his head, and the pastor prayed, and then, taking off their hands, laid them on again, and, speaking to him by his name, they did ||[4]thenceforth|| design him to the said office, in the name of the Holy Ghost, and did give him the charge of the congregation, and did

||except|| ||[2]recorded|| ||[3]except|| ||[4]thereby||

---

indeed, within a day's journey of the Merrimack; but the passage of Indian canoes into that river, over land, could never have been from the Great Lake. It may have been, with a short portage, from the St. Lawrence. All the beaver trade between Virginia and Canada, by which name is designated the great river of Niagara, Cataraqui, or St. Lawrence, naturally took the direction of Hudson's River, and was therefore secured to the Dutch. It could not easily have been diverted to the Merrimack or the Potomack.

1 An omission to notice the fact, that this gentleman was father of the celebrated John Leverett, governour of Massachusetts, can only be accounted for by supposing, that Mather, Hutchinson, Holmes, Eliot and Allen, were all unacquainted with it. Yet our First Church Record mentions it, when announcing the admission of the son, 14 July, 1639. Of Thomas little is mentioned; but we may be sure he came with Cotton, and other gentlemen of Boston in Old England; for his entrance to the church was in October, 1633, he and his wife, Ann, being Nos. 169 and 170. The date of his death is unknown.

2 His place was enjoyed but a short time; for, at the town meeting, on 6 October next year, which is the earliest, whose proceedings are preserved in our Town Records, the preceding pages being all lost, Richard Bellingham, Esq. was chosen a selectman, they say, "in the place of Giles Firmin, deceased." He took the freemen's oath 4 March, 1633—4. Eliot has given, with minuteness, the biography of the son, who attended his father across the ocean, and in a few years removed to Ipswich, whence an excellent letter from him to Winthrop, dated 26 December, 1639, is preserved in Hutch. Coll. 108; but I must correct his mistake in making the son, instead of the father, deacon of our church. Giles, the younger, married a daughter of the famous Nathaniel Ward, and died in England, 1697, at a great age, having written several devotional pieces, of which some are, as is reported, read in our time.

thereby (as by a sign from God) indue him with the gifts fit for his office; and lastly did bless him. Then the neighbouring ministers, which were present, did (at the pastor's ||motion||) give him the right hands of fellowship, and the pastor made a stipulation between him and the congregation. When Mr. Cotton accepted of the office, he commended to the congregation such as were to come over, who were of his charge in England, that they might be comfortably provided for.

The same day, Mr. Grant, in the ship James, arrived at Salem, having been but eight weeks between Gravesend and Salem. He brought Capt. Wiggin and about thirty, with one Mr. ||2Leveridge,||[1] a godly minister to Pascataquack, (which the Lord Say and the Lord Brook had purchased of the Bristol men,) and about thirty for Virginia, and about twenty for ||3this|| place, and some sixty cattle. He brought news, that the Richard, a bark of fifty tons, which came forth with the Griffin, being come above three hundred leagues, sprang such a leak, as she was forced to bear up, and ||4was put in at|| Weymouth.

11.] A fast at Newtown, where Mr. Hooker was chosen pastor, and Mr. Stone teacher, in such a manner as before at Boston.

The wolves continued to do much hurt among our cattle; and this month, by Mr. Grant, there came over four Irish greyhounds, which were sent to the governour by Mr. Downing, his brother-in-law.

[Very large blank.]

November.] A great mortality among the Indians. Chick-

||notice|| ||2L——|| ||3that|| ||4put into||

1 Brief notice only of this gentleman can be given. William Leveridge joined our church 9 August, 1635, being No. 308. Hubbard, who calls him "an able and worthy minister," says, 221, that, for want of encouragement at Wiggin's plantation of Dover, "he removed more southward, towards Plimouth or Long Island." This want of precision in that historian is especially blameable, as the earlier writer, Johnson, lib. 3. c. 10, had mentioned his residence at Sandwich, and engagement in the pious service of instructing the Indians. At that place notice is taken of him by our author, sub an. 1640, as introducing a new practice in celebrating the eucharist. His departure from Sandwich is related by Judge Davis in his edition of Morton's Memorial; and Hazard, II. 372, 384, informs of his employment, by the commissioners of the United Colonies, as a missionary, in 1657. Seventeen years later, in a letter from Col. Matthias Nicolls of New York to Gov. Winthrop of Connecticut, I find him named thus: "I have given conveyance to your enclosed to Mr. Leveredge, which your honour saith related to some medicinal matter, but have received no return; probably he will find out some other way to give answer to it." He was then, I presume, stationed at Nantucket, with which the best mode of conveyance, from Hartford, was through New York, to whose jurisdiction our island, at that time, belonged.

atabot, the sagamore of Naponsett, died, and many of his people. The disease was the small pox. Some of them were cured by such means as they had from us; many of their children escaped, and were kept by the English.

Capt. Wiggin of Pascataquack wrote to the governour, that one of his people had stabbed another, and desired he might be tried in the bay, if the party ||died.|| The governour answered, that if Pascataquack lay within their limits, (as it was supposed,) they would try him.

A small ship of about sixty tons was built at Medford, and called the Rebecca.

This year a watermill was built at Roxbury, by Mr. Dummer.[1]

The scarcity of workmen had caused them to raise their wages to an excessive rate, so as a carpenter would have three shillings the day, a labourer two shillings and sixpence, &c.; and accordingly those who had commodities to sell advanced their prices sometime double to that they cost in England, so as it grew to a general complaint, which the court, taking knowledge of, as also of some further evils, which were springing out of the excessive rates of wages, they made an order, that carpenters, ||[2]masons,|| &c. should take but two shillings the day, and labourers but eighteen pence, and that no commodity should be sold at above four pence in the shilling more than it cost for ready money in England; oil, wine, &c. and cheese, in regard of the hazard of bringing, &c. [excepted.] The evils which were springing, &c. were, 1. Many spent much time idly, &c. because they could get as much in four days as would keep them a week. 2. They spent much in tobacco and strong waters, &c. which was a great waste to the commonwealth which, by reason of so many ||[3]foreign|| commodities expended, could not have subsisted to this time, but that it was supplied by the cattle and corn, which were sold to new comers at very dear rates, viz. corn at six shillings the bushel, a cow at £20,—yea, some at £24, some £26,—a mare at £35, an ewe goat at 3 or £4; and yet many cattle were every year brought out of England, and some from Virginia. Soon after order was taken for prices of commodities, viz. not to exceed the rate of four pence in the shilling above the price in England, except cheese and liquors, &c.

The ministers in the bay and Sagus did meet, once a fort-

||desired|| ||[2]masters|| ||[3]scarce||

---

1 Earlier in the year, the first watermill in the colony had been in Dorchester, by Stoughton. See 1 Hist. Coll. IX. 164.

night, at one of their houses by ||course,|| where some question of moment was debated. Mr. Skelton, the pastor of Salem, and Mr. Williams, who was removed from Plimouth thither, (but not in any office, though he exercised by way of prophecy,) took some exception against it, as fearing it might grow in time to a presbytery or superintendency, to the prejudice of the churches' liberties. But this fear was without cause; for they were all clear in that point, that no church or person can have power over another church; neither did they in their meetings exercise any such jurisdiction, &c.[1]

[Large blank.]

News of the taking of [2]Machias by the French. Mr. Allerton of Plimouth, and some others, had set up a trading wigwam there, and ||[2]left|| in it five men and store of commodities. [3]La Tour, governour of the French in those parts, making claim to the place, came to displant them, and, finding resistance, killed two of the men, and carried away the other three, and the goods.

[Large blank.]

Some differences fell out still, now and then, between the governour and the deputy, which yet were soon healed. It had been ordered in court, that all hands should help to the finishing of the fort at Boston, and all the towns in the bay had gone once over, and most the second time; but those of Newtown being warned, the deputy would not suffer them to come, neither did acquaint the governour with the cause, which was, for that Salem and Sagus had not brought in money for their parts. The governour, hearing of it, wrote friendly to him, showing him that the intent of the court was, that the work should be done by those in the bay, and that, after, the others should pay a proportionable sum for the house, &c. which must be done by money; and therefore desired him that he would send in his neighbours. Upon this,

||commission|| ||[2]lost||

---

1 By Emerson, in History of the First Church, this is considered as the origin of the Boston Association of Congregational Ministers. He censures the strange bitterness of Hubbard, 189, 190, on this subject.

2 Permanent establishment of settlers at that port was delayed one hundred and thirty years. See 1 Hist. Coll. III. 144.

3 Of this governour of Nova Scotia, to whom a grant of the country had been made by Sir William Alexander, 30 April, 1630, extracted from the Suffolk Registry of Deeds, III. 265, by Hazard, I. 307, and confirmed by Cromwell, 9 August, 1656, as in Hazard, I. 616, such perpetual mention will occur in the progress of this History, that it may be necessary to protract this note no farther than by reference, for what is not to be found in our author, to Hutchinson, I. 120—126.

Mr. Haynes and Mr. Hooker came to the governour to treat with him about it, and brought a letter from the deputy full of bitterness and resolution not to send till Salem, &c. The governour told them it should rest till the court, and withal gave the letter to Mr. Hooker with this speech: I am not willing to keep such an occasion of provocation by me. And soon after he wrote to the deputy (who had before desired to buy a fat hog or two of him, being somewhat short of provisions) to desire him to send for one, (which he would have sent him, if he had known when his occasion had been to have made use of it,) and to accept it as a testimony of his good will; and, lest he should make any scruple of it, he made Mr. Haynes and Mr. Hooker (who both sojourned in his house) partakers with him. Upon this the deputy returned this answer: "Your overcoming yourself hath overcome me. Mr. Haynes, Mr. Hooker, and myself, do most kindly accept your good will; but we desire, without offence, to refuse your offer, and that I may only trade with you for two hogs;" and so very lovingly concluded.—The court being two days after, ordered, that Newtown should do their work as others had done, and then Salem, &c. should pay for three days at eighteen pence a man.

11.] The congregation of Boston met to take order for Mr. Cotton's ||passage|| and house, and his and Mr. Wilson's maintenance. Mr. Cotton had disbursed eighty pounds for his ||2passage,|| and towards his house, which he would not have again; so there was about £60 raised (by voluntary contribution) towards the finishing of his house, and about £100 towards their maintenance. At this meeting there arose some difference between the governour and Mr. Cottington, who charged the governour, that he took away the liberty of the rest, because (at the request of the rest) he had named some men to set out ||3men's|| lands, &c. which grew to some heat of words; but the next Lord's day they both acknowledged openly their failing, and declared that they had been reconciled the next day.

[Large blank.]

26.] Mr. Wilson (by leave of the congregation of Boston, whereof he was pastor) went to Agawam to teach the people of that plantation, because they had yet no minister. Whiles he was there, December 4, there fell such a snow (knee deep) as he could not come back for [blank] days, and a boat, which went thither, was frozen up in the river.[1]

||pursage|| ||2pursage|| ||3minister's||

1 Nobody can pretend, I believe, that an equal severity of cold has been twice experienced, at so early a season, for the last hundred years.

December 5.] John Sagamore died of the small pox, and almost all his people; (above thirty buried by Mr. Maverick of Winesemett in one day.) The towns in the bay took away many of the children; but most of them died soon after.

James Sagamore of Sagus died also, and most of his folks. John Sagamore desired to be brought among the English, (so

---

The 4th of December, corresponding to the 15th by our supputation of the year, Stat. Geo. II. 24, very seldom witnesses, on the sea shore, more than three or four inches depth of snow; and that which falls before Christmas does not often lie longer than two days. The frost, in the text, we should now think more remarkable than the snow; and no boat has probably been frozen up in Ipswich harbour, by the middle of December, within the recollection of any inhabitant. There is distinct reference to a degree of frost, in the year before this, that "hindered the making ready" of the expedition against Bull, the pirate, which, in the present age, would be extraordinary. In 1631 nothing is said of the approach of winter, nor any mention of the weather until 27 January. But the first autumn our author passed here was quite favourable; for he remarks that, till the 24 December, or our 4 January, was, "for the most part, fair, open weather;" yet such severity of "bitter frost and snow," as kept three servants in his boat, without victuals, from 27 November to 1 December, (that is, by our reckoning, from 8 to 12 December,) among the islands of Boston harbour, and finally compelled them to run ashore in Braintree Bay, (see page 38,) would surprise us. Cold came on earlier, it will be observed, in the year after this, in the text; and the man frozen in the snow, in November, on Plumb Island, would, in our days, be unable to find credit for his tale. November, 1635, affords strong proof of severe cold in Connecticut and Plimouth. Even Mr. Webster should be struck with the circumstance of the freezing of the Connecticut so early as the 15 of that month, O. S., however he might disregard the deep snow of the following December. Of the winter of 1636 nothing is observed, and perhaps Winthrop forgot the temperature of the sky in the unnatural heat of the controversy about grace. The rigid season of the next year, we shall see, continued one hundred and thirty-nine days.

The opinion is general, but not universal, that our climate is less rigorous than it was known to be soon after the discovery of the country; and we find certainly the mildness of autumn is usually prolonged to the winter solstice. But those who are slow to believe the improvement of temperature in our sky, overpowered by the testimony that establishes the fact of retardation in the advance of winter, discern some compensation, as they imagine, in the later approach of spring. I am confident, however, that the complaint of backwardness in that season, though rendered common by the tenderness of valetudinarians, and the impatience of husbandmen, is generally unjust. If the instances of that duration of cold, in the winter of 1641—2, when the ice was strong enough to bear many passengers together, from Pullen Point to Boston in a straight line, on the day corresponding to our 28 February, continuing even to 4 March, and that great snow of 1644—5, which blocked up the roads three weeks in March, and prevented the court from meeting in Boston, remaining on the ground to the 10th of April, N. S., be undervalued in the estimate, as uncommon cases, from which conclusions may not safely be deduced,—it may be answered, that modern wonders in the atmosphere are not greater, and that the experience of Winthrop being short, no greater portion of time than his should now be assumed for a parallel. In the autumn of 1645 the cold came earlier than had ever been known, so that the genial season of that year was shortened at the beginning and end. The

he ||was;||) and promised (if he recovered) to live with the English and serve their God. He left one son, which he disposed to Mr. Wilson, the pastor of Boston, to be brought up by him. He gave to the governour a good quantity of wampompeague, and to divers others of the English he gave gifts, and took order for the payment of his own debts and his men's. He died in a persuasion that he should go to the Englishmen's God. Divers of them, in their sickness, confessed that the Englishmen's God was a good God; and that, if they recovered, they would serve him.

It wrought much with them, that when their own people forsook them, yet the English came daily and ministered to them; and yet few, *only two families,* took any ||2infection|| by it. Among others, Mr. Maverick of Winesemett is worthy of *a perpetual*[1] remembrance. Himself, his wife and servants, went daily to them, ministered to their necessities, and buried their dead, and took home many of their children. So did other of the neighbours.

This infectious disease spread to Pascataquack, where all the Indians (except one or two) died.

One Cowper of Pascataquack, going to an island, upon the Lord's day, to fetch some sack to be drank at the great house,

||agreed|| ||2instructions||

---

aggregate, or mean, of observations for many years, as given, above one hundred and forty years ago, by Hubbard, 20, is here transcribed, in order that every reader may, every season, do something, by observation of the phænomena, in aid of the solution of so interesting a question: "The frost here *useth* to visit the inhabitants so early in the winter, and *ordinarily* tarries so long before it takes its leave in the spring, that the difficulty of subsistence is much increased thereby; for it *commonly* begins to take possession of the earth about the middle of November, (26, N. S.) forbidding the husbandman to meddle therewith any more, till the middle or end of March, (26 March—10 April, N. S.) not being willing, till that time, to resign up its possession or the hold it hath taken for near two feet below the surface of the earth."

On this subject, which has of late received much elucidation, an Essay by an anonymous author, published at Philadelphia, 1809, will reward attentive perusal. A review of it, by the editor of this work, was printed in the Monthly Anthology, IX. 25. Some years before, a very elaborate, but skeptical dissertation had been offered to the Connecticut Academy of Arts and Sciences, by Noah Webster, Esq., for which, and other ingenious labours, the literary publick is more indebted to him than even for the former edition of this History. A learned and judicious examination of that tract, usually ascribed to Professor Farrar of Cambridge, may be seen in the General Repository, IV. 313.

1 That Maverick was not in full communion with our churches, was not, we may hope, the cause of striking a pen through this honourable epithet. No man seems better entitled by his deeds to the character of a Christian. The MS. appears to testify that the mutilation was not Winthrop's.

he and a boy, coming back in a canoe, (being both drunk,) were driven to sea and never heard of after.

At the same plantation, a company having made a fire at a tree, one of them said, Here this tree will fall, §and here will I lie;§ and accordingly it fell upon him and killed him.

It pleased the Lord to give special testimony of his presence in the church of Boston, after Mr. Cotton was called to office there. More were converted and added to that church, than to all the other churches in the bay,[1] (or rather the lake, for so it were more ||properly|| termed,[2] the bay being that part of sea without, between the two capes, Cape Cod and Cape Ann.) Divers profane and notorious evil persons came and confessed their sins, and were comfortably received into the bosom of the church. Yea, the Lord gave witness to the exercise of prophecy, so as thereby some were converted, and others much edified. Also, the Lord pleased greatly to bless the practice of discipline, wherein he gave the pastor, Mr. Wilson, a singular gift,[3] to the great benefit of the church.

After much deliberation and serious advice, the Lord directed the teacher, Mr. Cotton, to make it clear by the scripture, that the minister's maintenance, as well as all other charges of the church, should be defrayed out of a ||2stock,|| or treasury, which was to be raised out of the weekly contribution; which accordingly was agreed upon.[4]

||principally|| ||2chest||

---

1 Hubbard, 190, who, with sufficient accuracy, quotes his master, from whom a large part of his History is transcribed, enlarges the expression to "all the rest of the churches in the country." The reputation of Cotton needs no such exaggeration. From his arrival to this time, that is, three months, I was led by curiosity to ascertain from the Records the precise number intended by the text, and found thirty-seven added to the members of the church. The "profane and notorious evil persons" cannot be distinguished in the list; but perhaps, in several, the old disease broke out again. Temporal inducements operated too strongly to swell the company of communicants.

2 The governour first wrote, "so it shall be termed henceforth;" but the name could not be made popular in his day, and has never been thought of since. Yet the situation resembles much those arms of the sea, called lochs by the Scots, loughs by the Irish, and lagoons by the Spaniards.

3 Elder Leverett, as well as Wilson, is, by Hubbard, 190, blessed with this *singular gift* in "the practice of discipline." It certainly belonged to his office.

4 Cotton's arguments are lost, we may presume, for the custom of raising these charges of the church, which was made so clear from the scripture, is totally changed. Our fathers looked too much to a special divine appointment in their management of secular concerns, often forgetting that reason was no less the gift of God, than the ritual of Moses, and that a different state

27.] The governour and assistants met at Boston, and took into consideration a treatise, which Mr. Williams (then of Salem) had sent to them, and which he had formerly written to the governour and council of Plimouth, wherein, among other things, he disputes their right to the lands they possessed here, and concluded that, claiming by the king's grant, they could have no title, nor otherwise, except they compounded with the natives. For this, taking advice with some of the most judicious ministers, (who much condemned Mr. Williams's errour and presumption,) they gave order, that he should be convented at the next court, to be censured, &c. There were three passages chiefly whereat they were much offended: 1, for that he chargeth King James to have told a solemn publick lie, because in his patent he blessed God that he was the first Christian prince that had discovered this land; 2, for that he chargeth him and others with blasphemy for calling Europe Christendom, or the ||Christian|| world: 3, for that he did personally apply to our present king, Charles, these three places in the Revelations, viz. [blank.][1]

Mr. Endecott being absent, the governour wrote to him to let him know what was done, and withal added divers arguments to confute the said errours, wishing him to deal with Mr. Williams to retract the same, &c. Whereto he returned a very modest and discreet answer. Mr. Williams also wrote to the governour, and also to him and the rest of the council, very submissively, professing his intent to have been only to have written for the private satisfaction of the ||[2]governour,|| &c. of Plimouth, without any purpose to have stirred any further in it, if the governour ||[3]here|| had not required a copy of him; withal offering his book, or any part of it, to be burnt.

At the next court he appeared ||[4]*penitently*,|| and gave satisfaction of his intention and ||[5]loyalty.|| So it was left, and nothing done in it.

January 21.] News came from Plimouth, that Capt. Stone, who this last summer went out of the bay or lake, and so to

||church|| ||[2]gentlemen|| ||[3]there|| ||[4]privately|| ||[5]gilt||

existed in the church, from that which the apostles were compelled, by circumstances, not led by inspiration, to adopt.

1 Perhaps the same expressions, by another, would have given less offence. From Williams they were not at first received in the mildest, or even the most natural sense; though further reflection satisfied the magistrates, that his were not dangerous. The passages from the Apocalypse were probably not *applied* to the honour of the king; and I regret, therefore, that Winthrop did not preserve them. No complaint of such indiscretion would have been expressed ten years later, when the mother country far outran the colony in these perversions of scripture.

Aquamenticus, where he took in Capt. Norton, putting in at the mouth of Connecticut, in his way to Virginia, where the Pequins inhabit, was there cut off by them, with all his company, being eight.[1] The manner was thus: *Three of his men, being gone ashore to kill fowl, were cut off. Then the sachem, with some of his men, came aboard, and staid with Capt. Stone in his cabin, till Capt. Stone (being alone with him) fell on sleep. Then he knocked him on the head, and all the rest of the English being in the cook's room, the Indians took such pieces as they found there ready charged, and bent them at the English; whereupon one took a piece, and by accident gave fire to the powder, which blew up the deck; but most of the Indians, perceiving what they went about, shifted overboard, and after they returned, and killed such as remained, and burned the pinnace. We agreed to write to the governour of Virginia, (because Stone was one of that colony,) to move him to revenge it, and upon his answer to take further counsel.*[2]

20.] Hall and the two others, who went to Connecticut November 3, came now home, having lost themselves and endured much misery. They ||informed|| us, that the small pox was gone as far as any Indian plantation was known to the west, and much people dead of it, by reason whereof they could have no trade.

At Naragansett, by the Indians' report, there died seven hundred; but, beyond Pascataquack, none to the eastward.

24.] The governour and council met again at Boston, to consider of Mr. Williams's letter, &c. when, with the advice of Mr. Cotton and Mr. Wilson, and weighing his letter, and further considering of the aforesaid offensive passages in his book, (which, being written in very obscure and implicative phrases, might well admit of doubtful interpretation,) they found the matters not to be so evil as at first they seemed. Whereupon they agreed, that, upon his retractation, &c. or taking an oath of allegiance to the king, &c. it should be passed over.

[Very large blank.]

||assured||

---

1 It was first written *ten or twelve*.

2 A pen has been drawn diagonally across this narrative in the MS.; and in the margin this direction is given, "See after, November 6, 1634." But it is evident, that this is not superseded by that relation, in fulness of detail at least. Whether the first story were designed to be stigmatized as less credible than the other, when neither could come from the innocent, is left to the judgment of the reader. Both are worth preserving.

An Englishman of Sacoe, travelling into the country to trade, was killed by the Indians.

[Very large blank.]

30.] John Seales, who ran from his master to the Indians, came ||home|| again. He was at a place twelve miles off, where were seven Indians, whereof four died of the pox while he was there.

[Large blank.]

February 1.] Mr. Cradock's house at Marblehead was burnt down about midnight before, there being then in it Mr. Allerton, and many fishermen, whom he employed that season, who all were preserved by a special providence of God, with most of his goods therein, by a tailor, who sate up that night at work in the house, and, hearing a noise, looked out and saw the house on fire above the oven in the thatch.

This winter was very mild, little wind, and most S. and S. W. but ||2oft|| snows, and great. One snow, the 15th of this month, was near two feet deep all over.

[Large blank.]

Such of the Indians' children as were left were taken by the English, most whereof did die of the pox soon after, three only remaining, whereof one, which the governour kept, was called Know-God, (the Indians' usual answer being, when they were put in mind of God, Me no know God.)

[Large blank.]

22.] The [1]grampus came up towards Charlestown ||3against|| the tide of ebb.

[Large blank.]

This season Mr. Allerton fished with eight boats at Marble Harbour.

[Large blank.]

By this time seventeen fishing ships were come to Richman's Isle and the Isles of Shoals.

March 4.] By order of court a mercate was erected at Boston, to be kept upon Thursday, the fifth day of the week, being the lecture day. Samuel [2]Cole set up the first house for

||here|| ||2after|| ||3by||

1 Here some may imagine, as the former editor certainly did, that the name of a ship is intended; but to me it seems evident, that the author designed only to remark the early arrival of that species of fish in our shoal waters.

2 From his being so early a member of the church, No. 42, and his wife, Ann, who died no long time after arrival, standing next, I conclude they came over with Winthrop. His will, dated 21 December, 1666, was proved in the following February.

common entertainment, and John [1]Cogan, merchant, the first shop.

Upon offer of some new comers to give liberally towards the building of a galley for defence of the bay, and upon consultation with divers experienced seamen and others, it was thought fitter for our condition to build a vessel forty feet in length, and twenty-one in breadth, to be ||minion|| proof, and the upper deck musket proof, to have one sail, and to carry whole culverin and other smaller pieces, eight in all. This was found to be so chargeable, and so long time ere it could be finished, that it was given over.

At this court all swamps, above one hundred acres, were made common, &c. Also Robert Cole, having been oft punished for drunkenness, was now ordered to wear a red D about his neck for a year.

[Blank.]

7.] At the lecture at Boston a question was propounded about veils. Mr. Cotton concluded, that where (by the custom of the place) they were not a sign of ||2the women's subjection,|| they were not commanded by the apostle. Mr. Endecott opposed, and did maintain it by the general arguments brought by the apostle.[2] After some debate, the governour, perceiving it to grow to some earnestness, interposed, and so it brake off.

[Large blank.]

Among other testimonies of the Lord's gracious presence with his own ordinances, there was a youth of fourteen years of age (being the son of one of the magistrates) so wrought upon by the ministry of the word, as, for divers months, he was held under such affliction of mind, as he could not be brought to apprehend any comfort in God, being much humbled and broken for his sins, (though he had been a dutiful child, and not given up to the lusts of youth,) and especially for his blasphemous and wicked thoughts, whereby Satan buffeted him,

||cannon|| ||2a woman's sobriety||

1 This gentleman, who died in 1658, spelt his name with a double *g*. He left a good estate, of which five hundred acres in Woburn is valued in the inventory at ten pounds. From the Boston Records it appears, he was married, for the second time, as his former wife, Ann, is named in the Church Record of July, 1634, to Mrs. Martha Winthrop, undoubtedly the widow of the author of this History, on 10 March, 1651, by Gov. John Endecott.

2 In this opinion Endecott had been instructed by Williams, whose scruple on this subject is ridiculed by Hubbard, 204, 5. That historian makes Cotton preach a sermon at Salem one Sunday morning, which so enlightened the women, that "they appeared in the afternoon without their veils."

so as he went mourning and languishing daily; yet, attending to the means, and not giving over prayer, and seeking counsel, &c. he came at length to be freed from his temptations, and to find comfort in God's promises, and so, being received into the congregation, upon good proof of his understanding in the things of God, he went on cheerfully in a Christian course, falling daily to labour, as a servant, and as a younger brother of his did, who was no whit short of him in the knowledge of God's will, though his youth kept him from daring to offer himself to the congregation.[1]—Upon this occasion it is not im-

---

1 Conjecture would confidently apply this anecdote to the writer's own family; for such minute relation could only be expected from a party. The "younger brother" was, no doubt, Deane, born March, 1622—3. Stephen, the governour's son, chiefly alluded to in the text, was, on 16 of this month, received as a member of the church. By his wife, Judith, he had, as I learn from Boston Records, two children, Stephen, born 7 November, 1644, and John, 24 May, 1646. They, probably, both died young. He went to England, as will be seen in the sequel of this History, either in the latter part of 1645, or in 1646, whence he did not return, I believe, but for a short period. I find a power of attorney from him to his brother John, 20 July, 1653, and a deed of 28 February, 1654—5, both executed here. He had before been a deputy, and was exposed in England to suit, because he had been *recorder* of a court, which gave an unsatisfactory judgment in the case of Alderman Berkley. In England he got forward in military and political life. He commanded a regiment, was a member of parliament in Oliver's time, for Scotland, as by letter of George Monk, 30 August, 1656, in Thurloe's State Papers, V. 366, appears; and, being a gentleman of sobriety, was much trusted by the protector. Roger Williams, in a letter to Gov. John of Connecticut, 21 February, 1655—6, gives him the news from England, "Your brother succeeds Major General Harrison." This was the exquisite enthusiast, who troubled Cromwell so much with his anticipation of a kingdom of the saints. He died early; for in our Registry of Deeds is one of 20 May, 1659, to John Leverett, from Judith in England, therein styled "relict of Stephen Winthrop."

I had supposed, when I wrote the note for his brother John, that the royal gratitude had been expressed to Stephen for assisting the preparation for the great change of 1660, knowing his influence so short a time before the restoration, and therefore postponed to this place the introduction of the following curiosity:

Letter of King Charles II. to . . . .

Brusselles, 6 *or* 8 *April*, 1660.

I have so good information of the many good offices you have done for me, that I cannot doubt but you will continue the same affection, till you have perfected the work you have begun, which, you may be most assured, will be accompanied with such an acknowledgment from me, that all the world shall take notice of the sense I have of your kindness, and how great an instrument you have been in promoting the happiness of your country. I have no more to ask of you, but to proceed in the same way and method your own understanding suggests to you, and that you will believe I will always be

Your affectionate friend,

CHARLES R.

pertinent (though no credit nor regard be to be had of dreams in these days) to report a dream, which the father of these children had at the same time, viz. that, coming into his chamber, he found his wife (she was a very gracious woman) in bed, and three or four of their children lying by her, with most sweet and smiling countenances, with crowns upon their heads, and *blue ribbons about their leaves.* When he awaked, he told his wife his dream, and made this interpretation of it, that God would take of her children to make them fellow heirs with Christ in his kingdom.

[Large blank.]

Satan bestirred himself to hinder the progress of the gospel, as, among other practices, appeared by this:[1] He stirred up a spirit of jealousy between Mr. James, the pastor of Charlton, and many of his people, so as Mr. Nowell, and some others, who had been dismissed from Boston, began to question their fact of breaking from Boston, and it grew to such a principle of conscience among them, as the advice of the other ministers was taken in it, who, after two meetings, could not agree about their continuance or return.

[Large blank.]

One Mr. [2]Morris, ensign to Capt. Underhill, taking some

The foregoing is folded in the common style of letters, but not superscribed, though it bears the royal signet on its wax. It has been since labelled, "Regis Angliæ Epistola," and in another place, by a different hand, "King Charles II. Letter to Gov. Winthrop." This letter, which is wholly in the king's hand-writing, has been preserved in the Winthrop family; but, the envelope being lost, it cannot be *known* to whom the honour was addressed. I now presume it was to John, the governour of Connecticut. As he had not been absent from New England, the service rendered must have been here, and the acknowledgment is, therefore, more honourable to him and to the sovereign.

[1] It is to be regretted, that any jealousy arose in the infant church of Charlestown; yet if Nowell and others doubted the propriety of their separation from the brethren of Boston, we may ascribe their dissatisfaction to finding their pastor to be a man of less useful talents or amiable temper than had been expected. Few in the present age would attribute such a misfortune to the agency of Satan, who has been, says Jortin, "charged with many things, which perhaps he never did." But in our indictments for capital offences, we retained, until very recently, the absurd allegation, "being moved and seduced by the instigation of the devil."

[2] Richard Morris was a person of some consequence in the colony, and probably accompanied Winthrop in the fleet; for he and his wife early became members of the Boston church, being Nos. 64 and 5. He was in the military service, when a body of men, or at least of officers, was kept in pay, in 1632 and 3, as appears from the original account of William Pynchon, the treasurer, and became a deputy in the general court of March, 1635—6, I presume from Roxbury. Being unhappily of that party in religion, which

distaste in his office, requested the magistrates, that he might be discharged of it, and so was, whereby he gave offence to the congregation of Boston, so as, being questioned and convinced of sin in forsaking his calling, he did acknowledge his fault, and, at the request of the people, was by the magistrates chosen lieutenant to the same company, for he was a very stout man and an experienced soldier.

April 1.] Order was taken for ministering an oath to all house keepers and sojourners, being twenty years of age and not freemen, and for making a survey of the houses and lands of all freemen.

Notice being sent out ||of|| the general court to be held the 14th day of the third month, called May, the freemen deputed two of each town to meet and consider of such matters as they were to take order in at the same general court; who, having met, desired a sight of the patent, and, conceiving thereby that all their laws should be made at the general court, repaired to the governour to advise with him about it, and about the abrogating of some orders formerly made, as for killing of swine in corn, &c. He told them, that, when the patent was granted, the number of freemen was supposed to be (as in like corporations) so few, as they might well join in making laws; but now they were grown to so great a body, as it was not possible for them to make or execute laws, but they must choose others for that purpose: and that howsoever it would be necessary hereafter to have a select company to intend that work, yet for the present they were not furnished with a sufficient number of men qualified for such a business, neither could the commonwealth bear the loss of time of so many as must intend it. Yet this they might do at present, viz. they might, at the general court, make an order, that, once in the year, a certain number should be appointed (upon summons from the governour)

||to||

---

favoured Wheelwright and his sister, Mrs. Hutchinson, he signed the petition in favour of the preacher, about which great controversy arose a few years after; and the legislature, 20 November, 1637, had ordered him, with the other dangerous schismaticks, to be disarmed, as in the history of that time will appear. On 6 September of next year, Col. Rec., I. 227, informs us, "Lieut. Morris had leave to depart, (having offended in subscribing the petition or remonstrance,) being advised to forbear meddling with our people in the matters of opinion, least they be farther dealt with; and was advised not to sit down within our limits, and was wished to warn the rest not to sit down within our limits." From this banishment, so gently expressed, for signing a memorial to the court eighteen months before, I know not that he returned. His retreat was Exeter, where, with many of his persecuted brethren, he formed the association, 4 October, 1639, which is preserved in Hazard, I. 463.

to revise all laws, &c. and to reform what they found amiss therein; but not to make any new laws, but prefer their grievances to the court of assistants; and that no assessment should be laid upon the country without the consent of such a committee, nor any lands disposed of.[1]

---

1 No country on earth can afford the perfect history of any event more interesting to its own inhabitants than that which is here related. Winthrop seems to have spoken like an absolute sovereign, designing to grant a favour to his subjects, by admitting them to a representation at court. Such was the origin of most of the assemblies, in other nations, of delegates of the people, by whom some influence of the majority is imparted to the government. The enlargement of this kind of civil liberty to that perfect measure, enjoyed in Great Britain and our country, may be traced, with tolerable distinctness, for about five hundred years; but its commencement is very dimly discerned through the mists of antiquity. A long controversy on the origin of parliaments is indeed now at an end; but it terminated with a general acquiescence in that opinion, which assigned their beginning to nearly the same motives as our general courts of deputies.

A natural inquiry arises, what induced this concert among the several towns to send deputies, or why the NOTICE mentioned in the text was given? Since nothing can be found in the Records, previous to this meeting of the deputies, the answer must be left to conjecture; and perhaps no conjecture can be more satisfactory, than that the assistants were become weary of the exercise of all the powers of government, and desired others to participate in the responsibility. For this, however cautious the language of our author, it appears to me very evidently designed. The very humble powers, he proposed that the representative should receive from his constituent, it is hardly necessary to add, were immediately transcended; and the assembly, as it ought, was ever afterwards by itself thought competent to the enaction of any regulation for the publick welfare.

It seems proper to transcribe here the earliest mention in our Colony Records, I. 115, of any representation, other than that to raise a publick stock, of which ample notice is heretofore taken, in pages 70, 76: "It was further ordered, that it shall be lawful for the freemen of every plantation to choose two or three of each town, before every general court, to confer of and prepare such publick business as by them shall be thought fit to consider of at the next general court; and that such persons as shall be hereafter so deputed by the freemen of [the] several plantations, to deal in their behalf in the publick affairs of the commonwealth, shall have the full power and voice of all the said freemen derived to them for the making and establishing of laws, granting of lands, &c. and to deal in all other affairs of the commonwealth, wherein the freemen have to do, the matter of election of magistrates and other officers only excepted, wherein every freeman is to give his own voice." This is one of the first acts of the representatives.

The proceedings of this *first* general court of delegates, 14 May, 1634, begin on the preceding page, in the margin of which are the names of twenty-four persons, who were, I have no doubt, deputies from only eight towns, being not *two*, as the text has it, but three for each town. As the occasion is so interesting, it may be agreeable to the reader to have here inserted the names of the FIRST representatives of Massachusetts, in the same order as in the Record: "MR. GOODWIN, MR. SPENCER, MR. TALCOTT; MR. FEAKES, MR. BROWN, MR. OLDHAM; MR BEECHER, MR. PALMER, ROBERT MOULTON; MR. COXEALL, EDMOND QUINSEY, CAPT. JOHN UNDERHILL; JOHN JOHNSON, WILLIAM HEATH, MR. ALCOCK; MR. ISRAEL STOUGHTON, WILLIAM FELPES, GEORGE HULL; CAPT. TURNER, MR. WILLIS, MR. EDWARD

3.] The governour went on foot to Agawam, and, because the people there wanted a minister, spent the Sabbath with them, and exercised by way of prophecy, and returned home the 10th.

20.] John [1]Coggeshall, gentleman, being dismissed from the church of Roxbury to Boston, though he were well known and

---

TOMLINS; MR. HOLGRAVE, MR. CONANT, FRANCIS WESTON." The first three were of Newtown; the others of Watertown, Charlestown, Boston, Roxbury, Dorchester, Sagus and Salem, in equal numbers, according to this order. But, in this assignment of the individuals to the several towns, I have followed my own judgment; in making up which, the most patient inquiry was rewarded, for all but two or three, with perfect certainty. No specification of the places, from which the deputies came, is inserted, for many years, in the margin of the volume, wherein their names are contained.

Having taken a copy of the names of members in the first *twenty-two* courts, I may add, that the places in the lists are filled without regard to rank of the person, or age of the town. Hingham stands at the top as often as Salem; and those of the same town are not always written next to each other, though so much regularity is commonly found. Perhaps they were often entered by the secretary, as they came in to take their seats. At the courts in May, September, and November, 1637, all the Boston members are named last. This, I presume, was a punishment of their heresy, and regret, that it was not the only punishment.

The ninth town, that sent deputies, was Ipswich, on 4 March next; and the right was extended to Weymouth at the court, 2 September following. Hingham members appear 25 May, 1636. In September after one from Newbury is found among the representatives; and in April following Concord has a place.

1 This gentleman was of high consideration, represented Boston in the first, second, third, sixth, seventh, eighth and ninth courts, in the Records of which his name is sometimes written by the secretary, as it was probably pronounced, Coxeall. He was elected for the twelfth, but, with Aspinwall, as we find, Col. Rec. I. 202, "affirming that Mr. Wheelwright is innocent, and that he was persecuted for the truth, was in like sort dismissed from being a member of the court, and order was given for two new deputies to be chosen by the town of Boston." Perhaps the ceremony, mentioned in the text, would have been dispensed with for himself; but his wife and a maid servant, Ann Shelley, were received, at the same time, from the neighbouring church, as I learn from the Records of our own. In general, communicants from other churches were received, in early times, with the same liberality as now prevails. At the same court from which he was expelled, 2 November, 1637, "being convented for disturbing the publick peace," he "was disfranchised, and enjoined not to speak any thing to disturb the publick peace, upon pain of banishment." He was exiled in March following, and retired with his blameless associates to Rhode Island, which they had just before purchased from the natives. In that peaceable settlement he became an assistant, and, in 1647, presided over the colony with a spirit of heterodox charity. See Callender, 30, 42. His son I presume to be the clerk of the general assembly of that colony in 1676. 2 Hist. Coll. VII. 112. Descendants in a right line remain to this day. In 1817 one was a representative in Massachusetts from Somerset, bordering on the state of Rhode Island; and, from some neighbouring ports, several masters of ships of this name have of late years been noticed.

approved of the church, yet was not received but by confession of his faith, &c.

[Very large blank.]

May 3.] News came of the death of Hockin and the Plimouth man at Kenebeck, (and of the arrival of the ship at Pemaquid, which brought thirty passengers for this place.)

The occasion of the death of those men at Kenebeck was this: The Plimouth men had a grant, from the grand patentees of New England, of Kenebeck, with liberty of sole trade, &c. The said Hockin came in a pinnace, belonging to the Lord Say and Lord Brook at Pascataquack, to trade at Kenebeck. Two of the magistrates ||of|| Plimouth, being there, forbad him; yet he went up the river; and, because he would not come down again, they sent three men in a canoe to cut his cables. Having cut one, Hockin presented a piece, and sware he would kill him that went to cut the other. They ||[2]bad|| him do if he durst, and went on to cut it. Thereupon he killed one of them, and instantly one in the Plimouth pinnace (which rode by them, and wherein five or six men stood with their pieces ready charged) shot and killed Hockin.

15.] At the general court at Boston, upon the complaint of a kinsman of the said Hockin, John [1]Alden, one of the said magistrates of Plimouth, who was present when Hockin was slain, being then at Boston, was called and bound with sureties not to depart out of our jurisdiction without leave ||[3]had;|| and withal we wrote to Plimouth to certify them what we had done, and to know whether they would do justice in the cause, (as belonging to their jurisdiction,) and to have a speedy answer, &c. This we did, that notice might be taken, that we did disavow the said action, which was much condemned of all men, and which was feared would give occasion to the king to send a general governour over; and besides had brought us all and the gospel under a common reproach of cutting one another's throats for beaver.[2]

[Blank.]

||at|| ||[2]told|| ||[3]&c.||

[1] While the Memorial of Plimouth Colony survives, the name of Alden, a brief account of whom is found in Eliot and Allen, cannot be forgotten. Many of his descendants are in honourable place in various parts of the United States, of whom one is an indefatigable antiquary, the president of a college at Meadville in Pennsylvania, to whose Collection of Epitaphs many acknowledgments are due. The ancestor and his genealogical series, down to the present hour, are found in vol. III. 264—274.

[2] Bradford's relation is a little more full; and, as he was a patentee, the reader will find, with pleasure, that his pen was guided by truth, as well as interest. See Appendix to Hutchinson, II. 418, 19. A little farther onward in this History, more will be found on the same subject.

By this time the fort at Boston was in defence, and divers pieces of ordnance mounted in it.

[Large blank.]

Those of Newtown complained of straitness for want of land, especially meadow, and desired leave of the ||court|| to look out either for enlargement or removal, which was granted; whereupon they sent men to see Agawam and Merimack, and gave out they would remove, &c.

[Large blank.]

14.] At the general court, Mr. Cotton preached, and delivered this doctrine, that a magistrate ought not to be turned into the condition of a private man without just cause, and to be publickly convict, no more than the magistrates may not turn a private man out of his freehold, &c. without like publick trial, &c. This falling in question in the court, and the opinion of the rest of the ministers being asked, it was referred to further consideration.[1]

The court chose a new governour,[2] viz. Thomas Dudley, Esq. the former deputy; and Mr. Ludlow was chosen deputy; and John Haines, Esq. an assistant, and all the rest of the assistants chosen again.

At this court it was ordered, that four general courts should be kept every year, and that the whole body of the freemen should be present only at the court of election of magistrates, &c. and that, at the other three, every town should send their deputies, who should assist in making laws, disposing lands, &c.[3] Many good orders were made this court. It held three days, and all things were carried very peaceably, notwithstanding that some of the assistants were questioned by the freemen for some errours in their government, and some fines imposed, but remitted again before the court brake up. The court was kept in the meeting-house at Boston, *and the new governour and the assistants *were together entertained* at the house of the old governour, as before.*

||council||

---

1 Expediency should have kept Cotton silent; for the people are more likely to become jealous, when such a principle is preached, than when it is put in practice. The reverend teacher took his freeman's oath at this court, and had not sufficient experience in the affairs of the country to authorize so strong an expression of his opinion, unless he believed himself directed from on high. Any of his friends could have led him to doubt the suggestion, however, had he pretended such; but he was delivering a sincere opinion of his own forming.

2 *Chosen by papers*, is written in the margin of our MS.

3 *Mr. Cottington chosen treasurer*, is in the margin.

The week the court was, there came in six ships, with store of passengers and cattle.

[Large blank.]

Mr. [1]Parker, a minister, and a company with him, being about one hundred, went to sit down at Agawam, and divers others of the new comers.

[Very large blank.]

One [blank,] a godly minister, upon conscience of his oath and care of the commonwealth, discovered to the magistrates some seditious speeches of his own son, delivered in private to himself; but the court thought not fit to call the party in question then, being loath to have the father come in as a publick accuser of his own son, but rather desired to find other matter, or other witness against him.

24.] Mr. Fleming, master of a ship of Barnstable, went hence to the eastward to cut masts there, and so to return to England. There returned with him Ensign Motham and another.

[Large blank.]

These ships, by reason of their short passage, had store of provisions left, which they put off at easy rates, viz. biscuit at 20*s*. the hundred; beef at £6 the hogshead, &c.

[Blank.]

Newtown men, being straitened for ground, sent some to Merimack to find a fit place to transplant themselves.

[Blank.]

June 1.] The Thunder, which went to Bermuda the 17th October, now returned, bringing corn and goats from Virginia, (for the weavils had taken the corn at Bermuda before they came there.) Ensign [2]Jenyson went in her for pilot, and related, at his return, that there was a very great change in Bermuda since he dwelt there, divers lewd persons ||being|| become good Christians. They have three ministers, (one a Scotchman,)

||having||

---

1 Of Thomas Parker, a learned theologian, pupil of the great Archbishop Usher, notice will often arise in the progress of this work. He was a bachelor, but stood in place of a father to many divines of the succeeding generation. One who desires to know more of him, may consult Hubbard, 193, the Magnalia, Eliot, Allen, and 1 Hist. Coll. VI. 273, and IX. 48. An errour may be corrected in a note to *James* Parker's letter, in Hutch. Coll. 155, where it is supposed, "*he* was *afterwards* one of the ministers of Newbury," which was the place of usefulness assigned to our Thomas. James had preached at Portsmouth *before* going to Barbados. 1 Hist. Coll. X. 39.

2 William Jennison was of Watertown, from which he was a deputy in the second and many subsequent courts, with higher titles than in the text, as lieutenant and captain.

who ||take|| great pains among them, and had lately (by prayer and fasting) dispossessed one possessed ||2with|| a devil. They obtained his recovery while the congregation were assembled.[1]

He brought news, also, of a great ship arrived in Patomack River in Virginia, with a governour and colony sent by the Lord [2]Bartimore, who was expected there shortly himself, and that they resisted those of Virginia, who came to trade in that river.

It appeared after, that the king had written to Sir John [3]Harvy, ||3knight,|| governour of Virginia, to give all assistance to that new plantation, which was called Maryland by the queen of England; and those who came over were, many of them, Papists, and did set up mass openly.

July.] The Hercules of Dover returned by St. George's to cut masts to carry to England.

The last month arrived here fourteen great ships, and one at Salem.

Mr. Humfrey and the lady Susan, his wife, one of the Earl of Lincoln's sisters, arrived here. He brought more ordnance,

||took|| ||2of|| ||3king's||

1 If this be the story of the traveller, not the belief of the author, giving it civilly, without throwing any shadow on it, we should rejoice at the completeness of the narrative, rather than exhibit regret for its credulity. The miracle wrought by the prayer and fasting of three ministers at Bermuda, has never, to my knowledge, been brought up against Protestantism, though it may be rejected with as much contempt as the numerous ones produced, at a later day, by the Jansenists in France. It has been remarked by a disbeliever, that, while the church of Rome asserts, from its foundation to our times, the regular succession of miraculous gifts of all kinds, the reformed are contented with exorcisms. What kind of *possession* this was, thus exorcised at Bermuda, we know not, unless we infer, from the mode of cure, that the operators attempted a recovery of that species (epilepsy) related by Matthew, xvii. 21, and Mark, ix. 29. Better signs, or better proof, are wanted in such cases, if, for our reception, a modern instance of hearing prayer in heaven is offered; though the weak and the cunning, the deluded or the deluders, have, in all ages, abounded in such impositions. The credibility of the evangelists is supported by the very means, which, to a careless observer, might seem to detract from it; and the truth is more resplendent, when the counterfeit is detected.

2 Cecil, son of George, Lord Baltimore, against whom nothing can be learned from history but the father's conscientious conversion, and the heir's adherence, to the Romish religion. For their just deserts, which the liberal inhabitants of Maryland will never forget, the reader is referred to Belknap's American Biography, II. 363—380. Candour must be extended to some passages of this History, in which the spirit of the age will appear more prominently than justice.

3 This gentleman, who had been named by King James, in his last year, of the council for the immediate government of Virginia, Haz. I. 189, was, by Charles, appointed governour, 26 March, 1627. Ib. 234. A new commission for the same place was given him nine years after. Ib. 400.

muskets and powder, bought for the publick by moneys given to that end; for godly people in England began now to apprehend a special hand of God in raising this plantation, and their hearts were generally stirred to come ||over.|| Among others, we received letters from a godly preacher, Mr. Levinston, a Scotchman in the north of Ireland, whereby he signified, that there were many good Christians in those parts resolved to come hither, if they might receive satisfaction concerning some questions and propositions which they sent over. Likewise, Mr. Humfrey brought certain [1]propositions from some persons of great quality and estate, (and of special note for piety,) whereby they discovered their intentions to join with us, if they might receive satisfaction therein. It appeared further, by many private letters, that the departure of so many of the best, both ministers and Christians, had bred sad thoughts in those behind of the Lord's intentions in this work, and an apprehension of some evil days to come upon England. ||[2]Then|| it began now to be apprehended by the archbishops, and others of the council, as a matter of state, so as they sent out warrant to stay the ships, and to call in our patent; but, upon petition of the ship masters, (||[3]attending|| how beneficial this plantation was to England) in regard of the Newfoundland fishing, which they took in their way homeward, the ships were at that time released. But Mr. Cradock (who had been governour in England before the government was sent over) had strict charge to deliver in the patent; whereupon he wrote to us to send it home. Upon receipt of his letter, the governour and council consulted about it, and resolved to answer Mr. Cradock's letter, but not to return any answer or excuse to the council at that time.

[Very large blank.]

§For the success of the passengers and cattle in the ships:§ Divers of the ships lost many cattle; but the two which came from Ipswich, of more than one hundred and twenty, lost but seven. None of the ships lost any passengers, but the Eliza-

||to us|| ||[2]yea|| ||[3]alleging||

[1] For these propositions of certain peers, and others of the English nobility, with the answers, drawn with great *discretion*, returned two years after, the curious are indebted to Hutchinson's Mass. I. Appendix, 433—436. Following them is a letter of Cotton, to enforce our answers, addressed to the Puritan Lord Say. He says, "Democracy I do not conceive that ever God did ordain as a fit government, either for church or commonwealth. If the people be governours, who shall be governed? As for monarchy, and aristocracy, they are both of them clearly approved, and directed in scripture, yet so as referreth the sovereignty to himself, and setteth up theocracy in both, as the best form of government in the commonwealth, as well as in the church."

beth Dorcas, which, having a long passage, and being hurt upon a rock at Scilly, and very ill victualled, she lost sixty passengers at sea, and divers came sick on shore, who all recovered, (through the mercy of God,) except

[Large blank.]

Mr. Humfrey brought sixteen heifers given by a private friend, viz. Mr. Richard [1]Andrews, to the plantation, viz. to every of the ministers one, and the rest to the poor, and one half of the increase of the ministers' to be reserved for other ministers. Mr. Wilson, so soon as he had his, gave it to Mr. Cotton. By Mr. Humfrey's means much money was procured, and divers promised yearly pensions.

[Large blank.]

Six of Newtown went in the Blessing, (being bound to the Dutch plantation,) to discover Connecticut River, intending to remove their town thither.

9.] Mr. Bradford and Mr. Winslow, two of the magistrates of Plimouth, with Mr. Smith, their pastor, came to Boston by water, to confer with some of our magistrates and ministers about their case of Kenebeck. There met hereabout Mr. Winthrop, Mr. Cotton and Mr. Wilson, and after they had sought the Lord, they fell first upon some passages which they had taken some offence at, but those were soon cleared. Then for the matter itself, it fell into these two points: 1, whether their right of trade there were such, as they might lawfully hinder others from coming there; 2, admitting that, whether, in point of conscience, they might so far stand upon their right as to take away or hazard any man's life in defence of it.

For the first, their right appeared to be good; for that, besides the king's grant, they had taken up that place as vacuum domicilium, and so had continued, without interruption or claim of any of the natives, for divers years; and also had, by their charge and providence, drawn down thither the greatest part of the trade, by carrying wampampeage thither, which none of the English had known the use of before. For the second, they ||alleged,|| that their servant did kill Hockin to save other of their men, whom he was ready to have shot. Yet they acknowledged, that they did hold themselves under guilt of the breach of the sixth commandment, in that they did hazard ||2man's life|| for such a cause, and did not rather wait to preserve

||allowed|| ||2men's lives||

[1] Of the liberality of this distinguished friend of Massachusetts and Plimouth colonies, further notice will occur in our progress. He became mayor of London.

their right by other means, which they rather acknowledged, because they wished it were not done; and hereafter they would be careful to prevent the like.

The governour and Mr. Winthrop wrote their letters into England to mediate their peace, and sent them by Mr. ||Winslow.||

Sir Ferdinando Gorges and Capt. Mason sent [blank] to Pascataquack and Aquamenticus, with two sawmills, to be erected, in each place one.[1]

[Blank.]

Mr. Cradock wrote to the governour and assistants, and sent a copy of the council's order,[2] whereby we were required to send over our patent. Upon long consultation whether we should return answer or not, we agreed, and returned answer to Mr. Cradock, excusing that it could not be done but by a general court, which was to be holden in September next.

[Blank.]

Mr. Winthrop, the late governour, received a letter from the Earl of Warwick, wherein he congratulated the prosperity of our plantation, and encouraged our proceedings, and offered his help to further us in it.

29.] The governour and council, and divers of the ministers, and others, met at Castle Island, and there agreed upon erecting two platforms and one small fortification, to secure ||²them both,||³ and, for the present furtherance of it, they agreed to lay out £5 a man till a ||³rate|| might be made at the next general court. The deputy, Roger Ludlow, was chosen overseer of this work.

August 2.] Mr. Samuel Skelton, pastor of Salem, died.

4.] At the court, the new town at Agawam was named Ipswich, in acknowledgment of the great honour and kindness done to our people which took shipping there, &c.; and a day of thanksgiving appointed, a fortnight after, for the ||⁴prosperous arrival of the others,|| &c.

A ⁴letter §was delivered§ to Mr. Winthrop by Mr. Jeffe-

||Wilson|| ||²the city|| ||³rule|| ||⁴particular revival of the times||

---

1 Belknap's New Hampshire, Appendix VIII. contains a letter of Mason about these mills, to erect which he sent people with Josselyn, brother of John, the voyager.

2 A copy of this order is in Hazard, I. 341, taken from Hubbard, 153.

3 By the errour of the former edition, Dr. Holmes was led to remark, Annals, I. 278, that the "metropolis has never *yet* been incorporated with hat name."

4 Never were feelings of triumph more openly, and, as the event showed, incautiously displayed, than in this epistle, for which the author smarted

ry,[1] an old planter, written to him from Morton, wherein he related, how he had obtained his long suit, and that a commission was granted for a general governour to be sent over, with many railing speeches and threats against this plantation, and Mr. Winthrop in particular. Mr. Winthrop acquainted the governour and council with it, and some of the ministers.

[Blank.]

This summer was hotter than many before.

[Blank.]

12.] About midnight, one Craford, (who came this summer,) with his brother and servant, having put much goods in a small boat in Charles River, over against Richard Brown his house, overset the boat with the weight of some hogsheads, (as was supposed,) so as they were all three drowned; yet one of them could swim well, and though the neighbours came running forth, instantly, upon their cry, yet none could be saved.

[Large blank.]

Our neighbours of Plimouth and we had oft trade with the Dutch at Hudson's River, called §by them§ New Netherlands. We had from them about forty sheep, and beaver, and brass pieces, and sugar, &c. for sack, strong waters, linen cloth, and other commodities. They have a great trade of beaver—about nine or ten thousand skins in a year. Our neighbours of Plimouth had great trade also this year at Kenebeck, so as Mr. Winslow carried with him into England, this year, about twenty hogsheads of beaver, the greatest part whereof was traded for wampampeage.

One pleasant passage happened, which was acted by the Indians. Mr. Winslow, coming in his bark from Connecticut to

---

ten years after, as in our History of that time, in our second volume, will be seen. The original deformity is there exhibited. Hubbard, 428, copied it, and most subsequent writers imagined, that to his page, not Winthrop's, were they indebted for the curiosity.

1 William Jeffery, or Jeffries, was a person of some distinction, settled in our colony before the arrival of the first company of Endecott, sent by the patentees in 1628. His admission as a freeman is noticed among the earliest who were received. Col. Rec. I. 73. I can assign his residence, only by guess, to Weymouth. See note 2, on page 43. He was named, with Blackstone, by Sir Ferdinando Gorges's son, in his abortive grant to Oldham, attorney to give possession of Massachusetts. Conf. Haz. I. 259 and 268. Such a letter Morton could not have sent, without supposing his correspondent would agree with him in dislike of the men, on whom he lavished so bold abuse; and it may almost seem treachery in the receiver to give it up. Perhaps Jeffery was afraid of discovery, or else the Merry Mount rioter was deceived in judging one his friend, who had six years before joined the formidable alliance for his overthrow.

Nariganset,—and he left her there,—and intending to return by land, he went to Osamekin the sagamore, his old ally, who offered to conduct him home to Plimouth. But, before they took their journey, Osamekin sent one of his men to Plimouth to tell them that Mr. Winslow was dead; and directed him to show how and where he was killed. Whereupon there was much fear and sorrow at Plimouth. The next day, when Osamekin brought him home, they asked him why he sent such word, &c. He answered, that it was their manner to do so, that they might be more welcome when they came home.

[Blank.]

19.] Mr. Bradford and Mr. [1]Collier of Plimouth came to Boston, having appointed a meeting here the week before, but by reason of foul weather were driven back. They had written to Capt. Wiggin of Pascataquack about the meeting for hearing the cause of Hockin's death.

[Large blank.]

Corn was this year at four shillings the bushel, and some at three shillings, and some cheaper.

[Large blank.]

29.] The ||Dove,|| a pinnace of about fifty tons, came from Maryland upon Patomack River, with corn, to exchange for fish and other commodities. The governour, Leonard [2]Calvert, and two of the commissioners, wrote to the governour here, to make offer of trade of corn, &c. and the governour of Virginia wrote also on their behalf, and one Capt. Young wrote to make offer to deliver cattle here. Near all their company came sick hither, and the merchant died within one week after.

[Blank.]

||D——||

---

1 Honourable mention must ever be made of William Collier, Esq. who came over to Plimouth only the year before that of the text. He was chosen an assistant in 1634, and thenceforward until 1666, every year, except 1638, 52 and 53, when he was probably absent, and was one of the two first delegates to the congress of the United Colonies, in 1643. For more particular account of this gentleman, the student will turn with pleasure to Judge Davis's edition of Morton's Memorial.

2 This gentleman was the brother of Cecil, Lord Baltimore, mentioned in the note on page 134, sent by the patentee as his governour. His name will recur in the progress of this History; but I regret that any information of the events of his administration is confined to its policy, applauded by Belknap, and the minute, but imperfect narrative in Bozman's History of Maryland. The Hon. Charles Calvert, governour of Maryland, a descendant, died 2 February, 1732. A tomb, erected at Annapolis, bore inscriptions in honour of himself and wife, which may be seen in the American Magazine, printed at Boston, 1743, page 74. I believe reputable descendants of this family perpetuate its fame in Maryland.

September 4.] The general court [1]began at Newtown, and continued a week, and then was adjourned ||fourteen|| days. Many things were there agitated and concluded, as fortifying in Castle Island, Dorchester and Charlestown; also against tobacco, and costly apparel, and immodest fashions; and committees appointed for setting out the bounds of towns; with divers other matters, which do appear upon record. But the main business, which spent the most time, and caused the adjourning of the court, was about the removal of Newtown. They had leave, the last general court, to look out some place for enlargement or removal, with promise of having it confirmed to them, if it were not prejudicial to any other plantation; and now they moved, that they might have leave to remove to Connecticut. This matter was debated divers days, and many reasons alleged pro and con. The principal reasons for their removal were, 1. Their want of accommodation for their cattle, so as they were not able to maintain their ministers, nor could receive any more of their friends to help them; and here it was alleged by Mr. Hooker, as a fundamental errour, that towns were set so near each to other.

2. The fruitfulness and commodiousness of Connecticut, and the danger of having it possessed by others, Dutch or English.

3. The strong bent of their spirits to remove thither.

[Large blank.]

Against these it was said, 1. That, in point of conscience, they ought not to depart from us, being knit to us in one body, and bound by oath to seek the welfare of this commonwealth.

2. That, in point of state and civil policy, we ought not to give them leave to depart. 1. Being ||[2]we|| were now weak and in danger to be assailed. 2. The departure of Mr. Hooker would not only draw many from us, but also divert other friends that would come to us. 3. We should expose them to evident peril, both from the Dutch (who made claim to the same river, and had already built a fort there) and from the Indians, and also from our own state at home, who would not endure

||eleven|| ||[2]new||

1 By the Col. Records, I. 126, the day of assembling is the 3d, not 4th, of September. But it is more important to observe, that no names of deputies appear; so that I regard it only as a second session of the court, adjourned in May, and therefore give the distinction of *second* court to that in March following. Many new members appeared then, and so we find the fact in every succeeding meeting for many years. Perhaps one or more new delegates appeared at this court from some town not represented at the May session.

they should sit down without a patent in any place which our king lays claim unto.

3. They might be accommodated at home by some enlargement which other towns offered.

4. They might remove to Merimack, or any other place within our patent.

5. The removing of a candlestick is a great judgment, which is to be avoided.

Upon these and other arguments the court being divided, it was put to vote; and, of the deputies, fifteen were for their departure, and ten against it.[1] The governour and two assistants were for it, and the deputy and all the rest of the assistants were against it, (except the secretary, who gave no vote;) whereupon no record was entered, because there were not six assistants in the vote, as the patent requires. Upon this grew a great difference between the governour and assistants, and the deputies. They would not yield the assistants a negative voice, and the others (considering how dangerous it might be to the commonwealth, if they should not keep that strength to balance the greater number of the deputies) thought it safe to stand upon it. So, when they could proceed no further, the whole court agreed to keep a day of humiliation to seek the Lord, which accordingly was done, in all the congregations, the 18th day of this month; and the 24th the court met again. Before they began, Mr. Cotton preached, (being desired by all the court, upon Mr. Hooker's instant excuse of his unfitness for that occasion.) He took his text out of Hag. ii. 4, &c. out of which he laid down the nature or strength (as he termed it) of the magistracy, ministry and people, viz.—the strength of the magistracy to be their authority; of the people, their liberty; and of the ministry, their purity; and showed how all of these had a negative voice, &c. and that yet the ultimate resolution, &c. ought to be in the whole body of the people, &c. with answer to all objections, and a declaration of the people's duty

---

1 The errour of Hutchinson, in reporting this division of the deputies, and his mistake of the name of the deputy governour, he owed to Hubbard, 173, 4, who copied our author with carelessness surprising even in him. He almost literally transcribed from our text the very form of the argument and partition of the subject; and the numerals are here as plain as in any part of the original MS. On so important a question, we might, a priori, conclude, that every one of the deputies was present; and since their number, at the *first* general court when representatives appeared, was twenty-four, and so small a body never appears again, we may confidently presume, there were now twenty-five, though the enumeration of the body cannot be given precisely, because the Records, in this solitary instance, omit their names. See the last note. Ludlow was the deputy governour.

and right to maintain their true liberties against any unjust violence, &c. which gave great satisfaction to the company. And it pleased the Lord so to assist him, and to bless his own ordinance, that the affairs of the court went on cheerfully; and although all were not satisfied about the negative voice to be left to the magistrates, yet no man moved aught about it, and the congregation of Newtown came and accepted of such enlargement as had [1]formerly been offered them by Boston and Watertown; and so the fear of their removal to Connecticut was removed.

At this court Mr. [2]Goodwin, a very reverend and godly man, being the elder of the congregation of Newtown, having, in heat of argument, used some unreverend speech to one of the assistants, and being reproved for the same in the open court, did gravely and humbly acknowledge his fault, &c.

---

1 Hubbard, 175, read this word *freely*.

2 William Goodwin is known to us, for many years, only by this notice of his language, as a deputy in the court. The occasion of his disrespect to the assistant, no doubt, arose from the projected migration of his townsmen. He did not represent Newtown in any following legislature, and removed, probably, the next year but one, with a large portion of his constituents, to Connecticut. Nothing more is heard of him until 1654, when a controversy sprang up in the church of Hartford, where Goodwin was ruling elder, between him and Stone, the teacher, which lasted several years, baffling the attempts of the legislature to calm it, and drawing New Haven and Massachusetts into the idle examination. The humble importance of such mighty agitation occupies many pages in Trumbull, I. 311 and following; but Mather, book III. says, the origin of it "has been rendered almost as obscure as the rise of Connecticut River." That author, in his usual diffuse manner, follows up his illustration with allusions to the force of the stream, and the width of its overflow; yet he has omitted the important parallel, of enriching the soil by its inundation. Goodwin was honoured by Gov. Hopkins, by being made a trustee in his will.

I have seen, among the Hutchinson Papers, in the archives of our Historical Society, a tract, of eight and a half folio pages, entitled "The Sentence of the Council held at Boston, September 26, 1659, concerning the long, sad, and afflicting Controversy between the rev. teacher, Mr. Samuel Stone, the honoured and dearly beloved brethren of the church of Hartford, on the one part, and the honoured and dearly beloved brethren, the withdrawers from the said church, on the other part, since the relapse after the pacification, May 3, 1657." It bears date 7 October, and is signed by Wilson, Chauncey, R. Mather, Allen, Symmes, Norton, Eliot, Edm. Browne, Cobbet, Sherman, Hubbard, Danforth, Mitchell and Shepard, among the divines; and R. Russell, Edw. Tyng, and Isaac Heath, of the laity. It appears to be the handwriting of *matchless* Mitchell; but though it refers to "the great labour of the reverend council held at Hartford in '56; the poor service of the church messengers from hence in '57; the several occasional letters from the elders of these parts before and since; and, lastly, the travels of this present assembly," with earnest entreaty for healing the scandalous divisions,—I hope it may not be imputed to any disesteem of the council or the subject, that my curiosity was not sufficiently strong to encounter the labour of perusal of so venerable a manuscript.

18.] At this court were many laws made against tobacco, and immodest fashions, and costly apparel, &c. as appears by the Records; and [1]£600 raised towards fortifications and other charges, which were the more hastened, because the Griffin and another ship now arriving with about two hundred passengers and one hundred cattle, (Mr. [2]Lothrop and Mr. [3]Simmes, two godly ministers, coming in the same ship,) there came over a copy of the [4]commission granted to the two archbishops and ten others of the council, to regulate all plantations, and power given them, or any five of them, to call in all patents, to make laws, to raise tythes and portions for ministers, to remove and punish governours, and to hear and determine all causes, and inflict all punishments, even death itself, &c. This being advised from our friends to be intended specially for us, and that there were ships and soldiers provided, given out as for the carrying the new governour, Capt. Woodhouse, to Virginia, but suspected to be against us, to compel us, by force, to receive

---

1 The apportionment is worth transcribing from the Records, I. 128, as, we may be confident, it represents the relative wealth of the settlements: "Boston, Dorchester and Newtown, each, £80; Roxbury, £70; Watertown, £60; Sagus and Ipswich, each, £50; Salem and Charlestown, each, £45; Meadford, £26; Wessaguscus, £10; Barecove, £4."

2 With the excellence of the Rev. John Lathrop, we could form little acquaintance in a place, to which every reader would most naturally resort, the Description of Barnstable, in 1 Hist. Coll. III. But the extraordinary errours of that tract, pages 15, 16, or any other writer's deficiency, are all forgotten on perusal of one of the amplest memoirs of him and his posterity, by a descendant, found in 2 Hist. Coll. I. 163. Eliot has afforded two pages to him, and his name is excluded from Allen only by some less desirable matter. A great, great grandson, one of the most sincere and benevolent men of his time, who died since furnishing that narrative of his ancestor, after a long life of devotion to his duties, will long be remembered as pastor of the Second Church of Boston. The patriarchal divine at West Springfield, whose sermons have justly been more in repute than those of equal volume by any other American, who deceased since the preparation of these notes began, deduced his origin from this first clergyman of Scituate. A very numerous line of descendants is found in our country.

3 Zechariah Symmes, the worthy teacher of the church at Charlestown, is sufficiently commemorated in Eliot's Dictionary, where the time of his death is erroneously given 1676, for February 4, 1670—1. Johnson has honoured him, and especially his wife, above most of the ministers in the land, lib. I. c. 32. In this History his service to the community is often mentioned; and at the last election of Winthrop, as governour, narrated in this work, he preached the sermon. His descendants, at different times, have been honoured in church and state.

The famous Mrs. Ann Hutchinson came over in the same ship with Symmes, as was given in evidence on her trial. See Hutchinson's Mass. II. Appendix.

4 See the commission in Hubbard, 264.

a new governour, and the discipline of the church of England, and the laws of the commissioners,—occasioned the magistrates and deputies to hasten our fortifications, and to discover our minds each to other; which grew to this conclusion,[1] viz.

Large blank.

At this court, as before, the assistants had their ||diet|| at the governour's at Newtown, and the first day all the deputies. He had £100 allowed him for his charges, and £500 more was raised towards fortifications, &c.

30.] About this time one Alderman, of Bear Cove, being about fifty years old, lost his way between Dorchester and Wessaguscus, and wandered in the woods and swamps three days and two nights, without taking any food, and, being near spent, God brought him to Scituate; but he had torn his legs much, &c. Other harm he had none.

October 5.] It being found, that the four lectures did spend too much time, and proved ||[2]over|| burdensome to the ministers and people, the ministers, with the advice of the magistrates, and with consent of their congregations, did agree to reduce them to two days, viz. Mr. Cotton at Boston one Thursday, or the 5th day of the week, and Mr. Hooker at Newtown the next 5th day, and Mr. Warham at Dorchester one 4th day of the week, and Mr. Welde at Roxbury the next 4th day.

Mr. Lathrop, who had been pastor of a private congregation in London, and for the same kept long time in prison, (upon refusal of the oath ex-officio,) being at Boston upon a sacrament day, after the sermon, &c. desired leave of the congregation to be present at the administration, &c. but said that he durst not desire to partake in it, because he was not then in order, (being dismissed from his former congregation,) and he thought it not fit to be suddenly admitted into any other, for example sake, and because of the deceitfulness of man's heart. He went to Scituate, being desired to be their pastor.

14.] It was informed the governour, that some of our people, being aboard the bark of Maryland, the sailors did revile them, calling them holy brethren, the members, &c. and withal did curse and swear most horribly, and use threatening speeches against us. The governour wrote to some of the assistants about it, and, upon advice with the ministers, it was

||dues|| ||[2]very||

[1] What the conclusion was, we may easily judge from the opinion of the ministers, obtained at a meeting 19 January following, as, a few pages onward, will appear.

agreed to call them in question; and to this end (because we knew not how to get them out of their bark) we apprehended the merchant of the ship, being ||on shore,|| and committed him to the marshal, till Mr. Maverick came and undertook that the offenders should be forthcoming.[1] The next day (the governour not being well) we examined the witnesses, and found them fall short of the matter of threatening, and not to agree about the reviling speeches, and, beside, not able to design certainly the men that had so offended. Whereupon (the bark staying only ||[2]upon|| this) the bail was discharged, and a letter written to the master, that, in regard such disorders were committed aboard his ship, it was his duty to inquire out the offenders and punish them; and withal to desire him to bring no more such disordered persons among us.

Mr. Wilson's hay, being stacked up not well dried, fell on fire, to his great prejudice at this season; fired by his own servants, &c. as they intended to prevent firing.

The weather was very fine and hot, without rain, near six weeks.

The Lords Say and Brook wrote to the governour and Mr. [2]Bellingham, that howsoever they might have sent a man of

||one Store|| ||[2]for||

---

1 The process was more effectual than regular.

2 Gov. Richard Bellingham's worth is exhibited in the annals of his country, of which he was the last surviving patentee named in the charter, "having spun," says Hubbard, 610, "a long thread of above eighty years." His talents were adapted less for eloquence than advice, as the same writer expresses it, "like a vessel whose vent holdeth no good proportion with its capacity." Hubbard, after observing that his qualifications, as a governour, were rather lessened by his melancholy humour, continues: "He had been bred a lawyer, yet turned strangely, although upon very pious considerations, as some have judged, out of the ordinary road thereof, in the making of his last will and testament, which defect, if there were any, was abundantly supplied by the power of the general court, so as that no prejudice did arise to his successors about his estate." A fact inconsistent with the correctness of the closing suggestion, is, by the recent editor, in the note to Hutch. I. 247, asserted. Bellingham and his wife, Elizabeth, who died in a few years, were received into Boston church, 3 August of this year, so that a wrong date of his arrival is given by Eliot; but more observation is deserved by a casual sentence about this gentleman from the same author. He calls him "a very learned man, compared with his contemporaries in New England." This is uttered without the caution that usually distinguishes our New England biographer. Several of the laity were equals, in my opinion, of Bellingham; and—without naming some of the worthies of Plimouth, Rhode Island, Connecticut or New Haven—both the Winthrops, Bradstreet and Saltonstall his superiours. I speak confidently, but advisedly, that, if we include the clergy, who surely had as good a share of letters as their brethren educated at the same universities of Oxford and Cambridge, there were in New England, at any time between 1630 and 1690, as many sons of those two famous nurseries of learning as would be found in a proper-

war to beat down the house at Kenebeck, for the death of Hockin, &c. ||yet|| they thought better to take another course; and therefore desired that some of ours might be joined with Capt. Wiggin, their agent at Pascataquack, to see justice done, &c.

20.] Six men of Salem, going on fowling in a canoe, were overset near Kettle Island, and five of them drowned.

November 5.] At the court of assistants complaint was made by some of the country, (viz. Richard Brown of Watertown, in the name of the rest,) that the ensign at Salem was defaced, viz. one part of the red cross taken out. Upon this, an attachment was awarded against Richard [1]Davenport,

||that||

---

tionate number of their fellow subjects in the mother country. Besides which our own college sent out streams, of which several flowed to make glad the land of their fathers.

In the eulogium of this worthy, by Hubbard, "a notable hater of bribes" is part; and in the Granary burial ground, in this city, over his tomb, which now belongs to the family of the late Gov. Sullivan, that honour is repeated:

"Virtue's fast friend within this tomb doth lie,
A foe to bribes, but rich in charity."

Surely the character of the age forbids us to consider these clean hands as *distinguishing* him from other magistrates.

He was of a good family in England, and perhaps Richard Bellingham, who was recorder of Boston in 1625, was his father. In our Registry of Deeds, lib. VIII. 297, is evidence of a gift from the governour to Angola, a negro, of a piece of land on the highway leading to Roxbury, fifty feet square, to him and his children forever, with the language of the donor: "He was the only instrument that, under God, saved my life, coming to me with his boat, when I was sunk in the river between Boston and Winisimet, several years since, and laid hold of me and got me into the boat he came in, and saved my life; which kindness of him I remember."

Something from the will, 28 November, 1672, in Prob. Rec. VII. 271, is worth copying: "Among many other undeserved favours of God towards me, this is none of the least, that, for so long a time, I have lived under the special government of Christ in his church, not without some soul satisfaction through the gracious presence of Christ, who hath walked in the midst of these churches, which I judge have been constituted according to his mind. That I may testify the engagement of my heart to the Lord, being now of perfect memory and understanding, I do dispose," &c. After various devises, he says, "I do freely and willingly dispose and give (after mine and my wife's decease) the farms she hath during her life, and (after the decease of my son and his daughter) my whole estate in Winnisimet, to be an annual encouragement to some godly ministers and preachers, and such as may be such, who shall be by my trustees judged faithful to those principles in church discipline, which are owned and practised in the First Church of Christ in Boston, of which I am a member; a main one whereof is, that all ecclesiastical jurisdiction is committed by Christ to each particular organical church, from which there is no appeal, visible saintship being the matter, and express covenanting the form, of the church." Bellingham was warm in his opposition to the Third, now Old South, Church.

[1] This person rose to higher rank, and was several years commander at

ensign-bearer, to appear at the next court to answer. Much matter was made of this, as fearing it would be taken as an act of rebellion, or of like high nature, in defacing the king's colours; though the truth were, it was done upon this opinion, that the red cross was given to the king of England by the pope, as an ensign of victory, and so a superstitious thing, and a relique of antichrist. What proceeding was hereupon, will appear after, at next court, in the first month; (for, by reason of the great snows and frosts, we used not to keep courts in the three winter months.)

The Rebecka came from Narigansett with five hundred bushels of corn given to Mr. John Oldham. The Indians had promised him ||one thousand|| bushels, but their store fell out less than they expected. They gave him also an island in the Narigansett Bay, called Chippacursett, containing about *one thousand acres,* six miles long, and two miles broad. This is a very fair bay, being above twelve leagues square, with divers great islands in it, a deep channel close to the shore, being rocky. Mr. Peirce took the height there, and found it forty-one degrees, forty-one minutes, being not above half a degree to the southward of us. In his voyage to and fro, he went over the shoals, having, most part, five or six fathom, within half a mile and less of the shore from the north part of Cape Cod to Natuckett Island, which is about twenty leagues—and, in the shallowest place, two and an half fathom. The country on the west of the Bay of Naragansett is all champaign for many miles, but very stony, and full of Indians. He saw there above one thousand men, women and children, yet the men were many abroad on hunting. Natuckett is an island full of Indians, about ten leagues in length east and west.

6.] There came to the deputy governour, about fourteen days since, a messenger from the Pekod sachem, to desire our friendship. He brought two bundles of sticks, whereby he signified how many beaver and ||²otter|| skins he would give us for that end, and great store of wampompeage, (about two bushels, by his description.) He brought a small present with him, which the deputy received, and returned a moose coat of as good value, and withal told him, that he must send persons of greater quality, and then our governour would treat with them.

||100|| ||²other||

Castle Island in Boston harbour, where, Clap and Hubbard, 642, inform us, he was killed by lightning in July, 1665, to which Hutchinson, I. 232, adds some particulars. Capt. Roger Clap, the next month, was appointed successor. From his Memoirs something may be learned of the spirit and manners of the early settlers, if not of their deeds.

And now there came two men, who brought another present of wampompeage. The deputy brought them to Boston, where most of the assistants were assembled, by occasion of the lecture, who, calling to them some of the ministers, grew to this treaty with them: That we were willing to have friendship, &c. but because they had killed some Englishmen, viz. Capt. Stone, &c. they must first deliver up ||those who|| were guilty of his death, &c. They answered, that the sachem, who then lived, was slain by the Dutch, and all the men, who were guilty, &c. were dead of the pox, except two, and that if they were worthy of death, they would move their sachem to have them delivered, (for they had no commission to do it;) but they excused the fact, saying that Capt. Stone, coming into their river, took two of their men and bound them, and made them show him the way up the river, which when they had done, he, with two others and the two Indians, (their hands still bound,) went on shore, and nine of their men watched them, and when they were on ||[2]sleep|| in the night, they killed them; then going towards the pinnace to have taken that, it suddenly blew up into the air. This was related with such confidence and gravity, as, having no means to contradict it, we inclined to believe it. But, the governour not being present, we concluded nothing; but some of us went with them the next day to the governour.

The reason why they desired so much our friendship was, because they were now in war with the Naragansetts, whom, till this year, they had kept under, and likewise with the Dutch, who had killed their old sachem and some other of their men, for that the Pekods had killed some Indians, who came to trade with the Dutch at Connecticut; and, by these occasions, they could not trade safely any where. Therefore they desired us to send a pinnace with cloth, and we should have all their trade.

They offered us also all their right at Connecticut, and to further us what they could, if we would settle a plantation there.

When they came to the governour, they agreed, according to the former treaty, viz. to deliver us the two men, who were guilty of Capt. Stone's death, when we would send for them; to yield up Connecticut; to give us four hundred fathom of wampompeage, and forty beaver, and thirty otter skins; and that we should presently send a pinnace with cloth to trade with them, §and so should be at peace with them, and as friends to trade with them,[1]§ but not to defend them, &c.

||such as|| ||[2]shore||

---

1 A cause of the omission, in the former edition, of this member of the sentence is very easily found. The eye of the transcriber, turning from his

The next morning news came, that two or three hundred of the Naragansetts were come to Cohann, viz. Naponsett, to kill the Pekod ambassadours, &c. Presently we ||met at|| Roxbury, and raised some few men in arms, and sent to the Naragansett men to come to us. When they came there were no more but two of their sachems, and about twenty ||2more,|| who had been on hunting thereabouts, and came to lodge with the Indians at Cohann, as their manner is. So we treated with them about the Pekods, and, at our request, they promised they should go and come to and from us in peace, and they were also content to enter further treaty of peace with them; and in all things showed themselves very ready to gratify us. So the Pekods returned home, and the Naragansetts departed well satisfied; only they were told in private, that if they did make peace with the Pekods, we would give them part of that wampompeage, which they should give us; (for the Pekods held it dishonourable to offer them any thing as of themselves, yet were willing we should give it them, and indeed did offer us so much for that end.[1])

The agreement they made with us was put in writing, and the two ambassadours set to their marks—one a bow with an arrow in it, and the other a hand.

13.] The Regard, a ship of Barnstable, of about two hundred tons, arrived with twenty passengers and about fifty cattle.

One thing I think fit to observe, as a witness of God's providence for this plantation. There came in this ship one Mans-

||sent out to|| ||2men||

copy to the original MS. caught, in the latter branch, the words, "trade with them," which close each part, and he supposed it was what he had already transferred to his sheet. Several errours of that edition, as will appear in the progress of our labour, were occasioned in this way. Collations of ancient MSS. afford criticks frequent opportunity of detecting such faults, arising from the ὁμοιοτέλευτον, which forms a class of cases excepted from the general rule, that the shorter reading should be preferred. By such a cause the loss of the famous spurious text, 1 John, v. 7, from all the MSS. was formerly, in vain, attempted to be explained.

1 If any doubt has ever been entertained, in Europe or America, of the equitable and pacifick principles of the founders of New England, in their relations with the Indians, the secret history, in the foregoing paragraph, of this negotiation, should dissipate it. By the unholy maxims of vulgar policy the discord of these unfriendly nations would have been encouraged, and our European fathers should have employed the passions of the aborigines for their mutual destruction. On the contrary, an honest artifice was resorted to for their reconciliation, and the tribute received by us from one offending party was, by a Christian deception, divided with their enemies to procure mutual peace. Such mediation is more useful than victory, and more honourable than conquest.

field, a poor godly man of Exeter, being very desirous to come to us, but not able to transport his family. There was in the city a rich merchant, one Marshall, who, being troubled in his dreams about the said poor man, could not be quiet till he had sent for him, and given him £50, and lent him £100, willing him withal, that, if he wanted, he should send to him for more. This Mansfield grew suddenly rich, and then lost his godliness, and his wealth soon after.[1]

18.] About this time an open pinnace of one Mr. [2]Sewall of Ipswich, going deep laden from Boston, was cast away upon the rocks at the head of Cape Ann, in a N. E. storm; but all the men were saved.

21.] One [3]Willys, a godly man, and member of Boston church, and one Dorety, an honest man, and two boys, going over to Noddle's Island to fetch wood, in a small boat, and none of them having any skill or experience, were cast away in a N. E. tempest, as they came home in the night laden, being then ebbing water. We sent two boats on the Lord's day, (so soon as they were missing, being the 23d,) but they could not find men, or boat, or wood, in any ||part|| of the bay. Three days after the boat was found at Muddy River overturned.

27.] The assistants met at the governour's, to advise about the defacing of the cross in the ensign at Salem, where (taking advice with some of the ministers) we agreed to write to Mr. Downing in England, of the truth of the matter, under all our hands, that, if occasion were, he might show it in our excuse; for therein we expressed our dislike of the thing, and our purpose to punish the offenders, yet with as much wariness as we might, being doubtful of the lawful use of the cross in an ensign, though we were clear that fact, as concerning the manner, was very unlawful.

||place||

---

1 The last sentence is an addition, by the author, at a later time. Perhaps that providence, which sent us a man, who soon lost his character and his property, had better been reverenced in silence.

2 This ancestor of one of the most venerated families, which has given three of its members to preside in the highest court of civil and criminal jurisdiction in Massachusetts, was one of the first settlers at Newbury. The biographies of Eliot and Allen, and especially the copious Collection of American Epitaphs, by Alden, II. 115, have well perpetuated the memory of his descendants. Henry died at Rowley, 1654; and in Hutchinson, I. Appendix xii. is a letter from Richard Cromwell, during his short enjoyment of the title of Lord Protector, to our governour and magistrates, in favour of the son, who was a minister in Hampshire, and came over about his father's estate.

3 John and Jane Willis are, in the Records of Boston church, numbered 135, 6; and against their names is written, *dead since.*

It was then informed us, how Mr. Eliot, the teacher of the church of Roxbury, had taken occasion, in a sermon, to speak of the peace made with the Pekods, and to lay some blame upon ||the ministry|| for proceeding therein, without consent of the people, and for other failings (as he conceived.) We took order, that he should be dealt with by Mr. Cotton, Mr. Hooker, and Mr. Welde, to be brought to see his errour, and to heal it by some publick explanation of his meaning; for the people began to take occasion to murmur against us for it.

It was likewise informed, that Mr. Williams of Salem had broken his promise to us, in teaching publickly against the king's patent, and our great sin in claiming right thereby to this country, &c. and for usual terming the churches of England antichristian. We granted summons to him for his appearance at the next court.

The aforesaid three ministers, upon conference with the said Mr. Eliot, brought him to acknowledge his errour in that he had mistaken the ground of his doctrine, and that he did acknowledge, that, for a peace only, (whereby the people were not to be engaged in a war,) the magistrates might conclude, plebe inconsulto, and so promised to express himself in publick next Lord's day.

24.] One Scott and Eliot of Ipswich were lost in their way homewards, and wandered up and down six days, and eat nothing. At length they were found by an Indian, being almost senseless for want of rest, &c.

About the same time one [blank] was twenty-one days upon Plumb Island, and found by chance frozen in the snow, yet alive, and did well. He had been missing twenty days, and himself said he had no food all that time.

December 4.] Was an extraordinary tempest of wind and snow, at N. N. E. which continued twenty-four hours, and after that such frost as, within two days, the whole bay was frozen over, but free again before night.

11.] The lectures at Boston and Newtown returned again to their former course, because the weather was many times so tedious as people could not travel, &c.

This day, after the lecture, the inhabitants of Boston met to choose seven men who should divide the town lands among them.[1] They chose by papers, and in their choice left out

||our measures||

[1] In his index the former editor seems to have considered this paragraph as affording an account of the "origin of selectmen in Boston;" and the same errour is followed even by so careful a writer as Holmes, Annals, I. 279. This, and most other of the towns, had before been governed by such officers,

Mr. *Winthrop,* Coddington, and other of the chief men; only they chose one of the elders and a deacon, and the rest of the inferiour sort, *and Mr. Winthrop had the greater number before one of them by a voice or two.*[1] This they did, as fearing that the richer men would give the poorer sort no great proportions of land, but would rather leave a great part at liberty for new comers and for common, which Mr. Winthrop had oft persuaded them unto, as best for the town, &c. Mr. Cotton and divers others were offended at this choice, because they declined the magistrates; and Mr. Winthrop refused to be one upon such an election as was carried by a voice or two, telling them, that though, for his part, he did not apprehend any personal injury, nor did doubt of their good ||affection|| towards him, yet he was much grieved that Boston should be the first who should shake off their magistrates, especially Mr. Coddington, who had been always so forward for their enlargement; adding further reason ||[2]of|| declining this choice, to blot out so bad a precedent. Whereupon, at the motion of Mr. Cotton, who showed them, that it was the Lord's order among the Israelites to have all such businesses committed to the elders, and that it had been ||[3]nearer|| the rule to have chosen some of each sort, &c. they all agreed to go to a new election, which was referred to the next lecture day.[2]

The reason why some were not willing that the people should have more land in the bay than they might be likely to use in some reasonable time, was partly to prevent the neglect of trades, and other more necessary employments, and partly that there might be place to receive such as should come after; seeing it would be very prejudicial to the commonwealth, if men should be forced to go far off for land, while others had much, and could make no use of it, more than to please their eye with it.

||offering|| ||[2]for|| ||[3]never||

---

though the title was different. See note 2 on p. 114. That which continues to our times is first used in Boston Records in 1645. See Shaw's Description of Boston, 147.

1 The author's modesty erased the conclusion of the sentence, and his own name, in the former part.

2 Our Town Records take no notice of the first election of these seven; but, on the 18th, Winthrop, Coddington, Bellingham, Cotton, Oliver, Colburn, and Baulstone, were chosen "to divide and dispose of all such lands, belonging to the town, as are not yet in the lawful possession of any particular person, to the inhabitants of the town, according to the order of the court, leaving such portions in common, for the use of new comers, and the further benefit of the town, as, in their best discretion, they shall think fit. The islands hired by the town to be also included in this order."

One Abigail Gifford, widow, being kept at the charge of the parish of Wilsden in Middlesex, near London, was sent by Mr. Ball's ship into this country, and being found to be sometimes distracted, and a very burdensome woman, the governour and assistants returned her back by warrant, 18, to the same parish, in the ship Rebecca.

22.] A fast was kept by the church of Charlton, and Mr. Symmes chosen their teacher.

By a letter from Plimouth it was certified, that the Dutch of Hudson's River had been at Connecticut, and came in warlike manner to put the Plimouth men out of their house there; but when they stood upon their defence, they departed, without offering any violence.[1]

[2]11 mo. 13.] The church of Boston kept a day of humiliation for the absence of their pastor and other brethren, gone to England, and like to be troubled and detained there, and for that the Lord had made a breach upon them by those four which were drowned, as is before set down; at which fast Mr. Cotton preached out of Numbers xxxv. 13, and one of the members taught out of that in ||Lamentations||[3] iii. 39: Wherefore doth a living man complain?

||Samuel||

---

1 In Haz. II. 262, the invaluable proceedings of the commissioners of the United Colonies preserve the Dutch relation of this affair. We must regret to find in Trumbull, I. 36, too much of the feeling of a partisan on this subject. A very judicious explanation of the controversy may be seen in the North American Review, VIII. 85.

2 Here is discovered the first instance of changing the name of the month, which arose from a weak scruple, as if there were something heathenish in following the Roman nomenclature. Our fathers departed gradually from the church of England, and perhaps their tendency to separation increased faster in the wilderness than it would have done at home. It will be observed, that this work begins on Easter Monday, and, in his margin, that great festival of the church is duly honoured by our historian. A slight errour, as to the commencement of this change, is found in Hutchinson, I. 377, who seems to attribute it to the Puritanical severity of Vane; but, before his coming, the settlers were well cured of their fondness for the forms, in which they had been educated. From this place, our original MS. usually employs this new enumeration of the great divisions of time, though we may occasionally observe a backsliding to the errours of the author's earlier years. The fantastical custom was maintained for nearly two generations in New England; and the gradual abrogation of it was, no doubt, regarded by the elder planters as a modern defection; for, in Johnson's Wonder-working Providence, lib. I. c. 27, we are informed, that the practice was designed "of purpose to prevent the heathenish and popish observation of days, months and years, that they may be forgotten among the people of the Lord."

3 The strange errour of the former edition, in giving here a wrong book in the Bible, is easily accounted for in note 1 on page 74. The editor was almost as well acquainted with scripture texts as Winthrop, who, we may be sure, is referred to by the passage above.

19.] All the ministers, except Mr. [1]Ward of Ipswich, met at Boston, being requested by the governour and assistants, to consider of these two cases: 1. What ||we ought to do,|| if a general governour should be sent out of England? 2. Whether it be lawful for us to carry the cross in our banners?—In the first case, they all agreed, that, if a general governour were sent, we ought not to accept him, but defend our lawful possessions, (if we were able;) otherwise to avoid or protract. For the matter of the cross, they were divided, and so deferred it to another meeting.

About the middle of this month, Mr. Allerton's pinnace came from the French about Port Royal. They went to fetch the two men, which had been carried by the French from Machias, and to demand the goods taken, &c. But Mr. La Tour made them answer, that he took them as lawful prize, and that he had authority from the king of France, who challenged all from Cape Sable to Cape Cod, wishing them to take notice, and to certify the rest of the English, that, if they traded to the east of Pemaquid, he would make prize of them. Being desired to show his commission, he answered, that his sword was commission sufficient, where he had strength to overcome; where that wanted, he would show his commission.

In the end of this month, three men had their boat frozen up at [2]Bird Island, as they were coming from Deer Island, so as they were compelled to lodge there all night; and in the morning they came over the ice to Noddle's Isle, and thence to Molten's Point in Charlestown, and thence over the ice, by Mr. Hoffe's, to Boston. At the same time six others were kept a week at the Governour's Garden; and in the end

||ought to be done||

---

1 Of Nathaniel Ward, the author of the celebrated "Simple Cobler of Agawam," almost enough will be found in the course of this History, in the biographies of Eliot and Allen, and in the books cited by the latter, to excuse me from saying more. He was in the church of Standon in Hertfordshire, about twenty-seven miles from London, and favoured the cause of New England some years before coming over. His work is very attractive for its humour, and curious for its execrable spirit.

2 This island is not remembered by any person now alive, I believe, as a spot on which men might lodge, although some soil, covered at high tide, permitted a coarse vegetation of grass within thirty-five years. That soil is now so washed away, that the rocks, on which it rested, are not visible till near low water. Better evidence of the devastation of the ocean, if better were wanted, will be found in a comparison of the modern state of Nix's Mate, so called, on which is barely room for a sea mark, with what it must have been in September, 1636, when the general court granted "twelve acres of land to John Gallop, upon Nixe's Island, to enjoy to him and his heirs forever, *if the island be so much.*"

gate with their boat to Mattapan Point; for, near all that time, there was no open place between the Garden and Boston, neither was there any passing at Charlestown for two or three days, the wind about the N. W. three weeks, with much snow and extreme frost.

[Very large blank.]

Mo. 12.] About the middle of this month, a ||proper|| young man, servant to Mr. Bellingham, passing over the ice to Winnesemett, fell in, and was drowned. Divers others fell in, in that and other places, but, by God's providence, were saved.

14.] Capt. Wiggin, governour at Pascataquack, under the Lords Say and Brook, wrote to ||[2]our|| governour, desiring to have two men tried here, who had committed sodomy with each other, and that on the Lord's day, in time of publick exercise. The governour and divers of the assistants met and conferred about it, but did not think fit to try them here.[1]

[Large blank.]

Mo. 1. 4.] A general court at Newtown. Mr. Hooker preached, and showed the three great evils.[2]

[Very large blank.]

At this court, [3]one of the deputies was questioned for deny-

||promp|| ||[2]the||

---

[1] It is apparent, from inspection of the MS., that the last sentence of this paragraph was written at a later time than the preceding. The desire of Wiggin seems to imply a defect of criminal jurisdiction; but the refusal, on our part, to accept it, was a very prudent measure.

[2] Perhaps these evils were evanescent, though it may be otherwise; but posterity, I believe, is deprived of the light shown to our fathers.

[3] The name was partly written in the author's MS. but erased. It appears, however, a few pages onward. An explanation worth transcribing is found in Col. Rec. I. 137: "Whereas Mr. Israel Stoughton hath written a certain book, which hath occasioned much trouble and offence to the court; the said Mr. Stoughton did desire of the court, that the said book might forthwith be burnt, as being weak and offensive." Such almost unexampled modesty, in an author, did not, however, propitiate the severe justice of the assembly; for on the same page appears an order, "that Mr. Israel Stoughton shall be disabled for bearing any publick office in the commonwealth, within this jurisdiction, for the space of three years, for affirming the assistants were not magistrates." But his disability was removed or overlooked before the expiration of the sentence; for, in December of the year 1636, he was again a deputy, and being orthodox on the subject of the antinomian controversy, was chosen an assistant the following spring. He commanded the forces in the Pequod expedition in the same year. The General Index to 1 Hist. Coll. X. 295, must be wrong in ascribing to *Thomas* Stoughton the erection of the mill at Neponsit; for our Col. Rec. I. 111, mentions, that *Israel* had liberty granted "to build a mill, a wear and a bridge over Neponsit River, and is to sell the alewives he takes there at five shillings the thousand."

Thomas was, I presume, brother of Israel, and, probably, came first to New

ing the magistracy among us, affirming that the power of the governour was but ministerial, &c. ||He|| had also much opposed the magistrates, and ||[2]slighted|| them, and used many weak arguments against the negative voice, as himself acknowledged upon record. He was adjudged by all the court to be disabled for three years from bearing any publick office.

One[1] of the assistants was called to the lower end of the table to answer for refusing to pay towards a rate made by the court, and was fined £5, which was after released.

Mr. Endecott was called to answer for defacing the cross in the ensign; but, because the court could not agree about the thing, whether the ensigns should be laid by, in regard that many refused to follow them, the whole cause was deferred till the next general court; and the commissioners for military affairs gave order, in the mean time, that all the ensigns should be laid aside, &c.

At this court brass farthings were forbidden, and musket bullets made to pass for farthings.

A ||[3]commission|| for military affairs was established, ||[4]which|| had power of life and limb, &c.[2]

[Very large blank.]

||and|| ||[2]stigmatized|| ||[3]commissioner|| ||[4]who||

England; for he was admitted freeman in May, 1631, while the same Records show that Israel took the oath 5 November, 1633.

In the latter part of this History it will be found, that Stoughton went to England, and became a lieutenant colonel in the parliament's service, and died during the civil war. He was father of the celebrated William Stoughton, first lieutenant governour named by the crown under the charter of William and Mary, and chief justice in the trial of the witches. In that lamentable delusion his agency may well be forgiven, by future generations, for his munificence to Harvard College, in which one of the halls perpetuates his memory. His epitaph, closely imitated from that of Pascal, is in 1 Hist. Coll. II. 10. A bachelor seldom attained such honours in the infancy of our country.

1 Pynchon was the offender. For the same cause fines were imposed, at the same time, on the towns of Sagus and Salem, and all were released together.

2 From the greatness of the powers granted to this body, a fuller account than Winthrop has given may reasonably be extracted from Col. Rec. I. 139: "It is ordered, that the present governour, deputy governour, John Winthrop, John Humfrey, John Haynes, John Endecott, William Coddington, William Pynchon, Increase Nowell, Richard Bellingham, Esquires, and Simon Bradstreet, or the major part of them, who are deputed by this court to dispose of all military affairs whatsoever, shall have full power and authority to see all former laws concerning all military men and munition executed; and also shall have full power to ordain or remove all military officers, and to make and tender to them an oath suitable to their places; to dispose of all companies, to make orders for them, and to make and tender to them a suitable oath, and to see that strict discipline and trainings be observed, and to com-

15.] Two of the elders of every church met at Sagus, and spent there three days. The occasion was, that divers of the brethren of that church, not liking the proceedings of the pastor, and withal making question, whether they were a church or not, did separate from church communion. The pastor and other brethren desired the advice and help of the rest of the churches, who, not thinking fit to judge of the cause, without hearing the other side, offered to meet at Sagus about it. Upon this the pastor, &c. required the separate members to deliver their grievances in writing, which they refusing to do, the pastor, &c. wrote to all the churches, that, for this cause, they were purposed to proceed against them as persons excommunicated; and therefore desired them to stay their journey, &c. This letter being read at a lecture at Boston, (where some of the elders of every church were present,) they all agreed (with consent of their churches) to go presently to Sagus, to stay this hasty proceeding, &c. Accordingly, being met, and both parties (after much debate) being heard, it was agreed, that they were a true church, though not constituted, at first, in due order, yet after consent and practice of a church estate had supplied that defect; and so all were reconciled.

[Large blank.]

Mo. 2.] Some of our people went to Cape Cod, and made some oil of a whale, which was cast on shore. There were three or four cast up, as it seems there is almost every year.

26.] An alarm was raised in all our towns, and the governour and assistants met at Boston, and sent forth a shallop to Cape Ann, to discover what ships were there. For the fishermen had brought in word to Marblehead, that two ships had been ||hovering|| upon the coast all the day; one of about four hundred tons, and the other three hundred and fifty, and were gone in to Cape Ann. But it proved to be only one ship of eighty tons, bound for Richman's Isle, and the other a small pinnace of ten tons.

30.] The governour and assistants sent for Mr. Williams.

||heaving||

mand them forth upon any occasion they think meet; to make either offensive or defensive war; as also to do whatsoever may be farther behoofeful for the good of this plantation, in case of any war that may befal us; and, also, that the aforesaid commissioners, or the major part of them, shall have power to imprison or confine any that they shall judge to be enemies to the commonwealth; and such as will not come under command or restraint, as they shall be required, it shall be lawful for the said commissioners to put such persons to death. This order to continue to the end of the next general court." It was prolonged from court to court, several times, and some new members were occasionally added.

The occasion was, for that he had taught publickly, that a magistrate ought not to tender an oath to an unregenerate man, for that we thereby have communion with a wicked man in the worship of God, and cause him to take the name of God in vain. He was heard before all the ministers, and very clearly ||confuted.|| Mr. Endecott was at first of the same opinion, but he gave place to the ||[2]truth.||

Mo. 3. 6.] A general court was held at Newtown, where John Haynes, Esq. was chosen governour, Richard Bellingham, Esq. deputy governour, and Mr. Hough and Mr. Dummer chosen [1]assistants to the former; and Mr. Ludlow, the late deputy, left out of the magistracy. The reason was, partly, because the people would exercise their absolute power, &c. and partly upon some speeches of the deputy, who protested against the election of the governour as void, for that the deputies of the several towns had agreed upon the election before they came, &c. But this was generally ||[3]discussed,|| and the election adjudged good.

Mr. Endecott was also left out, and called into question about the defacing the cross in the ensign; and a committee was chosen, viz. every town chose one, (which yet were voted by all the people,) and the magistrates chose four, who, taking the charge to consider of the offence, and the censure due to it, and to certify the court, after one or two hours ||[4]time,|| made report to the court, that they found his offence to be great, viz. rash and without discretion, taking upon him more authority than he had, and not seeking advice of the court, &c.; ||[5]uncharitable,|| in that he, judging the cross, &c. to be a sin, did content himself to have reformed it at Salem, not taking care that others might be brought out of it also; laying a blemish also upon the rest of the magistrates, as if they would suffer idolatry, &c. and giving occasion to the state of England to think ill of us;—for which they adjudged him worthy admonition, and to be disabled for one year from bearing any publick office; declining any heavier sentence, because they were persuaded he did it out of tenderness of conscience, and not of any evil intent.[2]

||confessed|| ||[2]teacher|| ||[3]distrusted|| ||[4]they|| ||[5]unwarrantable||

---

1 The other assistants were Winthrop, Dudley, Humfrey, Coddington, Pynchon, Nowell, Bradstreet, and Winthrop, jun.

2 Had his conscience been as enlightened as it was tender, he would have conformed to the harmless custom; but, next year, men of soberer judgment were found ready to refuse compliance with bearing the standard of their country, and almost willing to imitate the outrage of Endecott. A tract of nearly thirteen pages, in defence of the cross, by the celebrated Hooker, is

Some petitions of grievances were tendered to the court in the beginning of it, but the court refused to hear any, or to meddle in any ||courses|| but making freemen, until the elections were passed.[1] The governour and deputy were elected by papers, wherein their names were written; but the assistants were chosen by papers, without names, viz. the governour propounded one to the people; then they all went out, and came in at one door, and every man delivered a paper into a hat. Such as gave their vote for the party named, gave in a paper with some figures or scroll in it; others gave in a blank.

The new governour, in his speech to the people, declared his purpose to spare their charge towards his allowance this year, partly in respect of their love showed towards him, and partly for that he observed how much the people had been pressed lately with publick charges, which the poorer sort did much groan under.[2]

A petition was preferred by many of Dorchester, &c. for

||causes||

---

among the MSS. of our Historical Society; but I have neither courage nor curiosity enough to study it. We may not imagine, that our ancestors had carefully scrutinized the ecclesiastical fable of the holy sign in Constantine's vision, or were sufficiently instructed to repudiate the consecrated Labarum of the first Christian emperour; and perhaps an Englishman of our times may presume, that there was as much policy, as abhorrence of idolatry, in their dread of the banner of St. George. Yet this presumption would be unfounded. Though there appears, in September preceding, something like prepared opposition to expected tyranny, I do not discover, in these weak scruples about the ensign, any affectation of independence, to which, a few years later, their circumstances offered very powerful inducements.

In the flag of the United States are exhibited white stars in a blue field; but the most punctilious imitator of the severe simplicity of the fathers of New England has never compared our service under it to the heathenish abomination of worshipping the host of heaven. An anecdote of a politick use of these emblems by Barlow, when negotiating at Algiers, proves that a diseased conscience might entertain this scruple, because the imagination can thus apply the object. He said to the minister of the Dey, There ought to be friendship between our countries, since you worship the moon, and we the stars.

1 One of these petitions was on the matter of Endecott's censure. The wisdom of this resolution of the court, in which was now assembled all the people entitled to vote for governour and assistants, except those in towns which sent proxies, was strongly exhibited two years later, when, in the contest for the election between Vane and Winthrop, the precedent was followed. A full examination of that subject, with others, may be found in four tracts preserved in Hutch. Coll. 63—101.

2 The assessment at this court was £200, only one third of the amount in the autumn before, and it was apportioned thus:—to Dorchester, Boston, and Newtown, £27.6.8, each; Roxbury and Watertown, £20, each; Charlestown, Salem and Sagus, £16, each; Medford, £10; Ipswich and Newbury, £8, each; Wessaguscus, £4. Col. Rec. I. 152.

releasing the sentence against Mr. Stoughton the last general court; but it was rejected, and the sentence affirmed by the country to be just.

Divers jealousies, that had been between the magistrates and deputies, were now cleared, with full satisfaction to all parties.

The matter of altering the cross in the ensign was referred to the next meeting, (the court being adjourned for three weeks,) it being propounded to turn it to the red and white rose, &c. and every man was to deal with his neighbours, to still their minds, who stood so stiff for the cross, until we should fully agree about it, which was expected, because the ministers had promised to take ||pains|| about it, and to write into England to have the judgments of the most wise and godly there.[1]

The deputies having conceived great danger to our state, in regard that our magistrates, for want of positive laws, in many cases, might proceed according to their discretions, it was agreed, that some men should be appointed to frame a body of grounds of laws, in resemblance to a Magna Charta, which, being allowed by some of the ministers, and the general court, should be received for fundamental laws.

At this general court, some of the chief of Ipswich desired leave to remove to Quascacunquen, to begin a town there, which was granted them, and it was named Newberry.

Also, Watertown and Roxbury had leave to remove whither they pleased, so as they continued under this government. The occasion of their desire to remove was, for that all towns in the bay began to be much straitened by their own nearness to one another, and their cattle being so much increased.

21.] A Dutch ship of one hundred and sixty tons arrived at Marblehead. Capt. Hurlston came merchant. She came from Christopher Island. She brought one hundred and forty tons of salt, and ten thousand weight of tobacco.

[Blank.]

This island lies in eighteen degrees, and is about thirty miles in compass, inhabited by two colonies, one English and another French. There is in it about four thousand persons. They have three English churches, but the people are very wicked, as the merchant (who dwelt there five years) complained. The salt is made with the sun in a ||2natural|| pan, half a mile from the sea. Their rain begins in September, and continues till February.

||prayers|| ||2watering||

1 Answers of these "most wise and godly" in England have not fallen in my way. The tract of Hooker, before-mentioned, in note on page 158, from very slight examination, appears to contain a temperate censure of Endecott.

Mo. 4. 3.] Here arrived two Dutch ships, who brought twenty-seven Flanders mares, at £34 a mare, and three horses; sixty-three heifers, at £12 the beast; and eighty-eight sheep at 50*s*. the sheep. They came from the Tessell in five weeks three days, and lost not one beast or sheep. Here arrived also, the same day, the James, a ship of three hundred tons, with cattle and passengers, which came all safe from Southampton within the same time. Mr. Graves was master, who had come every year for these seven years. 7. The Lord's day there came in seven other ships, and one to Salem, and four more to the mouth of the bay, with store of passengers and cattle. They came all within six weeks.

For preventing the loss of time, and drunkenness, which sometimes happened, by people's running to the ships, and the excessive prices of commodities, it was ordered, that one in each town should buy for all, &c. and should ||retain|| the same within twenty days at five per hundred, if any came to buy in that time. But this took no good effect; for most of the people would not buy, except they might buy for themselves; and the merchants appointed could not disburse so much money, &c.; and the seamen were much discontented, yet some of them brought their goods on shore and sold them there.

16.] A bark of forty tons arrived, set forth with twenty servants, by Sir Richard Saltonstall, to go plant at Connecticut.

By a letter from the Lord Say, and report of divers passengers, it was certified to us, that Capt. Mason and others, the adversaries of this colony, had built a great ship to send over the general governour, &c. which, being launched, fell in sunder in the midst.

It appeared likewise, by a copy of a petition sent over to us, that they had divided all this country of New England, viz. between St. Croix in the east, and that of Lord Bartimore, called Maryland, into twelve provinces, disposed to twelve in England, who should send each ten men to attend the general governour coming over; but ||2the project [took] not effect.|| The Lord frustrated their design.[1]

Two carpenters, going to wash themselves in the river between Mount Woollaston and Wessaguscus, were carried away with the tide, and drowned.

[Large blank.]

||return|| ||2this proved not effectual||

[1] This idle division of American provinces may be seen in Hubbard, 228.

24.] Mr. Graves, in the James, and Mr. Hodges, in the Rebecka, set sail for the Isle of Sable for sea-horse (which are there in great number) and wild cows. Mr. John Rose, being cast ashore there in the [Mary and Jane] two years since, and making a small pinnace of the wreck of his ship, sailed thence to the French upon the main, being thirty leagues off, by whom he was detained prisoner, and forced to pilot them to the island, where they had great store of sea-horse ||teeth,|| and cattle, and ||[2]store|| [of] black foxes; and they left seventeen men upon the island to inhabit it. The island is thirty miles long, two miles broad in most places, a mere sand, yet full of fresh water in ponds, &c. He saw about eight hundred cattle, small and great, all red, and the largest he ever saw, and many foxes, whereof some perfect black. There is no wood upon it, but store of wild peas and flags by the ponds, and grass. In the middle of it is a pond of salt water, ten miles long, full of plaice, ||[3]soles,|| &c. The company, which went now, carried twelve landmen, two mastiffs, a ||[4]house,|| and a shallop.

August 26.] They returned from their voyage. They found there upon the island sixteen Frenchmen, who had wintered there, and built a little fort, and had killed some black foxes. They had killed also many of the cattle, so as they found not above one hundred and forty, and but two or three calves. They could kill but ||[5]few|| sea-horse, by reason they were forced to travel so far in the sand as they were too weak to stick them, and they came away at such time as they use to go up ||[6]highest|| to eat green peas. The winter there is very cold, and the snow above knee deep.

Mo. 5. 8.] At the general court, Mr. Williams of Salem was summoned, and did appear. It was laid to his charge, that, being under question before the magistracy and churches for divers dangerous opinions, viz. 1, that the magistrate ought not to punish the breach of the first table, otherwise than in such cases as did disturb the civil peace; 2, that he ought not to tender an oath to an unregenerate man; 3, that a man ought not to pray with such, though wife, child, &c.; 4, that a man ought not to give thanks after the sacrament nor after meat, &c.; and that the other churches were about to write to the church of Salem to admonish him of these errours; notwithstanding the church had since called him to [the] office of a teacher. Much debate was about these things. The said opinions were adjudged by all, magistrates and ministers, (who were desired to be present,) to be erro-

||blank|| ||[2]some|| ||[3]blank|| ||[4]horse|| ||[5]five|| ||[6]heights||

neous, and very dangerous, and the calling of him to office, at that time, was judged a great contempt of authority. So, in fine, ||time|| was given to him and the church of Salem to consider of these things till the next general court, and then either to give satisfaction to the court, or else to expect the sentence; it being professedly declared by the ministers, (at the request of the court to give their advice,) that he who should obstinately maintain such opinions, (whereby a church might run into heresy, apostacy, or tyranny, and yet the civil magistrate could not intermeddle,) were to be removed, and that the other churches ought to request the magistrates so to do.[1]

At this court Wessaguscus was made a plantation, and Mr. [2]Hull, a minister §in England,§ and twenty-one families with him, allowed to sit down there—after called Weymouth.

A plantation was likewise erected at Bear's Cove, after called ||[2]Hingham.||[3]

12.] Mr. Luxon arrived here in a small pinnace. He fished

||there|| ||[2]Kingham||

1 We ought not to censure more the declaration of the clergy, than the policy of the court in asking their advice. Church and state were too often playing into each other's hands—if so irreverent a phrase may be allowed—and thus sanctifying principles and conduct, which either would not have, singly, ventured to adopt or enforce.

2 Of this reverend gentleman no further account can easily be obtained, except that, in the MS. journal of Hobart, first minister of Hingham, on 5 May, 1639, I find "Mr. Hull gave his farewell sermon." Perhaps it was he, whom Mather, in Magnalia, mentions as minister at the Isles of Shoals. Conf. Magn. book III. with 1 Hist. Coll. VII. 254, which places him there two years after Hobart's notice of removal. It may be the same person, who, in this History, 3 month, 1643, is called "an excommunicated person, and very contentious;" yet, in the Magnalia, book VII., Mather, describing the perils of Mrs. Heard at the famous assault by the Indians on Cocheco, in 1689, makes her "daughter of Mr. Hull, a reverend minister, formerly living at Piscataqua." In our second volume, some failure, in propriety, it will be seen, is attributed to his son.
A careful history of Weymouth is much wanted.

3 By this establishment, or erection, of a plantation, we must not understand, that settlements were then first made at the spot, but that a municipal government was permitted there, or that the place was allowed to have deputies in the general court. Wessaguscus had, at the last general court, been assessed; and, at the same time, Joseph Andrews was "sworn constable of Barecove." Many of the inhabitants were made freemen of the colony in the preceding year. The spelling of the name varies between the Colony Records and this History, and each, in different places, has different orthography. Perhaps it sometimes was thought a natural resort of bears; perhaps sometimes the appearance of the cove, at low water, regulated the letters used to express the same sound. The new name was given by general court 2 September, 1635, because the pastor and most of his flock came from a small town called Hingham, in Norfolk, England.

at the Isle of Shoals, as he had done many years, and, returning to sell his fish at market, was taken in foggy weather and carried into the bay of Port Royal, and there wrecked upon a small island about [blank] leagues from the main. So he built a pinnace, and came hither in her.

[Blank.]

Salem men had preferred a petition, at the last general court, for some land in Marblehead Neck, which they did challenge as belonging to their town; but, because they had chosen Mr. Williams their teacher, while he stood under question of authority, and so offered contempt to the magistrates, &c. their petition was refused till, &c. Upon this the church of Salem write to other churches, to admonish the magistrates of this as a heinous sin, and likewise the deputies; for which, at the next general court, their deputies were not received until they should give satisfaction about the letter.[1]

Mo. 6, Aug. 16.] The wind having blown hard at S. and S.W. a week before, about midnight it came up at N. E. and blew with such violence, with abundance of rain, that it blew down many hundreds of trees, §near the towns,§ overthrew some houses, [and] drave the ships from their anchors. The Great Hope, of Ipswich, being about four hundred tons, was driven on ground at Mr. Hoffe's Point, and brought back again presently by a N. W. wind, and ||ran|| on shore at Charlestown. About eight of the clock the wind came about to N. W. very strong, and, it being then about high water, by nine the tide was fallen about three feet. Then it began to flow again about one hour, and rose about two or three feet, which was conceived to be, that the sea was grown so high §abroad§ with the N. E. wind, that, meeting with the ebb, it forced it back again.

§This tempest was not so far as Cape Sable, but to the south more violent, and made a double tide all that coast.§

In this tempest, the James of Bristol, having one hundred [2]passengers, honest people of Yorkshire, being put into the Isle of Shoals, lost there three anchors; and, setting sail, no can-

||came||

---

1 This denial, or perversion of justice, by postponement of a hearing, on a question of temporal right, for some spiritual deficiency in the church or pastor, will not permit us to think, that the judges of Williams were free from all blame in producing his schism.

2 Among the number were Richard Mather and Jonathan Mitchell, the latter quite a youth, both famous names with the early divines of Massachusetts. See Hubbard, 199, who, probably, had his information from Increase Mather, son of Richard. Increase, in his Life of his father, pages 21, 2, has related the circumstances of his preservation, as also in Remarkable Providences, 312.

vass nor ropes would hold, but she was driven within a cable's length of the rocks ||at|| Pascataquack, when suddenly the wind, coming to N.W., put them back to the Isle of Shoals, and, being there ready to strike upon the rocks, they ||2let|| out a piece of their mainsail, and weathered the rocks. In the same tempest a bark of Mr. Allerton's was cast away upon Cape Ann, and twenty-one persons drowned; among the rest one Mr. ||3Avery,||[1] a minister in Wiltshire, a godly man, with his wife and six small children, were drowned. None were saved but one Mr. [2]Thacher and his wife, who were cast on shore, and preserved by a powder horn and a bag with a flint, and a goat and a cheese, cast on shore after them, and a truss of bedding, and some other necessaries: and the third day after a shallop came thither to look for another shallop, which was missing in the storm, and so they were preserved. So as there did appear a miraculous providence in their preservation. The general court gave Mr. Thacher £26.13.4, towards his losses, and divers good people gave him besides. The man was cast on shore, when he had been (as he ||4thought||) a quarter of an hour beaten up and down by the waves, not being able to swim one stroke; and his wife sitting in the scuttle of the bark, the deck was broke off, and brought on shore, as she stuck in it. One of the children was then cast dead on shore, and the rest never found.

§Gabriel lost at Pemaquid; and Mr. Witheridge and the Dartmouth ships cut all their masts at St. George. The tide

||of|| ||2cut|| ||3Anvey|| ||4supposed||

---

1 This gentleman, whose fate was designed by his companion in adversity to be forever remembered in the name given to the outer rock, Avery's Fall, was cousin of Anthony Thacher, of whom slight notice is taken in the next note. From a folio page, in double column, of the Magnalia, book III. p. 77, we learn no more of the life of Avery than his latest hours. His baptismal name was John.

2 An admirable letter from this sufferer to his brother Peter, a clergyman of the city of Salisbury, relates all the particulars of this shipwreck, one of the most disastrous that ever afflicted the iron-bound coast of New England. It is the first article in Increase Mather's Remarkable Providences, and gives to that work its chief value. The vessel was returning from Ipswich to Marblehead. Anthony's nephew, Thomas, first pastor of the *Third* Church in Boston, who avoided the peril of his uncle by coming round on land, was progenitor of all, I think, who have rendered this name, in church and state, illustrious in Massachusetts. Of the last deceased pastor of the New South Church in this city, Samuel C. Thacher, the companion and friend of my studies from childhood, no language is too powerful to express my admiration. Animæ dimidium meæ. A memoir of his father, the Rev. Dr. Peter Thacher, late of Brattle Street Church, drawn by one who knew well his duty and his undertaking, contains very minute genealogical details. See 1 Hist. Coll. VIII. 277.

rose at Naragansett fourteen feet higher than ordinary, and drowned eight Indians flying from their wigwams.§[1]

At this time a French ship came with commission from the king of France, (as they pretended,) and took Penobscott, a Plimouth trading house, and sent away the men which were in it, but kept their goods and gave them bills for them, and bad them tell all the plantations, as far as forty degrees, that they would come with eight ships, next year, and displant them all. But, by a letter which the captain wrote to the governour of Plimouth, it appeared they had commission from Mons. Roselly, commander at the fort near Cape Breton, called La Havre, to displant the English as far as Pemaquid, and by it they professed all courtesy to us here.

Mr. Williams, pastor of Salem, being sick and not able to speak, wrote to his church a protestation, that he could not communicate with the churches in the bay; neither would he communicate with them, except they would refuse ||communion|| with the rest; but the whole church was grieved herewith.

[Large blank.]

The Dorchester men being set down at Connecticut, near the Plimouth trading house, the governour, Mr. Bradford, wrote to them, complaining of it as an injury, in regard of their possession and purchase of the Indians, whose right it was; and the Dutch sent home into Holland for commission to deal with our people at Connecticut.

September 1.] At this general court was the first grand jury, who presented above one hundred offences, and, among others, some of the magistrates.[2]

At this court Mr. Endecott made a protestation in justification of the letter formerly sent from Salem to the other churches, against the magistrates and deputies, for which he was committed; but, the same day, he came and acknowledged his fault, and was discharged.[3]

||communication||

1 Hubbard has expanded this account of the tempest, 199—201. Morton's Memorial informs us, that the marks were visible many years; but his "many hundred thousands of trees" are by Hubbard reduced to "*some thousands*." Though the more moderate number be generally preferable, we need not fear, in this instance, to follow the original historian rather than the copyer. Such extent of devastation in the forest has been equalled within our memories, especially from the gale at the autumnal equinox of 1815.

2 At this court the rate assessed is found in our Colony Records, I. 161, as follows:—Newtown and Dorchester, £26.5, each; Boston, £25.10; Watertown, £19.10; Roxbury, £19.5; Salem, £16; Charlestown, £15; Ipswich, £14; Sagus, £11; Medford, £9.15; Newbury, £7.10; Hingham, £6; Weymouth, £4; in all, £200.

3 Mention is made of the letter on a former page. To show the degree

Divers lewd servants (viz. six) ran away, and stole a skiff and other things. A commission was granted, at the general court, to Capt. [1]Trask to fetch them and other such from the eastward. He pursued them to the Isle of Shoals, and so to Pascataquack, where, in the night, he surprised them in a house, and brought them to Boston. At next court they were severely whipped, and ordered to pay all charges, &c.

At this court there was granted to Mr. [2]Buckly and [blank] merchant, and about twelve more families, to begin a town at Musketaquid, for which they were allowed six miles upon the river, and to be free from publick charges three years; and it was named Concord. A town was also begun above the falls of Charles River.[3]

[Large blank.]

At the Dutch plantation, this summer, a ship's long boat was overset with a gust, and five men in her, who gat upon ||her|| keel, and were driven to sea four days, in which time three of them dropt off and were drowned; and the fifth day the fourth, being sore beaten, and ||[2]pained|| with hunger and thirst, wilfully

||the|| ||[2]parched||

of moderation, with which our civil rulers treated ecclesiastical subjects, I give an extract from Col. Rec. I. 163: "Whereas Mr. Roger Williams, one of the elders of the church of Salem, hath broached and divulged divers new and dangerous opinions, against the authority of magistrates; as also writ letters of defamation, both of the magistrates and churches here, and that before any conviction, and yet maintaineth the same without any retraction; it is therefore ordered, that the said Mr. Williams shall depart out of this jurisdiction within six weeks now next ensuing; which, if he neglect to perform, it shall be lawful for the governour and two of the magistrates to send him to some place out of this jurisdiction, not to return any more without license from the court."

"Mr. Samuel Sharpe is enjoined to appear at the next particular court, to answer for the letter that came from the church of Salem, as also *to bring the names of those that will justify the same*, or else to acknowledge his offence, under his own hand, for his own particular."

1 He was of Salem, in the History of which town, 1 Hist. Coll. VI. 253, it is related, that he was out in the Pequod war, by which we must, I suppose, understand Stoughton's, not Endecott's, expedition. His baptismal name was William, as the Colony Records give it among the deputies at all the general courts, from the fourth to the tenth inclusive.

2 Such is the orthography of the original MS. though the head of this family always spelt the name Bulkeley. The Rev. Peter Bulkley is a character so well known by the reader of our early books, and the labours of Eliot and Allen have so successfully transferred to their pages the truth, which a succession of reverend descendants had preserved, that it were supererogation for me to enlarge this note. See President Stiles's opinion, in 2 Hist. Coll. II. 260. There is a good letter of Bulkley in 3 Hist. Coll. I. 47.

3 It is not easy to imagine, that any other settlement is here meant than Sudbury, though it had not sufficiently increased to attain the honour of a name for three or four years more. See Hubbard, 236.

fell off and was drowned. Soon after the wind came up at S. E. and carried the boat, with the fifth man, to the Long Island, and, being only able to creep on shore, he was found by the Indians, and preserved. He was grown very poor, and almost senseless, with hunger and watching, and would say, that he saw such and such come to give him meat, &c.[1]

The Plimouth men had hired the Great Hope, to go to displant the French, and regain their possession at Penobscott. The master, Mr. ||Girling,|| was to have for it £200. They sent ||[2]their bark|| with him and about twenty men; but when they came, they found the French had notice, and had so strongly intrenched themselves, (being eighteen,) as, having spent near all their powder and shot, the bark left the ship there, and came here to advise with us what further to do; for they had lately lost another bark laden with corn, and could not spare this to send back again. The general court, being assembled, agreed to aid them with men and munition, and therefore wrote to them to send one with commission to treat with us about it, resolving to drive them out, whatsoever it should cost, (yet first to put them to bear the charge, if it might be;) for we saw that their neighbourhood would be very dangerous to us.[2]

The next week they sent Mr. ||[3]Prence||[3] and Capt. ||[4]Standish|| to us, with commission to treat. Four of the commissioners

||Grig|| ||[2]her back|| ||[3]Pierce|| ||[4]S——||

---

1 Mather, in book VI. of the Magnalia, appropriately called by him Thaumaturgus, has a little decorated this narrative of mental alienation.

2 Good union followed from the common danger of the two colonies, whose preceding transactions evidently exhibit a mutual jealousy. I subjoin, from Colony Records, 162, September court, all that is there found of this important essay towards an alliance: "Agreed, that Plimouth shall be aided with men and munition to supplant the French at Penobscot. And it was ordered, that Capt. *Sellanova* shall be sent for, to confer with about this business, and recompensed out of the treasury for his pains, if he be not employed." The hard name of the engineer is quite strange to all our antiquaries of this age. It is manifestly a foreign one, probably of some Dutchman, who had seen service at home, and was now thought a fit antagonist for the enemies of the common religion. In a letter of Gov. Winthrop to his son, John, June, 1636, in our Appendix, the same person is mentioned as being arrived in the West Indies. I know not whether he was employed. The expulsion of the French was reserved for the vigorous administration of Cromwell, in 1654, when Sedgwick and Leverett succeeded with little difficulty.

3 This distinguished gentleman, whose name, though commonly in books spelt Prince, is always, as Judge Davis informs me, by himself written as Winthrop has given it, was long governour of Plimouth colony. He will be forever remembered in the pages of the new edition of Morton's Memorial. Every author, who treats of New England, is full of his praise, and my humble efforts are not needed to extend it.

gave them a meeting, which grew to this issue,—that they refused to deal further in it, otherwise than as a common cause of the whole country, and so to contribute their part. We refused to deal in it, otherwise than as in their aid, and so at their charge; for indeed we had then no money in the treasury, neither could we get provision of victuals, on the sudden, for one hundred men, which were to be employed. So we deferred all to further counsel.

Mo. 8. 6.] Two shallops, going, laden with goods, to Connecticut, were taken in the night with an easterly storm, and cast away upon Brown's Island, near the Gurnett's Nose, and the men all drowned.[1]

Here arrived two great ships, the Defence and the Abigail, with Mr. Wilson, pastor of Boston, Mr. [2]Shepard, Mr. [3]Jones, and [4]other ministers; amongst others, Mr. [5]Peter, pastor of the English church in Rotterdam, who, being persecuted by the English ambassadour,—who would have brought his and other churches to the English discipline,—and not having had his health these many years, intended to advise with the ministers here about his removal.

The special ||goodness|| of the Lord appeared in this, that the passengers came safe and hale in all [the] ships, though some of them long passages,—the Abigail ten weeks from

||providence||

---

1 A note in 1 Hist. Coll. VIII. 220, by the most accurate geographer of New England, remarks, that this island is become a shoal.

2 It would probably be an unsuccessful, and certainly a needless task, for me to add any thing about Shepard to what is already known in Eliot and Allen, and the authors referred to by the latter.

3 Little could be expected from my diligent inquiries, respecting this person, by one that finds nothing but his name known to Mather, who inserts it in his first classis of ministers, or Trumbull, I. 194. Both seem to be ignorant of any thing but what they learn from Winthrop. Perhaps, before removing to Fairfield, Conn. he was the pastor of Concord. See, in this History, 5 of 5 month, 1636, and 6 of 2 month, 1637. This conjecture I have found confirmed by the great authority of President Stiles, quoted by Holmes, Annals, I. 336, note 3.

4 Probably Flint, Carter, and Walton, mentioned by Johnson, lib. I. c. 31, as coming over this year, are here intended. Perhaps, in his work, the name of Walton is a misprint for *Waltham*, as thus Mather calls a minister, who came from England, with the prænomen William, settled at Marblehead. Flint was admitted of Boston church 15 November, this year, a fortnight after Vane.

5 The unhappy celebrity of Hugh Peters, or Peter, as he wrote it himself, will excuse me from giving more than a reference to some of the innumerable books, which furnish evidence of his labours, his errours, and his sufferings. He was executed 16 October, 1660.

Plimouth, with two hundred and twenty persons, and many cattle, infected also with the small pox; yet, &c.

There came also John Winthrop, the younger, with [1]commission from the Lord Say, Lord Brook, and divers other great persons in England, to begin a plantation at Connecticut, and to be governour there. They sent also men and ammunition, and £2000 in money, to begin a fortification at the mouth of the river.

Here came also one Mr. Henry [2]Vane, son and heir to Sir Henry Vane, comptroller of the king's house, who, being a young gentleman of excellent parts, and had been employed by his father (when he was ambassadour) in foreign affairs; yet, being called to the obedience of the gospel, forsook the honours and preferments of the court, to enjoy the ordinances of Christ in their purity here. His father, being very averse to this way, (as no way savouring the power of religion,) would hardly have consented to his coming hither, but that, acquainting the king with his son's disposition and desire, he commanded him to send him hither, and gave him license for three years' stay here.

This noble gentleman, having order from the said lords and others, treated with the magistrates here, and those who were to go to Connecticut,[3] about the said design of the lords, to this issue,—that either the three towns gone thither should give place, upon full satisfaction, or else sufficient room must be found there for the lords and their companies, &c. or else they would divert their thoughts and preparations some other ways.

[Large blank.]

November 1.] Mr. Vane was admitted a member of the church of Boston.

October.] At this general court Mr. Williams, the teacher of Salem, was again convented, and all the ministers in the bay being desired to be present, he was charged with the said two letters,—that to the churches, complaining of the magistrates for

---

1 See the commission in Trumbull, I. 497.

2 Few men have done less good with greater reputation than this statesman, whose fame rings in history too loudly to require my aid in its diffusion. The brief, but busy exercise of his faculties here, is exhibited with sufficient minuteness by our author, in whose page is found no deficiency of respect towards the fanatick, who was too much honoured when exalted as the rival of the father of Massachusetts.

3 In the Appendix may be seen the propositions, of which the original draft is preserved in the Historical Society's library, Trumbull Papers, vol. XIX. page 213.

injustice, extreme oppression, &c. and the other to his own church, to persuade them to renounce communion with all the churches in the bay, as full of antichristian pollution, &c. He justified both these letters, and maintained all his opinions; and, being offered further conference or disputation, and a month's respite, he chose to dispute presently. So Mr. Hooker was appointed to dispute with him, but could not reduce him from any of his errours. So, the next morning, the court sentenced him to depart out of our jurisdiction within six weeks, all the ministers, save one, approving the sentence; and his own church had him under question also for the same cause; and he, at his return home, refused communion with his own church, who openly disclaimed his errours, and wrote an humble submission to the magistrates, acknowledging their fault in joining with Mr. Williams in that letter to the churches against them, &c.

[Large blank.]

15.] About sixty men, women, and little children, went by land towards Connecticut with their cows, ||horses|| and swine, and, after a tedious and difficult journey, arrived safe there.

[Very large blank.]

The pinnace, which Sir Richard Saltonstall sent to take possession of a great quantity of land at Connecticut, was, in her return into England, cast away upon the Isle Sable.[1] The men were kindly entertained by the French there, and had passage to Le Havre, some twenty leagues east of Cape Sable, where Monsieur commander of Roselle was governour, who entertained them very courteously, and furnished them with a shallop to return to us, and gave four of their company passage into France, but made them pay dear for their shallop; and in their return, they put into Penobscot, at such time as Girling's ship lay there; so that they were kept prisoners there till the ship was gone, and then sent to us with a courteous letter to our governour. A little before, our governour had written to him (viz. Mons. [2]D'Aulnay) to send them home to us; but they were come before.

||heifers||

1 Saltonstall attributes the loss to her detention, both at Boston and at Connecticut River. He thought he had a just claim for satisfaction. See his interesting letter, which I copied for 2 Hist. Coll. VIII. 42, 3.

2 Enough, the reader will probably imagine, about the French governour of that part of Acadia west of the St. Croix, or the eastern half of the present state of Maine, will be found in this History, both of his disappointments and ultimate success. A brief sketch of the whole subject of controversy between

It is useful to observe, as we go along, such especial providences of God as were manifested for the good of these plantations.

Mr. Winslow, the late governour of Plimouth, being this year in England, petitioned the council there for a commission to withstand the intrusions of the French and Dutch, which was likely to take effect, (though undertaken by ill advice, for such precedents might endanger our liberty, that we should do nothing hereafter but by commission out of England;) but the archbishops, being incensed against him, as against all these plantations, informed the rest, that he was a separatist, &c. and that he did marry, &c. and thereupon gate him committed; but, after some few months, he petitioned the board, and was discharged.

[Very large blank.]

Another providence was in the voyage of Mr. Winthrop, the younger, and Mr. Wilson into England, who, returning in the winter time, in a small and weak ship, bound for Barnstaple, were driven by foul weather upon the coast of Ireland, not known by any in the ship, and were brought, through many desperate dangers, into Galloway, where they parted, Mr. Winthrop taking his journey over land to Dublin, and Mr. Wilson by sea, and being come within sight of Lundy, in the mouth of Severn, they were forced back by tempest to Kinsale, where some ships perished in their view. Mr. Wilson, being in Ireland, gave much satisfaction to the Christians there about New England.

Mr. Winthrop went to Dublin, and from thence to Antrim in the north, and came to the house of one Sir John [1]Clotworthy, the evening before the day when divers godly persons were appointed to meet at his house, to confer about their voyage to New England, by whom they were thoroughly informed of all things, and received great encouragement to proceed on in their intended course. From thence he passed over into Scotland, and so through the north of England;

---

him and La Tour, in which many of our people were unhappily involved, may be seen in Hutchinson, I. 120—126. See also note 3 on page 117.

1 This gentleman became a strenuous assertor of liberty in the long parliament, and, being too easily satisfied with deliverance from tyranny to coincide with the designs of Cromwell, was, by that hypocrite, with many other early associates, committed to prison. From the text we may not conclude positively, that Clotworthy was one of those, who thought of coming to our country; though many, of equal or higher rank and fortune, had such designs, in which most of them were prevented by the government, that had good reason afterwards, says Hume, to repent of such exercise of authority.

and all the way he met with persons of quality, whose thoughts were towards New England, who observed his coming among them as a special providence of God.

9ber. 3.] At the court of assistants, John [1]Pratt of Newtown was questioned about the letter he wrote into England, wherein he affirmed divers things, which were untrue and of ill report, for the state of the country, as that here was nothing but rocks, and sands, and salt marshes, &c. He desired respite for his answer to the next morning; then he gave it in in writing, in which, by making his own interpretation of some passages, and acknowledging his errour in others, he gave satisfaction. This was delivered in under his own hand, and the hands of Mr. Hooker and some other of the ministers, and satisfaction acknowledged under the hands of the magistrates.

Mr. Winthrop, jun. the governour appointed by the lords for Connecticut, sent a bark of thirty tons, and about twenty men, with all needful provisions, to take possession of the mouth of Connecticut, and to begin some building.

9.] About this time an open pinnace, returning from Connecticut, was cast away in Manemett Bay; but all the men (being six) were saved, and came to Plimouth, after they had wandered ten days in extreme cold and deep snow, not meeting with any Indian or other person.

26.] There came twelve men from Connecticut. They had been ten days upon their journey, and had lost one of their company, drowned in the ice by the way; and had been all starved, but that, by God's providence, they lighted upon an Indian wigwam. Connecticut River was frozen up the 15th of this month.

Mr. Hugh Peter, preaching at Boston and Salem, moved the country to raise a stock for fishing, as the only probable means to ||free|| us from that oppression, which the seamen and others held us under.

28.] Here arrived a small §[2]Norsey§ bark, of twenty-five

||save||

---

1 Notice of his death will occur in our second volume, sub an. 1645. The answer, in the text alluded to, was so equivocal, that, in an epistle preserved in Hutch. Coll. 106, Sir William Martin says to Winthrop, "in the main I find little difference therein from his letter." This curious apology was transcribed by me from the Colony Records, and printed in 2 Hist. Coll. VII. 126. Pratt had made a contract, in 1629, with our company in London, to come out as a surgeon for the plantation, on a salary. He removed, with most other Newtown people, to Connecticut, in company with Gov. Haynes, as I presume, from finding the same name at their first assembly of deputies in 1639. See Trumbull, I. 103.

2 I never saw this word before; but cannot doubt that it is the same gentilitial as Norwegian, or, of the North Country. *Norse* is common with the poets and others.

tons, sent by the Lords Say, &c. with one [1]Gardner, an expert engineer or work base,[2] and provisions of all sorts, to begin a fort at the mouth of Connecticut. She came through many great tempests; yet, through the Lord's great providence, her passengers, §twelve men, two women,§[3] and goods, all safe. Mr. Winthrop had sent, four days before, a bark, with carpenters and other workmen, to take possession of the place, (for the Dutch intended to take it,) and to raise some buildings.

A great shallop, coming from Pascataquack in a N. E. wind with snow, lost her way, and was forced into Anasquam; and going out with a N. W. wind, through the unskilfulness of the men, was cast upon the rocks, and lost £100 worth of goods.

A shallop of William [4]Lovell, laden with goods to Salem, worth £100, was, by foul weather, put into Plimouth, and, coming out, the men went aboard a small bark by the way, and their shallop brake loose and was lost, and, about two months after, was found about [5]Nawset, not much hurt, and the goods were, most of them, saved by some Plimouth men, who had notice of it by the Indians.[6]

[Large blank.]

---

1 From this person, whose name of baptism was David, I conceive Gardner's Island and Bay receive their names. Trumbull, I. 61, refers to manuscripts of his, and they certainly might have assisted him with some important illustrations of the origin of the war with the Pequods, during which he commanded the fort at Saybrook. He is also spoken of with respect by Saltonstall, in the letter mentioned in our note on page 171, and by Mason in his History of that war. But Mason calls him Lyon Gardner, spelling the sirname as in the text of our author.

2 A confession of inability to explain this phrase is made, without any reservation for the obscurity of the MS.

3 This addition to the text of the former edition is from Winthrop's margin.

4 He was, probably, of Dorchester, and from him Lovell's Island, in our harbour, I presume, receives its name.

5 Plimouth people settled there about nine years after, and it has been since called Eastham. See 1 Hist. Coll. VIII. 163.

6 Of the kindness and justice, with which the colonists of Plimouth and Massachusetts had universally treated their uncivilized neighbours, this proof of the honest and friendly conduct of the aborigines towards them is the stronger, because indirect evidence. We ought not to forget, that the native inhabitants of this very spot had indulged a peculiar hatred against the English name, on account of the perfidious conduct, twenty years before, of Hunt, in kidnapping twenty of their tribe, whom he transported for sale in Spain. See the narrative in most of the books on the earlier affairs of America, from Purchas to Holmes. The invaluable work of the latter annalist quotes I. Mather, sub an. 1675, to prove that Christian blood had not been shed in hostility, before that time, in Massachusetts.

10ber, 10.] The ship Rebecka, about sixty tons, came from Connecticut, and brought in her about seventy men and women, which came down to the river's mouth to meet the barks, which should have brought their provisions; but, not meeting them, they went aboard the Rebecka, which, two days before, was frozen twenty miles up the river, but a small rain falling set her free; but coming out, she ran on ground at the mouth of the river, and was forced to unlade. They came to Massachusetts in five days, which was a great mercy of God, for otherwise they had all perished with famine, as some did.

While the Rebecka lay there, the Dutch sent a ||sloop|| to take possession of the mouth of the river; but our men gate two pieces on shore, and would not suffer them to land.

The 2d and 3d of this month fell a snow about knee deep, with much wind from the N. and N. E.[1]

Mr. [2]Norton, a godly man, and a preacher in England, coming with his family to the Massachusetts, the ship, wherein he was, was by contrary winds put into Plimouth, where he continued preaching to them all the winter; and although Mr. Smith, their pastor, gave over his place, that he might have it, and the church used him with all respect, and large offers, &c. yet he left them and came to Massachusetts, alleging that his spirit could not close with them, &c.

[Large blank.]

11 mo. January.] The governour and assistants met at Boston to consider about Mr. Williams, for that they were credibly informed, that, notwithstanding the injunction laid upon him (upon the liberty granted him to stay till the spring) not to go about to draw others to his opinions, he did use to entertain company in his house, and to preach to them, even of such points as he had been censured for; and it was agreed to send him into England by a ship then ready to depart. The reason was, because he had drawn above twenty persons to his opinion, and they were intended to erect a plantation about the Naragansett Bay, from whence the infection would easily spread into these churches, (the people being, many of them, much taken with the apprehension of his godliness.) Whereupon

||ship||

---

1 Such depth of snow, at so early a season, though common enough in the interiour, among the hills, has not been known on the seacoast for many years.

2 The history of church and state affords abundant materials for a biography of John Norton, one of the most learned divines that came early to our country, and it has been compiled by Dr. Eliot with more than usual felicity. Mather and Emerson are more copious.

a warrant was sent to him to come presently to Boston, to be shipped, &c. He returned answer, (and divers of Salem came with it,) that he could not come without hazard of his life, &c. Whereupon a pinnace was sent with commission to Capt. Underhill, &c. to apprehend him, and carry him aboard the ship, (which then rode at Natascutt;) but, when they came at his house, they found he had been gone three days before; but whither they could not learn.[1]

He had so far prevailed at Salem, as many there (especially of devout women) did embrace his opinions, and separated from the churches, for this cause, that some of their members, going into England, did hear the ministers there, and when they came home the churches here held communion with them.

This month one went by land to Connecticut, and returned safe.[2]

Mr. Hugh Peter went from place to place labouring, both publickly and privately, to raise up men to a publick frame of spirit, and so prevailed, as he procured a good sum of money to be raised to set on foot the fishing business, to the value of [blank,] and wrote into England to raise as much more. The intent was to set up a magazine of all provisions and other necessaries for fishing, that men might have things at hand, and for reasonable prices; whereas now the merchants and seamen took advantage to sell at most excessive rates, (in many things two for one, &c.)

Mr. Batchellor of Sagus was convented before the magistrates. The cause was, for that, coming out of England with a small body of six or seven persons, and having since received in many more at Sagus, and contention growing between him and the greatest part of his church, (who had, with the rest, received him for their pastor,) he desired dismission for himself and his first members, which being granted, upon supposition that he would leave the town, (as he had given out,) he with the said six or seven persons presently ||renewed|| their old ||[2]covenant,|| intending to raise another church in Sagus; whereat the ||[3]most|| and chief of the town being offended, for that it would cross their intentions of calling Mr. Peter or some other minister, they complained to the magistrates, who, foreseeing

||removed|| ||[2]covert|| ||[3]rest||

1 Abundant cause for rejoicing at the failure of this tyrannical order, by which the services of Williams would have been transferred to England, is found in the progress of the life of the founder of Providence.

2 If it be intended by the author to mention this as matter of felicitation, it probably was because the journey was performed alone.

the distraction which was like to come by this course, had forbidden him to proceed in any such church way, until the cause were considered by the other ministers, &c. But he refused to desist. Whereupon they sent for him, and upon his delay, day after day, the marshal was sent to fetch him. Upon his appearance and submission, and promise to remove out of the town within three months, he was discharged.

18.] Mr. Vane and Mr. Peter, finding some distraction in the commonwealth, arising from some difference in judgment, and withal some alienation of affection among the magistrates and some other persons of quality, and that hereby factions began to grow among the people, some adhering more to the old governour, Mr. Winthrop, and others to the late governour, Mr. Dudley,—the former carrying matters with more lenity, and the latter with more severity,—they procured a meeting, at Boston, of the governour, deputy, Mr. Cotton, Mr. Hooker, Mr. Wilson, and there was present Mr. Winthrop, Mr. Dudley and themselves; where, after the Lord had been sought, Mr. Vane declared the occasion of this meeting, (as is before noted,) and the fruit aimed at, viz. a more firm and friendly uniting of minds, &c. especially of the said Mr. Dudley and Mr. Winthrop, as those upon whom the weight of the affairs did lie, &c. and therefore desired all present to take up a resolution to deal freely and openly with the parties, and they each with other, that nothing might be left in their breasts, which might break out to any jar or difference hereafter, (which they promised to do.) Then Mr. Winthrop spake to this effect: that when it pleased Mr. Vane to acquaint him with what he had observed, of the dispositions of men's minds inclining to the said faction, &c. it was very strange to him, professing solemnly that he knew not of any breach between his brother Dudley and himself, since they were reconciled long since, neither did he suspect any alienation of affection in him or others from himself, save that, of late, he had observed, that some new comers had estranged themselves from him, since they went to dwell at Newtown; and so desired all the company, that, if they had seen any thing amiss in his government or otherwise, they would deal freely and faithfully with him, and for his part he promised to take it in good part, and would endeavour, by God's grace, to amend it. Then Mr. Dudley spake to this effect: that for his part he came thither a mere patient, not with any intent to charge his brother Winthrop with any thing; for though there had been formerly some differences and breaches between them, yet they had been healed, and, for his part, he was not willing to renew them again; and so left it to others to utter their own complaints. Whereupon the governour, Mr. Haynes, spake to this effect: that Mr. Winthrop and himself had been always in good terms, &c.; therefore he was loath to give any offence to him, and he hoped that, considering what the end of this meeting was, he would take it in good part, if he did deal openly and freely, as his manner ever was. Then he spake of one or two passages, wherein he conceived, that [he] dealt too remissly in point of justice; to which Mr. Winthrop answered, that his speeches and carriage had been in part mistaken; but withal professed, that it was his judgment, that, in the infancy of plantations, justice should be administered with more lenity than in a settled state, because people were then more apt to transgress, partly of ignorance of new laws and orders, partly through oppression of business and other straits; but, if it might be made clear to him, that it was an errour, he would be ready to take up a stricter course. Then the ministers were desired to consider of the question by the next morning, and to set down a rule in the case. The next morning they delivered their several reasons, which all ||sorted|| to this conclusion, that strict discipline, both in criminal offences and in martial affairs, was more needful in plantations than in a settled state, as tending to the honour and safety of the gospel. Whereupon Mr. Winthrop acknowledged, that he was convinced that he had failed in over much lenity and remissness, and would endeavour (by God's assistance) to take a more strict course hereafter. Whereupon there was a renewal of love amongst them, and articles drawn to this effect:

1. That there should be more strictness used in civil government and military discipline.

2. That the magistrates should (as far as might be) ripen their consultations beforehand, that their vote in publick might bear (as the voice of God.)

3. That, in meetings out of court, the magistrates should not discuss the business of parties in their presence, nor deliver their opinions, &c.

4. That trivial things, &c. should be ||[2]ended|| in towns, &c.

5. If differences fall out among them in publick meetings, they shall observe these rules:

1. Not to touch any person differing, but speak to the cause.

2. To express their difference in all modesty and due respect to the court and such as differ, &c.

||served|| ||[2]ordered||

3. Or to propound their difference by way of question.
4. Or to desire a deferring of the cause to further time.
5. After sentence, (if all have agreed,) none shall intimate his dislike privately; or, if one dissent, he shall sit down, without showing any further distaste, publickly or privately.
6. The magistrates shall be more familiar and open each to other, and more frequent in visitations, and shall, in tenderness and love, admonish one another, (without reserving any secret grudge,) and shall avoid all jealousies and suspicions, each seeking the honour of another, and all, of the court, not opening the nakedness of one another to private persons; in all things seeking the safety and credit of the gospel.
7. To honour the governour in submitting to him the main direction and ordering the business of the court.
8. One assistant shall not seem to gratify any man in undoing or crossing another's proceedings, without due advice with him.
9. They shall grace and strengthen their under officers in their places, &c.
10. All contempts against the court, or any of the magistrates, shall be specially noted and punished; and the magistrates shall appear more solemnly in publick, with attendance, apparel, and open notice of their entrance into the court.[1]

[Very large blank.]

Mo. 12. 1.] Mr. Shepherd, a godly minister, come lately out of England, and divers other good Christians, intending to raise a [2]church body, came and acquainted the magistrates therewith, who gave their approbation. They also sent to all the neighbouring churches for their elders to give their assist-

---

1 Though several principles of sound policy were established, the general result of this conference must, I think, be regretted. When the administration of Winthrop was impeached by Gov. Haynes for too great lenity, it seems natural that such severe tempers as Dudley, and Vane, and Peter, should unite in the attack; and as the rest of the clergy probably agreed with their ardent brother Peter, the maxims of the first governour of the colony would be overruled; but when their united influence was strong enough to compel him to acknowledge his remissness in discipline, we are bound, as in our early history we often are, to lament the undue dictation of the church. It should be remembered, that Haynes and Hooker were, at this very time, preparing to establish themselves as the Moses and Aaron of a new plantation; and they might *decently* have left Massachusetts to be governed by rules, which, though not always observed, had been found beneficial by the earlier inhabitants.

2 As the former church preferred to remove to Connecticut in its corporate state, a new church was gathered, of necessity, in their place at Newtown. The same formality, it will be seen, was followed at Dorchester. Yet I cannot doubt, that several old members of both remained.

ance, at a certain day, at Newtown, when they should constitute their body. Accordingly, at this day, there met a great assembly, where the proceeding was as followeth:

Mr. Shepherd and two others (who were after to be chosen to office) sate together in the elder's seat. Then the elder of them began with prayer. After this, Mr. Shepherd prayed with deep confession of sin, &c. and exercised out of Eph. v. —that he might make it to himself a holy, &c.; and also opened the cause of their meeting, &c. Then the elder desired to know of the churches assembled, what number were needful to make a church, and how they ought to proceed in this action. Whereupon some of the ancient ministers, conferring shortly together, gave answer: That the scripture did not set down any certain rule for the number. Three (they thought) were too few, because by Matt. xviii. an appeal was allowed from three; but that seven might be a fit number. And, for their proceeding, they advised, that such as were to join should make confession of their faith, and declare what work of grace the Lord had wrought in them; which accordingly they did, Mr. Shepherd first, then four others, then the elder, and one who was to be deacon, (who had also prayed,) and another member. Then the covenant was read, and they all gave a solemn assent to it. Then the elder desired of the churches, that, if they did approve them to be a church, they would give them the right hand of fellowship. Whereupon Mr. Cotton, (upon short speech with some others near him,) in the name of their churches, gave his hand to the elder, with a short speech of their assent, and desired the peace of the ||Lord Jesus|| to be with them. Then Mr. Shepherd made an exhortation to the rest of his body, about the nature of their covenant, and to stand firm to it, and commended them to the Lord in a most heavenly prayer. Then the elder told the assembly, that they were intended to choose Mr. Shepherd for their pastor, (by the name of the brother who had exercised,) and desired the churches, that, if they had any thing to except against him, they would impart it to them before the day of ordination. Then he gave the churches thanks for their assistance, and so left them to the Lord.

At the last general court it was referred to the military commissioners to appoint colours for ||2every|| company; who did accordingly, and left out the cross in all of them,[1] appointing

||Lord's presence|| ||2each||

1 When the parliament, in arms against the king, continued the use of this idolatrous emblem, by order of our court, in a few years, the red cross was

the king's arms to be put into that of Castle Island, and Boston to be the first company.

[Large blank.]

3.] Mr. John Maverick, teacher of the church of Dorchester, died, being near sixty years of age. He was a [blank] man of a very humble spirit, and faithful in furthering the work of the Lord here, both in the churches and civil state.

24.] Mr. Winslow of Plimouth came to treat with those of Dorchester about their land at Connecticut, which they had taken from them. It being doubtful whether that place ||were|| within our patent or not, the Plimouth men, about three years since, had treaty with us about joining in erecting a plantation and trade there. We thought not fit to do any thing then, but gave them leave to go on. Whereupon they bought a portion of land of the Indians, and built a house there, and the Dorchester men (without their leave) were now setting down their town in the same place; but, after, they desired to agree with them; for which end Mr. ||2Winslow|| came to treat with them, and demanded one sixteenth part of their lands, and £100, which those of Dorchester not consenting unto, they brake off, those of Plimouth expecting to have due recompense after, by course of justice, if they went on. But divers resolved to quit the place, if they could not agree with those of Plimouth.[1]

[Large blank.]

25.] The distractions about the churches of Salem and Sagus, and the removal of other churches, and the great scarcity of corn, &c. occasioned a general fast to [be] proclaimed, which, because the court was not at hand, was moved by the elders of the churches, and assented unto by the ministers. The church of Boston renewed their covenant this day, and made a large explanation of that which they had first entered into, and acknowledged such failings as had fallen out, &c.

Mo. 1. 8.] A man's servant in Boston, having stolen from his master, and being threatened to be brought before the magistrates, went and hanged himself. Herein three things ||3were|| observable: 1. That he was a very profane fellow, given to cursing, &c. and did use to [go] out of the assembly,

||was|| ||2Wilson|| ||3are||

---

restored, " till the state of England shall alter the same, which we much desire." Hazard, I. 554. I suppose the desire abated as the royal cause was depressed; for the banner was the same of the godly and the malignants.

1 Some reasonable satisfaction to the Plimouth people, as we learn from Trumbull, I. 66, flowed from this high sense of equity.

upon the Lord's day, to rob his master. 2. The manner of his death, being with a small codline, and his knees touching the floor of the chamber, and one coming in when he was scarce dead, (who was a maid, and while she went to call out, &c. he was past recovery.) 3. His discontent, arising from the long time he was to serve his master, (though he were well used.) The same day came a letter from his father, out of the Bermuda, with money to buy out his time, &c.

The Rebecka came from Bermuda with thirty thousand weight of potatoes, and store of oranges and ||limes,|| which were a great relief to our people; but their corn was sold to the West Indies three months before. Potatoes were bought there for two shillings and eight pence §the bushel,§ and sold here for two pence the pound.[1]

11.] Some occasions of difference had fallen out between the church of Charlton and Mr. James, their pastor. The teacher, Mr. Simmes, and the most of the brethren, had taken offence at divers speeches of his, (he being a very melancholick man, and full of causeless jealousies, &c.) for which they had dealt with him, both privately and publickly; but, receiving no satisfaction, they wrote to all the neighbouring churches for their advice and help in the case, who, sending chosen men, (most elders,) they met there this day, and finding the pastor very faulty, yet because they had not proceeded with him in a due order,—for of the two witnesses produced, one was the accuser,—they advised, that, if they could not comfortably close, himself and such as stood on his part, (if they would,) should desire dismission, which should be granted them, for avoiding extremities; but if he persisted, &c. the church should cast him out.

30.] Mr. Allerton returned in his pinnace from the French at Penobscott. His bark was cast upon an island, and beat out her keel, and so lay ten days; yet he gate help from Pemaquid, and mended her, and brought her home.

Mr. Wither, in a vessel of fifty tons, going to Virginia, was cast away upon Long Island with a W. N. W. wind. The company (being about thirty) were, most of them, very profane persons, and in their voyage did much reproach our colony, vowing they would hang, drown, or, &c. before they would come hither again. Seven were drowned in landing; some gate in a small boat to the Dutch plantation; two were killed by the Indians, who took all such goods as they left on shore.

||lemons||

---

1 For so small a vessel, this was a very good adventure.

Those who escaped, went towards Virginia in a Dutch bark, and were never heard of after ; but were thought to be wrecked, by some Dutch pails, &c. which were found by the Indians thereabout.

Mo. 2. 1.] Mr. [1]Mather and others, of Dorchester, intending to begin a new church there, (a great part of the old one being gone to Connecticut,) desired the approbation of the other churches and of the magistrates ; and, accordingly, they assembled this day, and, after some of them had given proof of their gifts, they made confession of their faith, which was approved of ; but proceeding to manifest the work of God's

---

1 This was the father of Increase Mather, president of Harvard College, who was father of the more celebrated Cotton Mather, a name that will forever be perpetuated, while the strange contents of the Magnalia, in which are equally striking his voracious appetite and ill digestion of learning, excites the curiosity of antiquaries. Of all three sufficient accounts will be found in the Biographical Dictionary of Allen, and better still in that of Eliot. Three other sons of Richard, the gentleman named in our text, were clergymen, and are mentioned in these works, as is also a great grandson, who was a minister in Boston ; but on them Allen is more minute than Eliot. Richard and his wife, Katharine, were received into Boston church 25 October preceding. He married, in his old age, the widow of the *great* Cotton, and his son, Increase, married a daughter, whence the author of the Magnalia obtained his name of baptism. From the Records of Dorchester First Church I extract this notice :

"*Richard Mather. Anagram, A third Charmer.*

Third in New England's Dorchester
Was this ordained minister ;
Second to none for fruitfulness,
Ability and usefulness.
Divine his charms, years seven times seven,
Wise to win souls from earth to heaven.
Prophet's rewards he gains above,
But great's our loss by his remove.

Epitaph.

Sacred to God, his servant Richard Mather ;
Sons like him, good and great, did call him father.
Hard to discern a difference in degree
'Twixt his bright learning and high piety.
Short time his sleeping dust lies covered down ;
So can't his soul, or his deserved renown.
From's birth six lustres and a jubilee
To his repose ; but laboured hard in thee,
O Dorchester, four more than thirty years.
His sacred dust with thee thine honour rears.

Obiit April 22, 1669."

Other lines, of equal value, may be seen in Johnson, lib. I. c. 32.

grace in themselves, the churches, by their elders, and the magistrates, &c. thought them not meet, at present, to be the foundation of a church; and thereupon they were content to forbear to join till further consideration. The reason was, for that most of them (Mr. Mather and one more excepted) had ||builded|| their comfort of salvation upon unsound grounds, viz. some upon dreams and ravishes of spirit by fits; others upon the reformation of their lives; others upon duties and performances, &c.; wherein they discovered three special errours: 1. That they had not come to hate sin, because it was filthy, but only left it, because it was hurtful. 2. That, by reason of this, they had never truly closed with Christ, (or rather Christ with them,) but had made use of him only to help the imperfection of their sanctification and duties, and not made him their sanctification, wisdom, &c. 3. They expected to believe by some power of their own, and not only and wholly from Christ.

Those of Dorchester, who had removed their cattle to Connecticut before winter, lost the greatest part of them this winter; yet some, which came late, and could not be put over the river, lived very well all the winter without any hay. The people also were put to great straits for want of provisions. They eat acorns, and malt, and grains. They lost near £2000 worth of cattle.

7.] At a general court it was ordered, that a certain number of the magistrates should be chosen for life;[1] (the reason was, for that it was showed from the word of God, &c. that the principal magistrates ought to be for life.) Accordingly, the 25th of the 3d mo. John Winthrop and Thomas Dudley were chosen to this place, and Henry Vane, by his place of governour, was president of this council for his year.[2] It was likewise ordered, that quarter courts should be kept in several places for ease of the people, and, in regard of the ||[2]scarcity||

||burdened|| ||[2]streights||

---

[1] Only three years did this council for life subsist. The occasion of the establishment failed with the increase of the troubles in England; and though *the word of God* showed its propriety, jealousy was caused against the body of the magistrates, who easily avoided the unpopularity. See Hubbard, 244, who, however, copied but partially the account furnished by our author of the proceedings of the court in May, 1639. The object of this change in the constitution, I discover, not in the holy scriptures, but in Cotton's epistle to Lord Say. It was, to tempt over here some of the peers, and other leading men, who might expect at home, in due season, to be raised to the upper house, by assuring them of an equal tenure of power on this side of the ocean.

[2] This sentence is in Winthrop's margin.

of victuals, the remote towns should send their votes by proxy[1] to the court of elections; and that no church, &c. should be allowed, &c. that was gathered without consent of the churches and the magistrates.

Mr. [2]Benjamin's house burnt, and £100 in goods lost.

12.] The Charity of Dartmouth, of one hundred and twenty tons, arrived here laden with provisions. She came in with a strong N. W. wind, and was in great danger to have been lost between Allerton Point and Natascott; but the Lord, in mercy to his people, delivered her, after she had struck twice, and upon the ||ebb.|| Mr. Peter bought all the provisions at fifty in the hundred,[3] (which saved the country £200,) and distributed them to all the towns, as each town needed.

The church of Salem was still infected with Mr. Williams his opinions, so as most of them held it unlawful to hear in the ordinary assemblies in England, because their foundation was antichristian, and we should, by hearing, hold communion with them; and some went so far as they were ready to separate from the church upon it. Whereupon the church sent two brethren, and a letter, to the elders of the other churches, for their advice in three points: 1. Whether (for satisfying the weak) they might promise not to hear in England any false

||cliff||

---

1 It should be remembered, that the general court, for choice of governour and assistants, had formerly consisted of the whole body of the freemen of the jurisdiction assembled at one place, but that proxies were directed at the court in March preceding to be now received, as the Records show: "It is ordered, that the general court, to be holden in May next, for election of magistrates, &c. shall be holden at Boston, and that the towns of Ipswich, Newbury, Salem, Sagus, Weymouth and Hingham, shall have liberty to stay so many of their freemen at home, for the safety of their towns, as they judge needful; and that the said freemen, that are appointed by the town to stay at home, shall have liberty, for this court, to send their voices by proxy."

Another order, immediately following, is worth transcription: "Also it is agreed, that all other towns that are nearer shall send ten of their members out of each town to the said court, completely armed with muskets, swords, shots, &c."

2 Of this person, who, from the title given him by Winthrop, and the amount of his loss by the casualty, was, we may be certain, of some consideration in the colony, I have no other information, but that he was admitted free of the company, 6 November, 1632, lived at Watertown, and died in June, 1645. His will, made in that month, and proved in the next, is in our first volume of Probate Records, and the inventory in the second. The eldest son is named John, after his father. I presume the second or third generation removed to Norwich, Connecticut, or its neighbourhood, and perhaps the alderman of that name, in this city, may be a descendant.

3 I suppose fifty per cent. advance is meant. A letter, in the Appendix to this volume, from our author to his son, John, of 26 of this month, takes notice of this purchase, and the amount of provisions.

church. This was not thought safe, because then they would draw them to the like towards the other churches here, who were all of opinion that it was lawful, and that hearing was not ||church|| communion. 2. If they were not better, to grant them dismission to be a church by themselves. This was also opposed, for that it was not a remedy of God's ordering; neither would the magistrates allow them to be a church, being but three men and eight women; and besides it were dangerous to raise churches upon such grounds. 3. Whether they ought then to excommunicate them, if they did withdraw, &c. This was granted, yet, withal, that if they did not withdraw or run into contempt, they ought, in these matters of difference of opinion in things not fundamental nor scandalous, &c. to bear each with other.

[Very large blank.]

Mo. 3. 15.] Mr. Peter, preaching at Boston, made an earnest request to the church for [blank] things: 1. That they would spare their teacher, Mr. Cotton, for a time, that he might go through the Bible, and raise marginal notes upon all the knotty places of the scriptures. 2. That a new book of ||2martyrs|| might be made, to begin where the other had left. 3. That a form of church government might be drawn according to the scriptures. 4. That they would take order for employment of people, (especially women and children, in the winter time;) for he feared that idleness would be the ||3ruin|| both of church and commonwealth.

Here arrived a ship, called the St. Patrick, belonging to Sir Thomas [1]Wentworth, deputy of Ireland, one Palmer master. When she came near Castle Island, the lieutenant of the fort went aboard her, and made her strike her flag, which the master took as a great injury, and complained of it to the magistrates, who, calling the lieutenant before them, heard the cause, and declared to the master, that he had no commission so to do. And because he had made them strike to the fort, (which had then no colours ||4abroad||,) they tendered the master such satisfaction as he desired, which was only this, that the lieutenant, aboard their ship, should acknowledge his errour, that so all the ship's company might receive satisfaction, lest the lord deputy should have been informed, that we had offered that discourtesy to his ship, which we had never offered to any before.

||holding|| ||2blank|| ||3vice|| ||4aboard||

---

1 This friend of New England was afterwards the great Earl of Strafford, with whose labours the king was better pleased than the commons. He expiated his unpopularity on the scaffold; and the success of the unconstitutional means employed for his destruction, gave encouragement to the illegal proceedings against his master.

25.] Henry Vane, Esq. before mentioned, was chosen governour; and, because he was son and heir to a privy counsellor in England, the ships congratulated his election with a volley of great shot. The next week he invited all the masters (there were then fifteen great ships, &c.) to dinner. After they had dined, he propounded three things to them: 1. That all ships, which should come after this year, should come to an anchor before they came at the fort, except they did send their boat before, and did satisfy the commander that they were friends. 2. That, before they offered any goods to sale, they would deliver an invoice, &c. and give the governour, &c. twenty-four hours' liberty to refuse, &c. 3. That their men might not stay on shore (except upon necessary business) after sunset.—These things they all willingly condescended unto.

31.] Mr. Hooker, pastor of the church of Newtown, and the ||most|| of his congregation, went to Connecticut. His wife was carried in a horse litter; and they drove one hundred and sixty cattle, and fed of their milk by the way.

The last winter Capt. Mason died. He was the chief mover in all attempts against us, and was to have sent the general governour, and for this end was providing shipping; but the Lord, in mercy, taking him away, all the business fell on sleep, so as ships came and brought what and whom they would, without any question or controul.[1]

Divers of the ships this spring, both out of the Downs and from Holland, came in five weeks; and Mr. Ball his ship went from hence to England the 16th of January, and saw land there in eighteen days.

One Miller, master's mate in the Hector, spake to some of our people aboard his ship, that, because we had not the king's colours at our fort, we were all traitors and ||[2]rebels,|| &c. The governour sent for the master, Mr. Ferne, and acquainted him with it, who promised to deliver him to us. Whereupon we

||rest|| ||[2]robbers||

[1] We must always be careful to distinguish between the opinions and the principles of our fathers. The spirit of the age, in which religious controversy had borne or was bearing all its evil fruits, was not a spirit of charity; and the judgment of heaven was, by each party, perpetually invoked against the other. In the wilderness the errour increased, but it increased faster at home; and, much as we regret the fanaticism of the two first ages of New England, the examples of its baleful influence are more numerous and more shocking, though for a shorter season, in the native land of our ancestors. The disaster of Mason will be mentioned hereafter in more detail. Perhaps his dying declaration, of good will to our country, prevented a heavier condemnation at the tribunal of our author, as it has and will do in the judgment of later times.

sent the marshal and four serjeants to the ship for him, but the master not being aboard, they would not deliver him; whereupon the master went himself and brought him to the court, and, the words being proved against him by two witnesses, he was committed. The next day the master, to pacify his men, who were in a great tumult, requested he might be delivered to him, and did undertake to bring him before us again the day after, which was granted him, and he brought him to us at the time appointed. Then, in the presence of all the rest of the masters, he acknowledged his offence, and set his hand to a submission,[1] and was discharged. Then the governour desired the masters, that they would deal freely, and tell us, if they did take any offence, and what they required of us. They answered, that, in regard they should be examined upon their return, what colours they saw here, they did desire that the king's colours might be ||spread|| at our fort. It was answered, that we had not the king's colours. Thereupon two of them did offer them freely to us. We replied, that for our part we were fully persuaded, that the cross in the ensign was idolatrous, and therefore might not set it in our ensign; but, because the fort was the king's, and maintained in his name, we thought that his own colours might be ||[2]spread|| there. So the governour accepted the colours of Capt. Palmer, and promised they should be set up at Castle Island. We had conferred over night with Mr. Cotton, &c. about the point. The governour, and Mr. Dudley, and Mr. Cotton, were of opinion, that they might be set up at the fort upon this distinction,

||suspended|| ||[2]suspended||

---

1 If we should infer, from the language of this submission, that it was prepared by some *friendly* hand, we may still derive, from the incident, strong illustration of the regular discipline or severe police maintained by our fathers over the most refractory persons. I find it in Col. Rec. I. 179: "Whereas I, Thomas Millerd, have given out most false and reproachful speeches against his majesty's loyal and faithful subjects, dwelling in the Massachusetts Bay in America, saying that they were all traitors and rebels, and that I would affirm so much before the governour himself, which expressions I do confess (and so desire may be conceived) did proceed from the rashness and distemper of my own brain, without any just ground or cause so to think or speak, for which my unworthy and sinful carriage being called in question, I do justly stand committed,—my humble request therefore is, that, upon this my full and ingenuous recantation of this my gross failing, it would please the governour and the rest of the assistants to accept of this my humble submission, to pass by my fault, and to dismiss me from further trouble; and this my free and voluntary confession I subscribe with my hand this 9th June, 1636. Thomas Millerd." A new scribe appears in the Records for one or two pages preceding this, and the change of the culprit's name might be charged to him as fairly as to our author. But in another page he has given it like Winthrop.

that it was maintained in the king's name. [1]Others, not being so persuaded, answered, that the governour and Mr. Dudley, being two of the council, and being persuaded of the lawfulness, &c. might use their power to set them up. Some others, being not so persuaded, could not join in the act, yet would not oppose, as being doubtful, &c.

Mo. 5. 9.] The governour, &c. went to Salem.

Many ships lying ready at Natascott to set sail, Mr. Peter went down and preached aboard the Hector, and the ships going forth met with an east wind, which put them in again; whereupon he stayed and kept the sabbath with them.

5.] Mr. Buckly and Mr. Jones, two English ministers, appointed this day to gather a church at Newtown, to settle at Concord. They sent word, three days before, to the governour and deputy, to desire their presence; but they took it in ill part, and thought not fit to go, because they had not come to them before, §(as they ought to have done, and as others had done before,)§ to acquaint them with their purpose.

[Very large blank.]

§Mr. Winthrop, jun. gave £5 towards the building of the meeting-house at Charlton. I sent it by James Brown.§

20.] John Gallop, with one man more, and two little boys, coming from Connecticut in a bark of twenty tons, intending to put in at Long Island to trade, and being ||at|| the mouth of the harbour, ||[2]were|| forced, by a sudden change of the wind, to bear up for Block Island or Fisher's Island, lying before Naragansett, where they espied a small pinnace, which, drawing near unto, they found to be Mr. Oldham's (an old planter, and a member of Watertown congregation, who had been long out a-trading, having with him only two English boys, and two Indians of Naragansett.) So they hailed ||[3]him,|| but had no answer; and the deck was full of Indians, (fourteen in all,) and a canoe was gone from her full of Indians and goods. Whereupon they suspected they had killed John Oldham, and the rather, because the Indians let slip and set up sail, being two miles from shore, and the wind and tide being off the shore of the island, whereby they drove towards the main at Naragansett. Whereupon they went ahead of them, and having but two pieces and two pistols, and nothing but duck shot, they bear up near the Indians, (who stood ready armed with guns, pikes and swords,) and let fly among them, and so

||near|| ||[2]was|| ||[3]them||

---

[1] Among these others, I am sorry to observe, was Winthrop himself. See Addenda.

galled them ||as|| they all gate under hatches. Then they stood off again, and returning with a good gale, they stemmed her upon the quarter and almost overset her, which so frighted the Indians, as six of them leaped overboard and were drowned. Yet they durst not board her, but stood off again, and fitted their anchor, so as, stemming her the second time, they bored her ||2bow|| through with their anchor, and so sticking fast to her, they made divers shot through her, (being but inch board,) and so raked her fore and aft, as they must needs kill or hurt some of the Indians; but, seeing none of them come forth, they gate loose from her and stood off again. Then four or five more of the Indians leaped into the sea, and were likewise drowned. So there being now but four left in her, they boarded her; whereupon one Indian came up and yielded; him they bound and put into hold. Then another yielded, whom they bound. But John Gallop, being well acquainted with their skill to untie themselves, if two of them ||3be|| together, and having no place to keep them asunder, he threw him bound into [the] sea; and, looking about, they found John Oldham under an old seine, §stark naked,§ his head cleft to the brains, and his hand and legs cut as if they had been cutting them off, and yet warm. So they put him into the sea; but could not get to the other two Indians, who were in a little room underneath, with their swords. So they took the goods which were left, and the sails, &c. and towed the boat away; but night coming on, and the wind rising, they were forced to turn her off, and the wind carried her to the Naragansett shore.[1]

26.] The two Indians, which were with Mr. Oldham, and one other, came from Canonicus, the chief sachem of Naragansett, with a letter from Mr. Williams to the governour, to certify him what had befallen Mr. Oldham, and how grievously they were afflicted, and that Miantunnomoh was gone, with seventeen canoes and ||4two hundred||[2] men, to take revenge, &c. But, upon examination of the Indian who was brought [3]prisoner

||that|| ||2boom|| ||3were|| ||4twenty||

[1] Prince, though usually accurate in chronology to a proverb, in his introduction to Mason's History of the Pequot war, printed at Boston, 1736, republished in our 2 Hist. Coll. VIII. has, page 123, made the murder of Oldham a year earlier.

[2] It would have been no bold exertion of conjectural criticism, to change the reading of the former edition in this place, since a fleet of seventeen sail, even of canoes, would, by *twenty* persons, be weakly manned for warlike revenge; but I assure the reader the MS. is plain.

[3] He is, I presume, the one whom Gallop brought, the *first* taken, the next being thrown overboard.

to us, we found that all the sachems of the Naragansett, except Canonicus and Miantunnomoh, were the contrivers of Mr. Oldham's death; and the occasion was, because he went to make peace, and trade with the Pekods last year, as is before related. The prisoner said also, that Mr. Oldham's two Indians were acquainted with it; but, because they were sent as messengers from Canonicus, we would not imprison them. But the governour wrote back to Mr. Williams to let the Naragansetts know, that we expected they should send us the two boys, and take revenge upon the islanders; and withal gave Mr. Williams a caution to look to himself, if we should have occasion to make war upon the Naragansetts, for Block Island was under them. And the next day, 27, he wrote to Canonicus by one of those two Indians, and that he had suspicion of him, &c. yet he had sent him back, because he was a messenger, but did expect that, if he should send for the said two Indians, he should send them to us to clear themselves.

30.] Mr. Oldham's two boys were sent home by one of Miantunnomoh his men, with a letter from Mr. Williams, signifying that Miantunnomoh had caused the sachem of Niantick to send to Block Island for them; and that he had near one hundred fathom of wampom and other goods of Mr. Oldham's, which should be reserved for us; and that three of the seven, which were drowned, were sachems; and one of the two, which were hired by the sachem of Niantick, was dead also. So we wrote back to have the rest of those, which were accessory, to be sent to us, and the rest of the goods, and that he should tell Canonicus and Miantunnomoh, that we held them innocent; but that six other under-sachems were guilty, &c.

Mo. 6. 3.] Samuel Maverick, who had been in Virginia near twelve months, now returned with two pinnaces, and brought some fourteen heifers, and about eighty goats, (having lost ||above|| twenty goats by the way.) One of his pinnaces was about forty tons, of cedar, built at ||[2]Barbathes,|| and brought to Virginia by Capt. Powell, who there dying, she was sold for a small matter. There died in Virginia, (by his relation,) this last year, above eighteen hundred, and corn was there at twenty shillings the bushel, the most of the people having lived a great time of nothing but purslain, &c. It is very strange, what was related by him and many others, that, above sixty miles up James River, they dig nowhere but they find the ground full of oyster shells, and fishes' bones, &c.; ||[3]yea,|| he affirmed that he saw the bone of a whale taken out of the earth (where they digged for a well) eighteen feet deep.

||about|| ||[2]blank|| ||[3]yet||

8.] Lieut. Edward [1]Gibbons, and John [2]Higginson, with Cutshamekin, the sagamore of Massachusetts, were sent to Canonicus, to treat with him about the murder of John Oldham. 13. They returned, being very well accepted, and good success in their business. They observed in the sachem much state, great command over his men, and marvellous wisdom in his answers and the carriage of the whole treaty, clearing himself and his neighbours of the murder, and offering assistance for revenge of it, yet upon very safe and wary conditions.[3]

25.] The governour and council, having lately assembled the rest of the magistrates and ministers, to advise with them about doing justice upon the Indians for the death of Mr. Oldham, and all agreeing that it should be attempted with expedition, did this day send forth ninety men, distributed to four commanders,—Capt. John Underhill, Capt. Nathaniel [4]Turner, Ensign Jenyson, and Ensign Davenport; and over them all, as general, John Endecott, Esq. one of the assistants, was sent. They were embarked in three pinnaces, and carried two shallops and two Indians with them. They had commission to put to death the men of Block Island,[5] but to spare the women and

---

1 Edward Gibbons is named with honour in Eliot's, but not in Allen's Dictionary. He was early admitted into the Boston church, being No. 113, and his piety was probably more approved, because he had belonged to the irregular adventurers of Mount Wollaston. His name very frequently occurs in this History. He was deputy, several years, for Boston, made major general of all our forces, and, in 1650,—not 1644, as Eliot has it,—attained to the high rank of being an assistant. Death closed his services 9 December, 1654. In our Probate Records, II. 147, the inventory of his estate shows a considerable fortune for those times,—£535.6.7; yet the next information is of a special commission, resembling much those of our days, on account of its insolvency. He had been too adventurous in the great undertakings of La Tour, and was, beside, unfortunate in trade.

2 Of this gentleman, who became afterwards a minister of high respectability in his father's place at Salem, and survived all of his generation in the pulpit, good accounts are furnished by Eliot and Allen.

3 From the minuteness of his description of the Indian court, I think Johnson must have accompanied these ambassadours. See book II. c. 6, of the Wonder-working Providence.

4 He was representative, in the six first general courts, from Sagus or Lynn; but we have not, except his disaster by fire, mentioned by our author under date of January, 1636—7, any further account of him, than the present service with Endecott.

5 No degree of veneration for our fathers can lead to hesitation in coinciding with a remark I find in a copy of the first part of this History, formerly owned by Dr. Belknap, that these were "sanguinary orders." The numbers on the island must have been so small, that it was not matter of necessity; and perhaps we may attribute the cruel direction chiefly to the limited knowledge of the new governour.

children, and to bring them away, and to take possession of the island; and from thence to go to the Pequods to demand the murderers of Capt. Stone and other English, and one thousand fathom of wampom for damages, &c. and some of their children ||as|| hostages, which if they should refuse, they were to obtain it by force. No man was impressed for this service, but all went voluntaries.

26.] Miantunnomoh, sachem of Naragansett, sent a messenger to us, with a letter from Mr. Williams, to signify to us, that they had taken one of the Indians, who had broken prison and was escaped away, and had him safe for us, when we would send for him, (we had before sent to him ||2to|| that end;) and the other (being also of Block Island) he had sent away, (not knowing, as it seemed, that he had been our prisoner,) according to their promise, that they would not entertain any of that island, which should come to them. But we conceived it was rather in love to him; for he had been his servant formerly.

We sent for the two Indians. One was sent us; the other was dead before the messengers came.

A ship of one hundred and twenty tons was built at Marblehead, and called the Desire.[1]

7ber, 8.] At a general court, a levy was made of £1200 to pay the country's debts.[2]

The trade of beaver and wampom was to be farmed, and all others restrained from trading.

||for|| ||2for||

---

[1] Being furnished with the original bill of particulars for part of the outfits of this ship, signed William *Peirse*, I transcribe it: "The ship Desire, or the owners thereof, are debited to account of the bark Warwick, or her owners, for these particulars following, taken by order of the Gov. Winthrop:

1636.	Three falcons and one falconet, cwt. 38.3.0, with the old carriages, at 10*s*.6, per cwt	£21.5.10
	An old poop lanthorn, 5*s*. and a small crow of iron, 2*s*.6.	7. 6
	Two spindles for vanes, 18*d*. a pump bolt and a wooden brake, all	2. 2
	A small anchor stock, 4*s*. a pistol barrel, 6*d*. and three small tackle hooks, 12*d*. all is	5. 6
	A copper funnel, 6*s*. 2 sponge staves, a rammer and a ladle, all	11. 0
	Eleven falcon shot, 4*s*. a small bell, 3*s*	7. 0
	A small anchor, esteemed at	2.0. 0
		£24.19. 0

[2] The apportionment upon the several towns does not appear, it being left to the discretion of a committee. So heavy a contribution could not be made at once, and the order of court was, "one half at three months, and the other at a time to be appointed at the next session."

23.] A new church was gathered at Dorchester, with approbation of the magistrates and elders, &c.[1]

August 24.] John Endecott, Esq. and four captains under him, with twenty men a-piece, set sail. They arrived at Block Island the last of the same. The wind blowing hard at N. E. there went so great a surf, as they had much to do to land; and about forty Indians were ready upon the shore to entertain them with their arrows, which they shot ||oft|| at our men; but, being armed with ||[2]corslets,|| they had no hurt, only one was lightly hurt upon his neck, and another near his foot. So soon as ||[3]one man|| leaped on shore, they all fled. The island is about ten miles long, and four broad, full of small hills, and all overgrown with brush-wood of oak,—no good timber ||[4]in|| it,—so as they could not march but in one file and in the narrow paths.[2] There were two plantations, three miles in sunder, and about sixty wigwams,—some very large and fair,—and ||[5]above|| two hundred acres of corn, some gathered and laid on heaps, and the rest standing. When they had spent two days in searching the island, and could not find the Indians, they burnt their wigwams, and all their matts, and some corn, and staved seven canoes, and departed. They could not tell what men they killed, but some were wounded and carried away by their fellows.

Thence they went to the mouth of Connecticut, where they lay wind-bound four days, and taking thence twenty men and two shallops, they sailed to the Pequot harbour, where an Indian came to them in a canoe, and demanded what they were, and what they would have. The general told him, he came from the governour of Massachusetts to speak with their sachems. He told him, Sassacus was gone to Long Island. Then he bad him go tell the other sachem, &c. So he departed; and in the mean time our men landed, but with much danger, if the Indians had made use of their advantage,

||off|| ||[2]croslets|| ||[3]our men were|| ||[4]on|| ||[5]about||

[1] Being written in the margin, with the day, but not the month, given, this sentence left an uncertainty, from inspection, whether August, to which the subsequent paragraph refers, or September, which had accidentally obtained precedence, were the true date. But the Dorchester Records prove it to be the earlier month. The author wished to bring into one view the whole story of Endecott's expedition, and therefore, after the report of proceedings at September court, inserted the story of the campaign with the marginal date of the day when the fleet departed. Hubbard, 274, copying it, made a careless transcript of the day of the court in the above recital, and neglected, as he usually did, to seek collateral information.

[2] Dr. Stiles, president of Yale College, one of the most diligent antiquaries our country has furnished, made a hasty collation of some parts of the former edition with the original MS. and in this place read *passes*. I am convinced of the correctness of the text.

for all the shore was high, rugged rocks, &c. Then the messenger returned, and the Indians began to gather about our men till there were about three hundred of them; and some four hours passed while the messenger went to and fro, bringing still excuses for the sachem's not coming. At ||last|| the general told the messenger, and the rest of the Indians near, the particulars of his commission, and sent him to tell the sachem, that if he would not come to him, nor yield to those demands, he would fight with them. The messenger told him, that the sachem would meet him, if our men would lay down their arms, as his men should do their bows, &c. When the general saw they did but dally, to gain time, he bad them be gone, and shift for themselves; for they had dared the English to come fight with them, and now they were come for that purpose. Thereupon they all withdrew. Some of our men would have made a shot at them, but the general would not suffer them; but when they were gone out of musket shot, he marched after them, supposing they would have stood to it awhile, as they did to the Dutch. But they all fled, and shot at our men from the thickets and rocks, but did us no harm. Two of them our men killed, and hurt others. So they marched up to their town, and burnt all their wigwams and matts, but their corn being standing, they could not spoil it. At night they returned to their vessels, and the next day they went ashore on the west side of the river, and burnt all their wigwams, and spoiled their canoes; and so set sail and came to the Naragansett, where they landed their men, and, the 14th of 7ber, they came all safe to Boston, which was a marvellous providence of God, that not a hair fell from the head of any of them, nor any sick or feeble person among them.[1] As they came by Naragansett, Cutshamakin, an Indian, who went with them for an interpreter, who, being armed with a ||2corslet|| and a piece, had crept into a swamp and killed a Pequot, and having flayed off the skin of his head, he sent it to Canonicus, who presently sent it to all the sachems about him, and returned many thanks to the English, and sent four fathom of wampom to Cutshamakin.

The soldiers who went were all voluntaries, and had only their victuals provided, but demanded no pay. The whole charge of the voyage came to about £200. The seamen had all wages.

||length|| ||2croslet||

---

[1] Yet I find, at the general court in October, a grant of £5 to "George Munnings, in regard of the loss of his eye in the voyage to Block Island;" and an addition to that grant was made, on the same day, of the fines imposed upon members in that session of four days, for absence at the hour of meeting in the morning, amounting to £3 more.

The Naragansett men told us after, that thirteen of the Pequods were killed, and forty wounded; and but one of Block Island killed.[1]

At the last general court, order was taken to restrain the trade with the Indians, and the governour and council appointed to let it to farm, for a rent to be paid to the treasury.

The inhabitants of Boston, who had taken their farms and lots at Mount Woollaston, finding it very burdensome to have their business, &c. so far off, desired to gather a church there. Many meetings were about it. The great let was, in regard it was given to Boston for upholding the town and church there, which end would be frustrate by the removal of so many chief men as would go thither. For helping of this, it was propounded, that such as dwelt there should pay six-pence the acre, yearly, for such lands as lay within a mile of the water, and three-pence for that which lay further off.

[Very large blank.]

A ship of Barnstaple arrived here with eighty heifers.

Another from Bristol arrived, a fortnight after, with some cattle and passengers; §but she had delivered most of her cattle and passengers§ at Pascataquack for Sir Ferdinando Gorge[2] his plantation at Aquamenticus.

Canonicus sent us word of some English, whom the Pequods had killed at Saybrook; and Mr. Williams wrote, that the Pequods and Naragansetts were at ||truce,|| and that Miantunnomoh told him, that the Pequods had laboured to persuade them, that the English were minded to destroy all Indians. Whereupon we sent for Miantunnomoh to come to us.

[Very large blank.]

Another windmill was erected at Boston, and one at Charlestown; and a watermill at Salem, and another at Ipswich, and another at Newbury.[3]

[Very large blank.]

||war||

---

1 One prisoner was, by order of court, made a slave for life. If a man, he was preserved contrary to the instructions of the troops, and perhaps against his own desire.

2 I take this opportunity of printing the name as Winthrop wrote it, though usually spelt as two syllables. Probably the family had, in early times, as the old books and Collins's Peerage give it occasionally, used the writing of Gorge; and the old grammar, for the possessive case, employing the pronominal *his*, led them and all others to dignify it by the final *s*.

3 With this paragraph closes the regular sequence of narrative in the first volume of MS. For the many happy hours and days spent upon it, no slight share of veneration is by me felt and acknowledged.

§A CONTINUATION

OF THE

HISTORY

OF

NEW ENGLAND.§

1636.

8ber.] AFTER Mr. Endecott and our men were departed from the Pequod, the twenty men of Saybrook lay wind-bound there, and went to fetch some of the Indians' corn; and having fetched every man one sackful to their boat, they returned for more, and having loaded themselves, the Indians set upon them. So they laid down their corn and gave fire upon them, and the Indians shot arrows at them. The place was open for the distance of musket shot, and the Indians kept the covert, save when they ||came|| forth, about ten at a time, and discharged their arrows. The English put themselves into a single file, and some ten only (who had pieces ||[2]which|| could reach them) shot; the others stood ready to keep them from breaking in upon our men. So they continued the most part of the afternoon. Our men killed some of them, as they supposed, and hurt others; and they shot only one of ours, and he was armed,[1] all the rest being without arms. He was shot through the leg. Their arrows were all shot compass, so as our men, standing single, could easily see and avoid them; and one was employed to gather up their arrows. At last they emptied their sacks, and retired safe to their boat.

About two days after, five men of Saybrook went up the river about four miles, to fetch hay in a meadow on Pequot

||ran|| ||[2]that||

1 The meaning is, with defensive armour. Back and breast pieces of iron were then commonly worn. Those *without* arms had muskets.

side. The grass was so high as some Pequots, being hid in it, set upon our men, and one, that had hay on his back, they took; the others fled to their boat, one of them having five arrows in him, (but yet recovered.) He who was taken was a godly young man, called [blank] Butterfield; (whereupon the meadow was named Butterfield Meadow.)[1] About fourteen days after, six of Saybrook, being sent to keep the house in their corn-field, about two miles from the fort, three of them went forth on fowling, (which the lieutenant had *strictly* forbidden them.) Two had pieces, and the third only a sword. Suddenly about one hundred Indians ||came|| out of the covert, and ||[2]set|| upon them. ||[3]He|| who had the sword brake through them, (and received only two shot, not dangerous,) and escaped to the house, which was not a bow-shot off, and persuaded the other two to follow him; but they stood still till the Indians came and took them, and carried them away with their pieces. Soon after they burnt down the said house, and some outhouses and haystacks within a bow-shot of the fort, and killed a cow, and shot divers others; but they all came home with the arrows in them.

21.] Miantunnomoh, the sachem of Naragansett, (being sent for by the governour,) came to Boston with two of Canonicus's sons, and another sachem, and near twenty sanaps. Cutshamakin gave us notice the day before. The governour sent twenty musketeers to meet him at Roxbury. He came to Boston about noon. The governour had called together most of the magistrates and ministers, to give countenance to our proceedings, and to advise with them about the terms of peace. It was dinner time, and the sachems and their council dined by themselves in the same room where the governour dined, and their sanaps were sent to the inn. After dinner, Miantunnomoh declared what he had to say to us in [blank] propositions, which were to this effect: That they had always loved the English, and desired firm peace with us: That they would continue in war with the Pequods and their confederates, till they were subdued; and desired we should so do: They would deliver our enemies to us, or kill them: That if any of theirs should kill our cattle, that we would not kill them, but cause them to make satisfaction: That they would now make a firm peace, and two months hence they would send us a present.

||rose|| ||[2]shot|| ||[3]the man||

---

[1] Hubbard, 252, after faithful transcription of this narrative of the fate of Butterfield, has added from Ovid, Icarus Icariis nomina *dedit* aquis. We should be well pleased, did other parts of his volume show equal attention to the reader's gratification.

The governour told them, they should have answer the next morning.

In the morning we met again, and concluded the peace upon the articles underwritten, which the governour subscribed, and they also subscribed with their marks, and Cutshamakin also. But because we could not well make them understand the articles perfectly, we agreed to send a copy of them to Mr. Williams, who could best interpret them to them. So, after dinner, they took leave, and were conveyed out of town by some musketeers, and dismissed with a volley of shot.

THE ARTICLES.

1. A firm peace between us and our friends of other plantations, (if they consent,) and their confederates, (if they will observe the articles, &c.) and our posterities.

2. Neither party to make peace with the Pequods without the other's consent.

3. Not to harbour, &c. the Pequods, &c.

4. To put to death or deliver over murderers, &c.

5. To return our fugitive servants, &c.

6. We to give them notice when we go against the Pequods, and they to send us some guides.

7. Free trade between us.

8. None of them to come near our plantations during the wars with the Pequods, without some Englishman or known Indian.

9. To continue to the posterity of both parties.

The governour of Plimouth wrote to the deputy,[1] that we had occasioned a war, &c. by provoking the Pequods, and no more, and about the peace with the Naragansetts, &c. The deputy took it ill, (as there was reason,) and returned answer accordingly, and made it appear, 1. That there was as much done as could be expected, considering they fled from us, and we could not follow them in our armour, neither had any to guide us in their country. 2. We went not to make war upon them, but to do justice, &c.; and having killed thirteen of them for four or five, which they had murdered of ||ours,|| and destroyed sixty wigwams, &c. we were not much behind with them. 3. They had no cause to glory over us, when they saw that they could not save §themselves nor§ their houses and corn from so few of ours. 4. If we had left but one hun-

||us||

[1] Winthrop had not mentioned his own election to the second place.

dred of them living, those might have done us as much hurt as they have or are likely to do. 5. It was very likely they would have taken notice of our advantage against them, and would have sitten still, or have sought peace, if God had not deprived them of common reason.

About the middle of this month, John Tilley, master of a bark, coming down Connecticut River, went on shore in a canoe, three miles above the fort, to kill fowl; and having shot off his piece, many Indians arose out of the covert and took him, and killed one other, who was in the canoe. This Tilley was a very stout man, and of great understanding. They cut off his hands, and sent them before, and after cut off his feet. He lived three days after his hands were cut off; and themselves confessed, that he was a stout man, because he cried not in his torture.

About this time two houses were burnt, and all the goods in them, to a great value; one was one Shaw at Watertown, and the other one Jackson of Salem, both professors, and Shaw the day before admitted of the former church. This was very observable in [1]Shaw, that he concealed his estate, and made show as if he had been poor, and ||was|| not clear of some unrighteous passages.

One Mrs. [2]Hutchinson, a member of the church of Boston, a woman of a ready wit and bold spirit, brought over with her two dangerous errours: 1. That the person of the Holy Ghost dwells in a justified person. 2. That no sanctification can help to evidence to us our justification.—From these two grew many branches; as, 1, Our union with the Holy Ghost, so as a Christian remains dead to every spiritual action, and hath no gifts nor graces, other than such as are in hypocrites, nor any other sanctification but the Holy Ghost himself.

[Large blank.]

||went||

1 In the original first stood *both*, instead of *Shaw; they*, instead of *he; their*, instead of *his; they*, instead of *he;* and *were*, instead of *was*, in the progress of the sentence. The alteration was made by Winthrop. We may therefore conclude, that the report against Jackson's character was unfounded, and that he did not *deserve* to have his house and goods burnt by accident.

2 Being descended from this lady, the editor feels not at liberty to indulge his pen in a memoir, of which all benefit is indeed anticipated by the more honourable labours of a nearer relative, the late Gov. Hutchinson. Time has abated all the venom of the accusations against her, and the futility of most of them will forever forbid the inquiry of reason. Mather, in the middle age, and Eliot, of the present, 1 Hist. Coll. IX. 28—30, give her great credit, as in our text, for powers of mind; and all are strengthened by the orthodox contemporary, Johnson, lib. I. c. 42, who calls her "the masterpiece of women's wit."

There joined with her in these opinions a brother of hers, one Mr. [1]Wheelwright, a silenced minister sometimes in England.

[Large blank.]

25.] The other ministers in the bay, hearing of these things, came to Boston at the time of ||a|| general court, and entered conference in private with them, to the end they might know the certainty of these things; that if need were, they might write to the church of Boston about them, to prevent (if it were possible) the dangers, which seemed hereby to hang over that and the rest of the churches. At this conference, Mr. Cotton was present, and gave satisfaction to them, so as he agreed with them all in the point of sanctification, and so did Mr. Wheelwright; so as they all did hold, that sanctification did help to evidence justification. The same he had ||[2]delivered|| plainly in publick, divers times; but, for the indwelling of the person of the Holy Ghost, he held that still, *as some others of the ministers did,* but not ||[3]union|| with the person of the Holy Ghost, *(as Mrs. Hutchinson and others did,)* so as to amount to a personal union.

[Blank.]

||the|| ||[2]declared|| ||[3]very man||

---

1 A just estimate of this distinguished gentleman may readily be formed from the pages of this History and the volumes of Hutchinson and Eliot. His long life afforded him a triumph over the injustice of intolerance, which attempted hardly any other cure for his errours than banishment. Hubbard marks his death about 1681. Some pleasure may be derived from a jeu de mot of Johnson, to whom we are usually obliged to refer for less valuable qualities. In his verses to the honour of Wilson, alluding to the opposition he encountered from the supporters of Mrs. Hutchinson, the author of Wonder-working Providence of Zion's Saviour says,

"They thee deprave, thy ministry despise;
By thy thick utterance seek to call men back
From hearing thee: but Christ for thee did rise,
And turned the *wheel-right* over them to crack."

From our Town Records I find, that a daughter of Wheelwright was, in December, 1660, married to Samuel Maverick, soon after one of the royal commissioners to New England. Cotton Mather says, Belknap's New Hampshire, III. Appendix 1., that a daughter of this pilgrim informed him, that her father came in the same ship with Whiting of Lynn; and if this were his first appearance in our country, the authenticity of the famous Indian deed to him, for which, in the same letter, the credulous author of the Magnalia argues, must be rejected. That letter is well worth reading, as an admirable specimen of feeble argument; but the other evidence in the cause is irresistible; and it is not necessary to found an opinion on the incompetency of the advocate. Wheelwright and his wife, Mary, were admitted of Boston church 12 June, 1636, which was soon after arrival.

Mr. Cotton, being requested by the general court, with some other ministers, to assist some of the magistrates in compiling a body of fundamental laws, did, this court, present a model of Moses his judicials, compiled in an exact method, which were taken into further consideration till the next general court.

30.] Some of the church of Boston, being of the opinion of Mrs. Hutchinson, had laboured to have Mr. Wheelwright to be called to be a teacher there. It was propounded the last Lord's day, and was moved again this day for resolution. [1]One of the church stood up and said, he could not consent, &c. His reason was, because the church being well furnished already with able ministers, whose spirits they knew, and whose labours God ||had|| blessed in much love and sweet peace, he thought it not fit (no necessity urging) to put the welfare of the church to the least hazard, as he feared they should do, by calling in one, whose spirit they knew not, and one who seemed to dissent in judgment, and instanced in two points, which he delivered in a late exercise there: 1. That a believer was more than a creature. 2. That the person of the Holy Ghost and a believer were united. Hereupon the governour spake, that he marvelled at this, seeing Mr. Cotton had lately approved his doctrine. To this Mr. Cotton answered, that he did not remember the first, and desired Mr. Wheelwright to explain his meaning. He denied not the points, but showed upon what occasion he delivered them. Whereupon, there being an ||[2]endeavour|| to make a reconciliation, the first replied, that, although Mr. Wheelwright and himself might likely agree about the point, and though he thought reverendly of his godliness and abilities, so as he could be content to live under such a ministry; yet, seeing he was apt to raise doubtful disputations, he could not consent to choose him to that place. Whereupon the church gave way, that he might be called to a new church, to be gathered at Mount Woollaston, ||[3]now|| Braintree.[2]

Divers of the brethren took offence at the said speech against Mr. Wheelwright; whereupon the same brother spake in the congregation the next day to this effect: That, hearing that some of the brethren were offended at his former speech, and for that offences were dangerous, he was desirous to give satisfaction. The offence he said was in three things: 1. For

||hath|| ||[2]indication|| ||[3]near||

---

[1] This, we cannot doubt, was Winthrop himself.

[2] A later hand, I suspect Mather's, wrote the two last words.

that he had charged the brother in publick, and for a thing so long since delivered, and had not first dealt with him privately. For this he acknowledged it was a failing; but the occasion was, that, when he heard the points delivered, he took them in a good sense, as spoken figuratively, seeing the whole scope of his doctrine was sound, and savouring of the spirit of God; but hearing, very lately, that he was suspected to hold such opinions, it caused him to think, he spake as he meant. The 2d cause of offence was, that in his speech appeared some bitterness. For that he answered, that they well knew his manner of speech ||was|| always earnest in things, which he conceived to be serious; and professed, that he did love that brother's person, and did ||[2]honour|| the gifts and graces of God in him. The 3d was, that he had charged him to have held things which he did not. For this he answered, that he had spoken since with the said brother; and for the two points,—that ||[3]a|| believer should be more than a creature, and that there should be a personal union between the Holy Ghost and a believer,—he had denied to hold either of them; but by necessary consequence, he doth hold them both; for he holds, (said he,) that there is a real union with the person of the Holy Ghost, and then of necessity it must be personal, and so a believer must be more than a creature, viz. God-man, even Christ Jesus. For though, in a true union, the two terms may still remain the same, &c. as between husband and wife, he is a man still, and she a woman, (for the union is only in sympathy and relation,) yet in a real or personal union it is not. Now, whether this were agreeable to the doctrine of the church or not, he left to the church to judge; hoping that the Lord would direct our teacher to clear these points fully, as he had well done, in good measure, already. Withal he made this request to the ||[4]brother,|| (which he said he did seriously and affectionately,) that, seeing these ||[5]variances|| grew (and some estrangement withal) from some words and phrases, which were of ||[6]human invention,|| and tended to doubtful disputation, rather than to edification, and had no footing in scripture, nor had been in use in the purest churches for three hundred years after Christ,—that, for the peace of the church, &c. they might be forborn; (he meant, person of the Holy Ghost, and real union;) and concluded, that he did not intend to dispute the matter, (as not having place or calling thereunto then;) yet, if any brother desired to see what light he walked by, he would be ready to impart it to him. How this was

||as|| ||[2]know|| ||[3]the|| ||[4]teacher|| ||[5]uneasinesses|| ||[6]known intention||

taken by the congregation, did not appear, for no man spake to it.[1]

A day or two after, the same brother wrote his mind fully, with such scriptures and arguments as came to hand, and sent it to Mr. Cotton.

(9.) 8.] A new church was gathered at Sagus, now Lynn. The governour and deputy were not there, being letted by the coming in of a ship, and other occasions. It held the company two days, Mr. [2]Whiting, who was to be the pastor, being very unskilful in church matters, and those who were to be members not fit for such a work. At last six were accepted, with Mr. Whiting, but with much ado.

12.] A commission was sent out of the chancery in England to some private men here, to examine witnesses in a cause depending ||there;|| but nothing was done in it, nor any return made.[3]

[Large blank.]

||here||

---

1 On this subject the prudent advice of our author has, in general, prevailed in New England; and the personality of the Holy Spirit, with other metaphysical or barbarous terminology "of human invention," has seldom, before the present age, entered into the controversial labours of our divines, for whom the language of the scriptures, in their original tongues, has appeared sufficient. But Winthrop was less judicious in his conduct than in advice; for, having obtained from Wheelwright a denial of his holding the two dangerous points, that a believer was more than a creature, and that there was a personal union between the Holy Spirit and a believer, he should have been contented. Unhappily he proceeded to prove, that, by *necessary consequence*, both opinions were maintained by the heresiarch of Braintree. We shall never have peace in the church, if muddy-headed religionists are to be made answerable for inferences, which themselves do not deduce from their dogmas. "*Calvinism run to seed*" became, in the view of many Christians, a convenient periphrase for antinomianism; and the creed of the predestinarian, to which one or more of the articles of the Church of England makes near, and the catechism of the Westminster Assembly a nearer approach, is often charged with all the dangerous absurdities of the heathen notions of fate.

2 We may be very confident, that this notion of our author, of the *unskilfulness* in church matters of the Rev. Samuel Whiting, is an errour. He had been in the country but a few months, and Winthrop probably contracted a prejudice against him from his going so soon to join the company of poor Bachellor, which had been subjected to animadversion for its irregularities. It is strange, that Eliot omitted him in his Dictionary; but his memory is duly honoured by Hubbard, 194, Johnson, lib. I. c. 38, and, above all, Mather, III. 156. In the great controversy about the Third, or Old South Church, in Boston, he and his son, Samuel, the minister of Billerica, were much engaged. See Hutch. I. 247—251. He is miscalled Lambert by Neal, History of Puritans, II. 304. It was from regard to Whiting, perhaps, that the town received its name of Lynn, as he had been a preacher in the borough of Lynn Regis in Norfolk.

3 An unreasonable, though natural jealousy, may be imagined as the ground of this neglect. It might have come to private men from any court of a foreign nation.

17.] Two ships arrived here from London, and one a week before. They were full of passengers,—men, women and children. One of them had been from London twenty-six weeks, and between land and land ||eighteen|| weeks; (the other two something less time;) their beer all spent and leaked out a month before their arrival, so as they were forced to stinking water (and that very little) mixt with sack or vinegar, and their other provisions very short and bad. Yet, through the great providence of the Lord, they came all safe on shore, and most of them sound, and well liking. They had continual tempests, and when they were near the shore, (being brought two or three days with a ||[2]strong|| east wind,) the weather was so thick all that time, ||[3]as|| they could not make land, and the seamen were in great perplexity, when on ||[4]the|| sudden the fog cleared, so as they saw Cape Ann fair on their starboard bow, and presently grew thick again; yet by their compass they made their harbour. There were aboard that ship two godly ministers, Mr. Nathaniel [1]Rogers and Mr. [2]Partridge,

||sixteen|| ||[2]stronger|| ||[3]that|| ||[4]a||

---

1 Hubbard, 554, thinks "it might be honour enough to say, that he was the son of Mr. John Rogers, the famous preacher of Dedham." His probable descent from one of the most celebrated of that "noble army of martyrs" affords less cause for our veneration, than we should readily bestow on the progenitor of a numerous list of men, who, in several generations, are esteemed among the worthies of New England. His son, John, was president of Harvard College; and a grandson and great grandson were ministers of the same church in Ipswich, which was thus, by three degrees, supplied for over one hundred and twenty years. Other descendants have been distinguished for useful services. Eliot, who is very copious on this family of learned men, quoting the Magnalia, refers to a particular publication of the first Nathaniel; but the highest subject of praise in it is omitted. The tract is in the abundant collection at the Boston Athenæum. It is a letter written from this country to a member of parliament, 17 December, 1643; and though, of course, it favoured the cause of liberty and reformation, yet it contains a few lines of merited censure against the dishonourable aspersions on the king by Mercurius Britannicus. In that inflammatory gazette,—a perfect copy of which, containing 130 numbers, from 29 August, 1643, to 18 May, 1646, perhaps a unique in America, and certainly very rare in England, is in my possession,—the number 46, 5 August, 1644, bestows some vulgar abuse on the moderation of our peacemaker. Though Rogers's letter was printed under the authority of parliament, being licensed by Calamy, one of the great Westminster divines, the newspaper affects to consider it as part of an Oxford or royal plot, and insinuates, that the king had agents in New England. Such is the reception of truth and decency in a civil war. Mather's name is written in the first page of this curious belligerent volume; but perhaps the author of the Magnalia, in his life of Rogers, thought it unworthy of the amiable pilgrim to record with honour the gentle remonstrance in favour of his sovereign.

2 This gentleman is honoured in the Magnalia, Morton's Memorial, and Eliot's and Allen's Dictionaries. He was the first minister of Duxbury, and

and many good people in that and the other ships; and we had prayed earnestly for them; (for a small pinnace of thirty tons, which came out with them, and was come in three weeks before, brought us news of their coming.) In one of the other ships the passengers had but half a pint of drink for a day, fourteen days together; yet, through the Lord's mercy, did all well. One of the ships was overset in the night by a sudden gust, and lay so half an hour, yet righted of herself.

Cattle were grown to high rates;—a good cow, £25 or £30; a pair of bulls or oxen, £40. Corn was ||now|| at 5*s.* the bushel, and much rye was sown with the plough this year, for about thirty ploughs were at work. ||[2]Bread||[1] was at 9 and 10*s.* the C.; carpenters at 3*s.* the day, and other ||[3]workmen|| accordingly.

Things went not well at Connecticut. Their cattle did, many of them, cast their young, as they had done the year before.

[Large blank.]

Mons. D'Aulney, captain of Penobscott or Pentagonett, returned answer to the governour's letter, wherein he professed, that they claimed no further than to Pemaquid, nor would, unless he had further order; and that he supposed, that the cause why he had no order, &c. was, that the English ambassadour had dealt effectually with the cardinal of France for settling the limits for our peace, &c.

The governour, Mr. Vane, a wise and godly gentleman, held, with Mr. Cotton and many others, the indwelling of the person of the Holy Ghost in a believer, and went so far beyond the rest, as to maintain a personal union with the Holy Ghost; but the deputy, with the pastor and divers others, denied both; and the question proceeded so far by disputation, (in writing, for the peace sake of the church, which all were tender of,) as at length they could not find the person of the Holy Ghost in scripture, nor in the primitive churches three hundred years after Christ. So that, all agreeing in the chief matter of substance, viz. that the Holy Ghost is God, and that he doth dwell in the believers, (as the Father and Son both

||near|| ||[2]Board|| ||[3]work||

needs only the mention, which Judge Davis has given him. Johnson bestows on him and Rogers verses of less value for their beauty than justice. An honourable descendant at Duxbury is well known for his services in our revolutionary war.

1 I make this alteration by conjecture; for the MS. looks very much like the reading of the former edition, which was ridiculous.

are said also to do,) but whether by his gifts and power only, or by any other manner of presence, seeing the scripture doth not declare it,—it was earnestly desired, that the word person might be forborn, being a term of human invention, and tending to doubtful disputation in this case.

[Large blank.]

10ber.] The governour, receiving letters from his friends in England, which necessarily required his presence there, imparted the same to the council[2] and some others; and, being thereupon resolved of his return into England, called a court of deputies, to the end he might have free leave of the country, &c. They, being assembled in court, and himself declaring the necessity of his departure, and those of the council affirming the reasons to be very urgent, though not fit to be imparted to the whole court, they desired respite to consider thereof till the morning; when one of the assistants using some pathetical passages of the loss of such a governour in a time of such danger as did hang over us, from the Indians and French, the governour brake forth into tears, and professed, that howsoever the causes propounded for his departure were such as did concern the utter ruin of his outward estate, yet he would rather have hazarded all, than have gone from them at this time, if something else had not pressed him more, viz. the inevitable danger he saw of God's judgments to come upon us for these differences and dissensions, which he saw amongst us, and the scandalous imputations brought upon himself, as if he should be the cause of all; and therefore he thought it best for him to give place for a time, &c. Upon this the court concluded, that it would not be fit to give way to his departure upon these grounds. Whereupon he recalled himself, and

---

1 So much evil has not been caused in New England, as in most other Protestant countries, by the "*terms of human invention*," not found in the scriptures, nor in the three earliest centuries of the Christian church. Our exemption is chiefly owing to the separation of church and state, which gradually proceeded after the second generation. The early *forbearing* of the personality of the Holy Ghost in their technical theology, after examination of the ante-Nicene fathers, is not more a proof of the learning, than of the moderation of the clerical leaders of Massachusetts.

2 Hubbard, 256, adds, "which at that time consisted but of two, besides himself." In this I doubt the historian of Ipswich is mistaken, and that Vane consulted with the body of assistants, not merely the standing council for life, who were part of the council of assistants. When the house of deputies assembled, as in the next sentence is told, "*those of the council*" must mean the men to whom the governour *imparted* his letters; and no suggestion can be perceived, that it was two, instead of ten or more, who had thus been honoured.

professed, that the reasons concerning his own estate were sufficient to his own satisfaction for his departure, and therefore desired the court he might have leave to go; as for the other passage, it slipped him out of his passion, and not out of judgment. Upon this the court consented, silently, to his departure. Then the question was about supply of his place. Some were of opinion, that it should be executed by the deputy; but this scruple being cast in, that if the deputy should die, then the government would be vacant, and none have power to call any court, or to preside therein, &c. it was agreed to call a court of elections for a new governour and deputy, in case the present deputy should be chose governour; and an order was made, (in regard of the season,) that such as would might send their votes by proxy, in papers sealed up and delivered to the deputies. And so this court was adjourned four days, and two days after the court of elections was to assemble. These things thus passed, divers of the congregation of Boston met together, and agreed that they did not apprehend the necessity of the governour's departure upon the reasons alleged, and sent some of them to declare the same to the court; whereupon the governour expressed himself to be an obedient child to the church, and therefore, notwithstanding the license of the court, yet, without the leave of the church, he durst not go away.

Whereupon a great part of the court and country, who understood hereof, declared their purpose to continue him still in his place, and therefore, so soon as the day of election came, and the country were assembled, it was thought the best way for avoiding trouble, &c. not to proceed to election, but to adjourn the court to the great general court in May. And so the court of deputies, &c. continued still, (for the other court was not called.)

At this court the elders of the churches were called, to advise with them about ||discovering|| and pacifying the differences among the churches in point of opinion.[1] The governour having declared the occasion to them, Mr. Dudley desired, that men would be free and open, &c. Another of the magistrates spake, that it would much further the end they came for, if men would freely declare what they held different from others, as himself would freely do, in what point soever he

||discontinuing||

[1] Notice of this consultation is not contained in the publick records, and the community would, probably, have been more quiet, had the court done no more than their secretary has preserved.

should be opposed. The governour said, that he would be content to do the like, but that he understood the ministers were about it in a church way, &c. which he spake upon this occasion: the ministers had met, a little before, and had drawn into heads all the points, wherein they suspected Mr. Cotton did differ from them, and had propounded them to him, and pressed him to a direct answer, affirmative or negative, to every one; which he had promised, and taken time for. This meeting being spoke of in the court the day before, the governour took great offence at it, as being without his privity, &c. which this day Mr. Peter told him as ||plainly|| of, (with all due reverence,) and how it had sadded the ministers' spirits, that he should be jealous of their meetings, or seem to restrain their liberty, &c. The governour excused his speech, as sudden and upon a mistake. Mr. Peter told him also, that *before he came,* within less than two years since, the churches were in peace, &c. The governour answered, that the ||2light|| of the gospel brings a sword, and the children of the bondwoman would persecute those of the freewoman. Mr. Peter also besought him humbly to consider his ||3youth,|| and short experience in the things of God, and to beware of péremptory conclusions, which he perceived him to be very apt unto. He declared further, that he had observed, both in the Low Countries and here, three principal causes of new opinions and divisions thereupon: 1. Pride, new notions lift up the mind, &c. 2. Idleness. 3. [blank.]

Mr. Wilson made a very sad speech[1] of the condition of our churches, and the ||4inevitable|| danger of separation, if these differences and alienations among brethren were not speedily remedied; and laid the blame upon these new opinions risen up amongst us, which all the magistrates, except the governour and two others, did confirm, and all the ministers but two.

In this discourse ||5one question|| arose about sanctification. Mr. Cotton, in his sermon that day, had laid down this ground, that evident sanctification was an evidence of justification, and thereupon had taught, that in cases of ||6spiritual|| desertion, true desires of sanctification was found to be sanctification; and further, if a man were laid so flat upon the ground, as he could see no desires, &c. but only, as a bruised reed, did wait at the feet of Christ, yet here was matter of comfort for this, as found to be true.

||protimely|| ||2liberty|| ||3hasty|| ||4invoidable|| ||5two questions|| ||6special||

---

[1] His speech was approved by the court, as from the record, of only two lines, about the whole controversy, at the next session, appears.

The question here grew, whether any of these, or evident sanctification, could be evidence to a man without a concurrent sight of his justification. The governour and Mr. Cotton denied it.

The speech of Mr. Wilson was taken very ill by Mr. Cotton and others of the same church, so as he and divers of them went to admonish him. But Mr. Wilson and some others could see no breach of rule, seeing he was called by the court about the same matter with the rest of the elders, and ||exhorted|| to deliver their minds freely and faithfully, both for discovering the danger, and the means to help; and the things he spake of were only in general, and such as were under a common ||²fame.|| And being questioned about his intent, he professed he did not mean Boston church, nor the members thereof, more than others. But this would not satisfy, but they called him to answer publickly, 31; and there the governour pressed it violently against him, and all the congregation, except the deputy and one or two more, and many of them with much bitterness and reproaches; but he answered them all with words of truth and soberness, and with marvellous wisdom. It was strange to see, how the common people were led, by example, to condemn him in that, which (it was very probable) divers of them did not understand,[1] nor the rule which he was supposed to have broken; and that such as had known him so long, and what good he had done for that church, should fall upon him with such bitterness for justifying himself

||expected|| ||²form||

---

1 That the subject was not well understood, may be, in our days, thought the very occasion of the bitterness, as in theological controversies is often experienced. Charity should be expected rather from those, who well comprehend any matter of doubt in the faith of the church; for only they know the reasons for both sides, and the difficulty of forming a judgment. Winthrop and Cotton, on opposite sides, were moderate. Wilson's exculpation of himself, in the text, that he did not mean the members of his own church, more than others, appears something like equivocation; for that church was the only one in the colony, wherein any considerable part of the worshippers held these deadly, unintelligible opinions. Some palliation for his timidity is easily found in the unhappy circumstance of all but two or three of the congregation being vexed at his speech, and ready to proceed hastily to censure him for it. The difference, it will be seen, in several passages of this History, was very slight between the orthodox and heretical doctrine, even when men's wits were sharpened to discover that difference; and the indistinct shadows of meaning have, in our time, almost wholly vanished. Perhaps the language of neither would now be employed in definition of the nature or extent of divine influences on the human soul. By then imputing to Cotton what he did not teach,—though his gifted hearers, Vane and Mrs. Hutchinson, might so understand him,—opportunity was afforded, however, for a synod, to perform the important service of settling, as they supposed, the faith of future generations.

in a good cause; for he was a very holy, upright man, and for faith and love inferiour to none in the country, and most dear to all men. The teacher joined with the church in their judgment of him, (not without some appearance of prejudice,) yet with much wisdom and moderation. They were eager to proceed to present censure, but the teacher staid them from that, telling them he might not do it, because some opposed it, but gave him a grave exhortation. The next day Mr. Wilson preached, notwithstanding, and the Lord so assisted him, as gave great satisfaction, and the governour himself gave publick witness to him.

One of the brethren[1] wrote to Mr. Cotton about it, and laid before him divers failings, (as he supposed,) and some reasons to justify Mr. Wilson, and dealt very plainly with him. Mr. Cotton made a very ||loving|| and gentle answer, clearing his intentions, and persisting in his judgment of Mr. Wilson's offence, laying down divers arguments for it. The said brother replied to him in like loving manner, and desired leave to show his letter to Mr. Wilson, which he readily assented unto. But for answer to his arguments, he forbore to reply to Mr. Cotton, (because he was overburdened with business,) but wrote to the two ruling elders, (whom the matter most concerned,) and, by way of defence of Mr. Wilson, answered all Mr. Cotton's arguments.

Upon these publick occasions, other opinions brake out publickly in the church of Boston,—as that the Holy Ghost dwelt in a believer as he is in heaven; that a man is justified before he believes; and that faith is no cause of justification. And others spread more secretly,—as that the letter of the scripture holds forth nothing but a covenant of works; and that the covenant of grace was the spirit of the scripture, which was known only to believers; and that this covenant of works was given by Moses in the ||2ten commandments;|| that there was a seed (viz. Abraham's carnal seed) went along in this, and there was a spirit and life in it, by virtue whereof a man might attain to any sanctification in gifts and graces, and might have ||3spiritual|| and ||4*continual*|| communion with Jesus Christ, and yet be damned. After, it was granted, that faith was before justification, but it was only passive, an empty vessel, &c.; but in conclusion, the ground of all was found to be assurance by immediate revelation.

||long|| ||2tenth commandment|| ||3special|| ||4blank||

---

1 Winthrop, by this periphrase, beyond any doubt, means himself.

All the congregation of Boston, except four or five, closed with these opinions, or the most of them; but one of the brethren wrote against them, and bore witness to the truth, together with the pastor, and very few others joined with them.

About this time the rest of the ministers, taking offence at some doctrines delivered by Mr. Cotton, and especially at some opinions, which some of his church did broach, and for he seemed to have too good an opinion of, and too much familiarity with those persons, drew out sixteen points, and gave them to him, entreating him to deliver his judgment directly in them, which accordingly he did, and many copies thereof were dispersed about. Some doubts he well cleared, but in some things he gave not satisfaction. The rest of the ministers replied to these answers, and at large showed their dissent, and the grounds thereof; and, at the next general court, held 9th of the 1st, they all assembled at Boston, and agreed to put off all lectures for three weeks, that they might bring things to ||some|| issue.

One Mr. Glover of Dorchester, having laid sixty pounds of gunpowder in bags to dry in the end of his chimney, it took fire, and some went up the chimney; other of it filled the room and passed out at a door into another room, and blew up a gable end. A maid, which was in the room, having her arms and neck naked, was scorched, and died soon after. A little child, in the arms of another, was scorched upon the face, but not killed. Two men were scorched, but not much. Divers pieces, which lay charged in several places, took fire and went off, but did no harm. The room was so dark with smoke, as those in the house could neither find door nor window, and when neighbours came in, none could see each other a good time for smoke. The house was thatched, yet took not fire; yet when the smoke was gone, many things were found burnt. Another great providence was, that three little children, being at the fire a little before, they went out to play, (though it were a very cold day,) and so were preserved.

12 mo. 22.] The lieutenant ||2of|| Saybrook, at the mouth of Connecticut, going out with nine men, armed with swords and pieces, they started three Indians, whom they pursued till they were brought into an ambush of fifty, who came upon them, and slew four of their men, and had they not drawn their swords and retired, they had been all slain. The Indians were so hardy, as they came close up to them, notwithstanding their pieces.[1]

||an|| ||2at||

[1] Trumbull, I. 76, says it was in March.

(11.) 10.] Capt. Turner's house in Sagus took fire by an oven about midnight, and was burnt down, with all that was in it, save the persons. About fourteen days since, a ship called the George of Bristol, laden with cattle and passengers, (having been some time at the Western Islands,) and having spent her mainmast about Cape Cod, and after come near Brewster's Islands, was, by N. W. winds, forced to put into Plimouth.

20.] A general fast was kept in all the churches. The occasion was, the miserable estate of the churches in Germany; the calamities upon our native country, the bishops making havock in the churches, putting down the faithful ministers, and advancing popish ceremonies and doctrines, the plague raging exceedingly, and famine and sword threatening them; the dangers of those at Connecticut, and of ourselves also, by the Indians; and the dissensions in our churches.

The differences in the said points of religion increased more and more, and the ministers of both sides (there being only Mr. Cotton of one party) did publickly declare their judgments in some of them, so as all men's mouths were full of them. And there being, 12 mo. 3, a ship ready to go for England, and many passengers in it, Mr. Cotton took occasion to speak to them about the differences, &c. and willed them to tell our countrymen, that all the strife amongst us was about magnifying the grace of God; one party seeking to advance the grace of God within us, and the other to advance the grace of God towards us, (meaning by the one justification, and by the other sanctification;) and so bade them tell them, that, if there were any among them that would strive for grace, they should come hither; and so declared some particulars. Mr. Wilson spake after him, and declared, that he knew none of the elders or brethren of the churches, but did labour to advance the free grace of God in justification, so far as the word of God required; and spake also about the doctrine of sanctification, and the use and necessity, &c. of it; by occasion whereof no man could tell (except some few, who knew the bottom of the matter) where any difference was: which speech, though it offended those of Mr. Cotton's party, yet it was very seasonable to clear the rest, who otherwise should have been reputed to have opposed free grace. Thus every occasion increased the contention, and caused great alienation of minds; and the members of Boston (frequenting the lectures of other ministers) did make much disturbance by publick questions, and objections to their doctrines, which did any way disagree from their opinions; and it began to be as common here to distinguish between men, by being under a covenant of grace or a covenant of works, as in other countries between Protestants and Papists.

February 6.] A man of Weymouth (but not of the church) fell into some trouble of mind, and in the night cried out, "Art thou come, Lord Jesus?" and with that leaped out of his bed in his shirt, and, breaking from his wife, leaped out at a high window into the snow, and ran about seven miles off, and being traced in the snow, was found dead next morning. They might perceive, that he had kneeled down to prayer in divers places.

(1.) 9.] The general court began. When any matter about these new opinions was mentioned, the court was divided; yet the greater number far were sound. They questioned the proceeding against Mr. Wilson, for his speech in the last court, but could not fasten upon such as had prejudiced him, &c.; but, by the vote of the greater party, his speech was approved, and declared to have been a seasonable advice, and no charge or accusation.

The ministers, being called to give advice about the authority of the court in things concerning the churches, &c. did all agree of these two things: 1. That no member of the court ought to be publickly questioned by a church for any speech in the court, without the license of the court. The reason was, because the court may have sufficient reason that may excuse the sin, which yet may not be fit to acquaint the church with, being a secret of state. The second thing was, that, in all such heresies or errours of any church members as are manifest and dangerous to the state, the court may proceed without tarrying for the church; but if the opinions be doubtful, &c. they are first to refer them to the church, &c.

At this court, when Mr. Wheelwright was to be questioned for a sermon, which seemed to tend to sedition, &c. near all the church of Boston presented a petition to the court for two things: 1. That as freemen they might be present in cases of judicature. 2. That the court would declare, if they might deal in cases of conscience before the church, &c. This was taken as a groundless and presumptuous act, especially at this season, and was rejected with this answer: That the court had never used to proceed §judicially,§ but it was openly; but for matter of consultation and preparation in causes, they might and would be private.

One Stephen ||Greensmith,||[1] for saying that all the ministers,

||Green||

[1] Greensmith was a person of some consequence, as we should infer from the names of his sureties, which may be seen in Addenda.

except [1]A. B. C., did teach a covenant of works, was censured to acknowledge his fault in every church, and fined £40.

Mr. Wheelwright, one of the members of Boston, preaching at the last fast, inveighed against all that walked in a covenant of works, as he described it *to be,* viz. such as maintain sanctification as an evidence of justification, &c.[2] and called them antichrists, and stirred up the people against them with much bitterness and vehemency. For this he was called ||into|| the court, and his sermon being produced, he justified it, and confessed he did mean all that walk in such a way. Whereupon the elders of the rest of the churches were called, and asked whether they, in their ministry, did walk in such a way. They all acknowledged they did. So, after much debate, the court adjudged him guilty of sedition, and also of contempt, for that the court had appointed the fast as a means of reconciliation of the differences, &c. and he purposely set himself to kindle and increase them.[3] The gover-

||before||

---

1 From the Records of the general court, I find the names to be, Cotton, Wheelwright, "and, as he thought, Mr. Hooker." His sentence required also sureties in £100. Of the payment of the fine notice will appear in Addenda.

2 This explanation is in the margin.

3 In the archives of the Historical Society, I discovered, some years since, the larger part, being the last thirty-three pages, of this inflammatory discourse, which has never been printed, and probably not read more than once or twice for a hundred and sixty years. Having no acquaintance with the hand-writing of Wheelwright, though it is an ancient MS., I am not able to ascertain, whether it be copy or original; yet it is probably original, for some comparatively modern preserver has written on a blank leaf, that it "was left in the hands of Mr. John Coggeshall, who was a deacon of the church in Boston." The character of the sermon is, however, of more importance; and I unhesitatingly say, that it was not such as can justify the court in their sentence for *sedition* and *contempt*, nor prevent the present age from regarding that proceeding as an example and a warning of the usual tyranny of ecclesiastical factions. The author's conduct is by himself judged with sufficient severity in two letters, which will appear in this History sub an. 1644. Similar, and often much heavier artillery of reproach, is too often employed in that fortress, within which the brave defenders fear no answer of an adversary's fire.

The followers of Cotton, supporters of Wheelwright, and admirers of Mrs. Hutchinson, have been usually stigmatized as antinomians; and I am well satisfied, that the tendency of their doctrines was, by unscriptural representations of grace, to disparage the value of good works. But by many the same opinion is entertained of the tendency in teaching of the great body of their antagonists. We should never impute conclusions from the premises of one party, drawn by the adversary. With all his ardour against the errours of that time, Winthrop, who well understood them, has not used this term of reproach, though Welde and other inquisitors have trusted much to the influence of an odious name. It is the most common artifice of the

nour and some few more (who dissented) tendered a protestation, which, because it wholly justified Mr. ||Wheelwright,||[1] and condemned the proceedings of the court, was rejected. The church of Boston also tendered a petition in his behalf, justifying Mr. Wheelwright's sermon. The court deferred sentence till the next court, and advised with the ministers, &c. whether they might enjoin his ||[2]silence,|| &c. They answered, that they were not clear in that point, but desired rather, that he might be commended to the church of Boston to take care of him, &c. which accordingly was done, and he enjoined to appear at the next court. Much heat of contention was this court between the opposite parties; so as it was moved, that the next court might be kept at Newtown. The governour refused

||Wilson|| ||[2]sentence||

"exquisite rancour of theological hatred." Though we may presume it was given, the deluded did not adopt the denomination. I shall not be blamed for an extract from this sermon, which Hutchinson, I. 59, I fear, without having read it, characterizes as "carrying antinomianism to the height." It contains this exhortation: "Thirdly, let us have a care, that we do show ourselves holy in all manner of good conversation, both in private and publick; and, in all our carriages and conversations, let us have a care to endeavour to be holy as the Lord is; let us not give occasion to those that are coming on, or manifestly opposite to the ways of grace, to suspect the way of grace; let us carry ourselves, that they may be ashamed to blame us; let us deal uprightly with those with whom we have occasion to deal, and have a care to guide our families and to perform duties that belong to us; and let us have a care that we give not occasion to others to say, we are libertines or antinomians."

A perfect copy of this sermon, from the state house, with a great body of other old papers, supposed formerly to have belonged to Gov. Hutchinson, has been presented lately to the Historical Society; and from this I find no reason to alter the foregoing opinion. The text was, for the views of his party, admirably chosen from Matt. ix. 15.

Mather, book VII. chap. iii. sect. 3, says, of Wheelwright, "he published a vindication of himself against the wrongs, that by Mr. Welde and by Mr. Rutherford had been done unto him." The probable loss of this tract induces me to enlarge my quotation from the Magnalia: "In this vindication, he not only produces a speech of Mr. Cotton, *I do conceive and profess, that our brother Wheelwright's doctrine is according to God in the points controverted;* but also a declaration from the whole general court of the colony, signed by the secretary, August 24, 1654, upon the petition of Mr. Wheelwright's church at Hampton, in which declaration they profess, that, hearing that Mr. Wheelwright is, by Mr. Rutherford and Mr. Welde, rendered, in some books printed by them, as heretical and criminous, they now signify, that Mr. Wheelwright hath, for these many years, approved himself a sound, orthodox and profitable minister of the gospel, among these churches of Christ."

1 By following the absurd reading of the first edition, substituting the chief of one party for the head of the other, Emerson, History of First Church, 38, has puzzled his readers in a maze, from which they may now easily be extricated.

to put it to the vote; the deputy was loath to do it, except the court would require him, because he dwelt in Boston, &c. So the court put it to Mr. Endecott.

21.] Miantunnomoh, &c. sent twenty-six, with forty fathom of wampom and a Pequod's hand. We gave four of the chief ||each|| a coat of ||2fourteen|| shillings price, and deferred to return our present till after, according to their manner.

Mo. 2. 1.] Those of Connecticut returned answer to our publick letters, wherein they showed themselves unsatisfied about our former expedition against the Pequods, and their expectation of a further prosecution of the war, to which they offer to send men, and signify their unpreparedness to declare themselves in the matter of government, in regard of their engagement to attend the answer of the gentlemen of Saybrook about the same matter.

10.] Capt. Underhill was sent to Saybrook, with twenty men, to keep the fort, both in respect of the Indians, and especially of the Dutch, who, by their speeches and supplies out of Holland, gave ||3cause|| of suspicion, that they had some design upon it. The men were sent at the charge of the gentlemen of Saybrook, and lent by order of the council here, for fear any advantage should be taken by the adverse party, through the weakness of the place.

6.] The church of Concord kept a day of humiliation at Newtown, for ordination of their elders, and they chose Mr. Buckly teacher, and Mr. Jones pastor. Upon a question moved by one sent from the church of Salem, it was resolved by the ministers there present, that such as had been ministers in England were lawful ministers by the call of the people there, notwithstanding their acceptance of the call of the bishops, &c. (for which they humbled themselves, acknowledging it their sin,[1] &c.) but being come hither, they accounted themselves no ministers, until they were called ||4to|| another church, and that, upon election, they were ministers before they were solemnly ordained.

The governour, and Mr. Cotton, and Mr. Wheelwright, and the two ruling elders of Boston, and the rest of that church,

||sachems|| ||2nineteen|| ||3occasion|| ||4by||

1 Ordination by a bishop in England must have been thought valid, for by that rite it was, that all the other ministers asserted their claims to office, as we may see at the election, in August, 1630, of Wilson to the First Church of Boston. The people also equally respected it. But how it should be a sin, yet a valid entrance or admission to the Christian ministry, can be explained only by such timid casuists as humbled themselves for their act in submitting to it.

which were of any note, did none of them come to this meeting. The reason was conceived to be, because they accounted these as legal preachers, and therefore would not give approbation to their ordination.

3. 2.] Mr. Haynes, one of our magistrates, removed with his family to Connecticut.

12.] We received a letter from him and others, being then at Saybrook, that the Pekods had been up the river at Weathersfield, and had killed six men, being at their work, and twenty cows and a mare, and had killed three women, and carried away two maids.

Mr. Winslow was sent from the governour and council of Plimouth to treat with us about joining against the Pequods. He declared first their willingness to aid us; but that they could not do any thing till their general court, which was not till the first Tuesday in the 4th month. Then he made some objections: as, 1. Our refusal to aid them against the French. 2. Our people's trading at Kenebeck. 3. The injury offered them at Connecticut by those of Windsor, in taking away their land there. 4. Their own poverty, and our ability, which needed not any help from them.

To this answer was made by our governour and deputy: that, 1. We did not desire them to afford aid unto us, but to join against the common enemy, who, if he were not subdued, would prove as dangerous to them as to us, and, he prevailing, would cause all the Indians in the country to join to root out all the English. 2. For our refusal to aid them against the French, the case was not alike, for it was their private quarrel, and they were supposed to have commission from the king of France, and we thought it no wisdom for us to engage ourselves in a war with the king of France; §yet we acknowledged some failing in it.§[1] For our people's trading at Kenebeck, we answered, that we gave no allowance to it, nor had we heard of more than a boat or two that had been there. For the injury done them at Connecticut, we had dealt with them to give satisfaction, but it was not in our power to do them justice in it. ||He|| alleged also, that this war did not concern them, seeing the Pequods had not killed any of theirs. We answered, that Capt. Stone, &c. for whom this war was begun, were none of ours neither. ||²He|| alleged further, that, in our first undertaking, they were not acquainted with it till two or three days

||They|| ||²They||

[1] This clause is brought from the margin.

before our forces were to go forth. We answered, we intended at the first to send only to Block Island, and for that we thought it not needful to trouble them, and our sending them thence to the Pequods was with hope to draw them to parley, and so to some quiet end. We concluded to write further to them from our next court. And whereas they propounded to have us promise to aid them in all their occasions, &c. we answered, that, seeing, when we now treated with them about joining with us, they were at liberty and might withhold, except they saw reason to move them; so we desired to be left free, that we might judge of the reason of any such occasion as might fall out. According hereunto we writ to them the 20th of the 3d month, and gave them some considerations, why they should join with us: as, 1. because, if we should be overcome, it would cost them more to help us, and be less acceptable; 2. if we should prevail without them, it would occasion ill thoughts in our people towards theirs, &c. So we left it to them.

17.] Our court of elections was at Newtown. So soon as the court was set, being about one of the clock, a petition was preferred by those of Boston. The governour would have read it: but the deputy said it was out of order; it was a court ||for|| elections, and those must first be despatched, and then their petitions should be heard. Divers others also opposed that course as an ill precedent, &c.; and the petition, being about pretence of liberty, &c. (though intended chiefly for revoking the sentence given against Mr. Wheelwright,) would have spent all the day in debate, &c.; but yet the governour and those of that party would not proceed to election, except the petition were read. Much time was already spent about this debate, and the people crying out for election, it was moved by the deputy, that the people should divide themselves, and the greater number must carry it. And so it was done, and the greater number by ||2many|| were for election. But the governour and that side kept their place still, and would not proceed. Whereupon the deputy told him, that, if he would not go to election, he and the rest of that side would proceed. Upon that, he came from his company, and they went to election;[1] and Mr. Winthrop was chosen governour, Mr. Dudley deputy, and Mr. Endecott of the standing council;[2] and Mr. Israel

||of|| ||2much||

[1] A pleasant story of the exertion of Wilson to secure this election is told by Hutchinson, I. 62.

[2] He held this place, without re-election, till the change of the constitution in 1639.

Stoughton and Mr. Richard Saltonstall were called in to be assistants; and Mr. Vane, Mr. Coddington, and Mr. Dummer, (being all of ||that|| faction,) were left quite out.

There was great danger of a tumult that day; for those of that side grew into fierce speeches, and some laid hands on others; but seeing themselves too weak, they grew quiet. They expected a great advantage that day, because the remote towns were allowed to come in by proxy;[1] but it fell out, that there were enough beside. But if it had been otherwise, they must have put in their deputies, as other towns had done, for all matters beside elections. Boston, having deferred to choose deputies till the election was passed, went home that night, and the next morning they sent Mr. Vane, the late governour, and Mr. Coddington, and Mr. Hoffe, for their deputies; but the court, being grieved at it, found a means to send them home again, for that two of the freemen of Boston had not notice of the election. So they went all home, and the next morning they returned the same gentlemen again upon a new choice; and the court not finding how they might reject them, they were admitted.

Upon the election of the new governour, the serjeants, who had attended the old governour to the court, (being all Boston men, where the new governour also dwelt,) laid down their halberds and went home; and whereas they had been wont to attend the former governour to and from the meetings on the Lord's days, they gave over now, so as the new governour was fain to use his own servants to carry two halberds before him; whereas the former governour had never less than four.[2]

||the||

---

1 The admission of proxies was justified by experience at the election of the former year, and at the general court in December preceding this course was adopted, as by the record appears: "This court, taking into serious consideration the great danger and damage that may accrue to the state by all the freemen's leaving their plantations to come to the place of elections, have therefore ordered it, that it shall be free and lawful for all freemen to send their votes for elections by proxy, the next general court in May, and so for hereafter, which shall be done in this manner: the deputies, which shall be chosen, shall cause the freemen of their towns to be assembled, and then to take such freemen's votes as please to send by proxy for every magistrate, and seal them up severally, subscribing the magistrate's name on the back side, and so to bring them to the court sealed, with an open roll of the names of the freemen that so send by proxy."

2 Many writers, looking only to the tone of this paragraph in our author, have considered, that the officers showed a special discourtesy to him. A strict examination of the complaint, perhaps, may show that it was not very well founded, and, certainly, exempt these serjeants from the obloquy. The Colony Records, I. 145, instruct us, that, at the general court in March,

Divers writings were now published about these differences. Among the rest, the magistrates ||set|| forth an apology to justify the sentence of the court against Mr. Wheelwright, which the adverse party had much opposed and spoken evil of, and did also set forth a remonstrance to that end, in which they did not deal fairly; for, in abbreviating Mr. Wheelwright his sermon, they clear altered both the words and meaning of such passages in it, whereat the offence was taken, and which were the ground of the court's sentence.

Mr. Wheelwright also himself set forth a small ||[2]tractate|| about the principal doctrine of his sermon, viz. about the covenant of grace, which was also differing from his sermon.

The other ministers also set out an answer to his sermon, confuting the same by many strong arguments.

Mr. Cotton also replied to their answer very largely, and stated the differences in a very narrow scantling; and Mr. Shepherd, preaching at the day of election, brought them yet nearer, so as, except men of good understanding, and such as knew the bottom of the tenents of those of the other party, few could see where the difference was; and indeed it seemed so small, as (if men's affections had not been formerly alienated, when the differences were formerly stated as fundamental) they might easily have come to reconciliation. For in these particulars they agreed: 1. that justification and sanctification were both together in time; 2. that a man must know himself to be justified, before he can know himself to be sanctified; 3. that the spirit never witnesseth justification without a ||[3]word|| and a work.

The difference was, whether the first assurance be by an absolute promise always, and not by a conditional also, and whether a man could have any true assurance, without sight

||sent|| ||[2]treatise|| ||[3]wonder||

1635, it was ordered, "that at every general court there shall be six men appointed by the governour for the time being, out of the town where he lives, to attend with halberds and swords upon the person of the governour, and the rest of the members of the court, during the space of the first day of every general court; and that there shall be two men appointed by the governour to attend in like manner at every particular court at the publick charges." When Haynes was afterwards chosen, the officers for this service, appointed by him, of course belonged to Newtown; when Vane succeeded, he was required to appoint men of Boston; and at this election, after Winthrop was sworn in, he might have appointed the same or others of the same town. But those, whose office ceased with the authority of Vane, are not, it seems to me, to be blamed for declining, without commission anew, to wait on his successor.

of some such work in his soul as no hypocrite could attain unto.[1]

At the court Mr. Wheelwright, according as he was enjoined, did appear; but, because a general day of humiliation was appointed, and it was agreed, that all the churches should choose certain men to meet and confer about the differences, the court gave him respite to the next session, (which was appointed the first Tuesday in August,) to bethink himself, that, retracting and reforming his errour, &c. the court might show him favour, which otherwise he must not expect. His answer was, that if he had committed sedition, then he ought to be put to death; and if we did mean to proceed against him, he meant to appeal to the king's court; for he could retract nothing. The court told him, that they were clear in the justice of their proceeding, and should judge of his offence as they had done, if it were to do again; but if, upon the conference among the churches, the Lord should discover any further light to them than as yet they had seen, they should gladly embrace it.

The intent of the court in deferring the sentence was, that, being thus provoked by their tumultuous course, and divers insolent speeches, which some of that party had uttered in the court, and having now power enough to have crushed them, their moderation and desire of reconciliation might appear to all.

Having received intelligence from Miantunnomoh, that the Pequods had sent their women and children to an island for their safety, we presently sent away forty men by land to the Nariganseits, and there to take in Miantunnomoh, (and he offered to send sixteen men with ||ours,||) and so, in the night, to set upon them.

We also provided to send one hundred and sixty[2] more

||us||

---

[1] Upon such a harmony of the creeds, without want of reverence for the wisdom and sincerity of our ancestors, we may well refer to the language of Solomon, Prov. i. 6,—"the words of the wise and their dark sayings." The simplicity of the gospel seems utterly obscured by this controversy about the priority of sanctification or justification, which may be thought profound, or only absurd, according to the reader's education and ability to "darken counsel by words without knowledge."

[2] Of this number, the proportion to be raised by the several towns was as follows: Boston, 26; Salem, 18; Ipswich, 17; Sagus, 16; Watertown, 14; Dorchester, 13; Charlestown, 12; Roxbury, 10; Newtown, 9; Newbury, 8; Hingham, 6; Weymouth, 5; Medford, 3; Marblehead, 3. The note in Hutchinson, on I. 76, is wrong by one figure. It will be seen, in a comparison of the several notes on this subject, that the relative population and wealth of our settlements frequently changed.

after them to prosecute the war; and Mr. Stoughton, one of the magistrates, was sent with them, and Mr. Wilson, the pastor of Boston. These two were chosen thus in the open court: Three magistrates were set apart, and one was designed by a lot; also the elders set apart two; and a lot was cast between them in a solemn publick invocation of the name of God.

22.] Miantunnomoh sent us word, that Capt. Mason, with a company of the English upon the river, had surprised and slain eight Pequods, and taken seven squaws, and with some of them had redeemed the two English maids.

24.] By letters from Mr. Williams we were certified, (which the next day was confirmed by some who came from Saybrook,) that Capt. Mason[1] was come to Saybrook with eighty English and one hundred Indians; and that the Indians had gone out there, and met with seven Pequods; five they killed; one they took alive, whom the English put to torture; and set all their heads upon the fort. The reason was, because they had tortured such of our men as they took alive.[2]

The Dutch governour sent a sloop to Pequod to redeem the two English maids by what means soever, though it were with breach of their peace with the Pequods.[3] The sloop of-

---

At the general court, in August following, a rate of £400 was thus assessed: Boston, £59.4; Salem, £45.12; Dorchester, £42.6; Charlestown, £42.6; Ipswich, £34.12; Watertown, £30.8; Roxbury, £30.8; Newtown, £29.12; Sagus, £28.16; Medford, £24.12; Newbury, £16.18; Hingham, £8.10; Weymouth, £6.16. Property and numbers, in a very short period, appear to have been quite unequally distributed between Medford and Marblehead.

1 An ample account of Mason is given by Allen, and it seems strange, that Eliot omitted so distinguished a name. That he arrived in 1630, with the first settlers of Dorchester, as Allen asserts, from Trumbull, I. 322, may be an errour, as his name is not found before December, 1632, when he went in the expedition after the pirate Bull, of which notice in this volume, 96, 97, may be compared with 2 Hist. Coll. VIII. 232. I *presume* he came in that year, and *know*, that he was admitted a freeman 4 March, 1634—5. Prefixed to his own History of the Pequot War, in which he deserves the principal honour, reprinted 2 Hist. Coll. VIII. 120—153, is a life by the diligent hand of Prince, who would not assign an earlier arrival. His son, John, a captain, was wounded, 19 December, 1675, in the great battle with the Narragansetts, and died in September following. Descendants of this energetick warriour are found in New England, of whom one is the present Jeremiah Mason of Portsmouth, New Hampshire. Abundant correspondence with J. Winthrop of Connecticut is preserved.

2 It was, probably, a mistaken policy, however justifiable the practice of retaliation may be with nations of nearer similarity of manners. Savages are hardly tamed by kindness; never by severity.

3 This kindness of the Dutch I wish had been longer remembered by their neighbours of Connecticut, especially as mutual charges, without proof, of incitement of the barbarians, are so frequently made by all civilized nations.

fered largely for their ransom; but nothing would be accepted. So the Dutch, having many Pequods aboard, stayed six of them, (the rest leaped overboard,) and with them redeemed the two maids, who had been well used by the Pequods, and no violence offered them.[1]

The former governour and Mr. Coddington, being discontented that the people had left them out of all publick service, gave further proof of it in the congregation; for they refused to sit in the magistrates' seat, (where Mr. Vane had always sitten from his first arrival,) and went and sate with the deacons, although the governour sent to desire them to come in to him. And upon the day of the general fast, they went from Boston to keep the day at the Mount with Mr. Wheelwright.

Another occasion of their discontent, and of the rest of that party, was an order, which the court had made, to keep out all such persons as might be dangerous to the commonwealth, by imposing a penalty upon all such as should retain any, &c. above three weeks, which should not be allowed by some of the magistrates; for it was very probable, that they expected many of their opinion to come out of England from Mr. ||Brierly|| his church, &c.[2]

This order, and other differences between the new governour and them, was the cause, that, at his return to Boston, none of them met him; and the serjeants, which had constantly attended the former governour to all publick meetings with four halberds, did now refuse to do any such office to the new, alleging that they had done it to the former voluntarily, in respect of his person, not his place. To which it was answered, that there was a double errour; 1. because the place drowns the person, be he honourable or base; 2. in that any compliment of honour, being once conferred upon an office, (though voluntarily,) cannot after be taken away without contempt and injury. The country, taking notice of this, offered to send in

||B.||

---

1 No instance of the worst violence to woman has ever been told of our aborigines. Johnson, lib. II. c. 1, who makes them the "seed of the serpent," says the Indians questioned these maids "to know whether they could make gunpowder."

2 In Cotton's Way of Congregational Churches Cleared, in answer to Bayley, one of the assertors of Presbyterian divine right, he says, speaking of this arbitrary order: "I saw by this means we should receive no more members into our church, but such as must profess themselves of a contrary judgment to what I believed to be a truth." He designed to remove out of the jurisdiction with Davenport, but was dissuaded.

Three tracts on this subject,—A Defence, The Answer, and Replication,—are found in Hutchinson's Coll. 67—100.

some from the neighbouring towns to carry the halberds by course; and upon that the town of Boston offered to send some men, but not the serjeants; but the governour chose rather to make use of two of his own servants.[1]

25.] Our English from Connecticut, with their Indians, and many of the Naragansetts, marched in the night to a fort of the Pequods at Mistick, and, besetting the same about break of the day, after two hours' fight they took it, (by firing it,) and slew therein two chief sachems, and one hundred and fifty fighting men, and about one hundred and fifty old men, women and children, with the loss of two English, *whereof but one was*[2] killed by the enemy. Divers of the Indian friends were hurt by the ||English,||[3] *because they had not some mark to distinguish them from the Pequods, as some of them had.* The story is more fully described in the next leaf.[4]

Presently upon this came news from the Naragansett, that all the English, and two hundred of the Indians, were cut off in their retreat, for want of powder and victuals. Three days after, this was confirmed by a post from Plimouth, with such probable circumstances, as it was generally believed. But, three days after, Mr. Williams, having gone to the Naragansetts to discover the truth, found them mourning, as being confident of it; but that night some came from the army, and assured them all was well, and that all the Pequods were fled, and had forsaken their forts. The general defeat of the Pequods at Mistick happened the day after ||[2]our|| general fast.

Mo. 4. 3.] Two ships arrived here out of England, (Mr. Peirce was one.) In them came the copy of a commission, from the commissioners for New England, to divers of the magistrates here, to govern all the people in New England till further

||Pequods|| ||[2]the||

---

1 By the extract from the Records, in a former note on this subject, five pages back, it will be seen, that it was no part of the provision, that those who carried the halberds should be of the rank of serjeants.

2 Mason says, two were killed outright; and thus our author corrects his first relation.

3 The governour had erased *English*, and written *Pequods;* but that is manifestly an errour, if the following clause be part of the report, which was probably false.

4 It will not be found, though the author intended to furnish an account. This storming of the Indian fort at Mistick, between New London and Norwich, was an affair reflecting much credit on the commander, whose report, in the History of the war, is very full, accurate and animated; but he makes the loss of the enemy six or seven hundred, "as some of themselves confessed," and "only seven taken captive, and about seven escaped."

order, &c. upon this pretence, that there was no lawful authority in ||force|| here, either mediate or immediate, from his majesty.

Upon the news from Mr. Williams, that the Pequods were dispersed, and some come in and submitted to the Naragansetts, (who would not receive them ||2before he|| had sent to know our mind,) the governour and council thought it needless to send so many men, and therefore sent out ||3warrants|| only for one half of the two hundred; but some of the people liked not of it, and came to the governour to have all sent. He took it ill; and though three of the ministers came with them to debate the matter, he told them, that if any one, ||4discerning|| an errour in the proceedings of the council, had come, in a private manner, to acquaint ||5him|| therewith, &c. it had been well done; but to come, so many of them, in a publick and popular way, was not well, and would bring authority into contempt. This they took well at his hands, and excused their intentions. So it was thought fit to send about forty men more, which was yielded rather to satisfy the people, than for any need that appeared.

Upon our governour's letter to Plimouth, our friends there agreed to send a pinnace, with forty men, to assist in the war against the Pequods; but they could not be ready to meet us at the first.

15.] There was a day of thanksgiving kept in all the churches for the victory obtained against the Pequods, and for other mercies.

About this time came home a small pinnace of thirty tons, which had been forth eight months, and was given for lost.[1] She went to the Bermuda, but by continual tempests was kept from ||6thence,|| and forced to bear up for the West Indies, and, being in great distress, arrived at Hispaniola, and not daring to go into any inhabited place there, but to go ashore in obscure places, and lived of turtles and *hogs*, &c. At last they were forced into a harbour, where lay a French man-of-war with his prize, and had surely made prize of them also,

||form|| ||2till they|| ||3word|| ||4discovering|| ||5them|| ||6hence||

[1] The marginal note is, "Capt. Gib. and Mr. Hill at W. Indies." When we recollect how minute Winthrop usually is in his narrative of such disasters, we may judge how the tale of distress gained by frequent telling, till it grew up to "the wonderful story of Major Gibbons" in the Magnalia, lib. VI. chap. i. § 3. It would with difficulty be understood to refer to the same event in our text, were not the sufferer's name, and his relief by a French *pirate*, sufficient marks of identity to turn us from Mather's Thaumaturgus back to the first relation, probably received from the adventurers' mouths.

but that the providence of God so disposed, as the captain, one ||Petfree,|| had lived at Pascataquack, and knew the merchant of our bark, one Mr. Gibbons. Whereupon he used them courteously, and, for such commodities as she carried, ||2freighted|| her with tallow, hides, &c. and sent home with her his prize, which he sold for a small price to be paid in New England. He brought home an aligarto, which he gave the governour.

20.] Three ships arrived here from Ipswich, with three hundred and sixty passengers. The last being loath to come to an anchor at Castle Island, though hailed by the castle boat, and required, &c. the gunner made a shot, intending to shoot before her for a warning, but the powder in ||3the|| touch hole being wet, and the ship having fresh way with wind and tide, the shot took place in the shrouds and killed a passenger, an honest man. The next day the governour charged an inquest, and sent them aboard with two of the magistrates (one of them being deputed coroner) to take view of the dead body, and who, upon hearing all the evidence, &c. found that he came to his death by the providence of God.

23.] The governour went to Sagus, and so to Salem and to Ipswich, at all which places the men of the towns met him, and guarded him from town to town, (though not desired nor expected by him,) to show their respect to their governour, and also for his safety, in regard it was reported the Pequods were come this way.[1] He returned again the 28th, being forced to travel all the night by reason of the heat, which was so extreme, as divers of those, who were new come on shore, died in their travel a few miles.

26.] There arrived two ships from London, the Hector, and the [blank.] In these came Mr. [2]Davenport and

||Peterfore|| ||2furnished|| ||3her||

---

1 Fear of the enemy's enterprise may to us seem unreasonable, considering the numerous plantations between Pequot and Salem ; but the inhabitants were few, except on the seaboard. Yet we may believe, that their apprehension for his safety operated much less than a desire to show respect to the governour, especially under the circumstances of slight from those less sound in the faith.

2 Of this celebrated divine, who had been a priest in one of the parishes of London, ample memorials are preserved by all the writers on the early affairs of our country. A sermon preached by him in 1629 is found at the Boston Athenæum. His conduct in concealing the regicides has ever been eulogised in Connecticut, and was admired by many, who dared not imitate it in Massachusetts. He succeeded Wilson in the First Church of Boston, being the fourth minister in that place, all whose names were John. But his coming from New Haven occasioned one of the most disagreeable contro-

[1]another minister, and Mr. [2]Eaton and Mr. [3]Hopkins, two merchants of London, men of fair estate and of great esteem for religion and wisdom in outward affairs.

---

versies, with which the affairs of the church have ever troubled our country. Descendants have often vindicated their claim to the enjoyment of the talents of their progenitor.

1 We learn from Trumbull, who erroneously marks the arrival in July, instead of June, that this other minister was Samuel, brother of Gov. Eaton. That author might have read in Mather, that Samuel Eaton died, 9 January, 1665, at Denton in Lancashire.

2 No character in the annals of New England is of purer fame than that of Theophilus Eaton, governour of the colony of New Haven from its settlement to his death, by twenty annual elections,—the only instance of such an honour ever conferred. That his talents were adequate to the station, might be confidently concluded from the fact of his prior service, several years, as representative of Charles I. at the court of Denmark; and the long administration of an infant state without a rival, is irrefragable proof of his prudence and virtue. All the original writers of our history are abundant in his praise, and the later and more judicious inquirers are satisfied with their evidence. The errour of Trumbull, I. 99—100 and 231, in asserting that Eaton was three years in the East Indies, and sometime deputy governour of the company trading thither, arose probably from the appellation of *East Country*, used by Mather, from the universal custom of England, for the regions bordering on the Baltick. It had been avoided by Eliot, Holmes and Allen; but my respect for the venerable historiographer of Connecticut led me unhesitatingly to adopt his authority, till I saw the cause of his mistake in the Magnalia. On this pilgrim's character and death, Hubbard, 329, 330, is more valuable and minute than about any other. His death was 7 January, 1657—8.

3 Edward Hopkins was son-in-law of Gov. Eaton, and, alternately with Haynes, for many years, governour of the colony of Connecticut, in which station Eliot erroneously asserts he died. He went to England, probably, in 1652, whence he did not return; though, after the decease of Haynes, he was again chosen governour, in 1654. The time of his death was March, 1657, a few months before his friend Eaton. He was then serving in parliament, and also as a commissioner of the army and navy. His liberality to New England was abundantly shown in his will, made 7 or 17 March, 1656—7. Extracts will interest the present age: "For my estate in New England, (the full account of which I left clear in book there, and the care and inspection whereof was committed to my loving friend, Capt. John Cullick,) I do in this manner dispose: Item, I do give and bequeath unto the eldest child of Mrs. Mary Newton, wife to Mr. Roger *Newton of Farmington, and daughter to Mr. Thomas Hooker, deceased, the sum of £30; as also the sum of £30 unto the eldest child of Mr. John Cullick by Elizabeth his present wife. Item, I do give and bequeath to Mrs. Sarah Wilson, the wife of Mr. John Wilson, preacher of the gospel, and daughter of my dear pastor, Mr. Hooker, my farm at Farmington, with all the houses, outhouses, buildings, lands, &c. belonging thereunto, to the use of her and the heirs of her body forever. I do also give unto Mrs. Susan Hooker, the relict of Mr. Thomas Hooker, all such debts as are due to me from her, upon the account I left in New England. And the residue of my estate there I do hereby give and bequeath to my father, Theophilus Eaton, Esq. Mr. John Davenport,

* *First minister of Farmington.*

In the Hector came also the Lord Ley, son and heir of the Earl of Marlborough, being about nineteen years of age, who

---

Mr. John Cullick, and Mr. William Goodwin, in full assurance of their trust and faithfulness in disposing of it according to the true intent and purpose of me the said Edward Hopkins, which is, to give some encouragement in those foreign plantations for the breeding up of hopeful youths, both at the grammar school and college, for the publick service of the country in future times. For the estate the Lord hath given me in *this* England, I thus dispose, and my wish is, that £150 per annum be yearly paid per my executor to Mr. David Yale, brother to my dear distressed wife, for her comfortable maintenance, and to be disposed of per him for her good, she not being in a condition fit to manage it herself; and I do heartily entreat him to be careful and tender over her; and my will is, that this be paid quarterly by £37.10 each quarter, and to continue to the end of the quarter after the death of my said wife, and that my executor give good security for a punctual performance hereof. My will also is, that the £30 given me per the will and testament of my brother Henry Hopkins, lately deceased, be given to our sister Mrs. Judith [unknown,] during her natural life, and that it be made up £50 per annum during her life. I do give to my sister Mrs. Margaret Thomson the sum of £50, to be paid her within one year after my decease. I do give unto my nephew Henry Thomson £800, whereof £400 to be paid within sixteen months after my decease, and the other £400 within six months after the decease of my wife. I do likewise give and bequeath to my niece Katherine Thomson, but now Katherine James, (over and above the portion of £500 formerly given her,) £100. I do also give and bequeath unto my nieces Elizabeth and Patience Dalley, unto each of them, £200, provided they attend the direction of their brother or aunts, or such as are capable to give them advice in the dispose of themselves in marriage. I give unto my brother Mr. David Yale £200 ; to my brother Mr. Thomas Yale £200, and to my sister Mrs. Hannah Eaton £200. My farther mind and will is, that, within six months after the decease of my wife, £500 be made over into New England, according to the advice of my loving friends Major Robert Thomson and Mr. Francis Willoughby, and conveyed into the hands of the trustees before mentioned, in farther prosecution of the aforesaid publick ends, which, in the simplicity of my heart, are for the upholding and promoting the kingdom of the Lord Jesus Christ in those parts of the earth. I do farther give unto my beloved wife a bed, with all furniture belonging unto it, for herself to lie on, and another for the servant maid that waits on her, and £20 in plate for her present use, besides one third part of all my household goods. I give unto Mr. John Davenport, Mr. Theophilus Eaton, Mr. Cullick, each of them, £20, to be made over to them into New England where they are ; and my will and pleasure is, that £20 be put into a piece of plate, and presented in my name to my honoured friend Dr. Wright, to whom I owe more than that, being much engaged, desiring him to accept it only as a testimony of my respects. I do give unto my servant James Porter £10 ; unto my maid Margaret £5 ; unto my maid Mary £2. I do give unto my honoured and loving friends Major Robert Thomson and Mr. Francis Willoughby £20 a-piece, in a piece of plate, as a token of my respects unto them ; and I do give unto my servant Thomas Haytor £20. I do give unto my sister Yale, the wife of Mr. David Yale, £20 ; as also to John Lollor, a youth now with my sister Eve, £20, to farther him out to be an apprentice to some good trade, and £20 more at the time of his coming to his own liberty, to encourage him to set up his trade, if he continue living so long. I do give unto my nephew Henry Dalley, master of arts in Cambridge, my land in the county of Essex ; and, for the payment of all

came only to see the country. He was of very sober carriage, and showed much wisdom and moderation in his lowly and familiar carriage, especially in the ship, where he was much disrespected and unworthily used by the master, one Ferne, and some of the passengers; yet he bare it meekly and silently. When he came on shore the governour was from home, and he took up his lodging at the common inn. When the governour returned, he presently came to his house. The governour offered him lodging, &c. but he refused, saying, that he came not to be troublesome to any, and the house where he

---

debts, dues and legacies, do give unto him all my personal estate, and, by these presents, renouncing and making void all other wills and testaments, do declare, constitute and make him my sole executor, and my good friends Major Robert Thomson and Mr. Francis Willoughby overseers, of this my last will and testament. Signed, sealed, declared and published by the said Edward Hopkins, Esq. at his house at London, on the 17th day of March in the year of our Lord 1657, to be his last will and testament."

Mention of the distress of his wife, named Ann, which was by loss of her reason, will occur in our second volume. She died 17 December, 1698. Trumbull, I. 233, says, Hopkins's estate, "given in New England, was estimated at about £1000 sterling, and was appropriated to the support of the grammar schools in New Haven, Hartford and Hadley. The money originally belonged to New Haven and Hartford; but as a considerable number of the people of Hartford afterwards removed to Hadley, and were principal settlers of that town, they received their proportion of the donation."

In six months after the wife's decease, which was above forty years later than the testator's, the £500 out of the English property should have been paid. But the executor and residuary devisee being dead, process in chancery was necessary against *his* executor. Under a final decree by Sir Simon Harcourt, lord keeper, Harvard College has enjoyed, jointly with the grammar school in Cambridge, since 1714, a fund, of which Gov. Dudley and other principal persons, civil and ecclesiastical, to the number of twenty-one, were made first trustees. As the direction from the chancery was to invest the same in lands, a purchase was made, under authority of an act of the province, from the Natick Indians, being about thirteen thousand acres, comprising, with an additional grant from the province, the flourishing town of Hopkinton in Middlesex county,—having its name from this liberal benefactor of New England,—and part of the town of Upton in the county of Worcester. The rent charge of these lands, for many years secured by the commonwealth, amounted to $222,22 annually, until March, 1823, and from thence forward, forever, $666,67 annually, being at the rate of one penny sterling per acre for the first ninety-nine years of the leases, and three pence sterling afterwards. Being one of the trustees, the editor knows the faithful and judicious employment of this charity. The fund, which, notwithstanding the evils of paper money, and occasional injurious denial of rent by some of the tenants, has been increased, now exceeds the sum of $18000, besides the original investment.

Several letters of Gov. Hopkins to J. Winthrop, jun. are preserved in vol. XIX. of Trumbull MSS. and there is one to our author, 21 June, 1648, printed in Hutchinson's Collection, 225, showing a disposition to return to England, controlled by affection towards his adopted country. It is written with more perspicuity than is usually found in papers of that age.

was was so well governed, that he could be as private there as elsewhere.

We had news of a commission granted in England to divers gentlemen here for the governing of New England, &c.; but instead thereof we received a commission from Sir Ferdinando Gorges to govern his province of New Somersetshire, which is from Cape Elizabeth to Sagadahoc, and withal to oversee his servants and private ||affairs ;|| which was observed as a matter of no good discretion, but passed in silence. We excused our not intermeddling, &c. because, being directed to six or five of them, and one of their names being mistaken, and another removed to Connecticut, there were but four in the country; as also for that it did not appear to us what authority he had to grant such a commission. As for the commission from the king, we received only a copy of it, but the commission itself staid at the seal for want of paying the fees.

Mo. 5.] The party, who procured the commission, one George ||2Cleves,||[1] brought also a protection under the privy signet for searching out the great lake of Iracoyce, and for the sole trade of beaver, and the planting of Long Island, by §articles of§ agreement between the Earl of Sterling, Viscount Canada, and him. Thus this and other gentlemen in England get large circuits of lands, &c. in this country, and are very ready to grant them out to such as will become their tenants, and, to encourage them, do procure commissions, protections, &c. which cost them nothing, but will be at no charge in any right way of plantation, which should be by coming themselves, or sending some of their children, &c.; but now, as they adventure little, so they are sure to lose nothing but their vain hope.[2]

Capt. Stoughton and his company, having pursued the Pe-

||officers|| ||2Chever||

---

1 Cleves was a person of some importance, as, in the second volume of this History, will appear. He was agent or governour under Alexander Rigby, a member of parliament; and in Hazard, I. 570, is a letter from Edward Rigby, son of Alexander, to the inhabitants of Laconia, 19 July, 1652, taking notice of Cleves being in England, and expressing a design to send him back. I should consider it as an approbation, though Sullivan, History of Maine, 315, says, Cleves "was an equivocal character, and acted with great duplicity. He obtained a letter of agency from Sir Ferdinando Gorges, acted as deputy governour to both, and sold lands under the title of each, as appears from the registry of deeds, which he executed." On his next page he remarks on Cleves's unfaithfulness to the son, after the death of the father. I know not whether Cleves lived in Maine afterwards.

2 This opinion of Winthrop has, in all succeeding times, been confirmed, being not more founded on reason, than verified by experience.

quots beyond Connecticut, and missing of them, returned to Pequot River, where they were advertised, that one hundred of them were newly come back to a place some twelve miles off. So they marched thither by night, and surprised them all. They put to death twenty-two men, and reserved two sachems, hoping by them to get Sasacus, (which they promised.) All the rest were women and children, of whom they gave the Naragansetts thirty, and our Massachusetts Indians three, and the rest they sent hither.

A pinnace, returning, took a canoe with four Indians near Block Island. We sent to Miantunnomoh to know what they were, and after we discharged all save one, who was a Pequod, whom we gave Mr. Cutting to carry into England.

[Large blank.]

The differences grew so much here, as tended fast to a separation; so as Mr. Vane, being, among others, invited by the governour to accompany the Lord Ley at dinner, *not only* refused to come, (alleging by letter that his conscience withheld him,) *but also, at the same hour, he went over to Nottle's Island to dine with Mr. Maverick, and carried the Lord Ley with him.*[1]

6.] There were sent to Boston forty-eight women and children. There were eighty taken, as before is expressed. These were disposed of to particular persons in the country. Some of them ran away and were brought again by the Indians our neighbours, and those ||we|| branded on the shoulder.

12.] Ayanemo, the sachem of Niantick, came to Boston with seventeen men. He made divers propositions, which we promised to give answer unto the next day; and then, understanding he had received many of the Pequods, submitting to him since the former defeat, we first demanded the delivery of them, which he sticking at, we refused further conference with him; but, the next morning, he came and offered what we desired. So the governour referred him to treat with our captains at the Pequod, and wrote instructions to them how to deal with him, and received his present of ten fathom of wampom. He was lovingly dismissed, with some small things given him.

Here came over a brother of Mrs. Hutchinson, and some other of Mr. Wheelwright's friends, whom the governour thought not fit to allow, as others, to sit down among us, with-

||men||

---

1 I have no doubt, that every reader will be pleased with the preservation of this anecdote, though erased by the governour; for it strengthens his remark very much.

out some trial of them. Therefore, to save others from the danger of the law in receiving of them, he allowed them for four months. This was taken very ill by those of the other party, and many hot speeches given forth about it, and about their removal, &c.

13.] Mr. Stoughton, with about eighty of the English, whereof Mr. Ludlow, Capt. Mason, and [blank,] of Connecticut, were part, sailed to the west in pursuit of Sasacus, &c. At Quinepiack, they killed six, and took two. At a head of land a little short they beheaded two sachems; whereupon they called the place Sachem's Head. About this time they had given a Pequod his life to go find out Sasacus. He went, and found him not far off; but Sasacus, suspecting him, intended to kill him, which the fellow perceiving, escaped in the night, and came to the English. Whereupon Sasacus and Mononotto, their two chief sachems, and some twenty more, fled to the Mohawks. But eighty of their stoutest men, and two hundred others, women and children, were at a place within twenty or thirty miles of the Dutch, whither our men marched, and, being guided by a Divine Providence, came upon them, where they had twenty wigwams, hard by a most hideous swamp, so thick with bushes and so quagmiry, as men could hardly crowd into it. Into this swamp they were all gotten. Lieut. Davenport and two or three more, that entered the swamp, were dangerously wounded by the Indian arrows, and with much difficulty were fetched out. Then our men surrounded the swamp, being a mile about, and shot at the Indians, and they at them, from three of the clock in the afternoon till they desired parley, and offered to yield, and life was offered to all that had not shed English blood. So they began to come forth, now some and then some, till about two hundred women and children were come out, and amongst them the sachem of that place, and thus they kept us two hours, till night was come on, and then the men told us they would fight it out; and so they did all the night, coming up behind the bushes very near our men, and shot many arrows into their hats, sleeves and ||stocks,|| yet (which was a very miracle) not one of ours wounded. When it was near morning, it grew very dark, so as such of them as were left crept out at one place and escaped, being (as was judged) not above twenty at most, and those like to be wounded; for in the pursuit they found some of them dead of their wounds.[1] Here our men gat some booty of kettles, trays,

||stockings||

1 For a larger account of this swamp fight, see Mason's History.

wampom, &c. and the women and children were divided, and sent some to Connecticut and some to the Massachusetts. The sachem of the place, having yielded, had his life, and his wife and children, &c. The women, which were brought home, reported, that we had slain in all thirteen sachems, and that there were thirteen more left. We had now slain and taken, in all, about seven hundred. We sent fifteen of the boys and two women to Bermuda, by Mr. Peirce; but he, missing it, carried them to Providence Isle.[1]

Mo. 6.] Mr. Stoughton sailed, with some of his company, from Pequod to Block Island. They came thither in the night, yet were discovered, and our men having killed one or two of them, and burnt some of their wigwams, &c. they came to parley, and, submitting themselves to become tributaries in one hundred fathom wampompeague, and to deliver any that should be found to have any hand in Mr. Oldham's death, they were all received, and no more harm done them.

3.] At our general court, one Greensmith, being censured for saying, that all the elders, &c. except two, did preach a covenant of works, &c. he did appeal to the king; but the court, notwithstanding, committed him till, &c.

The Lord Ley, being told that one Ewre had spoken treason against the king, sent for the party, one Brooks, and inquiring of him, he told him that Ewre had said, about twelve months before, that, if the king did send any authority hither against our patent, he would be the first should resist him. This coming to the governour's knowledge, he sent for the parties, and bound them over to the general court. When they came there, Brooks brought his wife to witness with him; but her testimony agreed not with his; also three others (whom he had told it unto) reported it otherwise. So at length they all agreed, and set it under their hands, that Ewre said, that, if there came any authority out of England contrary to the patent, he would withstand it. Now, because here was no mention of the king, and because he never informed any of the magistrates of it, and for that it was evident that he bare malice ||to|| the said Ewre, we saw no cause to take any other of the parties informing, (the rather because themselves did

||of||

---

1 We cannot fail, I think, to lament this enslaving of the prisoners, by sale in a foreign country, however it might be excused by a pretended necessity. In that day it was probably justified by reference to the practice or institution of the Jews. Yet that cruel people never sent prisoners so far.

urge it, and she refused longer to speak at all, except she might be put to her oath,) nor any offence, which deserved punishment, seeing it is lawful to resist any authority, which was to overthrow the lawful authority of the king's ||grant;|| and so the governour did openly declare, in the court, as justifiable by the laws of England.[1]

3.] The Lord Ley and Mr. Vane went from Boston to the ship, riding at Long Island, to go for England. At their departure, those of Mr. Vane's party were gathered together, and did accompany him to the boat, (and many to the ship;) and the men, being in their arms, gave him divers vollies of shot, and five pieces of ordnance, and he had five more at the castle. But the governour was not come from the court, but had left order with the captain for their honourable dismission.[2]

There was an old woman in Ipswich, who came out of England blind and deaf, yet her son could make her understand any thing, and know any man's name by her sense of feeling. He would write upon her hand some letters of the name, and by other such motions would inform her. This the governour himself had ||[2]trial of|| when he was at Ipswich.

5.] Mr. Hooker and Mr. Stone came, with Mr. Wilson, from Connecticut by Providence; and, the same day, Mr. Ludlow, Mr. Pincheon, and about twelve more, came the ordinary way by land, and brought with them a part of the skin and lock of hair of Sasacus and his brother and five other Pequod sachems, who, being fled to the Mohawks for shelter, with their wampom, being to the value of ||[3]five hundred pounds,||[3] were by them surprised and slain, with twenty of their best men. Mononottoh was also taken, but escaped wounded. They brought news also of divers other Pequods, which had been slain by other Indians, and their heads brought to the English; so that now there had been slain and taken between eight and nine hundred. Whereupon letters were sent to Mr. Stoughton and the rest, to call them all home.[4]

||patent|| ||[2]tried often|| ||[3]£500||

1 Here is perhaps to be understood an indirect censure of Lord Ley for his interference, and a direct maintenance of the freedom of speech on *such* a topick.

2 A rate of £400 was by this court apportioned as follows: Boston, £59.4; Salem, £45.12; Charlestown and Dorchester, each, £42.6; Ipswich, £34.12; Roxbury and Watertown, each, £30.8; Newtown, £29.12; Sagus, £28.16; Medford, £24.12; Newbury, £16.18; Hingham, £8.10; Weymouth, £6.16.

3 Weight, not money, appears to me the meaning.

4 A despatch, from Stoughton on service, will be found in the Appendix.

A woman of Boston congregation, having been in much trouble of mind about her spiritual estate, at length grew into ||utter|| desperation, and could not endure to hear of any comfort, &c., so as one day she took her little infant and threw it into a well, and then came into the house and said, now she was sure she should be damned, for she had drowned her child; but some, stepping presently forth, saved the child.[1] See more after.

Mr. Hooker and the rest of the elders, meeting divers days, they agreed (with consent of the magistrates) upon a day of humiliation to be kept in all the churches the 24th of this month; the day for the conference to be the 30th day. At their private meetings some reconciliation was made between Mr. Cotton and Mr. Wheelwright and Mr. Wilson, he professing, that, by his speech in the court, he did not intend the doctrine of Mr. Cotton or Mr. Wheelwright delivered in the publick congregation, but some opinions, (||2naming|| three or four,) which were privately carried in Boston and other parts of the country; and accordingly Mr. Cotton declared so much in the congregation the Lord's day following. And for the rest of his speech, it was agreed by all the elders to be inoffensive, considering his call thereto by the court. This sudden change was much observed by some, who were privy that Mr. Wilson had professed as much before, both privately, to the elders, and publickly, in the congregation, and that the said opinions had been delivered to the elders of Boston in writing as those which Mr. Wilson intended.[2]

17.] Mr. Davenport preached at Boston (it being the lecture day) out of that in 1 Cor., I exhort you brethren, &c. that there be no divisions among you, &c.; wherein, as he fully set forth the nature and danger of ||3divisions, and the disorders|| which were among us, &c., so he clearly discovered his judgment against the new opinions and bitter practices, which were sprung up here.

||bitter|| ||2meaning|| ||3disorders and the divisions||

---

1 In the margin is written, "Hett's wife distracted." A similar instance of her insanity, in attempting to destroy another of her children, is found in this History five years later.

2 Nothing is more refreshing, in the violence of these contests, which grew more violent as the matter of contest was unintelligible to the many, and the diversity of opinions not very striking to the few, than the same church retaining, for their Christian instructers, the heads of the opposite parties, Cotton and Wilson. The fact proves, stronger than any argument, the prudence of the pastor and the temper of the teacher.

Mr. Cotton, expounding that in 2 Chron. [blank] of the defection of the ten tribes from Rehoboam, and his preparations to recover them by war, and the prophet's prohibition, &c. proved from that in Numbers, 27. 21, that the rulers of the people should consult with the ministers of the churches upon occasion of any war to be undertaken, and any other weighty business, though the case should seem never so clear, as David in the case of Ziglag, and the Israelites in the case of Gibeah. Judges, &c.

26.] The captain and soldiers returned all from Pequod, having lost but one man, and he died of a flux, and another fell sick of an old infirmity, an asthma. The Indians about sent in still many Pequods' heads and hands from Long Island and other places, and [blank] sachems of Long Island came voluntarily, and brought a tribute to us of twenty fathom of wampom, each of them; and Miantunnomoh sent here some Pequod squaws, which had run from us.

31.] The Naragansetts sent us the ||hands|| of three Pequods,—one the chief of those who murdered Capt. Stone.

[Very large blank.]

Twenty men went in a pinnace to kill sea horse at the Isle of Sable, and after six weeks returned home, and could not find the island; but, after another month, viz. about the [blank] of September, they set forth again with more skilful seamen, with intent to stay there all winter.

Mr. Eaton, and some others of Mr. Davenport's company, went to view Quinepiack, with intent to begin a plantation there. They had many offers here and at Plimouth, and they had viewed many places, but none could content.

[Large blank.]

Some of the magistrates and ministers of Connecticut being here, there was a day of meeting appointed to agree upon some articles of confederation, and notice was given to Plimouth, that they might join in it, (but their warning was so short as they could not come.) This was concluded after. See (3.) 1643.

[Very large blank.]

30.] The synod, called the assembly, began at Newtown. There were all the teaching elders through the country, and some ||2new|| come out of England, not yet called to any place here, as Mr. Davenport, &c.

The assembly began with prayer, made by Mr. Shepherd, the pastor of Newtown. Then the erroneous opinions, which were

||heads|| ||2were||

spread in the country, were read, (being eighty[1] in all;) next the unwholesome expressions;[2] then the scriptures abused. Then they chose two moderators for the next day, viz. Mr. Buckly and Mr. Hooker, and these were continued in that place all the time of the assembly. There were about eighty opinions, some blasphemous, others erroneous, and all unsafe, condemned by the whole assembly; whereto near all the elders, and others sent by the churches, subscribed their names; but some few liked not subscription, though they consented to the condemning of them.

Some of the church of Boston, and some others, were offended at the producing of so many errours, as if it were a reproach laid upon the country without cause; and called to have the persons named, which held those errours. To which it was answered and affirmed by many, both elders and others, that all those opinions could be proved, by sufficient testimony, to be held by some in the country; but it was not thought fit to name the §parties, because this assembly had not to do with§ persons, but doctrines only. Yet this would not satisfy some, but they oft called for witnesses; and, because some of the magistrates declared to them, (when they refused to forbear speech unseasonably, though the moderators desired them,) that, if they would not forbear, it would prove §a civil§ disturbance, and then the magistrate must interpose, they objected against this, as if the magistrate had nothing to do in this assembly. So as he was forced to tell one of them, that, if he would not forbear, but make trial of it, he might see it execut-

---

1 If any in our times have such insatiable curiosity, as to desire more particular information of the incomprehensible jargon contained in these errours, the exact numeration of which was eighty-two, imputed to the followers of Cotton and supporters of Wheelwright, with the antinomian explanations of Mrs. Hutchinson, that she denied, the whole is written in "A short Story of the Rise, Reign and Ruin of Antinomians, Familists and Libertines, that infected the Churches of New England," by Thomas Welde, who was one of the chief inquisitors. The edition, London, 1644, published by the author, is in the Boston Athenæum; a second edition, London, 1692, in Harvard College Library. The work has not, I presume, been often quoted within a century. It was relied upon in the famous "Testimony of the Pastors of the Churches in the Province of Massachusetts Bay at the Annual Convention in Boston, 25 May, 1743," protesting against the spreading of many antinomian and familistical errours, occasioned by the itinerant labours of Whitefield, Tennent, and their disciples, by which, for some years, was produced the greatest religious excitement ever known in New England. It was happy that the government did not employ the same means of conversion as in 1637.

2 They amounted to nine, in stating which, with their confutation, three pages of Welde's book is occupied.

ed. Upon this some of Boston departed from the assembly, and came no more.[1]

After the errours condemned, there were five points in question, between Mr. Cotton and Mr. Wheelwright on the one part, and the rest of the elders on the other part, *which were after reduced to three,* and those after put into such expressions as Mr. Cotton and they agreed, but Mr. Wheelwright did not:

1. The first was about our union with Christ. The question was, whether we were united before we had active faith. The consent was, that there was no marriage union with Christ before actual faith, which is more than habitual.

2. The second was, about evidencing justification §by sanctification.§ The consent was, that some saving sanctifications (as faith, &c.) were coexistent, concurrent, and coapparent (or at least might be) with the witness of the Spirit always.

3. That the new creature is not the person of a believer, but a body of saving graces in such a one; and that Christ, as a head, doth enliven or quicken, preserve and act the same, but Christ himself is no part of this new creature.

4. That though, in effectual calling, (in which the answer of the soul is by active faith, wrought at the same instant by the Spirit,) justification and sanctification be all together in them; yet God doth not justify a man, before he be effectually called, and so a believer.

5. That Christ and his benefits may be offered and exhibited to a man under a covenant of works, but not in or by a covenant of works.[2]

In the first handling of these questions, either party delivered their arguments in writing, which were read in the assembly, and, after, the answers to them, which spent much time without any effect; but after they came to open dispute, the questions were soon determined; for so they came to understand each other better.

Mo. 7.] The last day of the assembly other questions were debated and resolved:

---

1 Perhaps it may seem reasonable, to doubt the usefulness of such a declaration of errours, that might not, at least many of them, have entered into the heads of the speculatists, unless they had been thus branded. But, "'tis glorious sport, to see the engineer hoist with his own petard."

2 We must regret, rather than wonder, that consent in the faith, after a synod on high points of doctrine, not deduced simply, perhaps not deducible, from the scriptures, is generally obtained by expressing the propositions in language, either unintelligible or designedly ambiguous. The peace of the church is restored by darkness.

1. That though women might meet (some few together) to pray and ||edify|| one another; yet such a set assembly, (as was then in practice at Boston,) where sixty or more did meet every week, and one woman (in a prophetical way, by resolving questions of doctrine, and expounding scripture) took upon her the whole exercise, was agreed to be disorderly, and without rule.[1]

2. Though a private member might ask a question publickly, after sermon, for information; yet this ought to be very wisely and sparingly done, and that with leave of the elders: but questions of ||[2]reference,|| (then in use,) whereby the doctrines delivered were reproved, and the elders reproached, and that with bitterness, &c., was utterly condemned.

3. That a person, refusing to come to the assembly, to abide the censure of the church, might be proceeded against, though absent; yet it was held better, that the magistrates' help were called for, to compel him to be present.

4. That a member, differing from the rest of the church in any opinion, which was not fundamental, ought not for that to forsake the ordinances there; and if such did desire dismission to any other church, which was of his opinion, and did it for that end, the church whereof he was ought to deny it for the same end.[2]

22.] The assembly brake up; and it was propounded by the governour, that they would consider, that, seeing the Lord had been so graciously present in this assembly, that matters had been carried on so peaceably, and concluded so comfortably in all love, &c., if it were not fit to have the like meeting once a year, or, at least, the next year, to settle what yet remained to be agreed, or if but to nourish love, &c. This motion was well liked of all, but it was not thought fit to conclude it.[3]

||advise|| ||[2]blank||

---

[1] A *prophetical way* has been often followed, at meetings of women in Boston, and is, I think, in our days, without censure. The conduct of the female assembly in 1637, however, so much resembles party making, that the resolution of the synod is approved by the editor, though it bears hard on his great, great, great, great grandmother.

[2] Such resolutions as the two last must, by modern Congregationalists, be thought very tyrannical; and any proceedings of churches conformable to them would be utterly disregarded by the aggrieved. The law would now protect one, instead of compelling him, in case of refusal to go to church to hear his own censure.

[3] General experience in Christendom, since the council at Jerusalem in the days of the apostles, has shown, that, instead of tending to "*nourish love*," synods have served only to engender strife and debate, to rend anew

There was a motion made also by the governour, that, whereas there was difference among the churches about the maintenance of their ministers, it might be agreed what way was most agreeable to the rule of the gospel; but the elders did not like to deal in that, lest it should be said, that this assembly was gathered for their private advantage.[1]

26.] Mr. Davenport (as he had been before requested by the assembly) preached out of Phil. 3. 16, wherein he laid down the occasions of differences among Christians, &c. and declared the effect and fruit of the assembly, and, with much wisdom and sound argument, persuaded to unity, &c.

The diet of the assembly was provided at the country's charge, as also the fetching and sending back of those, which came from Connecticut. It came to, in all, [blank.[2]]

[Large blank.]

28.] Two men were hanged at Boston for several murders. The one, John Williams, a ship carpenter, who, being lately come into the country, and put in prison for theft, brake out of prison with one John Hoddy, ||whom,|| near the great pond, in the way to Ipswich, beyond Salem, he murdered, and took away his clothes and what else he had, and went in them to Ipswich, (where he had been sent to prison,) and was there again apprehended; and though his clothes were all bloody, yet he would confess nothing till, about a week after, that the body of Hoddy was found by the kine, who, smelling the blood, made such a roaring, as the cow keeper, looking about, found the dead body covered with a heap of stones.

The other, William Schooler, was a vintner in London, and had been a common adulterer, (as himself did confess,) and had wounded a man in a duel, for which he fled into the Low Country, and from thence he fled from his captain and came into this country, leaving his wife (a handsome, neat woman) in England. He lived with another fellow at Merrimack, and

||when||

the seamless coat of their master, and in his name to utter a new commandment, that men hate one another. If this first synod of New England produced peace, as we cannot but acknowledge it did, it was by the encouragement of the magistrate to the evangelical process of banishment, which was soon inflicted by the civil arm, after the ecclesiastical head had failed in its remedies.

1 This disinterested spirit of the assembly, when invited by the chief civil authority of the colony to consider of their own maintenance, must never be recollected without honour.

2 From the Colony Records, where we ought to look, I am unable to supply this blank.

there being a poor maid at Newbury, one Mary Sholy, who had desired a guide to go with her to her master, who dwelt at Pascataquack, he inquired her out, and agreed, for fifteen shillings, to conduct her thither. But, two days after, he returned, and, being asked why he returned so soon, he answered, that he had carried her within two or three miles of the place, and then she would go no further. Being examined for this by the magistrates ||at|| Ipswich, and no proof found against him, he was let go. But, about a year after, being impressed to go against the Pequods, he gave ill speeches, for which the governour sent warrant for him, and being apprehended, (and supposed it had been for the death of the maid, ||[2]some|| spake what they had heard, which might occasion suspicion,) he was again examined, and divers witnesses produced about it. Whereupon he was committed, arraigned and condemned by due proceeding. The ||[3]effect|| of the evidence was this :

1. He had ||[4]lived|| a vicious life, and now lived like an atheist.

2. He had sought out the maid, and undertook to carry her to a place, where he had never been.

3. When he crossed Merrimack, he landed in a place three miles from the usual path, from whence it was scarce possible she should get into the path.

4. He said he went by Winicowett house, which he said stood on the contrary side of the way.

5. Being, as he said, within two or three miles of Swamscote, ||[5]where|| he left her, he went not thither to tell them of her, nor staid by her that night, nor, at his return home, did tell any body of her till he was demanded of her.

6. When he came back, he had above ten shillings in his purse, and yet he said she would give him but seven shillings, and he carried no money with him.

7. At his return he had some blood upon his hat, and on his skirts before, which he said was with a pigeon, which he killed.

8. He had a scratch on the left side of his nose, and, being asked by a neighbour how it came, he said it was with a bramble, which could not be, it being of the breadth of a small nail ; and being asked after by the magistrate, he said it was with his piece, but that could not be on the left side.

9. The body of the maid was found by an Indian, about half a year after, in the midst of a thick swamp, ten miles short of the place he said he left her in, and about three miles from the place where he landed by Merrimack, (and it was after seen

||of|| ||[2]soon|| ||[3]estate|| ||[4]led|| ||[5]when||

by the English,) the flesh being rotted off it, and the clothes laid all on an heap by the body.

10. He said, that, soon after he left her, he met with a bear, and he thought that bear might kill her, yet he would not go back to save her.

11. He brake prison, and fled as far as Powder Horn Hill, and there hid himself out of the way, for fear of pursuit, and after, when he arose to go forward, he could not, but (as himself confessed) was forced to return back to prison again.

At his death he confessed he had made many lies to excuse himself, but denied that he had killed or ravished her. He was very loath to die, and had hope he should be reprieved; but the court held him worthy of death, in undertaking the charge of a shiftless maid, and leaving her (when he might have done otherwise) in such a place, as he knew she must needs perish, if not preserved by means unknown. Yet there were some ministers and others, who thought the evidence not sufficient to take away his life.[1]

(8.) 7.] The Wren, a small pinnace, coming from Connecticut, was taken in a N. E. storm, and forced to anchor near Conyhassett, where she drave upon the rocks, and was wrecked, but all the men were saved.

12.] A day of thanksgiving kept in all the churches for ||our victories|| against the Pequods, and for the success of the assembly; but, by reason of this latter, some of Boston would not be present at the publick exercises. The captains and soldiers, who had been in the late service, were feasted, and, after the sermon, the magistrates and elders accompanied them to the door of the house where they dined.

[Large blank.]

(9.) 1.] Miantunnomoh, the Naragansett sachem, came to Boston. The governour, deputy and treasurer treated with him, and they parted upon fair terms. He acknowledged that all the Pequod country and Block Island were ours, and promised that he would not meddle with them but by our leave. We gave him leave to right himself for the ||[2]wrongs,|| which ||[3]Janemoh and Wequash Cook|| had done him; and for the wrong they had done us, we would right ourselves in our own time.

A young man, coming alone in a skiff from Newtown,

||a victory|| ||[2]injuries|| ||[3]J. and N. Cook||

[1] Doubts might reasonably be entertained; for the first and last circumstances, to say nothing of more than half of the others, are of very uncertain tendency.

in a N. E. storm of wind and snow, was found dead in his boat, with a half crown piece in his mouth.

One Jewell, master of a bark, was drowned. The manner was this. He was bound to the Isle of Sable, to relieve our men there. His bark had lain near a week at Natascott, waiting for him, but he staid at Boston drinking, and could not be gotten away. Mo. x. When he went, there was committed to his care a rundlet of strong water, sent to some there, he promising, that, upon his life, it should not be touched; but, as he went down in his bark's skiff, he went on shore at the castle, and there drank out about a gallon of it, and at night went away; but, it being very cold and dark, they could not find their bark, and Jewell his hat falling into the water, as they were ||rowing|| back to look for it, he fell into the water, near the shore, where it was not six feet deep, and could not be recovered.

There was great hope, that the late general assembly would have had some good effect in pacifying the troubles and dissensions about matters of religion; but it fell out otherwise.[1] For though Mr. Wheelwright and those of his party had been

||coming||

1 By this generation an erroneous zeal for God in their fathers should be regarded with tenderness. We are not much endangered in this respect by their example; yet it is proper to look at their conduct, for it may be a warning. If the state had left this obscure controversy, where it belonged, to the unsound heads but pure hearts of the deluded, it might soon have subsided in silence. Hutchinson, I. 73, thinks posterity might have been ignorant that such a woman as his ancestor ever existed. The proceedings of the first council of Ephesus, A. D. 431, which condemned Nestorius and his harmless errours, may be found in Gibbon's Decline and Fall, chap. XLVII. Metaphysical doctrines then influenced, as they have often since, the concerns of the state, and the rights of citizens were judged by their opinions on religion; while the supreme magistrate, instead of an impartial arbiter, became the furious leader or blind follower of the dominant faction. "Ephesus, the city of the Virgin, was defiled with rage and clamour, with sedition and blood; the rival synods darted anathemas and excommunications from their spiritual engines; and the court of Theodosius was perplexed by the adverse and contradictory narratives of the Syrian and Egyptian factions. During a busy period of three months, the emperour tried every method, except the most effectual means of indifference and contempt, to reconcile this theological quarrel."

The deliberations at Ephesus terminated in the establishment of a dogma about the double nature of the founder of our religion; but this benefit, for which the unholy assembly has since been venerated under the title of the third œcumenical council, appears rather the result of passion than of argument, and relies more on the fraud of man than the authority of scripture. Similar indecencies may not be found in the ecclesiastical assemblies of New England; but there is some parallelism in the object and the result; and the sarcasms of the adversary are in some degree justified. For seventeen centuries, the occasions to blaspheme are almost as numerous as the synods.

clearly confuted and confounded in the assembly, yet they persisted in their opinions, and were as busy in nourishing contentions (the principal of them) as before. Whereupon the general court, being assembled in the 2 of the 9th month, and finding, upon consultation, that two so opposite parties could not ||contain|| in the same body, without apparent hazard of ruin to the whole, agreed to send away some of the principal; and for this a fair [1]opportunity was offered by the remonstrance or petition, which they preferred to the court the 9th of the 1st month, wherein they affirm Mr. Wheelwright to be innocent, and that the court had condemned the truth of Christ, with divers other scandalous and seditious speeches, (as appears at large in the proceedings[2] of this court, which were faithfully collected and published soon after the court brake up,) subscribed by more than sixty of that faction, whereof one ||[2]William|| Aspinwall, being one, and he that drew the said petition, being then sent as a deputy for Boston, was for the same dismissed, and after called to the court and disfranchised and banished.[3] John Coggeshall was another deputy, who,

||continue|| ||[2]Mr.||

---

1 *Pretence* would have been as proper a word as *opportunity*, and a strange pretence it seems. If by the remonstrance an indignity were offered to the March court, by all rules of proceeding, either of reason or practice, the same body, and not another, should have passed its animadversion on the contempt. Yet a new court was chosen in May, and held, as our author shows, a second session in August, without taking any notice of the previous offence. Perhaps it might have been imprudent to punish, before Sir H. Vane and Lord Ley departed; and such a probable inference is fortified by a passage in Welde's preface. There was still another general court, in September after the dissolution of the synod, and Aspinwall was a member of that court; yet, though it must have been known, that the foul spirit exhibited in the petition was not purged away by the scientifick confutation, the sleeping honour of the March legislature remained without vindication.

2 Unless my opinions be as much perverted by prejudice as those of the majority of the court appear to me, this account of the remonstrance is very unjust; but that every reader may form his own judgment of this "seditious libel," as it was called by authority, I have transcribed it from Welde, p. 23—25, and given it a place in the Appendix.

3 The petition was suddenly drawn up, as the audience withdrew from the court, after their censure of Wheelwright; and sentence of banishment was passed on Aspinwall, before it was known that he was the penman. Welde, 32, considers it "an overruling hand of God; for, the *next day*, it was discovered, that he was the man that did frame the petition, and drew many to subscribe to it, and some had their names put to it without their knowledge, and in his first draught there were other passages so foul, as he was forced to put them out, and yet many had not subscribed but upon his promise, that it should not be delivered without advice of Mr. Cotton, which was never done." Perhaps the passages erased before presenting were an aggravation of the crime in the opinion of the reverend casuist, whose judgment is so blinded by passion, that

though his hand ||were|| not to the petition, yet, professing himself to approve of it, &c. was also dismissed, and after disfranchised. Then the court sent warrant to Boston to send other deputies in their room; but they intended to have sent the same men again; but Mr. Cotton, coming amongst them, dissuaded them with much ado.[1] Then the court sent for Mr. Wheelwright, and, he persisting to justify his sermon, and his whole practice and opinions, and refusing to leave either the place or his publick exercisings, he was disfranchised and banished. Upon which he appealed to the king, but neither called witnesses, nor desired any act to be made of it. The court told him, that an appeal did not ||[2]lie;|| for by the king's grant we had power to hear and determine without any reservation, &c. So he relinquished his appeal, and the court gave him leave to go to his house, upon his promise, that, if he were not gone out of ||[3]our|| jurisdiction within fourteen days, he would render himself to one of the magistrates.[2]

The court also sent for Mrs. Hutchinson, and charged her with divers matters, as her keeping two publick lectures every week in her house, whereto sixty or eighty persons did usually resort, and for reproaching most of the ministers (viz. all except Mr. Cotton) for not preaching a covenant of free grace, and that they had not the seal of the Spirit, nor were able ministers of the New Testament; which were clearly proved against her, though she sought to shift it off. And, after many speeches to and fro, at last she was so full as she could not contain, but vented her revelations; amongst which this was one, that she had it revealed to her, that she should come into New England, and should here be ||[4]persecuted,|| and that God

||was|| ||[2]lay|| ||[3]the|| ||[4]presented||

---

he seems an unfortunate advocate, rather than an impartial reporter. Of the misrepresentation about Cotton, and of the forged signatures, no light is obtained from Winthrop or the publick records.

1 Coddington was the other representative of Boston, and probably did not sign the remonstrance; yet he approved it, I suppose, as much as Coggeshall. In place of Aspinwall and Coggeshall, the Town Records inform us, that, 6 November, William Colbron and John Oliver were chosen; but, at the same court, the latter was "dismissed from being a deputy for justifying the seditious libel, called a remonstrance or petition." Col. Rec. I. 203. The town had spirit enough to forbear further exercise of their right for that session; but Oliver and Hough, who was of the same party, were members of the two following courts. This John Oliver, I presume, was brother of Thomas, the ruling elder.

2 Hubbard, 368, almost confesses, that the government "had overdone in passing the sentence." This treacherous candour, had Wheelwright died thirty years sooner, might not have been observed.

would ruin us and our posterity, and the whole state, for the same. So the court proceeded and banished her; but, because it was winter, they committed her to a private house,[1] where she was well provided, and her own friends and the elders permitted to go to her, but none else.

The court called also Capt. Underhill, and some five or six more of the principal, whose hands were to the said petition; and because they stood to justify it, they were disfranchised, and such as had publick places were put from them.[2]

The court also ordered, that the rest, who had subscribed the petition, (and would not acknowledge their fault, and which near twenty[3] of them did,) and some others, who had been chief stirrers in these contentions, &c. should be disarmed. This troubled some of them very much, especially because they were to bring them in themselves; but at last, when they saw no remedy, they obeyed.[4]

---

1 It will be seen, a few pages onward, that this house was in Roxbury. The Colony Record of her banishment, I. 203, informs us, that she "was committed to Mr. Joseph Welde," probably one of the deputies from that town, and brother of the clergyman there, Thomas, the sad historian of the controversy, who had shown himself sufficiently desirous of convincing her of her errours, and was not a little soured by his ill success.

2 Underhill excused himself, like a soldier, but in vain. "He insisted much," says Welde, "upon the liberty which all states do allow to military officers for free speech, &c. and that himself had spoken sometimes as freely to Count Nassau."

3 Only *ten* names of those, who "acknowledged their sin in subscribing the seditious writing, and desired to have their names crossed out," are found in the Records of that session; and one of *them*, Ralph Mousall, a representative at the court in September, 1638, "for speeches formerly spoken by him in approbation of Mr. Wheelwright, was dismissed from being a member of this court." Rec. I. 227. We are left then to the supposition, that the governour enlarges the number of the converts, or else that, at a future day, when the violence of party was assuaged, reconciliation with the offended majesty of a *different* court was encouraged, without noticing the fact in their proceedings. Yet there is entered, so late as 13 May, 1640, the submission of "Mr. Henry Flint." But the victory over him was well deserving of notice, as he was a distinguished young man, then chosen minister at Braintree, where his settlement, which should have taken place at the same time with Thomson's, 24 September, 1639, was delayed till 17 March after. No doubt this postponement was, to afford him liberal opportunity for this recantation. The commendation of him by Johnson, lib. I. c. 37, and again, lib. II. c. 18, for his industry against the same "sinful opinions" appears, to us who know the whole, rather ludicrous. Mather's biography of Flint, Magnalia, III. c. 19, is remarkable, even in him, for its nothingness.

4 In no part of the history of any of the United States, perhaps, can a parallel be found for this act, the remarkable circumstances of which justify a long transcript from the Colony Records, vol. I. 207—8.

"Whereas the opinions and revelations of Mr. Wheelewright and Mrs. Hutchinson have seduced, and led into dangerous errours, many of the people

All the proceedings of this court against these persons were set down at large, with the reasons and other observations, and

---

heare in Newe England, insomuch as there is just cause of suspition, that they, as others in Germany, in former times, may, upon some revelation, make some suddaine irruption upon those that differ from them in judgment: for prevention whereof, it is ordered, that all those, whose names are underwritten, shall, (upon warning given or left at their dwelling houses,) before the 30th day of this month of November, deliver in at Mr. Cane's house at Boston all such guns, pistols, swords, powder, shot and match, as they shall bee owners of, or have in their custody, upon paine of tenn pound for evry default to bee made thereof; which armes are to bee kept by Mr. Cane till this court shall take further order therein. Also it is ordered, upon like penalty of X £, that no man, who is to render his armes by this order, shall buy or borrow any guns, swords, pistols, powder, shot or match, untill this court shall take further order therein."

"The names of Boston men to bee disarmed: Capt. John Underhill, Mr. Thomas Oliver, William Hutchinson, William Aspinwall, Samuel Cole, William Dyer, Edward Rainsfoard, John Button, John Sanfoard, Richard Cocke, Richard Fairbanks, Thomas Marshall, Oliver Mellows, Samuel Wilbore, John Oliver, Hugh Gunnison, John Biggs, Richard Gridley, Edward Bates, William Dinely, William Litherland, Mathewe Iyans, Henry Elkins, Zaccheus Bosworth, Robert Rice, William Townsend, Robert Hull, William Pell, Richard Hutchinson, James Johnson, Thomas Savage, John Davy, George Burden, John Odlin, Gamaliel Wayte, Edward Hutchinson, William Wilson, Isaack Grosse, Richard Carder, Robert Hardings, Richard Wayte, John Porter, Jacob Eliot, James Penniman, Thomas Wardell, William Wardell, Thomas Matson, William Baulston, John Compton, Mr. Parker, William Freeborn, Henry Bull, John Walker, William Salter, Edward Bendall, Thomas Wheeler, Mr Clarke, Mr. John Coggeshall."

"The like order is taken for other towns, changing the names of those who shall deliver their armes, and keepe them.

"The names of Salem men to bee disarmed: Mr. Scrugs, Mr. Alfoot, Mr. Commins, goodman Robert Moulton, goodman King, to deliver their arms to Leift. Damfort.

"The names of Neweberry men to bee disarmed are Mr. Dummer, Mr. Easton, Mr. Spencer, to bee delivered to the constable of the towne.

"The names of Roxberry men to bee disarmed are Mr. Edward Denison, Richard Morris, Richard Bulgar and William Denison, Philip Sherman, to bee delivered to goodman Johnson.

"The names of Ipswich men to bee disarmed are Mr. Foster and Samuel Sherman, which are to deliver their armes to Mr. Bartholomewe.

"The names of Charlestowne men to bee disarmed are Mr. George Bunker and James Browne, who are to deliver their armes to goodman Thomas Line."

"It was ordered, that if any that are to bee disarmed acknowledge their sinn in subscribing the seditious libell, or do not justify it, but acknowledge it evill to two magistrates, they shall bee thereby freed from delivering in their armes according to the former order."

"The towne of Roxberry is required to take order for the safe custody of Mrs. Hutchinson, and if any charge arise, to be defrayed by her husband."

The full and overflowing measure of an honourable and Christian revenge, for this indignity to the lineal ancestor of the editor, was enjoyed by him, little more than thirty-seven years after, when he was commander in chief of all the Massachusetts forces, in the beginning of King Philip's war, and the

were sent into England to be published there, to the end that *all* our godly friends might not be discouraged from coming to us, &c.[1]

After this, many of the church of Boston, being highly offended with the governour for this proceeding, were earnest with the elders to have him called to account for it; but they were not forward in it, and himself, understanding their intent, thought fit to prevent such a publick disorder, and so took occasion to speak to the congregation to this effect:

1. That if he had been called, &c. he would have desired, first, to have advised with the elders, whether the church had power to call in question the proceedings of the civil court.

2. He would have consulted with the rest of the court, whether he might discover the ||counsels|| of the court to this assembly.

3. Though he knew, that the elders and some others did know, that the church could not inquire into the justice and proceedings of the court, &c.; yet, for the ||[2]satisfaction|| of such as did not, and were willing to be satisfied, he would declare his mind herein.

4. He showed, that, if the church had such power, they must have it from Christ, but Christ had disclaimed it in his practice ||[3]and|| by rule, as Luke [blank,] Matt. [blank;] and the scripture holds not out any rule or example for it; and though Christ's kingly power be in his church, yet that is not that kingly power whereby he is King of kings and Lord of lords, for by that kings reign and princes, &c. It is true, indeed, that magistrates, as they are church members, are accountable to the church for their failings, but that is when they are out of their calling; for we have examples of the highest magistrates in the same kind, as Uzzia, when he would go offer incense in the temple, the officers of the church called him to account,

||concerns|| ||[2]sanctification|| ||[3]as||

blood of his sons was shed for his country. He was of the council in 1680, and until his death, 14 February, 1682.

Another of these disarmed gentlemen, Edward Hutchinson, son of the prophetess, and brother-in-law of Savage, fell in battle, the same year, in an honourable rank. His will is in our Probate Records, vol. VI. 95. His son, the Hon. Elisha Hutchinson, who died 10 December, 1717, aged 77, was father of Hon. Thomas, born 30 January, 1674, who died 3 December, 1739. This last was father of Thomas, born 9 September, 1711, H. C. 1727, the celebrated historian and unhappy governour of Massachusetts, who died 3 June, 1780. Of this latter Eliot gives an account more full and judicious than of any other in his admirable volume.

1 In the margin is written, "This was printed by Mr. Wells about seven years after." The misrepresentation of the author's name is strange.

and withstood him. But when Asa put a prophet in prison, and when Salam put out Abiathar from the priesthood, (the one being a good act and the other ill,) yet the officers of the church did not call either of them to account for it. If a magistrate shall, in a private way, take away a man's goods or his servant, &c. the church may call him to account for it; but if he doth thus in pursuing a course of justice, (though the thing be unjust,) yet he is not accountable, &c.

5. For himself, he did nothing in the cases of the brethren, but by the advice and direction of our teacher and other of the elders. For in the oath, which was administered to him and the rest, &c. there was inserted, by his advice, this clause,—In all causes wherein you are to give your vote, &c. you are to give your vote as in your judgment and conscience you shall see to be most for the publick good, &c.; and so for his part he was persuaded, that it would be most for the glory of God, and the publick good, to pass sentence as they did.

6. He would give them one reason, which was ||a|| ground for his judgment, and that was, for that he saw, that those brethren, &c. were so divided from the rest of the country in their judgment and practice, as it could not stand with the publick peace, that they should continue amongst us. So, by the example of Lot in Abraham's family, and after Hagar and Ishmael, he saw they must be sent away.[1]

Mo. 11.] The church at Roxbury dealt with divers of their members, (who had their hands to the petition,) and spent many days in publick meetings to have brought them to see their sin in that, as also in the corrupt opinions, which they held, but could not prevail with them. So they proceeded to two or three admonitions, and, when all was in ||[2]vain,|| they cast them out of the church. In their dealing with them, they took some of them in plain lies and other foul distempers.

[Blank.]

9.] Divers of the elders went to Weymouth, to reconcile the differences between the people and Mr. [2]Jenner, whom

||the|| ||[2]union||

[1] That such examples from the private history of the Jewish patriarchs were alleged as justification of the intolerance of the ruling party, should not lessen our esteem of the general prudence of Winthrop, which, on the main subject of inquiry before the church, is exhibited with great happiness, and must have satisfied, or silenced, all opponents.

[2] Thomas Jenner remained not long at Weymouth, though he represented the town in general court, May, 1640; for, in Hutchinson's Coll. 111, is a letter, and a good one, from him, early in 1641, at Saco. He had been made free of the colony 8 December, 1636. Lechford, 45, speaks of him as residing in Maine. Weymouth seems to have been peculiarly unfortunate in its minis-

they had called thither with intent to have him their pastor. They had good success of their prayers.

13.] About thirty persons of Boston going out in a fair day to Spectacle Island to cut wood, (the town being in great want thereof,[1]) the next night the wind rose so high at N. E. with snow, and after at N. W. for two days, and then it froze so hard, as the bay was all frozen up, ||save|| a little channel. In this twelve of them gate to the Governour's Garden, and seven more were carried in the ice in a small skiff out at Broad Sound, and kept among Brewster's Rocks, without food or fire, two days, and then, the wind forbearing, they gate to Pullin Point, to a little house there of Mr. Aspenwall's. Three of them gate home the next day over the ice, but their hands and feet frozen. Some lost their fingers and toes, and one died. The rest went from Spectacle Island to the main, but two of them fell into the ice, yet recovered again.

In this extremity of weather, a small pinnace was cast away upon Long Island by Natascott, but the men were ||[2]saved,|| and came home upon the ice.

[Large blank.]

16.] The powder and arms of the country, which were kept at Boston, were, by order of the last court, carried to Roxbury and Newtown.[2]

This year a plantation was begun at Tecticutt by a gen-

||except|| ||[2]found||

---

ters, the first five having all been transplanted. Hull, Jenner and Lenthall, appear in this History; Newman removed to Rehoboth; and when they were happy with Thacher, in the second generation, he was, in 1669, transferred to Boston. I presume Jenner went home to England; for, in Hazard, II. 78, a letter of Edward Winslow, London, 17 April, 1651, speaks of a purchase of his library for Harvard College, he being poor, and then living in Norfolk.

[1] It may seem strange, that a scarcity of wood should occur so soon after the settlement of the town; but we must remember its narrow dimensions within the peninsula, and presume that none was brought in from the country. By the accident which befel one of elder Oliver's sons cutting wood *on the neck* in January, 1632—3, we see there was then wood enough for the occasions of the people; and the Town Records, for three or four years later, contain frequent regulations of the manner and quantity in which the inhabitants might there be supplied. The forest was *now* probably exhausted, and in a letter, giving an account of the same disaster recorded in the text, the governour says to his son, " we at Boston were almost ready to break up for want of wood." Still there was plenty on the islands in the harbour. The continuance of our city has never been materially endangered since 1637 for want of fuel.

[2] We can assign no other reason for this measure than the religious opinions of the majority of Boston, by which the condition of the other party was rendered unsafe. As their faith was so unsound as to require the government to disarm them, there was little need of powder in the magazine.

tlewoman, an ancient maid, one Mrs. [1]Poole. She went late thither, and endured much hardship, and lost much cattle. Called, after, Taunton.[2]

[Blank.]

---

1 She was probably encouraged in her perilous undertaking by the Rev. William Hooke, who was the spiritual guide of the new settlement until he removed to New Haven. This was no long time, yet it is variously given, as are also the circumstances of ordination or installation, by Trumbull, I. 280, 286, 296, 493.

Hooke was *teacher* at New Haven, after the return of Samuel Eaton, but went home in 1656. I presume both of them were overshadowed by the powers of Davenport, the pastor. Yet the talents of Hooke were respectable. A very interesting letter from him to Winthrop of Connecticut, about the private intrigues and difficulties of Cromwell, with whom he was in great favour, is preserved in 3 Hist. Coll. I. 181, from vol. XIX. of Trumbull MSS. Whalley, the regicide, was, I find from MS., brother of his wife, which circumstance may partly account for the devotion shown to him and Goffe at New Haven. Hooke died 21 March, 1667, says Trumbull, but Mather makes it 1678.

In the Records of Taunton proprietors, which I have examined, in setting out Mrs. Poole's lot, May, 1639, reference is made to Hooke's lot. She was, I think, accompanied by some relatives; for in the town books is found, "Timothy Poole, the son of Mr. William Poole, died the 15th of December, 1667. He was drowned in a little pond at Nesquabinausit, where it was thought he did swim in after a goose, which he had shot." In this most ancient town of Bristol county, the curious traveller may see a fair slab, formerly laid over the grave of this virgin mother of Taunton, now removed to the common burial ground, having this inscription:

"Here rest the remains
of Mrs. Elizabeth Pool,
a native of Old England,
of good family, friends and prospects,
all which she left, in the prime of her life,
to enjoy the religion of her conscience
in this distant wilderness;
a great proprietor of the township
of Taunton,
a chief promoter of its settlement
and its incorporation 1639—40,
about which time she settled near this spot;
and, having employed the opportunity
of her virgin state
in piety, liberality,
and sanctity of manners,
died, May 21st, A. D. 1654, aged 65;
to whose memory
this monument is gratefully erected
by her next of kin,
John Borland, Esquire,
A. D. 1771."

2 A town so early settled as Taunton should have some history; and as it is not included in Prince's list of deficiencies, I presume, that, in the immense collection of that most diligent antiquary, three fourths of a century since, one was contained, but now gone, with his other MS. treasures, to the winds

Another plantation was begun (and called Sandwich) about fifteen miles beyond Plimouth, towards Cape Cod, by many families, which removed from Sagus, otherwise Lynn.[1]

[Blank.]

Upon occasion of the censures of the court upon Mrs. Hutchinson and others, divers other foul errours were discovered, which had been secretly carried by way of inquiry, but after were maintained by Mrs. Hutchinson and others; and so many of Boston were tainted with them, as Mr. Cotton, finding how he had been abused, and made (as himself said) their stalking horse, (for they pretended to hold nothing but what Mr. Cotton held, and himself did think the same,) did spend most of his time, both publickly and privately, to discover those errours, and to reduce such as were gone astray. And also the magistrates, calling together such of the elders as were near, did spend two days in consulting with them about the way to help the growing evils.

Some of the secret opinions were these:

That there is no inherent righteousness in a child of God.

That neither absolute nor conditional ||promises|| belong to a Christian.

That we are not bound to the law, not as a rule, &c.

That the Sabbath is but as other days.

That the soul is mortal, till it be united to Christ, and then it is annihilated, and the body also, and a new given by Christ.

That there is no resurrection of the body.

[Very large blank.]

Mo. 12.] Divers gentlemen and others, being joined in a military company, desired to be made a corporation, &c. But the council, considering (from the example of the Pretorian band among the Romans, and the Templars in Europe) how dangerous it might be to erect a standing authority of military men, which might easily, in time, overthrow the civil power, thought fit to stop it betimes. Yet they were allowed to be a company, but subordinate to all authority.[2]

||praises||

---

or the flames. The first volume of Bristol county's Registry of Deeds contains a more recent confirmation of lands of Titicut, purchased in 1637, by Mrs. Poole, in behalf of the town of Taunton.

1 If no other lover of the things of old will undertake to set in order the annals of Sandwich, the publick may well expect the favour from the historian of Plimouth. The possession of the faculty is evidence of the call to such a work.

2 A reason for this jealousy will appear in the course of a few paragraphs

About this time the Indians, which were in our families, were much frighted with Hobbamock (as they call the devil) appearing to them in divers shapes, and persuading them to forsake the English, and not to come at the assemblies, nor to learn to read, &c.

26.] Mr. Peirce, in the Salem ship, the Desire, returned from the West Indies after seven months. He had been at Providence, and brought some cotton, and tobacco, and negroes,[1] &c. §from thence,§ and salt from Tertugos. Dry fish and strong liquors are the only commodities for those parts. He met there two men-of-war, set forth by the lords, &c. of Providence with letters of mart, who had taken divers prizes from the Spaniard, and many negroes.

Mo. 1.] While Mrs. Hutchinson continued at Roxbury, divers of the elders and others resorted to her, and finding her to persist in maintaining those gross errours beforementioned, and many others, to the number of thirty or thereabout, some of them wrote to the church at Boston, offering to make proof of the same before the church, &c. 15; whereupon she was called, (the magistrates being desired to give her license to come,) and the lecture was appointed to begin at ten. (The general court being then at Newtown, the governour and the treasurer, being members of Boston, were permitted to come down, but the rest of the court continued at Newtown.) When she appeared, the errours were read to her. The first was, that the souls of men are mortal by generation, but, after, made immortal by Christ's purchase. This she maintained a long time; but at length she was so clearly convinced by reason and scripture, and the whole church agreeing that sufficient had been delivered for her conviction, that she yielded she had been in an errour. Then they proceeded to three

---

onward; but this company, now known as the Ancient and Honourable Artillery, soon triumphed over such scruples, and has enjoyed, in a remarkable manner, the countenance of the government of colony, province and commonwealth. The History of this military band was published, in 1820, by Zechariah G. Whitman, Esq. Keayne, its first captain, was orthodox, as we see from the order in a preceding note, page 248, that the arms of the disaffected of Boston were ordered to be surrendered at his house. His creed was more correct than his practice, on which a few remarks by the historian, and some exemplification by the editor, will appear.

1 Perhaps the unavoidable conclusion from this passage is, that slaves were brought here for sale. It was an unhappy exchange for the Indians—fifteen boys and two women—he had carried out, (see page 234;) though perhaps the blacks were happier than their red brethren. A few years later, we shall see a very honourable testimony of our fathers against the horrible practice of taking the negroes from their native land.

other errours: 1. That there was no resurrection of these bodies, and that these bodies were not united to Christ, but every person united hath a new body, &c. These were also clearly confuted, but yet she held her ||own ;|| so as the church (all but two of her sons) agreed she should be admonished, and because her sons would not agree to it, they were admonished also.[1]

||error||

[1] Bating what is incomprehensible, and may be rejected rather as nonsense than heresy, we should easily imagine, that a construction in the mildest sense would have found little damnable errour in these opinions. It was well that the projector of such novelties was not branded as an atheist, or Sadducee, denying the resurrection and future life altogether. Controversialists easily impute to the dogmas of their opponents consequences drawn only by the imputers, and then fasten on the new doctrines the opprobrium of their false inferences.

The doctrine of resurrection of the body, apparently of heathen origin, though incautiously asserted in words by Christians of many communions, I am glad to find so early disputed in Massachusetts. The materialists have indeed the majority on their side from a very early age of our religion, the Author and Finisher of which, in giving instruction to the poor, deemed it unnecessary to explain, what could hardly, in those times, be made intelligible, —the manner of existence in the future state. This part of the creed is not taught in the scriptures. But, in his first letter to the church of Corinth, xv. 35—51, the greatest of the apostles has illustrated, as far as the original and *acquired* ignorance of his correspondents could receive the explanation, the subject of a resurrection in a manner perfectly consistent with the refined intellectual philosophy of the spiritualists. Yet he strongly marks the folly of the question, "How are the dead raised, and with what bodies do they come?"

Hutchinson, I. 422, in a note to his chap. 6, which treats of the Indians, quotes Roger Williams as saying, "that when he had discoursed of the creation, of the soul, of the danger of it, and the saving of it, they assented; but when he spake of the resurrection of the body, they cried out, We will never believe this." On that passage a gentleman, distinguished in the civil history of our country in its latest age, had made a remark like this: "This doctrine of the resurrection of the body is, it seems, so absurd as to stagger even the credulity of Indians." Having sent to Washington, for the purpose of verifying this quotation, I find, from my friend's reply, that the words "*had been most carefully scratched out with a penknife.*" To me it seems a proof of more timid than useful friendship.

The future restoration of the *flesh*, as well as the soul, though asserted by speculative expounders of our religion in the second or third age after the apostles, did not become a necessary symbol of faith before the middle of the fourth century. A dignitary of the church of England, higher in learning than station, left, to be published after his death, "An Enquiry when the Resurrection of the Body, or Flesh, was first inserted into the publick Creeds," London, 1757. When the reader learns, that A. A. SYKES was the author, he will need no other recommendation of this modest tract.

A profound and original philosopher, to whom revelation owes much for his aid, in "The Light of Nature Pursued," vol. III. 425, offers a striking observation, which shall close this note: "As to the vulgar notion of a resurrection in the same form and substance we carry about at present, the various ways in which it has been expounded, and many difficulties raised

Mr. Cotton pronounced the sentence of admonition with great solemnity, and with much zeal and detestation of her errours and pride of spirit. The assembly continued till eight at night, and all did acknowledge the special presence of God's spirit therein; and she was appointed to appear again the next lecture day.

While the general court sate, there came a letter, directed to the court, from John [1]Greene of Providence, who, not long before, had been imprisoned and fined, for saying that the magistrates had usurped upon the power of Christ in his church, and had persecuted Mr. Williams and another, whom they had banished for disturbing the peace by divulging their opinions against the authority of the magistrates, &c.; but upon his submission, &c. his fine was remitted; and now, by his letter, he retracted his former submission, and charged the court as he had done before. Now, because the court knew, that divers others of Providence were of the same ill affection to the court, and were probably suspected to be confederate in the same letter, the court ordered, that, if any of that plantation were found within our jurisdiction, he should be brought before one of the magistrates, and if he would not disclaim the charge in the said letter, he should be sent home, and charged to come no more into this jurisdiction, upon pain of imprisonment and further censure.

At this court, divers of our chief military officers, who had declared themselves favourers of the familistical persons and opinions, were sent for, and being told, that the court having

---

upon them all, sufficiently declare it untenable: and the reason ordinarily given, because the body, being partaker in the deed, ought to share in the reward, as well requires a resurrection of the sword a man murders with, or the bank note he gives to charitable uses; for our mind is the sole agent, and our hands are as much instruments as any thing we hold in them."

[1] He is, probably, the same gentleman, of whom much will be found in our second volume, as a chief planter of Warwick, with Gorton and Holden; and from whom the highly respectable family in Rhode Island, of which was the celebrated General Greene, derives its descent. Like most other dwellers in that colony, he was subject to vexation from our government; for, in the Record of proceedings at our court, 1 August, 1637, I observe, "Mr. John Greene of New Providence, having spoken against the magistrates contemptuously, stands bound, in one hundred marks, to appear at the next quarter court to be held the first Tuesday of the 7th month ensuing;" and on 19th of *that* month he was fined £20, and forbid to come into this jurisdiction on pain of fine and imprisonment. His religious opinions seem not to have attracted the wrath of heaven to shorten his days, for he was deputy governour of the heterodox colony in 1700. See Callender, 35, 37, 43, 93.

some jealousy of them for the same, and therefore did desire some ||good|| satisfaction from them, they did ingenuously acknowledge, how they had been deceived and misled by the pretence, which ||2was|| held forth, of advancing Christ, and debasing the creature, &c. which, since, they had found to be otherwise, and that their opinions and practice ||3tended|| to disturbance and delusions; and so blessed God, that had so timely discovered their errour and danger to them.

At this court, a committee was appointed, of some magistrates, some ministers, and some others, to compile a body of fundamental laws.

Also the elders (who had been requested to deliver their judgments concerning the law of adultery, about which three had been kept long in prison) returned their answer, with the reasons thereof, to this effect: That, if the law had been sufficiently published, they ought to be put to death. Whereupon the court, considering that there had been some ||4defect|| in that point, and especially for that it had been oft questioned among the deputies and others, whether that law were of force or not, being made by the court of assistants by allowance of the general court; therefore it was thought safest, that these three persons should be whipped and banished;[1] and the law was confirmed and published.

The Castle Island being found to be very chargeable to maintain the garrison there, and of little use, but only to have some command of ships, which should come hither with passengers, &c. there was a committee appointed to dispose of the ammunition there, &c.[2]

22.] Mrs. Hutchinson appeared again; (she had been licensed by the court, in regard she had given hope of her repentance, to be at Mr. Cotton's house, that both he and Mr. Davenport might have the more opportunity to deal with her;) and the articles being again read to her, and her answer required, she delivered it in writing, wherein she made a retractation of near all, but with such explanations and circumstances as gave no satisfaction to the church; so as she was required to speak further to them. Then she declared, that it was just with God to leave

||general|| ||2had been|| ||3led|| ||4dispute||

1 On pain of death for returning, the Colony Record has it.

2 The rate levied by this court, of £1500, shows a considerable variance from the proportions in August preceding: Boston, £233.10; Ipswich, £180; Salem, £172.10; Dorchester, £140; Charlestown, £138; Roxbury, £115; Watertown, £110; Newtown, £106; Lynn, £105; Newbury, £75; Medford, £52.10; Hingham, £36; Weymouth, £27; and Mr. Theophilus Eaton, £20.

her to herself, as he had done, for her slighting his ordinances, both magistracy and ministry; and confessed, that what she had spoken against the magistrates at the court (by way of revelation) was rash and ungrounded; and desired the church to pray for her. This gave the church good hope of her repentance; but when she was examined about some particulars, as that she had denied inherent righteousness, &c. she affirmed that it was never her judgment; and though it was proved by many testimonies, that she had been of that judgment, and so had persisted, and maintained it by argument against divers, yet she impudently persisted in her affirmation, to the astonishment of all the assembly. So that, after much time and many arguments had been spent to bring her to see her sin, but all in vain, the church, with one consent, cast her out. Some moved to have her admonished once more; but, it being for manifest evil in matter of conversation, it was agreed otherwise; and for that reason also the sentence was denounced by the pastor, matter of manners belonging properly to his place.

After she was excommunicated, her spirits, which seemed before to be somewhat dejected, revived again, and she gloried in her sufferings, saying, that it was the greatest happiness, next to Christ, that ever befel her.[1] Indeed, it was a happy day to the churches of Christ here, and to many poor souls, who had been seduced by her, who, by what they heard and saw that day, were (through the grace of God) brought off quite from her errours, and settled again in the truth.

At this time the good providence of God so disposed, divers of the congregation (being the chief men of the party, her husband being one) were gone to Naragansett to seek out a

---

1 Welde, 68, calls her the American Jezabel, and is surprised, in the simplicity of his bigotry, at her hardness of heart in slighting the excommunication, "as she is not affected with any remorse, but glories in it, and fears not the vengeance of God, which she lies under; as if God did work contrary to his own word, and loosed from heaven what his church had bound upon earth." The sober ecclesiastical historian closes his book with these appropriate remarks. But the blood of this Jezabel,—the reader will see the propriety of this hard name, when, in a very few years, she and most of her family were murdered by the Indians on Long Island, as the author of Rise, Reign and Ruin exultingly relates,—the blood of this Jezabel, besides being licked by the dogs, was, in two generations, mixed, by intermarriage, with the more orthodox 'ιχωρ of Thomas Welde. His grandson, of the same name, first pastor of the church of Dunstable, gathered 16 December, 1685, took to wife a great granddaughter of this same outcast from heaven and from the church of Boston. The sin of the progenitor was, I presume, exhausted by subdivision, or neutralized by admixture; for their son, Habijah S. Welde, was minister of Attleborough. See Alden's Collection of Epitaphs, I. 110, with III. 41.

new place for plantation, and taking liking of one in Plimouth patent, they went thither to have it granted them; but the magistrates there, knowing their spirit, gave them a denial, but consented they might buy of the Indians an island in the Naragansett Bay.[1]

After two or three days, the governour sent a warrant to Mrs. Hutchinson to depart this jurisdiction before the last of this month, according to the order of court, and for that end set her at liberty from her former constraint, so as she was not to go forth of her own house till her departure; and upon the 28th she went by water to her farm at the Mount, where she was to take water, with Mr. Wheelwright's wife and family, to go to Pascataquack; but she changed her mind, and went by land to Providence, and so to the island in the Naragansett Bay, which her husband and the rest of that sect had purchased of the Indians, and prepared with all speed to remove unto. For the court had ordered, that, except they were gone with their families by such a time, they should be summoned to the general court, &c.

30.] Mr. Davenport, and Mr. [2]Prudden, and a brother of Mr. Eaton, (being ministers also,) went by water to Quinepiack; and with them many families removed out of this jurisdiction to plant in those parts, being much taken with the opinion of the fruitfulness of that place, and more safety (as they conceived) from danger of a general governour, who was feared to be sent this summer; which, though it were a great weakening to these parts, yet we expected to see a good providence of God in it, (for all possible means had been used to accommodate them here: Charlestown offered them largely, Newbury their whole town, the court any place which was free,) both for possessing those parts which lay open for an enemy, and for strengthening our friends at Connecticut, and for making room here for many, who were expected out of Eng-

---

1 The *denial* was matter of inference, for the adventurers were resolved to go free of Plimouth as well as Massachusetts; and the *consent* was the advice of equals, not the dictate of superiours. See Callender, 30, who informs us, that these purchasers of Rhode Island formed their civil compact 7 March, and that the cession by the Indian sachems was of the 24th of same month. As twelve of these eighteen associates were members of the church of Boston, the advantage taken of their absence, by "the good providence of God," would be thought, in a day of less ferment, disadvantageous to a cause, or dishonourable to its supporters.

2 Peter Prudden, who was first minister of Milford, Conn. was useful in his place, and of high esteem in the colony of New Haven, but nothing more can be learned of him than Dr. Trumbull, I. 294, supplying in part the deficiency of Mather, has told.

land this year, and for diverting the thoughts and intentions of such in England as intended evil against us, whose designs might be frustrate by our scatterings so far; and such as were now gone that way were as much in the eye of the state of England as we here.[1]

There came letters from Connecticut to the governour of the Massachusetts, to desire advice from the magistrates and elders here about Sequin and the Indians of the river, who had, underhand, (as was conceived,) procured the Pequods to do that ||onslaught|| at Weathersfield the last year. The case fell out to be this: Sequin gave the English land there, upon ||[2]contract|| that he might sit down by them and be protected, &c. When he came to Weathersfield, and had set down his wigwam, they drave him away by force. Whereupon, he not being of strength to repair this injury by open force, he secretly draws in the Pequods. Such of the magistrates and elders as could meet on the sudden returned this answer, viz. That, if the cause were thus, Sequin might, upon this injury first offered by them, right himself either by force or fraud, and that by the law of nations; and though the damage he had done them had been one hundred times more than what he sustained from them, that is not considerable in point of a just war; neither was he bound (upon such an open act of hostility publickly maintained) to seek satisfaction first in a peaceable way; it was enough, that he had complained of it as an injury and breach of covenant. According to this advice, they proceeded and made a new agreement with the Indians of the river.

Another plantation was now in hand at Mattakeese,[2] six miles beyond Sandwich. The undertaker of this was one Mr. Batchellor, late pastor at Sagus, (since called Lynn,) being about seventy-six years of age; yet he walked thither on foot in a very hard season.

He and his company, being all poor men, finding the difficulty, gave it over, and others undertook it.

||blank|| ||[2]Connecticut||

---

1 An excellent letter of Davenport and Gov. Eaton, the fathers of New Haven colony, giving the reasons of their removal, may be seen in the Appendix. It was copied by me from the original, in the handwriting of the first signer.

2 "Now Yarmouth," is written in the margin. Of that town a collection of Memorabilia is contained in 1 Hist. Coll. V. 54—60. Some correction of a slight errour in that tract will be found in a note on Marmaduke Matthews.

27.] The Indians of Block Island sent three men with ten fathom of wampom for part of their tribute.

The [1]wife of one William Dyer, a milliner in the New Exchange, a very ||proper|| and fair woman, and both of them notoriously infected with Mrs. Hutchinson's errours, and very censorious and troublesome, (she being of a very proud spirit, and much addicted to revelations,) had been delivered of [a] child some ||[2]few|| months before, §October 17,§ and the child buried, (being stillborn,) and viewed of none but Mrs. Hutchinson and the midwife, one Hawkins's wife, a rank familist also; and another woman had a glimpse of it, who, not being able to keep counsel, as the other two did, some rumour began to spread, that the child was a monster. One of the elders, hearing of it, asked Mrs. Hutchinson, when she was ready to depart; whereupon she told him how it was, and said she meant to have it chronicled, but excused her concealing of it till then, (by advice, as she said, of Mr. Cotton,) which coming to the governour's knowledge, he called another of the magistrates and that elder, and sent for the midwife, and examined her about it. At first she confessed only, that the head was defective and misplaced, but being told that Mrs. Hutchinson had ||[3]revealed|| all, and that he intended to have it taken up and viewed, she made this report of it, viz. It was a woman child, stillborn, about two months before the just time, having life a few hours before; it came hiplings till she turned it; it was of ordinary bigness; it had a face, but no head, and the ears stood upon the shoulders and were like an ape's; it had no forehead, but over the eyes four horns, hard and sharp; two of them were above one inch long, the other two shorter; the eyes standing out, and the mouth also; the nose hooked upward; all over the breast and back full of sharp pricks and scales, like a thornback; the navel and all the belly, with the distinction of the sex, were where the back should be, and the back and hips before, where the belly should have been; be-

||promp|| ||[2]four|| ||[3]recalled||

[1] Her name was Mary. She had been, with her husband, admitted of Boston church 13 December, 1635. After long enjoying her revelations, in quiet, at Rhode Island, she was unhappily led, about twenty-one years làter, again to visit Boston, probably bringing more light, when she was condemned to death as a Quaker. Winthrop, governour of Connecticut, oùr author's eldest son, inheriting the natural mildness of his father, attempted to save her life; but the bigotry of the age had acquired a severer character, and, for a second return, in June, 1660, she suffered. See Hutchinson, I. 184. Yet her son, at that very time, held an important office in the neighbouring colony. The influence of such cruelty could not be favourable.

hind, between the shoulders, it had two mouths, and in each of them a piece of red flesh sticking out; it had arms and legs as other children; but, instead of toes, it had on each foot three claws, like a young fowl, with sharp talons.[1]

The governour speaking with Mr. Cotton about it, he told him the reason why he advised them to conceal it: 1. Because he saw a providence of God in it, that the rest of the women, which were coming and going in the time of her travail, should then be absent. 2. He considered, that, if it had been his own case, he should have desired to have had it concealed. 3. He had known other monstrous births, which had been concealed, and that he thought God might intend only the instruction of the parents, and such other to whom it was ||known,|| &c. The like apology he made for himself in publick, which was well accepted.[2]

||shown||

---

1 From this disgusting story we are authorized by Welde to derive profit, less indeed for doctrine than for reproof. In his preface he favours us with the means of deliverance from the antinomian heresy,—preaching, conferences, the synod, the exertions of the magistrates in disfranchising, fining, or banishing the deluded, and, lastly, the misfortunes of Mrs. Dyer and Mrs. Hutchinson. He thus relates the ultimate cause of success:

"Then God himself was pleased to step in with his casting voice, and bring in his own vote and suffrage from Heaven, by testifying his displeasure against their opinions and practices, as clearly as if he had pointed with his finger, in causing the two fomenting women, in the time of the height of the opinions, to produce out of their wombs, as before they had out of their brains, such monstrous births, as no chronicle (I think) hardly ever recorded the like." He after asserts, "He that runs may read their sin in these judgments."

This "suffrage from heaven" is introduced in the wrong place, by Welde, as proxy or attorney of the Most High, such is the character he claims; for it appears by the text, that Mrs. Dyer's premature delivery was between the time of the synod and that of the general court, possibly occasioned by the result of the former and the expectation of the latter.

Another New England divine, of purer spirit as of greater name, has left a sermon, to which we may often turn for refreshment, when sickened with these uncharitable denunciations. Buckminster, XXIV. In the foul records of ecclesiastical history, one is frequently shocked with discoveries of the anger of Providence, asserted with higher presumption and directness than by the Temanite in his *questions* to his afflicted friend: "Remember, I pray thee, who ever perished, being *innocent?* Or where were the *righteous* cut off?" This execrable spirit belongs not to any particular communion; and that church, which must reproach itself with fewest instances, may still have enough to regret. On occasion of the sudden death of Jovian, Cardinal Baronius, "as being one of the privy council of Heaven, declares, that this emperour was taken out of the world by a divine judgment, because he had made a decent funeral for his predecessor Julian." Jortin's Eccl. Hist.

2 Apology to Cotton ought to have been made for the inquiry, rather than by him for the concealment, if the suspicion, under which he lay, had been entertained by a people less jealous for the honour of God, and less careful to

(2.)] The governour, with advice of some other of the magistrates and of the elders of Boston, caused the said monster to be taken up, and though it were much corrupted, yet most of those things were to be seen, as the horns and claws, the scales, &c. When it died in the mother's body, (which was about two hours before the birth,) the bed whereon the mother lay did shake, and withal there was such a noisome savour, as most of the women were taken with §extreme vomiting and purging, so as they were forced to depart; and others of them their children were taken with§ convulsions, (which they never had before nor after,) and so were sent for home, so as by these occasions it came to be concealed.

Another thing observable was, the discovery of it, which was just when Mrs. Hutchinson was cast out of the church. For Mrs. Dyer going forth with her, a stranger asked, what young woman it was. The others answered, it was the woman which had the monster; which gave the first occasion to some that heard it to speak of it. The midwife, presently after this discovery, went out of the jurisdiction; and indeed it was time for her to be gone, for it was known, that she used to give young women oil of mandrakes and other stuff to cause conception; and she grew into great suspicion to be a witch, for it was credibly reported, that, when she gave any medicines, (for she practised physick,) she would ask the ||party,|| if she did believe, she could help her, &c.[1]

Another observable passage was, that the father of this monster, coming home at this very time, was, the next Lord's day, §by an unexpected providence,§ questioned in the church for divers monstrous errours, as for denying all inherent

||patient||

---

vindicate it, as they supposed, by ascribing to his displeasure the cross accidents, that befel their opponents.

1 She did not go voluntarily, as by the text we might be led to infer; for our Colony Rec. I. 219, looks very much like banishment: "Jane Hawkins, the wife of Richard Hawkins, had liberty till the beginning of the third month, called May, and the magistrates (if she did not depart before) to dispose of her; and, in the mean time, she is not to meddle in surgery or physick, drink, plaisters, or oils, nor to question matters of religion, except with the elders for satisfaction." I suppose her oil of antinomianism was more dreaded than her oil of mandrakes.

Her "*suspicion to be a witch*," above, is elegantly expanded, in the History of Welde, to "notorious for familiarity with the devil;" and I am very sorry to remark, that Winthrop himself, at a later period, 1640, gives countenance to the same absurdity. Such intercourse, however, was not made capital for several years, or Welde might then have enjoyed, as *suspicion* of such a crime must be equal to full proof, the delight imputed to some of his brethren of the clergy, two generations after, in the delusion of 1692.

righteousness, &c. which he maintained, and was for the same admonished.

12.] A general fast was kept through all the churches, by advice from the court, for seeking the Lord to prevent evil, that we feared to be intended against us from England by a general governour; for the safe arrival of our friends from thence, (very many being expected;) and for establishment of peace and truth amongst us.

21.] Owsamekin, the sachem of Acooemeck, on this side Connecticut, came to the governour and brought a present of eighteen skins of beaver from himself and the sachems of Mohegan beyond Connecticut and Pakontuckett. The occasion was, (as he said,) it was reported, that we were angry with him, and intended to war upon them; so they came to seek peace. The governour received the present, and (having none of the other magistrates at hand to advise with) answered them, that if they had done no wrong to the English, nor aided our enemies, we would be at peace with them; and accordingly signified so much to the magistrates at Connecticut. They took this answer well, and departed with the letter.

23.] This was a very hard winter. The snow lay, from November 4th to March 23d, ||half a|| yard deep about the Massachusetts, and a yard deep beyond Merrimack, and so the more north the deeper, and the spring was very backward. This day it did snow two hours together, (after much rain from N. E.) with flakes as great as shillings. This was in the year 1637.

§ 24.] The governour and deputy went to Concord to view some land for farms, and, going down the river about four miles, they made choice of a place for one thousand acres for each of them. They offered each other the first choice, but because the deputy's was first granted, and himself had store of land already, the governour yielded him the choice. So, at the place where the deputy's land was to begin, there were two great stones, which they called the Two Brothers, in remembrance that they were brothers by their children's marriage, and did so brotherly agree, and for that a little creek near those stones was to part their lands. At the court in the 4th month after, two hundred acres were added to the governour's part.§[1]

||one and an half||

---

1 This paragraph is marked by a line down the margin, and "This may be left out" written in the same hand. I prefer to disregard the author's modesty, for the anecdote is interesting, and derives importance from the act of the general court, adopting *the name of the rocks* given by the grantees on their selection of these lands. See Col. Rec. I. 222.

26.] Mr. Coddington (who had been an assistant from the first coming over of the ||government,|| being, with his wife, taken with the familistical opinions) removed to Aquiday Island in the Naragansett Bay.

(3.) 2.] At the court of elections, the former governour, John Winthrop, was chosen again. The same day, at night, he was taken with a sharp fever, which brought him near death; but many prayers were put up to the Lord for him, and he was restored again after one month.

This court the name of Newtown was altered, and it was called Cambridge.[1]

The spring was so cold, that men were forced to ||[2]plant|| their corn two or three times, for it rotted in the ground; but, when we feared a great dearth, God sent a warm season, which brought on corn beyond expectation.

(4.) 1.] Between three and four in the afternoon, being clear, warm weather, the wind westerly, there was a great earthquake. It came with a noise like a continued thunder, or the rattling of coaches in London, but was presently gone. It was at Connecticut, at Naragansett, at Pascataquack, and all the parts round about. It shook the ships, which rode in the harbour, and all the islands, &c. The noise and the shakings continued about four minutes. The earth was unquiet twenty days after, by times.[2]

5.] Unkus, alias Okoco, the Monahegan sachem in the twist of Pequod River, came to Boston with thirty-seven men. He came from Connecticut with Mr. Haynes, and tendered the governour a present of twenty fathom of wampom. This was at the court, and it was thought fit by the council to refuse it, till he had given satisfaction about the Pequods he kept, &c. Upon this he was much dejected, and made account we would have killed him; but, two days after, having received good satis-

||governor|| ||[2]replant||

---

[1] In compliment to the place, where so many of the civil and clerical fathers of New England had received their education, this venerable name (may it ever be preserved!) was undoubtedly bestowed. There were probably, at that time, forty or fifty sons of the University of Cambridge in Old England—one for every two hundred or two hundred and fifty inhabitants—dwelling in the few villages of Massachusetts and Connecticut. The sons of Oxford were not few.

[2] Johnson, lib. II. c. 12, gives very unsatisfactory accounts of this earthquake. He was more engaged in the shaking of the people out of their antinomianism, in which those of his party went, perhaps, as far from propriety as the others from truth. Morton, in his Memorial, is more particular; yet it is evident his pen was not so careful as modern accuracy requires, for he says, "*about* the second of June."

faction of his innocency, &c. and he promising to submit to the order of the English touching the Pequods he had, and the differences between the Naragansetts and him, we accepted his present. And, about half an hour after, he came to the governour, and entertained him with these compliments: This heart (laying his hand upon his breast) is not mine, but yours; I have no men; they are all yours; command me any difficult thing, I will do it; I will not believe any Indians' words against the English; if any man shall kill an Englishman, I will put him to death, were he never so dear to me. So the governour gave him a fair, red coat, and defrayed his and his men's ||diet,|| and gave them corn to relieve them homeward, and a letter of protection to all men, &c. and he departed very joyful.

Many ships arrived this year, with people of good quality and estate, notwithstanding the council's order, that none §such§ should come without the king's license; but God so wrought, that some obtained §license,§ and others came away without. The troubles which arose in Scotland about the book of common prayer, and the canons, which the king would have forced upon the Scotch churches, did so take up the king and council, that they had neither heart nor leisure to look after the affairs of New England; yet, upon report of the many thousands, which were preparing to come away, the archbishops caused all the ships to be stayed. But, upon the petition of the masters, and suggestion of the great ||2damage|| it would be to the commonwealth in hindering the Newfoundland trade, which brought in much money, &c. they were presently released. And in this and other passages it plainly appeared, that near all the lords of the council did favour this plantation; and all the officers of the custom house were very ready to further it, for they never made search ||3for|| any goods, &c. but let men bring what they would, without question or controul. For ||4sure the Lord awed their hearts, and|| they and others (who savoured not religion) were amazed to see men of all conditions, rich and poor, servants and others, offering themselves so readily for New England, when, for furnishing of other plantations, they were forced to send about their stalls, and when they had gotten any, they were forced to keep them as prisoners from running away.

Mo. (6.) 3.] In the night was a very great tempest or hiracano at S. W. which drave a ship on ground at Charlestown, and brake down the windmill there, and did much other harm. It flowed twice in six hours, and about Naragansett it

||due|| ||2danger|| ||3of|| ||4since the Lords avowed their party, &c.||

raised the tide fourteen or fifteen foot above the ordinary spring tides, upright.

Janemoh, the sachem of Niantick, had gone to Long Island and rifled some of those Indians, which were tributaries to us. The sachem complained to our friends of Connecticut, who wrote us about it, and sent Capt. Mason, with seven men, to require satisfaction. The governour of the Massachusetts wrote also to Mr. Williams to treat with Miantunnomoh about satisfaction, or otherwise to bid them look for war.

Upon this Janemoh went to Connecticut, and made his peace, and gave full satisfaction for all injuries.

Two ships, which came over this year much pestered, lost many passengers, and some principal men, and many fell sick after they were landed, and many of them died.[1]

Four servants of Plimouth ran from their masters, and, coming to Providence, they killed an Indian. He escaped, after he was deadly wounded in the belly, and gat to other Indians. So, being discovered, they fled and were taken at the Isle Aquiday. Mr. Williams gave notice to the governour of Massachusetts, and desired advice. He returned answer, that, seeing they were of Plimouth, they should certify Plimouth of them, and, if they would send for them, to deliver them; otherwise, seeing no English had jurisdiction in the place where the murder was committed, neither had they at the island any ||government|| established, it would be safest to deliver the principal, who was certainly known to have killed the party, to the Indians his friends, with caution that they should not put him to torture, and to keep the other three to further consideration.[2]

||governor||

1 One of the ships so *pestered* was probably that, in which came John Josselyn, gentleman; for five of the passengers died on board. His book is a curiosity, sometimes worth examining, but seldom to be implicitly relied on. Where he speaks, page 20, of Boston as a village of "not above twenty or thirty houses," I suspect the right hand cypher was lost from his manuscript, or memory; for he printed thirty-six years after. The population, I am confident, required the number of dwellings I have supposed, and, in this eighth year of its existence, the log huts, that he *might* scorn to honour with the name of houses, were very few.

2 A directly opposite course of political motives is assigned by Morton. In the Plimouth secretary's Memorial, our author's advice was not given because the criminals belonged to Plimouth, nor because the English had not jurisdiction where the murder was committed, nor because they of Rhode Island were without any government; but "the Massachusetts refused this trial, as being committed in the jurisdiction of Plimouth, and they of Rhode Island, having apprehended them, delivered them to the aforesaid jurisdiction of Plimouth *on the same grounds*." Both writers evidently desire to depreciate the new schismatick colony, or colonies, if Providence and Rhode

After this, Plimouth men sent for them, (but one had escaped,) and the governour there wrote to the governour here for advice, especially for that he heard they intended to appeal into England. The governour returned answer of encouragement to proceed notwithstanding, seeing no appeal did lie, for that they could not be tried in England, and that the whole country here were interested in the case, and would expect to ||have|| justice done. Whereupon they proceeded as appears after.

Many of Boston and others, who were of Mrs. Hutchinson's judgment and party, removed to the Isle of Aquiday; and ||2others,|| who were of the rigid separation, and savoured anabaptism, removed to Providence, so as those parts began to be well peopled.

[Large blank.]

There came over this summer twenty ships, and at least ||3three thousand||[1] persons, so as they were forced to look out new plantations. One was begun at Merrimack, and another four or five miles above Concord, and another at Winicowett.

[Large blank.]

The three prisoners, being brought to Plimouth, and there examined, did all confess the murder, and that they did it to get his wampom, &c.; but all the question was about the death of the Indian, for no man could witness that he saw him dead. But Mr. Williams and Mr. [2]James of Providence made oath, that his wound was mortal, &c. At last two Indians, who, with much difficulty, were procured to come to the trial, (for they still feared that the English were conspired to kill all the In-

||see|| ||2many|| ||3three hundred||

Island be counted two. Winthrop, however, would not deny their independence. In 3 Hist. Coll. I. 171—173, is a very full account, in the original letter of Williams, of all the circumstances of this aggravated and cowardly murder.

1 Dr. Holmes, Ann. I. 305, followed the former edition without scruple, though his excellent judgment must have observed the probability of errour in this number, since the text immediately adds, all the established plantations would not afford room for so many passengers. In the ship with Josselyn were one hundred and sixty-four; and if the others were as full, the corrected reading of our author, which is plain enough in his MS., is within the limits. Hubbard, 242, when transcribing from this part of Winthrop, seems to have been afraid to number either the ships or the passengers. He often avoids the most valuable incidents of his story.

2 I know nothing more of this gentleman than Williams, in his letter, 3 Hist. Coll. I. 172, mentions of his humane endeavours for the sufferer; and in another letter in MS., early in 1649, he notices his return from England, with a full cargo of goods, which were saved from the wreck of the vessel on Rhode Island.

dians,) made oath after this manner, viz. that, if he were not dead of that wound, then they would suffer death. Upon this they three were condemned and executed. Two of them died very penitently, especially Arthur Peach, a young man of good parentage and fair conditioned, and who had done very good service against the Pequods.

The fourth escaped to Pascataquack. The governour sent after him, but those of Pascataquack conveyed him away and openly withstood his apprehension. It was their usual manner (some of them) to countenance, &c. all such lewd persons as fled from us to them.

(7.)] The general court was assembled, in which it was agreed, that, whereas a very strict order was sent from the lords commissioners for plantations for the sending home our patent, upon pretence that judgment had passed against it upon a quo warranto, a letter should be written by the governour, in the name of the court, to excuse our not sending of it; for it was resolved to be best not to send it, because then such of our friends and others in England would conceive it to be surrendered, and that thereupon we should be bound to receive such a governour and such orders as should be sent to us, and many bad minds, yea, and some weak ones, among ourselves, would think it lawful, if not necessary, to accept a general governour. The copy of the letter is reserved, &c. in form of a petition. See the after fol. 74.[1]

At this court a law was made about such as should continue excommunicated six months, and for publick thanksgiving for the arrival of the ships, and for the coming on of harvest beyond expectation, &c. This law was after repealed.[2]

At this court, also, Capt. Underhill (being about to remove to Mr. Wheelwright) petitioned for three hundred acres of land promised him formerly; by occasion whereof he was questioned about some speeches he had used in the ship lately, in his return out of England, viz. that he should say, that we were zealous here, as the Scribes and Pharisees were, and as Paul was before his conversion, &c. which he denying, they were proved to his face by a sober, godly woman, whom he

---

1 The reference is to the page of the governour's MS. but the letter will not be found in this work.

2 A rate of £400 was levied by this court in the following proportions: Boston, £57.14.9; Ipswich, £46.10; Salem, £44.11.3; Dorchester, £36.16.3; Charlestown, £35.13; Cambridge, 34.17.6; Roxbury and Lynn, each, £31; Watertown, £29.1.3; Newbury, £27.2.6; Hingham, £11.2.10; Weymouth, £7.15; and Medford, £6.15.8.

had seduced in the ship, and ||drawn|| to his opinions, (but she was after freed again.) Among other passages, he told her how he came to his assurance, and that was thus: He had lain under a spirit of bondage and a legal way five years, and could get no assurance, till at length, as he was taking a pipe of tobacco, the Spirit set home an absolute promise of free grace with such assurance and joy, as he never since doubted of his good estate, neither should he, though he should fall into sin. He would not confess nor deny this, but took exceptions at the court for crediting one witness against him, &c. and withal said, that he was still of the same opinion he had been, &c. Whereupon he was demanded, if he were of the same opinion he had been in about the petition or remonstrance. He answered, yes, and that his retractation was only of the manner, not of the matter. Whereupon his retractation (which he had lately delivered to the governour, to be presented to this court) was read, wherein he professeth how the Lord had brought him to see his sin in condemning the court, and passing the bounds of modesty and submission, which is required in private persons, &c. and in what trouble of spirit he had been for it, &c. Upon this, the court committed him for abusing the court with a show of retractation, and intending no such thing; and the next day he was called again and banished. The Lord's day following, he made a speech in the assembly, showing that, as the Lord was pleased to convert Paul as he was in persecuting, &c. so he might manifest himself to him as he was taking the moderate use of the creature called tobacco. He professed withal, that he knew not wherein he had deserved the sentence of the court, and that he was sure, that Christ was his, &c. The elders reproved him for this speech; and Mr. Cotton told him, that he brake a rule in condemning publickly the sentence of the court, before he had privately convinced the magistrates, or some of them; and told him also, that, although God doth often lay a man under a spirit of bondage, when he is walking in sin, as Paul was, yet he never sends such a spirit of comfort but in an ordinance, as he did to the same Paul by Ananias; and ||[2]ergo|| advised him well to examine the revelation and joy which he had.

The next Lord's day, the same Capt. Underhill, having been privately dealt with upon suspicion of incontinency with a neighbour's wife, and not hearkening to it, was publickly questioned, and put under admonition. The matter was, for that the woman being young, and beautiful, and withal of a jovial spirit and behaviour, he did daily frequent her house, and was

||drew|| ||[2]so||

divers times found there alone with her, the door being locked on the inside. He confessed it was ill, because it had an appearance of evil in it; but his excuse was, that the woman was in great trouble of mind, and sore temptations, and that he resorted to her to comfort her; and that when the door was found locked upon them, they were in private prayer together. But this practice was clearly condemned also by the elders, affirming, that it had not been of good report for any of them to have done the like, and that they ought, in such case, to have called in some brother or sister, and not to have locked the door, &c. They also declared, that once he procured them to go visit her, telling them that she was in great trouble of mind; but when they came to her, (taking her, it seems, upon the sudden,) they perceived no such thing. See the issue of this after, (9,) 1638, and (10,) 13, 38.

[Large blank.]

Mrs. Hutchinson, being removed to the Isle of Aquiday, in the Naragansett Bay, after her time was fulfilled, that she expected deliverance of a child, was delivered of a monstrous birth, which, being diversly related in the country, (and, in the open assembly at Boston, upon a lecture day, declared by Mr. Cotton to be twenty-seven ||several lumps of man's seed, without any alteration, or mixture of any thing from the woman,|| and thereupon gathered, that it might signify her errour in denying inherent righteousness, but that all was Christ in us, and nothing of ours in our faith, love, &c.) hereupon the governour wrote to Mr. [1]Clarke, a physician and a preacher to those of the

||singula frusta vel globulos seminis masculini sine ulla mutatione aut mixtura de femina||

---

1 John Clarke was one of the most distinguished gentlemen of Rhode Island, of which colony he was long agent in England, during the *reigns* of Oliver, Richard, and part of that of Charles II. The Baptist church of Newport owns him for its father. He published, in 1652, a book, entitled "Ill News from New England, or a Narrative of New England's persecution, wherein is declared, that, while Old England is becoming New, New England is becoming Old," &c. &c. &c. in which he introduced the substance of a tract, issued the preceding year, called "A Brief Discourse touching New England, and particularly Rhode Island; as also a faithful and true relation of the prosecution of Obadiah Holmes, John Crandall, and John Clarke, merely for conscience towards God, by the principal members of the church or commonwealth of the Massachusetts in New England, which rules over that part of the world." This tract was probably by the same hand.

Some light may be derived by us from a petition of the sufferer, of which the original is preserved, from the colony files, in the Historical Society's library: "To the honoured court assembled at Boston. Whereas it pleased this honoured court, yesterday, to condemn the faith and order which I hold and practise; and, after you had passed your sentence upon me for it, were

island, to know the certainty thereof, who returned him this answer: Mrs. Hutchinson, six weeks before her delivery, perceived her body to be greatly distempered, and her spirits failing, and in that regard doubtful of life, she sent to me, &c. and not long after (in ||immoderato fluore uterino||) it was brought to light, and I was called to see it, where I beheld, first unwashed, (and afterwards in warm water,) several lumps, every one of them greatly confused, and if you consider each of them according to the representation of the whole, they were altogether without form; but if they were considered in respect of the parts of each lump of flesh, then there was a representation of innumerable distinct bodies in the form of a globe, not much unlike the swims of some fish, so confusedly knit together by so many several strings, (which I conceive were the beginning of veins and nerves,) so that it was impossible either to number the small round pieces in every lump, much less to discern from whence every string did fetch its original, they were so snarled one within another. The small globes I likewise opened, and perceived the matter of them (setting aside the membrane in which ||[2]it was involved,||) to be partly wind and partly water. Of these several lumps there were about twenty-six, according to the relation of those, who more narrowly

||immoderate fluor and urine|| ||[2]they were involumed||

pleased to express, I could not maintain the same against your ministers, and thereupon publickly proffered me a dispute with them; be pleased by these few lines to understand, I readily accept it, and therefore do desire you would appoint the time when, and the person with whom, in that publick place where I was condemned, I might, with freedom, and without molestation of the civil power, dispute that point publickly, where I doubt not but, by the strength of Christ, to make it good out of his last will and testament, unto which nothing is to be added, nor from which nothing is to be diminished. Thus, desiring the Father of lights to shine forth by his power to expel the darkness, I remain your well wisher, John Clarke. From the prison, this 1. 6. 51," i. e. 1 August, 1651.

In 1653 was published "The Civil Magistrate's Power in Matters of Religion modestly debated, &c. &c. &c. with a brief answer to a certain slanderous pamphlet, called Ill News from New England, &c. by Thomas Cobbett of Lynn in N. E." This was written in the violent temper of that day, thought necessary for the orthodox, but now so universally reprobated. Clarke's book is exceedingly rare, perhaps irrecoverably lost. A copy was in Prince's New England library, but cannot be found now, nor could I hear of the work even in Rhode Island. Cobbett's answer, which could certainly be better spared, is preserved, but is very scarce, only a single copy having ever fallen into my reach. Clarke died, says Benedict, I. 495, in 1676, in the sixty-sixth year of his age, without children. Callender, who is very full in his account of Clarke, 2, 16, 21, 29, 45, 52, 62, 63, 93, marks his death 20 April of that year. From three of his brothers are descended the large family in Rhode Island bearing that name. The article CLARKE, JOHN, in Allen's Biographical Dictionary, is the best in that laborious work.

searched into the number of them. I took notice of six or seven of some bigness; the rest were small; but all as I have declared, except one or two, which differed much from the rest both in matter and form; and the whole was like the [blank] of the liver, being simular and every where like itself. When I had opened it, the matter seemed to be ||blood|| congealed. The governour, not satisfied with this relation, spake after with the said Mr. Clarke, who thus cleared all the doubts: The lumps were twenty-six or twenty-seven, distinct and not joined together; there came no secundine after them; six of them were as great as his fist, and one as great as two fists; the rest each less than other, and the smallest about the bigness of the top of his thumb. The globes were round things, included in the lumps, about the bigness of a small Indian bean, and like the pearl in a man's eye. The two lumps, which differed from the rest, were like liver or congealed blood, and had no small globes in them, as the rest had. Mr. Cotton, next lecture day, acknowledged his errour, &c. and that he had his information by a letter from her husband, &c.[1]

21.] A ship of Barnstaple arrived with about eighty passengers, near all western people. There came with them a godly minister, one Mr. [2]Matthews.

||hard||

---

1 Having been favoured with the original letter of Clarke, I testify that the author's transcription is sufficiently accurate, and nearly literal. It might be unnecessary to add, on this nauseous subject, the introduction of which, at a religious lecture, it seems hardly possible to justify, that Clarke says, he was sent to once and again, and that he considered her condition was both doubtful and dangerous, and that he was somewhat unwilling to meddle, at least before her delivery, but only advised to procure some medicines from the bay proper for the occasion; for "I conceived," he adds, "if it were a child, it was dead, but rather that it was not, but such a thing as afterward it proved." It is strange, that the word, which the governour leaves blank, is, plainly, *lobe* in the original letter. On the margin of the letter, the governour has added what Clarke told him, nearly as given in the text, with this slight variation: "the globes were like pearls, about the bigness of a sloe."

2 Very diligent inquiry has been followed with some success in tracing the course of this clergyman, of whom most of our early books take very slight notice. Lechford, 41, mentions him as living in Plimouth patent. He was probably at Yarmouth, where there is a tradition, that he was one of their first ministers. See 1 Hist. Coll. V. 59. The diligent author of that tract is certainly mistaken in supposing, that Miller was the *first*, and Matthews (whose given name was Marmaduke) the *second* minister there. Miller, who was at Yarmouth when Johnson wrote, preached first at Rowley; and we may safely conclude, that he did not go to Yarmouth before Matthews left it. I am quite confident it was not before 1642. Matthews had removed from that place, and spent some time at Hull, about the year 1650, whence, though, as Johnson says, he "lost the approbation of some able, understanding men, among both magistrates and ministers, by weak and unsafe ex-

Here arrived a small Spanish frigate with hides and tallow. She was a prize taken by Capt. Newman, who was set out with letters of mart by the lords, &c. of the Isle of Providence.

This year there came a letter from Mr. Thomas ||Mewtis,|| clerk of the council in England, directed to Mr. Winthrop, (the present governour,) and therein an order from the lords commissioners for foreign plantations, (being all of the council,) wherein they straightly required the patent to be sent home by the first ship, &c. This letter and order were produced at the general court last past, and there agreed not to send home the patent, but to return answer to the lords by way of humble petition, which was drawn up and sent accordingly. These instruments are all among the governour's papers, and the effect of them would be here inserted.[1]

25,] Being the third day of the week, and two days before the change, the wind having blown at N. E. all the day, and rainy in the night, was a mighty tempest, and withal the highest tide, which had been seen since our coming into this country; but, through the good providence of God, it did little harm. About fourteen days after, the wind having been at N. W. and then calm ||[2]here,|| came in the greatest eastern sea, which had been in our time. Mr. Peirce (who came in a week after) had that time a very great tempest three days at N. E.

A remarkable providence appeared in a case, which was tried at the last court of assistants. Divers neighbours of Lynn, by agreement, kept their cattle by turns. It fell out to the turn of one Gillow to keep them, and, as he was driving them forth, another of these neighbours went along with him, and kept him so earnestly in talk, that his cattle strayed and gate in the corn. Then this other neighbour left him, and would not help him recover his cattle, but went and told another how he had kept Gillow in talk, that he might lose his cattle, &c. The cattle, getting into the Indian corn, eat so much ere they could be gotten out, that two of them fell sick of it, and one of them

||M || ||[2]turn||

---

pressions in his teaching," he was, nevertheless, called to the church at Malden. A very humble confession of his darkness, and ignorance, and weak expressions, signed by him, though written by another, of 28 October, 1651, is preserved in the archives of the Historical Society, and, with other papers on the subject, of prior date, is printed in 3 Hist. Coll. I. 29—32. The hints of the author of Wonder-working Providence are more expressive than his verses usually are, lib. III. c. 7. He was one of the magistrates appointed for a scrutiny of the faith and doctrines of Matthews.

1 Hubbard, 268—271, has laid us under obligation by preserving both documents.

died presently; and these two cows were that neighbour's, who had kept Gillow in talk, &c. The man brings his action against Gillow for his cow, (not knowing that he had witness of his speech;) but Gillow, producing witness, &c. barred him of his action, and had good costs, &c.

The court, taking into consideration the great disorder ||general|| through the country in costliness of apparel, and following new fashions, sent for the elders of the churches, and conferred with them about it, and laid it upon them, as belonging to them, to redress it, by urging it upon the consciences of their people, which they promised to do. But little was done about it; for divers of the elders' wives, &c. were in some measure partners in this general disorder.[1]

[Large blank.]

8ber.] About two years since one Mr. Bernard, a minister at Batcomb in Somersetshire in England, sent over two books in writing, one to the magistrates, and the other to the elders, wherein he laid down arguments against the manner of our gathering our churches, &c. which the elders could not answer till this time, by reason of the many troubles about Mrs. Hutchinson's opinions, &c. Mr. Cotton also answered another book sent over in defence of set form of prayer. This I suppose was Mr. Ball's book.[2]

About this time was very much rain and snow, in six weeks together; scarce two days without rain or snow. This was observed by some as an effect of the earthquake.[3]

(9.) 8.] A church was gathered at Dedham with good approbation; and, 28th, Mr. [4]Peck ordained teacher at Hingham.

||proceeding||

---

1 The wives of clergymen have been, since that day, generally exempt from such charges.

2 It will not be expected, that an account of Bernard's books should be given here, especially as they were not, I believe, printed, one of them, probably, being too good for the character of the age. See Eliot, in 1 Hist. Coll. IX. 16.

3 To mark the relation of cause and effect in atmospherick phenomena, is a dangerous exercise of imagination. Example may, however, serve, better than precept, to dissuade from such idle philosophy as that in the text. One of the books, blending practical wisdom with amusement, by which Miss Edgeworth has favoured our age, makes a venerable observer of events regard "Tenderden steeple as the cause of Goodwin sands." I think there is evidence, that this anecdote belongs to the famous Sir Thomas More.

4 Little can be learned of this reverend gentleman, except from old records in Hingham, from which I find, he had been a preacher at Hingham in Norfolk in Old England, whence came almost all of the progenitors of the present inhabitants of that ancient town, preserving the same name in Massa-

By order of the last general court, the governour wrote a letter to Mr. [1]Burdet, Mr. Wiggin, and others of the plantation of Pascataquack, to this effect: That, whereas there had been good correspondency between us formerly, we could not but be sensible of their entertaining and countenancing, &c. some that we had cast out, &c. and that our purpose was to survey our utmost limits, and make use of them. Mr. Burdet returned a scornful answer, and would not give the governour his title, &c. This was very ill taken, for that he was one of our body, and sworn to our government, and a member of the church of Salem; so as the governour was purposed to summon him to appear at our court to answer his contempt; but, advising with the deputy about it, he was dissuaded from it, the rather for that, if he should suffer in this cause, it would ingratiate him more with the archbishops, (with whom he had intelligence, &c.) but his council was rather to undermine him by making him thoroughly known, &c. to his friends in Pascataquack, and to take them from him. Whereupon the governour wrote to Edward Hilton, declaring his ill dealing, (and sent a copy of his letter,) and advising them to take heed how they put themselves ||into|| his power, &c. but rather to give us a proof of their respect towards us, &c.—He intimated withal how ill it

||under||

chusetts. The teacher was Robert Peck; but the contemporary MS. of Hobart, the pastor, collated by me, informs, that, 27 October, 1641, he sailed for England, and, another ancient writing adds, "with his wife and son Joseph." I presume he found religion so free at home, that he had no inducement to return. He and Joseph Peck, probably a brother, were made freemen here 13 March, 1638—9. Both have the appropriate Mr. prefixed. Joseph was very soon after a representative in the general court. Notice of his removal from the jurisdiction will occur in our second volume.

Hubbard, 279, though literally extracting this paragraph, in his usual manner, has thrown the chronology into strange confusion, making it 1640, by disregard of Winthrop's arrangement of dates. Johnson, lib. II. c. 9, has made the gathering of Dedham church a year too early.

[1] Of the few instances, in which any advantage is derived from Hubbard, our acquaintance with this person is one. He was minister at Dover; and the historian of Ipswich informs us, 221, 353, that Burdet, "upon a pretended quarrel with the bishops and ceremonies of the church of England, had, about the year 1634, left Yarmouth in England," and came "to Salem, where he was received a member of their church, and was employed to preach among them for a year or more, being an able scholar, and of plausible parts and carriage. But finding the discipline of the church as much too strict for his loose conscience as the other was in pretence too large, he left his brethren at Salem, out of love to his friends at Piscataqua, where he continued for some time in good esteem (as least in appearance) with Mr. Wiggans, that had the power of a governour thereabouts, until he declared himself of what sort he was." Our Records show his admission as a freeman 2 September, 1635. The conclusion of his doings in America will appear in this History, 1640.

would relish, if they should advance Capt. Underhill, whom we had ||thrust|| out for abusing the court with ||2feigning|| a retractation both of his seditious practice and also of his corrupt opinions, and after denying it again, and for casting reproach upon our churches, &c.; signifying withal, that he was now found to have been an unclean person, (for he was charged by a godly young woman to have solicited her chastity under pretence of Christian love, and to have confessed to her, that he had his will oftentimes of the cooper's wife, and all out of strength of love,) and the church had sent for him, and sent him a license to come and go, under the hands of the governour and deputy; but he refused to come, excusing himself, by letters to the elders, that the license was not sufficient, &c. and, by letters to the governour, that he had no rule to come and answer to any offence, except his banishment were released; but to the matter he was charged with, he gave no answer, but sought an evasion. Pascataquack men had chosen him their governour before the letter came to them.

13.] The governour went by water to Salem, where he was entertained with all the respect that they could show him. The ||312|| he returned by land, and they sent six of their chief military officers with carbines to guard him to Boston.[1]

17.] Roger [2]Herlakenden, one of our magistrates, about

||cast|| ||2framing|| ||3 14th||

1 Both dates are plain in the MS., but it is not certain where the correction should be made. The former edition, assuming the first to be correct, and that the governour returned next day, altered the second date to 14. To me it seems more probable, that the day of return, being in the body of the paragraph, is right. Perhaps he went on the 10th, and spent Sunday with Endecott, returning on Monday, 12th.

2 The brother of this gentleman, Richard, is, by Dr. Holmes, from the Cambridge Records, 1 Hist. Coll. VII. 10, mentioned as one of the earliest proprietors. Roger had arrived in 1635, Hubbard, 233, says, in the same ship with Vane. He was admitted freeman 3 March, 1635—6, with Shepherd, Peter, Vane, and other distinguished men, and, on 25 May following, at the general election, chosen one of the assistants, to which place he was reelected in the two following years. It is proof of the solid judgment of so young a man. In the questions about Mrs. Hutchinson he took a part, as appears in that most curious and minute article of the Appendix to History of Massachusetts, II. 423. Some humble verses in honour of Harlackenden are afforded by Johnson, lib. I. c. 32. His will, in our Probate Records, I. 13, without date, was probably made two years or more before his death, since he makes Gov. Haynes one of his executors with his brother Richard. In it he takes notice of his estate in England, called "Colne Park, or the Little Lodge," and of one daughter only, though provision is made for the probability of another child. He was, I believe, a cousin of Lord Roper, and had, probably, been brought up under the ministry of Shepherd in his native country. See Neal's Puritans, II. 282. To enjoy the spiritual aid of the same gentleman, he purchased Dudley's estate at Newtown.

thirty years of age, second son of [blank] Herlakenden of ‖Earl's Colne‖ in Essex, Esq. died at Cambridge of the small pox. He was a very godly man, and of good use both in the commonwealth and in the church. He was buried with military honour, because he was lieutenant colonel. He left behind a virtuous *gentlewoman* and two daughters. He died in great peace, and left a sweet memorial behind him of his piety and virtue.

§10. 2.] Ezekiel [1]Rogers, son of Richard Rogers of Weathersfield in Essex, a worthy son of so worthy a father, lying at Boston with some who came out of Yorkshire with him, where he had been a painful preacher many years, being desirous to partake in the Lord's supper with the church of Boston, did first impart his desire to the elders, and having given them satisfaction, they acquainted the church with it, and before the sacrament, being called forth by the elders, he spoke to this effect, viz. that he and his company (viz. divers families, who came over with him this summer) had, of a good time, withdrawn themselves from the church communion of England, and that for many corruptions which were among them. But, first, he desired, that he might not be mistaken, as if he did condemn all there; for he did acknowledge a special presence of God there in three things: 1, in the soundness of doctrine in all fundamental truths; 2, in the excellency of ministerial gifts; 3, in the blessing upon the same, for the work of conversion and for the power of religion, in all which there appeared more, &c. in England than in all the known world besides. Yet there are such corruptions, as, since God let them see some light therein, they could not, with safe conscience, join any longer with them. The first is, their national church; second, their hierarchy, wholly antichristian; third, their dead service; fourth, their receiving (nay, compelling) all to partake of the seals; fifth, their abuse of excommunications, wherein they enwrap many a godly minister, by causing him to pronounce their sentence, &c. they not knowing that the *fear* of the excommunication lies in that. Hereupon they bewailed before the Lord their sinful partaking so

‖Karlscoke‖

---

1 No inadequate notices of Ezekiel Rogers may be found in the progress of our History, in Johnson, lib. II. 11, and, above all, in Mather's Magnalia. Eliot and Allen have well abbreviated these authorities; but the former misdates his death. He was a man of very high influence for a portion of his life, and his epitaph on *our* Hooker is thought by Hubbard, 541, worthy of preservation. The tardy justice of our age erected a monument to Rogers in 1805.

long in those corruptions, and entered a covenant together, to walk together in all the ordinances, &c.

1639. 10. 3.] Being settled at [1]Rowley, they renewed their church covenant, and their call [blank] of Mr. Rogers to the office of pastor, according to the course of other churches, &c.§

(10.) 6.] Dorothy Talbye was hanged at Boston for murdering her own daughter, a child of three years old. She had been a member of the church of Salem, and of good esteem for godliness, &c.; but, falling at difference with her husband, through melancholy or spiritual delusions, she sometimes attempted to kill him, and her children, and herself, by refusing ||meat,|| saying it was so revealed to her, &c. After much patience, and divers admonitions not prevailing, the church cast her out. Whereupon she grew worse; so as the magistrate caused her to be whipped. Whereupon she was reformed for a time, and carried herself more dutifully to her husband,[2] &c.; but soon after she was so possessed with Satan, that he persuaded her (by his delusions, which she listened to as revelations from God) to break the neck of her own child, that she might free it from future misery. This she confessed upon her apprehension; yet, at her arraignment, she stood mute a good space, till the governour told her she should be pressed to death, and then she confessed the indictment. When she was to receive judgment, she would not uncover her face, nor stand up, but as she was forced, nor give any testimony of her repentance, either then or at her execution. The cloth, which should have covered her face, she plucked off and put between the rope and her neck. She desired to have been beheaded, giving this reason, that it was less painful and less shameful. After a swing or two, she catched at the ladder. Mr. Peter, her late pastor, and Mr. Wilson, went with her to the place of execution, but could do no good with her. Mr. Peter gave an exhortation to the people to take heed of revelations, &c. and of despising the ordinance of excommunication as she had done; for, when it was to have been denounced against her, she turned her back, and would have gone forth, if she had not been stayed by force.

||water||

---

1 No doubt this name was adopted from the place in Yorkshire in Old England, where their pastor had laboured, and most of themselves had enjoyed his services.

2 The unfortunate husband, whose life had been attempted by her, was, after her execution, excommunicated "for much pride and unnaturalness to his wife." See the letter of Hugh Peter in Hutch. I. 371. The original has been seen by me. Perhaps Peter regretted his treatment of Talby, after his own wife was distracted.

One Capt. Newman, being set forth with commission from the Earl of Holland, governour of the Westminster company, and the Earl of Warwick and others of the same company, to spoil the Spaniard within the limits of their grant in the West Indies, after he had taken many of their small vessels, &c. returned home by the Massachusetts in a small pinnace, with which he had taken all ||his|| prizes (for his great ship was of no use for that purpose.) He brought many hides and much tallow. The hides he sold here for £17.10 the ||2score;||[1] the tallow at 29*s.* the hundred; and set sail for England (10,) 1. He was after cast away at ||3Christopher's|| with a very rich prize, in the great hyrracano, 1642.

13.] A general fast was kept upon the motion of the elders to the governour and council. The chief occasion was, the much sickness of pox and fevers spread through the country, (yet it was to the east and south also,) the apparent decay of power of religion, and the general declining of professors to the world, &c. Mr. Cotton, in his exercise that day at Boston, did confess and bewail, as the churches', so his own security, sloth and credulity, whereupon so many and dangerous errours had gotten up and spread in the church; and went over all the particulars, and showed how he came to be deceived; the errours being framed (in words) so ||4near|| the truths which he had preached, and the falsehood of the maintainers of them, who usually would deny to him what they had delivered to others, &c. He acknowledged, that such as had been seducers of others (instancing in some of those of the Island, though he named them not) had been justly banished. Yet he said, that such as had been only misled, and others, who had done any thing out of a misguided conscience, (not being ||5grossly|| evil,) should be borne withal, and first referred to the church, and if that could not heal them, they should rather be imprisoned, fined, or, &c. than banished, ||6*qua*|| it was likely no other church would receive them.

Those who were gone with Mrs. Hutchinson to Aquiday fell into new errours daily. One Nicholas [2]Easton, a tanner,

||the|| ||2stone|| ||3blank|| ||4were|| ||5greatly|| ||6tho'||

---

1 Having the printed copy before me, as I collated the MS., the errour of the former edition, it must be confessed, escaped me at two readings; but happening to reflect on the extreme disproportion of price and value, a closer inspection of the original easily undeceived me, and led to the restoration of the true text, though vexed with a bad chirography.

2 "One Milton, a blind man," derogates nothing from the author of Paradise Lost, though it proves a childish enmity in the writer of the Memoirs. Nicholas Easton is distinguished, with only four others, out of a list of fifty-

taught, that gifts and graces were that antichrist mentioned Thess., and that which withheld, &c. was the preaching of the law; and that every of the elect had the Holy Ghost and also the devil indwelling. Another, one Herne, taught, that women had no souls, and that Adam was not created in true holiness, &c. for then he could not have lost it.

Those who went to the falls ||at|| Pascataquack, gathered a church, and wrote to our church to desire us to dismiss Mr. Wheelwright to them for an officer; but, because he desired it not himself, the elders did not propound it. Soon after came his own letter, with theirs, for his dismission, which thereupon was granted. Others likewise (upon their request) were also dismissed thither.

The governour's letter to Mr. Hilton, about Mr. Burdet and Capt. Underhill, was by them intercepted and opened; and thereupon they wrote presently into England against us, §discovering what they knew of our combination to resist any authority, that should come out of England against us, &c.;§ for they were extremely moved ||2at|| the governour's letter, but could take no advantage by it, for he made account, when he wrote it, that Mr. Hilton would show it them. And, upon this, Capt. Underhill wrote a letter to Mr. Cotton, full of high and threatening words against us; but he wrote another, at the same time, to the governour in very fair terms, entreating an obliterating of all that was past, and a bearing with human infirmities, &c. disavowing all purpose of revenge, &c. See after, (1,) 1639.

The devil would never cease to disturb our peace, and to raise up ||3instruments|| one after another. Amongst the rest, there was a woman in Salem, one Oliver his wife, who had suffered somewhat in England for refusing to bow at the name of Jesus, though otherwise she was conformable to all their orders. She was (for ability of speech, and appearance of zeal and devotion) far before Mrs. Hutchinson, and so the

||of|| ||2by|| ||3insurgents||

---

four freemen admitted at a general court, 3 September, 1634, by the title of respect. It may be seen, Colony Rec. I. 113, that the Rev. Messieurs Parker and Noyes were admitted at the same time, and I conclude, that he accompanied them. In March after, Easton was deputy from Ipswich, and he probably followed his spiritual guide to Newbury. From his occupation, mentioned in the text, no conclusion to his discredit can be drawn; for that employment, in a new country, is found the most useful and profitable for men of good education and estate. Large capital is often invested in that business, and we need not suppose it was mere handicraft. He was governour at Rhode Island four years, and the station was five years filled by one, whom I presume to be his son, John Easton. See 1 Hist. Coll. VI. 144, 145, and Callender, 42, 93.

fitter instrument to have done hurt, but that she was poor and had little acquaintance. She took offence at this, that she might not be admitted to the Lord's supper without giving publick satisfaction to the church of her faith, &c. and covenanting or professing to walk with them according to the rule of the gospel; so as, upon the sacrament day, she openly called for it, and stood to plead her right, though she were denied; and would not forbear, before the magistrate, Mr. Endecott, did threaten to send the constable to put her forth. This woman was brought to the court for disturbing the peace in the church, &c. and there she gave such peremptory answers, as she was committed till she should find sureties for her good behaviour. After she had been in prison three or four days, she made ||means|| to the governour, and submitted herself, and acknowledged her fault in disturbing the church; whereupon he took her husband's bond for her good behaviour, and discharged her out of prison. But he found, after, that she still held her former opinions, which were very dangerous, as, 1. That the church is the heads of the people, both magistrates and ministers, met together, and that these have power to ordain ministers, &c. 2. That all that dwell in the same town, and will profess their faith in Christ Jesus, ought to be received to the sacraments there; and that she was persuaded, that, if Paul were at Salem, he would call all the inhabitants there saints. 3. That excommunication is no other but when Christians withdraw private communion from one that hath offended.[1]

About five years after, this woman was adjudged to be whipped for reproaching the magistrates. She stood without tying, and bare her punishment with a masculine spirit, glorying in her suffering. But after (when she came to consider the reproach, which would stick by her, &c.) she was much dejected about it. She had a cleft stick put on her tongue half an hour, for reproaching the elders, (6,) 1646.[2]

At Providence, also, the devil was not idle. For whereas, at

||blank||

---

1 A favourable construction would certainly find no deadly errours in these opinions; and certainly imprisonment appears not very appropriate means for conviction. I doubt that the apostle pointed at much more blameable notions, and even practices, in the church of Corinth, than he would have found at Salem, though he bestows the epithet *saints* on the members of the former. Mrs. Oliver thought, probably, there was too much power assumed by the elders.

2 This paragraph comes in where the author had long left a blank. I fear more reproach attached to the elders, with all who pitied the sufferer, than if her tongue had been left loose.

their first coming thither, Mr. Williams and the rest did make an order, that no man should be molested for his conscience, now men's wives, and children, and servants, claimed liberty hereby to go to all religious meetings, though never so often, or though private, upon the week days; and because one ||Verin||[1] refused to let his wife go to Mr. Williams so oft as she was called for, they required to have him censured. But there stood up one [2]Arnold, a witty man of their own company, and withstood it, telling them that, when he consented to that order, he never intended it should extend to the breach of any ordinance of God, such as the ||[2]subjection|| of wives to their husbands, &c. and gave divers solid reasons against it. Then one Greene (who hath married the wife of one [3]Beggerly, whose husband is living, and no divorce, &c. but only it was said, that he had lived in adultery, and had confessed it) he replied, that, if they should restrain their wives, &c. all the women in the country would cry out of them, &c. Arnold answered him thus: Did you pretend to leave the Massachusetts, because you would not offend God to please men, and would you now break an ordinance and commandment §of God§ to please women? Some were of opinion, that if ||[3]Verin|| would not suffer his wife to have her liberty, the church should dispose her to some other man, who would use her better. Arnold told them, that it was not the woman's desire to go so oft from home, but only Mr. Williams's and others. In ||[4]conclusion,|| when they would have censured ||[5]Verin,|| Arnold told them, that it was against their own order, for ||[6]Verin|| did ||[7]that he did|| out of conscience; and their order was, that no man should be censured for his conscience.

Another plot the old serpent had against us, by sowing jealousies and differences between us and our friends at Con-

||Udrin|| ||[2]submission|| ||[3]Udrin|| ||[4]court after|| ||[5]Udrin|| ||[6]Udrin|| ||[7]that, and did it||

---

1 Of this unusual name I have met with no recurrence, except in Hutchinson, I. 187, where he informs us of the trial and imprisonment of Philip Verin, as a Quaker.

2 Benedict Arnold was governour of Rhode Island thirteen years. 1 Hist. Coll. VI. 144, 145. In 1657, with Gov. Coddington, he purchased Cononicut Island. 1 Hist. Coll. V. 217. He will often be mentioned in this History as a great friend of Massachusetts, especially in negotiation with the Indians, whose language was better known to him and his son, of the same name, than most other of our people. I do not ascertain whether the anecdote in the text belongs to him or William Arnold. See Callender, 35, 43, 80, 93.

3 The circumstances of the separation, which may be seen in Addenda, sub an. 1636, will excuse our belief, that the charge against Greene is altogether invidious.

necticut, and also Plimouth. This latter was about our bounds. They had planted Scituate, and had given out all the lands to Conyhassett. We desired only so much of the marshes there, as might accommodate Hingham, which being denied, we caused Charles River to be surveyed, and found it come so far southward as would fetch in Scituate and ||more ;|| but this was referred to a meeting between us.[1]

The differences between us and those of Connecticut were divers; but the ground of all was their ||2shyness|| of coming under our government, which, though we never intended to make them subordinate to us, yet they were very jealous, and therefore, in the articles of confederation, which we propounded to them, and whereby order was taken, that all differences, which might fall out, should be ended by a way of peace, and never to come to a necessity or danger of force,—they did so alter the chief article, as all would have come to nothing. For whereas the article was, That, upon any matter of difference, two, three, or more commissioners of every of the confederate colonies should assemble, and have absolute power (the greater number of them) to determine the matter,—they would have them only to meet, and if they could agree, so; if not, then to report to their several colonies, and to return with their advice, and so to go on till the matter might be agreed; which, beside that it would have been infinitely tedious and extreme chargeable, it would never have attained the end; for it was very unlikely, that all the churches in all the plantations would ever have accorded upon the same propositions.[2]

||Concord|| ||2sickness||

---

1 Relative to this survey of Charles River, and the line between Plimouth and Massachusetts colonies, which frequently was matter of controversy, the earliest notice in our Colony Records, I. 228, is 6 September, 1638: "The town of Dedham is desired to spare two that are most fit to go with goodman Woodward and goodman Johnson, (if he can spare time,) or another to be got in his room, to lay out the most southermost part of Charles River, and to have five shillings a day a piece." Woodward was often employed in such business, and, at the same court, was ordered to survey the line north of Merrimack. He was admitted of Boston church 8 December, 1633, being No. 194.

2 If the liability to disagreement in the consultations of the churches had been regarded as an objection against submitting to them other matters of state, we might not so frequently have to lament the proceedings of our fathers. Whenever any course, that might proceed to a result of extreme injustice, cruelty, or tyranny, was contemplated by the civil rulers, the sanction of the churches or of the elders was usually solicited, and too often obtained. Such is the consequence of uniting the wisdom of magistrates and ecclesiasticks in concerns belonging exclusively to either. See the last article of Addenda.

These articles, with their alterations, they sent to our general court at Newtown, the [blank] of the 5th, by Mr. Haynes, Mr. Pincheon and John [1]Steele. The court, finding their alteration, and the inconveniences thereof, would take the like liberty to add and alter; (for the articles were drawn only by some of the council, and never allowed by the court.) This they excepted against, and would have restrained us of that liberty, which they took themselves; and one of their three commissioners, falling in debate with some of our deputies, said, that they would not meddle with any thing that was within our limits; which being reported to the court, they thought it seasonable we should stand upon our right, so as, though we were formerly willing that Agawam (now Springfield) should have fallen into their government, yet, seeing they would not be beholden to us for any thing, we intended to keep it; and accordingly we put it in as an article, that the line between us should be, one way, the Pequod River, (viz. south and north,) and the other way, (viz. east and west,) the limits of our own grant. And this article we added: That we, &c. should have liberty to pass to and fro upon Connecticut, and they likewise. To these articles all their commissioners offered to consent, but it was thought by our court, (because of the new articles,) that they should first acquaint their own court with it. And so their commissioners departed.

After this, we understood that they went on to exercise their authority at Agawam. Whereupon the governour wrote to ||them|| to desire them to forbear until the line were laid out, with advice about some other things, as by the copy of the letter appears. After a long time, Mr. Ludlow (in the name of their court) returned answer, which was very harsh; and in fine declared, that they thought it not fit to treat any further before they had advice from the gentlemen of Saybrook, &c. The governour acquainted the council and magistrates with this

||him||

1 Steele was one of the first settlers of Hartford, called Newtown, because the early inhabitants went from that town with Hooker and Haynes; but the Connecticut village changed its name very soon, probably before that in our neighbourhood. Windsor was first called Dorchester, and Weathersfield Watertown, after the chief fountains of their blood in Massachusetts. This gentleman was a deputy in our general court 4 March, 1634—5, and again in September following; and was also one of those appointed by the authority of Massachusetts to administer justice among the people of the new colony until they formed a government for themselves. See Hutchinson, I. 96, from the Colony Records. He was *now* one of the magistrates or assistants of Connecticut, and, when their first court of deputies assembled, in 1639, was one of that body. Trumbull, I. 79, 103. The time of his death is unknown to me. I suppose descendants are numerous.

letter; and, because they had tied our hands (in a manner) from replying, he wrote a private letter to Mr. Haynes, wherein he lays open their mistakes (as he called them) and the apparent causes of offence, which they had given us; as by ||disclaiming|| to their Naragansetts to be bound by our former agreement with them, (which they would never make till the wars were ended,) by making a treaty of agreement with the Naragansetts and Monhigans, without joining us, or mentioning us to that end, (though we had by letter given them liberty to take us in,) and by binding all the Indians (who had received any Pequods) to pay tribute for them all to them ||²at|| Connecticut, &c. (All these things are clearly to be seen in the letters.) *These and the like miscarriages in point of correspondency were conceived to arise from these two errours in their government: 1. They chose divers *scores* men, who had no learning nor judgment, which might fit them for those affairs, though otherwise men holy and religious. 2. By occasion hereof, the main burden for managing of state businesses fell upon some one or other of their ministers, (as the phrase and style of these letters will clearly discover,) who, though they were men of singular wisdom and godliness, yet, stepping out of their course, their actions wanted that blessing, which otherwise might have been expected.*[1]

15,] The wind at N. E., there was so great a tempest of wind and snow all the night and the next day, as had not been since our time. Five men and youths perished between Mattapan and Dorchester,[2] and a man and a woman[3] between Bos-

||disinclining|| ||²of||

[1] These lines were so effectually erased, that, for some years, my desire of decyphering them was baffled; but, after twice abandoning the task, I gradually obtained, with the aid of a gentleman much skilled in reading difficult MS., a sufficient confidence in all but one word.

[2] Our information cannot denote the line between the English and the Indian places, the names of which are commonly applied indiscriminately. The historian of Dorchester leaves me to conjecture; and my supposition is, that the neck, of old called Dorchester Neck, now annexed to the metropolis by the designation of South Boston, was Mattapan. The early settlement of the English was made near the present *first* church, and between that and South Boston the face of the country was bad enough for one to be lost in without an extreme tempest of snow. It is to be understood from the text, that the disaster occurred by land, not water.

[3] A very full relation of these persons perishing with cold on Boston Neck is given by Johnson, with characteristick deficiency of precision as to date, against which all readers should perpetually guard, lib. II. c. 15. "To end this year, 1639, the Lord was pleased to send a very sharp winter, and more especially in strong storms of weekly snows, with very bitter blasts. And here the reader may take notice of the sad hand of the Lord against two persons,

ton and Roxbury. ||Anthony|| [1]Dick, in a bark of thirty tons, cast away upon the head of Cape Cod. Three were starved to death with the cold; the other two got some fire and so lived there, by such food as they saved, seven weeks, till an Indian found them, &c. Two vessels bound for Quinipiack were cast away at Acquiday, but the people saved. Much other harm was done in staving of boats, &c. and by the great tides, which exceeded all before. This happened the day after a general fast, which occasioned some of our ministers to stir us up to seek the Lord better, because he seemed to discountenance the means of reconciliation. Whereupon the next general court, by advice of the elders, agreed to keep another day, and to seek further into the causes of such displeasure, &c.; which accordingly was performed.

(11.) 14.] The earthquake, which had continued at times since the 1st of the 4th, was more generally felt, and the same noise heard in many places.

30.] A church was gathered at Weymouth with approbation of the magistrates and elders. It is observable, this church, having been gathered before, and so that of Lynn, could not hold together, nor could have any elders join or hold with them. The reason appeared to be, because they did not begin according to the rule of the gospel, which when Lynn had found and humbled themselves for it, and began again upon a new foundation, they went on with a blessing.

The people of this town of Weymouth had invited one Mr. ||[2]Lenthall||[2] to come to them, with intention to call him to be

||Arthur|| ||[2]Leathall||

who were taken in a storm of snow, as they were passing from Boston to Roxbury, it being much about a mile distant, and a very plain way. One of Roxbury sending to Boston his servant maid for a barber-chirurgeon to draw his tooth, they lost their way in their passage between, and were not found till many days after, and then the maid was found in one place, and the man in another, both of them frozen to death; in which sad accident this was taken into consideration by divers people, that this barber was more then ordinary laborious to draw men to those sinful errours, that were formerly so frequent, and now newly overthrown,—by the blessing of the Lord upon the endeavour of his faithful servants with the word of truth,—he having a fit opportunity, by reason of his trade, so soon as any were set down in his chair, he would commonly be cutting of their hair and the truth together; notwithstanding some report better of the man, the example is for the living; the dead is judged of the Lord alone."

1 I know nothing more of this man than that Capt. Clap, in his Memoirs, mentions his having been taken by the pirate Bull, and that Clap received his information from Dick's own mouth.

2 Hubbard, 275, carefully copies his master, but neglects to enlarge our knowledge of this clergyman. I learn from Lechford, that he, soon after,

their minister. This man, though of good report in England, coming hither, was found to have drank in some of Mrs. Hutchinson's opinions, as of justification before faith, &c. and opposed the gathering of our churches in such a way of mutual stipulation as was practised among us. From the former he was soon taken off upon conference with Mr. Cotton; but he stuck close to the other, that only baptism was the door of entrance into the church, &c. so as the common sort of people did eagerly embrace his opinions, and some laboured to get such a church on foot as all baptized ones might communicate in without any further trial of them, &c. For this end they procured many hands in Weymouth to a blank, intending to have Mr. ||Lenthall's|| advice to the frame of their call; and he likewise was very forward to become a minister to them in such a way, and did openly maintain the cause. But the magistrates, hearing of this disturbance and combination, thought it needful to stop it betimes, and ||[2]ergo|| they called Mr. ||[3]Lenthall,|| and some of the chief of the faction, to the next general court in the 1 month, where Mr. ||[4]Lenthall,|| having before conferred with some of the magistrates and of the elders, and being convinced both of his errour in judgment, and of his sin in practice to the disturbance of our peace, &c. did openly and freely retract, with expression of much grief of heart for his offence, and did deliver his retractation in writing, under his hand, in the open court; whereupon he was enjoined to appear at the next court, and in the mean time to make and deliver the like recantation in some publick assembly at Weymouth. So the court stopped for any further censure by fine, or, &c. though it was much urged by some.

At the same court one Smith was convicted and fined £20

||Leathall's|| ||[2]so|| ||[3]Leathall|| ||[4]Leathall||

---

found him at Newport, "out of office and employment, and lives very poorly." From the proceedings in our Colony Records, I. 241, we find his name of baptism was Robert. Callender, 62, gives all the further information, that can be obtained, and confirms my conjecture, that he returned home: "They procured [for a religious teacher] Mr. Lenthal of Weymouth, who was admitted a freeman here August 6, 1640. And, August 20, Mr. Lenthal was by vote called to keep a publick school for the learning of youth, and for his encouragement there was granted to him and his heirs one hundred acres of land, and four more for an house lot. It was also voted, that one hundred acres should be laid forth, and appropriated for a school, for encouragement of the poorer sort to train up their youth in learning; and Mr. Robert Lenthal, while he continues to teach school, is to have the benefit thereof. But this gentleman did not tarry here very long. I find him gone to England the next year but one." It seems the New Lights of Rhode Island were willing to have advantage of the old light.

for being a chief stirrer in the business; and one Silvester was disfranchised; and one Britton, who had spoken reproachfully of the answer, which was sent to Mr. Barnard his book against our church covenant, and of some of our elders, and had sided with Mr. ||Lenthall,|| &c. was openly whipped, because he had no estate to answer, &c.[1]

Mo. 1.] A printing house was begun at Cambridge by one Daye, at the charge of Mr. Glover, who died on sea hitherward. The first thing which was printed was the freemen's oath; *the next was an almanack made for New England by Mr. William Peirce, mariner;* the next was the Psalms newly turned into metre.[2]

§A plantation was begun by Sandwich, and was called Yarmouth, in Plimouth jurisdiction.§

Another plantation was begun upon the north side of Merrimack, called Sarisbury, §now Colchester;§ another at Winicowett, called Hampton, which gave occasion of ||2some|| dif-

||Leathall|| ||2sore||

---

1 Of this extraordinary tyranny (I can appropriate no milder word) all that our court has left on record is here extracted from vol. I. 240:

"13 of 1, 1638—9, John Smyth, for disturbing the publick peace by combining with others to hinder the orderly gathering of a church at Weymouth, and to set up another there, contrary to the orders here established, and the constant practice of all our churches, and for undue procuring the hands of many to a blank for that purpose, is fined £20, and committed during the pleasure of court or the council.

"Richard Silvester, for going with Smyth to get hands to a blank, was disfranchised, and fined £2.

"Mr. Ambrose Marten, for calling the church covenant a stinking carrion, and a human invention, and saying he wondered at God's patience, feared it would end in the sharp, and said the ministers did dethrone Christ and set up themselves; he was fined £10, and counselled to go to Mr. Mather, to be instructed by him.

"Mr. Thomas Makepeace, because of his novel disposition, was informed, we were weary of him, unless he reform."

These two latter offenders are supposed by me to be among the conspirators for a free church, because their offences and sentences are related next after the former, and Mather was the minister nearest to Weymouth. It is observable, that nothing is said of Britton's crime or punishment. It was, probably, thought unnecessary to burden the record with such a case, though we should, in modern times, think very differently. Lechford says, "he was whipped eleven stripes," and his guilt is by that author represented as "saying that some of the ministers in the bay were Brownists."

2 The history of printing, at least in America, has been illustrated with exemplary diligence, in two amusing volumes, by Isaiah Thomas, who treats of his own profession with equal skill and affection. The place, where it was first practised in these English colonies, has been ever since devoted to the cause of letters, by the establishment of a College, having the widest fame of any on this side of the Atlantick, though long intervals have elapsed without the exercise of the press.

ference between us and some of Pascataquack, which grew thus: Mr. Wheelwright, being banished from us, gathered a company and sat down by the falls of Pascataquack, and called their town Exeter; and for their enlargement they dealt with an Indian there, and bought of him Winicowett, &c. and then wrote to us what they had done, and that they intended to lot out all these lands in farms, except we could show a better title. They wrote also to those whom we had sent to plant Winicowett to have them desist, &c. These letters coming to the general court, they returned answer, that they looked at this their dealing as against good neighbourhood, religion and common honesty; that, knowing we claimed Winicowett as within our patent, or as vacuum domicilium, and had taken possession thereof by building an house there above two years since, they should now go and purchase an unknown title, and then come to ||inquire|| of our right. It was in the same letter also manifestly proved, that the Indians having only a natural right to so much land as they had or could improve, so as the rest of the country lay open to any that could and would improve it, as by the said letter more at large doth appear.[1]

In this year one James ||[2]Everell,||[2] a sober, discreet man, and two others, saw a great light in the night at Muddy River. When it stood still, it flamed up, and was about three yards square; when it ran, it was contracted into the figure of a swine: it ran as swift as an arrow towards Charlton, and so up and down about two or three hours. They were come down in their lighter about a mile, and, when it was over, they found themselves carried quite back against the tide to the place they came from. Divers other credible persons saw the same light, after, about the same place.[3]

[Blank.]

||deny|| ||[2]Everett||.

---

1 From this paragraph my suspicion was first excited of the authenticity of the Indian deed to Wheelwright, the first article in Appendix to Belknap's New Hamp. I. The scrutiny has convinced me, that it is a forgery; but the length of the inquiry renders it expedient to postpone it to the Appendix.

2 He was a man of reputation, activity and good estate in Boston many years afterwards. With his wife, Elizabeth, he had been received into Boston church 20 of July, 1634, being Nos. 239, 240. His will, made 11 December, 1682, proved 2 February following, is found in our Probate Registry, vol. VI. 400.

3 This account of an ignis fatuus may easily be believed on testimony less respectable than that which was adduced. Some operation of the devil, or other power beyond the customary agents of nature, was probably im-

The general court, in the 7th mo. last, gave order to the governour to write to them of Pascataquack, to signify to them, that we looked at it as an unneighbourly part, that they should encourage and advance such as we had cast out from us for their offences, before they had inquired of us the cause, &c. (The occasion of this letter was, that they had aided Mr. Wheelwright to begin a plantation there, and intended to make Capt. Underhill their governour in the room of Mr. Burdett, who had thrust out Capt. Wiggin, set in there by the lords, &c.) Upon this, Capt. Underhill (being chosen governour there) wrote a letter to a young gentleman, (who sojourned in the house of our governour,) wherein he reviles ||the|| governour with reproachful terms and imprecations of vengeance upon us all. This letter being showed to the governour and council, the governour, by advice, wrote the letter to Edward Hilton as is before mentioned, page [blank,] mo. 10, 13. The captain was so nettled with this letter, and especially because his adulterous life with the cooper's wife at Boston was now discovered, and the church had called him to come and make answer to it; but he made many excuses, as want of liberty, being a banished man, (yet the governour and council had sent him a safe conduct,) and upon his pretence of the insufficiency of that, the general court sent him another for three months. But, instead of coming, he procured a new church at Pascataquack of some few loose men (who had chosen one Mr. [1]Knolles,

||our||

agined by the relaters and hearers of that age, and the wonder of being carried a mile against the tide became important corroboration of the imagination. Perhaps they were wafted, during the two or three hours' astonishment, for so moderate a distance, by the wind; but, if this suggestion be rejected, we might suppose, that the eddy, flowing always, in our rivers, contrary to the tide in the channel, rather than the meteor, carried their lighter back.

1 Hanserd Knollys is a name of considerable repute among the early Baptists in England, where, like the other divines of our first settlers, he had been episcopally ordained. After a residence of a few years in our country, the account of which, little creditable to his morals, will appear in other parts of this History, he returned home. Something of his sufferings, for the new doctrines, at the hands of the persecuting parliament and Independents, during the great age of anarchy, will be found in Toulmin's edition of Neal's Puritans, III. 551, 2, 3. He was persecuted by the other side, in the following age of prelatical domination, and his sufferings were probably of use to him. Hubbard, 356, has preserved the famous Bastwick's play upon his name,—Absurdo Knowless. His reputation was so much improved in his latter days, that Mather, III. calls him *godly*, and assures us he died "a good man in a good old age." Belknap, N. H. I. 45, with precision, notices his years and death, "Sept. 19, 1691, Ætat. ninety-three." Eliot includes him, but Allen does not.

a weak minister, lately come out of England, and rejected by us for holding some of Mrs. Hutchinson's opinions) to write to our church at Boston in his commendation, wherein they style him the right worshipful, their honoured governour; all which notwithstanding, the church of Boston proceeded with him; and, in the mean time, the general court wrote to all the chief inhabitants of Pascataquack, and sent them a copy of his letters, (wherein he professeth himself to be an instrument ordained of God for our ruin,) to know, whether it were with their privity and consent, that he sent us such a defiance, &c. and whether they would maintain him in such practices against us, &c.

Those of Pascataquack returned answer to us by two several letters. Those of the plantation disclaimed to have any hand in his miscarriages, &c. and offered to call him to account, &c. whensoever we would send any to inform against him. The others at the river's mouth disclaimed likewise, and showed their indignation against him for his insolences, and their readiness to join in any fair course for our satisfaction; only they desired us to have some compassion of him, and not to send any forces against him.

After this, Capt. Underhill's courage was abated, for the chiefest in the river fell from him, and the rest little regarded him, so as he wrote letters of retractation to divers; and, to show his wisdom, he wrote a letter to the deputy and the court, (not mentioning the governour,) wherein he sent the copies of some of the governour's letters to Pascataquack, supposing that something would appear in them either to extenuate his fault, or to lay blame upon the governour; but he failed in both, for the governour was able to make good what he had written.

[Large blank.]

16.] There was so violent a wind at S. S. E. and S. as the like was not since we came into this land. It began in the evening, and increased till midnight. It overturned some new, strong houses; but the Lord miraculously preserved old, weak cottages.[1] It tare down fences—people ||ran|| out of their houses in the night, &c. There came such a rain withal, as raised the waters at Connecticut twenty feet above their meadows, &c.

||came||

[1] If the new houses were higher, we may reasonably doubt the *miracle*. The oak breaks and the willow bends, according to the laws of nature, not by their suspension.

The Indians near Aquiday being pawwawing in this tempest, the devil came and fetched away five of them. Quere.[1]

At Providence things grew still worse; for a sister of Mrs. Hutchinson, the wife of one [2]Scott, being infected with Anabaptistry, and going last year to live at Providence, Mr. Williams was taken (or rather emboldened) by her to make open profession thereof, and accordingly was rebaptized by one [3]Holyman, a poor man[4] late of Salem. Then Mr. Williams rebaptized him and some ten more. They also denied the baptizing of infants, and would have no magistrates.[5]

At Aquiday, also, Mrs. Hutchinson exercised publickly, and she and her party ([6]some three or four families) would have no magistracy. She sent also an admonition to the church of Boston; but the elders would not read it publickly, because she was excommunicated. By these examples we may see how dangerous it is to slight the censures of the church; for it was

---

1 The last word seems to be of a later date. *Perhaps* the story staggered the credulity of Mather. But if the author meant only, that a violent flood, raised by the prince of the power of the air, carried off these natives and drowned them, we may regret the consequence, at least as much as we deride the manner of expression. A greater loss from such cause is related in this volume, 166, August, 1635.

2 Richard Scott, shoemaker, had been admitted of Boston church 28 Aug. 1634, being No. 265, and is, I presume, the same person, who, with Greene, Holliman, the two Arnolds, and others, derived title in the lands of Providence under Williams. Callender, 43.

3 Ezekiel Holliman, founder, with eleven others, of the first Baptist church in America, is well spoken of, as a man of gifts and piety, by those who knew him best. See Benedict. At our general court, March, 1637—8, being summoned, "because he did not frequent the publick assemblies, and for seducing many, he was referred by the court to the ministers for conviction." Of the execution of such a sentence, to the uttermost, we should in vain look for a record, and perhaps it may be thought a reward rather than a punishment. They who are found guilty of entertaining other notions than the court are seldom in a good temper for conviction after judgment. The dissenter thanked his judges, I suppose, for the opportunity of a conference.

4 Hubbard, 338, in transcribing this passage, candidly changes "poor man" into "mean fellow." The ministers failed, probably, to enlighten his conscience.

5 If the like assertion of rejecting magistracy, which, in the text immediately after, is made about Rhode Island, be untrue, as will be clearly proved, we may doubt this alleged insanity of the people at Williams's plantation. When shall we have a true history of Rhode Island, with the temper of Callender and the opportunities of Hutchinson?

6 *Save* is given by Hubbard instead of "some;" but although the MS. has not become more legible in the intervening hundred and forty years, I prefer my eyesight to his, as may our readers the sense of the passage.

apparent, that God had given them up to ||strange|| delusions. Those of Aquiday also had entertained two men, whom the church of Roxbury had excommunicated, and one of them did exercise publickly there. For this the church of Boston called in question such of them as were yet their members; and Mr. Coddington, being present, not freely acknowledging his sin, (though he confessed himself in some fault,) was solemnly admonished.

This is further to be observed in the delusions which this people were taken with: Mrs. Hutchinson and some of her adherents happened to be at prayer when the earthquake was at Aquiday, &c. and the house being shaken thereby, they were persuaded, (and boasted of it,) that the Holy Ghost did shake it in coming down upon them, as he did upon the apostles.

[Blank.]

(2.)] A plantation was begun between Ipswich and Newbury. The occasion was this: Mr. Eaton and Mr. Davenport having determined to sit down at Quinipiack, there came over one Mr. Ezekiel Rogers, second son of that truly faithful servant of God, Mr. Richard Rogers of Weathersfield in England, and with him some twenty families, godly men, and most of them of good estate. This Mr. Rogers, being a man of special note in England for his zeal, piety, and other parts, they laboured by all means to draw ||2with them|| to Quinipiack, and had so far prevailed with him, being newly come, and unacquainted with the state of the country, as they had engaged him; yet, being a very wise man, and considering that many of [1]quality in England did depend upon his choice of a fit place for them, he agreed upon such ||3propositions|| and cautions, as, though they promised to fulfill them all, (whereupon he sent divers of his people thither before winter,) yet, when it came to, they were not able to make good what they had promised. Whereupon he consulted with the elders of the bay, and, by their advice, &c. holding his former engagement released, he and his people took that place by Ipswich; and because some farms had been granted by Ipswich and Newbury, which would be prejudicial to their plantation, they bought out the owners, disbursing therein about £800; and he sent a pinnace to Quinipiack to fetch back the rest of his people; but Mr. Eaton and Mr. Davenport, and others of Connecticut, (being impatient of the loss of him and his people,) staid the pinnace, and sent a mes-

||strong|| ||2him|| ||3proposals||

1 Mather mentions two names of persons, Sir William Constable and Sir Matthew Boynton, who designed to accompany him.

senger with letters of purpose to recover him again. This made him to desire the elders to assemble again, and he showed them the letters they sent, (which wanted no arguments, though some [1]truth;) but he made the case so clear, by letters which had passed between them, &c. as they held him still free from all engagement; and so he returned answer to them, and went on with his plantation.

[Large blank.]

The Indians of Block Island sent, for their tribute this year, ten fathom of wampompeak.

One Mr. [2]Howe, of Lynn, a godly man, and a deputy of the last general court, after the court was ended, and he had dined, being in health as he used to be, went to pass over to Charlestown, and, being alone, he was presently after found dead upon the strand, being there (as it seemed) waiting for the boat, which came soon after.

(3.) 2.] Mr. Cotton, preaching out of the 8 of Kings, 8, taught, that, when magistrates are forced to provide for the maintenance of ministers, &c. then the churches are in a declining condition. There he showed, that the ministers' maintenance should be by voluntary contribution, not by lands or revenues, or tithes, &c.; for these ||have|| always been accompanied with pride, contention and sloth, &c.[3]

11.] The two chief sachems of Naragansett sent the governour a present of thirty fathom of wampom, and Sequin, the sachem of Connecticut, sent ten fathom.

At Aquiday the people grew very tumultuous, and put out Mr. Coddington and the other three magistrates, and chose Mr. William Hutchinson only, a man of a very mild temper and weak parts, and wholly guided by his wife, who had been the

||things had||

1 The exertions of the New Haven gentlemen to acquire so important a confederate, as Rogers, might lead to a little exaggeration; but the insinuation of falsehood against such characters, as Eaton and Davenport, needs not to be repelled. As they harmonized in symbols of doctrine and church forms with our colonists, so rude a charge upon them is more extraordinary than many suggestions we find against the lovers of episcopacy or the latitudinarians of Rhode Island.

2 Edward Howe had been representative in all the courts the year preceding. There was, in Lynn, another Howe, perhaps brother of Edward, named Daniel, of whom, in the progress of this History, something will be told.

3 Cotton did not often preach more sound doctrine, though I am not satisfied with the pertinency of the text, which was, undoubtedly, in the second book.

beginner of all the former troubles in the country, and still continued to breed disturbance.[1]

---

[1] Here I may redeem the pledge, given in note 5, on page 293, of showing this relation erroneous. The Hon. Samuel Eddy, many years secretary of the state of Rhode Island, and a consistent asserter of the doctrine of religious liberty, for which his fellow citizens may feel as great obligation, as I do for his antiquarian diligence in furnishing the State Papers, 2 Hist. Coll. VII. 75—113, besides other valuable information, has supplied me the evidence. In a letter of 18 January, 1817, now before me, after quoting from Hubbard, 338, 9, what that historian had copied from our text, he adds: "Now this, not to notice the contradiction, is altogether without foundation, and contrary to the whole tenor of the records, which admit of no such construction. On the first settlement of the island, they chose Coddington (7th 1st month, 1638, the day of their incorporation) their judge. He remained sole judge until the 2d of the 11th month, 1638, when they chose three elders to his assistance, viz. Nicholas Easton, John Coggeshall and William Brenton. These all continued in office until the 12th of the 1st month, 1640, when they ordered their chief magistrate to be called governour, the next, deputy governour, and Easton, Coggeshall, *William Hutchinson* and John Porter assistants, for one year. This was the only time that William Hutchinson was chosen to office. The four following years, Coddington and Brenton were re-elected. 1641, Coggeshall, Robert Harding, William Balston and John Porter were chosen assistants. The three following years, they were all re-elected. In 1642, according to Hutchinson, (vol. I. p. 72,) William Hutchinson died on Rhode Island. The same year, according to Hubbard, Mrs. Hutchinson and family 'removed to some place under the Dutch,' and were destroyed by the Indians."

"The fact, in itself, is, to be sure, of not much importance; though it removes from Mrs. Hutchinson a part of the evidence of her being a meddling and troublesome woman. But, so far as it shows the materials from which the historian composed his narrative, it is of considerable importance. Vague reports ought never to be adopted in opposition to records. Neither ought they to be adopted at all, but *as such;* and not then, until the proper sources of information have been examined. I am apprehensive, that much of what has been said, and continues to be said, of the first settlers of this state, is founded on the same kind of authority. I purpose hereafter to show something of this in the case of Gorton, who appears to have been the common butt of all the early, and some late writers, than whom, I am persuaded, no one of the first settlers of this country has received more unmerited reproach, nor any one suffered so much injustice. His opinions on religious subjects were, probably, somewhat singular, though certainly not more so than those of many at this day. But that was *his* business: his opinions were his own, and he had a *right* to them."

When my correspondent fulfils his promise of giving the *true* character and life of Gorton, he will render an acceptable service to his country; but if my desire could influence him, it should impose not only that calumniated individual, but the whole colony, upon a gentleman so well able to vindicate its reputation. But he must be told, that Hubbard is *innocently* chargeable with following materials, from which he did not so much *compose*, as compile, or rather copy, his work. To prevent him and all succeeding writers from looking into the historian of Ipswich, as an *original* authority, for any fact which Winthrop had related, I subjoin to this protracted note two considerations, from which the just value of his book may be ascertained.

1. Hutchinson, the most diligent and exact of all writers of colonial history, since Winthrop, whose work he could not see, at the opening of his labours, mentions his apparatus: "among the rest a manuscript history of Mr.

They also gathered a church in a very disordered way; for they took some excommunicated persons, and others who were members of the church of Boston and not dismissed.[1]

WILLIAM HUBBARD, which is carried down to the year 1680, but, *after* 1650, contains *but few facts*." Now our author's work brings the series of events to 1649, when he died. Yet, though Hubbard was in the prime of life for the thirty years following, he seems to have slighted most of the occurrences, in which he should have felt the deepest interest, if he had not also felt his incapacity to appear the relater of them. A small part of his volume was, certainly, compiled from several scarce tracts relative to the discovery of our coast and the early voyages to it; and, for any thing of date preceding 1630, his information is sometimes authentick, and often curious. A collation with Morton's Memorial will, however, prove the facility, with which Hubbard transcribed whole pages in succession, even from a printed book. But from the time when Winthrop came to his aid, he generously relies on him, and deems the labour of copying sufficient. So that more than seven eighths of his volume, between 1630 and 1650, is borrowed, usually by specifick extracts, occasionally with unimportant changes, from the text of the Father of Massachusetts. It must be acknowledged, however, that, sometimes, he wisely abbreviates; though, much more frequently, he slides over circumstances, as dates or numbers, in which the chirography of the MS. would have given him too much trouble to be accurate. I would recommend to any studious lover of our early history to go through from pages 128 to 536 of Hubbard, and in his margin to note the corresponding passages from this History.

2. Dr. Holmes, in his invaluable Annals, a work which almost compensates our loss of the accuracy of Prince, has referred, between pages 255 and 347 of vol. I. narrating events within the limits of time, for which Winthrop could and did afford assistance, not less than one hundred and seven times to the MS. of Hubbard. Now fifty-six of these citations are of passages taken literally by Hubbard from our History, and three fourths of the remaining fifty-one are such as the Ipswich historian adopted, with alterations utterly trivial, from the same authority. Printing, therefore, lamentably reduced the value of that MS., as all antiquaries, it may be presumed, would acknowledge higher veneration for written than printed evidence. Yet the scrupulous annalist may easily be absolved from censure; for, when his volumes were put forth, it had never been considered, whence Hubbard derived his treasures. Those which could not be found in the former printed volume of Winthrop, must have been sought in Hubbard; and of the fourteen last citations by Dr. Holmes, within the space abovementioned, eleven will be seen, from the part of the History now first published, to be literal extracts. All this process of verification, the work of a few hours, if not too easily credited by my readers, will afford, to any who attempt it, sufficient amusement, and at the same time furnish infallible means of ascertaining the relative value of the testimony furnished by each of the witnesses, Hubbard and Winthrop.

1 Those members of Boston church, who had been driven by intolerance to the new region, if they gathered a church at all, must do it in a disordered way; for they might well apprehend, that an application for dismission would be rejected, and perhaps punished by excommunication. The anathema against the outcasts, I suppose, belongs also to all who receive them. In 2 Hist. Coll. X. 184, is a long letter of Cotton, in the name of the church of Boston, to Francis Hutchinson, at Acquettinck, or Rhode Island, refusing dismission, though it appears to have been solicited on two grounds, of his remote situation rendering it impossible for him to perform the duties of his covenant at Boston, and also of his natural obligation to attend upon his parents.

6.] The two regiments in the bay were mustered at Boston, to the number of one thousand soldiers, able men, and well armed and exercised. They were ||led,|| the one by the governour, who was general of all, and the other by the deputy, who was colonel, &c. The captains, &c. showed themselves very skilful and ready in divers sorts of skirmishes and other military actions, wherein they spent the whole day.[1]

One of Pascataquack, having opportunity to go into Mr. Burdet his study, and finding there the copy of his letter to the archbishops, sent it to the governour, which was to this effect: That he did delay to go into England, because he would fully inform himself of the state of the people here in regard of allegiance; and that it was not discipline that was now so much aimed at, as sovereignty; and that it was accounted ||2perjury|| and treason in our general courts to speak of appeals to the king.

The first ships, which came this year, brought him letters from the archbishops and the lords commissioners for plantations, wherein they gave him thanks for his care of his majesty's service, &c. and that they would take a time to redress such disorders as he had informed them of, &c. but, by reason of the much business now lay upon them, they could not, at present, accomplish his desire. These letters lay above fourteen days in the bay, and some moved the governour to open them; but himself and others of the council thought it not safe to meddle with them, nor would take any notice of them; and it fell out well, by God's good providence; for the letters (by some means) were opened, (yet without any of their privity or consent,) and Mr. Burdett threatened to complain of it to the lords; and afterwards we had knowledge of the contents of them by some of his own friends.

The governour received letters from Mr. Cradock, and in them another order from the lords commissioners, to this effect: That, whereas they had received our petition upon their former order,[2] &c. by which they perceived, that we were taken with some jealousies and fears of their intentions, &c. they did accept of our answer, and did now declare their

||headed|| ||2piracy||

[1] Wonder-working Providence is chiefly valued for its account of the military array of the people in their several settlements, lib. II. c. 26, the author having been better acquainted with the use of the sword than the Bible, though so frequently ambitious of exhibiting his dexterity in handling the word.

[2] See page 269.

intentions to be only to regulate all plantations to be subordinate to the said commission; and that they meant to continue our liberties, &c.; and therefore did now again peremptorily require the governour to send them our patent by the first ship; and that, in the mean time, they did give us, by that order, full power to go on in the government of the people until we had a new patent sent us; and, withal, they added threats of further course to be taken with us, if we failed.

This order being imparted to the next general court, some advised to return answer to it. Others thought fitter to make no answer at all, because, being sent in a private letter, and not delivered by a certain messenger, as the former order was, they could not proceed upon it, because they could not have any proof that it was delivered to the governour; §and order was taken, that Mr. Cradock's agent, who delivered the letter to the governour, &c. should, in his letters to his master, make no mention of the letters he delivered to the governour,§ seeing his master had not laid any charge upon him to that end.

Mr. Haynes, the governour of Connecticut, and Mr. Hooker, &c. came into the bay, and staid near a month. It appeared by them, that they were desirous to renew the treaty of confederation with us, and though themselves would not move it, yet, by their means, it was moved ||to|| our general court, and accepted; for they were in some doubt of the Dutch, who had lately received a new [1]governour, a more discreet and sober man than the former, and one who did complain much of the injury done to them at Connecticut, and was very forward to hold correspondency with us, and very inquisitive how things stood between us and them of Connecticut, which occasioned us the more readily to renew the former treaty, that the Dutch might not take notice of any breach or alienation between us.

22.] The court of elections was; at which time there was a small eclipse of the sun. Mr. Winthrop was chosen governour again, though some labouring had been, by some of the elders §and others§ to have changed, not out of any dislike of him, (for they all loved and esteemed him,) but out of their fear lest it might make way for having a governour for life, which some had propounded as most agreeable to God's institution and the practice of all well ordered states. But neither the governour

||by||

1 His name was William Kieft; and of him frequent notice will occur in the interminable negotiations between the Dutch and our New England colonies. It is hardly necessary to refer the reader, for amusement at his expense, to Knickerbocker's New York.

nor any other attempted the thing; though some jealousies arose, which were increased by two occasions. The first was, there being want of assistants, the governour and other magistrates thought fit (in the warrant for the court) to propound three, amongst which Mr. Downing, the governour's brother-in-law, was one, which they conceived to be done to strengthen his party, and therefore, though he were known to be a very able man, &c. and one who had done many good offices for the country for these ten years, yet the people would not choose him.[1] Another occasion of their jealousy was, the court, finding the number of deputies to be much increased by the addition of new plantations, thought fit, for the ease both of the country and the court, to reduce all towns to two deputies.[2] This occasioned some to fear, that the magistrates intended to make themselves stronger, and the deputies weaker, and so, in time, to bring all power into the hands of the magistrates; so as the people in some towns were much displeased with their deputies for yielding to such an order. Whereupon, at the next session, it was propounded to have the number of deputies restored; and allegations were made, that it was an infringement of their liberty; so as, after much debate, and such reasons given for diminishing the number of deputies, and clearly proved that their liberty consisted not in the number, but in the thing, divers of the deputies, who came with intent to reverse the last order, were, by force of reason, brought to uphold it; so that, when it was put to the vote, the last order for two deputies only was confirmed. Yet, the next day, a petition was brought to the court from the freemen of Roxbury, to have the ||third deputy|| restored. Whereupon the reasons of the court's proceedings were set down in writing, and all objections answered, and sent to such towns as were unsatisfied, with this advice, that, if any could take away those reasons, or bring us

||three deputies||

---

[1] It is by no means remarkable, that this measure caused some jealousy. For the exact phraseology employed, on this occasion, by the assistants, see Addenda. Yet I find this memorandum on the last page of our first volume of Colony Records, in 1641: "Mr. Flint, Mr. Symonds, Mr. Dummer, Mr. Tyng, Mr. Downing, and Mr. Pyncheon, are to be propounded to the towns for new magistrates."

[2] Foresight, rather than experience, must have led to the adoption of this remedy; for the number of deputies, at the court in March preceding, amounted only to thirty-three, and had never been greater. But, in fact, the smaller towns had not exercised their full right, and the change was probably made, because two might represent either of the other towns as well as three. Perhaps it was thought, that not more than two fit men could be found in some towns.

better for what they did desire, we should be ready, at the next court, to repeal the said order.[1]

The hands of some of the elders (learned and godly men) were to this petition, though suddenly drawn in, and without due consideration, for the lawfulness of it may well be questioned: for when the people have chosen men to be their rulers, and to make their laws, and bound themselves by oath to submit thereto, now to combine together (a lesser part of them) in a publick petition to have any order repealed, which is not repugnant to the law of God, savours of resisting an ordinance of God; for the people, having deputed others, have no power to make or alter laws, but are to be subject; and if any such order seem unlawful or inconvenient, they ||were|| better prefer some reasons, &c. to the court, with manifestation of their desire to move them to a review, than peremptorily to petition to have it repealed, which amounts to a plain reproof of those whom God hath set over them, and putting dishonour upon them, against the tenour of the fifth commandment.

There fell out at this court another occasion of increasing the people's jealousy of their magistrates, viz.: One of the elders, being present with those of his church, when they were to prepare their votes for the election, declared his judgment, that a governour ought to be for his life, alleging for his authority the practice of all the best commonwealths in Europe,

||had||

1 Early practice and law seem to have established the equality of representation from towns; though it was, after a few years, restricted in some degree. Towns having less than twenty freemen were allowed but one deputy, and those less than ten, none, though the freemen of such towns were permitted to unite in election with the next towns. A "liberty of sending or not sending deputies" was very early exercised by the towns, and allowed by the house. It has constantly been enjoyed since, subject, however, to a discretion of the body in imposing fines for neglect; and, though a little more restricted under the provincial than the colony government, is perfectly well settled under our present constitution as an independent state. From the date in the text, Boston, like most of the other towns, sent only two members. In 1680 the number was increased again to three, and, after the first session under the charter of William and Mary, was raised to four. This was our complement, nearly ninety years, till the commencement of our national independence. By the charter of William and Mary, every town was authorized in the first house to have two representatives; but that first general court was by the charter empowered to declare and fix the apportionment to each town. In the exercise of this authority, leave was granted to towns of thirty freeholders to have one member; towns of one hundred and twenty freeholders, two members; and Boston, alone, four. A complete list of representatives from Boston to the commencement of the revolution in 1775 is given in 2 Hist. Coll. X. 23—29. I believe one or two additions for vacancies might, however, be made to it, had I leisure to spend as many hours as the formation of it cost.

and especially that of Israel by God's own ordinance.[1] But this was opposed by some other of the elders with much zeal, and so notice was taken of it by the people, not as a matter of dispute, but as if there had been some plot to put it in practice, which did occasion the deputies, at the next session of this court, to deliver in an order drawn to this effect: That, whereas our sovereign lord, King Charles, &c. had, by his patent, established a governour, deputy and assistants, that therefore no person, chosen a counsellor *for life,* should have any authority as a magistrate, except he were chosen in the annual elections to one of the said places of magistracy established by the patent. This being thus bluntly tendered, (no mention being made thereof before,) the governour took time to consider of it, before he would put it to vote. So, when the court was risen, the magistrates advised of it, and drew up another order to this effect: That whereas, at the court in [blank,] it was ordered, that a certain number of magistrates should be chosen to be a standing council for life, &c. whereupon some had gathered that we had erected a new order of magistrates not warranted by our patent, this court doth therefore declare, that the intent of the order was, that the standing council should always be chosen out of the magistrates, &c.; and therefore it is now ordered, that no such counsellor shall have any power as a magistrate, nor shall do any act as a magistrate, &c. except he be annually chosen, &c. according to the patent; and this order was after passed by vote. That which led those of the council to yield to this desire of the deputies was, because it concerned themselves, and they did more study to remove these jealousies out of the people's heads, than to preserve any power or dignity to themselves above others; for till this court those of the council, viz. Mr. Endecott, had stood and executed as a magistrate, without any annual election, and so they had been ||reputed|| by the elders and all the people till this present. But the order was drawn up in this form, that it might be of less observation and freer from any note of injury to make this alteration rather by way of explanation of the fundamental order, than without any cause shown to repeal that which had been established by serious advice of the elders, and had been in practice two or

||reported||

---

[1] Who gave such impolitick counsel, supported by the preposterous analogies, is unknown to me. The ministers were perpetually meddling with the regimen of the commonwealth; and we have frequent occasion to regret, that their references to the theocracy of Israel were received as authority, rather than illustration.

three years without any inconvenience.[1] And here may be observed, how strictly the people would seem to stick to their patent, where they think it makes for their advantage, but are content to decline it, where it will not warrant such liberties as they have taken up without warrant from thence, as appears in their strife for three deputies, &c. when as the patent allows them none at all, but only by inference, &c. voting by proxies, &c.

The governour acquainted the general court, that, in these two last years of his government, he had received from the Indians, in presents, to the value of about £40, and that he had spent about £20 in entertainment of them and in presents to their sachems, &c. The court declared, that the presents were the governour's due, but the tribute was to be paid to the treasurer.[2]

[Blank.]

15.] Mr. Endecott and Mr. Stoughton, commissioners for us, and Mr. Bradford and Mr. Winslow for Plimouth, met at Hingham about deciding the difference between us concerning our bounds. Our commissioners had full power to determine, &c.; but theirs had not, although they had notice of it long before, and themselves had appointed the day. Whereupon the court ordered, that those of Hingham should make use of all the land near Conyhassett to the ||creek|| next Scituate, till the court should take further order; and a letter was directed to the governour ||2of|| Plimouth to the same effect, with declaration of the reasons of our proceeding, and readiness to give them a further meeting. The charges of their commissioners' diet ||3was|| defrayed by us, because they met us within our own jurisdiction.

Those of Exeter replied to our answer, standing still to maintain the Indians' right, and their interest thereby. But, in the mean time, we had sent men to discover Merrimack, and found

||crook|| ||2at|| ||3were||

---

1 This appears a very idle scruple of the assistants. Since they consented to give up the substance, it was unwise to permit any jealousy about the form. Election for life has, in no other instance, I believe, obtained for any legislative or executive office in our country. Annual choice gives admirable opportunity for our people to show their stability; and a gentleman is much longer in office usually in the New England states than in those where the people vote only at periods of two or three years.

2 A rate of £1000, levied by this court, Rec. I. 250, was thus assessed: Boston, £144.10.1; Ipswich, £111.18.11; Salem, 111.13.11; Dorchester, £93.7.9; Cambridge, £91.19.9; Charlestown, £85.15.10; Watertown, £81.17.1; Lynn, £79.19.6; Roxbury, £74.12.6; Newbury, 67.8.3; Hingham, £33.14.5; Weymouth, £23.2.

some part of it about Penkook to lie more northerly than forty-three and a half. §So§ we returned answer to them, that, though we would not relinquish our interest by priority of possession for any right they could have from the Indians, yet, seeing they had professed not to claim any thing which should fall within our patent, we would look no further than that in respect of their claim.

One Mr. [1]Ryall, having gotten a patent at Sagadahoc out of the grand [2]patent, wrote to our governour and tendered it to our government, so as we would send people to possess it. The governour acquainted the general court with it, but nothing was done about it, for we were not ready for such a business, having enough ||to do|| at home.

[Large blank.]

26.] Mr. Hooker being to preach at Cambridge, the governour and many others went to hear him, (though the governour did very seldom go from his own congregation upon the Lord's day.)[3] He preached in the afternoon, and having gone on, with much strength of voice and intention of spirit, about a quarter of an hour, he was at a stand, and told the people, that God had deprived him both of his strength and matter, &c. and so went forth, and about half an hour after returned again, and went on to very good purpose about two hours.

There was at this time a very great ||[2]drouth|| all over the country, both east and west, there being little or no rain from the 26th of the 2d month to the 10th of the 4th; so as the corn generally began to wither, and great fear there was it would all

||besides|| ||[2]dearth||

---

1 In a diligent search amidst all accessible stores of information, very little knowledge on the subject of this gentleman's grant has been acquired, and, of this little, not a word from Gorges, under whom the title was derived. Very short and unsatisfactory reference is made to it in some proceedings under the authority of President Danforth, acting by power from Massachusetts, above forty years after, which may be seen in Sullivan's History of the District of Maine, 182—4. The name of Royal's River in North Yarmouth is, probably, deduced from this person, whose descendants, of the male line, pronouncing the name as it is spelt in the text, I am informed, are still remaining in the neighbourhood of their early domain.

2 By this *grand patent* is not intended, I presume, the original patent of 18 Jac. I., 3 November, usually called the Plimouth Charter, but one of much narrower limits, 15 Car. I., 3 April, which may be found in Haz. I. 442—455. Royal's letter must have been written immediately after the king's grant, in anticipation of which he, probably, had made his arrangements with Gorges.

3 Gov. Winthrop's travelling on Sunday, for such a purpose, must not, I suppose, be considered unnecessary. His example would justify the many others. Such instances are now unknown.

be lost. Whereupon the general court conferred with the elders, and agreed upon a day of humiliation about a week after. The very day after the fast was appointed there fell a good shower, and, within one week after the day of humiliation was past, we had such store of rain, and so seasonably, as the corn revived and gave hope of a very plentiful harvest. When the court and the elders were met about it, they ||considered|| of such things as were amiss, which might provoke God against us, and agreed to acquaint their churches therewith, that they might be stirred up to bewail and reform them.

(4.)] We were much afraid this year of a ||[2]stop|| in England, by reason of the complaints which had been sent against us, and the great displeasure which the archbishops and others, the commissioners for plantations, had conceived and uttered against us, both for those complaints, and also for our not sending home our patent. But the Lord wrought for us beyond all expectation; for the petition, which we returned in answer of the order sent for our patent, was read before the lords and well accepted, as is before expressed; and ships came to us from England and divers other parts with great store of people and provisions of all sorts.

About this time our people came from Isle Sable. A bark went for them, on the 2 of the 1 month, but by foul weather she was wrecked there, and of her ruins they made a small one, wherein they returned. It was found to be a great errour to send thither before the middle of the 2 month. They had gotten store of seal oil and skins, and some horse teeth and black fox skins; but the loss of the vessel, &c. overthrew the hope of the design.

The island is very healthful and temperate. We lost not one man in two years, nor any sick, &c.

(5.)] The rent at Connecticut grew greater, notwithstanding the great pains, ||[3]which|| had been ||[4]taken|| for healing it; so as the church of Weathersfield itself was not only divided from the rest of the town, &c., but, of those seven which were the church, four fell off; so as it was conceived, that thereby the church was dissolved, which occasioned the church of Watertown here (which had divers of ||[5]their|| members there, not yet dismissed) to send two of their church to look after their members, and to take order with them. But the contention and alienation of minds was such, as they could not bring them to any other accord than this, that the one party must remove to some other place, which they both consented to, but still the difficulty remained; for those three, who pretended themselves

||conferred|| ||[2]step|| ||[3]we|| ||[4]taking|| ||[5]her||

to be the church, pleaded that privilege for their stay, and the others alleged their multitude, &c. so as neither would give place, whereby it seemed, that either they minded not the example of Abraham's offer to Lot, or else they wanted Abraham's spirit of peace and love.

This controversy having called in Mr. Davenport and others of Quilipiack, for mediation, and they not according with those of Connecticut about the case, gave advantage to Satan to ||sow|| some seeds of contention between those plantations also; but, being godly and wise men on both parts, things were easily reconciled.[1]

In this month there arrived two ships ||2at|| Quilipiack. One was of three hundred and fifty tons, wherein came Mr. [2]Fenwick and his lady and family to make a plantation at Saybrook upon the mouth of Connecticut. Two other plantations were begun beyond Quilipiack, and every plantation intended a peculiar government.

There were also divers new plantations begun this summer here and at Plimouth, as [3]Colchester upon Merrimack, Sudbury by Concord, (Winicowett was named Hampton,) Yarmouth and Barnstaple by Cape Cod.

[Large blank.]

Capt. Underhill, having been dealt with and convinced of his great sin against God and the churches and state here, &c. returned to a better mind, and wrote divers letters to the governour and deputy, &c. bewailing his offences, and craving pardon. See after, (1,) 5, 39, and (7,) 3, 40.

There was sent to the governour ||3the|| copy of a letter written into England by Mr. Hansard Knolles of Pascataquack, wherein he had most falsely slandered this government, as that it was worse than the high commission, &c. and that here was

||straw|| ||2of|| ||3a||

---

1 From Trumbull, I. 120, 1, it appears, the reconciliation was not very easy, and was at last effected by the separation of the dissonant parts. Stamford was settled in consequence.

2 George Fenwick, Esq. would surely deserve more consideration than he has received from the writers about our country, neither Eliot nor Allen having thought his name required insertion in their volumes, and even Trumbull being apparently negligent of one of the principal fathers of Connecticut. This probably resulted from his return to England, and there ending his days in high office, of which some influence will appear in our second volume. Hutchinson, I. 97, 8, gives the fullest account of him and his friendly regards to our country. He died early in 1657.

3 At the court in October, 1640, this place was ordered to be called Salisbury. This seems, from page 289, to have been its first name.

nothing but oppression, &c. and not so much as a face of religion. The governour acquainted one of Pascataquack, Mr. Knolles his special friend, with it. Whereupon Mr. Knolles became very much perplexed, and wrote to the governour, acknowledging the wrong he had done us, and desired that his retractation might be published. The governour sent his letter into England, and kept a copy of it. See more of this after, (12,) 20, 1639.

At Providence matters went after the old manner. Mr. Williams and many of his company, a ||few|| months since, were in all haste rebaptized, and denied communion with all others, and now he was come to question his second baptism, not being able to derive the authority of it from the apostles, otherwise than by the ministers of England, (whom he judged to be ill authority,) so as he conceived God would raise up some apostolick power. Therefore he bent himself that way, expecting (as was supposed) to become an apostle; and having, ||[2]a little|| before, refused communion with all, save his own wife, now he would preach to and pray with all comers. Whereupon some of his followers left him and returned back from whence they went.

(6.) 27.] Here came a small bark from the West Indies, one Capt. ||[3]*Jackson*|| in her, with commission from the Westminster company to take prize, &c. from the Spaniard. He brought much wealth in money, plate, indico and sugar. He sold his indico and sugar here for £1400, wherewith he furnished himself with commodities, and departed again for the West Indies.

A fishing trade was begun at Cape Ann by one Mr. ||[4]Maurice|| [1]Tomson, a merchant of London; and an order was made, that all stocks employed in fishing should be free from publick charge for seven years. This was not done to encourage foreigners to set up fishing among us, (for all the gains would be returned to the place where they dwelt,) but to encourage our own people to set upon it, and in expectation that Mr. Tomson, &c. would, ere long, come settle with us.

||some|| ||[2]no title|| ||[3]Sackett|| ||[4]Maverick||

1 Of this gentleman I know very little. Francis Kirby, in a letter to John Winthrop, jun. 26 December, 1631, says: "Capt. B. who was employed by my cousin, Maurice Thomson and company, for the trade of beaver in the River of Canada, is now arrived here......He hath brought in here about three thousand pounds weight of beaver, and they are now hastening to set forth a small ship only for that river, hoping to be there before Capt. Kirk, who (I hear) is to fetch his men from Quebeck, and yield up the castle again to the French this next summer." Probably Thomson was not tempted to come to New England.

(7.)] Here was such store of exceeding large and fat mackerel upon our coast this season, as was a great benefit to all our plantations. Some one boat with three men would take, in a week, ten ||hogsheads,|| which was sold at Connecticut for £3.12 the ||[2]hogshead.||

There were such swarms of small flies, like moths, came from the southward, that they covered the sea, and came flying like drifts of snow; but none of them were seen upon the land.[1]

(7.) 17.] A church was gathered at the Mount.

4.] At the general court at Boston, one Mr. Nathaniel [2]Eaton, brother to the ||[3]merchant|| at Quilipiack, was convented and censured. The occasion was this: He was a schoolmaster, and had many scholars, the sons of gentlemen and others of best note in the country, and had entertained one Nathaniel [3]Briscoe, a gentleman born, to be his usher, and to do some other things for him, which might not be unfit for a scholar. He had not been with him above three days but he fell out with him for a very small occasion, and, with reproachful terms, discharged him, and turned him out of his doors; but, it being then about eight of the clock after the Sabbath, he told him he should stay till next morning, and, some words growing between them, he struck him and pulled him into his house. Briscoe defended himself, and closed with him, and, being parted, he came in and went up to his chamber to lodge there. Mr.

||hundreds|| ||[2]hundred|| ||[3]magistrate||

[1] In 2 Hist. Coll. IV. 230, a large account of the mackerel fishery on the south shore of Massachusetts Bay informs us, that the appearance of such insects is "a welcome herald to the fisherman." That memoir is worth consulting by all the curious.

[2] Slight mention of this unhappy man will be found in Addenda. He had been admitted a freeman of our colony 9 June of the preceding year. What became of him, after 1646, is known only from Mather, who says, he went from Virginia to England, there lived privately until the restoration, then conformed to the ceremonies of the church by law established, was settled at Biddeford, persecuted the dissenters, from whom he had *apostatized*, and died in prison for debt. He undoubtedly had very high encouragement to continue at the head of the newly established college; for, in the Court Records, I. 252, of May preceding the date in the text, I find a grant "to Mr. Nathaniel Eaton five hundred acres, if he continue his employment for his life, to be to him and his heirs." Further evidence of the resolution of the government in supporting that institution, is found, at the same court, in two orders: 1. "That a letter should be sent to Mr. Humfrey to send in the £100, which is in his hand, to further the college." 2. "Mr. Endecott, Mr. Downing and Mr. Hawthorne are to dispose of the house, which Mr. Peters bought, as they can, and return the money for the college."

[3] Of him I know nothing, unless he be the author of a very curious letter from England, 7 Sept. 1652, on which proceedings more curious were had here by our government. See 3 Hist. Coll. I. 32—35.

Eaton sent for the constable, who advised him first to admonish him, &c. and if he could not, by the power of a master, reform him, then he should complain to the magistrate. But he caused his man to fetch him a cudgel, which was a walnut tree plant, big enough to have killed a horse, and a yard in length, and, taking his two men with him, he went up to Briscoe, and caused his men to hold him till he had given him two hundred stripes about the head and shoulders, &c. and so kept him under blows (with some two or three short intermissions) about the space of two hours, about which time Mr. Shepherd and some others of the town came in at the outcry, and so he gave over. In this distress Briscoe gate ||out|| his knife, and struck at the man that held him, but hurt him not. He also fell to prayer, (supposing he should have been murdered,) and then Mr. Eaton beat him for taking the name of God in vain. After this Mr. Eaton and Mr. Shepherd (who knew not then of these passages) came to the governour and some other of the magistrates, complaining of Briscoe for his insolent speeches, and for crying out murder and drawing his knife, and desired that he might be enjoined to a publick acknowledgment, &c. The magistrates answered, that they must first hear him speak, and then they would do as they should see cause. Mr. Eaton was displeased at this, and went away discontented, &c. and, being after called into the court to make answer to the information, which had been given by some who knew the truth of the case, and also to answer for his neglect and cruelty, and other ill usage towards his scholars, one of the elders (not suspecting such miscarriages by him) came to the governour, and showed himself much grieved, that he should be publickly produced, alleging, that it would derogate from his authority and reverence among his scholars, &c. But the cause went on notwithstanding, and he was called, and these things laid to his charge in the open court. His answers were full of pride and disdain, telling the magistrates, that they should not need to do any thing herein, for he was intended to leave his employment. And being asked, why he used such cruelty to Briscoe his usher, and to other his scholars, (for it was testified by another of his ushers and divers of his scholars, that he would give them between twenty and thirty stripes at a time, and would not leave till they had confessed what he required,) his answer was, that he had this rule, that he would not give over correcting till he had subdued the party to his will. Being also questioned about the ill and scant diet of his boarders, (for, though their friends gave large allowance, yet their diet was ordinarily

||at||

nothing but porridge and pudding, and that very homely,) he put it off to his wife.[1] So the court dismissed him at present,

---

1 An examination of the lady followed, I presume, for the former secretary of the commonwealth furnished me a paper, which can hardly refer to any other transaction than this. Some overseer of the college, probably, either magistrate or clergyman, wrote it from the confession or dictation of the accused party: "For their breakfast, that it was not so well ordered, the flower not so fine as it might, nor so well boiled or stirred, at all times that it was so, it was my sin of neglect, and want of that care that ought to have been in one that the Lord had intrusted with such a work. Concerning their beef, that was allowed them, as they affirm, which, I confess, had been my duty to have seen they should have had it, and continued to have had it, because it was my husband's command; but truly I must confess, to my shame, I cannot remember that ever they had it, nor that ever it was taken from them. And that they had not so good or so much provision in my husband's absence as presence, I conceive it was, because he would call sometimes for butter or cheese, when I conceived there was no need of it; yet, forasmuch as the scholars did otherways apprehend, I desire to see the evil that was in the carriage of that as well as in the other, and to take shame to myself for it. And that they sent down for more, when they had not enough, and the maid should answer, if they had not, they should not, I must confess, that I have denied them cheese, when they have sent for it, and it have been in the house; for which I shall humbly beg pardon of them, and own the shame, and confess my sin. And for such provoking words, which my servants have given, I cannot own them, but am sorry any such should be given in my house. And for bad fish, that they had it brought to table, I am sorry there was that cause of offence given them. I acknowledge my sin in it. And for their mackerel, brought to them with their guts in them, and goat's dung in their hasty pudding, it's utterly unknown to me; but I am much ashamed it should be in the family, and not prevented by myself or servants, and I humbly acknowledge my negligence in it. And that they made their beds at any time, were my straits never so great, I am sorry they were ever put to it. For the Moor his lying in Sam. Hough's sheet and pillow-bier, it hath a truth in it: he did so one time, and it gave Sam. Hough just cause of offence; and that it was not prevented by my care and watchfulness, I desire [to] take the shame and the sorrow for it. And that they eat the Moor's crusts, and the swine and they had share and share alike, and the Moor to have beer, and they denied it, and if they had not enough, for my maid to answer, they should not, I am an utter stranger to these things, and know not the least footsteps for them so to charge me; and if my servants were guilty of such miscarriages, had the boarders complained of it unto myself, I should have thought it my sin, if I had not sharply reproved my servants, and endeavoured reform. And for bread made of heated, sour meal, although I know of but once that it was so, since I kept house, yet John Wilson affirms it was twice; and I am truly sorry, that any of it was spent amongst them. For beer and bread, that it was denied them by me betwixt meals, truly I do not remember, that ever I did deny it unto them; and John Wilson will affirm, that, generally, the bread and beer was free for the boarders to go unto. And that money was demanded of them for washing the linen, it's true it was propounded to them, but never imposed upon them. And for their pudding being given the last day of the week without butter or suet, and that I said, it was miln of Manchester in Old England, it's true that I did say so, and am sorry, they had any cause of offence given them by having it so. And for their wanting beer, betwixt brewings, a week or half a week together, I am

and commanded him to attend again the next day, when, being called, he was commanded to the lower end of the table, (where all offenders do usually stand,) and, being openly convict of all the former offences, by the oaths of four or five witnesses, he yet continued to justify himself; so, it being near night, he was committed to the marshal till the next day. When the court was set in the morning, many of the elders came into the court, (it being then private for matter of consultation,) and declared how, the evening before, they had taken pains with him, to convince him of his faults; yet, for divers hours, he had still stood to his justification; but, in the end, he was convinced, and had freely and fully acknowledged his sin, and that with tears; so as they did hope he had truly repented, and therefore desired of the court, that he might be pardoned, and continued in his employment, alleging such further reasons as they thought fit. After the elders were departed, the court consulted about it, and sent for him, and there, in the open court, before a great assembly, he made a very solid, wise, eloquent and serious (seeming) confession, condemning himself in all the particulars, &c. Whereupon, being put aside, the court consulted privately about his sentence, and, though many were taken with his confession, and none but had a charitable opinion of it; yet, because

---

sorry that it was so at any time, and should tremble to have it so, were it in my hands to do again."

The above is an exact copy of all that is written by that hand; but on the next page is found, in a more difficult, but uncommonly beautiful chirography, "and whereas they say, that sometimes they have sent down for more meat, and it hath been denied, when it have been in the house, I must confess, to my shame, that I have denied them oft, when they have sent for it, and it have been in the house."

In the archives of the State House it is not probable that any document more minute or entertaining can be preserved; nor would this seem of importance and gravity appropriate to this work, were it not connected with the history of the college, and highly illustrative of our author's text. That no complaints against Mrs. Eaton had been brought down from antiquity, when her husband suffered perpetual malediction, is perhaps owing to the gallantry of our fathers. Her accomplishments as a housewife appear equal to the gentleness of the head of the college. Her adherence to the religion, in which she was educated, might have been as frail as his, had she not been lost on a voyage with her children to Virginia the next year. The commons of the students have often been matter of complaint, but, I believe, have never since occupied the attention of the government of the state.

Of the two young men referred to by Mrs. Eaton, Wilson was son of the pastor of Boston, graduated in the first class, 1642, and, Mather says, "continued, unto old age, a faithful, painful, useful minister of the gospel" in Medfield. Hough was, probably, son of Atherton, the assistant, and was the second minister of Reading. Why he received not the usual degree is unknown. See Johnson, lib. II. c. 25. In our Town Records I find, "Mr. Samuel Haugh, pastor of the church at Reading, deceased at Mr. Hezekiah Usher's house in Boston, 30 March, 1662." The Moor was probably a slave.

of the scandal of religion, and offence which would be given to such as might intend to send their children hither, they all agreed to censure him, and put him from that employment. So, being called in, the governour, after a short preface, &c. declared the sentence of the court to this effect, viz. that he should give Briscoe £30, fined 100 ||marks,|| and debarred teaching of children within our jurisdiction. A pause being made, and expectation that (according to his former confession) he would have given glory to God, and acknowledged the justice and clemency of the court, the governour giving him occasion, by asking him if he had ought to say, he turned away with a discontented look, saying, "If sentence be passed, then it is to no end to speak." Yet the court remitted his fine to £20, and willed Briscoe to take but £20.

The church at Cambridge, taking notice of these proceedings, intended to deal with him. The pastor moved the governour, if they might, without offence to the court, examine other witnesses. His answer was, that the court would leave them to their own liberty; but he saw not to what end they should do it, seeing there had been five already upon oath, and those whom they should examine should speak without oath, and it was an ordinance of God, that by the mouths of two or three witnesses every matter should be established. But he soon discovered himself; for, ere the church could come to deal with him, he fled to Pascataquack, and, being pursued and apprehended by the governour there, he again acknowledged his great sin in flying, &c. and promised (as he was a Christian man) he would return with the messengers. But, because his things he carried with him were aboard a bark there, bound to Virginia, he desired leave to go fetch them, which they assented unto, and went with him (three of them) aboard with him. So he took his truss and came away with them in the boat; but, being come to the shore, and two of them going out of the boat, he caused the boatsmen to put off the boat, and, because the third man would not go out, he turned him into the water, where he had been drowned, if he had not saved himself by swimming. So he returned to the bark, and presently they set sail and went out of the harbour. Being thus gone, his creditors began to complain; and thereupon it was found, that he was run in debt about £1000, and had taken up most of this money upon bills he had charged into England upon his brother's agents, and others whom he had no such relation to. So his estate was seized, and put into commissioners' hands, to be divided among his creditors, allowing somewhat for the present maintenance of his wife and chil-

||blank||

dren. And, being thus gone, the church proceeded and cast him out. He had been sometimes initiated among the Jesuits,[1] and, coming into England, his friends drew him from them, but, it was very probable, he now intended to return to them again, being at this time about thirty years of age, and upwards. See after.

7. 17.] Mount Woollaston had been formerly laid to Boston; but many poor men having lots assigned them there, and not able to use those lands and dwell still in Boston, they petitioned the town first to have a minister there, and after to have leave to gather a church there, which the town at length (upon some small composition) gave way unto. So, this day, they gathered a church after the usual manner, and chose one Mr. [2]Tomson, a very gracious, sincere man, and Mr. Flint, a godly man also, their ministers.[3]

Mo. 9.] At a general court holden at Boston, great complaint was made of the oppression used in the country in sale of foreign commodities; and Mr. Robert [4]Keaine, who kept a shop in Bos-

---

1 His cruelty and injustice might have been as great, if the Jesuits had had no share in his education; though, I fear, the author intended to refer the fruits to the soil, rather than the tree.

2 Satisfactory accounts of William Thomson may be seen in Eliot's and Allen's Dictionaries, in the Magnalia, III., Johnson, lib. II. c. 7, 10 and 18, and lib. III. c. 1 and 11, larger in Morton, sub. an. 1666, the year of his death, and, best of all, in the century sermon of Hancock, his successor in the church of Braintree, now of Quincy. He had been some years in the country, perhaps; for the Records of Dorchester, which I have inspected, according to the views of the historian of that town, 1 Hist. Coll. IX. 191, reckon him among their members in 1636. But I suspect that was two years before his admission. The scrutinizing author must have concluded, that he was a different person from the future minister of the adjoining town; for he adds, of him "I cannot obtain any information." He was admitted freeman 13 May, 1640. Most of the materials used by later writers were found in our author, the most interesting event in his pilgrimage here being the mission to Virginia, of which a full account will be found in the next volume. The first mention of him, after that in the text, will show, that he "had been an instrument of much good at Acomenticus." The Braintree Records mention the birth of his son, Joseph, 1 May, 1640, Benjamin, 14 July, 1642, and death of his wife in January, 1642. Benjamin was graduated at Harvard College in 1662. Him I consider the author of the verses in praise of Whiting, which are, probably, the best in the Magnalia. A tribute in verse, of greater justice than beauty, is entered in the Roxbury Church Records on the lamentable death of Thomson's wife, while he was absent on the service of his master. It is supposed, that the celebrated Benjamin Thomson, Count Rumford, is descended from this first pastor of Braintree.

3 Our MS. had first "*their pastor*," after "Tomson," and "*teacher*" to end the sentence; and, as the alteration is by the governour, I infer that the distinction was disregarded at the election.

4 This gentleman is, probably, the same with one, whose name is the last signed to a letter of encouragement of the plantation at Plimouth, 7 April,

ton, was notoriously above others observed and complained of; and, being convented, he was charged with many particulars; in

---

1624, preserved by Gov. Bradford in 1 Hist. Coll. III. 28, and who united with others, in all forty-two, in a loan of £1800 sterling, by which its life was preserved. Ib. 48. Being received into Boston church 20 March, 1635—6, we may conclude, he had come over in the preceding autumn, probably with Wilson in October. At the general election, in May following, he was admitted to the freeman's oath, at the same time with Samuel Appleton, Henry Flint, and Daniel Maude, who alone, out of sixty-two that day sworn, have the prefix of respect.

Of the curious subject, introduced to our notice by the text, inquiry had, at the former session of the same court, in September, been instituted; and, from the language of the Record, I. 269, "Capt. Keayne was willed to return Sarah King her necessary clothes again," we may presume, the case was a flagrant one. It is evident, however, that much more tenderness was shown towards him than delinquents usually received; for we find, at the assistants' quarter court, four pages later, in the same volume, this note: "There is £10 delivered the governour by one that had failed by taking too great prices for his commodities. He hath satisfied the parties, whom he sold the commodities unto." At the general court in May after the date in the text, I find, Col. Rec. I. 276, "Mr. Robert Keayne had £120 of his fine remitted him; so that there remains only £80 to be paid by him." He was not the only person of eminence liable to this animadversion, though the proceedings against him went further than in any other case within my knowledge. Indeed, the attempt to prevent demand of high price for any commodity, however willing the purchaser may be to give it, is preposterous and destructive to all commerce between man and man. Sedgwick was admonished for a like frailty, in asking the money's worth for his goods. Before this scandal, Keayne had been four times chosen from Boston to the general court; and, after the evil report had passed over, was several times elected, and became speaker in October, 1646, but only for one day. Unhappily, he fell under obloquy again: a less probable, though more injurious accusation was preferred, of which a very particular relation is, in subsequent pages, given by our author. He certainly stood high in the estimation of the government; for, in May, 1639, a grant of four hundred acres had been made to him, when others of no larger quantity were made to several gentlemen of the first rank in the colony.

Keayne died 23 March, 1655—6. His will, proved 2 May after, written with his own hand,—for no other hand could have been so patient,—at different times, beginning 1 August 1653, is a most extraordinary instrument, commencing on page 116 of our first volume of Records in Probate office, and filling one hundred and fifty-eight folio pages. It would be an idle affectation to say, that it has been all studied by me, though most parts were cursorily examined; for no reader of this work would exact of its editor such an unprofitable labour. An abridgment of several pages could easily be afforded here, for it was made; but when thirty pages of the will are occupied about the animadversion of the court on his extortion, as explained in our text, with inculpation of his prosecutor for cruel and unfounded allegations in that and another affair, and thirty pages more given to explanation of his accounts in many different books, with the order and reasons, plentiful enough, of dividing his estate,—the most minute antiquary becomes weary with the trifles. Yet there are several curious parts. The ample declaration of his correct faith, that fills two of the early pages, hardly compensates, however, for the anxiously refined, but equivocal, morality, by which, towards the end, he excuses himself. Between his only son, Benjamin, and a daughter of Dudley,

some, for taking above six-pence in the shilling profit; in some above eight-pence; and, in some §small§ things, above two for one; and being hereof convict, (as appears by the records,) he was fined £200, which came thus to pass: The deputies considered, apart, of his fine, and set it at £200; the magistrates agreed but to £100. So, the court being divided, at length it was agreed, that his fine should be £200, but he should pay but £100, and the other should be respited to the further consideration of the next general court. By this means the magistrates and deputies were brought to an accord, which otherwise had not been likely, and so much trouble might have grown, and the offender escaped censure. For the cry of the country was so great against oppression, and some of the elders and magistrates had declared such detestation of the corrupt practice of this man (which was the more observable, because he was wealthy and sold dearer than most other tradesmen, and for that he was of ill report for the like covetous practice in England, that incensed the deputies very much against him.) And ||sure|| the course was very evil, especial circumstances considered: 1. He being an ancient professor of the gospel: 2. A man of eminent parts: 3. Wealthy, and having but one child: 4. Having come over for conscience sake, and for the advancement of the gospel here: 5. Having been formerly dealt with and admonished, both by private friends and also by some of the magistrates and elders, and having promised reformation; being a member of a church and commonwealth now in their infancy, and under the curious observation of all churches and civil states in the world. These added much aggravation to his sin in the judgment of all men of understanding. Yet most of the magistrates (though they dis-

||since||

"an unhappy and uncomfortable match" is spoken of in this will; and that union, perhaps, with other disagreeable circumstances, compelled the son to return to the land of his fathers, where he died, I presume, in 1668. In August of that year, administration of the estate was granted to his son-in-law. The male line ended with Benjamin.

The chief claims of Robert to be remembered, must arise from his activity in founding the Artillery Company, of which he was captain, and which is fondly remembered in the endless testament. See the History of that institution for other particulars. A large 4to MS. of his is preserved in the archives of the Historical Society, chiefly composed of the sermons or expositions of Cotton, as taken, probably in church, by the owner. It contains, besides, two very curious cases of ecclesiastical discipline, in which all the church members deliver their opinions on the matters,—one against Mrs. Hibbins, the other against Serjeant Richard Wait. The lady was cast out; the serjeant continued in the affection of the body. The report of brethren sent to Rhode Island, to warn the dwellers there of contumacy, is also given; and a few other trifles. He left, among other liberal bequests, a large one to Harvard College, still preserved in their exhibit.

cerned of the offence clothed with all these circumstances) would have been more moderate in their censure: 1. Because there was no law in force to limit or direct men in point of profit in their trade. 2. Because it is the common practice, in all countries, for men to make use of advantages for raising the prices of their commodities. 3. Because (though he were chiefly aimed at, yet) he was not alone in this fault. 4. §Because all men through the country, in sale of cattle, corn, labour, &c. were guilty of the like excess in prices. 5.§ Because a certain rule could not be found out for an equal rate between buyer and seller, though much labour had been bestowed in it, and divers laws had been made, which, upon experience, were repealed, as being neither safe nor equal. Lastly, and especially, because the law of God appoints no other punishment but ||double|| restitution; and, in some cases, as where the offender freely confesseth, and brings his offering, only half added to the principal. After the court had censured him, the church of Boston called him also in question, where (as before he had done in the court) he did, with tears, acknowledge and bewail his covetous and corrupt heart, yet making some excuse for many of the particulars, which were charged upon him, as ||[2]partly|| by pretence of ignorance of the true price of some wares, and chiefly by being misled by some false principles, as, 1. That, if a man lost in one commodity, he might help himself in the price of another. 2. That if, through want of skill or ||[3]other occasion,|| his commodity cost him more than the price of the market in England, he might then sell it for more than the price of the market in New England, &c. These things gave occasion to Mr. Cotton, in his publick exercise the next lecture day, to lay open the errour of such false principles, and to give some rules of direction in the case.

Some false principles were these:

1. That a man ||[4]might|| sell as dear as he can, and buy as cheap as he can.

2. If a man lose by casualty ||[5]of|| sea, &c. in some of his commodities, he may raise the price of the rest.

3. That he may sell as he bought, though he paid too dear, &c. and though the commodity be fallen, &c.

4. That, as a man may take the advantage of his own skill or ability, so he may of another's ignorance or necessity.

5. Where one gives time for payment, he is to take like recompense of one as of another.

The rules for trading were these:

1. A man may not sell above the current price, i. e. such a

||two|| ||[2]particularly|| ||[3]otherwise|| ||[4]may|| ||[5]at||

price as is usual in the time and place, and as another (who knows the worth of the commodity) would give for it, if he had occasion to use it; as that is called current money, which every man will take, &c.

2. When a man loseth in his commodity for want of skill, &c. he must look at it as his own fault or cross, and therefore must not lay it upon another.

3. Where a man loseth by casualty of sea, or, &c. it is a loss cast upon himself by providence, and he may not ease himself of it by casting it upon another; for so a man should seem to provide against all providences, &c. that he should never lose; but where there is a scarcity of the commodity, there men may raise their price; for now it is a hand of God upon the commodity, and not the person.

4. A man may not ask any more for his commodity than his selling price, as Ephron to Abraham, the land is worth thus much.

[Large blank.]

The cause being debated by the church, some were earnest to have him excommunicated; but the most thought an admonition would be sufficient. Mr. Cotton opened the causes, which required excommunication, out of that in 1 Cor. 5. 11. The point now in question was, whether these actions did declare him to be such a covetous person, &c. Upon which he showed, that it is neither the habit of covetousness, (which is in every man in some degree,) nor simply the act, that declares a man to be such, but when it appears, that a man sins against his conscience, or the very light of nature, and when it appears in a man's whole conversation. But Mr. Keaine did not appear to be such, but rather upon an errour in his judgment, being led by false principles; and, beside, he is otherwise liberal, as in his hospitality, and in church communion, &c. So, in the end, the church consented to an admonition.[1]

Upon this occasion a question grew, whether an admonition did bar a man from the sacrament, &c. Of this more shall be spoken hereafter.

---

[1] For this unusual instance of moderation in the church, whose corrective hand, in such an offence, had been more appropriately exercised than that of the magistrate, we may find two reasons: 1, that Keayne's principal accuser belonged to the country; the sympathies of Boston people, of whom many, being traders, must have felt the futility of several of the allegations against their craft, were therefore less strongly excited; 2. Wilson, the pastor of the church, was his brother-in-law. Keayne, in his will, says, Winthrop was prejudiced against him, but changed his opinion on the matter shortly before his death, and designed to have moved the court for restitution of the fine.

Being now about church matters, I will here insert another passage in the same church, which fell out about the same time. Their old meeting-house, being decayed and too small, they sold it away, and agreed to build another, which workmen undertook to set up for £600. Three hundred they had for the old, and the rest was to be gathered by voluntary contributions, as other charges were. But there grew a great difference among the brethren, where this new one should stand. Some were for the green, (which was the governour's first lot, and he had yielded it to the church, &c.;) others, viz. the tradesmen, especially, who dwelt about the market place, desired it might stand still ||near|| the market, lest in time it should divert the chief trade from thence. The church referred it to the judgment and determination of [1]five of the brethren, who agreed, that the fittest place (all things considered) would be near the market; but, understanding that many of the brethren were unsatisfied, and desired rather it might be put to a lot, they declared only their opinions in writing, and respited the full determination to another general meeting, thinking it very unsafe to proceed with the discontent of any considerable part of the church. When the church met, the matter was debated to and fro, and grew at length to some earnestness, &c.; but, after Mr. Cotton had cleared it up to them, that the removing it to the green[2] would be a damage to such as dwelt by the market, who had there purchased and built at great charge, but it would be no damage to the ||[2]rest|| to have it by the §market, because it would be no less, but rather more convenient for them, than where the former stood, they all yielded to have it set by the§ market place; and, though some remained still in their opinion, that the green were the fitter place, yet, for peace sake, they yielded to the rest by keeping silence while it passed. This good providence and overruling hand of God caused much admiration and acknowledgment of special mercy to the church, especially considering how long the like contention had held in some other churches, and ||[3]with what|| difficulty they had been accorded.

(7.) At the court of assistants, one Marmaduke Perry, of

||nearer|| ||[2]most|| ||[3]which without||

---

1 Instead of "five of the brethren," was originally written "*the governour and four others.*" We easily understand the cause of the change.

2 The green, the governour's first lot, was the corner of the street, part of which was afterwards taken for the Third, or Old South Church. Prince, who was minister of that church above a hundred years after,—Advertisement to Annals, II.—says, Winthrop "deceased in the very house I dwell in."

Salem, was arraigned for the death of one [blank,] his apprentice. The great inquest found the bill for murder; the jury of life and death could not agree; so they were adjourned to the next court, and Perry was let to bail by the governour and some other of the magistrates, after the court. At the court in 10ber, the prisoner appeared, and the jury, being called, had further evidence given them, which tended to the clearing of Perry; yet two of the jury dissented from the rest, who were all agreed to acquit him. In the end it had this issue, that these two were silent, and so the verdict was received. The cause was this: The boy was ill disposed, and his master gave him unreasonable correction, and used him ill in his diet. After, the boy gate a bruise on his head, so as there appeared a fracture in his scull, being dissected after his death. Now, two things were in the evidence, which made the case doubtful; one, the boy his charging his master, before his death, to have given him that wound with his meatyard and with a broomstaff (for he spake of both at several times;) the other was, that he had told another, that his hurt came with the fall of a bough from a tree; and other evidence there was none.

4.] At the general court, &c. the inhabitants of the upper part of Pascataquack, viz. Dover, &c. had written to the governour to offer themselves to come under our government. Answer was returned them, that, if they sent two or three of their company, with full commission, under all their hands, to conclude, &c. it was like the court would agree to their propositions. And now, at this court, came three with commission to agree upon certain articles annexed to their commission, which being read, the court appointed three to treat with them; but, their articles being not reasonable, they stood not upon them, but confessed that they had absolute commission to conclude by their discretion. Whereupon the treaty was brought to a conclusion to this effect: That they should ||be|| as Ipswich and Salem, and have courts there, &c. as by the copy of the agreement remaining with the recorder doth appear. This was ratified under ||2our|| publick seal, and so delivered to them; only they desired a promise from the court, that, if the people did not assent to it, (which yet they had no fear of,) they might be at liberty, which was granted them.[1]

Those of Exeter sent the like propositions to the court; but not liking (it seems) the agreement, which those of Dover had

||fare|| ||2a||

1 Much more of the terms, on which these settlements were taken under our jurisdiction, will appear two or three years later.

made, they repented themselves, and wrote to the court, that they intended not to proceed.

[Large blank.]

At this court there fell out some contestation between the governour and the [1]treasurer. Nicholas [2]Trerice being defendant in a cause, wherein Mr. [3]Hibbins, brother-in-law to the treasurer, was plaintiff, for £500, which the searchers took from him in the ship, whereof Trerice was master, and the defendant having answered upon oath to certain interrogatories ministered unto him, (and which were read to him before he took his oath,) and the treasurer pressing him again with the same interrogatory, the governour said, he had answered the same directly before. The treasurer thereupon said, (angerly,) Sir, I speak not to you. The governour replied, that time was very precious, and, seeing the thing was already answered, it was fit to proceed. Thereupon the treasurer stood up, and said, if he might not have liberty to speak, he would no longer sit there. The governour replied, that it was his place to manage the proceedings of the court, &c. The treasurer then said, You have no more to do in managing the business here than I. At which the governour took offence, as at an injury done to his place, and appealed to the court to declare, whether he might not enjoin any of the magistrates silence, if he saw cause. The deputy governour, at first apprehension, gainsaid it; but, presently, both himself and the rest of the magistrates (for the deputies were without, staying till this cause should be ended) did agree, that he might so do for a particular time; and if the party, so enjoined silence, were unsatisfied, he might appeal to the whole court, who might give him liberty to speak, though the governour had restrained him. So the governour pressed it no further, yet expected that the court would not have suffered such a publick affront to the governour to have passed without due reproof, &c. But nothing was done, save only the secretary and some one other spake somewhat of their dislike

---

1 The marginal note is, "Difference between the governour and Mr. Bellingham."

2 He was of Charlestown, as, from a deed in the first volume of our Registry, I ascertained, as also from Charlestown Records.

3 Of the services of William Hibbins much will appear in the progress of this work. He was a deputy from Boston in the autumn of the following year, though admitted only in May a freeman, and again in 1641 and 1643. In this latter he was chosen an assistant. Hutchinson, I. 173, gives as much of his character as can well be ascertained beyond the means furnished by Winthrop. He died 23 July, 1654.

of it; neither did it occasion any falling out between the governour and treasurer, for the governour held himself sufficiently discharged, after he had referred it to the consideration of the court, so as, if they did not look at it as a publick injury, he was willing to account of it accordingly.[1]

There happened a memorable thing at Plimouth about this time. One Keysar, of Lynn, being at Plimouth in his boat, and one Dickerson with him, a professor, but a notorious thief, was coming out of the harbour with the ebb, and the wind southerly, a fresh gale; yet, with all their skill and labour, they could not, in three hours, get the boat above one league, so as they were forced to come to an anchor, and, at the flood, to go back to the town; and, as soon as they were come in, the said Dickerson was arrested upon suspicion of a gold ring and some other pieces of gold, which, upon search, were found about him, and he was there whipped for it.[2]

The like happened at Boston about two years before. Schooler, who was executed for murder, as before is mentioned, had broke prison and was escaped beyond Winisemett, but there he was taken with such an astonishment, &c. as he could go no further, but was forced to return to Boston. These and

---

1 A strange and lamentable consequence of this controversy, in which Hibbins was cast, may be seen in Hubbard, 574. Some have said, he remarks, that the loss "so discomposed his wife's spirit, that she scarce ever was well settled in her mind afterward, but grew very turbulent in her passion and discontented, on which occasions she was cast out of the church, and then charged to be a witch, giving too much occasion, by her strange carriage, to common people so to judge." The unhappy woman might, perhaps, have been early cured by a ducking stool. A long controversy, in 1640, before the church, about some scolding, which terminated in a publick admonition and subsequent excommunication, is recorded in Keayne's MS. before mentioned; but to me it is not, and to others would not probably appear, a very attractive subject. Hutchinson, I. 173, informs us, that, though the magistrates refused to accept the verdict, yet it was the general court that condemned her for witchcraft; and the common people afterwards, with their accustomed manner, implied the judgments of God in the disasters of those who had given way, so unjustly, to the opinions of the same people. For the facts in support of his remark, he is indebted to Hubbard, ut supra. She suffered the punishment of death, for the ridiculous crime, the year after her husband's decease; her brother, Bellingham, not exerting, perhaps, his highest influence for her preservation. Her will, made in prison, immediately follows, in the Records, that of Keayne, who could not have been pleased with her.

2 It is in vain to regret, that such paragraphs are preserved in this History. The spirit of the age had prepared the people for such false impressions, and, in the perpetual glooms of the wilderness, their imagination gradually stole away the supremacy from judgment. The subsequent paragraph, remarking the *likeness* of the event there related, which is natural enough, would induce us to refer the astonishment, by which the escape of the criminal was prevented, to the *boat*, rather than the offender.

many other examples of discovering hypocrites and other lewd persons, and bringing them under their deserved punishments, do (among other things) show the presence and power of God in his ordinances, and his blessing upon his people while they endeavour to walk before him with uprightness.

At Kennebeck, the Indians wanting food, and there being store in the Plimouth trading house, they conspired to kill the English there for their provision; and some Indians coming into the house, Mr. [1]Willet, the master of the house, being reading in the Bible, his countenance was more solemn than at other times, so as he did not look cheerfully upon them, as he was wont to do; whereupon they went out and told their fellows, that their purpose was discovered. They asked them, how it could be. The others told them, that they knew it by Mr. Willet's countenance, and that he had discovered it by a book that he was reading. Whereupon they gave over their design.

The people had long desired a body of laws, and thought their condition very unsafe, while so much power rested in the discretion of magistrates. Divers attempts had been made at former courts, and the matter referred to some of the magistrates and some of the elders; but still it came to no effect; for, being committed to the care of many, whatsoever was done by some, was still disliked or neglected by others. At last it was referred to Mr. Cotton and Mr. Nathaniel [2]Warde, &c. and each of them framed a model, which were presented to this general court, and by them committed to the governour and deputy and some others to consider of, and so prepare it for the court in the 3d month next. Two great reasons there were, which caused most of the magistrates and some

---

1 From New England's Memorial we learn, that Capt. Thomas Willet was highly esteemed in Plimouth colony, being, in 1651, elected an assistant; and, by the choice for thirteen successive years to the same office, in that most strictly republican jurisdiction, we may be confident of his well deserving the affections of the people. It is unnecessary for me to add more than a reference to Judge Davis's edition of that work, in which his services with the Dutch, and settlement afterwards at New York, are particularly related. Descendants are, I believe, known in honourable stations.

2 In December, 1641, the labours of these legislators were perfected, as this History will show. The result was printed in London immediately after. An Abstract may be found by the curious in 1 Hist. Coll. V. 171—192, with an account of a second edition by Aspinwall. We may be sure, that Winthrop could not be mistaken in ascribing to Ward the principal honour of the work, though Cotton has often enjoyed it. Perhaps any one of twenty, in the civil or clerical line, had contributed as much as Cotton, though his name would carry the greatest weight.

of the elders not to be very forward in this matter. One was, want of sufficient experience of the nature and disposition of the people, considered with the condition of the country and other circumstances, which made them conceive, that such laws would be fittest for us, which should arise pro ||re nata|| upon occasions, &c. and so the laws of England and other states grew, and therefore the fundamental laws of England are called ||[2]customs, consuetudines.|| 2. For that it would professedly transgress the limits of our charter, which provide, we shall make no laws repugnant to the laws of England, and that we were assured we must do. But to raise up laws by practice and custom had been no transgression; as in our church discipline, and in matters of marriage, to make a law, that marriages should not be solemnized by ministers, is repugnant to the laws of England; but to bring it to a custom by practice for the magistrates to perform it, is no law made repugnant, &c. At length (to satisfy the people) it proceeded, and the two models were digested with divers alterations and additions, and abbreviated and sent to every town, (12,) to be considered of first by the magistrates and elders, and then to be published by the constables to all the people, that if any man should think fit, that any thing therein ought to be altered, he might acquaint some of the deputies therewith against the next court.

[Large blank.]

By this time there appeared a great change in the church of Boston; for whereas, the year before, they were all (save five or six) so affected to Mr. Wheelwright and Mrs. Hutchinson, and those new opinions, as they ||[3]slighted|| the present governour and the pastor, looking at them as men under a covenant of works, and as their greatest enemies; but they bearing all patiently, and not withdrawing themselves, (as they were strongly solicited to have done,) but carrying themselves lovingly and helpfully upon all occasions, the Lord brought about the hearts of all the people to love and esteem them more than ever before, and all ||[4]breaches|| were made up, and the church was saved from ruin beyond all expectation; which could hardly have been, (in human reason,) if those two had not been guided by the Lord to that moderation, &c. And the church (to manifest their hearty affection to the governour, upon occasion of some strait he was brought into through his bailiff's unfaithfulness) sent him £200.

There was now a church gathered at the Mount, and Mr.

||rei natura|| ||[2]custos consuetusdinis|| ||[3]perceived|| ||[4]breeches||

Tomson (a very holy man, who had been an instrument of much good at Acomenticus) was ordained the pastor the 19th of the 9th month.

(10.)] At the general court, an order was made to abolish that vain custom of drinking one to another, and that upon these and other grounds:

1. It was a thing of no good use.

2. It was an inducement to drunkenness, and occasion of quarrelling and bloodshed.

3. It occasioned much waste of wine and beer.

4. It was very troublesome to many, especially the masters and mistresses of the feast, who were forced thereby to drink more oft than they would, &c. Yet divers (even godly persons) were very loath to part with this idle ceremony, though (when disputation was tendered) they had no ||list,|| nor, indeed, could find any arguments, to maintain it. Such power hath custom, &c.

Mr. Ezekiel Rogers, of whose gathering of a church in England, mention was made before, being now settled with his company at ||[2]Rowley,|| was there ordained pastor, &c.

3.] There were so many lectures now in the country, and many poor persons would usually resort to two or three in the week, to the great neglect of their affairs, and the damage of the publick. The assemblies also were (in divers churches) held till night, and sometimes within the night, so as such as dwelt far off could not get home in due season, and many weak bodies could not endure so long, in the extremity of the heat or cold, without great trouble, and hazard of their health. Whereupon the general court ordered, that the elders should be desired to give a meeting to the magistrates and deputies, to consider about the length and frequency of church assemblies, and to make return to the court of their determinations, &c. This was taken in ill part by most of the elders and other of the churches, so as that those who should have met at Salem, did not meet, and those in the bay, when they met with the magistrates, &c. at Boston, expressed much dislike of such a course, alleging their tenderness of the church's liberties, (as if such a precedent might enthrall them to the civil power, and as if it would cast a blemish upon the elders, which would remain to posterity, that they should need to be regulated by the civil magistrate, and also raise an ill savour of the people's coldness, that would complain of much preaching, &c.—when as liberty for the ordinances was the main end (||[3]professed||) of our coming hither.) To which it was answered, 1. That the or-

||life|| ||[2]Roxbury|| ||[3]proposed||

der was framed with as much tenderness and respect as might be, in general words, without mentioning sermons or lectures, so as it might as well be taken for meetings upon other occasions of the churches, which were known to be very frequent. 2. It carried no command, but only an expression of a desire. 3. ||It|| concluded nothing but only to confer and consider. 4. The record of such an order will be rather an argument of the zeal and forwardness of the elders and churches, as it was of the Israelites', when they offered so liberally to the service of the tabernacle, as Moses was forced to restrain them.[1] Upon this interpretation of the court's intent, the elders were reasonably satisfied, and the magistrates finding how hardly such propositions would be digested, and that, if matters should be further pushed, it might make some breach, or disturbance at least, (for the elders had great power in the people's hearts, which was needful to be upheld, lest the people should break their bonds through abuse of liberty, which divers, having ||[2]surfeited of,|| were very forward to incite others to raise mutinies and foment dangerous and groundless jealousies of the magistrates, &c. which the wisdom and care of the elders did still prevail against; and indeed the people themselves, generally, through the churches, were of that understanding and moderation, as they would easily be guided in their way by any rule from scripture or sound reason:) in this consideration, the magistrates and deputies, which were then met, thought it not fit to enter any dispute or conference with the elders about the number of lectures, or for appointing any certain time for the continuance of the assemblies, but rested satisfied with their affirmative answer to these two propositions: 1. That their church assemblies might ordinarily break up in such season, as people that dwell a mile or two off might get home by daylight. 2. That, if they were not satisfied in the declaration of our intentions in this order of court, that nothing was attempted herein against the church's liberties, &c. they would truly acquaint us with the reasons of their unsatisfiedness; or, if we heard not

||I|| ||[2]forfeited||

---

1 "Much more than enough for the service of the work which the Lord commanded," Exodus xxxvi. 5, was the occasion of the order by Moses to restrain the free offerings. Yet it seems, from the history, they were brought only in the *morning*. In the ten preceding chapters, the contribution exacted, under that remarkable economy of the house of Israel, appears sufficiently burdensome. Pious services were, however, by our ancestors, given, in many instances, with greater liberality than by the chosen people; but the reference to their theocracy, in the text, will be thought, I presume, the most valuable and ingenious of all those that occur in our early history.

from them before the next court, we should take it for granted, that they were fully satisfied. They desired, that the order might be taken off the record; but for that it was answered, that it might not be done without consent of the general court; only it was agreed unto, that the secretary might defer to enter it in the book till the mind of the court might be known.

(12.) 20.] One Mr. Hanserd Knolles, a minister in England, who came over the last summer in the company of our familistical opinionists, and so being suspected and examined, and found inclining that way, was denied residence in the Massachusetts; whereupon he went to Pascataquack, where he began to preach; but Mr. Burdett, being then their governour and preacher, inhibited him. But, he being after removed to Acomenticus, the people called Mr. Knolles, and in short time he gathered some of the best minded into a church body, and became their pastor, and Capt. Underhill being their governour, they called ||their|| town Dover. But this Mr. Knolles, at his first coming thither, wrote a letter to his friends in London, wherein he bitterly inveighed against us, both against our magistrates and churches, and against all the people in general, (as by the copy of his letter sent over to our governour may appear.) The governour gave him notice thereof, and, being brought to a better judgment by further consideration and more experience, he saw the wrong he had done us, and was deeply humbled for it, and wrote to the governour to that effect, and desired a safe conduct, that he might come into the bay to give satisfaction, &c. for he could have no rest in his spirit until, &c.; which being sent him under the governour his hand, (with consent of the council,) §he came,§ and, upon a lecture day at Boston, (most of the magistrates and elders in the bay being there assembled,) he made a very free and full confession of his offence, with much aggravation against himself, so as the assembly were well satisfied. He wrote also a letter to the same effect to his said friends in England, which he left with the governour to be sent to them.

Capt. Underhill, also, being struck with horrour and remorse for his offences, both against the church and civil state, could have no rest till he had obtained a safe conduct to come and give satisfaction; and accordingly, (1,) 5, at a lecture at Boston, (it being then the court time,) he made a publick confession both of his living in adultery with Faber's wife, (upon suspicion whereof the church had before admonished him,) and attempting the like with another woman, and also the injury he had done to our state, &c. and acknowledged the justice of the

||this||

court in their proceeding against him, &c. Yet all his confessions were mixed with such excuses and extenuations, as did not give satisfaction of the truth of his repentance, so as it seemed to be done rather out of policy, and to pacify the sting of his conscience, than in sincerity. But, however, his offences being so foul and scandalous, the church presently cast him out; which censure he seemed to submit unto, and, for the time he staid in Boston, (being four or five days) he was very much dejected, &c.; but, being gone back, he soon recovered his spirits again, or, at least, gave not that proof of a broken heart, as he gave hope of at Boston. For (to ingratiate himself with the state of England, and with some gentlemen at the river's mouth, who were very zealous that way, and had lately set up common prayer, &c.) he sent thirteen men armed to Exeter to fetch one Gabriel Fish, who was detained in the officer's hands for speaking against the king, the magistrates of Exeter being then in the bay to take advice what to do with him; and besides, when the church and people of Dover desired him to forbear to come to the next court, till they had considered of his case, and he had promised so to do, yet, hearing that they were consulting to remove him from his government, he could not refrain, but came and took his place in the court; and though he had offered to lay down his place, yet, when he saw they went about it, he grew passionate, and expostulated with them, and would not stay to receive his dismission, nor would be seen to accept it, when it was sent after him. Yet they proceeded, and chose one [1]Roberts to be president of the court, and, soon after, they returned back Fish to Exeter, which was considerately done §of them,§ for it had been a dangerous precedent against them, being a weak plantation, if the commissioners from the lords of the council, who were daily expected, should have taken occasion to have done the like by them, though they held themselves to be out of that province, which was granted to Sir Ferdinando Gorges. Besides this, in the open court, he committed one of his fellow magistrates for rising up and saying he would not sit with an adulterer, &c. But the chief matter, ||which they produced|| against him, was, that, whereas he himself was the mover of them to break off their agreement with us, he had written to

||for which they proceeded||

1 Of this gentleman nothing is known to me, unless he be the John Roberts appointed marshal, in 1680, under the new administration by royal commission in that year, Belknap's N. H. I. 144, and who next year resigned, Ib. 149, 191, or Thomas Roberts, one of the principal landholders of Dover. Ib. 159.

our governour, and laid it upon the people, especially upon some among them; and for this they produced against him a letter from our governour, written to one of their commissioners in answer to a letter of his, wherein he had discovered the captain's proceeding in that matter. Soon after this the captain came by water into the bay to tender (as he said) satisfaction to the church. This was taken by some of the magistrates as a very presumptuous act, and they would have had him imprisoned, supposing that his safe conduct would not bear him out, having been once here and returned back again; but that ||counsel|| was not approved, because the time of his safe conduct was not expired, and it was thought very dangerous to our reputation to give the least occasion of reproach in this kind, seeing it might be objected against us to our great prejudice, ||2where|| we should not have opportunity to clear our innocency. But the church, not being satisfied of his repentance, would not admit him to publick speech. So, after one week, he returned home.

In this winter, in a close, calm day, there fell divers flakes of snow of this form *, very thin, and as exactly pointed as art could have cut them in paper, or, &c.

(1.) 24.] The church of Boston sent three brethren, viz. Capt. Edward Gibbons, Mr. Hibbins, and Mr. [1]Oliver the

||council|| ||2when||

[1] John, son of the ruling elder, is, probably, the gentleman intended. Notice of his death will appear in our second volume, sub an. 1646. In Keayne's MS. it appears, that, in our church, early in 1640, "a motion was made by such as have farms at Rumney Marsh, that our brother Oliver may be sent to instruct their servants, and to be a help to them, because they cannot many times come hither, nor sometimes to Lynn, and sometimes nowhere at all." On this much debate followed. His father spoke first: "I desire what calling my son hath to such a work, or by what rule of God's word may the church send out any of her members to such as are not of the church." Cotton answered, at some length. Two of the lay brethren proposed objections, to which Wilson briefly replied, and the subject was postponed. On 23 March, Wilson made a full statement of the general consent of the church, and the candidate closed thus: "Serjeant Oliver. I desire to speak a word or two to the business of Rumney Marsh. I am apt to be discouraged in any good work, and I am glad, that there is a universal consent in the hearts of the church; for if there should have been variety in their thoughts, or compulsion of their minds, it would have been a great discouragement. But, seeing a call of God, I hope I shall employ my weak talent to God's service; and, considering my own youth and feebleness to so great a work, I shall desire my loving brethren to look at me as their brother, to send me out with their constant prayers." From his will, I find, he married a daughter of John Newgate, and left three children, two sons, and a daughter, who afterwards married a gentleman of the name of Wiswell. Rumney Marsh is now Chelsea. It is a little strange, that a people, settled on a spot so difficult to have religious instruction at the neighbouring parishes, should have continued so long a time out of church state. The first sen-

younger, with letters to Mr. Coddington and the rest of our members at Aquiday, to understand their judgments in divers points of religion, formerly maintained by all, or divers of them, and to require them to give account to the church of their unwarrantable practice ||in|| communicating with excommunicated persons, &c. When they came, they found that those of them, who dwell at Newport, had joined themselves to a church there newly constituted, and thereupon they refused to hear them as messengers of our church, or to receive the church's letters.[1] Whereupon, at their return, the elders and most of the church would have cast them out, as refusing to hear the church; but, all being not agreed, it was deferred.

18.] Mr. [2]Norris was ordained teacher of the church of

||of||

tence of the Records of the Chelsea parish is, October 19, 1715, "This day the church was gathered at Rumney Marsh, and Mr. Thomas Cheever was ordained their pastor." For this information I am indebted to the kindness of the present pastor, Dr. Joseph Tuckerman. Undoubtedly the population was small, as it has ever since continued.

1 By Keayne's MS. it appears, the place was called Portsmouth, a name since appropriated to another town, of much less magnitude, on the island. Coggeshall, for the refractory brethren, it seems, inquired of these spiritual commissioners, "what power one church hath over another church?" Oliver relates, that "they denied our commission, and refused to let our letter be received; and they conceive, one church hath not power over the members of another church, and do not think they are tied to us by our covenant. So we were fain to take all their answers by going to their several houses. Mr. Hutchinson told us, he was more nearly tied to his wife than to the church: he thought her to be a dear saint and servant of God. We came then to Mrs. Hutchinson, and told her, that we had a message to do to her from the Lord and from our church. She answered, There are lords many, and gods many; but I acknowledge but one Lord. Which lord do you mean? We answered, we came in the name but of one Lord, and that is God. Then, saith she, so far we agree; and where we do agree, let it be set down. Then we told her, we had a message to her from the church of Christ in Boston. She replied, she knew no church but one. We told her, in scripture the Holy Ghost calls them churches. She said, Christ had but one spouse. We told her, he had in some sort as many spouses as saints. But for our church, she would not acknowledge it any church of Christ." The report of this unprofitable mission was made 16 March.

2 Edward Norris is commemorated with due honours in Eliot's Biographical Dictionary. Our regret, that so important a name eluded the search of Allen, though a descendant of our age is well remembered for his pious liberality, will not be vain, if the second edition of that gentleman's volume, which has been long preparing, supply the deficiency, and go beyond his predecessor. Norris arrived in our country, probably, the year before his ordination, which was the period that the church had to form their estimate of his merit. He was not admitted a freeman till May, 1640. He had been a minister in England, yet Johnson has not named him. Much influence in the state was exerted by him, of which evidence will appear in this History; and, four years after Winthrop's death, in the famous schism of the commissioners of the four United Colonies, he took side against the principles of the

Salem, there being present near all the elders of the other churches, and much people besides.

21.] The White Angel, a small ship of Bristol, went from hence, and arrived there in twenty-four days; and, the same year, the Desire, a ship built at Marblehead, of one hundred tons, went from hence in the summer, and arrived at Gravesend, in the Thames, in twenty-three days.

Our neighbours of Plimouth had procured from hence, this year, one Mr. [1]Chancey, a great scholar, and a godly man, intending to call him to the office of a teacher; but, before the fit time came, he discovered his judgment about baptism, that the children ought to be dipped and not sprinkled; and, he being an active man, and very vehement, there arose much trouble about it. The magistrates and the other elders there, and the most of the people, withstood the receiving of that practice, not for itself so much, as for fear of worse consequences, as the annihilating our baptism, &c. Whereupon the church there wrote to all the other churches, both here and at Connecticut, &c. for advice, and sent Mr. Chancey's arguments. The churches took them into consideration, and ||returned|| their several answers, wherein they showed their dissent from him, and clearly confuted all his arguments, discovering withal some great mistakes of his about the judgment

||wrote||

Massachusetts court, who resisted the war with the Dutch. War had been raging two years between the respective mother countries; yet our people were wise enough to keep at peace on this side of the Atlantick. Those who hoped to gain by a war were very eager for its declaration, and charged the pacifick temper of Massachusetts to any thing but its true cause. Norris was, happily, unsuccessful, though he quoted the curse against Meroz, which religious or political enthusiasm has commonly found effectual. See his letter of 3 May, 1653, in Hazard, II. 256. The president of the council, the amiable Bradstreet, was averse to war; but Norris's parishioner, Hawthorne, the other commissioner of Massachusetts, was urgent for it.

1 An excuse for neglecting great labour of inquiry about this celebrated scholar, who, after the honour conferred on him of two professorships by his alma mater, the University of Cambridge in England, became head of our own College, is afforded by the elaborate biography, written by a descendant of great name, preserved in 1 Hist. Coll. X. 171. Perhaps, however, the ancestor's doctrines are a little softened in that tract. He was of Trinity College. Mather mentions his verses on the death of Queen Ann, 1619. I have seen, in the Boston Athenæum, the Cantabrigiensium Dolor et Solamen, on the death of James and accession of Charles, 1625, containing his Greek and Latin verses, signed Car. Chauncy, Coll. Trin. Bac. Theol. His two unimportant opinions, relative to the time of celebrating the eucharist, and the mode of baptism, were no obstacles to his advancement, even in that age of narrow and scrupulous formality. It is a little remarkable, that the two first presidents of Harvard College adopted opinions on the form of baptism adverse to that of all the other divines and laicks of the colony.

and practice ot antiquity.[1] Yet he would not give over his opinion; and the church of Plimouth, (though they could not agree to call him to office, yet,) being much taken with his able parts, they were very loath to part with him. He did maintain, also, that the Lord's supper ought to be administered in the evening, and every Lord's day; and the church at Sandwich (where one Mr. Leveridge was minister) fell into the practice of it; but that being a matter of no great ill consequence, save some outward inconvenience, there was little stir about it. This Mr. Chancey was after called to office in the church of Scituate.

One [2]Palmer, of Hingham, and two others, (being ancient and skilful seamen,) being in a shallop of ||ten|| tons, in an easterly wind, by Peddock's Island, were overset; yet one of them had the sheet in his hand, and let fly; but it was too late, having but little ballast in her; yet it pleased God, there came by, soon after, a pinnace, which espied them sitting upon her ||[2]side,|| yet deep in the water, and took them up, but the shallop was not heard of after.

Many men began to inquire after the southern parts; and the great advantages supposed to be had in Virginia and the West Indies, &c. made this country to be disesteemed of many; and yet those countries (for all their great wealth) have sent hither, both this year and formerly, for supply of clothes and other necessaries; and some families have forsaken both Providence and other the Caribbee Islands and Virginia to come live here. And though our people saw what meagre, unhealthful countenances they brought hither, and how fat and well liking

||100|| ||[2]shrouds||

---

1 If nothing of greater value, than these answers of the churches, were lost by us, we should less regret the extent of our ignorance of the thoughts and actions of our fathers. From Keayne's MS. it appears, that answer by Boston church was made, 21 June, to a question and desire from the church of Plimouth, "whether it be lawful to use sprinkling in baptism, or rather dipping; Mr. Chauncy being of the mind, that it is a violation of an ordinance to use sprinkling instead of dipping." In the illustrious descendant's Life of his ancestor, there may be some mistake on this point. Yet an equal errour is, perhaps, discernible in the text, as to the confutation, and finding mistakes about "the judgment and practice of antiquity." Fortunately, it is a matter, on which little depends; and the churches here would do wisely to allow, as a large part of the antipædobaptists in England are liberal enough to do, that the substance of Christianity is of infinitely higher importance than this form of expressing our devotion to it, and that a controversy, which cannot be settled, had better be dropped.

2 Hingham Records show, that John Palmer came over in September, 1635, and those of the colony, that he was made free 13 March, 1638—9. Nothing more of him is known by me.

they became soon, yet they were so taken with the ease and plenty of those countries, as many of them sold their estates here to transport themselves to Providence; among whom the chief was John Humfrey, Esq. a gentleman of special parts of learning and activity, and a godly man, who had been one of the first beginners in the promoting of this plantation, and had laboured very much therein. He, being brought low in his estate, and having many children, and being well known to the lords of Providence, and offering himself to their service, was accepted to be the next governour. Whereupon he laboured much to draw men to join with him. This was looked ||at, both|| by the general court, and also by the elders, as an unwarrantable course; for though it was thought very needful to further plantation of churches in the West Indies, and all were willing to endeavour the same; yet to do it with disparagement of this country, (for they gave out that they could not subsist here,) caused us to fear, that the Lord was not with them in this way. And, withal, some considerations were propounded to them by the court, which diverted some of them, and made others to pause, upon three points especially: 1. How dangerous it was to bring up an ill report upon this good land, which God had found out and given to his people, and so to discourage the hearts of their brethren, &c. 2. To leave a place of rest and safety, to expose themselves, their wives and children, to the danger of a potent enemy, the Spaniard. 3. Their subjection to such governours as those in England shall set over them, &c. Notwithstanding these considerations, divers of them persisted in their resolutions, and went about to get some ship or bark to transport them; but they were still crossed by the hand of God.[1]

Mo. 3. 17.] Joseph [2]Grafton set sail from Salem, the 2d day in the morning, in a ||[2]ketch|| of about forty tons, (three men and a boy in her,) and arrived at Pemaquid (the wind easterly) upon the third day in the morning, and there took in some twenty

||upon|| ||[2]Cavye||

---

1 "That the Lord was not with them," in their design to draw off people from Massachusetts to the West Indies for a permanent plantation, we may as confidently believe, as did Winthrop and the majority who remained; yet it is desirable to disavow the notion, that their difficulties in the attempt prove, that they "were still crossed by his hand."

2 He had been made free at the general election in May, 1637. The relation in the text proves the prosperity of the plantation at Pemaquid, no less than the activity of Grafton. In the next volume it will be seen, that his vessel, carrying provisions to La Tour, was taken by D'Aulney, and the crew were very ill treated. Grafton died at Barbados, February, 1670. Descendants are known, among whom is one of the same name in this city.

cows, oxen, &c. with hay and water for them, and came to an anchor in the bay the 6th[1] day, about three after noon.

It came over by divers letters and reports, that the Lord Say did labour, by disparaging this country, to divert men from coming to us, and so to draw them to the West Indies; and, finding that godly men were unwilling to come under other governours than such as they should make choice of themselves, &c. they condescended to articles somewhat suitable to our form of government, although they had formerly declared themselves much against it, and for a ||meer aristocratie,|| and an hereditary magistracy to be settled upon some great persons, &c.

The governour also wrote to the Lord Say about the report aforesaid, and therein showed his lordship, how evident it was, that God had chosen this country to plant his people in, and therefore how displeasing it would be to the Lord, and dangerous to himself, to hinder this work, or to discourage men from supplying us, by abasing the goodness of the country, which he never saw, and persuading men, that here was no possibility of subsistence; whereas there was a sure ground for his children's faith, that, being sent hither by him, either he saw that the land was a good land, and sufficient to maintain them, or else he intended to make it such, &c. To this letter his lordship returned answer, (not denying that which was reported of him, nor the evidence of the Lord's owning the work, but) alleging, that this was a place appointed only for a present refuge, &c. and that, a better place being now found out, we were all called to remove thither.

[Very large blank.]

||more aristocratic||

---

1 Days of the week, probably, are meant. The same scruple, which led to change of the months, caused the names of the days to be offensive, and induced the fathers to reckon the less, as well as greater divisions of time, by numerals. Adherence to this custom distinguishes the Quakers.

APPENDIX.

A 1.

[The date of this letter is uncertain; probably as early as 1621 or 2.]

My good Wife,

I WROTE to thee this week by Roger Mather, but shall expect no other letter from thee, because of thy journey to Maplested, from whence I hope thou art safely returned. Blessed be the Lord, our good God, who watcheth over us in all our ways to do us good, and to comfort us with his manifold blessings, not taking occasion by our sins to punish us as we deserve. Through his mercy it is, that I continue in health, and that, to my great joy, I hear well of thee and our family. The Lord teach us the right use of all his blessings, and so temper our affections towards the good things of this life, as our greatest joy may be, that our names are in the book of life, that we have the good will of our heavenly Father, that Christ Jesus is ours, and that by him we have right to all things. Then, come what will, we may have joy and confidence.

My sweet wife,—I am sorry that I cannot now appoint the time, that I hope to return, which cannot be the next week; though, it is like, my sister Fones, or some of her company, will come down then; but you shall hear more the beginning of next week.

For news I have but one to write of, but that will be more welcome to thee than a great deal of other. My office is gone, and my chamber, and I shall be a saver in them both. So, as I hope, we shall now enjoy each other again, as we desire. The Lord teach us to improve our time and society to more use for our mutual comfort, and the good of our family, &c. than before.

Mr. Fowle.

It is now bed time; but I must lie alone; therefore I make less haste. Yet I must kiss my sweet wife; and so, with my blessing to our children, and salutation to all our friends, I commend thee to the grace and blessing of the Lord, and rest

Thy faithful husband,
JO. WINTHROP.

My brother D. and sister, and sister F. commend them to thee.

To his very loving wife, Mrs. WINTHROP,
at her House in Groton.

A 2.

Dear Son,

THOUGH I have received no letters yet from you, I cannot pass by any opportunity, without some testimony of my fatherly affection, and care of your welfare, for which respect I am content to have you absent from me in so far a distance; for I know, that, in respect of yourself, patria ubicunque bene, and in respect of the Almighty, his power and providence is alike in all places; and for mine own comfort, it shall be in your prosperity and well-doing wheresoever.

Because I cannot so oft put you in mind of those things, which concern your good, as if you were nearer to me, it must be your care the better to observe and ruminate those instructions, which I give you, and the better to apply the other good means, which you have. Especially labour, by all means, to imprint in your heart the fear of God, and let not the fearful profaneness and contempt of ungodly men diminish the reverent and awful regard of his Great Majesty in your heart. But remember still, that the time is at hand, when they shall call the [mountains to] hide them from the face of Him, whom now they slight and neglect, &c.

I have written to you more largely by one Mr. Southwell, and now am at little leisure. When you write back, let me know the state of your college, &c. and how you like, &c., and remember my love to your reverend tutor. Your grandfather, grandmother, and mother, salute and bless you. Your brothers and sister are in health, (I praise God.) The Lord, in mercy, season your heart with his grace, and keep you from the lusts of youth and the evil of the times. So I rest

Your loving father,

JOHN WINTHROP.

GROTON, *August* 6, 1622.

To my beloved Son, JOHN WINTHROP, *at the College in Dublin, d'd.*

A 3.

My beloved Son,

I BESEECH the Lord to bless thee with grace and peace. I give him thanks for thy welfare, and hope, through his mercy, that this infirmity, which is now upon thee, shall turn to thy health. I received two letters from thee, written (I perceive) in haste; but they were welcome to me and the rest, to your grandmother, mother, &c. who all rejoice in your good liking. I sent you two letters, a good while since, which I hope will not miscarry, though they be long in going. The further you are from me, the more careful I am of your welfare, both in body and soul; the chief means whereof lyeth in your own endeavour. Your friends may pray for you and counsel you, but your own diligence and watchfulness must be added to make you blessed. God hath provided you a liberal portion of outward good things. You must labour to use them soberly, and to consider, that your happiness lyeth not in meat, drink and bodily refreshings, but in the favour of God for your part in a better life. I purposed to send you, by this bearer, such books as you writ for; only Aristotle I cannot, because your uncle Fones is not at London to buy it; and I know not whether you would have Latin or Greek. I purpose also to send you some cloth for a gown and suit; but for a study gown, you were best buy some coarse Irish cloth. I shall (if God will) write to you again by Mr. Olmsted. For the carriage of such things as I send you by John Hutton, you must remember to pay him, because I cannot tell here what they will come to. I have written to your uncle to send over my gelding. If you see that he forget it, you may put him in mind. Your grandfather and grandmother will write to you. Your mother salutes you with her blessings. We are all in health, (I praise God.) Remember my love to your good tutor. The Lord in mercy bless and keep you, and direct and prosper your study. Amen. So I rest

Your loving father,

JOHN WINTHROP.

GROTON, *August* 31, 1622.

To my beloved Son, JOHN WINTHROP, *at the College near Dublin.*

A 4.

My dearly beloved Son,

I DO usually begin and end my letters with that, which I would have the A and Ω of all thy thoughts and endeavours, viz. the blessing of the Almighty to be upon thee, not after the common valuation of God's blessings, like the warming of the sun to a hale, stirring body; but that blessing, which faith finds in the sweet promises of God and his free favour, whereby the soul hath a place of joy and refuge in all storms of adversity. I beseech the Lord to open thine eyes, that thou mayest see the riches of this grace, which will abate the account of all earthly vanities: and if it please him to give thee once a taste of the sweetness of the true wisdom, which is from above, it will season thy studies, and give a new temper to thy soul. Remember, therefore, what the wisest saith, The fear of the Lord is the beginning of wisdom. Lay this foundation, and thou shalt be wise indeed.

I am very glad to hear, that you like so well in Ireland. If your profiting in learning may be answerable, it will much increase my comfort. I was not greatly troubled to hear that your body did break out, but rather occasioned to bless God, that sent you so good a means of future health. I must needs acknowledge the great care and kindness of your uncle and aunt towards you. It may be much to your good, if you be careful to make right use of it, as I hope you do; for I hear you love your study well. You must have special care, that you be not ensnared with the lusts of youth, which are commonly covered under the name of recreations, &c. I remember the counsel of a wise man, Quidquid ad voluptatis seminarium pullulat, venenum puta. Think of it, (dear son,) and especially that of Paul to Timothy, Exhort young men that they be sober minded.

I sent you some books by J. Hutton. I could not then buy the rest, nor such cloth, &c. which I would have sent you, because your uncle Fones was not then in London; and I have no friend else, that I can make bold with. I have now a piece of cloth to make your doublet and hose, if I can send it by Mr. Olmested; if not, then desire your uncle to fit you there; it is only some little more in the price; and I have found, that, except one send by some friend, the carriage and custom (besides the hazard) costs so much, as there will be little saved. You may line your gown with some warm baize, and wear it out, for else you will soon outgrow it; and if you be not already in a frieze jerkin, I wish you to get one speedily; and howsoever you clothe yourself when you stir, yet be sure to keep warm when you study or sleep. I send you no money, because you may have of your uncle what you need. I hope you will be honestly frugal, and have respect to my great charge and small means, which I shall willingly extend to the utmost to do you good. Your grandfather, grandmother and mother salute and bless you. We all, with your brothers and sister, are in health, (I praise God.) Forth is at Bury; but he fell so between two forms, as he had like, between both, to have fallen back to Boxford.

Your uncle Gostlin and aunt are in health, and he means to write to you. Your good host and hostess at Bury inquire much of you, and desire always to be remembered to you; so did your master there, when I last saw him.

I purpose to write two or three lines to your good tutor, in token of my thankful acceptance of his loving pains with you.

We are daily in expectation of Mr. Olmested's coming by us, who appointed to have set forth on his journey above a fortnight since; otherwise I had adventured some letters by London before this, though we received none from you since John Hutton came to us.

I hear not yet of my gelding. It will be fit, that, at the quarter's end, (if your uncle forget it,) you ask him money for your tutor. The Lord bless you ever. So I rest

Your loving father,

JOHN WINTHROP.

October 16, 1622.

Commend me to Mr. Downes the stationer.

To my beloved Son, JOHN WINTHROP, *at Trinity College in Dublin*, *Ireland*, *d'd.*

A 5.

My sweet Wife,

Blessed be God, by whose providence and protection I am come safe to London. Here I find them all in health, and a great deal of kind welcome; only thy company is wanting, which they much desire.

I doubt my brother's coming to Ipswich will be deferred till the spring; for Mr. Hore (who should hire his house) and he are broken off. Thus man purposeth, but God disposeth. O, that we could learn, at length, to trust his wisdom, love, power, &c. and cast our care upon him, and leave our own carnal wisdom, fear, confidence, &c. Then should it go well with us assuredly; then should we have our rest in that true peace, which passeth understanding. But it is our wretched infidelity that keeps good things from us. Let us, therefore, pray earnestly, and labour for this precious faith; it will recompense all our cost.

For such news as is here, this bearer can sufficiently inform you, and so may spare my labour; and, besides, I am hasted into the city about my business. When I shall return, I cannot yet tell, but thy love will make me lose no time. Therefore, for the present, with my brother's and sister's kind salutations to thee and to my parents, to whom I commend my love and duty, I heartily commend thee and our little ones, and all our family, to the gracious protection and blessing of the Lord. So I rest

Thy faithful, loving husband,

JOHN WINTHROP.

London, *October* 19, 1622.

A 6.

My dear Son,

I received your letters, with the bill of charges inclosed, &c. I bless God for the continuance of your health, but especially for the good seed of his true fear, which I trust is planted, and grows daily in you. I perceive you lose not your time, nor neglect your study, which, as it will be abundantly fruitful to my comfort, so much more to your own future and eternal happiness, and especially to the glory of him, who hath created you to this purpose. I pray continually, that God will please to establish your heart, and bless these good beginnings. For the money, which you have spent, I will pay it, and what else your uncle shall appoint me, so soon as I receive my rents. And for your expenses, seeing I perceive you are considerate of my estate, I will have as great regard of yours; and so long as your mind is limited to a sober course, I will not limit your allowance less than to the uttermost of mine own estate. So as, if £20 be too little, (as I always accounted it,) you shall have £30; and when that shall not suffice, you shall have more. Only hold a sober and frugal course, (yet without baseness,) and I will shorten myself to enlarge you. For your apparel, desire your uncle to furnish you for this present; and, if I can find out a means to send you things against winter at a more easy rate, I will provide for you, as I would have done before this, but that I thought (the charges of sending and hazard considered) you were as good provide them there. Your mother is lately delivered of another son, (his name is Deane,) and is reasonable well, (I praise God,) with your grandmother, brothers, sister, uncle and aunt Gostlin, &c.; but your grandfather is very weak, and (we fear) in his last sickness. They all salute you, and rejoice in your welfare. Goodman Hawes was here, and salutes you also. Remember my love to your tutor, &c. The Lord bless you always. Amen.

Your loving father,

J. WINTHROP.

I wrote to you lately, and to your uncle and aunt; and, since, I wrote another letter to your aunt.

March 25, 1623.

To my beloved Son, JOHN WINTHROP, *at Trinity College, in Dublin, d'd, Ireland*....Rec'd April 26.

A 7.

Son John,

THE blessing of the Lord be upon thee, and upon thy studies unto a most happy success. I received divers letters from thee since Christ-tide, and I have written three. I hope thou hast received them before this. I bless God, and am heartily refreshed to hear of thy health and good liking; especially to see those seeds of the fear of God, which (I hope and daily pray) will arise to timely fruit. He, who hath begun that good in you, will perfect it unto the day of the Lord Jesus; only you must be constant and fervent in the use of the means, and yet trust only to God's blessing.

I was purposed to defer writing to you till your uncle Gostlin should have come; but his journey being put off on the sudden, I am enforced to borrow of the night to write these few lines unto thee. Concerning thy charges, I have written my mind in a former letter; but, lest that hath miscarried, know that my good persuasion of thy tender regard of my estate, and confidence of a sober course, shall make me to extend myself to the farthest of my ability for thy good, be it £30 per annum, or more, if occasion be. And though I have sent over no money all this time, it was not through my neglect of thee, but upon that assurance, which I had of thy uncle and aunt their care of thee, he himself willing me to send no money till he sent for it; and now, since Mr. Good is dead, I know not to whom to pay it. But make you no question, for (God willing) I will discharge every groat. And for your apparel and books, I find it so difficult and troublesome, &c. to send things over, as I would wish you to provide there for the present.

I have written to your uncle of the change, that it hath pleased the Lord to make in our family.[1] The Lord give us and you to make a right use of it. Time will not permit me to write more. Your grandmother and mother salute and bless you. Remember me very kindly to your good tutor and Mr. Downes, &c.

Your loving father,

J. WINTHROP.

April 20, 1623.

Send me word, in your next, how Mr. Olmsted and that plantation prospers. I wish oft God would open a way to settle me in Ireland, if it might be for his glory there.

Commend me to my little cousins, and to my god-daughter, Susannah Mitton, to Richard, and the rest of the family.

To my loving Son, John Winthrop, *at the College in Dublin, Ireland.*

A 3.

My well beloved Son,

I received thy letters of the 26 of May this 26 of June; and, the messenger being presently to return, I cannot satisfy myself in writing to thee as I desire. Let it suffice for the present, that I humbly praise our heavenly Father for his great mercy towards thee, in all respects; especially for the hope, which I conceive, that he hath pleased to make thee a vessel of glory for thy salvation in Christ Jesus. And I heartily rejoice, that he hath withdrawn thy mind from the love of those worldly vanities, wherewith the most part of youth are poisoned, and hath given thee to discern of, and exercise thyself in, things that are of true worth. I see by your epistle, that you have not spent this year past in idleness, but have profited even beyond my expectations. The Lord grant that thy soul may still prosper in the knowledge of Jesus Christ, and in the strength of the Spirit, as thy mind is strengthened in wisdom and learning; for this gives the true lustre and beauty to all gifts, both of nature and industry, and is as wisdom with an inheritance. I am sure, before this, you have knowledge of that, which, at the time when you wrote, you were ignorant of, viz. the departure of your grandfather;[2] (for I wrote over

---

1 This refers, probably, to the death of Gov. Winthrop's father.

2 Adam, born 10 August, 1548.

twice since.) He hath finished his course, and is gathered to his people in peace, as the ripe corn into the barn. He thought long for the day of his dissolution, and welcomed it most gladly. Thus is he gone before, and we must go after in our time. This advantage he hath of us, he shall not see the evil, which we may meet with ere we go hence. Happy those, who stand in good terms with God and their own conscience: They shall not fear evil tidings; and in all changes they shall be the same.

The rest of us (I praise God) are in health. Your grandmother and mother salute and bless you in the Lord. We all think long to see you; and, it is like, myself shall (if it please God) go over to you, before I shall be willing you should take so great a journey, and be so long withdrawn from your happy studies to come to us. It satisfieth me, that I know you are well, and can want nothing, and that (I believe) God blesses you. I shall continue to pray for you, and will not be wanting, to my power, to further your good in every thing; and know this, that no distance of place, or length of absence, can abate the affection of a loving father towards a dutiful, well-deserving child. And in that I have not sent you money all this time, it is upon that assurance, which I have of your uncle's and aunt's care of you, and his free offer to forbear me till he should send. But I have written to him to receive £30, or £40, of some of Dublin, who have occasion to use money in London, and they shall not fail to receive it again at my brother Fones his [house,] upon the first demand. For Cooper's Dictionary,[1] I will send it you so soon as I can; but it is so difficult and hazardable, (especially now, since Mr. Good died,) as I cannot tell how to convey that, or any thing else to thee. Remember my kind love to your good tutor. And so, in haste, I end; and, beseeching daily the Lord Jesus Christ to be with thee and bless thee, I rest

Your loving father,

JOHN WINTHROP.

GROTON, *June* 26, 1623.

To my [torn off] JOHN WINTHROP, *at Trinity College in Dublin*, *Ireland*....Rec'd Aug. the 1st.

A 9.

My dear Son,

THE Lord bless thee, and multiply his graces in thee, to the building up of that good work, which (I well hope) is truly begun in thee, and wherein I rejoice daily, and bless God, who hath pleased to call thee and keep thee in that good course, which yields hope to all the friends of thy future happiness. Be watchful, good son, and remember, that, though it be true, in some cases, that principium est

---

1 This dictionary is now in the library of the Historical Society.

dimidium totius, yet, in divinity, he who hath attained beyond the middest, must still think himself to have but new begun; for, through the continual instigation of Satan, and our own proneness to evil, we are always in danger of being turned out of our course; but God will preserve us to the end, if we trust in him, and be guided by his will.

I received no letters from you since that in Latin, wherein you wrote for Cooper's Dictionary, which I sent you since by London; and I have wrote twice since. I purpose to send by this bearer, Samuel Gostlin, a piece of Turkey grogram, about ten yards, to make you a suit; and I shall have a piece of good cloth against winter, to make you a gown; all my care is how to get it well conveyed. I would have sent you some other things, with some remembrancers to your aunt and cousins, but that the occasion of sending this messenger was so sudden as I could not provide them. If your uncle come over to Chester, you may come with him, and there I hope to see you. Be directed by him and your tutor; for, though I much desire to see you, yet I had rather hear of your welfare than hazard it. And if your uncle mean to come further than Chester, I would wish you not to come over now, for I am not willing you should come to Groton this year, except your uncle shall much desire your company. Remember my kind love to your good tutor, and to Mr. Downes, and excuse me to your aunt, that I write not to her, for I have not leisure; and, if occasion be, impart my joy in her safe deliverance, which we long much to hear of. What remains, this bearer can inform you of all our affairs. Put him in mind (as from me) to be sober, and beware of company. Your grandmother and mother salute and bless you; your uncle Gostlin and aunt salute you; your master at Bury, (to whom I wish you to write at leisure,) your good host and hostess, salute you also.—Vale.

JOHN WINTHROP.

Groton, *August* 12, 1623.

You shall receive by Samuel a twenty-two shilling piece, if he have not occasion to spend it by the way.

[The superscription of this letter is wanting.]

A 10.

My well beloved Son,

I beseech our God and heavenly Father, through Christ, to bless thee; and I humbly praise his holy name for his great mercy towards thee hitherto, which is a great occasion of my rejoicing: For there is nothing in this world, that can be like cause of private comfort to me as to see the welfare of my children; especially when I may have hope, that they belong to Christ, and increase his kingdom, and that I shall meet them in glory, to enjoy them in life eternal, when this shade of life shall be vanished. Labour (my dear son) to have in highest esteem the favour of this God, whose blessing is better than life, and reacheth to eternity. Make him thy joy, by trusting in him with all thy heart; and nourish the peace of a pure conscience in an undefiled body. I am glad also to hear, that thou declinest the evil company and manners of the place thou livest in, and followest thy study with good fruit. Go on, and God will still prosper thee. To fall back will be far worse than never to have begun; but I hope better of thee. Your grandmother, mother, brothers and sister are in health, (I praise God.) How we do all here at London, this bearer can tell you. Your uncle (Fones) wishes well to you. I would have you write him a Latin epistle at your leisure. You must be careful to visit your aunt, and help her to be cheerful in this time of your uncle's absence. Commend me heartily to your reverend tutor; and think not of seeing England till you may bring a hood at your back.

It shall satisfy me, in the mean time, to hear of your welfare, which I daily pray for. And so I commend thee to the Lord, and rest

Your loving father,

JOHN WINTHROP.

LONDON, *October 3d*, 1623.

I send two books by Richard. One of them is for your aunt; the other for yourself. Read it over and again, and God give a blessing with it.

To my beloved Son, JOHN WINTHROP, *at Trinity College in Dublin, Ireland, d'd*....Rec'd Nov. 14, 1623.

A 11.

[A fragment of a letter.]

I SENT you in January last the books, which you wrote for. Imagines Deorum is very dear and hard to get. I could not find a second in London. It is a book that may be of some use, for the praise and antiquity of the monuments, abused by the superstition of succeeding times; but you must read it with a sober mind and sanctified heart. Your grandmother and mother are in health, (I bless God,) and do salute and bless you. Your brothers and sister, and the rest of your friends, are likewise in health; only Adam hath a sore ague. Let me hear, by your next, how your aunt bears this long absence of your uncle, and how things agree in Ireland, at Mont Wealy, and elsewhere; and what success hath been of the proclamation. Our parliament here is begun with exceeding much comfort and hope. The treaty about the Spanish match is now concluded, by king, prince and parliament, to be at an end; and, it is very like, we shall not hold long with Spain. The Duke of Richmond and Lenox died suddenly that morning the parliament should have begun. The Duke of Buckingham hath quit himself worthily, and given great satisfaction to the parliament. God send a good end to these happy beginnings. This bearer comes suddenly upon me, and is but a stranger. Therefore I end; and, with loving salutations to your reverend tutor, and your kind friend, his substitute, with Mr. Downes, your little cousins, Richard, &c. I rest

Your loving father,
JOHN WINTHROP.

GROTON, *March 7*, 1623.

To my loving Son, JOHN WINTHROP, *at Trinity College, in Dublin, Ireland, d'd*....Rec'd March 29, 1624.

A 12.

Most dear and loving Husband,

I CANNOT express my love to you, as I desire, in these poor, lifeless lines; but I do heartily wish you did see my heart, how true and faithful it is to you, and how much I do desire to be always with you, to enjoy the sweet comfort of your presence, and those helps from you in spiritual and temporal duties, which I am so unfit to perform without you. It makes me to see the want of you, and wish myself with you. But I desire we may be guided by God in all our ways, who is able to direct us for the best; and so I will wait upon him with patience, who is all-sufficient for me. I shall not need to write much to you at this time. My brother Gostling can tell you any thing by word of mouth. I praise God, we are all here in health, as you left us, and are glad to hear the same of you and all the rest of our friends at London. My mother and myself remember our best love to you, and all the rest. Our children remember their duty to you. And thus, desiring to be remembered in your prayers, I bid my good husband good night. Little Samuel thinks it is time for me to go to bed; and so I beseech the Lord to keep you in safety, and us all here. Farewell, my sweet husband.

Your obedient wife,
MARGARET WINTHROP.

[Probably 1624 or 1625.]

A 13.

My good Son,

I RECEIVED your letter, and do bless God for the continuance of your health and of all our good friends at London; but I had no letters from any of them. For the matter which you write of, I can give you no advice; for I must deal plainly and faithfully with all men, and especially with my inward friends. So it is, that I have had lately some speech with my cousin Waldegrave, about matching you with his younger daughter, which I have referred to your own liking; but yet I cannot in honesty enter treaty for another till he hath some determinate answer. It is a religious and a worshipful family; but how the woman will like you, I know not, for she is somewhat crooked. I will neither persuade you to that, nor dissuade you from this or any other, which you shall desire, that may be fitting for my estate, and hopeful of comfort to you, which is not to be judged of only by wealth and person, but by meet parts and godly education. I trust you will mind well that saying, Deliberandum est diu, quod statuendum est semel.

I praise God, we continue all in health, as you left us, and, when you are weary of London, will be glad to see you and your sister at home; but take your own time before the holidays. Your grandmother and mother salute and bless you and your sister. Your mother thanks you for the things, which you sent her. Remember us very kindly to your uncles and aunts, and to all our cousins and good friends. The good Lord guide, protect and bless you in all your ways.

Your loving father,

JOHN WINTHROP.

November 21, 1626.

I pray buy me a pair of stirrup stocks, the warmest you can get; and when you go near the bridge, on Fish Street Hill dwells one, that sells lines and packthread—buy some lines to raise up the long net, and some packthread to do it. A hair line were best for the leads.

To my loving Son, JOHN WINTHROP, *d'd.*

A 14.

My good Son,

I WROTE the last week so far as my paper would reach. I hope you received my letters, which I desire to understand from you, for Jarvice his man had them. I bless God for your health and welfare; but we now think long to have you at home, for your brother is to return to Cambridge, and then we shall be alone; but if there be any good occasion to stay you still, I will not urge your hasty return. Touching the matter of Mr. Pettuall, (though I can give no direct answer where nothing is propounded, yet) thus much in general, where I may have more money, I can depart with the more land. I pray God give you wisdom and grace to discern of meet gifts and disposition, that may promise hope of a comfortable life in the fear of God; otherwise (if you can so content your own mind) you were best live as you are. But I commit this, and all other our affairs, to the only wise providence of our heavenly Father.

We have had much ado for a minister, since Mr. Simonds refused it. Groton church did not afford such variety of gifts in divers years before. We have many suitors, that would take it at a mean rate; but for such as are worthy, all the difficulty is to get maintenance enough. We are now (by God's providence) like to fasten upon a godly man, one Mr. [1]Lea, a curate at Denston in Suffolk, a man of very good parts, but of a melancholick constitution, yet as sociable and full of good discourse as I have known. All the parish are very earnest with me to take him; but I have taken a little respite, because he is but a stranger to me, but well known to divers in the town. He was Mr. Simonds's pupil. I purpose to send up £10 for my A. B. if I can hear of any fit party; if not, you should receive some money of your uncle Downing for Mr. John Brande. Lay out £10 of that, and I will restore it, for I have the money by me. Be not known to any body of any money you receive for Mr. Brande; but fail not to write me word this week of the receipt of it. You may speak to your uncle about it, lest he should forget it. Mr. Rogers hath set forth a little book of faith. Buy it. I want a pair of plain, ordinary knives, and some leaf tobacco and pipes. You may buy these things at your leisure; as likewise some packthread and lines, hemp ones, if you will. Your grandmother and mother salute and bless you. The good Lord bless you ever. Farewell.

Your loving father,

JOHN WINTHROP.

January 9, 1626.

I should have sent up some fowls this week, if they had been fat.

To my loving Son, JOHN WINTHROP, *at the House of Mr. Downing*, *at the Sign of the Bishop*, *over against the Conduit*, *in Fleet Street*, *London*, *d'd.*

A 15.

My good Son,

I RECEIVED your letter from Gravesend, and do bless God for your safe arrival there; but I heard not from you since, which I impute to the sudden departure of your captain out of the Downs

---

[1] He was afterwards settled there. The name was William Leigh. I have had a letter of 13 May, 1628, from him at Groton "to the worshipful, his most loving patron, John Winthrop, Esq. at London," announcing the birth of a son, and his baptism, by the name of John, on Sunday preceding, at which Mrs. Winthrop, our governour's wife, stood godmother. Calamy calls him fellow of Christ College, Cambridge, and says, he was "a serious, single-hearted man, of good abilities, very laborious in the work of the ministry; one of the classis of Manchester. He was grievously afflicted with the stone, which at last cut him off in 1664, about fifty years of age. He wrote an English elegy on the death of Dr. Samuel Bolton, and one in Latin on the death of Mr. Bright of Emanuel." There is an errour, manifestly, either in his age, or time of his death.

upon the duke's coming thither. But I hope to hear from you soon, for I long to understand how you fare, and what entertainment you find with your captain, that accordingly I may be stirred up to prayer for you, and to bless God for his mercies towards you. I know not what further advice to give you, than you have already received, and your own observation, upon occasion, shall direct you. Only be careful to seek the Lord in the first place, and with all earnestness, as he who is only able to keep you in all perils, and to give you favour in the sight of those, who may be instruments of your welfare; and account it a great point of wisdom, to keep diligent watch over yourself, that you may neither be infected by the evil conversation of any, that you may be forced to converse with, neither that your own speech or behaviour be any just occasion to hurt or ensnare you. Be not rash, upon ostentation of valour, to adventure yourself to unnecessary dangers; but, if you be lawfully called, let it appear, that you hold your life for him, who gave it you, and will preserve it unto the farthest period of his own holy decree. For you may be resolved, that, while you keep in your way, all the cannons or enemies in the world shall not be able to shorten your days one minute. For my part, as a father, who desires your welfare as mine own, I cease not daily to commend you to God, beseeching him to preserve, prosper and bless you, that I may receive you again in peace, and have assurance of enjoying you in a better life, when your course here shall be finished. Your friends here (I praise God) are all in health, and are daily mindful of you. Let me hear from you so soon and oft as you may conveniently. Remember my love and service to your good captain. The Lord bless you ever. So I rest

Your loving father,

JOHN WINTHROP.

LONDON, *June* 6, 1627.

To my loving Son, JOHN WINTHROP, *attending upon Capt. Best, in his Majesty's Ship the Due Repulse, at Portsmouth, d'd.*

[The Duke of Buckingham sailed from Portsmouth 27 June.]

A 16.

Mine own dear Heart,

I PRAISE God, we are all in health at Chelmsford this morning. My son F. came to us last night about ten of the clock. Our two boys are lusty travellers, and God's providence hath fitted them with so good means for their carriage, as we could not desire better. I thank thee for thy kind tokens. I have nothing to return thee but love and prayers for thee and thine. The blessing of the Lord be upon thee and them. My son Hen. must go by Maplested. Pray him to call to my brother [1]Tindale for £100, and bring it with him. It is in gold. Send John Hardinge when thou wilt. Commend us to all our friends, broth. G. and sister, Mr. Leigh, goodwife Cole, all at Castleins, and all that love us. We all here salute you all. You must divide it at leisure, with my love and blessing to all our children and the rest in our family. Farewell, my sweet wife, and be of good comfort. The Lord is with us. He hath sent his servants to bless us, and we shall be blessed. Kiss me, my sweet wife. Farewell.

Thy faithful husband,

JO. WINTHROP.

This Saturday morning.

Nov. 1627. *To* Mrs. Marg. Winthrop, *at Groton, with haste.*

A 17.

Loving Son,

I received your letter, and I bless God for your welfare, begging of him daily, that your soul may prosper as your body doth; and if this care be in your heart, (as I hope it is,) you shall do well, for this rule God hath set us to walk by,—first to seek the kingdom of heaven, then will he see to us for other things. So as I dare avouch it for infallible truth, that he who doth otherwise takes a preposterous course to happiness, and shall not prosper. Should not a man trust his Maker, and rest upon the counsel of his Father, before all other things? Should not the promise of the holy Lord, the God of truth, be believed above all carnal, false fears and shallow ways of human wisdom? It is just with God to harden men's hearts in their distrust of his faithfulness, because they dare not rely upon him. But such as will roll their ways upon the Lord, do find him always as good as his word. I bless his name, we all continue in health, and this day I expect your brother from Cambridge. I wish you could meet with some safe means to send to your brother Henry. I have found two sturdy youths, that would go to him. If Capt. Powell return not soon, I shall fear he hath miscarried, and then shall we see God's providence, that your brother returned not with him.

---

1 Sir John Tindal, a master in chancery, was, probably, the father of this gentleman and of Gov. Winthrop's third wife. He was assassinated 12 November, 1616, for making a report against a suitor, in a cause of comparatively trifling amount. The murderer was examined 16 November, and the next day hanged himself in prison. See the Works of Bacon, Lord Chancellor, V. 452—455, and VI. 133.

I cannot come up till the week after Easter; but you may know Mr. Featherstone's resolution in the mean time. I pray, inquire how things go in the parliament, and write to me of them; but things which are doubtful, let pass. If the commission for the navy be dissolved, what employment hath your captain then? for it seems he was lately put into it. When you see him or her, commend me kindly to them.

We want a little tobacco. I had very good, for seven shillings a pound, at a grocer's, by Holburn Bridge. There be two shops together. It was at that which is farthest from the bridge, towards the Conduit. If you tell him, it is for him that bought half a pound of Verina and a pound of Virginia of him last term, he will use you well. Send me half a pound of Virginia. I would gladly hear of a chamber in the Temple, or in some other convenient place; for that I have is much too dear.

I have many letters to write: therefore I end; and, with my love and blessing to you, I commend you to the protection and good government of the Lord, and rest

Your loving father,

JO. WINTHROP.

March 18, 1627.

I think to send my brother Downing a greyhound.

To my loving Son, JOHN WINTHROP, *at the House of Mr. Downing, near the Conduit, in Fleet Street, London, d'd.*

A 18.

My good Sister,

I HAVE been too long silent to you, considering mine own consciousness of that great debt, which I owe you for your love and much kindness to me and mine. But, I assure you, it is not through want of good will to you; but having many letters to write weekly, I take my ease, to include you in my brother's.

I partake with you in that affliction, which it pleaseth the Lord still to exercise you and my good brother in. I know God hath so fitted and disposed your mind to bear troubles, as your friends may take the less care for you in them. He shews you more love, in enabling you to bear them comfortably, than you could apprehend in the freedom from them. Go on cheerfully, (my good sister,) let experience add more confidence still to your patience. Peace shall come. There will be a bed to rest in, large and easy enough for you both. It is preparing in the lodging appointed for you in your Father's house. He that vouchsafeth to wipe the sweat from his disciples' feet, will not disdain to wipe the tears from those tender, affectionate eyes. Because you have been one of his mourners in the house of

FAC SIMILE OF PART OF A LETTER FROM GOV. WINTHROP TO HIS WIFE.— See Vol. I. P. 368. 9. Appendix A. 41.

And now (my sweet soule) I must once againe
take my last farewell of thee in old England;
it goeth verye neere to my heart to leave thee but
I know to whom I haue committed thee, euen to him, who
loves thee much better than any husband can, who hath
taken account of the haires of thy head, & putts all thy
teares in his bottle, who can, & (if it be for his glorye)
will bringe us togither againe wth peace & comfort.
oh how it refresheth my heart to thinke that I shall
yet againe see thy sweet face in the lande of the
livinge: that lovely countenance, that I have so much
delighted in, & beheld wth so great content! I have
hitherto been so taken up wth businesse, as I could
seldome looke backe to my former happinesse, but
now when I shalbe at some leysure, I shall not
avoid the remembrance of thee nor the greife for
thy absence: thou hast thy share wth me, but I
hope, the course we haue agreed upon wilbe
some ease to us both, mundayes & frydayes at 5:
of the clocke at night, we shall meet in spiritt
till we meet in pson. yet if all these hopes should
faile, blessed be or God, that we are assured, we shall
meet one day, if not as husband & wife, yet in a
better condition, let that staye & comfort thy heart,
neither can the sea drowne thy husband, nor enemyes
destroye, nor any adversity deprive thee of thy husband or
children. therefore I will onely take thee now & my sweet
children in mine armes, & kisse & embrace you all &
so leave you wth my God. farewell farewell. I blesse
you all in the name of the Lord Jesus; I salute
my daughter Winth: Matt: Nan & the rest & all my
good neighbors & friends pray all for us. farewell.

Commend my blessinge to my sonne John, I cannot now write to him, but tell him
I haue committed thee & thine to him, labour to drawe him yet nearer to God, &
he wilbe the surer staffe of comfort to thee. I cannot name the rest of my good
friends, but thou canst supply it. I wrote a weeke since to thee & mr Leigh &
diverse others.

Thine wheresoeuer Jo: Winthrop

from aboard the Arbella rydinge at the Cowes march 28 1630.

tribulation, you shall drink of the cup of joy, and be clothed with the garment of gladness, in the kingdom of his glory. The former things, and evil, will soon be passed; but the good to come shall neither end nor change. Never man saw heaven, but would have passed through hell to come at it. Let this suffice as a test of my true love to you, and of the account I make of the happiness of your condition. I commend you to his good grace, who is all-sufficient; and so, with my mother's, my wife's and mine own salutation to yourself, and my good brother, and all my cousins, I rest

Your loving brother,
JO. WINTHROP.

March 25, 1628.

I pray remember my love to your brother, Mr. Burgesse.

I pray tell my brother, that his tenant Gage desires him to forbear him £10 till Whitsuntide.

To my very loving Sister, Mrs. Fones, *at her House in the Old Bailey, London, d'd.*

A 19.

Son John,

I received your letter and the books you sent, for which I do thank you. I bless God for the continuance of your health and welfare, which, through his mercy, we all here also enjoy; only myself have a sore hand, which makes me that I cannot write. For the note, which you mentioned in your letter, I received it not. I desire to hear from you concerning Mr. Featherstone's resolution, and whether you have inquired out a chamber for me, or else to take order, that I may have that I had before. I pray send me down six of Mr. Egerton's cattle. For the stuff for the gowns, you may buy it of some olive colour, or such like. Either let there be several colours, or else the velvet for the capes of several colours. Remember us all to your uncles and aunts and the rest of our friends. Pray your uncle Downing to send me an answer of my last week's letter, and thank your aunt Downing for her kind love and prayers, and excuse my not writing to them all, for my hand is so as I am not able. Your grandmother and mother salute and bless you. So, with my love and blessing to you, I commend you to the protection, direction and good providence of our heavenly Father, and rest

Your loving father,
JOHN WINTHROP.

March 31, 1628.

To my very loving Son, John Winthrop, *d'd, London.*

A 20.

Son John,

I RECEIVED your letter, with the things you sent. I do praise God for the continuance of your health and welfare. For myself, my hand is so ill as I know not when I shall be able to travel. It hath pleased God to make it a sharp affliction to me. I hope he will dispose it for my good, and, in his due time, send me deliverance. For your journey intended, seeing you have a resolution to go to sea, I know not where you should go with such religious company, and under such hope of blessing; only I am loath you should think of settling there, as yet, but to be going and coming are best, and afterward to do as God shall offer occasion. You may adventure somewhat in the plantation at the present, and hereafter more, as God shall give enlargement. If Mr. Featherstone will not deal, I will look no further; but your uncle Fones shall have it, and the odd £50 may be for your occasions. Commend me heartily to all your uncles and aunts. Desire them to be mindful of me in their prayers. Thank your aunt Downing for her kind letter. Tell her I see she now means to work upon the advantage in setting me upon the score for letters when I want my hand to free myself. Put your uncle Downing in mind again of my chamber, and tell him, that this day my brother Gostling and another shall go about the business he did write of. Tell him also, that Peter Alston is dead. Commend me to Edward, and desire him to get me out a privy seal against John Carver Clarcke and Eliza his wife, at the suit of Mr. Attorney, on the behalf of Thomas Foule. In the business concerning your voyage, I pray be advised by your uncle and other your worthy friends, who are experienced in these affairs; but, above all, seek direction and blessing from God. And so, being forced to use another's pen, so as I am not at that freedom to write as I would, I end; and, with your grandmother's and mother's salutation and blessing unto you, I commend you to the gracious providence, direction and rich blessing of the Almighty. Farewell.

Your loving father,

JOHN WINTHROP.

April 7, 1628.

As soon as I am able to stir about the house, I will look out those geometrical instruments and books, and send them unto you, and any thing else that you will write for.

To his loving Son, Mr. JOHN WINTHROP, *at Mr. Fones's House in the Old Bailey, London, d'd.*

A 21.

My most sweet Husband,

How dearly welcome thy kind letter was to me, I am not able to express. The sweetness of it did much refresh me. What can be more pleasing to a wife, than to hear of the welfare of her best beloved, and how he is pleased with her poor endeavours! I blush to hear myself commended, knowing my own wants. But it is your love that conceives the best, and makes all things seem better than they are. I wish that I may be always pleasing to thee, and that those comforts we have in each other may be daily increased, as far as they be pleasing to God. I will use that speech to thee, that Abigail did to David, I will be a servant to wash the feet of my lord. I will do any service wherein I may please my good husband. I confess I cannot do enough for thee; but thou art pleased to accept the will for the deed, and rest contented.

I have many reasons to make me love thee, whereof I will name two: First, because thou lovest God; and, secondly, because that thou lovest me. If these two were wanting, all the rest would be eclipsed. But I must leave this discourse, and go about my household affairs. I am a bad housewife to be so long from them; but I must needs borrow a little time to talk with thee, my sweet heart. The term is more than half done. I hope thy business draws to an end. It will be but two or three weeks before I see thee, though they be long ones. God will bring us together in his good time; for which time I shall pray. I thank the Lord, we are all in health. We are very glad to hear so good news of our son Henry. The Lord make us thankful for all his mercies to us and ours. And thus, with my mother's and my own best love to yourself and all the rest, I shall leave scribbling. The weather being cold, makes me make haste. Farewell, my good husband; the Lord keep thee.

Your obedient wife,

MARGARET WINTHROP.

Groton, *November* 22.[1]

I have not yet received the box; but I will send for it. I send up a turkey and some cheese. I pray send my son Forth such a knife as mine is. Mrs. Hugen would pray you to buy a cake for the boys.

I did dine at Groton Hall yesterday; they are in health, and remember their love. We did wish you there, but that would not bring you, and I could not be merry without thee. Mr. Lee and his wife were there; they remember their love. Our neighbour Cole and goodman Newton have been sick, but somewhat amended again. I fear thy cheese will not prove so good as thou didst expect. I have sent it all, for we could not cut it.

---

1 It might seem as early as 1621 or 2, before the death of Adam, lord of the manor of Groton; but the mention of Lee or Leigh, would certainly make it as late as 1627, and the news from Henry must make it 1628.

A 22.

Right Honourable,

After the exhibition of my service to your lordship and my lady, I crave pardon, if these rude lines presume to kiss your honour's hands. My duty and respect to your honour urgeth me to givē some testimony thereof; and your noble favours have obliged me to present this as a small earnest of my thankfulness, and the service which I owe, and desire to perform, whensoever your lordship shall please to command. Here is no news worth your honour's intelligence. We are this day setting sail from the Castles. So, wishing your honour a happy beginning, and prosperous continuance of this new year, and many more to succeed, I humbly take my leave, resting, &c.

Castles of Hellespont, *December* 26, 1628.

[The above is a rough draught of a letter "To Sir Peter Wich, Lord Ambassadour at Constantinople," found among papers of John Winthrop, jun. The same paper contains, in cypher, probably the same words. It is mentioned, that he was sailing "for Venice," which words are erased, that fact being known to his correspondent. The writer had, no doubt, accompanied this very celebrated minister, either as secretary of legation, or private secretary; most likely the latter.]

A 23.

Son Henry,

It is my daily care to commend you to the Lord, that he would please to put his true fear into your heart, and the faith of the Lord Jesus Christ, that you may be saved, and that your ways may be pleasing in his sight. I wish also your outward prosperity, so far as may be for your good. I have been sick, these seven or eight weeks, near unto death; but the Lord hath had mercy on me to restore me; yet I am not able to go abroad.

I sent you by Capt. Powell a letter, and in it a note of such things as I likewise sent you by him, in a chest with two locks, whereof the keys were delivered to his brother, who went master of the ship. The things cost me about £35; but, as yet, I have received nothing towards it. I sent divers times to Capt. Powell about your tobacco, but my man could never see it, but had answer, I should have it, or money for it. But there was ten pounds of it, by your appointment, to be delivered to one, and the worth of four paid to another, which made me that I knew not what course to take; besides, I found, by the rolls you sent to me and to your uncles, that it was very ill-conditioned, foul, and full of stalks, and evil coloured; and your uncle Fones, taking the judgment of divers grocers, none of them would give five shillings a pound for it. I desired Capt. Powell, (coming one day to see me,) that he would help me with money for it, which he promised to do; but, as yet, I hear not from him. I would have sent you some other things by Mr. Randall; but, in truth, I have no money, and I am so far in debt already, to both your uncles, as I am ashamed to borrow any more. I have disbursed a great deal of money for you, more than my estate will bear. I paid for your debts since you went, above £30, besides £4.10s. to Annett and Dixon, and now £35. Except you send commodity to raise money, I can supply you no further. I have many other children that are unprovided, and I see my life is uncertain. I marvel at your great undertakings, having no means, and knowing how much I am in debt already. Solomon saith, He who hasteth to be rich, shall surely come to poverty. It had been more wisdom and better becoming your youth, to have contained yourself in a moderate course, for your three years; and by that time, by your own gettings and my help, you might have been able to have done somewhat. But this hath been always the fruit of your vain, overreaching mind, which will be your overthrow, if you attain not more discretion and moderation with your years. I do wonder upon what ground you should be led into so gross an errour as to think, that I could provide ten such men as you write for, and disburse a matter of £200, (when I owe more already than I am able to pay, without sale of my land,) and to do this at some two or three months warning. Well, I will write no more of these things. I pray God, make you more wise and sober, and bring you home in peace in his due time. If I receive money for your tobacco before Mr. Randall go, I will send you something else; otherwise you must be content to stay till I can. Your brother (as I wrote to you) hath been in the Levant above this half year, and I look not for him before a year more. Your friends here are all in health. Your uncles and aunts commend them to you; but they will take none of your tobacco; only your uncle Tindale and aunt (whom you write your kinswoman upon the outside of your tobacco) thank you for theirs. I sent you, also, two boys, (for men I could get none,) such as Capt. Powell carried over; but I knew not what to do for their binding, being not able then either to walk or write, and they being but youths. For news, here is little but what, I suppose, this bearer can tell you. We shall have peace with France. The Dutch have taken from the Spaniard, in the West Indies, a very great prize of silver, gold, &c. and have brought it safe home. The king of Bohemia, and his oldest son, going aboard to see it, in their return were cast away. The king was saved, but the prince and many others were lost.

Sir Nathaniel Barnardiston, and Sir William Springe, are knights of the parliament for Suffolk. All the gentlemen have been long since set at liberty. Sir Francis Barington is at rest in the Lord. Sir Henry Mildmay, of Graces, is sheriff of Essex, and Mr. Gurdon for Suffolk.

I have staid sending my letter above a week since I wrote it, expecting some money from Capt. Powell, according to his promise, that I might have sent you some other things; but I hear of none.

Therefore I will end, and defer till some other occasion. So, again, I commend you to the blessing, protection and direction of the Lord, and rest

Your loving father,

JO. WINTHROP.

LONDON, *this* 30 *of January*, 1628.

A 24.

My good Wife,

ALTHOUGH I wrote to thee last week by the carrier of Hadleigh, yet, having so fit opportunity, I must needs write to thee again; for I do esteem one little, sweet, short letter of thine (such as the last was) to be well worthy two or three from me. How it is with us, these bearers can inform thee, so as I may write the less. They were [1]married on Saturday last, and intend to stay with thee till towards the end of the term; for it will be yet six weeks before they can take their voyage. Labour to keep my son at home as much as thou canst, especially from Hadleigh. I began this letter to thee yesterday at two of the clock, thinking to have been large, but was so taken up by company and business, as I could get but hither by this morning. It grieves me that I have not liberty to make better expression of my love to thee, who art more dear to me than all earthly things; but I will endeavour that my prayers may supply the defect of my pen, which will be of best use to us both, inasmuch as the favour and blessing of our God is better than all things besides. My trust is in his mercy, that, upon the faith of his gracious promise, and the experience of his fatherly goodness, he will be our God to the end, to carry us along through this course of our pilgrimage, in the peace of a good conscience, and that, in the end of our race, we shall safely arrive at the haven of eternal happiness. We see how frail and vain all earthly good things are. There is no means to avoid the loss of them in death, nor the bitterness which accompanyeth them in the cares and troubles of this life. Only the fruition of Jesus Christ and the hope of heaven can give us true comfort and rest. The Lord teach us wisdom to prepare for our change, and to lay up our treasure there, where our abiding must be forever. I know thou lookest for troubles here, and, when one affliction is over, to meet with another; but remember what our Saviour tells us: BE OF GOOD COMFORT, I HAVE OVERCOME THE WORLD. See his goodness: He hath conquered our enemies beforehand, and, by faith in him, we shall assuredly prevail over them all. Therefore, (my sweet wife,) raise up thy heart, and be not dismayed at the crosses thou meetest with in family affairs or otherwise; but still fly to him, who will take up thy burden for thee. Go thou on cheerfully, in obedience to his holy will, in the course he hath set thee. Peace shall

---

1 Was this Henry?

come. Thou shalt rest as in thy bed; and, in the mean time, he will not fail nor forsake thee. But my time is past; I must leave thee. So I commend thee and all thine to the gracious protection and blessing of the Lord. All our friends here salute thee; salute thou ours from me. Farewell, my good wife. I kiss and love thee with the kindest affection, and rest

Thy faithful husband,

JO. WINTHROP.

April 28, 1629.

Let John Bluet be satisfied for his horse.

A 25.

The largeness and truth of my love to thee makes me always mindful of thy welfare, and set me on work to begin to write before I hear from thee. The very thought of thee affords me many a kind refreshing: What will then the enjoying of thy sweet society, which I prize above all worldly comforts?

Yet, such is the folly and misery of man, as he is easily brought to contemn the true good he enjoys, and to neglect the best things, which he holds only in hope, and both upon an ungrounded desire of some seeming good, which he promiseth to himself. And if it be thus with us, that are Christians, who have a sure word to direct us, and the holy faith to live by, what is the madness and bondage of those, who are out of Christ? Oh! the riches of Christ! Oh! the sweetness of the word of grace! It ravisheth my soul in the thought hereof, so as, when I apprehend but a glimpse of the dignity and felicity of a Christian, I can hardly persuade my heart to hope for so great happiness. Let men talk what they will of riches, honours, pleasures, &c.; let us have Christ crucified, and let them take all besides. For, indeed, he who hath Christ, hath all things with him; for he enjoyeth an all-sufficiency, which makes him abundantly rich in poverty, honourable in the lowest abasements, full of joy and consolation in the sharpest afflictions, living in death, and possessing eternity in this vale of misery. Therefore bless we God for his free and infinite mercy, in bestowing Christ upon us. Let us entertain and love him with our whole hearts; let us trust in him, and cleave to him with denial of ourselves, and all things besides, and account our portion the best in the world; that so, being strengthened and comforted in his love, we may put forth ourselves to improve our life and means to do him service. There are very few hours left of this day of our labour: then comes the night, when we shall take our rest. In the morning we shall awake unto glory and immortality, when we shall have no more work to do; no more pain or grief to endure; no more care, fear, want, reproach or infirmity; no more sin, corruption or temptation.

I am forced to patch up my letters, here a piece and there another. I have now received thine, the kindly fruits of thy most sweet affections. Blessed be the Lord for the welfare of thyself and all our family.

I received letters from my two sons with thee. Remember my love and blessing to them, and to my daughter Winthrop, for whose safety I give the Lord thanks. I have so many letters to write, as I cannot write to them now. Our friends here are in reasonable health, and desire to be kindly remembered to you all. Commend me to all my good friends, my loving neighbours, goodman Cole and his wife, to whom we are always much beholden. I will remember M——— her gown and petticoat, and the children's girdles. So, with my most affectionate desires of thy welfare, and my blessing to all our children, I kiss my sweet wife, and commend thee and all ours to the gracious protection of our heavenly Father, and rest

Thy faithful husband,
still present with thee in his most unkind absence,
JO. WINTHROP.

May 8, 1629.

I am sorry for my neighbour Bluet's horse; but he shall lose nothing by him. Tell my son Henry I will pay the money he writes of.

A 26.

Most loving and good Husband,

I HAVE received your letters. The true tokens of your love and care of my good, now in your absence, as well as when you are present, make me think that saying false, Out of sight out of mind. I am sure my heart and thoughts are always near you, to do you good and not evil all the days of my life.

I hope, through God's blessing, your pains will not be altogether lost, which you bestow upon me in writing. Those serious thoughts of your own, which you sent me, did make a very good supply instead of a sermon. I shall often read them, and desire to be of God's family, to whom so many blessings belong, and pray that I may not be one separated from God, whose conscience is always accusing them. I shall not need to write to you of any thing this week. My son and brother Gostling can tell you how we are. And I shall think long for your coming home. And thus, with my best love to you, I beseech the Lord to send us a comfortable meeting in his good time. I commit you to the Lord.

Your loving and obedient wife,
MARGARET WINTHROP

For my very loving Husband, JOHN WINTHROP, Esq. *these deliver.*

[Probably in May, 1629.]

A 27.

My sweet Husband,

I REJOICE in the expectation of our happy meeting; for thy absence hath been very long in my conceit, and thy presence much desired. Thy welcome is always ready; make haste to entertain it. I was yesterday at a meeting at goodman Cole's, upon the going of the young folk to Dedham, where many thanks were given to God for the reformation of the young man, and amendment of his life. We had also a part in their prayers. My dear husband, I will now leave writing to thee, hoping to see thee shortly. The good Lord send us a comfortable meeting. And thus, with my due respect to thyself, brother and sister D. sister Fanny, son John and the rest. My daughter remembers her duty to you all; thinks long for her husband. I received the things you sent, and thank you heartily for them. I will take order with my man to buy some trimming for my gown. And so I bid my good husband farewell, and commit him to the Lord.

Your loving and obedient wife,

MARGARET WINTHROP.

I pray buy a Psalter for Deane. I can get none here.

To my very loving Husband these deliver.

[Probably, 1629.]

A 28.

Sir,

My humble duty remembered to you and my mother, may you please to understand, that I received your letters, that by William Ridley on Wednesday, and your other yesterday, rejoicing much to hear of your welfare, with the rest of our good friends, which I desire much with my own eyes to behold. Therefore I purpose, God willing, to make all haste down the next week, hoping to accept of Mr. Gurdon's kind offer, if I can. For the business of New England, I can say no other thing, but that I believe confidently, that the whole disposition thereof is of the Lord, who disposeth all alterations, by his blessed will, to his own glory and the good of his; and, therefore, do assure myself, that all things shall work together for the best therein. And for myself, I have seen so much of the vanity of the world, that I esteem no more of the diversities of countries, than as so many inns, whereof the traveller that hath lodged in the best, or in the worst, findeth no difference, when he cometh to his journey's end; and I shall call that my country, where I may most glorify God, and enjoy the presence of my dearest friends. Therefore herein I submit myself to God's will and yours, and, with your leave, do dedicate myself (laying by all desire of other employments whatsoever) to the service of God and the company herein, with the whole endeavours, both of body and mind. The CONCLUSIONS, which you sent down, I showed my uncle and aunt, who like them well. I think they are unanswerable; and it cannot but be a prosperous action, which is so well allowed by the judgments of God's prophets, undertaken by so religious and wise worthies of Israel, and indented to God's glory in so special a service. My aunt Goulding remembereth her love to you. She saith, it is not yet discharged, that she knoweth. Here is certain news, that the Dutch have taken Wesel. So, desiring your prayers and blessing, I commend you to the Almighty's protection, and rest

Your obedient son,

JOHN WINTHROP.

LONDON, *August* 21, 1629.

I pray remember my love to my brothers and sisters and all our friends, whom I hope shortly to see.

[The father's letters, referred to by the son, are not preserved. From our own Colony Records we know, that, on 28 July preceding, at the meeting, or general court, of the company, in London, Gov. Cradock proposed, that, for the advancement of the plantation, the inducing persons of worth and quality to transplant themselves and families thither, and other weighty reasons, to transfer the government to those, who shall inhabit there, and not continue the same subordinate to the company here. Prince, I. 189, 190; and see page 2, note 2. At the meeting, August 28, a special committee was raised to debate this subject, pro and con, and, the next day, the resolution was adopted, the benefit of which has been felt every day from that to the present. The CONCLUSIONS spoken of by the son were, no doubt, a paper of considerations for the plantation, with an answer to several objections, printed in Hutchinson's Coll. 27—31, probably drawn by our author. I have had in my possession the larger part of the original. An agreement to transport themselves and families to New England, was this month made at Cambridge, by Sir Richard Saltonstall, Thomas Dudley, William Vassall, Nich. West, Isaac Johnson, John Humfrey, Thomas Sharp, Increase Nowell, John Winthrop, William Pynchon, Kellam Browne, William Colburn, which may be seen in Hutchinson's Coll. 25.]

A 29.

My dear Wife,

I PRAISE the Lord that I hear of thy welfare, and of the rest of our family. I thank thee for thy most kind letter, and especially that sweet affection, from whence it flows. I am sorry I cannot come down to thee, as I hoped; but there is no remedy. The Lord so disposeth as I must stay yet (I doubt) a fortnight, but, assure thyself, not one day more than I must needs.

I pray thee have patience. God, in his due time, will bring us together in peace. We are now agreed with the merchants, and stay only to settle our affairs. I have not one quarter of an hour's time to write to thee. Therefore thou must bear with me, and supply all defects of remembrances. The Lord bless thee, my sweet wife, and all ours. Farewell.

Thy faithful husband,
JO. WINTHROP.

Send not up my horses till I send for them.

October.
[Early in the month, and, no doubt, 1629.]

A 30.

Son,

I RECEIVED your letter, and do heartily bless the Lord for the continuance of your welfare, beseeching him to sanctify you more and more, for his glory and your own salvation.

For the business you write of, concerning your brother, I have conferred with him, and shall be as glad as any of his stay here, if he can take any good order for his estate there. What he will do, I know not yet; but I think he will be with you soon. I would gladly have you here betimes next week; but, being it will be Monday sennight before we shall get forth of town, it will be chargeable to keep all the horses here so long. Therefore, if you can find any company to come up with, you may be here on Tuesday or Wednesday; otherwise, you may stay a day or two the longer, and let John come with you; for I would not have you ride alone. I have sent down all the late news from New England. I would have some of you read it to your mother, and let Forth copy out the observations and all that follows from the ☞, and the letter in the end, and show it Mr. Mott and others, that intend this voyage. Your uncle and aunts are all in health, and salute you and the rest of ours, &c. Commend me to your uncle G. and a. and all the rest of our loving friends, that ask of me. So, with my love and blessing to yourself, your brothers and sister, salutations to our young company, I end, and rest

Your loving father,
JO. WINTHROP.

October 9, 1629.

[*To*] *his loving Son*, JOHN WINTHROP, *at Groton*, *Suffolk*, *d'd.*

A 31.

My dear Wife,

I MUST needs write to thee by this bearer, though I can write little, in regard of my much business. I praise God, I came safe hither, where I found all in health, and so (through his mercy) we continue. I have sent down my horses, because I am like to stay somewhat longer than I made account of; but I shall make what haste I can back. Here is much news: Divers great personages questioned and committed; but the cause yet uncertain. St. Christopher's is taken by the Spaniard, and the English there honestly sent home. The same is reported of the Barbethes, but not so certain; but, if it be, the people are all safe. Some would discourage us with this news; but there is no cause, for neither are we in the like danger; and, besides, God is with us, and will surely keep us. I shall take time to write to thee again in the end of the week. So, for this time, with all our hearty salutations to thyself, my good sister Fones, and the rest of our friends, with my love and blessing to all our children, I commend thee to the Lord. So I kiss my sweet wife, and rest

Thy faithful husband,

JO. WINTHROP.

November 11, 1629.

My son remembers his duty to thee and his aunt, and love to all, &c.

To his very loving Wife, Mrs. WINTHROP *the elder*, *at Groton*, *Suffolk*, *d'd.*

A 32.

My dear Wife,

I HAVE many things to thank thee for this week,—thy most kind letter, fowls, puddings, &c.; but I must first thank our heavenly Father, that I hear of thy health and the welfare of all our family; for I was in fear, because I left thee not well. But thus is the Lord pleased still to declare his goodness and mercy to his unworthy servants. Oh that we could learn to trust in him, and to love him as we ought!

For my care of thee and thine, I will say nothing. The Lord knows my heart, that it was one great motive to draw me into this course. The Lord prosper me in it, as I desire the prosperity of thee and thine. For this end, I purpose to leave £1500 with thy friends, if I can sell my lands, which I am now about, but, as yet, have done nothing. I purpose (if God will) to be at home the next week. I am forced to keep John here for my business, which now comes so heavy upon me, as I can spare no time for aught else. The Lord in mercy bring us well through all our troubles, as I trust he will. Thou must bear with my brevity. The Lord bless and keep thee, and all our children and company. So I kiss my sweet wife, and rest

Thy faithful husband,

JO. WINTHROP.

My brother and sister salute you all. Let the cow be killed against I come home; and let my son Henry provide such peas as will porridge well, or else none.

January 15, 1629.

A 33.

My dear Wife,

I PRAISE God, we came safe to London, and continue in health, and found all well here. Thus it pleaseth the Lord to follow us with his blessings, that we might love him again. I find here so much to do, as I doubt I shall not come down these three weeks; but, thou mayest be sure, I will stay no longer than my occasions shall enforce me.

I must now begin to prepare thee for our long parting, which grows very near. I know not how to deal with thee by arguments; for if thou wert as wise and patient as ever woman was, yet it must needs be a great trial to thee, and the greater, because I am so dear to thee. That which I must chiefly look at in thee, for a ground of contentment, is thy godliness. If now the Lord be thy God, thou must show it by trusting in him, and resigning thyself quietly to his good pleasure. If now Christ be thy Husband, thou must show what sure and sweet intercourse is between him and thy soul, when it shall be no hard thing for thee to part with an earthly, mortal, infirm husband for his sake. The enlargement of thy comfort in the communion of the love and sweet familiarity of thy most holy, heavenly and undefiled Lord and Husband, will abundantly recompense whatsoever want or inconvenience may come by the absence of the other. The best course is to turn all our reasons and discourse into prayers; for he only can help, who is Lord of sea and land, and hath sole power of life and death.

It is now near eleven of the clock, and I shall write again ere long (if God will.) The good Lord bless thee and all thy company. My broth. and sister salute you all. Commend my hearty love to my good sister F. and all the rest. Tell her I wrote to Mr. Dummer so soon as I came to town; and, if I can, I will speak with him, before John go down. So I kiss my sweet wife, and rest

Thy frail, yet faithful husband,

JO. WINTHROP.

January 31, 1629.

A 34.

My most dear Husband,

I SHOULD not now omit any opportunity of writing to thee, considering I shall not long have thee to write unto. But, by reason of my unfitness at this time, I must entreat thee to accept of a few lines from me, and not to impute it to any want of love, or neglect of my duty to thee, to whom I owe more than I shall ever be able to express. My request now shall be to the Lord to prosper thee in thy voyage, and enable thee and fit thee for it, and give all graces and gifts for such employments as he shall call thee to. I trust God will once more bring us together before you go, that we may see each other with gladness, and take solemn leave, till we, through the goodness of our God, shall meet in New England, which will be a joyful day to us. I send thee here enclosed letters from Mr. P. My good sister F. remembers her love to you, and, it seemeth, hath written so earnestly to Mr P. not to come, that he doth forbear to come till he hear more. I think she would have you send him word to come as soon as he can, being desirous to speak with him before you go; but it must not come from herself, for she will write to him to stay still. She saith, that he shall not need to provide any thing but a house, for she will furnish it herself. And thus, with my best wishes to God for thy health and welfare, I take my leave, and rest

Thy faithful, obedient wife,

MARGARET WINTHROP.

January the last.

[The superscription of this letter, written, without doubt, 1629—30, is wanting.]

A 35.

My sweet Wife,

THE opportunity of so fit a messenger, and my deep engagement of affection to thee, makes me write at this time, though I hope to follow soon after. The Lord our God hath oft brought us together with comfort, when we have been long absent; and, if it be good for us, he will do so still. When I was in Ireland, he brought us together again. When I was sick here at London, he restored us together again. How many dangers, near death, hast thou been in thyself! and yet the Lord hath granted me to enjoy thee still. If he did not watch over us, we need not go over sea to seek death or misery: we should meet it at every step, in every journey. And is not he a God abroad as well as at home? Is not his power and providence the same in New England that it hath been in Old England?
Job 5. If our ways please him, he can command deliverance and safety in all places, and can make the stones of the field and the beasts, yea, the raging seas, and our very enemies, to be in league with us.

But, if we sin against him, he can raise up evil against us out of our own bowels, houses, estates, &c. My good wife, trust in the Lord, whom thou hast found faithful. He will be better to thee than any husband, and will restore thee thy husband with advantage. But I must end, with all our salutations, with which I have laden this bearer, that he may be the more kindly welcome. So I kiss my sweet wife, and bless thee and all ours, and rest

Thine ever,

February 14, 1629. JO. WINTHROP.

Thou must be my valentine, for none hath challenged me.

To MARG. WINTHROP, *the elder, at Groton.*

A 36.

Mine own sweet Self,

I BLESS God, our heavenly Father, we are all come safe to Maplested, where we find all in health. I have nothing to write to thee, but an expression of my dearest and most faithful affection to thee, and my dear children and friends with thee. Be comfortable and courageous, my sweet wife. Fear nothing. I am assured the Lord is with us, and will be with thee. Thou shalt find it in the needful time. Cleave to thy faithful Lord and Husband, Christ Jesus, into whose blessed arms I have put thee, to whose care I have and do commend thee and all thine. Once again I kiss and embrace my sweet wife. Farewell; the Lord bless thee and all thy company. Commend me to all, and to all our good friends and neighbours, and remember Monday and Friday between five and six.

Thy faithful husband,

JO. WINTHROP.

My son Henry must come by Maplested to seal a writing, which I left there.

To my very loving Wife, Mrs. WINTHROP, *at Groton.*

[Dated, probably, latter part of February, 1629—30.]

A 37.

LONDON, *March* 2, 1629.

Mine own dear Heart,

I MUST confess, thou hast overcome me with thy exceeding great love, and those abundant expressions of it in thy sweet letters, which savour of more than an ordinary spirit of love and piety. Blessed be the Lord our God, that gives strength and comfort to thee to undergo this great trial, which, I must confess, would be too heavy for thee, if the Lord did not put under his hand in so gracious a measure. Let this experience of his faithfulness to thee in this first trial, be a ground to establish thy heart to believe and expect his help in all that may follow. It grieveth me much, that I want time and freedom of mind to discourse with thee (my faithful yokefellow) in those things, which thy sweet letters offer me so plentiful occasion for. I beseech the Lord, I may have liberty to supply it, ere I depart; for I cannot thus leave thee. Our two boys and James Downing, John Samford and Mary M. and most of my servants, are gone this day towards South Hampton. The good Lord be with them and us all. Goodman Hawes was with me, and very kindly offers to bring his wife to Groton about the beginning of April, and so stay till thyself and my [1]daughter be in bed; so as thou shalt not need take care for a midwife. Ah, my most kind and dear wife, how sweet is thy love to me! The Lord bless thee and thine with the blessings from above and from beneath, of the right hand and the left, with plenty of favour and peace here, and eternal glory hereafter. All here are in health, (I praise God,) and salute thee. Remember my love and blessing to our children, and my salutations to all as thou knowest. So I kiss and embrace thee, and rest

Thine ever,

JO. WINTHROP.

A 38.

Mine only Best-beloved,

I NOW salute thee from South Hampton, where, by the Lord's mercy, we are all safe; but the winds have been such as our ships are not yet come. We wait upon God, hoping that he will dispose all for the best unto us. I supposed I should have found leisure to have written more fully to thee by this bearer; but here I meet with so much company and business, as I am forced to borrow of my sleep for this. I purpose to redeem this loss before I go hence, and to write to divers of my friends. I must entreat thee to supply this defect by remembering me in the kindest manner to them all. And now (my dear wife) what shall I say to thee? I am full of matter and affection towards thee, but want time to express it. I beseech the good Lord to take care of thee and thine; to seal up his loving kindness to thy soul; to fill thee with the sweet comfort of his presence, that may uphold thee in this time of trial; and grant us this mercy, that we may see the faces of each other again in the time expected. So, loving thee truly, and tender of thy welfare, studying to bestow thee safe, where I may have thee again, I leave thee in

---

[1] I suppose this was Henry's wife.

the arms of the Lord Jesus, our sweet Saviour, and, with many kisses and embracings, I rest

Thine only, and ever thine,

JO. WINTHROP.

SOUTH HAMPTON, *March* 14, 1629.

The good Lord bless our children and all thy company.

Do thou bless these here, and pray pray for us.

Give Mrs. Leigh many thanks for her horse, and remember to requite it.

A 39.

My dear Wife,

I WROTE to thee, when I went from South Hampton, and now I must salute thee and take leave together from the ship. God be blessed, the wind is come very fair, and we are all in health. Our [1]children remember their duties, and desire thy blessing. Commend me to all our good friends, as I wrote in my former letter, and be comfortable, and trust in the Lord, my dear wife, pray, pray. He is our God and Father; we are in covenant with him, and he will not cast us off. So, this once more, I kiss and embrace thee and all my children, &c. &c.

Thy faithful husband,

JO. WINTHROP.

From aboard the Arbella, riding at the COWES, *March* 22, 1629.

A 40.

My good Son,

WE are now going to the ship, under the comfort of the Lord's gracious protection and good providence. I pray have care so to walk with God in faith and sincerity, as, by his blessing, we may meet with joy. There is newly come into our company, and sworn an assistant, one Sir Brian Janson of London, a man of good estate, and so affected with our society, as he hath given £50 to our common stock, and £50 to the joint stock. He desires to be acquainted with you.

I pray pay Bulbrooke of Wenham such money as his provisions cost him, about 30 or 40*s.* and receive £12 of goodman Pond for the rest of his son's two cows, (I had £10 before,) and ask him for their passage £10. You shall receive £5 for Edward Palsford, which John S. hath order for. I pray pay Mr. Goffe such money as you shall receive direction for from your uncle Downing.

---

[1] Henry, and, probably, Adam.

We are now come safe (I praise God) to the Cowes. The wind is now very fair, (God be praised,) and we are preparing to set sail this night. The Lord in mercy send us a prosperous voyage. Farewell, my dear son. The Lord bless you and all my children and friends. Commend me to them all, as if I named them; for I am in great straits of leisure. So I rest

Your loving father,
JO. WINTHROP.

March 22, 1629.

To my very loving Son, Mr. JOHN WINTHROP, *at Groton, Suffolk, d'd.*

A 41.

My faithful and dear Wife,

IT pleaseth God, that thou shouldest once again hear from me before our departure, and I hope this shall come safe to thy hands. I know it will be a great refreshing to thee. And blessed be his mercy, that I can write thee so good news, that we are all in very good health, and, having tried our ship's entertainment now more than a week, we find it agree very well with us. Our boys are well and cheerful, and have no mind of home. They lie both with me, and sleep as soundly in a rug (for we use no sheets here) as ever they did at Groton; and so I do myself, (I praise God.) The wind hath been against us this week and more; but this day it is come fair to the north, so as we are preparing (by God's assistance) to set sail in the morning. We have only four ships ready, and some two or three Hollanders go along with us. The rest of our fleet (being seven ships) will not be ready this sennight. We have spent now two Sabbaths on shipboard very comfortably, (God be praised,) and are daily more and more encouraged to look for the Lord's presence to go along with us. Henry Kingsbury hath a child or two in the Talbot sick of the measles, but like to do well. One of my men had them at Hampton, but he was soon well again. We are, in all our eleven ships, about seven hundred persons, passengers, and two hundred and forty cows, and about sixty horses. The ship which went from Plimouth carried about one hundred and forty persons, and the ship which goes from Bristowe carrieth about eighty persons. And now (my sweet soul) I must once again take my last farewell of thee in Old England. It goeth very near to my heart to leave thee; but I know to whom I have committed thee, even to him who loves thee much better than any husband can, who hath taken account of the hairs of thy head, and puts all thy tears in his bottle, who can, and (if it be for his glory) will bring us together again with peace and comfort. Oh, how it refresheth my heart, to think, that I shall yet again see thy sweet face in the land of the living!—that lovely countenance, that I have so much delighted in, and beheld with so great content! I have hitherto been so taken up with business, as I could seldom look back to my former happiness; but now, when I shall be at some leisure, I shall not avoid the remembrance of thee, nor the grief for thy absence. Thou hast thy share with me, but I hope the course we have agreed upon will be some ease to us both. Mondays and Fridays, at five of the clock at night, we shall meet in spirit till we meet in person. Yet, if all these hopes should fail, blessed be our God, that we are assured we shall meet one day, if not as husband and wife, yet in a better condition. Let that stay and comfort thy heart. Neither can the sea drown thy husband, nor enemies destroy, nor any adversity deprive thee of thy husband or children. Therefore I will only take thee now and my sweet children in mine arms, and kiss and embrace you all, and so leave you with my God. Farewell, farewell. I bless you all in the name of the Lord Jesus. I salute my daughter Winth. Matt. Nan. and the rest, and all my good neighbours and friends. Pray all for us. Farewell. Commend my blessing to my son John. I cannot now write to him; but tell him I have committed thee and thine to him. Labour to draw him yet nearer to God, and he will be the surer staff of comfort to thee. I cannot name the rest of my good friends, but thou canst supply it. I wrote, a week since, to thee and Mr. Leigh and divers others.

Thine wheresoever,

JO. WINTHROP.

From aboard the Arbella, riding at the COWES, *March* 28, 1630.

I would have written to my brother and sister Gostling, but it is near midnight. Let this excuse; and commend my love to them and all theirs.

To MARG. WINTHROP, *the elder, at Groton.*

A 42.

My Love, my Joy, my faithful One,

I SUPPOSE thou didst not expect to have any more letters from me till the return of our ships; but so is the good pleasure of God, that the winds should not serve yet to carry us hence. He will do all things in his own time, and that shall be for the best in the end. We acknowledge it a great mercy to us, that we went not out to sea on Monday, when the wind was fair for one day; for we had been exposed, ever since, to sore tempests and contrary winds. I praise God, we are all in good health, and want nothing. For myself, I was never at more liberty of body and mind these many years. The Lord make me thankful and wise to improve his blessings for the furtherance of his own work. I desire to resign myself wholly to his gracious disposing. Oh that I had an heart so to do, and to trust perfectly in him for his assistance in all our ways. We find him still going along with us. He hath brought in the heart of the master of our ship to afford us all good respect, and to join with us in every good action. Yesterday he caused his seamen to keep a fast with us, wherein the Lord assisted us and our minister very comfortably; and when five of the clock came, I had respite to remember thee, (it being Friday,) and to parley with thee, and to meet thee in spirit before the Lord. After supper, we discovered some notorious lewd persons of our own company, who, in time of our fast, had committed theft, and done other villanies, for which we have caused them to be severely punished.

I am uncertain whether I shall have opportunity to send these to thee; for, if the wind turn, we shall soon be gone. Therefore I will not write much. I know it will be sufficient for thy present comfort, to hear of our welfare; and this is the third letter I have written to thee, since I came to Hampton, in requital of those two I received from thee, which I do often read with much delight, apprehending so much love and sweet affection in them, as I am never satisfied with reading, nor can read them without tears; but whether they proceed from joy, sorrow or desire, or from that consent of affection, which I always hold with thee, I cannot conceive. Ah, my dear heart, I ever held thee in high esteem, as thy love and goodness hath well deserved; but (if it be possible) I shall yet prize thy virtue at a greater rate, and long more to enjoy thy sweet society than ever before. I am sure thou art not short of me in this desire. Let us pray hard, and pray in faith, and our God, in his good time, will accomplish our desire. Oh, how loath am I to bid thee farewell! but, since it must be, farewell, my sweet love, farewell. Farewell, my dear children and family. The Lord bless you all, and grant me to see your faces once again. Come, (my dear,) take him and let him rest in thine arms, who will ever remain,

Thy faithful husband,

JO. WINTHROP.

Commend my love to all our friends at Castleins, Mr. Leigh and his wife, my neighbour Cole and his wife, and all the rest of our good friends and neighbours, and our good friends at Maplested, when you see them, and those our worthy and kind friends at Assington, &c. My brother Arthur hath carried himself very soberly since he came on shipboard, and so hath Mr. Brand's son, and my cousin Ro. Sampson. I hope their friends shall hear well of them.

From aboard the Arbella, riding before YARMOUTH, *in the* ISLE OF WIGHT, *April* 3, 1630.

To my very loving Wife, Mrs. WINTHROP, *the elder, at Groton, in Suffolk, d'd.*

A 43.

My good Son,

I RECEIVED two letters from you since I came to Hampton, and this is the second I have written back to you. I do much rejoice and bless God for that goodness I find in you towards me and mine. I do pray, and assuredly expect, that the Lord will reward it plentifully into your bosom; for it is his promise to prolong their days, (which includes all outward prosperity,) who give due honour to their parents. Trust him, son, for he is faithful. Labour to grow into nearer communion and acquaintance with him, and you shall find him a good God, and a master worth the serving. Ask of any who have tried him, and they will justify him in his kindness and bounty to his servants. Yet we must not look that he should always give us what we think might be good for us; but wait, and let him take his own way, and the end will satisfy our expectation.

Our ship and the Talbot are now at Yarmouth; but the Jewell and Ambrose are put back unto the Cowes. We have had very tempestuous weather, with the wind at S. W. so as some ships, which went out at the Needles before us, are driven back again; and we intend not to stir till we see the wind settled. I would wish women and children not to go to sea till April, and then to take shipping at London. If we had done so, it had eased us of much trouble and charge. There lie now at Cowes two ships of Holland, bound, one to the Streights, and the other to the East Indies, of one hundred tons a piece, which, putting to sea in February, spent their masts, and, with much difficulty, and loss of near one hundred men, are come in hither. There came in lately by us a ship from Virginia, laden with tobacco. The master came aboard us, and told us, that they want corn there. She was fourteen weeks outward, and yet lost but one man. I pray certify me, by the next occasion, what the wine cost for the common use, and if you have laid out any more in that kind, that I may perfect my account.

I pray prepare money so soon as you can, that I may be clear with Mr. Goffe and others, and that my part in the joint stock may be made up.

Sir Nath. Barnardiston desired to put in money into our joint stock. Remember my love and respect to him, and if he will put in £50, take it as part of the £200, which I have put in already, except you have money enough to supply more.

Yesterday we kept a fast aboard our ship and in the Talbot. Mr. Phillips exercised with us the whole day, and gave very good content to all the company, as he doth in all his exercises, so as we have much cause to bless God for him.

In the Talbot a woman was lately delivered of a son, and both like to do well.

For other things, which concern my affairs at home, I refer them to your care and the good providence of the Almighty.

Commend my love to all our good friends, as you have occasion,—to my daughter Winthrop, your sister and cousin, and to Mr. Leigh,

Mr. Nutt and that family, and to all at Castleins, and the rest, whom I can't now name; and the Lord bless, direct and prosper you in all your ways. So farewell, my good son.

Your loving father,
JO. WINTHROP.

From aboard the Arbella, riding before YARMOUTH, *April* 5, 1630.

Our long stay here hath occasioned the expense of much more money than I expected, so as I am run much in Mr. Goffe's debt. I pray get up some money so soon as you can, and pay him £150, or so much as you can get.

To [*my very loving Son,*] Mr. [JOHN WINTHROP,] *Groton, in Suffolk, d'd.*

A 44.

CHARLETON *in* NEW ENGLAND, *July* 16, 1630.

My dear Wife,

BLESSED be the Lord, our good God and merciful Father, that yet hath preserved me in life and health to salute thee, and to comfort thy long longing heart with the joyful news of my welfare, and the welfare of thy beloved children.

We had a long and troublesome passage, but the Lord made it safe and easy to us; and though we have met with many and great troubles, (as this bearer can certify thee,) yet he hath pleased to uphold us, and to give us hope of a happy issue.

I am so overpressed with business, as I have no time for these or other mine own private occasions. I only write now, that thou mayest know, that yet I live and am mindful of thee in all my affairs. The larger discourse of all things thou shalt receive from my brother Downing, which I must send by some of the last ships. We have met with many sad and discomfortable things, as thou shalt hear after; and the Lord's hand hath been heavy upon myself in some very near to me. My son Henry! my son Henry! ah, poor child! Yet it grieves me much more for my dear daughter. The Lord strengthen and comfort her heart, to bear this cross patiently. I know thou wilt not be wanting to her in this distress. Yet, for all these things, (I praise my God,) I am not discouraged; nor do I see cause to repent or despair of those good days here, which will make amends for all.

I shall expect thee next summer, (if the Lord please,) and by that time I hope to be provided for thy comfortable entertainment. My most sweet wife, be not disheartened; trust in the Lord, and thou shalt see his faithfulness. Commend me heartily to all our kind friends at Castleins, Groton Hall, Mr. Leigh and his wife, my neighbour Cole, and all the rest of my neighbours and their wives, both rich and poor. Remember me to them at Assington Hall, and Codenham Hall, Mr. Brand, Mr. Alston, Mr. Mott, and their wives, goodman Pond, Charles Neale, &c. The good Lord be with thee and bless thee and all our children and servants. Commend my love to them all. I kiss and embrace thee, my dear wife, and all my children, and leave thee in his arms, who is able to preserve you all, and to fulfil our joy in our happy meeting in his good time. Amen.

Thy faithful husband,

JO. WINTHROP.

I shall write to my son John by London.

To my very loving Wife, Mrs. Winthrop, *the elder, at Groton in Suffolk, near Sudbury. From* New England.

A 45.

My good Son,

The blessing of God all-sufficient be upon thee ever. Amen. It hath pleased the Lord to bring us hither in peace, (blessed be his name.) For the course of our voyage, and other occurrents, you shall understand them by a journal, which I send with my letters to your uncle D. We had a comfortable passage, and I found that love and respect from Capt. Milburne our master, as I may not forget. I pray (if he be returned before you come hither) take occasion to see him, and remember my kind salutations to him and his wife.

It is like you shall hear (before this come to you) how the Lord hath disposed of your brother Hen. The Lord teach you and the rest by it to remember your Creator in the days of your youth, and to improve your time to his service, while it lasts.

The unexpected troubles and necessities, which are fallen upon us, will bring a great deal of business and care upon thee; but be not discouraged. It is the Lord, who hath cast it upon thee, and he will uphold and deliver thee.

We are forced to send to Bristowe for supply of provisions, by Mr. Peirce and Mr. Allerton, for which I have given them a bill of exchange. You must needs take order, the money may be provided presently for them, for they can't stay. If all means fail, Mr. Revel hath promised to help me with £100. He hath a bill also for money for provisions, which I took up of him here; so have divers others, which you must take care to see paid.

For the freight for the ships, you shall receive some bills from Sir Richard, Mr. Johnson and Mr. Dudley; but it is doubtful whether their moneys will be ready. What you can provide of theirs and mine, be sure the Talbot be first discharged, for they will not tarry.

There is much likewise to be paid to Mr. Beecher, which may stay awhile. There are other moneys to be paid to Mr. Peirce, which must be provided. If all means fail, you may try Doctor Wright; but I hope you have sold the land, and then that care is at an end. For Mr. Goffe, he hath failed exceedingly in his undertaking, so as he is in debt to many of us, and hath had a great deal more of me than his due. Therefore pay him no more. I will send you the account for him and rest, whom I undertook for.

I shall expect your mother and you and the rest of our company here the next spring, if God will. For directions for your passage, I have written about it to your uncle D. and your mother, and I am tired out with writing and much business. Commend my love and blessing to your brother Forth, and your sister M., my neice, Matt. and the rest of our family, and my kind salutations to all my good friends and neighbours, who inquire of us, and to Mr. Nicolson.

For your sister Winthrop, if she will come over, I will provide for her as mine own; if not, she hath a bond of £400. Yet you know there is not so much due to her; for your brother had much money of me out of the £400 I had of him, besides what he ought to your sister Mary. Yet, if it be to be had, I would pay it her, as it can be raised; but then she must give me a general release.

If money be brought to you or your uncle Downing for goodman Lockwood, let Mr. Peirce be paid his bill of provisions for him, and bring the rest with you.

For Forth's coming over, I leave it to my sister Painter her disposing. If they come, they shall be welcome. These afflictions we have met with need discourage none, for the country is exceeding good, and the climate very like our own; only people must come well provided, and not too many at once. Pease may come, if he will, and such other as you shall think fit, but not many, and let those be good, and but few servants, and those useful ones.

Take order that a copy of my relation, &c. be sent to Sir Nath. Barnardiston, and my excuse of not writing to him and Sir Wm. Spring, with my salutations to them both; and if Sir Nath. hath put in no money, let him forbear still.

You must call to Mr. Andrews in Bowe Lane for £20, which Mr. Pincheon hath appointed for you, and you are to pay it, and £30 more, to Mr. Rich. Andrews, at the Mermaid in Cheapside; but you must first inquire if it were lent to us, as we were promised at Hampton. It may be paid soon after Michaelmas next. There is also £208 to be paid to Mr. Cradock, or Mr. Woodward at his house in St. Bartl. near the Exchange, September 8, for which Mr. Johnson and I stood bound; but, if it be not ready, I think Mr. Cradock will get it continued.

Here is a barrel of neat of Bulbrooke's of Wenham. If I did not pay for it, let it be paid.

If you reckon with Mr. Wall, thus it stands: You receive of him by Mr. Chamber (to whom I desire to be kindly remembered)

The passage for himself, his wife and a servant, comes to £16.10
For one cow...15.02
For tonnage of his goods...11.00

42.12

Demand the rest of him, and certify me of it.

Henry Kingsbury hath appointed money to be paid to you by [blank.]

John Warren hath appointed money to be paid to you by the bond he left with you. He owes beside £10, beside his present provisions.

Demand of Stone and Bragge of Neyland, £15. You have bond for it.

Mr. Goffe's and my account stands thus:

He received of me in England at several payments..........£642.00
More of me for my brother Downing.................................107.02
You have paid him since, by my direction from Hampton
He is to discount for two mares and a horse, (one Mr. Brand's,) which died by the way..27.00
He is allowed for ninety-six passengers, at £4......................384.00
For twenty-four cows, (ten being for my broth. D.)..............361.00
For thirty-two tons of goods, at £3.

I must end. The Lord God Almighty bless you, and send you all hither in peace. Farewell, my dear son,

Your loving father,
JO. WINTHROP.

Commend me to old Pond, and tell him both his sons are well, and remember their duty to him. He must needs send his son John some more provisions, for much of that he brought was spoiled by the way. You must demand money of him. His reckoning stands thus:

His passage and goods come to......................................£27.00
One cow..15.00

I had of him, £10.04. 42.00
Rest due...............32.00.

CHARLTON, *July* 23, 1630.

For the country itself, I can discern little difference between it and our own. We have had only two days, which I have observed more hot than in England. Here is as good land as I have seen there, but none so bad as there. Here is sweet air, fair rivers, and plenty of springs, and the water better than in England. Here can be no want of any thing to those, who bring means to raise out of the earth and sea.

To my very loving Son, Mr. JOHN WINTHROP,
at Groton, *in Suffolk*, *d'd.*

A 46.

Charleton *in* New England, *August* 14, 1630.

My good Son,

I received your letters by Mr. Huson's ship, and do much rejoice, and bless the Lord for the good news of all your welfares. For our condition here, and our voyage hither, I wrote to you, about a fortnight since, by Mr. Revel, but more fully in a journal and relation, which I sent to your uncle Downing; yet I could [not] make any perfect relation, for want of time and leisure, and I am still as much straitened as before, so as I must refer you and all my friends to my former report as it is. Withal I sent a card of our voyage at sea, which Capt. Milborne drew for me. I wrote, also, how the Lord's hand had been very heavy upon our people in these parts, and that which I conceived to be the reason why so many fell sick, and so many died, and what course you should take when your mother is to come hither, &c. I can now only write a word or two for direction about our affairs; and so I shall leave my blessing with you. First, for the land, (if it be not already sold,) you must sell it speedily, for much debt will lie upon us. For Mr. Appleton, take no money of him, for he can have no cows: there came not on shore one half of them. I had £15 of Mrs. Sands for a cow for her brother Goffe; but he could have none now: ergo, if she will not have him have it at next return, let her have her money again.

Pay Mr. Goffe no more money, but require the remainder; and, if he refuse to pay it, it were well his bond were put in suit. If you have money to spare, send over some more cows and goats, and bring £100 with you, or 2.

The beef we had of Mr. Stretton is as sweet and good as if it were but a month powdered. You shall know of other things by your mother's letters. We have powder and pieces enough, but want flints and bird-shot and store of chalk. But I must end. The Lord bless you, and send you hither in safety. Farewell, my good son.

Your loving father,

JO. WINTHROP.

To my very loving Son, Mr. John Winthrop, *at Groton*, *Suffolk*, *d'd.*

A 47.

My dear Wife,

The blessing of God all-sufficient be upon thee and all my dear ones with thee forever.

I praise the good Lord, though we see much mortality, sickness and trouble, yet (such is his mercy) myself and children, with most of my family, are yet living, and in health, and enjoy prosperity enough, if the afflictions of our brethren did not hold under the comfort of it. The lady Arbella is dead, and good Mr. Higginson, my servant, old Waters of Neyland, and many others. Thus the Lord is pleased still to humble us; yet he mixes so many mercies with his corrections, as we are persuaded he will not cast us off, but, in his due time, will do us good, according to the measure of our afflictions. He stays but till he hath purged our corruptions, and healed the hardness and errour of our hearts, and stripped us of our vain confidence in this arm of flesh, that he may have us rely wholly upon himself. The French ship, so long expected, and given for lost, is now come safe to us, about a fortnight since, having been twelve weeks at sea; and yet her passengers (being but few) all safe and well but one, and her goats but six living of eighteen. So as now we are somewhat refreshed with such goods and provisions as she brought, though much thereof hath received damage by wet. I praise God, we have many occasions of comfort here, and do hope, that our days of affliction will soon have an end, and that the Lord will do us more good in the end than we could have expected, that will abundantly recompense for all the trouble we have endured. Yet we may not look at great things here. It is enough that we shall have heaven, though we should pass through hell to it. We here enjoy God and Jesus Christ. Is not this enough? What would we have more? I thank God, I like so well to be here, as I do not repent my coming; and if I were to come again, I would not have altered my course, though I had foreseen all these afflictions. I never fared better in my life, never slept better, never had more content of mind, which comes merely of the Lord's good hand; for we have not the like means of these comforts here, which we had in England. But the Lord is all-sufficient, blessed be his holy name. If he please, he can still uphold us in this estate; but, if he shall see good to make us partakers with others in more affliction, his will be done. He is our God, and may dispose of us as he sees good.

I am sorry to part with thee so soon, seeing we meet so seldom, and my much business hath made me too oft forget Mondays and Fridays. I long for the time, when I may see thy sweet face again, and the faces of my dear children. But I must break off, and desire thee to commend me kindly to all my good friends, and excuse my not writing at this time. If God please once to settle me, I shall make amends. I will name now but such as are nearest to thee, my broth. and sister Gostlin, Mr. Leigh, &c. Castleins, my neighbour Cole and his good wife, with the rest of my good neighbours, tenants and servants. The good Lord bless thee and all our children and family. So I kiss my sweet wife and my dear children, and rest

Thy faithful husband,

JO. WINTHROP.

I would have written to Maplested, if I had time. Thou must excuse me, and remember me kindly to them all.

This is the third letter I have written to thee from New England.

September 9, 1630.

A 48.

My good Son,

THE good Lord bless you ever.

I have written to your mother and to your uncle Downing at large of all things here, to which I must refer you, in regard of my much business and little leisure here.

I shall expect your mother and you and the rest of my company here next spring, (if God will.) I pray take order (if it be possible) to make even reckoning with all before you come over, and get a good ship and forty hogsheads of meal at least, well cleansed from the bran, and laid abroad three or four days before it be packed; peas and oatmeal, well dried, as much as you can; good store of dry, Suffolk cheese, brought loose, or packed in very dry malt; butter and tried suet; sugar and fruit; pepper and ginger; store of coarse rugs, both to use and sell; a hogshead of wine vinegar, and another of verjuice, both in good casks and iron-bound. We have lost much by bad casks. Bestow every thing in even hogsheads, if you can; for it will save much in the charge of freight. Bring some good oil, pitch and tar, and a good piece of an old cable to make oakum; for that which was sent is much lost. Some more cows would be brought, especially two new milch, which must be well mealed and milked by the way, and some goats, especially sheep, (if they can be had.) Bring some store of garlick and onions, and conserve of red roses, alum, and aloes, oiled skins, both calf and sheep, and some worsted ribbing of several sizes. This is the third letter I have written to you from here. Commend me to all our friends. My love and blessing to your brother and sisters, your sister Winthrop and cousin Matt. My love and service to Mr. Gurdon and his wife. Salutations to Mr. Jacy, Mr. Chamber, and the rest of the good ministers, Mr. Nott and Mr. Brand. I laid out £15 to Mr. Goffe for a cow for his son. Commend me to all my good neighbours, Mr. Jarrold, William Pond, and the rest. Those who were to have cows delivered here, and failed, must have their money again, my cousin [blank] of Battlesden, £20. I can think of no other, but Mrs. Sands, £15. Commend me to her; and if you see them at Graces, remember me to them. The Lord bless you. Farewell.

Your loving father,

JO. WINTHROP.

September 9, 1630.

A 49.

My sweet Wife,

THE blessing of the Almighty be upon thee and thine forever.

There is a ship arrived at Plimouth, some thirty miles from us, which came from London the 10th of August, and was twelve weeks at sea in such tempests as she spent all her masts; yet, of sixty passengers, she lost but one. All the rest (through the Lord's great mercy) are safe and in health. Edy of Boxted, who came in her, told me, a fortnight since, that he had many letters in the ship for me; but I hear not yet of them, which makes me now (having opportunity to send to Plimouth) to write these few lines to thee, lest the ship should be gone before I have received my letters, and can return answer to them. Thou shalt understand by this, how it is with us since I wrote last, (for this [is] the third or fourth letter I have written to thee since I came hither,) that thou mayest see the goodness of the Lord towards me, that, when so many have died, and many yet languish, myself and my children are yet living and in health. Yet I have lost twelve of my family, viz. Waters and his wife, and two of his children, Mr. Gager and his man Smith of Buxall and his wife and two children, the wife of Taylor of Haverill and their child: my son H. makes the twelve. And, besides many other of less note, as Jeff. Ruggle of Sudbury, and divers others of that town, (about twenty,) the Lord hath stripped us of some principal persons, Mr. Johnson and his lady, Mr. Rossiter, Mrs. Phillips and others unknown to thee. We conceive, that this disease grew from ill diet at sea, and proved infectious. I write not this to discourage thee, but to warn thee and others to provide well for the sea, and, by God's help, the passage will be safe and easy, how long soever. Be careful (I entreat thee) to observe the directions in my former letters; and I trust that that God, who hath so graciously preserved and blessed us hitherto, will bring us to see the faces of each other with abundance of joy. My dear wife, we are here in a paradise. Though we have not beef and mutton, &c. yet (God be praised) we want them not; our Indian corn answers for all. Yet here is fowl and fish in great plenty. I will here break off, because I hope to receive letters from thee soon, and to have opportunity of writing more largely. I will say nothing of my love to thee, and of my longing desires towards thee. Thou knowest my heart. Neither can I mention salutations to my good friends, other than in general. In my next, I hope to supply all. Now the Lord, our good God, be with thee and all my children and company with thee. Grace and peace be with you all. So I kiss my sweet wife and all my dear children, and bless you in the Lord. Farewell.

and one of L. Kedby his sons.

Thy faithful husband,

JO. WINTHROP.

BOSTON, *in* MATTACHUSETS,
November 29, 1630.

Thou must excuse my not writing to my son John and other of my friends at this time; for I defer it till I receive my letters.

To MARG. WINTHROP, *the elder*,
at Groton, *d'd.*

A 50.

My dear Wife,

I HAVE small hope, that this should come to thy hands, in regard of the long stay of the ship here, so as thou mayest be well onward of thy way hither before these can come to England. Therefore I write little to thyself and my son, and those whom I expect to see here shortly, if it shall so please the Lord. And blessed be his holy and glorious name, that he hath so far magnified his mercy towards us, that, when so many have been laid in their graves since we parted, yet he hath pleased to preserve us unto this hope of a joyful meeting, that we may see the faces of each other again, the faces of our children and sweet babes. These things I durst scarce think of heretofore; but now I embrace them oft, and delight my heart in them, because I trust, that the Lord, our God, who hath kept me and so many of my company in health and safety among so many dead corpses, through the heat of the summer and the cold of winter, and hath also preserved thee in the peril of childbirth, and upheld thy heart in the midst of so many discouragements, with the life of all thy company, will, of his own goodness and free mercy, preserve us and ours still, that we shall meet in joy and peace, which I daily pray for, and shall expect in the Lord's good time; who still continue his favour and blessing upon thee and our sweet babes and all thy company. For our little daughter, do as thou thinkest best. The Lord direct thee in it. If thou bringest her, she will be more trouble to thee in the ship than all the rest. I know my sister will be tender of her, till I may send for her. Bring Amy and Ann Gostlin with thee, if thou canst. If they come not, they will much wrong themselves. They need fear no want here, if they will be guided by God's word; otherwise they can look to prosper nowhere. I praise God, I want nothing but thee and the rest of my family. Commend my love and blessing to them all, and to all my neighbours and friends; but I have desired my brother Gostlin to perform that. Remember to bring juice of lemons to sea with thee, for thee and thy company to eat with your meat as sauce. But of these things, my son hath direction. So again I kiss thee, my sweet wife, and commend thee and all ours to the Lord, and rest

Thine,

March 28, 1631. JO. WINTHROP.

A 51.

My good Son,

THE blessing of the Almighty be upon thy soul and life forever.

Among many the sweet mercies of my God towards me in this strange land, where we have met many troubles and adversities, this is not the least, and that which affords much comfort to my heart, that he hath given me a loving and dutiful son. God all-sufficient reward thee abundantly for all thy care and pains in my affairs, and for all that love and duty thou hast showed to thy good mother. I doubt not but thou shalt find it in outward blessings, for thou art under the promise of having thy days prolonged; but I desire especially thou mayest find it in the manifestation of the good will of the Lord towards thee, and in those spiritual blessings, which may fatten thy soul.

This ship staying so long here, I am almost out of hope, that my letters should come to thy hands; for, though I think very long till I see you all here, yet I would rather you stayed, though it were two or three months, to come with Mr. Peirce, partly because of his skill and care of his passengers, and partly that we might be the better provided of housing, &c. to entertain you. For we are much straitened yet that way, and we have had divers houses burnt, and now, within these two days, Mr. Sharpe and Mr. Colburne, both of our town, had their houses burnt to the ground, and much goods lost. Thus it pleaseth the Lord still to humble us. I doubt not but he will do us the more good at the last.

I have written to your uncle D. concerning all our business, fearing you should be come away. I have sent the assignment sealed. I left all my bonds and writings in my cupboard at Groton, or else at London.

Bring no provision with you, but meal, and peas, and some oatmeal, and sugar, fruit, figs, and pepper, and good store of saltpetre, and conserve of red roses, and mithridate, good store of pitch, and ordinary suet or tallow. Bring none but wine vinegar, and not much of that, and be sure that the cask be good; store of oiled calves-skins of the largest; and the strongest welt leather shoes and stockings for children; and hats of all sizes. If you could bring two or three hundred sheep-skins and lamb-skins, with the wool on, dyed red, it would be a good commodity here; and the coarsest woollen cloth, (so it be not flocks,) and of sad colours, and some red; millstones, some two foot and some three foot over, with bracings ready cast, and rings, and mill-bills; store of shoemakers' thread and hobnails; chalk and chalk-line; and a pair or two, or more, of large, steel compasses; store of coarse linen; some birdlime.

When you have cleared all things in England, if you have any money left, you may bring some with you, (not above £100,) and the rest leave with your uncle D. or dispose of it as your own occasions may require. Anywise, Matt. must have £400, and there will be much due to your sister Winthrop, which were best to be left in England. But you must advise with your uncle D. about these things; for I am so full of business here, as I can't think of mine own affairs as I should. You must also consider what you would have for yourself, and how you would employ it.

I never had letter yet from your brother F. If he intends to come hither, it were good he sold his land, and paid his sister her £100, which he promised when I put over his land to him. You shall need bring no more cows, for I have enough. The good Lord bless you, and bring you and all my company hither in safety. So I rest

Your loving father,

JO. WINTHROP.

MASSACHUSETTS, *March* 28, 1631.

I hope the Lord hath provided a good husband for your sister Winthrop. Mr. Coddington is well affected to her. If he proceed, I wish you to further it; for he is a godly man, and of good estate.

To my very loving Son, Mr. JOHN WINTHROP, *at London*, *d'd*.
If he be come away, my brother Downing may open this letter.

A 52.

My dear Son,

BLESSED be our good God, who hath not failed us, but hath given us cause of most unspeakable joy, for the good news, which we have heard out of New England. Mr. Wilson had been with me before thy letters came to my hands, but brought me no letter. He speaks very well of things there, so as my heart and thoughts are there already. I want but means to carry my body after them. I am now fully persuaded, that it is the place wherein God will have us to settle in; and I beseech him to fit us for it, that we may be instruments of his glory there. This news came very seasonable to me, being possessed with much grief for thee, hearing how things went concerning thy wife's jointure. But now I have cast off that, and hope God will turn all to the best. If thou canst but send me over when Mr. Wilson goeth back, I shall be very, very glad of his company. If thy manifold employments will not suffer thee to go with me, I shall be very sorry for it; for I would be glad to carry all my company with me. But I will not say any more of this till I hear from thee, how things may be done. I pray consider of it, and give me the best counsel you can. Mr. Wilson is now in London, and promised me to come and see you. He cannot yet persuade his wife to go, for all he hath taken this pains to come and fetch her. I marvel what mettle she is made of.[1] Sure she will yield at last, or else we shall want him exceedingly in New England. I desire to hear what news

[1] I believe she could not be induced to come till her husband had made a second voyage to England, and, on his third coming, in November, 1635, she probably attended him. Her admission to Boston church is of 20 March, 1635—6.

my brother Downing hath; for my husband writ but little to me, thinking we had been on our voyage. And thus, with my love to thyself, my daughter, and all the rest of my good friends, I desire the Lord to bless and keep you, and rest

Your loving mother,
MARGARET WINTHROP.

I received the things you sent down by the carrier this week, and thank my daughter for my band. I like it well. I must, of necessity, make me a gown to wear every day, and would have one bought me of some good strong black stuff, and Mr. Smith to make it of the civilest now in use. If my sister Downing would please to give him some directions about it, he would make it the better.

[May or June, 1631.]

A 53.

My worthy and beloved Brother,

I AM told by my mother,—and she showed me a letter, which you have very kindly written to my father,—that you will repay certain money, that was taken up in London, by reason of my troubles occasioned by God's providence in that my so much desired match with your dearest brother, which the Lord otherwise ordered, and brought his estate into your hands. The Lord prosper it unto you and yours. I shall truly pray for you, and desire your prayers may be before the Lord for me, who am left to pass through the miseries of a troublesome pilgrimage. I thank you for the continuance of your love. My father and mother are very kind unto me, and will not be wanting, I know, in their love. But, though the Lord should greatly increase your estate by the loss of my dearest friend, and the lessening of my poor portion, and laying other hindrances upon me, yet shall I never think my love ill settled upon one, that loved me so dearly, though he could leave me nothing but his prayers for me and the interest I have in your love, whose kindness is so clearly manifested, like the kindness of Ruth, to the living and to the dead. The £30 you writ of was taken up of my uncle Talley; besides which, the £10 my father's man brought with him, and the £5 of Mr. Brinscely, and £8 from my uncle Downing, goeth out of that sum of £50 in his hands, which my father Paynter was willing mother should add to my portion, which was but £250 before, for your brother. And now that is all spent, excepting very little. But in all this I do submit myself patiently to the will of God, and take it as the least part of that great affliction. I do not mention any of this to press you, good brother; neither are you bound, but as the consideration of God's dealing, both with you and your brother and me, shall move you. Your promises were your kindness. I could not deserve them, forlorn and desolate as I was. Yet they were comfortable in that case, and I still thank you, and pray the Lord to reward you.

The mare I confess I should desire to get down, if it might stand with your good liking. I hope to ride to Sutton upon her shortly. Mr. Brinscely knows how to send her down by the carrier. I am ashamed to put all these things in a letter, which your well known love and ready kindness would prevent me in, if I could but see you, nay, hath prevented. My father and mother desire to see you all, if it be possible, though they have little hope, by reason of my father's employments. Pray remember my unfeigned love to my sister your wife, and my sister Elizabeth Winthrop. Pray certify her, that I received her loving letter, and excuse me to her, that I have not now written to her. I should be very thankful, if you would be pleased to let me hear from you, the messenger of your welfare being always welcome, and much rejoicing the heart of me.

Your ever-loving sister,
URSULA SHERMAN.

My mother remembereth her love to yourself and your wife, and thanks you both for your kind tokens you sent her by me. She desires to be excused for not writing you at this time.

From EXETER, *June* 18, 1631.

To my worthy and very loving Brother, Mr. JOHN WINTHROP, *at Groton in Suffolk*, *d'd.*

[Does this letter come from a maiden betrothed to Forth? I know nothing of *him*, but that he was left in England, when his father came over; and his first letter to John in England leaves it to his sister Painter's disposing, whether Forth should come or not. Another, of March, 1631, mentions him. F. was old enough then to be married, and, I imagine, died that spring of 1631. Henry Painter, of Exeter, was one of the celebrated Assembly of Divines at Westminster, and my conjecture is, that he married the mother of the above-mentioned lady. There would, therefore, have been a double connexion between Gov. Winthrop and Painter, by the marriage of the governour's eldest son, John, with Elizabeth, daughter of Painter, and by the marriage of his third son, Forth, with Ursula Sherman, daughter of Painter's wife.]

A 54.

My dear Son,

I HOPE the Lord hath carried you safe to England, with our most dear Mr. [1]Warner, and the rest of our good brethren and friends. There is nothing befallen since your departure, but Mr. Peirce came from Naraganset, three days after, with five hundred bushels of corn only. At the court it was informed, that some of Salem had

---

[1] Undoubtedly Wilson is meant.

taken out a piece of the cross in their ensign; whereupon we sent forth an attachment to bring in the parties at the next court, where they are like to be punished for their indiscreet zeal, for the people are generally offended with it. Mrs. [1]W. was at first very much affected with her husband's departure, but she is now well pacified. I intend to send this letter by Capt. Underhill, who hath leave to go see his friends in Holland. If he come to you, he can inform you of all things here. As I was writing this, Richard came in and told me, the dogs had killed an old wolf this morning in our neck. She made more resistance than both the former. I have many things to write to you about, for such necessaries as are to be provided and sent over; but this occasion is sudden, and I can't think of them, but shall write more largely by Mr. P. if the Lord will. Yourself know what will be needful, and therefore may consider accordingly. Remember copperas, white and green, and two or three pounds of Paracelsus's plaister, and some East Indian bezoar, store of sail cloth, nails, cordage, pitch, tallow and wick, steel spades and shovels, two hand saws and small axes, the best of all, whatever they cost. Commend us to all our good friends where you be come, Mr. W. and the rest, your uncles, aunts, &c. Advise Mr. W. to keep close by all means, and make haste back. The good Lord bless and prosper you, that we may see your face with joy. Your mother, &c. salute and bless you. Farewell.

November 6, 1634.

To my loving Son, Mr. JOHN WINTHROP, *d'd, at Mr. Downing his Chamber, in the Inner Temple Lane, London.*

A 55.

My good Son,

THE Lord bless thee ever.

I wrote to you by Capt. Underhill, who went hence in Mr. Babb's ship; since which time here arrived a ship from Barnstable of two hundred tons, Mr. Packers master. She brought about twenty passengers and forty cattle. She lost but two, and yet was seventeen weeks outward bound, whereof five in Ireland. She now returns empty with Mr. Peirce, by whom I send these.

All things continue as when you left us; only Mrs. Warham is dead, and Mr. Hooker's young son, (who died of the small pox, which are very rife at Newton,) and two men of our town, Willys and Doretye; and two lads were cast away in a great tempest at N. E. on Friday, November 21, in the night, between Noddle's Island and Boston, in a small boat, which they had overladen with wood. Myself and divers others were in the same tempest, not without

---

1 Perhaps this means Wilson's wife; but see note on p. 382.

some peril, but the Lord preserved us. Mr. Sewall's boat was then in the cove at the head of Cape Ann, and broken to pieces, but the men and goods saved. The pestilent fever hath taken away some at Plimouth; among others, Mr. Prence the governour his wife, and Mr. Allerton's wife.

We met the last week, to consider about the business of the ensign at Salem, and have written a letter to my brother Downing, wherein, under our hands, we signify our dislike of the action, and our purpose to punish the offenders.[1]

I wrote to you in my former letter about divers things, which we should have need of, which I will here insert also, with addition of some others.

The Pekods sent two embassies to us. The first time, they went away without answer. The next time, we agreed a peace with them, (for friendly commerce only,) which was that they desired, having now war with the Dutch and Narigansetts, upon these terms, viz. that they should deliver us those men, who killed Capt. Stone, &c. and surrender up to us their right in Conecticott, which they willingly agreed unto, and offered us a great present of wampompeag, and beavers, and otter, with this expression, that we might, with part thereof, procure their peace with the Narigansetts, (themselves standing upon terms of honour, not to offer any thing of themselves.)

Winter hath begun early with us. The bay hath been frozen all over, but is now open again; and we had a snow last week of much depth in many places. It came with so violent a storm, as it put by our lecture for that day. I wish that, in your return, you would observe the winds and weather, every day, that we may see how it agrees with our parts.

Mr. Ward continues at your house this winter, and Mr. Clerk (to give him content) in his own. Mr. Cl. finds much fault with your servants John and Sarah, and tells me they will not earn their bread, and that Ned is worth them all.

Spades and shovels.
Felling axes, and other small axes.
Nails of 6, 10 and 20.
Piercer bitts.
Sithes for grass, and two brush sithes.
Copperas, white and green.
Emplastrum Paracelsi, two or three lb.
Emplastrum de mim.
Trading cloth, good store, if money may be had.
Brown thread, and hair buttons, and a hogshead of twine for herring nets.
Shoes, two soaled, strong, and the best Irish stockings and wash leather stockings.

---

[1] Six lines are here perfectly erased, possibly at the time of writing, but it may be since.

Strong cloth suits, unlinen and linen suits of canvas.
Suet, tallow, and wick.
A carpenter, and a husbandman, and a rope-maker, and a cooper.
Some muskets.
Store of brimstone.
A brake for hemp.

Bring the more of all necessaries, because this is the last we shall have without custom.

If my brother Tindale would let you have £100, you may give him assurance of so much in cattle here, to be presently set out for my wife and her children, with the increase, or for £200, if he will.

Commend us to all our good friends, your aunt Downing and uncle G. and aunts, those at Maplested, Graces, Assington, Groton, Charter-House, Sir Richard S. and his son, and all the rest, as you have occasion, Mr. Kirby, &c. and Mr. Howes; and make haste back. And if there be any matter of importance, write by the first fishing ships. Direct your letters to Capt. Wiggin, or Mr. Hilton. Your mother and the rest are in health, (I praise God.) We all salute you. The good Lord direct, keep and bless you. Farewell, my good son.

December 12, 1634.

To my dear Son, Mr. JOHN WINTHROP, *at the House of Mr. Downing, in Lincoln's Fields, near the Golden Lion Tavern, London, d'd.*

A 56.

Son,

I WENT to Ten Hills this morning, with your mother and your wife, to have seen goodman Bushnell; but the Lord had taken him away half an hour before we came there. So I made haste down to send you notice of it; but the ship was under sail before I came, which gives me no time to write further to you, for I must send the boat presently after her. You shall receive of Mr. Hodges the key of one of his chests, where the seeds are; the key of the other can't be found; so you must break it open. There is in one of them a rundlet of *honey*, which she desires may be sent to her against she lie down. She desires you to take an inventory of all he hath there. We are all in health, I praise God for it. Your two men you left sick, your wife and mother, and all of us, salute you and your good company. The Lord bless and prosper you. Farewell, my good son.

This 28 *of the* 1 *mo.* 1636.

To my very loving Son, Mr. WINTHROP, Jun. *Governour of Conecticott, d.*

A 57.

Son,

Blessed be the Lord, who hath preserved and prospered you hitherto.

I received your letters by the Blessing, which arrived here the 14 of this present, and is to return to you with Mr. Pincheon's goods, so soon as she can be laden. By her I shall (God willing) write to you of other things, which I may now omit. Your wife and all our family (I praise God) are in health. I think you will have no letter from her till the Blessing come. It hath been earnestly pressed to have her go to Virginia for Mr. Maverick and his corn; but I have no heart to it at this season, being so perilous both to the vessel, (for worms,) and especially the persons. I will never have any that belong to me come there, if I can avoid it; but Mr. Mayhew hath taken order the Rebecca shall go, if she can be met with.

The Lord, in much mercy, sent us a ship the 12 of this present with provisions; but she had put in at Pascataqua, and sold much there; for she brought only thirty-nine hogsheads of meal, twenty-five of peas, eight of oatmeal, forty of malt, and some beef, and prunes and aquavitæ, eighteen thousand of [unknown.] My brother Peter bought it all, and divided it among all the

[Here about sixteen lines are gone, the paper being torn.]

Queen of Bohemia her eldest son is in England, and no speech of any stop of shipping hither, nor of the general governour, more than divers years before. This ship came in eight weeks from Dartmouth, and saith, there had not been an easterly wind in England fourteen weeks before.

For home news—the general court hath ordained a standing council for life, and quarterly courts to be kept at Ipswich, Salem, Newtown and Boston; and four courts in the year at Boston, for greater causes, and for appeals. Mr. Allerton is returned, but had a very ill voyage. His bark lay ten days upon the rock, and beat out all her keel; and so, the second time, Mr. Mayhew and he could get but little provisions, and at extreme rates, but six hogsheads of bread, and few peas. I can get but one barrel of peas of Mr. Allerton, which I will send you. Some pork they brought, but so lean as I have not seen the like salted. The Indians killed up all their swine, so as Capt. Lovell had none; but you shall have beef instead of it. I have sent to Ipswich for your cattle and your servant; for it will be great loss to keep them there. I will take the others from Mr. Mayhew so soon as grass is up.

[The same deficiency as above mentioned.]

I sent you two letters lately, one by Mr. Hodges, and the other by Mr. Oldham, wherein I certified you of the death of goodman Bushnell, one whom you will miss above all the rest. I had him down to Boston, to do him what honour I could at his burial. Your carpenter and the other fellow (who, I think, truly fears God) are recovering, and, I hope, shall be able to come to you in the Blessing. I pray send me some saltpetre; for I suppose it was a means, through God's blessing, to save one of their lives, being far spent in a fever.

I purpose to send you some milch goats and swine. The prunes I suppose you may sell such of them as you can't spend. The butt cost £10, and should weigh near one thousand pounds. The aquavitæ was put aboard by my brother Peter's order, without my appointment. It cost £22. What you will not spend of it, you may sell to the Dutch for profit enough.

I sent you two letters by Mr. Tilly. [A line and a half erased.] Your brother Stephen was desirous to come to you. If you have any employment for him, you may keep him; otherwise you may return him back.

This ship is bound for the Isle of Sable. If you will send the Blessing with her, she may be here time enough a month hence. But two things I fear: first, that here will be no men nor provisions to set her forth with: the second, that both of them will not be of sufficient strength against the French; for this ship hath not above fourteen men. Neither would I send any of ours without taking leave of the French.

I think the bark goeth away in the morning. Therefore I here end, with salutations to all our friends with you, Mr. Gardiner and his wife, &c. Your mother saluteth you; your wife writes. The Lord in mercy preserve, guide, prosper and bless you in all your ways. Farewell, my good son.

Mr. Hooker and his company intend to set forth three weeks hence.

This 26 *of the* 2 *mo.* 1636.

This night we hear of a ship arrived at Pemaquid, and of twenty-four ships upon the seas, bound hither.

To my very loving Son, Mr. Winthrop, Jun. *Governour of the new Plantation upon Connecticut, d'd.*

A 58.

Queneticut, *May* 16, 1636.

Sir,

John Wood being returned without any corn, I shall now desire, that I may be supplied, by the first shipping that arrive with any store of provisions, with ten or twelve hogsheads of meal, five or six hogsheads of peas, two or three barrels of oatmeal, two hogsheads of beef; for, if we should want, I see no means to be supplied here; and a little want may overthrow all our design.

I send home the Bachelor, and desire your help for her disposing. I must, of necessity, have her return here, for I may shortly have much use of her; but I desire they may go for shares, and victual themselves, which John Wood and his company are willing to do. I cannot find, that the miscarriage of his voyage was through his default, but contrary winds. Therefore I am desirous he should and that company go still in her, so they will go for shares, and victual themselves. The Blessing I would sell, if any will buy her at £160, or £150—she cost £145, besides some new sail and rigging, and a new cable, above £20—the cable is special good; except you should foresee any occasion, that she should rather be kept still; or if there be employment to Sable for her. But, if she continues still to go upon any design, I desire she should go likewise for her share, the men to find themselves; otherwise I would have her laid up at Boston till further occasion. The men I desire should be discharged, as soon as ever they come ashore, and their wages paid them. I thank you for the bread you sent. You write of eight hundred, but there is not above three hundred and an half, at most, delivered, besides one hundred they keep still aboard. The rest I cannot learn what become of it, but that it hath been wastefully spent. They had, besides, half an hogshead of bread of their own, which was likewise spent, and they were but two [torn,] eleven persons, they say, most of that time, [much torn;] for they pillaged her the time they had her to Salem pitifully, that she hath neither blocks nor braces, nor running ropes, which the bolt Will saith, that Mr. Holgrave cut them off. He saw him. Therefore I have agreed with John Wood, Frederick and George, to take her to thirds. Thus, with my duty remembered, I rest

Your obedient son,

JOHN WINTHROP.

A 59.

Son,

Mr. Hooker went hence upon Tuesday the last of May, by whom I wrote to you, and sent all your letters, with one from England, and all such news as came to hand; and with that company, viz. by Tho. Bull and a man of mine own, I sent six cows, four steers and a bull. I left it to James and Thomas Skidmore to send such as might be fittest both for travel and for your use. I now send this by the Rebecca, in which you shall find such provisions as are here expressed on the other side. Mr. Fenwick of Gray's Inn (one of those who employ you) hath written to you by Mr. Hooker, and intends, about a month hence, with my brother P. to be with you. The gentlemen seem to be discouraged in the design here; but you shall know more when they come to you.

I received a very loving letter from my Lord S. wherein he expresseth a great deal of satisfaction in your proceedings; but saith withal, that those up the river have carved largely for themselves, which, he thinks, they will after repent, when they see what helps they have deprived themselves of. The ship, which went to Ireland for sheep, lost all her sheep, being five hundred, and so bare up when she was near this coast. Capt. Mason is dead; and thereupon all their designs against us are (through God's great mercy) fallen asleep. But, of all these things, you shall hear more fully when my other letters come to you. Here are come for you, from my sister Downing, divers chests of commodities, and many firkins of butter and suet, which I have bestowed till I hear what you will have done with them. There is a great glut of all provisions, so as they are not like to fall in haste.

We had nine pieces of ordnance to the Rebecca her side; but all the means could be used could not get one into her. Sir Nath. Boynton hath sent more cattle, and two servants. I intend to send his servants to Ipswich to provide for them against winter; for here is not hay to be had. His letters to you come by Mr. Hooker. Sir A. Hazlerig hath refused my brother P. his bills, which is great damage both to him and Mr. Endecott.

I pray deliver this letter enclosed to John Friend, and if he pay you the money, deliver him his bill, (which is here also enclosed;) if not, I pray return it to me again.

Here was an anvil, with a beak horn at the end of it, which I think was carried to Con. If it be, I pray send it back, for it is challenged.

I paid Mr. Garsford of Salem £5 for a buff coat for Mr. Gardiner, which you must remember to put upon his account. Your wampompeak I put off for £30, to be paid in England for the provisions I send you.

Solling and his wife will come to you by the next, if he hear not to the contrary. I know not what to write more on the sudden. I think your wife writes, but she is now at the Garden with my cousin Mary. The Lord bless and prosper you. Your mother salutes you. Farewell.

Provisions sent in the Rebecca.

A hogshead of oatmeal.
Two hogsheads of meal...£8.02
Five casks of peas...10.08
Seven barrels of beef...14.14
A hogshead of pork, which my brother P. puts in............14.07.7
A frail of figs, which I send to yourself, (in the barrel of raisins.)
[1]Two kilderkins of butter, put in by Mr. Peirce for Serjeant Willes.
A barrel of raisins of the sun, (the figs are in the end that hath your mark in black lead,) about two cwt. at 45*s*. the cwt. which is about four pounds and a half.
Four barrels of meal.
A rundlet of sack, of [blank] gallons.
Biscuit in two great bags, at 30*s*. the cwt.

[1] I have paid for them £7.4.4, which he is to pay you.

This 10 of the 4 *mo.* 1636.

To my very loving Son, Mr. JOHN WINTHROP, *Governour of the Plantation upon the mouth of the Conecticott*, *d'd.*

A 60.

Son,

I WROTE to you by Mr. Hooker, and sent you, withal, the letters out of England, and six cows, four steers, and one bull I wrote since by Mr. Hodges in the Rebecca, and sent many provisions, as by my letter did appear; since which time the Wren came in, and one brought me your letter, but being very busy with divers friends, I desired him to come to me again at dinner; but I never heard of him since, nor of any other of that vessel, so as I know not what they intend to do with the clay you sent. The potter saith, that you sent formerly is very good. I shall take order with him about your store, &c. I have spoke with Mr. Wilson and Mr. Coddington for money, but can get none. I will send you what I have or can borrow by John Gallop, (£10,) and some wether goats. The Bachelor is to come to you next week with Mr. Peirce's goods, and the lighter, with some ordnance [in] Mr. Peirce his pinnace. Mr. Fenwick, my brother Peter, &c. set forth on horseback on the 27 of this month, and will expect your shallop at the upper towns to carry them down the river, and so will go in Mr. Peirce's pinnace to Long Island, Hudson's River, &c. I would have sent you some ship beer, but Mr. Fleming hath provided a butt brought in John Gallop. Goodwife B. is delivered of a daughter, and abroad again in a week. Your wife grows big, but as lively as any woman in the house, God be praised.

I do not send you George, because they are speaking of putting off servants, &c. I suppose, when they come to you, they will consider of the widow Bushnell and of the other widows at Ten Hills, widow Briskowe, who hath been sick ever since you went abroad, and is a great burden to us.

We hear that Scilla Nova is at the West Indies; but we hear nothing of the Pied Cow.

I must end, with remembrance of mine own and your mother's love and blessing to you and to Stephen. Farewell, my good son.

23 *of the* 4*th mo.* 1636.

I send you two small sugar loaves by J. Gallop.

Mr. W.'s debt is £310. I showed him his bill, with all the several sums, and of whom he received them. I have laid out, since you went, in provisions, &c. and for seamen's wages, near £200.

John Gallop hath a pair of stockings for Stephen, and shoes and stockings for Hen. Smith.

Serjeant Willes's two kilderkins of B. cost 7.4.4, at 7*d.* the pound. If you have more peas and beef than you need, you may send back some.

If you write into England, send your letters by the first return, and I shall convey them.

I have taken order with Mr. Coggeshall for Mr. Oldham, &c.

To my very loving Son, Mr. WINTHROP, *Governour of the new Plantation upon Connecticut, d'd.*

A 61.

Dear in my thoughts,

I BLUSH to think how much I have neglected the opportunity of presenting my love to you. Sad thoughts possess my spirits, and I cannot repulse them; which makes me unfit for any thing, wondering what the Lord means by all these troubles among us. Sure I am, that all shall work to the best to them that love God, or rather are loved of him. I know he will bring light out of obscurity, and make his righteousness shine forth as clear as the noon day. Yet I find in myself an adverse spirit, and a trembling heart, not so willing to submit to the will of God as I desire. There is a time to plant, and a time to pull up that which is planted, which I could desire might not be yet. But the Lord knoweth what is best, and his will be done. But I will write no more. Hoping to see thee tomorrow, my best affections being commended to yourself, the rest of our friends at Newton, I commit thee to God.

Your loving wife,
MARGARET WINTHROP.

Sad BOSTON, 1637.

[Probably May, or other session of the general court, or at the synod.]

To her honoured Husband,
these be delivered.

A 62.

My good Son,

I RECEIVED your letter, and do heartily rejoice and bless the Lord for his merciful providence towards us all, in delivering your wife from so great a danger. The Lord make us truly thankful. And I hope it will teach my daughter and other women to take heed of putting pins in the mouth, which was never seasonable to be fed with such morsels. I can write you no news, only we had letters from Conectacott, where they were shut up with snow above a month since, and we at Boston were almost ready to break up for want of wood, but that it pleased the Lord to open the bay, (which was so frozen as men went over it in all places,) and mitigate the rigour of the season; blessed be his name. On Friday was fortnight, a pinnace was cast away upon Long Island by Natascott, and Mr. Babbe and others, who were in her, came home upon the ice. We have had one man frozen to death, and some others have lost their fingers and toes. Seven men were carried out to sea in a little, rotten skiff, and kept there twenty-four hours, without food or fire, and at last gat to Pullen Point.

We have appointed the general court the 12 of the 1 month. We shall expect you here before the court of assistants. So, with all hearty salutations from myself and your mother to yourself and wife, and little Betty, and all our good friends with you, I commend you to the blessing of the Lord, and rest

Your loving father,

JO. W.

I send you herein the warrant for Ipswich and Newbury. Commend me to your brother and sister Dudley.

XI*th*, 22, 1637.

To his very loving Son, Mr. JOHN WINTHROP, *at Ipswich, d'd.*

A 63.

Son,

I RECEIVED your letter, and do bless the Lord for your recovery and the welfare of your family. You must be very careful of taking cold about the loins; and, when the ground is open, I will send you some pepper-wort roots. For the flux, there is no better medicine than the cup used two or three times, and, in case of sudden torments, a clyster of a quart of water boiled to a pint, which, with the quantity of two or three nutmegs of saltpetre boiled in it, will give present ease.

For the pills, they are made of grated pepper, made up with turpentine, very stiff, and some flour withal; and four or five taken fasting, and fast two hours after. But, if there be any fever with the flux, this must not be used till the fever be removed by the cup. This bearer is in great haste, and so am I. So, with our blessing to you and yours, and salutations to all, &c. I rest

Your loving father,

JO. WINTHROP.

This bearer can tell you all the news, which is come from England by the fishing ships, &c.

To my loving Son, Mr. JOHN WINTHROP, *at Ipswich.*
Salutem tibi tuæque plurimam in Christo Jesu.
JOHN WILSON.

A 64.

My dear Wife,

WHEN my brother Stephen went hence, I was not up, nor well, so that I could not write to thee. I thank God I am now much better than I was when he left me. Though I much desire to enjoy thy company, yet I would not have thee cross thy intentions, in staying till that time be past. I hoped to fetch thee home myself, but am yet prevented.

I can get no garden enclosed nor digged; but I hear, that, in new ground, it is best to begin when the weeds are sprung up; for then they will be all killed and grow no more that year. Put my brother Stephen in mind to send me my carbine, as he promised me. So, with my best affections and love to thee, I commend thee to the Lord, and rest

Thine, in my best affections,

J. WINTHROP.

From the Salt House, Monday Morning.

My duty to my mother; my love to my brothers and all friends; forget not. My blessing to Betty and Fitz.

My brother Stephen hath promised to bring thee home, when thou comest.

To my dear Wife, Mrs. ELIZABETH WINTHROP, *at Boston.*

[Written not probably after the death of his father, though he is not mentioned, but not later than 1645, for in that year Stephen went to England, whence he came not back, before John went to Pequod. It can hardly be doubted, that it was written in May, 1638 or 1639, before the birth of any other children than Betty and Fitz.]

B.

The Accompt of John Winthrop, Esq. late Governour.

WHEREAS, by order of the last general court, commissioners were appointed, viz. Roger Ludlow, Esq. the deputy governour, and Mr. Israel Stoughton, gent. to receive my accompt of such things as I have received and disbursed for publick use in the time of my government; in all due observance and submission to the order of the said court, I do make this declaratory accompt ensuing:

First, I affirm, that I never received any moneys or other goods committed to me in trust for the commonwealth, otherwise than is hereafter expressed.

Item, I acknowledge I have in my custody certain barrels of common powder, and some match and drumheads, with some things belonging to the ordnance; which powder, being landed at Charlestown, and exposed to the injury of the weather, I took and bestowed first in a tent, which I made of mine own broadcloth, (being then worth eight shillings the yard, but in that service much spoiled.) After, I removed it to my storehouse at Boston, where it still remains, save that some of it hath been spent in publick service, and five barrels delivered to Dorchester, and four to Roxbury, and three barrels I sold to some ships that needed them, which I will allow powder or money for. The rest I am ready to deliver up to such as shall be appointed to receive them. I received also some meal and peas, from Mr. White of Dorchester in England, and from Mr. Roe of London, which was bestowed upon such as had need thereof in the several towns ; as also £10 given by Mr. Thomson. I received also from Mr. Humfrey, some rugs, frieze suits, shoes and hose, (the certain value whereof I must know from himself,) with letters of direction to make use of the greatest part thereof, as given to help bear out my charge for the publick. I paid for the freight of these goods, and disposed of the greatest part of them to others; but how, I cannot set down. I made use, also, of two pair of carriage wheels, which I will allow for: I had not meddled with them, but that they lay useless for want of the carriages, which were left in England. For my disbursements, I have formerly delivered to the now deputy a bill of part of them, amounting to near £300, which I disbursed for publick services divers years since, for which I have received in corn, at six shillings the bushel, (and which will not yield me above four shillings,) about £180, or near so much. I disbursed also for the transportation of Mr. Phillips his family, which was to be borne by the government till he should be chosen to some particular congregation.

Now, for my other charges, by occasion of my place of governour, it is well known I have expended much, and somewhat I have received towards it, which I should have rested satisfied with, but that, being called to accompt, I must mention my disbursements with my receipts, and, in both, shall refer myself to the pleasure of the court.

I was first chosen to be governour without my seeking or expectation, (there being then divers other gent. who, for their abilities every way, were far more fit.) Being chosen, I furnished myself with servants and provisions accordingly, in a far greater proportion than I would have done, had I come as a private man, or as an assistant only. In this office I continued four years and near an half, although I earnestly desired, at every election, to have been freed. In this time, I have spent above £500 per annum, of which £200 per annum would have maintained my family in a private condition. So as I may truly say, I have spent, by occasion of my late office, above £1200. Towards this I have received, by way of benevolence, from some towns, about £50, and, by the last year's allowance, £150, and, by some provisions sent by Mr. Humfrey, as is before mentioned, about £50, or, it may be, somewhat more.

I also disbursed, at our coming away, in England, for powder and great shot, £216, which I did not put into my bill of charges formerly delivered to the now deputy, because I did expect to have paid myself out of that part of Mr. Johnson's estate, which he gave to the publick; but, finding that it will fall far short, I must put it to this accompt.

The last thing, which I offer to the consideration of the court, is, that my long continuance in the said office hath put me into such a way of unavoidable charge, as will be still as chargeable to me as the place of governour will be to some others. In all these things, I refer myself to the wisdom and justice of the court, with this protestation, that it repenteth me not of my cost or labour bestowed in the service of this commonwealth; but do heartily bless the Lord our God, that he hath pleased to honour me so far as to call for any thing he hath bestowed upon me for the service of his church and people here, the prosperity whereof, and his gracious acceptance, shall be an abundant recompense to me. I conclude with this one request, (which in justice may not be denied me,) that, as it stands upon record, that, upon the discharge of my office, I was called to accompt, so this my declaration may be recorded also; lest hereafter, when I shall be forgotten, some blemish may lie upon my posterity, when there shall be nothing to clear it, &c.

JOHN WINTHROP.

September 4*th*, 1634.

[The foregoing was copied for me by direction of Alden Bradford, Esq. then secretary of the commonwealth. It is extremely interesting to observe the diffidence of the author, and his prudence in guarding from imputations, *when he should be forgotten*, against his posterity. No distinct reference can be found, in the text of the History, to the circumstances, by which I could have been justified in denoting the place of this document in the Appendix.]

C. Page 170.

Dear Friends,

Whereas there is a patent granted to certain persons of quality (friends to New England) of the River of Connecticut, with the places adjoining, together with liberties and prerogatives as in such cases are usual, so that, by virtue thereof, they conceive they have full power, right and authority to govern and dispose of all persons and affairs that shall fall within the circuit and limits of the said grant; it is therefore conceived requisite, by the agents of the said patentees now present in New England, to lay forth the claims and rights of the said personages to such as here in New England it may concern, to the end, if any thoughts or designs of others have been heretofore, or may be hereafter prejudicial or injurious to the right or possessions of the said patentees, they may so far take notice of the same, as, whatever hath happened in the bypast, or may befall for the future, any way derogating from the former claims, may seasonably meet with a loving and friendly prevention; at least, every one that seems to be interested herein may declare and give reasons of their titles and pretensions thereto, that so, in so weighty an enterprise, the business may be carried an end with order, justice, peace, and joint power and strength for the accomplishing of the same, and fruition of it with blessing and love.

Upon consideration of the premises, we conceive, that the present face of affairs of Connecticut, as it now appears, will admit or require a punctual and plain answer to these necessary queries from the towns, that are lately removed from the Massachusetts Bay to take up plantation within the limits of the foresaid patent.

Imprimis, whether they do acknowledge the rights and claims of the said persons of quality, and in testimony thereof will and do submit to the counsel and direction of their present governour, Mr. John Winthrop the younger, established by commission from them in those parts.

Secondly, under what right and pretence they have lately taken up their plantations within the precincts forementioned, and what government they intend to live under, because the said country is out of the claim of the Massachusetts patent.

Item, what answer and reasons we may return to the said patentees, if the said towns intend to intrench upon their rights and privileges, and justify the same.

These things we tender to you as our truly respected brethren, and do desire you earnestly to take them into your serious and Christian consideration, with as much secrecy as may be, so that we may receive your speedy and loving resolutions, that, by the present opportunities, which now present themselves for returning your answers into England, we discharge our trust, which we have lately been put in mind of. And thus we commend you to the guidance and protection of our good God, and remain

Your loving friends,

H. VANE, Jun.
JOHN WINTHROP.
HUGH PETER.

To our loving and much respected Friends, Mr. Ludlow, Mr. Maverick, Mr. Newberry, Mr. Stoughton, *and the rest of our Friends engaged in the business of Connecticut Plantations in the Town of Dorchester*, *d'd.*

D. Page 235.

Sir,

Yours by Robinson we have received, and careful we shall be (I trust) to observe your instructions, and to hasten home as fast as the cause will permit. We are now in a readiness for Block Island; only we wait for a fair wind. We are informed of many Indians there; so we expect the toughest work we have yet met. But we are assured our cause is good, and so we commend ourselves to God's mercy and power. By reason you sent for Mr. Wilson to come with Mr. Hooker, we being willing to show our loyalty to you, and love to the common cause, we have, without gainsaying, dismissed him, albeit we conceived we had special interest in him, and count ourselves naked without him, and therefore expect supply, if we be required to abide by it. Upon consideration that Mr. Wilson going along in the vessel to Connecticut might the more engage Mr. Hooker and expedite his journey to you, and for that, being to go to Block Island, we could enjoy him but one Sabbath more, we dismissed him at first view of your letter.

We do thankfully acknowledge your care and tenderness toward us, signified by your writings, and sending my provisions, &c. and desire we may deserve it. *For* the hardship you conceive you put us to, and pity us for, for my part, what I endure is so *little thought of*, that it is not worthy pity, neither doth it trouble me, and therefore I desire it may trouble none of my friends. It is what I have been acquainted with in part before; and if I be never more put to it for God's cause sake, it is much less than I have expected. Whiles we *enjoy* part in what is there to be had, I hope we shall be satisfied.

We hear not of Miantonimo, nor any of the Narrigansets nor Nianticks that were with you, concerning the Pequids they have, or any thing else, albeit we have sent for Miantonimo to come to us. The last day of the week, (being to go to Block Island, and) wanting a guide, we sent Tho. Stanton and twenty men, with Lieut. How, towards the Narragansets to get one, who found divers people in Pequid corn, and desired speech with some of them, but by no means could not obtain it, for they ran all away. Still they endeavoured after it, and to know the reason of their running, especially seeing we had formerly expressly told them, they must not use that, for we should then take them for Pequids. At length, they told, that Englishmen had some of them in prison in the bay, and they knew not what Englishmen meant towards them. But we were also told by a squaw, that they were mixt, Pequids and Narragansets together; *and were besides* signs of two rendezvous; she said, one was the Pequids. So, there being twenty *canoes*, ours brought two away, with one kettle and beans, that were at the Pequids' rendezvous, but told them, let them come hither, and, if they were Narragansets, they should have all without any damage.

We conceive you do well, in keeping them to strict, just terms, as also in that you refer them to us in the matters specified; for we conceive, being in the field, with our swords in our hands, we shall do better with them than when the sword is sheathed, and all peace.

Concerning Pequids harboured by them, we have thoughts (after return from Block Island) to require every one of them from those that have them, for these reasons:

1. Their flying to them is no submission to us, but of purpose to avoid it; so that they bear the same good will to us as formerly;

that is, they stand enemies, only use the Narragansetts and others as their covering.

2. Standing thus, we can expect no other but that they will do us mischiefs as opportunity serves; and, besides, be as spurs to the Narragansetts to provoke them to it, and as captains to aid and strengthen them in it, when, &c.

3. Under the vizor of a Narragansett, they will come amongst us, and do us mischiefs.

4. And when a mischief is done, then it will be fathered upon some renegado Pecot, that will have no master to own him; but it will be said, such a one did it, or such a one, &c.

Therefore, if they will not deliver all to us, according to their covenant, we cannot think their intentions to be good toward us, and shall accordingly declare ourselves towards them; though we will not *so* use like faith with them, but first advise with you, unless we be constrained. And if God do harden their hearts, I doubt not but it will be to their perdition. Only I pray for the contrary, if it be the Lord's will.

For Wequash, we fear he is killed; and if he be, 'tis a mere wicked plot, and, seeing he showed faithfulness to us, and for it is so rewarded, it is hard measure to us-ward; and what is meet to be done therein, is difficult to me to conclude; I shall therefore desire your speedy advice.

After return from Block Island, we shall fall upon destroying corn. Near to us it fails much by the weeds, and far from us it will do us little good. The Naragansetts do gather beans in abundance, and we are silent at it; yet, if they should turn enemy, it would be to our great damage. But my opinion is, that they will be twice advised before they will fall out *with us*. Only they will let us bear their injuries as long as we will, and, if they see us in good earnest, I believe they will think upon it, especially whiles the terrour of our sword and our God's doings is upon them.

There be many Pequids yet living, and such as will do much mischief. It will be found therefore necessary for one pinnace, one shallop, and some sixty men, to abide here to take opportunities, partly at Long Island, and elsewhere upon the coasts, (for they lie mostly upon the coast, except such as are under the wing of other Indians.) Else I see not many need stay. For, for this place, it is scarce worthy much cost. As for plantation, here is no meadow I see or hear of near; the upland good, but rocky and unfit for ploughs for the most part. Indeed, were there no better, 'twere worthy the best of us, the upland being, as I judge, stronger land than the bay upland.

But if you would enlarge the state, and provide for the poor servants of Christ, that are yet unprovided, (which I esteem a worthy work,) I must speak my conscience. I confess the place and places whither God's providence carried us, that is, to Quillipeage River, and so beyond to the Dutch, is before this, or the bay either, (so far as I can judge,) abundantly. But unless great necessity, or approved policy, require such undertakings, I would be loath to have a hand in, or that my pen should further them, for I affect not scattering, but would rather part stakes at home; yet, so far as it may tend to publick utility, and the enlargement of Christ's kingdom, I hope I should not hinder so good a work, though it be to self's disadvantage. It seems to me, God hath much people to bring hither, and the place is too strait, most think. And if so, then, considering, 1st, the goodness of the land, 2d, the fairness of the title, 3d, the neighbourhood of Connecticut, 4th, the good access that may be thereto, wherein it is before Connecticut, even in the three forementioned considerations, (for the land Connecticut men so judge,) and, 5th, that an ill neighbour may possess it, if a good do not,—I should readily give it my good word, if any good souls have a good liking to it.

I am willing, for my own particular, to stay here so long as yourself and the council, or general court, shall see just cause to require me. Yet I also am as willing to be at home so soon as it may be permitted; and, for my part, when some few things more are over, I see nothing against but that I may come home, and therefore shall wait to know your minds therein.

Thus, with my due respect remembered to yourself, *the honoured council,* and the rest of the magistrates, desiring your prayers, I humbly *commend* you to God.

Yours, as in duty I am bound,
ISRAEL STOUGHTON.

From PEQUID, *the 2d day of the 6th week of our warfare.*

To his much honoured in the Lord, the Governour and Council of the Massachusetts, these present.

[This was probably written 14 August, 1637. They reached home 26th.]

E. Page 245.

[*Remonstrance or Petition by Members of Boston Church, in favour of Wheelwright, March,* 1637. *Copied from the Book of their Antagonist, Thomas Welde, pp.* 23—5.]

WE, whose names are underwritten, have diligently observed this honoured court's proceedings against our dear and reverend brother in Christ, Mr. Wheelwright, now under censure of the court for the truth of Christ. We do humbly beseech this honourable court to accept this remonstrance or petition of ours, in all due submission tendered to your worships.

For, first, whereas our beloved brother, Mr. Wheelwright, is censured for contempt by the greater part of this honoured court, we desire your worships to consider the sincere intention of our brother to promote your end in the day of fast; for whereas we do perceive your principal intention the day of fast looked chiefly at the publick peace of the churches, our reverend brother did, to his best strength, and as the Lord assisted him, labour to promote your end, and therefore endeavoured to draw us nearer unto Christ, the head of our union, that so we might be established in peace, which we conceive to be the true way, sanctified of God, to obtain your end, and therefore deserves no such censure, as we conceive.

Secondly, whereas our dear brother is censured of sedition, we beseech your worships to consider, that either the person condemned must be culpable of some seditious fact, or his doctrine must be seditious, or must breed sedition in the hearts of his hearers, or else we know not upon what grounds he should be censured. Now, to the first, we have not heard any that have witnessed against our brother for any seditious fact. Secondly, neither was the doctrine itself, being no other but the very expressions of the Holy Ghost himself, and therefore cannot justly be branded with sedition. Thirdly, if you look at the effects of his doctrine upon the hearers, it hath not stirred up sedition in us, not so much as by accident; we have not drawn the sword, as sometimes Peter did, rashly, neither have we rescued our innocent brother, as sometimes the Israelites did Jonathan, and yet they did not seditiously. The covenant of free grace held forth by our brother hath taught us rather to become humble suppliants to your worships; and, if we should not prevail, we would rather with patience give our cheeks to the smiters. Since, therefore, the teacher, the doctrine and the hearers be most free from sedition, (as we conceive,) we humbly beseech you, in the name of the Lord Jesus Christ, your Judge and ours, and for the honour of this court and the proceedings thereof, that you will be pleased either to make it appear to us, and to all the world, to whom the knowledge of all these things will come, wherein the sedition lies, or else acquit our brother of such a censure.

Farther, we beseech you, remember the old method of Satan, the ancient enemy of free grace, in all ages of the churches, who hath raised up such calumnies against the faithful prophets of God. Elijah was called the troubler of Israel, 1 Kings, 18. 17, 18. Amos was charged for conspiracy, Amos 7. 10. Paul was counted a pestilent fellow, or mover of sedition, and a ringleader of a sect, Acts 24. 5; and Christ himself, as well as Paul, was charged to be a teacher of new doctrine, Mark 1. 27. Acts 17. 19. Now, we beseech you, consider, whether that old Serpent work not after his old method, even in our days.

Farther, we beseech you, consider the danger of meddling against the prophets of God, Psalm 105. 14, 15; for what ye do unto them the Lord Jesus takes as done unto himself. If you hurt any of his members, the head is very sensible of it; for so saith the Lord of

Hosts, He that toucheth you toucheth the apple of mine eye, Zech. 2. 8. And better a millstone were hanged about our necks, and that we were cast into the sea, than that we should offend any of these little ones, which believe on him, Matt. 18. 6.

And, lastly, we beseech you consider, how you should stand in relation to us, as nursing fathers, which gives us encouragement to promote our humble requests to you, or else we would say with the prophet, Isa. 22. 4, Look from me, that I may weep bitterly; Labour not to comfort me, &c.; or as Jer. 9. 2, Oh that I had in the wilderness a lodging place of a way-faring man!—And thus have we made known our griefs and desires to your worships, and leave them upon record with the Lord and with you, knowing that, if we should receive repulse from you, with the Lord we shall find grace.

F.

Beloved Brethren,

I MET lately with the remonstrance subscribed by yourselves with others. I must confess I saw it once before, but had not then time to read it advisedly, as now I have. I hope soon (by God's assistance) to make it appear, what wrong hath been done to the court, yea, and to the truth itself, by your rash, unwarranted and seditious delinquency. In the mean time, I thought fit to advertise you of some miscarriages therein; and though your countenancing of others in the like practice leaves me small hope, that you will hearken to my counsel in this, yet, in discharge of my duty and brotherly respect towards you, I have given this attempt, and shall leave the success to God.

1. In this you have broke the ends of your calling, that you did publish such a writing, when you were no members of the court.

2. In that you tax the court with injustice.

3. In that you affirm, that all the acts of that major part of that court are void, whereby you go about to overthrow the foundation of our commonwealth and the peace thereof, by turning all our magistrates out of office, and by nullifying all our laws.

4. In that you invite the body of the people to join with you in your seditious attempt against the court and the authority here established, against the rule of the apostle, who requires every soul to be subject to the higher powers, and every Christian man to study to be quiet and to meddle with his own business.

I earnestly desire you to consider seriously of these things, and if it please the Lord to open your eyes to see your failings, it will be much joy to me, and (I doubt not but) the court will be very ready to pass them by, and accept of your submission, and it may be a means of a further and firm reconciliation; which the Lord grant, and in his good time effect. So I rest

Your loving brother,

J. W.

XI*th*, 15, 1637.

To my worthy Friends and beloved Brethren, Mr. Coddington, Mr. Coggeshall, *and* Mr. Colburn.

[No reference is made in my notes to this document, because no fit place was afforded by the text. The exasperation of the controversy did not, as usual, turn to gall Winthrop's gentleness of temper, though it seems to me to have had an injurious influence on his judgment.]

G. Page 260.

It may please the worthy and much honoured governour, deputy, and assistants, and, with them, the present court, to take knowledge, that our desire of staying within this patent was real and strong, if the eye of God's providence (to whom we have committed our ways, especially in so important an enterprise as this, which, we confess, is far above our capacities) had guided us to a place convenient for our families and for our friends. Which, as our words have often expressed, so, we hope, the truth thereof is sufficiently declared by our almost nine months' patient waiting in expectation of some opportunity to be offered us, for that end, to our great charge and hindrance many ways. In all which time we have, in many prayers, commended the guidance of our apprehensions, judgments, spirits, resolutions and ways into the good hand of the only wise God, whose prerogative it is to determine the bounds of our habitations, according to the ends for which he hath brought us into these countries; and we have considered, as we were able, by his help, whatsoever place hath been propounded to us, being ready to have, with contentment, accepted (if by our stay any publick good might be promoved) smaller accommodations, and upon dearer terms (if they might be moderately commodious) than, we believe, most men, in the same case with us, in all respects, would have done. And whereas a place for an inland plantation, beyond Watertown, was propounded to us, and pressed with much importunity by some, whose words have the power of a law with us, in any way of God, we did speedily and seriously deliberate thereupon, it being the subject of the greatest part of a day's discourse. The conclusion was, that, if the upland should answer the meadow ground in goodness and desirableness, (whereof yet there is some ground of doubting,) yet, considering that a boat cannot pass from the bay thither, nearer than eight or ten miles distance, and that it is so remote from the bay, and from any town, we could not see how our dwelling there would be advantageous to these plantations, or compatible with our conditions, or commodious for our families, or for our friends. Nor can we satisfy ourselves, that it is expedient for ourselves, or for our friends, that we choose such a condition, wherein we must be compelled to have our dwelling houses so far distant from our farms as Boston or Charlestown is from that place, few of our friends being able to bear the charge thereof, (whose cases, nevertheless, we are bound to consider,) and some of them, that are able, not being persuaded that it is lawful for them to live continually from the greatest part of their families, as, in this case, they would be necessitated to do. The season of the year, and other weighty considerations, compelled us to hasten to a full and final conclusion, which we are, at last, come unto, by God's appointment and direction, we hope, in mercy, and have sent letters to Connectacutt for a speedy transacting the purchase of the parts about Quillypieck from the natives, which may pretend title thereunto. By which act we are absolutely and irrevocably engaged that way; and we are persuaded, that God will order it for good unto these plantations, whose love so abundantly, above our deserts or expectations, expressed in your desire of our abode in these parts, as we shall ever retain in thankful memory, so we shall account ourselves thereby obliged to be any way instrumental and serviceable for the common good of these plantations as well as of those, which the divine providence hath combined together in as strong a bond of brotherly affection, by the sameness of their condition, as Joab and Abishai were, whose several armies did mutually strengthen them both against several enemies, 2 Sam. 10. 9, 10, 11, or rather they are joined together, as Hippocrates his twins, to stand and fall, to grow and decay, to flourish and wither, to live and die, together. In witness of the premises, we subscribe our names,

JOHN DAVENPORTE.
THEOPH. EATON.

The 12th day of the 1st month, 1638.

To the much honoured, the Governour, Deputy and Assistants, &c.

H. Page 290.

Authenticity of the Deed *of four Indian Sagamores to Rev. John Wheelwright and others,* 17 *May,* 1629.

Before the 13th June, 1820, I had no more suspicion of the truth of the deed to Wheelwright and four others, of 17 May, 1629, which is the first article of Appendix in Belknap's N. H., I. and may also be seen in Hazard, I. 271—274, than of the charter of 4 March, 1628—9, for the colony of Massachusetts Bay, or of any other undisputed document. On that day, casually perusing Gov. Winthrop's

History, page 172 of the first edition, after having twice, in former years, collated the whole with the original MS. without perceiving any inconsistency with an instrument, that indeed had no necessary connexion with my text, I was struck with the improbability, that Wheelwright and his associates, in 1639, should not have mentioned their *ancient* title, when so severely censured by their former brethren of Massachusetts for *now* "dealing with an Indian there, and buying Winicowet." See page 290 of this volume.

To remove or confirm my doubts, I considered immediately several circumstances, and on the same day wrote for advice to N. A. Haven, jun. Esq. of Portsmouth, competent counsel in such a cause. To aid him in supplying an early answer on some suspicious points, I mentioned, 1. The wretched argument of Cotton Mather, the first article of Appendix in Belknap's N. H., III. 2. The names of the grantees, not generally known, except Wheelwright, who did not probably come over till seven years after, and Wentworth, who was probably too young. 3. The absence of Samuel Sharp, on the ocean, just parted from England, when he is made witness to the signing of the deed. 4. The seven witnesses of delivery of possession, on the same day with execution, not one of whom witnessed the signing; and the doubts raised in 1707, when the handwriting of several, perhaps of all, these seven, could so easily be proved. 5. The argument from History of Winthrop, which seemed irrefragable. I asked, if the original deed were visible, that my own eyes might judge, whether "it has almost as many marks of 1629 as there be years in the number," which was the authoritative declaration of Mather, without seeing the instrument, probably from the overbearing impulse of a celestial vision. My further question was, "When was it last seen? or heard of?" In conclusion, I begged him to inquire of Hon. Jeremiah Mason, or any other competent person, and to answer every particular.

Mr. Haven replied, 20 July, 1820, "I cannot better answer your letter of June 13, than by enclosing a communication from Mr. Nathaniel Adams, to which it gave occasion. Mr. Adams procured for Belknap the copy of Wheelwright's deed, which had been filed among the records of the superiour court in 1707, in the case of Allen vs. Waldron. The papers in this case he examined a few years ago, but afterwards mislaid them in the office. They are not now on the regular files. He remembers, that Dr. Belknap inquired in vain for the original deed. If it exist at all, it must be among the heirs of Wheelwright, their executors, administrators, or assigns,—

"Ignari hominumque locorumque,
Erramus."

The communication of Mr. Adams follows:

"Portsmouth, *July 3d,* 1820.

"My dear Sir,

"I have read with some attention Mr. Savage's letter upon the Indian deed to Wheelwright, as well as the deed itself in the Appendix to Belknap's New Hampshire, vol. I. and cannot discover the many suspicious circumstances, with which Mr. Savage thinks it 'pregnant;' and as he is methodical in pointing out his objections, I will pursue the same order in answering them.

"First, with respect to the grantees, three of whom, he says, are unknown in his researches. It appears from the Records of Exeter, that, in the year 1639, soon after the settlement of the town, the brethren of the church there, and the other inhabitants, made a combination, as they called it, or form of government, which was signed by all the inhabitants, and the names of all the grantees in the deed are amongst them. When they came to this country does not appear. William Wentworth was one of the first settlers in Exeter, and continued there as long as their combination lasted, and then removed to Dover. He assisted in defending Heard's garrison in 1689. If he was born 1609, he was twenty years old at the time of executing the deed, eighty at the attack on Heard's, and eighty-eight when he died. His mode of securing the gate at Heard's did not require more muscular strength than many men of that age possess. I see nothing improbable in his being one of the grantees, on account of his age.

"That Wheelwright was not in this country till 1636, is a mistake; for Neal and Wiggin, in a letter to John Mason, Esq. dated August 13th, 1633, say, 'We have treated with a gentleman, who has purchased a trackt of land of the Indians at Squamscott Falls—the gentleman's name being Wheelwright.' Belknap, vol. I. Appendix, No. 6. If Mrs. Pierson's account is correct, that Mr. Wheelwright came over, *with his family*, in the same ship with Samuel Whiting, in 1636, then, as Cotton Mather says, 'he might step over hither to see how the land lay before his transportation of his family.' Belknap, vol. III. Appendix, No. 1.

"2d. Concerning the two English witnesses, Oldham and Sharp. It is acknowledged, that Oldham was in the country at the time, and was not killed till seven years afterwards. But Mr. Savage says, 'that Sharp was, that very day, on the ocean, just parted from England in company with Higginson,' and refers to Prince's N. E. Chronology, I. 185. Prince does not any where assert, that Sharp came over with Higginson. He says that, on the 30th of April, 1629, at a general court of the Massachusetts company in London, it was ordered, 'that thirteen in their plantation shall have the sole ordering of the affairs and government there, by the name of the Governour and Council of London's Plantation in the Massachusetts Bay in New England.' And, at the same court, Sharp was elected a member of this council; but it does not follow, that he was then in England. Endicott was, at the same time, elected governour, although he was in Massachusetts; for he came over in 1628, as appears from Prince's N. E. Chronology, 174; and, as others were sent over with him to begin a plantation, probably Sharp was one of them.

"3d. As to the witnesses to the delivery of possession. This, in my mind, is a corroborative circumstance of the authenticity of the deed. The grantees, desirous of having every thing conducted in the most fair and open manner, procured not only two very respectable witnesses to the execution of the deed, but seven of the first characters in the neighbouring plantations to witness the transaction, and to endorse on the deed the delivery of the possession, which they supposed equivalent to the endorsement of livery of seizin in England. Three of these very witnesses, four years afterwards, recognize the deed in question, as appears by Belknap, I., Appendix, No. 6, above referred to; and two of them were directly interested in the suppression of it, if it had been a forgery.

"A copy of the deed, certified by Jos. Hammond, register of deeds for the county of York, was used in the trial of the cause Allen vs. Waldron, in the year 1707, although it was not recorded there until 1713. I cannot say why it was lodged in the register's office for the county of *York*, unless it was, because the heirs of Wheelwright lived in that county. After the record of the deed, his heirs took it into their possession; for, in the year 1720, the people, who settled at Londonderry, then called Nutfield, purchased of Col. Wheelwright of Wells his Indian right. The Rev. Mr. Macgregore, in his letter to Gov. Shute, says, 'His deed, being of ninety years standing, and conveyed from the chief sagamores between the Rivers Merrimack and Pascataqua, with the consent of the whole tribes of the Indian nation, and well executed, is the most authentick we have seen.' Belknap, III., Appendix, No. 4.

"I have not Gov. Winthrop's Journal; but as he did not arrive in this country until 12th June, 1630, it is not surprising, that he did not mention the transaction of Wheelwright's purchase, which took place fifteen months before, and especially as it did not relate to the society, over which he came to preside.

"I shall be gratified if the foregoing observations have any tendency to investigate the truth. If I am mistaken, receive with candour the attempt of

"Your friend,

"NATHANIEL ADAMS."

On 1 August, 1820, I replied, with much fuller evidence of the falsity of the deed, but not so full as shall be added to this article. Here the matter rested until 22 November, 1823, when appeared in the Portsmouth Journal an article, under the editor's head, giving several reasons for the opinion, that the deed "is, without doubt, a forgery." In the Historical Collections of New Hampshire, I. 299—304, is a defence of the instrument from the former governour of that state, which is here copied:

"*Remarks on the Authenticity of the Wheelwright Deed.*

"It has been recently affirmed, by a writer in one of our publick papers,[1] that this deed 'is, without doubt, a forgery.' The reasons

[1] Portsmouth Journal, November 22, 1823.

he assigns in support of this opinion are, that Wheelwright was not heard of in this country till 1636, seven years after the date of the deed; that Samuel Sharpe, one of the subscribing witnesses, was then on the ocean; that, of the seven witnesses to the delivery of possession, no one of them witnessed the execution of the deed, though made the same day; as some of these witnesses were officers and agents of Laconia, it is incredible they should have lent their names to an act destructive of their own title; that Wheelwright, in 1634, four years after the purchase from the Indians, claimed only about a mile square at Squamscott Falls; that, when Wheelwright and the other gentlemen at Exeter were censured, in 1639, by Massachusetts, for dealing with an Indian and buying Winnicomett, they made no mention of the grant from the four sagamores; that no trace of Augustine Story, Thomas Wite and Thomas Levitt is to be found in the history of Massachusetts or New Hampshire; that William Wentworth, one of the supposed grantees, died in 1697; if he was only twenty-one years old when the deed was executed, he must have been eighty-one when he performed the astonishing feat of strength, that Belknap records of him; and that the original deed cannot now be found.

"Though these reasons may merit consideration, they do not, in my opinion, prove that *the deed from the four sagamores is a forgery*. We have no evidence, that Wheelwright did not come to this country till the year 1636. Though he came *with his family* in that year to New England, he might, before that time, have visited and resided in it some time *without* his family, and that appears to be the opinion of one of our early historians, Dr. Cotton Mather, as is expressed in his letter of 1708 to Vaughan.[1] But we have more conclusive evidence to this point: Neale and Wiggin, who laid out the four first towns in New Hampshire, in their return to John Mason, of August 13, 1633, explicitly state the fact of Wheelwright's having previously purchased of the Indians a tract of land at Squamscott Falls, which, when settled, was to be called *Exeter*.[2]

"The second objection is, that Samuel Sharpe, one of the subscribing witnesses, was on the ocean the very day the deed is dated; and to prove this, the reader is referred to 1 Prince's N. E. Chronology, 185. But, in the passage referred to, there is no evidence that Sharpe was on the ocean that day any more than that John Endicott was, who in fact arrived in Massachusetts the preceding summer, and was then governour of that colony. All that Prince states is, that Endicott, on the 30th of April, 1629,[3] was, by the company in England, appointed governour of Massachusetts, and Sharpe a member of the council in that colony, and not that either of them were then in England, or on the ocean. There is, however, better and more conclusive authority than Prince. I will state the facts, though one of them favours the

1 "3 Belknap's N. H. Appendix, No. 1." 2 "Ditto, Appendix, No. 6."

3 "He and Sharpe were appointed at an earlier day, but probably sometime in that month."

writer upon the point under consideration. A letter from the council in England, dated April 17—21st, 1629, states, that, previous to its date, they had received a letter from Gov. Endicott, written by him in New England, dated September 13th, 1628; and that they [the council in England] had *re-appointed* him governour, and appointed Samuel Sharpe counsellor, &c. and that they then thought Sharpe, who had embarked for New England, was detained, by bad weather, on the coast of England.[1] But, what is of most importance, neither the letter last mentioned, Prince, or the writer in the Journal, afford any evidence that the Samuel Sharpe to whom they refer was the same man who appears as one of the subscribing witnesses. On the day that deed was executed, Samuel Sharpe, the counsellor, was probably on the ocean; but another man, of the same name, might then be in this country, and in fact subscribe as a witness. The writer appears to admit, that John Oldham, the other English subscribing witness, was then in this country; for he says he was murdered by the Indians in 1736.

"It is not objected to the witnesses of the delivery of possession, that they were not then in this country, but that it was incredible that some of them should be witnesses to a deed that was destructive of their own title. I can see nothing incredible or improper in Neale, Vaughan, and Gibbons, who were agents, and perhaps owners, under the Laconia company, subscribing as witnesses to an Indian chief's delivering possession of part of the tract which the company claimed. If they were present when possession was delivered, they must know it, and their certifying it in writing could not operate against them or their employers. Their act neither confirmed Wheelwright's title, or impaired that of the company. Four years after the execution of the deed, two of those witnesses, in their report to Mason, appear to consider Wheelwright's claim to the lands, or some part of them, as good.[2] But the writer, to evade the force of this fact, says, it was only about one mile square; and cites Winthrop's Journal, p. 172, to shew, that, when Massachusetts, in 1639, complained of Wheelwright and his associates for purchasing Winnicomett of the Indians, he did not then state his claim to the large tract conveyed by the deed of 1629. But what necessity was there for his doing it? If a man is required to defend his title to *one* tract of land, is he obliged to assert and vindicate his claim to *two?* According to Winthrop, the complaint of Massachusetts against Wheelwright was not on account of the purchase and settlement of Exeter, but Winnicomett, that is, Hampton. Wheelwright might, within four years from the execution of the first deed, be induced, from motives, which, after the lapse of near two centuries, we are unable to discover, to abandon his right to a great portion of the land described in the deed. We have reason to believe, he had neither the means to settle the whole, or support a controversy with Mason and others.

"Another objection to the authenticity of the deed is, that no trace of three of the grantees named in the deed, to wit, Augustine Story,

---

1 "Hazard's State Papers, 256—268." 2 "1 Belk. N.H. Appendix, No. 6."

Thomas Wite, and Thomas Levitt, can be found in the history of Massachusetts or New Hampshire, and that it is remarkable their names should never again occur. Whoever reads the deed must be convinced, that it was obtained by the labour and expense of Wheelwright, and not by those of his associates, and that possession of the premises was delivered to him, and not them. But it is not a fact that we hear no more of the associates; for, in the year 1639, an agreement was made by the settlers at Exeter, for the government of themselves and their concerns. This agreement is signed by thirty-five persons, of whom are John Wheelwright, William Wentworth, and *Thomas Levitt,* three of the five grantees; and, as to the other two, it is highly probable they also settled at Exeter, and signed the contract, but spelled their names different from what they were written in the deed, a circumstance that frequently occurs in the old documents relating to this country. In the deed, their names were written Augustine Story and Thomas Wite, but, in signing the agreement, Augustine Starr and Thomas Wright.[1] And the remark respecting William Wentworth, that, if he had been but twenty-one years of age at the time of the purchase in 1629, he must have been eighty-one when he performed the extraordinary feat of strength recorded in Belknap, does not appear to me to impair the authenticity of the Indian deed. In the first place, there is no evidence, that Wentworth, in 1629, was twenty-one years old, for though minors are not capable of giving, they are of receiving deeds. But, admitting he was of that age, the feat of strength, which Belknap states Wentworth performed in 1689, was not greater, if so great, as what he affirms was effected by Waldron, who, he says, was then 'advanced in life to the age of eighty years.'[2] History affords many instances of men, older than either of these, who performed greater feats of strength and activity.

"The last objection is, that the original deed has disappeared. Considering the long period of time, that has elapsed since it was given, and the number of generations, that have passed away, its preservation would have been more extraordinary than its loss. The deed itself was produced in court in 1707 and 1708, in the case of Allen vs. Waldron; it was on the ancient files in the county of York on the 28th of January, 1713, and was then recorded in the records of deeds in that county.

"There are many other considerations, which support the authenticity of the deed, but it appears unnecessary to state them. I will only add, that, if the deed was forged, Wheelwright must have been privy to it; but the goodness of his character repels the charge: and, if it was forged, it would be incredible, that a man of so much understanding and knowledge as he possessed, should select the names of the officers and agents of the company of Laconia as witnesses, who, of all others, were most interested in detecting and exposing the fraud.

"WILLIAM PLUMER."

---

1 "1 Hazard's State Papers, 463." 2 "1 Belknap's N. H. 248, 249."

My first remarks will be on the internal evidence.

1. No Indian deed, in my knowledge, and I have examined many, was ever drawn so long, formal and precise. Conveyances between the English were not, for a long space of years, artificially written on our side of the Atlantick. This deed was, it will be said, drawn by one of the grantees. But who could have done it in so clerklike length and beauty, more than a year before any lawyer, except Thomas Morton of Merry Mount, came to the country, and half a century before any lawyers here drew such solemn assurances?

2. The names of the sachems are suspicious. Passaconaway was, probably, not sagamore of Penecook alone, but of much more of the country, confined however to the Merrimack, certainly superiour lord of Pentucket; yet the deed appears to show an equality with him of Runnaawit, sagamore of Pentucket, and of the two others. There is, in 2 Hist. Coll. IV. 169, a *true* deed of Haverhill, 15 November, 1642, in which Passaquo and Saggahew, "with the consent of Passaconaway," sell Pentucket, and they, without their paramount, affix their marks. I know it may be objected, that, in this very instrument, the grantors describe "Passaconaway our chief sagamore;" but this is one of the strongest marks of fabrication. He was chief sagamore on the Merrimack, and Runnaawit, if there ever were such a person, sagamore of Pentucket, had therefore done well to express his fealty; but he was not chief of Squamscot, much less of Nuchawanuck, that ever I heard of, nor does it appear from any other paper. The force of this remark must not be evaded, by referring the fact of his superiority, acknowledged apparently by Wahangnonawitt and Rowls, only to the other grantor, because the payment, annually, from each township within the limits, of "one coat of trucking cloth," is reserved to the *chief* alone. Besides this objection, the names of all the other three sagamores are unknown in any other transaction. It may indeed be thought, that Rowls is an easy mistake of transcription for Knowles, who, it is known, was sachem of Nuchawanack, and, in 1643, granted to Humphrey Chadbourne lands still remaining in that family, and, in 1650, to Spencer. See Sullivan's Maine, 143. I have two partial answers to this fact: One, that, in these deeds, he takes no notice of his liege lord, Passaconaway; and the other, that it is probably an English adopted name. But this practice of taking our names was not, in 1629, used by the Indians. Who were the two other strange sachems?

3. In the preamble to the deed, the sachems are made to declare their inclination "to have the English inhabit amongst us, as they are amongst our countrymen in the Massachusetts Bay; by which means we hope, in time, to be strengthened against our enemy, the Tarateens, who yearly doth us damage." This is quite inconsistent with truth, but might readily be suggested to an Englishman of a later age, composing a fictitious document. The shore Indians expressed such fear to Plimouth people in 1621. The Tarrateens did, in 1631, *surprise* the Indians at Agawam on the sea-side; but what fear could the martial tribes of the upper Merrimack, of Squamscot, and of Nuchawanack, entertain of such *un-*

known enemies. The English settlements at Dover and Portsmouth, of six years standing, were their shields, if any could have been needed. Yet this instrument refers to the humble settlement of Massachusetts Bay, i. e. Salem, eight months old, where Higginson *afterwards* found about ten houses and one hundred settlers.

4. The grantees, five in number, "all of the Massachusetts Bay," are all unheard of for some years; yet, if the men, women and children at Salem amounted but to one hundred, and there were not, in which I am confident, half as many more in the bay, some one of these five names should have appeared in the governour and company's letters to Endecott, or in his to them. Especially does this apply to Wheelwright, in the deed called "late of England, a minister of the gospel." We know the ships, in which most of our principal fathers severally came, and the day of arrival of each. Remarkably is this verified of the early ministers, except Blackstone. He, we know, was not accordant with our Puritans; but Wheelwright was of the straitest sect. This reverend gentleman did not visit Plimouth or Salem in their destitute state, wanting the bread of life. Did he leap, with his associates, from the anchoring ground thirty miles into the country, without accepting congratulations of the settlers on the coast? and leap back from Squamscot to England, without a farewell to his friends, coming and going without being seen?

5. These four liberal sagamores "give, grant, bargain, sell, release, ratify and confirm unto J. W. &c. all that part of the main land bounded by the River of Piscataqua, and the River of Merimack, that is to say, to begin at Nuchawanack Falls in Piscataqua River aforesaid, and so down said river to the sea, and so alongst the seashore to Merimack River, and so up along said river to the falls at Pantucket aforesaid, and from said Pantucket Falls, upon a northwest line, twenty English miles into the woods, and from thence to run upon a straight line, north-east and south-west, till [it] meet with the main rivers, that runs down to Pantucket Falls and Nuchawanuck Falls; and the said rivers to be the bounds of the said lands from the thwart line, or head line, to the aforesaid falls, and the main channel of each river, from Pentucket and Nuchawanack Falls to the main sea, to be the side bounds, and the main sea, between Piscataqua River and Merimack River, to be the lower bounds, and the thwart or head line, that runs from river to river, to be the upper bounds; together with all islands within said bounds, as also the Isles of Shoals, so called by the English, together with all profits, advantages and appurtenances whatsoever, to the said tract of land belonging, or in any wise appertaining, reserving to ourselves liberty of making use of our old planting land, as also free liberty of hunting, fishing and fowling." Now it may seem, that, after such a grant in 1629, Passaconaway should not have *consented* to another sale of Pentucket in 1642, by sachems, who acknowledged his sovereignty. But a much stronger objection is, that, at the very time, and even six years before, according to the authentick history of the contemporary Gov. Winslow, settlements were made at Portsmouth

and Dover, which both continued without interruption, under the grants to Gorges, the whole of whose pretended rights, and those in actual enjoyment, on the sea between Merimack and Piscataqua, and up the river close to Nuchawanack, must be defeated by this deed. In view of all the foregoing particulars, one can hardly avoid the conclusion, that this deed, which, we may soon see reason to believe, was not made for more than seventy years after its assumed date, was made with a special reference to the grant of the president and council of New England to John Mason, 7 Nov. 1629, because its lines in the two rivers are the same, and the Indian deed is made to include Isles of Shoals, which were embraced (not indeed by name) in Mason's, and had not been in Gorges's grant. But the including those islands is a very strong objection to the deed. What possible claim of title could these inland Indians have to islands they never saw, or probably heard of? Wheelwright could not, as an *honest* man, which he assuredly was, take their grant of lands of great extent, of which the Hiltons and others at Dover, and the dwellers at Portsmouth, had long been in peaceable enjoyment; but he must have been as *foolish* as dishonest, to take in the isles of the ocean, to which the sagamore of Ipswich, or Squidrayset, beyond Saco, had much more reasonable claims than his supposed grantors.

6. Of the conditions, or provisoes, the bearing of most is to lessen the credibility of the instrument. The first, that "the said John Wheelwright shall, within *ten years* after the date hereof, set down with a company of English, and begin a plantation at Squamsquott Falls," looks more like accommodation of a pre-existent fact to a desired hypothesis, than a real bargain by children of the forest. Savages are not accustomed to postpone enjoyment or revenge. It looks cunning, but it defeats itself. The plantation did begin in ten years, but ought not to have been delayed as many months.—The second is of the same character. It was desirable, less than eighty years after, "that what other inhabitants shall come and live on said tract of land, from time to time, and at all times, shall have and enjoy the same benefits as the said Wheelwright." But what reason could the grantors have for imposing such a condition? Was not Wheelwright, like any other purchaser, to sell out parcels of his right?—The third is altogether foreign from any imaginable object of the Indians.—The fourth is still more so, and seems borrowed from a habit, that grew a few years after in the Massachusetts court in making grants. It has also a strong likeness to the erection of townships designed in a letter of Neal and Wiggin, more than four years after, which has been hastily thought to confirm this deed, which, in fact, it falsifies.—The fifth seems utterly destructive of the verity of the transaction. Why should the Indians require, that their grantees, "to avoid contentions amongst them," should be subject to "the government of the colony of the Massachusetts, their neighbours, and to observe their laws and orders until they have a settled government amongst themselves?" What can be more irreconcilable to us, who know the precise cir-

cumstances of the colony, then covering only a few acres at Salem? Why should orders by Capt. Endecott, who had not then his commission from the governour and company, extend to regions far beyond the bounds of the company's purchase of the preceding year, and confirmed by the charter a few weeks before this date? Is it not apparent, that the penman of this deed knew the subsequent assertion and exercise of jurisdiction, by Massachusetts, over that region, but had forgotten, or hoped others would forget, that it did not begin till twelve years after?—The sixth is idle repetition of the reservation in the premises. People, who could waste time in the wilderness for such forms, might as well have settled there at once, and would soon have learned better employment.—The seventh is divisible. The first member, providing, that each township should pay to Passaconaway and his successors forever "one coat of trucking cloth a year," "for an acknowledgment," seems indeed to show a reasonable object of the grantors' care, though, as before hinted, under the second head of these remarks, it leaves all but one without any such equivalent. But what should have led to the second member, "and also shall pay to Mr. John Wheelwright aforesaid, his heirs and successors forever, two bushels of Indian corn a year?" Why should the grantors have taken any care to enforce payment to their grantee by those, who purchased of him? It would be no difficult matter, if the deed had been true, to show payment of this yearly "coat of trucking cloth;" for the Indians were quite punctual, and always have been so, in asking for their annuities.

7. After the habendum et tenendum, with warranty, come the seals and signatures, with two Indian witnesses, whose names are as little known as those of two, at least, of the grantors. But the signing is the remarkable point. All the six marks are different, yet not one is an Indian mark. Those, who are conversant with the habits of the aborigines, in this particular, know their pride is exhibited by animal or other devices, on the same principle of human nature, that led civilized men to "the boast of heraldry," to put family or fancy arms and mottoes on their seals. It may be said, that exact copies of the marks should not be expected, because we have only copy, not original of the deed, given by Belknap, and that Hazard has not distinguished the marks. I should not insist much on this circumstance, more than on Hazard's omission of the signature of one of the grantors, but that the copy, in Belknap, which has six different marks, was "corrected by a copy on file, in the superiour court of New Hampshire, in the case of Allen vs. Waldron, which copy is attested by the" register of the original deed. Could any one have made for the supreme court a copy, without these *imposing* marks from the original?

8. Perhaps the strongest circumstance of intrinsick evidence is the attestation, on the *same* "day of May, one thousand six hundred twenty and nine, in the fifth year of our sovereign lord, Charles, king of England, Scotland, France and Ireland, defender of the faith," &c. by *seven* English gentlemen of reputation, five of whom were then *directly*, and the two others *indirectly*, as agents of

Gorges in another plantation, interested against the effect of said deed, that Wahangnonaway, sagamore of Squamsquott, "in behalf of himself and the other sagamores *then present*," did "deliver quiet and peaceable possession of all the lands mentioned in the within-written deed unto the within-named John Wheelwright," and that the deed "was signed, sealed, and delivered in our presence." Yet there are two other English, gentlemen of reputation also, witnesses to signing, sealing and delivering. Now, why did not the seven, or some of them, sign as witnesses to the first solemnity? Or why did not one or both of the witnesses to the first solemnity sign as witnesses to the last? Where was the deed executed? in the wilderness of Squamscot? or in the English settlements of Dover or Portsmouth? Wherever it was, it was all one transaction. All the nine English are made to say, they saw it signed, sealed and delivered; yet seven only witness delivery of possession, not one of whom sign in the proper place as witnesses of signing and sealing. All the sachems are said to be present at delivery of possession, as well as at execution of the deed; yet the two English witnesses of signing and sealing say nothing of possession. They were far from home, and might stay out the after ceremony as well as the others. It is usual at Indian treaties for all parties and witnesses to remain to the end of the solemnities, especially if they occupy but one day.

I now turn to the extrinsick evidence.

Mr. Adams says, the grantees were all here 4 October, 1639. This is to him satisfactory proof of the genuineness, to me of the falsity, of the instrument. There can be no doubt, that, if this deed be a forgery, the maker knew of Exeter combination by thirty-five persons at that time, as taken from their records by Hazard, I. 463; for his grantees' names are those of the *four first* signers with the thirty-first. But it is beyond credibility, that all five, there in October, 1639, were there, and no others, in May, 1629; for in no other instance, in the whole Atlantick coast of this union, will five men, on any spot at the *first* opening of the country, be found on the same spot ten years after. At Plimouth, *half* died in *three months.* Prince, I. 85, 86. At Salem, we know, there was much mortal sickness in Endecott's little company the first year, and worse the second, after Higginson's fleet of three ships increased the colony. A melancholy tale is told by Winthrop of his companions, in the letters, Appendix, A 47 and 49. Of our twelve first assistants in the summer of 1630, only five remained next spring, Johnson being dead in less than three months, Rossiter in less than four, Saltonstall, Coddington, Revell, T. Sharp and Vassall gone to England. Coddington and Vassall did indeed return to America; but the former, within the *fatal* ten years, had left Boston forever, to found a new state at Rhode Island; and Vassall could not even live in Massachusetts. Ludlow and Pynchon, too, were gone within ten years. Though the latter was within the jurisdiction, at Springfield, he was too remote to continue in office. So that nine out of twelve were missing in less than the same period that all our five grantees continue to enjoy life at Exeter.

But Mr. Adams supposes, that all the grantees were here in May, 1629, and that my proof of Wheelwright's coming in 1636, for the *first* time, is a mistake. He refers to Neal and Wiggin's letter to John Mason, 13 August, 1633, Belknap's N. H., I., Appendix, 6: "Because you would have four towns named as you desired, we have treated with a gentleman, who has purchased a tract of land of the Indians at Squamscut Falls, and your land running up to the said falls on one side of the river from the falls about a mile downward, said gentleman having a mind to said land on your side to a certain creek, and one mile backward from the river, which we agreed on, and the creek is called Wheelwright's, the gentleman's name being Wheelwright, and he was to name said plantation (when settled) Exeter." This letter is verified, seven days *after*, by Vines and Jocelyn. Now this letter, so far from supporting the deed, tends to its overthrow. 1. Because it refers to Mason's *recent* desire about four towns, yet the deed, four years before, contemplates division into townships. 2. The purchase was just then made; for in the letters of 24 June and 13 July, 1633, or any former letters of the agents to their principals, notice is not taken of it. 3. The purchase is of "a tract of land at Squamscut Falls," and "about a mile downward;" not the whole province between Merimack and Piscataqua, thirty or forty miles back, down to the sea, and Isles of Shoals. This Wheelwright was not, probably, our John, though it may have been his father, uncle, brother or cousin, here in the *summer of* 1633, after as many thousands of English had come over to New England as there were hundreds in the *spring of* 1629. I cannot believe his *character* would have been omitted in that letter, "late of England, a minister of the gospel," of course ordained by one of the bishops, friends of their employer. Mrs. Pierson, his daughter, "the more sensible and capable of the two" "very incompetent witnesses to determine the time of their father's *first* coming over into America," told Cotton Mather, "that her father's coming over with his family was in the same ship with Mr. Samuel Whiting the minister of Lynn, and others," and he adds of *them*, "who, we are all sure, came in 1636;" and that she never heard her father speak of visiting America before. Now I leave it to *judges* of probability, not to Mather, who, instead of weighing evidence, had not discretion enough to be trusted to wipe the scales, whether Wheelwright, who lived with his children for thirty-four years from 1636, can be presumed to have mentioned *particularly* his coming in 1636, when the country was comparatively thriving and well filled, and to have omitted the fact of his coming, in 1628, to a wilderness, which he saw, in his latter days, blossoming as the rose. I say 1628, not 1629, for no vessel in *this* year had yet brought over men to make a treaty with inland Indians. The *minute* information of the daughter was accurate. Whiting left England in April, arrived 26 May, says Mather's Life, in one of the "fifteen great ships," no doubt, mentioned by Winthrop, all in our harbour together. On 12 of June, little more than a fortnight after, our Church Records have "John Wheelwright and Mary his wife" admitted, Nos. 354, 5. In October after, he is mentioned in this History, as "a brother of Mrs. Hutchinson, one Mr. Wheelwright, a silenced minister sometimes in England." I should be pleased with a *probable* explanation of this clergyman's neglect, either to join some of our churches sooner, if he remained a few months after his purchase, or to bring over his family earlier than 1636, if, as the exquisite casuist suggests, "he had stepped over hither to see how the land lay, before his transportation of them." If he had gone back in 1629, why did he not return, if not before, at least, in the ship with his sister, Mrs. Hutchinson, and the Rev. Messieurs Lathrop and Symmes, with other good company, arriving September, 1634? See this History of that date, compared with Symmes's evidence in Hutchinson, II. 430 and 440.

Passing over, for the present, several other remarks of Mr. Adams, which will be amply answered hereafter, when the *trial of the witnesses* comes, I observe his difficulty about copy and original. "A copy was used in the trial of the cause in 1707," certified by the register, though the original was not recorded till 1713. Now, when we remember, that this cause was the cause involving every title in the province, why was not the original brought from the other side of the river, in York county? Why should the register, if the original was too precious to be trusted from one town to the next, postpone six years the recording of such a valuable instrument? How he could certify, except from his record, or how he could know the original, never heard of before, to be genuine, are questions of very little concern in that time, when the jury would believe any thing, and distinguish no more between copy and original, than if Mather had been their foreman. The power of the court was, of course, nothing.

The language of Macgregore and others, settlers of Londonderry, proves nothing but their innocence. They were not arrived till some years after the death of Allen, when this or any other forged deed, of ninety years old, became as good as a true one, nobody appearing to dispute, and every body asserting, its authenticity. The Col. Wheelwright, of whom they purchased, was probably grandson of our John; but grandson or son might believe the deed authentick. His right to grant may have been under the purchase of 1633, or that in 1639; but, if it were under neither, it is very clear, it could not be under the deed, of which his father knew no more than he did of my present argument. I am as well satisfied, that he was dead twenty-five years before that deed was made, as that he lived fifty years after its pretended date.

Mr. Adams wholly avoids or mistakes my argument about Gov. Winthrop's silence, which is not, that the governour said nothing about the transaction, "which took place fifteen months before" his arrival; but that Wheelwright and his associates, when, in March, 1638—9, complained of by our court for buying Winicowett of *an* Indian, knowing that we claimed and had taken possession of it, "by building an house there above *two* years since," said nothing about the transaction, did not triumphantly reply, We bought, *ten years* since, all the lands of *four* Indian sachems, from Merrimack to Piscataqua; we bought, last month, of this poor Indian, only his actual enjoyment of Winicowet, but from the sovereigns of the soil more than thirty times Winicowet, before one in seventy of your people came over the ocean. See page 290, and compare it with page 303. Who made the instrument, is not known to me. It was heard of first in 1707, but not in any of the former numerous trials of the same title. The counsel for defendant were John Pickering and Charles Story. Was Story an heir of the grantee of that name? On their side were court, witnesses, jury, and spectators, with their ears open to hear all the pathetick obtestations of the tenant for his cause and their own, and their eyes closed against any offensive sights of the adversary's strength, or their own weakness. For the honour of God's people, and their protection against the Egyptians, this imposition of a spurious deed, if known to a few, would seem no worse than perjury, which every lawsuit, involving such interests, furnishes like a hotbed.

In reply to the observations of Gov. Plumer, most of what is said above, in answer to Mr. Adams, will be equally pertinent; and very few remarks are necessary, before the following inquiries about the witnesses. Mr. Plumer's question, "If a man is required to defend his title to *one* tract of land, is he obliged to assert and vindicate his claim to *two?*" is very wide of the point. My complaint is, that he does *not* defend his title to *the one* tract, that is Winicowet, as he would naturally do, if this deed were in existence, by saying, Winicowet is in our great purchase ten years ago. The *elder* title, I say, would have been alleged. Again, Mr. Plumer says, "the deed itself was produced in court in 1707." Now this is contrary to Mr. Adams, who says, "a copy of the deed, certified, &c. was used in the trial." This is probable; for the copy is certified by the *register* of York, not by the *clerk* of New Hampshire tribunal, in which original had been produced at the trial, but was now withdrawn. Mr. Plumer's acquaintance with law processes will satisfy him, that a court does not permit copy of a deed, after original has been used in a suit, to be substituted for original, with the verification of register of a county in a foreign province, instead of its own clerk. But, if it were original, not copy, that was used, I better understand the management, which Mather piously considers "a remarkable display and instance of the Providence of Heaven in the finding of this instrument *just before* the sitting of your last court," so that scrutiny of signatures of men, dead many years, could not be had. For so remarkable a gift of Providence, it would have been respectful to have incurred the expense of recording; but it seemed dangerous, I suppose, for the next five years and a half. Did those, whose title materially depended on this deed, expect Providence to continue to favour them, by preserving the deed against their own negligence; or did they think the evil of keeping it secret was much less than that of showing it? Mr. Plumer, too, repeats, from C.

Mather, the assertion, "if the deed was forged, Wheelwright must have been privy to it; but the goodness of his character repels the charge." I presume the paper was forged twenty-six years or more after his death; but whether it were earlier or later, there is no privity necessary, probable, presumable, or hardly possible. The character of Wheelwright is valued by me as highly as by Dr. Mather or Gov. Plumer; and I think it is vindicated, by showing, that he was too sensible, as well as too honest, to take or make such a conveyance. But when the pretended deed is shown to be a forgery, and never heard of till it was wanted, and could be in some degree safely produced, a quarter of a century after he was in his grave, how can any stain attach to his character? No doubt there is guilt somewhere, but it may be too late to ascertain, whether it belong to the counsel in the cause, or to the agent of the province, who applied to the ambiguous oracle at Boston, or to some other dealer in such spells and necromancy.

Of the nine English witnesses, in whose presence this deed is attested to be signed, sealed, and delivered, 17 May, 1629, I believe we may entertain strong doubts, whether more than one was then in this country.

1. John Oldham is first mentioned in 1624, by Bradford, in Prince, I. 149, and Morton's Memorial, 74, from which latter Hubbard, 92—94, takes his narrative. In 1625 he lived at Nantasket, (Hubbard, 107,) having, in March, undergone ludicrous and severe punishment for his injurious treatment of Plimouth colony, (Bradford in Prince, I. 153.) The next year his character, or at least his conduct, changed, "and we give him liberty," says Bradford, Ib. 158, "to come and converse with us when he pleases." So high did he stand, next year, with the saints he had formerly persecuted, that Gov. Bradford, sending to his majesty's council, from Plimouth, 9 June, 1628, the letter about arrest and sending home of Morton, the anarchist, says in it, "this bearer, Mr. John Oldham, who can give your honours further information upon his oath, if need so require, whom we have sent with the prisoner, and to attend your lordships' pleasures," 1 Hist. Coll. III. 63. Morton, we are told, came back next year; but I shall now show, that Oldham, before May, at least, did *not:* 1. It is *highly improbable*, from Sullivan's Maine, 219, reciting the grant in 1629, from the Earl of Warwick, Lord Gorges, Sir Ferd. Gorges and Thomas Smith, of the territory between Cape Elizabeth and Cape Porpoise, to John Oldham and Richard Vines, of which livery of seizin was given in 1630, in which grant their undertaking to transport fifty persons thither, must imply their presence in England. 2. It is *impossible;* for, in our venerable Colony Records, then kept in London, at a meeting of the governour and company, 2 March, 1628—9, is this passage: "Touching John Oldham, the governour was ordered to confer with him upon any indifferent course, that might not be prejudicial to the company." Three days after is this record: "5 March. A new proposition being made in the behalf of Mr. Oldham, to be entertained by this company, it was deferred to farther consideration." On 10 of same month,

only five days later, the names are given of a large committee "once more to confer with Mr. John Oldham." On "11 May, 1629. This day Mr. Oldham propounded unto Mr. White, that he would have his patent examined, and it's agreed by the court, not to have any treaty with him about it, by reason it's thought, he doth it not out of love, but out of some sinister respect." Certainly John Oldham was all this time in London. For these extracts, the New Hampshire gentlemen may rely on my accuracy. But in Hazard, I. 256—268, is the general letter of our governour and company in London to their agent, John Endecott, at Salem, 17 April, 1629, from Gravesend, in which, page 258, may be read, "Mr. John Oldham came from New England not long before your arrival there," [E. arrived September, 1628,] "by whom we have had no small distraction in our business, having been cast behind, at the least, two months time in our voyage, through the variety of his vast conceits of extraordinary gain," &c. &c. The voyage was that of the three ships, with Skelton, Higginson, Samuel Sharp, &c. by whom came this letter. They proceed, "Finding him" [Oldham] "a man altogether unfit for us to deal with, we have at last left him to his own way; and, as we are informed, he, with some others, *are providing a vessel, and is minded, as soon as he can despatch, to come* for New England," &c. &c. through forty lines it cannot be necessary to transcribe. There is a P. S. to said letter of 21 April, and from the postscript to the P. S. page 268, probably by Gov. Cradock, I am sure every one would infer, that Oldham was still there. Now, what becomes of the confidence, that Oldham *might* have witnessed the deed 17 May of that year? Our ships arrived in the latter part of June.

2. Samuel Sharp was passenger, with Samuel Skelton, in the George Bonadventure, one of the abovementioned three ships, and she was detained at the Isle of Wight till 4 May, and arrived at Salem 23 June. See in the foregoing letter, in Haz. I. page 262, "We have caused a common seal to be made, which we send you by Mr. Sharpe," and, page 265, "If, at the arrival of *this* ship, Mr. Endecott should be departed this life, (which God forbid,) or should happen to die before the other ships arrive, we authorize you," [by whom this letter is carried?] "Mr. Skelton and Mr. Samuel Sharpe, to take care of our affairs, and to govern the people," &c. The P. S. of 21 April, page 266, "The aforewritten is, for the most part, the copy of our general letter, sent you, together with our patent, under the broad seal, and the company's seal in silver, by Mr. Samuel Sharpe, passenger in the George, who, we think, is yet riding in the Hope; but, by means of stormy weather, the Talbot and the Lion's Whelp are yet at Blackwall. By these ships, that are to follow, we intend," &c. See, also, the next letter of our governour and company, "London, 28 May, 1629," with P. S. Gravesend, 3 June, Haz. I. 277—285: "Our last unto you was of the 17th and 21st April, sent by the last ships, viz. the George Bonadventure, Thomas Cox master, who set sail from the Isle of Wight the 4th of this month, and seconded by the Talbot, Thomas Beecher master, and

the Lion's Whelp, John Gibbs master, who set sail also from the Isle of Wight about the 11th of this month," &c. This letter came by a new expedition of three ships, in one of which, perhaps, John Oldham might have passage, though probably his views, adverse to our company, led him to seek other conveyance, it may be in the vessel he was providing. We have Higginson's own journal in print, kept with the exactness of a log book for each day. It is republished in the invaluable Collection of Hutchinson, pages 32—44. In page 35, the sailing of the Talbot, in which he was embarked, and the Lion's Whelp together, on 11 May, from the Isle of Wight, is recorded; and on page 44, Tuesday, 30 June, "being come into the harbour" [of Salem,] "we saw the George, to our great comfort, then," [quere *there?*] "being come on Tuesday, which was seven days before us." Now Mr. Plumer, as every body else, must see, that our Samuel Sharp, in the George Bonadventure, coming from the Isle of Wight to Salem, between 4 May and 23 June, could not sign his name to this instrument 17 of the same May. But I am filled with admiration at his suggestion against the identity, that "another man of the same name might then be in this country, and in fact subscribe as a witness." What! *two* Samuel Sharps in New England before the first of July, 1629! I beg the gentlemen of the other side to inquire, how few more on that day than eight hundred English there were on the whole continent, between Newfoundland and Virginia. The computation may take infant Salem, as the most populous, except Plimouth, then nine years and a half old, two hundred; the rest of Massachusetts, one hundred and fifty, (Higginson, in Hutch. Coll. 47, makes "in all, old and new planters, three hundred," and I give in sixteen per cent.;) Plimouth, "near three hundred," is the boast of their friends, Prince, I. 197; and there was less than one hundred and fifty in the rest of one thousand miles of Atlantick coast, counting from five to fifty at Pemaquid, Portsmouth, Dover, Cape Ann, Weymouth, and any other cabin east of Virginia. There are now one million and three quarters of people in New England alone, of whom I beg an enumeration of all that bear the exact name of Samuel Sharp. Will there be four thousand? or four hundred? or forty? It is not, and never was, a common English *sirname;* and the name of baptism is not, probably, united with this sirname more than once in twenty. Of the representatives of New Hampshire in 1824, eleven in two hundred and eleven, are Samuels. Mr. Plumer has no hesitation in proving *John* Wheelwright's purchase in May, 1629, when there were not five hundred English between Virginia and Canada, by a letter of Neal and Wiggin, about *Mr.* Wheelwright, 13 August, 1633, when there were near five thousand; but he thinks *a* Samuel Sharp might have been a witness on that first day, though we prove, that the only one of that name, ever heard of in our early history, was then on the ocean. If it were to be regarded, however, as a possibility, that there was a Samuel Sharp at Piscataqua or its neighbourhood 17 May, 1629, how infinitely multiplied are the chances against *another* John Oldham,—a name of much rarer occurrence!

Yet these are the formal witnesses to signing, sealing and delivering a deed, when each was some thousands of miles distant. I say each was absent, for the identity of both these, so well known persons, must be presumed. How many hundreds of millions to one against the presumption, is not a matter for my arithmetical powers. Something like such a calculation may be seen in the letters of Herbert Marsh, the present Bishop of Llandaff, a d Margaret Professor of Divinity, to Travis, the unhappy archdeacon, whose blunders were the occasion of calling out from Porson the most extraordinary union of perspicacious argument, witty sarcasm and profound erudition, that our language can exhibit. Can an alibi be better made out? Can a forgery of near two hundred years old be better detected?

3. "Walter Neal, governour," "came in the bark Warwick this summer" [1630] "to Pascataqua, sent as governour there for Sir F. Gorges and others." See page 39 of this History, compared with page 7. It may be guessed, that he had been there before, and went back to England soon after 17 May, 1629. Might we not presume, he had not before been "governour," the title of the verification? I say, he had never been there at all, though, unless he were governour, the deed must fall; and quote the language, "humbly presented and submitted by the governour and company of Massachusetts Bay to the king's most excellent majesty," 6 September, 1676, on the solemn subject of our exercise of jurisdiction over New Hampshire adverse to Gorges and Mason, Belknap's N. H., I., Appendix, 14: "Our first exercise of jurisdiction being in the year 1641, eight years after Capt. Neale, agent for Mr. Mason, had wholly deserted the improvement of land and the government of the country, which, indeed, he never used but one year; for in the year 1630 *he first came over*, and in the year 1634 he quitted the place, and in the interim neglected the same, in making a voyage for England," &c.

4. "George Vaughan, factor," seems liable to part of the objection against Neal, governour. I know not when he came first to our country, but presume it was not so early. He left in August, 1634, and there is nothing to be found, but this deed, to render it probable, he had then passed three years here. The very next article to this famous deed, in the Appendix, is a letter from Eyre, of the "company of Laconia, to Mr. Gibbons, their *factor*," dated last of May, 1631. Eyre's letter informs Gibbons, that they now "send you a factor to take charge of the trade goods." Was not this factor, coming out in July, 1631, George Vaughan? In the disputed attestation, Gibbons is called trader, as Neal is governour, and Vaughan factor, "for the company of Laconia." Now, if Neal were not sent governour by the company until 1630, it may be presumed, the factor *and* trader had not their appointments sooner. It appears probable, contrary to Belknap, N. H., I. 14, that the company of Laconia was not formed till six months after the date of this deed.

5. "Ambrose Gibbons, trader," came with Neal in the bark Warwick, having written to Eyre, 8 April, 1630, from Plimouth in Old

England, 21 July and 14 August, 1630, from Piscataqua. See Eyre's letter in Belknap's N. H., I., Appendix, 2. I conclude, he then came for the *first* time, because his "wife and children" were sent next year; and if he had been here, with appointment from Mason or Gorges, in 1629, then gone to England, and come back, he would, on his *second* voyage, have brought them.

6 and 7. "Richard Vines, governour, and Richard Bonighton, assistant, of the plantation at Saco." What a goodly *outside* falsehood hath! But this outside is decorated in such a manner as to lead to detection. Had the names *alone* been given, some doubt might have remained about these persons. But the offices and the residence are both fatal. Vines was here, as an explorer, many years before any settlement, according to Belknap, Amer. Biog. I. 354—356, and his back might be thought broad enough to carry Bonighton, who is never heard of till long after this deed. But Vines, with Oldham, was, I think, in England, in 1629, taking grant of land here, not possession, till 1630. The appointment of Vines as governour, and of Bonighton, as assistant, of the plantation, which is the important point, was not made till 2 September, 1639. See the commission in Hazard, I., 458—462. Sir Thomas Josselyn, who stands before Vines, did not come over. I know, that that commission from Sir F. Gorges is for the province of Maine "from the entrance of Piscataqua harbour unto the River of Sagadahock;" but I deny, that Vines was governour and Bonighton assistant under any other commission. Further, Saco was not settled till some years after this deed. See 2 Hist. Coll. IV. 187, and Hubbard, 214.

8. "Thomas Wiggin, agent," was not here, probably, for two years after this signing his name. Hubbard, 221, makes him *begin* his plantation in 1631; and when the exact truth is found out by the New Hampshire gentlemen, perhaps, it will show Hubbard's correctness.

9. "Edward Hilton, steward," was, probably, at Piscataqua, and the only one of these nine witnesses, who, we may reasonably believe, was there 17 May, 1629. But we may as reasonably doubt his signature, as that of the others. If the other signatures are disbelieved, in any degree, on account of the description given, by themselves, of themselves, in the attestation, Hilton's is equally suspicious. Our only account of him, for several years, is from Hubbard, 214, and if Wiggin and the others did not come before May, 1629, Hilton was entitled to be called governour, instead of steward; for Mason had not sent over any body superiour to him.

I close this examination without making any remarks, though very much more presumptive evidence of the fabrication of this instrument, long after its date, could easily be furnished, and may be imagined. An apology is, perhaps, due to all my readers for its great length. But two gentlemen, at least, in New Hampshire, will not complain of the deference shown by me to their opinions, nor slight the labour bestowed in proving them erroneous.

END OF VOL. I.

THE

HISTORY

OF

NEW ENGLAND

FROM

1630 TO 1649.

BY JOHN WINTHROP, ESQ.

FIRST GOVERNOUR OF THE COLONY OF THE MASSACHUSETTS BAY.

FROM

HIS ORIGINAL MANUSCRIPTS.

WITH NOTES

TO ILLUSTRATE

THE CIVIL AND ECCLESIASTICAL CONCERNS, THE GEOGRAPHY, SETTLEMENT AND INSTITUTIONS OF THE COUNTRY, AND THE LIVES AND MANNERS OF THE PRINCIPAL PLANTERS.

BY JAMES SAVAGE,

MEMBER OF THE MASSACHUSETTS HISTORICAL SOCIETY.

VOL. II.

Sæpe audivi, Q. Maximum, P. Scipionem, præterea civitatis nostræ præclaros viros, solitos ita dicere, cum majorum imagines intuerentur, vehementissime sibi animum ad virtutem accendi. *Sallust, Bell. Jugurth. c. iv.*

Boston:

PRINTED BY THOMAS B. WAIT AND SON

No. 90, Court Street.

1826.

THE

HISTORY

OF

NEW ENGLAND.

(3.) 13.] THE court of elections was at Boston, and Thomas Dudley, Esq. was chosen governour. Some trouble there had been in making way for his election, and it was obtained with some difficulty; for many of the elders laboured much in it, fearing lest the long continuance of one man in the place should bring it to be for life, and, in time, hereditary. Beside, this gentleman was a man of approved wisdom and godliness, and of much good service to the country, and therefore it was his due to ||share|| in such honour and benefit as the country had to bestow. The elders, being met at Boston about this matter, sent some of their company to acquaint the old governour with their desire, and the reasons moving them, clearing themselves of all dislike of his government, and seriously professing their sincere affections and respect towards him, which he kindly and thankfully accepted, concurring with them in their motion, and expressing his unfeigned desire of more freedom, that he might a little intend his private occasions, wherein (they well knew) how much he had lately suffered (for his bailiff, whom he trusted with managing his farm, had engaged him £2500 without his privity) in his outward estate.[1] This they had heard of, and were much affected therewith, and all the country in general, and took course, (the elders agreeing upon it at that meeting,) that supply should be sent in from the several towns, by a voluntary contribution, for freeing of those engagements; and the court (having no money to bestow, and

||serve||

---

1 See Appendix, I. 2. for a notice of this misfortune by the author in revoking his will.

being yet much indebted) gave his wife three thousand acres of land, and some of the towns sent in liberally, and some others promised, but could perform but little, and the most nothing at all. The whole came §not§ to £500 whereof near half came from Boston, and one gentleman of Newbury, Mr. Richard Dummer, propounded for a supply by a more private way, and for example, himself disbursed £100.[1]

This first court there fell some difference between the governour and some of the deputies about a vote, upon a motion to have the fine of £200 imposed upon Mr. Robert Keaine to be abated. Some would have had it at £100—others at 100 ||marks,|| others at 50, and because the governour put the lowest to the vote first, whereas divers called for the highest, they charged the governour with breach of order, whereupon he grew into some heat, professing that he would not suffer such things, &c. The deputies took this as a menacing, and much offence they took at it; but the next day he cleared his intention to them, and all was quiet.[2]

[Blank.]

Mo. 4.] Divers of the inhabitants of Linne, finding themselves straitened, looked out for a new plantation, and going to Long Island, they agreed with the Lord Sterling's agent there, one Mr. [3]Forrett, for a parcel of the isle near the west end, and

||mills||

---

1 This unexampled liberality to Winthrop, in his distress, is a more satisfactory proof of the high estimation, in which he stood, than could be afforded by the most elaborate eloquence of eulogy. But the generosity of Dummer is above all praise. His contribution is fifty per cent. above the whole tax of his town, and equal to half the benevolence of the whole metropolis; yet he had been a sufferer under the mistaken views of Winthrop, and the other triumphant sound religionists, as set forth in our note on Vol. I. 248.

At this court, a rate of £1200 was agreed on for the year in these proportions: Boston, £179; Ipswich, £120; Salem, £115; Cambridge, £100; Dorchester, £95; Charlestown and Watertown, each, £90; Lynn, £85; Roxbury, £75; Newbury, £65; Concord, £50; Hingham, £35; Dedham, £30; Braintree, £25; Weymouth, £21; Colchester, £15; Hampton, £10. But it was found, by the depreciation of estates, at a subsequent court, that the change rendered it impossible to collect a large portion of the tax.

2 We may recollect, that Dudley was brother-in-law of the delinquent, and that three fifths of the fine was abated, Vol. I. 314, in note. Six or seven years later, Benjamin Keayne, husband of Dudley's daughter, being in London, repudiated his wife, writing to her father, and his spiritual guides, Wilson and Cotton, in terms of the strongest reprobation of her conduct. These letters are preserved in our first volume of Registry of Deeds, where one would hardly look for such scandal; but it is so disgusting, that I must leave them, with the character of the lady, in oblivion.

3 Either Forrett, whose name is strangely *printed* in Hubbard, 245, had not granted leave to settle without some conditions, or the people from

agreed with the Indians for their right.[1] The Dutch, hearing of this, and making claim to that part of the island by a former pur-

Lynn had, in his opinion, violated their engagements; for he came, next year, to Boston, and made a very formal protest against their proceedings in these words:

"Know all men by these presents, that whereas Edward Tomlyns and Timothy Tomlyns, together with one Hansard Knowles and others, have lately entered and taken possession of some part of the Long Island in New England, which was formerly granted by the letters patent of our sovereign lord, king Charles, to the right honourable William, Earl of Stirling, and his heirs,—I, James Forrett, gentleman, by virtue of a commission under the hand and seal of the said earl to me made, for the disposing and ordering of the said Long Island, do hereby protest and intimate, as well to the said Edward Tomlyns and others the said intruders, as to all others, whom it may concern, that neither they, nor any of them, nor any other person or persons (not claiming by or from the said earl) have, or shall have, or enjoy any lawful right, title or possession of, in, or to the said island, or any part thereof, but that the said earl, his heirs or assigns may, and will at all times, when they please, implead or eject either by course of law, or lawful force, if need be, all the said intruders, their servants, tenants or assigns, and may and will recover against them, and every of them, all damages and costs in this behalf sustained, any colour of title or pretence of right by grant from the governour of New England, or any other, notwithstanding. In testimony whereof, I have made and published this protest and intimation before John Winthrop, one of the magistrates and council of the Massachusetts in New England aforesaid, and have desired, that the same may be recorded there and in other jurisdiction in those parts, and have published and showed the same to the said Edward Tomlyns, in the presence of the witnesses under named. Dated at Boston, 28 day of the 7 month, An. Dom. 1641, an. Regis Domini nostri Caroli Angliæ, &c. decimo septimo."

"The above named James Forrett, gentleman, did make this protestation the 28 of the said month in the year aforesaid, at Boston, in the Massachusetts aforesaid. Before me,

JOHN WINTHROP."

It is a little singular, that, in the volume of our Records, the signature of Winthrop is an original. But it is more strange, that no notice of this solemn instrument is found in Wood's Sketch of the settlement of Long Island, or any other book, to my knowledge.

Edward Tomlyns had been, it will be remembered, representative in the first court for Lynn, and afterwards served in September, 1635, and September, 1639. Timothy, who may be supposed his brother, was deputy in eleven courts, between March, 1634—5, and May, 1640.

1 Trumbull's account, I. 119, is not very satisfactory, though it assists our topography: "Capt. Howe and other Englishmen, in behalf of Connecticut, purchased a large tract of the Indians, the original proprietors on Long Island. This tract extended from the eastern part of Oyster Bay to the western part of Home's or Holmes's Bay to the middle of the great plain. It lay on the northern part of the island, and extended southward about half its breadth. Settlements were immediately begun upon the lands, and by the year 1642 had made considerable advancement." Some mistake of the reverend historian is here observable; for, in coincidence with Winthrop, he mentions, on the third page after, the breaking up of this settlement, and imprisoning some, and driving the rest away. I doubt, also, that the purchase was not made *in behalf of Connecticut*. Trumbull takes no notice of

chase of the Indians, sent men to take possession of the place, and set up the arms of the Prince of Orange upon a tree. The Linne men sent ten or twelve men with provisions, &c., who began to build, and took down the prince's arms,[1] and, in place thereof, an Indian had drawn an unhandsome face. The Dutch took this in high displeasure, and sent soldiers and fetched away their men, and imprisoned them a few days, and then took an oath of them [blank] and so discharged them.[2] Upon this the Linne men (finding themselves too weak, and having no encouragement to expect aid from the English) ||deserted|| that place, and took another at the east end of the same island; and, being now about forty families, they proceeded in their plantation, and called one Mr. [3]Pierson, a godly learned man, and a member of the church of Boston, to go with them, who with some seven or eight more of the company gathered (9) into a church body at Linne, (before they went,) and the whole company entered into a civil combination (with the advice of some of our magistrates) to become a corporation.

Upon this occasion, the Dutch governour, one William Kyfte, (a discreet man,) wrote to our governour complaint of the English usurpations, both at Connecticut, and now also at Long Island, and of the abuse offered to the Prince's arms, &c. and thereupon excused his imprisoning our men. To which the governour returned answer, (*in Latin, his letter being in the same,*) that our

||desisted||

---

the negotiation with Lord Stirling's agent. He has, besides, forgotten to mention the English afterwards setting down on the eastern point of the island, nearly a hundred miles from their former habitation. Thinking only of the wrongs of Connecticut, he carelessly took a very brief statement of the commissioners of the United Colonies from Hazard, II. 164. But the right appears to me to have been on the side of the Dutch.

1 Lechford, 44, says, "Lieut. Howe pulled down the Dutch arms." His name was Daniel, and he was deputy for Lynn, I think, in the courts, May and September, 1636; in April, May, September and November, 1637.

2 Wood, in his Sketch of Long Island, 9, says, in a note, "13 May, 1640, Gov. Kieft sent Cornelius Van Ten Hoven, the secretary, the under sheriff, a sergeant and twenty-five soldiers, to Scout's Bay, to break up a settlement of the English, who had torn down the state's arms, and carved a fool's head on the tree. The party set out the 14th, and returned the 15th. They found a company of eight men, and a woman with an infant, who had erected one house, and were engaged in erecting another. The party brought six of the men to the governour. On examination, it appeared, that they came from Lynn, near Boston, under Andrew Forrester, a Scotchman, agent for Lord Stirling, who had returned to New Haven. After they had been examined, and signed an agreement to leave the place, they were dismissed." Andrew Forrester is an odd perversion of James Forrett.

3 Rev. Abraham Pierson, after serving these settlers at Southampton, re-

desire had always been to hold peace and good correspondency with all our neighbours; and though we would not maintain any of our countrymen in any unjust action, yet we might not suffer them to be injured, &c. As for our neighbours of Connecticut, &c., he knew they were not under our government, and for those at Long Island, they went voluntarily from us, &c.

This year there came over great store of provisions, both out of England and Ireland, and but few passengers, (and those brought very little money,) which was occasioned by the store of money and quick markets, which the merchants found here the two or three years before, so as now all our money was drained from us, and cattle and all commodities grew very cheap, which enforced us at the next general court, in the 8th month, to make an order, that corn should pass in payments of new debts; Indian at 4*s*. the bushel; rye at 5*s*. and wheat at 6*s*.; and that, upon all executions for former debts, the creditor might take what goods he pleased, (or, if he had no goods, then his lands,) to be appraised by three men, one chosen by the creditor, one by the debtor, and the third by the marshal.[1]

One of the ships, which came this summer, struck upon a whale with a full gale, which put the ship a stays; the whale struck the ship on her bow, with her tail a little above water, and brake the planks and six timbers and a beam, and staved two hogsheads of vinegar.

(7.)] There was some rumour of the Indians plotting mischief against the English; and, to strengthen this, the governour of

---

moved, in 1644, to Branford in New Haven colony, whence he departed in 1665, it is supposed, for Newark in New Jersey. His son, of the same name, graduated at Harvard College, 1668, became the first ruler of the college at New Haven. See Trumbull, the Biographical Dictionaries, and a chapter in Mather, that contains very little.

[1] It seems best here to give the transcript from our Records, I. 291, "Whereas many men in the plantation are in debt, and here is not money sufficient to discharge the same, though their cattle and goods should be sold for half their worth, as experience has showed upon some late executions, whereby a great part of the people in the country may be undone, and yet their debts not satisfied, though they have sufficient, upon an equal valuation, to pay all, and live comfortably upon the rest; It is therefore ordered, that upon every execution of debts past, the officer shall take land, houses, corn, cattle, fish, or other commodities, and deliver the same, in full satisfaction to the creditor, at such prices, as the same shall be valued at by three understanding and indifferent men, to be chosen, the one by the creditor, and another by the debtor, and the third by the marshal. And the creditor is at liberty to take his choice of what goods he will, and if he hath not sufficient goods to discharge it, then he is to take his house, or land, as aforesaid." Our great legal antiquary, in tracing the mode of levy on land from this *peculiar* law, begins in 1647, and has not gone so far back as its origin. See Dane's Gen. Abr. and Dig. of Am. Law, ch. 136,

Plimouth, a Mr. Bradford, wrote a letter to this effect: that he was informed, (and did believe it,) that the Naragansett sachem, Miantunnomoh, had sent a great present of wampom to the Mohawks to aid him against the English, and that it was accepted, and aid promised. The like news was brought by Mr. Haynes, one of the magistrates upon Connecticut, and many words were taken up from some Indians among us, which our fears interpreted the same way. The governour and council gave no great credit to these suspicions, yet they thought fit to take order, strengthening the watches in all towns, and caused them to be ordered by the military officers, (being before committed to the constables' charge,) and withal sent Capt. Jenyson with three men and an Indian interpreter to the Naragansett sachems, to know the truth of their intentions, &c. They were very kindly entertained, but they would not speak with him in the presence of his Indian interpreter, §because he was a Pequod, and a servant, and their enemy, and might discover their counsels. So he made use of another interpreter.§ They denied all confederations with the Mohawks, &c. and professed their purpose to continue friendship with us, and not to use any hostility towards the English, except they began, &c. and promised to come to Boston (as he was desired) if Mr. Williams might come with him, (but that we had denied.) Only Janemoh, the Niantick sachem, carried himself proudly, and refused to come to us, or to yield to any thing, only he said he would not harm us, except we invaded him[1].

The governour and council took from Cutshamekin the powder and shot they had bought of our people, with promise to pay for it, or restore it, &c.

This summer there came divers godly men, as they pretended, from ||Christophers|| with their families. The occasion was, one Mr. [2]Collins, a young scholar, full of zeal, &c. preaching in the

||papers||

art. 14, Vol. v. 23. The morals of our people did not suffer by the short continuance of this regulation, as far as chattels are concerned. The necessity will not justify, however, their policy.

Ancient charters and laws, p. 173, compiled by the same laborious student, has an error in the date, August, instead of October, which, no doubt, arose from the numeral of the month, 8th, being used in the record. August *was* the sixth month.

1 No information on the matter of this paragraph can be derived from Morton's Memorial, where we should naturally seek it, and very little from the historian of Connecticut.

2 Relative to this gentleman, no light has dawned upon me from any quarter, beyond what is contained in this narrative of the tyrannical proceedings against him, in the following year, to which it may be reasonably suspected, that his

island, it pleased God, divers were wrought upon by him, but he and they being ||persecuted,|| and their liberty restrained, they came away and brought all their substance in tobacco, which came at so dead a market, as they could not get above two pence the pound (the freight came to one penny, ||²observe,||) nor could sell half at that rate. They arrived first at Quilipiack, (since called New Haven,) and so dispersed themselves here and there, and some returned to Ireland. Mr. Collins and one Mr. [1]Hales (a young man very well conceited of himself and censorious of others) went to Aquiday, and so soon as Hales came acquainted with Mrs. Hutchinson, he was taken by her and became her disciple. Mr. Collins was entertained at Hartford to teach a school, and hearing of Mrs. Hutchinson's opinions, &c. wrote to Mr. Hales to beware of her. Mr. Hales returned him answer, and the next morning he went away, without taking leave, and being come to Mrs. Hutchinson, he was also taken with her heresies, and in great admiration of her, so as these, and other the like before, when she dwelt at Boston, gave cause of suspicion of witchcraft, for it was certainly known, that Hawkins's wife (who continued with her, and was her bosom friend) had much familiarity with the devil in England, when she dwelt at St. Ives, where divers ministers and others resorted to her and found it true.

This summer here arrived one Mr. Thomas [2]Gorge, a young

||presented|| ||²the pound||

---

marriage of a daughter of Mrs. Hutchinson was as strong an inducement, as the letter written by him, then made ground of complaint. His unfortunate death, in 1643, was of course viewed as a judicial punishment, like that of those on whom the tower of Siloam fell.

1 I have been as unsuccessful in seeking information about this person, as about the scholar whom he seduced from Hartford.

2 For his labours the province of Maine is under high obligation to Thomas Gorges, who resided three years, not *about two*, as Belk. Biog. I. 385, has it, in that part of our country. Hutchinson, Coll. 114, where is preserved a letter to our Winthrop of 28 June, 1643, calls him son of Sir Ferdinando, but the charter from the patentee names him cousin. He writes, in that letter, he supposes he shall soon go for England in a ship then lying there, but seems not certain. After that, nothing is heard of him, except his grant, on 14 July following, of the township of Wells, 1 Hist. Coll. III. 138. His commission to be of the council of Maine, and secretary of that board, dated 10 March, 1639, that is 1640, N. S. immediately before he came over, is copied from the York Records into Sullivan's Maine Apx. VI. It recites, that in September last his kinsman had given a commission, which Sullivan prints next, as if, because bearing date 2 September, 1639, it were subsequent, though really six months earlier. Similar errours are often committed by writers of more care than that distinguished gentleman, through failure of recollecting the ancient computation, persevered in by English protestants of that and four succeeding ages refusing to adopt the Gregorian style.

gentleman of the inns of court, a kinsman to Sir Ferdinand Gorge, and sent by him with commission for the government of his province of Somersetshire. He was sober and well disposed; he staid a few days at Boston, and was very careful to take advice of our magistrates how to manage his affairs, &c. When he came to Acomenticus, *now called Bristol*, he found all out of order, for Mr. Burdett ruled all, and had let loose the reins of liberty to his lusts, that he grew very notorious for his pride and adultery; and the neighbours now finding Mr. Gorge well inclined to reform things, they complained of him, and produced such foul matters against him, as he was laid hold on, and bound to appear at their court at Sacoe: but he dealt so with some other of the commissioners, that, when the court came, Mr. [1]Vines and two more stood for him, but Mr. Gorge having the greater party on his side, and the jury finding him guilty of adultery and other crimes, with much labour and difficulty he was fined (under £30.) He appealed unto England, but Mr. Gorge would not admit his appeal, but seized some of his cattle, &c. Upon this Mr. Burdett went into England, but when he came there he found the state so changed, as his hopes were frustrated, and he, after taking part with the cavaliers, was committed to prison.[2]

[blank]

One Baker, master's mate of the ship, [blank] being in drink, used some reproachful words of the queen.[3] The governour and

---

1 Richard Vines, Esquire, had been employed by the famous Sir F. Gorges, according to Belknap, a long time before the settlement at Plimouth; and from the continuance of his office in Maine, we may be confident, he deserved the approbation of his superiors. He lived at Winter harbour, near the Saco. Sullivan 218, 224. Power to him and six others to be of the council was given by the commission, mentioned in the last note, which may be seen in Haz. I. 458: when Gorges was added, there were eight. So that Vines and two others standing for Burdett, five would have been against him. Sullivan says, that, on account of his adherence to the king, it was inconvenient for Vines to remain in America after 1645. But in that year he was chosen deputy governour, that is, I presume, chief magistrate, of the Province, for the proprietory governour was in England. Two letters from him, of 19 July, 1647, and 29 April, 1648, to our Gov. Winthrop, preserved in Hutch. Coll. 222, 3, show he was well settled at Barbados, and, besides the profit of his plantation, gained by the practice of medicine. By them his regard for our country appears too great to permit us to suppose him to have been a high royalist.

2 A strange error is found in Sullivan, 238. Of York he says, "we do not find that they ever had a preacher there under the government of Gorges. In the year 1660, one Burdett, who had been expelled from Exeter, for misdemeanours, became a preacher, &c." Yet on the next page he copies from our author's text the whole preceding paragraph with its date. The circumstances, under which his history was composed, were very adverse to accuracy, and the author was constantly engaged in more important labours.

3 Had his reproaches been uttered against our magistrates or churches, per-

council were much in doubt what to do with him, but having considered that he was distempered and sorry for it, &c. and being a stranger and a chief officer in the ship, and many ships were then in harbour, they thought it not fit to inflict corporal punishment upon him, but after he had been two or three days in prison, he was set an hour at the whipping post with a paper on his head, and so dismissed.

Mo. 5. 27.] Being the second day of the week, the Mary Rose, a ship of Bristol, of about 200 tons, her master one Capt. [blank] lying before Charlton, was blown in pieces with her own powder, being 21 barrels; wherein the judgment of God appeared, for the master and company were many of them profane scoffers at us, and at the ordinances of religion here; so as, our churches keeping a fast for our native country, &c. they kept aboard, at their common service, when all the rest of the masters came to our assemblies; likewise the Lord's day following; and a friend of his going aboard next day and asking him, why he came not on shore to our meetings, his answer was, that he had a family of his own, &c. and they had as good service aboard as we had on shore. Within two hours after this (being about dinner time) the powder took fire (no man knows how) and blew all up, viz. the captain and nine or ten of his men and some four or five strangers. There was a special providence that there were no more, for many principal men were going aboard at that time, and some were in a boat near the ship, and others were diverted by a sudden ||shower|| of rain, and others by other occasions. There was one man saved, being carried up in the scuttle, and so let fall in the same into the water, and being taken up by the ferry boat, near dead, he came to himself the next morning, but could not tell any thing of the blowing up of the ship, or how he came there. The rest of the dead bodies were after found much bruised and broken. Some goods were saved, but the whole loss was estimated at £2,000. A 20*s*. piece was found sticking in a chip, for there was above £300 in money in her, and 15 tons of lead, and 10 pieces of ordnance, which a year after were taken up, and the hull of the ship drawn ashore.[1]

||storm||

haps his punishment would have been heavier. It will not escape observation, that drunkenness was received as a mitigation of the offence, and perhaps our ancestors were right in such judgment; but we must remember, that the state of intoxication was of itself punishable. Could we approach nearer to their sanctity of manners, our popular maxim, that such a circumstance is an aggravation, might justly bear a qualification, if not a reversal.

1 That Hubbard, who transcribes from our text whole pages of less remarkable circumstances, has omitted this casualty, which is the most striking re-

This judgment of God upon these scorners of his ordinances and the ways of his servants (for they spake very evil of us, because they found not so good a market for their commodities as they expected, &c.) gives occasion to mention other examples of like kind, which fell out at this and other times, by which it will appear how the Lord hath owned this work, and preserved and prospered his people here beyond ordinary ways of providence.

One Capt. Mason of London, a man in favour at court, and a professed enemy to us, had a plantation at Pascataquack; which he was at great charge about, and set up a sawmill, but nothing prospered. He provided a ship, which should have been employed to have brought ||a|| general governour, or in some other design to our prejudice, but in launching of it, her back was broken. He also employed Gardiner, and Morton and others to prosecute against us at council table, and by a quo warranto, &c. so as Morton wrote divers letters to his friends here, insulting against us, and assuring them of our speedy ruin, &c. But the Lord still ||2disappointed|| them and frustrated all their designs. As for this ||3Mason|| he fell sick and died soon after, and in his sickness he sent for the minister, and bewailed his enmity against us, and promised, if he recovered, to be as great a friend to New England as he had formerly been an enemy.

Sir Ferdinand Gorge also had sided with our adversaries against us, but underhand, pretending by his letters and speeches to seek our welfare: but he never prospered. He attempted great matters, and was at large expenses about his province here, but he lost all.

One [1]Austin (a man of good estate) came with his family in the year 1638 to Quinipiack, and not finding the country as he expected, he grew discontented, saying that he could not subsist here, and thereupon made off his estate, and with his family and £1000 in his purse, he returned for England in a ship bound for Spain, against the advice of the godly there, who told him he would be taken by the Turks; and it so fell out, for in Spain he embarked

||the|| ||2disapproved|| ||3Morton||

---

corded by Winthrop, is the more curious, since it was ascribed, in the erroneous temper of the age, to a judgment of God; and the Ipswich historian partially extracts the next following paragraph about Mason. Johnson, lib. III. c. 9. slightly mentions the destruction of the ship.

1 A family of the same name has long been very respectable in the city of New Haven, or its neighborhood; but of this sufferer I can learn nothing more, than his fault in being discontented with the country, and returning home. We may safely disagree with our author's judgment, that so slight an errour deserved so heavy an infliction.

himself in a great ship bound for England which[1] carried £200,000 in money, but the ship was taken by the Turks, and Austin and his wife and family were carried to Algiers and sold there for slaves.

The Lord showed his displeasure against others, though godly, who have spoken ill of this country, and so discouraged the hearts of his people; even the Lords and others of Providence having spoken too much in that kind, thinking thereby to further their own plantation. They set out a ship the last year with passengers and goods for Providence, but it was taken by the Turks. Captain Newman, the same year, having taken good prizes in their service, returning home, when he was near Dover, was taken by a Dunkirker, and all lost. Mr. Humfrey, who was now for Providence with his company, raised an ill report of this country, were here kept, in spite of all their endeavours and means to have been gone this winter, and his corn and all his hay to the value of £160 were burnt by his own servants[2] who made a fire in his barn, and by gunpowder, which accidently took fire, consumed all; himself having at the court before petitioned for some supply of his want, whereupon the court gave him £250. Soon after also Providence was taken by the Spaniards, and the Lords lost all their care and cost to the value of above £60,000.

Mo. 7. 3.] Captain Underhill being brought, by the blessing of God in this church's censure of excommunication, to remorse for his foul sins, obtained, by means of the elders, and others of the church of Boston, a safe conduct under the hand of the governour and one of the council to repair to the church. He came at the

---

1 [Here ends the perfect text of the second venerable MS. of the author, which began in my Vol I. p 197. On the morning of the 10th November last, the original was destroyed by fire, and my copy, on which the labour of collation, equally faithful and pleasant, had been bestowed by me, three times, in different years, was also lost. Another copy, designed for the printers, shared the same fate, except that the few pages foregoing, having been sent to the press, were preserved. From this place to the end of the second volume of the original MS. the boast of a pure text, with correction of the grosser errours denoted in the margin, and supplying of omissions in the former edition, must be abandoned. In some few places my memory preserves what the destructive element ravished from my possession; but I shall be cautious of trusting so frail a resource. Nearly all my notes are preserved for that part of the present volume, which had been printed in 1790, and all that is found in this part of my work, written since the disaster, will be seen, like the present note in brackets.]

2 From our Col. Rec. I. 295, at the Quarter Court of Assistants, 1 November following, the blame of the negligence appears to be cast on *one*, for it stands: "Henry Stevens for firing the barn of his master, Mr. John Humfrey, he was ordered to be servant to Mr. Humfrey for 21 years from this day, toward recompensing the loss."

time of the court of assistants; and upon the lecture day, after sermon, the pastor called him forth and declared the occasion, and then gave him leave to speak: and indeed it was a spectacle which caused many weeping eyes, though it afforded matter of much rejoicing to behold the power of the Lord Jesus in his own ordinances, when they are dispensed in his own way, holding forth the authority of his regal sceptre in the simplicity of the gospel. He came in his worst clothes (being accustomed to take great pride in his bravery and neatness) without a band, in a foul linen cap pulled close to his eyes; and standing upon a form, he did, with many deep sighs and abundance of tears, lay open his wicked course, his adultery, his hypocrisy, his persecution of God's people here, and especially his pride (as the root of all, which caused God to give him over to his other sinful courses) and contempt of the magistrates. He justified God and the church and the court in all that had been inflicted on him. He declared what power Satan had of him since the casting out of the church; how his presumptuous laying hold of mercy and pardon, before God gave it, did then fail him when the terrors of God came upon him, so as he could have no rest, nor could see any issue but utter despair, which had put him divers times upon resolutions of destroying himself, had not the Lord in mercy prevented him, even when his sword was ready to have done the execution. Many fearful temptations he met with beside, and in all these his heart shut up in hardness and impenitency as the bondslave of Satan, till the Lord, after a long time and great afflictions, had broken his heart, and brought him to humble himself before him night and day with prayers and tears till his strength was wasted; and indeed he appeared as a man worn out with sorrow, and yet he could find no peace, therefore he was now come to seek it in this ordinance of God. He spake well, save that his blubbering &c. interrupted him, and all along he discovered a broken and melting heart, and gave good exhortations to take heed of such vanities and beginnings of evil as had occasioned his fall; and in the end he earnestly and humbly besought the church to have compassion of him, and to deliver him out of the hands of Satan. So accordingly he was received into the church again; and after he came into the court, (for the general court began soon after) and made confession of his sin against them &c. and desired pardon, which the court freely granted him so far as concerned their private judgment. But for his adultery they ||would|| not pardon that for example sake, nor would restore him to freedom, though they released his banishment, and declared the former law against adultery to

||could||

be of no force; so as there was no law now to touch his life, for the new law against adultery was made since his fact committed. He confessed also in the congregation that though he was very familiar with that woman, and had gained her affection &c. yet she withstood him six months against all his solicitations (which he thought no woman could have resisted) before he could overcome her chastity, but being once overcome, she was wholly at his will. And to make his peace the more sound, he went to her husband (being a cooper) and fell upon his knees before him in the presence of some of the elders and others, and confessed the wrong he had done him, and besought him to forgive him, which he did very freely, and in testimony thereof he sent the captain's wife a token.[1]

4. 5. 6.] It rained three days and nights together, and the tides were extraordinary high.

Mo. 9.] It is before declared, how the church of Boston sent messengers and a letter to their members at Aquiday, and how they refused to hear them, pretending themselves to be no members, being now so far removed. Whereupon the elders and most of the church intended to have cast them out, as refusers to hear the church; but some others desired that the church would write to them once again, which accordingly was done, and the letter drawn by Mr. Cotton, wherein he fully repeated all former proceedings, both of the church and of the court, and justified both, and condemned their errours and disturbance of the peace here, and their remonstrance, and Mr. Wheelwright's sermon, (which formerly, among other his failings, being misled by their subtilty &c. he had justified and commended) and showed how the church had been wronged by them.

Miantunomoh, the sachem of Naragansett, came, and was met at Dorchester by Captain Gibbons and a guard of twelve musketeers, and well entertained at Roxbury by the governour; but when we came to parley he refused to treat with us by our Pequod interpreter, as he had done before to Captain Jenyson, and the

---

1 The tone of this long paragraph, which contains some of the author's best delineation of manners, leads me to doubt, that Winthrop suspected the sincerity of Underhill's penitence. We are presented, in a note on p. 34 of Wood's Sketch of Long Island, with a more copious account of this adventurer, than I was able to afford in Vol. I. 55, n. 2: "He had served as an officer in the British forces in the Low Countries, in Ireland, and at Cadiz, and he acted a distinguished part in the war with the Pequots, during the years 1636 and 1637. After the termination of that war he removed to Connecticut, and settled at Stamford. He was a delegate from that town to the general court at New Haven, in 1643, and was appointed an assistant justice there. During that year, he was sent for by the Dutch governour, to take a command in the war which the Dutch were about to commence with the Indians, situated north of the

governour being as resolute as he, refused to use any other interpreter, thinking it a dishonour to us to give so much way to them.[1] Whereupon he came from Roxbury to Boston, departing in a rude manner, without showing any respect or sign of thankfulness to the governour for his entertainment, whereof the governour informed the general court, and would show him no countenance, nor admit him to dine at our table, as formerly he had done, till he had acknowledged his failing &c. which he readily did, so soon as he could be made to understand it, and did speak with our committees and us by a Pequod maid who could speak English perfectly. But it was conceived by some of the court that he kept back such things as he accounted secrets of state, and that he would carry home in his breast, as an injury, the strict terms he was put to both in this, and the satisfaction he was urged to for not observing our custom in matter of manners, for he told us that when our men came to him they were permitted to use their own fashions, and so he expected the same liberty with us. So as he departed and nothing agreed, only the former articles of peace were read to him and allowed by him with this addition, that if any of his men did set traps in our jurisdiction &c. they should be liable to satisfy all damages, &c.

Mo. 8.] The elders had moved at a general court before, that the distinction between the two jurisdictions might be set down, that the churches might know their power, and the civil magistrate his. The same had been moved by the magistrates formerly, and now at this court they presented a writing to that effect to be considered by the court, wherein they declared that the civil magistrate should not proceed against a church member before the church had dealt with him, with some other restraints which the court did not allow of. So the matter was referred to

---

Sound and west of the Connecticut settlements, which lasted till the summer of 1646, and was terminated by a great battle at Strickland's plain in Horseneck, in which the Dutch with difficulty obtained the victory. After the conclusion of this war, in which he acted a principal part, he settled at Flushing on Long Island. He had some agency in detecting and exposing the intrigues of the Dutch treasurer with the Indians in 1653. He wrote to the commissioners of the united colonies, tendered them his services, and may have acted under their orders in attacking Fort Neck. In 1665, he was a delegate from the town of Oyster Bay to the assembly held at Hempstead by governour Nicolls, and was appointed by him under sheriff of the north riding of Yorkshire, or Queens county. In 1667 the Matinecoc Indians gave him 150 acres of land, which has remained in the family ever since, and is now in possession of one of his descendants that bears his name. It is supposed Captain Underhill died in 1672, at Oyster Bay."

1 Dudley, if he knew the objection to the use of a Pequod interpreter, made by Miantunnomoh two months before, showed more resolution than good policy.

further consideration, and it appeared indeed that divers of the elders did not agree in those points.[1]

At this court Mr. Ezekiel Rogers, pastor of the church in Rowley, being not kindly dealt with, nor justly, as he alleged, concerning the limits of their town, moved for further enlargement for taking in a neck of land upon Merrimack near Cochitawit,[2] for which end they desired their line might run square from Ipswich line. This line was granted, and he said it should satisfy, but within an hour after it was discovered that he was mistaken, and that such a line would not reach the neck, whereupon he came again and confessed his mistake, and still demanded the neck. The court was very doubtful what to do in it, having formerly granted a plantation at Cochitawit, and did not yield his request. Whereupon he pleaded justice, upon some promises of large accommodations, &c. when we desired his sitting down with us, and grew into some passion, so as in departing from the court, he said he would acquaint the elders with it. This behaviour, being menacing, as it was taken, gave just cause of offence to the court, so as he was sent for, not by the officer, but by one of Rowley deputies. Before he came, he wrote to the governour, wherein he confessed his passionate distemper, declared his meaning in those offensive speeches, as that his meaning was that he would propound the case to the elders for advice only about the equity of it, which he still defended. This would not be accepted, but the court would have him appear and answer: only they left him to take his own time, so the next day he came, not accompanied with any other of the elders, though many were then in town, and did freely and humbly blame himself for his passionate distemper; and the court knowing that he would not yield from the justice of his cause, (as he apprehended it,) they

1 Nothing could have been proposed, more effectual than the measure advised by some of the elders, to enlarge the clerical power, which was already too great. For ecclesiastical delinquencies, indeed, it is proper enough that the church should proceed before the criminal administration interferes, and perhaps such offences should be left only to the church. In England, after excommunication, civil penalties and disabilities are added.

2 The Indian name of a plantation, afterwards called Andover, one of the best agricultural districts in the state. It is sometimes written Cochituit, and Coojetowick, and more often Cochichawick, and thus it appears in the earliest mention of it by our records. At an adjourned meeting of the general court, Sept. 24, 1634, "it is ordered that the land about Cochichawick shall be reserved for an inland plantation, and that whosoever will go inhabit there shall have three years immunity from all taxes, levies, public charges and services whatsoever, military discipline only excepted." A committee, consisting of Winthrop, Bellingham, and Coddington, was at the same time authorized "to license any that they think meet to inhabit there, and that it shall be lawful for no person to go thither without their consent or the major part of them."

would not put him upon any temptation, but accepted his satisfaction, and freely granted what he formerly desired.

A commission had formerly been granted to Mr. Endecott and Mr. Stoughton for joining with the commissioners §of Plimouth§, who met the second time at Scituate, and there came to a full agreement, which was certified this court, and recorded to this effect: That the bounds should be ||that branch|| of Conyhassett creek nearest to Scituate, with 60 acres of marsh in the south side.[1]

The scarcity of money made a great change in all commerce. Merchants would sell no wares but for ready money, men could not pay their debts though they had enough, prices of lands and cattle fell soon to the one half and less, yea to a third, and after one fourth part.

Mo. 10. 9.] The church of Watertown ordained Mr. Knolles,[2] a godly man and a prime scholar, pastor, and so they had now two pastors and no teacher, differing from the practice of the other churches, as also they did in their privacy, not giving notice thereof to the neighbouring churches, nor to the magistrates, as the common practice was.[3]

||the beach||

---

1 In vol. I. 284, is transcribed what I then thought the earliest notice in our colony records of any inquiry about the bounds of the two jurisdictions; but the Rec. I, 192, at the general court in May, 1637, has the following: "Mr. Timothy Hatherley and Mr. . . . . . Tilden, with Mr. William Aspinwall and Joseph Andrews were appointed to view the bounds between us and Plimouth, and make return how they find them lie to both courts." Tilden, Nathaniel, was of Scituate, and a respectable mention of him is made in 2 Hist. Coll. IV. 242.

2 Both by Eliot and Allen the Rev. John Knowles is overlooked, yet he seems entitled to a place in their works, at least, as much as many who are thus honoured. In a later period of this history, his name will occur in connexion with a memorable mission to Virginia, of which an account may be seen in Eliot's Eccl. Hist. 1 Hist. Coll. IX. 46, abbreviated from our author. Johnson has given a fuller relation of the result, Lib. III. c. 11, and in his usual manner L. II. c. 15, bestows on Knowles appropriate verses. Hutch. Coll. 447 and 514 contains two letters to Gov. Leverett from Knowles, in London, 1674 and 1677, from which we learn how strongly he continued an attachment to our colony, and especially to Harvard College. In 3 Hist. Coll. I. 62, 65, are other valuable letters from him. I am dissatisfied, as curious readers often are, with Hubbard 410, 411, for adding nothing to what he borrowed of Winthrop, when he ought to have learned much about one of his brethren in the ministry many years after our author's decease, and had better means than Hutchinson.

3 Our congregational societies of christians assert the *right* of each body of worshippers to elect and ordain, without any assistance from others, its own pastor, though the fellowship of the churches, as *equal* members of the mystical body, is requested. They design to stand fast in the liberty, which forbids them to call any man on earth master. When a clergyman so distinguished as Phillips, and well acquainted with the discipline of his sect, (see Vol. I. p. 14, n. 1.)

At the court of assistants one Hugh Bewett was banished for holding publicly and maintaining that he was free from original sin and from actual also for half a year before, and that all true christians after [1] are enabled to live without committing actual sin.[2]

15.] A pinnace called the Coach, being in her voyage to New Haven (late Quinipiack) between Salem and Cape Cod, sprang a leak, so as in the morning they found her hold half filled with water; whereupon the seamen and passengers betook themselves to their skiff, being a very small one, and the wind then growing very high at S.W. Only one Jackson, a godly man and an experienced seaman, would not leave the vessel before he had tried the utmost, so getting them in again, and ||laying|| the bark upon the contrary side, they fell to getting out the water, which, it pleased God, they overcame, and having a fine fresh gale, they got safe back to Salem.

Mr. Pelham's[3] house in Cambridge took fire in the dead of the night by the chimney. A neighbour's wife hearing some noise

||tying||

---

received a colleague, we may be confident, no deficiency in the delegation of pastoral duties and privileges was designed or permitted. The fact related in the text confirms my doubt of the very great distinction between the offices of pastors and teachers, Vol. I. p. 31.

[1 This blank had been filled by me, but it is impossible now to recover the exact words. The loss is very trifling, as the next note may convince any other reader than myself.]

2 Hubbard, 277, adds to the narrative a profound reflection: "it being justly to be feared, that if he had staid still, he would have made himself, and others too, guilty of more actual sin than his neighbours, (as is ordinarily found by experience of those great pretenders to perfection and holiness.") But in his compilation, part of Bewett's heresy, that all true christians after some exercise of faith may live without actual transgression, is omitted. Emerson, in his history of First Church, 70, has more candidly said: "In this avowal he seemed desirous of gaining no peculiar reputation for sanctity." The names of the jury are given in our Col. Rec. I. 295, and their verdict, "guilty of heresy, and that his person and errours are dangerous for infection of others." The sentence "ordered, that the said Hugh Buet should be gone out of our jurisdiction by the 24th present upon pain of death, and not to return upon pain of being hanged." This was rather milder than common, though removal in December might be uncomfortable. The first named juryman was Edward Rainsford, who was, says Hutchinson I, 238, brother of the Lord Chief Justice of that name. An Island in our harbour is called after him. Bewett went to Providence, the common resort of those who had too weak or too strong a faith for Massachusetts. 3 Hist. Coll. I. 4.

3 We can hardly doubt, that this is Herbert Pelham, Esq. the same gentleman mentioned in Vol. I. p. 8, n. 1. He had been of the company in England in 1629, Hubbard, 122, and in the common stock of the colony advanced 100 pounds. He was first treasurer of Harvard College, appointed by our govern-

among her hens, persuaded her husband to arise, which, being very cold, he was loth to do, yet through her great importunity he did, and so espied the fire, and came running in his shirt, and had much to do to awake any body, but he got them up at last, and so saved all. The fire being ready to lay hold upon the stairs, they had all been burnt in their chambers, if God had not by his special providence sent help at that very instant.

About this time a pinnace called the Make Shift, (§so called§ because she was built of the wreck of a greater vessel[1] at the Isle of Sable, and by that means the men saved,) being on a voyage to the southward, was cast away upon a ledge of rocks near Long Island, the goods were all lost, but the men were saved. No winter but some vessels have been cast away in that voyage.

About this time there fell out a thing worthy of observation. Mr. Winthrop the younger, one of the magistrates, having many books in a chamber where there was corn of divers sorts, had among them one wherein the Greek testament, the psalms and the common prayer were bound together. He found the common prayer eaten with mice, every leaf of it, and not any of the two other touched, nor any other of his books, though there were above a thousand.[2]

§ Quere, of the child at Cambridge killed by a cat.§

Mo. 8.] We received a letter at the general court from the magistrates of Connecticut and New Haven and of Aquiday, wherein they declared their dislike of such as would have the Indians rooted out, as being of the cursed race of ||Ham,|| and their desire of our mutual accord in seeking to gain them by justice and kindness, and withal to watch over them to prevent any danger by them, &c. We returned answer of our consent with them in all things

||Shem||

---

ment before the charter; and was honoured with the offices of assistant and commissioner of the United Colonies. Johnson Lib. II. c. 13, says Pelham came over in 1639, and pays him a tribute of verse, chiefly valuable for its information, that he went home Hutchinson makes him of the same family as the Duke of Newcastle in his time.

1 Cast away in April of the preceding year. See Vol. I. p. 305.

2 Such an anecdote looks too much like superstitious belief in the relater. It is apparently introduced as a pointing from heaven against the service of the Episcopal church, but is susceptible of an harmless explanation: the mice, not liking psalmody, and not understanding Greek, took their food from another part of the volume. Our age will believe that the book, which alone was injured among a thousand, was fortuitously attacked by these humble mischief-makers. The succeeding paragraph, omitted by the former editor, is surely of equal value, whether true or not. If the cat had been in Winthrop's library, she might have prevented the stigma on the common prayer.

propounded, only we refused to include those of Aquiday in our answer,or to have any treaty with them.[1]

Mo. 10.] About the end of this month a fishing ship arrived at Isle of Shoals, and another soon after, and there came no more this season for fishing. They brought us news of the Scots entering into England, and the calling of a parliament, and the hope of a thorough reformation, &c. whereupon some among us began to think of returning back to England. Others despairing of any more supply from thence, and yet not knowing how to live there, if they should return, bent their minds wholly to removal to the south parts, supposing they should find better means of subsistence there, and for this end put off their estates here at very low rates. These things, together with the scarcity of money, caused a sudden and very great abatement of the prices of all our own commodities. Corn (Indian) was sold ordinarily at three shillings the bushel, a good cow at seven or eight pounds, and some at £5,— and other things answerable (see the order of court in 8ber. about these things) whereby it came to pass that men could not pay their debts, for no money nor beaver were to be had, and he who last year, or but three months before was worth £1000 could not now, if he should sell his whole estate, raise £200, whereby God taught us the vanity of all outward things, &c.

One Taylor of Linne, having a milch cow in the ship as he came over, sold the milk to the passengers for 2d the quart, and being

---

1 By giving the order of court, to which our text refers, I shall not deserve the condemnation of exposing the nakedness of our fathers: "It is ordered, that the letter lately sent to the governour by Mr. Eaton, Mr. Hopkins, Mr. Haynes, Mr. Coddington, and Mr. Brenton, but concerning also the general court, shall be thus answered by the governour, that the court doth assent to all the propositions laid down in the aforesaid letter; but that the answer shall be directed to Mr. Eaton, Mr. Hopkins, and Mr. Haynes only, excluding Mr. Coddington and Mr. Brenton, as men not to be capitulated withal by us, either for themselves, or the people of the island, where they inhabit, as their case standeth." This is the most exalted triumph of bigotry. Papists, Jews, Musselmans, idolators, or atheists, may be good parties to a civil compact, but not erroneous Protestant brethren, of unimpeachable piety, differing from us in explication of unessential, or unintelligible, points of doubtful disputation. It was not enough, that the common charities of life were broken off, but our rulers proved the sincerity of their folly, in abhorring the opinions entertained at Rhode Island, by refusing connexion in a just and necessary course of policy, which demanded the concurrence of all the plantations on our coast. Our father's conduct, also, appears little more civil, than prudent; for when those of Aquiday were associated by the gentlemen of Connecticut and New Haven in their address, the answer should have been directed to all without scruple.

The errour of the former edition in giving the name of that son of Noah, upon whom the curse was fastened or denounced, will seem ludicrous to such as know the universal acquaintance of the people of Connecticut, learned or illiterate, with the scriptures of the Old Testament.

after at a sermon wherein oppression was complained of, &c. he fell distracted. §Quere, of the price, for 2d the quart was not dear at sea.[1]§

This evil was very notorious among all sorts of people, it being the common rule that most men walked by in all their commerce, to buy as cheap as they could, and to sell as dear.

A great ship called the Charles of above 300 tons brought passengers hither this year. The master was a plain quiet man, but his company were very wicked, and did wrong the passengers much, and being at Pascataquack to take in clapboards with another ship wherein Mr. Peter by occasion preached one Lord's day, the company of the Charles did use all the means they could to disturb the exercise, by hooting and hallooing, but in their return they were set upon by the Turks and divers of them killed.

A wicked fellow, given up to bestiality, fearing to be taken by the hand of justice, fled to Long Island, and there was drowned. He had confessed to some that he was so given up to that abomination, that he never saw any beast go before him but he lusted after it.

Mr. Nathaniel Eaton, of whom mention is made before, being come to Virginia, took upon him to be a minister, but was given up of God to extreme pride and sensuality, being usually drunken, as the custom is there.[2] He sent for his wife and children. Her friends here persuaded her to stay a while, but she went notwithstanding, and the vessel was never heard of after.

Mo. 12. 2.] The church of Dorchester being furnished with a very godly and able pastor, one Mr. Mather, and having invited to them one Mr. Burr,[3] who had been a minister in England, and of

---

1 This is a refreshing sentence, as it shows, that our author would not always consider misfortune to be proof of guilt.

2 Our neighbours of Virginia will not, I hope, be disconcerted at this report of customary drunkenness; or they must, at least, recollect that the materials of their infant colony were less select than those of New England. If the imputation be intended, as appears not improbable, to apply only to the ministers of religion, the author's gradually acquired prejudice against the church of England will afford explanation of the phrase, and their charity must supply the deficiency of his.

3 Ample memorials of the Rev. Jonathan Burr will be found in the Magnalia, Book III, whose author was grandson of his colleague, in Harris's History of Dorchester, and in Allen's Dictionary. His short course, for he died the next year after that of our text, does not fully excuse the omission of him by Eliot. At which of the English universities he was educated is unknown to me, but it is certain, he studied at one of them between three and four years. His widow married Richard Dummer of Newbury, by whom his son, Jonathan, was brought up at Harvard College, received its honours 1651, and was a physician at Bristol, Eng. died 25 July, 1691. Peter Burr, H. C. 1690, son of the last named, a Judge of the Superior Court of Connecticut, was father of President Burr of Princeton College, a distinguished name in the history of our country.

very good report there for piety and learning, with intent to call him also to office, after he was received a member in their church, and had given good proofs of his gifts and godliness to the satisfaction of the church, they gave him a call to office, which he deferring to accept, in the mean time he delivered some points savouring of familism, wherein the church desiring satisfaction, and he not so free to give it as was meet, it was agreed that Mr. Mather and he should confer together, and so the church should be informed wherein the difference lay. Accordingly Mr. Burr wrote his judgment in the points in difference, in such manner and terms as from some of his propositions there could no other be gathered but that he was erroneous; but this was again so qualified in other parts as might admit of a charitable construction. Mr. Mather reports to the church the errours which might be collected, without mentioning the qualification, or acquainting Mr. Burr with it before. When this was published, Mr. Burr disclaimed the errours, and Mr. Mather maintained them from his writings; whereupon the church was divided, some joining with the one, and some with the other, so as it grew to some heat and alienation, and many days were spent for reconciliation, but all in vain. In the end they agreed to call in help from other churches, so this day there was a meeting at Dorchester of the governour and [1]another of the magistrates, and about ten of the elders of the neighbouring churches, wherein four days were spent in opening the cause, and such offences as had fallen out in the prosecution; and in conclusion the magistrates and elders declared their judgment and advice in the case to this effect; that both sides had cause to be humbled for their failings, more particularly Mr. Burr for his doubtful and unsafe expressions, and backwardness to give clear satisfaction, &c. and Mr. Mather for his inconsideration both in not acquainting Mr. Burr with his collections before he had published them to the church, and in not certifying the qualifications of those errours which were in his writings: for which they were advised to set a day apart for reconciliation. Upon this Mr. Mather and Mr. Burr took the blame of their failings upon themselves, and freely submitted to the judgment and advice given, to which the rest of the church yielded a silent assent, and God was much glorified in the close thereof; and Mr. Burr did again fully renounce those erroneous opinions of which he had been suspected, confessing that he was in the dark about these points, till God, by occasion of this agitation, had cleared them to him, which he did with much meekness and many tears.

---

[1] The author designates himself by this modest expression.

The church of Boston were necessitated to build a new meeting house, and a great difference arose about the place of situation, which had much troubled other churches on the like occasion, but after some debate it was referred to a committee and was quietly determined. It cost about £.1000, which was raised out of the weekly voluntary contribution without any noise or complaint, when in some other churches which did it by way of rates, there was much difficulty and compulsion by ||levies|| to raise a far less sum.[1]

The general fear of want of foreign commodities, now our money was gone, and that things were like to go well in England, set us on work to provide shipping of our own, for which end Mr. Peter, being a man of a very public spirit and singular activity for all occasions, procured some to join for building a ship at Salem of 300 tons, and the inhabitants of Boston, stirred up by his example, set upon the building another at Boston of 150 tons. The work was hard to accomplish for want of money, &c. but our shipwrights were content to take such pay as the country could make. The shipwright at Salem, through want of care of his tackle, &c. occasioned the death of one Baker[2], who was desired with five or six more to help hale up a piece of timber, which, the rope breaking, fell down upon them. The rest by special providence were saved. This Baker, going forth in the morning very well, after he had prayed, told his wife he should see her no more, though he could not foresee any danger towards him.

The court having found by experience that it would not avail by any law to redress the excessive rates of labourers' and workmen's wages, &c. (for being restrained, they would either remove to other places where they might have more, or else being able to live by

||laws||

1 By this paragraph we are compelled to dissent from the inscription in front of the first church, rebuilt 1808. The time of finishing the edifice must certainly be received as this year, not, as that monument bears, 1639. Cotton Mather, who has published more errours of carelessness than any other writer on the history of New England, which he professed to understand better than all his contemporaries, in his discourse on occasion of the great fire of 1711, by which the edifice, whose erection is commemorated in the text, was consumed, utters this strange statement: "I suppose my grandfather preached the first sermon in it, sixty-five or six years ago." It was at least seventy-one years, as he might, on slight calculation, have ascertained.

2 Of this sufferer I cannot easily learn any thing, but the name of baptism. A remarkable instance of the judicial policy of our fathers is found in their animadversion upon the shipwright; for in Col. Rec. I. 297, at the court 2d March following, may be read, "Richard Hollingworth, upon occasion of the death of Robert Baker, was fined 10 pound, to be paid to the wife and children of the said Baker, his negligence being the occasion of his death."

planting and other employments of their own, they would not be hired at all,) it was therefore referred to the several towns to set down rates among themselves. This took better effect, so that in a voluntary way, by the counsel and persuasion of the elders, and example of some who led the way, they were brought to more moderation than they could be by compulsion. But it held not long.

Upon the great liberty which the king had left the parliament to in England, some of our friends there wrote to us advice to send over some to solicit for us in the parliament, giving us hope that we might obtain much, &c. But consulting about it, we declined the motion for this consideration, that if we should put ourselves under the protection of the parliament, we must then be subject to all such laws as they should make, or at least such as they might impose upon us; in which course though they should intend our good, yet it might prove very prejudicial to us.[1] But upon this occasion the court of assistants being assembled, and advising with some of the elders about some course to serve the providence of God in making use of present opportunity of a ship of our own being ready bound for England, it was thought fit to send some chosen men in her with commission to negotiate for us, as occasion should be offered, both in furthering the work of reformation of the churches there which was now like to be attempted, and to satisfy our countrymen of the true cause why our engagements there have not been satisfied this year, as they were wont to be in all former time since we were here planted; and also to seek out some way, by procuring cotton from the West Indies, or other means that might be lawful, and not dishonourable to the gospel, for our present supply of clothing, &c. for the country was like to afford enough for food, &c. The persons designed hereto were Mr. Peter, pastor of the church of Salem, Mr. ||Welde|| the pastor of the church of Roxbury, and Mr. Hibbins of Boston. For this end the governour and near all the rest of the magistrates and some of the elders wrote a letter to the church of Salem acquainting them with our intentions, and desiring them to spare their pastor for that service. The governour also moved the church of

||Wade||

---

1 Upon this passage, transcribed for his letter to Baron Van der Capellan, a distinguished Dutch statesman, in 1779, Governour Trumbull, one of the most deliberate asserters of the American revolution, remarks: "Here observe, that, as at this time, so it hath been ever since, that the colonies, so far from acknowledging the parliament to have a right to make laws binding on them in all cases whatsoever, they have denied it in any case." 1 Hist. Coll. VI. 156. Cradock, the first governour of the company of Massachusetts, was a member, of the parliament then sitting, for the city of London.

Roxbury for Mr. Welde, whom, after some time of consideration, they freely yielded. But when it was propounded to the church of Salem, Mr. Endecott, being a member thereof, and having formerly opposed it, did now again the like in the church. Some reasons were there alleged, as that officers should not be taken from their churches for civil occasions, that the voyage would be long and dangerous, that it would be reported that we were in such want as we had sent to England to beg relief, which would be very dishonourable to religion, and that we ought to trust God who had never failed us hitherto, &c. But the main reason, indeed, which was privately intimated, was their fear lest he should be kept there, or diverted to the West Indies, for Mr. Humfrey intended to go with him, who was already engaged that way by the lord Say, &c. and therefore it was feared he should fall under strong temptations that way, being once in England; and Mr. Humfrey discovered his intentions the more by falling §foul§ upon Mr. Endecott in the open assembly at Salem for opposing this motion, and with that bitterness as gave great offence, and was like to have grown to a professed breach between them, but being both godly, and hearkening to seasonable counsel, they were soon reconciled, upon a free and public acknowledgment of such failings as had passed. But the church, not willing to let their pastor go, nor yet to give a plain denial to the magistrates' request, wrote an answer by way of excuse, tendering some reasons of their unsatisfiedness about his going, &c. The agitation of this business was soon about the country, whereby we perceived there would be sinister interpretations made of it, and the ship being suddenly to depart, we gave it over for that season.

Mo. 2. 13.] A negro maid, servant to Mr. Stoughton of Dorchester, being well approved by divers years' experience, for sound knowledge and true godliness, was received into the church and baptized.[1]

Some agitation fell out between us and Plimouth about Seacunk. Some of our people finding it fit for plantations, and thinking it out of our patent, which Plimouth men understanding, forbad them, and sent to us to signify that it was within their grant, and that we would therefore forbid ours to proceed. But the planters having acquainted us with their title, and offering to yield it to our jurisdiction, and assuring us that it could not be in the Plimouth patent, we made answer to Plimouth accordingly, and encouraged our neighbours to go on, so as divers letters passing between us,

---

[1] Similar instances have been common enough ever since.

and ||they|| sending some to take possession for them, at length we sent some to Plimouth to see their patent, who bringing us a copy of so much as concerned the thing in question, though we were not fully satisfied thereby, yet not being willing to strive for land, we sat still.

There fell out much trouble about this time at Pascataquack. Mr. Knolles had gathered a church of such as he could get, men very raw for the most part, &c. Afterwards there came amongst them one Mr. Larkham,[1] who had been a minister at Northam near Barnstable in England, a man not savouring the right way of church discipline, but being a man of good parts and wealthy, the people were soon taken with him, and the greater part were forward to cast off Mr. Knolles their pastor and to choose him, for they were not willing nor able to maintain two officers, so Mr. Knolles gave place to him, and he being thus chosen, did soon discover himself. He received into the church all that offered themselves, though men notoriously scandalous and ignorant, so they would promise amendment, and fell into contention with the people, and would take upon him to rule all, even the magistrates (such as they were;) so as there soon grew sharp contention between him and Mr. Knolles, to whom the more religious still adhered, whereupon they were divided into two churches. Mr. Knolles and his company excommunicated Mr. Larkham, and he again laid violent hands upon Mr. Knolles. In this heat it began to grow to a tumult, some of their magistrates joined with Mr. Larkham and assembled a company to fetch Capt. Underhill (another of their ma-

||the||

1 Belknap, in N. H. I. 43, 51, has given as much of Thomas Larkham, as can probably be ascertained, though he refers to Hubbard MS. rather than the original text of Winthrop, sub. an. 1642. Notwithstanding the suspicious case there introduced, Larkham is reported, in his later years, as "well known for a man of great piety and sincerity" in England, when ejected under the statute of 1662. He died, aged 68, in 1669. Lechford's account of the dispute varies a little from that above: "They two fell out about baptising children, receiving of members, burial of the dead; and the contention was so sharp, that Knowles and his party rise up and excommunicated Mr. Larkham and some that held with him; and further, Mr. Larkham flying to the magistrates, Mr. Knowles and Captain Underhill raised arms, and expected help from the Bay, Mr. Knowles going before the troop with a bible upon a pole's top, and giving forth that their side were Scots and the other English Whereupon the gentlemen of Sir F. Gorge's plantation came in, and kept court with the magistrates of Piscataqua, who have also a patent, being weak of themselves, and they fined all those that were in arms for a riot, by indictment, jury, and verdict formally: nine of them were censured to be whipped, but that was spared; Mr Knowles, and the captain, their leaders, were fined 100 pounds apiece, which they were not able to pay." The antagonist excommunications of the rival synods must have given much scandal to disinterested spectators, if there were any.

gistrates and their captain) to their court, and he also gathered some of the neighbours to defend himself, and to see the peace kept; so they marched forth towards Mr. Larkham's, one carrying a bible upon a staff for an ensign, and Mr. Knolles with them armed with a pistol. When Mr. Larkham and his company saw them thus provided, they proceeded no further, but sent to Mr. [1]Williams, who was governour of those in the lower part of the river, who came up with a company of armed men and beset Mr. Knolles' house, where Capt. Underhill then was, and there they kept a guard upon them night and day; and in the mean time they called a court, and Mr. Williams sitting as judge, they found Capt. Underhill and his company guilty of a riot, and set great fines upon them, and ordered him and some others to depart the plantation. The cause of this eager prosecution of Capt. Underhill was, because he had procured a good part of the inhabitants there to offer themselves again to the government of the Massachusetts, who being thus prosecuted, they sent a petition to us for aid.

The governour and council considered of their petition, and gave commission to Mr. Bradstreet, one of our magistrates, Mr. Peter and Mr. Dalton[2] two of our elders, to go thither and to endeavour to reconcile them, and if they could not effect that, then to inquire how things stood, and to certify us, &c. They went accordingly, and finding both sides to be in fault, at length they brought matters to a peaceable end. Mr. Larkham was released of his excommunication and Capt. Underhill and the rest from their centures, and by occasion of these agitations Mr. Knolles was discovered to be an unclean person, and to have solicited the chastity of two maids, his servants, and to have used filthy dalliance with them, which he acknowledged before the church there, and so was dismissed, and removed from Pascataquack. This sin of his was the more notorious, because the fact, which was first discovered, was the same night after he had been exhorting the people by reasons and from scripture, to proceed against Capt. Underhill for his adultery. And it is very observable how God gave up these

---

1 Francis Williams, Esquire, was governour of the settlements at Portsmouth, and Dover, appointed, after Neal's return to England, by Gorges and Mason, and continued in office by the people. Belk. N. H. I. 26. Soon after this disturbance, Hutch. I. 102, says, he removed to Barbados.

2 Very little notice can be found of this reverend gentleman, except in Johnson lib. II. c. 13, who has given the usual complement of rhyme. His name was Timothy, and his descendants have been honoured with much public confidence in our time. Samuel, whom I presume to be his son, was an early representative from Hampton.

two, and some others who had held with Mrs. Hutchinson, in crying down all evidence from sanctification, &c. to fall into these unclean courses, whereby themselves and their erroneous opinions were laid open to the world.

Mr. Peter and Mr. Dalton, with one of Acomenticus, went from Pascataquack, with Mr. John Ward,[1] who was to be entertained there for their minister; and though it be but six miles, yet they lost their way, and wandered two days and one night without food or fire, in the snow and wet. But God heard their prayers, wherein they earnestly pressed him for the honour of his great name, and when they were even quite spent, he brought them to the sea side near the place they were to go to, blessed forever be his name.

Not long before a godly maid of the church of Linnė, going in a deep snow from Meadford homeward, was lost and some of her clothes found after among the rocks.

One John Baker, a member of the church of Boston, removing from thence to Newbury for enlargement of his outward accommodation, being grown wealthy from nothing, grew there very disordered, fell into drunkenness and such violent contention with another brother, maintaining the same by lying, and other evil courses, that the magistrates sent to have him apprehended. But he rescued himself out of the officer's hands and removed to Acomenticus, where he continued near two years, and now at this time he came to Boston, and humbled himself before the church confessing all his wickedness, with many tears, and showing how he had been followed with satan, and how he had laboured to pacify his conscience by secret confessions to God, &c. but could have no peace, yet could not bring his heart to return and make public acknowledgment, until the hand of God fell upon one Swain his neighbour, who fell into despair, and would often utter dreadful speeches against himself, and cry out that he was all on fire under the wrath of God, but would never discover any other heinous sin, but that having gotten about £40 by his labour, he went into England and there spent it in wicked company, and so continued, and after a small time hanged himself. This Baker coming in, and seeing him thus dead, was so struck with it as he could have no rest, till he came and made his peace with the church and court.

---

1 John, son of Nathaniel Ward, mentioned in my note 1, Vol. I. 154, is remembered in Eliot and Allen. He was born at Haverhill, in old England, where his grandfather, John, was the pastor; and in compliment to him the place of his descendant's residence in our country was named. All that could be interesting about him is supplied by the history of Haverhill, in 2 Hist. Coll. IV. Johnson has given him, lib. III. c. 1. some rugged verses.

Upon his confession the church was doubtful whether they ought not to cast him out, his offences being so scandalous, notwithstanding they were well persuaded of the truth of his repentance: but the judgment of the church was, that seeing he had excommunicated himself by deserting the church, and Christ had ratified it by giving him up to satan, whereby the ordinance had had its proper effect, therefore he ought now to be received and pardoned, whereto the church agreed. Yet this man fell into gross distempers soon after.

Mr. Cotton out of that in Revelations 15. none could enter into the temple until, &c. delivered, that neither Jews nor any more of the Gentiles should be called until Antichrist were destroyed, viz. to a church estate, though here and there a proselyte.

Upon the Lord's day at Concord two children were left at home alone, one lying in a cradle, the other having burned a cloth and fearing its mother should see it, thrust it into a hay stack by the door (the fire not being quite out) whereby the hay and house were burned and the child in the cradle before they came from the meeting. About the same time two houses were burned at Sudbury.[1]

By occasion of these fires I may add another of a different kind, but of much observation. A godly woman of the church of Boston, dwelling sometimes in London, brought with her a parcel of very fine linen of great value, which she set her heart too much upon, and had been at charge to have it all newly washed and curiously folded and pressed, and so left it in press in her parlour over night. She had a negro maid went into the room very late and let fall some snuff of the candle upon the linen, so as by the morning all the linen was burned to tinder, and the boards underneath, and some stools and a part of the wainscot burned, and never perceived by any in the house, though some lodged in the chamber over head, and no ceiling between. But it pleased God that the loss of this linen did her much good, both in taking off her heart from worldly comforts, and in preparing her for a far greater affliction by the untimely death of her husband who was slain not long after at Isle of Providence.[2]

---

1 An extraordinary errour in Vol. I. 167, n. 3, may here be corrected. The settlement above the falls of Charles river, here alluded to, was undoubtedly Dedham, and Sudbury was not planted before 1639, *ib.* 306. I paid too much attention to Hubbard, and neglected to reflect, that the latter town lies on Concord, not Charles, river. Dr. Holmes had been led by the same guide to the same errour, Ann. I. 281, but he corrected it more happily than myself, ib. 311.

2 The wife of Capt. William Peirce is probably the object of this paragraph.

Mo. 4. 2.[1]] The court of elections, Richard Bellingham, Esq. chosen governour. See more a few leaves after.

This year the two ships were finished, one at Salem of 300 tons and another at Boston of 160 tons.

The parliament of England setting upon a general reformation both of church and state, the earl of Strafford being beheaded, and the archbishop (our great enemy) and many others of the great officers and judges, bishops and others, imprisoned and called to account, this caused all men to stay in England in expectation of a new world, so as few coming to us, all foreign commodities grew scarce, and our own of no price. Corn would buy nothing: a cow which cost last year £20 might now be bought for 4 or £5, &c. and many gone out of the country, so as no man could pay his debts, nor the merchants make return into England for their commodities, which occasioned many there to speak evil of us. These straits set our people on work to provide fish, clapboards, plank, &c. and to sow hemp and flax (which prospered very well) and to look out to the W. Indies for a trade for cotton. The general court also made orders about payment of debts, setting corn at the wonted price, and payable for all debts which should arise after a time prefixed. They thought fit also to send some chosen men into England to congratulate the happy success there, and to satisfy our creditors of the true cause why we could not make so current payment now as in former years we had done, and to be ready to make use of any opportunity God should offer for the good of the country here, as also to give any advice, as it should be required, for the settling the right form of church discipline there, but with this caution, that they should not seek supply of our wants in any dishonourable way, as by begging or the like, for we were resolved to wait upon the Lord in the use of all means which were lawful and ||honourable||. The men chosen were Mr. Hugh Peter, pastor of the church in Salem, Mr. Thos. Welde, pastor of the church in Roxbury, and Mr. William Hibbins of Boston. There being no ship which was to return right for England, they went to Newfoundland, intending to get a passage from thence in the fishing fleet. They departed hence the 3d of the 6th month, and with them went one of the magistrates Mr. John

||humble||

[1] It has been too hastily thought, that our general election always came nearly at the same time as is fixed by our modern constitution. Careful readers, observing its occurrence in these volumes at different dates, as in 1640, on 13 May, and in 1641, on 2 June, will find the explanation in the charter of 1629, providing that the general court be held on "the last Wednesday in Easter term yearly." By the new charter of William and Mary, 7 Oct. 1691, the last Wednesday of May was established.

Winthrop, jun. This act of the court did not satisfy all the elders, and many others disliked it, supposing that it would be conceived we had sent them on begging; and the church of Salem was unwillingly drawn to give leave to their pastor to go, for the court was not minded to use their power in taking an officer from the church without their consent, but in the end they and the other churches submitted to the desire of the court. These with other passengers to the number of forty went to Newfoundland, expecting to go from thence in some fishing ships. They arrived there in 14 days, but could not go altogether, so were forced to divide themselves and go from several parts of the island, as they could get shipping. The ministers preached to the seamen &c. at the island, who were much affected with the word taught, and entertained them with all courtesy, as we understood by letters from them which came by a fishing ship to the Isles of Shoals about the beginning of October.

21.] A young man, a tanner in Boston, going to wash himself in a creek, said jestingly, I will go and drown myself now, which fell out accordingly, for by the slipperiness of the earth, he was carried beyond his depth, and having no skill to swim, was drowned, though company were at hand, and one in the water with him.

Letters came from the governour, &c. of Connecticut for advice about the difference between them and the Dutch. The Dutch governour had pressed them hard for his interest in all Hartford, &c. as far as one might see from their house, alleging he had purchased so much of the Pequods, and threatened force of arms. They of the river alleged their purchase of other Indians, the true owners of the place, &c. with other arguments from our patent and that of Say-brook. We returned answer without determining of either side, but advising to a moderate way, as the yielding some more land to the Dutch house (for they had left them but 30 acres.) But the Dutch would not be thus pacified, but prepared to send soldiers to be billeted at their house. But it pleased the Lord to disappoint their purpose, for the Indians falling out with them, killed four of their men at their fort Orange, whereof three were English who had gone to dwell among them, whereby they were forced to keep their soldiers at home to defend themselves; and Mr. Peter going for England, and being well acquainted with the chief merchants in Holland, undertook to pacify the West India company, but for want of commission from those of Hartford, the company there would not treat with him.

About this time three boys of Summer's Islands stole away in an open boat or skiff, and having been eight weeks at sea, their boat was cast away upon a strand without Long Island, and themselves were saved by the Indians.[1]

A church being gathered at Providence in the West Indies, and their pastor, Mr. Sherwood, and another minister being sent prisoners into England by one Carter, the deputy governour, the rest of the church, being but five, wrote to our churches complaining of the persecution of their magistrates and others, and desiring our prayers and help from us, which moved the churches and magistrates more willingly to further those who were already resolved and preparing for that Island. Whereupon two small vessels, each of about 30 tons, with divers families and goods, so many as they could bestow, 30 men, 5 women and 8 children set sail for the Island, and touching at Christophers, they heard that a great fleet of Spanish ships was abroad, and that it was feared they had taken Providence, so as the master, Mr. Peirce, a godly man and most expert mariner, advised them to return, and offered to bear part of the loss. But they not hearkening to him, he replied, then am I a dead man. And coming to the Island they marvelled they saw no colours upon the fort, nor any boat coming towards them, whereupon he was counselled to drop an anchor. He liked the advice, but yet stood on into the harbour, and after a second advice, he still went on; but being come within pistol shot of one fort and hailing, and no answer made, he put ||his bark|| a stays, and being upon the deck, which was also full of passengers, women and children, and hearing one cry out, they are traversing a piece at us, he threw himself in at the door of the cuddy, and one Samuel Wakeman[2], a member of the church of Hartford, who was sent with goods to buy cotton, cast himself down by him, and presently a great shot took them both. Mr. Peirce died within an hour, the other, having only his thighs tore, lived ten days. Mr. Peirce had read to the company that morning (as it fell in course) that in Genesis the last, lo I die, but God will surely visit you and bring you back; out of which words he used godly exhortations to them.[3] Then they shot from all parts about thirty great shot,

||her back||

1 Many less striking stories of preservation at sea are given by Mather, who neglects this. How the boys found food, is a natural inquiry ; and the author of the Magnalia might have furnished the aid of the prophet Elijah. Perhaps it was stolen with the boat.

2 He was admitted a freeman of Massachusetts 7 Aug 1632, and probably before removing to Hartford, lived at Cambridge, for which town he was, I think, a deputy at the third court, May 1635.

3 Johnson, lib. II. c. 20, has given an account of this disastrous expedition, in which a strange lack of sympathy for the sufferers is observable.

besides small, and tore the sails and shrouds, but hurt not the bark, nor any person more in it. The other vessel was then a league behind, which was marvelled at, for she was the better sailer, and could fetch up the other at pleasure; but that morning they could not by any means keep company with her. After this the passengers, being ashamed to return, would have been set on shore at Cape Grace de Dios, or Florida, or Virginia, but the seamen would not, and through the wonderful providence of God they came all safe home the 3d of 7ber following. This brought some of them to see their errour and acknowledge it in the open congregation, but others were hardened. There was a special providence in that the ministers were sent prisoners into England before the Island was taken, for otherwise it is most probable they had been all put to the sword, because some Spaniards had been slain there a little before by the deputy governour his command, after the lieutenant had received them upon quarter, in an attempt they had made upon the Island, wherein they were repulsed with the loss of two or three ||hundred[1]|| men. They took it after and gave the people quarter and sent them home.

A like providence there was, though not so safe, in that divers godly people, in their voyage to the Island the year before, were taken prisoners by the Turks, and so their lives saved, paying their ransom.

This year divers families in Linne and Ipswich having sent to view Long Island, and finding a very commodious place for plantations, but challenged by the Dutch, they treated with the Dutch governour to take it from them. He offered them very fair terms, as that they should have the very same liberties, both civil and ecclesiastical, which they enjoyed in the Massachusetts, only liberty for appeal to the Dutch, and after ten years to pay the 10th of their corn. The court were offended at this, and sought to stay them, not for going from us, but for strengthening the Dutch, our doubtful neighbours, and taking that from them which our king challenged and had granted a patent of, with Martha's Vineyard and other Islands thereby, to the earl of Sterling, especially for binding themselves by an oath of fealty; whereupon divers of the chief being called before the general court in 8ber, and reasons laid down to dissuade them, they were convinced and promised to desist.

This summer the merchants of Boston set out a vessel again to the isle of Sable, with 12 men, to stay there a year. They sent

||thousand||

1 The original MS. is plain enough.

again in the 8th month, and in three weeks the vessel returned and brought home 400 pair of sea horse teeth, which were esteemed worth £300, and left all the men well and 12 ton of oil and many skins, which they could not bring away, being put from the island in a storm.

I must here return to supply what was omitted concerning the proceedings of the last court of elections.[1] There had been much labouring to have Mr. Bellingham chosen, and when the votes were numbered he had six more than the others; but there were divers who had not given in their votes, who now came into the court and desired their liberty, which was denied by some of the magistrates, because they had not given them in at the doors. But others thought it was an injury, yet were silent, because it concerned themselves, for the order of giving in their votes at the door was no order of court, but only direction of some of the magistrates; and without question, if any freeman tender his vote before the election be passed and published, it ought to be received.

Some of the freemen, without the consent of the magistrates or governour, had chosen Mr. Nathaniel Ward to preach at this court, pretending that it was a part of their liberty. The governour (whose right indeed it is, for till the court be assembled the freemen are but private persons) would not strive about it, for though it did not belong to them, yet if they would have it, there was reason to yield it to them. Yet they had no great reason to choose him, though otherwise very able, seeing he had cast off his pastor's place at Ipswich, and was now no minister by the received determination of our churches. In his sermon he delivered many useful things, but in a moral and political discourse, grounding his propositions much upon the old Roman and Grecian governments, which sure is an errour, for if religion and the word of God makes men wiser than their neighbours, and these times have the advantage of all that have gone before us in experience and observation, it is probable that by all these helps, we may better frame rules of government for ourselves than to receive others upon the bare authority of the wisdom, justice, &c. of those heathen commonwealths. Among other things, he advised the people to keep all their magistrates in an equal rank, and not give more

1 "*Mr. B. chosen unduly*" is the marginal note of our MS. Of the manner of election no evidence is furnished by the records; but I find in them this vote, showing, perhaps, that the court was less friendly than the people to Bellingham: "The order formerly made for allowing 100 pounds per annum to the governour is repealed." At this general court, it was "ordered that John Humfrey, Esq. shall be sergeant major general." Col. Rec. I. 308. This is a fact not usually known; Hubbard 373, and most writers after him suppose the organization of the militia to be three years later.

honour or power to one than to another, which is easier to advise than to prove, seeing it is against the practice of Israel (where some where rulers of thousands, and some but of tens) and of all nations known or recorded. Another advice he gave, that magistrates should not give private advice, and take knowledge of any man's cause before it came to public hearing. This was debated after in the general court, where some of the deputies moved to have it ordered. But it was opposed by some of the magistrates upon these reasons: 1. Because we must then provide lawyers to direct men in their causes. 2. The magistrates must not grant out original process, as now they do, for to what end are they betrusted with this, but that they should take notice of the cause of the action, that they might either divert the suit, if the cause be unjust, or direct it in a right course if it be good. 3. By this occasion the magistrate hath opportunity to end many differences in a friendly way, without charge to the parties, or trouble to the court. 4. It prevents many difficulties and tediousness to the court to understand the cause aright (no advocate being allowed, and the parties being not able, for the most part, to open the cause fully and clearly, especially in public.) 5. It is allowed in criminal causes, and why not in civil. 6. ||Whereas|| it is objected that such magistrate is in danger to be prejudiced, answer, if the thing be lawful and useful, it must not be laid aside for the temptations which are incident to it, for in the least duties men are exposed to great temptations.[1]

||Where||

---

1 The advice of the preacher was good, notwithstanding the above formidable array of arguments against it. A denial to parties of right to employ advocates, was one cause of the absurd and dangerous practice of obtaining opinions from judges on ex parte hearing Lechford, of Clement's Inn, in the character of whose book Hutchinson, I. 398, has too liberally shown his patriotic sensibility, for the author respected our rulers and wished well to the country, was compelled to return home after vainly trying his fortune near three years in this colony. His rare book will vindicate my judgment. In Col. Rec. I. 294, I find this curiosity in legislative and judicial economy: "At a quarter court, 1 Dec. 1640, Mr. Thomas Lechford, acknowledging he had overshot himself, and is sorry for it, promising to attend his calling, and not to meddle with controversies, was dismissed." Yet the very calling, by which he sought to earn his bread, was that of an attorney, and the following year, finding that his labour as a scrivener would not maintain him, the poor lawyer returned to England. Of his tract, called "Plain Dealing, or News from England," in 80 pages, London 1642, I have never seen any copy but that in the Ebeling collection of Harvard College library, nor heard of any more than one, in possession of Hon. Francis Baylies, of Taunton. It is remarkable, that a considerable part of his most valuable matter is in a beautiful ancient MS. in the archives of our Historical Society. From the peculiar spelling, sometimes more correct than in the printed volume, and from the use of short hand in several of the notes, it appears to me to be the autograph of Lechford. His description of our ancient forms of trial is interesting:

At this court it was ordered that the elders should be desired to agree upon a form of catechism which might be put forth in print.

Offence being taken by many of the people that the court had given Mr. Humfrey £250, the deputies moved it might be ordered that the court should not have power to grant any benevolences; but it was considered that the court could not deprive itself of its honour, and that hereby we should lay a blemish upon the court, which might do more hurt to the country by weakening the reputation of the wisdom and faithfulness of the court in the hearts of the people, than the money saved would recompense. Therefore it was thought better to order it by way of declaration, as if it were to deter importunity of suitors in this ||kind||, that the court would give no more benevolences till our debts were paid, and stock in the treasury, except upon foreign occasions, &c.

There arose a question in the court about the punishment of single fornication, because, by the law of God, the man was only to marry the maid, or pay a sum of money to her father; but the case falling out between two servants, they were whipped for the wrong offered to the master in abusing his house, and were not able to make him other satisfaction. The like difficulty arose about a rape, which was not death by the law of God, but because it

||hand||

" Twice a year, in the said great quarter courts, held before the general courts, are two grand juries sworn for the jurisdiction, one for one court, and the other for the other; and they are charged to inquire and present offences, reduced by the governour, who gives the charge, most an end, under the heads of the ten commandments. Matters of debt, trespass, and upon the case, and equity, yea and of heresy also, are tried by a jury, which, although it may seem to be indifferent, and the magistrates may judge what is law and what is equal, and some of the chief ministers inform what is heresy, yet the jury may find a general verdict, if they please; and seldom is there any special verdict found by them with deliberate arguments made thereupon, which breeds many inconveniences. The parties be warned to challenge any juryman, but because there is but one jury in court for trial of causes, and all parties not present at their swearing, the liberty of the challenge is much hindered, and some inconveniences do happen thereby. Juries are returned by the marshal; he was at first called the Beadle of the society. Seldom is there any matter of record, saving the verdict, many times at random taken and entered, which is also called the judgment. The parties in all causes speak themselves for the most part, and some of the magistrates, where they think cause requireth, do the part of advocates without fee or reward."

Many of our magistrates, as Winthrop, Bellingham, Humfrey, and probably Pelham and Bradstreet had been bred lawyers at home, and were well able to administer justice to the infant community; but no judge can be wise enough to decide always with satisfaction to both parties, after privately hearing, and of necessity, as it were, undertaking the cause of one before issuing of process.

was committed by a boy upon a child of 7 or 8 years old, he was severely whipped. Yet it may seem by the equity of the law against sodomy, that it should be death, for a man to have carnal copulation with a girl so young, as there can be no possibility of generation, for it is against nature as well as sodomy and buggery.

At this court the gentlemen, who had the two patents of Dover and Strawberry bank at Pascataquack in the name of the lords and ||themselves||, granted all their interest of jurisdiction, &c. to our court, reserving the most of the land to themselves. Whereupon a commission was granted to Mr. ||2Bradstreet|| and Mr. Simonds[1], with two or three of Pascataquack, to call a court there and assemble the people to take their submission, &c. but Mr. Humfrey, Mr. Peter, and Mr. Dalton had been sent before to understand the minds of the people, to reconcile some differences between them, and to prepare them. See more.[2]

Mrs. Hutchinson and those of Aquiday island broached new heresies every year. Divers of them turned professed anabaptists, and would not wear any arms, and denied all magistracy among christians, and maintained that there were no churches since those founded by the apostles and evangelists, nor could any be, nor any pastors ordained, nor seals administered but by such, and that the church was to want these all the time she continued in the wilderness, as yet she was. Her son Francis and her son in law Mr. Collins (who was driven from Barbadoes where he had preached a time and done some good, but so soon as he came to her was infected with her heresies) came to Boston and were there sent for to come before the governour and council. But they refused to come, except they were brought; so the officer led him, and being come (there were divers of the elders present) he was charged with a letter he had written to some in our jurisdiction, wherein he charged all our churches and ministers to be antichristian, and many other reproachful speeches, terming our

||these|| ||2Bradford||

1 Hubbard, 372, calls Samuel Symonds, Esquire, "a gentleman of an ancient and worshipful family, from Yeldham in Essex;" but he falls into an errour of the date of his election as an assistant. He was a deputy from Ipswich, in May 1638 and after, and was, of course, a parishioner of Hubbard. A letter from him to Gov. Winthrop, relative to the petition for enlargement of privileges, encouraged by Vassall, Dr. Child, Yale and others, of which so much will be seen in the later part of this volume, is printed in Hutch. Coll. 218. He always enjoyed high consideration with the people whom he served, in 1673 succeeded Leverett, as deputy governour, and was continued in that office until his death in 1678.

2 This was mentioned in a former part of the narrative for this year, page 28.

king, king of Babylon, and sought to possess the people's hearts with evil thoughts of our government and of our churches, &c. He acknowledged the letter, and maintained what he had written, yet sought to evade ||by|| confessing there was a true magistracy in the world and that christians must be subject to it. He maintained also that there were no gentile churches (as he termed them) since the apostles times, and that none now could ordain ministers, &c. Francis Hutchinson did agree with him in some of these, but not resolutely in all; but he had reviled the church of Boston (being then a member of it) calling her a strumpet. They were both committed to prison; and it fell out that one Stoddard,[1] being then one of the constables of Boston, was required to take Francis Hutchinson into his custody till the afternoon, and said withal to the governour, sir, I came to observe what you did, that if you should proceed with a brother otherwise than you ought, I might deal with you in a church way. For this insolent

||the||

[1] It should be constantly remembered, that the constables, being chosen by the general court, were in early times among the chief people in their several towns. Edward Tyng had served before in this office for Boston. Anthony Stoddard, linen-draper, was allowed to become a citizen, or townsman, of Boston, 26 August 1639, and 27 January following a hundred acres of land at Mount Wollaston was granted him. He was admitted to the freeman's oath 13 May 1640. In the first volume of our county registry of deeds, p. 30, is a bond in Latin, Ant. Stoddard to "John Eliot, Joshua Huns, Isaac Heath, Thomas Bell, Edward Clap, William Paete and John Johnson de Roxbury, supervisoribus testamenti Jos. Welde," to the use of Barbara Welde, "viduae predicti Jos. Welde." The condition, in English, reciting that said Ant. Stoddard purposeth to enter into marriage with B. W. widow of Joseph Welde, with whom he is to receive the dowry left by her said husband, if therefore A. S. leave said B. at his death 500 pounds, lawful money or money's worth, then to be void. It is dated 24th of 6. 1647. On 18 March 1649-50, he was chosen recorder of Boston, and next May a representative. Many of the later years of his life he filled the same place. His son, Solomon, born of a former marriage from that above mentioned, was a distinguished divine, of whose powers abundant records are known. His mother was daughter of Emanuel Downing, Winthrop's brother-in-law. Other descendants have served the community in honourable stations even to our days. A very short letter from him, in a collection of Winthrop papers, but without superscription, seems worth transcribing:

Northampton 25 Aug. '73.

Hon. S.—I was desired by John Earle, who was sometime your servant, to convey to you the enclosed money. He has acknowleged to me, that while he was in your service, he wronged you of a bushel and half of wheat. God has been pleased to discover to him the evil of his practice, and he begs your forgiveness, and has sent six shillings in way of restitution. I doubt not but you will be ready to pass by his offence, and beg forgiveness of his sin from God.

We have no late intelligence to send, therefore I shall not further trouble your honour, but leaving you to the blessing of God, I take leave, and rest

Your humble servant,

SOL. STODDARD.

behaviour he was committed, but being dealt with by the elders and others, he came to see his errour, which was that he did conceive that the magistrate ought not to deal with a member of the church before the church had proceeded with him. So the next Lord's day in the open assembly, he did freely and very affectionately confess his errour and his contempt of authority, and being bound to appear at the next court, he did the like there to the satisfaction of all. Yet for example's sake he was fined 20*s.* which though some of the magistrates would have had it much less, or rather remitted, seeing his clear repentance and satisfaction in public left no poison or danger in his example, nor had the commonwealth or any person sustained danger by it. At the same court Mr. Collins was fined £100 and Francis Hutchinson £50, and to remain in prison till they gave security for it. We assessed the fines the higher, partly that by occasion thereof they might be the longer kept in from doing harm, (for they were kept close prisoners,) and also because that family had put the country to so much charge in the synod and other occasions to the value of £500 at least:[1] but after, because the winter drew on, and the prison was inconvenient, we abated them to £40 and £20. But they seemed not willing to pay any thing. They refused to come to the church assemblies except they were led, and so they came duly. At last we took their own bonds for their fine, and so dismissed them.

Other troubles arose in the island by reason of one Nicholas ||Easton|| a tanner, a man very bold, though ignorant. He using to teach at Newport, where Mr. Coddington their governour lived, maintained that man hath no power or will in himself, but as he is acted by God, and that seeing God filled all things, nothing could be or move but by him, and so he must needs be the author of sin, &c. and that a christian is united to the essence of God. Being showed what blasphemous consequences would follow hereupon, they professed to abhor the consequences, but still defended the propositions, which discovered their ignorance, not apprehending how God could make a creature as it were in himself, and yet no part of his essence, as we see by familiar instances: the light is in the air, and in every part of it, yet it is not air, but a distinct thing from it. There joined with Nicholas ||Easton|| Mr. Coddington,

||Eason||

1 Such arbitrary conduct cannot be overlooked by faithful history in silence; yet nothing can be more clear, than that our magistrates thought they were doing God service. The subsequent relaxation appears to be told without any design of gaining credit for clemency. From our Col. Rec. may be learned, that the delinquents were forbidden to come again into this jurisdiction under pain of death.

Mr. Coggeshall[1] and some others, but their minister, Mr. Clark, and Mr. Lenthall, and Mr. Harding,[2] and some others dissented and publicly opposed, whereby it grew to such heat of contention, that it made a schism among them.

Mo. 7.] Captain Underhill, coming to Boston, was presently apprehended by the governour's warrant to appear at the next court, and bound for his good behaviour in the mean time, which was ill taken by many, seeing he did not stand presented by any man, and had been reconciled to the church and to the court, who had remitted his sentence of banishment, and showed their willingness to have pardoned him fully, but for fear of offence. And it was held by some of the magistrates, that the court, having reversed the sentence against him for former misdemeanors, had implicitly pardoned all other misdemeanors before that time, and his adultery was no more then but a misdemeanor; but to bind a man to his good behaviour, when he stands reconciled to the church and commonwealth, was certainly an errour, as it was also to commit such an one, being not presented nor accused. So easily may a magistrate be misled on the right hand by the secret whisperings of such as pretend a zeal of justice and the punishment of sin. The governour caused him to be indicted at the next court, but he was acquitted by proclamation.

Mo. 7. 11.] It being court time, about 7 or 8 in the evening there appeared to the southward a great light, about 30 or 40 feet in length; it went very swift, and continued about a minute. It was observed by many in the bay and at Plimouth and New Haven, &c. and it seemed to all to be in the same position.

15.] A great training at Boston two days. About 1200 men were exercised in most sorts of land service; yet it was observed that there was no man drunk, though there was plenty of wine and strong beer in the town, not an oath sworn, no quarrel, nor any hurt done.[3]

---

1 All three of these wilful heretics were gentlemen of high esteem in civil life, and at different times governours of the colony.

2 My only information of Robert Harding induces me to believe him a companion in the fleet with Winthrop, as he is the *eleventh* member of the Boston church, and admitted among the earliest freemen, 18 May 1631. He was disarmed for his heterodoxy in 1637, Vol. I. 248. In 1641 he was an assistant at Rhode Island, Callender 42.

3 Drunkenness was, however, known on other days, as from the frequent animadversion of the courts on the delinquents is apparent. Some credit may well be deserved by the community, whose moral sense drives such depravity from public view. Perhaps at our military reviews in modern times there is just claim for a similar commendation, especially if regard be had to the diversity of cir-

The parliament in England falling so readily to reform all public grievances, some of our people being then in London preferred a petition to the Lords' house for redress of that restraint which had been put upon ships and passengers to New England, whereupon an order was made, that we should enjoy all our liberties, &c. according to our patent, whereby our patent, which had been condemned and called in upon an erroneous judgment in a quo warranto, was now implicitly ||revived|| and confirmed. This petition was preferred without warrant from our court,

7. 2.] A day of thanksgiving was kept in all our churches for the good success of the parliament in England.

This year men followed the fishing so well that there was about 300,000 dry fish sent to the market.

The lords and gentlemen that had two patents at Pascataquack, finding no means to govern the people there, nor to restrain them from spoiling their timber, &c. agreed to assign their interest to us (reserving the greatest part of the propriety of their lands.) So commissioners being sent thither, the whole river agreed to come under our jurisdiction under two propositions. 1. If we took them in upon a voluntary submission, then they would have liberty to choose their own magistrates, &c. 2. If we took them in as being within the line of our patent, they would then submit to be as Ipswich and Salem, &c. and would have such liberties for felling timber, &c. as they had enjoyed, &c. and so referred it to the next general court; and to have courts there as Ipswich and Salem had. And accordingly at the general court in the 3d month next, they sent two deputies, who, being members of the church there, were sworn freemen, and order made for giving the oath to others at their own court, the like liberty to other courts for ease of the people.

Mo. 9. 8.] Monsieur Rochett, a Rocheller and a protestant, came from Monsieur La Tour, planted upon St. John's river up the great bay on this side Cape Sable. He brought no letters with him, but only letters from Mr. Shurt of Pemaquid, where he left his men

||received||

---

cumstances, by which the proportion of spectators is now much increased. Formerly all were soldiers.

In Vol. 1. 298, we have an account of the military muster 6 May 1639, when 1000 men appeared, and in the intervening two years and four months, the number is increased twenty per cent. Probably the addition of new comers, as not many arrived in 1639, and few in 1640, did not exceed the emigration to Long Island, New Haven and other parts. With such a rate of increase for thirty-five years the people would have multiplied more than fifteen fold before the beginning of Phillip's war, making the period of doubling not quite nine years. This ratio could last but a very short time, while the first young brood were coming up to maturity.

and boat. He propounded to us, 1. Liberty of free commerce. This was granted. 2. Assistance against D'Aulnay of Penobscott, whom he had war with. 3. That he might make return of goods out of England by our merchants. In these two we excused any treaty with him, as having no letters or commission from La Tour. He was courteously entertained here, and after a few days departed.

9.] Query, whether the following be fit to be published.

The governour, Mr. Bellingham, was married, (I would not mention such ordinary matters in our history, but by occasion of some remarkable accidents.) The young gentlewoman was ready to be contracted to a friend of his, who lodged in his house, and by his consent had proceeded so far with her, when on the sudden the governour treated with her, and obtained her for himself. He excused it by the strength of his affection, and that she was not absolutely promised to the other gentleman. Two errours more he committed upon it. 1. That he would not have his contract published where he dwelt, contrary to an order of court.[1] 2. That he married himself contrary to the constant practice of the country. The great inquest presented him for breach of the order of court, and at the court following, in the 4th month, the secretary called him to answer the prosecution. But he not going off the bench, as the manner was, and but few of the magistrates present, he put it off to another time, intending to speak with him privately, and with the rest of the magistrates about the case, and accordingly he told him the reason why he did not proceed, viz. being unwilling to command him publicly to go off the bench, and yet not thinking it fit he should sit as a judge, when he was by law to answer as an offender. This he took ill, and said he would not go off the bench, except he were commanded.[2]

Archibald Thomson[3], of Marblehead,[4] carrying dung to his

---

1 By statute in 1639 the intention of the parties should have been published three times. Our present law differs very little from the old A registry of all marriages was required, but that of Boston, prior to 1651, being lost, it is out of my power to ascertain the name of the "young gentlewoman," who jilted the friend of the governour to obtain a more dignified establishment.

2 "*I did command him*" was originally written, instead of the last three words. In June, 1642, the *new* governour was Winthrop. No wonder the people were scandalized at such a breach of order in their chief magistrate.

3 All my knowledge of this person is derived from the inexhaustible stores of that thorough antiquary, John Farmer, Esquire, of Concord, N. H. who quotes for me from the Salem records: "1. 11. 1637, the inhabitants of Marblehead to be rated," and adds that Arch. Tomson was rated 40 shillings.

4 A valuable Memoir, historical and topographical, of Marblehead is preserved in 1 Hist. Coll. VIII. 54—78.

||ground|| in a canoe upon the Lord's day, in fair weather and still water, it sunk under him in the harbour near the shores and he was never seen after.

One Knore, of Charlestown, coming down Mistick in a small boat laden with wood, was found dead in it: a good caveat for men not to go single in boats in such a season of the year, for it was very stormy weather.

9. 12.] A great tempest of wind and rain from the S. E. all the night, as fierce as an hurricane. It continued very violent at N. W. all the day after. Divers boats and one bark were cast away in the harbour, but (which was a wonder to all) no dwelling house blown down, nor any person killed; and the day after it came to S. E. again, and continued all the night with much wind and rain; and thereupon (it being about the new moon) followed the highest tide which we had seen since our arrival here.

The summer past was very cool and wet, so as much Indian corn never ripened, though some stood till the 20th of this month. It was observed, that people who fed upon that corn were extraordinarily infected with worms in their bodies all the year following, which in some was well prevented by leaving their bread and feeding upon salt fish.

The Charles of Dartmouth, of 400 tons, lying at Pascataquack to take in pipe staves, was forced from her anchors in the last tempest and driven upon the rocks; yet all her masts were before taken down to be new masted. There rode by her a small ship which was safe. This small ship was before despised by the men of the greater, and they would needs unrig their ship upon the Lord's day, though they were admonished not to do it. In the same great tempest a shallop of 3 tons rode it out all night at the head of Cape Anne, and came in safe after.

Mr. Stephen Batchellor, the pastor of the church at Hampton, who had suffered much at the hands of the bishops in England, being about 80 years of age, and having a lusty comely woman to his wife, did solicit the chastity of his neighbour's wife, who acquainted her husband therewith; whereupon he was dealt with, but denied it, as he had told the woman he would do, and complained to the magistrates against the woman and her husband for slandering him. The church likewise dealing with him, he stiffly denied it, but soon after, when the Lord's supper was to be administered, he did voluntarily confess the attempt, and that he did intend to have defiled her, if she would have consented. The church, being moved with his free confession and tears, silently forgave him, and communicated with him: but after, finding how

||garden||

scandalous it was, they took advice of other elders, and after long debate and much pleading and standing upon the church's forgiving and being reconciled to him in communicating with him after he had confessed it, they proceeded to cast him out. After this he went on in a variable course, sometimes seeming very penitent, soon after again excusing himself, and casting blame upon others, especially his fellow elder Mr. Dalton, (who indeed had not carried himself in this cause so well as became him, and was brought to see his failing, and acknowledged it to the elders of the other churches who had taken much pains about this matter.) So he behaved himself to the elders when they dealt with him. He was off and on for a long time, and when he had seemed most penitent, so as the church were ready to have received him in again, he would fall back again, and as it were repent of his repentance. In this time his house and near all his substance was consumed by fire. When he had continued excommunicated near two years, and much agitation had been about the matter, and the church being divided, so as he could not be received in, at length the matter was referred to some magistrates and elders, and by their mediation he was released of his excommunication, but not received to his pastor's office. Upon occasion of this meeting for mediation, Mr. Wilson, pastor of Boston, wrote this letter to him, (the letter is worthy inserting.)[1]

§This year there was discovered a very foul sin, committed by three persons, who the year following came under censure for the same. The case was thus: One Daniel Fairfield (an half Dutchman) about forty years of age, and his wife a lusty young woman, dwelling at Salem near a farm of Mr. Humfrey (one of the magistrates) who much neglected his children, leaving them among a company of rude servants, two of them being young girls (the eldest not seven) came oft to this Fairfield's house, and were by him abused very often, especially upon the Lord's days and lecture days, by agitation and effusion of seed, and after by entering the body of the elder, as it seemed; for upon search she was found to have been forced, and in this course he continued about two years. These girls were after put to board and school to one Jenkin[2] Davis of Lynn, (who had been servant to Mr. Humfrey,) a member of the church there, and in good esteem for piety and sobriety. His wife being quick with child, and scrupulous of hav-

---

1 Were it in my power, I would supply the author's deficiency by copying Wilson's letter on so tender a subject.

2 This wretched member of the christian community had been received to the freeman's oath, 9 March 1637.

ing fellowship with her husband in that condition, he was hurried by the strength of lust to abuse the elder of these girls, (being then about 9 years of age,) but constantly denied any entrance of her body, and continued this wicked course near a year, but with much striving against the temptation, so as he would oft entreat his wife, when she went forth, to carry the children with her, and put up a bill to the elders, to pray for one, who was strongly tempted to a foul sin.

There was also one John Hudson, a lusty young man, an household servant to Mr. Humfrey, who working sometimes at the farm, the elder girl being there, and having no woman to lodge with, came to bed to him, and then he abused her, (she was then about 8 years of age,) and after this he did abuse her many times, so as she was grown capable of man's fellowship, and took pleasure in it.

All this time the girl never discovered any of this wickedness, nor was there any suspicion thereof, till her father was gone into England, which was (8) 26, 41. Then she told her sister (who was newly married) how Fairfield had abused her, and being brought before the governour, and examined, she charged them all three, and declared how they used her from time to time. She also accused two of her own brothers to have used such dalliance with her. (They were so young, as they could not use any semination, and so were referred to private correction.) Thus was this family secretly polluted, and brake not out, till Mr. Humfrey had left the country, which he had plotted two or three years before, against the advice of his best friends.

The offenders, being brought to examination, presently confessed all but entrance of her body; and being committed to prison, and the judgment of the case referred to the general court, it was a great question what the kind of this sin was, whether sodomy, or rape, or &c. which caused the court to seek to know the mind of God by the help of all the elders of the country, both our own, and Plymouth, and Connecticut, New Haven, &c. They took it into consideration divers months, and at last returned different answers. Most of our own agreed in one, viz. that it was a rape, though she consented, in regard she was unripe and not of understanding fit to give consent, and that before God they were guilty of death; but because there was no express law in the word of God for such a sentence, nor any law made and published in the country, they referred it to the wisdom of the court, &c. They agreed also that penetration must necessarily be concluded, (if the body of the child be found to have been opened,) though the parties deny it. So also if man and woman be taken in such a manner, (as in bed together, or their naked bodies joined, &c.) as in common intendment the act was committed, it is testimony sufficient, for it is not possible to see further. Those of Connecticut and New Haven agreed with the former in point of rape of an unripe girl. Some of the elders of Plymouth concurred with the rest; others, both there, and in the bay, were of different judgment, not thinking it to be capital, (but there were but few of that judgment.)

One of the questions put to the elders was, an contactus et fricatio usque ad effusionem seminis sit sodomia morte plectenda? To this most of them answered negatively, and that there must be such an act as must make the parties one flesh.

Another question was, how far a magistrate might exact a confession from a delinquent in capital cases? To this it was answered by the most, that where such a fact is committed, and one witness or strong presumptions do point out the offender, there the judge may examine him strictly, and he is bound to answer directly, though to the peril of his life. But if there be only light suspicion, &c. then the judge is not to press him to answer, nor is he to be denied the benefit of the law, but he may be silent, and call for his accusers. But for examination by oath or torture in criminal cases, it was generally denied to be lawful.

A third question was, whether two vocal witnesses be always necessary for conviction and sentencing an offender? The answer of the most to this was; 1, that where the fact itself speaks, or the offender freely confesseth, there needs no other witness, for witness is to clear hid or doubtful cases; 2, one clear witness with concurrent and concluding circumstances are instead of two witnesses.

A fourth question was, about presumptuous sins. To this, all made not answer; but the judgment of some of the chief [was], that such sins as are not capital in themselves, yet if committed with open contempt of authority, they are presumptuous capital sins, as Deut. 17, 12. So when a man goeth on in riot, whoredom, theft, &c. notwithstanding all restraint of civil authority, &c.

The help of the elders being presented to the general court, held in the 3 month 1642, the court proceeded against the said offenders, (Mr. Winthrop being again chosen governour at this court, and Mr. Thomas [1]Flint of Concord newly elected to be an assistant, so as there were now in all nine magistrates.) The court was much divided about the sentence. The foulness of the

---

1 He brought into the country an estate of 2000 pounds, and was a very useful ruler, dying poor in 1655. See 3 Hist. Coll. I. 48.

sin, and their long continuance in it, wrought strongly with many to put them to death, (especially Fairfield;) but after much dispute, (and some remaining doubtful,) the court agreed upon another sentence. The only reason that saved their lives, was, that the sin was not capital by any express law of God, but to be drawn only by proportion; nor was it made capital by any law of our own, so as we had no warrant to put them to death, and we had formerly refrained (by the advice of the elders) upon the same ground, in a case of manifest adultery, and rape of a child under 7 by a boy of about 17.

The sentence against Fairfield was, that he should be severely whipped at Boston and at Salem, and confined to Boston neck, upon pain of death, if he went out, &c. he should have one nostril slit and seared at Boston, and the other at Salem, and to wear an halter about his neck visibly all his life, or to be whipped every time he were seen abroad without it, and to die, if he attempted the like upon any person, and £40 to Mr. Humfrey.[1]

Jenkin Davis was to be whipped at Boston and Lynn, to wear an halter during the pleasure of the court, confined to Lynn, and not to attempt the like upon any child upon pain of death, and to pay £40 to Mr. Humfrey.

John Hudson to be whipped at Boston and Lynn, and to pay Mr. Humfrey £20 within two years.

This sentence was accordingly executed. The parties received their punishment very patiently, without any striving or complaining, (though they had near 40 stripes,) and acknowledged their sins to be greater than their punishment, &c.

As people increased, so sin abounded, and especially the sin of uncleanness, and still the providence of God found them out. One [blank] Hackett, a servant in Salem, about 18 or 20 years of age, was found in buggery with a cow, upon the Lord's day. He was discovered by a woman, who being detained from the public assembly by some infirmity that day, and by occasion looking out at her window, espied him in the very act; but being affrighted at it, and dwelling alone, she durst not call to him, but at night made it known, so as he was apprehended, and brought before the magistrate, to whom he confessed the attempt and some entrance, but denied the completing of the fact. The trial was deferred to the general court, and much scruple there was with

1 On the humble petition of Fairfield and his wife, probably accompanied with certificates of his good behaviour, they and their children were permitted, some years after, to leave the jurisdiction, on condition of wearing again the opprobrious rope, if he returned. A previous request for relief from the badge had been refused.

many, because there was but one witness; but in the end the court agreed, that his confession of some entrance was sufficient testimony with the woman (for more cannot be proved by testimony); so the major part condemned him to die. But the then governour, Mr. Bellingham, being doubtful of the evidence, refused to pronounce the sentence; so the deputy governour, Mr. Endecott, performed it. The boy remained stiff in his denial, and seemed not affected with the apprehension of death, (for he was noted always to have been a very stupid, idle, and ill-disposed boy, and would never regard the means of instruction, either in the church or family;) but after his condemnation, divers of the elders and other christians resorting to him, and labouring by the word of God to convince him of his sin, and the present danger of his soul, (the elders also of Boston applying themselves to him in their public ministry,) it pleased the Lord so to bless his own ordinances, that his hard heart melted. He freely confessed the full completing this foul fact, and attempting the like before, with other wickedness he had been guilty of, and fell into much horrour of conscience, and after being shut up in an inner room within the prison, his keeper (a very godly man) hearing him speaking, drew near the wall, and, perceiving he was praying, attended carefully by the space of [blank] with much amazement to hear one, who but a few days before was so ignorant and blockish, to pray now with such understanding and affection, confessing and bewailing his sins, judging himself for them with their due aggravations, justifying the Lord, appealing to his mercy by the death of his son, and pressing him with strong arguments from the word, &c. The keeper acquainting the elders herewith, they repaired to him, and finding that the Lord had begun a gracious work upon his soul, (the day of his execution being appointed on the morrow,) they obtained of the governour, &c. that it was respited a week longer, in which time he well improved, and gave good testimony of the truth of that work. He desired not much company, nor would use much speech to those who came to him, but would intreat his keeper sometimes to let nobody come to him, that he might be at liberty to speak with God. (11.) 13. When the day of execution came, after he had been at the lecture, he went to the place of execution sadly and silently, and being up the ladder, he said nothing; but the cow (with which he had committed that abomination) being brought forth and slain before him,[1] he brake

[1] If any one would require any addition of mine to the disgusting relation of this and one or two preceding paragraphs, he must have a depraved appetite. From Col. Rec. it is known, that the last criminal was named William, and that the

out into a loud and doleful complaint against himself, bewailed his sinful course of life, his disobedience to his parents, his slighting and despising their instructions and the instructions of his dame, and other means of grace God had offered him, &c. Then Mr. Wilson, the pastor of Boston, (the rest of the elders and people there present joining with him,) prayed earnestly to the Lord for him a good space. He attended duly thereto, and prayed also himself, crying oft and earnestly for mercy; yet with a trembling body, and amazed with the apprehension of death so near at hand, to which he quietly yielded himself, when he was required. There is no doubt to be made but the Lord hath received his soul to his mercy; and he was pleased to lift up the light of his countenance so far towards him, as to keep him from despair, and to hold him close to his grace in a seeking condition; but he was not pleased to afford him that measure of peace and comfort as he might be able to hold out to others, lest sinful men, in the love of their lusts, should set mercy and repentance at too low a rate, and so miss of it when they vainly expect it.§

The general court held in the 10th month past was full of uncomfortable agitations and contentions. The principal occasion (for history must tell the whole truth) was from the governour, who, being a gentleman of good repute in England for wisdom and godliness, finding now that some other of the magistrates bare more sway with the people than himself, and that they were called to be of the standing council for life, and himself passed by, was so taken with an evil spirit of emulation and jealousy (through his melancholic disposition) as he set himself in an opposite frame to them in all proceedings, which did much retard all business, and was occasion of grief to many godly minds, and matter of reproach to the whole court in the mouths of others, and brought himself low in the eyes of those with whom formerly he had been in honour. Some instances I will give.

There fell out a case between Mr. Dudley, one of the council, and Mr. Howe, a ruling elder of the church of Watertown, about a title to a mill. The case is too long here to report, but it was so clear on Mr. Dudley's part, both in law and equity, (most of the magistrates also and deputies concurring therein,) as the elders, being desired to be present at the hearing of the case, they also consented with the judgment of the court, before the case was put to vote, and some of them humbly advised the court that

---

cow was sentenced to be burnt. Since the change in our laws, which regard offences against nature no longer as capital crimes, we seldom hear of their perpetration.

it would be greatly to their dishonour, and an apparent injustice, if they should otherwise determine. Notwithstanding, he still laboured to have the cause carried against Mr. Dudley, reproved some of the elders for their faithful advice, took upon him to answer all the arguments, but so weakly as many were ashamed at it, and in reading an order of court whereupon the issue of the case chiefly depended, he sought to help himself by such unworthy shifts, as interpreting some things against the very letter and common sense, wholly omitting the most material part, &c. refusing to put things to the vote that made against his purpose, &c. that all might see by what spirit he was led.[1]

Another case fell out about Mr. Maverick of Nottles Island, who had been formerly fined £100 for giving entertainment to Mr. Owen and one Hale's wife, who had escaped out of prison, where they had been put for notorious suspicion of adultery[2],

---

1 Nothing can be learned of this controversy from the records. It is a little remarkable, that a dispute on title to real estate should rise before the country had been eleven years occupied. The opponent of Dudley was a respectable man, as of course must be presumed from his office in the church, before entering on which he was, I believe, a deputy from Watertown in May and Sept. 1635, in Sept. and Dec. 1636, and again May 1639. His name of baptism was Edward. In our Probate Records I. 31 his will, made 13 June 1644, is proved 25 July after.

2 The character of Maverick induces me to believe, that he supposed the parties innocent, which probably influenced Winthrop and the majority to a mitigation of the penalty. Hospitality was a distinguished virtue of this gentleman, see Vol. I. 27, n. 4, but our fathers sometimes viewed its excess in him, as a failing, for at the general court 4 March 1634–5, I find this among their records I. 142: "It is ordered that Mr. Samuel Maverick shall before the last of December next remove his habitation for himself and his family to Boston, and in the mean time shall not give entertainment to any strangers for longer times than one night, without leave from some assistant, and all this to be done under the penalty of 100 pound." Happily this order was repealed in Sept. following. My opinion of Maverick's conduct, reported in the text, gains confirmation from the implication of many others in the escape of the offenders. Our Col. Rec. I. 314 has: "At a quarter court at Boston 7 of 7, 1641, Thomas Owen, for his adulterous practices, was censured to be sent to the gallows with a rope about his neck, and to sit upon the ladder an hour, the rope's end thrown over the gallows, and so to return to prison.

Sarah Hales, the wife of William Hales, was censured for her miscarriage to be carried to the gallows with a rope about her neck, and to sit an hour upon the ladder, the rope's end flung over the gallows, and after to be banished."

A few lines lower is found: "Mr. Samuel Maverick, being found guilty of a confederacy with Thomas Owen to break prison, concealing of it, and letting be upon his island, was fined one hundred pounds.

Mr. Chidley for confederating and concealing was fined 13 pounds 6. 8.
Mr. Ducket for confederating and concealing was fined 13 pounds 6. 8.
Mr. Wollaston for concealing, being privy, was fined 13 pounds 6. 8.
Mr. Oateley for concealing was fined 13 pounds 6. 8.
Thorne for concealing, hiding and supplying, was fined 6 pounds 13. 6.

as shall after be showed.[1] The court upon his petition had referred it to the usual committee, who made return that their opinion was, the court might do well to remit it to £60, which he knew would please some of the council well, who had often declared their judgment that fines should be so imposed as they might upon occasion be moderated. So when the petition was returned to him, he takes it and alters the sum from £60 to £80 without acquainting the court therewith, nor would say that he had done it, when the committee informed the court of the alteration, before the secretary charged him with it. Then he said, he did it in jest, and when the secretary said he had reformed it, and the court called to have it put to the vote, he refused, and stirred up much heat and contention about it, so in the end the court required the deputy to put it to the vote.

Upon these and other miscarriages the deputies consulted together, and sent up their [2]speaker, with some others, to give him

---

William Cope for concealing was fined 6 pounds 13. 6.

Mary Wilbee for concealing and consenting was fined 6 pounds 13. 6.

Thomas Owen for escaping out of prison was fined 20 pounds, to be paid within a week, or to be severely whipped.

Sarah Hales for escaping to pay 13 pounds 6. 8, or to be whipped and banished.

Mr. Dutchfield, Mr. Williams, and Mr. Hale were admonished to take heed of the like concealment."

It will be observed, that seven of the men, besides Maverick, have the prefix of dignity, and it is not very unlikely that Mr. Hale was the husband of the female charged.

1 It is not to be found in any part of this history.

2 A natural inference would be, I believe, that this phrase denotes the presiding officer of the deputies; yet it must be erroneous, if the governour and assistants still continued to sit with them in the same apartment, and generally to act as one assembly. The separation of magistrates and deputies was first provided for at the general court 7 of March 1643-4, as may be seen in Col. Rec. II. 44-5 and in the proper place of this history. Previous to that event, we must presume, that the governour presided, or the deputy in the governour's absence, and such appears to be the current of evidence. At the general court 7 Oct. 1640, "it is ordered that no man in the general courts shall speak above three times to any cause, without leave from the governour or court, upon pain of twelve pence a time; and that if any be speaking about private business, whilst the business of the court is in hand, he shall forfeit twelve pence in like sort." The enforcement of the latter branch of this rule would present a great change in our deliberative bodies.

For explanation of the text I suggest, that the deputies "consulted together" *apart*, and chose one of their number speaker pro hac vice, as a fit person for the extraordinary service of solemn admonition. The records have nothing of this curious piece of history. Notice of the first election of a speaker occurs at the general court in May 1644, when William Hawthorne was chosen. In the third paragraph of the text after the above, this gentleman is said by the governour to be "usually one of their speakers." In this connexion it means;

a solemn admonition, which was never done to any governour before, nor was it in their power without the magistrates had joined.

---

in my opinion, only, one of those who usually spoke, and is rather corroborative of the above suggestion.

By the kindness of the former secretary of the commonwealth, Alden Bradford, Esq. I have been furnished with the names of all the speakers to the period of our revolution, mentioned in the records; and where the records are, as for some years they unhappily are, defective, persevering search of my own, with the assistance of the present treasurer, Nahum Mitchell, Esq. has enabled me to render complete this list, which the reader will be pleased to peruse with these observations, that the beginning only of a term of service is noted, the same person having been continued in office till the following date, and that where the month is not mentioned, it is always May.

1644 William Hawthorne of Salem,
Oct. 1645 George Cooke of Cambridge,
1646 William Hawthorne,
Oct. . . . Robert Keayne of Boston, but only for the first day,
. . . Robert Bridges of Lynn,
1647 Joseph Hill of Malden,
1648 William Hawthorne,
Oct. . . . Richard Russell of Charlestown,
1649 Daniel Denison of Ipswich,
1650 William Hawthorne,
Oct. . . . Richard Russell,
1651 Daniel Gookin of Cambridge,
Oct. . . . Daniel Denison,
1653 Humphrey Atherton of Springfield,*
1654 Richard Russell,
1655 Edward Johnson of Woburn,
. . . Richard Russell,
1657 William Hawthorne,
1658 Richard Russell,
1659 Thomas Savage of Boston,
Dec. 1660 William Hawthorne,
1662 Thomas Clark of Boston,
1663 John Leverett of Boston,
1665 Thomas Clark,
1666 Richard Waldron of Dover,
1669 Thomas Clark,
1671 Thomas Savage of Andover,*
1672 Thomas Clark,
1673 Richard Waldron,

---

* Atherton belonged to Dorchester; Savage to Boston. Before 1694 our towns had not been restrained from choosing any person to represent them in the general court, other than freeholders and residents within such towns. See Hutch. II. 77. 78 from which it appears, that it was the high court party, in their vain support of the arbitrary conduct of Sir William Phipps, which, by a majority of two, drove out the independent, non resident members, because many belonged to Boston, and knew the governour's conduct too well. It was certainly a violation of the existing rights of the country towns, and an abridgment of their liberty for the future; but its ultimate result was beneficial. This part of our ancient constitution has been too much overlooked.

These continual oppositions and delays, tending to the hindrance and perverting of justice, afforded much occasion of grief

---

Jan. 1674 Joshua Hobart of Hingham,
. . . Richard Waldron,
Feb. 1676 Peter Bulkley of Concord,
1677 Thomas Savage,
1679 Richard Waldron,
Feb. 1680 John Richards of Dorchester,
. . . Daniel Fisher of Dedham,
1683 Elisha Cooke of Boston,
1684 John Waite of Malden,
1685 Isaac Addington of Boston,
1686 John Saffyn of Boston,
usurpation of Andros,
1689 Thomas Oakes of Boston,
Feb. 1690 John Bowles of Roxbury,
. . . Penn Townsend of Boston,
Oct. 1691 William Bond of Watertown,
1692 Penn Townsend,
June . . . under new charter of William and Mary, William Bond,
Nov. 1693 Nathaniel Byfield of Bristol,
1694 Nehemiah Jewett of Ipswich,
1695 William Bond,
Feb. 1696 Penn Townsend,
1698 Nathaniel Byfield,
1699 James Converse of Woburn,
1700 John Leverett of Cambridge,
1701 Nehemiah Jewett,
1702 James Converse,
1705 Thomas Oakes,
1707 John Burrill of Lynn,
1708 Thomas Oliver of Cambridge,
1709 John Clark of Boston,
1711 John Burrill,
1720 Elisha Cooke of Boston, negatived, and the court dissolved for refusing to choose any but him,
July, . . . Timothy Lindall of Salem,
1721 John Clark,
1724 William Dudley of Roxbury,
1729 John Quincy of Braintree,
1739 Paul Dudley of Roxbury, negatived, and then
. . . John Quincy,
1741 William Fairfield of Wenham,
1742 Thomas Cushing of Boston,
1746 Thomas Hutchinson of Boston,
1749 Joseph Dwight of Brookfield,
1750 Thomas Hubbard of Boston,
1759 Samuel White of Taunton,
1760 James Otis of Barnstable,
1762 Timothy Ruggles of Hardwick,
1764 Samuel White, and in his absence, pro. tem.
June . . . Thomas Clap of Dorchester,
1765 Samuel White,
1766 James Otis, jr. of Boston, negatived, and then
. . . Thomas Cushing of Boston, and in his sickness, pro. tem.

to all the magistrates, especially to Mr. Dudley, who being a very wise and just man, and one that would not be trodden under foot of any man, took occasion (alleging his age &c.) to tell the court that he was resolved to leave his place, and therefore desired them against the next court of elections to think of some other. The court was much affected with it, and entreated him, with manifestation of much affection and respect towards him, to leave off these thoughts, and offered him any ease and liberty that his age and infirmities might stand in need of, but he continued resolute. Thereupon the governour also made a speech, as if he desired to leave his place of magistracy also, but he was fain to make his own answer, for no man desired him to keep, or to consider better of it.

This session continued three weeks, and established 100 laws, which were called the Body of Liberties. They had been composed by Mr. Nathaniel Ward, (sometime pastor of the church of Ipswich: he had been a minister in England, and formerly a student and practiser in the course of the common law,) and had been revised and altered by the court, and sent forth into every town to be further considered of, and now again in this court, they were revised, amended and presented, and so established for three years, by that experience to have them fully amended and established to be perpetual.

At this session Mr. [1]Hathorn, one of the deputies, and usually one of their speakers, made a motion to some other of the deputies of leaving out [2]two of their ancientest magistrates, because they were grown poor, and spake reproachfully of them under that motion. This coming to Mr. Cotton his knowledge, he took occasion from his text, the next lecture day, to confute, and sharply (in his mild manner) to reprove such miscarriage, which he termed a slighting or dishonouring of parents, and told the country, that such as were decayed in their estates by attending the

---

April 1770 John Hancock of Boston, negatived, and then
. . . . . . James Warren of Plimouth,
. . . Thomas Cushing.

1 William Hathorne, or Hawthorne, as the Secretary in the public records usually spells the name, to conform to the sound, was a distinguished man in Salem, where his posterity have always enjoyed influence. Sufficient account of him may be found in Eliot and in the history of Salem, 1 Hist. Coll. VI. But the author of that tract, more celebrated for his amiable temper and multifarious learning, than for correctness or method in exhibiting facts, has left his reader to presume, that Hathorne was not a deputy before 1643; and Eliot, following Hutchinson, dates his first election as speaker in 1650. He came deputy in May 1635, in Sept. 1637, and very often after.

2 Probably Winthrop was one.

service of the country ought to be maintained by the country, and not set aside for their poverty, being otherwise so well gifted, and approved by long experience to be faithful. This public reproof gave such a check to the former motion as it was never revived after. Yet by what followed it appeared, that the fire, from which it brake out, was only raked up, not quenched, as will be showed anon.

Mr. Hathorn and some others were very earnest to have some certain penalty set upon lying, swearing, &c. which the deputy and some other of the magistrates opposed, (not disliking to have laws made against ||these|| or any other offences, but in respect of the certain punishment,) whereupon Mr. Hathorn charged him with seeking to have the government arbitrary, &c. and the matter grew to some heat, for the [1]deputy was a wise and a stout gentleman, and knew Mr. Hathorn his neighbour well, but the strife soon fell, and there was no more spoken of it that court. Yet this gave occasion to some of the magistrates to prepare some arguments against the course intended, of bringing all punishments to a certainty. The scope of these reasons was to make good this proposition, viz. All punishments, except such as are made certain in the law of God, or are not subject to variation by merit of circumstances, ought to be left arbitrary to the wisdom of the judges.

Reason 1. God hath left a pattern hereof in his word, where so few penalties are prescribed, and so many referred to the judges; and God himself varieth the punishments of the same offences, as the offences vary in their circumstances; as in manslaughter, in the case of a riotous son proving incorrigible, in the same sin aggravated by ||[2]presumption||, theft, &c. which are not only rules in these particular cases, but to guide the judges by proportion in all other cases: as upon the law of adultery, it may be a question whether Bathsheba ought to die by that law, in regard to the great temptation, and the command and power of the kings of Israel. So that which was capital in the men of Jabesh Gilead, Judges [xxi. 10] in not coming up to the princes upon proclamation, was but confiscation of goods, &c. in Ezra 10. 8. See 2d Sam. 14. 6. 11.

Reason 2. All punishments ought to be just, and, offences varying so much in their merit by occasion of circumstances, it would be unjust to inflict the same punishment upon the least as upon the greatest.

||theft|| ||[2]presumptuous||

---

[1] Endecott.

3. Justice requireth that every cause should be heard before it be judged, which cannot be when the sentence and punishment is determined before hand.

4. Such parts and gifts, as the word of God requires in a judge, were not so necessary, if all punishments were determined beforehand.

5. God hath not confined all wisdom, &c. to any one generation, that they should set rules for all others to walk by.

6. It is against reason that some men should better judge of the merit of a cause in the bare theory thereof, than others (as wise and godly) should be able to discern of it pro re nata.

7. Difference of times, places, &c. may aggravate or extenuate some offences.

8. We must trust God, who can and will provide as wise and righteous judgment for his people in time to come, as in the present or forepassed times; and we should not attempt the limiting of his providence, and frustrating the gifts of others, by determining all punishments, &c.

Objection. In theft and some other cases, as cases capital, God hath prescribed a certain punishment.

Ans. 1. In theft, &c. the law respects the damage and injury of the party, which is still one and the same, though circumstances may aggravate or extenuate the sin. 2. In capital cases death is appointed as the highest degree of punishment which man's justice can reach.

Objection. Then we might as well leave all laws arbitrary at the discretion of the judge.

Ans. 1. The reason is not like. 1. God gave a certain law where he left the punishment arbitrary, so as we have a clear rule to guide the law where the punishment may be uncertain. The varying of the offence in the circumstances doth not vary the ground or equity of the law, nor the nature of the guilt, as it doth the measure of the reward. He is as ||fully|| guilty of theft who steals a loaf of bread for his hunger, as he that steals an horse for his pleasure

Objection. The statutes in England set down a certain penalty for most offences.

Ans. 1. We are not bound to make such examples ourselves. 2. The penalty, commonly, is not so much as the least degree of that offence deserves: 12*d.* for an oath, 5*s.* for drunkenness, &c.

Mo. 11.] Those of Providence, being all anabaptists, were divided in judgment; some were only against baptizing of infants; others denied all magistracy and churches, &c. of which [1]Gorton,

||freely||

[1] Of Samuel Gorton, a distinguished fanatick "in the most high and palmy

state" of fanaticism on each side of the ocean, a perfect biography would require more examination than I have leisure to bestow, and would probably be thought by the reader a labour little rewarded by the result. Allen and Eliot in their dictionaries have adequately commemorated him, and the latter in his candid essays on Eccl. Hist. 1 Hist. Coll. IX. 35—38, has dilated upon the injurious treatment he received. Hutchinson is also explicit in his opinion against it. From the long narrative, in this volume, of the proceedings relative to the claim of lands purchased by him and others at Narraganset, will be discerned equal degrees of injustice and cruelty in the rulers of Massachusetts: any one, whose curiosity is eager enough to look at a defence, may find satisfaction in the bloody bigotry of Johnson, lib. II. c. 23, 24. Allen would not include this author in his references. As the heretic had not been in his grave perhaps twenty years, when Mather wrote, the Magnalia of course contains the maledictions furnished by Morton and Hubbard, whose enmity is less censurable, because contemporary. Callender, 36—38, has spoken with his usual candour of both parties; and from a more inquisitive antiquary than Callender I had encouragement to expect a correction of many of the idle scandals against Gorton, as in my note Vol. I. 296 is expressed. That valued correspondent, in answer to a letter of 30 June 1820, writes, 16 October of the same year:

"I did intend, when I wrote the letter accompanying the papers sent to the Historical Society, to have given a sketch of the life of Gorton, whom I still think has been much abused, and had made minutes for that purpose. But my feelings at present are widely different from what they were at that time. I mean not by this that I have lost all curiosity for these subjects, but I have lost nearly all confidence as to the truth of what is related I see in my own times, that I cannot get at the truth of what passes before my own eyes. How then can I know what took place 200 years ago, when I have no evidence but that which is distorted by the worst passions? I mean not this charge for one side more than another; and I at the same time acknowledge that these considerations ought not to deter us from using our exertions to come at the truth, and preserve it for the benefit of others. But still, such are my feelings. As to Gorton, he was undoubtedly, in religion, a wild enthusiast. I obtained from his descendants a manuscript volume, from which I expected to have learnt something of his history. But it contained nothing but the wildest and most extravagant whimsies. He spiritualized every thing, and one would almost have thought that he had taken the tour of Sweedenbergh. At any rate, I believe there is no one at this time sufficiently skilled in *mysteries* to interpret his meaning. You must know that, in a conveyance to his son on record, he calls himself 'Professor of the mysteries of Christ.' Before this, in a release from John Duckingfield, he is called by the more humble title of 'Samuel Gorton of London, clothier.' It is said that Gorton was banished, 1637, from the colonies of Massachusetts, Plymouth and Rhode Island I presume the Island of Rhode Island is meant, though it was not settled till the year after. There is no evidence of that fact on record as relates to Rhode Island. It does not appear that he was ever a freeholder or freeman of that Island. 20th, 4th, 1638 he was admitted an inhabitant. In March 1642, Randall Houlden, Richard Carder and others were disfranchised the Island. These, Backus says, *followed* Gorton to Newport from Plymouth, though Carder and Houlden were two of the original purchasers of the Island, and both signed the original act of incorporation. Houlden, with R. Williams, witnessed the deed to Coddington, &c. dated 24th, 1st month, 1637. I mention these facts to show how easy it is to write carelessly about men whom we hate or despise. Some writers say he was whipped, others corrected, at Newport. Which is true, if by correction is meant other than whipping, I know not. There is no evidence on record of either. But admit he was both whipped and corrected. It was not for *crime*. An immoral act, as far as I know, has not been charged upon him. His offences

who had lately been whipped at Aquiday, as is before [1]mentioned, was their instructer and captain. These, being ||too|| strong for the other party, provoked them by injuries, so as they came armed into the field, each against other, but Mr. Williams pacified them for the present. This occasioned the weaker party to write a letter, under all their hands, to our governour and magistrates, complaining of the wrongs they suffered, and desiring aid, or, if not that, counsel from us. We answered them that we could not levy any war, &c. ||[2]without|| a general court. For counsel we told them, that except they did submit themselves to some jurisdiction, either Plimouth or our's, we had no calling or warrant to interpose in their contentions, but if they were once subject to any, then they had a calling to protect them. After this answer we heard no more from them for a time.[2]

||two|| ||[2]with||

---

were his opinions. On whom then does the odium of whipping fall? on him who unjustly suffered, or him who unrighteously inflicted the unjust punishment? I esteem not the less the character of Obadiah Holmes, from whom, on the maternal side, I have been lately told I am descended, for having been most cruelly whipped. Now, any man of common sense, would be ashamed to avow the principles which actuated his accusers in bringing him to the post. We should all much rather share with the sufferer, than his judges, the odium of the punishment.

I have read, I believe, almost every word that is legible of the record of this colony, from its first settlement till after the death of Gorton. From the first establishment of government, he was almost constantly in office; and during a long life there is no instance of record, to my knowledge, of any reproach or censure cast upon him, no complaint against him, although history furnishes abundance of evidence that there was no lack of enemies to his person, principles or property. This can hardly be said of any other settler in the colony of any standing. It was this fact that fixed my opinion of the general tenour of his conduct, and the uprightness of his character. I remember an instance in which he applied to be excused from serving in the court of commissioners, and assigned his long services as a reason. It would be a remarkable fact, that a man should be an enemy to *magistracy*, to religion, in short a bad man, and yet constantly enjoy the confidence of his fellow townsmen and receive from them the highest honours in their gift."

1 I find no former mention of this punishment by Winthrop, but learn from Lechford, an author, whom my friend, whose letter gives its chief value to the last note, had not probably seen, that "there lately they whipt one Mr. Gorton, a grave man, for denying their power, and abusing some of their magistrates with uncivil terms; the governour, Mr. Coddington, saying in court, you that are for the king lay hold on Gorton, and he again on the other side called forth, all you that are for the king lay hold on Coddington, whereupon Gorton was banished the island. So with his wife and children he went to Providence. They began about a small trespass of swine, but it is thought some other matter was ingredient."

2 The original matter of complaint by the Providence people is published by

The frost was so great and continual this winter that all the bay was frozen over, so much and so long, as the like, by the Indians' relation, had not been these 40 years, and it continued from the 18th of this month to the 21st of the 12th month; so as horses and carts went over in many places where ships have sailed. Capt. Gibbons and his wife, with divers on foot by them, came riding from his farm at Pullen point, right over to Boston, the 17th of the 12th month, when it had thawed so much as the water was above the ice half a foot in some places; and they passed with loads of wood and six oxen from Muddy river to Boston, and when it thawed it removed great rocks of above a ton or more weight, and brought them on shore. The snow likewise was very deep, especially northward about Acomenticus, above three feet, and much more beyond. It was frozen also to sea so far as one could well discern.

To the southward also the frost was as great and the snow as deep, and at Virginia itself the great bay was much of it frozen over, and all their great rivers, so as they lost much cattle for want of hay, and most of their swine.

There was a shallop with eight men to go from Pascataquack to Pemaquid about the beginning of the frost, they would needs set forth upon the Lord's day, though forewarned, &c. They were taken with a N. W. tempest and put to sea about 14 days: at length they recovered Monhigen. Four of them died with cold, the rest were discovered by a fisherman a good time after and so brought off the Island.

There was great fear lest much hurt might have been done upon the breaking up of the frost, (men and beasts were grown so ||bold||,) but, by the good providence of God, not one person miscarried save one Warde of Salem, an honest young man, who going to show a traveller the safest passage over the river, as he thought, by the salthouse, fell in, and, though he had a pitch fork in his hand, yet was presently carried under the ice by the tide. The traveller fell in with one leg while he went to help the other, but God preserved him. He had about him all the letters from England which were brought in a ship newly arrived at the isle of Shoals, which sure were the occasion of God's preserving him, more than any goodness of the man.[1] Most of the bridges were broken down and divers mills.

||cold||

me in 3 Hist. Coll. I. 2. It is not strange, that after the answer of our rulers, they heard no more for a time.

1 We should think, unless otherwise instructed, that the life of the messenger might have been as precious, as his despatches, in the view of heaven. Per-

About this time one Turner of Charlestown, a man of about 50 years of age, having led a loose and disorderly life, and being wounded in conscience at a sermon of Mr. Shepherd's, he kept it in and did not discover his distress to such as might have offered him help, &c. nor did attend upon the public means as he ought to have done, and after a good space he went out from his wife on the Lord's day at night, having kept at home all that day, and drowned himself in a little pit where was not above two feet water.

At New Haven there was a sow, which among other pigs had one without hair, and some other human resemblances, it had also one eye blemished, just like one eye of a loose fellow in the town, which occasioned him to be suspected, and being examined before the magistrates, he confessed the fact, for which, after they had written to us, and some other places for advice, they put him to death.[1]

Three men coming in a shallop from Braintree, the wind taking them short at Castle Island, one of them stepping forward to hand the sail, caused a fowling piece with a French lock, which lay in the boat, to go off. The whole charge went through the thigh of one man within one inch of his belly, yet missed the bone, then the shot (being goose shot) scattered a little and struck the second man under his right side upon his breast, so as above 40 shot entered his body, many into the capacity of his breast. The third man being now only able to steer, but not to get home the boat, it pleased God the wind favoured him so as he did fetch the governour's garden, and there being a small boat and men at that time, they brought them to Boston before they were too far spent with cold and pain, and beyond all expectation, they were both soon perfectly recovered, yet he who was shot in the breast fell into a fever and spit blood.

One John [2]Turner, a merchant's factor of London, had gone from hence to the West Indies the year before in a small pinnace of 15 tons, and returned with great advantage in indigo, pieces of

---

haps there is some danger in our author's construction of this providence, as Warde, who is well spoken of, was lost under the ice.

1 The confession, we ought to presume, was very full. This absurd paragraph is transcribed to swell the follies of the Magnalia, book VI. called Thaumaturgus.

2 It is presumed, that this person became a planter at Barbados, and kept up a correspondence with his old friends here. In our registry of deeds Vol. II. 27, is entered a bond from one of the same name to John Richards of Boston, dated 16 Aug. 1653 for "22,848 lbs. of good, dry, well-cured muscovado sugar, to be delivered at the Indian Bridge, or at some convenient store house at the hole in this Island of Barbados, free of storage, at or before the last day of April next." It was recorded after it was payable, of course,on request of obligee.

8, &c. He said he got them by trade, but it was suspected he got them by prize. He prepared a bigger vessel and well manned in the beginning of winter, and putting to sea was forced in again three times. 1. By a leak. 2. By a contrary wind; and 3. he spent his mast in fair weather, and having gotten a new at Cape Anne, and towing it towards the bay, he lost it by the way, and so by these occasions and by the frost, he was kept in all winter. Thereupon he gave over his voyage and went to Virginia, and there sold his vessel and shipped himself and his commodities in a Dutch ship for the West Indies.

Mo. 1. 27.] Mr. William Aspenwall, who had been banished, as is before declared, for joining with Mr. Wheelwright, being licensed by the general court to come and tender his submission, &c. was this day reconciled to the church of Boston. He made a very free and full acknowledgment of his errour and seducement, and that with much detestation of his sin. The like he did after, before the magistrates, who were appointed by the court to take his submission, and upon their certificate thereof at the next general court, his sentence of banishment was released.

It is observable how the Lord doth honour his people and justify their ways, even before the heathen, when their proceedings are true and just, as appears by this instance. Those at New Haven, intending a plantation at Delaware, sent some men to purchase a large portion of land of the Indians there, but they refused to deal with them. It so fell out that a Pequod sachem (being fled his country in our war with them, and having seated himself with his company upon that river ever since) was accidentally there at that time. He, taking notice of the English and their desire, persuaded the other sachem to deal with them, and told him that howsoever they had killed his countrymen and driven him out, yet they were honest men, and had just cause to do as they did, for the Pequods had done them wrong, and refused to give such reasonable satisfaction as was demanded of them. Whereupon the sachem entertained them and let them have what land they desired.

2. 14.] A general fast was kept for our native country and Ireland and our own occasions.

The spring began very early, and the weather was very mild, but the third and fourth month proved very wet and cold, so that the low meadows were much spoiled, and at Connecticut they had such a flood as brake their bridges and killed all their winter corn, and forced them to plant much of their Indian over.

The last [1]winter divers vessels were cast away to the southward,

---

[1] Hubbard, 422, has a strange mistake of the date of these misfortunes.

one at Long Island, wherein 8 or 9 persons were drowned. These were loose people who lived by trucking with the Indians.

Mo. 3. 9.] The ship Eleanor of London, one Mr. ||Inglee|| master, arrived at Boston. She was laden with tobacco from Virginia, and having been about 14 days at sea, she was taken with such a tempest, as though all her sails were down and made up, yet they were blown from the yards, and she was laid ||2over|| on one side two and a half hours, so low as the water stood upon her deck, and the sea over-raking her continually, and the day was as dark as if it had been night, and though they had cut her masts, yet she righted not till the tempest assuaged. She staid here till the 4th of the (4) and was well fitted with masts, sails, rigging and victuals at such reasonable rates as the master was much affected with his entertainment, and professed that he never found the like usage in Virginia where he had traded these ten years.

Captain Underhill, finding no employment here that would maintain him and his family, and having good offers made him by the Dutch governour, (he speaking the Dutch tongue and his wife a Dutch woman,) had been with the governour, and being returned desired the church's leave to depart. The church, understanding that the English, at Stamford near the Dutch, had offered him employment and maintenance, (after their ability,) advised him rather to go thither, seeing they were our countrymen and in a church estate. He accepted this advice. His wife, being more forward to this, consented, and the church furnished him out, and provided a pinnace to transport him; but when he came there he changed his mind, or at least his course, and went to the Dutch.

18.] The court of elections was. Mr. Winthrop was again chosen governour, and Mr. Endecott deputy governour. This being done, Mr. Dudley went away, and though he were chosen an assistant, yet he would not accept it. Some of the elders went to his house to deal with him. His answer was, that he had sufficient reasons to excuse and warrant his refusal, which he did not think fit to publish, but he would impart to any one or two of them whom they should appoint, which he did accordingly. The elders acquainted the court with what they had done, but not with the reasons of his refusal, only that they thought them not sufficient. The court sent a magistrate and two deputies to desire him to come to the court, for as a counsellor he was to assist in the general court. The next day he came, and after some excuse he consented to accept the place, so that the court would declare that if at any time he should depart out of the jurisdiction,

||Jugle|| ||2only||

(which he ||protested|| he did not intend,) no oath, either of officer, counsellor or assistant should hold him in any bond ||[2]where|| he stood. §This§ he desired, not for his own satisfaction, but that it might be a satisfaction to others who might scruple his liberty herein. After much debate the court made a general order which gave him satisfaction.

One Mr. [1]Blinman, a minister in Wales, a godly and able man, came over with some friends of his, and being invited to Green's [2]Harbour, near Plimouth, they went thither, but ere the year was expired there fell out some difference among them, which by no means could be reconciled, so as they agreed to part, and he came with his company and sat down at Cape Anne, which at this court was established to be a plantation, and called Gloucester.

A book was brought into the court, wherein the institution of the standing council was pretended to be a sinful innovation. The governour moved to have the contents of the book examined, and then, if there appeared cause, to inquire after the author. But the greatest part of the court, having some intimation of the author, of whose honest intentions they were well persuaded, would not consent, only they permitted it to be read, but not to be spoken unto, but would have inquiry first made how it came into the court. Whereupon it was found to have been made by Mr. Saltonstall, one of the assistants, and by him sent to Mr. Hathorn (then a deputy of the court) to be tendered to the court, if he should approve of it. Mr. Hathorn did not acquaint the court with it, but delivered it to one of the freemen to consider of, with whom it remained about half a year, till he delivered it to Mr. Dudley. This discovery being made, the governour moved again that the matter of the book might be considered, but the court could not agree to it except Mr. Saltonstall were first acquit from any censure concerning the said book. This was thought to be

||professed|| ||[2]which||

[1] Richard Blinman, whom Johnson means not to disparage, when he spells his name Blindman, lib. II. c. 20, is well remembered by Allen in Biog. Dict. and by Eliot, in Eccl. Hist. 1 Hist. Coll. IX. 39. After sixteen years passed in our country, at four several vineyards, viz. Marshfield, Gloucester, New London and New Haven, he returned to England, and continued in the service at Bristol, having declined offers to settle at Newfoundland, where he stopped on his way. This I learn from a letter of Davenport, mentioning receipt of one, written 22 Aug. 1659, by Blinman from that island, and see Holmes I. 346.

[2] Marshfield is the corporate name, though it was first called Rexham by the Plimouth government. See 1 Hist. Coll. IV. 111. by which it appears their first minister was Edward Bulkley, though the name is given Buckley there, and in 2 Hist. Coll. X. 65. But Hubbard spells it, 663, as I do. He was, probably, son of the first teacher of Concord.

a course out of all order, and upon that some passages very offensive and unwarrantable were mentioned, about which also the court being divided, the governour moved to take the advice of the elders concerning the soundness of the propositions and arguments. This the court would not allow neither, except the whole cause were referred also, which he thought sure they would have accepted, for the cause being of a civil nature, it belonged to the court, and not to the elders, to judge of the merit thereof. In the end, a day or two after, when no further proceeding was otherwise like to be had, it was agreed, that in regard the court was not jealous of any evil intention in Mr. Saltonstall, &c. and that when he did write and deliver it, (as was supposed,) there was an order in force, which gave liberty to every freeman to consider and deliver their judgments to the next court about such fundamental laws as were then to be established, (whereof one did concern the institution and power of the council,) therefore he should be discharged from any censure or further inquiry about the same, which was voted accordingly, although there were some expressions in the book which would not be warranted by that order, as that the council was instituted unwarily to satisfy Mr. Vane's desire, &c. whereas it was well known to many in the court, as themselves affirmed, that it was upon the advice and solicitation of the elders, and after much deliberation from court to court. Other passages there were also, which were very unsound, reproachful and dangerous, and was manifested by an answer made thereunto by Mr. Dudley, and received at the next session of the court, and by some observations made by Mr. Norris, a grave and judicious elder, teacher of the church in Salem, (and with some difficulty read also in court,) who, not suspecting the author, handled him somewhat sharply according to the merit of the matter.

This summer ||five|| ships ||[2]more were|| built, ||[3]three|| at Boston, and one at Dorchester, and one at Salem.

A cooper's wife of Hingham, having been long in a sad melancholic distemper near to phrensy, and having formerly attempted to drown her child, but prevented by God's gracious providence, did now again take an opportunity, being alone, to carry her child, aged three years, to a creek near her house, and stripping it of the clothes, threw it into the water and mud. But, the tide being low, the little child scrambled out, and taking up its clothes, came to its mother who was set down not far off. She carried the child again, and threw it in so far as it could not get out; but then it pleased God, that a young man, coming that way,

||three|| ||[2]were new|| ||[3]one||

saved it. She would give no other reason for it, but that she did it to save it from misery, and withal that she was assured, she had sinned against the Holy Ghost, and that she could not repent of any sin. Thus doth satan work by the advantage of our infirmities, which should stir us up to cleave the more fast to Christ Jesus, and to walk the more humbly and watchfully in all our conversation.

At this general court appeared one Richard [1]Gibson, a scholar, sent some three or four years since to Richman's Island to be a minister to a fishing plantation there belonging to one Mr. ||Trelawney|| of Plimouth in England. He removed from thence to Pascataquack, and this year was entertained by the fishermen at the Isle of Shoals to preach to them. He, being wholly addicted to the hierarchy and discipline of England, did exercise a ministerial function in the same way, and did marry and baptize at the Isle of Shoals which was now found to be within our jurisdiction. This man being incensed against Mr. Larkham, pastor of the church at Northam, (late Dover,) for some speeches he delivered in his sermon against such hirelings, &c. he sent an open letter to him, wherein he did scandalize our government, oppose our title to those parts, and provoke the people, by way of arguments, to revolt from us (this letter being showed to many before it came to Mr. Larkham.) Mr. Gibson being now showed this letter, and charged with his offence, he could not deny the thing, whereupon he was committed to the marshall. In a day or two after he preferred a petition, which gave not satisfaction, but the next day he made a full acknowledgment of all he was charged with, and the evil thereof, submitting himself to the favour of the court. Whereupon, in regard he was a stranger, and was to depart the country within a few days, he was discharged without any fine or other punishment.

Mo. 4. 8.] One Nathaniel [2]||Briscoe[2],|| a godly young man, newly admitted a member of the church of Boston, being single, he kept with his father, a godly poor man, but minded his own advantage more than his father's necessity, so as that his father, desir-

||Tretaway|| ||[2]Bristoe||

---

1 No just ground of complaint, I suppose, appeared against Gibson, who probably did good service to the poor fishermen, at least by his marrying them. A curious absurdity may be seen in 1 Hist. Coll. VII. 250, from which it seems, that women were forbidden to live at the Isle of Shoals; but it was then under a different jurisdiction.

2 We cannot presume, that this godly young member of the church of Boston, who disregarded his poor father's request, was the same so shockingly beaten by the head of the college, Vol. I. 308.

ing in the evening to have his help the next day, he neglected his father's request, and rose very early next morning to go help another man for wages, and being loading a boat in a small creek, he fell into the water and was drowned.

About this time the adventurers to the Isle of Sable fetched off their men and goods all safe. The oil, teeth, seal and horse hides, and some black fox skins came to near £1500.

One Darby Field,[1] an Irishman, living about Pascataquack, being accompanied with two Indians, went to the top of the white hill.[2] He made his journey in 18 days. His relation at his return was, that it was about ||one hundred|| miles from Saco, that after 40 miles travel he did, for the most part, ascend, and within 12 miles of the top was neither tree nor grass but low ||[2]savins,|| which they went upon the top of sometimes, but a continual ascent upon rocks, on a ridge between two valleys filled with snow, out of which came two branches of Saco river, which met at the foot of the hill where was an Indian town of some 200 people. Some of them accompanied him within 8 miles of the top, but durst go no further, telling him that no Indian ever dared to go higher, and that he would die if he went. So they staid there till his return, and his two Indians took courage by his example and went with him. They went divers times through the thick clouds for a good space, and within 4 miles of the top they had no clouds, but very cold.

||160|| ||[2]blank||

---

1 Field was one of the earliest members of the church of Exeter, Haz. I. 263.

2 This was, undoubtedly, the first visit of any European to the White mountains. Belknap has erroneously, N. H. I. 22–24, made Neal, "in company with Josselyn and Darby Field," in 1632, the discoverers; and magnifies his error by this note. "Mr. Hubbard, and after him Gov. Hutchinson, place this discovery of the White Hills in 1642. But as Neal had positive orders to discover the lakes, and tarried but three years in the country, employing great part of his time in searching the woods, it is probable that Mr. Hubbard mistook one figure in his date." Here, as he has often done elsewhere, Hubbard might indeed have mistaken a figure, but he faithfully copied Winthrop, whose work was unknown to Dr. Belknap, when his history of N. H. was published. A greater mistake is however chargeable on Belknap, in making Josselyn the companion of Neal, who was gone home four years before Josselyn came over. Nor did Josselyn make the journey, according to his own account, before his second voyage to New England in 1663. That Neal ever went to the White mountains, is not rendered probable by any authorities cited by Belknap; and as the circumstance would have been for him a great matter of boasting, we may be confident of the first journey of Field, as in the text above. The great lake of Iroquois, which the grandson of Sir F. Gorges writes about as *ascertained* by Neal to be 90 or 100 miles by land from Pascataquack settlement, was, I am satisfied, the Winipiseogee. Distances were always magnified in the wilderness; and poor Neal was lost in the woods, not far from home, when "the discovery wanted but one day's journey of being finished."

By the way, among the rocks, there were two ponds, one a blackish water and the other reddish. The top of all was plain about 60 feet square. On the north side there was such a precipice, as they could scarce discern to the bottom. They had neither cloud nor wind on the top, and moderate heat. All the country about him seemed a level, except here and there a hill rising above the rest, but far beneath them. He saw to the north a great water which he judged to be about 100 miles broad, but could see no land beyond it. The sea by Saco seemed as if it had been within 20 miles. He saw also a sea to the eastward, which he judged to be the gulph of Canada: he saw some great waters in parts to the westward, which he judged to be the great lake which Canada river comes out of.[1] He found there much muscovy glass, they could rive out pieces of 40 feet long and 7 or 8 broad. When he came back to the Indians, he found them drying themselves by the fire, for they had a great tempest of wind and rain. About a month after he went again with five or six in his company, then they had some wind on the top and some clouds above them which hid the sun. They brought some stones which they supposed had been diamonds, but they were most crystal. See after, another relation more true and exact.

Mo. 4. 22.] In the time of the general court, in a great tempest of thunder and lightning, in the evening, the lightning struck the upper sail of the windmill in Boston by the [2]ferry, and shattered it in many pieces, and, missing the stones, struck into the standard, rived it down in three parts to the bottom, and one of the spars; and the main standard being bound about with a great iron hoop, fastened with many long spikes, it was plucked off, broken in the middle, and thrown upon the floor, and the boards upon the sides of the mill rived off, the sacks &c. in the mill set on fire, and the miller being under the mill, upon the ground, chopping a piece of board, was struck dead, but company coming in, found him to breathe, so they carried him to an house, and within an hour or two he began to stir, and strove with such force, as

1 Perhaps it is hardly necessary to observe, that the great waters seen north, east, and west, by this traveller, to that elevated spot, on the first visit, were delusions, probably fog banks in the valleys.

2 Our windmill continued, it seems, as it was left by Wood nine years before, on Copp's hill, from near the foot of which was the ferry to Charlestown. This and other ferries were regulated early by the government, as may be seen from the records. At the general court 18 May 1631, Vol. I. 72 is found: "Thomas Williams hath undertaken to set up a ferry betwixt Winnettsemit and Charlton, for which he is to have *3d*, a person, and from Winnettsemit to Boston, *4d*, a person." In the Addenda will be seen an account of the ferry between Boston and Charlestown.

six men could scarce hold him down. The next day he came to his senses, but knew nothing of what had befallen him, but found himself very sore on divers parts of his body. His hair on one side of his head and beard was singed, one of his shoes torn off his foot, but his foot not hurt.[1]

The Indians at Kennebeck, hearing of the general conspiracy against the English, determined to begin there, and one of them knowing that Mr. Edward Winslow did use to walk within the palisadoes, prepared his piece to shoot him, but as he was about it, Mr. Winslow not seeing him nor suspecting any thing, but thinking he had walked enough, went suddenly into the house, and so God preserved him.

At the same general court there fell out a great business upon a very small occasion. Anno 1636, there was a stray sow in Boston, which was brought to Captain Keayne: he had it cried divers times, and divers came to see it, but none made claim to it for near a year. He kept it in his yard with a sow of his own. Afterwards one Sherman's wife, having lost such a sow, laid claim to it, but came not to see it, till Captain Keayne had killed his own sow. After being showed the stray sow, and finding it to have other marks than she had claimed her sow by, she gave out that he had killed her sow. The noise hereof being spread about the town, the matter was brought before the elders of the church as a case of offence; many witnesses were examined, and Captain Keayne was cleared. She not being satisfied with this, by the instigation of one George [2]Story, a young merchant of London, who kept in her house, (her husband being then in England,) and had been brought before the governour upon complaint of Captain Keayne as living under suspicion, she brought the cause to

---

1 I have not found any rate for 1641. But in Coll. Rec. II. 10, is the following:

At the adjourned session 14 June 1642, Mr. William Tyng, goodman Thomas Line, goodman Heath, Lieutenant Duncan, goodman Cheesbrough, Mr. Parker, Mr. Peck, Mr. Sparhawk, Mr. Ayres, Mr. Noyse, Lieutenant Willard, Mr. Allen, Captain Bridges, Mr. Batter, Mr. Whipple, goodman Boyse, Mr. Rawson, John Saunders, and goodman Hayward were appointed a committee to levy and proportion a rate of 800 pounds, which they agreed as followeth;

Boston, 120 pounds; Ipswich, 82 pounds; Salem, 75 pounds; Cambridge, 67 pounds, 10; Charlestown, 60 pounds; Dorchester, 58 pounds, 10; Watertown, 55 pounds; Roxbury, 50 pounds; Lynn, 45 pounds; Newbury, 30 pounds; Concord, 25 pounds; Hingham, 20 pounds; Dedham, 20 pounds; Rowley, 15 pounds; Sudbury, 15 pounds; Weymouth, 14 pounds; Braintree, 14 pounds; Salisbury, 12 pounds, 10; Medford, 10 pounds; Gloucester, 6 pounds, 10; Hampton, 5 pounds.

2 My search for any traces of this man has been unsuccessful.

the inferiour court at Boston, where, upon a full hearing, Captain Keayne was again cleared, and the jury gave him £3 for his cost, and he bringing his action against Story and her for reporting about that he had stolen her sow, recovered £20 damages of either of them. Story upon this searcheth town and country to find matter against Captain Keayne about this stray sow, and got §one§ of his witnesses to come into Salem court and to confess there that he had forsworn himself; and upon this he petitions in Sherman's name, to this general court, to have the cause heard again, which was granted, and the best part of seven days were spent in examining of witnesses and debating of the cause; and yet it was not determined, for there being ||nine magistrates|| and thirty deputies, no sentence could by law pass without the greater number of both, which neither plaintiff nor defendant had, for there were for the plaintiff two magistrates and fifteen deputies, §and for the defendant seven magistrates, and eight deputies[1]§, the other seven deputies stood doubtful. Much contention and earnestness there was, which indeed did mostly arise from the difficulty of the case, in regard of cross witnesses, §and some prejudices§ (as one ||2professed||) against the person, which blinded some men's judgments that they could not attend the true nature and course of the evidence. For all the plaintiff's witnesses amounted to no more but an evidence of probability, so as they might all swear true, and yet the sow in question might not be the plaintiff's. But the defendant's witnesses gave a certain evidence, upon their certain knowledge, and that upon certain grounds, (and these as many and more and of as good credit as the others,) so as if this testimony were true, it was not possible the sow should be the plaintiff's. Besides, whereas the plaintiff's wife was admitted to take her oath for the marks of her sow, the defendant and his wife (being a very godly sober woman) was denied the like, although propounded in the court by Mr. Cotton, upon that rule in the law   he shall swear he hath not put his hands to his neighbour's goods. Yet they both in the open court solemnly, as in the presence of God, declared their innocency, &c. Further, if the case had been doubtful, yet the defendant's lawful possession ought to have been preferred to the plaintiff's doubtful title, for in equali jure melior est conditio possidentis. But the defendant being of ill report in the country for a hard dealer in his

||one magistrate|| ||2protested||

---

1 It is strange how the former editor could have suffered the mutilated sentence to pass.

course of trading, and having been formerly censured in the court and in the church also, by admonition for such offences, carried many weak minds strongly against him. And the truth is, he was very worthy of blame in that kind, as divers others in the country were also in those times, though they were not detected as he was; yet to give every man his due, he was very useful to the country both by his hospitality and otherwise. But one dead fly spoils much good ointment.[1]

There was great expectation in the country, by occasion of Story's clamours against him, that the cause would have passed against the captain, but falling out otherwise, gave occasion to many to speak unreverently of the court, especially of the magistrates, and the report went, that their negative voice had hindered the course of justice, and that these magistrates must be put out, that the power of the negative voice might be taken away. Thereupon it was thought fit by the governour and other of the magistrates to publish a declaration of the true state of the cause, that truth might not be condemned unknown. This was framed before the court brake up; for prevention whereof, the governour tendered a declaration in nature of a pacification, whereby it might have appeared, that, howsoever the members of the court dissented in judgment, yet they were the same in affection, and had a charitable opinion of each other; but this was opposed by

---

1 Frequent animadversions are found in our records on cases of real or supposed overcharge for labour and commodities. A ludicrous one, mentioned by Hubbard, 248, is more satisfactorily stated in our records of the colony I. 250, at a general court 22 of 3, 1639: "Edward Palmer, for his extortion, taking 1 pound 13.7, for the plank and wood-work of Boston stocks, is fined 5 pounds, and censured to be set an hour in the stocks." Afterwards the fine was "*remitted* to ten shillings." The remainder of the sentence, I fear, was executed. Our Ipswich chronicler is almost facetious about this part: he "had the honour to sit an hour in them himself, to warn others not to offend in the like kind."

The unhappy subject of the controversy in the text was exposed to very general blame, and several particular complaints. I have seen an original affidavit of Thomas Wiltshire, that for work done at Captain Keayne's house there was due to the deponent 38 shillings, and that K. sold him a piece of broad cloth, "which he said was Spanish broad cloth, and delivered for payment to this deponent at seventeen shillings per yard, the which cloth this deponent showed to Henry Shrimpton, and he said it was not worth above ten shillings per yard, for it was but cloth rash, and so said goodman Read, and his wife showed a waistcoat of the same kind of cloth, which cost but nine shillings per yard, and in this deponent's judgment was better cloth; and this deponent showed the same cloth to Mr. Rock, and he said it was worth but ten shillings per yard, for it was but cloth rash, and this deponent showed it also to Mr. Stoddard, and he said likewise that it was cloth rash, and was not worth above ten shillings per yard, and was dear enough of that price, or words to that effect." Such was the dangerous form and matter of judicial investigations in the early days.

some of the plaintiff's part, so it was laid by. And because there was much labouring in the country upon a false supposition, that the magistrate's negative voice stopped the plaintiff in the case of the sow, one of the magistrates published a declaration of the necessity of upholding the same. It may be here inserted, being but brief.

Mo. 5. 7.] From Maryland came one Mr. Neale[1] with two pinnaces and commission from Mr. Calvert, the governour there, to buy mares and sheep, but having nothing to pay for them but bills charged upon the Lord Baltimore in England, no man would deal with him. One of his vessels was so eaten with worms that he was forced to leave her.

Mr. Chancey of Scituate persevered in his opinion of dipping in baptism, and practised accordingly, first upon two of his own, which being in very cold weather, one of them swooned away. Another, having a child about three years old, feared it would be frightened, (as others had been, and one caught hold of Mr. Chancey and had near pulled him into the water,) she brought her child to Boston, with letters testimonial from Mr. Chancey, and had it baptized there.

21.] A general fast was kept by order of the general court and advice of some of the elders. The occasion was principally for the danger we conceived our native country was in, and the foul sins which had broken out among ourselves, &c.

23.] Osamaken, the great sachem of Pakanocott in Plimouth jurisdiction, came, attended with many men and some other sagamores accompanying him, to visit the governour, who entertained him kindly, &c.

The Mary Rose, which had been blown up and sunk with all her ordnance, ballast, much lead, and other goods, was now weighed and brought to shore by the industry and diligence of one Edward Bendall[2] of Boston. The court gave the owners above a

---

1 Of this agent of the governour of Maryland I know nothing. One of the protested bills is recorded in our registry of deeds, so that, probably, one person had dealt with him, and found his payment illusory, no doubt, arising from the civil convulsions in England.

2 He was so early a member of Boston church, being No. 77, that I presume he came with Winthrop. Credit is due to him for a great share of enterprise, of which the relation in the text is sufficient proof. The dock, or cove, which was in early times the principal seat of trade in Boston, was long called by his name, because he owned part of the upland around it, and had a ware house on it. It has since been called the town dock, but the exact boundaries, north and south, cannot probably be explained. Bendall lived, I think, to good old age, for administration of his estate was granted 2 May 1682, to William Phil-

year's time to recover §her§ and free the harbour, which was much damnified by her; and they having given her over and never attempting to weigh her, Edward Bendall undertook it upon these terms, viz. if he freed the harbour, §he should have the whole, otherwise§ he should have half of all he recovered. He made two great tubs, bigger than a butt, very tight, and open at one end, upon which were hanged so many weights as would sink it to the ground (600wt.) It was let down, the diver sitting in it, a cord in his hand to give notice when they should draw him up, and another cord to show when they should remove it from place to place, so he could continue in his tub near half an hour, and fasten ropes to the ordnance, and put the lead, &c. into a net or tub. And when the tub was drawn up, one knocked upon the head of it, and thrust a long pole under water, which the diver laid hold of, and so was drawn up by it; for they might not draw the open end out of water for endangering him, &c.[1] The case of the money, shot out of one of the guns, which came to a trial in the court at Boston, (8) 27, see in the next leaf.

5. 28.] A Dutch ship of 300 tons arrived here, laden with salt from the West Indies, which she sold here for plank and pipe staves. She brought two Spanish merchants, who being taken at sea, while they went in a frigate from Domingo to find an English ship which they had freighted there, and was by their agreement stolen out of the harbour, where she had been long embarred, they hired this Dutchman to bring them hither where they had appointed their ship to come, not daring to go into Spain or England. They staid here about a month, but their ship came not, so they went away again. We heard after that their ship had been 14 days beating upon our coast, and being put back, still, by N. W. winds, she bare up, and went for England, and arriving at Southampton, the parliament made use of the treasure.

God would not suffer her to come to us, lest our hearts should have §been taken with her wealth, and so have§ caused the Spaniard to have an evil eye upon us.

Some of the elders went to Concord, being sent for by the church there, to advise with them about the maintenance of their elders, &c. They found them wavering about removal, not finding their plantation answerable to their expectation, and the maintenance of two elders too heavy a burden for them. The elders'

---

lips, senr. Fregrace Bendall, who was many years register of deeds in our county, was perhaps brother of Edward.

1 If the diving bell had by ingenious or philosophical men been earlier invented, I doubt that no instance of its successful application can be found before this.

advice was, that they should continue and wait upon God, and be helpful to their elders in labour and what they could, and all to be ordered by the deacons, (whose office had not formerly been improved this way amongst them,) and that the elders should be content with what means the church was able at present to afford them, and if either of them should be called to some other place, then to advise with other churches about removal.

One Wequash Cook, an Indian, living about Connecticut river's mouth, and keeping much at Saybrook with Mr. Fenwick, attained to good knowledge of the things of God and salvation by Christ, so as he became a preacher to other Indians, and laboured much to convert them, but without any effect, for within a short time he fell sick, not without suspicion of poison from them, and died very comfortably.

There was about £30 put into one of the guns of the Mary Rose, which was known all abroad. The guns being taken up and searched, they pulled out of one of them a wad of rope yarn. They handled it and found it very heavy, and began to undo it, but being very wet and foul they threw it down; and about 8 or 9 days after, coming to try one of the guns, and finding this wad lying there, they thrust it in after the powder, and shot it off into the channel, but perceived part of it to break and fall short, and the rest fell into the middle of the channel. But the next low water there was taken up several pieces of gold and some silver. This was in a place where people passed daily, and never any found there before that time. Those who found the money refused to restore it to him who had bought and taken up the wreck. Whereupon he brought his action, and the money was adjudged to him.

Two ships arrived from England, but brought not above five or six passengers, save our own people, and very few goods, except rigging, &c. for some ships which were building here.[1]

---

1 We are told by Johnson, lib. II. c. 21, "the number of freemen added were about 1232" this year, which is so far beyond the average annual addition, or indeed the increase of any single year, that it is strange so careful a compiler as Dr. Holmes transcribed it for his Ann. I. 324, without hinting a suspicion, that the first or last figure was an errour of the London press. In the two preceding years it is known from our author, pp. 7, 31 of this volume, that the "reformation both of church and civil state" had "caused all men to stay in England in expectation of a new world;" of course, that few passengers came over to the colonies. But as the young men, coming of age here yearly, might have supplied a large increase of freemen, I have diligently examined the records of their admission, and find in May 113, in June 6, in September 2, in December, at Salem, 9, in February 7=137. Following the advice of a most patient antiquary of New Hampshire, John Farmer, Esquire, I have resolved to transcribe from our colony lists the names of all those who took the freeman's oath before

Now came over a book of Mr. Cotton's sermons upon the seven vials. Mr. Humfrey had gotten the notes from some who had took them by characters, and printed them in London, *he had 300 copies for it,* which was a great wrong to Mr. Cotton, and he was much grieved at it, for it had been fit he should have perused and corrected the copy before it had been printed.

Mo. 6.] Mr. Welde, Mr. Peter, and Mr. Hibbins, who were sent the last year into England, had procured £500 which they sent over in linen, woollen, and other useful commodities for the country, which, because the stock might be preserved and returned this year for a further supply, were put off together, for about eighty pounds profit, and the principal returned by Mr. Stoughton in the next ship.

By their means also, Mr. Richard Andrews,[1] an haberdasher in Cheapside, London, a godly man, and who had been a former benefactor to this country, having 500 pounds due to him from the governour and company of Plimouth, gave it to this colony to be laid out in cattle, and other course of trade, for the poor.

Two fishermen drowned in a shallop, which was overset near Pascataquack.

24.] The ship Trial, about 200 tons, built at Boston by the merchants there, being now ready to set sail, (Mr. Thomas ||Coytmore[2]|| master, and divers godly seamen in her,) Mr. Cotton was

||blank||

Winthrop's death. These are probably ancestors of near three fourths of the present inhabitants of the six New England states, with almost half of New York and Ohio. See Appendix K. But I must not be charged with some errours of the secretary, nor are we permitted to be confident, that *all* the freemen's names are inserted in the records. Those adventurers, in the company, were free before coming from England, and therefore were not sworn. Yet I doubt several were received, in whose favour no record remains.

1 Great liberality of this gentleman is noticed in Vol. I. 136. The observation, that he became mayor of London, is erroneous; he was an alderman. Thomas Andrews was mayor in 1651. Richard had been one of the London associates for aid to the Plimouth colony in 1626. See governour Bradford in 1 Hist. Coll. III. 46-73. The poverty of that settlement for many years prevented the full effect of his benefaction to ours, for it was long before the adjustment was made. See a letter of his dated from Rotterdam in 1645, in answer to one of governour Winthrop's, probably in reply to this proof of liberality in the text, 3 Hist. Coll. I. 21.

2 Mr. Thomas Coytmore was a deputy from Charlestown in Oct. 1640, and some following courts, and seems to have been a gentleman of good estate. The manner of his death will be seen in a later part of this work. In Dec. 1647, his widow became the fourth wife of our author, and the marriage settlements, preserved in the records of our general courts, Vol. II. 197-9, seem worthy of preservation. See appendix L.

desired to preach aboard her, &c. but upon consideration that the audience would be too great for the ship, the sermon was at the meeting house.

A plantation was begun the last year at Delaware Bay by those of New Haven, and some 20 families were transported thither, but this summer there fell such sickness and mortality among them as dissolved the plantation. The same sickness and mortality befell the Swedes also, who were planted upon the same river. The English were after driven out by the Swedes.

Mo. 7.] Mr. William Hibbins, who was one of those who were sent over into England the year before, arrived now in safety, with divers others who went over then also. He made a public declaration to the church in Boston, of all the good providences of the Lord towards him in his voyage to and fro, &c. wherein it was very observable what care the Lord had of them, and what desperate dangers they were delivered from upon the seas, such as the eldest seamen were amazed; and indeed such preservations and deliverances have been so frequent, to such ships as have carried those of the Lord's family between the two Englands, as would fill a perfect volume to report them all.

6] There came letters from divers Lords of the upper house, and some 30 of the house of commons, and others from the ministers there, who stood for the independency of churches, to Mr. Cotton of Boston, Mr. Hooker of Hartford, and Mr. Davenport of New Haven, to call them, or some of them, if all could not, to England, to assist in the synod there appointed, to consider and advise about the settling of church government. Upon this such of the magistrates and elders as were at hand met together, and were most of them of opinion that it was a call of God, yet took respite of concluding, till they might hear from the rest. Whereupon a messenger was presently despatched to Connecticut, and New Haven, with the letters, &c. Upon return, it was found that Mr. Hooker liked not the business, nor thought it any sufficient call for them to go 3,000 miles to agree with three men, (meaning those three ministers who were for independency, and did solicit in the parliament, &c.) Mr. Davenport thought otherwise of it, so as the church there set apart a day to seek the Lord in it, and thereupon came to this conclusion, that seeing the church had no other officer but himself, therefore they might not spare him.

Mr. Cotton apprehended strongly a call of God in it, though he were very averse to a sea voyage, and the more because his ordinary topic in Acts 13, led him to deliver that doctrine of the interest all churches have in each other's members for mutual helpfulness, &c. But soon after came other letters out of England, upon the breach between the king and parliament, from one of the former Lords, and from Mr. Welde and Mr. Peter, to advise them to stay till they heard further; so this care came to an end.[1]

There arrived another ship with salt, which was put off for pipe staves, &c. so by an unexpected providence we were supplied of salt to go on with our fishing, and of ships to take off our pipe staves, which lay upon men's hands.

There fell out a very sad accident at Weymouth. One Richard Sylvester,[2] having three small children, he and his wife going to the assembly, upon the Lord's day, left their children at home. The eldest was without doors looking to some cattle; the middlemost, being a son about five years old, seeing his father's fowling piece, (being a very great one,) stand in the chimney, took it and laid it upon a stool, as he had seen his father do, and pulled up the cock, (the spring being weak,) and put down the hammer, then went to the other end and blowed in the mouth of the piece, as he had seen his father also do, and with that stirring the piece, being charged, it went off, and shot the child into the mouth and through his head. When the father came home he found his child lie dead, and could not have imagined how he should have been so killed, but the youngest child, (being but three years old, and could scarce speak,) showed him the whole manner of it.

There arrived in a small pinnace one Mr. Bennet,[3] a gentleman of Virginia, with letters from many well disposed people of the upper ||new farms|| in Virginia to the elders here, bewailing their

||blank||

---

1 That these celebrated divines, chiefs in their profession of the three colonies where they lived, remained here, instead of obeying this call, is perhaps one of the most fortunate circumstances in our early history. Probably they would have been made members of the famous Westminster assembly, which opened 1 July 1643, and maintained, through the wretched intrigues and convulsions of the civil war, and the fluctuations of anarchy, an unequal existence of five years, six months, and twenty-two days. In New England a high regard has always been shown to the doctrinal decisions of this council, but with still greater unanimity has its assertion of the divine right of Presbyterian government been opposed. Our three members would have found few superiors among their clerical brethren; yet their voice must have been drowned in that of the immense majority, who borrowed their ecclesiastical polity from the Northen impulse of sectarian ambition; and thus might we have seen introduced, for the simplicity of our present church discipline, a regimen at least as offensive as that from which it had just before escaped.

2 It may be remembered, from vol. I. 289, that this person had suffered in the petty persecution of some of the Weymouth people.

3 Johnson, lib. III. c. 11, increases our knowledge of this gentleman by calling him Philip.

sad condition for want of the means of salvation, and earnestly entreating a supply of faithful ministers, whom, upon experience of their gifts and godliness, they might call to office, &c. Upon these letters, (which were openly read in Boston upon a lecture day,) the elders met, and set a day apart to seek God in it, and agreed upon three who might most likely be spared, viz. Mr. Phillips of Watertown, Mr. Tompson of Braintree, and Mr. Miller of Rowley, for these churches had each of them two. Having designed these men, they acquainted the general court herewith, who did approve thereof, and ordered that the governour should commend them to the governour and council of Virginia, which was done accordingly. But Mr. Phillips being not willing to go, Mr. Knolles, his fellow elder, and Mr. Tompson, with the consent of their churches, were sent away, and departed on their way 8ber 7. to Taunton, to meet the bark at Narragansett. Mr. Miller did not accept the call.[1] The main argument, which prevailed with the churches to dismiss them to that work, and with the court to allow and further it, was the advancement of the kingdom of Christ in those parts, and the confidence they had in the promise, that whosoever shall part with father, &c. for my sake and the gospel's, shall receive an hundred fold. We were so far from fearing any loss by parting with such desirable men, as we looked at them as seed sown, which would bring us in a plentiful harvest, and we accounted it no small honour that God had put upon his poor churches here, that other parts of the world should seek to us for help in this kind. For about the same time, two of our vessels which had been gone near a year, and were much feared to be lost, returned home with a good supply of cotton, and brought home letters with them from Barbadoes and other islands in those parts, intreating us to supply them with ministers. But, understanding that these people were much infected with familism, &c. the elders did nothing about it, intending to inquire further by another vessel, which was preparing for those parts.

Mo. 7. 1.] There came letters from the court at Connecticut, and from two of the magistrates there, and from Mr. Ludlow, near the Dutch, certifying us that the Indians all over the country had combined themselves to cut off all the English, that the time was

1 Hubbard, 410, adds to this information by assigning the reason of Miller's declining the call "because of his bodily weakness." It seems, however, that his people at Rowley could *spare* him, for we learn from the same author, 663 that he was next year established in Plimouth colony. Johnson, lib. II. c. 11, honours him with verses, that teach us little more, than that he was low of stature, but his prose assures us he continued at Yarmouth in 1651. •Mather gives his name of baptism, John.

appointed after harvest, the manner also, they should go by small companies to the chief men's houses by way of trading, &c. and should kill them in the houses and seize their weapons, and then others should be at hand to prosecute the massacre; and that this was discovered by three several Indians, near about the same time and in the same manner; one to Mr. Eaton of New Haven, another to Mr. Ludlow, and the third to Mr. Haynes. This last being ||hurt|| near to death by a cart, &c. sent after Mr. Haynes, and told him that Englishman's God was angry with him, and had set Englishman's cow to kill him, because he had concealed such a conspiracy against the English, and so told him of it, as the other two had done. [1]Upon this their advice to us was, that it was better to enter into war presently, and begin with them, and if we would send 100 men to the river's mouth of Connecticut, they would meet us with a proportionable number.

Upon these letters, the governour called so many of the magistrates as were near, and being met, they sent out summons for a general court, to be kept six days after, and in the mean time, it was thought fit, for our safety, and to strike some terrour into the Indians, to disarm such as were within our jurisdiction. Accordingly we sent men to Cutshamekin, at Braintree, to fetch him and his guns, bows, &c. which was done, and he came willingly, and being late in the night when they came to Boston, he was put in the prison; but the next morning, finding upon examination of him and divers of his men, no ground of suspicion of his partaking in any such conspiracy, he was dismissed.

Upon the warrant which went to Ipswich, Rowley and Newbury, to disarm Passaconamy, who lived by Merrimack, they sent forth 40 men armed the next day, being the Lord's day. But it rained all the day, as it had done divers days before, and also after, so as they could not go to his wigwam, but they came to his son's and took him, which they had warrant for, and a squaw and her child, which they had §no§ warrant for, and therefore order was given so soon as ||[2]we|| heard of it, to send them home again. They, fearing his son's escape, led him in a line, but he taking an opportunity, slipped his line and escaped from them, but one very indiscreetly made a shot at him, and missed him narrowly. Upon

||quite|| ||[2]he||

1 No light on the subject of their fears is given by the historian of the people of Connecticut. Good sense and honest policy is observable in the reception by the Massachusetts rulers of these complaints against the Indians, which were certainly extravagant, and probably unfounded.

the intelligence of these unwarranted proceedings, and ||considering|| that Passaconamy would look at it as a manifest injury, (as indeed we conceived it to be, and had always shunned to give them any just occasion against us,) the court being now assembled, we sent Cutshamekin to him to let him know that what was done to his son and squaw was without order, and to show him the occasion whereupon we had sent to disarm all the Indians, and that when we should find that they were innocent of any such conspiracy, we would restore all their arms again, and to will him also to come speak with us. He returned answer that he knew not what was become of his son and his squaw, (for one of them was run into the woods and came not again for ten days after, and the other was still in custody,) if he had them safe again, then he would come to us. Accordingly about a fortnight after he sent his eldest son to us, who delivered up his guns, &c.

Mo. 7. 8.] The general court being assembled, we considered of the letters and other intelligence from Connecticut, and although the thing seemed very probable, yet we thought it not sufficient ground for us to begin a war, for it was possible it might be otherwise, and that all this might come out of the enmity which had been between Miantunnomoh and Onkus, who continually sought to discredit each other with the English. We considered also of the like reports which had formerly been raised almost every year since we came, and how they proved to be but reports raised up by the opposite factions among the Indians. Besides we found ourselves in very ill case for war, and if we should begin, we must then be forced to stand continually upon our guard, and to desert our farms and business abroad, and all our trade with the Indians, which things would bring us very low; and besides, if upon this intelligence we should kill any of them, or lose any of our own, and it should be found after to have been a false report, we might provoke God's displeasure, and blemish our wisdom and integrity before the heathen. Further it was considered, that our beginning with them could not secure us against them: we might destroy some part of their corn and wigwams, and force them to fly into the woods, &c. but the men would be still remaining to do us mischief, for they will never fight us in the open field. Lastly, it was considered that such as were to be sent out in such an expedition were, for the most part, godly, and would be as well assured of the justice of the cause as the warrant of their call, and then we would not fear their forwardness and courage, but if they should be sent out, not well resolved, we might fear the success.

||concerning||

According to these considerations, we returned answer to Connecticut, and withal we sent two men with two interpreters, an Englishman and an Indian, to Miantunnomoh, to let him know what intelligence we had of his drawing the rest of the Indians into a confederation against us, and of his purpose to make his son sachem of Pequod, and of other things which were breaches of the league he made with us, and to desire him to come by such a time to give us satisfaction about them. If he refused to come, and gave them ||no|| satisfactory answer, then to let him know that if he regarded not our friendship, he would give us occasion to right ourselves. And instruction was given them, that if he gave them occasion, they should tell him the reason of our disarming the Indians, and excuse the injury done to Passaconamy, to be a mistake and without our order. The messengers coming to him, he carried them apart into the woods, taking only one of his chief men with him, and gave them very rational answers to all their propositions, and promised also to come over to us, which he did within the time prefixed.[1]

When he came, the court was assembled, and before his admission, we considered how to treat with him, (for we knew him to be a very subtile man,) and agreed upon the points and order, and that none should propound any thing to him but the governour, and if any other of the court had any thing material to suggest, he should impart it to the governour.

Being called in, and mutual salutations passed, he was set down at the lower end of the table, over against the governour, and had only two or three of his counsellors, and two or three of our neighbouring Indians, such as he desired, but would not speak of any business at any time, before some of his counsellors were present, alleging, that he would have them present, that they might bear witness with him, at his return home, of all his sayings.

In all his answers he was very deliberate and showed good understanding in the principles of justice and ||[2]equity,|| and ingenuity withal. He demanded that his accusers might be brought forth, to the end, that if they could not make good what they had charged him with, they might suffer what he was worthy of, and must have expected, if he had been found guilty, viz. death. We

||a|| ||[2]amity||

1 The magnanimity of the sachem is more consistent with his innocence than with the justice of the accusations from Connecticut. Most earnestly have we to deplore, that the firmness manifested by our government, in rejecting the delusive evidence of treachery in the natives, was not maintained the following year.

answered, we knew them not, nor were they within our power, nor would §we§ give credit to them, before we had given him knowledge of it, according to our agreement with him. He replied, if you did not give credit to it, why then did you disarm the Indians. We answered, for our security, and because we had been credibly informed that some of the eastern Indians had lately robbed divers Englishmen's houses at Saco, and taken away their powder and guns. This answer satisfied ||him||. He gave divers reasons, why we should hold him free of any such conspiracy, and why we should conceive it was a report raised by Onkus, &c., and therefore offered to meet Onkus at Connecticut, or rather at Boston, and would prove to his face his treachery against the English, &c. and told us he would come to us at any time; for though some had dissuaded him, assuring him, that the English would put him to death, or keep him in prison, yet he being innocent of any ill intention against the English, he knew them to be so just, as they would do him no wrong, and told us, that if we sent but any Indian to him that he liked, he would come to us, and we should not need to send any of our own men. He urged much, that those might be punished, who had raised this slander, and put it to our consideration what damage it had been to him, in that he was forced to keep his men at home, and not suffer them to go forth on hunting, &c. till he had given the English satisfaction, and the charge and trouble it had put the English unto, &c. We spent the better part of two days in treating with him, and in conclusion he did accommodate himself to us to our satisfaction; only some difficulty we had, to bring him to desert the Nianticks, if we had just cause of war with them. They were, he said, as his own flesh, being allied by continual intermarriages, &c. But at last he condescended, that if they should do us wrong, as he could not draw them to give us satisfaction for, nor himself could satisfy, as if it were for blood, &c. then he would leave them to us.

When we should go to dinner, there was a table provided for the Indians, to dine by themselves, and Miantunnomoh was left to sit with them. This he was discontented at, and would eat nothing, till the governour sent him meat from his table. So at night, and all the time he staid, he sat at the lower end of the magistrate's table. When he departed, we gave him and his counsellors coats and tobacco, and when he came to take his leave of the governour, and such of the magistrates as were present, he returned, and gave his hand to the governour again, saying, that was for the rest of the magistrates who were absent.

||them||

The court being adjourned for a few days, till we might hear from Miantunnomoh, (it was assembled again at such time as he came to Boston,) there came letters from Connecticut, certifying us of divers insolencies of the Indians, which so confirmed their minds in believing the former report, as they were now resolved to make war upon the Indians, and earnestly pressing us to delay no longer to send forth our men to join with them, and that they thought they should be forced to begin before they could hear from us again.

Upon receipt of these letters, the governour assembled such of the magistrates and deputies, as were at hand, and divers of the elders also, (for they were then met at Boston upon other occasions,) and imparted the letters to them, with other letters sent from the governour of Plimouth, intimating some observations they had, which made them very much to suspect, that there was such a plot in hand, &c. We all sat in consultation hereabout all the day, and in the end concluded, 1. That all these informations might arise from a false ground, and out of the enmity which was between the Naragansett and Monhigen. 2. Being thus doubtful, it was not a sufficient ground for us to war upon them. 3. That all these particular insolencies and wrongs ought to be revenged and repaired by course of justice, if it might be obtained, otherwise we should never be free from war. And accordingly, letters were sent back to our brethren at Connecticut, to acquaint them with our opinions, and to dissuade them from going forth, alleging how dishonourable it would be to us all, that, while we were upon treaty with the Indians, they should make war upon them, for they would account their act as our own, seeing we had formerly professed to the Indians, that we were all as one, and in our late message to Miantunnomoh, had remembered him again of the same, and he had answered that he did so account us. Upon receipt of this our answer, they forbare to enter into war, but (it seemed) unwillingly, and as not well pleased with us.[1]

---

1 [Here should have been inserted a passage of complaint, that the Connecticut brethren refused to furnish any evidence of the justice of their suspicions of the Naragansett sachem, or something like it, the loss of which I deeply lament. The governour had indeed drawn his pen through the original passage, but its import was probably as powerful as in such a case is possible. The curious reader will judge for himself, after reading the residue of this note, written while the venerable MS. was before me.]

In preserving this piece of information, probably erased after the unhappy triumph of the prejudices of our brethren in the neighbouring colony, we have some reason to confirm our doubts of the correctness of their insinuations or charges. When the complainants are silent, and the accused voluntarily ap-

Although we apprehended no danger, yet we continued our military watches, till near the end of 8ber, and restored the Indians all their arms we had taken from them: for although we saw it was very dangerous to us, that they should have guns, &c. yet we saw not in justice how we could take them away, seeing they came lawfully by them, (by trade with the French and Dutch for the most part,) and used them only for killing of fowl and deer, &c. except they brought themselves into the state of an enemy, therefore we thought it better to trust God with our safety than to save ourselves by unrighteousness.

At this court we were informed of some English to the eastward, who ordinarily traded powder to the Indians, and lived alone under no government; whereupon we granted warrant to a gentleman, that upon due proof, &c. he should take away their powder, leaving them sufficient for their own occasion.

This court also took order, that every town should be furnished with powder out of the common store, paying for it in country commodities; likewise for muskets, and for military watches, and alarms, &c. Presently upon this, there arose an alarm in the night upon this occasion. (7.) 19. A man, travelling late from Dorchester to Watertown, lost his way, and being benighted and in a swamp about 10 of the clock, hearing some wolves howl, and fearing to be devoured of them, he cried out help, help. One that dwelt within hearing, over against Cambridge, halloed to him. The other still cried out, which caused the man to fear that the Indians had gotten some English man and were torturing him, but not daring to go to him, he discharged a piece two or three times. This gave the alarm to Watertown, and so it went as far as Salem and Dorchester, but about one or two of the clock no enemy appearing, &c. all retired but the watch.

At this court also, four of Providence, who could not consort with Gorton and that company, and therefore were continually injured and molested by them, came and offered themselves and their lands, &c. to us, and were accepted under our government and protection. This we did partly to rescue these men from unjust violence, and partly to draw in the rest in those parts, either under ourselves or Plimouth, who now lived under no government, but grew very offensive, and the place was likely to be of use to us, especially if we should have occasion of sending out against any Indians of Naragansett §and likewise for an outlet into the

---

pears, before a tribunal most favourable to the accuser, there is just ground for acquittal after more suspicious circumstances than can be perceived in the case of Miantunnomoh.

Naragansett§ Bay, and seeing it came without our seeking, and would be no charge to us, we thought it not wisdom to let it slip.[1]

The English of Southampton, on Long Island, having certain intelligence of one of those Indians who murdered Hammond, who was put ashore there with others, when their pinnace was wrecked, sent Captain Howe, and eight or ten men to take him. He being in the wigwam, ran out, and with his knife wounded one of the English in the breast, and so behaved himself as they were forced to kill him.

22.] The court, with advice of the elders, ordered a general fast. The occasions were, 1. The ill news we had out of England concerning the breach between the king and parliament. 2. The danger of the Indians. 3. The unseasonable weather, the rain having continued so long, viz. near a fortnight together, scarce one fair day, and much corn and hay spoiled, though indeed it proved a blessing to us, for it being with warm easterly winds, it brought the Indian corn to maturity, which otherwise would not have been ripe, and it pleased God, that so soon as the fast was agreed upon, the weather changed, and proved fair after.

At this court, the propositions sent from Connecticut, about a combination, &c. were read, and referred to a committee to consider of after the court, who meeting, added some few cautions and new articles, and for the taking in of Plimouth, (who were now willing,) and Sir Ferdinand Gorges' province, and so returned them back to Connecticut, to be considered upon against the spring, for winter was now approaching, and there could be no meeting before, &c.[2]

The sudden fall of land and cattle, and the scarcity of foreign commodities, and money, &c. with the thin access of people from England, put many into an unsettled frame of spirit, so as they concluded there would be no subsisting here, and accordingly they began to hasten away, some to the West Indies, others to the Dutch, at Long Island, &c. (for the governour there invited them by fair offers,) and others back for England. Among others who returned thither, there was one of the magistrates, Mr. Humfrey, and four [3]ministers, and a schoolmaster. These would needs go

---

1 The record is "William Arnold, and Robert Coale, William Carpenter and Benedict Arnold, his company, upon their petition were taken under our government and protection. William Arnold is to see to keep the peace in their lands." Vol. II. 22.

2 An unreasonable jealousy next year prevented us from permitting the junction of Maine in this admirable alliance.

3 These were probably returning home, on the change of times, with expec-

against all advice, and had a fair and speedy voyage, till they came near England, all which time, three of the ministers, with the schoolmaster, spake reproachfully of the people and of the country, but the wind coming up §against them,§ they were tossed up and down, (being in 10ber,) so long till their provisions and other necessaries were near spent, and they were forced to strait allowance, yet at length the wind coming fair again, they got into the Sleeve, but then there arose so great a tempest at S. E. as they could bear no sail, and so were out of hope of being saved (being in the night also.) Then they humbled themselves before the Lord, and acknowledged God's hand to be justly out against them for speaking evil of this good land and the Lord's people here, &c. Only one of them, Mr. [1]Phillips of Wrentham, in England, had not joined with the rest, but spake well of the people, and of the country; upon this it pleased the Lord to spare their lives, and when they expected every moment to have been dashed upon the rocks, (for they were hard by the Needles,) he turned the wind so as they were carried safe to the Isle of Wight by St. [2]Helen's: yet the Lord followed them on shore. Some were exposed to great straits and found no entertainment, their friends forsaking them. [3]One had a daughter that presently ran mad, and two other of his daughters, being under ten years of age, were discovered to have been often abused by divers lewd persons, and filthiness in his family. The schoolmaster had no sooner hired an house, and gotten in some scholars, but the plague set in, and took away two of his own children.

Others who went to other places, upon like grounds, succeeded no better. They fled for fear of want, and many of them fell into it, even to extremity, as if they had hastened into the misery which they feared and fled from, besides the depriving themselves

---

tation of better employment, than they had found here, where I imagine they had not been encouraged by any settlement.

1 In Mather's list, I find a Phillips of Dedham, without baptismal name, whom, if it could be ascertained from the unknown annals of that town, that he died not in our country, we might conjecture to be the same. John Phillips of Wrentham was one of the Westminster assembly of divines. But the member of Dedham church, was named Henry, perhaps son of John, or his brother. A deacon of that church declined some time to undertake his office, out of regard to Mr. Phillips in England. See century sermon of Rev. Samuel Dexter, grand father of the late Hon. Samuel Dexter.

2 Without admitting the consequence our author draws, we may be equally grateful for their preservation.

3 He was Humfrey, of whose misfortunes we had relation of a large part a few pages before.

of the ordinances and church fellowship, and those civil liberties which they enjoyed here; whereas, such as staid in their places, kept their peace and ease, and enjoyed still the blessing of the ordinances, and never tasted of those troubles and miseries, which they heard to have befallen those who departed. Much disputation there was about liberty of removing for outward advantages, and all ways were sought for an open door to get out at; but it is to be feared many crept out at a broken wall. For such as come together into a wilderness, where are nothing but wild beasts and beastlike men, and there confederate together in civil and church estate, whereby they do, implicitly at least, bind themselves to support each other, and all of them that society, whether civil or sacred, whereof they are members, how they can break from this without free consent, is hard to find, so as may satisfy a tender or good conscience in time of trial. Ask thy conscience, if thou wouldst have plucked up thy stakes, and brought thy family 3000 miles, if thou hadst expected that all, or most, would have forsaken thee there. Ask again, what liberty thou hast towards others, which thou likest not to allow others towards thyself; for if one may go, another may, and so the greater part, and so church and commonwealth may be left destitute in a wilderness, exposed to misery and reproach, and all for thy ease and pleasure, whereas these all, being now thy brethren, as near to thee as the Israelites were to Moses, it were much safer for thee, after his example, to choose rather to suffer affliction with thy brethren, than to enlarge thy ease and pleasure by furthering the occasion of their ruin.[1]

Nine bachelors commenced at Cambridge; they were young men of good hope, and performed their acts, so as gave good proof of their proficiency in the tongues and arts. (8.) 5. The general court had settled a government or superintendency over the college, viz. all the magistrates and elders over the ||six|| nearest churches and the president, or the greatest part of these. Most of them were now present at this first commencement, and dined at the college with the scholars' ordinary commons, which was done of purpose for the students' encouragement, &c. and it gave good content to all.[2]

||three||

[1] Few passages in this history are more gratifying than this faithful exhibition of the feelings, by which the early planters of New England were characterised. Unlike the American colonists from all other nations, and of the English settlers in all other quarters of the world, they seem to have transferred at once the whole ardour of their patriotism to this country of their own creation.

[2] We must regret, that Winthrop has taken no notice of the ever-honoured

At this commencement, complaint was made to the governours of two young men, of good quality, lately come out of England, for foul misbehaviour, in swearing and ribaldry speeches, &c. for which, though they were ||adulti,|| they were corrected in the college, and sequestered, &c. for a time.

6.] Here came in a French shallop with some 14 men, whereof one was La Tour his lieutenant. They brought letters from La Tour to the governour, full of compliments, and desire of assistance from us against Monsieur D'Aulnay. They staid here about a week, and were kindly entertained, and though they were papists, yet they came to our church meeting; and the lieutenant seemed to be much affected to find things as he did, and professed he never saw so good order in any place. One of the elders gave him a French testament with ||2Marlorat's|| notes, which he kindly accepted, and promised to read it.

13.] Six ships went hence, laden with pipe staves and other commodities of this country; four went a little before. Of these, four were built in the country this year. Thus God provided for us beyond expectation.

||adult|| ||2blank||

---

name of Rev. John Harvard, except in the loose memoranda, at the end of his MSS. From our Col. Rec. I find, he was made free 2 Nov. 1637, at the same time with Rev. John Fiske. By a most diligent antiquary, John Farmer, Esq. of Concord, N. H. this information is given me from Rev. Samuel Danforth's Almanack for 1648: "7mo. 14 day 1638, John Harvard, Master of Arts, of Emmanuel College in Cambridge, deceased, and by will gave the half of his estate, (which amounted to about 700 pounds,) for the erecting of the college." My correspondent adds: "I do not recollect, that any other authority gives the exact *time* of his death, or the *college* at which he was educated." Johnson, lib. II. c. 12 and 19, has favoured us with more than any other book. It is peculiarly vexatious to learn from Mather, of the founder of the college, which he so much and so often desired, happily in vain, to rule, only the amount of his bequest, and that he died of consumption. The sons of the oldest university in our country will be pleased with my extract from our Col. Rec. I. 179, of the first motion in this blessed work: "The court agreed to give 400 pounds towards a school or college, whereof 200 pounds to be paid the next year, and 200 pounds when the work is finished, and the next court to appoint where and what building." This was in October 1636, in the midst of the war with the Pequots, and the beginning of the Antinomian controversy; and we should remember, that the appropriation was equal to a year's rate of the whole colony. Subsequently the income of the ferry between Boston and Charlestown was given, and an annual rate of 100 pounds was ordered for the college. In later days, liberal grants have been made at various times; and the claims of this venerable institution, especially for its library, may soon, I hope be further acknowledged. Harvard's will was, probably, nuncupative, as it is nowhere recorded. Gladly should we give fifty pages of Keayne's for one of this other benefactor, who left, I suppose, no other progeny but this posthumous university.

6.] Mention is made before of the white hills, discovered by one Darby Field. The report he brought of ||shining|| stones &c. caused divers others to travel thither, but they found nothing worth their pains. Amongst others, Mr. Gorge and Mr. Vines, two of the magistrates of Sir Ferdinand Gorge his province, went thither about the end of this month. They went up Saco river in birch canoes, and that way, they found it 90 miles to Pegwaggett, an Indian town, but by land it is but 60. Upon Saco river, they found many thousand acres of rich meadow, but there are ten falls, which hinder boats, &c. From the Indian town, they went up hill (for the most part) about 30 miles in woody lands, then they went about 7 or 8 miles upon shattered rocks, without tree or grass, very steep all the way. At the top is a plain about 3 or 4 miles over, all shattered stones, and upon that is another rock or spire, about a mile in height, and about an acre of ground at the top. At the top of the plain arise four great rivers, each of them so much water, at the first issue, as would drive a mill, Connecticut river from two heads, at the N. W. and S. W. which join in one about 60 miles off, Saco river on the S. E, Amascoggen which runs into Casco Bay at the N. E. and Kennebeck, at the N. by E. The mountain runs E. and W. 30 or 40 miles, but the peak is above all the rest. They went and returned in 15 days.[1]

8. 18.] All the elders met at Ipswich; they took into consideration the book which was committed to them by the general court, and were much different in their judgments about it, but at length they agreed upon this answer in effect.

Whereas in the book, there were three propositions laid down, and then the application of them to the standing council, and then the arguments enforcing the same: the propositions were these:

1. In a commonwealth, rightly and religiously constituted, there is no power, office, administration, or ||[2]authority,|| but such as are commanded and ordained of God.

2. The powers, offices, and administrations that are ordained of God, as aforesaid, being given, dispensed, and erected in a christian commonwealth by his good providence, proportioned ||[3]by|| his rule to their state and condition, established by his power

||strange|| ||[2]duty|| ||[3]to||

[1] Here a map, drawn with tolerable accuracy, of the courses of the rivers flowing from the vicinity of the White Hills, is inserted in the original MS. The most satisfactory account of these mountains is found in the New England Journal of Medicine and Surgery, Vol. V. 321—338, Jan. 1816.

against all opposition, carried on and accompanied with his presence and blessing, ought not to be by them either changed or altered, but upon such grounds, for such ends, in that manner, and only so far as the mind of God may be manifested therein.

3. The mind of God is never manifested concerning the change or alteration of any civil ordinance, erected or established by him as aforesaid in a christian commonwealth, so long as all the cases, counsels, services and occasions thereof may be duly and fully ended, ordered, executed and performed without any change or alteration of government.

In their answer they allowed the said propositions to be sound, with this distinction in the 1st. viz. That all lawful powers are ordained, &c. either expressly or by consequence, by particular examples or by general rules.

In the applications they distinguished between a standing council invested with a kind of transcendent[1] authority beyond other magistrates, or else any kind of standing council distinct from magistrates; the former they seem implicitly to disallow; the latter they approve as necessary for us, not disproportionable to our estate, nor of any dangerous consequence for disunion among the magistrates, or factions among the people, which were the arguments used by the author against our council. Some passages they wish had been spared, and other things omitted, which, if supplied, might have cleared some passages, which may seem to reflect upon the present councils, which they do think not to be of that moment, but that the uprightness of his intentions considered, and the liberty given for advice, according to the rules of religion, peace and prudence, they would be passed by.

Lastly, they declare their present thoughts about the moulding and perfecting of a council, in four rules.

1. That all the magistrates, by their calling and office, together with the care of judicature, are to consult for the provision, protection, and universal welfare of the commonwealth.

2. Some select men taken out from the assistants, or other freemen, being called thereunto, be in especial, to attend by way of council, for the provision, protection, and welfare of the commonwealth.

3. This council, as counsellors, have no power of judicature.

4. In cases of instant danger to the commonwealth, in the interim, before a general court can be called, (which were meet to be done with all speed,) what shall be consented unto and con-

---

[1] Hubbard, 388, absurdly gives this word *transient*.

cluded by this council, or the major part of them, together with the consent of the magistrates, or the major part of them, may stand good and firm till the general court.

9. 7.] Some of our ||merchants|| sent a pinnace to trade with La Tour in St. John's river. He welcomed them very kindly, and wrote to our governour letters very gratulatory for his lieutenant's entertainment, &c. and withal a relation of the state of the controversy between himself and Monsieur D'Aulnay. In their return they met with D'Aulnay at Pemaquid, who wrote also to our governour, and sent him a printed copy of the arrest against La Tour, and threatened us, that if any of our vessels came to La Tour, he would make prize of them.

22.] The village at the end of Charlestown bounds, was called Woburn, where they had gathered a church, and this day Mr. [1]Carter was ordained their pastor, with the assistance of the elders of other churches. Some difference there was about his ordination; some advised, in regard they had no elder of their own, nor any members very fit to solemnize such an ordinance, they would desire some of the elders of the other churches to have performed it; but others supposing it might be an occasion of introducing a dependency of churches, &c. and so a presbytery, would not allow it. So it was performed by [2]one of their own members, but not so well and orderly as it ought.[3]

||magistrates||

1 My acquaintance with Thomas Carter is very limited, yet a little better than Mather's, who leaves us ignorant of his name of baptism, though Johnson, who was one of his flock, lib. II. c. 22, repeats it three times. The same writer lib. I. c. 37, informs us, he came over in 1635. From his silence, I concluded, that Carter was still alive, when, in 1651, the book was sent to England, and from an old almanack I find, that he died 5 Sept. 1684, but Woburn records, say 1 Dec. See notes to Chickering's sermon, which however do not change my faith in the almanack.

2 Johnson, lib. II. c. 22, says " two persons," I presume he was one, " in the name of the church, laid their hands upon his head, and said, We ordain thee, Thomas Carter, to be Pastor unto this church of Christ; then one of the Elders Priest [present?] being desired of the church, continued in prayer," &c.

3 Wonder working Providence, as cited in last note, is very full on the matter of gathering a church in Woburn on 24 of August preceding, but the town records say 14, which is undoubtedly the true date. Cotton and Wilson of Boston, Allen and Symmes of Charlestown, Shepherd and Dunster of Cambridge, Knowles of Watertown, Allen of Dedham, Eliot of Roxbury, and Mather of Dorchester, some of whom by vicious punctuation are represented as belonging to respective churches in other order, were assistants at the solemnity. It will be seen that 24 August, Cotton was aiding at a different labour in Boston. Very little confidence should be reposed in Johnson's Arabic numerals. Correction of the date of Woburn church must be made in the note Vol. I. 96, but the order may remain.

Divers houses were burnt this year, by drying flax. Among others one ||Briscoe,|| of Watertown, a rich man, a tanner, who had refused to let his neighbour have leather for corn, saying he had corn enough, had his barn, and corn, and leather, &c. burnt, to the value of 200 pounds.

Mr. Larkam of Northam, alias Dover, suddenly discovering a purpose to go to England, and fearing to be dissuaded by his people, gave them his faithful promise not to go, but yet soon after he got on ship board, and so departed. It was time for him to be gone, for not long after, a widow which kept in his house, being a very handsome woman, and about 50 years of age, proved to be with child, and being examined, at first refused to confess the father, but in the end she laid it to Mr. Larkam. Upon this the church of Dover looked out for another elder, and wrote to the elders to desire their help.[1]

There arrived at Boston a small ship from the Madeiras with wine and sugar, &c. which were presently sold for pipe staves, and other commodities of the country, which were returned to the Madeiras: but the merchant himself, one Mr. Parish, staid divers months after. He had lived at the Madeiras many years among the priests and jesuits, who told him, when he was to come hither, that those of New England were the worst of all heretics, and that they were the cause of the troubles in England, and of the pulling down the bishops there. When he went away, he blessed God for bringing him hither, professing that he would not lose what he had gotten in New England for all the wealth in the world. He went away in a pinnace built here, intending a speedy return. By the way his pinnace (being calked in the winter) proved very leaky, so as all the seamen, being tired out with pumping, gave her over, but Mr. Parish continued the pump, and so kept her up, till it pleased God they espied land, and so they came safe to Fayal.

10.] Those of the lower part of the river Pascataquack invit-

||blank||

---

1 Hubbard, 364, informs us, they obtained "one Mr. Maud, whom they enjoyed many years for their minister, who was a good man, and of a serious spirit, and of a peaceable and quiet disposition. He continued with them to his death." Dr. Belknap, the admirable successor of Maude in our days, following the Magnalia, says "he had been a minister in England." Some may wonder at the omission of his name of baptism by Mather, when they hear that he was, on the same day with Richard Mather and his wife, admitted a member of Boston church, 25 Oct. 1635, being No. 316. Belknap N. H. I. 51 calls him Daniel. Before going to Dover, he had been employed as a schoolmaster in Boston.

ed one Mr. James [1]Parker of Weymouth, a godly man and a scholar, one who had been many years a deputy for the public court, to be their minister. He, by advice of divers of the magistrates and elders, accepted the call, and went and taught among them this winter, and it pleased God to give great success to his labours, so as above 40 of them, whereof the most had been very profane, and some of them professed enemies to the way of our churches, wrote to the magistrates and elders, acknowledging the sinful course they had lived in, and bewailing the same, and blessing God for calling them out of it, and earnestly desiring that Mr. Parker might be settled amongst them. Most of them fell back again in time, embracing this present world.[2]

This winter was the greatest snow we had, since we came into the country, but it lay not long, and the frost was more moderate than in some other winters.

12.] News came out of England, by two fishing ships, of the civil wars there between the king and the parliament, whereupon the churches kept divers days of humiliation. But some of the magistrates were not satisfied about the often reiteration of them for the same cause, but they would not contend with the elders about it, but left the churches to their liberty.

1. 5.] At 7 in the morning, being the Lord's day, there was a great earthquake. It came with a rumbling noise like the former, but through the Lord's mercy it did no harm.

The churches held a different course in raising the ministers' maintenance. Some did it by way of taxation, which was very offensive to some. Amongst others, one Briscoe of Watertown, who had his barn burnt, as before mentioned, being grieved with that course in their town, the rather because himself and others, who were no members, were taxed, wrote a book against it, wherein, besides his arguments, which were ||naught||, he cast reproach upon the elders and officers. This book he published underhand, which occasioned much stir in the town. At length, he and two more were convented before the court, where he acknowledged his fault in those reproachful speeches, and in publishing it, whereas it had been his duty to have acquainted the court or magistrates with his grievance, &c. (but for the arguments in the

||weighty||

1 He first appears at our general courts in May 1639. Belknap, N. H. I. 48, correcting an errour of Hutchinson about him, makes him soon after remove to Barbados.

2 This sentence, it is evident, was added some time after the preceding.

point, there was nothing required of him,) and was fined 10 pounds for that, and some slighting of the court, and one of the publishers, 40 shillings.[1]

Corn was very scarce all over the country, so as by the end of the 2d. month, many families in most towns had none to eat, but were forced to live of clams, muscles, cataos, dry fish, &c. and ||sure|| this came by the just hand of the Lord, to punish our ingratitude and covetousness. For corn being plenty divers years before, it was so undervalued, as it would not pass for any commodity: if one offered a shop keeper corn for any thing, his answer would be, he knew not what to do with it. So for labourers and artificers; but now they would have done any work, or parted with any commodity, for corn. And the husbandman, he now made his advantage, for he would part with no corn, for the most part, but for ready money or for cattle, at such a price as should be 12d. in the bushel more to him than ready money. And indeed it was a very sad thing to see how little of a public spirit appeared in the country, but of self-love too much. Yet there were some here and there, who were men of another spirit, and were willing to abridge themselves, that others might be supplied/ The immediate causes of this scarcity were the cold and wet summer, especially in the time of the first harvest; also, the pigeons came in such flocks, (||2above|| 10,000 in one flock,) that beat down, and eat up a very great quantity of all sorts of English grain; much corn spent in setting out the ships, ketches, &c.; lastly, there were such abundance of mice in the barns, that devoured much there. The mice also did much spoil in orchards, eating off the bark at the bottom of the fruit trees in the time of the snow, so as never had been known the like spoil in any former winter. So many enemies doth the Lord arm against our daily bread, that we might know we are to eat it in the sweat of our brows.

1. 30.] The Trial, Mr. Coytmore master, arrived, and a week after one of the ketches. He sailed first to Fayal, where he found an extraordinary good market for his pipe staves and fish. He took wine and sugar, &c. and sailed ||3thence|| to ||4Christophers|| in the West Indies, where he put off some of his wine for cotton and tobacco, &c. and for iron, which the islanders had saved of the ships which were there cast away. He obtained license, also, of the governour, Sir Thomas Warner, to take up what ordnance, anchors, &c. he could, and was to have the one half; and by the

||since|| ||2about|| ||3hence|| ||4Pt. Peters||

1 Of this dangerous book, or the sentence upon its author, I can find no trace in the records.

help of a diving tub, he took up 50 guns, and anchors, and cables, which he brought home, and some gold and silver also, which he got by trade, and so, through the Lord's blessing, they made a good voyage, which did much encourage the merchants, and made wine and sugar and cotton very plentiful, and cheap, in the country.

Two ketches also, which were gone to the West Indies for cotton, &c. arrived safe not long after, and made return with profit. Another ship also, called the Increase, sent to the Madeiras, returned safe, and two other ships, after, though they went among the Turks.

There was a piece of justice executed at New Haven, which, being the first in that kind, is not unworthy to be recorded. Mr. [1]Malbon, one of the magistrates there, had a daughter about [blank] years of age, which was openly whipped, her father joining in the sentence. The cause was thus.

[Large blank.]

The wife of one ||Onion|| of Roxbury died in great despair: she had been a servant there, and was very stubborn and self-willed. After she was married, she ||2proved|| very worldly, aiming at great matters. Her first child was still-born, through her unruliness and falling into a fever. She fell withal into great horrour and trembling, so as it shook the room, &c. and crying out of her torment, and of her stubbornness and unprofitableness under the means, and her lying to her dame in denying somewhat that in ||3liquorishness|| she had taken away, and of her worldliness, saying that she neglected her spiritual good for a little worldly trash, and now she must go to everlasting torments, and exhorted others to take heed of such evils, &c. and still crying out O! ten thousand worlds for one drop of Christ, &c. After she had then been silent a few hours, she began to speak again, and being exhorted to consider of God's infinite mercy, &c. she gave still this answer, "I cannot for my life," and so died.[2]

The three ministers which were sent to Virginia, viz. Mr. Tompson, Mr. Knolles, and Mr. James from New Haven, departed (8)

||Oymoe|| ||2grew|| ||3liquor||

---

1 The name of Richard Malbon is, I believe, found only in the historian of Connecticut, I. 106, as one of twelve, from whom the seven pillars of the church at New Haven should be taken.

2 We are often compelled to regret such accounts of the crying out of persons in delirium, to which, without hesitation, this case may be referred. The Roxbury records say, "Mary, the wife of Robert Onion, buried 4, (2) 1643. An infant also of Robert Onion buried in the 2d month."

7. and were eleven weeks before they arrived. They lay windbound sometime at Aquiday: then, as they passed Hellgate between Long Island and the Dutch, their pinnace was bilged upon the rocks, so as she was near foundered before they could run on the next shore.[1] The Dutch governour gave them slender entertainment; but Mr. Allerton of New Haven, being there, took great pains and care for them, and procured them a very good pinnace and all things necessary. So they set sail in the dead of winter, and had much foul weather, so as with great difficulty and danger they arrived safe in Virginia. Here they found very loving and liberal entertainment, and were bestowed in several places, not by the governour, but by some well disposed people who desired their company. In their way the difficulties and dangers, which they were continually exercised with, put them to some question whether their call were of God or not; but so soon as they arrived there and had been somewhat refreshed, Mr. Tompson wrote back, that being a very melancholic man and of a crazy body, he found his health so repaired, and his spirit so enlarged, &c. as he had not been in the like condition since he came to New England. But this was to strengthen him for a greater trial, for his wife, a godly young woman, and a comfortable help to him, being left behind with a company of small [2]children, was taken away by death, and all his children scattered, but well disposed of among his godly friends.

4. 20.] Mr. Knolles returned from Virginia, and brought letters from his congregation and others there to our elders, which were openly read in Boston at a lecture, whereby it appeared that God had greatly blessed their ministry there, so as the people's hearts were much inflamed with desire after the ordinances, and though the state did silence the ministers, because they would not conform to the order of England, yet the people resorted to them in private houses to hear them as before.

There fell out hot wars between the Dutch and the Indians

---

1 Perhaps the Episcopal church in Virginia reckoned it a judgment of heaven.

2 In addition to what is said in my note on p. 313 of Vol. I. of the children of this early New England missionary, I learn, that Joseph, the date of whose birth is there mentioned, lived at Billerica. For many years he was a selectman, town clerk, captain of the militia, schoolmaster, representative and deacon of the church, and died 13 October 1732, aged above 92 years and a half. His wife, whom he had married before removing from Braintree, died 9 October 1742, aged 91. Benjamin Tompson, many years a magistrate in Billerica, and Col. William Tompson, deacon of that church and a representative, were descendants of Joseph. William died 2 Septr. 1806 at the age of 83. These details are derived from John Farmer, Esquire, the most inquisitive genealogist of our country.

thereabout. The occasion was this. An Indian, being drunk, had slain an old Dutchman. The Dutch required the murderer, but he could not be had. The people called often upon the governour to take revenge, but he still put it off, either for that he thought it not just, or not safe, &c. It fell out that the Mowhawks, a people that live upon or near Hudson's river, either upon their own quarrel, or rather, as the report went, being set on by the Dutch, came suddenly upon the Indians near the Dutch and killed about 30 of them, the rest fled for shelter to the Dutch. One Marine, a Dutch captain, hearing of it, goeth to the governour, and obtains commission of him to kill so many as he could of them, and accordingly went with a company of armed men, and setting upon them, fearing no ill from the Dutch, he slew about 70 or 80 men, women and children. Upon this the Indians burnt divers of their farm houses and their cattle in them, and slew all they could meet with, to the number of 20 or more, of men, women and children, and pressed so hard upon the Dutch, even home to their fort, that they were forced to call in the English to their aid, and entertained Captain Underhill, &c. which Marine, the Dutch captain, took so ill, seeing the governour to prefer him before himself, that he presented his pistol at the governour, but was staid by a stander-by. Then a tenant of Marine discharged his musket at the governour, but missed him narrowly, whereupon the sentinel, by the governour's command, shot that fellow presently dead. His head was set upon the gallows, and the captain was sent prisoner into Holland. The people, also, were so offended at the governour for the damage they now sustained by the Indians, though they were all for war before, that the governour durst not trust himself among them, but entertained a guard of 50 English about his person, and the Indians did so annoy them by sudden assaults out of the swamps, &c. that he was forced to keep a running army to be ready to oppose them upon all occasions.

The Indians also of Long Island took part with their neighbours upon the main, and as the Dutch took away their corn, &c. so they fell to burning the Dutch houses. But these, by the mediation of Mr. Williams, who was then there to go in a Dutch ship for England, were pacified, and peace re-established between the Dutch and them. At length they came to an accord of peace with the rest of the Indians also.

23.] One John Cook, an honest young man, being in his master's absence to salute a ship, &c. in the vanity of his mind thought to make the gun give a great report, and accordingly said to some, that he would make her speak. Overcharging her, she brake all into small pieces and scattered round about some men a ||flight|| shot off. Himself was killed, but no hurt found about him, but only one hand cut off and beaten a good distance from the place where he stood. And there appeared a special providence of God in it, for although there were many people up and down, yet none was hurt, nor was any near the gun when she was fired, whereas usually they gather thither on such occasions.

One of our ships, the Seabridge, arrived with 20 children and some other passengers out of England, and 300 pounds worth of goods purchased with the country's stock, given by some friends in England the year before; and those children, with many more to come after, were sent by money given one fast day in London, and allowed by the parliament and city for that purpose.

The house of commons also made an order in our favour, which was sent us under the hand of H. ||2Elsynge,|| Cler. Parl. D. C. to this effect, viz. ||3Veneris|| 10 Martii [1]1642. Whereas the plantations in New England have, by the blessing of Almighty God, had good and prosperous success without any charge to this state, and are now likely to prove very happy for the propagation of the gospel in those parts, and very beneficial and commodious for this kingdom and nation, the commons now assembled in parliament do, for the better advancement of these plantations and encouragement of the planters, &c. ordain that all merchandizes, goods exported, &c. into New England to be spent, used or employed there, ||4or|| being of the growth of that country, shall §be§ imported hither, or put aboard to be spent, &c. in the voyage going or returning, and all and every the owners thereof, be free of all custom, &c. in England and New England, and all other ports, until this house shall take further order. This to be observed and allowed by all officers and persons whatsoever upon showing forth of this order, signed by the said clerk, without any other warrant.

Our general court, upon receipt of this order, caused the same, with our humble and thankful acknowledgment of so great a favour from that honourable assembly, to be entered verbatim among our records, in perpetuam rei memoriam.

One Richard [blank,] servant to one [blank] Williams of Dorchester, being come out of service, fell to work at his own hand

||slight|| ||2Effinge|| ||3blank|| ||4as||

1 Dr. Holmes Ann. I. 321, Hutchinson I. 114, and Chalmers, 174, who relies on Hutchinson, all seem to understand the date of this honourable testimony as *our* 1642, whereas it is evident that it should be reckoned of the following year. The tenth of March 1642 was Thursday, in 1643 Friday. Lady-day began the year, as explained in the preface to Vol. I. pp. vi. and vii.

and took great wages above others, and would not work but for ready money. By this means in a year, or little more, he had scraped together about 25 pounds, and then returned with his prey into England, speaking evil of the country by the way. He was not gone far, after his arrival, but the cavaliers met him and eased him of his money; so he knew no better way but to return to New England again, to repair his loss in that place which he had so much disparaged.

Mo. 3. 10.] Our court of elections was held, when Mr. Ezekiel Rogers, pastor of the church in Rowley, preached. He was called to it by a company of freemen, whereof the most were deputies chosen for the court, appointed, by order of the last court, to meet at Salem about nomination of some to be put to the vote for the new magistrates. Mr. Rogers, hearing what exception was taken to this call, as unwarrantable, wrote to the governour for advice, &c. who returned him answer: That he did account his calling not to be sufficient, yet the magistrates were not minded to strive with the deputies about it, but seeing it was noised in the country, and the people would expect him, and that he had advised with the magistrates about it, he wished him to go on. In his sermon he described how the man ought to be qualified whom they should choose for their governour, yet dissuaded them earnestly from choosing the same man twice together, and expressed his dislike of that with such vehemency as gave offence. But when it came to trial, the former governour, Mr. Winthrop, was chosen again, and two ||new|| magistrates, Mr. William Hibbins and Mr. Samuel Simons.

At this court came the commissioners from Plimouth, Connecticut and New Haven, viz. from Plimouth Mr. Edward Winslow and Mr. ||2Collier||, from Connecticut Mr. Haynes and Mr. Hopkins, with whom Mr. Fenwick of Saybrook joined, from New Haven Mr. Theophilus Eaton and Mr. Grigson.[1] Our court chose a committee to treat with them, viz. the governour and Mr. Dudley and Mr. Bradstreet, being of the magistrates; and of the deputies, Captain Gibbons, Mr. ||3Tyng||[2] the treasurer, and Mr. Ha-

||more|| ||2Collins|| ||3T. ||

[1] Grigson, whose christian name was Thomas, had come over in company with governours Eaton and Hopkins, Rev. J. Davenport and others, according to Trumbull, I. 95. They arrived 26 June 1637, as in our former volume is mentioned. He was, probably, the chief man in the colony of New Haven, after Eaton, filled the office of treasurer at the organization of government, and was very active in all its concerns. In a later part of this history will be mentioned his untimely death.

[2] William Tyng was a gentleman of high respectability, but not, I imagine,

thorn. These coming to consultation encountered some difficulties, but being all desirous of union and studious of peace, they readily yielded each to other in such things as tended to common utility, &c. so as in some two or three meetings they lovingly accorded upon these ensuing articles, which, being allowed by our court, and signed by all the commissioners, were sent to be also ratified by the general courts of other jurisdictions; only Plimouth commissioners, having power only to treat, but not to determine, deferred the signing of them till they came home, but soon after they were ratified by their general court also.

Those of Sir Ferdinando Gorge his province, beyond Pascataquack, were not received nor called into the confederation, because they ran a different course from us both in their ministry and civil administration; for they had lately made Acomenticus (a poor village) a corporation, and had made a taylor their ma or, and had entertained one Hull, an excommunicated person and very contentious, for their minister.

At this court of elections there arose a scruple about the oath which the governour and the rest of the magistrates were to take, viz. about the first part of it: "You shall bear true faith and allegiance to our sovereign Lord King Charles," seeing he had violated the privileges of parliament, and made war upon them, and thereby had lost much of his kingdom and many of his subjects; whereupon it was thought fit to omit that part of it for the present.

---

entitled to the merit, as is said 1 Hist. Coll. x. 180, of coming to our country "about the year 1630." His name is not embraced in my list of all the members of Boston church, to Sept. 1636; yet no long time after he must have been admitted, for in Sept. 1639, he was chosen a deputy for Boston, and served in eight following courts. He was continued treasurer of the colony, but "being absent for some space of time in England," as Johnson, lib. I. c. 45 informs, Richard Russell was chosen in his room. This, from the records, we learn was in 1645. William Tyng died, probably after his return here, early in 1653. The inventory of his estate, which was, I think, as large as any in the colony for those days, amounting to 2774 pounds 14, 4, preserved in our Probate records II. 99–107, was made on 25 May of that year. It is proved by his brother Edward. The titles of several of his books show an estimable curiosity in the possessor. He left no family. Edward Tyng, a person of great influence in the colony, from whom has descended a numerous line, lived to a greater age, dying 28 Sept. 1681. His will, made 25 Aug. 1677, proved 19 January 1681–2, Lib. VI. 380, distributes his property, as follows : 100 pounds to his son Edward, "having given him a considerable estate already," 500 pounds to his daughter Eunice, a debt remitted to his son, Jos. Dudley, afterwards the governour, 100 pounds to each of nine grand children, three Savages, four Dudleys, Samuel Searle and John Tyng, and all the residue to his wife, who was named executrix. His daughter Eunice, having received her portion on her marriage with Samuel Willard, pastor of the third church, afterwards head of Harvard College, on 7 Jan. 1680–1 her legacy was made void. For a full account of the services of some of his descendants see 1 Hist. Coll. x. 180–183.

About this time two plantations began to be settled upon Merrimack,* Pentuckett called Haverill, and ||Cochichawick|| called Andover.

The articles of confederation between the plantations under the government of the Massachusetts, the plantations under the government of New Plimouth, the plantations under the government of Connecticut and the government of New Haven, with the plantations in combination therewith:

WHEREAS we all came into these parts of America with one and the same end and aim, namely, to advance the kingdom of our Lord Jesus Christ, and to enjoy the liberties of the gospel in purity with peace: and whereas by our settling, by the wise providence of God, we are further dispersed upon the seacoasts and rivers than was at first intended, so that we cannot, according to our desire, with convenience communicate in one government and jurisdiction: and whereas we live encompassed with people of several nations and strange languages, which hereafter may prove injurious to us or our posterity; and for as much as the natives have formerly committed sundry insolences and outrages upon several plantations of the English, and have of late combined themselves against us, and seeing by reason of the sad distractions in England, (which they have heard of,) and by which they know we are hindered both from that humble way of seeking advice, and reaping those comfortable fruits of protection, which at other times we might well expect; we therefore do conceive it our bounden duty, without delay, to enter into a present consociation amongst ourselves for mutual help and strength in all future concernment, that, as in nation and religion, so in other respects, we be and continue one, according to the tenor and true meaning of the ensuing articles—

1. Wherefore it is fully agreed and concluded between the parties above named, and they jointly and severally do, by these presents, agree and conclude that they all be, and henceforth be called by the name of the United Colonies of New England.

2. These united colonies, for themselves and their posterities, do jointly and severally hereby enter into a firm and perpetual league of friendship and amity, for offence and defence, mutual advice and succour upon all just occasions, both for preserving and propagating the truth and liberties of the gospel, and for their own mutual safety and welfare.

3. It is further agreed, that the plantations which at present are, or hereafter shall be settled within the limits of the Massachusetts, shall be forever under the government of the Massachu-

||C

setts, and shall have peculiar jurisdiction amongst themselves in all cases as an entire body; and that Plimouth, Connecticut, and New Haven, shall each of them in all respects have like peculiar jurisdiction and government within their limits, and in reference to the plantations which are already settled, or shall hereafter be erected, and shall settle within any of their limits respectively; provided that no other jurisdiction shall hereafter be taken in as a distinct head or member of this confederation, nor shall any other, either plantation or jurisdiction in present being, and not already in combination or under the jurisdiction of any of these confederates, be received by any of them: nor shall any two of these confederates join in one jurisdiction, without consent of the rest, which consent to be interpreted as in the 6th ensuing article is expressed.

4. It is also by these confederates agreed, that the charge of all just wars, whether offensive or defensive, upon what part or member of this confederation soever they shall fall, shall, both in men and provisions and all other disbursements, be borne by all the parts of this confederation in different proportions, according to their different abilities, in manner following, viz. That the commissioners for each jurisdiction, from time to time as there shall be occasion, bring account and number of all the males in each plantation, or any way belonging to or under their several jurisdictions, of what quality or condition soever they be, from sixteen years old to sixty, being inhabitants there, and that according to the different numbers which from time to time shall be found in each jurisdiction upon a true and just account, the service of men and all charges of the war be borne by the poll; each jurisdiction or plantation being left to their own just course or custom of rating themselves and people according to their different estates, with due respect to their qualities and exemptions among themselves, though the confederation take no notice of any such privilege; and that, according to the different charge of each jurisdiction and plantation, the whole advantage of the war, (if it please God so to bless their endeavours,) whether it be in lands, goods or persons, shall be proportionably divided among the said confederates.

5. It is further agreed, that if any of these jurisdictions, or any plantation under or in combination with them, be invaded by any enemy whatsoever, upon notice and request of any three magistrates of that jurisdiction so invaded, the rest of the confederates, without any further notice or expostulation, shall forthwith send aid to the confederate in danger, but in different proportions, namely, the Massachusetts one hundred men sufficiently armed and provided for such a service and journey, and each of the rest

45 men so armed and provided; or any less number, if less be required, according to this proportion. But if such a confederate in danger may be supplied by their next confederate, not exceeding the number hereby agreed, they may crave help thence, and seek no further for the present; the charge to be borne as in this article is expressed, and at their return to be victualled, and supplied with powder and shot, if there be need, for their journey, by that jurisdiction which employed or sent for them; but none of the jurisdictions to exceed these numbers till by a meeting of the commissioners for this confederation a greater aid appear necessary; and this proportion to continue till upon knowledge of the numbers in each jurisdiction, which shall be brought to the next meeting, some other proportion be ordered. But in any such case of sending men for present aid, whether before or after such order or alteration, it is agreed that at the meeting of the commissioners for this confederation, the cause of such war or invasion be duly considered, and if it appear that the fault lay in the party invaded, that then that jurisdiction or plantation make just satisfaction both to the invaders whom they have injured, and bear all the charge of the war themselves without requiring any allowance from the rest of the confederates towards the same. And further, that if any jurisdiction see any danger of an invasion approaching, and there be time for a meeting, that in such case three magistrates of that jurisdiction may summons a meeting at such convenient place as themselves shall think meet, to consider and provide against the threatened danger; provided when they are met, they may remove to what place they please: only while any of these four confederates have but three magistrates in their jurisdiction, a request or summons from any two of them shall be accounted of equal force with the three mentioned in both the clauses of this article, till there may be an increase of magistrates there.

6. It is also agreed, that for the managing and concluding of all affairs peculiar to and concerning the whole confederation, commissioners shall be chosen by and out of each of these four jurisdictions, viz. two for the Massachusetts, two for Plimouth, two for Connecticut, and two for New Haven, all in church fellowship with us, which shall bring full power from their several general courts respectively, to hear, examine, weigh and determine all affairs of war or peace, leagues, aids, charges, and numbers of men for war, division of spoils, or whatever is gotten by conquest; receiving of more confederates or plantations into the combination with any of these confederates, and all things of like nature which are the proper concomitants or consequents of such

a confederation for amity, offence and defence, not intermeddling with the government of any of the jurisdictions, which by the 3d article is preserved entirely to themselves. But if those eight commissioners, when they meet, shall not agree, yet it is concluded that any six of the eight, agreeing, shall have power to settle and determine the business in question; but if six do not agree, that then such propositions, with their reasons, so far as they have been debated, be sent and referred to the four general courts, viz. the Massachusetts, Plimouth, Connecticut and New Haven: and if at all the said general courts the business so referred be concluded, then to be prosecuted by the confederation and all their members. It is further agreed, that these eight commissioners shall meet once every year (besides extraordinary meetings according to the 5th article) to consider, treat, and conclude of all affairs belonging to this confederation, which meeting shall ever be the first Thursday in 7ber. and that the next meeting after the date of these presents (which shall be accounted the second meeting) shall be at Boston in the Massachusetts, the third at Hartford, the fourth at New Haven, the fifth at Plimouth, §the sixth and seventh at Boston,§ and so in course successively, if in the mean time some middle place be not found out and agreed upon, which may be commodious for all the jurisdictions.

7. It is further agreed, that at each meeting of these eight commissioners, whether ordinary or extraordinary, they all, or any six of them agreeing as before, may choose their president out of themselves, whose office and work shall be to take care and direct for order and a comely carrying on of all proceedings in their present meeting, but he shall be invested with no such power or respect, as by which he shall hinder the propounding or progress of any business, or any way cast the scales otherwise than in the preceding articles is agreed.

8. It is also agreed, that the commissioners for this confederation hereafter at their meetings, whether ordinary or extraordinary, as they may have commission or opportunity, do endeavour to frame and establish agreements and orders in general cases of a civil nature wherein all the plantations are interested for preserving peace amongst themselves, and preventing, as much as may be, all occasions of war or differences with others, as about free and speedy passage of justice in each jurisdiction to all the confederates equally, as to their own, receiving those that remove from one plantation to another without due certificates, how all the jurisdictions may carry it towards the Indians, that they neither grow insolent nor be injured without due satisfaction, lest war break in upon the confederates through miscarriages. It is

also agreed, that if any servant run away from his master into any of these confederate jurisdictions, that in such case, upon certificate of one magistrate in the jurisdiction out of which the said servant fled, or upon other due proof, the said servant shall be delivered either to his master or any other that pursues and brings such certificate or proof: And that upon the escape of any prisoner or fugitive for any criminal cause, whether breaking prison or getting from the officer, or otherwise escaping, upon the certificate of two magistrates of the jurisdiction out of which the escape is made, that he was a prisoner or such an offender at the time of the escape, the magistrate, or some of them of the jurisdiction where for the present the said prisoner or fugitive abideth, shall forthwith grant such a warrant as the case will bear, for the apprehending of any such person and the delivery of him into the hand of the officer or other person who pursueth him; and if there be help required for the safe returning of any such offender, then it shall be granted unto him that craves the same, he paying the charges thereof.

9. And for that the justest wars may be of dangerous consequence, especially to the smaller plantations in these united colonies, it is agreed, that neither the Massachusetts, Plimouth, Connecticut nor New Haven, nor any of the members of any of them, shall at any time hereafter begin, undertake, or engage themselves or this confederation, or any part thereof in any war whatsoever (sudden exigencies with the necessary consequences thereof excepted, which are also to be moderated as much as the case will permit) without the consent and agreement of the aforenamed eight commissioners, or at least six of them, as in the 6th article is provided; and that no charge be required of any of the confederates, in case of a defensive war, till the said commissioners have met and approved the justice of the war, and have agreed upon the sum of money to be levied, which sum is then to be paid by the several confederates in proportion according to the 4th article.

10. That in extraordinary occasions, when meetings are summoned by three magistrates of any jurisdiction, or two, as in the 5th article, if any of the commissioners come not, due warning being given or sent, it is agreed that four of the commissioners shall have power to direct a war which cannot be ||delayed||, and to send for due proportions of men out of each jurisdiction, as well as six might do if all met; but not less than six shall determine the justice of the war, or allow the demands or bills of charges, or cause any levies to be made for the same.

||detained||

11. It is further agreed, that if any of the confederates shall hereafter break any of these present articles, or be otherway injurious to any one of the other jurisdictions, such breach of agreement or injury shall be duly considered and ordered by the commissioners for the other jurisdictions, that both peace, and this present confederation may be entirely preserved without violation.

12. Lastly, this perpetual confederation, and the several articles and agreements thereof being read and seriously considered both by the general court for the Massachusetts and the commissioners for the other three, were subscribed presently by the commissioners, all save those of Plimouth, who, for want of sufficient commission from their general court, deferred their subscription till the next meeting, and then they subscribed also, and were to be allowed by the general courts of the several jurisdictions, which accordingly was done, and certified at the next meeting held at Boston, (7) 7, 1643.

Boston, (3) 29,[1] 1643.

---

[1] This date is very plain in our original MS. yet a doubt can hardly exist, whether it should not be 19 May. Hazard, who professes to publish the records of the United Colonies, beginning with these articles of confederation, for which his book, with all its typographical errours or false readings, will always be one of the most valuable monuments of our early history, gives, II. 6, the earlier date. But though, at the first meeting of the commissioners, in Sept. after, the recital, ib. 7, contains the same date, and though the order of the Massachusetts general court, appointing its members of this congress, is said to be of xx. May 1643, and though ib. 11, the common form of commission for all acting under the United Colonies repeats the same, and though, at the opening of the conferences, 1647, the recital, ib. 75, and in fifteen other places, in which the acts of these annual assemblies severally begin, the same day is mentioned, and in one of them the printed word, *nineteenth*, instead of the Arabic figures, is used, yet in the solemn renewal of the articles, on account of Connecticut and New Haven uniting in one colony, proposed in 1670 and finally ratified an. 1672, the records, ib. 515, change the time to 29 May, as they do also in another draft of the same paper, ib. 520, and again, ib. 526. Morton, sub anno. has the earlier day. Unfortunately our MS. copy of these common records is lost, and Mr. Hazard is understood to have used the set which belonged to Plimouth colony. For the true period of this alliance, in this discrepance of citation from the authentic volumes of the high contracting parties themselves, we should then be left to conjecture, for Hubbard, Mather or Hutchinson could hardly be resorted to as any authorities on such a subject, where records are ambiguous. Our general court records for 1643, have no other notice of this matter than of the appointment of the committee mentioned in this volume. But in the following year, after notice of the choice of delegates to the autumnal congress, a copy of their commission is, happily, inserted, which relieves our doubts by reciting the true date of these celebrated articles, 19 May 1643. I can easily explain the confusion, which seems to have been introduced, at the renewal of the league in 1670, or in 1672, as above cited in Hazard, or in Mass. Anc. Chart. 726, by supposing, that this copy of Winthrop was referred to, instead of the records, and my suggestion is strengthened by finding the first signature that of his son, John, the governour of Connecticut, who had his father's MS.

4. 12.] Mr. La Tour arrived here in a ship of 140 tons and 140 persons. The ship came from Rochelle, the master and his company were protestants. There were two friars and two women sent to wait upon La Tour his lady. They came in with a fair wind, without any notice taken of them. They took a pilot out of one of our boats at sea, and left one of their men in his place. Capt. Gibbons' wife and children passed by the ship as they were going to their farm, but being discovered to La Tour by one of his gentlemen who knew ||her||, La Tour manned out a shallop which he towed after him to go speak with her. She seeing such a company of strangers making towards her, hastened to get from them, and landed at the governour's garden. La Tour landed presently after her, and there found the governour and his wife, and two of his sons, and his son's wife, and after mutual salutations he told the governour the cause of his coming, viz. that this ship being sent him out of France, D'Aulnay, his old enemy, had so blocked up the river to his fort at St. John's, with two ships and a galliot, as his ship could not get in, whereupon he stole by in the night in his shallop, and was come to crave aid to convey him into his fort. The governour answered that he could say nothing to it till he had conferred with other of the magistrates; so after supper he went with him to Boston in La Tour's boat, having sent his own boat to Boston to carry home Mrs. Gibbons. Divers boats, having passed by him, had given notice hereof to Boston and Charlestown, his ship also arriving before Boston, the towns betook them to their arms, and three shallops with armed men came forth to meet the governour and to guard him home. But here the Lord gave us occasion to take notice of our weakness, &c. for if La Tour had been ill minded towards us, he had such an opportunity as we hope neither he nor any other shall ever have the like again; for coming by our castle and saluting it, there was none to answer him, for the last court had given order to have the castle-Island deserted, a great part of the work being fallen down, &c. so as he might have taken all the ordnance there. Then, having the governour and his family, and Captain Gibbons' wife, &c. in his power, he might have gone and spoiled Boston, and having so many men ready, they might have taken two ships in the harbour, and gone away without danger or resistance, but his neglecting this opportunity gave us assurance of his true meaning. So being landed at Boston, the governour, with a sufficient guard, brought him to his lodging at Captain Gibbons'. This gave further assurance that he intended us no evil, because he voluntarily put his person in our power. The next day the go-

||him||

vernour called together such of the magistrates as were at hand, and some of the deputies, and propounding the cause to them, and La Tour being present, and the captain of his ship, &c. he showed his commission, which was fairly engrossed in parchment, under the hand and seal of the Vice Admiral of France, and grand prior, &c. to bring supply to La Tour, whom he styled his majesty's lieutenant general of L'Acadye, and also a letter from the agent of the company of France to whom he hath reference, informing him of the injurious practices of D'Aulnay against him, and advising him to look to himself, &c. and superscribed §to§ him as lieutenant general, &c. Upon this it appeared to us, (that being dated in April last,) that notwithstanding the news which D'Aulnay had sent to our governour the last year, whereby La Tour was proclaimed a rebel, &c. yet he stood in good terms with the state of France, and also with the company. Whereupon, though we could not grant him aid without advice of the other commissioners of our confederacy, yet we thought it not fit nor just to hinder any that would be willing to be hired to aid him; and accordingly we answered him that we would allow him a free ||mercate,|| that he might hire any ships which lay in our harbour, &c. This answer he was very well satisfied with and took very thankfully; he also desired leave to land his men that they might refresh themselves, which was granted him, so they landed in small companies, that our women, &c. might not be affrighted by them. This direction was duly observed.

But the training day at Boston falling out the next week, and La Tour having requested that he might be permitted to exercise his soldiers on shore, we expected him that day, so he landed 40 men in their arms, (they were all shot.) They were brought into the field by our train band, consisting of 150, and in the forenoon they only beheld our men exercise. When they had dined, (La Tour and his officers with our officers, and his soldiers invited home by the private soldiers,) in the afternoon they were permitted to exercise, (our governour and other of the magistrates coming then into the field,) and all ours stood and beheld them. They were very expert in all their postures and motions.[1]

||mercature||

1 [Here was inserted, in my lost copy, a transcript from the MS. of an account of one peculiar feat in arms, showed by La Tour's soldiers, of which my memory is not sufficiently tenacious, I sincerely regret, to give an adequate representation. In the midst of their exercise with muskets, they threw down their pieces, cast off their bandoleers, drew their swords and appeared to make a charge. Some alarm was excited among the women and children, and perhaps a little suspicion among full grown men.]

In the margin is written by our author, "*this were better left out;*" but the

When it was near night, La Tour desired our governour that his men might have leave to depart, which being granted, his captain acquainted our captain therewith, so he drew our men into a march, and the French fell into the middle. When they were to depart, they gave a volley of shot and went to their boat, the French showing much admiration to see so many men of one town so well armed and disciplined, La Tour professing he could not have believed it, if he had not seen it. Our governour and others in the town entertained La Tour and his gentlemen with much courtesy, both in their houses and at table. La Tour came duly to our church meetings, and always accompanied the governour to and from thence, who all the time of his abode here was attended with a good guard of halberts and musketeers. Those who engrossed the ships, understanding his distress, and the justice of his cause, and the magistrates' permission, were willing to be entertained by him.

But the rumour of these things soon spreading through the country, were diversly apprehended, not only by the common sort, but also by the elders, whereof some in their sermons spoke against their entertainment, and the aid permitted them; others spake in the justification of both. One [blank] a judicious minister, hearing that leave was granted them to exercise their men in Boston, out of his fear of popish leagues and care of our safety, spake as in way of prediction, that, before that day were ended, store of blood would be spilled in Boston. Divers also wrote to the governour laying before him great dangers, others charging sin upon the conscience in all these proceedings; so as he was forced to write and publish the true state of the cause and the reasons of all their proceedings, which satisfied many, but not all. Also, the masters and others, who were to go in the ships, desired advice about their proceedings, &c. whereupon the governour appointed another meeting, to which all the ||near|| magistrates and deputies, and the elders also were called, and there the matter was debated upon these heads.

1. Whether it were lawful for christians to aid idolaters, and how far we may hold communion with them?

2. Whether it were safe for our state to suffer him to have aid from us against D'Aulnay?

[1]To the first question, the arguments on the negative part were

||new||

reason having ceased, probably all readers of the curious anecdote will agree with me, that it had better be printed.

1 Our author writes in his margin, "*some of the ensuing arguments were not*

these. 1. Jehoshaphat is reproved for the like—wouldst thou help the wicked? The answer to this was, first, this must be meant only in such case as that was, not simply according to the words of that one sentence taken apart from the rest, for otherwise it would be unlawful to help any wicked man, though a professed protestant, and though our own countryman, father, brother, &c. and that in any case, though ready to be drowned, slain, famished, &c.; second, Jehoshaphat aided him in a brotherly league of amity and affinity: I am as thou art, my people as thy people, &c. 2. Ahab was declared a wicked man by God, and denounced to destruction. ||Answer||. Ahab was in no distress, and so needed no aid.

2. Argument. Jehoshaphat joining after with Ahazia in making ships, is reproved, &c. Answer. There is difference between helping a man in distress, which is a duty imposed, and joining in a course of merchandise where the action is voluntary; and it appears by this their joining, that the league of amity continued between the two kingdoms.

3. Argument. Josias did evil in aiding the king of Babylon against Pharaoh Necho. Answer 1. The king of Babylon was in no distress, nor did desire his help, nor is it said he intended his aid. 2. Josias, no doubt, did not break any known general rule, being so strict an observer of all God's commandments; for it was not lawful for him to stop Pharaoh's army from going through his country, but his sin was, that either he did not believe the message of God by Pharaoh in that particular case, or did not inquire further about it from his own prophets, and so it is expressed in that story.

4. Argument. Amaziah, king of Judah, is reproved for hiring an army out of Israel, because God was near with Israel. Answer. This is not to the question, which is of giving aid, and not of hiring aid from others, nor was Amaziah in any distress, but only sought to enlarge his dominion.

5. Argument. By aiding papists we advance and strengthen popery. Answer 1. We are not to omit things necessary and

||3||

---

used at that meeting, but in the agitation of the case at other times." Hume, Chap. LXII. speaking of the fanaticism in England from 1640 to 1660, says: "The Old Testament, preferably to the New, was the favourite of all the sectaries. The Eastern poetical style of that composition made it more easily susceptible of a turn which was agreeable to them." I am sorry to confirm his remark, though the practice was less observable in our country. Yet it seems civil polity was deeply influenced by quotations from the Hebrew Scriptures, which assuredly were not *given for our instruction* to the extent manifested in our text.

lawful for a doubtful ill consequence, which is but accidental. 2. Such aid may as well work to the weakening of popery by winning some of them to the love of the truth, as hath sometimes fallen out, and sometimes by strengthening one part of them against another, they may both be the more weakened in the end.

For the 2d question, whether it be safe, &c. the arguments on the negative part were these.

1. Papists are not to be trusted, seeing it is one of their tenets that they are not to keep promise with heretics. Answer. In this case we rely not upon their faith but their interest, it being for their advantage to hold in with us, we may safely trust them; besides we shall not need to hazard ourselves upon their fidelity, having sufficient strength to secure ourselves.

2. We may provoke the state of France against us, or at least D'Aulnay, and so be brought into another war. Answer. It appears by the commission and letter before mentioned, that La Tour stands in good terms with the state of France and the company, &c. It is usual in all states in Europe to suffer aid to be hired against their confederates, without any breach of the peace, as by the states of Holland against the Spaniards, and by both out of England, without any breach of the peace, or offence to either. As for D'Aulnay, he hath carried himself so, as we could look for no other but ill measures from him, if he were able, though we should not permit La Tour to have help from us, for he hath taken Penobscott from us with our goods to a great value. He made prize of our men and goods also at Isle Sable, and kept our men as slaves a good space, but never made satisfaction for our goods; likewise he entertained our servants which ran from us, and refuseth to return them, being demanded; he also furnisheth the Indians about us with guns and powder; and lastly, he wrote last year to our governour forbidding our vessels to pass beyond his fort in the open sea, and threatening to make prize if he should meet, &c. and if the worst should happen that can be feared, yet if our way be lawful, and we innocent from wrong, &c. we may and must trust God with our safety so long as we serve his providence in the use of such means as he affords us.

3. Argument. Solomon tells us, that he that meddleth with a strife which belongs not to him, takes a dog by the ear, which is very dangerous. Answer. This is a strife which doth belong to us, both in respect of La Tour seeking aid of us in his distress, and also in respect it so much concerns us to have D'Aulnay subdued or weakened: and it were not wisdom in us to stop the course of providence, which offers to do that for us without our

charge, which we are like otherwise to be forced to undertake at our own charge.

4. It is not safe to permit this aid to go from us, especially without advice of the general court, lest it should miscarry, and so prove a dishonour and weakening to us. Answer 1. For the general court, it could not have been assembled under fourteen days, and such delay, besides the necessary charge it would have put La Tour unto, and ourselves also by the strong watches we ||were|| forced to keep, it might have lost the opportunity of relieving him, or it might have put him upon some dangerous design of surprising our ships, &c. Besides, if the court had been assembled, we knew they would not have given him aid without consent of the commissioners of the other colonies, and for a bare permission, we might do it without the court; and to have deferred this needlessly, had been against that rule: say not ||2to|| thy neighbour go and come again, and tomorrow I will give thee, when there is power in ||3thine|| hands to do it. As for the danger of miscarriage, it is not so much as in other our voyages to Spain or England, or &c. and if the rule be safe that we walk by, the success cannot alter it.

5. We hear only one party, we should as well hear the other, otherwise we deal not judicially, and perhaps may aid a man in an unjust quarrel. Answer 1. We heard formerly D'Aulnay's allegations against La Tour, and notwithstanding all that, La Tour his cause appears just; for they being both the subjects of the same prince, the ship coming by permission from their prince's authority, D'Aulnay ought to permit him to enter peaceably. 2. Our men that go will first offer parley with D'Aulnay, and if La Tour his cause be unjust, they are not to offend the others. 3. La Tour being now in desperate distress, he is first to be succoured, before the cause be further inquired into, according to the example of Abraham, who, hearing of the distress of his kinsman Lot, staid not till he might send to Chedorlaomer to have his answer about the justice of his cause, yet there was strong presumption that his cause was just, and that Lot and all the rest were lawful prisoners, for they had been twelve years his subjects and were in rebellion at this time, but he stays not to inquire out the cause, the distress not permitting it, but goes personally to rescue them: As put case—an Englishman or Spaniard should be driven into our harbour by a pirate, and should come and inform us so, and desire us to let him have aid to convey him safe to sea, might we not lawfully send out aid with him, before we had sent to the pirate to understand the cause; it would be time enough to

||are|| ||2as|| ||3their||

demand that, when our aid came up with him. So if our neighbouring Indians should send to us to desire aid against some other Indians who were coming to destroy them, should we first send to the other Indians to inquire the justice of the cause? No, but we should first send to save them, and after examine the cause.

The arguments on the affirmative part are many of them touched in the former answers to the arguments on the other part. The rest are these.

1. By the ||royal|| law thou shalt love thy neighbour as thyself. If our neighbour be in distress, we ought to help him without any respect to religion or other quality; but an idolater in distress is our neighbour, as appears by that parable, Luke 10. where it is plainly concluded, that the Samaritan was neighbour to the distressed traveller, and our Saviour bids the lawyer, being a Jew, to do likewise, that is, even to a Samaritan, if in distress; and by the law of relations the distressed Jew was neighbour to the Samaritan, and the Samaritan in distress should have been so to him, though as opposite in religion as protestants and papists. If such an one be not our neighbour, then we have no relation to him by any command of the second table, for that requires us to love our neighbour only, and then we may deceive, beat, and otherwise damnify him and not sin, &c.

2. Argument out of Gal. 6. 10. Do good to all, but specially to the household of faith, by which it appears that under all, he includes such as were not believers, and those were heathen idolaters, and if we must do good to such, we must help them in distress.

3. We are exhorted to be like our Heavenly Father in doing good to the just and unjust, that is to all, as occasion is offered, even such as he causeth the sun to shine upon, and the rain to fall upon, though excommunicated persons, blasphemers and persecutors, yet if they be in distress, we are to do them good, and therefore to relieve them.

4. We may hold some kind of communion with idolaters, as 1. We may have peace with them, 2. Commerce: Ezek. 27. 17. speaking of Tyrus, who were idolaters, he sayeth, Judah were thy merchants in wheat, &c. and the Jews were not forbidden to trade with the heathen in Nehemiah's time, so it were not on the Sabbath. 3. In eating and drinking and such like familiar converse: 1. Cor. 10. if an heathen invite a christian to his table, he might go, &c. and so he might as well invite such to his table, as Solomon did the queen of Sheba, and the ambassadors of other princes round about him, who would not have resorted to him as they did, if he had not

||blank||

entertained them courteously; and he both received presents and gave presents to the queen of Sheba, and others who were then idolaters—and Neh. 5. 17. he sayeth, that with the Jews there were also at his table usually such of the heathen as came to him: so that it was not then (nor indeed at all by the law) unlawful for the Jews to eat with heathen, though the Pharisees made it unlawful by their tradition.

The fourth and last kind of communion is succour in distress.

To the second question, the arguments on the affirmative part were these, with others expressed before in the answers.

1. D'Aulnay is a dangerous neighbour to us; if he have none to oppose him, or to keep him employed at home, he will certainly be dealing with us, but if La Tour be not now helpen, he is undone, his fort, with his wife, children and servants will all be taken, he hath no place to go unto—this ship cannot carry back him and all his company to France, but will leave them on shore here, and how safe it will be for us to keep them, is doubtful, but to let them go will be more dangerous, for they must then go to D'Aulnay, and that will strengthen him greatly both by their number, and still also by their present knowledge of our state and place, which, in regard of our own safety, lays a necessity upon us of aiding La Tour, and aiding him so as he may subsist, and be able to make good his place against his enemy.

2. La Tour being in urgent distress, and therefore as our neighbour to be relieved, if it be well done of us, we may trust in God, and not be afraid of any terrour, 1 Peter 3. 6.

3. It will be no wisdom for D'Aulnay to begin with us, for he knows how much stronger we are than he, in men and shipping; and some experience we have had hereof, in that when our friends of Plimouth hired a ship in our harbour and therewith went and battered his house at Penobscott, yet he took no occasion thereby against us, nor ever attempted any thing against them, though their trading house at Kennebeck be an hindrance to him, and easy for him to take at his pleasure.

There were other instances brought to the lawfulness, both in Joshua his aiding the Gibeonites, who were Cananites and had deluded him, and he might hereupon have left them to be spoiled by their neighbours. So when Jehoshaphat aided Jehorim against Moab, (for he had put away Baal,) Elisha speaks honourably to him and doth not reprove him, but for his presence sake saves their house by miracle, &c.

The like rumours and fears were raised upon our first expedition against the Pequods, 1636. The governour of Plimouth wrote to Mr. Winthrop, the deputy governour, in dislike of our attempt, and in apprehension of the great danger we had incurred, that we had provoked the Pequods, and no more, and had thereby occasioned a war, &c. But we found, through the Lord's special mercy, that that provocation and war proved a blessing to all the English. Our brethren of Connecticut wrote also to us, declaring their fears, and the danger we had cast them into by warring upon the Pequods, &c. And indeed we committed an errour, in that we did not first give them notice of our intention, that they might take the more care of their own safety, but they could not be ignorant of our preparations.

The governour by letters informed the rest of the commissioners of the united colonies of what had passed about La Tour; but the reason why he did not defer him at first for his answer, till some more of the magistrates and deputies might have been assembled, and the elders likewise consulted with, was this. Conceiving that he stood still under the same sentence of the arrest from the state of France, there would have been no need of advice in the case, for we must have given him the same answer we gave his lieutenant the last year, and upon the same ground, viz. That however he might trade here for such commodities as he stood in need of, yet he could expect no aid from us, for it would not be fit nor safe for us to do that which might justly provoke the state of France against us. But being met, and seeing the commission from the vice admiral, &c. that occasion of danger being removed, we doubted not but we might safely give him such answer as we did, without further trouble to the country or delay to him. See more of this [blank] leaves after.

The sow business not being yet digested in the country, many of the elders being yet unsatisfied, and the more by reason of a new case stated by some of the plaintiff's side and delivered to the elders, wherein they dealt very ||partially||, for they drew out all the evidence which made for the plaintiff, and thereupon framed their conclusion without mentioning any of the defendant's evidence. This being delivered to the elders, and by them imparted to some of the other side, an answer was presently drawn, which occasioned the elders to take a view of all the evidence on both parties, and a meeting being procured both of magistrates and elders (near all in the jurisdiction) and some of the deputies, the elders there declared, that notwithstanding their former opinions, yet, upon examination of all the testimonies, they found ||2such|| contrariety and crossing of testimonies, as they did not see any ground for the court to proceed to judgment in the case, and therefore earnestly desired that the court might never be more

||particularly|| ||2much||

troubled with it. To this all consented except ||Mr. Bellingham|| who still maintained his former opinion, and would have the magistrates lay down their negative voice, and so the cause to be heard again. This stiffness of his and singularity in opinion was very unpleasing to all the company, but they went on notwithstanding, and because a principal end of the meeting was to reconcile differences and take away offences, which were risen between some of the magistrates by occasion of this sow business and the treatise of Mr. Saltonstall against the council, so as Mr. Bellingham and he stood divided from the rest, which occasioned much opposition even in open court, and much partaking in the country, but by the wisdom and faithfulness of the elders Mr. Saltonstall was brought to see his failings in that treatise, which he did ingenuously acknowledge and bewail, and so he was reconciled with the rest of the magistrates. They laboured also to make a perfect reconciliation between the governour and Mr. Bellingham. The governour offered himself ready to it, but the other was not forward, whereby it rested in a manner as it was. Mr. Dudley also had let fall a speech in the court to Mr. Rogers of Ipswich, which was grievous to him and other of the elders. The thing was this. Mr. Rogers being earnest in a cause between the town and Mr. Bradstreet, which also concerned his own interest, Mr. Dudley used this speech to him, "Do you think to come with your eldership here to carry matters," &c. Mr. Dudley was somewhat hard at first to be brought to see any evil in it, but at last he was convinced and did acknowledge it, and they were reconciled.

The deputies, also, who were present at this meeting and had voted for the plaintiff in the case of the sow, seemed now to be satisfied, and the elders agreed to deal with the deputies of their several towns, to the end that that cause might never trouble the court more. But all this notwithstanding, the plaintiff, (or rather one G. Story ||2her|| solicitor,) being of an unsatisfied spirit, and animated, or at least too much countenanced, by some of the court, preferred a petition at the court of elections for a new hearing, and this being referred to the committee for petitions, it was returned that the greater part of them did conceive the cause should be heard again, and some others in the court declared themselves of the same judgment, which caused others to be much grieved to see such a spirit in godly men, that neither the judgment of near all the magistrates, nor the concurrence of the elders and their mediation, nor the loss of time and charge, nor the settling of peace in court and country could prevail with

||blank|| ||2his||

§them§ to let such a cause fall, (as in ordinary course of justice it ought,) as nothing could be found in, by any one testimony, to be of criminal nature, nor could the matter of the suit, with all damages, have amounted to forty shillings. But two things appeared to carry men on in this course as it were in captivity. One was, the deputies stood only upon this, that their towns were not satisfied in the cause (which by the way shows plainly the democratical spirit which acts our deputies, &c.) The other was, the desire of the name of victory; whereas on the other side the magistrates, &c. were content for peace sake, and upon the elders' advice, to decline that advantage, and to let the cause fall for want of advice to sway it either way.

Now that which made the people so unsatisfied, and unwilling the cause should rest as it stood, was the 20 pounds which the defendant had recovered against the plaintiff in an action of slander for saying he had stolen the sow, &c. and many of them could not distinguish this from the principal cause, as if she had been adjudged to pay 20 pounds for demanding her sow, and yet the defendant never took of this more than 3 pounds, for his charges of witnesses, &c. and offered to remit the whole, if she would have acknowledged the wrong she had done him. But he being accounted a rich man, and she a poor woman, this so wrought with the people, as being blinded with unreasonable compassion, they could not see, or not allow justice her reasonable course. This being found out by some of the court, a motion was made, that some who had interest in the defendant would undertake to persuade him to restore the plaintiff the 3 pounds (or whatever it were) he took upon that judgment, and likewise to refer other matters to reference which were between the said Story and him. This the court were satisfied with, and proceeded no further.

There was yet one offence which the elders desired might also be removed, and for that end some of them moved the governour in it, and he easily consented to them so far as they had convinced him of his failing therein. The matter was this. The governour had published a writing about the case of the sow, as is herein before declared, wherein some passages gave offence, which he being willing to remove, so soon as he came into the general court, he spake as followeth, (his speech is set down verbatim to prevent misrepresentation, as if he had retracted what he had wrote in the point of the case:) "I understand divers have taken offence at a writing I set forth about the sow business; I desire to remove it, and to begin my year in a reconciled estate with all. The writing is of two parts, the matter and the manner. In the former I had the concurrence of others of my brethren, both magistrates and deputies; but for the other, viz. the manner, that was wholly mine own, so as whatsoever was blame-worthy in it I must take it to myself. The matter is point of judgment, which is not at my own disposing. I have examined it over and again by such light as God hath afforded me from the rules of religion, reason, and common practice, and truly I can find no ground to retract any thing in that, therefore I desire I may enjoy my liberty herein, as every of yourselves do, and justly may. But for the manner, whatsoever I might allege for my justification before men, I now pass it over: I now set myself before another judgment seat. I will first speak to the manner in general, and then to two particulars. For the general. Howsoever that which I wrote was upon great provocation by some of the adverse party, and upon invitation from others to vindicate ourselves from that aspersion which was cast upon us, yet that was no sufficient warrant for me to break out into any distemper. I confess I was too prodigal of my brethren's reputation: I might have obtained the cause I had in hand without casting such blemish upon others as I did. For the particulars. 1. For the conclusion, viz. now let religion and sound reason give judgment in the case; whereby I might seem to conclude the other side to be void both of religion and reason. It is true a man may (as the case may be) appeal to the judgment of religion and reason, but, as I there carried it, I did arrogate too much to myself and ascribe too little to others. The other particular was the profession I made of maintaining what I wrote before all the world, which, though it may modestly be professed, (as the case may require,) yet I confess it was now not so beseeming me, but was indeed a fruit of the pride of mine own spirit. These are all the Lord hath brought me to consider of, wherein I acknowledge my failings, and humbly intreat you will pardon and pass them by; if you please to accept my request, your silence shall be a sufficient testimony thereof unto me, and I hope I shall be more wise and watchful hereafter."

The sow business had started another question about the magistrates' negative vote in the general court. The deputies generally were very earnest to have it taken away; whereupon one of the magistrates wrote a small treatise, wherein he laid down the original of it from the patent, and the establishing of it by order of the general court in 1634, showing thereby how it was fundamental to our government, which, if it were taken away, would be a mere democracy. He showed also the necessity and usefulness of it by many arguments from scripture, reason, and common practice, &c. Yet this would not satisfy, but the deputies and common people would have it taken away; and yet it was apparent (as some of the deputies themselves confessed) the most did not understand it. An answer also was written (by one of the magistrates as was conceived) to the said treatise, undertaking to avoid all the arguments both from the patent and from the order, &c. This the deputies made great use of in this court, supposing they had now enough to carry the cause clearly with them, so as they pressed earnestly to have it presently determined. But the magistrates told them the matter was of great concernment, even to the very frame of our government; it had been established upon serious consultation and consent of all the elders; it had been continued without any inconvenience or apparent mischief these fourteen years, therefore it would not be safe nor of good report to alter on such a sudden, and without the advice of the elders: offering withal, that if upon such advice and consideration it should appear to be inconvenient, or not warranted by the patent and the said order, &c. they should be ready to join with them in taking it away. Upon these propositions they were stilled, and so an order was drawn up to this effect, that it was desired that every member of the court would take advice, &c. and that it should be no offence for any, either publicly or privately, to declare their opinion in the case, so it were modestly, &c. and that the elders should be desired to give their advice before the next meeting of this court. It was the magistrates' only care to gain time, that so the people's heat might be abated, for then they knew they would hear reason, and that the advice of the elders might be interposed; and that there might be liberty to reply to the answer, which was very long and tedious, which accordingly was done soon after the court, and [1]published to good satisfaction. One of the elders also wrote a small treatise, wherein scholastically and religiously he handled the question, laying down the several forms of government both simple and mixt, and the true form of our government, and the unavoidable change into a democracy, if the negative voice were taken away; and answered all objections, and so concluded for the continuance of it, so as the deputies and the people also, having their heat moderated by time, and their judgments better informed by what they had learned about it, let the cause fall, and he who had written the answer to the first defence, appeared no further in it.

Our supplies from England failing much, men began to look about them, and fell to a manufacture of cotton, whereof we had

---

1 Publishing does not here mean printing. The tract, written for circulation by Winthrop, is in our Historical Society's library, dated 5 of 4th mo, 1643. It contains sixteen pages, and is among the Hutchinson MSS.

store from Barbados, and of hemp and flax, wherein Rowley, to their great commendation, exceeded all other towns.

The governour acquainted the court with a letter he received from Mr. Wheelwright, to intreat the favour of the court that he might have leave to come into the Bay upon especial occasions, which was readily granted him for 14 days, whereupon he came and spake with divers of the elders, and gave them such satisfaction as they intended to intercede with the court for the release of his banishment. See more (3) 44.

Sacononoco and Pumham, two sachems near Providence, having under them between 2 and 300 men, finding themselves overborne by Miantunnomoh, the sachem of Naragansett, and Gorton and his company, who had so prevailed with Miantunnomoh, as he forced one of them to join with him in setting his hand or mark to a writing, whereby a part of his land was sold to Gorton and his company, for which Miantunnomoh received a price, but the other would not receive that which was for his part, alleging that he did not intend to sell his land, though through fear of Miantunnomoh he had put his mark to the writing, they came to our governour, and by ||Benedict|| Arnold, their interpreter, did desire we would receive them under our government, and brought withal a small present of wampom, about ten fathom. The governour gave them encouragement, but referred them to the court, and received their present, intending to return it them again, if the court should not accord to them; but at the present he acquainted another of the magistrates with it. So it was agreed, and they wrote to Gorton and his company to let them know what the sachems had complained of, and how they had tendered themselves to come under our jurisdiction, and therefore if they had any thing to allege against it, they should come or send to our next court. We sent also to Miantunnomoh to signify the same to him. Whereupon, in the beginning of the court, Miantunnomoh came to Boston, and being demanded in open court, before divers of his own men and Cutshamekin and other Indians, whether he had any interest in the said two sachems as his subjects, he could prove none. Cutshamekin also in his presence affirmed, that he had no interest in them, but they were as free sachems as himself; only because he was a great sachem, they had sometime sent him presents, and aided him in his war against the Pequots: and Benedict Arnold affirmed, partly upon his own knowledge, and partly upon the relation of divers Indians of those parts, that the Indians belonging to these sachems did usually pay their deer skins (which are a tribute belonging to the chief sachem) always to

||Benjamin||

them, and never to Miantunnomoh or any other sachem of Naragansett, which Miantunnomoh could not contradict. Whereupon it was referred to the governour and some other of the magistrates and deputies to send for the two sachems after the court, and to treat with them about their receiving in to us.[1]

But before this, Gorton and his company (12 in number) sent a writing to our court of four sheets of paper, full of reproaches against our magistrates, elders and churches, of familistical and absurd opinions, and therein they justified their purchase of the sachems' land, and professed to maintain it to the death. They sent us word also after, (as Benedict Arnold reported to us,) that if we sent men against them, they were ready to meet us, being assured of victory from God, &c. Whereupon the court sent two[2] of the deputies to speak with them, to see whether they would own that writing which was subscribed by them all. When they came, they with much difficulty came to find out Gorton and two or three more of them, and upon conference they did own and justify the said writing. They spake also with the two sachems, as they had commission, and giving them to understand upon what terms they must be received under us, they found them very pliable to all, and opening to them the ten commandments, they received this answer, which I have set down as the commissioners took it in writing from their mouths.

1. Quest. Whether they would worship the true God that made heaven and earth, and not blaspheme him? Ans. We desire to speak reverently of Englishman's God and not to speak evil of

---

1 It may be very difficult, perhaps impossible, to arrive at the whole truth in regard to this purchase by Gorton and his associates. A copy of the deed, 12 January 1642-3, found in Trumbull's MSS. xix. proves that "Myantonomy, chief sachem of the Narrhyganset, have sold unto the persons here named one parcel of lands, with all the rights and privileges thereof whatsoever, lying upon the west side of that part of the sea called Sawhames bay from Copessuatuxit over against a little island in the said bay, being the north bounds, and the utmost point of that neck of land called Shawhomet, being the south bounds from the sea shore of each border upon a strait line westward twenty miles, I say I have truly sold this parcel of land abovesaid, the proportion whereof is according to the map underwritten or drawn, being the form of it, unto Randall Houlden, John Greene, John Wickes, Francis Weston, Samuel Gorton, Richard Waterman, John Warner, Richard Carder, Sampson Shotten, Robert Potter, William Waddall, for one hundred and forty-four fathom of Wampompeague, I say I have sold it and possession of it given unto the men abovesaid, with the free and joint consent of the present inhabitants, being natives, as it appears by their hands hereunto annexed, dated, &c. being enacted upon the abovesaid parcel of lands in the presence of the sachem of Shaomet, Pumham, Jano, Totanoman, John Green, junior." The Indian witnesses affix marks, of which one is a hatchet, another a gun; the grantor's is a bow and arrow.

2 Humfrey Atherton and Edward Tomlyns, as I ascertain by the records.

him, because we see the Englishman's God doth better for them than other Gods do for others.

2. That they should not swear falsely. Ans. We never knew what swearing or an oath was.

3. Not to do any unnecessary work on the Lord's day within the gates of ||proper|| towns. Ans. It is a small thing for us to rest on that day, for we have not much to do any day, and therefore we will forbear on that day.

4. To honour their parents and superiours. Ans. It is our custom so to do, for inferiors to be subject to superiours, for if we complain to the governour of the Massachusetts that we have wrong, if they tell us we lie, we shall willingly bear it.

5. Not to kill any man but upon just cause and just authority. Ans. It is good, and we desire so to do.

6. 7. Not to commit fornication, adultery, bestiality, &c. Ans. Though fornication and adultery be committed among us, yet we allow it not, but judge it evil, so the same we judge of stealing.

8. For lying, they say it is an evil, and shall not allow it.

9. Whether you will suffer your children to read God's word, that they may have knowledge of the true God and to worship him in his own way? Ans. As opportunity serveth by the English coming amongst us, we desire to learn their manners.

After the court, the governour &c. sent for them, and they came to Boston at the day appointed, viz. the 22d of the 4th month, and a form of submission being drawn up, and they being by Benedict Arnold, their neighbour, and interpreter, (who spake their language readily,) made to understand every particular, in the presence of divers of the elders and many others, they freely subscribed the submission, as it here followeth verbatim. Being told that we did not receive them in as confederates but as subjects, they answered, that they were so little in respect of us, as they could expect no other. So they dined in the same room with the governour, but at a table by themselves; and having much countenance showed them by all present, and being told that they and their men should be always welcome to the English, provided they brought a note from Benedict Arnold, that we might know them from other Indians, and having some small things bestowed upon them by the governour, they departed joyful and well satisfied. We looked at it as a fruit of our prayers, and the first fruit of our hopes, that the example would bring in others, and that the Lord was by this means making a way to bring them to civility,

||blank||

and so to conversion to the knowledge and embracing of the gospel in his due time.[1]

Soon after their departure, we took order that Miantunnomoh and the English in those parts should have notice of their submission to us, that they might refrain from doing them injury.

Their submission was as followeth.

"This writing is to testify, That we Pumham, sachem of Shawomock, and Sacononoco, sachem of Patuxet,[2] &c, have, and by these presents do, voluntarily and without any constraint or persuasion, but of our own free motion, put ourselves, our subjects, lands and estates under the government and jurisdiction of the Massachusetts, to be governed and protected by them, according to their just laws and orders, so far as we shall be made capable of understanding them: and we do promise for ourselves and our subjects, and all our posterity to be true and faithful to the said government, and aiding to the maintenance thereof to our best ability, and from time to time to give speedy notice of any conspiracy, attempt, or evil intention of any which we shall know or hear of, against the same: and we do promise to be willing, from time to time, to be instructed in the knowledge and worship of God. In witness whereof," &c.

The lady Moodye,[2] a wise and anciently religious woman, being

---

1 We may rejoice in the benevolence, which attempted the civilization and conversion to christianity of these Indians, and certainly must honour the government, whose liberal treaty with their confederates is so diverse from the usual terms of stipulation with the natives; but it may be feared, that there was too much human policy at work in obtaining their *subjection*, and we must acknowledge that a territorial usurpation beyond the limits of our charter was the result, if not the motive, of the negotiation. Yet the act of submission in June could not invalidate the deed of January preceding.

2 Shawomock, or Shaomet, and Patuxet lie south of Providence, of course far without the bounds of Massachusetts charter.

3 My acquaintance with this lady is very slight. Hutchinson I. 21 mentions her purchase of Humfrey's plantation at Saugus, when he returned to England. At a general court 13 May 1640, probably before that transaction, I find from Col. Rec. I. 276: "The Lady Deborah Moody is granted 400 acres of land, where it may not hinder a plantation, nor any former grant." I fear we must infer from the text, that her perversion to anabaptism deprived her, in the writer's opinion, of the "anciently religious" character; as that was, undoubtedly, the reason of her expulsion from the church, as if it were a private society. She suffered from the Indians a little, as will appear a few pages onward, but her fortune was more happy than her neighbour, Mrs. Hutchinson's. Wood's Sketch of the settlement of Long Island, p. 41, relates the advantage of her aid obtained to an extraordinary degree by governour Stuyvesant. Having some trouble with the English planters of Gravesend, who were a majority in that town, he went thither 23d Nov. 1654, "and to effect his purpose, he was obliged to avail himself of the influence of Lady Moody, a connection of Sir Henry Moody, one

taken with the errour of denying baptism to infants, was dealt withal by many of the elders and others, and admonished by the church of Salem, (whereof she was a member,) but persisting still, and to avoid further trouble, &c. she removed to the Dutch against the advice of all her friends. Many others, infected with anabaptism, removed thither also. She was after excommunicated.

5. 5.] There arose a sudden gust at N. W. so violent for half an hour as it blew down multitudes of trees. It lifted up their meeting house at Newbury, the people being in it. It darkened the air with dust, yet through God's great mercy it did no hurt, but only killed one Indian with the fall of a tree. It was straight between Linne and Hampton.

2.] Here arrived one Mr. Carman,[1] master of the ship called [blank] of 180 tons. He went from New Haven in 10ber last, laden with clapboards for the Canaries, being earnestly commended to the Lord's protection by the church there. At the Island of Palma, he was set upon by a Turkish pirate of 300 tons and 26 pieces of ordnance and 200 men. He fought with her three hours, having but 20 men and but 7 pieces of ordnance that he could use, and his muskets were unserviceable with rust. The Turk lay cross his hawse, so as he was forced to shoot through his own hoodings and by these shot killed many Turks. Then the Turk lay by his side and boarded him with near 100 men and cut all his ropes, &c. but his shot having killed the captain of the Turkish ship and broken his tiller, the Turk took in his own ensign and fell off from him, but in such haste as he left about 50 of his men aboard him, then the master and some of his men came up and fought with those 50 hand to hand, and slew so many of them as the rest leaped overboard. The master had many wounds on his head and body, and divers of his men were wounded, yet but one slain; so with much difficulty he got to the island, (being in view thereof,) where he was very courteously entertained and supplied with whatsoever he wanted.

Continuation about La Tour.

The governour, with the advice of some of the magistrates and elders, wrote a letter to D'Aulnay, taking occasion in answer to

---

of the original patentees. He conceded the nomination of the magistrates that year to her, and her popularity reconciled the people to the measure, and produced submission to the arbitrary act of the governour."

1 Mention of his death in a very disastrous shipwreck will occur in the progress of this history.

his letter in 9ber last to this effect, viz. Whereas he found by the arrest he sent last autumn, that La Tour was under displeasure and censure in France, thereupon we intended to have no further to do with him than by way of commerce which is allowed, and if he had made prize of any of our vessels in that way, as he threatened, we should have righted ourselves so well as we could, without injury to himself or just offence to his ||majesty|| of France, whom we did honour as a great and mighty prince, and should endeavour always to behave ourselves towards his majesty and all his subjects as became us, &c. But La Tour coming now to us, and acquainting us how it was with him, &c. and here mentioning the vice admiral's commission and the letters, &c. though we thought not fit to give him aid, as being unwilling to intermeddle in the wars of any of our neighbours, yet considering his urgent distress, we could not in christianity or humanity deny him liberty to hire for his money any ships in our harbour, either such as came to us out of England or others. And whereas some of our people were willing to go along with him, (though without any commission from us,) we had charged them to labour by all means to bring matters to a reconciliation, &c. and that they should be assured, that if they should do or attempt any thing against the rules of justice and good neighbourhood, they must be accountable therefor unto us at their return.[1]

Beside the former arguments, there came since to Boston one Mr. Hooke,[2] a godly gentleman, and a deputy of the court for Salisbury, who related of the good usage and great courtesy which La Tour had showed to himself and other passengers, who were landed at his fort about nine years since as they came from England, and how the ship leaving them there, and only a small shallop to bring them to these parts, and a dangerous bay of 12 leagues to be passed over, he would not suffer them to depart before he had provided his own pinnace to transport them.

And whereas he was charged to have killed two Englishmen at Machias not far from his fort, and to have taken away their goods

||master||

---

1 In the course of a very short time we had trouble enough from this impolitick and unlawful interference. There was wisdom enough in the country to have prevented it; but Winthrop was probably prevailed on by the Boston merchants. See Hutch. Coll. 115—134.

2 William Hooke was a witness, 27 May 1633, to the delivery of possession, by Capt. Neale, to Aldworth and Elbridge of the Pemaquid grant from the Earl of Warwick and Sir Ferdinand Gorges, for the President and Council of New-England, Haz. I. 318; and by the charter of 2 Septr. 1639 was named by Sir F. to be one of his council, Haz. I. 458.

to the value of 500 pounds, Mr. Vines of Saco, who was part owner of the goods and principal trader, &c. being present with La Tour, the governour heard the cause between them, which was thus: Mr. Vines being in a pinnace trading in those parts, La Tour met him in another pinnace, and bought so many of his commodities as Mr. Vines received then of him 400 skins, and although some of Mr. Vines his company had abused La Tour, whereupon he had made them prisoners in his pinnace, yet at Mr. Vines' intreaty he discharged them with grave and good counsel, and acquainted Mr. Vines with his commission to make prize of all such as should come to trade in those parts, and thereupon desired him peaceably to forbear, &c. yet at his request he gave him leave to trade the goods he had left, in his way home, so as he did not fortify or build in any place within his commission, which he said he could not answer it if he should suffer it; whereupon they parted friendly. Mr. Vines landed his goods at Machias, and there set up a small wigwam, and left five men and two murderers to defend it, and a shallop, and so returned home. Two days after La Tour comes, and casting anchor before the place, one of Mr. Vines men came on board his pinnace, and while they were in parley, four of La Tour his men went on shore. One of the four which were in the house, seeing them, gave fire to a murderer, but it not taking fire, he called to his fellow to give fire to the other murderer, which he going to do, the four French retreated and one of their muskets went off, (La Tour sayeth it was by accident, and that the shot went through one of his fellow's clothes, but Mr. Vines could say nothing to that.) It killed two of the men on shore, which La Tour then professed himself innocent of, and very sorry for; and said further, that the five men were at that time all drunk, and not unlikely, having store of wine and strong water, for had they been sober, they would not have given fire upon such as they had conversed friendly with but two days before, without once bidding them stand, or asking them wherefore they came. After this La Tour coming to the house, and finding some of his own goods, (though of no great value,) which had a little before been taken out of his fort at St. Johns by the Scotch and some English of Virginia, (||when|| they plundered all his goods to a great value and abused his men,) he seized the three men and the goods and sent them into France according to his commission, where the men were discharged, but the goods adjudged lawful prize. Mr. Vines did not contradict any of this, but only that he did not build or fortify at Machias, but only set up a shelter for his men and goods. For the value of the goods Mr. Vines show-

||where||

ed an invoice which came to 3 or 400 pounds, but La Tour said he had another under the men's hands that were there, which came not to half so much. In ||conclusion|| he promised that he would refer the cause to judgment, and if it should be found that he had done them wrong, he would make satisfaction.

5. 14.] In the evening La Tour took ship, the governour and divers of the chief of the town accompanying him to his boat. There went with him four of our ships and a pinnace. He hired them for two months, the chiefest, which had 16 pieces of ordnance, at 200 pounds the month; yet she was of but 100 tons, but very well manned and fitted for fight, and the rest proportionable. The owners took only his own security for their pay. He entertained also about 70 land soldiers, volunteers, at 40*s*. per month a man, but he paid them somewhat in hand.[1]

Of the two friars which came in this ship, the one was a very learned acute man. Divers of our elders who had conference with him reported so of him. They came not into the town, lest they should give offence, but once, being brought by some to see Mr. Cotton and confer with him, and when they came to depart, the chief came to take leave of the governour and the two elders of Boston, and showed himself very thankful for the courtesy they found among us.

In the afternoon they set sail from Long Island, the wind N.

||courtesy||

---

1 Haz. I. 499—502 has transcribed from our registry of Suffolk Vol. I. 7, the articles of agreement, 30 June 1643, between La Tour and Captain Edward Gibbons and Thomas Hawkins, masters and part owners of the ship Seabridge, ship Philip and Mary, ship Increase and ship Greyhound, that the Seabridge shall be completely fitted with a master and 14 able seamen and a boy, with 14 pieces of ordnance, powder and shot, &c. for two months from 10 July next, the Philip and Mary the same number of men, &c. with 10 pieces of ordnance, &c. the Increase with 14 persons and 10 pieces of ordnance, the Greyhound with 4 murderers and 8 men, all to be ready to set sail from the roads of Boston and Charlestown on or before 10 July, and from thence "*by God's grace* shall directly sail in company with the ship Clement appurtaining to the said Monsieur La Tour, the danger of the seas excepted, as near unto the fort of the said M. La Tour, in the river of St. Johns, as the abovementioned ships may conveniently ride at anchor; and farther we promise to join with the said ship Clement in the defence of ourselves and the said M. La Tour against M. Dony's his forces, or any other that shall unjustly assault or oppose M. La Tour in his way to his fort as abovesaid, and for any further assistance, we promise no further than by a mutual consent of the said M La Tour, with the agent and his counsel by us appointed or the major part of them." Many extraordinary provisions on the part of La Tour show the proceeding to have been a most palpable violation of the neutrality we ought to have maintained. No doubt our rulers were confident of their integrity, as the governour makes apology for not advising with the elders.

and by W. amd went out at Broad Sound at half flood, where no ships of such burthen had gone out before, or not more than one.

Three errours the governour, &c. committed in managing this business. 1. In giving La Tour an answer so suddenly (the very next day after his arrival). 2. In not advising with any of the elders, as their manner was in matters of less consequence. 3. In not calling upon God, as they were wont to do in all public affairs, before they fell to consultation, &c.

The occasions of these errours were, first, their earnest desire to despatch him away, and conceiving at first they should have given him the same answer they gave his lieutenant the last year, for they had not then seen the Vice Admiral's commission. 2. Not then conceiving any need of counsel, the elders never came into the governour's thoughts. 3. La Tour and many of the French coming into them at first meeting, and some taking occasion to fall in parley with them, there did not appear then a fit opportunity for so solemn an action as calling upon God, being in the midst of their business before they were aware of it. But this fault hath been many times found in the governour to be oversudden in his resolutions, for although the course were both warrantable and safe, yet it had beseemed men of wisdom and gravity to have proceeded with more deliberation and further advice.

Those about Ipswich &c. took great offence at these proceedings, so as three of the magistrates and the elders of Ipswich and Rowley, with Mr. Nathaniel Ward, wrote a letter to the governour and assistants in the bay, and to the elders here, protesting against the proceedings, and that they would be innocent of all the evil which might ensue &c. with divers arguments against it, whereof some were weighty, but not to the matter, for they supposed we had §engaged§ the country in a war, as if we had permitted our ships &c. to go fight with D'Aulnay, whereas we only permitted them to be hired by La Tour to conduct him home. The governour made answer to this protestation, so did Mr. Dudley and the pastor of Boston.[1]

5.] Letters came to our governour from Mr. Haynes, governour at Hartford, certifying of a war begun between Onkus, sachem of Mohigen, and Sequasson, sachem upon Connecticut, and that upon Onkus' complaint of the other's assaulting him, &c. he sent for Sequasson and endeavoured to make them friends, but Sequasson chose rather to have war, so they were forced to leave

---

[1] These valuable papers, of both sides of the question, are preserved in Hutch. Coll. 115—134.

them to themselves, promising to be aiding to neither, &c. Soon after Onkus set upon Sequasson and killed seven or eight of his men, wounded 13, burnt his wigwams and carried away the booty. Upon this Miantunnomoh (being allied to Sequasson) sent to Mr. Haynes to complain of Onkus. He answered that the English had no hand in it, nor would encourage them, &c. Miantunnomoh gave notice hereof also to our governour by two of our neighbour Indians who had been with him, and was very desirous to know if we would not be offended, if he made war upon Onkus. Our governour answered, if Onkus had done him or his friends wrong and would not give satisfaction, we should leave him to take his own course.

5. 22.] A Dutch sloop arrived with letters in Latin, signed by the secretary there in the name and by the command of the governour and senate, directed to the governour and senate of U. P. of New England, wherein 1st, he congratulates our late confederation, then he complains of unsufferable wrongs done to their people upon Connecticut, more of late than formerly, and of misinformation given by some of ours to the States' ambassador in London, and desires to know by a categorical answer, whether we will aid or desert them, (meaning of Hartford,) that so they may know their friends from their enemies, &c. The governour appointed a meeting of some of the next magistrates on the second day next, but the rain hindering some of them, it was put off to the fifth day.

Here arrived a bark of the Earl of Warwick from Trinidado. She came for people and provisions, but our people, being well informed of the state of those places, were now become wiser, and could stay here where they were in better condition than they could be in those parts, so he altered his design and went towards Canada, and by the way guarded home a pinnace of La Tour's which came hither for provisions.

The wife of one [blank] Hett, of whom mention was made before, being cast out of the church of Boston, the Lord was pleased so to honour his own ordinance, that whereas before no means could prevail with her either to reclaim her from her wicked and blasphemous courses and speeches, &c. or to bring her to frequent the means, within a few weeks after her casting out, she came to see her sin and lay it to heart, and to frequent the means, and so was brought to such manifestation of repentance and a sound mind, as the church received her in again.

The day appointed for considering of the letter from the Dutch proved again so wet as but few met, and of those some would have another day appointed, and all the magistrates to be called to it, but others thought it not fit both in regard the messenger hasted away, and also, for that no direct answer could be returned without a general court. At length advising with some of the elders who were at hand, and some of the deputies, we returned answer to this effect, (in the name of the governour only) viz. After gratulation, &c. of their friendly respect and our earnest desire of the continuance of that good correspondency which hath been between themselves and us, ever since our arrival in these parts, That our chief council, to whom their letters were directed, being far dispersed, &c. he was necessitated, with the advice of some other of the magistrates, to return this answer to them for the present, being rather a declaration of their own conceptions than the determination of our chiefest authority, from which they should receive further answer in time convenient. We declared our grief for the difference between them and our brethren of Hartford, which we conceived might be composed by arbiters, either in England or Holland, or here; that by our confederation we were bound to seek the good and safety of each other as our own, which we hoped would not hinder the continuance of that amity and correspondency between themselves and us; and that the ground of their difference, being only for a small parcel of land, was a matter of so little value in this vast continent, as was not worthy to cause a breach between two people so nearly related, both in profession of the same protestant religion and otherwise; therefore we would seriously request them, as we would do also the others, that ||until|| the justice of the cause were decided by one of the ways before named, there might be abstinence on both sides from injury and provocation, and if any should happen on their part, that it might be duly examined, and we were assured (they being a people fearing God, they durst not allow themselves in any unrighteous course) they should receive equal satisfaction. See more page [blank.]

We received news of a great defeat given the Narragansetts by Onkus, and of 15 Dutch slain by the Indians, and much beaver taken, and of Mr. Lamberton,[1] &c.

6.] Onkus, being provoked by Sequasson, a sachem of Connecticut, who would not be persuaded by the magistrates there to

||when||

---

1 Very little more can be ascertained of him, than in this history will be seen of his controversy with the Swedes in the attempt to get a settlement, contrary to their right, and of his loss at sea in the early part of 1646. Trumbull, I. 122, calls him "a principal gentleman of New Haven," but I see no evidence of his dignity.

a reconciliation, made war upon him, and slew divers of his men and burnt his wigwams; whereupon Miantunnomoh, being his kinsman, took offence against Onkus, and went with near 1,000 men and set upon Onkus before he could be provided for defence, for he had not then with him above 3 or 400 men. But it pleased God to give Onkus the victory, after he had killed about 30 of the Narragansetts, and wounded many more, and among these two of Canonicus' sons and a brother of Miantunnomoh, who fled, but having on a coat of mail, he was easily overtaken, which two of his captains perceiving, they laid hold on him and carried him to Onkus, hoping thereby to procure their own pardon. But so soon as they came to Onkus, he slew them presently; and Miantunnomoh standing mute, he demanded of him why he would not speak. If you had taken me, sayeth he, I would have besought you for my life. The news of Miantunnomoh's captivity coming to Providence, Gorton and his company, who had bought of him the lands belonging to the sachems who were come under our jurisdiction, wrote a letter to Onkus, willing him to deliver their friend Miantunnomoh, and threatened him with the power of the English if he refused, *and they sent their letter in the name of the governour of Massachusetts*. Upon this Onkus carries Miantunnomoh to Hartford to take advice of the magistrates there, and at Miantunnomoh's earnest entreaty he left him with them, yet as a prisoner. They kept him under guard, but used him very courteously, and so he continued till the commissioners of the United Colonies met at Boston, who taking into serious consideration what was safest and best to be done, were all of opinion that it would not be safe to set him at liberty, neither had we sufficient ground for us to put him to death. In this difficulty we called in five of the most judicious elders, (it being in the time of the general assembly of the elders,) and propounding the case to them, they all agreed that he ought to be put to death. Upon this concurrence we enjoined secrecy to ourselves and them, lest if it should come to the notice of the Narragansetts, they might set upon the commissioners, &c. in their return, to take some of them to redeem him, (as Miantunnomoh himself had told Mr. Haynes had been in consultation amongst them;) and agreed that, upon the return of the commissioners to Hartford, they should send for Onkus and tell him our determination, that Miantunnomoh should be delivered to him again, and he should put him to death so soon as he came within his own jurisdiction, and that two English should go along with him to see the execution, and that if any Indians should invade him for it, we would send men to defend him: If Onkus should refuse to do it, then Miantunnomoh should be sent in a pinnace to Boston, there to be kept until further consideration.[1]

---

[1] Of several parts of this history many readers will perhaps form an unfavourable judgment, but none has been so painful in the whole progress of my labours, as this which relates the treatment of Miantunnomoh by our fathers. Such a case of perfidy, or cruelty, or both, it is impossible to pass without animadversion.

This prince had deserved of our people, it seems to me, at least, as highly as Onkus, who, after removal of his great rival, became a perpetual plague to the English of Connecticut. Miantunnomoh certainly showed an aptitude for policy in some things worthy of a great mind; and his advice, when a prisoner, to Governour Haynes, to guard against surprise by his subjects for obtaining his liberation, discloses as great magnanimity as he probably expected to find in his civilized friends. Something of the character of both these sachems may be learned from Roger Williams, their nearest neighbour and most unprejudiced judge, 3 Hist. Coll. I. 166, and from a comparison of his relation with that of our author, Vol. I. 265. He calls the inferiour Okace.

In May preceding the date in the text, the chief of the Narragansetts had been summoned to Boston, whither he came with confidence, to answer our demand, if he could prove any interest in Pumham and Sacononoco, who early in the same year had sold parcel of their lands to eleven men of somewhat different faith from that of the majority of Massachusetts. Our colony having prevailed on those sachems immediately after to submit themselves to us, thereupon denied most injuriously the right of Gorton, Holden, and the others, to the lands thus purchased, because the Indians had been induced to make the sale by Miantunnomoh, who asserted a superiority of some sort over them, and took part of the price.

We next hear of this chieftain in July, that, a feud breaking out between Onkus and Sequasson, a relative of Miantunnomoh, he complained against Onkus to the governours of Connecticut and Massachusetts, and desired them not to take offence, if he made war upon him. Hostile feelings, and injuries, perhaps mutual, had long subsisted between these barbarians, but to which of their confederates the first wrong might be imputed by the English, they certainly did not assume the part of avengers. The answer of Governour Winthrop to this complaint, see page 129, is a full declaration of neutrality: "If Onkus had done him *or his friends* wrong, and would not give satisfaction, we should leave him to take his course." Now the severest casuistry of christian belligerents is not yet so refined as to deny, that Onkus had wronged Sequasson, for he had defeated him, killed and wounded several of his men, burnt his wigwams, and carried away plunder.

Miantunnomoh, in the earliest prosecution of the war, was seized by the treachery of two of his captains, and delivered to his enemy, by whom, on his solicitation, he was carried to Hartford. It cannot be doubted, I presume, that the captive, having in vain pressed the conqueror to put him to death, expected friendship from the English, to which his former services and recent deference gave him no slight claim. The Narragansetts made presents to Onkus: by one party these gifts are represented as a reward for delivering his prisoner to the English, by the other, as a ransom for the life of their sovereign. See governour Hayne's letter to Winthrop, 3 Hist. Coll. I. 229. Perhaps the conqueror was persuaded to surrender his prey at Hartford through the influence of Gorton and his associates, for it was at first reported, that "they sent their letters in the name of the governour of Massachusetts;" but as this clause was afterwards struck out by Winthrop, it was probably a false report. Such a deception, for a benevolent purpose, might not be a heavy aggravation of the errours of

The reasons of this proceeding with him were these. 1. It was now clearly discovered to us, that there was a general conspiracy

---

ignorance, under which those hereticks sank. Whatever influence, however, moved Onkus, it seems hardly possible, that he could have anticipated the joyful result of the policy of his teachers in civilization, the deliberation of pious statesmen, by which his captive was restored to his hands, with an injunction to put him to death.

A judicial investigation of the case of this sachem should not have been undertaken; but as it was, we may look at the grounds of judgment. Trumbull, I. 130, makes part of his offence "without consulting the English according to agreement." Our author's narrative ought to have silenced such a pretence. Little importance need be attached to another allegation, "that he had promised us in the open court to send to Onkus the Pequod, who had shot him in the arm, yet in his way homeward he killed him;" nor indeed to any other part of the doubtful story about the traitorous slave of the Moheagan. By the acts of the commissioners, Haz. II. 8, we learn, that it was fully proved, from the Pequod's own mouth, that he was guilty, and therefore Miantunnomoh, if innocent, as our people, before his misfortunes, thought him, might believe his royal promise satisfactorily performed by putting to death the assassin, instead of returning him to his master. Perhaps his promise to the English, on this matter, was less distinctly understood than it might have been between contracting parties of the same language. If Onkus were, however, free from all blame, and the Narragansett chargeable with treachery, and every other vice of kings, our rulers had no cognizance of the cause, and their advice to the successful warriour was cruel; but their conduct to Miantunnomoh, who had so few years before been their ally against the Pequods, can hardly be regarded as less than a betraying of innocent blood. In the congress of the united colonies, whose doings in this behalf are briefly, but fairly, told by our author, its president, and may be seen at large in Haz. II. 11—13, it was too hastily, I think, resolved, "that it would not be safe to set him at liberty;" and as death was the alternative, in their want of counsel and confidence to come to such a shocking result, against an unarmed prisoner, who was in amity with them, advice was asked, yet of only five among fifty assembled, of the ministers of religion. The fate of Agag followed of course.

"In case Onkus shall refuse to *execute justice* upon Miantunnomoh," say our records, he was to be sent by water to Massachusetts. Such an unwelcome visit from one who had been often here in his prosperity and pride of independence was to be avoided. How much those of Connecticut desired his destruction, may easily be judged by their undertaking to send "12 *or* 14 *musketeers* home with Onkus to abide a time with him for his defence." If so low was their estimate of the peril from the subjects of the chieftain in revenge of his death, how slight must have been the danger from their want of gratitude for restoring him to liberty and power?

With profound regret I am compelled to express a suspicion, that means of sufficient influence would easily have been found for the security of themselves, the pacifying of Onkus, and the preservation of Miantunnomoh, had he not encouraged the sale of Shaomet and Patuxet to Gorton and his heterodox associates. This idea had been unwillingly entertained years before I knew the comment of Governour Stephen Hopkins, 2 Hist. Coll. IX. 202, with which I close this unhappy subject: "The savage soul of Uncas doubted, whether he ought to take away the life of a great king, who had fallen into his hands by misfortune; and to resolve this doubt, he applied to the christian commissioners of the four united colonies, who met at Hartford,* in September, 1644: They

* It should be Boston, 1643. Trumbull, I. 133. hastily says, the commissioners for Plimouth are not on record this year. Their names are signed to the acts.

among the Indians to cut off all the English, and that Miantunnomoh was the head and contriver of it. 2. He was of a turbulent and proud spirit, and would never be at rest. 3. Although he had promised us in the open court to send the Pequod to Onkus, who had shot him in the arm with intent to have killed him, (which was by the procurement of Miantunnomoh as it did probably appear,) yet in his way homeward he killed him. 4. He beat one of Pumham's men and took away his wampom, and then bid him go and complain to the Massachusetts.

According to this agreement the commissioners, at their return to Connecticut, sent for Onkus, and acquainted him therewith, who readily undertook the execution, and taking Miantunnomoh along with him, in the way between Hartford and Windsor, (where Onkus ||hath|| some men dwell,) Onkus' brother, following after Miantunnomoh, clave his head with an hatchet, some English being present.[1] And that the Indians might know that the English did approve of it, they sent 12 or 14 musketeers home with Onkus to abide a time with him for his defence, if need should be.

Mo. 6.] About the 20th of this month the ships which went with La Tour came back safe, not one person missing or sick. But the report of their actions was offensive and grievous to us;

||had||

were less scrupulous, and ordered Uncas to carry Myantonomo out of their jurisdiction, and slay him; but kindly added, that he should not be tortured; they sent some persons to see execution done, who had the satisfaction to see the captive king murdered in cold blood. This was the end of Myantonomo, the most potent Indian prince the people of New England had ever any concern with; and this was the reward he received for assisting them seven years before, in their war with the Pequots. Surely a Rhode Island man may be permitted to mourn his unhappy fate, and drop a tear on the ashes of Myantonomo, who, with his uncle Conanicus, were the best friends and greatest benefactors the colony ever had: They kindly received, fed, and protected the first settlers of it, when they were in distress, and were strangers and exiles, and all mankind else were their enemies; and by this kindness to them, drew upon themselves the resentment of the neighbouring colonies, and hastened the untimely end of the young king."

1 Trumbull I. 135, relates that "Uncas cut out a large piece of his shoulder, and ate it in savage triumph!" He said, "it was the sweetest meat he ever ate; it made his heart strong." This was the report, I suppose, of the two English, who were deputed to witness the butchery. From the same author, we learn, that Miantunnomoh was buried at the same place, and a great heap, or pillar, was erected on the spot; "this memorable event gave the place the name of Sachem's Plain." It is in the eastern part of the town of Norwich. This is strangely at variance with our history, which represents the place, as to me seems much the most probable, between Hartford and Windsor.

for when they drew near to La Tour's place, D'Aulnay, having discovered them, set sail with his vessels (being two ships and a pinnace) and stood right home to Port Royal. Ours pursued them, but could not fetch them up, but they ran their ships on ground in the harbour and began to fortify themselves: whereupon ours sent a boat to D'Aulnay with the governour's letter and a letter from Captain Hawkins, who by agreement among themselves was commander in chief. The messenger who carried the letters, being one who could speak French well, was carried blindfold into the house and there kept six or seven hours, and all D'Aulnay's company plied for their fortifying with palisadoes, and the friars as busy as any, and encouraging the women who cried pitifully, telling them we were infidels and hereticks. D'Aulnay would not open La Tour's letter, because he did not style him Lieutenant General, &c. but he returned answer to the governour and to Captain Hawkins, and sent him a copy of the arrest against La Tour, and showed the original to the messenger, but refused to come to any terms of peace. Upon this La Tour urged much to have our men to assault him, but they refused. Then he desired that some of ours might be landed with his to do some mischief to D'Aulnay. Captain Hawkins would send none, but gave leave to any that would go; whereupon some 30 of ours went with La Tour's men, and were encountered by D'Aulnay's men, who had fortified themselves by his mill, but were beaten out with loss of three of their men, and none slain on our side nor wounded, only three of La Tour's men were wounded. They set the mill on fire and burnt some standing corn and retired to their ships with one prisoner whom they took in the mill. D'Aulnay shot with his ordnance at their boats as they went aboard, but missed them, nor did our ships make one shot at him again, but set sail and went to La Tour's fort. While they lay there D'Aulnay's pinnace came, supposing he and his ships had been still there, and brought in her 400 moose skins and 400 beaver skins. These they took without any resistance and divided them; one third La Tour had and the pinnace, one third to the ships and the other to the men. So they continued there till their time was near expired, and were paid their hire and returned, one ship coming a good time before the other; and the pinnace went up John's River some 20 leagues and loaded with coal. They brought a piece of white marble, whereof there is great store near his fort, which makes very good lime.

Mo. 7. The Indians near the Dutch, having killed 15 men, as is before related, proceeded on and began to set upon the English who dwelt under the Dutch. They came to Mrs. Hutchinson's in way of friendly neighbourhood, as they had been accustomed, and taking their opportunity, killed her and Mr. Collins her son in law, (who had been kept prisoner in Boston, as is before related,) and all her family, and such of Mr. Throckmorton's and Mr. Cornhill's families as were at home; in all sixteen, and put their cattle into their houses and there burnt them.[1] By a good providence of God there was a boat came in there at the same instant, to which some women and children fled, and so were saved, but two of the boatmen going up to the houses were shot and killed.

These people had cast off ordinances and churches, and now at last their own people, and for larger accommodation had subjected themselves to the Dutch and dwelt scatteringly near a mile asunder: and some that escaped, who had removed only for want (as they said) of hay for their cattle which increased much, now coming back again to Aquiday, they wanted cattle for their grass[2]. These Indians having killed and driven away all the English upon the main as far as Stamford, (for so far the Dutch had gained possession by the English,) they passed on to Long Island and there assaulted the Lady Moodey in her house divers times, for there were 40 men gathered thither to defend it.

These Indians at the same time set upon the Dutch with an implacable fury, and killed all they could come by, and burnt their houses and killed their cattle without any resistance, so as the governour and such as escaped betook themselves to their fort at Monhaton, and there lived and eat up their cattle.

4.] There was an assembly at Cambridge of all the elders in the country, (about 50 in all,) such of the ruling elders as would were present also, but none else. They sat in the college, and

---

1 Welde's Rise, Reign and Ruin of the Antinomians contains this pious exultation at the destruction of Mrs. Hutchinson: "Now I am come to the last act of her tragedy, a most heavy stroak upon herself and hers, as I received it very lately from a godly hand in New England." "The Indians set upon them, and slew her, and all her family, her daughter, and her daughter's husband, and all their children, save one that escaped; (her own husband being dead before;) a dreadful blow. Some write that the Indians did burn her to death with fire, her house, and all the rest named that belonged to her; but I am not able to affirm by what kind of death they slew her, but slain it seems she is, according to all reports. I never heard that the Indians in those parts did ever before this commit the like outrage upon any one family, or families; and therefore God's hand is the more apparently seen herein, to pick out this woful woman, to make her, and those belonging to her, an unheard of heavy example of their cruelty above others."

2 Considering the gentle and catholic temper of Winthrop, who utters this sarcasm, we might presume, that others, of less amiable disposition, indulged in greater abuse of the inhabitants of Rhode Island, and may wonder at the humility of the seceders.

had their diet there after the manner of scholars' commons, but somewhat better, yet so ordered as it came not to above sixpence the meal for a person. Mr. Cotton and Mr. Hooker were chosen moderators. The principal occasion was because some of the elders went about to set up some things ||according|| to the presbytery, as of Newbury, &c. The assembly concluded against some parts of the presbyterial way, and the Newbury ministers took time to consider the arguments, &c.

7.] Upon the complaint of the English of Patuxet near Providence, who had submitted to our jurisdiction, and the two Indian sachems there, of the continual injuries offered them by Gorton and his company, the general court sent for them, by letter only, not in way of command, to come answer the complaints, and sent them letters of safe conduct. But they answered our messengers disdainfully, refused to come, but sent two letters full of blasphemy against the churches and magistracy, and other provoking terms, slighting all we could do against them. So that having sent three times, and receiving no other answer, we took testimonies against them both of English and Indians, and determined to proceed with them by force. And because they had told our messengers the last time, that if we had any thing to say to them, if we would come to them, they would do us justice therein, therefore we wrote to them to this effect, viz. To the end that our justice and moderation might appear to all men, we would condescend so far to them as to send commissioners to hear their answers and allegations, and if thereupon they would give us such satisfaction as should be just, we would leave them in peace, if otherwise, we would proceed by force of arms; and signified withal that we would send a sufficient guard with our commissioners. For seeing they would not trust themselves with us upon our safe conduct, we had no reason to trust ourselves with them upon their bare courtesy. And accordingly we sent the next week Captain George Cook,[1] Lieutenant Atherton,[2] and Edward Johnson with commis-

||undoing||

---

1 Johnson, lib. II. c. 26, says "*now* Colonel Cook in the wars of Ireland," that is 1651. I find him a deputy from Cambridge in May 1636, and not after for some years, though Joseph Cooke, perhaps his brother, often appears. He probably died in Oliver's service.

2 Humphrey Atherton deserves much honour in our early annals, though probably he had not come over long before his admission, as a freeman, 2 May 1638. In September after, he was a deputy for Dorchester, again in May 1639 and in June 1641. He had, I suppose, an interest at Springfield, for he represented that town in 1653, when he was chosen speaker, yet lived at Dorchester.

sion and instructions, (the instructions would here be inserted at large,) and with them 40 soldiers.

They came to Providence, and by the way received another letter from Gorton, of the like contents with the former, and told them plainly they were prepared for them, &c. Being come near, they found they had put themselves all into one house, which they had made musket proof with two flankers. But by the mediation

---

Next year he was chosen assistant, and major general about the same time, succeeding Sedgwick in that office. Johnson lib. I. c. 45, and lib. II. c. 26 honours him. He was much employed in the negotiations with the Indians, and made use of his influence with them in a great purchase for himself and private associates within the colony of Rhode Island; but after all his services there was something uncommonly melancholy in his death. Hubbard, 641, says "in the year 1665, Mr. Atherton, the chief military officer in New England, died suddenly by a *fall* from his horse, who likewise" [he had just before related the obloquy with which the Rev. John Norton was oppressed] "was called to conflict with the strife of tongues, and the manner of his death also noted as a judgment. Moses and Aaron must be stoned when the mixed multitude in Israel have not their will, who by the perverseness of their minds become the more obdurate in their errours by the solemn strokes of Providence, which if rightly improved might lead them to repentance, which is the use thereof." In this date, as in very many others, Hubbard is wrong. The tombstone, according to Alden I. 238, says he died September 16, 1661, and the contemporary Journal of Rev. Peter Hobart of Hingham, copy of which is in my possession, mentioning the fall from his horse *at Boston*, has the same date, "being Monday, buried Friday following." In our Probate records IV. 31 is written, "at a meeting at the governour's house, this 27 September, 1661, power of administration to the estate of the late Major General Humphrey Atherton is granted to Jonathan Atherton, his eldest son, and Timothy Mather, James Throwbridge and Obadiah Swift, three of his sons in law, in behalf of the widow, themselves and rest of the children, they bringing in an inventory of that estate to the next county court, and giving security to administer according to law." In the same volume p. 191, "at an adjournment of the county court in Boston 6 July, 1662, this court doth order that the estate of Major Humphrey Atherton lately deceased, his inventory amounting to 900 pounds, besides a farm of 700 acres near Worronoco, shall be divided in manner following, i. e. to the widow, his late mansion house with the land adjoining, and meadow at little neck, and the division on this side Naponsett, being all valued at about 204 pounds, the same to enjoy during her life, she maintaining the house and fences from time to time and at all times in good and sufficient repair, and her executors and administrators to stand bound to leave the same so at her decease; also to the said widow, besides the said house and lands, about 96 pounds 14., to be let her out of the goods and chattels and debts according to a schedule hereunto annexed; and the remainder of the said estate, all just debts being first paid, to be divided among the children of the said Major Atherton, to his eldest son a double portion, and the rest equally to be shares, and in like manner the reversion of the house and land assigned to the widow to be divided amongst the children after her decease, provided always such of the children as have received any part of their portions during their father's life shall be abated proportionably in the division of the said estate."

Hope Atherton, a son of the Major General, H. C. 1665, was the first minister of Hatfield. He was exposed to much suffering in the great Indian war of 1675 and 1676, and on 18 May of the latter year served as chaplain to the troops unof others of ||Providence,|| they came to parley, and then offered to refer their cause to arbitrators, (alleging that we were parties and so not equal judges,) so as some of them might be of Providence or of Aquiday, and offered their cattle for security to abide the order, &c. Our commissioners, through importunity of themselves and others of Providence, were content to send to us to know our minds about it. Their letter came to us, when a committee, appointed by the general court, were met about the tidings of Miantunnomoh's death; so calling into us five or six of the elders who were near at hand, we considered of the motion, and agreed that it was neither seasonable nor reasonable, neither safe nor honourable for us to accept of such a proposition. 1. Because they would never offer us any terms of peace before we had sent our soldiers. 2. Because the ground of it was false, for we were not parties in the case between the Indians and them, but the proper judges, they being all within our jurisdiction by the Indians and English their own grant. 3. They were no state, but a few fugitives living without law or government, and so not honourable for us to join with them in such a course. 4. The parties whom they

||providence||

der Captain Turner, who performed a memorable service against the enemy at the falls at Montague on Connecticut river. In the disastrous retreat "he was separated from the troops and lost in the woods. After wandering at random until next morning, despairing of finding the route home, he came to the resolution of delivering himself to the enemy, and the next day approaching a party, by signs he offered himself as a prisoner; but they refused to receive him. When he approached and called to them, they fled from his presence and none offered to molest him, or discovered the least hostility; fear seemed rather to predominate, and Mr. Atherton was left to his own fate. In this strange dilemma, he determined, if possible, to find the river, and follow it to Hatfield, and after a devious march of several days, of uncommon fatigue, hunger and anxiety, was restored to his people. This singular conduct of the Indians was attributed to some of their religious superstitions. Probably Mr. Atherton's dress indicated his profession; and having some knowledge of the sacredness of his office, these superstitious notions led them to consider him as a superior being." See the very interesting history of the Indian Wars by General Epaphras Hoyt, p. 133–4, whose narrative, in this part, is taken from the Appendix to Williams's Redeemed Captive and the sermon of Atherton preached the next Sunday after his return.

[By the benevolence of my friend, John Farmer, Esquire, my conjecture, as to the period of Atherton's coming over, is partially confirmed. He informs me, that Dorchester church records show, that A. signed the covenant in 1636. Perhaps some of the children, referred to in the order of court, were born before, for my informant gives me record of baptisms of Rest 26, 3, 1639, Increase 11, 2, 1641, Thankful 29, 2, 1644, Hope 30, 6, 1646, Watching 24, 6, 1651, Patience 2, 2, 1654. Charles Humphrey Atherton, H. C. 1794, a distinguished gentleman of Amherst, N. H. is not descended from the Major General, but from James, perhaps a brother of the principal subject of this note.]

would refer it unto were such as were rejected by us, and all the governments in the country, and besides, not men likely to be equal to us, or able to judge of the cause. 5. Their blasphemous and reviling writings, &c. were not matters fit to be compounded by arbitrament, but to be purged away only by repentance and public satisfaction, or else by public punishment.

And lastly the commission and instructions being given them by the general court, it was not in our power to alter them; so accordingly we wrote to our commissioners to proceed, which accordingly they did, and approached the house, where they had fortified themselves, with trenches so near as they might fire the house, which they attempted two or three times, but they within quenched it. At last three of them escaped out and ran away, and the rest yielded and were brought to Boston and were committed to the prison. It was a special providence of God that neither any of them nor of ours were slain or hurt, though many shot passed between them, but every man returned safe and hale. See more, page [blank].

Here wants the beginning which may be supplied out of the records. 64.

Other affairs were transacted by the commissioners of the United Colonies, as writing letters to the Swedish governour in Delaware river, concerning the foul injuries offered by him to Mr. Lamberton and those people whom New Haven had planted there, and also to the Dutch governour about the injuries his agent there had also offered and done to them, as burning down their trading house, joining with the Swedes against them, &c. But this was inserted in the letter which the general court sent to him in further answer of that which he sent to them, as is expressed herebefore; in which letter we declared the complaints which had been made by our confederates both of Hartford and New Haven, of their injurious dealings, as well at Hartford and New Haven as at Delaware: also our opinion of the justice of the cause of Hartford in respect of title of the land in question between them, which we could not change, except we might see more light than had yet appeared to us by the title the Dutch insisted upon, nor might we desert either of our confederates in a righteous cause. And we gave also commission to Mr. Lamberton to go treat with the Swedish governour about satisfaction for those injuries and damages, and to agree with him about settling their trade and plantation. This Swedish governour demeaned himself as if he had neither christian nor moral conscience, getting Mr. Lamberton into his power by feigned and false pretences, and keeping him prisoner and some of his men, labouring by promises and threats to draw them to accuse him to have conspired with the Indians to cut off the Swedes and Dutch, and not prevailing these ways, then by attempting to make them drunk, that so he might draw something from them: and in the end, (though he could gain no testimony,) yet he forced him to pay [blank] weight of beaver before he would set him at liberty. He is also a man very furious and passionate, cursing and swearing, and also reviling the English of New Haven as runagates, &c. and himself with his own hands put irons upon one of Mr. Lamberton's men, and went also to the houses of those few families planted there, and forced some of them to swear allegiance to the crown of Sweden, though he had no colour of title to that place, and such as would not, he drave away, &c. All these things were clearly proved by Mr. Lamberton's relation, and by other testimony upon oath, but this was ||before he was sent|| with commission.

About this time our governour received letters from Philip Bell, Esq. governour of Barbados, complaining of the distracted condition of that island in regard of divers ||²sects|| of familists sprung up there, and their turbulent practices, which had forced him to proceed against some of them by banishment, and others of mean quality by whipping; and earnestly desiring us to send them some godly ministers and other good people. The governour imparted the letter to the court and elders, but none of our ministers would go thither, and the governour returned answer accordingly.

8. 12]. The new sachem of Narraganset, Miantunnomoh's brother called Pesecus, a young man about 20, sent a present to our governour, viz. an otter coat and girdle of wampom, and some other wampom, in all worth about 15 pounds, and desired peace and friendship with us, and withal that we would not aid Onkus against him, whom he intended to make war upon in revenge of his brother's death. Our governour answered the messengers, that we were willing to have peace and friendship with him, and to that end had sent messengers to Canonicus, (whom it seemed they met with by the way,) but we desired withal that there might be peace with all Indians also, both Onkus and others, and that we had also sent to Ousamekin to that end; therefore except their sachem would agree to it, we could not receive his present. They replied that they had no instructions about the matter, but would return back and acquaint their sachem with it, and return to us again, and desired to leave their present with our governour in the mean time, which he agreed unto.

||sent before|| ||²sorts||

13.] Captain Cook and his company, which were sent out against Gorton, returned to Boston, and the captives, being nine, were brought to the governour his house in a military order, viz. the soldiers being in two files, and after every five or six soldiers a prisoner. So being before his door, the commissioners came in, and after the governour had saluted them, he went forth with them, and passing through the files, welcomed them home, blessing God for preserving and prospering them, and gave them all thanks for their pains and good carriage, and desired of the captain a list of their names, that the court, &c. might know them if hereafter there should be occasion to make use of such men. This good acceptance and commendation of their service gave many of them more content than their wages, (which yet was very liberal ||ten shillings|| per week, and they to victual themselves, and it is needful in all such commonwealths where the state desires to be served by volunteers.) Then having conferred privately with the commissioners, he caused the prisoners to be brought before him in his hall, where was a great assembly, and there laid before them their contemptuous carriage towards us, and their obstinacy against all the fair means and moderation we had used to reform them and bring them to do right to those of ours whom they had wronged, and how the Lord had now justly delivered them into our hands. They pleaded in their excuse that they were not of our jurisdiction, and that though they had now yielded themselves to come and answer before us, yet they yielded not as prisoners. The governour replied, they were brought to him as taken in war, and so our commissioners had informed, but if they could plead any other quarter or agreement our commissioners had made with them, we must and would perform it; to which they made no answer. So the governour committed them to the marshall to convey to the common prison, and gave order they should be well provided for both for lodging and diet. Then he went forth again with the captain, and the soldiers gave him three vollies of shot and so departed to the inn, where the governour had appointed some refreshing to be provided for them above their wages.

The next Lord's day in the forenoon, the prisoners would not come to the meeting, so as the magistrates determined they should be compelled.[1] They agreed to come, so as they might have li-

||blank||

---

1 Nothing marks more the habits of our fathers, than this perverse desire that prisoners of erroneous opinions should come to hear the orthodox preachers.

berty after sermon to speak, if they had occasion. The magistrates' answer was, that they did leave the ordering of things in the church to the elders, but there was no doubt but they might have leave to speak, so as they spake the words of truth and sobriety. So in the afternoon they came, and were placed in the fourth seat right before the elders. Mr. Cotton (in his ordinary text) taught ||then|| out of Acts 19. of Demetrius pleading for Diana's silver shrines or temples, &c. After sermon Gorton desired leave to speak, which being granted, he repeated the points of Mr. Cotton's sermon, and coming to that of the silver shrines, he said that in the church there was nothing now but Christ, so that all our ordinances, ministers, sacraments, &c. were but men's inventions for show and pomp, and no other than those silver shrines of Diana. He said also that if Christ lived eternally, then he died eternally; and it appeared both by his letters and examinations that he held that Christ was incarnate in Adam, and that he was that image of God wherein Adam was created, and that the chief work and merit was in that his incarnation, in that he became such a thing, so mean, &c. and that his being born after of the Virgin Mary and suffering, &c. was but a manifestation of his sufferings &c. in Adam. Likewise in his letters he condemned and reviled magistracy, calling it an idol, alleging that a man might as well be a slave to his belly as to his own species: yet being examined he would acknowledge magistracy to be an ordinance of God in the world as marriage was, viz. no other magistracy but what was natural, as the father over his wife and children, and an hereditary prince over his subjects.

When the general court was assembled, Gorton and his company were brought forth upon the lecture day at Boston, and there, before a great assembly, the governour declared the cause and manner of our proceeding against them, and their letters were openly read, and all objections answered. As 1. That they were not within our jurisdiction. To this was answered. 1. That they were either within Plimouth or Mr. Fenwick, and they had yielded their power to us in this cause. 2. If they were under no jurisdiction, then had we none to complain unto for redress of our injuries, and then we must either right ourselves and our subjects by force of arms, or else we must sit still under all their reproaches

||them||

It has in some parts of the country, and in former times here, been customary to carry criminals, condemned to death, on the Sunday preceding their execution, to the public service of the church; but it seems hard to compel the accused so to hear themselves condemned before trial.

and injuries, among which they had this insolent passage.—"We do more disdain that you should send for us to come to you, than you could do, if we should send for the chiefest among you to come up to us, and be employed according to our pleasure in such works as we should appoint you."

As for their opinions, we did not meddle with them for those, otherwise than they had given us occasion by their letters to us, and by their free and open publishing them amongst us, for we wrote to them only about civil controversies between them and our people, and gave them no occasion to vent their blasphemings and revilings, &c. And for their title to the Indians' land, we had divers times desired them to make it appear, but they always refused, even to our commissioners whom we sent last to them; and since they were in prison, we offered to send for any witnesses they would desire, but still they refused, so that our title appearing good, and we having now regained our possession, we need not question them any more about that. Their letters being read, they were demanded severally if they would maintain those things which were contained therein. They answered they would in that sense wherein they wrote them.

After this they were brought before the court severally to be examined, (divers of the elders being desired to be present,) and because they had said they could give a good interpretation of all they had written, they were examined upon the particular passages. But the interpretation they gave being contradictory to their expressions, they were demanded then if they would retract those expressions, but that they refused, and said still that they should then deny the truth. For instance in one or two; their letters were directed, one to their neighbours of the Massachusetts, and the other of them to the great honoured idol ||general|| of the Massachusetts, and by a messenger of their own delivered to our governour, and many passages in both letters particularly applied to our courts, our magistrates, our elders, &c. yet in their examinations about their reproachful passages, they answered, that they meant them of the corrupt estate of mankind in general and not of us, &c. So whereas in their letters they impute it to us as an errour, that we teach that Christ died actually only when he suffered under Pontius Pilate, and before only in types, upon their examination they say that their meaning was, that his death was actual to the faith of the fathers under the law, which is in effect no other than we hold, yet they account it an errour in us, and would not retract that charge. One of the elders had been in the prison with them, and had conferred with them about their

||gentleman||

opinions, and they expressed their agreement with him in every point, so as he intended to move for favour for them, but when he heard their answer upon their examination, he found how he had been deluded by them; for they excel the jesuits in the ||art|| of equivocation, and regard not how false they speak to all other men's apprehensions, so they keep to the rules of their own meaning. Gorton maintained, that the image of God wherein Adam was created was Christ, and so the loss of that image was the death of Christ, and the restoring of it in ||²regeneration|| was Christ's resurrection, and so the death of him that was born of the Virgin Mary was but a manifestation of the former.[1] In their letters, &c. they condemned all ordinances in the church, calling baptism an abomination, and the Lord's supper the juice of a poor silly grape turned into the blood of Christ by the skill of our magicians, &c. Yet upon examination they would say they did allow them to be the ordinances of Christ; but their meaning was that they were to continue no longer than the infancy of the church lasted, (and but to novices then,) for after the revelation was written they were to cease, for there is no mention of them, say they, in that book.

They were all illiterate men, the ablest of them could not write true English, no not common words, yet they would take upon them the interpretation of the most difficult places of scripture, and wrest them any way to serve their own turns: as to give one instance for many. Mr. Cotton pressing them with that in Acts 10. "Who can forbid water why these should not be baptized? so he commanded them to be baptized" they interpret thus. Who can deny but these have been baptized, seeing they have received the Holy Ghost, &c. so he allowed them to have been baptized. This shift they were put to that they might maintain their former opinion, That such as have been baptized with the Holy Ghost need not the outward baptism.[2]

||act|| ||²generation||

---

1 This last sentence, representing some of the strange notions of the chief prisoner, which seem hardly worthy to be called jesuitical, is written in the margin. It is not very closely connected with the preceding, and indeed requires some critic illuminated with the spirit of Gortonism to bring it to the *rule of their own meaning.*

2 The illiterate Gorton makes a very sensible justification against Morton's Memorial, Hutch. I. appx. xx. There was a universal dread of having any ministers, who had not been regularly educated, and some allowance must be made for the opinions of Winthrop and the rest of the magistrates on this account. But men who have enjoyed great advantages of education may be led to employ language inconsistent with scripture and shocking to reason, without

The court and the elders spent near a whole day in discovery of Gorton's deep mysteries which he had boasted of in his letters, and to bring him to conviction, but all was in vain. Much pains was also taken with the rest, but to as little effect. They would acknowledge no errour or fault in their writings, and yet would seem sometimes to consent with us in the truth.

After all these examinations the court began to consult about their sentence. The judgment of the elders also had been demanded about their blasphemous speeches and opinions, what punishment was due by the word of God. Their answer was first in writing, that if they should maintain them as expressed in their writings, their offence deserved death by the law of God. The same some of them declared after in open court. But before the court would proceed to determine of their sentence, they agreed first upon their charge, and then calling them all publicly they declared to them what they had to charge them with, out of their letter and speeches. Their charge was this, viz. They were charged to be blasphemous enemies of the true religion of our Lord Jesus Christ, and of all his holy ordinances, and likewise of all civil government among his people, and particularly within this jurisdiction. Then they were demanded whether they did acknowledge this charge to be just, and did submit to it, or what exceptions they had against it. They answered they did not acknowledge it to be just, but they took no particular exceptions to it, but fell into some cavilling speeches, so they were returned to prison again. Being in prison they behaved insolently towards their keeper, and spake evil of the magistrates. Whereupon some of the magistrates were very earnest to have irons presently put upon them. Others thought it better to forbear all such severity till their sentence were passed. This latter opinion prevailed.

After divers means had been used both in public and private to reclaim them, and all proving fruitless, the court proceeded to consider of their sentence, in which the court was much divided. All the magistrates, save three, were of opinion that Gorton ought to die, but the greatest number of the deputies dissenting, that vote did not pass. In the end all agreed upon this sentence, for seven of them, viz. that they should be dispersed into seven several towns, and there kept to work for their living, and wear

---

justly being liable to the charge of impious blasphemy. A few years since, in one of the largest churches of Boston, the teacher spoke of the crucifixion as Deicide, which in English must be rendered murder of God ; yet neither he nor his hearers suffered, I believe, in any degree.

irons upon one leg, and not to depart the limits of the town, nor by word or writing maintain any of their blasphemous or wicked errours upon pain of death, only ||with|| exception for speech with any of the elders, or any other licensed by any magistrate to confer with them; this censure to continue during the pleasure of the court.[1]

There were three more taken in the house with them, but be-

||the||

1 Silence might perhaps become the commentator on this lamentable delusion; but this narrative almost defies the power of comment to enhance or mitigate the injustice of our government. It is some consolation, however, that three of the magistrates and a majority of the deputies rejected the horrible judgment of the elders, that the offences deserved death. Ridicule they might have deserved, but neglect would have been the most appropriate sentence. We cannot doubt, that our fathers thought the prisoners were justly within our jurisdiction, and this first errour led to the invasion of their humble colony, which ought to have been as secure from process as ours was from them. After the usurpation, the civil wrong, which was the first pretence of complaint, seems to have merged in their theological pravity. Our rulers assumed the right of proceeding against them as heretics, because we had injuriously acquired the power of inquiry into the title of their lands. If only this History remained, an exact measure of justice could now be rendered to these unfortunate mysticks by one who reads only the tale of their persecutors. But the story of the sufferers written more than twenty years after, in a short petition to the royal commissioners, may be seen in 2 Hist. Coll. VIII. 68—70, and Governour Hopkins still later by a hundred years has embodied their wrongs in a very brief manner, 2 Hist. Coll. IX. 199—201. Both must be read by him who would know the whole truth. The consummation of the tyranny I extract from our records II. p. 39—41:

"Upon much examination and serious consideration of your writings, with your answers about them, we do charge you to be a blasphemous enemy of the true religion of our Lord Jesus Christ and his holy ordinances, and also of all civil authority among the people of God, and particularly in this jurisdiction.

It is ordered that Samuel Gorton shall be confined to Charlestown, there to be set on work, and to wear such bolts or irons, as may hinder his escape, and to continue during the pleasure of the court, provided that if he shall break his said confinement, or shall in the mean time, either by speech or writing, publish, declare or maintain any of the blasphemous or abominable heresies, wherewith he hath been charged by the general court, contained in either of the two books sent unto us by him, or Randall Houlden, or shall reproach or reprove the churches of our Lord Jesus Christ in these United Colonies, or the civil government or the public ordinances of God therein, (unless it be by answer to some question propounded to him, or conference with any elder, or with any other licensed to speak with him privately under the hand of one of the assistants,) that immediately upon accusation of any such writing or speech he shall, by such assistant to whom such accusation shall be brought, be committed to prison till the next court of assistants, then and there to be tried by a jury, whether he hath so spoken or written, and upon his conviction thereof shall be condemned to death and executed. Dated the 3d of the 9mo. 1643.

John Wicks, Randall Houlden, Robert Potter, Richard Carder, Francis Weston and John Warner are confined upon the same conditions.

cause they had not their hands to the letters, they were dismissed, two of them upon a small ransom, as captives taken in war, and the third freely, for that he was but in his master's house, &c. A fourth, being found to be an ignorant young man, was only enjoined to abide in Watertown upon pain of the court's displeasure only.

§At the next court they were all sent away, because we found that they did corrupt some of our people, especially the women, by their heresies.[1]§

About a week after, we sent men to fetch so many of their cattle as might defray our charges, both of the soldiers and of the court, which spent many days about them, and for their expenses in prison. It came to in all about 160 pounds. There were three who escaped out of the house; these being sent for to come in, two of them did so, and one of them, because his hand was not to the letters, was freely discharged, the other was sent home upon his own bond to appear at the next court, (only some of his cattle were taken towards the charges.) There was a fourth who had his hand to the first letter, but he died before our soldiers went, and we left his whole estate to his wife and children. Their arms were all taken from them, and of their guns the court gave one fowling piece to Pumham and another to Saconoco, and liberty granted them to have powder as being now within our jurisdiction.

The Lord Bartemore being owner of much land near Vir-

John Wicks to Ipswich, Randall Houlden to Salem, Robert Potter to Rowley, Richard Carder to Roxbury, Francis Weston to Dorchester, John Warner to Boston,	All these are upon same conditions that Samuel Gorton abovenamed is.

William Waddell is confined to Watertown during the pleasure of the court, and if he escape, to be punished, as this court or the court of assistants shall think meet.

Richard Waterman is dismissed for the present, so that what is taken of his is to go toward payment of the charge, and the rest of his estate is bound in an 100 pounds, that he shall appear at the general court the 3d mo. and not to depart without license, and to submit to the order of the court.

Nicholas Power appearing and denying that he set his hand to the first book, was dismissed with an admonition."

1 It is strange, that so important a part of the history, though given in the margin of the original MS. should have been omitted in the former edition, for it fills the measure of our ancestors' policy. Part of the truth is told indeed in a later paragraph, but the whole is better. Though death had been threatened for speaking, yet when they were known to have corrupted some of the flock, these misguided prisoners were liberated, because their keepers were in danger.

ginia, being himself a papist, and his brother Mr. Calvert the governour there a papist also, but the colony consisted both of protestants and papists, he wrote a letter to Captain Gibbons of Boston, and sent him a commission, wherein he made tender of land in Maryland to any of ours that would transport themselves thither, with free liberty of religion, and all other privileges which the place afforded, paying such annual rent as should be agreed upon; but our captain had no mind to further his desire herein, nor had any of our people temptation that way.

5. 13.] One Captain John Chaddock, son of him that was governour of Bermuda, a godly gentleman, but late removing from them with his family and about 100 more to Trinidado, where himself and wife and most of his company died, arrived here in a man of war of about 100 tons, set forth by the Earl of Warwick. He came hither for planters for Trinidado, (Mr. Humfry having told the Earl that he might be supplied from hence,) but here was not any that would enter upon that voyage, &c. So La Tour having a pinnace here at the same time, they hired Captain Chaddock for two months at 200 pounds the month, partly to convoy the pinnace home from the danger of D'Aulnay his vessels, and partly for other service against D'Aulnay there. But when they came, they found D'Aulnay gone into France, and a new fort raised at Port Royal, and a pinnace ready to go forth to trade, so they kept her in so long till the season was over and his two months out, and then he returned to Boston. When he was come in near the town, his men going up upon the main yard to hand in the sail, the main tie brake, and the yard falling down shook off five men into the sea, and though it were calm and smooth water, yet not having their boat out, three of them were drowned. One of these had taken some things out of the deserted castle, as they went out. Notwithstanding this sad accident, yet so soon as they came on shore, they fell to drinking, &c. and that evening, the cap-

---

From the terms of the court's order, which I extract from Vol. II. 44, it must be inferred that no place but England was left for the unhappy schismatics. To England they went, and we must rejoice that they obtained justice. "It is ordered that Samuel Gorton and the rest of that company, who now stand confined, shall be set at liberty, provided that if they, or any of them, shall after fourteen days after such enlargement come within any part of our jurisdiction, either in the Massachusetts, or in or near Providence, or any of the lands of Pumham or Sachonocho, or elsewhere within our jurisdiction, then such person or persons shall be apprehended, wheresoever they may be taken, and shall suffer death by course of law, provided also that during all their continuance in our bounds inhabiting for the said time of fourteen days, they shall be still bound to the rest of the articles of their former confinement upon the penalty therein expressed."

tain and his master being at supper and having drank too much, the captain began to speak evil of the country, swearing fearfully, that we were a base heathen people. His master answered that he had no reason to say so, for it was the best place that ever he came in. Upon these and other speeches the captain arose and drew his sword, and the master drew forth his pistol, but the company staying them from doing any mischief, the captain sware blood and wounds he would kill him. For this they were brought before the court, and the captain fined 20 pounds and committed to the marshall till he gave security for it. The master for that he was in drink, as he ingenuously acknowledged, &c. was fined only 10 shillings, but was set at liberty from the captain, who had formerly misused other of his men, and was a very proud and intemperate man. But because the ship was the Earl of Warwick's, who had always been forward to do good to our colony, we wrote to him, that the fine should be reserved to be at his lordship's disposing, when he should please to command or call for it. See the next page.

10. 27.] By order of the general court all the magistrates and the teaching elders of the six nearest churches were appointed to be forever governours of the college, and this day they met at Cambridge and considered of the officers of the college, and chose a treasurer, H. Pelham, Esq. being the first in that office.

This day five ships set sail from Boston; three of them were built here, two of 300 tons and the other of 160. One of them was bound for London with many passengers, men of chief rank in the country, and great store of beaver. Their adventure was very great, considering the doubtful estate of the affairs of England, but many prayers of the churches went with them and followed after them.

11. 2.] Captain Chaddock having bought from the French a pinnace of about 30 tons, (which La Tour sold him for ||a demiculverin|| and was the same which was taken before from D'Aulnay,) he had manned and fitted her to go in her to Trinidado, and riding before Boston ready to depart, and eight men aboard her, one striking fire with a pistol, two barrels of powder took fire and blew her up: five of the men being in the cabin were destroyed, and the other three being in the other part were much scorched and hurt, but got into their boat and were saved. The captain himself was then on shore at Boston. It is observable that these men making no use of the sudden loss of three of their company, but falling to drinking, &c. that very evening this judgment came thus upon them. It is also to be observed that two

||blank||

vessels have thus been blown up in our harbour, and both belonging to such as despised us and the ordinance of God amongst us. See more, page [blank].

About this time Captain Daniel Patrick was killed at Stamford by a Dutchman, who shot him dead with a pistol. This captain was entertained by us out of Holland (where he was a common soldier of the Prince's guard) to exercise our men. We made him a captain, and maintained him. After, he was admitted a member of the church of Watertown and a freeman. But he grew very proud and vicious, for though he had a wife of his own, a good Dutch woman and comely, yet he despised her and followed after other women; and perceiving that he was discovered, and that such evil courses would not be endured here, and being withal of a vain and unsettled disposition, he went from us, and sat §down§ within twenty miles of the Dutch, and put himself under their protection, and joined to their church, without being dismissed from Watertown: but when the Indians arose in those parts, he fled to Stamford and there was slain. The Dutchman who killed him was apprehended, but made an escape; and this was the ||fruit|| of his wicked course and breach of covenant with his wife, with the church, and with that state who had called him and maintained him, and he found his death from that hand where he sought protection. It is observable that he was killed upon the Lord's day in the time of afternoon exercise (for he seldom went to the public assemblies.) It was in Captain Underhill's house. The Dutchman had charged him with treachery, for causing 120 men to come to him upon his promise to direct them to the Indians, &c. but deluded them. Whereupon the captain gave him ill language and spit in his face, and turning to go out, the Dutchman shot him behind in the head, so he fell down dead and never spake. The murderer escaped out of custody.

10. 3.] The Hopewell, a ship of Boston, about 60 tons, arrived; the freight was wines, pitch, sugar, ginger, &c. She had her lading at Palma an island near Teneriffe. The Spaniards used our people courteously, but put them to give security ||[2]by|| some English merchants residing there to discharge their cargoes at Boston; for they would not have the Portugals of the ||[3]Madeiras|| to have any goods from them. She performed her voyage in four months. She went a second voyage thither soon after, but was never heard of. Her lading was corn in bulk.

At this time came over Thomas Morton, our professed old adversary, who had set forth a book against us, and written reproachful and menacing letters to some of us.

||first|| ||[2]to|| ||[3]blank||

Some of Watertown began a plantation at Martin's Vineyard beyond Cape Cod, and divers families going thither, they procured a young man, one Mr. [1]Green, a scholar, to be their minister, in hopes soon to gather a church there. He went not.[2]

Others of the same town began also a plantation at [3]Nashaway some 15 miles N. W. from Sudbury.

11. 18.] About midnight, three men, coming in a boat to Boston, saw two lights arise out of the water near the north point of the town cove, in form like a man, and went at a small distance to the town, and so to the south point, and there vanished away. They saw them about a quarter of an hour, being between the town and the governour's garden. The like was seen by many, a week after, arising about Castle Island and in one fifth of an hour came to John Gallop's point.

The country being weary of the charge of maintaining Castle

---

1 Notice of his early death, after being settled as the first minister of Reading only two and a half years, will be seen in the progress of this volume. Hubbard, 416, mentions his name of baptism, Henry, which Mather omitted. Johnson, lib. II. c. 25 honours him with verses, of which the first is, perhaps, the best in his book:

On earth's bed thou at noon hast laid thy head.

2 The church, however, was gathered, and Thomas Mayhew jr. ordained its pastor. It is remarkable, that so great neglect of the early history of the Vineyard is found in the original historians. Thomas Mayhew, the father of that colony, had been admitted a freeman 14 May 1634, at the same time with Governour Haynes, Cotton, Hooker, and Stone, whom I therefore presume he accompanied in the Griffin, which arrived in September preceding. He was a deputy from Watertown at the general court, 8 September 1636, again in May 1637, and in the eleven following courts. He lived to the mature age of ninety, governed Martha's vineyard many years, and is, with a numerous list of descendants, honoured in the highest rank of benevolent labourers in the divine employment of civilizing the Indians. Very full memorials of him and his posterity are to be seen in 2 Hist. Coll. III. from the pen of a most accurate and judicious enquirer. Of this family was the Rev. Jona. Mayhew, of Boston, one of the most distinguished asserters of civil and religious liberty.

3 Something more of this settlement will be found next year. Watertown was a hive, from which swarmed many new towns. It had been a matter of complaint, that towns were so thickly planted, as early as 1635, for the government at first permitted no man to live more than half a mile from the meeting house in his town; and Watertown people seem to have felt more than others this density of population. See Pratt's Apology in 2 Hist. Coll. VII. 126. By Tyler Bigelow, Esquire, of that town, I am furnished with one of their votes of that date, which explains their views of the evil: "Agreed by the consent of the freemen (in consideration there be too many inhabitants in the town, and the town thereby in danger to be ruinated) that no foreigner coming into the town, or any family arising among ourselves, shall have any benefit either of commonage, or land undivided, but what they shall purchase, except that they buy a man's right wholly in the town." Probably for a century and three quarters the fear has been removed.

Island, the last general court made an order to have it deserted and the ordnance fetched away; but Boston and other towns in the bay finding that thereupon the masters of some ships which came from England took occasion to slight us and to offer injury to our people, having liberty to ride and go out under no command, and considering also how easily any of our towns in the bay might be surprised, we having no strength without to stop them or to give notice of an enemy, they chose certain men out of the several towns who met at Boston to consider of some course of repairing and maintaining it at their proper charge: but the difficulty was, how to do it without offence to the general court who had ordered the deserting of it, &c.

The 18th of this month two lights were seen near Boston, (as is before mentioned,) and a week after the like was seen again. A light like the moon arose about the N. E. point in Boston, and met the former at Nottles Island, and there they closed in one, and then parted, and closed and parted divers times, and so went over the hill in the island and vanished. Sometimes they shot out flames and sometimes sparkles. This was about eight of the clock in the evening, and was seen by many. About the same time a voice was heard upon the water between Boston and Dorchester, calling out in a most dreadful manner, boy, boy, come away, come away: and it suddenly shifted from one place to another a great distance, about twenty times. It was heard by divers godly persons. About 14 days after, the same voice in the same dreadful manner was heard by others on the other side of the town toward Nottles Island.

These ||prodigies|| having some reference to the place where Captain Chaddock's pinnace was blown up a little before, gave occasion of speech of that man who was the cause of it, who professed himself to have skill in necromancy, and to have done some strange things in his way from Virginia hither, and was suspected to have murdered his master there; but the magistrates here had no notice of him till after he was blown up. This is to be observed that his fellows were all found, and others who were blown up in the former ship were also found, and others also who have miscarried by drowning, &c. have usually been found, but this man was never found.

12. 5.] Cutshamekin, and Agawam, and Josias, Chickatabot his heir, came to the governour, and in their own name and the names of all the sachems of Watchusett, and all the Indians from Merrimack to Tecticutt, tendered themselves to our government, and gave the governour a present of 30 fathom of wampom, and

||proceedings||

offered to come to the next court to make their acknowledgment, &c. The governour received their present to keep it till the court, &c. and if the court and they did agree, then to accept it. We now began to conceive hope that the Lord's time was at hand for opening a door of light and grace to those Indians, and some fruit appeared of our kind dealing with Pumham and Sacononoco, protecting them against the Narragansett, and righting them against Gorton, &c. who had taken away their land: for this example gave encouragement to all these Indians to come in and submit to our government, in expectation of the like protection and benefit.

16.] Pesacus, the Narragansett sachem, sent again a message to the governour with another present by Washose, a sachem who came before, and his errand was, that seeing they, at our request, had sitten still this year, that now this next year we would grant their request, and suffer them to fight with Onkus, with many arguments. The governour refused his present, and told him that if they sent us 1000 fathom of wampom and 1000 skins, yet we would not do that which we judged to be unjust, viz. to desert Onkus, but our resolution was, and that they must rest upon, that if they made war upon Onkus, the English would all fall upon them.

1. 23.] The Trial (the first ship built in Boston) being about 160 tons, Mr. Thomas Graves an able and a godly man master of her, was sent to Bilboa in the 4th month last, with fish, which she sold there at a good rate, and from thence she freighted to Malaga, and arrived here this day laden with wine, fruit, oil, iron and wool, which was a great advantage to the country, and gave encouragement to trade. So soon as she was fitted (3.) she was set forth again to trade with La Tour, and so along the eastern coast towards Canada.

One Mr. Rigby, a lawyer and a parliament man, wealthy and religious, had purchased the Plough Patent lying at Sagadahock, and had given commission to one Mr. Cleaves, as his deputy, to govern the people there, &c. He landing at Boston and knowing how distasteful this would be to the governour of Sir Ferdinand Gorges' province of New Somersetshire, who challenged jurisdiction in a great part of Ligonia or the Plough patent, petitioned the general court to write to them on his behalf, but the court thought not fit so to do, but rather that the governour should write in his own name only, which he did accordingly. But when Mr. Cleaves came to set his commission on foot, and called a court at Casco, Mr. Richard [1]Vines and other of Sir Ferdinand Gorges' commis-

[1] The strange errour of the press in Hubbard's Indian Wars 206, *Umes* for

sioners opposed, and called another court at Saco the same time: whereupon the inhabitants were divided; those of Casco, &c. wrote to Mr. Vines that they would stand to the judgment of the magistrates of the Bay till it were decided in England, to which government they should belong, and sent this letter by one Tucker. Mr. Vines imprisoned him, and the next day took his bond for his appearance at Saco and his good behaviour. Upon this Mr. Cleaves and the rest, about thirty persons, wrote to our governour for assistance against Mr. Vines, and tendered themselves to the consociation of the United Colonies. §The governour returned answer, that he must first advise with the commissioners of the United Colonies.§ And beside, they had an order not to receive any but such as were in a church way, &c.

Not long after, viz. (2.) 24, Mr. Vines came to Boston with a letter from himself and the other of Sir F. Gorges' commissioners and other inhabitants of the province, between 20 and 30.

Three fishermen of a boat belonging to Isle of Shoals were very profane men, and scorners of religion, and were drinking all the Lord's day, and the next week their boat was cast upon the rocks at the Isle of Shoals, and they drowned.

There was little rain this winter, and no snow till the 3d of the 1st month, the wind continuing W. and N. W. near six weeks, which was an occasion that very many houses were burned down, and ||much chattels|| (in some of them) to a greater value than in 14 years before.

1. 7.] Boston, Charlestown, Roxbury, Dorchester, Cambridge and Watertown, conceiving that the want of fortification at Castle Island would leave them open to an enemy, appointed a committee to consider how it might be fortified, and coming to some conclusion about it, they advised with the governour and some other of the magistrates, who encouraged them in it, as the elders also did in their sermons; but because the general court had given order for fetching off the ordnance, &c. it was thought fit not to attempt any thing without the advice of the same. It fell out also that five of the neighbouring Indian sachems came at the same time to the governour with a present of wampom about 30 fathom, worth some 8 pounds, and desired to come under our government as Pumham and Sacononoco had done. For these two occasions the governour summoned a general court to be held at

||many cattle||

Vines, is corrected in his history by Sullivan 312 et seq. but Hubbard's General History, 368, 9, faithfully copies Winthrop.

Boston this day (the court of assistants being to begin the 5th day before) where the committees of the said six towns exhibited a petition for fortifying of the said Island, craving help also from the country, though they had agreed to do it at their own charge rather than fail. The court refusing to undertake it, they gave in certain propositions whereby they craved some aid, at least for maintaining of the garrison, and some privileges and immunities. These coming to be debated in the court, some opposition there was, which had almost discouraged the committee. The arguments brought against it were chiefly these. 1. The great charge. 2. The little help it could afford against a strong enemy. 3. The opportunity left of another passage by Bird Island. But these objections were so far removed, as after much debate, the court voted for the fortification, and granted 100 pounds pay for the maintenance of it, when it should be in defence and a garrison of 20 men residing there; and 50 pounds towards the securing the other passage. And a committee was appointed to draw up a commission for him who should have command in chief, &c. But this allowance was yielded rather out of a willingness to gratify these six towns (being near one half of the commonwealth for number of people and substance) and to keep ||loving|| correspondency among all the towns, rather than out of any confidence of safety by it. Many also of good judgment did conceive that the fortifications would not be accomplished according to the dimensions propounded, nor so great a garrison maintained, for the people were known generally to be more willing and forward in such public engagements, than able, upon trial, to perform them: for in such cases, the major part, which carries the vote, is of such as can afford least help to the work.

The court finding that Gorton and his company did harm in the towns where they were confined, and not knowing what to do with them, at length agreed to set them at liberty, and gave them 14 days to depart out of our jurisdiction in all parts, and no more to come into it upon pain of death. This censure was thought too light and favourable, but we knew not how in justice we could inflict any punishment upon them, the sentence of the court being already passed, &c.

At this court Cutshamekin and ||2squaw sachem||, Masconomoco, Nashacowam and Wassamagoin, two sachems near the great hill to the west called ||3Wachusett||, came into the court, and according to their former tender to the governour, desired to be received under our protection and government upon the same terms that Pumham and Sacononoco were; so we causing them to un-

||living|| ||2Squasushen|| ||3Warehassett||

derstand the articles, and all the ten commandments of God, and they freely assenting to all, they were solemnly received, and then presented the court with 26 fathom more of wampom, and the court gave each of them a coat of two yards of cloth, and their dinner; and to them and their men every of them a cup of sack at their departure, so they took leave and went away very joyful.

At this court came letters from New Haven, and withal an answer from the Swedes and Dutch to the letters of the commissioners of the union, sent in the 7th month last. The Dutch still maintained their right to the land at Hartford, and their complaint of injuries. The Swedes denied what they had been charged with, and sent copies of divers examinations upon oath taken in the cause, with a copy of all the proceeding between them and our friends of New Haven from the first; and in their letters used large expressions of their respect to the English, and particularly to our colony. And Mr. Eaton desired a copy of our patent to show the Swedish governour (at his request) and a new commission from the commissioners of the union, allowing them to go on with their plantation and trade in Delaware river and bay (for the governour had told their agent that upon such a commission they should have liberty, &c.) This coming at the sitting of the general court, the commissioners advised with the court about it, who granted both, but the commission with a salvo jure: we were then informed also of a Dutch ship lately arrived at Hudson's river sent to the free boors at Fort Orange, which brought them 4,000 weight of powder, and 700 pieces to trade with the natives, which the Dutch governour having notice of, did seize and confiscate to the use of the company.[1]

We had the news also that the Dutch had entertained Captain Underhill, who with 120 men, Dutch and English, had killed 120 Indians upon Long Island, and 300 more upon the main, which was found to be a plot of the Dutch governour to engage the English in that quarrel with the Indians, which we had wholly declined, as doubting of the justice of the cause.

At this court of assistants one James Britton, a man ill affected both to our church discipline and civil government, and one Mary Latham, a ||proper|| young woman about 18 years of age, whose

||promp||

[1] A paragraph next but one to this on the same page of our MS. repeats the story of the ship from Holland, but it was properly erased by the author, because it contained only two more circumstances, one that the ship was "*not sent by the company, but by some private men,*" and of the dwellers at Fort Orange, "*these have liberty to trade by themselves,*" which were probably both erroneous.

father was a godly man and had brought her up well, were condemned to die for adultery, upon a law formerly made and published in print. It was thus occasioned and discovered. This woman, being rejected by a young man whom she had an affection unto, vowed she would marry the next that came to her, and accordingly, against her friends' minds, she matched with an ancient man who had neither honesty nor ability, and one whom she had no affection unto. Whereupon, soon after she was married, divers young men solicited her chastity, and drawing her into bad company, and giving her wine and other gifts, easily prevailed with her, and among others this Britton. But God smiting him with a deadly palsy and fearful horror of conscience withal, he could not keep secret, but discovered this, and other the like with other women, and was forced to acknowledge the justice of God in that having often called others fools, &c. for confessing against themselves, he was now forced to do the like. The woman dwelt now in Plimouth patent, and one of the magistrates there, hearing she was detected, &c. sent her to us. Upon her examination, she confessed he did attempt the fact, but did not commit it, and witness was produced that testified (which they both confessed) that in the evening of a day of humiliation through the country for England, &c. a company met at Britton's and there continued drinking sack, &c. till late in the night, and then Britton and the woman were seen upon the ground together, a little from the house. It was reported also that she did frequently abuse her husband, setting a knife to his breast and threatening to kill him, calling him old rogue and cuckold, and said she would make him wear horns as big as a bull. And yet some of the magistrates thought the evidence not sufficient against her, because there were not two direct witnesses; but the jury cast her, and then she confessed the fact, and accused twelve others, whereof two were married men. Five of these were apprehended and committed, (the rest were gone,) but denying it, and there being no other witness against them than the testimony of a condemned person, there could be no proceeding against them. The woman proved very penitent, and had deep apprehension of the foulness of her sin, and at length attained to hope of pardon by the blood of Christ, and was willing to die in satisfaction to justice. The man also was very much cast down for his sins, but was loth to die, and petitioned the general court for his life, but they would not grant it, though some of the magistrates spake much for it, and ques-

---

It may be supposed, that the ship was despatched by the company, and the dangerous commodities unduly put on board of her.

tioned the letter, whether adultery was death by God's law now. This Britton had been a professor in England, but coming hither he opposed our church government, &c. and grew dissolute, losing both power and profession of godliness.

1. 21.] They were both executed, they both died very penitently, especially the woman, who had some comfortable hope of pardon of her sin, and gave good exhortation to all young maids to be obedient to their parents, and to take heed of evil company, &c.

The Earl of Warwick and other lords, &c. being appointed by the parliament commissioners for regulating the West Indies and all other English plantations in [1]America, sent commission to Virginia to free them from all former taxations and all other charges but such as should be needful for their own occasions, and gave them liberty to choose their own governour; and sent command to all English ships there (which were then to the number of sixteen, most of them great ships) to assist them if need were. But the king sending a countermand to ||Sir Robert|| [2]Berkley, the gover-

||G. R.||

---

1 Under this supreme commission much controul of our proceedings will appear in the progress of this volume. The document may be seen in Haz. I 533. It empowers Robert, Earl of Warwick, Philip, Earl of Pembroke, Edward, Earl of Manchester, William, Viscount Say and Seal, Philip, Lord Wharton, John, Lord Roberts, of the peers, and Sir Gilbert Gerard, baronet, Sir Arthur Hazlerig, baronet, Sir Henry Vane, junr. knight, Sir Benjamin Rudyer, knight, John Pym, Oliver Cromwell, Denis Bond, Miles Corbet, Cornelius Holland, Samuel Vassall, John Rolles, and William Spurstow, of the house of commons, to exercise unlimited authority. The members were occasionally changed.

2 How Winthrop fell into the mistake, which he repeats a few passages onwards, of the baptismal name of the royal governour of Virginia, I am unable to explain. Of Sir William Berkeley a good account appears in Allen's Biog. Dict. but a remarkable errour is followed by that author, in making this governour successor to Sir John Harvey, on the authority of Sir William Keith's History of Virginia 144. Beverly, from whom Keith abridges his narrative, has the same mistake, and the diffuse and declamatory writer on their history, John Burk, has not corrected it. The great historian of Washington, in his brief introduction, seems ignorant of any intervening governour; and the only notice of such an one is found in a modest duodecimo of J. W. Campbell, 61, the only writer known to me who takes notice of the administration of Sir Francis Wyatt from 1639, when Harvey was superseded, to 1641, when Berkeley was appointed. Even Chalmers, whose accuracy is usually wonderful, says, 119, "Sir William Berkeley was appointed governour of Virginia in the beginning of 1639." The scrupulous diligence of Holmes Ann. I. 312, which had found the commission of Harvey, overlooked that of Berkeley in the same volume. Such is the manner in which errours are perpetuated. Yet the elegant Notes on Virginia, in the large collection of papers, 357, refers to Rymer's Foedera, xx. 484, for a commission of the governour and council of Virginia, dated 9 Aug. 1641, which,

nour, he withstood the parliament's commissioners, and drew most of the other magistrates to take oath upon the sacrament to maintain the king's authority, &c. so that the whole country was like to rise in parties, some for the king, and others for the parliament.

A proposition was made this court for all the English within the united colonies to enter into a civil ||agreement|| for the maintenance of religion and our civil liberties, and for yielding some more of the freeman's privileges to such as were no church members that should join in this government. But nothing was concluded, but referred to next court, and in the mean time, that letters should be written to the other colonies to advise with them about it. Nothing was effected for want of opportunity of meeting, &c.

At the same court in the first month, upon the motion of the deputies, it was ordered that the court should be divided in their consultations, the magistrates by themselves, and the deputies by themselves, what the one agreed upon they should send to the other, and if both agreed, then to pass, &c. This order determined the great contention about the negative voice.

Divers of the merchants of Boston being desirous to discover the great lake, supposing it to lie in the north west part of our patent, and finding that the great trade of beaver which came to all the eastern and southern parts, came from thence, petitioned the court to be a company for that design, and to have the trade which they should discover, to themselves for twenty-one years. The court was very unwilling to grant any monopoly, but perceiving that without it they would not proceed, granted their desire· whereupon, having also commission granted them under the public seal, (3) and letters from the governour to the Dutch and Swedish governours, they sent out a pinnace well manned and furnished with provisions and trading stuff, which was to sail up

||government||

had it been examined, would have cleared all difficulty. This commission, which is also given in Haz. I. 477, from Car. I. an. reg. 17, recites that the king had, January 11, an. reg. 14, i. e. 1639, appointed Sir Francis Wyatt to be his governour, whose commission he now revokes and makes him first member of the council. So that more than two and a half years, between the administrations of Harvey and Berkeley, was the period of Sir Francis Wyatt's government. Perhaps the authors of their annals considered it sufficient to honour Wyatt by reckoning him as governour many years before, when he was quite a young man. Berkeley's letter to England, in 1671, in which he says, "I thank God, there are no free schools, nor printing; and I hope we shall not have these hundred years," has been often subject of remark. No man in the world can differ from his reasons, more than the editor; and I regret to observe, that his hopes in regard to the first object have been so effectually satisfied.

Delaware river so high as they could go, and then some of the company, under the conduct of Mr. William Aspenwall, a good artist, and one who had been in those parts, to pass by small skiffs or canoes up the river so far as they could.

Many of Watertown and other towns joined in the plantation at Nashaway, and having called a young man, an ||university|| scholar, one Mr. ||[2]Norcross||, to be their minister, seven of them, who were no members of any churches, were desirous to gather into a church estate; but the magistrates and elders advised them first to go and build them habitations, &c. (for there was yet no house there,) and then to take some that were members of other churches, with the consent of such churches, as formerly had been done, and so proceed orderly. But the persons interested in this plantation, being most of them poor men, and some of them corrupt in judgment, and others profane, it went on very slowly, so as that in two years they had not three houses built there, and he whom they had called to be their minister left them for their delays.[1]

One Dalkin and his wife dwelling near [2]Meadford coming from

||universal|| ||[2]Nocroff||

---

1 The last sentence is added, probably by the governour, at a later time. From our Col. Rec. II. 57, I find "the petition of Mr. Nathaniel Norcross, Robert Childe, Stephen Day, John Fisher and others for a plantation at Nashawake is granted, provided that there shall not be more land allotted to the town, or particular men, (notwithstanding their purchase of land of the Indians,) than the general court shall allow." Day was the person, who first introduced printing in New England, see Vol. I. 289. He died in Cambridge, Dec. 22, 1668, aged about 58 years, see Thomas's History of Printing in America, I. 231. Of Norcross I know nothing more, and therefore, as his education was so liberal, presume he returned home. Childe is, perhaps, the same, whose exertions for extension of privileges so much disturbed our colony two years after. The name of Fisher, I think, has prevailed in Lancaster from its settlement.

2 Of so flourishing a town as Medford, the settlement of which had been made as early as that of any other, except Charlestown, in the bay, it is remarkable, that the early history is very meagre. From several statements of its proportion of public charges in the colony rates, it must be concluded, that it was, within the first eight years, superior in wealth at different times to Newbury, Ipswich, Hingham, Weymouth, all ancient towns, furnished with regular ministers. Yet the number of people was certainly small, and the weight of the tax was, probably, borne by the property of Governour Cradock, there invested for fishing and other purposes. When that establishment was withdrawn, I suppose, the town languished many years. A most diligent inspection of the records has been made by its present pastor, Rev. Andrew Bigelow, from which it appears that its first regularly ordained minister was Aaron Porter, in 1712. Some instruction had for several years preceding been regularly given by Benjamin Woodbridge, who died there 1710, and before him by Simon Bradstreet, H. C. 1689, whom Mather in his Hecatompolis makes the minister in 1696, but he

Cambridge, where they had spent their Sabbath, and being to pass over the river at a ford, the tide not being fallen enough, the husband adventured over, and finding it too deep, persuaded his wife to stay a while, but it raining very sore, she would needs adventure over, and was carried away with the stream past her depth. Her husband not daring to go help her, cried out, and thereupon his dog, being at his house near by, came forth, and seeing something in the water, swam to her, and she caught hold on the dog's tail, so he drew her to the shore and saved her life.

At the general court (8.) 4. there came a letter to the governour from Mr. Wheelwright, (who was now ||moved|| from Exeter to Wells, near Cape Porpoise, where he was pastor of a church,) the contents whereof were as followeth.

Right Worshipful.

Upon the long and mature consideration of things, I perceive that the main difference between yourselves and some of the reverend elders and me, in point of ||[2]justification|| and the evidencing thereof, is not of that nature and consequence as was then presented to me in the false glass of satan's temptations and mine own distempered passions, which makes me unfeignedly sorry that I had such an hand in those sharp and vehement contentions raised thereabouts to the great disturbance of the churches of Christ. It is the ||[3]grief|| of my soul that I used such vehement censorious speeches in the application of my sermon, or in any other writing, whereby I reflected any dishonour upon your worships, the reverend elders, or any of contrary judgment to myself. It repents me that I did so much adhere to persons of corrupt judgment, to the countenancing of them in any of their errours or evil practices, though I intended no such thing; and that in the synod I used such unsafe and obscure expressions falling from me as a man dazzled with the buffetings of satan, and that I did appeal from misapprehension of things. I confess that herein I have done very sinfully, and do humbly crave pardon of this honoured

||carried|| ||[2]jurisdiction|| ||[3]gift||

was not settled, and left the place early in 1697, soon after which Woodbridge was employed. Yet it appears that the celebrated James Noyes, afterwards teacher at Newbury, preached near a year at this place, on first coming over in 1634. See Magnalia III. c. 25, an excellent letter of his nephew, Nicholas Noyes, minister at Salem. The consequences of this destitution of the best means of religion were very unhappy. The town was poorly inhabited, the people much divided, occasionally prosecuted for their deficiencies, and long in a miserable condition. A long period of happiness at last arrived in the times of Turell and Osgood, and for more than a century Medford has appeared one of the most thriving villages in the vicinity of Boston.

state. If it shall appear to me, by scripture light, that in any carriage, word, writing or action, I have walked contrary to rule, I shall be ready, by the grace of God, to give satisfaction: thus hoping that you will pardon my boldness, I humbly take leave of your worship, committing you to the good providence of the Almighty; and ever remain, your worship's in all service to be commanded in the Lord.

||J.|| WHEELWRIGHT.

Wells, (7) 10—43.

Upon this letter the court was very well inclined to release his banishment; and thereupon ordered that he might have a safe conduct to come to the court, &c. Hereof the governour certified him by letter, and received this answer from him.

RIGHT WORSHIPFUL.

I have received the letter wherein you signify to me that you have imparted my letter to the honourable court, and that it finds good applause, for which I rejoice with much thankfulness. I am very thankful to your worship for the letter of safe conduct which I formerly received, as likewise for the late act of court, granting me the same liberty in case I desire letters to that end. I should very willingly, upon letters received, express by word of mouth openly in court, that which I did by writing, might I, without offence, explain my true intent and meaning more fully to this effect: that notwithstanding my failings, for which I humbly crave pardon, yet I cannot with a good conscience condemn myself for such capital crimes, dangerous revelations and gross errours, as have been charged upon me, the concurrence of which (as I take it) make up the very substance of the cause of all my sufferings. I do not see, but in so mixt a cause I am bound to use, may it be permitted, my just defence so far as I apprehend myself to be innocent, as to make my confession where I am convinced of any delinquency; otherwise I shall seemingly and in appearance fall under guilt of many heinous offences, for which my conscience doth acquit me. If I seem to make suit to the honourable court for relaxation to be granted, by an act of mercy, upon my sole confession, I must offend my conscience; if by an act of justice, upon mine apology and lawful defence, I fear lest I shall offend your worships. I leave all things to your wise and godly consideration, hoping that you will pardon my simplicity and plainness

||F.||

which I am forced unto by the power of an over-ruling conscience. I rest your worship's in the Lord.

||J.|| [1]WHEELWRIGHT.

Wells, (1) 1—43.

To this the governour replied to this effect, viz. that though his liberty might be obtained without his personal appearance, yet that was doubtful, nor did he conceive that a wise and modest apology would prejudice the acceptance of his free and ingenuous confession, seeing the latter would justify the sentence of the court, which looked only at his action, and yet by the former, he might maintain the liberty of his conscience in clearing his intention from those ill deserving crimes which the court apprehended by his action: and withal (because there might want opportunity of conveyance before the court) he sent him inclosed a safe conduct, &c. The next court released his banishment without his appearance.

3. 20.] A ship coming from Virginia certified us of a great massacre lately committed by the natives upon the English there, to the number of [2]300 at least, and that an Indian whom they had since taken confessed, that they did it because they saw the English took up all their lands from them, and would drive them out of the country, and they took this season for that they understood that they were at war in England, and began to go to war among themselves, for they had seen a fight in the river between a London ship which was for the parliament and a Bristol ship which was for the king. He confessed further that all the Indians within 600 miles were confederate together to root all strangers out of the country.

It was very observable that this massacre came upon them soon after they had driven out the godly ministers we had sent to them, and had made an order that all such as would not conform to the discipline of the church of England should depart the country by a certain day, which the massacre now prevented: and the governour (one Sir Robert Berkeley, a courtier, and very malignant towards the way of our churches here) and council had appointed a

||F.||

---

1 Some slight variations in Hubbard, 366, 7, show how differently he read the originals. [Such was the language used by me, while the exact copy of Winthrop was in my power to give, but my recollection can furnish very little, however severely taxed.]

2 In the original MS. the first figure has been changed from 3 to 5, or vice versa. The smaller number is more probable; but Beverley 49, and Keith 144, make it near five hundred.

fast to be kept through the country upon good Friday (as they call it) for the good success of the king, &c. and, the day before, this massacre began in the outparts of the country round about, and continued two days, for they killed all, by sudden surprisal, living amongst them, and as familiar in their houses as those of the family.[1] This massacre was accompanied with a great mortality. Upon these troubles divers godly disposed [2]persons came from thence to New England, and many of the rest were forced to give glory to God in acknowledging that this evil was sent upon them from God for their reviling the gospel and those faithful ministers he had sent among them.

A letter came to the governour, under the marks of Pesecus and Canonicus, the sachem of Narragansett, but written by Gorton's company, to this effect: That they were purposed to make war

---

1 No greater deficiency in the history of Virginia can be found than about the date and circumstances of this massacre; and I shall now show how much the writers on their affairs may be indebted to Winthrop of Massachusetts for the knowledge of one of the most interesting events that ever befel their colony. Beverley and Keith both represent this shocking catastrophe as occurring during the unhappy administration of Harvey, which closed in 1639, or during the irregularities, which immediately followed his removal. Burk in his copious history II. 54, after discussing the uncertainty and finding cause to doubt the earlier date which had been assigned to the disaster, concludes "there is reason to believe that this event took place in the winter of 1641, or the early part of the following year, before the colony had regained its tranquillity under the mild and able administration of Berkeley." In a place where we should not expect it, Holmes, Ann. I. 325, slightly mentions the event, with correct date, on authority of Hubbard, instead of Winthrop. From our author, who no doubt had his information directly from the puritans, who fled from the evil, it appears, the massacre began the day before Good Friday, which, I think, that year fell on 19 April. The massacre therefore began on 18 April, 1644.

2 Among these was, I presume, Captain Daniel Gookins, afterwards so well known as the last major general of our colony He had, no doubt, showed kindness in Virginia to Tompson and the other missionaries, for his admission as a freeman was on 29 May of this year, and the ship reached here only 20 of the same month. It was not common for one to be allowed to take his oath so soon after arriving within the jurisdiction, without strong recommendation. His reputation in the present age stands justly higher than it did during a part of his life, when his benevolent attempts to serve and save the Indians were misinterpreted, much obloquy was uttered against him, and he said on the bench of justice, that he was afraid for his life in walking the streets. See a most curious pamphlet of 1675, called the State of New England, preserved in the Boston Athenaeum. The memory of Gookin, or Gookins, or Gookings, is well preserved by Eliot and Allen, and especially in 1 Hist. Coll. I. 228. From the humble notice of Johnson, lib. I. c. 45 and lib. II. c. 26, to the highest authority of the records of our United Colonies, Haz. II. 474, 492, his great desert may be ascertained. Descendants have exhibited in several generations the same christian spirit, and the family name is still perpetuated in New Hampshire.

upon Onkus in revenge of the death of ||[1]Onkus|| and others of their people whom he had slain, and that they marvelled why we should be against it; that they had put themselves under the government and protection of the king of England, and so were now become our fellow subjects, and therefore if any difference should fall between us and them, it ought to be referred to him; professing withal their willingness to continue all friendly correspondency with us.

The general court being assembled, when Mr. Endecott was chosen governour and Mr. Winthrop deputy governour, they took this letter into consideration, together with another from Gorton's company to the same effect, and sent two messengers to the Narragansetts with instructions to this purpose, viz. to know whether they did own that letter, &c. and by whose advice they had done as they wrote, and why they would countenance and take counsel from such evil men and such as we had banished from us, and to persuade them to sit still, and to have more regard to us than such as Gorton, &c. When our messengers came to them, Canonicus would not admit them into his wigwam for two hours, but suffered them to stay in the rain. When he did admit them, he lay along upon his couch, and would not speak to them more than a few froward speeches, but referred them to Pesacus, who, coming after some four hours, carried them into an ordinary wigwam, and there had conference with them most part of the night. Their answers were witty and full to the questions; and their conclusion was, that they would presently go to war upon Onkus, but not in such manner as Miantunnomoh had done, by a great army, but by sending out parties of 20 or more or less, to catch his men, and keep them from getting their living, &c.

At this court Passaconaway, the Merrimack sachem, came in and submitted to our government, as Pumham &c. had done before.

4. 5.] Two of our ministers' sons, being students in the college, robbed two dwelling houses in the night of some 15 pounds. Being found out, they were ordered by the governours of the college to be there whipped, which was performed by the president himself—yet they were about 20 years of age; and after they were brought into the court and ordered to two fold satisfaction, or

||Miantonamoh||

1 I have chosen to preserve the errour of the original, which the former editor corrected. It can lead to no mistake.

to serve so long for it. We had yet no particular punishment for burglary.[1]

At this court there arose some troubles by this occasion. Those ||of|| Essex had procured at the court before, that the deputies of the several shires should meet before this court to prepare business, &c. which accordingly they did, and propounded divers things which they agitated and concluded among themselves without communicating them to the other shires, who conceived they had been only such things as had concerned the commonwealth, but when they came now to be put to this court, it appeared that their chief intent was to advantage their own shire. As 1. by drawing the government thither. 2. By drawing the courts thither. 3. By drawing a good part of the country stock thither. 4. By procuring four of those parts to be joined in commission with the magistrates. And for this end they had made so strong a party among the deputies of the smaller towns (being most of them mean men, and such as had small understanding in affairs of state) as they easily carried all these among the deputies. But when the [2]two bills came to the magistrates, they discerning the plot, and finding them hurtful to the commonwealth, refused to pass them, and a committee of both being appointed to consider the reasons of both sides, those of the magistrates prevailed.

But the great difference was about a commission which the deputies sent up, whereby power was given to seven of the magistrates and three of the deputies and Mr. Ward (some time pastor of Ipswich, and still a preacher) to order all affairs of the commonwealth in the vacancy of the general court, which the magistrates returned with this answer: That they conceived such commission did tend to the overthrow of the foundation of our government, and of the freemen's liberty, and therefore desired the deputies to consider of a way how this danger might be avoided and the liberty of the freemen preserved inviolable, otherwise they could not comfortably proceed in other affairs.

Upon this return all the deputies came to confer with the ma-

||at||

---

1 The names of these offenders it is impossible, I presume, to ascertain: they were, probably, expelled from the college, and cannot be found in the catalogue. Certainly the sons of ministers have not become worse since the first generation. The punishment of burglary was not, I believe, fixed till three years later, and the first date in Ancient Charters 56, at the bottom of the page, is erroneous.

2 Whether the numeral in our MS. were originally written 2 or 3, is now difficult to determine, for it has been altered. Hubbard, 392, wisely abbreviates our author, and omits the number.

gistrates. The exceptions the magistrates took were these. 1. That this court should ||create|| general ||[2]officers|| which the freemen had reserved to the court of elections. 2. That they should put out four of the magistrates from that power and trust which the freemen had committed to them. 3. At the commission itself, seeing they ought not to accept that power by commission which did belong to them by the patent and by their election. They had little to answer to this, yet they alleged a precedent or two where this court had ordered some of the magistrates and some others to be a council of war, and that we had varied from our patent in some other things, and therefore were not bound to it in this.

But they chiefly stood upon this, that the governour and assistants had no power out of court but what was given them by the general court. To this the magistrates replied. 1. That such examples as were against rules or common right were errours and no precedents. 2. That council was for ||[3]one|| particular case only and not of general extent. 3. In those things wherein we had varied from our patent we did not touch the foundation of our government. To the last it was said, that the governour and assistants had power of government before we had any written laws or had kept any courts; and to make a man a governour over a people, gives him, by necessary consequence, power to govern that people, otherwise there were no power in any commonwealth to order, dispose or punish in any case ||[4]where it|| might fall out, that there were no positive law declared in.

It was consented to that this court had authority to order and direct the power of these magistrates for time, place, persons, &c. for the common good, but not wholly to deprive them of it, their office continuing: so as these being chosen by the people, by virtue of the patent to govern the people, a chief part whereof consists in counsel, they are the standing council of the commonwealth, and therefore in the vacancy of this court, may act in all the affairs thereof without any commission.

Upon this they withdrew, and after a few hours came again, and then they tendered a commission for war only, and ||[5]none|| of the magistrates to be left out. But the magistrates refused to accept of any commission, but they would consent the same should pass by order so as the true power of the magistrates might be declared in it: or to a commission of association, to add three or [1]four others to the magistrates in that council: or to continue

||treat|| ||[2]affairs|| ||[3]our|| ||[4]which|| ||[5]more||

[1] In Hubbard, 394, this is absurdly given *nine*.

the court a week longer and send for the elders to take their advice in it; but none of these would be accepted. But they then moved, that we would consent that nothing might be done till the court met again, which was before agreed to be adjourned to the 28th of (8). To this was answered, that, if occasion required, they must act according to the power and trust committed to them; to which their speaker replied—You will not be obeyed.[1]

4. 23.] Two days after the court was broken up, Pumham sent two men to Boston to tell us that the Narragansetts had taken and killed six of Onkus' men and five women, and had sent him two hands and a foot to engage him in the war, but he refused to receive them and sent to us for counsel, &c. This occasioned such of the magistrates and deputies as were at hand (advising also with some of the near elders) to meet to consult about calling the court, and agreed, both in regard of this news from the Indians, and especially for speedy reconciling the magistrates and deputies, to write to the governour that the court might be called the 28th following, which the governour assented unto.

The court being assembled, they took order for ten men to be sent to Pumham according to his desire, to help him make a fort

---

1 This language of Mr. Speaker Hathorne, however extraordinary it now may appear, in spite of the immaturity of our constitution, or did then to those, who had exercised unquestioned powers of government for fourteen years, shows the liberality and profoundness of the principles, by which the popular body was actuated. Undoubtedly Winthrop and the magistrates were correct in asserting their right to govern in the vacancy of the general court; and the representatives were wrong in attempting to give to a special commission what the people had confided to the whole body of the assistants. But how much had been thus confided, was matter of perpetual dispute; and could only be determined, in the absence of a written constitution, by the two branches, under the sober construction of the charter, in circumstances, for which the charter was never designed. One of these branches, being the assistants, was thus of necessity to construe its own powers; and its negative voice of course would be interposed to prevent any diminution. There was indeed no lasting danger to popular rights, because all the officers were subject to annual elections; and from any adjudication in a particular case by the magistrates, an appeal lay to the whole court. But the constant tendency of the claims of the representatives to absorb all power by compelling the magistrates to forego their independent existence, as an equal branch of the government, and submit to the consolidation of a single assembly, proves how little the deputies regarded the theory of a balance in the legislation. Without the assistants, the governour would have been nothing; and with them, his power seems to have been hardly more than that of primus inter pares. Having been so long unadjusted, the balance was so greatly agitated in this controversy between the branches, in which it was very deeply as well as warmly argued, and nearly all of the most experienced and venerated men of the colony were on one side, while causes wholly unconnected with abstract politics gave a momentary strength to the other, that when it was settled the latter part of the year, it appears to have been settled forever.

of palisadoes, &c. but the men, being volunteers, asked 10*s*. per week for each man, and such spoil as they should get, if they were put to fight, and arms fixed and powder and shot. Whereupon the court, fearing it would be an ill precedent, staid and sent word to Pumham that the men were ready, but he must pay them, &c.

The commission also for the serjeant major general was agreed and sealed, and in it he was referred to receive his instructions, &c. from the council of the commonwealth, but who were this council was not agreed. Whereupon the magistrates (all save two) signed a declaration in maintenance of their authority, and to clear the aspersions cast upon them, as if they intended to bring in an arbitrary government, &c. This they sent first to the deputies, with intimation that they intended to publish it, whereupon the deputies sent to desire that it might not be published, and desired a committee might meet to state the difference between us, which was done, and the difference was brought under this question: ||whether|| the magistrates are by patent and election of the people the standing council of the commonwealth in the vacancy of the general court, and have power accordingly to act in all cases subject to government, according to the said patent and the laws of this jurisdiction; and when any necessary occasions call for action from authority, in cases where there is no particular express law provided, there to be guided by the word of God, till the general court give particular rules in such cases? This difference being thus stated, they drew up this following order and sent it to us, viz.

Whereas there is a difference between the governour, assistants and deputies in this court, concerning the power of the magistrates in the vacancy of the general court—we therefore (salvo jure) for the peace and safety of this colony do consent, that the governour and assistants shall take order for the welfare of this commonwealth in all sudden cases that may happen within our jurisdiction, until the next session of this court, when we desire this question may be determined.

This we accepted (with the salvo jure) but we had refused to accept of another they sent us before in these words—we do authorise those three which are of the standing council to proceed, &c.

Upon this agreement the magistrates consented, that the declaration should remain with the secretary, and not be published without the consent of the major part of the magistrates, which we intended not to do, except we were necessitated thereto by the deputies' misreport of our proceedings. And indeed some of the

||where||

magistrates did decline the publishing thereof, upon this apprehension, that it would cause a public breach throughout the country: and if it should come to that, the people would fall into factions, and the non-members would certainly take part with the magistrates, (we should not be able to avoid it,) and this would make us and our cause, though never so just, obnoxious to the common sort of freemen, the issue whereof must needs have been very doubtful.[1]

5. 2.] Mr. George Phillips was [2]buried. He was the first pastor of the church of Watertown, a godly man, specially gifted, and very peaceful in his place, much lamented of his own people and others.

Another great errour the deputies committed, which also arose out of the same false bottom, viz. the choosing one of the younger magistrates, (though a very able man,) Mr. [3]Bradstreet, and one

---

1 Here is disclosed a secret spring of policy, the force of which we cannot by any reflection fully estimate, and with which we might have been wholly unacquainted, unless our author had given us the information. That no others than church members could choose, or be chosen, to any office, or even serve as jurymen, was generally known to students of our history; but this fact alone is barren. Hutchinson, who was more thoroughly imbued, than any of his age, or any subsequent one, with the spirit of our antiquities, has, I. 30, given a quotation from Lechford, that throws much light on the text of Winthrop: "the most of the persons at New England are not admitted of their church, and therefore are not freemen; and when they come to be tried there, be it for life or limb, name or estate, or whatsoever, they must be tried and judged too by those of the church who are in a sort their adversaries. How equal that hath been or may be, some by experience do know, others may judge." A very slight relaxation was admitted in a few years, by which non-members were empowered to serve as jurymen, and even to vote in laying town taxes and choosing selectmen. But the severe policy was obstinately retained until, in 1665, the royal injunction of 1662, having been long evaded, could no longer be disobeyed. To us it will appear strange, that, in this contest between the two branches, the magistrates feared to have *most of the persons*, as Lechford says, on their side, because the minority elected *all* the deputies as well as themselves.

2 He died the day before. For some slight notice of him, the reader is referred to Eliot and Allen and my note Vol. I. 14. His will, in our Probate Rec. I. 33, mentions his son, Samuel, as being under age, and gives him a double portion of the estate. This Samuel, H. C. 1650, was minister of Rowley, and died 22 April, 1696, aet. 71. His son, George, H. C. 1686, became a minister at Brookhaven on Long Island, 1697, and died 1739. Another son, Samuel, was a goldsmith at Salem, who was father of Samuel, H. C. 1708, sufficiently commemorated in Allen's Dictionary. But this writer, in making him grandson of George, sinks one generation, in which errour he is followed by the diligent author of the Sketch of Haverhill, 2 Hist. Coll. IV. 155. The present Hon. William Phillips of Boston, whose name is mentioned whenever christian munificence is honoured, is great great great grandson of the first clergyman of Watertown.

3 Perhaps the desert of none of our early rulers, except the two Winthrops.

of the deputies, Mr. Hathorne, (the principal man in all these agitations,) a young man also, to be commissioners for the united colonies; both [1]eastern men, quite out of the way of opportunity of correspondency with the other confederates; whereas all the rest had chosen either their governours or other chief magistrates; and ourselves had formerly chosen the governour and Mr. Dudley. Thus usual it is for one errour in state to beget others.

This also was a failing in them, that, when the governour of Plimouth (our brethren and confederates) wrote earnestly to us, in their great want of powder, to supply them out of our store, and the magistrates had granted them two barrels, the deputies stopped it, and would not consent they might have liberty to buy for their money.

Those also of Aquiday Island, being in great fear of the Indians, wrote to us for some powder and other ammunition, but the court was then adjourned; and because the deputies had denied our

---

is equal to that of Governour Simon Bradstreet, whose labours equalled them both in duration. He was born 1603, had part of his education at Cambridge University, in Emanuel College, celebrated in those days as the Puritan College, and was chosen an assistant of Massachusetts, 18 March, 1629—30, at the same time with Sir Brian Janson and William Coddington. Having been elected fourteen times afterward to the same place, it hardly seems a fit objection of our author in the text, that he was one of the *younger* magistrates, when he was chosen a commissioner of the United Colonies. It is, indeed, added, that he with his colleague were *Eastern* men, and it was, probably, the undue influence of the Salem party that so early secured his elevation. But half of the magistrates, at least, were his juniors in the office. His epitaph, in 1 Hist. Coll. VI. 288, marks his death 27 March, 1697, and gives a character with justice and brevity. It has happened, that the talents of Governour Bradstreet have not been rated so highly, see Allen, as to me they seem to deserve, but the cause, probably, was his moderation in politics and religion. Our author calls him a very able man. His contemporaries, in 1662, designed to send one of the ablest men in the country, as companion with Norton, to effect the difficult purpose of conciliating the crown; and his success in that mission naturally dissatisfied some of the more eager spirits, whose disgust at the royal favour, thus obtained or promised, pursued Norton to the grave. The arguments about La Tour's business and his defence of our titles to lands against Andros's pretences give honourable evidence of talents. Several descendants of Bradstreet have been honoured in church and state; but in the direct male line they are nearly extinct.

1 Bradstreet then lived at Ipswich and Hathorne at Salem. The errour in state policy is not very great, for though, at the first meeting of the commissioners, each colony had chosen their principal men, yet Collier of Plimouth and Gregson of New Haven, who then served, cannot be reckoned superiors of these Massachusetts men for the second meeting. This meeting was to be held at Hartford, and, probably, the people would hardly have spared either of those who had served last year, nor would they have been willing to undertake such a journey. Two of the three other colonies did not choose for this year, till several weeks after our election.

confederates, the magistrates thought not fit to supply them: but certainly it was an errour (in state policy at least) not to support them, for though they were desperately erroneous and in such distraction among themselves as portended their ruin, yet if the Indians should prevail against them, it would be a great advantage to the Indians, and danger to the whole country by the arms, &c. that would there be had, and by the loss of so many persons and so much cattle and other substance belonging to above 120 families. Or, if they should be forced to seek protection from the Dutch, who would be ready to accept them, it would be a great inconvenience to all the English to have so considerable a place in the power of strangers so potent as they are.

Another errour also was this, that, when by the articles of confederation we were bound, if any of our confederates upon any pressing occasion should send to us for aid, we should forthwith send them such a number of men as is agreed upon in the articles, yet the deputies would not consent, that upon any such occasion the magistrates should raise any man, without calling a general court, which would put the country to great charge, and might occasion the loss of the opportunity; and when they should be assembled, there would be no use of council, the thing being already determined by the articles of confederation.

5. 15.] Upon the earnest importunity of Pumham who feared the Narragansetts because of their threatenings, that it might really appear that we did own them and would protect them, we sent 10 men and an officer, a discreet man, to command them, and gave them commission to stay there one, two, or three days, as &c. with charge not to enter into the limits of the Narragansett, nor to provoke them, &c. and if they were forced, to defend themselves, yet they should not pursue the enemy, if he retired, &c.

Two new ships, one of 250 [tons], built at Cambridge, the other of 200, built at Boston, set sail towards the Canaries laden with pipe staves, fish, &c.

The court, breaking up in haste, (it being on the evening of the fast appointed,) gave order to the magistrates in the bay to return answer to the Dutch governour's letter of (12) 11. which accordingly was done, to this effect, viz. Gratulation of his respect and correspondency with us, manifestation of our good will to him, and desire of continuance of all friendly intercourse, &c.—acknowledging that he had largely and prudently discoursed of the matters in difference: but we are also to attend the allegations on the other part. But seeing proofs were not yet had on either side, he could expect no further answer than before: but if he would please to send commissioners to Hartford to treat with the commissioners for the colonies, it would be very acceptable, and a hopeful means to prepare for a good issue.

Anabaptistry increased and spread in the country, which occasioned the magistrates, at the last court, to draw an order for banishing such as continued obstinate after due conviction. This was sent to the elders, who approved of it with some mitigations, and being voted, and sent to the deputies, it was after published.[1]

A poor man of Hingham, one Painter,[2] who §had§ lived at New Haven and at Rowley and Charlestown, and been scandalous and burdensome by his idle and troublesome behaviour to them all, was now on the sudden turned anabaptist, and having a child born, he would not suffer his wife to bring it to the ordinance of

---

1 With painful emotions is the history of the intolerance of our fathers read by those of their descendants, who hold them in the highest veneration. Nothing can be more unfair, as in our age it seems, than the preamble of this law, which Haz. I. 538 has given from our Col. Rec. as passed 13 November of this year: "Incendiaries of the commonwealths, and the infectors of persons in main matters of religion, and the troublers of churches in all places where they have been," are part of the inflammatory accusations, by which is introduced the penal enactment, "that if any person within this jurisdiction shall either openly condemn or oppose the baptising of infants, or go about secretly to seduce others from the approbation or use thereof, or shall purposely depart the congregation at the ministration of the ordinance, or &c. and shall appear to the court wilfully and obstinately to continue therein after due time and means of conviction, every such person shall be sentenced to banishment." Now these nursing fathers of the commonwealth knew very well, that some of the most sincere and orthodox christians, according with them even in "the mint, anise and cummin" of all forms, or rejection of forms, except this single one of paedobaptism, had gathered separate churches in England; yet they level their battery of insinuations and assertions against the direful delusions and execrable fanaticism of the savage reformers of Munster. The amiable and learned Jacie, the friend and correspondent of Winthrop, jr. see 3 Hist. Coll. I. 235—246, had thus far departed from the faith, three or four years before. This fatal errour of the rulers of Massachusetts was, undoubtedly, resisted by our author in his latter days, and it will be some mitigation of the reader's disgust, to learn from Hutch. I. 142, "that upon his death bed, when Mr. Dudley pressed him to sign an order of banishment of an heterodox person, he refused, saying, I HAVE DONE TOO MUCH OF THAT WORK ALREADY." Gladly would I adduce, were it in my power, the original authority for this golden commentary on the fatuitous legislation of the age. Hubbard and Mather are silent, perhaps from design. Unhappily Endecott and Dudley were less mild, and a very few years after Winthrop's death, Anabaptists were whipped and imprisoned in Boston for their religion. Passing from bad to worse, our rulers soon punished Quakers with death, the last extravagance to which sincere professors of our divine religion could proceed.

2 Thomas Painter was the man thus severely dealt with, before the passage of the law, by which his conduct was declared or directed to be considered an offence. Land in Hingham had been granted him by the town, 8 October 1637, and he probably was complained of by Rowley or Charlestown.

baptism, for she was a member of the church, though himself were not. Being presented for this, and enjoined to suffer the child to be baptized, he still refusing, and disturbing the church, he was again brought to the court not only for his former contempt, but also for saying that our baptism was antichristian; and in the open court he affirmed the same. Whereupon after much patience and clear conviction of his errour, &c. because he was very poor, so as no other but corporal punishment could be fastened upon him, he was ordered to be whipped, not for his opinion, but for reproaching the Lord's ordinance, and for his bold and evil behaviour both at home and in the court. He endured his punishment with much obstinacy, and when he was loosed, he said boastingly, that God had marvellously assisted him. Whereupon two or three honest men, his neighbours, affirmed before all the company, that he was of very loose behaviour at home, and given much to lying and idleness, &c. Nor had he any great occasion to gather God's assistance from his stillness under the punishment, which was but moderate, for divers notorious malefactors had showed the like, and one the same court.

5. 15.] Here arrived Monsieur La Tour, who understood by letters from his lady, that Monsieur D'Aulnay had prevailed against him in France, and was coming with great strength to subdue him: whereupon he came to desire some aid, if need should be.

Natascott being formerly made a town, and having ||now|| twenty houses and a minister, was by the last general court named Hull.[1]

||near||

---

[1] So called, I suppose, in honour of Joseph Hull of Hingham, who was admitted to the freeman's oath 2 September 1635, and, with Edmond Hobart senr., was by the general court 6 September 1638 chosen a commissioner to end small causes for that town. He was at the same time, and in March after, a deputy at the court.

Who was the minister referred to by our text in this secluded town of Hull, which has, I think, been never more populous than soon after 1644, must, probably, rest in conjecture. From the records of our general court we are authorized to suspect, that it was Mathews, for in Vol. III. 218, which contains the proceedings of the deputies, is found, at the May session 1649: "Received a petition from the inhabitants of Hull for the encouraging Mr. Mathews to go to them and preach amongst them," and in Vol. II. 235, recording the acts of the magistrates, at the same session, the following: "The court judge it no way meet to grant the inhabitants of Hull their desire for Mr. Mathews *returning* to them, nor residing with them, and do declare that they find several erroneous expressions, others weak, inconvenient and unsafe, for which it judgeth it meet to order, that the said Mr. Mathews should be admonished by the governour in the name of this court" Governour Endecott was a fit man to perform such a duty, but, I fear, the admonition was ineffectual. See

At this court Captain Jenyson, captain of the military company in Watertown, an able man who had been there from the first settling of that town, having a year before, (being then a deputy,) in private conference, questioned the lawfulness of the parliament's proceeding in England, was sent for by the deputies, and examined about it, and after before the magistrates. He ingenuously confessed his scruple, but took offence, that being a church member, and in public office, he should be openly produced merely for matter of judgment, not having been first dealt with in private, either in a church way or by some of the magistrates, which seemed to some of the court to have been a failing. The court was unwilling to turn him out of place, having been a very useful man, &c. yet not seeing how he might be trusted, being of that judgment, yet professing that he was assured that those of the parliament side were the more godly and honest part of the kingdom, and that though, if he were in England, he should be doubtful whether he might take their part against their prince, yet, if the king or any party from him should attempt any thing against this commonwealth, he should make no scruple to spend estate and life and all in our defence against them, he was dismissed to further consideration; and the court being broken up, he came soon after to some of the magistrates and told them, that this questioning in the court had occasioned him to search further into the

---

my note in Vol. I. 273. I doubt, that this ancient town has never had more than one minister to reside in it through his life. That one was Zechariah Whitman, H. C. 1668, ordained 13 September, 1670, died 5 November, 1726, aged 82. In April 1753, Samuel Veazie, H. C. 1736, was ordained at Hull, but dismissed July 1767, and, probably, the christian ordinances have never since been regularly administered for a continuous period.

Perhaps the interest felt by the reader in this ancient town, the least populous of any in Massachusetts, and the smallest in extent, except Newburyport, may excuse the extension of this note. From twelve to eighteen votes are usually given at the elections, and the editor had the honour, some year's since, of a seat in the same house of representatives, which contained a member from Hull. The following record is found in the doings of the general court 26 May 1647: "There being now divers fishermen and men of good ability in Hull, who may comfortably carry on the affairs of a town, they are enabled by the authority of this court to order the prudential affairs of that town according to former orders of this court and course of other plantations, provided that according to former orders of court they endeavour the advancement of fishing, and that such fishermen as are there already and others which shall come thither may have all such reasonable privileges and encouragement as the place will afford, and that such places as are fit for fishermen may be reserved for that purpose, and with this caution also that William Parks, Mr. Glover and Mr. Duncan, or any two of them, be appointed to see the order of court for advance of fishing duly observed." By the deputies III. 108. By the magistrates II. 163, Parks was of Roxbury, the two others of Dorchester.

point, and he was now satisfied that the parliament's cause was good, and if he were in England he would assist in defence of it.[1]

The contentions in Hampton were grown to a great height, the whole town was divided into two factions, one with Mr. Batchellor their late pastor, and the other with Mr. Dalton their teacher, both men very passionate, and wanting discretion and moderation. Their differences were not in matters of opinion but of practice. Mr. Dalton's party being the most of the church, and so freemen, had great advantage of the other, though a considerable party, and some of them of the church also, whereby they carried all affairs both in church and town according to their own minds, and not with that respect to their brethren and neighbours which had been fit. Divers meetings had been both of magistrates and elders, and parties had been reconciled, but brake out presently again, each side being apt to take fire upon any provocation. Whereupon Mr. Batchellor was advised to remove, and was called to Exeter, whither he intended to go, but they being divided, and at great difference also, when one party had appointed a day of humiliation to gather a new church, and call Mr. Batchellor, the court sent order to stop it, for they considered they were not in a fit condition for such a work, and beside, Mr. Batchellor had been in three places before, and through his means, as was supposed, the churches fell to such divisions, as no peace could be till he was removed. And at this court there came petition against petition both from Hampton and Exeter; whereupon the court ordered two or three magistrates to be sent to Hampton with full power to hear and determine all differences there.

At Wenham also there was a public assembly for gathering a church, but the magistrates and elders present, finding upon trial, that the persons appointed were not fit for foundation stones, they advised them not to proceed, which they obeyed.

4. & 5.] About this time, Mr. Vines of Saco, Mr. Short of Pemaquid, and Mr. [2]Wannerton of Pascataquack, went to La

---

1 Happy would it have been for our infant commonwealth, if the same moderation on the subject of its own factions had prevailed, as here seems to be manifested to the parties in the civil discord of their mother country.

2 Wannerton seems to have died as he lived. Josselyn in his Voyages, 26, mentions, that several of his friends at Piscataqua, or beyond, came to take leave of him 24 September 1639, and particularly commemorates "among the rest Captain Thomas Wannerton, who drank to me a pint of kill-devil, alias Rhum, at a draught." Fuller evidence of his habits I find in our Col. Rec. at a court at Newtown, 4 August 1635: "John Holland, being at the eastward, affirmeth, that Mr. Thomas Wannerton threatened to sink his boat, if he would not pay him a debt, that Henry Way ought him, and called him rogue and

Tour to call for some debts, &c. In their way they put in at Penobscott, and were there detained prisoners a few days; but after, for Mr. Short's sake, to whom D'Aulnay was in debt, they were dismissed: and going to La Tour, Mr. Wannerton and some other Englishmen of the eastern parts were entertained by him, and sent with some twenty of his men to try if they could not take Penobscot, for he understood the fort was weakly manned and in want of victual. They went first to a farm house of D'Aulnay's, about six miles off, and there Wannerton and two more went and knocked at the door, with their swords and pistols ready. One opens the door, and another presently shoots Wannerton dead, and a third shoots his second in the shoulder, but he withal discharged his pistol upon him that shot him, and killed him. Then other of Wannerton's company came in and took the house and the two men (for there were no more) prisoners, and they burnt the house and killed the cattle they found there, and so embarked themselves and came to Boston to La Tour. This Thomas Wannerton was a stout man, and had been a soldier many years: he had lived very wickedly in whoredom, drunkenness and quarrelling, so as he had kept the Pascataquack men under ||awe|| of him divers years, till they came under this government, and since that he was much restrained, and the people freed from his terrour. He had of late come under some terrours, and motions of the spirit, by means of the preaching of the word, but he had shaken them off, and returned to his former dissolute course, and so continued till God cut him off by this sudden execution. But this hostile action being led on by an Englishman of our jurisdiction, it was like to provoke D'Aulnay the more against us.

3. 3.] There was mention made before of a pinnace sent by the company of discoverers to Delaware river, with letters from the governour to the Dutch and Swedish governours for liberty to pass. The Dutch promised to let them pass, but for maintaining their own interest he must protest against them. When they came to the Swedes, the fort shot at them, ere they came up: whereupon they cast forth anchor, and the next morning, being

||care||

---

knave, and said they were all so in the bay, and that he hoped to see all their throats cut, and that he could find in his heart to begin with him, and thereupon struck him upon the head; and when the said Holland told him, if Way ought him any money, he might recover it by law, to which Wannerton answered, that they had no law for them but to starve them. The like Bray Wilkinson and Robert Elwell witnesseth against Wannerton. Whereupon it was ordered, that the said Wannerton should put in sufficient sureties for his good behaviour, and in the mean time to remain in durance."

the Lord's day, the lieutenant came aboard them and forced them to fall down lower; when Mr. Aspenwall came to the governour and complained of the lieutenant's ill dealing, both in shooting at them before he had hailed them, and in forcing them to weigh anchor on the Lord's day. The governour acknowledged he did ill in both, and promised all favour, but the Dutch agent, being come down to the Swedes' fort, showed express order from the Dutch governour not to let him pass, whereupon they returned. But before they came out of the river, the Swedish lieutenant made them pay 40 shillings for that shot which he had unduly made. The pinnace arrived at Boston (5) 20.—44. See page [1].

A Dutch ship came from the West Indies and brought to Monhatoes 200 soldiers from Curassou, which was taken by the Portugal and the Indians and 800 slain of the Dutch part, as was reported.

23.] La Tour having been with the governour at Salem, and made known his condition to him, he was moved with compassion towards him, and appointed a meeting of the magistrates and elders at Boston this day. In opening La Tour's case, it appeared that the place, where his fort was, had been purchased by his father of Sir William Alexander, and he had a free grant of it, and of all that part of New Scotland, under the great seal of Scotland, and another grant of a Scotch Baronetcy under the same seal; aud that himself and his father had continued in possession, &c. about thirty years, and that Port Royal was their's also, until D'Aulnay had dispossessed him of it by force within these five years. Most of the magistrates and some of the elders were clear in the case that he was to be relieved, both in point of charity, as a distressed neighbour, and also in point of prudence, as thereby to root out, or at least weaken, an enemy or a dangerous neighbour. But because many of the elders were absent, and three or four of the magistrates dissented, it was agreed the rest of the elders should be called in, and that another meeting should be at Salem the next week.

When they were met, the governour propounded the case to them, and it was brought to the two former questions. 1. Whether it were lawful for true christians to aid an antichristian. 2.

1 Hubbard, 443, has committed a wretched mistake, after transcribing the above paragraph. He applies to the expedition of this pinnace a disaster that befel *another*, whose crew were cut off by the Indians, as related by Winthrop, from whom also Hubbard borrowed that narrative, in a very distant part of this history. No less skilful, than affluent, in materials, was the Ipswich chronicler.

Whether it were safe for us in point of prudence. After much disputation, some of the magistrates and elders remaining unsatisfied, and the rest not willing to conclude any thing in this case without a full consent, a third way was propounded, which all assented unto, which was this, that a letter should be sent to D'Aulnay to this effect, viz. That by occasion of some commissions of his (which had come to our hands) to his captains to take our people, &c. and not knowing any just occasion we had given him, to know the reason thereof, and withal to demand satisfaction for the wrongs he had done us and our confederates in taking Penobscott, and our men and goods at Isle Sable, and threatening to make prize of our vessels if they came to Penobscot, &c. declaring withal that although our men, which went last year to aid La Tour, did it without any commission from us, or any counsel or act of permission of our state, yet if he made it appear to us that they had done him any wrong, (which yet we knew not of,) we should be ready to do him justice; and requiring his express answer by the bearer, and expecting that he should call in all such commissions, &c. We subscribed the letter with the hands of eight of the magistrates, and directed it to Monsieur D'Aulnay, Knight, General for the King of France in L' Acady at Port Royal. We sent it in English, because he had written to our governour in French, but understanding that he had been formerly scrupulous to answer letters in English, we therefore gave the messenger a copy of it in French. We sent also in the letter a copy of an order published by the governour and council, whereby we forbade all our people to use any act of hostility, otherwise than in their own defence, towards French or Dutch, &c. till the next general court, &c. In our letter we also mentioned a course of trade our merchants had entered into with La Tour, and our resolution to maintain them in it.

Before this letter was sent, we had intelligence from the West Indies, that D'Aulnay was met at sea by some Biscayers and his ship sunk, yet being not certain hereof, when La Tour went home, we sent the letter by a vessel of our own which accompanied him, to be delivered if occasion were. This news proved false, and no such thing was; and indeed it was so usual to have false news brought from all parts, that we were very doubtful of the most probable reports.

At the same meeting there were three other questions on foot. The first was upon this occasion.

Captain [1]Stagg arriving at Boston in a ship of London, of 24

---

1 By a probable conjecture, this is the same gentleman, who had a higher

pieces of ordnance, and finding here a ship of Bristol of 100 tons, laden with fish for Bilboa, he made no speech of any commission he had, but having put on shore a good part of his lading, which was wine from Teneriffe, he suddenly weighed anchor, and with the ||sea turn|| sailed from before Boston to Charlestown, and placed his ship between Charlestown and the ||[2]Bristol|| ship, and ||[3]moored|| himself ||[4]abreast|| her. Then he called the master of the ||[5]Bristol|| ship, and showed him his commission, and told him, if he would yield, himself and all his should have what belonged to them and their wages to that day, and turning up the half hour glass, set him in his own ship again, requiring to have his answer by that time of half an hour. The master coming aboard acquainted his men with it, and demanded their resolution. Two or three would have fought, and rather have blown up §their§ ship than have yielded; but the greater part prevailed, so she was quietly taken, and all the men save three sent to Boston, and there order was taken by the captain for their diet.

In this half hour's time much people gathered together upon Windmill hill to see the issue, and some who had interest in the ship, especially one Bristol merchant, (a very bold malignant person,) began to gather company and raise a tumult. But some of the people present laid hold of them and brought them to the deputy governour, who committed the merchant and some others who were strangers to a chamber in an ordinary, with a guard upon them, and others who were town dwellers he committed to prison, and sent the constable to require the people to depart to their houses; and then hearing that the ship was taken, he wrote to the captain to know by what authority he had done it in our harbour, who forthwith repaired to him with his commission, which was to this effect:

Robertus Comes Warwici, &c. magnus Admirallus Angliae, &c. ||[6]omnibus|| cujuscunque status honoris, &c. salutem. Sciatis quod in registro ||[7]curiæ Admiralitatis,|| &c.—and so recites the ordinance of parliament, in English, to this effect: That it should be lawful for all men, &c. to set forth ships and to take all vessels in or outward bound to or from Bristol, Barnstable, Dartmouth, &c. in hostility against the king and parliament, and to visit all ships in any port or creek, &c. by force, if they should

||blank|| ||[2]British|| ||[3]moved|| ||[4]aboard|| ||[5]British|| ||[6]orb : et|| ||[7]cuj : Admiralis||

commission in a few years later. See Thurloe's State Papers, I. 197 or Haz. I. 556, for his authority, jointly with three others, dated 26 September, 1651, to subdue Virginia to the authority of the commonwealth of England.

refuse, &c. and they were to have the whole prize to themselves, paying the ||tenth|| to the admiral, provided, before they went forth, they should give security to the admiral to observe their commission, and that they should make a true invoice of all goods, and not break bulk, but bring the ship to the admiral and two or three of the officers, and that they should not rob or spoil any of the parliament's friends, and so concludes thus: Stagg Capitaneus obligavit se, &c. in bis mille libris, &c. In cujus rei testimonium sigillum Admiralitatis ||2presentibus|| apponi feci.

Dat. March, 1644.

Upon sight of this commission, the deputy appointed Captain Stagg to bring or send it to the meeting at Salem; and the tumult being pacified, he took bond, with sureties, of the principal stirrers, to appear at the meeting and to keep the peace in the mean time. The captain brought his commission to Salem, and there it was read and considered. Some of the elders, the last Lord's day, had in their sermons reproved ||3this|| proceeding, and exhorted the magistrates, &c. to maintain the people's liberties, which were, they said, violated by this act, and that a commission could not supersede a patent. And at this meeting some of the magistrates and some of the elders were of the same opinion, and that the captain should be forced to restore the ship. But the greater part of both were of a different judgment.—Their reasons were these.

1. Because this could be no precedent to bar us from opposing any commission or other foreign power that might indeed tend to our hurt and violate our liberty; for the parliament had taught us, that salus populi is suprema lex.

2. The king of England was enraged against us, and all that party, and all the popish states in Europe: and if we should now, by opposing the parliament, cause them to forsake us, we could have no protection or countenance from any, but should lie open as a prey to all men.

3. We might not deny the parliament's power in this case, unless we should deny the foundation of our government by our patent; for the parliament's authority will take place in all peculiar and privileged places, where the king's writs or commissions will not be of force, as in the Dutchy of Lancaster, the Cinque ports, and in London itself, the parliament may fetch ||4out|| any man, even the Lord Mayor himself, and the reason is, because what the parliament doth is done by themselves, for they have their burgesses, &c. there; nor need they fear that the parliament will do any man wrong: and we have consented to hold our land of

||10 pounds|| ||2blank|| ||3his|| ||4at||

the manor of E. Greenwich, and so such as are burgesses or knights for that manor, are our burgesses also. This only might help us, that the king giving us land which was none of his, but we were forced to purchase it of the natives, or subdue it as vacuum domicilium, we are not bound to hold that of him which was not his. But if we stand upon this plea, we must then renounce our patent and England's protection, which were a great weakness in us, seeing their care hath been to strengthen our liberties and not overthrow them: and if the parliament should hereafter be of a malignant spirit, &c. then if we have strength sufficient, we may make use of salus populi to withstand any authority from thence to our hurt.

4. Again, if we who have so openly declared our affection to the cause of the parliament by our prayers, fastings, &c. should now oppose their authority, or do any thing that might make such an appearance, it would be laid hold on by those in Virginia and the West Indies to confirm them in their rebellious course; and it would grieve all our godly friends in England, or any other of the parliament's friends.

5. Lastly, if any of our people have any goods in the ship, it is not to be questioned, but upon testimony the parliament will take order for their satisfaction.

It was objected by some, that our's is perfecta respublica and so not subject to appeals, and consequently to no other power but among ourselves. It was answered, that though our patent frees us from appeals in cases of judicature, yet not in point of state; for the king of England cannot erigere perfectam rempublicam in such a sense: for nemo potest plus ||juris|| in alios transferre quam in se habet; he hath not an absolute power without the parliament.

Upon these and other considerations, it was not thought fit to oppose the parliament's commission, but to suffer the captain to enjoy his prize. But because some of our merchants had put goods aboard her, wherein they claimed property, they desired to try their right by action, to which the captain consented to appear. So a court was called of purpose, the issue whereof follows after.

The third matter which fell into consideration, at the said meeting at Salem, was about one Franklin, who at the last court of assistants was found guilty of murder, but, some of the magistrates doubting of the justice of the case, he was reprieved till the next court of assistants. The case was this. He had taken to ap-

||jure||

prentice one Nathaniel Sewell, one of those [1]children sent over the last year for the country; the boy had the scurvy, and was withal very noisome, and otherwise ill disposed. His master used him with continual rigour and unmerciful correction, and exposed him many times to much cold and wet in the winter season, and used divers acts of rigour towards him, as hanging him in the chimney, &c. and the boy being very poor and weak, he tied him upon an horse and so brought him (sometimes sitting and sometimes hanging down) to Boston, being five miles off, to the magistrates, and by the way the boy calling much for water, would give him none, though he came close by it, so as the boy was near dead when he came to Boston, and died within a few hours after. Those who doubted whether this were murder or not, did stick upon two reasons chiefly. 1. That it did not appear that the master's intention was to hurt him, but to reform him. 2. In that which was most likely to be the occasion or cause of his death, he was busied about an action which in itself was lawful, viz. the bringing of him before the magistrates; and murder cannot be committed but where the action and intention both are evil. To this it was answered, that this continual act of cruelty did bring him to death by degrees, and the last act was the consummation of it; and that this act, in regard to the subject, who, to the apprehension of all that saw him, was more fit to be kept in his bed than to be haled to correction, was apparently unlawful. As in case a man had a servant sick in bed of the small pox, newly come forth, and that his master knowing and seeing these upon his body should, against the physician's advice, hale him forth of his bed into the open air in frosty weather, upon pretence that he might ease nature, &c. this act, in regard of the state of the subject, were utterly unlawful, and if the servant should die under his hand, &c. it were murder in him. As for the intention, though prima intentio might be to reform him, yet sure proxima intentio was evil, because it arose from distemper of passion; and if a man in a sudden passion kill his dear friend or child, it is murder, though his prima intentio were to instruct or admonish him: and in some cases where there appears no intention to hurt, as where a man knowing his ox to have used to push, shall not keep him in, so as he kills a man, he was to die for it, though to keep an ox were a lawful act, and he did not intend hurt, but because he did not what he reasonably ought to prevent, &c. therefore he was a murderer. And that in Exodus if a master strike his ser-

1 For an account of these unfortunate settlers, the export of a land suffering by civil war, see p. 98 of this volume.

vant with a rod, which is a lawful action, and he die under his hand, (as this servant did,) he was to die for it:—And that in Deut. if a man strike with a weapon or with his hand, or any thing wherewith he may die, and he die, he is a murderer,—shows plainly, that let the means be what it may, if it be voluntarily applied to an evil intent, it is murder; according to that judgment given against her that gave a potion to one to procure his love, and it killed him, it was adjudged murder.

All the magistrates seeming to be satisfied upon this conference, warrant was signed by the governour for his execution a week after, which was not approved by some, in regard of his reprieval to the next court of assistants. But it was without any good reason, for a condemned man is in the power of the magistrate to be executed when he please, and the reprieval was no stipulation or covenant with him, but a determination among the magistrates for the satisfaction of some who were doubtful, which satisfaction being attained, currat lex &c. Pro. 22. He shall go to the pit, let no man hinder him.[1]

This man had been admitted into the church of Roxbury about a month before, and upon this he was cast out; but the church, in compassion to his soul, after his condemnation, procured license for him to come to Roxbury, intending to receive him in again before he died, if they might find him truly penitent. But though presently after his condemnation he judged himself, and justified God and the court, yet then he quarrelled with the witnesses, and justified himself, and so continued even to his execution, professing assurance of salvation, and that God would never lay the boy his death to his charge, but the guilt of his blood would lie upon the country. Only a little before he was turned off the ladder, he seemed to apprehend some hardness of heart, that he could not see himself guilty of that which others did.

A fourth matter then in consideration was upon a speech, which the governour made to this effect, viz. 1. That he could not but bewail the great differences and jarrings which were upon all

---

1 For disapproving the warrant *then* signed, we should now think, the reason was irrefragable. By the records of the court, Vol. II. p. 45, "William Franklin is referred to the magistrates; if they see cause, he may have a second trial for his life, the next quarter court." Now the same magistrates, by whom the first trial was holden, who had granted a reprieve to consider his case at another stated term, hold a meeting before the time of the next quarter court confessedly on other business, and yet act upon this case *against* the prisoner. No injustice was done, except by taking advisement, and passing sentence too soon. When irregularities in the administration of justice in capital causes occur, we may naturally expect other greater deviations from the rules which lie at the very foundation of society.

occasions, among the magistrates, and between them and the deputies; that the ground of this was jealousies and misreports; and thereupon some elders siding, &c. but not dealing with any of them in a way of God; but hearing them reproached and passing it in silence: also their authority questioned, as if they had none out of court but what must be granted them by commission from the general court, &c.—and the way to redress hereof was, that the place and power of magistrates and deputies might be known; and so the elders were desired (which they willingly assented to) to be mediators of a thorough reconciliation, and to go about it presently, and to meet at Boston two or three days before the next court to perfect the same. But indeed the magistrates did all agree very well together, except two only, viz. Mr. Bellingham and Mr. Saltonstall, who took part with the deputies against the other ten magistrates about their power, and in other cases where any difference was. And some of the elders had done no good offices in this matter, through their misapprehensions both of the intentions of the magistrates, and also of the matters themselves, being affairs of state, which did not belong to their calling.[1]

The merchants which had to do with the goods in the ship which was seized by Captain Stagg, being desirous to do their utmost to save their principals in England from damage, knowing them to be honest men and faithful to the parliament, intended to have a trial at law about it, and procured an attachment against the captain; but they were dissuaded from that course, and the deputy sent for Captain Stagg and acquainted him with it, and took his word for his appearance at the next court which was called of purpose. When the governour and six other of the magistrates were met, (for the governour did not send for such as dwelt far off,) and the jury, the merchants were persuaded not to put it to a jury, for the jury could find no more but the matter of fact, viz. whose the goods were, whether the merchants' in England, or theirs who shipped them, in regard they had not yet made any consignment of them, nor taken any bills of lading: and this the magistrates could as well determine upon proof, and certify accordingly: for it was resolved not to use any force against the parliament's authority; and accordingly they certified

---

1 Yet their advice *upon affairs of state, which did not belong to their calling*, was asked by the same magistrates, in points connected with these very misapprehensions. No doubt the opinions of the clergy were sincere, and, as they appear a few pages onward, will approve themselves to the sober judgment of impartial posterity; but it may be feared, that those opinions, certainly so far as formed by the principal members of the body, were previously known to the party, in whose favour they were given.

the Lord Admiral of the true state of the case, as they found it upon examination and oath of the factors.

The pinnace which went to Delaware upon discovery, returned with loss of their voyage. The occasion was, the Dutch governour made a protest against them, yet promised them leave to pass, &c. provided they should not trade with the Indians: also the Swedish governour gave them leave to pass, but would not permit them to trade; and for that end each of them had appointed a pinnace to wait upon our pinnace, but withal the master of their vessel proved such a drunken sot, and so complied with the Dutch and Swedes, as they feared, when they should have left the vessel to have gone up to the lake in a small boat, he would in his drunkenness have betrayed their goods, &c. to the Dutch, whereupon they gave over and returned home; and bringing their action against the master both for his drunkenness and denial to proceed as they required, and as by charter party he was bound, they recovered 200 pounds of him, which was too much, though he did deal badly with them, for it was very probable they could not have proceeded.

There fell out a troublesome business at Boston, upon this occasion. There arrived here a Portugal ship with salt, having in it two Englishmen only. One of these happened to be drunk, and was carried to his lodging, and the constable, (a godly man, and zealous against such disorders,) hearing of it, found him out, being upon his bed asleep, so he awaked him, and ||led|| him to the stocks, there being no magistrate at home. He being in the stocks, one of La Tour's gentlemen lifted up the stocks and let him out. The constable, hearing of it, went to the Frenchman, (being then gone and quiet,) and would needs carry him to the stocks; the Frenchman offered to yield himself to go to prison, but the constable, not understanding his language, pressed him to go to the stocks: the Frenchman resisted and drew his sword; with that company came in and disarmed him, and carried him by force to the stocks, but soon after the constable took him out and carried him to prison, and presently after took him forth again and delivered him to La Tour. Much tumult there was about this: many Frenchmen were in town, and other strangers, which were not satisfied with this dealing of the constable, yet were quiet. In the morning the magistrates examined the cause and sent for La Tour, who was much grieved for his servant's miscarriage, and also for the disgrace put upon him, (for in France it is a most ignominious thing to be laid in the stocks,) but yet he complained not of any injury, but left him wholly to the magistrates

||bade||

to do with him what they pleased. The magistrates told him, they were sorry to have any such occasion against any of his servants, but they must do justice, and therefore they must commit him to prison, except he could find sureties to be forth coming, to answer, &c. and to keep the peace. La Tour's gentlemen offered to engage themselves for him. They answered, they might not take security of strangers in this case, otherwise they would have desired no more than La Tour's own word. Upon this two Englishmen, members of the church of Boston, standing by, offered to be his sureties, whereupon he was bailed till he should be called for, because La Tour was not like to stay till the court. This was thought too much favour for such an offence by many of the common people, but by our law bail could not be denied him, and beside the constable was the occasion of all this in transgressing the bounds of his office, and that in six things. 1. In fetching a man out of his lodging that was asleep upon his bed, and without any warrant from authority. 2. In not ||putting|| a hook upon the stocks, nor setting some to guard them. 3. In laying hands upon the Frenchman that had opened the stocks, when he was gone and quiet, and no disturbance of the peace then appearing. 4. In carrying him to prison without warrant. 5. In delivering him out of prison without warrant. 6. In putting such a reproach upon a stranger and a gentleman, when there was no need, for he knew he would be forthcoming, and the magistrate would be at home that evening: but such are the fruits of ignorant and misguided zeal. It might have caused much blood and no good done by it, and justice might have had a more fair and safe way, if the constable had kept within his own bounds, and had not interfered upon the authority of the magistrate. But the magistrates thought not convenient to lay these things to the constable's charge before the assembly, but rather to admonish him for it in private, lest they should have discouraged and discountenanced an honest officer, and given occasion to the offenders and their abettors to insult over him. The constable may restrain, and, if need be, imprison in the stocks, such as he sees disturbing the peace, but, when the affray is ended and the parties departed and in quiet, it is the office of the magistrate to make inquiry and to punish it, and the persons so wrongfully imprisoned by the constable might have had their action of false imprisonment against him.

6. 26.] About nine in the evening there fell a great flame of fire down into the water towards Pullen Point; it lighted the air far about: it was no lightning, for the sky was very clear.

At Stamford an Indian came into a poor man's house, none being at home but the wife, and a child in the cradle, and taking

||getting||

up a lathing hammer as if he would have bought it, the woman stooping down to take her child out of the cradle, he struck her with the sharp edge upon the side of her head, wherewith she fell down, and then he gave her two cuts more which pierced into her brains, and so left her for dead, carrying away some clothes which lay at hand. This woman after a short time came to herself and got out to a neighbour's house, and told what had been done to her, and described the Indian by his person and clothes, &c. Whereupon many Indians of those parts were brought before her, and she charged one of them confidently to be the man, whereupon he was put in prison with intent to have put him to death, but he escaped, and the woman recovered, but lost her senses. A good time after the Indians brought another Indian whom they charged to have committed that fact, and he, upon examination, confessed it, and gave the reason thereof, and brought forth some of the clothes which he had stolen. Upon this the magistrates of New Haven, taking advice of the elders in those parts, and some here, did put him to death. The executioner would strike off his head with a falchion, but he had eight blows at it before he could effect it, and the Indian sat upright and stirred not all the time.

7. 7.] Here came a pinnace from Virginia with letters from the governour and council there, for procuring powder and shot to prosecute their war against the Indians, but we were weakly provided ourselves, and so could not afford them any help in that kind.[1]

9.] Mr. La Tour departed from Boston; all our train bands (it being then the ordinary training day) made a guard for him to his boat; and the deputy governour and many others accompanied him to the wharf. When he was aboard his bark, he weighed, and set sail and shot off all his guns, which were six, and our small shot gave him a volley and one piece of ordnance, and all the ships, viz. four, saluted him, each of them with three pieces.

At the court of assistants, Thomas Morton was called forth presently after the lecture, that the country might be satisfied of the justice of our proceeding against him. There was laid to his charge his complaint against us at the council board, which he denied. Then we produced the copy of the bill exhibited by Sir Christopher Gardiner, &c. wherein we were charged with treason, rebellion, &c. wherein he was named as a party or witness. He denied that he had any hand in the information, only was cal-

---

1 Winthrop seems to have doubted, in the following winter, of the goodness of this excuse, for the refusal was visited by a judgment of heaven in the destruction of our magazine.

led as a witness. To convince him to be the principal party, it was showed: 1. That Gardiner had no occasion to complain against us, for he was kindly used, and dismissed in peace, professing much engagement for the great courtesy he found here. 2. Morton had set forth a book against us, and had threatened us, and had prosecuted a quo warranto against us, which he did not deny. 3. His letter was produced, written soon after to Mr. Jeffery, his old acquaintance and intimate friend, in these words.

My very good Gossip,

If I should commend myself to you, you reply with this proverb, propria laus sordet in ore: but to leave impertinent salute, and really to proceed.—You shall hereby understand, that, although, when I was first sent to England to make complaint against Ananias and the brethren, I effected the business but superficially, (through the brevity of time,) I have at this time taken more deliberation and brought the matter to a better pass. And it is thus brought about, that the king hath taken the business into his own hands. The Massachusetts Patent, by order of the council, was brought in view; the privileges there granted well scanned upon, and at the council board in public, and in the presence of Sir Richard Saltonstall and the rest, it was declared, for manifest abuses there discovered, to be void. The king hath reassumed the whole business into his own hands, appointed a committee of the board, and given order for a general ||governour|| of the whole territory to be sent over. The commission is passed the privy seal, I did see it, and the same was ||[2]1 mo. Maii|| sent to the Lord Keeper to have it pass the great seal for confirmation; and I now stay to return with the governour, by whom all complainants shall have relief: So that now Jonas being set ashore may safely cry, repent you cruel separatists, repent, there are as yet but forty days. If ||[3]Jove|| vouchsafe to thunder, the charter and kingdom of the separatists will fall asunder. Repent you cruel ||[4]schismatics||, repent. These things have happened, and I shall see (notwithstanding their boasting and false alarms in the Massachusetts with feigned cause of thanksgiving) their merciless cruelty rewarded, according to the merit of the fact, with condign punishment for coming into those parts, like Sampson's foxes with fire-brands at their tails. The king and council are really possessed of their preposterous loyalty and irregular proceedings, and are incensed against them: and although they be so opposite to the catholic ||[5]axioms||, yet they will be compelled to perform them, or at ||[6]leastwise|| suffer them to be put in practice to their sorrow.

||government|| ||[2]10th May|| ||[3]you|| ||[4]blank|| ||[5]opinions|| ||[6]least must||

In matter of restitution and satisfaction, more than mystically, it must be performed visibly, and in such sort as may be subject to the senses in a very lively image. My Lord Canterbury having, with my Lord Privy Seal, caused all Mr. Cradock's letters to be viewed, and his apology in particular for the brethren here, protested against him and Mr. Humfrey, that they were a couple of imposterous knaves; so that, for all their great friends, they departed the council chamber in our view with a pair of cold shoulders. I have staid long, yet have not lost my labour, although the brethren have found their hopes frustrated; so that it follows by consequence, I shall see my desire upon mine enemies: and if John Grant had not betaken him to flight, I had taught him to sing clamavi in the Fleet before this time, and if he return before I depart, he will pay dear for his presumption. For here he finds me a second Perseus: I have uncased Medusa's head, and struck the brethren into astonishment. They find, and will yet more to their shame, that they abuse the word and are to blame to presume so much—that they are but a word and a blow to them that are without. Of these particulars I thought good, by so convenient a messenger, to give you notice, lest you should think I had died in obscurity, as the brethren vainly intended I should, and basely practised, abusing justice by their sinister practices, as by the whole body of the committee, una voce, it was concluded to be done, to the dishonour of his ||majesty||. And as for Ratcliffe, he was comforted by their lordships with the cropping of Mr. Winthrop's ears: which shows what opinion is held amongst them of King Winthrop with all his inventions and his Amsterdam fantastical ordinances, his preachings, marriages, and other abusive ceremonies, which do exemplify his detestation to the church of England, and the contempt of his ||²majesty's|| authority and wholesome laws, which are and will be established in those parts, invita Minerva. With these I thought fit to salute you, as a friend, by an epistle, because I am bound to love you, as a brother, by the gospel, resting your loving friend.[1] THOMAS MORTON.

Dated 1 mo. Maii, 1634.

||master|| ||²master's||

[1] See Vol. I. 137, n. 4, and 138, n. 1. In the writer's tone of exultation over the brethren of New England we must remember the circumstances, that he had been more than three years and a half claiming redress for his fancied wrongs, and wrote on the same day that the royal commission, the evidence of his triumph, passed the privy seal. A comparison of my reading with that of Hubbard, 428–430, will show his transcript of this very curious document to be much more correct than that of the former edition. [Unhappily my corrections are lost.]

The patent was called for An. 1634, by order of council.

Having been kept in prison about a year, in expectation of further evidence out of England, he was again called before the court, and after some debate what to do with him, he was fined 100 pounds, and set at liberty. He was a charge to the country, for he had nothing, and we thought not fit to inflict corporal punishment upon him, being old and crazy, but thought better to fine him and give him his liberty, as if it had been to procure his fine, but indeed to leave him opportunity to go out of the jurisdiction, as he did soon after, and he went to Acomenticus, and living there poor and despised, he died within two years after.

7. 16.] Here arrived a ship from Dartmouth. She was impressed into the king's service, and sent to sea in the Earl of Marlborough's fleet, but she left the fleet, and took in wine and salt at the Spanish Islands, and went to Virginia, where he left his merchants and divers of his men; and not putting off his goods there, he came to Boston, where the London ship, Captain Bayley commander, having commission from the parliament, would have taken him, but he stood upon his defence, and was able to keep his ship against the other. But another question arose about her, upon this occasion; our merchants of Boston had set out a small ship worth 1500 pounds, which, being trading in Wales, was taken by the king's ships, whereupon the merchants desired leave to seize this ship for their satisfaction. On the other side, the master, being come under our command, desired our protection. Our answer was, that, if he would deliver his sailors on shore, we would protect him till the court, &c. See more next leaf.

17.] The lady La Tour arrived here from London in a ship commanded by Captain Bayley. They had been six months from London, having spent their time in trading about Canada, &c. They met with D'Aulnay near Cape Sable, and told him they were bound for the Bay, and had stowed the lady and her people under hatches, so he not knowing it was Captain Bayley, whom he earnestly sought for, to have taken or sunk him, he wrote by the master to the deputy governour to this effect: That his master the king of France, understanding that the aid La Tour had here the last year was upon the commission he showed from the Vice Admiral of France, gave him in charge not to molest us for it, but to hold all good correspondency with us and all the English, which he professed he was desirous of, so far as might stand with his duty to his master, and withal that he intended to send to us so soon as he had settled his affairs, to let us know what further commission he had, and his sincerity in the business of La Tour, &c.

Here arrived also Mr. Roger Williams of Providence, and with him two or three families. He brought with him a letter from divers lords and others of the parliament, the copy whereof ensueth.

Our much honoured Friends.

Taking notice, some of us of long time, of Mr. Roger Williams his good affections and conscience, and of his sufferings by our common enemies and oppressors of God's people, the prelates, as also of his great industry and travail in his printed Indian labours in your parts, the like whereof we have not seen extant from any part of America, and in which respect it hath pleased both houses of parliament freely to grant unto him and friends with him a free and absolute ||[1]charter|| of civil government for those parts of his abode: and withal sorrowfully resenting, that amongst good men (our friends) driven to the ends of the world, exercised with the trials of a wilderness, and who mutually give good testimony each of other, as we observe you do of him, and he abundantly of you, there should be such a distance; we thought it fit, upon divers considerations, to profess our great desires of both your utmost endeavours of nearer closing, and of ready expressing of those good affections, which we perceive you bear each to other, in the actual performance of all friendly offices; the rather because of those bad neighbours you are like to find too near unto you in Virginia, and the unfriendly visits from the West of England and from Ireland: that howsoever it may please the Most High to shake our foundations, yet the report of your peaceable and prosperous plantations may be some refreshing to

Your true and faithful friends

Northumberland,	P. Wharton,
Rob. Harley,	Thos. Barrington,
Wm. Masham,	Ol. St. John,
John Gurdon,	Isaac Pennington,
Cor. Holland,	Gil. Pykering,
J. Blakiston,	Miles Corbet.

To the Right Worshipful the Governour and Assistants and the rest of our worthy friends in the plantation of Massachusetts Bay, in New England.

||character||

1 It bears date 14 March preceding, and may be seen in Haz. I. 538 or 2 Hist. Coll. IX. 185. Callender 44 erroneously gives the date 17 March. Williams probably came in the same ship with Lady La Tour.

19.] Two churches were appointed to be gathered, one at Haverhill and the other at Andover, both upon Merrimack river. They had given notice thereof to the magistrates and elders, who desired, in regard of their far remoteness and scarcity of housing there, the meeting might be at Rowley, which they assented unto, but being assembled, most of those who were to join, refused to declare how God had carried on the work of his grace in them, upon this reason, because they had declared it formerly in their admission into other churches; whereupon the assembly brake up without proceeding, &c.

The governour and others of the magistrates met at Boston upon two special occasions; the one was for trial of an action between the Lady La Tour and Captain Bayley for not carrying her &c. to her own place, and for some injuries done her aboard his ship. See more after.

The other was upon the request of some merchants of Boston, who, having a ship taken in Wales by the king's party, desired recompence by a ship of Dartmouth riding in our harbour. Whereupon we sent for the master of the Dartmouth ship, who delivered his ship into our hands till the cause should be tried, which he did the more willingly, for that some London ships of greater force, riding also in our harbour, had threatened to take him; and the next morning Captain Richardson (having commission from the Lord Admiral) fitted his ship to take her, notwithstanding that he had been forbidden over night by the deputy governour to meddle with her, being under our protection, and lying so before Boston as their shot must needs do harm. Whereupon the governour and the other magistrates (sitting then in court) arose and went to take order about it, and having over night given commission to some to make seizure of the Dartmouth ship, they went aboard her with their commission, and an officer was sent with warrant to stay Captain Richardson, but he being then come to anchor close by the other ship, he could not (or would not) stay, but suffered his men to enter the other ship, and the master coming aboard him at his request, he detained him prisoner. Whereupon the governour &c. sent two other masters of ships to him to command him ashore, but he seeing his men so unruly, and fearing they would fall to fight or pillage in his absence, (as he after told us,) excused himself for not coming upon that command. Upon which fire was given to a warning piece from the battery, which cut a rope in the head of his ship: and upon that one of his men, without any command, ran down hastily to fire upon our battery; but it pleased God that he hurt himself in the way, and so was not able to go on. A stranger also (unbidden) gave fire to another piece on the battery which was levelled at the bow of his ship, but it struck against the head of a bolt in the cutwater of the Dartmouth ship, and went no further. Then we sent forty men armed aboard the Dartmouth ship, and upon that Captain Richardson came ashore and acknowledged his errour, and his sorrow for what he had done, yet ||withal|| alleging some reasons for his excuse. So we only ordered him to pay a barrel of powder, and to satisfy the officers and soldiers we had employed &c. and dismissed him. The reason was, because (through the Lord's special providence) there was no hurt done, nor had he made one shot; for if he had, we were resolved to have taken or sunk him, which we might easily have done, lying close under our battery, so as we could have played upon him with whole culverin or demi culverin six hours together, nor had he yet showed to us or to the master of the Dartmouth ship any commission. But after, he showed only an ordinary commission from the Lord Admiral, not under the great seal, nor grounded upon any ordinance of parliament, as Captain Stagg's was: therefore we forbade him to meddle with any ship in our harbour, for he could not by that commission take a ship in any place exempt from the Admiral's jurisdiction.

Having thus seized this ship, we were to consult what to do with her. Upon examination, we found that the master and company were Dartmouth men, and that the ship had formerly been employed in the parliament's service, but, Dartmouth being taken by the king, she had been employed for taking a vessel or two of the parliament's under the same master, but a captain put over him and many soldiers, and was since sold to a merchant of ||2Christopher|| Island, and by his agent sent forth upon merchant affairs to divers places, and to repair at last to St. Maloes in France where the agent dwelt, who was an Englishman and had used to trade at Dartmouth, whose letter of advice and the bill of sale of the ship were produced by the master. It appeared further to us, that Dartmouth had been cordial to the parliament, and stood out seven days against 12,000 men; and after it was surrendered did generally refuse to take the oath to the king, and the master among others, and that they had many better ships there which lay still at home, and such as they sent forth they were not to come home but by advice. Yet it appeared after by divers testimonies, that she belonged to Dartmouth, and the charter party also, and that the master was part owner. Divers of the elders, being called in for advice, agreed (near all) that she might be seized to satisfy for our two ships which the king's party had taken from us, and accordingly commission was given by

||with|| ||2P——||

the governour and council to the merchant to seize and use her, giving security to be responsible and 8 pounds per 100 if she should be lawfully recovered within thirteen months, but the company to have their wages and goods.

While the governour and other of the magistrates were at Boston, a boat sent from Mr. D'Aulnay with ten men arrived at Salem, hearing that the governour dwelt there. There was in her one Marie, supposed to be a friar, but habited like a gentleman. He wrote a letter to our governour by a gentleman of his company to know where he should attend him: and upon our governour's answer to him, he came the next day to Boston, and with letters of credence and commission from Mr. D'Aulnay; he showed us the king of France his commission under the great seal of France, with the privy seal annexed, wherein the proceedings against La Tour were verified, and he condemned as a rebel and traitor &c. with command for the apprehension of himself and lady, who had fled out of France against special order, under &c. He complained also of the wrong done by our men the §last§ year in assisting of La Tour &c. and proffered terms of peace and amity. We answered to the 1. That divers of the ships and most of the men were strangers to us, and had no commission from us, nor any permission to use any hostility, and we were very sorry when we heard what had been done. This gave him satisfaction. To the other proposition we answered, that we could not conclude any league with him, without the advice of the commissioners of the united colonies; but if he would set down his propositions in writing, we would consider further of them: and withal we acquainted him with what we had lately written to Mr. D'Aulnay, and the injuries we had complained of to him. So he withdrew himself to his lodging at Mr. ||Fowle's||, and drew out both his propositions and answers to our complaints in French, and returned to us. He added two propositions more, one that we would aid him against La Tour, and the other that we would not assist him, and gave reasonable answer to our demands. Upon these things we discoursed half the day, sometimes with our governour in French and otherwhile with the rest of the magistrates in Latin. We urged much for a reconciliation with La Tour, and that he would permit his lady to go to her husband. His answer was, that if La Tour would voluntarily submit and come in, he would assure him his life and liberty, but if he were taken, he were sure to lose his head in France; and for his lady, she was known to be the cause of his contempt and rebellion, and therefore they could not let her go to him, but if we should send her in any of our vessels he must take her, and if we carried any

||Fowler's||

goods to La Tour he would take them also, but he would give us satisfaction for them. In the end we came to this agreement, which was drawn up in Latin in these words, and signed by the governour and six other magistrates and Mr. Marie, whereof one copy we kept and the other he carried with him. He came to Boston the sixth day very late, and made great haste away, so he departed on the third day following. We furnished him with horses and sent him to Salem well accompanied, and offered him a bark to carry him home, but he refused it. We entertained him with all courteous respect, and he seemed to be surprised with his unexpected entertainment, and gave a very liberal testimony of his kind acceptance thereof and assurance of Mr. D'Aulnay's engagement to us for it. The agreement between us was this.

The agreement between John Endecott, Esq. Governour of the Massachusetts in New England, and the rest of the magistrates there, and Mr. Marie, commissioner of Mr. D'Aulnay, Knight, Governour and Lieutenant General of his Majesty the king of France, in Acadie, a province of New France, made and ratified at Boston in the Massachusetts aforesaid, 8 die mensis 8 An. Dom. 1644.

The governour and the rest of the magistrates do promise to Mr. Marie, that they and all the English within the jurisdiction of the Massachusetts aforesaid shall observe and keep firm peace with Mr. D'Aulnay &c. and all the French under his command in Acadie: and likewise the said Mr. Marie doth promise for Mr. D'Aulnay, that he and all his people shall also keep firm peace with the governour and magistrates aforesaid, and with all the inhabitants of the jurisdiction of the Massachusetts aforesaid; and that it shall be lawful for all men, both French and English to trade each with other: so that if any occasion of offence shall happen, neither party shall attempt any thing against the other in any hostile manner before the wrong be first complained of, and due satisfaction not given. Provided always, the governour and magistrates aforesaid be not bound to restrain their merchants to trade with their ships with any persons, either French or other, wheresoever they dwell: provided also, that the full ratification and conclusion of this agreement be referred to the next meeting of the commissioners of the united colonies of New England, for the continuation or abrogation of the same; and in the mean time to remain firm and inviolate.[1]

---

1 Copy of the original, of which translation is below, may be seen in Haz. I. 536 with a solemn confirmation, also in Latin, by the congress of commissioners of the United Colonies. Probably Winthrop wrote the treaty, as from what is

By this agreement we were freed from the fear our people were in, that Mr. D'Aulnay would take revenge of our small vessels or out plantations, for the harm he sustained by our means the last year; and also from any further question about that business.

We were now also freed from as great a fear of war with the Narragansetts. For the commissioners, meeting at Hartford, sent for Onkus and some from Narragansett, (a sachem and a chief captain were sent,) and whereas the Narragansett's plea against Onkus was, that he had put their sachem to death after he had received a ransom for his life, it was clearly proved otherwise, and that the things he received were part of them given him for his courteous usage of the said Miantunnomoh and those sachems which were slain in the battle, and another part, that Miantunnomoh might be given to the English. In the end it was agreed by all parties, that there should be peace on all sides till planting time were over the next year; and then neither of them should attempt any hostile act against the other, without first acquainting the English &c. therewith.

The lady La Tour, being arrived here, commenced her action against Captain Bayley and the merchant, (brother and factor to Alderman Berkley who freighted the ship,) for not performing the charter party, having spent so much time upon the coast in trading, as they were near six months in coming and had not carried her to her fort as they ought and might have done: and upon a full hearing in a special court four days, the jury gave her 2,000 pounds. For had they come in any reasonable time, it might have been much more to her advantage in her trade and safety against D'Aulnay: whereas now it was like to occasion her utter ruin: for she knew not how to get home without hiring two or three ships of force.

La Tour, and a vessel of ours in his company laden with provision, went hence with a fair wind, which if he had made use of, he had met with D'Aulnay, and after he had touched at divers places by the way, and staid there some time, he passed by Penobscot soon after D'Aulnay was gone into the harbour, and so escaped, whereas if he had passed any time many days before, he must needs have been taken. This vessel of ours in her return was met by D'Aulnay, who stayed her, and taking the mas-

---

said above it may reasonably be concluded, that Endecott was not sufficiently versed in the learned language. An original rough draft, by Winthrop, in Latin, of the act of ratification by the commissioners, 3tio die 7bris Anno Domini 1645, is preserved in the Hutchinson MSS.

ter aboard his ship, manned the other with Frenchmen, and telling the master his intention, and assuring him of all good usage and recompense for the stay of his vessel, (all which he really performed,) he brought her with him to the mouth of St. John's river; and then §sent§ her boat with one gentleman of his own to La Tour to show his commission, and withal desired the master to write to La Tour to desire him to dismiss the messenger safely, for otherwise D'Aulnay would keep him for hostage (yet he assured him he would not do it.) So La Tour dismissed the messenger in peace, which he professed he would not have done but for our master's sake. D'Aulnay carried our ketch with him to Port Royal, where he used the master very courteously and gave him credit for fish, &c. he bought of him, and recompense for keeping his vessel, and so dismissed him. Presently after their return, we sent another vessel to trade with D'Aulnay, and by it the deputy governour wrote to D'Aulnay to show the cause of sending her, with profession of our desire of holding good correspondency with him &c. and withal persuading him by divers arguments to entertain peace with La Tour. That vessel found courteous entertainment with him, and he took off all her commodities, but not at so good rates as they expected.

The lady La Tour having arrested the captain and merchant of the ship, they were forced to deliver their cargo on shore to free their persons, by which means she laid her execution upon them to the value of 1100 pounds; more could not be had without unfurnishing the ship, which must have been by force, for otherwise the master and seamen would deliver none. The master petitioned the general court for his freight and wages, for which the goods stood bound by charter party. The general court was much divided about it, but the ||magistrates|| voted that none was due ||2here||, nor the goods bound for them; but the major part of the deputies being of another judgment, they made use of their negative vote, and so nothing was ordered. Whereupon the master brought his action at the next court of assistants. When it came to be tried, two of the assistants were of opinion that it ought not to be put to trial, because the general court had the hearing and voting of it: but it was answered by the rest, (the governour being absent,) that, seeing the general court had made no order in it, this court might hear and determine it, as if the general court had never taken cognizance of it. Accordingly it was put to the jury upon this issue: Whether the goods were security for the freight &c. And the jury found for the defendant, and yet in the charter party the merchants bound themselves, their executors, &c.

||major part|| ||2her||

and goods, as the owners had bound their ship &c. to the merchants.

This business caused much trouble and charge to the country, and made some difference between the merchants of Charlestown, (who took part with the merchants and master of the ship,) and the merchants of Boston, who assisted the lady, (some of them being deeply engaged for La Tour,) so as offers were made on both sides for an end between them. Those of Charlestown offered security for the goods, if upon a review within thirteen months the judgment were not reversed, or the parliament in England did not call the cause before themselves. This last clause was very ill taken by the court as making way for appeals &c. into England, which was not reserved in our charter. The other offered them all the goods save 150 pounds to defray the lady's expenses in town, and security for that, if the judgment was reversed, so as the other ||would give|| security to answer the whole 2,000 pounds if the judgment were not reversed, &c.

10. 8.] The parties not agreeing, the lady took the goods and hired three ships which lay in the harbour, belonging to strangers, which cost her near 800 pounds, and set sail for her fort. And the merchants, against whom she had execution for their bodies for satisfaction of the rest of the judgment, got into their ship and fell down beyond the castle, (where they were out of command,) and took aboard some thirty passengers, and so, (26,) in company of one of our own ships which carried about seventy passengers, they set sail for London.

When our ship, &c. arrived at London, Alderman Berkley arrested the goods of two of the passengers.[1]

||would not give||

1 Here ends the narrative of our second volume of MS. and all that purported to be published from a *correct copy* at Hartford in 1790. If my labour has not seemed to myself of too great value, this new edition will not be less cherished by the admirers of Winthrop than the succeeding part of this volume, which had never before been seen by the public.

A CONTINUATION

OF THE

HISTORY

OF

NEW ENGLAND.

1644.

17. 7.] THE Lady La Tour arrived here in a ship set forth from London by Alderman Berkley and Captain Bayley. They were bound for La Tour's fort, and set forth in the spring, but spent so much time in trading by the way &c. as when they came at Cape Sable, Monsieur D'Aulnay came up to them in a ship from France, so as they durst not discover what they were, but stood along for Boston. The lady, being arrived, brought her action against them for delaying her so long at sea, whereby she lost the opportunity of relieving her fort, and must be at excessive charges to get thither. The cause was openly heard at a special court at Boston before all the magistrates, and a jury of principal men impannelled, (most merchants and seamen,) and the charter party being read, and witnesses produced, it appeared to the court, that

1 My emotions, on coming again to the true text of the original historian, where others may follow my footsteps in the original MS. and scrutinize the faithfulness of the track, are very gratifying. The common reader, who feels the difference between the text, from page 13 of this volume to the last, wherein my memory and judgment only have contributed sometimes to its correctness, and that pure transcript extending from page 197 of the former volume to page 12 of this, ad fidem codicis, on which he may confidently rely, though the MS. is destroyed by fire, will rejoice in the new field that he now enters on, without participating my exultation in the hope that future scrupulous antiquaries will the more diligently, on account of the loss of the second, recur to the first and third volumes of Winthrop's autograph.

they had broken charter party, so as the jury gave her 2000 pounds damages. Whereupon the cargo of the ship was seized in execution, (so much of it as could be found,) and being meal, and peas, and trading stuff &c. and being appraised by four men, sworn &c. it was found to the value of about 1100 pounds. The defendants desired liberty till the next year to bring a review, pretending they had evidence in England &c. It was granted them, and they were offered to have all their goods again, (except 100 pounds for defraying the lady's present charges in Boston, for which they should have good security &c.) so as they would put in security to answer the whole 2000 pounds, if they did not reverse the judgment within the year. This they refused, and would give security for no more than what they should receive back; whereupon the execution proceeded. But the master of the ship brought his action upon the goods in execution for security for his freight and men's wages (which did amount to near the whole extended.) The jury found against him, whereupon at the next general court he petitioned for redress. A great part of the court was of opinion, that the goods, being his security by charter party, ought not to be taken from him upon the execution, and most of the deputies, and the deputy governour, and some others of the magistrates voted that way; but the greater part of the magistrates being of the other side, he would not be relieved. The lady was forced to give 700 pounds to three ships to carry her home.[1]

It may be of use to mention a private matter or two, which fell out about this time, because the power and mercy of the Lord did appear in them in extraordinary manner. One of the deacons of Boston church, Jacob [2]Eliot, (a man of a very sincere heart

---

1 In the margin is written, by Winthrop, "*this is before in the other book*," and diagonal cross lines are drawn from the top of the page to the bottom. But as some of this is *not* in the former book, I have thought the whole worth printing, at least as an abridged narrative.

2 He was, I presume, a relative of the great apostle of our American gentiles, for both were admitted freemen on the same day, soon after arrival of John, and, in the list of our first church members, Jacob is numbered 114, only four after the distinguished divine. That he was carried away with the delusions of Mrs. Hutchinson, with the majority of Boston people, appears in our Vol. I. 248. In his will, made 28 April 1651, proved 20 November after, in our Probate Rec. I. 58, he takes notice of only one son, Jacob, a minor, and of unmarried daughters, one of whom is, no doubt, referred to in our text. Mather, Lib. VI. c. 2, relates this disaster, and gives her name, Abigail, adding, that "she lived to be a mother of several children." The author of the Magnalia might have conversed with her, for she could be only twenty four or five years older than himself. Without feeling the reasonable distrust of his authority, which experience would justify, I have ascertained, from the will of Margery, widow of Jacob, made 31 October 1661, proved 7 November following, by

and an humble frame of spirit,) had a daughter of eight years of age, who being playing with other children about a cart, the hinder end thereof fell upon the child's head, and an iron sticking out of it struck into the child's head, and drove a piece of the skull before it into the brain, so as the brains came out, and seven surgeons (some of the country, very experienced men, and others of the ships, which rode in the harbour) being called together for advice &c. did all conclude, that it was the brains, (being about half a spoonful at one time, and more at other times,) and that there was no hope of the child's life, except the piece of skull could be drawn out. But one of the ruling elders of the church, an experienced and very skilful surgeon, liked not to take that course, but applied only plasters to it; and withal earnest prayers were made by the church to the Lord for it, and in six weeks it pleased God that the piece of skull consumed, and so came forth, and the child recovered perfectly; nor did it lose the senses at any time.

Another was a child of one [1]Bumstead, a member of the church, had a child of about the same age, that fell from a gallery in the meeting house about eighteen feet high, and brake the arm and shoulder, (and was also committed to the Lord in the prayers of the church, with earnest desires, that the place where his people assembled to his worship might not be defiled with blood,) and it pleased the Lord also that this child was soon perfectly recovered.

The differences which fell out in the court, and still continued [blank.]

A bark was set out from Boston with seven men to trade at Delaware. They staid in the river near the English plantation all the winter, and in the spring they fell down, and traded three

---

Rev. J. Wilson, and elders Colbron and Penn, that the children were Jacob and Asaph, Hannah Frary, Susannah, Mehitable and Sarah, with five grand children, issue, probably, of Hannah. There was an Abigail Eliot, but she was daughter of Francis, whose will, made 20 October 1677, proved 13 November after, is found in Rec. VI. 214. Jacob had a child of that name, born 7 April 1639, of course *now* only five years old; but the casualty, I suppose, befel Hannah, born 29 January 1636-7.

Another Eliot, Philip, a gentleman of some distinction at Roxbury, was brother of Rev. John, a deacon of his church, and made freeman 25 March 1636. In his will, made 21 October 1657, proved 11 February next after, found in our Probate Rec. I. 293, he mentions three daughters, and no son.

1 Thomas Bumstead's will, made 25 May 1677, proved 4 August after, which is contained in our Probate Rec. VI. 530, names a son, Jeremy, and three daughters, Hannah, wife of Thomas Sherwood, Mary, wife of Ambrose Dawes, and Mary, wife of Samuel Bosworth. I know nothing more of him, nor why he had the same name for two daughters.

weeks, and had gotten five hundred skins, and some otter &c. and being ready to come away, fifteen Indians came aboard, as if they would trade again, and suddenly they drew forth hatchets from under their coats, and killed the [1]master and three others, and rifled the bark, and carried away a boy, and another man, who was the interpreter; and when they came on shore, they gave him forty skins, and twenty fathom of wampom, and other things, and kept them till about six weeks after. The Swedish governour procured another sachem to fetch them to him, who sent them to New Haven by a bark of that place, and so they were brought to Boston (5) 14, 45, the man as a prisoner.

(8) 30. The general court assembled again, and all the elders were sent for, to reconcile the differences between the magistrates and deputies. When they were come, the first question put to them was that which was stated by consent the last session, viz.

Whether the magistrates are, by patent and election of the people, the standing council of this commonwealth in the vacancy of the general court, and have power accordingly to act in all cases subject to government, according to the said patent and the laws of this jurisdiction; and when any necessary occasions call for action from authority, in cases where there is no particular express law provided, there to be guided by the word of God, till the general court give particular rules in such cases.

The elders, having received the question, withdrew themselves for consultation about it, and the next day sent to know, when we would appoint a time that they might attend the court with their answer. The magistrates and deputies agreed upon an hour, but the deputies came not all, but sent a committee of four (which was not well, nor respectively, that when all the elders had taken so much pains at their request, some having come thirty miles, they would not vouchsafe their presence to receive their answer.) Their answer was affirmative on the magistrates' behalf, in the very words of the question, with some reasons thereof. It was delivered in writing by Mr. Cotton in the name of them all, they being all present, and not one dissentient.

Upon the return of this answer, the deputies prepared other questions to be propounded to the elders, and sent them to the magistrates to take view of. Likewise the magistrates prepared four questions, and sent them also to the deputies.

The magistrates' questions, with the elders' answers, were

---

[1] In the margin is written "*Luter killed by Indians,*" and a pen has been drawn twice across the paragraph, and "*See after* 35" is added.

1. Whether the deputies in the general court have judicial and magistratical authority?

2. Whether by patent the general court, consisting of magistrates and deputies, (as a general court) have judicial and magistratical authority?

3. Whether we may warrantably prescribe certain penalties to offences, which may probably admit variable degrees of guilt?

4. Whether a judge be bound to pronounce such sentence as a positive law prescribes, in case it be apparently above or beneath the merit of offence?

The elders answer to the two first.

1. The patent, in express words, giveth full power and authority, as to the governour and assistants, so to the freemen also assembled in general court.

2. Whereas there is a threefold power of magistratical authority, viz. legislative, judicial, and consultative or directive of the public affairs of the country for provision and protection. The first of these, viz. legislative is expressly given to the freemen, jointly with the governour and assistants. Consultative or directive power &c. is also granted by the patent as the other. But now for power of judicature, (if we speak of the constant and usual administration thereof,) we do not find that it is granted to the freemen, or deputies, in the general court, either by the patent, or the elections of the people, or by any law of the country. But if we speak of the occasional administration thereof, we find power of judicature administrable by the freemen, jointly with the governour and assistants upon a double occasion. 1, In case of defect or delinquency of a magistrate, the whole court, consisting &c. may remove him. 2, If by the law of the country there lie any appeal to the general court, or any special causes be reserved to their judgment, it will necessarily infer, that, in such cases, by such laws, the freemen, jointly with the governour and assistants, have power of judicature, touching the appellant's cause of appeal and those reserved cases. [1]What we speak of the power of freemen by patent, the same may be said of the deputies, so far forth as the power of the freemen is delegated to them by order of law.

To the third and fourth questions the elders answer.

1. Certain penalties may and ought to be prescribed to capital crimes, although they may admit variable degrees of guilt; as in case of murder upon prepensed malice, and upon sudden provocation, there is prescribed the same death in both, though murder

---

[1] The sense is quite changed by the punctuation in Hubbard, 397.

upon prepensed malice be of a far greater guilt than upon sudden provocation, Numb. 35. 16. 18 with 20. 21. Also in crimes of less guilt, as in theft, though some theft may be of greater guilt than other, (as for some man to steal a sheep, who hath less need, is of greater guilt, than for another, who hath more need,) the Lord prescribed the same measure of restitution to both.

2. In case that variable circumstances of an offence do so much vary the degrees of guilt, as that the offence is raised to an higher nature, there the penalty must be varied to an higher answerable proportion. The striking of a neighbour may be punished with some pecuniary mulct, when the striking of a father may be punished with death. So any sin committed with an high hand, as the gathering of sticks on the Sabbath day, may be punished with death, when a lesser punishment may serve for gathering sticks privily, and in some need.

3. In case circumstances do so vary a sin, as that many sins are complicated or wrapped up in it, the penalty is to be varied, according to the penalties of those several sins. A single lie may be punished with a less mulct, than if it be told before the judgment seat, or elsewhere, to the damage of any person, whether in his good name, by slander, or in his estate, by detriment in his commerce; in which case, a lie aggravated by circumstances is to be punished with respect both to a lie and to a slander and to the detriment which another sustaineth thereby.

4. In case that the circumstances, which vary the degrees of guilt, concern only the person of the offender, (as whether it were the first offence, or customary, whether he were enticed thereto, or the enticer, whether he were principal or accessory, whether unadvised, or witting or willing &c.) there it were meet the penalty should be expressed with a latitude, whereof the lowest degree to be expressed (suppose five shillings, or, as the case may be, five stripes) and the highest degree, twenty shillings or &c. or stripes more or less; within which compass or latitude it may be free to a magistrate to aggravate or mitigate the penalty &c. Yet even here also care would be taken, that a magistrate attend, in his sentence, as much as may be, to a certain rule in these circumstances, lest some persons, whose sins be alike circumstanced with others, if their punishment be not equal &c. may think themselves more unequally dealt withal than others.

5. In those cases wherein the judge is persuaded in conscience, that a crime deserveth a greater punishment than the law inflicteth, he may lawfully pronounce sentence according to the prescript penalty &c. because he hath no power committed to him by law to go higher. But where the law may seem to the conscience of

the judge to inflict a greater penalty than the offence deserveth, it is his part to suspend his sentence, till by conference with the lawgivers, he find liberty, either to inflict the sentence, or to mitigate it.

6. The penalties of great crimes may sometimes be mitigated by such as are in chief power, out of respect to the public good service which the delinquent hath done to the state in former times, as Solomon did by Abiathar, 1 Kings 2. 26. 27.

Questions propounded to the elders by the deputies.

1. Whether the governour and assistants have any power by patent to dispense justice in the vacancy of the general court, without some law or order of the same to declare the rule?

The elders' answer was negative; and further, they conceived it meet, the rule should be express for the regulating of all particulars, as far as may be, and where such cannot be had, to be supplied by general rules.

2. Quest. Whether any general court hath not power by patent, in particular cases, to choose any commissioners, (either assistants or freemen,) exempting all others, to give them commission, to set forth their power and places? By "any particular case" we mean in all things, and in the choice of all officers, that the commonwealth stands in need of between election and election; not taking away the people's liberty in elections, nor turning out any officer so elected by them, without showing cause.

The elders answer.

1. If the terms, "all things," imply or intend all cases of constant judicature and counsel, we answer negatively &c. because then it would follow, that the magistrates might be excluded from all cases of constant judicature and counsel, which are their principal work, whereby also the end of the people's election would be made frustrate.

2. But if these terms, "all things," imply or intend cases (whether occasional or others) belonging neither to constant judicature nor counsel, we answer affirmatively &c. which yet we understand with this distinction, viz. that if the affairs committed to such officers and commissioners be of general concernment, we conceive the freemen, according to patent, are to choose them, the general court to set forth their power and places; but if they be of merely particular concernment, then we conceive the general court may choose them, and set forth their power and places. Whereas we give cases of constant judicature and counsel to the magistrates, we thus interpret the word "counsel." Counsel consists of care and action. In respect of care, the magistrates are not limited; in respect of action, they are to be limited by the

general court, or by the supreme council. Finally, it is our humble request, that in case any difference grow in the general court, between magistrates and deputies, either in these, or any like weighty cases, which cannot be presently issued with mutual peace, that both parties will be pleased to defer the same to further deliberation for the honour of God and of the court.

Upon other propositions made by the deputies, the elders gave this further answer, viz.

That the general court, consisting of magistrates and deputies, is the chief civil power of this commonwealth, and may act in all things belonging to such a power, both concerning counsel, in consulting about the weighty affairs of the commonwealth, and concerning making of laws, also concerning judicatures, in orderly impeaching, removing and sentencing any officers, even the highest, according to law, likewise in receiving appeals, whether touching civil or criminal causes, wherein appeals are or shall be allowed by the general court; provided that all such appeals proceed orderly from an inferiour court to the court of assistants, and from thence to the general court; or if the case were first depending in the court of assistants, then to proceed from thence to the general court, in all such cases as are appealable, "as in cases "judged evidently against law, or in cases wherein the subject is "sentenced to banishment, loss of limb, or life, without an express "law, or in cases weighty and difficult, (not admitting small mat-"ters, the pursuit whereof would be more burdensome to the "court and country, than behoveful to the appellant, nor need-"lessly interrupting the ordinary course of justice in the court of "assistants, or other inferiour courts;) provided also, that if it do "appear, that the appeal proceed not out of regard of right, but "from delay of justice, or out of contention, that a due and just "punishment be by law ordained, and inflicted upon such appel-"lant."

That no magistrate hath power to vary from the penalty of any law &c. without consulting with the general court.

3. Quest. Whether the titles of governour, deputy, and assistants do necessarily imply magistratical authority, in the patent?

The elders answer was affirmative.

4. Quest. Whether the magistratical power be not given by the patent to the people or general court, and by them to the governour &c.

The elders answer, that magistratical power is given to the governour &c. by the patent. To the people is given, by the same patent, to design the persons to those places of government; and to the general court power is given to make laws, as the rules of their administration.

These resolutions of the elders were after put to vote, and were all allowed to be received, except those in the last page marked in the margin thus. " " Most of the deputies were now well satisfied concerning the authority of the magistrates &c. but some few leading men (who had drawn on the rest) were still fixed upon their own opinions. So hard a matter it is, to draw men (even wise and godly) from the love of the fruit of their own inventions.

There fell out at this court another occasion of further trouble. The deputy governour having formerly, and from time to time, opposed the deputies' claim of judicial authority, and the prescribing of set penalties in cases which may admit variable degrees of guilt, which occasioned them to suspect, that he, and some others of the magistrates, did affect an arbitrary government, he now wrote a small treatise about these points, showing what arbitrary government was, and that our government (in the state it now stood) was not arbitrary, neither in the ground and foundation of it, nor in the exercise and administration thereof. And because it is of public, and (for the most part) of general concernment, and being a subject not formerly handled by any that I have met with, so as it may be of use to stir up some of more experience and more able parts to bestow their pains herein, I have therefore made bold to set down the whole discourse, with the proceedings which happened about it, in a treatise by itself, with some small alterations and additions (not in the substance of the matter) for clearer evidence of the question. And I must apologize this to the reader, that I do not condemn all prescript penalties, although the argument seem to hold forth so much, but only so far as they cross with the rules of justice, and prudence, and mercy also, in such cases of smaller concernment, as wherein there may be lawful liberty allowed to judges to use admonition, or to respite an offender to further trial of reformation, &c.

At this court Mr. Saltonstall moved very earnestly that he might be left out at the next election, and pursued his motion after to the towns. It could not appear what should move him to it; only Mr. Bellingham and he held together, and joined with the deputies against the rest of the magistrates, but not prevailing, and being oft opposed in public, might put some discouragement upon his spirit, to see all differ from him save one. And indeed it occasioned much grief to all the elders, and gave great offence through the country; and such as were acquainted with other states in the world, and had not well known the persons, would have concluded such a faction here as hath been usual in the council of England and other states, who walk by politic principles only. But these gentlemen were such as feared God, and endeavoured to walk by the rules of his word in all their proceedings, so as it might be conceived in charity, that they walked according to their judgments and conscience, and where they went aside, it was merely for want of light, or their eyes were held through some temptation for a time, that they could not make use of the light they had, for in all these differences and agitations about them, they continued in brotherly love, and in the exercise of all friendly offices each to other, as occasion required.

One Cornish, dwelling some time in Weymouth, removed to Acomenticus, for more outward accommodation, and in the [blank] month last was taken up in the river, his head bruised, and a pole sticking in his side, and his canoe laden with clay found sunk. His wife (being a lewd woman, and suspected to have fellowship with one Footman) coming to her husband, he bled abundantly, and so he did also, when Footman was brought to him; but no evidence could be found against him. Then something was discovered against the son of Mr. Hull, their minister, and the woman was arraigned before the mayor, Mr. Roger Garde, and others of the province of Maine, and strong presumptions came in against her, whereupon she was condemned and executed. She persisted in the denial of the murder to the death, but confessed to have lived in adultery with divers. She charged two specially, the said Garde, the mayor, and one Edward Johnson, who confessed it openly at the time of her execution; but the mayor denied it, and it gave some likelihood that he was not guilty, because he had carried himself very zealously and impartially in discovery of the murder. But there might be skill in that; and he was but a carnal man, and had no wife in the country, and some witnesses came in against him of his acknowledgment to the woman &c.

12. 17.] Mr. Allerton coming from New Haven in a ketch, with his wife and divers other persons, were taken in a great storm at northeast with much snow, and cast away at Scituate, but the persons all saved.

12. 16.] The winter was very mild hitherto, and no snow lay, so as ploughs might go most part of the winter, but now there fell so great a snow in several days, as the ways were unpassable for three weeks, so as the court of assistants held not (the magistrates and juries not coming to Boston (1) 4 being the usual day for that court.) And withal the weather was cold, and the frost as fierce as is at any time of the winter; and the snow was not off the ground till the end of the first month.

1645.] 2. 6.] Two great fires happened this week, one at Salem; Mr. Downing having built a new house at his farm, he being gone to England, and his wife and family gone to the church meeting upon the Lord's day, the chimney took fire, and burnt down the house, and bedding, apparel and household to the value of 200 pounds. The other was at Roxbury this day. John Johnson,[1] the surveyor general of the ammunition, a very industrious and faithful man in his place, having built a fair house in the midst of the town, with divers barns and other out houses, it fell on fire in the day time, (no man knowing by what occasion,) and there being in it seventeen barrels of the country's powder and many arms, all was suddenly burnt and blown up, to the value of 4 or 500 pounds, wherein a special providence of God appeared, for he being from home, the people came together to help, and many were in the house, no man thinking of the powder, till one of the company put them in mind of it, whereupon they all withdrew, and soon after the powder took fire, and blew up all about it, and shook the houses in Boston and Cambridge, so as men thought it had been an earthquake, and carried great pieces of timber a great way off and some rags and such light things beyond Boston meeting house. There being then a stiff gale at south, it drove the fire from the other houses in the town, (for this was the most northerly,) otherwise it had endangered the greatest part of the town. This loss of our powder was the more observable in two respects, 1. because the court had not taken that care they ought to pay for it, having been owing for divers years; 2. in that, at the court before, they had refused to help our countrymen in Virginia, who had written to us for some for their defence against the Indians, and also to help our brethren of Plimouth in their want.

Mr. Wheelwright being removed from Exeter to Wells, the people remaining felt at variance among themselves. Some would gather a new church, and call old Mr. Batchellor from Hampton to be their pastor, and for that purpose appointed a day, and gave notice thereof to the magistrates and churches, but the court, understanding of their divisions and present unfitness for so solemn

---

1 As he was "chosen constable of *Rocksbury*" so early as 19 October 1630, testified by our Col. Rec. I. 62, we may confidently conclude he came with Winthrop. He was deputy in the three first, fifth, sixth and seventh courts, and in the eighth came in place of Isaac Heath on 13 December 1636, five days after opening, and continued to represent the town in all the courts to the fifteenth, except one, after which he is found only in the twenty-first. By his will, made 30 of 7th 1659, proved 15 of 8th in the same year, he gives dwelling house and lands to wife during her life, and after "unto my five children, to be equally divided, my eldest son having a double portion therein, ACCORDING TO THE WORD OF GOD."

and sacred a business, sent and wrote to them (by way of direction only) to desist for that time, and not to proceed until upon satisfaction given to this court, or the court at Ipswich, of their reconciliation, they might proceed with allowance of authority, according to order. To this they submitted, and did not proceed.

The question about Seacunk, now Rehoboth, being revived this court, whether it should belong to this jurisdiction (upon the submission of the purchasers &c.) or to Plimouth by right of their patent, the court (by order) referred it to the judgment of the commissioners of the union, who decreed it for Plimouth, with reservation, if better evidence should appear by the next meeting.

Some malignant spirits began to stir, and declare themselves for the king &c. whereupon an order was made to restrain such courses, and to prevent all such turbulent practices, either by action, word or writing.

The court ordered letters of thanks to be sent to Mr. Richard Andrews of London, haberdasher, for his gift of 500 pounds, and to the Lady Armine for her gift of 20 pounds per annum, and to the Lady Moulson for her gift, which was done accordingly by the committee appointed.

Upon advice from Mr. Weld, remaining still at London, a commission was sent under the publick seal to Mr. [1]Pocock and divers other our friends in London to this effect, 1. to answer for us upon all such occasions as may be presented to the parliament or any other court or officer, concerning us or our affairs, but not to engage us, without our consent, 2. to receive all letters and other despatches of public nature or concernment from us, 3. to advise us of all occurrents as may happen touching our colony, 4. to receive all moneys or other things due to us from any person in England, by gift or otherwise, and to dispose of them by direction under our publick seal.

Mr. John Winthrop, the younger, coming from England two years since, brought with him 1000 pounds stock and divers workmen to begin an iron work, and had moved the court for some encouragement to be given the undertakers, and for the court to join in carrying on the work &c. The business was well approved by the court, as a thing much conducing to the good of the country, but we had no stock in the treasury to give furtherance to it, only some two or three private persons joined in it, and the court granted the adventurers near all their demands, as a monopoly of it for twenty-one years, liberty to make use of any six

---

1 No doubt this is the gentleman, who had been chosen an assistant in May 1629, but he never came to our country.

places not already granted, and to have three miles square in every place to them and their heirs, and freedom from publick charges, trainings &c. and this was now sent them over under the publick seal this year.[1]

---

1 In searching for information on this important topick, the earliest I find is, in Boston Rec. I. 68, "at a general towns meeting upon publick warning, 19th of 11mo. 1643.

There is granted unto Mr. John Winthrop, junr. and his partners, and to their heirs and assigns forever, three thousand acres of the common land at Braintry, for the encouragement of an iron-work to be set up about Monotocot river: the said 3000 acres to be laid out in the land next adjoining, and most convenient for their said iron-work, by the direction of the select townsmen."

Ib. 82. "31 of 11mo. 1647. At a meeting this day of Wm. Colburn, Jacob Eliot, Anthony Stoddard, Thomas Marshall, James Everell, Wm. Davis, James Penn, the three thousand acres of land given by the town towards the encouragement of the iron-works at Braintry is laid out according to order."

Hubbard seems to have known very little of this great undertaking, for he treats the subject, 374-5, in a very slight way. But our colony records, at the court 7 March 1643-4, contain at great length the orders, which in our text are compressed into few lines. Again, on the 13th of 9th following, very encouraging resolutions were passed by the court, in which notice is taken of the 1000 pounds being "*already disbursed*," and ending with the following: "Mr. John Winthrop is granted the hill at Tantousque about 60 miles westward, in which the black lead is, with liberty to purchase some land there of the Indians." In May following, we find this remarkable order: "Whereas it is now found by sufficient proof, that the iron-work is very successful (both in the richness of the ore and the goodness of the iron) and like to be of great benefit to the whole country, especially if the inhabitants here should be interested therein in some good proportion, (one half at the least,) and whereas the time limited for adventurers to come in will be expired in the ninth month next, this court taking the same into serious consideration, and being careful that such an opportunity for so great advantage to the commonwealth might not be let slip, have taken order, that speedy notice thereof shall be given to every town within this jurisdiction, expecting that all such persons, as are of sufficient ability and *intend their own benefit* with the common good, will forthwith appear to come in to share in the work according to their abilities; and for their better instruction and direction herein, they are hereby to understand, that there is already disbursed between 1200 and 1500 pounds, with which the furnace is built with that which belongeth to it and good quantity of mine, coal and wood provided, and some tuns of sow iron cast, and some other things in readiness for the forge &c. They are also to know, that no adventurer is to put in less than 100 pounds, but divers may join together to make up that sum, so it come all under one name. There will be need of some 1500 pounds to finish the forge &c. which will be accepted in money, beaver, wheat, coal, or any such commodities as will satisfy the workmen, and these are to be paid in to Mr. Henry Webb of Boston by such direction as they may receive from the undertakers, Mr. John Winthrop, junr. Major Sedgwick, Mr. Henry Webb aforesaid, and Mr. Joshua Hewes. The new adventurers are also to know, that they must bear their part in such loss as is befallen the first stock by forbearance or otherwise to the time of the new adventurers paying in their adventures; and all such as will adventure are desired to hasten their resolutions, that the work may go on speedily." With this last extract, and a mass of other documents about the iron works at Lynn, I am furnished by my friend, the Rev. Dr. Jenks, whose

The court, finding that the over number of deputies drew out the courts into great length, and put the country to excessive charges, so as some one court hath expended more [than] 200 pounds &c. did think fit to have fewer deputies, and so to have only five or six out of every shire; and because the deputies were still unsatisfied with the magistrates' negative vote, the magistrates consented to lay it down, so as the deputies might not exceed them in number, and those to be the prime men of the country, to be chosen by the whole shires; but they agreed first to know the mind of the country. But upon trial, the greater number of towns refused it, so it was left for this time.[1]

At this court in the third month Passaconaway, the chief sachem of Merimack, and his sons came and submitted themselves and their people and lands under our jurisdiction, as Pumham and others had done before.

Mr. Shepherd, the pastor of the church in Cambridge, being at Connecticut when the commissioners met there for the United Colonies, moved them for some contribution of help towards the maintenance of poor scholars in the college, whereupon the commissioners ordered that it should be commended to the deputies of the general courts and the elders within the several colonies to raise (by way of voluntary contribution) one peck of corn or

---

lineal ancestor, the grandfather of Governour Joseph Jenks of Rhode Island, was probably one of the workmen brought over by Winthrop, junr. as mentioned in the text. From 1646, for several years, honourable mention and encouragement of Joseph Jenks are seen in our colony records, by grants of exclusive privilege of seven and of fourteen years for his ingenious inventions. But my knowledge is inadequate to determine the question, whether the forge alluded to in the court's order of 1645 were at Braintree, or Lynn, or at any other of the six places, with which the adventurers were to be rewarded. It may be, that a history of the town of Lynn, for which large preparation is made by A. Lewis, Esquire, a competent inquirer, will soon establish the right. Johnson, Lib. III. c. 6. takes notice of the investment by the English undertakers in the work at Braintree; but though more full, he is little more satisfactory than Hubbard. Neither of these writers mention but one place, so that from Hubbard we should learn nothing of Braintree forge, nor from Johnson of Lynn. From some powers of attorney given by the London undertakers, preserved in the Suffolk registry, Vol. III. 155, I find the interest was the same at both places. In the elder colony of Plimouth the celebrated iron works of the family of Leonard were established in 1652, as appears 1 Hist. Coll. III. 170.

[1] And for all succeeding time to the present. The complaint of too numerous a body of representatives is not kindly entertained by the people, who are wisely careful of preserving the right and often indifferent to the use of it. The restriction of each towns' privilege to two, instead of three deputies, had begun in May 1639, and it is not probable that the whole were more than three dozen, or about one twentieth of the congregation in 1811, or 1812, of which the Editor has strong recollection. The next court after Winthrop's above remarks, we learn from him, the amount was only 33.

twelve pence money, or other commodity, of every family, which those of Connecticut presently performed.

5. 3.] By order of the general court, upon advice with the elders, a general fast was kept. The occasions were, the miseries of England, and our own differences in the general court, and also for the great drought. In this latter the Lord prevented our prayers in sending us rain soon after, and before the day of humiliation came.

Divers free schools were erected, as at Roxbury (for maintenance whereof every inhabitant bound some house or land for a yearly allowance forever) and at Boston (where they made an order to allow forever 50 pounds to the master and an house, and 30 pounds to an usher, who should also teach to read and write and cipher, and Indians' children were to be taught freely, and the charge to be by yearly contribution, either by voluntary allowance, or by rate of such as refused &c. and this order was confirmed by the general court [blank].) Other towns did the like, providing maintenance by several means.[1]

---

[1] This is not the place to publish, had I leisure, patience and ability to write, a historical account in an hundred pages of the admirable system of free schools, in which, unless I greatly mistake, Massachusetts is superior to all the rest of the world, unless those states, neighbouring or remote, who have borrowed from her, may divide the honour. Provision is made by law for the education of every child in the state, and the obligation is as extensively felt by the several towns in their respective districts, as that for the maintenance of roads or support of the poor, and generally is better obeyed than either of the others. Legal enactment was, I think, first made effectually in 1647, and how precise and comprehensive it was may be seen in Ancient Charters, 136. Our fathers probably attempted, without coercion of law, to secure instruction for their children equal to that which themselves had enjoyed in England, and soon perceived the necessity of a sanction for this duty. In the voluntary support of schools perhaps Boston led the way; at least from the *third* surviving page of our records, we find 13 of 2, 1635 a vote "that our brother Philemon Pormont shall be intreated to become schoolmaster for the teaching and nurturing of children with us." In the admirable history of Boston, by Dr. Caleb H. Snow, p. 348, and in the Prize Book, No. IV. of the Public Latin School in Boston, very full memorials of the origin, course and progress of these invaluable institutions may be seen. The latter tract is given anew in that interesting periodical work, begun with the present year, called "American Journal of Education," p. 209. Pormont was an adherent of Wheelwright, and accompanied him to Exeter in 1638, Maude was called to Dover 1642. I shall attempt to add nothing to such labours but this subscription from our town records:

At the end of the first volume is a list with an introduction, of which the first line is worn off, but the second is "towards the maintenance of free-schoolmaster for Mr. Daniel Maude, being now also chosen thereunto." In the margin is "12th of the 6th Aug. 1636." "The Governour Mr. Henry Vane, Esq, 10 pounds. The deputy governour Mr. John Winthrop, 10 pounds. Mr. Richard Bellingham 10 pounds. Mr. Wm. Coddington 30 shillings. Mr. Winthrop, junr. 20. Mr. Wm. Hutchinson 20. Mr. Robert Keayne 20. Mr. Thomas Oliver 10. Thomas

* By agreement of the commissioners, and the motions of the elders in their several churches, every family in each colony gave one peck of corn or twelve pence to the college at Cambridge.*

1. 25.] Another strange accident happened by fire about this time. One Mr. [1]Peck and three others of Hingham, being about with others to remove to Seaconk, (which was concluded by the commissioners of the United Colonies to belong to Plimouth,) riding thither, they sheltered themselves and their horses in an Indian wigwam, which by some occasion took fire, and (although they were all four in it, and laboured to their utmost &c.) burnt three of their horses to death, and all their goods to the value of 50 pounds.

Also some children were killed, and others sore scorched with wearing cloaths of cotton, which was very apt to take fire, and hard to be quenched; so as one man of Watertown being so cloathed, and taking fire by endeavouring to save his house being on fire, was forced to run into a well to save his life.

2. 13.] Mr. Hopkins, the governour of Hartford upon Connecticut, came to Boston, and brought his wife with him, (a godly young woman, and of special parts,) who was fallen into a sad infirmity, the loss of her understanding and reason, which had been growing upon her divers years, by occasion of her giving herself wholly to reading and writing, and had written many books. Her husband, being very loving and tender of her, was loath to grieve her; but he saw his errour, when it was too late. For if she had attended her household affairs, and such things as belong to women, and not gone out of her way and calling to meddle in such things as are proper for men, whose minds are stronger &c. she had kept her wits, and might have improved them usefully and honourably in the place God had set her. He brought her to Boston, and left her with her brother, one Mr.

Leverett 10. Wm. Colborne 10. John Coggeshall 8. 4. John Coggan 20. Robt. Harding 8. 4. John Newgate 10. Richard Tuttle 10. Wm. Aspenwall 8. John Sampford 8. Samuel Cole 10. Wm. Balstone 6. 8. Wm. Brenton —. James Penn 6. 8. Jacob Eliot 6. 8. Nicholas Willys — Ralph Hudson 10. Wm. Hudson —. Wm. Peirce 20. John Audley 4. John Button 6. Edward Bendall 5. Isaac Grosse 5. Zach. Bosworth 4. Wm. Salter 4. James Penniman 5. John Pemberton 3. John Bigge 4. Sam. Wilbore 10. Mr Cotton —. Mr. Wilson 20. Richd. Wright 6. 8. Thomas Marshall 6. 8. Wm. Talmage 4. Richard Gridley 4. Thomas Savage 5. Edward Rainsford 5. Edward Hutchinson 4."

[1] An ancient memorandum at Hingham mentions, that Mr. Joseph Peck died at Rehoboth, 22 Dec. 1662, but the very exact contemporary journal of Hobart makes it Thursday, 22 Dec. 1663.

[1]Yale, a merchant, to try what means might be had here for her. But no help could be had.[2]

The governour and assistants met at Boston, to consider what might lawfully be done for saving La Tour and his fort out of the hands of D'Aulnay, who was now before it with all his strength both of men and vessels. So soon as we were met, word was brought us, that a [3]vessel sent by some merchants to carry provisions to La Tour was fallen into the hands of D'Aulnay, who had made prize of her, and turned the men upon an island, and kept them there ten days, and then gave them an old shallop (not above two tons) and some provisions to bring them home, but denied them their clothes &c. (which at first he had promised them) and

---

1 Much will be found, in the progress of this volume, of David Yale of Boston, brother of Thomas, who lived at New Haven. This latter was father of governour Elihu, the great benefactor of the celebrated college, which is honoured with his name. President Stiles has commemorated this patron of that flourishing institution in these terms, "Governour Yale descended from an ancient and wealthy family in Wales, which, for many generations, possessed the manor of Plas Grannow, and several other messuages, near the city of Wrexham, of the yearly value of 500 pounds. Thomas Yale, Esquire, the governour's father, for the sake of religion, came over to America, with the first settlers of New Haven, in 1638. Here the governour was born in 1648. He went to England, at the age of about ten years; to the East Indies, at about thirty; acquired a very great estate, was made governour of Fort St. George, and married an Indian lady of fortune, the relict of governour Hinmers, his predecessor. After his return to London, he was chosen governour of the East India Company, and made liberal donations to the newly founded college at Connecticut. He journeyed into Wales, and died July 8, 1721, at or near the seat of his ancestors." His eldest daughter, Catherine, was married to Dudley North, Esquire, whose only son, Mr Dudley North, was, in 1789, a member of parliament, and in possession of the ancestral seat at Glemham. See Holmes's Life of Stiles, 386. David was, probably, driven from Massachusetts by the intolerance of the age, for his estate here was sold by his attorneys.

2 Her life was prolonged to December 1698. See Vol. I. 230 in note. I had intended here to introduce the advice of John Winthrop, jr. on the lady's case, in answer to her husband's application, and extracts from two letters of Governour Hopkins in which he mentions it, that were found in Vol. XIX. of the Trumbull MSS. belonging to the Massachusetts Historical Society, but that volume perished, with many other treasures, in the sad conflagration of 10 November last.

3 From the margin of our original MSS. we are informed, that it was Grafton's ketch. See also the Commissioners' Acts in Haz. II. 52. A slight mistake in my former note about Grafton, Vol. I. 332, may here be corrected. By the kindness of the gentleman, William Gibbs, Esq. of Salem, from whom the relation of his death, at Barbadoes, in 1670, was derived, I am furnished with the facts, that it was Joseph, junr. who thus died at that time, and that at a court 26 September 1671, at Ipswich, "Joseph Grafton the grandfather" was made "guardian for the two children, and to take their part of the estate into his hands and improve it for them the said children till they come to age to choose a guardian for themselves."

any gun or compass, whereby it was justly conceived that he intended they should perish, either at sea, or by the Indians (who were at hand, and chased them next day &c.) Upon this news we presently despatched away a vessel to D'Aulnay with letters, wherein we expostulated with him about this act of his, complaining of it as a breach of the articles of our peace, and required the vessel and goods to be restored, or satisfaction for them. We gave answer also to some charges he laid upon us in a letter lately written to our governour, carried on in very high language, as if we had hired the ships, which carried home the lady La Tour, and had broken our articles by a bare sufferance of it &c. which caused us to answer him accordingly, that he might see we took notice of his proud terms, and were not afraid of him. And whereas he oft threatened us with the king of France his power &c. we answered that we did acknowledge him to be a mighty prince, but we conceived withal he would continue to be just, and would not break out against us, without hearing our answer, or if he should, yet New England had a God, who was able to save us and did not use to forsake his servants &c. So soon as he had set our men upon an island, in a deep snow, without fire, and only a sorry wigwam for their shelter, he carried his ship up close to La Tour's fort (supposing they would have yielded it up to him, for the friars and other their confederates, whom the lady presently upon her arrival had sent away, had persuaded him that he might easily gain the place, La Tour being come into the Bay, and not above fifty men left in it, and little powder, and that decayed also;) but after they had moored their ship, and began to let fly at the fort with their ordnance, they within behaved themselves so well with their ordnance, that they tare his ship so as he was forced to warp her on shore behind a point of land, to save her from sinking, (for the wind coming easterly, they could not bring her forth,) and they killed (as one of his own men reported) twenty of his men, and wounded thirteen more.

[Large Blank.]

The governour and assistants had used for ten or eleven years at least to appoint one to preach on the day of election, but about three or four years since the deputies challenged it as their right, and accordingly had twice made the choice, (the magistrates still professing it to be a mere intrusion &c.) and now at the last general court in October they had given order to call Mr. Norton to that service, (never acquainting the magistrates therewith,) and about some two months before the time, the governour and divers other of the magistrates (not knowing any thing of what the deputies had done) agreed upon Mr. Norris of Salem, and gave him notice of it. But at this meeting of the magistrates it grew a question, whether of these two should be employed, seeing both had been invited, and both were prepared. At last it was put to vote, and that determined it upon Mr. Norton. The reason was, the unwillingness of the magistrates to have any fresh occasion of contestation with the deputies. But some judged it a failing (especially in one or two who had already joined in calling Mr. Norris) and a betraying, or at least weakening the power of the magistrates, and a countenancing of an unjust usurpation. For the deputies could do no such act, as an act of court, without the concurrence of the magistrates; and out of court they had no power at all, (but only for regulating their own body,) and it was resolved and voted at last court, (according to the elders' advice,) that all occurrents out of court belong to the magistrates to take care of, being the standing council of the commonwealth.

One of our ships, which went to the Canaries with pipestaves in the beginning of November last, returned now, and brought wine, and sugar, and salt, and some tobacco, which she had at Barbadoes, in exchange for Africoes, which she carried from the Isle of Maio. She brought us news, that a ship of ours of about 260 tons, set out from Cambridge before winter, was set upon, near the Canaries, by an Irish man of war, which had seventy men and twenty pieces of ordnance, whereas ours had but fourteen pieces and not above thirty men, and the Irishman grappled with our ship, and boarded her, and fought with her, side by side, near a whole day, but falling off, a shot of ours had taken off their steerage,[1] so as they could not bring their ship to ours again, but we received a shot under water, which had near sunk our ship, but the Lord preserved her and our men, so as we had but two slain in all that time and some four wounded; but the damage of the ship and her merchandise was between 2 and 300 pounds.

We had tidings also of another of our ships of the like force, set out from Boston, which the Earl of Marlborough had lain in wait for at the Madeiras a good time, and with a ship of great force, but it pleased the Lord to send him away the very day before our ship arrived there.

The wars in England kept servants from coming to us, so as those we had could not be hired, when their times were out, but upon unreasonable terms, and we found it very difficult to pay their wages to their content, (for money was very scarce.) I may

1 Dr. Holmes, Ann I. 336, has here, I think, mistaken the meaning of Hubbard, 526, whose transcript from our text is not perfect.

upon this occasion report a [1]passage between one of Rowley and his servant. The master, being forced to sell a pair of his oxen to pay his servant his wages, told his servant he could keep him no longer, not knowing how to pay him the next year. The servant answered him, he would serve him for more of his cattle. But how shall I do (saith the master) when all my cattle are gone? The servant replied, you shall then serve me, and so you may have your cattle again.

A village was erected near Lynn, and called Reading; another village erected between Salem and Gloucester, and called Manchester.

Among other benefactors to this colony, one Union Butcher, a clothier, near Cranbrook in Kent, did (for divers years together, in a private way) send over a good quantity of cloth, to be disposed of to some godly poor people.

The government of Plimouth sent one of their magistrates, Mr. [2]Brown, to Aquiday Island to forbid Mr. Williams &c. to exercise any of their pretended authority upon the Island, claiming it to be within their jurisdiction.[3]

Our court also sent to forbid them to exercise any authority within that part of our jurisdiction at Patuxent and Mishaomet; and although they had boasted to do great matters there by virtue of their charter, yet they dared not to attempt any thing.

3. 14.] The court of elections was held at Boston. Mr. Thomas Dudley was chosen governour, Mr. Winthrop, deputy governour again, and Mr. Endecott, serjeant major general. Mr. Israel Stoughton,[4] having been in England the year before, and now gone again about his private occasions, was by vote left out, and Herbert Pelham, Esquire, chosen an assistant.

---

1 The word "insolent," being written in the margin, shows us, that the relation between master and servant was in those times such, that a witty reply to an inquiry by the superior was offensive, however appropriate.

2 John Brown is very honourably mentioned in Morton's Memorial, as having been acquainted with the desert of the pilgrims before they left Leyden. He became an assistant in 1636 and continued to serve in that station, with exception of the year 1646, until 1650. He was often a commissioner of the United Colonies from 1644 to 1655, and died in 1662. A son, James, who lived at Swanzea, was an assistant in 1665.

3 I rejoice in the defeat of this futile claim by Plimouth, and equally rejoice in the ill success of the attempt by our own people mentioned in the next paragraph.

4 He had made his will, which appears in Vol. I. p. 50 to 57 at great length, when in London, 17 July 1644. By it he gave 300 acres of land to Harvard College.

This court fell out a troublesome business, which took up much time. The town of Hingham, having one [1]Emes their lieutenant seven or eight years, had lately chosen him to be their captain, and had presented him to the standing council for allowance; but before it was accomplished, the greater part of the town took some light occasion of offence against him, and chose one [2]Allen to be their captain, and presented him to the magistrates (in the time of the last general court) to be allowed. But the magistrates, considering the injury that would hereby accrue to Emes, (who had been their chief commander so many years, and had deserved well in his place, and that Allen had no other skill, but what he learned from Emes,) refused to allow of Allen, but willed both sides to return home, and every officer to keep his place, until the court should take further order. Upon their return home, the messengers, who came for Allen, called a private meeting of those of their own party, and told them truly what answer they received from the magistrates, and soon after they appointed a training day, (without their lieutenant's knowledge,) and being assembled, the lieutenant hearing of it came to them, and would have exercised them, as he was wont to do, but those of the other party refused to follow him, except he would show them some order for it. He told them of the magistrates' order about it; the others replied that authority had advised him to go home and lay down his place honourably. Another asked, what the magistrates had to do with them? Another, that it was but three or four of the magistrates, and if they had been all there, it had been nothing, for Mr. Allen had brought more for them from the deputies, than the lieutenant had from the magistrates. Another of them professeth he will die at the sword's point, if he might not have the choice of his own officers. Another (viz. the clerk of the band) stands up above the people, and requires them to vote,

---

1 Eames, whose baptismal name was Anthony, lived at Hingham, I presume, not long after this controversy, in which a great majority revolted from his authority. He had been representative of that town in the general court, 18 April 1637, as also in the two next courts, and three times afterwards, but not later than March 1638-9.

2 Bozoun Allen, some few years after, removed to Boston, where he was engaged in trade. His will is preserved in our Prob. Rec. I. 88, made 9 Sept. 1652, he died 14, and his inventory is sworn to 22 of same month. The controversy seems not to have lessened his influence, for he was several times a representative, and next year was, with Eames, chosen a commissioner to end small causes in Hingham. In 1700, his son, Bezoun Allen, born 13 February 1653, was a representative of Boston. But a peculiar interest was at work, which brought in the whole delegation, and this person served only that year.

whether they would bear them out in what was past and what was to come. This being assented unto, and the tumult continuing, one of the officers (he who had told them that authority had advised the lieutenant to go home and lay down his place) required Allen to take the captain's place; but he not then accepting it, they put it to the vote, whether he should be their captain. The vote passing for it, he then told the company, it was now past question, and thereupon Allen accepted it, and exercised the company two or three days, only about a third part of them followed the lieutenant. He, having denied in the open field, that authority had advised him to lay down his place, and putting (in some sort) the lie upon those who had so reported, was the next Lord's day called to answer it before the church, and he standing to maintain what he had said, five witnesses were produced to convince him. Some of them affirmed the words, the others explained their meaning to be, that one magistrate had so advised him. He denied both. Whereupon the pastor, one Mr. [1]Hubbert, (brother

---

1 Peter Hobart, near forty five years the pastor, and for the larger part of the same time pastor and teacher of the church of Hingham, where he settled in September 1635, says in his diary he arrived with his wife and four children in New England 8 June of that year. No doubt his voyage was in one of those seven ships mentioned Vol. I. 161. He was a master of arts in the university at Cambridge, and happily outlived the evils that for a period darkened his reputation. He had a celebrated progeny of divines, viz. Joshua, born in England, H. C. 1650, settled as a minister at Southold, Long Island, died February 1717, aged 89, Jeremiah, born in England, H. C. 1650, first settled as a minister at Topsfield, Massachusetts, afterwards at Haddam, in Connecticut, 14 November, 1700, died March 1717, aged 87; Gershom, born at Hingham, December 1645, H. C. 1667, settled as a minister at Groton, Massachusetts, 26 November 1679, died 19 December 1707; Japhet, born April 1647, H. C. 1667, was employed, it is said, as surgeon of a ship bound to England, and was lost at sea; Nehemiah, born November 1648, H. C. 1667, was settled as a minister at Newtown, Massachusetts, 23 December 1674, died 25 August 1712. Their influence perhaps secured the father honourable mention in the Magnalia, Lib. III. c. 27. As usual, Mather proves his kindness more than his accuracy, for he speaks of Hobart as having been a minister at Haverhill in England, and without hesitation affirms, that he was earnestly invited to return thither, after he had been here some years. Hobart's own Journal does not encourage such a representation, and all other old writings in our Hingham uniformly claim the derivation of the pastor and flock from the village of the same name in Norfolk. This is, probably, a mere blunder, for the ecclesiastical historian, as he has sometimes been absurdly called, has repeated correctly some things, as that he was born 1604, and died 20 January 1678-9. Mather says, he took ship in the *summer* of 1635, when we know it was in April, and he adds, that on arriving at Charlestown "he found his desired relations got safe there before him." But his father had been here nearly two years, and two of his brothers, at least, not less than one year, so that he, no doubt, had letters from them before leaving home. From Mather too we might be in doubt, whether he had "four or five" sons in the ministry, though the author had certainly inquired of one of them. Such is the customary laxness of the Magnalia. Descendants of this pilgrim father are

to three of the principal in this sedition,) was very forward to have excommunicated the lieutenant presently, but, upon some opposition, it was put off to the next day. Thereupon the lieutenant and some three or four more of the chief men of the town informed four of the next magistrates of these proceedings, who forthwith met at Boston about it, (viz. the deputy governour, the serjeant major general, the secretary, and Mr. Hibbins.) These, considering the case, sent warrant to the constable to attach some of the principal offenders (viz. three of the Hubbards and two more) to appear before them at Boston, to find sureties for their appearance at the next court &c. Upon the day they came to Boston, but their said brother the minister came before them, and fell to expostulate with the said magistrates about the said cause, complaining against the complainants, as talebearers &c. taking it very disdainfully that his brethren should be sent for by a constable, with other high speeches, which were so provoking, as some of the magistrates told him, that, were it not for respect to his ministry, they would commit him. When his brethren and the rest were come in, the matters of the information were laid to their charge, which they denied for the most part. So they were bound over (each for other) to the next court of assistants. After this five others were sent for by summons (these were only for speaking untruths of the magistrates in the church.) They came before the deputy governour, when he was alone, and demanded the cause of their sending for, and to know their accusers. The deputy told them so much of the cause as he could remember, and referred them to the seoretary for a copy, and for their accusers he told them they knew both the men and the matter, neither was a judge bound to let a criminal offender know his accusers before the day of trial, but only in his own discretion, least the accuser might be taken off or perverted &c. Being required to give bond for their appearance &c. they refused. The deputy laboured to let them see their errour, and gave them time to consider of it. About fourteen days after, seeing two of them in the court, (which was kept by those four magistrates for smaller causes,) the deputy required them again to enter bond for their

---

very numerous. A grandson, Nehemiah, born 27 April 1697, H. C. 1714, was ordained first pastor of the second church in Hingham, now Cohasset, 13 December 1721, died 31 May 1740. Another grandson, brother of the last named, Noah, born 2 January 1705, H. C. 1724, was settled as a minister at Fairfield, Connecticut, 7 February 1732, died 6 December 1773. He married, 22 September 1735, Ellen Sloss, and was father of the late Judge Hobart of New York.

appearance &c. and upon their second refusal committed them in that open court.

The general court falling out before the court of assistants, the Hubberts and the two which were committed, and others of Hingham, about ninety, (whereof Mr. Hubbert their minister was the first,) presented a petition to the general court, to this effect, that whereas some of them had been bound over, and others committed by some of the magistrates for words spoken concerning the power of the general court, and their liberties, and the liberties of the church &c. they craved that the court would hear the cause &c. This was first presented to the deputies, who sent it to the magistrates, desiring their concurrence with them, that the cause might be heard &c. The magistrates, marvelling that they would grant such a petition, without desiring conference first with themselves, whom it so much concerned, returned answer, that they were willing the cause should be heard, so as the petitioners would name the magistrates whom they intended, and the matters they would lay to their charge &c. Upon this the deputies demanded of the petitioners' agents (who were then deputies of the court) to have satisfaction in those points, whereupon they singled out the deputy governour, and two of the petitioners undertook the prosecution. Then the petition was returned again to the magistrates for their consent &c. who being desirous that the deputies might take notice, how prejudicial to authority and the honour of the court it would be to call a magistrate to answer criminally in a cause, wherein nothing of that nature could be laid to his charge, and that without any private examination preceding, did intimate so much to the deputies, (though not directly, yet plainly enough,) showing them that nothing criminal &c. was laid to his charge, and that the things objected were the act of the court &c. yet if they would needs have a hearing, they would join in it. And indeed it was the desire of the deputy, (knowing well how much himself and the other magistrates did suffer in the cause, through the slanderous reports wherewith the deputies and the country about had been possessed,) that the cause might receive a public hearing.

The day appointed being come, the court assembled in the meeting house at Boston. Divers of the elders were present, and a great assembly of people. The deputy governour, coming in with the rest of the magistrates, placed himself beneath within the bar, and so sate uncovered. Some question was in court about his being in that place (for many both of the court and the assembly were grieved at it.) But the deputy telling them, that, being criminally accused, he might not sit as a judge in that cause, and if he were upon the bench, it would be a great disadvantage to him, for he could not take that liberty to plead the cause, which he ought to be allowed at the bar, upon this the court was satisfied.

The petitioners having declared their grievances &c. the deputy craved leave to make answer, which was to this effect, viz. that he accounted it no disgrace, but rather an honour put upon him, to be singled out from his brethren in the defence of a cause so just (as he hoped to make that appear) and of so publick concernment. And although he might have pleaded to the petition, and so have demurred in law, upon three points, 1, in that there is nothing laid to his charge, that is either criminal or unjust; 2, if he had been mistaken either in the law or in the state of the case, yet whether it were such as a judge is to be called in question for as a delinquent, where it doth not appear to be wickedness or wilfulness; for in England many erroneous judgments are reversed, and errours in proceedings rectified, and yet the judges not called in question about them; 3, in that being thus singled out from three other of the magistrates, and to answer by himself for some things, which were the act of a court, he is deprived of the just means of his defence, for many things may be justified as done by four, which are not warrantable if done by one alone, and the records of a court are a full justification of any act, while such record stands in force. But he was willing to waive this plea, and to make answer to the particular charges, to the end that the truth of the case, and of all proceedings thereupon might appear to all men.

Hereupon the court proceeded to examine the whole cause. The deputy justified all the particulars laid to his charge, as that upon credible information of such a mutinous practice, and open disturbance of the peace, and slighting of authority, the offenders were sent for, the principal by warrant to the constable to bring them, and others by summons, and that some were bound over to the next court of assistants, and others that refused to be bound were committed; and all this according to the equity of laws here established, and the custom and laws of England, and our constant practice here these fifteen years. And for some speeches he was charged with as spoken to the delinquents, when they came before him at his house, when none were present with him but themselves, first, he appealed to the judgment of the court, whether delinquents may be received as competent witnesses against a magistrate in such a case; then, for the words themselves, some he justified, some he explained so as no advantage could be taken of them, as that he should say, that the magistrates could try some criminal causes without a jury, that he knew no law of God or man, which required a judge to make known to the party his accusers (or rather witnesses) before the cause came to hearing. But two of them charged him to have said, that it was against the law of God and man so to do, which had been absurd, for the deputy professed he knew no law against it, only a judge may sometimes, in discretion, conceal their names &c. least they should be tampered with, or conveyed out of the way &c.

Two of the magistrates and many of the deputies were of opinion that the magistrates exercised too much power, and that the people's liberty was thereby in danger; and other of the deputies (being about half) and all the rest of the magistrates were of a different judgment, and that authority was overmuch slighted, which, if not timely remedied, would endanger the commonwealth, and bring us to a mere democracy. By occasion of this difference, there was not so orderly carriage at the hearing, as was meet, each side striving unseasonably to enforce the evidence, and declaring their judgments thereupon, which should have been reserved to a more private debate, (as after it was,) so as the best part of two days was spent in this publick agitation and examination of witnesses &c. This being ended, a committee was chosen of magistrates and deputies, who stated the case, as it appeared upon the whole pleading and evidence, though it cost much time, and with great difficulty did the committee come to accord upon it.

The case being stated and agreed, the magistrates and deputies considered it apart, first the deputies, having spent a whole day, and not attaining to any issue, sent up to the magistrates to have their thoughts about it, who taking it into consideration, (the deputy always withdrawing when that matter came into debate,) agreed upon these four points chiefly; 1. that the petition was false and scandalous, 2. that those who were bound over &c. and others that were parties to the disturbance at Hingham, were all offenders, though in different degrees, 3. that they and the petitioners were to be censured, 4. that the deputy governour ought to be acquit and righted &c. This being sent down to the deputies, they spent divers days about it, and made two or three returns to the magistrates, and though they found the petition false and scandalous, and so voted it, yet they would not agree to any censure. The magistrates, on the other side, were resolved for censure, and for the deputy's full acquittal. The deputies being thus hard held to it, and growing weary of the court, for it began (3) 14, and brake not up (save one week) till (5) 5, were content they should pay the charges of the court. After, they were drawn to consent to some small fines, but in this they would have drawn in lieutenant Emes to have been fined deeply, he being neither plaintiff nor defendant, but an informer only, and had made good all the points of his information, and no offence found in him, other than that which was after adjudged worthy of admonition only; and they would have imposed the charges of the court upon the whole trained band at Hingham, when it was apparent, that divers were innocent, and had no hand in any of these proceedings. The magistrates not consenting to so manifest injustice, they sent to the deputies to desire them to join with them in calling in the help of the elders, (for they were now assembled at Cambridge from all parts of the United Colonies, and divers of them were present when the cause was publickly heard, and declared themselves much grieved to see that the deputy governour should be called forth to answer as a delinquent in such a case as this was, and one of them, in the name of the rest, had written to him to that effect, fearing least he should apprehend over deeply of the injury &c.) but the deputies would by no means consent thereto, for they knew that many of the elders understood the cause, and were more careful to uphold the honour and power of the magistrates than themselves well liked of, and many of them (at the request of the elder and others of the church of Hingham during this court) had been at Hingham, to see if they could settle peace in the church there, and found the elder and others the petitioners in great fault &c. After this (upon motion of the deputies) it was agreed to refer the cause to arbitrators, according to an order of court, when the magistrates and deputies cannot agree &c. The magistrates named six of the elders of the next towns, and left it to them to choose any three or four of them, and required them to name six others. The deputies finding themselves now at the wall, and not daring to trust the elders with the cause, they sent to desire that six of themselves might come and confer with the magistrates, which being granted, they came, and at last came to this agreement, viz. the chief petitioners and the rest of the offenders were severally fined, (all their fines not amounting to 50 pounds,) the rest of the petitioners to bear equal share to 50 pounds more towards the charges of the court, (two of the principal offenders were the deputies of the town, Joshua Hubbert and Bozone Allen, the first was fined 20 pounds, and the other 5 pounds,) lieutenant Emes to be under admonition, the deputy governour to be legally and publickly acquit of all that was laid to his charge.

According to this agreement, (5) 3, presently after the lecture the magistrates and deputies took their places in the meeting house, and the people being come together, and the deputy governour placing himself within the bar, as at the time of the hearing &c. the governour read the sentence of the court, without speaking any more, for the deputies had (by importunity) obtained a promise of silence from the magistrates. Then was the deputy governour desired by the court to go up and take his place again upon the bench, which he did accordingly, and the court being about to arise, he desired leave for a little speech, which was to this effect.

I suppose something may be expected from me, upon this charge that is befallen me, which moves me to speak now to you; yet I intend not to intermeddle in the proceedings of the court, or with any of the persons concerned therein. Only I bless God, that I see an issue of this troublesome business. I also acknowledge the justice of the court, and, for mine own part, I am well satisfied, I was publickly charged, and I am publickly and legally acquitted, which is all I did expect or desire. And though this be sufficient for my justification before men, yet not so before the God, who hath seen so much amiss in my dispensations (and even in this affair) as calls me to be humble. For to be publickly and criminally charged in this court, is matter of humiliation, (and I desire to make a right use of it,) notwithstanding I be thus acquitted. If her father had spit in her face, (saith the Lord concerning Miriam,) should she not have been ashamed seven days? Shame had lien upon her, whatever the occasion had been. I am unwilling to stay you from your urgent affairs, yet give me leave (upon this special occasion) to speak a little more to this assembly. It may be of some good use, to inform and rectify the judgments of some of the people, and may prevent such distempers as have arisen amongst us. The great questions that have troubled the country, are about the authority of the magistrates and the liberty of the people. It is yourselves who have called us to this office, and being called by you, we have our authority from God, in way of an ordinance, such as hath the image of God eminently stamped upon it, the contempt and violation whereof hath been vindicated with examples of divine vengeance. I entreat you to consider, that when you choose magistrates, you take them from among yourselves, men subject to like passions as you are. Therefore when you see infirmities in us, you should reflect upon your own, and that would make you bear the more with us, and not be severe censurers of the failings of your magistrates, when you have continual experience of the like infirmities in yourselves and others. We account him a good servant, who breaks not his covenant. The covenant between you and us is the oath you have taken of us, which is to this purpose, that we shall govern you and judge your causes by the rules of God's laws and our own, according to our best skill. When you agree with a workman to build you a ship or house &c. he undertakes as well for his skill as for his faithfulness, for it is his profession, and you pay him for both. But when you call one to be a magistrate, he doth not profess nor undertake to have sufficient skill for that office, nor can you furnish him with gifts &c. therefore you must run the hazard of his skill and ability. But if he fail in faithfulness, which by his oath he is bound unto, that he must answer for. If it fall out that the case be clear to common apprehension, and the rule clear also, if he transgress here, the errour is not in the skill, but in the evil of the will: it must be required of him. But if the cause be doubtful, or the rule doubtful, to men of such understanding and parts as your magistrates are, if your magistrates should err here, yourselves must bear it.

For the other point concerning liberty, I observe a great mistake in the country about that. There is a twofold liberty, natural (I mean as our nature is now corrupt) and civil or federal. The first is common to man with beasts and other creatures. By this, man, as he stands in relation to man simply, hath liberty to do what he lists; it is a liberty to evil as well as to good. This liberty is incompatible and inconsistent with authority, and cannot endure the least restraint of the most just authority. The exercise and maintaining of this liberty makes men grow more evil, and in time to be worse than brute beasts: omnes sumus licentia deteriores. This is that great enemy of truth and peace, that wild beast, which all the ordinances of God are bent against, to restrain and subdue it. The other kind of liberty I call civil or federal, it may also be termed moral, in reference to the covenant between God and man, in the moral law, and the politic covenants and constitutions, amongst men themselves. This liberty is the proper end and object of authority, and cannot subsist without it; and it is a liberty to that only which is good, just and honest. This liberty you are to stand for, with the hazard (not only of your goods, but) of your lives, if need be. Whatsoever crosseth this, is not authority, but a distemper thereof. This liberty is maintained and exercised in a way of subjection to authority; it is of the same kind of liberty wherewith Christ hath made us free. The woman's own choice makes such a man her husband; yet being so chosen, he is her lord, and she is to be subject to him, yet in a way of liberty, not of bondage; and a true wife accounts her subjection her honour and freedom, and would not think her condition safe and free, but in her subjection to her husband's authority. Such is the liberty of the church under the authority of Christ, her king and husband; his yoke is so easy and sweet to her as a bride's ornaments; and if through frowardness or wantonness &c. she shake it off, at any time, she is at no rest in her spirit, until she take it up again; and whether her lord smiles upon her, and embraceth her in his arms, or whether he frowns, or rebukes, or smites her, she apprehends the sweetness of his love in all, and is refreshed, supported and instructed by every such dispensation of his authority over her. On the other side, ye know who they are that complain of this yoke and say, let us break their bands &c. we will not have this man to rule over us. Even so, brethren, it will be between you and your magistrates. If you stand for your natural corrupt liberties, and will do what is good in your own eyes, you will not endure the least weight of authority, but will murmur, and oppose, and be always striving to shake off that yoke; but if you will be satisfied to enjoy such civil and lawful liberties, such as Christ allows you, then will you quietly and cheerfully submit unto that authority which is set over you, in all the administrations of it, for your good. Wherein, if we fail at any time, we hope we shall be willing (by God's assistance) to hearken to good advice from any of you, or in any other way of God; so shall your liberties be preserved, in upholding the honour and power of authority amongst you.

The deputy governour having ended his speech, the court arose, and the magistrates and deputies retired to attend their other affairs. Many things were observable in the agitation and proceedings about this case. It may be of use to leave a memorial of some of the most material, that our posterity and others may behold the workings of satan to ruin the colonies and churches of Christ in New England, and into what distempers a wise and godly people may fall in times of temptation; and when such have entertained some false and plausible principles, what deformed superstructures they will raise thereupon, and with what unreasonable obstinacy they will maintain them.

Some of the deputies had seriously conceived, that the magistrates affected an arbitrary government, and that they had (or sought to have) an unlimited power to do what they pleased without control, and that, for this end, they did strive so much to keep their negative power in the general court. This caused them to interpret all the magistrates' actions and speeches (not complying exactly with their own principles) as tending that way, by which occasions their fears and jealousies increased daily. For prevention whereof they judged it not unlawful to use even extrema remedia, as if salus populi had been now the transcendant rule to walk by, and that magistracy must be no other, in effect, than a ministerial office, and all authority, both legislative, consultative, and judicial, must be exercised by the people in their body representative. Hereupon they laboured, equis et velis, to take away the negative vote. Failing of that, they pleaded that the magistrates had no power out of the general court, but what must be derived from the general court; and so they would have put upon them commissions, for what was to be done in the vacancy of the general court, and some of themselves to be joined with the magistrates, and some of the magistrates left out. This not being yielded unto, recourse was had to the elders for advice, and the case stated, with incredible wariness; but the elders casting the cause against them, (as is before declared,) they yet believed, (or at least would that others should,) that the elders' advice was as much for them in their sense as for the magistrates, (and if it were, they had no cause to shun the advice of the elders, as they have seemed to do ever since.) This project not prevailing, the next is, for such a body of laws, with prescript penalties in all cases, as nothing might be left to the discretion of the magistrates, (while in the mean time there is no fear of any danger in reserving a liberty for their own discretion in every case,) many laws are agreed upon, some are not assented unto by the magistrates not finding them just. Then is it given out, that the magistrates would have no laws &c. This gave occasion to the deputy governour to write that treatise about arbitrary government, which he first tendered to the deputies in a model, and finding it approved by some, and silence in others, he drew it up more at large, and having advised with most of the magistrates and elders about it, he intended to have presented it orderly to the court. But to prevent that, the first day of the court, the deputies had gotten a copy, which was presently read amongst them as a dangerous libel of some unknown author, and a committee was presently appointed to examine it, many false and dangerous things were collected out of it, all agreed and voted by them, and sent up to the magistrates for their assent, not seeming all this time to take any notice of the author, nor once moving to have his answer about it, for they feared that his place in the council would have excused him from censure, as well as the like had done Mr. Saltonstall for his book against the standing council not long before. But if they could have prevailed to have had the book censured, this would have weakened his reputation with the people; and so if one of their opposite had been removed, it would somewhat have facilitated their way to what they intended; but this not succeeding as they expected, they kept it in deposito till some fitter season. In this time divers occasions falling out, wherein the magistrates had to do in the vacancy of the general court, as the French business, the seizure of the Bristol ship by Captain Stagg, and of the Dartmouth ship by ourselves, as is before related, and other affairs, they would still declare their judgments contrary to the magistrates' practice; and if the event did not answer the counsel, (though it had been interrupted by themselves or others,) there needed no other ground to condemn the counsel; all which tended still to weaken the authority of the magistrates and their reputation with the people.

Then fell out the Hingham case, which they eagerly laid hold on, and pursued to the utmost, for they doubted not but they could now make it appear, either that the magistrates had abused their authority, or else that their authority was too great to consist with the people's liberty, and therefore ought to be reduced within narrower bounds. In pursuit whereof it may be observed,

1. That a cause, orderly referred to a trial, at a court of assistants, should be taken into the general court, before it had received a due proceeding in the proper court; the like having never been done before, nor any law or order directing thereto, but rather the contrary.

2. That a scandalous petition against some of the magistrates should be received by the deputies, and the magistrates often pressed to consent to a judicial hearing, and to give way that the deputy governour should be called to answer thereupon, as a delinquent, before any examination were first privately had, about the justice of the cause.

3. That the testimony, in writing, of the three chiefest officers of the commonwealth (in a case properly committed to their trust) should be rejected, by a considerable part of the court, as a thing of no credit.

4. That the same part of the court should vote manifest contradictions, and require assent to both.

5. That being clearly convinced, that the petition was false and scandalous, and so voted, they should yet professedly refuse to assent to any due censure.

6. That they should receive the testimony of two of those whom themselves judged delinquents and false accusers, and thereupon judge him, the deputy governour, an offender in words, against his own protestation, and other testimony concurring, and that in a matter of no moment, and against common reason, to be either spoken by him, or believed by others, in such sense as they were charged upon him.

7. That a mutinous and seditious practice, carried on with an high hand, to the open contempt of authority, attempting to make division in the town, and a dangerous rent in the highest court of the jurisdiction, should (by such a considerable part of the same court, looked at by others as the choice of the country for piety, prudence, and justice) be accounted as worthy of no censure, and in the conclusion not valued at so high a rate, as some offences have been of private concernment arising of common infirmity.

8. That this practice should hold forth an apprehension, that liberty and authority are incompatible, in some degrees; so as no other way can be found to preserve the one, but by abasing and abating the honour and power of the other.

9. That being entrusted with the care and means of the country's prosperity, we should waste our time and their estates and our own (for the charges of this court came to 300 pounds) in such agitations as tend only to the discountenancing and interrupting the ordinary means of our welfare.

10. That while we sympathize with our native country in their calamities, and confess our own compliance with them in the provocations of God's wrath, (as in many days of humiliation, and one even in the time of this court,) we should be hasting by all our skill and power to bring the like miseries upon ourselves.

11. That Bozon Allen, one of the deputies of Hingham, and a delinquent in that common cause, should be publickly convict of divers false and reproachful speeches published by him concerning the deputy governour, and the book he wrote about arbitrary government, as that it was worse than Gorton's letters, that it should be burnt under the gallows, that if some other of the magistrates had written it, it would have cost him his ears, if not his head, and other like speeches, and no censure set upon him for this, only he was fined 5 pounds among others, for their offences in general.

12. It is observable, that the deputies, being so divided, (for of thirty-three there was only the odd man who carried it in most of their votes,) remembered at length a law they had agreed to in such cases, viz. that in causes of judicature they would not proceed without taking an oath &c. whereupon the most of them took it among themselves, (quaere, quo jure?) but five of them came to the magistrates, who administered the oath to them.[1]

1 An unusual fairness, for a party, whose feelings had been so much engaged in the controversy, and who had been accused of permitting those feelings to give force to an erroneous judgment, is here shown by our author. The narrative is, I am satisfied, as nearly impartial as can ever be expected from the

We had intelligence from Pascataquack of a French ship of 200 tons, full of men, which hovered up and down, and would not take harbour, though a pilot had been offered them by a fisher's boat of Isle of Shoals; whereupon all concluded it was Monsieur

---

most honest and enlightened contemporary, were he an observer only, instead of a mover, of the occurrences. I have turned, however, to the records, especially the volume of the deputies' proceedings, and for some forms and some details, I trust, the following extracts will be considered worth transcription.

Vol. III. p. 10. "Several inhabitants of the town of Hingham, to the number of 81, petitioning this court for a redress of several evils which in their petition they complained of, as of their liberties being infringed &c. amongst them, Joshua Hubbard, John Faulsham, and John Tour, laying a charge on the deputy governour for illegal imprisoning of some of them, and forcing the first with others to give in bond with sureties to appear and answer at the next quarter court what should be laid against him and them. The petition was read and their request granted, that the whole cause should be heard and tried. The parties above named laid their charge above mentioned on the day of trial on John Winthrop, Esq deputy governour, who gave his answer, whereon the court proceeded to judgment."

Ib. p. 16—28 June. "The house of deputies did voluntarily enter into an oath of God, verbatim to the oath in the court's records, to deal uprightly in Hingham case, except Captain Keayne, Lieutenant Atherton, John Johnson, Thomas Lyne and William Parkes, who did take their oaths in this case before the magistrates. Witness Increase Nowell, Secretary."

The *first* order of the magistrates is, as follows: "fined the persons after named at such sums as hereafter are expressed, having been as moderate and gone as low as they any ways could with the holding up of authority in any measure, and the maintenance of justice, desiring the concurrence of the deputies herein, that at length an end may be put to this long and tedious business.

Joshua Hubbard is fined	L.20.00.00	
Edmond Hubbard,	5.00.00	
Thomas Hubbard,	2.00.00	
Edmond Gold,	1.00.00	
John Faulshame,	20.00.00	
John Towers,	5.00.00	
Daniel Cushin,	2.10.00	
William Hersey,	10.00.00	L.155.10
Mr. Bozon Allen,	10.00.00	
Mr. Peter Hubbard, that first subscribed the petition	2.00 00	
All the rest of the petitioners, being 81, out of which number are excepted three, viz. Mr. Peter Hubbard, John Foulshame and John Towres, the rest making 78, are fined 20 shillings a piece, the sum of which is		

We have also voted, that according to the order of the general court, for so long time as their cause hath been in handling, the petitioners shall bear the charge of the general court, the sum of which costs is to be cast up and agreed by the court, when the cause is finished."

"The house of deputies having issued the Hingham business before the judgment of our honoured magistrates upon the case came down, they have hereunder expressed their determinate censures upon such as they find delinquent in the case, viz.

D'Aulnay lying in wait for La Tour, and the wind continuing easterly, we had intelligence from Plimouth, that she was imbayed near Sandwich among the Shoals. The court consulted what was to be done. Some advised to take no notice of her, lest, if we should send out to her, we should be necessitated (in common courtesy) to invite him to Boston, and so put ourselves to a needless charge and interruption in our business; for being but one ship, there was no fear of any danger &c. But the major part prevailed to send out two shallops and the letter which we had ready to send to him; but before the shallops could get out, she was gone, and it was found after to be a fishing ship, which had lost her way, by contrary winds &c.

I should have mentioned in the Hingham case, what care and pains many of the elders had taken to reconcile the differences which were grown in that church. Mr. Hubbert, the pastor there, being of a Presbyterial spirit, did manage all affairs without the church's advice, which divers of the congregation not liking of, they were divided in two parts. Lieutenant Emes &c. having complained to the magistrates, as is before expressed, Mr. Hubbert, &c. would have cast him out of the church, pretending that he had told a lie, whereupon they procured the elders to write to the church, and so did some of the magistrates also, whereupon they stayed proceeding against the lieutenant for a day or two. But he and some twelve more of them, perceiving he was resolved to proceed, and finding no way of reconciliation, they withdrew from the church, and openly declared it in the congregation. This

---

Joshua Hubbard is fined	L.20 00.00	L.50
Anthony Eames,	5.00.00	
Thomas Hubbard,	4.00.00	
Edmond Hubbard,	10.00.00	
Daniel Cushan,	4.00 00	
William Hersey,	4.00.00	
Mr. Allen, beside his proportion with the train band,	1.00.00	
Edmond Gold,	2.00.00	

The rest of the train band of Hingham, that have an equal vote allowed them by law for the choice of their military officers, are fined 55 pounds to be paid by equal proportion, the which said sums of 50 and 55 pounds are laid upon the said delinquents for the satisfying of the charge of the court occasioned by the hearing of the cause, in case the said charge shall arise to the sum of 105 pounds. The deputies desire the consent of the magistrates herein."

Several discordant votes passed each branch, before the business was brought to its close, as related in our text.

Joshua, Edmond and Thomas Hobart were brothers of Rev. Peter, and the first, then and often afterwards, till 1681, a representative. He died 28 July, 1682. Daniel Cushing was a person of distinguished service in the town, was often representative before 1695, and especially deserving of regard for the manner in which he filled the office of town clerk from 1669 to 1700.

course the elders did not approve of. But being present in the court, when their petition against the deputy governour was heard, Mr. Hubbert, perceiving the cause was like to go against him and his party, desired the elders to go to Hingham to mediate a reconciliation (which he would never hearken to before, being earnestly sought by the other party, and offered by the elders) in the interim of the court's adjournment for one week. They readily accepted the motion, and went to Hingham, and spent two or three days there, and found the pastor and his party in great fault, but could not bring him to any acknowledgment. In their return by water, they were kept twenty four hours in the boat, and were in great danger by occasion of a tempest which arose in the night; but the Lord preserved them.

This year the Trial of Boston arrived from London, and brought many useful commodities from thence and from Holland. She had been preserved in divers most desperate dangers, having been on ground upon the sands by Flushing, and again by Dover, and in great tempests; but the Lord delivered him beyond expectation. Here arrived about ten ships more, (one of our own called the Endeavor of Cambridge,) which brought store of linen, woollen, shoes, stockings and other useful commodities, so as we had plenty of all things, and divers of the ships took pay in wheat, rye, peas &c. so as there went out of the country this year about 20,000 bushels of corn. Yet it was feared no ships would have come to us, because we had suffered the Bristol and Dartmouth ships to be taken in our harbour.

The parliament also had made an ordinance to free all goods from custom, which came to New England, which caused the magistrates to dispense with an order, made the last general court, for all ships to pay sixpence the ton, which we freed all parliament ships from; and good reason, for by that order we might have gotten 20 or 30 pounds this year, and by the ordinance of parliament we saved 3 or 400 pounds.

When one of the ships came near Cape Ann, 20 (6) 45, an hour and a half before night, there appeared to all the company a sun near the horizon, more bright than the true sun, (which was seen above it,) which continued near an hour, there being a small cloud between the true sun and that. This was affirmed by divers persons of credit, who were of this country and then in the ship. But it was not seen by any upon the shore. Captain Wall was master of the ship.

The merchants of Boston sent a pinnace the last winter to trade in Delaware Bay. She traded upon Maryland side, and had gotten a good parcel of beaver; at last the Indians came aboard, and while the English (who were about five and a boy) were trading with some of them, others drew out hatchets from under their coats, and killed the master and three others, and took the other and the boy, and carried them on shore, and rifled the pinnace of all her goods and sails &c. Soon after, other Indians came upon these and slew the sachem, and took away all their goods they had stolen. There was one Redman suspected to have betrayed their pinnace, for he being linkister, (because he could speak the language,) and being put out of that employment for his evil carriage, did bear ill will to the master, and the Indians spared him, and gave him a good part of the spoil, and he lived amongst them five or six weeks, till the Swedish governour procured other Indians to go fetch him and the boy to his fort, from whence they were brought to Boston, and then said Redman was tried for his life, and being found guilty by the grand jury, was deferred his farther trial in expectation of more evidence to come from Delaware.[1]

The governour, Mr. Endecott, having received a letter from Monsieur D'Aulnay in the spring, wherein he slighted us very much, and charged us with breach of covenant in entertaining La Tour, sending home his lady &c. We returned a sharp answer to him by Mr. [2]Allen, declaring our innocency, in that we sent not the lady home, but she hired three London ships &c. as is before related, page 218. When he had received this letter, he was in a great rage, and told Mr. Allen that he would return no answer; nor would he permit him to come within his fort, but lodged him in his gunner's house without the gate, and himself came daily, and dined and supped with him, but at last he wrote to our governour in very high language, requiring satisfaction for burning his mill &c. and threatening revenge &c. So the matter rested till the meeting of the commissioners in the seventh month next, and then their agreement to the peace was sent to him by a special messenger, Captain Robert [3]Bridges, as is hereafter declared.

---

1 From our court records it may be known, that he was ultimately acquitted. The carelessness of Hubbard in misappropriation of this calamity has been remarked in a former note p. 179. A petition for charity to the widow and orphans of Luter, or Luther, was offered in the general court.

2 Did not the admirable index to 2 Hist. Coll. identify this messenger with the delegate from Hingham, it might be unnecessary here to warn against such a conclusion. Our records show the carrier of these despatches to have been a shipmaster.

3 Of this gentleman I have learned little more than Winthrop has told, except from Alonzo Lewis, Esq. of Lynn. Johnson lib. II. c. 26, speaks of his

We understood for certain afterward that Monsieur La Tour's fort was taken by assault and scalado, that Monsieur D'Aulnay lost in the attempt twelve men, and had many wounded, and that he had put to death all the men (both French and English) and had taken the lady, who died within three weeks after, and her little child and her gentlewoman were sent into France. La Tour valued his jewels, plate, household, ordnance and other moveables at 10,000 pounds. The more was his folly to leave so much substance in so great danger, when he might have brought the most of it to Boston, whereby he might have discharged his engagements of more than 2500 pounds to Major Edward Gibbons, (who by this loss was now quite undone,) and might have had somewhat to have maintained himself and his men; for want whereof his servants were forced to go out of the country, some to the Dutch, and others to France, and he himself to lie at other men's charge. But in the spring he went to Newfoundland, and there was courteously entertained by Sir David Kirk, the governour, who promised him assistance &c. But he returned to Boston again by the vessel which carried him, and all the next winter was entertained by Mr. Samuel Maverick at Nottles Island.

Some of our merchants of Boston and Charlestown sent forth a ship and other vessels to Newfoundland upon a fishing voyage. They went not to Ferryland, (where they might have been in safety,) but to the Bay of Bulls, and when they had near made their voyage, Captain Firnes's ships (being of the king's party) came and took their ship and most of their fish; so the men returned safe, but lost their voyage. Firnes was hereby five ships strong, and so went to the Terceras, and there fought with two ships of London and a Scotch ship, who sunk two of Firnes's ships, and made him fly with the rest.

[Large Blank.]

Captain Thomas [1]Hawkins, a shipwright of London, who had

---

ability and good disposition to serve the public. He came over, I find, in 1643, with J. Winthrop, jr. and in the three following years was a deputy for Lynn. Having served in 1646 as speaker, he was elevated to the rank of assistant next year, and continued in the office till his death in 1656. Probably the interest in the iron works, with which he was inspired by Winthrop, was the cause of his coming to our country. By his intervention was caused the first punishment inflicted on the baptists, Clark, Crandall and Holmes. Having come from Rhode Island, they attempted, on a Sunday, to preach at Lynn, and by order of Bridges they were taken by two constables to hear Mr. Whiting preach in the established church in the afternoon, and next day sent to prison at Boston.

[1] It cannot be doubted, that he was distinguished for other valuable qualities as well as his enterprising spirit, for he had been in 1644 a representative of

lived here divers years, had built at Boston a ship of 400 tons and upward, and had set her out with much strength of ordnance, and ornament of carving, painting, &c. and called her the Seaiort, and the last year 23 (9) he set sail from Boston, accompanied with another ship of London, Mr. Kerman, master, laden with bolts, tobacco, &c. for Malago. When they came near the coast of Spain, in the evening, some of the company supposed they saw land, yet they sailed on all the night, with a fair gale, and towards the morning they saw a light or two, which they conceiving to have been in some ships, either Turks or others, they prepared their ships and stood on towards them. But some three hours before day [blank] (10ber.) both ships struck aground, and presently brake. Nineteen were drowned, whereof Mr. Kerman was one, and one Mr. Thomas Coytmore of Charlestown (a right godly man, and an expert seaman) was another, and Mr. Pratt and his wife. This man was above sixty years old, an experienced surgeon, who had lived in New England many years, and was of the first church at Cambridge in Mr. Hookers' time, and had good practice, and wanted nothing. But he had been long discontented, because his employment was not so profitable to himself as he desired, and it is like he feared lest he should fall into want in his old age, and therefore he would needs go back into England, (for surgeons were then in great request there by occasion of the wars,) but God took him away childless. The rest of the company (both women and children, who went passengers that way into England, choosing to go in that ship, because of her strength and conveniency, rather than in another ship, which went right for England, and arrived safe there) were all saved, upon pieces of the ships, and by the help of a rope which one of the seamen swam on shore with; and although the ships at first grounded two or three miles from the shore, yet (through the Lord's great mercy) they were heaved by the seas near to the dry land before they fell in pieces. This was five miles from Cales. In the morning the poor people of the island came down, and pillaged all they could come by, yea they took away some pieces of plate, which the passengers had saved. But when they came to the city, (naked and barefoot as they went frighted out of their

---

Boston. I suppose he died abroad. His inventory, taken 26 July 1654, presented by his wife Mary, is contained in our Probate Rec. III. 101. A house, barn, and 180 acres of land at Dorchester (over the water, which is an unknown site to me) are valued at 257 pounds, the house and land at Boston, 200 pounds, one half of ship Perigrine, in England, 75 pounds. The whole makes 900 pounds, and was divided between the widow, one son, Thomas, and four daughters.

cabins,) the Spaniards used them kindly, especially the women, and clothed them, and took them into their houses. There was an English ship then in the roads, whereof one Mr. Mariot was master: he entertained as many as his ship could stow, and clothed many of them with his own clothes, (the Lord reward him.) The governour of the island gave Captain Hawkins 500 pounds for the wreck of his ship.

The same Captain Hawkins going for London, found much favour with his creditors and others his friends there, so as the next year they employed him to Malago, to meet a New England ship called [blank], built at Cambridge, and freight for Malago with pipe staves, fish, and other commodities, which he was to freight thence with wine &c. for London, but as she was on her voyage, (Captain Hawkins being in her, and twelve other ships in company) being come out of the Streight's mouth, they were taken with such a violent tempest at south, as they were (five of them, whereof Captain Hawkins's ship was one) cast upon the same place at Cales, where his ship was wrecked the year before, and there all their ships were cast away, but all the men in Captain Hawkins's ship were saved, and most of the rest. This was 2 (12) 45.

The scarcity of good ministers in England, and want of employment for our new graduates here, occasioned some of them to look abroad. Three honest young men, good scholars, and very hopeful, viz. a younger [1]son of Mr. Higginson, to England, and so to Holland, and after to the East Indies, a younger [2]son of Mr. Buckley, a Batchelor of Arts to England, and Mr. George [3]Downing, son to Mr. Emanuel Downing of Salem, Batchelor of

---

1 The college catalogue does not contain the name of this young man, who must not, probably, be included in the author's term of graduates. Any further information has not been obtained by me. Two elder sons of the first minister of Salem, who left eight children, are commemorated by Eliot.

2 Hutchinson's note, I. 107, gives all the knowledge, I suppose, that any one can have, though very slight.

3 Every printed book has, I believe, hitherto called this most distinguished of the early sons of Harvard College, the son of Calibute Downing, a puritan divine. This errour is probably chargeable to honest Anthony Wood's Athenæ Oxonienses.

Another mistake is found in the famous Andrew Marvell. Among his works is "A seasonable argument to persuade all the grand juries of England to petition for a new parliament; or a list of the principal labourers in the great design of popery and arbitrary power, who have betrayed their country to the conspirators, and bargained with them to maintain a standing army in England, under the command of the bigotted popish D[uke] who by the assistance of the L.L's [Lord Lauderdale's] Scotch army, the forces in Ireland,

Arts also, about twenty years of age, went in a ship to the West Indies to instruct the seamen. He went by Newfoundland, and

---

and those in France, hopes to bring all back to Rome" Amsterdam, 1677. This curious tract contains a list of the members of the commons, arranged under the several counties in alphabetical order, with some account of the rewards to each for his service to the court. Our son of the first days at Harvard College is thus mentioned: "Northumberland. Morpeth. Sir George Downing, a poor child, bred upon charity; like Judas, betrayed his master. What then can his country expect? He drew and advised the oath of renouncing the king's family, and took it first himself. For his honesty, fidelity &c. rewarded by his majesty with 80,000 pounds at least, and is a commissioner of the customs, the house bell to call the courtiers to vote at six o'clock at night, an Exchequer teller."

Wood's Athenæ Oxonienses Vol. II. 27 in the account of Calybute Downing L. L. D. who died 1644 says "This Dr. Cal. Downing was father to a son of his own temper named George, a sider with all times and changes, well skilled in the common cant, and a preacher some times to boot, a man of note in Oliver's days, as having been by him sent resident to the Lord's States General of the United Provinces, a soldier in Scotland, and at length Scout Master General there, and a burgess for several corporations in that kingdom, in parliaments that began there in 1654 and 56. Upon a foresight of his mjaesty K. Ch. 2. his restoration, he wheeled about, took all opportunities to show his loyalty, was elected burgess for Morpeth in Northumberland, to serve in that parliament begun at Westminister, 8 May 1661, was about that time sent envoy extraordinary into Holland, where to show his zeal and love for his majesty, he seized on three Regicides at Delft named John Barkstead, John Okey and Miles Corbet, whom he forthwith sent into England to receive the reward of the gallows. Afterwards being made secretary to the treasury and one of his majesty's commissioners of the customs, was by the name of Sir George Downing of East Hatley in Cambridgeshire, Knight, created a baronet on the first of July 1663." In the same vol. p. 758–9, Wood repeats the story of Sir George's service in seizing the regicides at an alehouse at Delft in the beginning of March 1661, and in conclusion quotes the passage above from Marvell.

Now we know, that, being son of Emanuel Downing, and nephew of governour Winthrop, he was not a *poor child*, bred upon charity, as the indignation of Marvell represents. However undeserving of approbation his political character may be, which is fairly represented, I imagine, by Hutchinson I. 107 in the most amusing note of his history, his powers of rendering himself useful by aptitude for affairs of state and great assiduity in business could alone gain him the high employments which Oliver Cromwell bestowed. He was employed in negotiations with the Duke of Savoy in 1653, and at home in business of the army, and was specially chosen member of parliament in 1656 for the protector's purposes from the Scotch borough of Haddington in Scotland under Monk's instructions. But his great services for Oliver and the succeeding brief administrations was as minister in Holland, 1657–8, very abundant evidence of which is in Thurloe's State papers, especially vol. VII.

By the recently published Memoirs of Pepys, who was in Downing's office, at first, as a clerk, it appears that in the anarchy of 1659 the crafty politician was at home, near the Exchequer; and went over, in the most important juncture, end of January 1660, to wait for events at the Hague. He was knighted a week before the restoration. Of the arrest of the regicides Pepys writes in his Diary, 1662, March 12, "this morning we had news, that Sir G. Downing (like a perfidious rogue, though the action is good and of service to the king, yet he cannot with a good conscience do it) hath taken Okey, Corbet and Bark-

so to Christophers and Barbados and Nevis, and being requested to preach in all these places, he gave such content, as he had

---

stead at Delft in Holland, and sent them home in the Blackmore. Sir W. Penn talking to me this afternoon of what a strange thing it is for Downing to do this, he told me of a speech he made to the Lord's States of Holland, telling them to their faces that he observed that he was not received with the respect and observance, that he was when he came from the traitor and rebel Cromwell; by whom, I am sure, he hath got all he hath in the world, and they know it too." Vol. I. 134–5. He adds, under the date of 17th, mentioning the arrival of the prisoners, "the captain tells me, the Dutch were a good while before they could be persuaded to let them go, they being taken prisoners in their land. But Sir G. Downing would not be answered so; though all the world takes notice of him for a most ungrateful villain for his pains."

Pepys, probably, knew Downing's origin, but his noble editor, Lord Braybrooke, has repeated the story about Col. Downing being his father. We need not be surprised at this, for Hutchinson has not given any genealogy, and a relative of Downing, the late William Winthrop of Cambridge, in his catalogue of Harvard College, MS. belonging to the Historical Society, prolongs the delusion of Wood.

I may be excused for extending this note by farther extracts from one who knew him so well, as Pepys: "1667, May 27. The new commissioners of the treasury have chosen Sir G. Downing for their secretary; and I think in my conscience they have done a great thing in it; for he is active and a man of business, and values himself upon having of things do well under his hand; so that I am mightily pleased in their choice." Vol. II. 58.

"1668, December 27. Met with Sir G. Downing, and walked with him an hour talking of business, and how the late war was managed, there being nobody to take care of it; and he telling, when he was in Holland, what he offered the king to do if he might have power, and then upon the least word, perhaps of a woman, to the king, he was contradicted again, and particularly to the loss of all that we lost in Guinea. He told me that he had so good spies, that he hath had the keys taken out of De Witt's pocket when he was abed, and his closet opened and papers brought to him and left in his hands for an hour, and carried back and laid in the place again, and the keys put into his pocket again. He says he hath always had their most private debates, that have been but between two or three of the chief of them, brought to him in an hour after, and an hour after that hath sent word thereof to the king." Vol. II. 291.

A note to Bliss's edition of Wood mentions an epithalamium in 1654, in nuptias viri vere honoratissimi Georgii Downingi, campo-exploratoris generalissimi &c. et vere nobilissimae Franciscae Howardi equitis aurati et sororis illustrissimi Caroli Howardi de Naworth in Com. Cumbraei &c. This marriage probably extended his influence very much. His son, Sir George, married Catharine, eldest daughter of James, Earl of Salisbury. Their son, Sir George, grandson of the youth mentioned in our text was in three different parliaments, 1710, 1713, and 1727, and dying in 1747 without issue, left the most splendid perpetuation of his name, by a bequest for the foundation of a college at Cambridge, incorporated in 1800, by the name of Downing College, on a more liberal foundation than any other at that renowned university. See Dyer's History of the University of Cambridge, Vol. II. 440–447. The amount of the bequest is now valued at more than 150,000 pounds.

Our governour Bradstreet married a sister of Downing, and kept up a correspondence with him. But in our country, which harboured and favoured

large offers made to stay with them. But he continued in the ship to England, and being a very able scholar, and of a ready wit and fluent utterance, he was soon taken notice of, and called to be a preacher in Sir Thomas Fairfax his army, to Colonel Okye his regiment.

[Blank.]

The inhabitants of Boston, Charlestown, Cambridge, Roxbury and Dorchester, conceiving that the fortification at Castle Island (which by a late order of court was deserted) would be of great use for their defence against a foreign enemy, agreed among themselves (with leave of the court) to repair and fortify the same; and accordingly they chose a committee out of the several towns to raise means, and to get the work done. Whereupon the old earthwork was slighted, and a new work of pine trees, [blank] foot square, fourteen foot high, and [blank] foot thick, was reared, with four bulwarks, which cost in all [blank]. But finding the charge of the work and the maintenance of a garrison to be over heavy for them, they petitioned the general court in [blank] to afford assistance, which with much difficulty was at length obtained to this effect.

[Large Blank.]

In the beginning of the winter a Portugal ship lying at Natascot, (now called Hull,) the seamen stole divers goats off the islands there. Complaint thereof being made to the governour and council, they gave warrant to one Mr. Smith, who then lay with his ship in the same place, to require the Portugal to give satisfaction, or else to bring his ship up to Boston. Mr. Smith (who was a member of the church of Boston) sent one Thomas Keyser his mate with his long boat well manned, to require satisfaction, who coming to the Portugal did not reason the case with him, nor give him any time to consider, but presently boarded him, and took possession of his ship, and brought her up, and his men fell to rifling his ship, as if she had been a prize. The Portugal being brought to the magistrates, and the theft proved, he was ordered to make double restitution, (as our manner was,) and the seamen were made to restore what they had taken out of the ship. So the Portugal departed well satisfied.

The said Mr. James Smith with his mate Keyser were bound to Guinea to trade for negroes. But when they arrived there,

---

three of the regicides so many years, he, who betrayed, or at least seized in a foreign land, three others, with one of whom he had served, could hardly expect greater favour than such conduct deserves.

they met with some Londoners, with whom they consorted, and the Londoners having been formerly injured by the natives, (or at least pretending the same,) they invited them aboard one of their ships upon the Lord's day, and such as came they kept prisoners, then they landed men, and a murderer, and assaulted one of their towns and killed many of the people, but the country coming down, they were forced to retire without any booty, divers of their men being wounded with the negroes' arrows, and one killed. Mr. Smith, having taken in wine at Madeiras, sailed to Barbados to put off his wine. But being engaged there, and his wife being there also unprovided of maintenance, and his ship and cargo bound over to the said Keyser his mate and others of Boston who set out the ship, Keyser refused to let any of the wines go on shore, except he might have security for the proceeds to be returned on ship board. So the ship lay a week in the roads, and then Keyser fearing that the master would use some means by other ships which rode there to deprive him of the cargo, told him plainly that if he would not come aboard, and return to Boston, (which was the last port they were bound to,) he would carry away the ship, and leave him behind, which accordingly he did; and arriving at Boston about midsummer, he repaired to the magistrates and told them how he was come away, and tendered the cargo to them, who finding that it was engaged to himself and others, and that there would be great loss in the wines if they were not presently disposed, delivered them to the merchants and himself, taking bond of them to be responsible to Mr. Smith &c. A short time after, Mr. Smith came, and brought his action against Keyser and the other mariners for bringing away the ship, and by a jury of seamen and merchants recovered three or four times the value of what he was damnified, and the mate Keyser to lose not only his wages, but he and the rest of the merchants to lose the proceed or interest agreed for their stock and adventure, which was forty per cent. and all the mariners to lose their wages. But divers of the magistrates being unsatisfied with this verdict, (perceiving that the jury in their displeasure against Keyser &c. did not only regard Smith's satisfaction for his damages, but also the punishment of Keyser &c.) the defendants at the next court brought a review, and then another jury abated much of the former damages; whereupon the plaintiff Smith preferred a petition to the next general court.

[Large Blank.]

For the matter of the negroes, whereof two were brought home in the ship, and near one hundred slain by the confession of some of the mariners, the magistrates took order to have these two set at liberty, and to be sent home; but for the slaughter committed, they were in great doubt what to do in it, seeing it was in another country, and the Londoners pretended a just revenge. So they called the elders; and desired their advice.[1]

Mr. Israel Stoughton, one of the magistrates, having been in England about merchandize, and returned with good advantage, went for England again the last winter, with divers other of our best military men, and entered into the parliament's service. Mr. Stoughton was made lieutenant colonel to colonel Rainsborow, Mr. Nehemiah Bourne, a ship carpenter, was major of his regiment, and Mr. John [2]Leverett, son of one of the elders of the church of Boston, a captain of a foot company, and one William Hudson, ensign of the same company, Lioll, surgeon of the Earl

---

1 See Appendix M. By our Col. Rec. III. 45, at the session in October, I find this proceeeding was had: "Upon a petition of Richard Saltonstall, Esq. for justice to be done on Captain Smith and Mr. Keyser for their injurious dealing with the negroes at Guinea, the petition was granted and ordered that Captain Smith and Mr. Keyser be laid hold on and committed to give answer in convenient time thereabouts."

2 So much is generally known of this distinguished man, afterwards governour of Massachusetts, that I would willingly have permitted his name to pass without a note, had not a fact come to my knowledge, of which no mention is to be found in any place, and which probably was concealed by design. An original letter, "given at our court at Whitehall the 22d day of August 1676, in the 28th year of our reign," with the royal sign manual and the royal seal appendant, signed by secretary Williamson by his majesty's command, is preserved by one of the descendants, addressed "to our trusty and well beloved Sir John Leverett, Knight, governour of Massachusetts bay in New England." Whether this honour of knighthood were kept secret by the puritan, because he doubted of the stability of the government at home, from which it emanated, or because he was too nearly advanced to the other world to regard the vanities of this, or feared its publicity might render him less acceptable to his constituents, by whose suffrages he was annually elected, is perhaps not unworthy of conjecture. The letter is marked "received 2 June 1677," of course after the election, and the next year a different person was chosen.

Leverett was a representative for Boston in 1651, 2, and 3, then went to England again, and was employed by that government or ours chiefly till 1662. Next year he was chosen for Boston and served three years, being also speaker part of the time, then he became an assistant, and in 1671 deputy governour. He became governour in 1673, and was annually rechosen, until 1678, when Bradstreet succeeded. He died 16 March 1679. Great military talents fitted him for the place of serjeant major general several years, and in the higher station of governour, in the most perilous period Massachusetts ever knew, Philip's war, they were fully exerted. His son, Hudson, did not, says Hutchinson, support the reputation of his father; but his grandson, John, in his presidency of Harvard College, gave a character to that institution which it had never before attained.

of Manchester's life guard. These did good service, and were well approved, but Mr. Stoughton falling sick and dying at Lincoln, the rest all returned to their wives and families. But three of them went to England again about the end of this year, but came back again and settled themselves here, all save the surgeon.

[Blank.]

The Narragansetts having begun war upon Uncus, the Monheagan sachem, notwithstanding their covenant to the contrary and divers messages sent to them from the commissioners to require them to forbear, until a meeting might be had, and the cause heard. It was thought fit by the general court in the third month, that though the next meeting was in course to be at New Haven in the beginning of September, yet in regard of the danger Uncus was in, and our engagement to save him harmless from any damage from Miantonomo his death, as also in regard of the distressed condition of Monsieur La Tour, (who earnestly petitioned the court for relief &c.) the commissioners should be written to to meet at Boston in the 28 of the fifth month, which was done accordingly. The names of the commissioners and all their proceedings are at large set down in the books of their records, whereof every colony hath one.[1]

[Blank.]

At this general court, which continued from 14 (3), to 5 (5), the military officers prevailed with much importunity to have the whole power of those affairs committed to them; which was thought by divers of the court to be very unfit, and not so safe in times of peace; but a great part of the court being military officers, and others not willing to contend any further about it, the order passed, the inconvenience whereof appeared soon after, and will more in future time.[2]

The taking of the Bristol ship in our harbour by Captain Stagg

---

[1] See Appendix N.

[2] At this court in July, our Records III. 21, contain an order of "a rate of *L.*616,15, one half to be paid in three months, and one half by the end of the first month next, in cattle, corn, beaver or money, as towns please." It was assessed in the proportions following:—Boston, *L.*100.00.0; Ipswich, 61.10.0; Charlestown, 55.00.0; Salem, 45.00.0; Cambridge, 45.00.0; Dorchester, 43.17.6; Watertown, 41.05.0; Roxbury, 37.10.0; Lynn, 25.00.0; Newbury, 23.00.0; Dedham, 20.00.0; Concord, 15.00.0; Rowley, 15.00,0; Hingham, 15.00.0; Sudbury, 11.05.0; Weymouth 10.10.0; Braintree, 10.10.0; Salisbury, 10.00.0; Hampton, 10.00.0; Medford, 7.00.0; Wooburn, 7.00.0; Gloucester, 4.17.6; Wenham, 3.10.0.

occasioned much debate in the court. The deputies drew up a bill to give protection to all ships in our harbour, coming as friends. The magistrates foreseeing that this might put us upon a necessity of fight with some parliament ships, (which we were very unwilling to be engaged in,) and so might weaken that interest we had in the parliament, they refused the bill; and so divers bills passed from one to the other, before they could agree. At length (few of the magistrates being then in the court) a bill passed to that effect, but not so full as was desired. But to strengthen the same, and to secure all ships which should come as friends into our harbour, commission was given to major Gibbons for Boston, and major [1]Sedgwick for Charlestown to keep the peace in the said towns, and not to permit any ships to fight in the harbour without license from authority.[2]

14. 5.] A new watch house set up on the fort hill at Boston was smote with lightning, and the boards and timber at one end of it torn in pieces, and many of the shingles of the covering torn off.

25.] Monsieur La Tour having stayed here all the winter and thus far of the summer, and having petitioned the court for aid against Monsieur D'Aulnay, and finding no hope to obtain help that way, took shipping in one of our vessels which went on fishing to Newfoundland, hoping by means of Sir David Kirk, governour there, and some friends he might procure in England to obtain aid from thence, intending for that end to go from thence to England. Sir David entertained him courteously, and promised to do much for him; but no means of help appearing to answer his ends, he returned hither before winter, Sir David giving him passage in a vessel of his which came hither.

[Large Blank.]

Captain Bayley being returned into England, and informing Alderman Barkly of the proceedings here against him and Mr. Barkly his brother in the business of the Lady La Tour, withal he carried a certificate of the proceedings of the court under the

---

1 My earliest notice of Robert Sedgwick is 9 March 1636-7 when he was made free. The next month he appears among the deputies, and very often afterwards. He was employed by Cromwell in 1654, and afterwards in his great expedition against the Spanish West Indies, when Jamaica was taken. There he died 24 May 1656, having, as appears from Thurloe's State Papers V. 138, 154, been just advanced to the rank of Major General by the Protector.

2 Perhaps the scope of the policy was, to favour the parliament, without giving by the language of the enactment any offence to the king's party.

hands of divers persons of good credit here, who although they reported truth for the most part, yet not the whole truth, (being somewhat prejudiced in the case; they were called in question about it after, for the offence was great, and they had been censured for it, if proof could have been had for a legal conviction,) whereby the alderman was so incensed as he attached a [1]ship of ours being then arrived at London; but being persuaded to release the ship, he attached two of New England, viz. Mr. Stephen Winthrop, who was recorder of the court when the cause was tried, and Captain Joseph Weld, who was one of the jury, so as they were forced to find sureties in a bond of 4000 pounds to answer him in the court of admiralty. But it pleased God to stir them up such friends, viz. Sir Henry Vane, (who had sometime lived at Boston, and though he might have taken occasion against us for some dishonour which he apprehended to have been unjustly put upon him here, yet both now and at other times he showed himself a true friend to New England, and a man of a noble and generous mind &c.) and some others by Mr. Peter's means, so as (although he spared for no costs) yet he was forced to give over his suit in the admiralty, and then procured out of Chancery a ne exeat regno against them. But the cause being heard there, and they discharged, he petitioned the lords of the parliament (pretending great injuries, which he was not able to prove) for letters of reprisal. After he had tried all means in vain, he was brought at length to sit down and lose his charges, and they theirs.

[Large Blank.]

1. 5.] Many books coming out of England, some in defence of anabaptism and other errours, and for liberty of conscience as a shelter for their toleration &c. others in maintenance of the Presbyterial government (agreed upon by the assembly of divines in England) against the congregational way, which was practised here, the elders of the churches through all the United Colonies agreed upon a meeting at Cambridge this day, where they conferred their councils and examined the writings which some of them had prepared in answer to the said books, which being agreed and perfected were sent over into England to be printed. The several answers were these; Mr. Hooker in answer to Mr. Rutterford the Scotch minister about Presbyterial government,

---

[1] Fowle, of whom much will be seen a few pages onward, was owner of the ship, as I learn from the records. He, Winthrop and Weld, all petitioned our court for indemnity, but in vain.

(which being sent in the New Haven ship was lost.) [1]While Mr. Hooker lived, he could not be persuaded to let another copy go over, but after his death, a copy was sent, and returned in print (3) 48.

[Blank.]

A sad business fell out this year in Boston. [2]One of the brethren of the church there, being in England in the parliament service about two years, had committed the care of his family and business to another of the same church, (a young man of good esteem for piety and sincerity, but his wife was in England,) who in time grew over familiar with his master's wife, (a young woman no member of the church,) so as she would be with him oft in his chamber &c. and one night two of the servants, being up, perceived him to go up into their dame's chamber, which coming to the magistrates' knowledge, they were both sent for and examined, (but it was not discovered till about a quarter of a year after, her husband being then come home,) and confessed not only that he was in the chamber with her in such a suspicious manner, but also that he was in bed with her, but both denied any carnal knowledge; and being tried by a jury upon their lives by our law, which makes adultery death, the jury acquitted them of the adultery, but found them guilty of adulterous behaviour. This was much against the minds of many, both of the magistrates and elders, who judged them worthy of death; but the jury attending what was spoken by others of the magistrates, 1. that seeing the main evidence against them was their own confession of being in bed together, their whole confession must be taken, and not a part of it; 2. the law requires two witnesses, but here was no witness at all, for although circumstances may amount to a testimony against the person, where the fact is evident, yet it is otherwise where no fact is apparent; 3. all that the evidence could evince was but suspicion of adultery, but neither God's law nor ours doth make suspicion of adultery (though never so strong) to be death; whereupon the case seeming doubtful to the jury, they judged it safest in case of life to find as they did. So the court adjudged them to stand upon the ladder at the place of execution with halters about their necks one hour, and then to be whipped, or each of them to pay 20 pounds. The husband (although he condemned his wife's immodest behaviour, yet) was so confident of her inno-

---

1 This sentence was, of course, added long after the principal matter.

2 The margin, in Winthrop's hand writing, informs us his name was Hudson; no doubt the ensign mentioned before.

cency in point of adultery, as he would have paid 20 pounds rather than she should have been whipped; but their estate being but mean, she chose rather to submit to the rest of her punishment than that her husband should suffer so much for her folly. So he received her again, and they lived lovingly together. All that she had to say for herself upon her trial was the same which she had revealed to her husband as soon as he came home, before the matter had been discovered, viz. that he did indeed come into bed to her, which so soon as she perceived, she used the best arguments she could to dissuade him from so foul a sin, so as he lay still, and did not touch her, but went away again as he came; and the reason why she did not cry out, was because he had been very faithful and helpful to her in her husband's absence, which made her very unwilling to bring him to punishment or disgrace.

This punishment of standing upon the gallows was not so well approved by some of the magistrates; because the law of God appoints in case of whipping, that they should not exceed forty stripes, and the reason given is, lest thy brother should seem despised in thine eyes, and why this reason should not hold in all cases and punishments not capital doth not appear.

[Large Blank.]

29, 8.] The wind E.N.E. with rain, so great a tempest as it drave three ships upon the shore, and did very much harm besides in bilging boats, and breaking down wharfs; and the night after for the space of two hours the tempest arose again at S. with more wind and rain than before. In which tempest one of our vessels coming from Bermuda had two men fetched overboard with the sea, and the vessel was in great danger of being foundered.

At the general court held at Boston the first of this month there was a petition preferred by divers merchants and others about two laws, the one forbidding the entertaining of any strangers above three weeks, except such as should be allowed by two magistrates &c. (this was made in Mrs. Hutchinson's time;) the other for banishing anabaptists, made the last year. The petitioners complained to the court of the offence taken thereat by many godly in England, and that some churches there did thereupon profess to deny to hold communion with such of our churches as should resort thither. Whereupon they entreated the court that they would please to take the said laws into further consideration, and to provide as far as they might for the indemnity of such of ours as were to go into England. Many of the court well inclined for these and other considerations to have had the execution of those laws to have been suspended for a season. But many of the elders, hearing of it, went first to the deputies and after to the magistrates, and laying before them what advantage it would give to the anabaptists, (who began to increase very fast through the country here, and much more in England, where they had gathered divers churches and taught openly and had published a confession of their faith,) entreated that the law might continue still in force, and the execution of it not suspended, though they disliked not that all lenity and patience should be used for convincing and reclaiming such erroneous persons. Whereupon the court refused to make any farther order about the petition. See 60 a counter petition.

There came hither to Boston at the same time out of England one Captain Partridge, who had served the parliament, but in the ship he broached and zealously maintained divers points of antinomianism and familism, for which he was called before the magistrates and charged with the said opinions, to which he refused to give any answer. But before he departed, he was willing to confer with Mr. Cotton, which accordingly he did, and Mr. Cotton reported to the magistrates, that he found him corrupt in his judgment, but ignorant of those points which he had maintained, so as he perceived he had been but lately taken with them, and that upon argument he was come off from some of the worst of them, and he had good hope to reclaim him wholly; but some of the magistrates requiring a present renouncing of all under his hand, he the said captain was not willing to that before he were clearly convinced of his errour in them. It was moved by some of the magistrates, in regard he had made so hopeful a beginning, and that winter was now at hand, and it would be very hard to expose his wife and family to such hardships &c. to permit him to stay here till the spring, but the major part (by one or two) voting the contrary, he was forced to depart, and so went to Rhode Island. This strictness was offensive to many, though approved of by others. But sure the rule of hospitality to strangers, and of seeking to pluck out of the fire such as there may be hope of to be reduced out of errour and the snare of the devil, do seem to require more moderation and indulgence of human infirmity where there appears not obstinacy against the clear truth.

This year about twenty families (most of them of the church of Braintree) petitioned the court for allowance to begin a plantation at the place where Gorton and his company had erected three or four small houses upon the land of Pumham the Indian sachem by Narragansett who had submitted himself and country to this jurisdiction. The court readily granted their petition, promising all encouragement &c. (for it was of great concernment to all the English in these parts, that a strong plantation should be there as a bulwark &c. against the Narragansetts.) But Mr. John Browne, one of the magistrates of Plimouth, and then one of their commissioners for the United Colonies, dwelling at Rehoboth, and intending to drive a trade with the Indians in those parts, meeting with some of ours when they went to view the place and to take the bounds of it, forbade them in the name of the government of Plimouth to proceed in the said plantation, telling them that it belonged to Plimouth, and that it should be restored to the right owners, (meaning Gorton and his company.) Whereupon the planters (not willing to run any hazard of contention for place in a country where there was room enough) gave over their purpose, and disposed themselves otherwise; some removed more southward, and others staid where they were. This practice of Mr. Browne being complained of to the governour of the Massachusetts, Mr. Dudley, he informed the magistrates of Plimouth thereof by letter, who returned answer, that Mr. Browne had no order from their court to forbid the proceeding &c. for they should have been glad to have had the place planted by us, though the right of it were (as they conceived) in themselves, and for that end referred themselves to an order of the commissioners, wherein liberty is given to the Massachusetts to take course with Gorton and the lands they had possessed &c. and therein is a proviso, that it should not prejudice the right of Plimouth &c. But they took not the rest of the order, wherein it follows, that all such lands of English or Indians as had submitted themselves to the government of the Massachusetts should not be comprised in that proviso. Now this land where the plantation should have been erected was part of Pumham's land. And our general court wrote to the governour and council of Plimouth to the same effect, with desire to have their further answer about the same, and for satisfaction about Mr. Browne's carriage herein. The governour and three magistrates returned answer, that Mr. Browne had commission in general to forbid any to plant upon their jurisdiction within the Narragansett river without their leave, which, if any of ours would seek, they might have. But the case being after put to the commissioners for explanation of their said order, they resolved for the Massachusetts.

[Large Blank.]

8.] A church was gathered at Haverhill upon the north side of Merrimack, and Mr. John Ward chosen and ordained pastor. About the same time a church was also gathered at Andover upon the south side of Merrimack, and Mr. [1]Woodbridge ordained pastor.

5. 9.] A church was gathered at Reading, and Mr. Greene ordained pastor. He was a very godly man, and died (3) 48.

The village at Jeffry's creek was named Manchester, and the people there (not being yet in church state) had procured Mr. Smith (sometimes pastor of the church of Plimouth) to preach to them.

At the last general court it was ordered, that divers farmers belonging to Ipswich and Salem (but so far distant from either

---

1 John Woodbridge married a daughter of Governour Dudley, from whom a letter affords so much information, that I have thought it worth transcribing:

Son Woodbridge,

On your last going from Rocksbury, I thought you would have returned again before your departure hence, and therefore neither bade you farewell, nor sent any remembrance to your wife. Since which time I have often thought of you, and of the course of your life, doubting you are not in the way wherein you may do God best service. Every man ought (as I take it) to serve God in such a way whereto he hath best fitted him by nature, education, or gifts, or graces acquired. Now in all these respects I conceive you to be better fitted for the ministry, or teaching a school, than for husbandry. And I have been lately stirred up the rather to think hereof by occasion of Mr. Carter's calling to be pastor at Woburn the last week, and Mr. Parker's calling to preach at Pascattaway, whose abilities and piety (for aught I know) surmount not yours. There is a want of schoolmasters hereabouts, and ministers are, or in likelihood will be, wanting ere long. I desire that you would seriously consider of what I say, and take advice of your uncle, Mr. Noyse, or whom you think meetest, about it; withal considering that no man's opinion in a case wherein he is interested by reason of your departure from your present habitation is absolutely to be allowed without comparing his reason with others. And if you find encouragement, I think you were best redeem what time you may without hurt of your estate in perfecting your former studies. Above all commend the case in prayer to God, that you may look before you with a sincere eye, upon his service, not upon filthy lucre, which I speak not so much for any doubt I have of you, but to clear myself from that suspicion in respect of the interest I have in you. I need say no more. The Lord direct and bless you, your wife and children, whom I would fain see, and have again some thoughts of it, if I live till next summer. Your very loving father,

THOS. DUDLEY.

Rocksbury, November 28, 1642.

To my very loving son, Mr. John Woodbridge, at his house in Newbury.

Woodbridge followed the advice in this letter, and probably had the advantage of instruction from the celebrated Thomas Parker. For some time he taught the school in Boston. He was the first settled minister at Andover in Essex county, as above appears. There he remained not long, being induced to return to England. I have seen a letter from his father Dudley 8 July 1648 to him, "preacher of the word of God at Andover in Wiltshire," advising of the means he would follow to send his wife and children. On the expulsion of the nonconformists in 1662 he returned to our country, and a satisfactory account of him is seen in Allen's Biog. Dict.

town as they could not duly repair to the public ordinances there) should erect a village and have liberty to gather a church. This was much opposed by those of the town of Ipswich, pleading their interest in the land &c. But it was answered, that, when the land was granted to the town, it was not intended only for the benefit of the near inhabitants, or for the maintenance of the officers of that one church only, but of all the inhabitants and of any other church which should be there gathered; and a principal motive which led the court to grant them and other towns such vast bounds was, that (when the towns should be increased by their children and servants growing up &c.) they might have place to erect villages, where they might be planted, and so the land improved to the more common benefit.

15. 10.] There appeared about noon, upon the north side of the sun, a great part of a circle like a rainbow, with the horns reversed, and upon each side of the sun, east and west, a bright light. And about a month after were seen three suns, about the sun-setting; and about a month after that two suns at sunrising, the one continued close to the horizon, while the other (which was the true sun) arose about half an hour. This was the earliest and sharpest winter we had since we arrived in the country, and it was as vehement cold to the southward as here. Divers of our ships were put from their anchors with the ice and driven, on shore 25 (10), and one ketch carried out to sea, and wrecked upon Lovell's Island. At New Haven a ship bound for England was forced to be cut out of the ice three miles. And in Virginia the ships were frozen up six weeks.

At Ipswich there was a calf brought forth with one head, and three mouths, three noses and six eyes. What these prodigies portended the Lord only knows, which in his due time he will manifest.

There was beside so sudden a thaw in the spring, (the snow lying very deep,) and much rain withal, that it bare down the bridge at Hartford upon Connecticut, and brake down divers mills to the southward about New Haven, and did much other harm.

This winter also the Swedes' fort upon Delaware river and all the buildings in it were burnt down, and all their powder and goods blown up. It happened in the night, through the negligence of a servant who fell on sleep leaving a candle burning. Some houses at Hartford, and a barn with corn, were burnt also; and two houses at Hingham in the Massachusetts.[1]

---

1 Hobart's Diary mentions the disaster thus: " 1646 March 15. All the

1646. 26. (1.)] The governour and council met at Boston to take order about a rescue which they were informed of to have been committed at Hingham upon the marshal, when he went to levy the fines imposed upon Mr. Hubberd their pastor and many others who joined with him in the petition against the magistrates &c. and having taken the information of the marshal and others, they sent out summons for their appearance at another day, at which time Mr. Hubberd came not, nor sent any excuse, though it was proved that he was at home, and that the summons was left at his house. Whereupon he was sent for by attachment directed to the constable, who brought him at the day of the return. And being then charged with joining in the said rescue by animating the offenders, and discouraging the officer, questioning the authority of his warrant because it was not in the king's name, and standing upon his allegiance to the crown of England, and exemption from such laws as were not agreeable to the laws of England, saying to the marshal that he could never know wherefore he was fined, except it were for petitioning, and if they were so waspish that they might not be petitioned, he knew not what to say to it &c. All the answer he would give was, that if he had broken any wholesome law not repugnant to the laws of England, he was ready to submit to censure. So he was bound over to the next court of assistants.

The court being at Boston, Mr. Hubberd appeared, and the marshal's information and other concurrent testimony being read to him, and his answer demanded, he desired to know in what state he stood, and what offence he should be charged with, or what wholesome law of the land, not repugnant to the law of England, he had broken. The court told him, that the matters he was charged with amounted to a seditious practice and derogation and contempt of authority. He still pressed to know what law &c. He was told that the oath which he had taken was a law to him; and beside the law of God which we were to judge by in case of a defect of an express law. He said that the law of God admitted various interpretations &c. Then he desired to see his accusers. Upon that the marshal was called, who justified his information. Then he desired to be tried by a jury, and to have the witnesses produced viva voce. The secretary told him that two were present, and the third was sworn to his examination, (but in that he was mistaken, for he had not been sworn,) but to satisfy him, he was sent for and sworn in court. The matters

---

houses of Thomas Loring and John Pratt burnt to the ground, being the Sabbath day in the morning.

testified against him were his speeches to the marshal before thirty persons, against our authority and government &c. 1. That we were but as a corporation in England; 2. That by our patent (as he understood it) we could not put any man to death, nor do divers other things which we did; 3. That he knew not wherefore the general court had fined them, except it were for petitioning, and if they were so waspish (or captious) as they might not be petitioned &c. and other speeches tending to disparage our authority and proceedings. Accordingly a bill was drawn up &c. and the jury found that he seemed to be ill affected to this government, and that his speeches tended to sedition and contempt of authority. Whereupon the whole court (except Mr. Bellingham, who judged him to deserve no censure, and desired in open court to have his dissent recorded) adjudged him to pay 20 pounds fine, and to be bound to his good behaviour, till the next court of assistants, and then farther if the court should see cause. At this sentence his spirit rose, and he would know what the good behaviour was, and desired the names of the jury, and a copy of all the proceedings, which was granted him, and so he was dismissed at present.

The contention continuing between Mr. Cleves, deputy president of Ligonia for Mr. Rigby, and Mr. [1]Jocelin and other commissioners of Sir Ferdinando Gorge, they both wrote letters to the governour and council of the Massachusetts, complaining of injuries from each other, and Mr. Cleves desiring aid for his defence against open force threatened by the other part; the governour and magistrates returned answer to them severally, to this effect, to persuade them both to continue in peace, and to forbear all violent courses until some London ships should arrive here, by which it was expected that order would come from the commissioners for the colonies &c. to settle their differences. These letters prevailed so far with them, as they agreed to refer the cause to the determination of the court of assistants at Boston, which was to be held 3 (4), next. For Mr. Rigby came Mr. Cleves and Mr. Tucker; for the province of Maine came Mr. Jocelin and Mr. Roberts. The court appointed them a day for hearing their cause, and caused a special jury to be empannelled.

---

1 Henry Jocelin, or Josselyn, brother of John, the gentleman, voyager, poet and naturalist, lived at Black Point, now Scarborough. With his long acquaintance in the country, he was well selected, 21 June 1664, with others, as deputies of Ferdinando Gorges, son of John, son of Sir Ferdinando. He was chief of a commission, under authority of the royal commissioners in 1666, to hold a court at Casco.

Mr. Cleves was plaintiff, and delivered in a declaration in writing. The defendants (though they had a copy thereof before) pleaded to it by word only. Some of the magistrates advised not to intermeddle in it, seeing it was not within our jurisdiction, and that the agents had no commission to bind the interest of the gentlemen in England. Others (and the most) thought fit to give them a trial, both for that it was a usual practice in Europe for two states being at odds to make a third judge between them, and though the principal parties could not be bound by any sentence of this court, (for having no jurisdiction, we had no coercion, and therefore whatever we should conclude was but advice,) yet it might settle peace for the present &c. Upon a full hearing, both parties failed in their proof. The plaintiff could not prove the place in question to be within his patent, nor could derive a good title of the patent itself to Mr. Rigby, (there being six or eight patentees, and the assignment only from two of them.) Also the defendant had no patent of the province, but only a copy thereof attested by witnesses, which was not pleadable in law. Which so perplexed the jury, as they could find for neither, but gave in a non liquet. And because the parties would have it tried by a jury, the magistrates forbore to deal any further in it. Only they persuaded the parties to live in peace &c. till the matter might be determined by authority out of England.

This spring was more early and seasonable than many before it, yet many were taken with a malignant fever, whereof some died in five or six days, but if they escaped the eighth, they recovered; and divers of the churches sought the Lord by publick humiliation, and the Lord was entreated, so as about the middle of the third month it ceased. It swept away some precious ones amongst us, especially one Mr. John Oliver, a gracious young man, not full thirty years of age, an expert soldier, an excellent surveyor of land, and one who, for the sweetness of his disposition and usefulness through a publick spirit, was generally beloved, and greatly lamented. For some few years past he had given up himself to the ministry of the gospel, and was become very hopeful that way, (being a good scholar and of able gifts otherwise, and had exercised publickly for two years.)

There fell out also a loathsome disease at Boston, which raised a scandal upon the town and country, though without just cause. One of the town (blank) having gone cooper in a ship into, (blank), at his return his wife was infected with lues venerea,[1] which ap-

1 The two first blanks in this paragraph were once filled, the first probably with the person's name, the second with that of the place, but they have been

peared thus: being delivered of a child, and nothing then appearing, but the midwife, a skilful woman, finding her body as sound as any other, after her delivery, she had a sore breast, whereupon divers neighbours resorting to her, some of them drew her breast, and others suffered their children to draw her, and others let her child suck them, (no such disease being suspected by any,) by occasion whereof about sixteen persons, men, women, and children, were infected, whereby it came at length to be discovered by such in the town as had skill in physick and surgery, but there was not any in the country who had been practised in that cure. But (see the good providence of God) at that very season there came by accident a young surgeon out of the West Indies, who had had experience of the right way of the cure of that disease. He took them in hand, and through the Lord's blessing recovered them all (blank) in a short time. And it was observed that although many did eat and drink and lodge in bed with those who were infected and had sores &c. yet none took it of them, but by copulation or sucking. It was very doubtful how this disease came at first. The magistrates examined the husband and wife, but could find no dishonesty in either, nor any probable occasion how they should take it by any other, (and the husband was found to be free of it.) So as it was concluded by some, that the woman was infected by the mixture of so many spirits of men and women as drew her breast, (for thence it began.) But this is a question to be decided by physicians.

6. 3.) The court of elections was at Boston. Mr. Norris of Salem preached. Mr. Winthrop was chosen governour, Mr. Dudley, (the last governour,) deputy governour, Mr. Endecott, serjeant major general, and he and Mr. Pelham commissioners for the United Colonies. The magistrates and deputies had formerly chosen the commissioners, but the freemen, looking at them as general officers, would now choose them themselves, and the rather because some of the deputies had formerly been chosen to that office, which gave offence to our confederates and to many among ourselves. This court lasted near three weeks, and was carried on with much peace and good correspondency; and when the business was near ended, the magistrates and deputies met,

---

effectually erased. In such an unimportant narrative, it may be of little consequence, that it was first written, the man "infected his wife, and leaving her with child went to sea again; the woman knew all, but knew not what she ailed." So that reports were various. Whether the result, as stated in the text, be the truth or not, is of less consequence than to observe, how the ignorance of our fathers on this topick gives confirmation to the general opinion of their blameless manners.

and concluded what remained, and so departed in much love. The several committees for laws made return of their commissions, and brought in many laws which were read over, and some of them scanned, but finding much difficulty in digesting and agreeing them, and the court having much other business, another committee was chosen out of several parts of the jurisdiction in the vacancy of the court, which was adjourned to 7 (8), to extract out of the whole such as should be thought fit to be established, and so to reduce them into one volume, to agree with such as were already in force &c.

The last year the court had imposed ten shillings upon every butt of sack &c. to be landed in our jurisdiction, and this spring there came in four ships with sack, and landed about 800 butts, but the merchants being much offended at the impost, (having no intelligence of it before, for indeed there had not been a due course taken to give notice thereof to foreign parts,) after much debate &c. the court remitted the one half thereof for the present. See after, four leaves.

Captain Bridges was sent by the commissioners the last year to Monsieur D'Aulney with the articles of peace ratified by them, and with order to demand his confirmation of them under his hand, wherein also was expressed our readiness that all injuries &c. of either part might be heard and composed in due time and place, and the peace to be kept at the same time, so as he would subscribe the same. Monsieur D'Aulney entertained our messenger with all state and courtesy that he possibly could; but refused to subscribe the articles, until differences were composed, and accordingly wrote back, that he perceived our drift was to gain time &c. whereas if our messenger had been furnished with power to have treated with him, and conclude about the differences, he doubted not but all had been agreed; for we should find, that it was more his honour which he stood upon, than his benefit, therefore he would sit still till the spring, expecting our answer herein, and would attempt nothing against us, until he heard from us.[1]

The general court, taking this answer into consideration, (and there not being opportunity for the commissioners to meet in season, only they had been certified by letters of Monsieur D'Aulney's propositions &c. and consented to a course for hearing &c.) agreed to send the deputy governour, Mr. Dudley, Mr. Hawthorne,

---

1 For a very valuable paper relative to our injurious violation of all regard to neutrality, in 1644, between these French combatants, see appendix O.

and major [1]Denison with full power to treat and determine &c. and wrote a letter to him to that end, (assenting to his desire for the place, viz. Penobscot (which they call Pentagoet) and referring the time also to him, so it were in September. Some thought it would be dishonourable for us to go to him, and therefore would have had the place to have been Pemaquid. But others were of a different judgment, 1. for that he was lieutenant general to a great prince; 2. being a man of a generous disposition, and valuing his reputation above his profit, it was considered, that it would be much to our advantage to treat with him in his own house. This being agreed, a private committee was chosen to draw up instructions, which were not to be imparted to the court, in regard of secresy, (for we had found, that D'Aulney had intelligence of all our proceedings,) and the same committee had orders to provide all things for the commissioners' voyage and to draw up their commission &c. and it was ordered, that if the deputy governour (in regard of his age, being above 70) should not be fit for the voyage, then Mr. Bradstreet should supply his place.

One Mr. William [2]Vassall, sometimes one of the assistants of

---

1 Daniel Denison, who is commemorated with fondness by Hubbard, under whose spiritual guidance he lived at Ipswich, was a person of great distinction in our colony. He had come over early, and lived first, I believe, at Newtown, now Cambridge. See 1 Hist. Coll. VII. 10, and 2 Hist. Coll. VIII. 229. By the military rank, serjeant major general, or commander of all the troops, which he obtained, I suppose after the death of Atherton, we may judge of his talents for this line of publick service; and by his long continuance in the office of assistant, to which he rose in 1654, we must conclude that his services in civil life were not less acceptable. In 1651 he had a commission with others in the difficult duty of bringing the people of Maine to the allegiance of Massachusetts. For several years he was one of the two commissioners of the United Colonies, and in their proceedings in Hazard II. we may see how important regard was paid to his judgment in the agitations between New Haven and the Dutch in 1653, and in the less arduous concern of united proceedings against the Quakers in 1657. Danforth in 2 Hist Coll. VIII. 109, informs us of his politics in the distracted councils of 1666, and Randolph, in 1673, enumerates Denison among the few "popular and well principled men in the magistracy," in Hutch. Coll. 500 also Chalmers Pol. Ann. 434. The moderate spirit, by which he was usually actuated, had not a general spread, yet the continuance of his election to the same rank for many years, where his sympathy was not, in relation to the controversy with the crown, in unison with that of the people, is evidence of the strong hold his virtues and publick labours had acquired. He died 20 September 1682, and is one of the few authors of that early period, having left an "Irenicon, or salve for New England's sore," a curious tract, which those who are not satisfied with Eliot, in Biog. Dict. may see in the Historical Society's Library.

2 He had been one of the first assistants, chosen in England, 1629, and came over probably in the fleet with Winthrop, but returned in the Lyon with Revell.

the Massachusetts, but now of Scituate in Plimouth jurisdiction, a man of a busy and factious spirit, and always opposite to the civil governments of this country and the way of our churches, had practised with such as were not members of our churches to take some course, first by petitioning the courts of the Massachusetts and of Plimouth, and (if that succeeded not) then to the parliament of England, that the distinctions which were maintained here, both in civil and church estate, might be taken away, and that we might be wholly governed by the laws of England; and accordingly a petition was drawn up to the parliament, pretending that they being free born subjects of England were denied the liberty of subjects, both in church and commonwealth, themselves and their children debarred from the seals of the covenant, except they would submit to such a way of entrance and church covenant, as their consciences could not admit, and take such a civil oath as would not stand with their oath of allegiance, or else they must be deprived of all power and interest in civil affairs, and were subjected to an arbitrary government and extrajudicial proceedings &c. And now at this court at Boston a petition to the same effect, much enlarged, was delivered in to the deputies under the hands of Doctor [1]Childe, Mr. Thomas [2]Fowle, Mr. Sa-

---

See Dudley's letter, 1 Hist. Coll. VIII. 40. After his return to our country, which Hubbard, 500, says was in 1635, he settled himself at Scituate in Plimouth colony, where he was much respected, though of a less strait sect than most of the New England people. See the account of Scituate in 2 Hist. Coll. IV. For his engagement in this famous controversy Hubbard charges him with publishing the curious tract, New England's Jonas cast up at London, which was, however, according to the title page, by Major John Child, brother of Dr. Robert. An amusing anecdote of Vassall's readiness of wit is there told, 2 Hist. Coll. IV. 107. Perhaps, as he returned home with Fowle and other petitioners, Vassall abandoned his hopes of success, or at least of comfort and quiet, in New England, and turned his views to the West Indies a few years after. Mr. S. Davis says he died in Barbados 1655. Hutchinson I. 23, says " when Jamaica was taken by Cromwell, he laid the foundation of several estates there, enjoyed by his posterity to the present time." The present Lord Holland has part of his property, I think, and his name, Vassall, certainly, from this gentleman or his brother Samuel, another of our assistants, who never came over to us. This latter had great influence in parliament, of which he was a member, and deservedly became one of the commissioners for foreign plantations.

1 Hutch. I. 137 says " Child was a young gentleman just before come from Padua, where he studied physick, and as was reported, had taken the degree of doctor." From a curious letter of William White, in 2 Hist. Coll. IV. 198, it may be presumed, that Child had in view the exploring of mines in our country; but probably after the long vexation and arbitrary imprisonment suffered in consequence of this petition, his affection for our country was sufficiently cooled to induce him to remain at home, after his return in safety. His baptismal name was Robert.

2 Fowle was, it seems, a merchant. By the tyranny of our rulers he must

muel Maverick, Mr. Thomas Burton, Mr. John [1]Smith, Mr. David [2]Yale, and Mr. John [3]Dand, in the name of themselves and many others in the country, whereto they pressed to have present answer. But the court being then near at an end, and the matter being very weighty, they referred the further consideration thereof to the next session. And whereas a law was drawn up, and ready to pass, for allowing non-freemen equal power with the freemen in all town affairs, and to some freemen of such estate &c. their votes in election of magistrates, it was thought fit to defer this also to the next session.

4.] The Narragansetts having broken their covenants with us in three days of payment, so as there was now due to us above

---

have been convinced, that this was no place for a man of his opinions. The judgment of God fell upon him, as well as Child, according to the opinion of their opponents.

1 Smith was one of the church of Providence, associated with Roger Williams, probably, more than ten years before. See Governour Hopkins's History, 2 Hist. Coll. IX. 170. One of the same name, and, probably, the same person, was chief magistrate of the colony, under its first charter, in 1649. 1 Hist. Coll. VI. 144. My inquiries about Burton have been unsuccessful.

2 In addition to my former note, it may be mentioned, that our town records verify the birth of David, son of David Yale and Ursula his wife, 18 September 1645, and of Theophilus 14 January 1651. From our county records, Lib. II. p. 47, I extract the conveyance of one of the most beautiful estates in this or any other city, being the same now owned and occupied by my friend, Gardiner Greene, Esquire: "Be it known by these presents, that I, Edward Bendall, of Boston, planter, for good and valuable considerations by me in hand received, have given, granted, bargained and sold, and by these presents do give &c. unto David Yeale, of Boston aforesaid, merchant, a certain house and garden, with other lands thereunto belonging, be it in quantity two acres more or less, being bounded with Mr. John Cotton on the south, Sudbury street on the east, [blank] on the north, to have and to hold the said land to him and his heirs forever with warranty against all manner of persons. In witness whereof I have hereunto set my hand and seal this 23 (6) 1645. Edward Bendall. Sealed and delivered in the presence of Robert Loveland, Thomas Graves. Entered and recorded 8 September, 1654, pr. Edward Rawson, recorder. Endorsed, We Thomas Clarke and Thomas Lake of Boston in New England, merchants, being attorneys to Mr. David Yeale, late of the same place, have bargained, sold, granted, delivered and assigned all that his house and ground mentioned in this deed of sale unto Mr. Hezekiah Usher for the use of Captain John Wall of London, mariner. In witness whereof we have put to our hands September 8, 1653. Thomas Clarke and Thomas Lake. Entered and recorded as above."

3 Dand was, we may presume, a gentleman of some education, both from his association with these petitioners, and from the searching of his *study* in the violent proceedings against him. He probably remained not long, where his treatment was so ungentle, and, as nothing more is known of him, no doubt, he went home.

1300 fathom of wampom, they now sent us to Boston to the value of 100 fathom, (the *most* in old kettles,) excusing themselves by their poverty and by the Nianticks and others failing to contribute their parts. But the commissioners (who were then two of them at Boston) refused to accept so small a sum, and rebuking them sharply for breaking their covenants both in their payments [and] other acts, told them that if they were forced to fetch the rest, they could as well fetch this. So they sold their kettles to a brazier in Boston, and left the pay in his hands for us, if we would accept it, when they should bring the rest.[1]

One captain Cromwell (about ten years since a common seaman in the Massachusetts) had been out with captain Jackson in a man of war by commission from the Earl of Warwick divers years, and having a commission of deputation from his said captain, had taken four or five Spanish vessels, and in some of them great riches, and being bound hither with three ships, and about eighty men, (they were frigates of cedar wood of about sixty and eighty tons,) by a strong northwest wind they were forced into Plimouth, (divine providence so directing for the comfort and help of that town, which was now almost deserted,) where they continued about fourteen days or more, and spent liberally and gave freely to many of the poorer sort. It fell out, while they were there, that a desperate drunken fellow, one Voysye, (who had been in continual quarrels all the voyage,) on being reproved by his captain, offered to draw his rapier at him, whereupon the captain took it from him, and giving him some blows with it, as it was in the scabbard, he threw it away; Voysye gate it again, and came up to his captain, who taking it from him again, and throwing it away, when he could not make him to leave his weapon, nor forbear his insolent behaviour, he gave him a blow on the forehead with the hilt of it, which made a small wound, which the captain would presently to have been searched and dressed, but Voysye refused, and the next day went into the field to fight with another of his fellows, but their weapons being taken from them, no hurt was done; and the next day after, his wound putrifying immediately, he died. It was then the general court at Plimouth,

1 In Haz. II. 67, and following may be seen much of the dealing with these unhappy tributaries. Since Uncas, in whose cause we had involved ourselves in the irksome duty of restraining the more powerful Indians, was ungrateful to his benefactors, and the whole spirit of his adversaries was broken, I wish the Connecticut people had been more moderate in their assertion of the full terms of the contract. The records of the United Colonies speak of the Indians' tribute "as if they would put a scorn upon" us; but their poverty was real. A few years after great expense was incurred, Roger Williams thought, needlessly, to convince the Narragansetts of the English superiority.

and a jury being empannelled, they found that he died of the wound received from the captain, whereupon the captain was sent for on shore. He offered to put himself upon trial, so as he might not be imprisoned, and that he might be tried by a council of war, both which were granted him, and one of Plimouth, one of their chief men, but no magistrate, undertook for him, body for body, and some of the magistrates and other military officers were chosen a council of war, who, upon the evidence, and sight of his commission, by which he had power of martial law &c. acquitted him. The trained band accompanied the body to the grave, and the captain gave every one of them an eln of black taffeta for a mourning robe. After this he came 10 (4), with his three ships to Boston, and presented the governour with a sedan, which (as he said) was sent by the viceroy of Mexico to his sister. It was a very fair one, and could not be less worth than 50 pounds. He and all his men had much money, and great store of plate and jewels of great value; yet he took up his lodging in a poor thatched house, and when he was offered the best in the town, his answer was, that in his mean estate that poor man entertained him, when others would not, and therefore he would not leave him now, when he might do him good. He was ripped out of his mother's belly, and never sucked, nor saw father nor mother, nor they him.

At the last general court a bill was presented by some of the elders for a synod to be held in the end of the summer. The magistrates passed it, but the deputies sending some of themselves to confer with the magistrates about it, their objections were these, first, because therein civil authority did require the churches to send their messengers to it, and divers among them were not satisfied of any such power given by Christ to the civil magistrate over the churches in such cases; secondly, whereas the main end of the synod was propounded to be, an agreement upon one uniform practice in all the churches, the same to be commended to the general court &c. this seemed to give power either to the synod or the court to compel the churches to practise what should so be established. To these it was answered, 1. that the civil magistrate had power upon just occasion to require the churches to send their messengers to advise in such ecclesiastical matters, either of doctrine or discipline, as the magistrate was bound by God to maintain the churches in purity and truth in (which was assented unto,) 2. that the end of the synod was not to proceed by way of power, but only of counsel from the word of God, and the court was at liberty either to establish or disannul such agreement of the synod, as they should see cause, which could put no more power into the court's hands than it had by the word of God and our own Laws and Liberties established in that case. Whereupon it was ordered, that howsoever the civil magistrate had authority to call a synod when they saw it needful, yet in tender respect of such as were not yet fully satisfied in that point, the ensuing synod should be convened by way of motion only to the churches, and not by any words of command.

Mr. Eaton, the governour of New Haven, wrote to the governour of the Bay, to desire the advice of the magistrates and elders in a special case, which was this: one Plain of Guilford being discovered to have used some unclean practices, upon examination and testimony, it was found, that being a married man, he had committed sodomy with two persons in England, and that he had corrupted a great part of the youth of Guilford by masturbations, which he had committed, and provoked others to the like above a hundred times; and to some who questioned the lawfulness of such a filthy practice, he did insinuate seeds of atheism, questioning whether there were a God &c. The magistrates and elders (so many as were at hand) did all agree, that he ought to die, and gave divers reasons from the word of God.[1] And indeed it was horrendum facinus, and he a monster in human shape, exceeding all human rules and examples that ever had been heard of, and it tended to the frustrating of the ordinance of marriage and the hindering the generation of mankind.

A petition was presented to the court under many hands for the continuance of the two laws against anabaptists and other hereticks, which was done in reference to a petition presented at the former court concerning the same laws.[2]

A plantation was this year begun at Pequod river by Mr. John

---

1 The margin informs us "he was executed at New Haven."

2 A few pages back, it may be remembered, the reasonable petition was mentioned, but, I fear, this counter petition had more signers. Persons going to England, with hopes of employment in the parliament service, were probably desirous of recommending themselves by carrying evidence of a relaxation of the rigour of our laws, or at least of their own exertions to obtain it. But the erroneous policy of our court, encouraged by the support of the multitude, showed its strength in the abrupt and positive report on the subject, which is here extracted from our Col. Rec. Vol. III. p. 50. "In answer to the petition of Em. Downing, Nehem. Bourne, Robert Sedgwick, Thomas Foule, with others, for the abrogation or alteration of the laws against the anabaptists and the law that requires special allowance for new comers residing here, it is ordered, that the laws in their petition mentioned shall not be altered or explained at all." Bourne had lived in Boston, as I find record of two children born to him here; but after his return from the wars, before mentioned by Winthrop, I presume he removed.

Winthrop, junr. Mr. Thomas [1]Peter, a minister, (brother to Mr. Peter of Salem,) and this court power was given to them two for ordering and governing the plantation till further order &c. although it was uncertain whether it would fall within our jurisdiction or not, because they of Connecticut challenged it by virtue of a patent from the king, which was never showed us, so it was done de bene esse, quousque &c. for it mattered not much to which jurisdiction it did belong, seeing the confederation made all as one; but it was of great concernment to have it planted, to be a curb to the Indians &c.

Monsieur La Tour being returned from Newfoundland in a pinnace of Sir David Kirk, was (by some merchants of Boston) set forth in the same pinnace to the eastward with trading commodities to the value of 400 pounds. When he came at Cape Sable, (which was in the heart of winter,) he conspired with the master (being a stranger) and his own Frenchmen, being five, to go away with the vessel, and so forced out the other five English, (himself shooting one of them in the face with a pistol,) who, through special providence, having wandered up and down fifteen days, found some Indians who gave them a shallop, and victuals, and an Indian pilot. So they arrived safe at Boston in the third month. Whereby it appeared (as the scripture saith) that there is no confidence in an unfaithful or carnal man. Though tied with many strong bonds of courtesy &c. he turned pirate &c.

Mr. Lamberton, Mr. [2]Grigson, and divers other godly persons, men and women, went from New Haven in the eleventh month last in a ship of 80 tons, laden with wheat for London; but the ship was never heard of after. The loss was very great, to the value of some 1000 pounds; but the loss of the persons was very deplorable.

Monsieur D'Aulney, having received our letter, returned answer, that he saw now that we seriously desired peace, which he (for his part) did also, and that he accounted himself so highly honoured, that we would send such principal men of ours home to him &c. that he desired this favour of us, that he might spare

---

1 He is said, in a book of no authority, Peters's Hist. of Connecticut, to have come over in 1634 and settled at Saybrook with Fenwick. There, also, Mather places him. Very little is known of him, but that he was of a less sanguine temperament than Hugh.

2 Grigson's children were Richard and Mary, who resided in London, Anna, who married Stephen Daniels, Susan, who married ——— Crittenden, Sarah, who married ——— Whitehead, Phebe, who married Rev. John Whiting of Hartford, and three more daughters. His widow, Jane, lived to a great age.

us that labour, for which purpose he would send two or three of his to us to Boston about the end of August, to treat and determine &c. Upon receipt of this letter, the governour thought it expedient to call the general court (if it were but for one day) to have considered of commissioners to treat with his here, for he conceived that those who were *invited* to treat at Penobscot had not power to treat at home, and besides the court had declared their mind not to have chosen all these three, if they had been to have treated at home. But some other of the magistrates differing, he deferred it, and the harvest coming on, it was thought better to let it alone.

One Smith of Watertown had a son about five years old, who fell into the river near the mill gate, and was carried by the stream under the wheel, and taken up on the other side, without any harm. One of the boards of the wheel was fallen off, and it seems (by special providence) he was carried through under that gap, for otherwise if an eel pass through, it is cut asunder. The miller perceived his wheel to check on the sudden, which made him look out, and so he found the child sitting up to the waist in the shallow water beneath the mill.

[Blank.]

5.) Three of our elders, viz. Mr. Mather, Mr. [1]Allen and Mr. Eliot, took with them an interpreter, and went to the place where Cutshamekin, the Indian sachem [blank.]

A daughter of Mrs. Hutchinson was carried away by the Indians near the Dutch, when her mother and others were killed by them; and upon the peace concluded between the Dutch and the same Indians, she was returned to the Dutch governour, who restored her to her friends here. She was about eight years old, when she was taken, and continued with them about four years, and she had forgot her own language, and all her friends, and was loath to have come from the Indians.

Great harm was done in corn (especially wheat and barley) in this month by a caterpillar, like a black worm about an inch and a half long. They eat up first the blades of the stalk, then they eat up the *tassels*, whereupon the ear withered. It was believed

---

1 From his proximity to the residence of the Indian sovereign, I doubt not that this was John Allen of Dedham, of whom, as usual in Mather, parvum in multo may be seen in the Magnalia III. c. 22. Eliot and Allen have added very little to the original. Another Allen, Thomas, was minister at Charlestown as colleague with Symmes part of the time, but returned home in a few years.

by divers good observers, that they fell in a great thunder shower, for divers yards and other bare places, where not one of them was to be seen an hour before, were presently after the shower almost covered with them, besides grass places where they were not so easily discerned. They did the most harm in the southern parts, as Rhode Island &c. and in the eastern parts in their Indian corn. In divers places the churches kept a day of humiliation, and presently after the caterpillars vanished away.[1]

[Large Blank.]

The court had made an order in (8) last, for ten shillings to be paid upon every butt of Spanish wine landed &c. and now this spring arrived divers English ships, which brought about 800 butts; but having lost much by leakage, and coming to a bad market, they were very unwilling to pay the impost, and refused to give in an invoice of such wines as they had landed, whereupon they were forfeited by the order. But upon their petition the general court remitted the forfeiture and half the impost, (in regard the order was made so lately as they could not have notice of it in those parts from whence the wines came,) but this notwithstanding, they would not submit to the order, so as the auditor who had the charge of receiving the said impost was forced to break open the cellar doors where their wines lay, and took out of the best wines for the impost, which by the order he might do. But this also they took as a great injury, because their best wines being gone, the sale of the rest was much hindered, and they threatened to get recompense some other way.

The merchants of New Haven had purchased some land of the Indians about thirty miles to the northwest of them upon Pautucket river, and had set up a trading house. The Dutch governour made a protest against it, and sent it to Mr. Eaton, claiming the place to be theirs, and within ten Dutch miles of Fort Orange. Mr. Eaton answered the protest, acknowledging no right in the Dutch, but alleging their *purchase* and offering to refer the cause &c. The Dutch governour by letter complained of it to the governour of Massachusetts, and also of Mr. [2]Whiting for saying

---

1 Vexation of many days labour was necessary for a satisfactory transcription of this paragraph, the ink having spread through the paper, probably by injury from damp, so as it appears almost a perfect blot. On the word in italics I spent more study than in many pages of any other part of this work, and consulted more friends than in the whole of the residue.

2 William Whiting was one of the early settlers of Hartford, and was a member of the first general court of deputies of Connecticut, but not, as Ma-

that the English were fools in suffering the Dutch in the centre &c. The governour of Massachusetts informed Mr. Eaton hereof, (the commissioners being then to meet at New Haven,) and tendered it to their consideration, if it would not be expedient to call Mr. Whiting (then a magistrate at Hartford) to give account of these speeches, seeing the Dutch would expect satisfaction &c.

When the time of the synod drew near, it was propounded to the churches. The order was sent to the churches within this jurisdiction; and to the churches in other jurisdictions a letter was sent withal.

All the churches in this jurisdiction sent their messengers, except Boston, Salem, Hingham, Concord [blank]. Concord would have sent, if their elder had been able to come, or if they had had any other whom they had judged fit &c. Boston and Salem took offence at the order of court, 1. because by a grant in the Liberties the elders had liberty to assemble without the compliance of the civil authority, 2. it was reported, that this motion came originally from some of the elders, and not from the court, 3. in the order was expressed, that what the major part of the assembly should agree upon should be presented to the court, that they might give such allowance to it as should be meet, hence was inferred that this synod was appointed by the elders, to the intent to make ecclesiastical laws to bind the churches, and to have the sanction of the civil authority put upon them, whereby men should be forced under penalty to submit to them, whereupon they concluded that they should betray the liberty of the churches, if they should consent to such a synod. The principal men who raised these objections were some of Boston, who came lately from England, where such a vast liberty was allowed, and sought for by all that went under the name of Independents, not only the anabaptists, antinomians, familists, seekers &c. but even the most godly and orthodox, as Mr. Goodwin, Mr. Nye, Mr. Burrows &c. who in the assembly there had stood in opposition to the presbytery, and also the greater part of the house of commons, who by their commissioners had sent order to all English plantations in the West Indies and Summers Islands, that all men should enjoy their liberty of conscience, and had by letters intimated the same to us. To these did some others of the church of Boston adhere, but not above thirty or forty in all.

---

ther says, a magistrate in 1637. To that honour he rose in 1642, and next year was treasurer of that colony, but after 1647 Trumbull gives no light upon his situation.

1. To the particular objections, it was thus answered, viz. to the first, that that liberty was granted only for a help in case of extremity, if, in time to come, the civil authority should either grow opposite to the churches, or neglect the care of them, and not with any intent to practise the same, while the civil authority were nursing fathers to the churches. For the second, that it was not for the churches to inquire, what or who gave the court occasion to call the synod, but if they thought fit to desire the churches to afford them help of counsel in any matters which concerned religion and conscience, it was the churches' duty to yield it to them; for so far as it concerns their command or request it is an ordinance of man, which we are to submit unto for the Lord's sake, without troubling ourselves with the occasion or success. Ex malis moribus bonae leges: the laws are not the worse by being occasioned by evil men and evil manners. 3. Where the order speaks of the major part of the assembly, it speaks in its own language, and according to the court's practice, where the act of the major part is the act of the court; but it never intended thereby to restrain or direct the synod in the manner of their proceeding, nor to hinder them but that they might first acquaint the churches with their conclusions, and have their assent to them before they did present them to the court, for that is their care; the court's care was only to provide for their own cognizance. And for that inference which is drawn from that clause, that the court might give them such allowance as should be meet, it is without rule, and against the rule of charity, to infer from thence any such sanction of the court as is supposed. For if they say only they will give them such allowance as is meet, it cannot be inferred, that they will put any such sanction or stamp of authority upon them, as should be unmeet.

Two Lord's days this agitation was in Boston, and no conclusion made, by reason of the opposite party. So the elders sate down much grieved in spirit, yet told the congregation, that they thought it their duty to go notwithstanding, not as sent by the church, but as specially called by the order of court.

The assembly or synod being met at Cambridge, 1 (7), they wrote letters to the elders and brethren of the church of Boston, inviting them and pressing them also by arguments to send their elders and other messengers. Upon this, the ruling elders, being at home, assembled so many of the church, as they could upon the sudden, but the greater part being from home, and divers of those who were met still opposing, nothing could be done.

The next day was Boston lecture, to which most of the synod repaired, and Mr. Norton, teacher of the church of Ipswich, being procured to supply the place, took his text suitable to the occasion, viz. of Moses and Aaron meeting in the mount and kissing each other, where he laid down the nature and power of the synod, as only consultative, decisive, and declarative, not coactive &c. He showed also the power of the civil magistrate in calling such assemblies, and the duty of the churches in yielding obedience to the same. He showed also the great offence and scandal which would be given in refusing &c. The next Lord's day the matter was moved again, in three propositions; 1. whether the church would hold communion with the other churches &c. and desired them to express it by holding up their hands, which most of the church did, but some of the opposite party resisted and gave this reason, that though they did assent to the proposition, yet they could not vote it, because they knew not what would be inferred upon it; upon this the second proposition was mentioned, viz. whether they would exercise this communion in sending messengers to the synod, and if not, then the third proposition was, whether the church would then go themselves.

Exception was taken at this way of doing a church act by the major part, which had not been our practice in former times. To this it was answered, that in some cases (as the choice of officers &c.) it is needful to have every man's consent, but in other cases, as admission of a member &c. it was sufficient, if the major part assented; and for this practice of proceeding by erection of hands that in [2] Cor. [viii. 19] was alleged, where the Greek word χειρο[τονηθεις] signifies the same. And in the present case, it was necessary, because the order of court, and the letters of the synod to us, required (both in duty and civility) that the church should return answer, which the minor part could not do, therefore the major part (of necessity) must.

Then it was moved by some, that the third proposition might rather be intended and the church agree to go to the synod, rather than to send. To this it was answered, 1. that it would not be convenient nor of good report, to go in a singular way; 2. it would savour of disorder and tumult; 3. it might produce an impossibility, for if one man's conscience should bind him to attend, so might another man's, and then as well might every man's, and if all (or but the major part of our church) should go thither, it were almost impossible any business could proceed in due order. In the end it was agreed by vote of the major part, that the elders and three of the brethren should be sent as messengers &c.

The synod brake up and was adjourned to 8 (4), having continued but about fourteen days, in regard of winter drawing on, and few of the elders of other colonies were present.

Gorton and two others of his company, viz. John Greene and Randall [1]Holden, going into England, complained to the commissioners for Plantations &c. against us &c. who gave order, that some of ours then in England should be summoned to answer their petition; whereupon some appeared, but they having no instructions about the case, and the writings sent over to Mr. Welde the year before being either lost or forgotten, so as a full answer could not be given in the particular, and the petitioners being favoured by some of the commissioners, partly for private respects, and partly for their adhering to some of their corrupt tenets, and generally out of their dislike of us for our late law for banishing anabaptists, they seemed to be much offended with us for our rigorous proceeding (as they called it) against them, and thereupon (without sending to us to hear our answer &c.) they gave them this order following:

By the governour in chief Lord high admiral and commissioners appointed by parliament for the English plantations in America.

Seal Warwick Governour & Admiral.

Whereas we have thought fit to give an order for Mr. Samuel Gorton, Mr. Randall Holden, Mr. John Greene, and others, late inhabitants of a tract of land called the Narragansett Bay, near the Massachusetts Bay in New England, to return with freedom to the said tract of land, and there to inhabit and abide without interruption, these are therefore to pray and require you, and all others whom this may concern, to permit and suffer the said Samuel Gorton &c. with their company, goods and necessaries carried with them out of England, to land at any port in New England, where the ship wherein they do embark themselves shall arrive, and from thence to pass, without any of your lets or molestations, through any part of the continent of America, within your jurisdiction, to the said tract of land called Narragansett Bay, or any part thereof, they carrying themselves without offence, and paying according to the custom of the country, and their contract, for all things they shall make use of in their way, for victuals, carriage, or other accommodation. Hereof you may not fail; and this shall

---

1 I rejoice to find, that he lived long enough after these abuses to make them known to the royal commissioners in 1665. He and Greene were by them appointed justices of the peace within the Narragansett country, the object for which they had so many years toiled and suffered, 2 Hist. Coll. VII. 93.

be your warrant. Dated at Westminster this 15 of May, 1646.

To the governour and assistants of the English plantation in the Massachusetts Bay in New England, and to all other governours and other inhabitants of New England, and all others whom this may concern.

Nottingham,
Fra. Dacre,
Fer. Rigby,
Cor. Holland,
Sam. Vassall,
Geo. Fenwick,
Fran. Allein,
Wm. Purefoy,
Geo. Snelling.

13. (7.)] Randall Holden arrived here in a London ship, captain Wall master, and sent this order to the governour to desire leave to land &c. Accordingly the governour answered, that he could not give him leave of himself, nor dispense with an order of the general court; but the council were to meet within two or three days, and he would impart it unto them &c. and in the mean time he would not seek after him &c.

The council being met, they were of different judgments in the case, so as they agreed to take the advice of such of the elders, as were then met at the lecture at Boston (being about ten). The elders also differed, some were very earnest for his commitment till the general court &c. But the greater part, both of magistrates and elders, thought it better to give so much respect to the protection which the parliament had given him, (and whereupon he adventured his life &c.,) as to suffer him to pass quietly away, and when the general court should be assembled, (which would be within a month,) then to consider further about their repossessing the land they claimed.

20. (7.)] Being the Lord's day, and the people ready to go to the assembly after dinner, Monsieur Marie and Monsieur Louis, with Monsieur D'Aulney his secretary, arrived at Boston in a small pinnace, and major Gibbons sent two of his chief officers to meet them at the water side, who conducted them to their lodgings sine strepitu. The publick worship being ended, the governour repaired home, and sent major Gibbons, with other gentlemen, with a guard of musketeers to attend them to the governour's house, who, meeting them without his door, carried them into his house, where they were entertained with wine and sweetmeats, and after a while he accompanied them to their lodgings (being the house of major Gibbons, where they were entertained that night.) The next morning they repaired to the governour, and delivered him their commission, which was in form of a letter directed to the governour and magistrates. It was open, but had

a seal only let into the paper with a label. Their diet was provided at the ordinary, where the magistrates use to diet in court times; and the governour accompanied them always at meals. Their manner was to repair to the governour's house every morning about eight of the clock, who accompanied them to the place of meeting; and at night either himself or some of the commissioners accompanied them to their lodging. It was the third day at noon before our commissioners could come together. When they were met, they propounded great injuries and damages, sustained by captain Hawkins and our men, in assistance of La Tour, and would have engaged our government therein. We denied that we had any hand, either by commission or permission, in that action. We only gave way to La Tour to hire assistance to conduct his ship home, according to the request made to us in the commission of the vice admiral of France. And for that which was done by our men beyond our commission, we showed Monsieur D'Aulney's letter to our governour, by captain Bayley, wherein he writes, that the king of France had laid all the blame upon the vice admiral, and commanded him not to break with us, upon that occasion. We also alleged the peace formerly concluded without any reservation of those things. They replied, that howsoever the king of France had remitted his own interest, yet he had not nor intended to deprive Monsieur D'Aulney of his private satisfaction. Here they did stick two days. Their commissioners alleged damages to the value of 8000 pounds, but did not stand upon the value. They would have accepted of very small satisfaction, if we would have acknowledged any guilt in our government. In the end they came to this conclusion: we accepted their commissioner's answer, in satisfaction of those things we had charged upon Monsieur D'Aulney, and they accepted our answer for clearing our government of what he had charged upon us; and because we could not free captain Hawkins and the other voluntaries of what they had done, we were to send a small present to Monsieur D'Aulney in satisfaction of that, and so all injuries and demands to be remitted, and so a final peace to be concluded. Accordingly we sent Monsieur D'Aulney by his commissioners a very fair new sedan, (worth forty or fifty pounds where it was made, but of no use to us,) sent by the viceroy of Mexico to a lady his sister, and taken in the West Indies by Captain Cromwell, and by him given to our governour. This the commissioners very well accepted; and so the agreement being signed in several instruments, by the commissioners of both parts, on 28 day of the same month they took leave and departed to their pinnace, the governour and our commissioners accompanying them to their boat, attended with a guard of musketeers, and gave them five guns from Boston, three from Charlestown, and five from Castle Island, and we sent them aboard a quarter cask of sack and some mutton. They answered all our salutations with such small pieces as they had, and so set sail, major Sedgwick and some other gentlemen accompanying them as far as Castle Island. The Lord's day they were here, the governour, acquainting them with our manner, that all men either come to our publick meetings, or keep themselves quiet in their houses, and finding that the place where they lodged would not be convenient for them that day, invited them home to his house, where they continued private all that day until sunset, and made use of such books, Latin and French, as he had, and the liberty of a private walk in his garden, and so gave no offence &c. The two first days after their arrival their pinnace kept up her flag in the main top, which gave offence both to the Londoners who rode in the harbour and also to our own people, whereupon Monsieur Marie was put in mind of it. At first he excused it by a general custom for the king's ships, both French, English and Dutch &c. to use it in all places; but being now under our government, if we would so command, he would cause [it] to be taken down. We desired him not [to] put us to that, but seeing he knew our minds he would do it of himself. Whereupon he gave order to have it taken down.

[Blank.]

There fell a sad affliction upon the country this year, though it more particularly concerned New Haven and those parts.[1] A small ship of about 100 tons set out from New Haven in the middle of the eleventh month last (the harbour there being so frozen, as they were forced to hew her through the ice near three miles.) She was laden with pease and some wheat, all in bulk, with about

1 A strange errour in date, the cause of which I shall hereafter explain, has been most commonly applied to this melancholy event. That Mather, Lib. I. c. 6. §6, committed the mistake, though he had Winthrop's history by him, is not very remarkable, for he quotes Pierpont's letter for authority, and the correspondent was born only about sixteen or seventeen years after the event, and wrote the relation not more than fifty-three or four years later than the fact, and the author of the Magnalia could suppose such evidence better than a contemporary notice of the occurrence. But in our days Trumbull I. 161 and the East Haven Register, published in 1824, assign the event to 1647. Johnson, Lib. III. c. 8, has taken notice of the loss, but without exact reference to time. Hubbard, 322, follows correctly his master Winthrop, and gives it 1645 in the old style. Pierpont, and Mather after him, had a reason for making it, as will be seen, January 1648, according to our reckoning. On page 254 the difficulty of getting the ship out of the harbour was mentioned by our author.

200 West India hides, and store of beaver, and plate, so as it was estimated in all at [1]5000 pounds. There were in her about seventy persons, whereof divers were of very precious account, as Mr. Grigson, one of their magistrates, the wife of Mr. [2]Goodyear, another of their magistrates, (a right godly woman,) Captain [3]Turner, Mr. Lamberton, master of the ship, and some seven or eight others, members of the church there. The ship never went voyage before, and was very crank-sided, so as it was conceived, she was overset in a great tempest, which happened soon after she put to sea, for she was never heard of after.

[Blank.]

7.] Some few families being gone to the new plantation at Pequod, some of them kept in the Indians' wigwams there, while their own houses were building. Some of these Indians, accompanied with some English, went to hunt deer, Unkas, the Moheagen sachem, pretending they had hunted in his limits, came with 300 men, and set upon them, and beat some of the Indians, and took away some of their goods, putting them by force out of their wigwams, where the English kept. Complaint being made hereof to the commissioners, (who were then met at New Haven,) they sent for Unkas, and charged him with this outrage &c. He confessed he had done very ill, and said, he thought he was mad; so he promised to go to the English there, and acknowledge his offence, and make full satisfaction, and for time to come, would live peaceably with them &c.

[Large Blank.]

The merchants of New Haven had set up a trading house upon a small river some thirty miles up into the country, and some fifty miles from fort Orange.[4] The Dutch governour hearing thereof

---

1 This figure has been changed to a 6, perhaps by John Winthrop, junior.

2 Stephen Goodyear was one of the chief men at New Haven, but not, as Mather says, a magistrate in 1637, in 1641 was chosen deputy governour, and was generally continued in that office until 1656, in 1645 was one of the commissioners of the United Colonies. In 1657 he died in London. Trumbull says "he left a respectable family."

3 Nathaniel Turner was one of the principal among the first settlers of New Haven, says Trumbull. No doubt he is the same person, who was very early a freeman of Massachusetts, a captain in the Pequot war, and deputy from Sagus. I had less acquaintance with him in Vol. I. 192. He acquired a desire for New Haven in Stoughton's expedition, before that quarter of our country was settled by the English. See Vol. I. 400.

4 Mention was made of this subject of complaint, on p. 263. We must not

sent a protest there against it, claiming the place to be in New Netherland. Mr. Eaton returned answer by the same messenger.

[Large Blank.]

A woman of the church of Weymouth being cast out for some distempered speeches, by a major party, (the ruling elder and a minor party being unsatisfied therein,) her husband complained to the synod, which being then ready to break up, could do nothing in it, but only acquainted the pastor therewith privately. Whereupon complaint was made to the elders of the neighbouring churches, and request made to them to come to Weymouth and to mediate a reconciliation. The elders acquainted their churches with it. Some scrupled the warrantableness of the course, seeing the major party of the church did not send to the churches for advice. It was answered, that it was not to be expected, that the major party would complain of their own act, and if the minor party, or the party grieved, should not be heard, then God should have left no means of redress in such a case, which could not be. Some of the churches approved their going; the rest permitted it. So they went, and the church of Weymouth, having notice before hand, gave them a meeting, and first demanded, whether they were sent by their churches or not. Being certified, as before, they objected this, that except they had been sent by their churches, they should never know when they had done, for others might come still, and require like satisfaction &c. It was answered, the like objection would lie, if the churches had sent, for other churches might yet have required &c. but they came not in way of authority, but only of brotherly communion, and therefore impose nothing upon them, but only to give their advice as occasion should require. This and some other scruples being removed, the church consented to have the cause heard, and opened from the beginning, whereupon some failing was found in both parties, the woman had not given so full satisfaction as she ought to have done, and the major party of the church had proceeded too hastily against a considerable party of the dissenting brethren, whereupon the woman who had offended was convinced of her failing, and bewailed it with many tears, the major party also acknowledged their errour, and gave the elders thanks for their care and pains.

[Blank.]

---

doubt, I presume, that the river is the Housatonick. It is obvious, that the mensuration of either party was not very accurate, for the modern miles would be double between New Haven and Albany.

7.] One William Waldron, a member of the church of Dover upon Pascataquack, (received into the church in the corrupt beginning of it,) a man given to drunkenness and contention, being after cast out, and upon some formal repentance received in again, being also a good clerk, and a subtle man, was made their recorder,[1] and also recorder of the province of Maine under Sir Ferdinando Gorge, and returning from Saco about the end of September alone, passing over a small river at Kennebunk, was there drowned, and his body not found until near a month after.

(8.) 17.] A ship of 300 tons, built at Boston, was this day launched.

(9.) 4.] The general court (being adjourned from (8) began again, and that night was a most dreadful tempest at northeast with wind and rain, in which the lady Moodye her house at Salem, being but one story in height, and a flat roof with a brick chimney in the midst, had the roof taken off in two parts (with the top of the chimney) and carried six or seven rods off. Also one Cross of Connecticut had his pinnace cast away in Narragansett Bay, but the men and goods saved. Mr. Haines &c. taken in this tempest half way from Connecticut, and by providence brought casually in the night to an empty wigwam, where they found fire kindled, and room for themselves and horses, else had perished.

This court the business of Gorton &c. and of the petitioners, Dr. Child &c. were taken into consideration, and it was thought needful to send some able man into England, with commission and instructions, to satisfy the commissioners for plantations about those complaints; and because it was a matter of so great and general concernment, such of the elders as could be had were sent for, to have their advice in the matter. Mr. Hubbard of Hingham came with the rest, but the court being informed that he had an hand in a petition, which Mr. Vassall carried into England against the country in general, the governour propounded, that if any elder present had any such hand &c. he would withdraw himself. Mr. Hubbard sitting still a good space, and no man speaking, one of the deputies informed the court, that Mr. Hubbard was the man suspected, whereupon he arose, and said, that he knew nothing of any such petition. The governour replied, that seeing he was now named, he must needs deliver his

---

1 By our own general court, as the records prove. Richard Waldron, probably a brother of William, was a gentleman of high character, and employed in important business by our government. The family is perpetuated in Portsmouth and its neighbourhood, and has always been distinguished for publick service.

mind about him, which was, that although they had no proof present about the matter of the petition, and therefore his denial was a sufficient clearing &c. yet in regard he had so much opposed authority, and offered such contempt to it, as for which he had been lately bound to his good behaviour, he thought he would (in discretion) withdraw himself &c. whereupon he went out. Then the governour put the court in mind of a great miscarriage, in that our secretest counsels were presently known abroad, which could not be but by some among ourselves, and desired them to look at it as a matter of great unfaithfulness, and that our present consultations might be kept in the breast of the court, and not be divulged abroad, as others had been.

Then it was propounded to consideration, in what relation we stood to the state of England; whether our government was founded upon our charter, or not; if so, then what subjection we owed to that state. The magistrates delivered their minds first, that the elders might have the better light for their advice. All agreed that our charter was the foundation of our government, and thereupon some thought, that we were so subordinate to the parliament, as they might countermand our orders and judgments &c. and therefore advised, that we should petition the parliament for enlargement of our power &c. Others conceived otherwise, and that though we owed allegiance and subjection to them, as we had always professed, and by a copy of a petition which we presented to the lords of the privy council when they sent for our charter anno [blank] then read in the court, did appear, yet by our charter we had absolute power of government; for thereby we have power to make laws, to erect all sorts of magistracy, to correct, punish, pardon, govern and rule the people absolutely, which word implies two things, 1. a perfection of parts, so as we are thereby furnished with all parts of government, 2. it implies a self-sufficiency, quoad subjectam materiam, and ergo should not need the help of any superiour power, either general governour, or &c. to complete our government; yet we did owe allegiance and subjection, 1. because our commonwealth was founded upon the power of that state, and so had been always carried on, 2. in regard of the tenure of our lands, of the manor of East Greenwich, 3. we depended upon them for protection &c. 4. for advice and counsel, when in great occasions we should crave it, 5. in the continuance of naturalization and free liegeance of ourselves and our posterity. Yet we might be still independent in respect of government, as Normandy, Gascoyne &c. were, though they had dependence upon the crown of France, and the kings of England did homage &c. yet in point of government they were not dependent upon

France. So likewise Burgundy, Flanders &c. So the Hanse Towns in Germany, which have dependence upon the empire &c. And such as are subject to the imperial chamber, in some great and general causes, they had their deputies there, and so were parties to all orders there.

And for that motion of petitioning &c. it was answered, 1. that if we receive a new charter, that will be (ipso facto) a surrender of the old, 2. the parliament can grant none now, but by way of ordinance, and it may be questioned, whether the king will give his royal assent, considering how he hath taken displeasure against us, 3, if we take a charter from the parliament, we can expect no other than such as they have granted to us at Narragansett, and to others in other places, wherein they reserve a supreme power in all things.

The court having delivered their opinions, the elders desired time of consideration, and the next day they presented their advice, which was delivered by Mr. Allen, pastor of the church in Dedham, in divers articles, which (upon request) they delivered in writing as followeth. But first I should have mentioned the order of the commissioners, sent to us in the behalf of Gorton, which, together with their petition and declaration, were sent over to us by the commissioners. The order was in these words.

After our hearty commendations, we being specially entrusted by both houses of parliament with ordering the affairs and government of the English plantations in America, have some months since received a complaint from Mr. Gorton and Mr. Holden, in the name of themselves and divers others English, who have transported themselves into New England, and now are or lately were inhabitants of a tract of land called by the name of the Narragansett Bay, (a copy of which complaint the inclosed petition and narrative will represent to your knowledge,) we could not forthwith proceed to a full hearing and determination of the matter, it not appearing unto us, that you were acquainted with the particular charge, or that you had furnished any person with power to make defence in your behalf, nor could we conveniently respite some kind of resolution therein without a great prejudice to the petitioners, who would have lain under much inconvenience, if we had detained them from their families till all the formality and circumstances of proceeding (necessary at this distance) had regularly prepared the cause for a hearing. We shall therefore let you know in the first place, that our present resolution is not grounded upon an admittance of the truth of what is charged, we knowing well how much God hath honoured your government, and believing that your spirits and affairs are acted by principles of justice, prudence and zeal to God, and therefore cannot easily receive any evil impressions concerning your proceedings. In the next place, you may take notice, that we found the petitioners' aim and desire, in the result of it, was not so much a reparation for what past, as a settling their habitation for the future under that government by a charter of civil incorporation which was heretofore granted them by ourselves. We find withal that the tract of land, called the Narragansett Bay, (concerning which the question is arisen,) was divers years since inhabited by those of Providence, Portsmouth and Newport, who are interested in the complaint, and that the same is wholly without the bounds of the Massachusetts patent granted by his majesty. We have considered that they be English, and that the forcing of them to find out new places of residence will be very chargeable, difficult and uncertain.

And therefore upon the whole matter do hereby pray and require you to permit and suffer the petitioners and all the late inhabitants of Narragansett Bay, with their families and such as shall hereafter join with them, freely and quietly to live and plant upon Shawomett and such other parts of the said tract of land within the bounds mentioned in our said charter, on which they have formerly planted and lived, without extending your jurisdiction to any part thereof, or otherwise disquieting them in their consciences or civil peace, or interrupting them in their possession until such time as we shall have received your answer to their claim in point of title, and you shall thereupon have received our further order therein.

And in case any others, since the petitioners' address to England, have taken possession of any part of the lands heretofore enjoyed by the petitioners or any their associates, you are to cause them which are newly possessed, as aforesaid, to be removed, that this order may be fully performed. And till our further order neither the petitioners are to enlarge their plantations, nor are any others to be suffered to intrude upon any part of the Narragansett Bay.

And if they shall be found hereafter to abuse this favour by any act tending to disturb your right, we shall express a due sense thereof, so as to testify a care of your honour, protection, and encouragement.

In order to the effecting of this resolution, we do also require, that you do suffer the said Mr. Gorton, Mr. Holden, Mr. Greene, and their company, with their goods and necessaries, to pass through any part of that territory which is under your jurisdiction, toward the said tract of land, without molestation, they demeaning themselves civilly, any former sentence of expulsion or otherwise notwithstanding.

We shall only add that to these orders of ours we shall expect a conformity, not only from yourselves, but from all other governours and plantations in New England whom it may concern. And so commending you to God's gracious protection, we rest, your very loving friends.

From the governour in chief, Lord Admiral and Commissioners for foreign Plantations, sitting at Westminster, 15 May 1646.

Warwick, Governour and Admi. Jud.
Northumberland,
Pembroke and Montgomery,
Nottingham,
Manchester,
Fra. Dacre,
Sam. Vassall,
Corn. Holland,
Wm. Waller,
Wm. Purefoy,
Dennis Bond,
Geo. Snelling,
Ben. Rudyer.

Upon this order one question was, whether we should give the commissioners their title, least thereby we should acknowledge all that power they claimed in our jurisdiction as well as in other plantations, which had not so large a charter as we. It was considered withal, that whatever answer or remonstrance we presented to them, if their stile were not observed, it was doubted they would not receive it.

The advice of the elders was as follows.

Concerning the question of our dependence upon England, we conceive,

1. That as we stand in near relation, so also in dependence upon that state, in divers respects, viz. 1. We have received the power of our government and other privileges, derived from thence by our charter. 2. We owe allegiance and fidelity to that state. 3. Erecting such a government as the patent prescribes and subjecting ourselves to the laws here ordained by that government, we therein yield subjection to the state of England. 4. We owe unto that state the fifth part of gold and silver ore that shall &c. 5. We depend upon the state of England for protection and immunities of Englishmen, as free denization &c.

2. We conceive, that in point of government we have granted by patent such full and ample power of choosing all officers that shall command and rule over us, of making all laws and rules of our

obedience, and of a full and final determination of all cases in the administration of justice, that no appeals or other ways of interrupting our proceedings do lie against us.

3. Concerning our way of answering complaints against us in England, we conceive, that it doth not well suit with us, nor are we directly called thereto, to profess and plead our right and power, further than in a way of justification of our proceedings questioned, from the words of the patent. In which agitations and the issues thereof our agents shall discern the mind of the parliament towards us, which if it be propense and favourable, there may be a fit season to procure such countenance of our proceedings, and confirmation of our just power, as may prevent such unjust complaints and interruptions, as now disturb our administrations. But if the parliament should be less inclinable to us, we must wait upon providence for the preservation of our just liberties.

4. Furthermore we do not clearly discern, but that we may give the Earl of Warwick and the rest such titles as the parliament hath given them, without subjecting to them in point of our government.

5. Lastly we conceive that as the hazardous state of England, the case of the church of Bermuda, and so this weighty case of our liberties do call the churches to a solemn seeking of the Lord for the upholding of our state and disappointment of our adversaries.

The court had made choice of Mr. Edward Winslow, (one of the magistrates of Plimouth,) as a fit man to be employed in our present affairs in England, both in regard of his abilities of presence, speech, courage, and understanding, as also being well known to the commissioners, having suffered a few years before divers months imprisonment, by means of the last arch prelate, in the cause of New England. But it was now moved by one of the elders, to send one of our own magistrates and one of our elders. The motion and the reasons of it were well apprehended, so as the governour and Mr. Norton, teacher of the church in Ipswich, were named, and in a manner agreed upon; but upon second thoughts it was let fall, chiefly for these two reasons, 1. it was feared, in regard that Mr. Peter had written to the governour to come over and assist in the parliament's cause &c. that if he were there, he would be called into the parliament, and so detained, 2. many were upon the wing, and his departure would occasion more new thoughts and apprehensions &c. 3. it was feared what changes his absence might produce &c.

The governour was very averse to a voyage into England, yet he declared himself ready to accept the service, if he should be called to it, though he were then fifty-nine years of age, wanting one month; but he was very glad when he saw the mind of the Lord to be otherwise.[1]

The court conferred with the elders about the petition of Dr. Child &c. also, for it had given great offence to many godly in the country, both elders and others, and some answers had been made to it, and presented to the court, out of which one entire answer had been framed, in way of declaration of the court's apprehension thereof, not by way of answer, because it was adjudged a contempt, which declaration was after published. The elders declared their opinion about it, but gave no advice for censure &c. leaving that to the court.

There was a ship then ready to set sail for England, wherein Mr. Fowle (one of the petitioners) was to go &c. The court therefore sent for him, and required an account of him about it, before his departure, and also Mr. John Smith of Rhode Island, being then in town, and they were both required to find sureties to be responsal &c. whereupon they were troubled, and desired they might answer presently, in regard they were to depart, taking exception also, that the rest of the petitioners were not called as well as they. Whereupon Dr. Child &c. were sent for, and all appeared, save Mr. Maverick; and the Dr. (being the chief speaker) demanded what should be laid to their charge, seeing it was no offence to prefer a petition &c. It was answered, that they were not questioned for petitioning, but for such miscarriages &c. as appeared in their petition and remonstrance. The Doctor replied, desiring that they might know their charge. The court answered, they should have it in due time; it was not ready at present, nor had they called them then, had it not been, that some of them were upon their departure, and therefore the court required sureties for their forth coming &c. The Doctor &c. still demanded what offence they had committed, for which they should find sureties &c. Upon this pressing, one clause in their petition was read to them, which was this, our brethren of England's just indignation against us, so as they fly from us as from a pest &c. whereby they lay a great scandal upon the coun-

---

1 Almost any other man, than Winthrop, whose publick spirit would have sustained him through any sufferings for New England, might have discerned the mind of the Lord to be adverse to his embassy, because there was so little money in the publick chest, that it became necessary to borrow 100 pounds, as will appear in a few pages onward. The country was, besides, so poor that no tax was assessed for the year, and I regret the deficiency the more, since it served perhaps to inflame the fines which tyrannical rulers inflicted on such as differed from them but slightly in their notions of policy.

try &c. This was so clear as they could not evade it, but quarrelled with the court, with high terms. The Doctor said, they did beneath themselves in petitioning to us &c. and in conclusion appealed to the commissioners in England. The governour told them, he would admit no appeal, nor was it allowed by our charter, but by this it appeared what their aim was in their petition; they complained of fear of perpetual slavery &c. but their intent was, to make us slaves to them and such as themselves were, and that by the parliament and commissioners, (meaning, by threatening us with their authority, or calumniating us to them &c.). For ourselves, it was well known, we did ever honour the parliament, and were ready to perform all due obedience &c. to them according to our charter &c. The court let them know, that they did take notice of their contemptuous speeches and behaviour, as should further appear in due time. In conclusion Mr. Fowle and Mr. Smith were committed to the marshal for want of sureties, and the rest were enjoined to attend the court when they should be called. So they were dismissed, and Mr. Fowle &c. found sureties before night, and were set at liberty.

A committee was appointed to examine the petition, and out of it to draw a charge, which was done, as followeth:

The court doth charge Dr. Child &c. with divers false and scandalous passages in a certain paper entitled a remonstrance and petition (exhibited by them to this court in the third month last) against the churches of Christ and the civil government here established, derogating from the honour and authority of the same, and tending to sedition, as in the particulars following will appear:

1. They take upon them to defame our government, and to controul both the wisdom of the state of England in the frame of our charter, and also the wisdom and integrity of this court, in charging our government to be an ill-compacted vessel.

2. They lay open the afflictions, which God hath pleased to exercise us with, and that to the worst appearance, and impute it to the evil of our government.

3. They charge us with manifest injury to a great part of the people here, persuading them, that the liberties and privileges in our charter belong to all freeborn Englishmen, inhabitants here; whereas they are granted only to such as the governour and company shall think fit to receive into that fellowship.

4. They closely insinuate into the minds of the people, that those now in authority do intend to exercise unwarranted dominion and an arbitrary government, such as is abominable to the parliament and that party in England, thereby to make them

slaves; and (to hide themselves) they pretend it to be the jealousies of others, and (which tends to stir up commotion) they foretel them of intolerable bondage to ensue.

5. They go about to weaken the authority of our laws, and the reverence and esteem of them, and consequently their obedience to them, by persuading the people, that partly through want of the body of English laws, and partly through the insufficiency or ill frame of those we have, they can expect no sure enjoyment of their lives and liberties under them.

6. They falsely charge us with denying liberty of votes in such cases where we allow them, as in choice of military officers, which is common to the non-freemen with such as are free.

7. Their speeches tend to sedition, by insinuating into the people's minds, that there are many thousands secretly discontented at the government &c. whereby those who indeed were so might be emboldened to discover themselves, and to attempt some innovation, in confidence of so many thousands to join with them, and so to kindle a great flame, the foretelling whereof is a chief means to kindle it.

8. They raise a false report and foul slander upon the discipline of our churches, and upon the civil government, by inferring that the frame and dispensation thereof are such, as godly, sober, peaceable &c. men cannot live here like christians, which they seem to conclude from hence, that they desire liberty to remove where they may live like christians.

9. They do (in effect) charge this government with tyranny, in impressing their persons into the wars, committing them to prison, fining, rating &c. and all unjustly and illegally.

10. They falsely charge and slander the people of God, in affirming that christian vigilancy is no way exercised towards such as are not in church fellowship, whereas themselves know, and have had experience to the contrary. And if they had discerned any such failing, they ought first to have complained of it in private to the elders, or brethren of such churches where they have been so neglected, which (we may well think) they have not done, nor had any just cause thereof.

11. Having thrown all this dirt and shame upon our churches and government &c. they endeavour to set it on, that it might stick fast, so as all men might undoubtedly be persuaded of the reality thereof, by proclaiming it in their conclusion, that our own brethren in England have just indignation against us for the same, which they labour to confirm by the effect thereof viz. that for these evils amongst us these our own brethren do fly from us as from a pest.

12. Lastly, that it may yet more clearly appear, that these evils and obliquities, which they charge upon our government, are not the mere jealousies of others, but their own apprehensions (or pretences rather) they have publickly declared their disaffection thereto, in that, being called by the court, to render account of their misapprehensions and evil expressions in the premises, they refused to answer; but, by appealing from this government, they disclaimed the jurisdiction thereof, before they knew whether the court would give any sentence against them, or not.

Their petition being read, and this charge laid upon them, in the open court, before a great assembly, they desired time to make answer to it, which was granted. And giving the court notice that their answer was ready, they assembled again, and before all the people caused their answer to be read, which was large, and to little purpose, and the court replied to the particulars extempore, as they were read. The substance both of the answer and reply was, as followeth, with some little addition, which for want of time was then omitted.

Answer. To the first they answer, that they termed these plantations an ill compacted vessel, 1. comparatively, in respect of our native country, 2. in regard of the paucity of people, scattered &c. 3. for diversity of judgments amongst us, many being for presbyterial government, according to the reformation in England, others opposing it; some freemen, others not. Differences there are also about bounds of colonies, patents, privileges, &c.

Reply. To this was replied, 1. that the being of a thing, talis &c. lies in the perfection of parts, not degrees; a child of a year old is as truly a man, and as well compact, as one of sixty; a ship of forty tons may be as well compact a vessel, as the Royal Sovereign. And for the differences which are amongst us, (through the Lord's mercy,) they are not either in number or degree suitable to those in England, nor do they concern our esse or non esse; and those which are, are raised by such discontented and unquiet spirits as those petitioners.

To the second they answer negatively, which needed no reply, it being evident in their petition, that (though they speak of our sins in general, yet) they chiefly impute them to our evil government &c.

Answer. To the third, they deny the charge, but grant that the governour and company may have some peculiar privileges, as other corporations of England have, which corporation privileges, made for the most part for advancing mechanical professions, in some places are much slighted by the English gentry, unless in

London and some great cities, because freeborn privileges are far greater and more honourable &c.

Reply. To this it was replied, that we could not but take this as a scorn and slighting of us, (according to their former carriage,) allowing us no more than any ordinary corporation, and such privileges only as belong to mechanick men; but for greater and more gentile privileges, (as they term them,) those they would share in; and (which they impudently deny against the plain words of their petition) they would have all freeborn English to have as much right to them as the governour and company.

Answer. To the fourth they answer as in their petition, and a reason they give of their fear of arbitrary government is, that some speeches and papers have been spread abroad for maintenance thereof &c. and that a body of English laws hath not been here established, nor any other not repugnant thereto.

Reply. To this it was replied, 1. that the constant care and pains the court hath taken for establishing a body of laws, and that which hath been effected herein beyond any other plantation, will sufficiently clear our government from being arbitrary, and our intentions from any such disposition, 2. for the laws of England (though by our charter we are not bound to them, yet) our fundamentals are framed according to them, as will appear by our declaration, which is to be published upon this occasion, and the government of England itself is more arbitrary in their chancery and other courts than ours is, 3. because they would make men believe, that the want of the laws of England was such a grievance to them, they were pressed to show, what laws of England they wanted, and it was offered them, (before all the assembly, who were desired to bear witness of it,) that if they could produce any one law of England, the want whereof was a just grievance to them, the court would quit the cause, whereupon one of them instanced in a law used in London, (where he had been a citizen,) but that was easily taken away by showing that that was only a bye-law, or peculiar custom of the city, and none of the common or general laws of England.

Answer. They answer negatively to the fifth, alleging that they only commend the laws of England as those they are best accustomed unto &c. and therein they impudently and falsely affirm, that we are obliged to those laws by our general charter and oath of allegiance, and that without those laws, or others no way repugnant to them, they could not clearly see a certainty of enjoying their lives, liberties, and estates &c. according to their due natural rights, as freeborn English &c.

Reply. To this it was replied, that they charge us with breach of our charter and of our oaths of allegiance, whereas our allegiance binds us not to the laws of England any longer than while we live in England, for the laws of the parliament of England reach no further, nor do the king's writs under the great seal go any further; what the orders of state may, belongs not in us to determine. And whereas they seem to admit of laws not repugnant &c. if by repugnant they mean, as the word truly imports, and as by the charter must needs be intended, they have no cause to complain, for we have no laws diametrically opposite to those of England, for then they must be contrary to the law of God and of right reason, which the learned in those laws have anciently and still do hold forth as the fundamental basis of their laws, and that if any thing hath been otherwise established, it was an errour, and not a law, being against the intent of the law-makers, however it may bear the form of a law (in regard of the stamp of authority set upon it) until it be revoked.

Answer. To the sixth they confess, that non-freemen have a vote in choice of military officers, but they justify their assertion, in regard they must first take an oath of fidelity, which, they say, is not (as they conceive) warranted by our charter, and seems not to concur with the oath of allegiance and the later covenants, but detracts from our native country and laws, so as they cannot take it &c.

Reply. This needs no reply. An absolute denial, and a denial sub modo are not the same.

Answer. To the seventh they answer negatively only, which their petition will sufficiently clear, for (reply) the inference is so plain, as is obvious to any reasonable understanding.

Answer and reply. The like for the eighth.

Answer. To the ninth they confess the words in their petition, viz. that divers of the English subjects have been impressed for the wars, that rates are many and grievous, but charge them not with tyranny, or injustice, or illegal proceeding.

Reply. See what a manifest contradiction they have run themselves into. They complain of these impresses and rates, as an unsupportable grievance, and yet neither tyrannical, unjust, nor illegal; so as we must then conclude (as the very truth is indeed) that the exercise of lawful authority, justice and law, are a grievance to these men, if it come not in their own way.

Answer. To the tenth, they would shift off that slander upon our churches and brethren, by this distinction of christian vigilancy, properly and improperly so called; properly is in three respects, 1. of the church covenant, 2. of the term, brethren, 3. church censure. And all other christian vigilancy they account improper; and so this is not to be intended or comprised in this proposition, viz. christian vigilancy is no way exercised towards non-members.

Reply. This is so gross a fallacy, as needs no skill to discover it.

Answer. To the eleventh they answer by confessing the words, save that they say, they spake of their brethren, not our brethren. Reply. Who they challenge for their brethren peculiarly we know not, for all such there as in judgment of charity go for true christians in England, we do and have always accounted brethren, and in a common sense all of that nation we have accounted brethren; and further they justify that speech, that they have just indignation against us &c. for three reasons, 1. for not establishing the laws of England, 2. not admitting them to civil liberties, 3. not admitting them to the sacraments; and yet they dare affirm that they do not charge this upon the court &c. They also justify that speech, of flying from us as from a pest, by the like speeches some of them have heard from godly men in England, and by so many going from us, and so few coming to us. But admit all this to be true, yet what calling have these men to publish this to our reproach? And beside they know well, that as some speak evil of us, because we conform not to their opinions, in allowing liberty to every erroneous judgment, so there are many, no less godly and judicious, who do approve our practice, and continue their good affection to us.

Answer. To the twelfth (professing their ignorance of the meaning of the word, obliquities, to which was replied, that then they did not know rather what rectum was, for whatsoever is not rectum is obliquum) they make an apology for their appeal, as conceiving it lawful to appeal to the parliament, to which they were necessitated, some of them being hindered from their necessary occasions, and accounting it no offence to petition &c. nor had the parliament ever censured any for the like &c. And if this will not satisfy the court &c. some few queries to the parliament (the best arbiters in these cases) will (we hope) end all controversies &c. concluding that they hope we will censure all things candidly and in the best sense.

To which it was replied, that appeals did not lie from us, by our charter; and to appeal, before any sentence, was to disclaim our jurisdiction &c.

I should also have noted the Doctor's logick, who undertook to prove, that we were subject to the laws of England. His argument was this, every corporation of England is subject to the laws of England; but this was a corporation of England, ergo &c.

To which it was answered, 1. that there is a difference between subjection to the laws in general, as all that dwell in England are, and subjection to some laws of state, proper to foreign plantations, 2. we must distinguish between corporations within England and corporations of but not within England; the first are subject to the laws of England in general, yet not to every general law, as the city of London and other corporations have divers customs and by-laws differing from the common and statute laws of England. Again, though plantations be bodies corporate, (and so is every city and commonwealth,) yet they are also above the rank of an ordinary corporation.] If one of London should say before the mayor and aldermen, or before the common council, you are but a corporation, this would be taken as a contempt. And among the Romans, Grecians, and other nations, colonies have been esteemed other than towns, yea than many cities, for they have been the foundations of great commonwealths. And it was a fruit of much pride and folly in these petitioners to despise the day of small things.

These petitioners persisting thus obstinately and proudly in their evil practice, the court proceeded to consider of their censure, and agreed, that the Doctor (in regard he had no cause to complain, and yet was a leader to the rest, and had carried himself proudly &c. in the court) should be fined fifty pounds, Mr. Smith (being also a stranger) forty pounds, Mr. Maverick (because he had not as yet appealed) ten pounds, and the other four thirty pounds each.[1] So being again called before the court, they were exhorted to consider better of their proceedings, and take knowledge of their miscarriage, which was great, and that they had transgressed the rule of the Apostle [blank], study to be quiet and to meddle with your own business. They were put in mind

---

1 Surprise almost equals our indignation at this exorbitant imposition, for in this very year Fowle was associated with Winthrop as one of the selectmen of Boston, and Maverick was so much interested in the great work of fortifying Castle Island, that he advanced a large part of the outlay, and the metropolis engaged to save him harmless to a certain extent Union of the good spirit of the civilians, that dreaded all appeals to England for correction of any errour in our administration, with the evil spirit of the clergy, that would enforce uniformity in ceremonies and belief, produced the effect of preventing many from coming to Massachusetts, and drove away many who had already established here their domestic altars. All these petitioners, but Maverick, left the country, I believe. He had long experience enough of the habits of our rulers to know, that their intolerance sometimes yielded to interest, and that humanity often overpowered the perversity of their zeal for God's house, by which they might seem to be eaten up. How far the petitioners offended, the student of our history may learn from New England's Jonas cast up at London, printed in 2 Hist. Coll. IV. 107 et seq.

also of that sin of Corah &c. and of the near resemblance between theirs and that; they only told Moses and Aaron, that they took too much upon them, seeing all were the Lord's people &c. so these say, that the magistrates and freemen take too much upon them, seeing all the people are Englishmen &c. and others are wise, holy &c. They were offered also, if they would ingenuously acknowledge their miscarriage &c. it should be freely remitted. But they remaining obstinate, the court declared their sentence, as is before expressed.

Upon which they all appealed to the parliament &c. and tendered their appeal in writing. The court received the paper; but refused to accept it, or to read it in the court.[1]

Three of the magistrates, viz. Mr. Bellingham, Mr. Saltonstall, and Mr. Bradstreet dissented, and desired to be entered contradicentes in all the proceedings (only Mr. Bradstreet went home before the sentence.) Two or three of the deputies did the like. So the court was dissolved.

Dr. Child prepared now in all haste to go for England in the ship, which was to go about a week after, to prosecute their appeal, and to get a petition from the non-freemen to the parliament, and many high and menacing words were given forth by them against us, which gave occasion to the governour and council (so many of them as were then assembled, to hold the court of assistants) to consider what was fit to be done. Neither thought they fit to impart their counsel to such of the magistrates as had declared their dissent; but the rest of them agreed to stay the Doctor for his fine, and to search his trunk and Mr. Dand's study, but spake not of it till the evening before the Doctor was to depart. Then it was propounded in council, and Mr. Bellingham dissented, as before, (yet the day before he moved for stopping the Doctor, which was conceived to be to feel if there were any such intention,) and presently went aside, and spake privately with one, who we were sure would prevent our purpose, if it were possible. Whereupon (whereas we had agreed to defer it till he had been on shipboard) now perceiving our counsel was discovered, we sent the officers presently to fetch the Doctor, and to search his study and Dand's both at one instant, which was done accordingly, and the Doctor was brought, and his trunk, that was to be

1 Hutchinson I. 138, confounds the controversy raised by Child and others, about enlargement of privileges, in which the court was almost unanimous against the petitioners, with that of the Hingham military sedition, the preceding year, for which the majority of the deputies were with great difficulty brought to inflict any fines.

carried on shipboard (but there was nothing in that, which concerned the business.) But at Dand's they found Mr. Smith, who catched up some papers, and when the officer took them from him, he brake out into these speeches, viz. we hope shortly we shall have commission to search the governour's closet. There were found the copies of two petitions and twenty-three queries, which were to be sent to England to the commissioners for plantations. The one from Dr. Child and the other six petitioners, wherein they declare, how they had formerly petitioned our general court, and had been fined for the same, and forced to appeal, and that the ministers of our churches did revile them &c. as far as the wit or malice of man could &c. and that they meddled in civil affairs beyond their calling, and were masters rather than ministers, and ofttimes judges, and that they had stirred up the magistrates against them, and that a day of humiliation was appointed, wherein they were to pray against them &c. Then they mention (as passing by them) what affronts, jeers and despiteful speeches were cast upon them by some of the court &c. Then they petition, 1. for settled churches according to the reformation of England, 2. that the laws of England may be established here, and that arbitrary power may be banished, 3. for liberties for English freeholders here as in England &c. 4. that a general governour or some honourable commissioners be appointed for settling &c. 5. that the oath of allegiance may be commanded to be taken by all, and other covenants which the parliament shall think most convenient, to be as a touchstone to try our affections to the state of England and true restored protestant religion, 6. to resolve their queries &c. 7. to take into consideration their remonstrance and petition exhibited to the general court.

Their queries were chiefly about the validity of our patent, and how it might be forfeited, and whether such and such acts or speeches in the pulpits or in the court &c. were not high treason; concerning the power of our court and laws in divers particular cases; and whether they may be hindered by the order of this court from settling in a church way according to the reformation of England &c.

The other petition was from some non-freemen (pretending to be in the name, and upon the sighs and tears of many thousands.) In the preamble they show how they were driven out of their native country by the tyranny of the bishops &c. Then they petition for liberty of conscience &c. and for a general governour &c. They sent their agents up and down the country to get hands to this petition. But of the many thousands they spake of, we could hear but of twenty-five to the chief petition, and those were (for the most part) either young men who came over servants, and never had any show of religion in them, or fishermen of Marblehead, profane persons, divers of them brought the last year from Newfoundland to fish a season, and so to return again; others were such as were drawn in by their relations, men of no *reason* neither, as a barber of Boston, who, being demanded by the governour, what moved him to set his hand, made answer, that the gentlemen were his customers &c. and these are the men, who must be held forth to the parliament, as driven out of England by the bishops &c. and whose tears and sighs must move compassion.

Dr. Child, being upon this apprehended and brought before the governour and council, fell into a great passion, and gave big words, but being told, that they considered he was a person of quality, and therefore he should be used with such respect as was meet to be showed to a gentleman and a scholar, but if he would behave himself no better, he should be committed to the common prison and clapped in irons. Upon this he grew more calm; so he was committed to the marshal, with Smith and Dand, for two or three days, till the ships were gone. For he was very much troubled to be hindered from his voyage, and offered to pay his fine; but that would not be accepted for his discharge, seeing we had now new matter and worse against him (for the writings were of his hand.) Yet, upon tender of sufficient bail, he was set at liberty, but confined to his house, and to appear at the next court of assistants. His confinement he took grievously, but he could not help it. The other two were committed to prison, yet lodged in the keeper's house, and had what diet they pleased, and none of their friends forbidden to come to them. There was also one Thomas [1]Joy, a young fellow, a carpenter, whom they had employed to get hands to the petition; he began to be very busy, and would know of the marshal, when he went to search Dand's study, if his warrant were in the king's name &c. He was laid hold on, and kept in irons about four or five days, and then he humbled himself, confessed what he knew, and blamed himself for meddling in

---

1 Experience of the peril, from which so humble an individual could not escape, as easily as his superiors, by voluntary exile, nor buy off so quietly as the wealthy Maverick, perhaps made Joy a more quiet subject for time to come, but I doubt he was not thoroughly converted by being kept in irons so few days. He removed from Boston, I believe, to Hingham, where he could enjoy more sympathy of neighbours. There he built and owned the town mill. In our Probate registry VI. 281, his will, made 8 July 1677, proved 31 October, 1678, is signed with a *mark*. It remembers his sons, Joseph and Ephraim, daughters, Sarah, Elizabeth and Ruth.

matters belonging not to him, and blessed God for these irons upon his legs, hoping they should do him good while he lived. So he was let out upon reasonable bail. But Smith and Dand would not be examined, and therefore were not bailed; but their offence being in nature capital &c. bail might be refused in that regard.

For their trial at the general court in (4) 47, and the sentence against them &c. it is set down at large in the records of that court, with their petitions and queries intended for England, and all proceedings. Mr. Dand not being able to pay his fine of two hundred pounds, nor willing to acknowledge his offence, was kept in prison; but at the general court (3) 48, upon his humble submission, he was freely discharged.

Mr. Winslow being now to go for England &c. the court was troubled how to furnish him with money or beaver, (for there was nothing in the treasury, the country being in debt one thousand pounds, and what comes in by levies is corn or cattle,) but the Lord stirred up the hearts of some few persons to lend one hundred pounds, to be repaid by the next levy. Next we went in hand to draw up his commission and instructions, and a remonstrance and petition to the commissioners in England, which were as follows:

To the right honourable Robert, Earl of Warwick, governour in chief, lord admiral, and other the lords and gentlemen, commissioners for foreign plantations, the humble remonstrance and petition of the governour and company of the Massachusetts Bay in New England in America.

In way of answer to the petition and declaration of Samuel Gorton &c.

Whereas by virtue of his majesty's charter, granted to your petitioners in the fourth year of his highness's reign, we were incorporated into a body politick with divers liberties and privileges extending to that part of New England where we now inhabit, we do acknowledge (as we have always done, and as in duty we are bound) that, although we are removed out of our native country, yet we still have dependence upon that state, and owe allegiance and subjection thereunto, according to our charter, and accordingly we have mourned and rejoiced therewith, and have held friends and enemies in common with it, in all the changes which have befallen it. Our care and endeavour also hath been to frame our government and administrations to the fundamental rules thereof, so far as the different condition of this place and people, and the best light we have from the word of God will allow. And whereas, by order from your honours, dated May 15, 1646, we find that your honours have still that good opinion of us, as not to credit what hath been informed against us before we be heard, we render humble thanks to your honours for the same; yet forasmuch as our answer to the information of the said Gorton &c. is expected, and something also required of us, which (in all humble submission) we conceive may be prejudicial to the liberties granted us by the said charter and to our well being in this remote part of the world, (under the comfort whereof, through the blessing of the Lord, his majesty's favour, and the special care and bounty of the high court of parliament, we have lived in peace and prosperity these seventeen years,) our humble petition (in the first place) is, that our present and future conformity to your orders and directions may be accepted with a salvo jure, that when times may be changed, (for all things here below are subject to vanity,) and other princes or parliaments may arise, the generations succeeding may not have cause to lament, and say, England sent our fathers forth with happy liberties, which they enjoyed many years, notwithstanding all the enmity and opposition of the prelacy, and other potent adversaries, how came we then to lose them, under the favour and protection of that state, in such a season, when England itself recovered its own? In freto viximus, in portu morimur. But we confide in your honours' justice, wisdom and goodness, that our posterity shall have cause to rejoice under the fruit and shelter thereof, as ourselves and many others do; and therefore we are bold to represent to your honours our apprehensions, whereupon we have thus presumed to petition you in this behalf.

It appears to us, by the said order, that we are conceived, 1. to have transgressed our limits, by sending soldiers to fetch in Gorton &c. out of Shaomett in the Narragansett Bay, 2. that we have either exceeded or abused our authority, in banishing them out of our jurisdiction, when they were in our power. For the first we humbly crave (for your better satisfaction) that your honours will be pleased to peruse what we have delivered to the care of Mr. Edward Winslow, our agent or commissioner, (whom we have sent on purpose to attend your honours,) concerning our proceedings in that affair and the grounds thereof, which are truly and faithfully reported, and the letters of the said Gorton and his company, and other letters concerning them, faithfully copied out (not verbatim only, but even literatim, according to their own bad English.) The originals we have by us, and had sent them, but for casualty of the seas. Thereby it will appear what the men are, and how unworthy your favour. Thereby also will appear the wrongs and provocations we received from them, and our long patience towards them, till they became our professed enemies, wrought us disturbance, and attempted our ruin. In which case, our charter (as we conceive) gives us full power to deal with them as enemies by force of arms, they being then in such place where we could have no right from them by civil justice; which the commissioners for the United Colonies finding, and the necessity of calling them to account, left the business [to us] to do.

For the other particular in your honour's order, viz. the banishment of Gorton &c. as we are assured, upon good grounds, that our sentence upon them was less than their deserving, so (as we conceive) we had sufficient authority, by our charter, to inflict the same, having full and absolute power and authority to punish, pardon, rule, govern &c. granted us therein.

Now, by occasion of the said order, those of Gorton's company begin to lift up their heads and speak their pleasures of us, threatening the poor Indians also, who (to avoid their tyranny) had submitted themselves and their lands under our protection and government; and divers other sachems, following their example, have done the like, and some of them brought (by the labour of one of our elders, Mr. John Eliot, who hath obtained to preach to them in their own language) to good forwardness in embracing the gospel of God in Christ Jesus. All which hopeful beginnings are like to be dashed, if Gorton &c. shall be countenanced and upheld against them and us, which also will endanger our peace here at home. For some among ourselves (men of unquiet spirits, affecting rule and innovation) have taken boldness to prefer scandalous and seditious petitions for such liberties as neither our charter, nor reason or religion will allow; and being called before us in open court to give account of their miscarriage therein, they have threatened us with your honour's authority, and (before they knew whether we would proceed to any sentence against them, or not) have refused to answer, but appealed to your honours. The copy of their petition, and our declaration thereupon, our said commissioner hath ready to present to you, when your leisure shall permit to hear them. Their appeals we have not admitted, being assured, that they cannot stand with the liberty and power granted us by our charter, nor will be allowed by your honours, who well know it would be destructive to all government, both in the honour and also in the power of it, if it should be in the liberty of delinquents to evade the sentence of justice, and force us, by appeal, to follow them into England, where the evidence and circumstances of facts cannot be so clearly held forth as in their proper place; besides the insupportable charges we must be at in the prosecution thereof. These considerations are not new to your honours and the high court of parliament, the records whereof bear witness of the wisdom and faithfulness of our ancestors in that great council, who, in those times of darkness, when they acknowledged a supremacy in the bishops of Rome in all causes ecclesiastical, yet would not allow appeals to Rome &c. to remove causes out of the courts in England.

Beside, (though we shall readily admit, that the wisdom and experience of that great council, and of your honours, as a part thereof are far more able to prescribe rules of government, and to judge of causes, than such poor rusticks as a wilderness can breed up, yet,) considering the vast distance between England and these parts, (which usually abates the virtue of the strongest influences,) your counsels and judgments could neither be so well grounded, nor so seasonably applied, as might either be so useful to us, or so safe for yourselves, in your discharge, in the great day of account, for any miscarriage which might befal us, while we depended upon your counsel and help, which could not seasonably be administered to us. Whereas if any such should befal us, when we have the government in our own hands, the state of England shall not answer for it. In consideration of the premises, our humble petition to your honours (in the next place) is, that you will be pleased to continue your favourable aspect upon these poor infant plantations, that we may still rejoice and bless our God under your shadow, and be there still nourished (tanquam calore et rore coelesti;) and while God owns us for a people of his, he will own our poor prayers for you, and your goodness towards us, for an abundant recompense. And this in special, if you shall please to pass by any failings you may have observed in our course, to confirm our liberties, granted to us by charter, by leaving delinquents to our just proceedings, and discountenancing our enemies and disturbers of our peace, or such as molest our people there, upon pretence of injustice. Thus craving pardon, if we have presumed too far upon your honours' patience, and expecting a gracious testimony of your wonted favour by this our agent, which shall further oblige us and our posterity in all humble and faithful service to the high court of parliament and to your honours, we continue our earnest prayers for your posterity forever. By order of the general court.

(10) 46. Increase Nowell, *Secretary.*

John Winthrop, *Governour.*

The copy of the commission to Mr. Winslow.

Mattachusetts in New England in America.

Whereas Samuel Gorton, John Greene, and Randall Holden,

by petition and declaration exhibited to the right honourable the Earl of Warwick, governour in chief, and commissioners for foreign plantations, as members of the high court of parliament, have charged divers false and scandalous matters against us, whereof their honours have been pleased to give us notice, and do expect our answer for clearing the same, we therefore the governour and company of the Mattachusetts aforesaid, assembled in our general court, being careful to give all due respect to his lordship and the honourable commissioners, and having good assurance of the wisdom and faithfulness of you, our worthy and loving friend, Mr. Edward Winslow, do hereby give power and commission to you to appear before his lordship and commissioners, and presenting our most humble duty and service to their honours, for us and in our name to exhibit our humble remonstrance and petition, in way of answer to the said false and unjust charge of the said Gorton &c. and by the same and other writings and instructions delivered to you under the hand of Mr. Increase Nowell our secretary, to inform their honours of the truth and reason of all our proceedings with the said Gorton &c. so as our innocency and the justice of our proceedings may appear to their honours' satisfaction. And if any other complaints, in any kind, have been, or shall be, made against us before the said commissioners, or before the high court of parliament, you have hereby like power and commission to answer on our behalf according to your instructions. And we humbly crave of the high court of parliament and of the honourable commissioners, that they will vouchsafe our said commissioner free liberty of seasonable access, as occasion shall require, and a favourable hearing, with such credit to such writings as he shall present in our name, under the hand of our said secretary, as if we had presented them in person, upon that faith and credit, which we would not wittingly violate, for all worldly advantages; and that our said commissioner may find such speed and despatch, and may be under such safe protection, in his stay and return, as that honourable court useth to afford to their humble subjects and servants in like cases. In testimony hereof we have caused our common seal to be hereunto affixed, dated this 4 (10) 1646.

By order of the court.

Increase Nowell, *Secretary.*

John Winthrop, *Governour.*

Mr. Winslow his instructions were of two sorts; the one (which he might publish &c.) were only directions, according to his commission, and remonstrance and other writings delivered him. The other were more secret, which were these following.

If you shall be demanded about these particulars:

Obj. 1. Why we make not out our process in the king's name? you shall answer:

1. That we should thereby waive the power of our government granted to us, for we claim not as by commission, but by a free donation of absolute government, 2. for avoiding appeals &c.

Obj. 2. That our government is arbitrary.

Answer. We have four or five hundred express laws, as near the laws of England as may be; and yearly we make more, and where we have no law, we judge by the word of God, as near as we can.

Obj. 3. About enlarging our limits &c.

Answer. Such Indians as are willing to come under our government, we know no reason to refuse. Some Indians we have subdued by just war, as the Pequids. Some English also, having purchased lands of the Indians, have submitted to our government.

Obj. 4. About our subjection to England.

Answer 1. We are to pay the one fifth part of ore of gold and silver.

2. In being faithful and firm to the state of England, endeavouring to walk with God in upholding his truth &c. and praying for it.

3. In framing our government according to our patent, so near as we may.

Obj. 5. About exercising admiral jurisdiction.

Answer 1. We are not restrained by our charter.

2. We have power given us to rule, punish, pardon &c. in all cases, ergo in maritime.

3. We have power granted us to defend ourselves and offend our enemies, as well by sea as by land, ergo we must needs have power to judge of such cases.

4. Without this, neither our own people nor strangers could have justice from us in such cases.

Obj. 6. About our independency upon that state.

Answer. Our dependency is in these points: 1. we have received our government and other privileges by our charter, 2. we owe allegiance and fidelity to that state, 3. in erecting a government here accordingly and subjecting thereto, we therein yield subjection to that state, 4. in rendering the one fifth part of ore &c.

5. we depend upon that state for protection, and immunities as freeborn Englishmen.

Obj. 7. Seeing we hold of East Greenwich &c. why every freeholder of forty shillings per annum have not votes in elections &c. as in England.

Answer. Our charter gives that liberty expressly to the freemen only.

Obj. 8. By your charter, such as we transport are to live under his majesty's allegiance.

Answer. So they all do, and so intended, so far as we know.

Obj. 9. About a general governour.

Answer 1. Our charter gives us absolute power of government.

2. On the terms above specified, we conceive the patent, hath no such thing in it, neither expressed, nor implied.

3. We had not transported ourselves and families upon such terms.

4. Other plantations have been undertaken at the charge of others in England, and the planters have their dependence upon the companies there, and those planters go and come chiefly for matter of profit; but we came to abide here, and to plant the gospel, and people the country, and herein God hath marvellously blessed us.

(1.) At the court of assistants, three or four were sent for, who had been very active about the petition to the commissioners in procuring hands to it, (it being thought fit to pass by such as being drawn in had only subscribed the petition,) especially Mr. Samuel Maverick and Mr. Clerk of Salem, the keeper of the ordinary there and a church member. These having taken an oath of fidelity to the government, and enjoying all liberties of freemen, their offence was far the greater. So they were bound over to answer it at the next general court.

Mr. Smith and Mr. Dand (giving security to pay their fines, assessed upon the former petition, within two months) were bailed to the general court.

Dr. Child also was offered his liberty, upon bail to the general court, and to be confined to Boston; but he chose rather to go to prison, and so he was committed.

The reason of referring these and others to the general court was, both in regard the cause was of so great concernment, as the very life and foundation of our government, and also because the general court had cognizance thereof already upon the first petition.[1]

---

[1] On taking leave of this subject, which is more fully treated in this history

[Large Blank.]

Mr. Burton, one of the petitioners, being in the town meeting, when the court's declaration was read, was much moved, and spake in high language, and would needs have a copy of it, which so soon as he had, he went with it (as was undoubtedly believed) to Dr. Child, and in the way fell down, and lay there in the cold near half an hour, till company was gotten to carry him home in a chair, and after he continued in great pain, and lame divers months.

It is observable that this man had gathered some providences about such as were against them, as that Mr. Winslow's horse died, as he came riding to Boston; that his brother's son (a child of eight years old) had killed his own sister (being ten years of age) with his father's piece &c. and his great trouble was, least this providence which now befel him, should be imputed to their cause.

[Large Blank.]

There fell out at this time a very sad occasion. A merchant of Plimouth in England, (whose father had been mayor there,) called [blank] Martin, being fallen into decay, came to Casco Bay, and after some time, having occasion to return into England, he left behind him two daughters, (very proper maidens and of modest behaviour,) but took not that course for their safe bestowing in his absence, as the care and wisdom of a father should have done, so as the eldest of them, called Mary, twenty-two years of age, being in [the] house with one Mr. Mitton, a married man of Casco, within one quarter of a year, he was taken with her, and soliciting her chastity, obtained his desire, and having divers times committed sin with her, in the space of three months, she then removed to Boston, and put herself in service to Mrs. Bourne; and finding herself to be with child, and not able to bear the shame of it, she concealed it, and though divers did suspect it, and some told her mistress their fears, yet her behaviour was so modest, and so faithful she was in her service, as her mistress would not give ear to any such report, but blamed such as told her of it. But, her time being come, she was delivered of a woman child in a back room by herself upon the 13 (10) in the night, and the child was born alive, but she kneeled upon the head of it, till she thought it had been dead, and having laid it by, the child, being strong, recovered, and cried again.

than any where else, I ought perhaps to refer to Johnson Lib. III. c. 3, who is very severe upon the petitioners.

Then she took it again, and used violence to it till it was quite dead. Then she put it into her chest, and having cleansed the room, she went to bed, and arose again the next day about noon, and went about her business, and so continued till the nineteenth day, that her master and mistress went on shipboard to go for England. They being gone, and she removed to another house, a midwife in the town, having formerly suspected her, and now coming to her again, found she had been delivered of a child, which, upon examination, she confessed, but said it was still-born, and so she put it into the fire. But, search being made, it was found in her chest, and when she was brought before the jury, they caused her to touch the face of it, whereupon the blood came fresh into it. Whereupon she confessed the whole truth, and a surgeon, being called to search the body of the child, found a fracture in the skull. Before she was condemned, she confessed, that she had prostituted her body to another also, one Sears. She behaved herself very penitently while she was in prison, and at her death, 18 (1,) complaining much of the hardness of her heart. She confessed, that the first and second time she committed fornication, she prayed for pardon, and promised to commit it no more; and the third time she prayed God, that if she did fall into it again, he would make her an example, and therein she justified God, as she did in the rest. Yet all the comfort God would afford her, was only trust (as she said) in his mercy through Christ. After she was turned off and had hung a space, she spake, and asked what they did mean to do. Then some stepped up, and turned the knot of the rope backward, and then she soon died.

Mention was made before of some beginning to instruct the Indians &c. Mr. John Eliot, teacher of the church of Roxbury, found such encouragement, as he took great pains to get their language, and in a few months could speak of the things of God to their understanding; and God prospered his endeavours, so as he kept a constant lecture to them in two places, one week at the wigwam of one Wabon a *new* sachem near Watertown mill, and the other the next week in the wigwam of Cutshamekin near Dorchester mill. And for the furtherance of the work of God divers of the English resorted to his lecture, and the governour and other of the magistrates and elders sometimes; and the Indians began to repair thither from other parts. His manner of proceeding was thus; he would persuade one of the other elders or some magistrate to begin the exercise with prayer in English; then he took a text, and read it first in the Indian language, and after in English; then he preached to them in Indian about an hour; (but first I should have spoke of the catechising their children, who were soon brought to answer him some short questions, whereupon he gave each of them an apple or a cake) then he demanded of some of the chiefs, if they understood him; if they answered, yea, then he asked of them if they had any questions to propound. And they had usually two or three or more questions, which he did resolve. At one time (when the governour was there and about two hundred people, Indian and English, in one wigwam of Cutshamekin's) an old man asked him, if God would receive such an old man as he was; to whom he answered by opening the parable of the workmen that were hired into the vineyard; and when he had opened it, he asked the old man, if he did believe it, who answered he did, and was ready to *weep*. A second question was, what was the reason, that when all Englishmen did know God, yet some of them were poor. His answer was, 1. that God knows it is better for his children to be good than to be rich; he knows withal, that if some of them had riches, they would abuse them, and wax proud and wanton &c. therefore he gives them no more riches than may be needful for them, that they may be kept from pride &c. to depend upon him, 2. he would hereby have men know, that he hath better blessings to bestow upon good men than riches &c. and that their best portion is in heaven &c. A third question was, if a man had two wives, (which was ordinary with them,) seeing he must put away one, which he should put away. To this it was answered, that by the law of God the first is the true wife, and the other is no wife; but if such a case fell out, they should then repair to the magistrates, and they would direct them what to do, for it might be, that the first wife might be an adulteress &c. and then she was to be put away. When all their questions were resolved, he concluded with prayer in the Indian language.

The Indians were usually very attentive, and kept their children so quiet as caused no disturbance. Some of them began to be seriously affected, and to understand the things of God, and they were generally ready to reform whatsoever they were told to be against the word of God, as their sorcery, (which they call powwowing,) their whoredoms &c. idleness &c. The Indians grew very inquisitive after knowledge both in things divine and also human, so as one of them, meeting with an honest plain Englishman, would needs know of him, what were the first beginnings (which we call principles) of a commonwealth. The Englishman, being far short in the knowledge of such matters, yet ashamed that an Indian should find an Englishman ignorant of any thing, bethought himself what answer to give him, at last resolved upon this, viz. that the first principles of a commonwealth was salt, for (saith he) by means of salt we can keep our flesh and fish, to have it ready when we need it, whereas you lose much for want of it, and are sometimes ready to starve. A second principle is iron, for thereby we fell trees, build houses, till our land &c. A third is, ships, by which we carry forth such commodities as we have to spare, and fetch in such as we need, as cloth, wine &c. Alas (saith the Indian) then I fear, we shall never be a commonwealth, for we can neither make salt, nor iron, nor ships.[1]

It pleased God so to prosper our fishing this season, as that at Marblehead only they had taken by the midst of the (11) month about four thousand pounds worth of fish.

(10.) But the Lord was still pleased to afflict us in our shipping, for Major Gibbons and Captain Leverett having sent a new ship of about one hundred tons to Virginia, and having there freighted her with tobacco, going out of the river, by a sudden storm was forced on shore from her anchor, and much of the goods spoiled, to the loss (as was estimated) of above two thousand pounds.

I must here observe a special providence of God, pointing out his displeasure against some profane persons, who took part with Dr. Child &c. against the government and churches here. The court had appointed a general fast, to seek God (as for some other occasions, so) in the trouble which threatened us by the petitioners &c. The pastor of Hingham, and others of his church (being of their party) made light of it, and some said they would not fast against Dr. Child and against themselves; and there were two of them (one Pitt and Johnson) who, having a great raft of masts and planks (worth forty or fifty pounds) to tow to Boston, would needs set forth about noon the day before (it being impossible they could get to Boston before the fast;) but when they came at Castle Island, there arose such a tempest, as carried away their

---

1 Eliot's memory is embalmed in these benevolent deeds, the full development of which, with their consequences, deserve and have produced several volumes. The earliest notice, except an order in September 1646 for giving instruction in our laws to the Indians, if *times be safe*, once a year by interpreters, is in our records, vol. III. 108, general court 26 May 1647:

"It is ordered that ten pounds be given Mr. Eliot as a gratuity from this court in respect of his pains in instructing the Indians in the knowledge of God, and that order be taken that the twenty pounds per annum given by the lady Armine for that purpose may be called for and employed accordingly."

Waban is said to have been of the same age, 42, as Eliot. The first day of the apostle's instruction was 28 October. See 1 Hist. Coll. V. 256 et seq. and 1 Hist. Coll. VIII. 12, but the fullest account of the labours in preaching christianity to the natives is by Gookin in 1 Hist. Coll. I. 168 et seq.

raft, and forced them to cut their mast to save their lives. Some of their masts and planks they recovered after, where it had been cast on shore; but when they came with it to the Castle, they were forced back again, and were so oft put back with contrary winds &c. as it was above a month before they could bring all the remainder to Boston.[1]

Prescott, another favourer of the petitioners, lost a horse and his lading in Sudbury river; and a week after, his wife and children, being upon another horse, were hardly saved from drowning.

A woman of Charlestown having two daughters, aged under fourteen, sent them to the tide-mill near by with a little corn. They delivered their corn at the mill, and returning back (they dwelt towards Cambridge) they were not seen till three months after, supposed to be carried away by the tide, which was then above the marsh. This was 13 (11).

(1.) In the midst of this month a small pinnace was set out for Barbados with [blank] persons and store of provisions. It was her first voyage, and 2 (3) after she was put on shore at Scituate, the goods in her, but not a man, nor any of their clothes.

*[2]The merchants of Boston had set forth a small ship to trade about the Gulf of Canada, and they had certificate under the public seal to that end. They set sail from Boston the midst of the (1) month, and by tempest were forced into an harbour near Cape Sable, and having lost their boat, and forced to let slip their cables, were driven on ground, and having staid there about four days, Mr. D'Aulney having intelligence of them, sent eighteen men by land, who finding eleven of ours on shore, without weapons, surprised them, and after the ship, having but six men in

---

1 Unless we be careful always to consider the cause of any special providence, we may fail in our views of the displeasure of God. No doubt our author was satisfied of the ill desert of the Hingham people, who would not fast against Dr. Child and against themselves; but on page 236 of this volume, it may be seen, that the clergy, going to the same town to reduce the church members to sobriety, "were kept twenty-four hours in the boat, and were in great danger by occasion of a tempest." A sentence is worth extracting from Hubbard, 648, though the pastor sometimes "recks not his own rede;" "Let men take heed how they pass rash censures upon others, lest unawares they read their own destiny in pronouncing sentence upon their neighbours, and not be too forward, with the men of Miletum, to give an interpretation of the acts of providence, the beginnings of which we may see, but cannot foresee the issue and intendment thereof."

2 Diagonal lines are drawn across this paragraph in our original MS.; but I have preferred to retain it, as, if good for nothing else, it affords, in connexion with a subsequent one, two very different reports of the same transaction.

her; and being carried to Port Royal, he examined them upon oath, whether they had traded, which they had not done, only the merchant had received two beaver skins, given him by the sachem; for which, (notwithstanding he allowed their commission,) after he had kept them three weeks prisoners, he kept their ship and goods to the value of one thousand pounds, and sent them home in two shallops, meanly provided, and without any *lead* &c. This is more fully set down after, fol. 99.*

One [blank] of Windsor arraigned and executed at Hartford for a witch.[1]

[Large Blank.]

1647.] 30 (3.) In the evening there was heard the report as of a great piece of ordnance. It was heard all over the Bay, and all along to Yarmouth &c. and there it seemed as if it had been to the southward of them.

[Blank.]

26.] The court of elections was at Boston. Great labouring there had been by the friends of the petitioners to have one chosen governour, who favoured their cause, and some new magistrates to have been chosen of their side; but the mind of the country appeared clearly, for the old governour was chosen again, with two or three hundred votes more than any other, and no one new magistrate was chosen but only captain Robert Bridges.

Captain [2]Welde of Roxbury being dead, the young men of the town agreed together to choose one George [3]Denison, a young

---

1 Nothing of this is found in the History of Connecticut by Dr. Trumbull, yet it is deserving of melancholy commemoration, as the first instance of delusion in New England too soon infectious. We may presume the unhappy woman was *tried*, as well as arraigned before execution, if the wretched ceremonies in such cases deserve the name of trial. See Trumb. I. 8, in pref. where he says: "after the most careful researches, no indictment of any person for that crime, nor any process relative to that affair can be found."

2 It seems he was a merchant. The inventory of his estate, returned by his wife, Barbara, 4 (12) 1646 in our Prob. Rec. II. 29, amounts to *L*.2028.11.3, as appraised by Isaac Heath, Wm. Denison, John Johnson and William Parke. He appears as a deputy September 1636, and several times afterwards.

3 Probably a son of one of the Roxbury antinomians mentioned in my note, Vol. I. 248. William was a representative of that town in the second court, March 1635. Nothing more is known of George by me, except that the Roxbury records mention the birth of a daughter, 20 (1) 1641, and another, 20 (3) 1643, and the death of Bridget, his wife, in August, 1643. He certainly was not very young, but had, perhaps, received a taint in Oliver's army, that in the opinion of our rulers might render him unfit to be a captain of more orthodox soldiers.

soldier come lately out of the wars in England, which the ancient and chief men of the town understanding, they came together at the time appointed, and chose one Mr. [1]Prichard, a godly man and one of the chief in the town, passing by their lieutenant, fearing least the young Denison would have carried it from him, whereupon much discontent and murmuring arose in the town. The young men were over strongly bent to have their will, although their election was void in law, (George Denison not being then a freeman,) and the ancient men over-voted them above twenty, and the lieutenant was discontented because he was neglected &c. The cause coming to the court, and all parties being heard, Mr. Prichard was allowed, and the young men were pacified, and the lieutenant.

[Large Blank.]

4 (4.) Canonicus, the great sachem of Narragansett, died, a very old man.[2]

8 (4.) The synod began again at Cambridge. The next day Mr. Ezekiel Rogers of Rowley preached in the forenoon, and the magistrates and deputies were present, and in the afternoon Mr. Eliot preached to the Indians in their own language before all the assembly. Mr. Rogers in his sermon took occasion to speak of the petitioners, (then in question before the court,) and exhorted the court to do justice upon them, yet with desire of favour to such as had been drawn in &c. and should submit. He reproved also the practice of private members making speeches in the church assemblies to the disturbance and hindrance of the ordinances, also *the* call for the reviving the ancient practice in England of children asking their parents' blessing upon their knees &c. Also he reproved the great oppression in the country &c. and other things amiss, as long hair &c. Divers were offended at his zeal in some of these passages. Mr. Bradford, the governour of Plimouth, was there as a messenger of the church of Plimouth. But the sickness (mentioned here in the next leaf)

---

1 Of this gentleman, whose name of baptism was Hugh, I have learned nothing, but his employment next year in a mission mentioned by Winthrop, and from the records of his town, that a son, Zebadiah, was born to him 17 (8) 1643, and another, 13 (8) 1644. I presume he and his competitor for the military distinction removed from Roxbury.

2 Hubbard, 464, adds to our author's paragraph these words: "still leaving the hereditary quarrel entailed upon his successor. But Uncas was alive and well in the year 1680, and probably may live to see all his enemies buried before him." Canonicus deserved as well of the English, at least, as the Moheagan sachem. Hubbard makes the event a year too late, and has misled Dr. Holmes.

prevailed so as divers of the members of the synod were taken with it, whereupon they were forced to break up on the sudden.

[Very large blank.]

The success of Mr. Eliot's labours in preaching to the Indians appears in a small book set forth by Mr. Shepherd and by other observations in the country.

1646. 19, (1.) One captain Dobson in a ship of eighty tons, double manned and fitted for a man of war, was set forth from Boston to trade to the eastward. Their testimonial was for the gulf of Canada. But being taken with foul weather, and having lost their boat, they put into harbour at Cape Sable, and there shooting off five or six pieces of ordnance, the Indians came aboard them, and traded some skins; and withal Mr. D'Aulney had notice, and presently sent away twenty men over land, (being about thirty miles from Port Royal,) who lurking in the woods for their advantage, providence offered them a very fair one. For the ship, having bought a shallop of the Indians, and being under sail, in the mouth of the harbour, the wind came about southerly with such violence, as forced them to an anchor; and having lost all their anchors, they were forced on shore, yet without danger of shipwreck. Whereupon the master and merchant and most of the company went on shore (leaving but six men aboard) and carried no weapons with them, which the French perceiving, they came upon them and bound them, and carried the master to the ship's side, who commanded the men aboard to yield up the ship. The French being possessed of the ship, carried her to Port Royal, and left some of their company to conduct the rest by land. When they came there, they were all imprisoned, and examined apart upon oath, and having confessed that they had traded &c. the ship and cargo (being worth in all one thousand pounds) was kept as confiscated, and the men were put into two old shallops and sent home, and arrived at Boston 6 (3) 47. The merchants complained to the court for redress, and offered to set forth a good ship, to deal with some of D'Aulney's vessels, but the court thought it not safe nor expedient for us to begin a war with the French; nor could we charge any manifest wrong upon D'Aulney, seeing we had told him, that if ours did trade within his liberties, they should do it at their own peril. And though we judged it an injury to restrain the natives and others from trading &c. (they being a free people,) yet, it being a common practice of all civil nations, his seizure of our ship would be accounted lawful, and our letters of reprisal unjust. And besides there appeared an overruling providence in it, otherwise he could not have seized a ship so well fitted, nor could wise men have lost her so foolishly.

At Concord a bullock was killed which had in his maw a ten shilling piece of English gold, and yet it could not be known that any had lost it.

A barn at Salem was set on fire with lightning, and all the corn and hay consumed suddenly. It fell upon the thatch in the breadth of a sheet, in the view of people.

(4.) An epidemical sickness was through the country among Indians and English, French and Dutch. It took them like a cold, and a light fever with it. Such as bled or used cooling drinks died; those who took comfortable things, for most part recovered, and that in few days. Wherein a special providence of God appeared, for not a family, nor but few persons escaping it, had it brought all so weak as it did some, and continued so long, our hay and corn had been lost for want of help; but such was the mercy of God to his people, as few died, not above forty or fifty in the Massachusetts, and near as many at Connecticut. But that which made the stroke more sensible and grievous, both to them and to all the country, was the death of that faithful servant of the Lord, Mr. Thomas Hooker, pastor of the church in Hartford, who, for piety, prudence, wisdom, zeal, learning, and what else might make him serviceable in the place and time he lived in, might be compared with men of greatest note; and he shall need no other praise: the fruits of his labours in both Englands shall preserve an honourable and happy remembrance of him forever.[1]

14, (4.) In this sickness the governour's wife, daughter of Sir John Tindal, Knight, left this world for a better, being about fifty-six years of age: a woman of singular virtue, prudence, modesty and piety, and especially beloved and honoured of all the country.[2]

The meeting of the commissioners of the colonies should, in

---

1 An exact date of so important an event would perhaps have been given by our author, but for his private grief, as the next paragraph explains. Hubbard, 541, says it was 7 July.

2 The reader would not forgive me, if I attempted to add any thing to this character, equally observable for its brevity and elegance. Her own letters with those of her husband in the appendix to the former volume are ample and curious memorials of their mutual affection, with which any stranger can intermeddle only to disadvantage. For this extract from a MS. note in an almanac of 1647 belonging to S. Danforth, then probably a resident of Cambridge, with which J. Farmer, Esq. supplies me, no excuse can be necessary: JUNE, "15th day, Mrs. Winthrop, the governour his wife, was buried, who fell sick on the 13th day in afternoon and died the next morning."

course, have been at Plimouth in the sixth month next, but upon special occasion of the Indians there was a meeting appointed at Boston [blank] which continued to the 17 (6) next. The chief occasion was, that [1]Ninicraft, the sachem of Niantick, had professed his desire to be reconciled to the English &c. and that many Indians would complain of Uncas and his brother their falsehood and cruelty &c. if they might come to Boston to be heard there.

[Large Blank.]

The general court made an order, that all elections of governour &c. should be by papers delivered in to the deputies before the court, as it was before permitted. This was disliked by the freemen, and divers of the new towns petitioned for the repeal of it, as an infringement of their liberties; for when they consented to send their deputies with full power &c. they reserved to themselves matter of election, as appears by the record of the court [blank.] Upon these petitions the said order was repealed, and it was referred to the next court of elections to consider of a meet way for ordering elections, to the satisfaction of the petitioners and the rest of the freemen. But that court being full of business, and breaking up suddenly, it was put off farther.

[Large Blank.]

In the depth of winter, in a very tempestuous night, the fort at Saybrook was set on fire, and all the buildings within the palisado, with all the goods &c. were burnt down, captain Mason, his wife, and children, hardly saved. The loss was estimated at one thousand pounds, and not known how the fire came.

[2]Captain Bridges house at Lynn burt down 27 (2) 48.

At Newfoundland, towards the end of the fishing season, there was a great hiracano in the night, which caused a great wreck of ships and boats, and much fish blown off the shore into the sea. Some small vessels we had there, but through mercy none of them miscarried.

The United Colonies having made strict orders to restrain all trade of powder and guns to the Indians, by occasion whereof the

---

1 Of this sachem, whose name is as frequently spelt Ninegret, I am told, that a portrait is preserved at New York by the descendants of governour John Winthrop, jr. with the interesting tradition, that the life of their ancestor was once saved by him.

2 Blank space having been left after the last paragraph, probably for insertion of the cause of the disaster at Saybrook, this misfortune of Capt. Bridges, though it occurred above a year later, is by the author thrown in here.

greatest part of the beaver trade was drawn to the French and Dutch, by whom the Indians were constantly furnished with those things, though they also made profession of like restraint, but connived at the practice, so as our means of returns for English commodities were grown very short. It pleased the Lord to open to us a trade with Barbados and other Islands in the West Indies, which as it proved gainful, so the commodities we had in exchange there for our cattle and provisions, as sugar, cotton, tobacco and indigo, were a good help to discharge our engagements in England. And this summer there was so great a drouth, as their potatoes and corn &c. were burnt up; and divers London ships which rode there were so short of provisions as if our vessels had not supplied them, they could not have returned home; which was an observable providence, that whereas many of the London seamen were wont to despise New England as a poor, barren country should now be relieved by our plenty.

After the great dearth of victuals in these islands followed presently a great mortality, (whether it were the plague, or pestilent fever, it killed in three days,) that in Barbadoes there died six thousand, and in Christophers, of English and French, near as many, and in other islands proportionable.[1] The report of this coming to us, by a vessel which came from Fayal, the court published an order, that all vessels, which should come from the West Indies, should stay at the castle, and not come on shore, nor put any goods on shore, without license of three of the council, on pain of one hundred pounds, nor any to go aboard &c. except they continued there &c. on like penalty. The like order was sent to Salem and other haven towns.

But one goodman [2]Dell of Boston, coming from Christophers

---

1 In two or three histories of Barbados, into which I have looked, no mention of this epidemic is found. Hubbard, 532, has carelessly made the pestilence to *accompany* the drought, and Dr. Holmes in quoting him, Ann. I. 343, with a judicious abridgment, increases the perversion of the order of events.

2 The *goodman* Dell, who told the lie, to secure himself from the effect of our earliest quarantine regulation, left a will, made 3 November 1653. It is found in our registry of Probate, Vol. I. 110, and was made, without advice, probably abroad, since it recites, that he was "bound on a voyage to sea, from England to Ireland, and from Ireland to Virginia, and from Virginia to New England." He gives to his wife during her life one half of his estate, "moveables and unmoveables," and "one fourth to his two youngest sons, to be divided equally betwixt them." Difficulty in settling the residue might have arisen, but as the instrument had no witnesses, the court, 6 August 1655, granted administration to his wife Abigail, with an order to act "in reference to this imperfect will." The inventory of his estate, dated 6 September next following, amounts to *L.* 1506,14.7 1-2, including no small sum in silver and gold,

in a small pinnace, and being put in to Gloucester, and there forbidden to land, and informed of the order of court, yet coming into the Bay, and being hailed by the Castle boat, and after by the captain of the Castle, denied that he came from the West Indies, and having taken in three fishermen (whom the captain knew) who joined with him in the same lie, they were let pass, and so came on shore at Boston, before it was known. But such of the council as were near assembled the next day, and sent for some of the company, and upon examination finding that the sickness had been ceased at Christophers three months before they came forth, so as there could be no danger of infection in their persons, they gave them liberty to continue on shore; but for cotton and such goods as might retain the infection, they ordered them to be laid in an house remote, and for Dell, he was bound over to the next court to answer his contempt.

About fourteen days after came a ship from Malago, which had staid nine days at Barbados. She was stopped at the Castle. The captain brought the master and two others to Boston (which he ought not to have done.) Four magistrates examined them upon oath, and finding they were all well, save two, (who had the flux,) and no goods from Barbados but three bags of cotton, which were ordered to be landed &c. at an island, the ship was suffered to come up, but none to come on shore for a week after &c.

4. (6). There was a great marriage to be solemnized at Boston. The bridegroom being of Hingham, Mr. Hubbard's church, he was procured to preach, and came to Boston to that end. But the magistrates, hearing of it, sent to him to forbear. The reasons were, 1. for that his spirit had been discovered to be averse to our ecclesiastical and civil government, and he was a bold man, and would speak his mind, 2. we were not willing to bring in the English custom of ministers performing the solemnity of marriage, which sermons at such times might induce,[1] but if any

---

and one tenth of the ship Goodfellow and one tenth of the ship Starr. Our registry of births gives his sons, John, born October 1645, Samuel, 31 August 1647, Joseph, February 1649, Benjamin, 27 April 1652.

[1] Fear of this evil seems to have arisen, I think, more from the person who officiated in the present instance, than from abstract considerations of propriety. My opinion is confirmed by Mather, though his statement, that it was a custom in 1651, is made with his usual looseness: In his life of Sam. Danforth, Magn. IV. c. 3, §6, he says, "after his contraction, according to the *old usage* of New England, unto the virtuous daughter of Mr. Wilson, (whereat Mr. Cotton preached the sermon,) he was married unto that gentlewoman in the year 1651."

minister were present, and would bestow a word of exhortation &c. it was permitted.

The new governour of the Dutch, called Peter Stevesant, being arrived at the Monados, sent his secretary to Boston with letters to the governour, with tender of all courtesy and good correspondency, but withal taking notice of the differences between them and Connecticut, and offering to have them referred to friends here, not to determine, but to prepare for a hearing and determination in Europe; in which letter he lays claim to all between Connecticut and Delaware. The commissioners being then assembled at Boston, the governour acquainted them with the letter; and it was put to consideration what answer to return. Some advised, that seeing he made profession of much good will and desire of all neighbourly correspondency, we should seek to gain upon him by courtesy, and therefore to accept his offer, and to tender him a visit at his own home, or a meeting at any of our towns where he should choose. But the commissioners of those parts thought otherwise, supposing it would be more to their advantage to stand upon terms of distance &c. And answer was returned accordingly, only taking notice of his offer and showing our readiness to give him a meeting in time and place convenient. So matters continued, as they were.

26. (7.) But it appeared, that a Dutch ship from Holland, being in the harbour at New Haven, (where they had traded about a month,) was surprised by the Dutch governour, and carried to the Monhados. The manner was thus: The merchants of New Haven had bought a ship at the Monhados, which was to be delivered at New Haven. In her the Dutch governour put a company of soldiers, who, being under decks when the ship came into New Haven, took their opportunity afterward, upon the Lord's day, to seize the Dutch ship, and having the wind fair, carried her away. The governour of New Haven complained of the injury to the Dutch governour and made a protest &c. The Dutch governour justified the act by examples of the like in Europe &c. but especially by claiming the place and so all along the seacoast to Cape Codd. He pretended to seize the ship as forfeit to the West India Company by trading in their limits without leave or recognition. It fell out at the same time, that three of the Dutch governor's servants fled from him and came to New Haven, and being pursued, were there apprehended and put in prison. The Dutch governour writes to have them delivered to him, but directs his letter to New Haven in New Netherlands. Upon this the governour of New Haven refused to deliver them, and writes back to the Dutch, maintaining their right to the place,

both by patent from King James, and also by purchase from the natives, and by quiet possession and improvement many years. He wrote also to the governour of the Massachusetts, acquainting him with all that had passed, and desired advice. These letters coming to Boston about the time of the general court, he acquainted the court with them, and a letter was drawn and sent (as from the court) to this purpose, to the Dutch governour, viz. that we were very sorry for the difference which was fallen out between him and our confederates of New Haven; that we might not withhold assistance from them, in case of any injurious violence offered to them; that we accounted their title to the place they possessed to be as good as the Dutch had to the Monhados; that we would willingly interpose for a friendly reconciliation; and that we would write to New Haven to persuade the delivery of the fugitives &c. We wrote also to the governour of New Haven to the same purpose, intimating to him that our request he might deliver the fugitives without prejudice to their right or reputation. But this notwithstanding, they detained the fugitives still, nor would send our letter to the Dutch governour; whereupon he made proclamation of free liberty for all servants &c. of New Haven within his jurisdiction, and wrote to the governour of the Massachusetts, blaming the practice in the general, but excusing it in his particular case, as being enforced thereto &c. This course not prevailing, about the end of winter he wrote privately to the fugitives, and the minister of their church wrote also, whereby he gave such assurance to the fugitives, both of pardon of what was passed, and satisfaction otherwise, as they made an escape and returned home. So that it then appeared, that the advice sent from Boston had been better to have been put in practice in season, than their own judgment, in pursuit whereof this reproach and damage befel them.

(1.) After this the Dutch governour writes to our governour in Dutch, complaining of injuries from the governour of New Haven, (calling him the pretended governour &c.) particularly for wronging his reputation by slanderous reports, and proffers to refer all differences (as formerly he had done) to the two governours of the Massachusetts and Plimouth, Mr. Winthrop and Mr. Bradford, by name, and professing all good neighbourhood to all the rest of the colonies, with some kind of retractation of his former claim to New Haven &c. as if all claim by word or writing, protests &c. were of no value, so long as there is no invasion by force.

The governour of New Haven, Mr. Theophilus Eaton, he writes also about the same time, complaining of the Dutch governour, and informing of Indian intelligence of the Dutch his animating the natives to war upon the English, and of the excessive customs and other ill usage of our vessels arriving there, propounding withal a prohibition of all trade with the Dutch until satisfaction were given. These letters being imparted 15 (11), to the general court at Boston, they thought the matter more weighty and general to the concernment of all the country, than that any thing should then be determined about it, and more fit for the commissioners first to consider of &c. and returned answer to New Haven accordingly. See after 115.

About this time we had intelligence of an observable hand of God against the Dutch at New Netherlands, which though it were sadly to be lamented in regard of the calamity, yet there appeared in it so much of God in favour to his poor people here, and displeasure towards such as have opposed and injured them. as is not to be passed by without due observation and acknowledgment.[1] The late governour, Mr. William Kieft, (a sober and prudent man,) though he abstained from outward force, yet had continually molested the colonies of Hartford and New Haven, and used menacings and protests against them, upon all occasions, and had burnt down a trading house which New Haven had built upon Delaware river, and went for Holland in a ship of 400 tons, well manned and richly laden, to the value (as was supposed) of twenty thousand pounds, and carried away with him two of our people under censure, (the one condemned for rape,) though we pursued them &c. But in their passage in the (8th) month, the ship, mistaking the channel, was carried into Severn, and cast away upon the coast of Wales near Swansey, the governour and eighty other persons, drowned, and some twenty saved.

Complaint had been made to the commissioners of the colonies, at their last meeting, by Pumham and Sacononoco, against the Gortonists (who were now returned to Shaomett, and had named it Warwick) for eating up all their corn with their cattle &c. It was left to our commissioners, who wrote to some in those parts to view the damages, and require satisfaction. But Mr. Cogges-

---

1 Hubbard, 444–5, against whose carelesness in transcribing this relation and making the event fall in 1648 we must protest, though, in 546, he correctly remembers the date of Kieft's return, has enlarged Winthrop's construction of this disaster: "For though indeed God seemed not to favour the designs of those colonies [the Dutch] in the matter of their trade with the Indians, (the salvation of whose souls should have been their principal aim, and so their merchandize might have been holiness to the Lord of Hosts,) by his constant blasting their plantations, intended chiefly to carry on such designs, yet he seemed to be more highly offended with them, that without cause set themselves so violently to oppose them."

hall (who died soon after) and other of their magistrates of Rhode Island, came to Shaomett, and gave the praisers a warrant under their hands and one of their seals, forbidding them or any other to intermeddle &c. pretending it to be within their jurisdiction, whereupon the men returned, and did nothing. And upon another warrant from the president, in the name of the commissioners, there was nothing done neither; so as the poor Indians were in danger to be starved &c. Upon their farther complaints to us, the general court in the (1) month sent three messengers to demand satisfaction for the Indians, and for other wrongs to some English there, and to command them to depart the place, as belonging to us &c. They used our messengers with more respect than formerly, but gave no satisfaction, bearing themselves upon their charter &c. We could do no more at present, but we procured the Indians some corn in the mean time.

In the agitation of this matter in the general court, some moved to have an order (upon refusal of satisfaction &c.) to send forces presently against them; but others thought better to forbear any resolution until the return of our messengers, and the rather because we expected our agent out of England shortly, by whom we should know more of the success of our petition to the parliament &c. it being very probable, that their charter would be called in, as illegal &c. and this counsel prevailed.

It may be now seasonable to set down what success it pleased the Lord to give Mr. Winslow, our agent, with the parliament.

Mr. Winslow set sail from Boston about the middle of 10ber. 1646, and carried such commissions, instructions &c. as are before mentioned. Upon his arrival in England, and delivery of his letters to the Earl of Warwick, Sir Henry Vane &c. from the governour, he had a day appointed for audience before the committee, and Gorton and other of his company appeared also to justify their petition and information, which they had formerly exhibited against the court &c. for making war upon them, and keeping them prisoners &c. But after that our agent had showed the two letters they wrote to us from Shaomett, and the testimony of the court, and some of the elders, concerning their blasphemous heresies and other miscarriages, it pleased the Lord to bring about the hearts of the committees, so as they discerned of Gorton &c. what they were, and of the justice of our proceedings against them; only they were not satisfied in this, that they were not within our jurisdiction &c. to which our agent pleaded two things, 1. that they were within the jurisdiction of Plimouth or Connecticut, and so the orders of the commissioners of the United Colonies had left them to us, 2. the Indians (upon whose lands they dwelt) had subjected themselves and their land to our government. Whereupon the committee made this order following, which they directed in form of a letter to Massachusetts, Plimouth and Connecticut, (one to each) viz.

After our hearty commendations,

In our late letter of 25 May &c. we imparted how far we had proceeded upon the petition of Mr. Gorton and Mr. Holden &c. We did by our said letter declare our tenderness of your just privileges, and of preserving entire the authority and jurisdiction of the several governments in New England, whereof we shall still express our continued care. We have since that taken further consideration of the petition, and spent some time in hearing both parties, concerning the bounds of those patents under which yourselves and the other governments do claim, to the end we might receive satisfaction, whether Shaomett and the rest of the tract of land, pretended to by the petitioners, be actually included within any of your limits. In which point (being matter of fact) we could not, at this distance, give a resolution, and therefore leave that matter to be examined and determined upon the place, if there shall be occasion, for that the boundaries will be there best known and distinguished. And if it shall appear, that the said tract is within the limits of any of the New England patents, we shall leave the same, and the inhabitants thereof to the proper jurisdiction of that government under which they fall. Nevertheless, for that the petitioners have transplanted their families thither, and there settled their residences at a great charge, we commend it to the government, within whose jurisdiction they shall appear to be, (as our only desire at present in this matter,) not only not to remove them from their plantations, but also to encourage them, with protection and assistance, in all fit ways; provided that they demean themselves peaceably, and not endanger any of the English colonies by a prejudicial correspondency with the Indians, or otherwise, wherein if they shall be found faulty, we leave them to be proceeded with according to justice. To this purpose we have also written our letters of this tenour to the governments of New Plimouth and Connecticut, hoping that a friendly compliance will engage these persons to an inoffensive order and conformity, and so become an act of greater conquest, honour and contentment to you all, than the scattering or reducing of them by an hand of power. And so, not doubting of your concurrence with this desire, as there shall be occasion, we commend you to the grace of Christ, resting

Your very affectionate friends,

From the Committee, &c.
22 of July, 1647.

Warwick, Gov'r. and Admiral,
Pembroke and Montgomery,
Manchester,
Arth. Heselrige,
John Rolle,
Hen. Mildmay,
Geo. Fenwick,
Wm. Purefoy,
Rich. Salway,
Miles Corbet,
Cor. Holland,
Geo. Snelling.

The first letter from the committee after Mr. Winslow had delivered our petition and remonstrance, which should have been inserted before the former.

After our hearty commendations &c.

By our letter of May 15, 1646, we communicated to you our reception of a complaint from Mr. Gorton and Mr. Holden &c. touching some proceedings tried against them by your government. We also imparted to you our resolutions (grounded upon certain reasons set forth in our said letter) for their residing upon Shaomett, and the other parts of that tract of land, which is mentioned in a charter of civil incorporation heretofore granted them by us, praying and requiring you to permit the same accordingly, without extending your jurisdiction to any part thereof, or disquieting them in their civil peace, or otherwise interrupting them in their possession, until we should receive your answer to the same in point of title, and thereupon give further order. We have since received a petition and remonstrance from you by your commissioner, Mr. Winslow, and though we have not yet entered into a particular consideration of the matter, yet we do, in the general, take notice of your respect, as well to the parliament's authority, as your own just privileges, and find cause to be further confirmed in our former opinion and knowledge of your prudence and faithfulness to God and his cause. And perceiving by your petition, that some persons do take advantage, from our said letter, to decline and question your jurisdiction, and to pretend a general liberty to appeal hither, upon their being called in question before you for matters proper to your cognizance, we thought it necessary (for preventing of further inconveniences in this kind) hereby to declare, that we intended not thereby to encourage any appeals from your justice, nor to restrain the bounds of your jurisdiction to a narrower compass than is held forth by your letters patent, but to leave you with all that freedom and latitude that may, in any respect, be duly claimed by you; knowing that the limiting of you in that kind may be very prejudicial (if not destructive) to the government and public peace of the colony. For your further satisfaction wherein, you may remember, that our said resolution took rise from an admittance, that the Narragansett Bay (the thing in question) was wholly without the bounds of your patent, the examination whereof will, in the next place, come before us. In the mean time we have received advertisement, that the place is within the patent of New Plimouth, and that the grounds of your proceedings against the complainants was a joint authority from the four governments of Massachusetts, Plimouth, Connecticut and New Haven, which if it falls in upon proof, will much alter the state of the question.

And whereas our said direction extended not only to yourselves, but also to all the other governments and plantations in New England, whom it might concern, we declare, that we intended thereby no prejudice to any of their just rights, nor the countenancing of any practice to violate them; and that we shall for the future be very ready to give our encouragement and assistance in all your endeavours for settling of your peace and government, and the advancement of the gospel of Jesus Christ, to whose blessing we commend your persons and affairs.

Your very loving friends,

From the committee of Lords and Commons, &c. 25 May, 1647.

Warwick, Gov'r. and Admiral,
Bas. Denbigh,
Edw. Manchester,
Wm. Say and Seale,
Fr. Dana,
Wm. Waller,
Arthur Heselrige,
Miles Corbet,
Fr. Allen,
Wm. Purefoy,
Geo. Fenwick,
Cor. Holland.

The committee having thus declared themselves to have an honourable regard of us and care to promote the welfare of the four United Colonies and other English plantations to the eastward, (for they had confirmed Mr. Rigby his patent of Ligonia, and by their favourable interpretation of it had brought it to the sea-side, whereas the words of the grant laid it twenty miles short, and had put Sir Ferdinando Gorge out of all as far as Saco,) our agent proceeded to have the charter (which they had lately granted to those of Rhode Island and Providence) to be called in, as lying within the patent of Plimouth or Connecticut.

[Blank.]

1648.] 10, (3.) The court of elections was at Boston. Mr. Symmes, pastor of Charlestown, preached. Mr. Winthrop was chosen governour again, and Mr. Dudley, deputy governour, Mr. Endecott, sergeant major, and he and Mr. Bradstreet, commissioners &c.

[Blank.]

(3.) Here arrived three ships from London in one day. By the passengers we understood, as also by letters from Mr. Winslow &c. how the hopes and endeavours of Dr. Child and other the petitioners &c. had been blasted by the special providence of the Lord, who still wrought for us. Dr. Child had a brother, a major of a regiment in Kent, who, being set on by his brother and William Vassall, (who went from Scituate to petition against the country &c.) set out a pamphlet, wherein he published their petition, exhibited to our general court, and other proceedings of the court. This was answered by Mr. Winslow in a book, entitled the Salamander, (pointing therein at Mr. Vassall, a man never at rest, but when he was in the fire of contention,) wherein he cleared the justice of our proceedings. As for those who went over to procure us trouble, God met with them all. Mr. Vassall, finding no entertainment for his petitions, went to Barbados.

Dr. Child preferred a petition to the committee against us, and put in Mr. Thomas Fowle his name among others; but he, hearing of it, protested against it, (for God had brought him very low, both in his estate and in his reputation, since he joined in the first petition.) After this the Doctor, meeting with Mr. [1]Willoughby

1 Francis Willoughby became deputy governour in 1665, and died 3 April, 1671. He was entrusted with some agency in England for the colony, probably at a later date than that of our text. For I am furnished with an extract from our records of the general court, 15 October 1669, as follows: "The court considering that our honoured deputy governour Francis Willoughby, Esq. hath yet had no acknowledgment of the country's respect to him by grant of lands or otherwise, as has been shown to some others that have not done that public service which he hath done for this place as well in England as here, do therefore grant him one thousand acres of land to be laid out in any place that may not prejudice a plantation." In 2 Hist. Coll. VIII. 99–100 may be seen, among the earnest debates in council, 1666, about submission to the power at home, how decided was Willoughby against prerogative. Charlestown re-

upon the exchange, (this Mr. Willoughby dwelt at Charlestown, but his father was a colonel of the city,) and falling in talk about New England, the Doctor railed against the people, saying they were a company of rogues and knaves; Mr. Willoughby answered, that he who spake so &c. was a knave, whereupon the Doctor gave him a box on the ear. Mr. Willoughby was ready to have closed with him &c. but being upon the exchange, he was stayed, but presently arrested him. And when the Doctor saw the danger he was in, he employed some friends to make his peace, who ordered him to give five pounds to the poor of New England, (for Mr. Willoughby would have nothing of him,) and to give Mr. Willoughby open satisfaction in the full exchange, and to give it under his hand, never to speak evil of New England men after, nor to occasion any trouble to the country, or to any of the people, all which he gladly performed; and besides God had so blasted his estate, as he was quite broken &c.

Samuel Gorton arrived here. The court, being informed of it, made an order, that he should be apprehended &c. but he sending us the Earl of Warwick's letter, desiring only that he might have liberty to pass home, the court recalled their former order, and gave him a week's liberty to provide for his departure. This was much opposed by some; but the most considered, that, it being only at the Earl's request, (no command,) it could be no prejudice to our liberty, and our commissioner being still attending the parliament, it might much have disadvantaged our cause and his expedition, if the Earl should have heard that we had denied him so small a request. Yet it was carried only by a casting voice.

The Gortonists of Shaomett, hearing how matters were like to go against them in England, and [[1]illegible] by Aquiday, began to consider how they might make their peace with us, and for that end sent two of their company to petition our general court &c. but these messengers being come to Dedham, and hearing that the court was adjourned, they came no further; but one of them wrote a letter to our governour, in this tenour following:

---

cords notice birth of his daughter, Hannah 17 of 3d. 1643, who died 4 September following, and sons Nehemiah, born 18 of 4th, 1644, and Jeremiah 29 of 5th, 1647.

1 Curious readers will unite in my regret for the loss of a word, or at most two, in this place, but on turning to Hubbard, 511, they may find reason to presume that the passage in our MS. was not less obscure one hundred and forty-five years back.

To the right worshipful Mr. John Winthrop, Governour of the Massachusetts,

Humbly presented to your worship's consideration,

That whereas I, with another, was chosen by the general court held at Providence the eighteenth of this month, and sent with an humble request to this honourable state concerning Shaomett business, but when we came at Dedham, hearing that the general court was adjourned, I your suppliant (being an inhabitant of Shaomett) seriously weighing my present condition there, I made bold to advise with Mr. [1]Powell concerning the same, who advised me to repair to your worship, which (on consideration) I could not, till I had some knowledge of your worship's favourable acceptation. My humble request therefore is, that your worship would be pleased to send me your mind in a few lines concerning the premises. So, craving your worship's favourable construction, I remain,

Yours, most humbly,

Dedham, May 22, 1648. Rufus Barton.

---

1 Michael Powell kept the ordinary, as from the general court records I find, in the town of Dedham, and was of course an orthodox man, not likely to be corrupted by the schismatic. He removed next year to Boston, and was one of the founders of the second church of Boston. The people would gladly have ordained him as their pastor, or teacher, being unable, I suppose, to afford compensation at first, to more than one. But, after long agitation of the matter, the magistrates, having authority under a recent act of the legislature, forbade the union, in 1653, with such "a well gifted, though illiterate person." See Hubbard, 551. But he was made ruling elder, and exercised as an instructer in sacred things, and received pay for his services. An exquisite curiosity, illustrative of the habits of our fathers in their ecclesiastical administrations, subordinate to the civil authority in too great a degree, may be read in 3 Hist. Coll. I. 45–47. It is a memorial from Powell to the governour and assistants, in which he says: "I had rather be followed to my grave than unto that which crosses the rule of Christ, or disturbs the peace of the churches. Honoured fathers of this commonwealth, my humble request is that you would not have such hard thoughts of me, that I would consent to be ordained to office without your concurrence; nor that our poor church would attempt such a thing without your approbation." The date is 6 September 1653. It gives a fuller account of the origin of the second religious society of the metropolis than can elsewhere be found; but for sufficient and most interesting history of its progress to this time two sermons by its present pastor with copious notes leave nothing to be supplied. Of Powell Mr. Ware says, that he was "incapacitated for all labour by a paralytic affection" soon after being ordained as ruling elder, "and his office being vacant, I do not find that it was ever again filled." In a note he adds: "He died January 28, 1672-3." Our Probate records VII. 281 contain the inventory of his estate, taken 8 February after, the amount of which, *L.*72.15, I am less particular to mention, than these two items: "a bed, bedstead and furniture *L.*14," and all his library, "three bibles, a concordance, with other books, *L.*2." It is almost as monstrous as Sir John's "half penny worth of bread" to five and eight pence of sack. No wonder the government

This year corn was very scarce, and so it was in all countries of Europe. Our scarcity came by occasion of our transporting much to the West Indies, and the Portugal and Spanish islands. The magistrates sent out to have a survey of the corn in the country, and finding it to fall very short, the next general court made an order to prohibit transportation except of such as should be brought in from other parts and such as were sold before to be transported &c. Yet this restraint notwithstanding &c. the price did not rise 12d. in the bushel, nor (through the good providence of the Lord) was the scarcity much felt among the people.

Mr. Eaton having again moved the governour to know the mind of the court touching the Dutch governour's proceedings, the court appointed a committee to consider of it, (after the court was adjourned,) and withal to consider of the articles of confederation, and some of the commissioners' orders; for there was some murmuring among the people about the inequality of some articles, as that we bearing more than half the charge upon all occasions &c. should yet have no more commissioners than the smallest of the others, and that all charges should be levied by the poll, considering how great a part of our people were labourers and craftsmen, and of theirs the most were farmers and well stocked &c.

28, (3.) Soon after the court was adjourned, the governour received two letters from the Dutch governour, holding forth much assurance of his sincere affection to a firm peace and neighbourly compliance with all the English, and that upon these grounds, 1. our unity in the true religion, 2. the ancient league between the two nations, 3. the community in danger, in respect of the common enemy, both Spaniards and Indians, 4. the reconciling former differences and preventing future, 5. the benefit of a mutual league, both offensive and defensive, against a common enemy; and offered to meet Mr. Bradford, the governour of Plimouth, and Mr. Winthrop, the governour of the Massachusetts, at Connecticut, at such time as we should appoint, and to refer all to us.

The governour returned answer to him, of what gladness he conceived in his forwardness to peace, and had no reason to doubt of his cordial intentions &c. promising to further the meeting what lay in his power &c.

There was some reason, why the Dutch governour's spirit should begin to fall, both in regard of the weakness the state of

interposed to prevent such a scandal to the office. Dedham records mention birth of daughters, Elizabeth 10 of 4th, 1641, and Dorothy 11 of 5th, 1643, and son Michael 12 of 8th, 1645.

Holland (especially the West India Company) were fallen into, (which was not the least occasion of their late peace with Spain,) and also in respect of the doubts which he was fallen into at this time, both from his own unruly people, and also of their neighbour Indians, for neither would his people be restrained from furnishing the Indians with guns, powder &c. nor would the Indians endure to be without that trade; and the great loss the company had sustained by late wreck of three ships, and the old governour and many principal men with him, made him doubtful of any great supply from Holland.

4. (4). Here arrived one [1]Sir Edmund Plowden, who had been in Virginia about seven years. He came first with a patent of a county Palatine for Delaware Bay, but wanting a pilot for that place, he went to Virginia, and there having lost the estate he brought over, and all his people scattered from him, he came hither to return to England for supply, intending to return and plant Delaware, if he could get sufficient strength to dispossess the Swedes.

This year a new way was found out to Connecticut, by Nashua, which avoided much of the hilly way.

The magistrates, being informed at a court of assistants that four or five Indians, who lived upon the spoil of their neighbours, had murdered some Indians of Nipnett, who were subject to this government, and robbed their wigwam, sent twenty men to Nashua to inquire of the truth of the matter, and to apprehend the murderers, if they could be found; but being fled to Narragansett, they returned, and informed us certainly of the persons murdered, and of the actors &c. which was of this good use, (though they could not apprehend them,) that the Indians saw our care of them, and readiness to protect them, and revenge their wrongs.

After this, two Indians, of Cutshamekins' procuring, offering themselves to apprehend some of the murderers, we gave them commission, and withal wrote to Mr. Pincheon to assist them &c. (they being near Springfield.) Mr. Pincheon offered his assistance, but wrote to the governour, that the Indians murdered, nor yet the murderers, were not our subjects, and withal that it would endanger a war; whereupon the governour advising with the de-

---

[1] In Haz. I. 160–170 may be seen a grant to this gentleman, of as singular character as any of the grants by royal authority, dated 21 June 1634. Two following documents in the same volume relate to the same grant. Plantations are referred to in these papers as having been formed two years before, but it is a little remarkable, that no book of American history has taken notice of the labours and success of Sir Edmund Plowden in Maryland. He called his country New Albion, and himself Lord Palatine of New Albion.

puty &c. wrote back presently to Mr. Pincheon, that then he should proceed no further, but send back the Indians &c.[1]

At this court one Margaret Jones of Charlestown was indicted and found guilty of witchcraft, and hanged for it. The evidence against her was, 1. that she was found to have such a malignant touch, as many persons, (men, women and children,) whom she stroked or touched with any affection or displeasure or &c. were taken with deafness, or vomiting, or other violent pains or sickness, 2. she practising physick, and her medicines being such things as (by her own confession) were harmless, as aniseed, liquors &c. yet had extraordinary violent effects, 3. she would use to tell such as would not make use of her physick, that they would never be healed, and accordingly their diseases and hurts continued, with relapses against the ordinary course, and beyond the apprehension of all physicians and surgeons, 4. some things which she foretold came to pass accordingly; other things she could tell of (as secret speeches &c.) which she had no ordinary means to come to the knowledge of, 5. she had (upon search) an apparent teat in her secret parts as fresh as if it had been newly sucked, and after it had been scanned, upon a forced search, that was withered, and another began on the opposite side, 6. in the prison, in the clear day-light, there was seen in her arms, she sitting on the floor, and her clothes up &c. a little child, which ran from her into another room, and the officer following it, it was vanished. The like child was seen in two other places, to which she had relation; and one maid that saw it, fell sick upon it, and was cured by the said Margaret, who used means to be employed to that end. Her behaviour at her trial was very intemperate, lying notoriously, and railing upon the jury and witnesses &c. and in the like distemper she died. The same day and hour she was executed, there was a very great tempest at Connecticut, which blew down many trees[2] &c.

4.] The wife of one Willip of Exeter was found in the river dead, her neck broken, her tongue black and swollen out of her mouth, and the blood settled in her face, the privy parts swollen &c. as if she had been much abused &c.

---

1 See Appendix P.

2 Perhaps this tempest, and several other of the pieces of evidence against the poor witch, are as strong proof of innocence as guilt. In Danforth's Almanack for this year, Mr. Farmer writes me, a note is set against 15 June: "*Alice* Jones was executed at Boston for witchcraft." The errour of the name is observable. But I am unable to find any thing in our records about the trial, except an order for a strict watch on her in prison, the good effect of which is observable in the text.

[Large Blank.]

A vessel of Connecticut being the last winter at Quorasoe, in the possession of the Dutch, found there a negro, who had lost his legs, and had been sent thither out of Holland to perform such service to the governour &c. as he was fit for (having been trained up to some learning in Holland.) This man had attained to some good savour of religion, so as he grew weary of the Dutch of the island, who were very debauched, (only one man he found some piety in,) and there being some Indians in the island, he acquainted himself with them, and having attained some skill in their language, he began to instruct them and their children in the knowledge of God &c. and the Lord so blessed his endeavours, as the Indians began to hearken to him, and yielded themselves to be taught at certain times which this negro appointed. This negro told the master of the English vessel, one Bull, a godly and discreet man, of all his proceedings, and what comfort he had in that one godly Dutchman, saying that he never was in his company but he found Jesus Christ warming him at the heart. He inquired of Bull about New England and our religion and churches, and asked if we were of those christians, who advanced the doctrine of merits &c. and much rejoiced when he heard the truth of our doctrine &c. and showed himself very desirous to see New England; and so he left him at that time.

28.] The Welcome, of Boston, about 300 tons, riding before Charlestown, having in her eighty horses and 120 tons of ballast, in calm weather, fell a rolling, and continued so about twelve hours, so as though they brought a great weight to the one side, yet she would heel to the other, and so deep as they feared her foundering. It was then the time of the county court at Boston, and the magistrates hearing of it, and withal that one Jones (the husband of the witch lately executed) had desired to have passage in her to Barbados, and could not have it without such payment &c. they sent the officer presently with a warrant to apprehend him, one of them saying that the ship would stand still as soon as he was in prison. And as the officer went, and was passing over the ferry, one said to him, you can tame men sometimes, can't you tame this ship. The officer answered, I have that here that (it may be) will tame her, and make her be quiet; and with that showed his warrant. And at the same instant, she began to stop and presently staid, and after he was put in prison, moved no more.[1]

---

1 Our fathers must not be charged with any partiality, I presume, in passing over what Mather would call the nefandous witchcraft of this man, though tes-

There appeared over the harbour at New Haven, in the evening, the form of the keel of a ship with three masts, to which were suddenly added all the tackling and sails, and presently after, upon the top of the poop, a man standing with one hand akimbo under his left side, and in his right hand a sword stretched out towards the sea. Then from the side of the ship which was from the town arose a great smoke, which covered all the ship, and in that smoke she vanished away; but some saw her keel sink into the water. This was seen by many, men and women, and it continued about a quarter of an hour.[1]

---

timony to support it was apparent to the whole community in the diabolical motion of the ship. The acuteness, at least, of one of the judges, who foretold the security of the ship, as a necessary consequence of that precaution, before he who was refused passage in her was committed to prison, certainly entitled him to great influence in such a trial; but the escape of the husband undoubtedly was owing to a mistake in philosophy and law, that such powerful enchantments could be perpetrated only by female influence. Forty-four years later his sex would not have given him security, for so impudent was the devil then become by his success, as to make addresses sometimes even to men, though unhappily much more often to women.

1 Here is the first known relation of that atmospherical phenomenon, out of which the unhappy mourners of relatives lost in the ship near two years and a half before, possibly, in their gloomy and solitary state, worked up their imaginations to shape some application to the cause of their suffering, and which tradition and credulity certainly magnified to one of the most portentous meteors that was ever witnessed in a land of marvels. How could the date of an occurrence of so much interest, as the sailing of the New Haven bark, be brought down two years later than the truth? Probably by many minds the exact period was forgotten, before the strange illusion in the clouds had attracted attention. After this appearance, in the lapse of a very few years, the story of the apparition would be told more frequently, if not more impressively, than that of the unheard of shipwreck, which preceded it; and as the time of the meteorological splendour was probably marked, and this had become with the majority the principal event, though in frequent repetition connected with that as a cause, it became natural to bring cause and effect into greater propinquity. Few other subjects of conversation were so safe and interesting in that humble colony for many years; yet it was never, I believe, exhibited in full blown magnificence, till the happy eye of Mather having been blessed with a momentary vision, he kindly solicited from Reverend James Pierpont an imperishable representation. How precise was the relation at so distant a day, even of "the most credible, judicious and curious surviving observers of it," we can well judge without the aid of the author of the Magnalia or his correspondent. Pierpont was graduated at H. C. 1681, settled at New Haven in 1685. Hubbard, 322, says the ship, besides being ill built and very crank, was, "to increase the inconveniency thereof, ill laden, the lighter goods at the bottom; so that understanding men did even beforehand conclude in their deliberate thoughts a calamitous issue." It was not, then, quite so remarkable, perhaps, as Pierpont thought, that Mr. Davenport "in prayer with an observable *emphasis* used these words: Lord, if it be thy pleasure to bury these our friends in the bottom of the sea, they are thine: save them," especially since he also notes, "that the

[Large Blank.]

Divers letters passed between our governour and the Dutch governour about a meeting for reconciling the differences between our confederates of New Haven &c. and him. But Mr. Bradford, the governour of Plimouth, (being one of the two whom the Dutch governour desired to refer the differences unto,) being sent unto about it, came to Boston, and there excused himself, by bodily infirmities and other reasons, that he could not go to Hartford that summer, but promised (the Lord assisting) to prepare against the middle of the (4) next summer. So the governour (Mr. Hopkins being then also at Boston) despatched away letters presently to the Dutch governour to certify him thereof, who re-

---

master (Lamberton) often said she would prove their grave." Hubbard, who wrote in 1682, and is copious enough about the disaster, has nothing about the air-drawn picture of it; and thus I am led to conclude that it was so justly told by our author, as to be thought by him, as our own judgment also makes it, too trivial an occurrence for such vast combinations to be united with.

The account of this air-ship has been so often republished from the Magnalia, that my regard for the people of New Haven induces me to request a perusal of that fictitious relation, which, though wonderfully amplified by their former clergyman, hardly contains any part of the modest particulars in our text: After perusal of the counterfeit, they must make a comparison with the original. Pierpont indeed has enriched the narrative with glowing appendages, as I. after failure of news of their ship from England in the following spring, "prayers, both public and private," of the distressed people, "that the Lord would (if it was his pleasure) let them hear what he had done with their dear friends, and prepare them with a suitable submission to his holy will" II. "a great thunder storm arose out of the northwest" III. "the ship sailing against the wind" IV. "the very children cried out, there's a brave ship" V. the pertinacity of the apparition, "crowding up as far as there usually was water sufficient for such a vessel, and so near some of the spectators, as that they imagined a man might hurl a stone on board her," VI. "her maintop seemed to be blown off, but left hanging in the shrouds, then her mizen top, then all her masting seemed blown away by the board." VII. the certainty and satisfaction enjoyed from this cloudy exhibition, "Mr. Davenport in public declared to this effect: that God had condescended, for the quieting of their afflicted spirits, this extraordinary account of his sovereign disposal of those for whom so many fervent prayers were made continually." It is very reasonable that the late version of his correspondent, worthy of Mather himself, who had our author's MS. in possession, having suppressed the actual circumstances as related at the time, should have furnished superiour beauty to the narrative fifty years later. The duration of the appearance, in our text, is doubled, at least, in the modern story, which makes it sail "against the wind for the space of half an hour."

Were we in these days as skilful in penetrating the counsels of heaven by the signs of the sky, it might be thought that this play of the clouds in June 1648 at New Haven had as much relation to the loss in November 1657 of Garret's ship, wherein was Mr. Davis, H. C. 1651, one of the best scholars of New Haven, as to the loss of Lamberton in January 1646. The circumstances of each were nearly similar. See Gookin in 1 Hist. Coll. I. 202, 3. Providence might have some purpose in *foreshowing*, but could be less distinctly reverenced in so uncertain a *reflection*.

turned answer soon after, that he was very sorry the meeting did not hold, and professed his earnest inclination to peace, and that he never had any thought of war, and desired that in the mean time all things might remain as they were, neither encroaching upon others' pretended limits, desiring withal that he might meet the commissioners of the colonies also to treat with them about the Indian trade, which was much abused &c.

[Large Blank.]

15. (6.) The synod met at Cambridge by adjournment from the (4) last. Mr. Allen of Dedham preached out of Acts 15,[1] a very godly, learned, and particular handling of near all the doctrines and applications concerning that subject, with a clear discovery and refutation of such errours, objections and scruples as had been raised about it by some young heads in the country.

It fell out, about the midst of his sermon, there came a snake into the seat, where many of the elders sate behind the preacher. It came in at the door where people stood thick upon the stairs. Divers of the elders shifted from it, but Mr. Thomson, one of the elders of Braintree, (a man of much faith,) trode upon the head of it, and so held it with his foot and staff with a small pair of grains, until it was killed. This being so remarkable, and nothing falling out but by divine providence, it is out of doubt, the Lord discovered somewhat of his mind in it. The serpent is the devil; the synod, the representative of the churches of Christ in New England. The devil had formerly and lately attempted their disturbance and dissolution; but their faith in the seed of the woman overcame him and crushed his head.

The synod went on comfortably, and intended only the framing

---

1 Probably the whole chapter, as it contains the admirable history of the council of Jerusalem, almost the only one since the foundation of our religion, whose result in matter of general doctrine and practice can be venerated, afforded the theme of the preacher. But if any particular part were more largely commented on, than another, considering the manner of our fathers' dissent from the church of England, then in its humiliation, we may fancy that with reverential tenderness the 10 and 11 verses were handled, though the chief application was undoubtedly to resist the presbyterian form of government of the churches, established by the Westminster assembly :

Now therefore why tempt ye God, to put a yoke upon the neck of the disciples, which neither our fathers nor we were able to bear?

But we believe that through the grace of the Lord Jesus we shall be saved, even as they.

This synod erected the famous Cambridge platform, which, with slight occasional departures, required by the lapse of time, continued the rule of our ecclesiastical polity until the constitution of the commonwealth in 1780, and is still of some influence in construction of difficult topics.

of a confession of faith &c. and a form of church discipline (not entertaining any other business.) For the first, they wholly agreed with that which the assembly in England had lately set forth. For the other, viz. for discipline, they drew it by itself, according to the general practice of our churches.[1] So they ended in less than fourteen days.

This month, when our first harvest was near had in, the pigeons came again all over the country, but did no harm, (harvest

---

1 No more proper place can, perhaps, be found for a correction of an errour as to the number of New England congregational churches, which the authority of so distinguished a name as Dr. Stiles might irretrievably confirm.

He observes "there is no body of Christians on earth in such a rapid increase, and in so flourishing a state, as the congregationalists of New England. The present state of our denomination as to numbers, for the year 1760, is nearly this: In Massachusetts are above three hundred congregational churches; in Connecticut one hundred and seventy; in New Hampshire forty-three; which with those in this colony, [Rhode Island] form a body of about five hundred and thirty churches. In 1650 there were about thirty six churches already founded, several of which were small beginnings, requiring many years to fill up. In 1696 there were but one hundred and thirty congregational churches in all New England. And being A. D. 1760 increased to five hundred and thirty the proportion of doubling is once in thirty years. A. D. 1643 there had arrived in two hundred and ninety-eight transports, about four thousand two hundred planters with their families, making about twenty-one thousand people for all New England. Since that time more have gone from us to Europe, than have arrived from thence hither. The present inhabitants, therefore, of New England are justly to be estimated a natural increase by the blessing of heaven on the first twenty-one thousand that arrived by the year 1643."

Holmes' Life of Stiles, 93.

First, I doubt he is too easily satisfied, as to the number in 1696, which he makes one hundred and thirty, when it is probable there were more. He relied on the Magnalia, but inquiry has convinced me, as it will any one else, of an observation, that may soon become an axiom: put not your faith in Mather.

More pertinent however to the narrow limits, within which this work is confined, is the result of my investigation as to the churches already founded in 1650, which the learned president of Yale College makes "*about* 36." The latitudinarianism of the phrase, about, on such a subject, is to be abhorred. I make more than half as many again, and prove my computation, as follows: Massachusetts proper, see Vol. I. 95, 6, in note, 29, Martha's Vineyard, 1. Maine, scil. York, and Wells, 2, New Hampshire, scil. Portsmouth, Dover, Exeter, and Hampton, 4, Plimouth, scil. Plimouth, Scituate, Duxbury, Barnstable, Marshfield, Yarmouth, Sandwich, Taunton, Eastham, and Rehoboth, 10, Connecticut, scil. Hartford, Windsor, Weathersfield, New Haven, Milford, New London, Guilford, Stratford, Fairfield, Saybrook, Stamford, and Branford, 12, total 58.

As to the ships that brought planters to New England, it should always be remembered, the *authority* is no weaker, and after some week's labour on the matter, I am qualified to say, the *reason* is stronger for the number 198, than 298. But I have not room to give the reasons for my opinion, that would occupy several pages.

being just in,[1]) but proved a great blessing, it being incredible what multitudes of them were killed daily. It was ordinary for one man to kill eight or ten dozen in half a day, yea five or six dozen at one shoot, and some seven or eight. Thus the Lord showed us, that he could make the same creature, which formerly had been a great chastisement, now to become a great blessing.

About the midst of this summer, there arose a fly out of the ground, about the bigness of the top of a man's little finger, of brown colour. They filled the woods from Connecticut to Sudbury with a great noise, and eat up the young sprouts of the trees, but meddled not with the corn. They were also between Plimouth and Braintree, but came no further. If the Lord had not stopped them, they had spoiled all our orchards, for they did some few.

At the last meeting of the commissioners at New Haven, information was given them, that Sequashin, a sachem near Hartford, would have hired an Indian to kill some of the magistrates of Hartford, whereupon he was sent for, but came not; and being among other Indians about Pacomtuckett, they sent for Unkas, who undertook to fetch him in, which he not being able to do by force, he surprised him in the night, and brought him to Hartford,

---

1 Our author's note of time is not very precise, inasmuch as the whole month of August is given. What harvest he intends is conjectural. I suppose English, not Indian, corn, as wheat, rye, barley, &c. is meant. My indefatigable correspondent, John Farmer, Esquire, has furnished me with the following extracts from the notes in the interleaved Almanacks for 1646 and 1647 of Danforth, that may to some extent indicate the progress of vegetation.

1646, August	1.	The great pears ripe.
	3.	The long apples ripe.
	12.	Blackston's apples gathered.
	15.	Tankerd apples gathered.
	18.	Kreton pippins, Long red apples, } gathered.
1647, July	5.	We began to cut the peas in the field.
	14.	We began to shear rye.
Aug.	2.	We mowed barley. The same week we shear summer wheat.
	7.	The great pears gathered.
Sept.	15.	The Russetins gathered and Pearmaines.
1648, May	26.	Sown 1 peck of peas, the moon in the full. Observe how they prove.
July	28.	Summer apples gathered.
1646, July	20.	Apricoks ripe.

Mr. Farmer remarks in a note: "Josselyn says under date of October 11, 1638, that he was presented with a score of *pippins* from Governor's Island, and that there was not one apple tree nor pear tree planted yet, in no part of the country, but upon that Island." Perhaps Josselyn was mistaken.

where he was kept in prison divers weeks. But there not being sufficient proof to convict him &c. he was discharged. Yet the Indians, from whom he was taken, took it so to heart against Uncas, as they intended to make war upon him, and the Narragansett sent wampom to them to encourage them; and accordingly in this month, there were gathered together from divers parts about one thousand Indians armed, three hundred or more having guns, powder and bullets, and were at Pacomtuckett preparing &c. which the magistrates of Hartford hearing of, they sent three horsemen to them (one being very expert in the Indian language) to know their intent, and to tell them, that if they made war upon Uncas, the English must defend him. The Indian sachems entertained the messengers courteously; and having heard their message, they took time to give their answer, which was this, viz. they knew the English to be a wise and warlike people, and they intended not to fall out with them, therefore for the present they would desist, and consider further of the matter. And God had so disposed, as at the same instant they had intelligence of a defeat given to some of their confederates by other Indians, which called them to their aid, and also the Narragansett had failed to send them all the wampom he had promised. Thus the Lord delivered us from that war, which must needs have been very dangerous, especially to our brethren of Connecticut.

The Narragansett and Niantick dealing thus underhand contrary to their covenant, and being yet behind near one thousand fathom of the wampom they should have paid us long since, the commissioners, sitting at Plimouth, (7) ordered four men to be sent to them, with an interpreter, with instructions how to treat with them, both concerning their hiring other Indians to war upon Uncas, and also about the wampom behind. Captain Atherton and Captain Prichard, assisted with two others, voluntarily undertook this service, and went hence, 3 (8). They were to have taken Benedict Arnold for their interpreter; but he being from home, they went to Mr. Williams, who sent for the sachems. But they had heard that many horsemen were come to take them, which made Pessicus fly over to Rhode Island. Then our messengers went to Niantick, where Ninicraft entertained them courteously, (there they staid the Lord's day,) and came back with them to Mr. Williams, and then Pessicus and Canonicus' son, being delivered of their fear, came to them, and being demanded about hiring the Mohawks against Uncas, they solemnly denied it; only they confessed, that the Mohawks, being a great sachem, and their ancient friend, and being come so near them, they sent some twenty fathom of wampom for him to tread upon, as the manner of Indians is. And Canonicus' son called [blank] used this asseveration, viz. Englishman's God doth know, that we did not send to stir up or hire the Mohawks against Uncas. Then they further promised, that they would not meddle with Uncas, nor stir up any other against him, before they had paid all their debt of wampom to the English, and then they would require satisfaction for all the wrongs Uncas had done them, and if the English would not see them satisfied, they would consider what to do. And for their wampom behind &c. they desired the English to bear with them, in regard their want of corn last winter had made them lay out their wampom to the English for corn; but in the spring they would provide part of it, and the rest so soon as they could.

(8.) A shallop having been fishing at Monhigen, and returning with other boats, and being to put in at Damarells' cove, the other boats fell to their oars (the wind failing) and called upon this boat to do the like, that they might be harboured before night; but they were slothful, and neglected &c. whereupon she missed her way, and was split upon a rock, and all the men (being four, and one Indian) and all the goods perished.

20.] In the time of our general court here arrived from Virginia one Mr. Haryson, pastor of the church of Nanseman there, and reported to us, that their church was grown to one hundred and eighteen persons, and many more looking towards it, which had stirred up the governour there, Sir William Berkley, to raise persecution against them, and he had banished their elder Mr. Durand, and himself (viz. Mr. Haryson) was to depart the country by the third ship at furthest, which had caused [him] to come now to take advice of the magistrates and elders here about the matter. First he spake with the magistrates, and propounded two things, 1. whether their church ought not to remove, upon this persecution, 2. whither we would advise them to remove.

To the first our answer was, that seeing God had carried on his work so graciously hitherto &c. and that there was so great hope of a far more plentiful harvest at hand, (many of the council being well inclined &c. and one thousand of the people by conjecture,) they should not be hasty to remove, as long as they could stay upon any tolerable terms. 2. For the place they should remove to, if necessitated, Mr. Haryson acquainted us with a place allowed and propounded to them, and the occasion of it, which was thus: Captain Wm. [1]Sayle of Summers Islands, having been

1 By a reasonable conjecture, this is the same gentleman, who first planted South Carolina, about twenty years after, with a commission as governour.

lately in England, had procured an ordinance of parliament for planting the Bahamas Islands (now called Eleutheria) in the mouth of the gulf of Florida, and wanting means to carry it on, had obtained of divers parliament men and others in London to undertake the work, which they did, and drew up a covenant and articles for all to enter into, who would come into the business. The first article was for liberty of conscience, wherein they provided, that the civil magistrate should not have cognisance of any matter which concerned religion, but every man might enjoy his own opinion or religion, without controul or question, (nor was there any word of maintaining or professing any religion or worship of God at all;) and the commission (by authority of the ordinance of parliament) to captain Sayle to be governour three years was with limitation, that they should be subject to such orders and directions as from time to time they should receive from the company in England &c. Upon these terms they furnished him with a ship and all provisions and necessaries for the design, and some few persons embarked with him, and sailed to the Summers Islands, where they took in Mr. Patrick Copeland, elder of that church, a godly man of near eighty years of age, and so many other of the church there, as they were in the ship in all seventy persons. But in the way to Eleutheria, one captain Butler, a young man who came in the ship from England, made use of his liberty to disturb all the company. He could not endure any ordinances or worship &c. and when they arrived at one of the Eleutheria Islands, and were intended there to settle, he made such a faction, as enforced captain Sayle to remove to another island, and being near the harbour, the ship struck and was cast away. The persons were all saved, save one, but all their provisions and goods were lost, so as they were forced (for divers months) to lie in the open air, and to feed upon such fruits and wild creatures as the island afforded. But finding their strength to decay, and no hope of any relief, captain Sayle took a shallop and eight men, and with such provisions as they could get, and set sail, hoping to attain either the Summers Islands, or Virginia, or New England; and so it pleased the Lord to favour them, that in nine days they arrived in Virginia, their provisions all spent &c. Those of the church relieved them, and furnished them with a bark and provisions to return to relieve their company left in Eleutheria. Captain Sayle, finding the church in this state, persuaded them to remove to Eleutheria, which they began to listen unto; but after they had seen a copy of his commission and articles &c. (though he undertook to them, that the company in England would alter any thing they should desire, yet) they paused upon it (for the church were very orthodox and zealous for the truth) and would not resolve before they had received advice from us. Whereupon letters were returned to them, dissuading them from joining with that people under those terms.[1]

[Large Blank.]

(9) 2.] Here arrived a Dutch hoy of about 30 tons, with cordage and other goods, seven men in her. She came from the Isle of Wight hither in five weeks.

18.] One Bezaleel [2]Payton of the church of Boston, coming from Barbados in a vessel of 60 tons, was taken with a great storm of wind and rain at east in the night, between Cape Cod and the bay, so as he was forced to put out two anchors; but the storm increasing, they were put from their anchors, and seeing no way but death before their eyes, they commended themselves to the Lord, who delivered them marvellously, for they were carried among Conyhasset rocks, yet touched none of them, and put on shore upon a beach, and presently there came a mighty sea, which lifted their vessel over the beach into a smooth water, and after the storm was over, they used means, and gate her safe out.

The like example of the blessing of prayer fell out not long after in saving a small open vessel of ours, wherein was one Richard [3]Collicut of the church of Dorchester, who being eastward about trading was carried by a violent storm among the rocks, where they could find no place to get out. So they went to prayer, and

---

1 Hubbard 522-4, with very trifling qualifications, copies all this statement about the church of Virginia, and its invitation to Eleutheria; but of Durand, Sayle, Copeland or Butler he adds no information, and but this little of Harrison: "Mr. Harrison tarried a year or two in New England, and then went to England, and at last settled in Ireland, having taken the degree of a doctor; but what became of the church of Virginia or the planters of Eleutheria, there was no certain report, but it is to be feared they were so nipped in the bud, they never flourished much afterwards." Johnson, Lib. III. c. 11 mentions Harrison, and Copeland, and Durand, but his remarks about Virginia are very curious.

2 Bezaleel Payton's Inventory, Vol. II. 56, was taken 21 (9) 1651. Our records show birth of daughters, Sarah 9 (6) 1643, and Mary 7 (3) 1646. I believe he had a son of the same christian name.

3 Collicot was early settled there, see 2 Hist. Coll. VIII. 231, and the records of that town mention birth of Experience, daughter of him and Thomasin his wife, 29 (7) 1641, and of Dependence, their son, 5 (5) 1643. A former wife, Joanna, died 5 (6) 1640. He removed, after some years, to Boston, where the records contain entry of birth of his son, Ebenezer 6 September 1659. But I believe there were other children, and one of them was named, I think, Mary, and another, Preserved. He lived long, for his will, contained in our Prob. Rec. XI. 17-18, was made 23 April 1686, and proved 26 August after. In it he mentions his lands on the Merrimack, at Dunstable, given by the colony, and others on the Kennebeck, purchased of the Indians and English.

presently there came a great sea, and heaved their vessel over into the open sea, in a place between two rocks.

11, (11.) About eight persons were drowned this winter, all by adventuring upon the ice, except three, whereof two (one of them being far in drink) would needs pass from Boston to Winisemett in a small boat and a tempestuous night. This man (using to come home to Winisemett drunken) his wife would tell him, he would one day be drowned &c. but he made light of it. Another went aboard a ship to make merry the last day at night, (being the beginning of the Lord's day,) and returning about midnight with three of the ship's company, the boat was overset by means of the ice, they guiding her by a rope, which went from the ship to the shore. The seamen waded out, but the Boston man was drowned, being a man of good conversation and hopeful of some work of grace begun in him, but drawn away by the seamen's invitation. God will be sanctified in them that come near him. Two others were the children of one of the church of Boston. While their parents were at the lecture, the boy, (being about seven years of age,) having a small staff in his hand, ran down upon the ice towards a boat he saw, and the ice breaking, he fell in, but his staff kept him up, till his sister, about fourteen years old, ran down to save her brother (though there were four men at hand, and called to her not to go, being themselves hasting to save him) and so drowned herself and him also, being past recovery ere the men could come at them, and could easily reach ground with their feet. The parents had no more sons, and confessed they had been too indulgent towards him, and had set their hearts over much upon him.

This puts me in mind of another child very strangely drowned a little before winter. The parents were also members of the church of Boston. The father had undertaken to maintain the mill-dam, and being at work upon it, (with some help he had hired,) in the afternoon of the last day of the week, night came upon them before they had finished what they intended, and his conscience began to put him in mind of the Lord's day, and he was troubled, yet went on and wrought an hour within night. The next day, after evening exercise, and after they had supped, the mother put two children to bed in the room where themselves did lie, and they went out to visit a neighbour. When they returned, they continued about an hour in the room, and missed not the child, but then the mother going to the bed, and not finding her youngest child, (a daughter about five years of age,) after much search she found it drowned in a well in her cellar; which was very observable, as by a special hand of God, that the child should go out of that room into another in the dark, and then fall down at a trap door, or go down the stairs, and so into the well in the farther end of the cellar, the top of the well and the water being even with the ground. But the father, freely in the open congregation, did acknowledge it the righteous hand of God for his profaning his holy day against the checks of his own conscience.[1]

---

1 Here ends the MS. history of the venerable father of Massachusetts. As my notes have been abundant, beyond measure, I shall be excused readily from any such service as portraying his character. He died, Hobart's Diary says, on 26 March, being Monday, about noon, and was buried on Tuesday 3 April, 1649. The notices from the colony records will, I hope, be acceptable:

In the first volume of the deputies acts, which I call Vol. III. page 221, on 7 May, 1649, "it was unanimously agreed and voted that two hundred pounds should be given to the infant of our late honoured governour John Winthrop, Esquire, out of the next country levy."

In the doings of the other branch, Vol. II. 234 is this vote: "Forasmuch as our late honoured governour upon his death bed did express his tender desires towards his wife and youngest child, that if the country did think meet to bestow upon him any thing for his service done, that it should be to the said child, and remain in the hands of his wife for its education, and the stock preserved entire for the child's use, and forasmuch as the court hath not provided for the disposing of that estate in case of the death of the child, the court doth conceive it just, that in case the infant dies before it attain the age of 21 years, the one third part thereof should accrue to the widow of our late honoured governour, and the other two thirds, one third to Mr. Deane Winthrop, and the other to Mr. Samuel Winthrop, they as yet having had no portions out of the late governour's estate, nor like to have."

This infant was, as our first church records show, "baptised 17 (10) 1648, being about five days old." He was son of the fourth wife, though Mather, nor any other writer I have ever seen, had not any knowledge of such an union. The paternal regard of the colony was ineffectual. Our town records mention, that "Joshua Winthrop, youngest son of the late Mr. John Winthrop, Esquire, died 11 (11) 1651."

Mather says, Winthrop was born on June 12, 1587, and though he has more correctly given the date of his death, yet one of his enigmatical sentences, about the coming of the "grand climacterical," has made most of his successors represent the year of our author's age, when he died, as the sixty-third. It is plain enough, from the record mentioned Vol. I, 63, that he was 61 years, 2 months, and 14 days old, having been born 12 January, 1588.

I was once asked by a descendant of gov. Winthrop, since deceased, whether his ancestor had, probably, received news of the beheading of his old master, Charles I. The reply was not prompt, but I have now before me a letter of Roger Williams "to his honoured kind friend, Mr. John Winthrop at Nameag," that is lettered on the back "Mr. Williams of the high news about the king," from which it is very evident that our chief magistrate was spared that distress. Its date is Narragansett 26 3. 1649, of course two months after the governour's death. He says: "Sir, tidings are high from England; many ships from many parts say, and a Bristol ship come to the Isle of Shoals within few days confirms, that the king and many great lords and parliament men are beheaded: London was shut up on the day of execution, not a door to be opened &c. The States of Holland and the Prince of Orange (forced by them) consented to proceedings; It is said Mr. Peters preached (after the fashion of England) the funeral sermon to the king after sentence out of the terrible denunciation to the king of Babylon, Is. 14, 18, &c."

ADDENDA.

There are appended to each of the three MS. volumes of Governour Winthrop's History certain memoranda in his hand writing, some of which are sufficiently important for publication. It is very evident that he designed most of them for publication, because two or three paragraphs, in the regular sequence of the history, are distinguished by marginal annotations directing them to be transferred to the other end. Such articles are now inserted with the others in the ends of the several MSS. Of these the two articles, in the beginning of the first volume, are directions to make a strong boat, and to cover a house, which, however valuable in that time, may now seem unnecessary. At the other end of the first volume, the earliest writing is a citation of several passages of scripture. The next page is here copied :

December 7, 1630.] I have in all 15 cows and [illegible], whereof 5 are my brother Downing's, marked on the left horn with the brand of a [illegible]. Two of these cows I bought of the company; one at [blank] and the other at [blank].

I have also 14 she goats, whereof 3 I bought of the company at 30 shillings a piece. There be two wether goats here, not yet divided.

I have 2 sows bought from Plimouth.

I had more, of Kingsbury one cow, and of Lamb (which he could not pay for) one cow, and of Mr. Johnson's 9 cows, 2 at Boston, and of Mr. *Huysons* one brought to Boston.

I received more, of Mr. Allerton for my brother D. 5 heifers, which have a knotting in one horn, and 3 for Mr. Haynes, which have their tails tipped at the end.

Next is this remark :

The agreement for the Arbella *L*.750, whereof to be paid in hand [blank] the rest upon certificate of our safe arrival.

Agreed with [Thomas] Keene of Southwark, baker, for 20,000 of biscuit, 15,000 of brown, and 5,000 of white.

Next,

Mr. Stretton of Eastcheap, butcher, agreed with for beef at 19 shillings the cwt. for pork at 20 pence the stone, neats tongues at 14 pence a piece.

The sides of beef, being 29 sides, with 50 pieces of Mr. Beecher's beef, weighed 79,,2,,15 (cwt. q. lb.). The beef is in 15 hogsheads, the shanks in one hogshead, and the necks with 16 pieces of pork in a tierce, and are marked as followeth. Beef, No. 1 to 15 con-

cwt. q. lb.
taining &c. Pork 6 hogsheads weighing in all 28. 2. 23, Salt for all this viz.

White salt,	$16\frac{1}{2}$	bushels,	*L*2. 6.8
Spanish salt,	13	bushels,	2.12.0
Bay salt,	3	bushels,	13.6

The charge of salting *L*.2.11.2. 5.12.2

Next follows a catalogue, I presume, of those who in February designed to come over, and of whom the greater part embarked and arrived It is probable, the author designed by spaces between the columns to distinguish the passengers in the several ships; but I cannot detect his distribution perfectly. Perhaps the last names in the second column are not of persons designing to embark, but only of proprietors.

Sir Rich. Saltonstall,
Mr. Johnson,
Mr. Winthrop,
Mr. Dudley,
Mr. Coddington,
Mr. Ludlow,
Mr. Bradstreet,
Mr. Rossiter,
Mr. Pincheon,
Mr. Vassall,
Mr. Sharpe,
Mr. Burrow,
Mr. Brand,
Colburne,
Lockwood,
Sergeant,
Warren,
Firmin,
Sterne,
Cuttin,
Wood,
Hen. Kingsbury,
Thos. Kingsbury,
Hawke,
Weed,
Page,
Hutchinson,
Finch,
Raynold,
Mr. Revell,
Mr. Dutton,
Mr. [blank],
Mr. Wilson.

Mr. Fines,
Mr. Humfry.,
Mr. Pelham,
Mr. Hen. Winthrop,
Mr. Sam. Dudley,
Mr. Palgrave,
Mr. Gager,
Mr. Ball,
Johnson,
Richardson,
Child,
Pond,
Mr. Burrows,
Mr. Hosier,
Mr. Parke,
Hodson,
Lambe,
Goffe,
Nicoles,
Mr. Wade,

Sir Wm. Brereton,
Mr. Cradock,
Mr. Downing,
Mr. Rowe,
Mr. Webb,
Mr. [blank.]

Salter.

2 ministers.
Mr. Hoffe.
Ro. Cole.
John Cole.
Simpson.
Sale.
Bolston.
Penn.
John Ruggle.
Milles.
Waterbury.
Jef. Ruggles.
Hawkins.
Gosnold.
Hammond.
Reeder.
Redby.

The next three pages are occupied with plans for a house and offices, and for forts, of which the latter seem to be of a later date than the body of the work, perhaps drawn by the second John Winthrop.

Next comes:

A note of provisions set down for the ship Arbella for her voyage, 1629, by Mr. Beecher.

42 tons of beer,
10 M of bread,
16 hogsheads of beef, neat,
600 of haberdyne,
40 bushels of peas,
30 bushels of oatmeal,
11 firkins of butter,
3 way of cheese,
14 tons of water cask,
1 hogshead of vinegar,
2 hogsheads of cider,
1½ bushels of mustard seed,
1 barrel of flour,
100 weight of suet,
1 barrel of salt,
8 M of burning wood,
6 dozen of candles.

The cook's store.
100 platters,
4 trays,
2 wooden bowls,
4 lanthorns,
4 pumps for water and beer,
3½ doz. of quarter cans,
3 doz. of small cans,
13 doz. of wooden spoons,
3½ doz. bread baskets,
3½ doz. mustard dishes,
2½ doz. butter dishes,
3 or 4 doz. trenchers,
1 doz. cod lines,
3 doz. of codhooks,
½ doz. mackerel lines,
1½ doz. mackerel hooks,
12 leads,
6 small leads.

Next follows a circular perpetual calendar for each day of the week, month and year, much like such as are now common.

Next follows large instruction for making salt petre, and then a receipt for making gunpowder with minute particulars.

Next a small chart of Cape Ann, which is of no value, but the remarks shows the author's diligence in observation:

About the E. point of Cape Ann lie 3 or 4 islands, which appear above water, and a ledge of rocks under water lyeth to the eastward of the bigger E. island, which ridge stretcheth about half a mile to the E. but a mile or two to the S. of the said islands is deep water above 30 fathoms. The most northeast of all the said islands is a small rock, bare, without weed or aught upon it; the rest have shrubs. Within 5 or 6 leagues of Cape Ann are store of mackerel. The Isles of Shoals are woody.

The addenda at the beginning of the second volume are as follows:

Gifts bestowed upon the colony since 1634.

1635. Dec. 10.] Denis Geere of Sagus gave by his will (at the motion of Mr. Hugh Peter) *L*.300.

Mr. Robert Houghton of Southwark, brewer, and others, gave to this colony, at the motion of Captain Underhill, 10 barrels powder.

John Allen of Surslingham, minister, in Norfolk, gave *L*.25 to the treasury, sent by Thomas Fisher of Winton.

Sir Simonds Dewes, Knight, gave a debt of one Hannel of *L*.30, but only *L*.10 could be gotten.

Mr. [blank] Freeman of Sagus gave 20 corslets.

Brampton Gurdon, Esq.	*L*.10,	Bestowed in 5 sheets of lead for the Castle at the island. Mr. Tyng gave the freight in the William and John 9ber. 1636.
Sir William Spring, Knight,	*L*. 5,	
Emanuel Downing, Esq.	50*s*.	
Mr. Smith, a tailor, London,	50*s*.	

Mr. Graves of Lynn gave near *L*.300 left to Mr. Peters' order.

[A pen is drawn through this last sentence, and I cannot be certain of the benefactor's name.]

About *L*.500 procured in London by Mr. Welde, Mr. Peter &c. and sent in goods.

Mr. Parker, of Weymouth, his brother *L*.300, *L*.50 to Mr. Parker and Mr. Stone their disposing.

Mr. Harvard gave to the college about *L*.800.

Mr. Richard Andrews gave many cattle, by Mr. Humfry, and *L*.544 by Mr. Peter &c.

1641.] Mr. Welde and Mr. Peter &c. procured from Mr. Houghton, the king's brewer, and divers others *L*.500, which was bestowed in commodities &c.

After two blank pages, is added :

Mr. Thomas Graves, a member of Dorchester, and a very understanding man, would needs leave the church, and go to Virginia against all counsel &c. He and his wife and divers of his children died, and his whole family was ruined about a year after. Only one daughter escaped, who, being left a maid with a good estate, married after to that apostate, Nathaniel Eaton, who, having spent all she had, fled away, and left her miserable, 1646.

At the other end of the same volume, the four first papers, being a form of a warrant to the constable to call together the freemen of his town to choose deputies to the next general court, a form of a warrant to give notice of the court of elections, a form of a commission for marriages "to be duly, lawfully and solemnly accomplished," and a form of marriage contract, may all be omitted.

Next follows this memorandum :

This clause was put in beneath the warrant for the general court of elections, 1639, viz.

Upon conference with others of the magistrates, it is thought fit to give notice that there will be need of a supply of the number of assistants, for which end it may be of use to name to the freemen some of those of best note amongst us, (as Mr. D. of S. Mr. H. of C. Mr. S. of J. &c.) not with intent to lead their choice in these, or to divert it from any other, but only to propound them to consideration, (which any freeman may do,) and so leave them to use their liberty according to their consciences. This was looked at by the people as dangerous to their liberty, and therefore they would choose none of these.

After by order of court [blank] the court of elections was to assemble without warrant.

From the next article the relation between state and church will partly appear:

To the constable of Salem.

Whereas we are credibly informed, that divers persons, (both men and women,) within your town, do disorderly assemble themselves both upon the Lord's day and at other times, and contemptuously refusing to come to the solemn meetings of the church there, (or being some of them justly cast out,) do obstinately refuse to submit themselves, that they might be again received; but do make conventions and seduce divers persons of weak capacity, and have already withdrawn some of them from the church, and thereby have caused much (not only disturbance in the church, but also) disorder and damage in the civil state, so as if they be suffered to go on, your town is like to be deserted of many of the chief and most useful members, to the great dishonour of God; these are therefore to require you forthwith to repair unto all such disordered persons, (taking assistance of two or three honest neighbours,) and signify unto them that their said course is very offensive to the government here, and may no longer be suffered, and therefore command them from us to refrain all such disordered assemblies and pretended church meetings, and either to confine themselves to the laws and orders of this government, being established according to the rule of God's word, or else let them be assured, that we shall by God's assistance take some such strict and speedy course for the reformation of these disorders and preventing the evils which may otherwise ensue, as our duty to God and charge over this people do call for from us. And when you have given them this admonition, you shall diligently attend how it is observed, and certify us accordingly, as you will answer your neglect herein at your peril.

H. Vane, Gov'r.
Jo. Winthrop, Dept.
Tho. Dudley.

From Boston this 30 of the 3 month, 1636.

All the following articles seem to have regular sequence of time.

1636, mo. 4. 2.] Governour and council and assistants heard the cause between Richard Beggerly and his wife, who had been here six years, and he in England. She charged him with adultery &c and so great were the presumptions, as though we held them not sufficient to ground a divorce upon, yet we ordered he should remain separate from her till she might send into England for further proof, and appointed him twenty shillings from her to set him to work &c.

16.] The governour with consent of Mr. Dudley gave warrant to lieutenant Morris to spread the king's colours at Castle Island, when the ships passed by. It was done at the request of the masters of the ten ships, which were then here, yet with this protestation, that we held the cross in the ensign idolatrous, and therefore might not set it up in our own ensigns; but this being kept as the king's fort, the governour and some others were of opinion, that his own colours might be spread upon it. The colours were given us by captain Palmer, and the governour in requital sent him three beaver skins. But the deputy allowed not of this distinction.

16th of the 4th mo.] To lieutenant Howe of Sagus, and to the military officers and company there. Whereas we have formerly given you command of the trained band in Sagus, we do hereby require you to see them duly exercised according to the orders of court, and we do also require you, the military company there, that you diligently attend with your complete arms at such times and places as your said lieutenant shall appoint, and that all you, the officers and soldiers of the said company, be obedient to all such commands as by authority of this place or order from us you shall receive from him, so as you may be well trained and fitted for such future service as you may be called unto; hereof not to fail.

Hen. Vane, Gov'r.
Jo. Winthrop, Dept.

18.] We granted Mr. Palmer a demi-culverin in exchange for a sacre of Mr. Walton's, which was ready mounted at Castle Island, being by the opinion of Mr. Peirce and some others better for us than the demi-culverin. We had 100 wt. of shot and some *wires* and spunges into the bargain.

21.] One of the seamen of the ship Prudence being at Mr. *Longs* at Charlestown stole a beaver skin. He was apprehended and kept all night in the bolts, and next morning being brought before us, we ordered him to make double restitution, viz. 20*s*.

H. Vane, Gov'r.
J. W. Dept.

28.] The governour and John Winthrop returned a letter of thanks to Mr. Robert Houghton of Southwark, brewer, and Mr. Wm. Hiccock &c. for ten barrels of gunpowder, which they sent to this colony the last year upon the motion of captain Underhill.

30.] Warrant to the constable of Dorchester to inventory and appraise the rigging &c. of the bark Warwick, cast away &c. until some came to demand them, or till further order &c.

By advice with other of the assistants, we ordered, that the present sent us by the Pequott should be forthwith returned, as being the price of blood.

Mo. 5. 14.] Nic. Simpkin brought before the governour and John Winthrop for braving the lieutenant Morris, and telling him in public, that he lied &c. He confessed the words, but refused to acknowledge it a fault, or to ask his pardon in the mercate place. So we committed him.

16.] Upon his submission and acknowledgment, that he had done ill, we took his bond in twenty pounds, to appear at the next court, and left him at liberty. Besides he was ill, and we feared he would grow distracted &c.

21.] John Newgate brought John *Gurney*, his apprentice, before us. He had gotten away his indentures. So we ordered, he should serve him till he were 24 years of age, viz. for 3 years from the 29 of 7ber next.

Walter Palmer sworn constable of Charlestown.

28.] Sebastian Paulmin brought over by Nic. Simpkin and upon a covenant of his to bind him with Mr. Robert Keayne for ten years, but because it appeared to us by the witness of Mr. Jeyner, that Nic. Simpkin being his uncle had no power to put him apprentice, and for that Mr. Keayne had disbursed money about him, we ordered that the country should pay him his money (Mr. Simpkin having long promised it, but not paid it) and so dispose of him till we heard from his mother.

Warrant to the constables of Watertown &c. at Connecticut to seize and inventory Mr. Oldham's goods for payment of his debts &c.

Mo. 6. 8.] Lieutenant Edward Gibbons and John Higginson with one to attend them, and some Massachusetts Indians, were sent to Canonicus and Miantinomoh to treat with them about justice to be done upon those who were guilty of the murder of John Oldham.

9.] The deputy granted license to [blank] Andrews of Ipswich to sell wine by retail for six months, provided he did not wittingly sell to such as were like to abuse it by drunkenness.

11. [Blank] a boy of Mr. Oldham's, whom he bought of

[blank] for *L.*8, we restored to his old master for *L.*4, in regard he had no clothes, and had spent the most of the summer with Mr. Oldham &c.

12.] John White, merchant, *L.*10, to appear at next court to answer for drunkenness &c.

22.] John Newgate sworn constable of Boston for a year.

7. 3.] Mr. William Pincheon took the oath of assistant.

22.] Ezekiah Holle entertained to serve at Castle Island for a year at *L.*10 per annum.

24.] Mr. Jones *L.*10 to appear at next court for drunkenness.

29.] Edward Grove entertained to serve at the fort from the 24 of July at *L.*10 per annum.

Richard Paul entertained for the same from this day at *L.*10 per annum.

Thomas Tredwell *L.*20 to appear at next court for misdemeanour &c. Mr. Hill prosecutes.

8ber. 13.] Serjeant Willard appointed to exercise the military company at Concord.

Vincent Potter entertained to serve at the fort for one year at *L.*10 wages.

18.] Thomas Gilbert brought before us. He was drunk at Serjeant Baulston's, and the constable being sent for, he struck him. He was kept in the prison all night, and next day his father, John Gilbert and his brother John Gilbert of Dorchester undertook in *L.*40 that John Gilbert the younger would appear at court to answer for him and perform the order of the court &c. The reason was, for that he was to go into England presently, and not known to have been any way disordered, and was his father's oldest son, who was a grave honest gentleman &c. They did undertake also, that he should acknowledge his fault openly to the constable &c.

9. 10.] Alice Benfield, an orphan of the age of three years, being left upon the charge of the country, (her parents dying ere they were settled &c.) was put apprentice to Emanuel White of Watertown and Katharine, his wife, for fifteen years, and in consideration of *L.*10 to be paid to him by the treasurer (for which he had warrant) they are to educate her as their own child during her minority, and after to employ and maintain her as a servant during the rest of the term; and if she die within these twelve months, he is to repay so much of the money, as we shall judge equal.

11.] Robert [blank] a freeman is bound in *L.*5 to appear at next court at Boston to answer for drunkenness.

19.] *Letters* to John Cogan ad colligenda bona Daniel Norcott, who went in the Pied Cow last year, and not heard of.

Wm. Sanders, carpenter, sent to me by the governour, and Mr. Bellingham came with him, and having agreed before the governour, that, to satisfy the debt which he owed to Mr. Bellingham and Mr. Gibbins, he should serve them for three years, with this proviso, that if at any time he should satisfy so much as should remain of their several debts, that then the governour and council or any two of them might set him free.

12. 4.] Willington is to bring in his man to the next court to answer for stealing stuff, being a tailor &c. His master promised to give satisfaction &c.

1637.] 2. 13.] Edward Mellhouse sworn constable of Charlestown.

28.] Being about full moon, about ten of the clock in the evening, in a clear sky, a perfect moon was seen about a flight shoot northerly from the true moon. It was seen so about half an hour, and then vanished with dim flashings. It was more dim than the true moon.

3. 11.] Anderson, master of a small pinnace, coming by our fort, stood out three shot before he would come to an anchor; and then three of our men going aboard him, he weighed and carried them to Boston, and used braving speeches. We sent for him and committed him, and the next day took security for his appearance at the next court, and ordered him to pay for the powder and shot &c.

22.] Math. Bridge, for killing, by careless discharging a pistol at Concord, one John Abbot, John Bridge his father of Newton undertook in *L*.40 for his appearance at next court.

4. 12.] Nathan Bircher and Philip Squance, taken vagrant at Muddy river, and having taken away Mr. Mayhew's skiff, and divers things at the governour's garden, Mr. Bellingham and myself caused them to be whipped and sent home.

5. 3.] Henry Wood, a seaman in Mr. Tillet his ship, brought by the constable of Charlestown, and Mr. Nowell with him, for suspicion of ravishing Ann Brakerbourne, a child of nine years of age. The child said, he did lie upon her, and did hurt her; and one Thomas Sheepy, hearing a child cry, went towards the place, and saw the said Henry arise from off her. But her mother and those who searched the child found no signs, whereby it might appear, that any act had been committed. We committed the *fellow* to prison, and after whipped him.

3.] Rich. Serle, servant to Elias Parkman of Dorchester, charged with giving his master insolent speeches, for which he taking up a stick to correct him, he ran within him, and laid violent hands upon him, which he confessed, and it was witnessed by Thomas Millet, who was present &c. and it appeared to have been his manner before. Mr. *Bellingham* consenting, he was whipped.

20.] John Hobby, brought before me by the constable of Dorchester, confesseth that about fourteen days since, lying at Sam. Cole's, he saw beaver bound up in a bag there, whereof he took two skins and a half, (the beaver was Phil. White's,) which he carried to Mr. Cutting's ship, and put it away there for twenty-four shillings, (it weighed four and a half pounds,) but he denies that he took any more. But after he confessed he had three skins more, which he laid in the backside.

6. 15.] Richard Knight of Weymouth undertook for Robert Corbin, master of the Speedwell, to appear at the next court to answer the action of Edward Wyatt, and to abide the order of the court.

7. 25.] James Penn and Edward Bendall of Boston did bind themselves, their heirs and executors, to pay unto the treasurer within three months forty pounds for the fine of Stephen Greensmith.

[Marks are drawn across this paragraph, but it is evident that it was designed by the author only to express the discharge of the obligation, for in the margin is written :]

Paid by *L.*20 in wampom and *L.*20 by debt to Robert Saltonstall.

William Tuttle of Charlestown five pounds to prosecute suit against Robert Shorthose next court at Newtown for unlawful impounding his mare.

8. 19.] John Dotteris brought before me by Edward Andrews at the complaint of Henry Larmore. He was apprentice to Mr. Taylor of London, and sent by him in a ship to Virginia, and there fell sick, and left with Mr. *Letherbee* to take care of him &c. He employs him in a bark hither. The boy goeth to his mother, the wife of the said Andrews, so as finding that Mr. *Letherbee* had no power to send him apprentice, his mother entreats us the last term, and so I wrote to Mr. *Letherbee* that the boy remains with her.

Job Tiler, servant to Richard Baldwin of Mount Wollaston, brought before me, and the treasurer, secretary &c. He confessed he did attempt to have carnal knowledge of the body of Jane, the daughter of the said Richard, two times, but could not. Women had searched her, and found no act committed. We committed him to prison &c.

21.] John Stringer, servant to Mrs. Knight, brought before me and the deputy and secretary for divers miscarriages towards his mistress and Mr. Stoughton, and for running away &c. We caused him to be whipped.

9. 28.] The governour and treasurer, by order of the general court, did demise to Edward Converse the ferry between Boston and Charlestown, to have the sole transporting of passengers and cattle from one side to the other, for three years from the first day of the next month, for the yearly rent of forty pounds to be paid quarterly to the treasurer: Provided that he see it be well attended and furnished with sufficient boats; and that so soon as may be in the next spring he set up a convenient house on Boston side, and keep a boat there, as need shall require. And he is allowed to take his wonted fees, viz. 2d. for a single person, and pence a piece, if there be more than one, as well on lecture days as at other times; and for every horse and cow with the man which goeth with them 6d. and for a goat 1d. and a swine 2d. And if any shall desire to pass, before it be light in the morning, or after it is dark in the evening, he may take recompence answerable to the season and his pains and hazard, so it be not excessive. Edward Converse.[1]

1638. 1. 30.] Edward Seale of Marblehead twenty pounds for his wife's appearance when she shall be called for after her delivery.

2. 30.] Anne, ux. Richard Walker, being cast out of the church of Boston for intemperate drinking from one inn to another and for light and wanton behaviour, was the next day called before the governour and the treasurer, and convict by two witnesses upon oath of the same misdemeanour, and was stripped naked one shoulder, and tied to the whipping post; but because she was with child, her punishment was respited.

6. 28.] In my letter to Mr. Hooker, I complain of three things:

1. That they told the Narragansetts, that they were not tied to the agreement we made with the Indians; and that they did this, to advance their own reputation with the Indians, and to abase ours; that it was a point of state policy in them not to dissent, while the war was at their doors, for they had need of our help &c. that it was done without any pressing occasion; that it was

---

1 This is an original signature of the lessee, however strange the place may seem in the middle of a page in the history, where is written, "this should have been put in the other end." By our colony records I. 80, I learn, that Converse had, 14 June, 1631, "undertaken to set up a ferry betwixt Charlton and Boston, for which he is to have 2d. for every single person, and 1d. a piece, if there be two or more."

done unseasonably, after their own commissoners had propounded that before the Indians we should in all things appear as one.

2. That they altered the articles of confederation in the most material point, and all because some preeminence was therein yielded to the Massachusetts, and being again agreed, (only referred to consent &c.) in three months we had no answer from them; that the way which they would have taken, of referring differences to the churches, would occasion infinite trouble and expense, and yet leave the issue to the sword.

I expostulated about the unwarrantableness and unsafeness of referring matter of counsel or judicature to the body of the people, quia the best part is always the least, and of that best part the wiser part is always the lesser. The old law was, choose ye out judges &c. and thou shalt bring the matter to the judge &c.

3. That they did still exercise jurisdiction at Agawam, though one of their commissioners disclaimed to intermeddle in our line, and thither we challenged our right, and it was agreed so, and I had wrote to them to desire them to forbear until &c. that Mr. Pincheon had small encouragement to be under them; that if his relation were true, I could not see the justice of their proceeding against him &c.

That the end of my writing to him was, that he might help quench these sparks of contention; that I did open our grievances to him in their most true and reasonable intendment; that though I be strict for our right in public, quia their magistrates are so, yet I am willing to listen to advice, and my aim is the common good.

Nothing is found worth transcription in the addenda of the third volume.

APPENDIX.

A 65.

My good Son,

The comfortable season God was pleased to send after thy departure from us, and the fair S. E. wind the last day of the week, gives me hope, that you are all safe arrived at your new habitation. Upon the said last day of the week at evening here came in captain Hawkins in a ship of 220 tons, set forth by one Mr. Roberts a merchant of London. Her lading is linen, woollen, shoes, stockings &c. and 40 tons of coal, and is bound from hence to Malago. Captain Hawkins is commander of her. Here came no more in her but my sister, Peter, (who is now as she used to be,) and Mr. Clerk. Your brother hath again sent for his wife, and it seems means to stay in England with his brother Rainsborow, who is governour of Worcester, and he is captain of a troop of horse. The army intended for Ireland is put off. I suppose it is upon the king's refusing to comply with the parliament, which is all the news we have, except that that the sickness began to spread much in London. I send you herein your letters, which I thought best to open least there might be any occasion from them to write back by this next ship. We are all as you left us, I praise God. We all salute you and all yours. The blessing of the Lord be upon you, and he protect and guide you in this great undertaking. Farewell.

Your loving father,
JO. WINTHROP.

26 (8) 46.

To my very good son, Mr. Jo. Winthrop,
at Fisher's Island, near Pequod River.

A 66.

My good Son,

I received your letter &c. from Rhode Island, and returned another to you by Mr. Cowley; and having another opportunity by captain Malbone, I thought fit to write again. We bless God for the good hope we have of your safe arrival at your own place, which we much desire a further confirmation of. We all continue in health as you left us (blessed be God). Waitstill is with our sister Truesdale. They make much of him, and he likes so well, as he desires no change. Mary is with goodwife Child. They are in love with her, and she likes them well. Betty and Luce are still with us. John Robertson (I hope) is come to you; he went hence a week after you in C. Dunham's vessel. I purpose to write to your brother Stephen, and press him to satisfy those two debts. The Rainbow went hence the 10th of this present with eighty passengers; but Mr. Peters is resolved to go by Malago with captain Hawkins. Major Bourne's ship will be ready within this fourteen days. Here arrived yesterday a Dutch ship of 300 tons, with 250 tons of salt, sent by Mr. Onge from Lisbon, so as salt was abated in a few hours from 36 to 16 a hogshead. We look at it as a singular providence and testimony of the Lord's care of us. Mr. Haynes is come safe to us, but in great danger to have perished in the tempest, but that beyond expectation, wandering in the night, God brought him to an empty wigwam, where they found two fires burning and wood ready for use. There they were kept two nights and a day, the storm continuing so long with them, with much snow as well as rain. Mrs. Peters went three days since to Salem, and Mrs. Mary Fenwick and Mrs. Lake and her daughter with her. This is all the news I can impart. It was to admiration, that in such a tempest (than which I never observed a greater) so little harm was done, and no person hurt. At Salem the lady Moody's house being a flat roof and but nine feet high, the roof was taken off, and so much of the chimney as was above it, and carried in two parts six or eight rods off. Ten persons lay under it, and knew not of it till they arose in the morning. I had thought we should only have declared our apprehensions concerning the petition, without questioning the petitioners, but the deputies called upon it, whereupon Mr. Fowle was forced to put in bond to answer &c. and the rest being called, did presently appeal to the parliament &c. so as we are like to proceed to some censure for their appeal, if not for the petition. I have no more at present, but commend you and my good daughter and your children and Deane and all your company in your plantation (whom I desire to salute) to the gracious protection and blessing of the Lord. I rest your loving father.

Your mother, brother and sister salute you all.

JO. WINTHROP.

Boston, 16 (9) 46.

To my loving son Mr. Jo. Winthrop, *at Fisher's Island near Pequod river, d'd.*

A 67.

My good Son,

I HAVE written two letters to you, one by Wm. Cowley, and the other by New Haven. I received your letter from Rhode Island, and do bless God for your safety so far, and the hope of your safe arrival at Fisher's Island. I think very long to hear certainly from you, for the tempest was most violent Some hurt was done here, especially by the tide the second day after, which was the greatest we ever had; much fish and salt lost at eastward, and terrible loss thereabout as is feared. We are all in health, I praise God. Wait is with sister Truesdale, and Mary at sister Child's. This gentleman, Mr. Malbone, can inform you of all, or in my other letters you may meet with more. So with your mother's and brother and sister's salutes to yourself and wife and children and Deane, I commend thee to the precious blessing of the Lord.

Your loving father,

JO. WINTHROP.

19 (9) 46.

To my loving son Mr. Jo. WINTHROP, *at Fisher's Island,*

A 68.

My good Son,

To your last by Willys I returned answer by the Indians who came with them, together with letters to Mr. Eaton enclosed, which (I hope) you have sent away before this; and from them, it is like, you will hear of the time of the commissioners' meeting here before us. For such things as have befallen us here, in the wreck of a new pinnace bound for Barbados two months since with nine persons in her, whereof Mr. Stoughton's son was one, and Mr Ruck's another, and the taking of our trading ship at Cape Sable by Mr. D'Aulney to the value of *L.*1000 &c.

Here came in this morning a ship from Virginia with captain Gookin and some others. She was bought by him [of] the governour there. She came out ten days since, and we hear by her, that Mr. Whiting's pinnace is safe there, and another of Connecticut.

Your mother hath been very ill lately, but (I praise God) she is upon recovery. Your brother Adam is like to lose *L.*60 by this ship that D'Aulney took. Thus the Lord is pleased to keep us under, and all in love, and for our good, that he may wean us from this world, and draw our hearts more after Christ Jesus and those riches which will endure to eternity.

I hear that Colonel Rainsborow is gone for Ireland, and, I fear, your brother Stephen is then gone with him. We shall hear no certainty till a ship come from England. Captain Harding arrived at Bristol 19 (10). They went from here 9 (9), and had a very tempestuous voyage, and were carried among the rocks at Scilly, where never ship came. Our pinnaces had very good receipts in the West Indies. I received letters by them from your brother Samuel. He is well (I praise God) and desires to be remembered to you. He writes that there was great loss in your brother's fish and corn; and that there was lately a great volcano in Palma, which brake out into seven fires, and they saw them every night at Teneriffe, which is sixty miles distant, and the ashes were blown thither in their faces. He sent some of them to me. It melted the stones &c. so as they ran down like streams of molten lead. It threw forth mighty rocks, and let in the sea 300 fathom deep.

I hear that Unkas is much at Connecticut soliciting &c. Seeing he is your neighbour, I would wish you would not be averse to reconciliation with him, if they of Connecticut desire it. The wampom which he received for me never came to my hands, as I wrote you in my last.

Your neighbours refusing to help drive the cattle hath discharged Deane from coming at present. Your hogs will be lost or killed, for they lie in the neighbours' corn.

The receipt for ink [may be omitted].

We will see if a cooper can be had, but salt here is none now to be sold. You write not, whether you received the hogshead of salt I sent you by Captain Smith.

I can think of no more at present. Your mother and brother and sisters are at the garden. The Lord bless you and my good daughter and children. So I salute you all, and rest

Your loving father,

JO. WINTHROP.

14 (3) 47. Received May 22.

I send you a little box with my daughter's glasses. two are still behind. I could not bestow them. You write nothing about the stray mare. Gold's wife at Tenhills is dead.

To my very good son Mr. Jo. Winthrop, *at Nameage upon Pequod River, d'd.*

A 69.

My good Son,

I BLESS the Lord, and rejoice with thee in the safe delivery of my dear daughter, and the comfort of your little Martha. We find by frequent experience, that where the Lord withholds the ordinary means, he supplies with the greater blessing upon such as he affords us. I hope you will find the like gracious goodness, in spiritual blessings, upon such means as you can attain, until you may be supplied with a publick ministry. There were three hopeful young men commenced masters of arts this last commencement, one is schoolmaster at Concord, another at Hartford, and a third at [blank]. Your neighbour Lathrop came not at me (as I expected) to advise about it; but went away without taking leave &c. Only inquiring after him, I sent my letters to the house where he wrought, the day before his departure.

The auditor hath received the wampom, being but 88 fathom, and so small as no man will receive it by the penny &c. I shall acquaint the commissioners with what you write, and so leave it. The meeting is at Plimouth the first 5th of the (7). The last week we were at Salem, where they are all in health, and gave us very kind entertainment. Henry Pease, my old servant, died this day senight. Mrs. Bellingham was delivered of a daughter which died lately. The iron work goeth on with more hope. It yields now about 7 tons per week, but it is most out of that brown earth which lies under the bog mine. They tried another mine, and after 24 hours they had a sum of about 500, which when they brake, they conceived to be a 5th part silver. There is a grave man of good fashion come now over to see how things stand here. He is one who hath been exercised in iron works. I have no more at present, but my love and blessing to you all, yourself and my good daughter and all your children (little Martha also). My wife salutes you all. Your brothers and sisters &c. are all abroad. In haste farewell.

Your loving father,

JO. WINTHROP.

BOSTON, 14 (6) 48. Some two hours after I received yours.

To my good son Mr. Jo. WINTHROP, *at Pequod, d'd.*

A 70.

My good Son,

RETURNING this afternoon from Ipswich, I heard of this opportunity of writing to you, which I would not let slip. I have been ill of a fever these six weeks, yet (I praise God) I have been able to go abroad every day. At Ipswich they are all in health (God be praised). Your sister Symonds is delivered of a daughter. All the other magistrates being absent, save your brother Symonds, there was some necessity of my going, and (through God's mercy) it was not useless. The news out of England is very sad: all the counties are for the king, save Yorkshire. Kent raised about 20,000. The general went against them with about 10,000, and soon routed them. Cromwell is gone against them in the west, and carries all before him, and will give no quarter. Some ten or more of the parliament's ships revolted to the king.

Our news is sad at home also: God hath visited our family and taken from us your good sister Adam. She died at the garden. Divers young children die here. Our neighbour Sherman his daughter died this day. They are well at Salem, and your uncle is now beginning to distil. We have looked for you long. Mr. Endecott hath found a copper mine in his own ground. Mr. Leader hath tried it. The furnace runs 8 tons per week, and their bar iron is as good as Spanish. The adventurers in England sent over one Mr. Dawes to oversee Mr. Leader &c. but he is far short of Mr. Leader for &c. They could not agree, so he is returned by Teneriffe.

I can think of no more at present. I end with my blessing to you and my good daughter and all our children and my love to Mrs. Lake. My wife salutes you all. So I rest

Your loving father,

JO. WINTHROP.

30 (7) 48. Received Oct. 7.

To my good son Mr. Jo. Winthrop,
at Pequod, d'd.

A 71.

My good Son,

I received your letter by Mr. Brewster, and am glad to hear of the welfare of all your family. For that which you write about a minister, I understand by my brother Dudley, that his son D. finding that Mr. B. is offended with his teaching at the new town, is now resolved to remove, and if he have a call from your people and assurance of reasonable maintenance at present, and what likelihood of competency afterward, he will come to you. The messenger stays for this, therefore for other things I must refer you to my other letter by the Roxbury butcher. So with all our loving salutations to you all and mine own blessing I rest

Your loving father,

JO. WINTHROP.

16 (8) 48. Received Nov. 9.

To my good son Mr. Jo. Winthrop,
at Pequod, d'd.

A 72.

My good Son,

We have now received full and certain intelligence from England by Captain Hawkins's ship, (God was pleased to change his voyage and send him to heaven by the way.) I send you herewith some books, 13 in all. I received also a letter from your brother Stephen, who was in all those northern wars against the Scots, and (I perceive) did good service; and the Lord was graciously pleased to preserve him, that he was come safe to London 7 (7), and I hope his heart is with the Lord, for he writes christianly; and he and his wife sit down meekly under the Lord's correction in taking away their two children by the small pox at London, after they had been driven from Deal to Harwich and so to Ipswich and then to London for fear of Goring's army. I had letters also from your brother Samuel, who is married in Holland to a Dutch woman, and intends to come this way and so to Barbados.

Trerice his ship was taken in the Downs by the Prince and carried to Holland, with other merchants' ships, but there is hope of her recovery. Mr. Fenwick is made a colonel and governour of Tinmouth Castle. The books will tell you more. I am in much streights of time. The Lord bless you and all yours. My wife salutes you all. So I rest

Your loving father,

JO. WINTHROP.

7 (9) 48.

My brother Peter took the Duke of Hamilton prisoner.

I 1.

John Winthrop,

[seal.]

In the name of God, amen, this tenth day of May in the year of our Lord God 1620, and in the eighteenth year of the reign of our sovereign Lord King James of England &c. and of Scotland the 53, I, John Winthrop of Groton in the county of Suffolk, Esquire, being (I praise God) of sound mind and memory, and in good health of body, (upon serious consideration of the frailty and uncertainty of this momentary life, occasioned by the Lord's watchword, and frequent examples of such as I have observed to have been snatched away suddenly and in their best health and strength,) do make and declare by these presents my last will and testament in manner following:

First I commend my soul into the hands of God who made me, and redeemed me, and hath renewed me into the image of Christ Jesus, by whom only I am washed from my sins, and adopted to be the child of God and an heir of everlasting life, and that of the mere and free favour of God, who hath elected me to be a vessel of glory for the only manifestation of his infinite mercy, and accordingly hath called me outwardly by his word, and inwardly and effectually by his holy spirit, into this grace wherein now I stand and rejoice under the hope of the glory to come. My body I yield to the earth,† there to be decently bestowed, as waiting for the hope of the resurrection of the just. Now for such temporal goods as I shall leave behind me I do commit them to the care and disposition of Margaret my wife, *Mr. Adam Winthrop my father, Anne Winthrop my mother,* and John Winthrop my son, whom I do make and ordain executors of this my last will and testament to this end and upon this confident persuasion, that they will have a mutual love and due regard each to other and to all the rest of our family, and that they will faithful perform this my last will and testament. Item I give unto my said wife all those my lands and tenements which I lately purchased of William Forthe of Neyland, gentleman, viz. the two tenements and six acres of land lying by Leven heath in the occupation of [blank] Coker and ten acres of woodland lying near the same tenements, which land and woods are called by the several names of Masterman's Cross, Masterman's Grove, Stubbins Cross, Stubbins Grove, and Homylie's Grove, or by what other names soever; and also one close of pasture ground, called little pond field containing about eight acres lying at the end of Neyland town towards Buers; and also three acres of meadow lying in Lowe's meadow in the parish of Assington just by the said end of Neyland town; all which said parcels of land, meadow and wood are more particularly expressed in a certain deed of feoffment from the said William Forthe to me made, bearing date the 27th day of July 1617. To have and to hold the said tenements, land, meadows, pastures and woods unto my said wife for term of her life, and after her decease to remain to Adam my son and to his heirs. Item I give unto my said son John all that messuage wherein I now dwell, together with all the appurtenances, and all that indenture of lease or term of years which I have in the same and in certain acres of land therewith let, being now in my occupation situate in Groton aforesaid, and being parcel of the rectory of the same parish. Item, whereas I have one parcel of land called Upper Crabtreewent containing about twelve acres, lying in Groton aforesaid, and now in the occupation of Philip Gostlin the elder, which I have left out of former conveyances to this end that I might lay it unto the parsonage of Groton, in satisfaction of the like quantity of land which I have of the same, I do hereby admonish my said son and streightly charge him before the Lord, that he so dispose hereof as may be best to God's glory, the peace of his own conscience, and the due recompence of the faithful incumbent, as myself purpose to do, if God spare me life to a fit opportunity.

Item for Mary my daughter I will that my executors shall pay her

† I desire to be laid near my godly and loving wives, if conveniently it may be.

her grandfather Forthe his legacy of *L*.240 to be paid her at her age of eighteen years, and withal I do commit her to the care of my executors to be well and christianly educated with such goods as I shall leave unto them. *Item I will that my said executors shall pay unto Luce Winthrop my sister one hundred and twenty pounds, one hundred whereof is due to her upon an agreement between my father and me upon the setting over his whole estate unto me. Item I will that they shall pay unto Ezekiel Bonde three score pounds and [blank] that which is behind and due to him of such legacies as my said father was to pay unto him.* Item I will that my son *s Henry and* Forthe shall be brought up and disposed of by my executors in learning, *or else in some honest calling such as they shall prove most fit for,* out of the rents and profits as they are to have by the will and testament of their said grandfather Mr. Forthe, when they shall attain to certain ages, as in the said will is expressed. My other two sons Stephen and Adam I commend to the care of their mother to be brought up in the fear of God by the help of such lands and goods as I shall leave unto her. Item I will that my executors shall pay my son Henry *L* 13.6.8d yearly out of those lands which should fall to him by his grandfather Forthe's will at his age of twenty-four years. Item I make my loving wife and John my son executors of this my last will and testament, entreating and charging them that they will provide that all my debts may be truly paid and satisfied out [of] such lands and goods as I shall leave unto them, for performance whereof I do give unto my said son John the lease of the house I dwell in with the lands thereunto belonging and therewith occupied.

Published in the presence of
HENRY WINTHROP,
SAMUEL GOSTLIN.

I 2. Page 3.

I, JOHN WINTHROP of Boston in New England being (through the blessing of the Lord) in good health, yet considering my change approaching and the uncertainty thereof, and desiring (according to the good pleasure of the Lord) so to settle the affairs of my family, as when the Lord shall call me to himself, I may neither be troubled with the care of these outward things, nor for want thereof may leave any occasion of strife or evil report behind me, do in the name and fear of the Lord ordain this my last will and testament, though I can't make it so full and exact as I would in many particulars, in regard of those engagements which now lie upon me, and the incertainty of my estate in England, yet my intent is that this shall stand for the present to be some direction to my executors &c till God may please to give opportunity of altering the same in a more clear way.

First my care is that all my debts and duties be paid, and for that end I give power to my executors to sell the house I dwell in at Boston, and the land beyond Powder-horn hill, and any of my stock and moveables, corn on the ground, my part of the windmill, and interest at the wear at Mistick. And for my dear wife, who hath been a faithful help to me, though I left an estate for her in England, yet being doubtful what may become of that, and having had *L.*400 of it already, my will is, she should be maintained in a comfortable and honourable condition, according to her place, and as my estate will bear, therefore I give unto her half my farm Tenhills during her life, with the use of such stock as shall be left upon it (my debts &c. paid.)

And for my good son John, who hath always been most loving and dutiful to me, and to my wife, as if she had been his natural mother, and hath cheerfully departed with all his interest both in his mother's inheritance and mine, to a great value, and that without any recompence, I do commend him to the Lord in all that the blessing of a father may obtain for an abundant recompence upon him and his; and I do give unto him the other moiety of my farm Tenhills, with the stock thereupon, and after the decease of my wife the whole, to remain to him and his heirs forever.

I give to my son Adam my island called the Governour's Garden, to have to him and his heirs forever; not doubting but he will be dutiful and loving to his mother, and kind to his brethren in letting them partake in such fruits as grow there. I give him also my Indians there and my boat and such household as is there.

I give to my son Stephen my moiety of the Isle Prudence in Narragansett Bay, which with his part of the reversion of his mother's estate in England will be a good portion, for it will be fit she should dispose some part of it to her other sons, according to our first intention, and I hope they will all rest satisfied at their mother's disposal thereof.

I give to my son Deane and his heirs my land at Pullen Point with the 40 acres of marsh on the other side the hill there; and I must leave him to his mother's care to furnish him with some stock; and if my land beyond Powder-horn hill shall not be sold &c. then I give it to him and his heirs.

I give to my son Samuel my lot at Concord, which I intend to build upon, if God give life and means, and the half of my farm of 1200 acres upon Concord river, and my 3 oxen in Ephr. Child's keeping.

All the rest of my land undisposed of (there being above 2000 acres still due to me from the country) I give to my son John and his heirs, whom together with my wife I make executors of this my last will and testament, and my will is that all my plate and other (8) 29, 1639,] household, and books shall be equally divided between them; and my wife to dispose of her part (besides her own jewels and other peculiar things fit for her own use) as herself shall think fit.

I will that John Gager shall have a cow, one of the best I shall have, in recompence of a heifer his father bought of me, and 2 ewe goats and 10 bushels of Indian corn.

[In a later hand.]

My estate becoming since much decayed through the unfaithfulness of my servant Luxford, so as I have been forced to sell some of my land already, and must sell more for satisfaction of *L*.2600 debts, whereof I did not know of more than *L*.300, when I intended this for my testament, I am now forced to revoke it, and must leave all to the most wise and gracious providence of the Lord, who hath promised not to fail nor forsake me, but will be an husband to my wife and a father to our children, as he hath hitherto been in all our struggles. Blessed be his holy name.

JO. WINTHROP.

(4) 25, 1641.

K. page 75.

General Court, 19 *October*, 1630. Vol. I. p. 62.

"The names of such as desire to be made freemen."

[Some went home, several died before being admitted, and some were absent at the next court, and took the oath at a later one.]

Mr. Samuel Maverick,
Mr. Edward Johnson,◊
Mr. Edward Gibbons,◊
Mr. William Jeffries,◊
Mr. John Burslin,◊
Mr. Samuel Sharpe,
Mr Thomas Graves,◊
Mr. Roger Conant,◊
John Woodbury,◊
Peter Palfry,◊
Mr. Nath'l Turner,
Mr. Samuel Freeman,
Ephraim Child,◊
John Grinoway,◊
Christopher Gibson,
John Benham,◊
Thomas Williams,◊ alias Harris,
Richard Garrett,
John Howman,
John Crabb,
Capt. Walter Norton,◊
Mr. Alex. Wignall,◊
Mr. William Jennison,◊
Mr. Thomas Southcoate,◊
Mr. Richard Southcoate,
James Pemberton,
Mr. John Dillingham,◊
John Johnson,◊
George Alcocke,◊
Mr. Robert Coles,◊
John Burr,◊
Thomas Rawlins,◊
Rich. Bugby,◊
Richard Hutchins,
Ralph Mushell,◊
Mr. William Clerke,◊
Mr. Abraham Palmer,◊
John Page,◊
Mr. Robert Feake,◊
Mr. William Pelham,
Mr. Benj. Brand,
Mr. William Blackstone,◊
Mr. Edmond Lockwood,◊
Mr. Richard Browne,◊
John Stickland,◊
Ralph Sprague,◊
Mr. George Ludlow,
James Penn,
Mr. George Phillips,◊
Mr. John Wilson,
Mr. John Maverick,◊
Mr. John Warham,◊
Mr. Samuel Skelton,◊
Mr. William Colbron,◊
Mr. William Aspinwall,
Edward Converse,◊
Mr. Richard Palgrave,◊
John Taylor,◊
Richard Church,
Rich. Sylvester,
Will. Balstone,◊
Robert Abell,◊
Thomas Lamb,◊
William Frothingham,
William Chase,
[*Richard?*] Foxwell,◊
Mr. Charles Gott,◊
Henry Harwood,
William Brakenbury,
John Drake,
John Balche,◊

Mr. Samuel Coole,§
Mr. William Traske,
Henry Wolcott,
Thomas Stoughton,§
William Phelps,§
George Dyer,§
John Hoskins,§
Thomas Ford,§
Nich. Upsall,§
Stephen Terry,§
Henry Smyth,§
Roger Williams,§
John Woolridge,
Thomas Lumberd,§
Bigot Egglestone,§
Mr. Giles Sexton,§
Robert Seely,§
John Mills,
John Cranwell,
Mr Ralph Glover,
William Hubbard,
Edmond James,
John Phillips,
Nath. Bowman,
John Doggett,§
Laurence Leach,§
Daniel Abbot,§
Charles Chadwick,§
William Gallard,§
William Rockwell,§
Henry Herrick,§
Samuel Hosier,§
Rich. Myllet,
Mr. Abraham Pratt,
William James,
William Allen,§
Samuel Archer.

[On p. 73, are "the names of such as took the oath of freemen," General Court, 18 May, 1631, besides those above marked with a section (§).

Capt. Daniel Patrick,
Capt. John Underhill,
Mr. Geo. Throckmorton,
Sergeant Morris,
John Horne,
Mr. John Oldham,
Rich. Sprague,
Francis Johnson,
Bray Rossiter,
William Noddle,
William Agar,
Nich. Stower,
Robert Harding,
William Woods,
Robert Moulton,
Mr. Edward Belchar,
John Edmonds,
John Moore,
Math. Grant,
Simon Hoyt,
William Parks,
William Hudson,
Walter Palmer,
Jonas Weed,
Mr. Edward Tomlyns,
Mr. Rich. Saltonstall,
Isaac Sterne,
John Ferman,
Richard Bulgar,
Anthony Dix,
John Warren,
Davy Johnson,
William Bateman,
Daniel Finch,
Mr. John Masters,
Roger Mawry,
John Goffe,
John Perkins,
Francis Smyth,
John Peirce,
Griffin Crofte,
Thomas Moore,
Ezekiel Richardson,
Thomas Dexter,
Mr. Edward Jones,
William Cheesebrough,
Francis Aleworth.

On 6 March, 1631-2.

Mr. John Eliot,
Jacob Eliot,
Abraham Browne,
James Penniman,
Isaac Perry,
Gregory Baxter,
William Frothingham,§
Samuel Moore,
John Black,
John Mills.§

On 3 April, 1632.

Mr. John Winthrop, jr.
Mr. William Aspinwall,§
John Sampeford,
William Hulbert.

On July 3, 1633.

Mr. Nath. Turner,§
John Ruggles,
Elias Stileman,
Mr. William Dennison,
Mr. Samuel Sharpe,§
Mr. John Wilson,§
John Moore.

On August 7, 1632.

John Phillips, §
Valentine Prentice,
John Hull,
Samuel Wakeman.

On October 2, 1632. Mr. Samuel Maverick.§

On 6 November 1632.

Mr. Thomas Weld,
Mr. Thomas James,
Mr. John Willust,
Mr. John Coggeshall,
Mr. Rich. Dummer,
Mr. Thomas Oliver,
Mr. John Branker,
Mr. Thomas Beecher,
Thomas French,
William Goodwin,
John Benjamin,
John Talcot,
James Olmstead,
John Clerke,
William Leawis,
Nath. Richards,
William Wadsworth,
Rich. Webb.

On 4 March 1632–3.

William Curtis,
Thomas Uffot,
John Perry,
Isaac Morrall,
William Heath,
George Hull,
Henry Harwood,§
William Brackenbury,§
Eltweed Pummery,
Nich. Denslowe,
Giles Gibbs,
John Newton,
John White,
William Spencer,
Richard Collocott,
John Smith,
John Kirman,
Timothy Tomlyns.

On 1 April 1633.

Sergeant Greene,
Rise Coles,
William Dady.

On 11 June 1633.

William Stilson,
Rich. Millett,§
Rich Lyman,
Jespar Rawling,
Thomas Smyth,
David Wilton,
John Witchfield,
Elias Maverick.

On November 5, 1633.

Mr. Israel Stoughton,
Mr. John Coggin,
Mr. William Hill,
Mr. John Moody,
John Porter,
Francis Weston,
John Matson,
John Holgrave.

On 4 March 1633–4.

Thomas Grubb,
Edmond Hubbert,
Edward Hutchinson,
Mr. Thomas Leverett,
Mr. Giles Firman,
Edmond Quinsey,
William Collishaw,
Thomas Minor,
Mr. Atherton Hough,
William Andrews,
Thomas Howlett,
John Gage,
Samuel Wilboare,
John Levens,
John Cranwell,§
Edward Mellowes,
James Brown,
Mr. John Woolridge,§
Rich. Walker,
George Ruggles,
Joshua Hewes,
Robert Turner,
John Biggs,
Thomas Matson,
Walter Merry,
Rich Tappin,
Mr. Nich. Parker.

On 1 April 1634.

Mr. Daniel Dennison,
George Minot,
Rich. Gridley,
Thomas Reade,
George Hutchinson,
Robert Roise,
John Pemerton,
Bernard Lumbert,
Henry Wolcott,§
Rich. Hull,
John Gallop,
Rich. Silvester,§
William Horseford.

On 14 May 1634.

John Haynes, Esq.
Philip Sherman,
Daniel Brewer,
Thos. Gouldthait,
Robt. Gamlyn, senr.
Thomas Hale,
Edward Riggs,
John Walker,
Thomas Wilson,
Samuel Bass,
Thomas Pigg,
William Hill,
Edward Howe,
John Steele,
George Steele,
Edwd Must,
John Haward,
Thomas Hatch,

Joseph Reddings,
Francis Plummer,
James Rawlyns,
Stephen Hart,
Thomas Fairweather,
Peter Wolfe,
Mr. John Cotton,
Miles Reddin,
Mr. Thomas Mayhew,
Thomas Holcombe,
James Parker,
Edmd. Harte,
Christopher Hussey,
Rich. Raymond,
James Tompson,
John Baker,
Francis Dent,
Samuel Finch,
George Williams,
Edward Giles,
William Dixy,
George Norton,
Thomas Eborne,
Daniel Wray,
Abraham Mellowes,
John Oliver,
Robert Hale,
Thomas Cakebread,
Thomas Squire,
Bartholomew Greene,
Edm. Stebbins,
Rich. Butler,
Rich. Goodman,
Andrew Ward,
George Whitehand,
Anthony Colby,
Humphrey Pynney,
Jacob Barny,
Jeffery Massy,
William Hedges,
William Chase,
Nath. Gillet,
John Eales,
Robt. Walker,
Thos. Dewey,
Walter Filer,
William Hathorne,
Edwd. Bendall,
Jonathan Wade,
Thomas Hubbard,
Mr. Wm. Brenton,
Henry Feakes,
Robert Houlton,
John Odlyn,
Roger Clap,
Joshua Carter,
Thomas Talmage,
Richard Fairbanks,
Philip Tabor,
Gregory Taylor,
John Chapman,
Wm. Learned,
Mr. Thomas Hooker,
Mr. Samuel Stone,
Rich. Wright,
Andrew Warner,
Thomas Spencer,
John Pratt,
Joseph Twitchwell,
Jerad Hadden,
John Bosworth,
Bray Wilkins,
Thomas Lowthrop,
Richard Brakenbury,
John Hoskins,
Wm. Talmidge,
Daniel Howe,
Mr Wm. Peirce,
Philip Randill,
Thomas Jeffrey,
John Haydon,
Stephen French,
John Button,
Thomas Coldham,
John Hall,
John Capen,

On September 3, 1634.

Benjamin Hubbard,
Edmond Hubbard,
Oliver Mellowes,
Joseph Rawlyns,
Wm. Freeborne,
Jonathan Negos,
Henry Pease,
Edwd. Hutchinson,
Moses Maverack,
Henry Short,
Abraham Finch,
Martin Underwood,
John Edy,
Nathaniel Foote,
John Pope,
Robert Reynolls,
Thomas Thorneton,
Mr. Nicholas Easton,
John Mousell,
Wm. Baker,
Robt. Gamlyne,
John Stowe,
Wm. Perkins,
Nicholas Willust,
Samuel Crumwell,
John Sibley,
Mr. John Spencer,
Philip Fowler,
Anthony Peirce,
Samuel Smyth,
Robt. Abbitt,
Rich. Davenport,
John Hawkes,
Robt. Potter,
Matthias Sension,
Mr James Noise,
Wm. Nash,
Thomas Goble,
Ralph Hiningway,
John Cumpton,
James Everill,
Alex. Becke,
Joseph Rednape,
Hugh Hillyard,
Robt. Mussey,
Bryan Pendleton,
John Bernard,
John Browne,
Robt. Coe,
Mr. Thomas Newbery,
Ralph Fogg,
John Handy,
Mr. Thomas Parker,
Joshua Hubbard.

On March 4, 1634-5.

Capt. John Mason,
Hugh Mason,
George Munings,
John Brandish,
Samuel Hubbert,
Edward Dix,
Thomas Bartlett,
George Buncar,
Robt. Blott,
Rich. Kettle,
Wm Johnson,
Thomas Lynd,
Mr. Wm. Andrews,
Wm. Westwood,
Mathew Allen,

Guy Bambridge,
Wm. Pantry,
Thomas Fisher,
Thomas Scott,
John Webster.
Wm Bartholomew,
James Davis,
Thomas Marshall,
Thomas Wardall,
Gamaliel Wate,
Robert Parker,
Thomas Standley,
John Hopkins,
John Bridge,
Wm. Kelsey,
John Bernard,
James Ensign,
Samuel Greenhill,
Timothy Stanley,
Rich. Lord,
John Prince,
Thomas Boreman,
Hugh Sheratt,
Thomas Dorman,
John Newgate,
Rich. Cooke,
Rich. Hutchinson,
Rich. Trusedale,
Joseph Easton,
Edward Winship,
Samuel Greene,
Joseph Clerke,
John Wulcott,
Abraham Newell,
Rich. Popp,
Isaac Johnson,
Christopher Peakes,
Thomas Woodford,
Roger Lankton,
Joseph Metcalfe,
Rich. Kent,
Mr. Wm. Hutchinson,
Wm. Netherland,
Francis Hutchinson,
Edwd. Hitchin,
John Tylley.

On 6 May 1635.

Philemon Portmonte,
Henry Elkins
Christopher Marshall,
Edmond Jackling,
Mr. Zechariah Symmes,
John Reynolls,
John Lethermore,
John Clerke,
Thomas Hosmer,
George Stockin,
Jeremy Adams,
Samuel Allen,
John Gay,
Thomas Marshall,
Robert Andrews,
Thomas Gun,
Elias Parkman,
Joseph Morse,
Wm. Moody,
Rich. Jacob,
Boniface Burton,
Wm. Edmonds,
George Farr,
Edmond Bulckley,
Edward Browne,
Jarrett Bourne,
John Sebley,
Barnaby Wynes,
Henry Bright,
John Batchelor,
Thomas Swift,
Wm. Butler,
Nathaniel Ely,
Joseph Maggott,
Humfry Bradstreet,
George Strange,
Thomas Hoskins,
Henry Wright,
Robert Dibell,
John Blackleach,
Edward Garfield,
Christopher Osgood,
Aaron Cooke,
Robert Bootefish,
John Ravensdale,
Robert Cotty,
Wm Pell,
Benjamin Gillam,
Thomas Alcocke,
Thomas Peirce,
Jeffery Fernis,
Thomas Hastings,
John Tompson,
Robert Wincall,
John Arnoll,
Robert Day,
John Hall,
Thomas Pyne,
Nathaniel Duncan,
Rich. Kemball,
Jonathan Jellett,
Henry Fowkes,
Daniel Morse,
Rich. Browne,
Thomas Buckland,
George Phelpes,
Robert Driver,
John Legge,
Mr. Stephen Batchelor.

On 2 September 1635.

Wm. Blumfield,
Joseph Hull,
Wm. Smyth,
Mr. George Burditt,
Mr. John Faunce,
Wm. Read,
Rich. Adams,
Rich. Woodward,
Mr. Townsend Bishop,
Thomas Scruggs,
John Upham,
Robert Lovell,
Peter Hubbert,
Philip Verein.

On 3 March 1635-6.

Mr. Clement Chaplain,
Wm Moss,
Robert Lord,
Clement Bates,
Wm Norton,
John Otis,
David Phippin,
John Whitney,
Wm. Dyer,
Joseph Wells,
Wm. Walton,
John Astwood,
George Ludkin,
Nicholas Baker,
Edmond Batter,
Wm. Swayne,
John Cogswell,
Richard Tuttle,

Thomas Loring,
Thomas Wakely,
George Marsh,
Nicholas Jacob,
Philemon Dolbon,
Henry Kingman,
Thomas White,
John Levett,
Mr. Joseph Cooke,
Thomas Marryott,
Simon Crosby,
Passevil Greene,
Edmond Frost,
Thomas Ewer,
Joseph Andrews,
Angel Holland,
Thomas Rawlyns,
Mr. George Cooke,
Mr. Samuel Shepheard,
Thomas Cheeseholme,
Mr. Hugh Peters,
Mr. Thomas Shepheard,
Thomas Bridgden,
John Kingsbury,
Roger Harlackenden, Esq.
Mr. Nicholas Danforth,
Wm. French,
John Russell,
Thomas Bloyett,
Henry Vane, Esq.
Michael Bastowe.

On 25 May 1636.

Joseph Gun,
Isaac Heath,
Wm. Webb,
John Knight,
Robert Long,
Bernard Capon,
Mr. Robert Keaine,
Thomas Hassard,
George Bate,
Wm. Townsend,
Mr. Henry Flint,
Zaccheus Bosworth,
Wm. Salter,
Rich. Champneys,
John Smythe,
John Coolidge,
George Hepburne,
Rich. Carder,
Thomas Dimmock,
Edward Bennett,
Edmond Jackson,
Thomas Bell,
Philip Eliot,
Edward Woodman,
Richard Knight,
Robert Hawkins,
Wm. Hammond,
Mr Daniel Maude,
James Johnson,
Nathaniel Heaton,
Richard Bracket,
Wm. Courser,
Mathias Ines,
Anthony Harker,
Edmond Lewis,
John Eaton,
Gregory Stone,
Wm. King,
John Higginson,
John Lovering,
Thomas Mekyn, junr.
Bernaby Doryfall,
Mr. Samuel Appleton,
Adam Mott,
Thomas Judd,
Anthony Mosse,
Edward Carington,
John Saunders,
Ralph Hudson,
John Davy,
Wm. Bensley,
Thomas Savage,
James Browne,
Wm. Wilson,
Edward Goffe,
John Stowers,
Edmond Sherman,
Simon Stone,
Augustine Clement,
John Mylam,
Wm. Wilcocks,
Hugh Gunnison.

On 7 December 1636.

James Bate,
Edward Clapp,
John Smythe,
Robert Scott,
Gilbert Crackborne,
Wm. Wilcockson,
Thomas Atkinson,
Edward White,
David Peirce,
George Aldridge,
Stephen Winthrop,
Samuel Whiting,
Wm. Beadesley,
John Holland,
Oliver Purchase,
John Webb,
Alex. Winchester,
Wm. Goodhue,
Thomas Brooke,
Alex. Knolls,
Walter Nicholas.

On 8 December 1636.

Mr. Thomas Jenner,
John Cooper,
Francis Lightfoot,
John More,
Edward Howe,
Thomas Beale.

On 9 March 1636-7.

Edward Ketcham,
John Hassell,
Samuel Warde,
Nicholas Hudson,
Robert Lockwood,
Edward Bates,
Gerret Spencer,
Robert Sedgwick,
John Strong,
Rich. Wayte,
Wm. Dinny,
Richard Root,
Richard Betsham,
Thomas Hammond,
John Winchester,
Wm. Barsham,
Jenkin Davies,
Thomas Tilestone,

James Heyden,
Thomas Carter,
Robert Hull,
Thomas Meakins,
Joseph Isaac,
Anthony Eames,
Thomas Underwood,
Abraham Shaw,
Rich. Beares,
Matthew West,
Henry Collins,
Thomas Samford,
Joseph Armitage,
Richard Wade.

On 18 April 1637.

Thomas Parish,
Wm. Towne,
John Ruggles,
Giles Pason,
Thomas Brigham,
John Gore,
Laurence Whitamore,
George King,
Wm. Cutter,
Robert Sever,
John Graves.

On 17 April 1637.

I know not why the secretary entered the last first.

Christopher Foster,
Wm. Dodge,
Edward Dinny,
Nath. Woodward,
Thomas Wheeler,
Thomas Browning,
Francis Smythe,
Wm. Dineley,
John Smythe,
John Lawrence,
Simon Eyre,
Nath. Porter,
Francis East,
Edward Rainsford,

On 17 May 1637.

Thomas Olney,
Henry Bartholomew,
Henry Seawell, junr.
Nicholas Noise,
Robert Pike,
George Hunn,
Thomas Dible,
John Syverens,
Thomas Bircher,
John Sharman,
Richard Johnson,
Thomas Gardner,
Joseph Grafton,
Henry Bull,
Archelaus Woodman,
Thomas Coleman,
Wm. Sumner,
Philip Drinker,
Thomas Wells,
Edward Porter,
John Rogers;
Themas Parker,
Joseph Pope,
Francis Skerry,
Thomas Smythe,
James Browne,
Matthew Chafe,
George Proctor,
John Cheney,
John Perkins,
James Howe,
Miles Nutt,
John Hawchet,
Wm. Bound,
Edmond Marshall,
Nicholas Holt,
John Bartlett,
George Burden,
Thomas Millet,
John Norton,
Wm. Lampson,
Thomas Rogers,
James Osmer,
John Gibson,

On 7 September 1637,

Mr. George Moxam,
Mr. Timothy Dalton.

On 2 November 1637.

Nathaniel Wales,
Mr. John Harvard,
Edward Sale,
Wm. Casely,
Mr. John Fiske.

In March 1637-8. Day not mentioned.

Thomas Spooner,
Henry Skerry,
Michael Spencer,
Samuel Symonds,
George Haywood,
Henry Rust,
Thomas Lincoln,
Thomas Venner,
Joseph Bachiler,
John Pearce,
Mr. Thomas Flint,
Thomas Fox,
David Fiske,
Henry Tuttle,
James Moulton,
John Symonds,
Nicholas Busby,
Rich. Griffin,
George Hochens,
Wm. Harsey,
James Haynes,
John Gedney,
Ralph Woodward,
John Evart,
Edward Rawson,
Wm. Ludkin.

On 2 May 1638.

Samuel Richardson,
John Brimsmeade,
Henry Dow,
John Tatman,
Ralph Tomkins,
Michael Willes,
Edward Hall,
Mark Symonds,
George Taylor,
Wm. Ballard,
John Browne,
Robert Cutter,
Isaac Mixer,
Nicholas Byram,
Robert Williams,
Richard Hawes,
John Sill,
Mr. Wm. Hubbard,§
Thomas Rawlinson,
John Gould,
Wm. Thorne,
Henry Burdsall,
Thomas Richardson,
Henry Kemball,
Samuel Hackburne,
Humfry Atherton,
Alex. Miller,
George Willis,
Rich. Lumkin,
Thomas Carter,
Thomas Cobbet,
Abraham Tappin,
Edward Johnson,
Wm. Nickerson,
Abraham Howe,
Gabriel Meade,
Joseph Wilson,
Thomas Sweetman,
Wm. Warrener,
Wm. Knight,
Daniel Peirce,
Henry Lunt.

On 9 June 1638.

Mr. Nathaniel Eaton was made free.

On 6 September 1638.

The magistrates of Ipswich had order to give Mr. Nath. Rogers the oath of freedom.

On 7 September 1638.

Thomas Hale,
Zachary Fitch,
Rich. Singletery,
Thomas Treadwell,
Stephen Fosditch,
George Giddings,
Nicholas Browne.

On 13 December 1638.

Mr. John Allen,
Mr. Edward Alleyne,
Mr. Ralph Wheelock,
Mr. Wm. Tyng,
John Leuson,
John Fraye,
Eleazer Lusher,
John Hunting,
Robert Hinsdall
Edward Kempe,
John Dwite,
Henry Phillips,
Mr. Joseph Peck,
Henry Smythe,
Edward Gilman,
Thomas Cooper,
John Beale,
Henry Chamberlin,
Thomas Clapp,
John Palmer,
John Tower,
Henry Webb,
James Mattucks,
John Tuttle,
Theophilus Wilson,
John Rogers,
Edmond Greenliffe,
Robert Meriam,
Wm. Eastowe,
Thomas Jones,
Jeremy Belcher,
Christopher Batte,
Thomas Bulkley,
James Bennett,
Thomas Moulton,
Wm. Cockerom,
Samuel Newman,
Luke Potter,
John Whiteman,
Rich. Swayne,
Edward Bates,
Mr. Robert Peck,
Ephraim Wheeler,
Wm. Palmer,
Wm. Wakefield.

On 14 December 1638.

Nicholas Butler,
Rich. Wells,
Wm. Langley,
Robert Parsons,
Godfrey Armitage,
Hezekiah Usher,
Edward Burcham,
Wm. Basse,
John Miles,
John Maudsley,
Thomas Dickerman,
Mr. Thomas Wills,
Mr. Edward Holiock,
Mr. Rich. Sadler,
Mr. Edward Howell,
Thomas Townsend,
Christopher Cayne,
Joseph Meriam,
Henry Brooke,
Seth Switzer,
Joseph Farnworth,
Thomas Clarke,
Edward Baker,
Henry Gaynes,
Arthur Geeree,
Joseph Pell,
Thomas Layton,

Robert Steedman,
Thomas Browne,
Henry Farewell,
Isaac Cole,
Wm. Reed,
Nicholas Batter,
James Boutwell,
Wm. Partridge,
Roger Shaw,
Robert Dannell,
George Keezar,
George Fowle,
Roger Draper,
John Wisewall,
Wm Blake.

Mr Endecot and Mr. John Winthrop, jr. had order to give Mr. Emanuel Downing the oath of freedom.

On 22 May 1639.

Mr. Wm. Sergeant,
Mr. Thomas Hawkins,
John Goffe,
John Mussellwhit,
Thomas Ruggles,
Wm. Bowstreete,
Thomas Says,
Richard Hollige,
Benjamin Felton,
Edmond Bloise,
Mathew Boyse,
Edward Bridge,
Thomas Firman,
Hugh Laskin,
Mr. Samuel Freeman,
Thomas Marten,
Stephen Kent,
John Rimmington,
Joseph Shaw,
Hopestill Foster,
John Alderman,
John Clarke,
Jarves Garfoard,
Wm. Osborne,
James Astwood,
Walter Blackborne,
Nath. Chappell,
John Smythe,
Nicholas Guy,
Mr. Samuel Winsley,
Thomas Browne,
John Moulton,
Francis More,
Thomas Scotto,
Griffin Bowen,
Giles Firman,
Edward Breck,
John Miller,
John Robert,
Joseph Jewet,
John Skot,
Henry Swan,
Stephen Dummer,
John Osgood,
Hulling,
Richard Waters,
Walter Edmonds,
Wm. Adams,
John Spooer,
Joshua Todd,
Wm. Clarke,
George Holmes,
Rich. Pococke,
Roger Porter,
James Buck.

On 23 May 1639.

Mr Ezekiel Rogers,
Mr. Thomas Nelson,
Mr. Nath. Rogers,
Robert Saunders,
Mr. Nath. Sparhawk.

On 6 June 1639.

Stephen Paine,
James Garrett.

On 6 September 1639.

Mr. Thomas Ginner,
Lawrence Southick,
Luke Heard,
Mr. Benj. Keayne,
John Cross,
Anthony Sadler,
Job Swinnerton,
John Roffe,
Thomas Masie,
Wm. Lord,
John Ellsley.

On 7 September 1639.

Edmond Bridge,
Richard Mellen,
Robert Tuck,
Robert Saunderson.

On 13 of May 1640.

Mr. Wm. Worcester,
Henry Munday,
John Saunders,
Thomas Bradberry,
Thomas Dummer,
Thomas Barker,
Thomas Mighill,
Maximi. Jewet,
Francis Parrat,
Richard Swan,
John Oliver (new br.
Mr. Edward Norris,
Richard Withington,
Robert Haseldine,
John Haseldene,
Francis Lambert,
Wm. Scales,
John Burbank,

Wm. Bointon,
John Jarrat,
Michael Hopkinson,
George Kilborne,
Edward Woode,
James Standige,
Mr. Thomas Ruck,
Rich. Syckes,
Mr. Thomas Coytemore,
Mr. Thomas Graves,
Mr. Francis Willoughby,
Edward Larkin,
Thom. Caule,
John Penticus,
John Martin,
Wm. Fillips,
Abraham Hill,
Mr. Wm. Paine,
John Whipple,
Mr. Wm. Stevens,
Clement Tapley,
John Fairfield,
John Bachilor,
Robert Elwell,
Thomas Watson,
Mark Formais,
Thomas Waterhouse,
Jeremy Howchenes,
Jonas Humphreyes,
Thomas Toleman,
George Weekes,
John Farnum,
Rich. Lipincote,
Gawin Anderson,
John Bowelis,
John Trumbell,
John Chandler,
George Browne,
John Harding,
Thomas Bayly,
Robert Titus,
Thomas Arnoll,
Arthur Clarke,
Walter Hayne,
John Bent,
John Ruddyk,
Valentine Hill,
John Leveritt,
Samuel Sherman,
George Rowes,
Gregory Belchar,
Edward Spolden,
Wm. Andrews,
John Trumball,
Nathan Aldish,
Wm. Bullard,
Daniel Fisher,
Edward Passon,
Edward Bumstead,
Simon Rogers,
John Norwick,
Wm. Carpenter,
Samuel Butterworth,
Thomas Richards,
Wm. Haward,
James Davis,
Edmond Rice,
Edmond Goodnoe,
John Howe,
Francis Seyle,
Peter Oliver,
George Curtis,
Stephen Kinseley,
Thomas Place,
Wm. Allise,
John Stidman,
Wm. Manning,
Michael Medcalfe,
John Bullard,
Joshua Fisher,
Wm. Chanler,
Joseph Wheeler,
Michael Wood,
Edmond Pitts,
John Holbroke,
Robert Marten,
Henry Greene,
Abraham Perkins,
Mr. Edmond Browne.
Thomas White,
Thomas Islin,
Mr. Wm. Hibbens,
John Hurd,
John Kenerick,
Cotton Flack.
John Dassette,
James Copie,
Martin Saunders,
Edmond Anger,
Edward Collins,
Ferdinando Adams,
Henry Smythe,
Rich. Barbore,
John Hall,
Timothy Wheeler,
John Merrill,
Francis Smyth,
Nicholas Fillips,
Matthew Prat,
Wm. Godfree,
Jeffery Mingy,
Peter Noyse,
John Parmenter,
John Wood,
Arthur Perry,
Nath. Williams,
Anthony Stoddard,
Mr. Wm. Tompson,
Wm. Potter,
Thomas Flackman,
John Reade,
Richard Frances,
Rich. Hogg,
Francis Chickering,
John Mose,
John Scarbrow.

On 7 October, 1640.

Mr. Samuel Dudley,
Henry Sands,
Josias Cobbit,
Robert Hunter,
Edmond Gardner,
Wm. Stickney,
James Barker.

On 8 October 1640.

John Page,
Samuel Morse,
Thomas Weight.

On 9 October 1640.

Robert Ring,
Isaac Buswell.

On 12 October 1640.

Wm. Hudson,	James Oliver,	Thomas Painter,
Mr. Wm. Bellingham,	Mr. Wm. Hooke,	Edward Fletcher.

On 2 June 1641.

Mr. Henry Dunster,	Edward Browne,	Wm. Brisco,
Mr. Richard Russell,	Robert Day,	Charles Glover,
Mr. John Allen,	Henry Chickry,	John Jackson,
John Maies,	Wm. Barnes,	John Knowlton,
Samuel Bidfield,	John Harrison,	Jacob Leager,
Nicholas Wood,	John Lowell,	Joseph Kingsbury,
Robert Holmes,	Thomas Davies,	John Roaper,
Wm. Woodberry,	Abel Kelly,	Benjamin Smyth,
John Robinson,	Thomas Lake,	Henry Wilson,
Thomas Gould	Rich. Cutter,	Abel Parr,
Robert Fuller,	Philemon Dickinson,	Josias Firman,
Samuel Corning,	Thomas Marston,	Benjamin Turney,
Wm. Browne,	Rich. Robinson,	John Viall,
Thomas Davenish,	Bozoun Allen,	Arthur Gill,
Philip Verin,	Rich. Pattengell,	George Wheeler,
Nehemiah Bourne,	Christo. Stanley,	Nath. Coalborne,
Robert Cooke,	Ellis Barrow,	Austin Kilham,
Rich. Sanford,	Rich. Parker,	Samuel Bullen,
Robert Paine,	Robert Bridges,	Benjamin Ward,
John Deane,	Wm. Tiff,	Wm. Cop,
Simon Tompson,	Henry Archer,	Rich. Rice,
George Bullard,	Michael Katherick,	Thomas Buttolph,
Rich. North,	Daniel Warner,	Thomas Clipton,
John Seir,	Andrew Hodges,	Obediah Wheeler,
John Stevens,	Michael Powell,	John Ellis,
Mr. Adam Winthrop,	John Emery,	Thomas Payne,
Francis Eliot,	Samuel Plummer,	Wm. Fuller,
John Harbert,	Moses Payne,	Wm. Hunt,
Goulden More,	Daniel Weld,	Nath. Halsteed,
Wm. Geares,	Jacob Wilson,	James Blood,
Thomas Gardner,	Andrew Pitcher,	Francis Dowse,
Thomas Wilder,	John Fessenden,	George Merriam,
Wm. Blanchard,	Esdras Read,	Francis Bloyce,
Jonathan Porter,	Rich. Bartelmew,	Edward Richards,
Samuel Chapin,	John Marston,	Timothy Dwight,
Walter Harris,	Miles Ward,	Evan Thomas,
John Palmer,	John Goodnow,	Wm. Bateman,
Francis Lawes,	John Harrison,	Nath. Billing,
Henry Dawson,	Wm. Parker,	Thomas Clarke,
Augustine Walker,	Edward Tyng,	John Sweete,
John Baker,	John Baker,	John Heald.

On 4 June 1641.

Thomas Marshall.

On 7 October 1641.

Mr. Richard Blindman, Thomas Wheeler.

On 18 May 1642.

Mr. Francis Norton,	Robert Button,	Thomas Putman,

James Fiske,
Elias Stileman,
John Bulfinch,
Robert Bradford,
John Ingoldsbey,
Daniel Briscow,
Rich. Taylor,
Thomas Oakes,
John Coggan, junr.
John Hill,
Rich. Taylor,
Hugh Chaplin,
John Greene,
Wm. Ripley,
John Stodder,
Rich. Baker,
Thomas Bliss,
John Cooper,
Thomas Bateman,
John Stevens,
Wm. Berry,
Peter Woodward,
Robert Page,
Henry Ambrose,
John Withman,
Benjamin Vermaes,
John Cooke,
George Byam,
John Tomkins, junr.
Joseph Boyse,
Hugh Williams,
Robert Howen,
John Search,
Philip Taylor,
Edward Gooding,
John Clough,
Richard Wody,
Edward Carleton,
Rich. Lowder,
Isaac Comins,
Matthew Hawkes,
Wm. Robinson,
Robert Pond,
Benjamin Albee,
Wm. Dickson,
Wm. Alline,
Wm. Stevens,
Samuel Guile,
John Brock,
Francis Peabody,
Walter Roper,
Gawdy James,
Thomas Antrum,
Phineas Fiske,
Rich. Bishop,
Ananias Conkling,
Samuel Grimes,
Rich. Crichley,
Thomas Snow,
John Baker,
John Bulkeley,
Sampson Shore,
John Witherell,
John Mathis,
Humphrey Keyne,
John Burrage,
Allen Pearley,
Hugh Pritchard,
Robert Peirce,
John Rigbey,
Roger Bancroft,
Moses Wheat,
Thomas Wheller,
Anthony Somersbey,
Abel Howes,
Nathaniel Whiting,
Isaac Perkins,
Henry Kibbey,
John March,
Michael Shaflin,
Wm. Fiske,
Allen Kenniston,
John Neale,
Theodore Atkinson,
John Guttering,
Thomas Foster,
Rich. Knight,
Edward Oakes,
Wm. Torrey,
Samuel Thatcher,
Wm. Lowell,
Hugh Smith,
Solomon Phips,
Thomas Thaxter,
Thomas Lincoln,
Thomas Davenport,
George Right,
Rich. Eckels,
Robert Edwards,
Wm. Hartwell,
Henry Somersbey,
John Swett,
Michael Metcalfe,
Thomas Worde,
David Zullesh.

On 19 May 1642.

John Sadler,
Wm. Walderne,
Walter Tybbot,
Obediah Brown,
Wm. Hilton.

On 22 June 1642.

Henry Palmer,
Wm. White,
Joseph Peaseley,
Thomas Dowe,
Rich. Pid,
Wm. Titcombe.

On 14 September 1642.

Thomas Het.

On 21 September 1642.

Wm. English.

On 27 December 1642. At Salem.

Walter Price,
Robert Looman,
Hugh Cawkin,
Robert Gutch,
Thomas More,
George Gardner,
Thomas Tresler,
Rich. Prence,
Wm. Robinson.

On 28 February 1642-3.

Thomas Edwards, John Kitchin, Henry Harwood.

And at Salem same day.

Rich. More, Thomas Avery,
Hugh Stacey, Edward Beachamp.

On 10 May 1643.

Mr. Thomas Wallis,	Jeffrey Tnrner,	Rich. Hildrick,
Gideon Sister,	Rich. Evans,	Andrew Stephenson,
John Parmenter,	Nath. Howard,	John Wright,
Christo. Smyth,	Francis James,	John Hollister,
John Jackson,	John Woode,	Nath. Herman,
Thomas Beard,	Rich. Rawlen,	Wm. Phese,
Nich. White,	Wm. Blanton,	John Ward,
Wm. Ware,	Robert Pepper,	Henry Looker,
Henry Woodworth,	Thomas Danforth,	John Thurston,
John Mansfield,	John Tydd,	John Knights,
Wm. Vincen,	Nicholas White,	John Pratt,
George Barrell,	Peter Bracket,	James Prest,
Isaac Colimer,	John Whetley,	Laurence Smyth,
James Morgan,	Isaac Wheeler,	John Gurnell,
Daniel Stone,	Robert Dauts,	Robert Williams,
Henry Simonds,	John Newton,	Wm. Fletcher,
Edward Winn,	John Plunton,	Robert Mader,
John Albye,	George Parkhurst,	John Sanderbank,
John Hastings,	John Hollister,	Nath. Norcross,
Thomas Adams,	Roger Billings,	Edward Shepard,
John Scot,	Wm. Trescott,	Wm. Manning,
Thomas Goodnow,	Rich. Way,	Benj. Butterfield,
Wm. Ward,	Robert Proctor,	James Prest,
John Guile,	Henry Bridgham,	Sam. Adams,
Nathan Fiske,	Strong Furnell,	John Shephard.
John Arnol,	Miles Tarne,	

On 29 May 1644.

Capt. Daniel Gookins,	John Lake,	Stephen Streete,
Wm. Bachilor,	Nicholas Boulton,	Shefield,
Thomas Marshall,	Edward Wilder,	Allen Converse,
George Spear,	John Gay,	Faintnot Wines,
Robert Gowing,	Baptize Smeedley,	Robert Field,
Rich. Haule,	Rich. Wooddy,	Timothy Prout,
Thomas Dyer,	John Russell,	Thomas Webster,
Jasper Rush,	James Parker,	John French,
Thos. Fox,	Robert Leach,	Nath. Partridge,
Philip Torry,	Wm. Greene,	John Blake,
Thomas Chamberlin,	Edward Witheridge,	John Smedley,
John Carter,	Henry Powning,	John Maynard,
Faithful Rouse,	Thomas Trott,	James Jones,
Wm. Smith,	Henry Cunlithe,	Lambert Sutton.
Roger Toule,	Joseph Phippen,	
Simon Bird,	Rich. Goard,	

In May 1645.

Herbert Pelham,	Thos. Line,	Hugh Griffin,
Abr. Hackburne,	Thos. Holbrook,	Jeremy More,
George Davies,	Samuel Stow,	James Umphryes,

Samuel Davies,
Thos. Barrill,
Lambert Genery,
Ralph Day,
Henry Firnam,
Edward Devotion,
Joseph Underwood,
Wm. Wenbane,
Joseph Hill,
Samuel Fellows,
Rich Newberry,
Anth. Fisher,
George Allen,
Edward Jackson,
John Langford,
Peter Aspinwall,
Rich. Black,
Rich. Bullock,
John Morley,
John Gay,
Mich. Medcalfe,
Thos. Roberts,
Henry Chamberlin,
Henry Evans,
John Bird,
Matthew Smith,
George Halsall,
Nath. Bishop,
Thos. Richards,
Wm. Davies,
Nich. Wife,
Rich. Newton,
Edward Wyatt,
James Nash,
Abr. Harding,
Henry Black,
Sam. Miles,
Sam. Sendall,
Robert Jenison,
Vincent Ruth,
John Fownell,
Harman Atwood,
Abr. Hawkins,
Abr. Parker,
John Stimson,
Wm. Pardon,
John Jones, stud.
John Watson,
John Toll,
Rich. Leeds,
Benj. Thwing,
Christopher Webb,
Edward Gilman,
John Daming,
Wm. Hely,
John Warren,
Thos. Barnes,
Sam. Bright,
Nath. Greene,
Francis Grissell,
Robert Long,
Henry Aldridge,
John Rydeat,
Thos Reeves,
Wm. Patten,
Wm Parsons,
Nich. Chelett,
Elijah Corlet,
Thos. Thacher,
George Dowdy.

On 6 May 1646.

Matthew Day,
Francis Heman,
Thos. Buckmaster,
Benj. Crispe,
Joel Jenkins,
John Wincoll,
Richard Everard,
Anthony Fisher,
John Lewes,
John Gingen,
Alex. Baker,
Wm. Pary,
Henry Thorpe,
Wm. Douglas,
Joshua Kent,
Thos. Jones,
Nath. Hadlock,
John Haynes,
Thomas Collier,
Wm. Dawes,
George Woodward,
Peter Place,
Robert Onion,
Isaac Walker,
John Hill,
John Looker,
Thos. Gardner,
Henry Modsley,
Chas. Stearns,
John Collins,
Andrew Dewing.

On 26 May 1647.

Ro. Chaulkly,
Manus Sally,
John Wayte,
Mr. John Wilson, junr.
Thos. Tayer,
Moses Payne,
John Harris,
Daniel Kemster,
Barth. Chever,
George Munjoy,
Ro. Wares,
Henry Wight,
Thos. Dunn,
Thos. Paget,
James Greene,
James Pike,
Law. Dowse,
Wm. Harvy,
John Niles,
David Fiske,
Thomas Boyden,
Jonah Clooke,
John Miriam,
Rich. Hassall,
Thos. Jorden,
James Allen,
Thos. Foster,
George Davies,
Thos. Carter, junr.
Richard Harrington,
Wm. Bridges,
Wm. Kirby,
John Stebbin,
David Stone,
Mr. Samuel Danford,
Thos. Huit,
Francis Kendall,
Wm. Buttrick,
John Metcalfe,
Nath. Adams,
Thomas Pratt,
John Peirson,
Mighil Smith,
Samuel Carter,
Edward White,
Richard Newton,
John Whitney, junr.
Philip Cooke,
Wm. Ames,
John Smith,
Wm. Cotton,
George Barber,
John Baker,
Wm. Holbrook,
Robert Rendell.

The court in October authorized Mr. Pincheon "to make freemen in the town of Springfield, of those that are in covenant and live according to their profession." A few pages after is recorded "made free at Springfield 13 April 1648."

John Pynchon,	Elizur Holioak,	Henry Burt,
Samuel Wright,	Wm. Branch,	Roger Pritchard.

On 10 May 1648.

Mr. Edward Denison,	Samuel Bass,	Rich. Hardier,
Thomas Hartshorn,	Henry Rice,	James Pemberton,
George Denison,	John Staple,	Mr. Samuel Mather,
Thomas Kendall,	Simon Tomson,	Henry Allen,
Thomas Osburn,	Wm. Daniel,	Wm. Needam,
Wm. Hooper,	John Chickley,	Philemon Whale,
Benj. Negus,	Mr. Samuel Danforth,	Alex. Adams,
Edward Tayler,	Benj. Negus,	John Peerce.
Rich. Holbrook,	Barth. Porsune,	

Those marked with a section (§) had applied for admission in 1630.

I must earnestly beg the reader not to make me responsible for any omissions, or other errours of the records. Several gentlemen, who *desired* admission, have left no proof of the fulfilment of their request. Perhaps they were stockholders in England of the company, and therefore their oaths were not required. At least we are confident of the employment in most responsible offices of some, to whom we have not evidence that the oath of fidelity was ever administered.

L. Page 75.

Colony Records, II. p. 197—199.

THESE presents witnesseth I Martha Coytemore of Charles towne widow executrix unto my late husband Thom: Coytemore deceased, in and for the more sure accomplishment of his said last will and testament bearing date the 25th of the 6th mo. 1642 by which he did bequeath and give his whole estate unto myself and child his sonne Thom: Coytemore, as by the said will doth appeare, which estate did amount unto the sume of twelve hundred sixty six pounds nyne shillings seaven pence, as by the inventory thereof doth appear, and now being purposed, by the providence and permission of God, to enter marrige, (with) John Winthropp, Esq. govr. of the Massachusets, intending, respect also to my said child and other considerations mee thereunto moveing with the advice and consent of my beloved brother Mr. Increase Nowell, one of the overseers of the said will, as also by the direction and with the good liking of the said John Winthropp have agreed and do hereby covenant graunt and agree, that all and every the particulers hereafter mentioned shall henceforth be, and be accounted the proper estate of my said child as his halfe part of the estate come to my hands, by vertue of the said last will and testament and also to ordaine and appoint my beloved brethren Mr. Increase Nowell Mr. William Ting Mr. Joseph Hill, and Wm. Stitson as feoffees in trust and trustees in the behalf of my s'd child, into whose hands and power to the onely use and behoof of my s'd child, I do hereby estate and intrust all the particulers hereafter mentioned, as aforesaid, as well lands, houses, mills and other goods, in nothing to be alienated, allessed, or diminished by me or any other person or persons whatsover, without the order and consent of the s'd feoffees or the major part of them, or the survivers of them under their hands in writing, and that to the benefit of the s'd child, which s'd division I also agree to, and desire it may be ratified by the next general corte and confirmed, and the s'd feoffees authoriz-ed to do, execute, provide, and performe on the behalfe of my s'd child in all things according to the true intent and meaning of this present agreement, and according to the last will and testament afore-s'd; provided, nevertheless, that all the revenue of the s'd hous-ing, lands, mills, and cattle, as also so much of the other estate hereafter mention'd, as shall be put into land or other improvement for annual advantage, or incombe shalbe and remaine to my owne use and benefit, and for education of my s'd child, until he shall come the age of discretion; and further, till he shall accomplish the age of twenty-one yeares, unles he shall before (being capable thereof) make choyce of some other guardian, till he shall attaine his full age afores'd: provided, also, that if it so come to passe, that any part of the s'd estate shalbe disposed unto my mother Mrs. Catherine Coytemore as is provided in the s'd will, then the feoffees shall pay out of the estate of my s'd child in proportion, as is provided in the s'd will notwithstanding the agreement and division hereby made and express'd. In witness whereof I have hereunto put my hand and seale the 20th of the 10th mo 1647.

1 new feather bed, boulster and pillow,	(—)	4 00 00
2 blankets, 1 green rug, and coverlet,	(—)	1 18 00
1 chest of drawers,	(—)	2 00 00
1 trunk and 2 Holland skirts,	(—)	1 02 00
9 towels, 5s. $3\frac{1}{4}$ duss napkins, $32\frac{1}{2}$s.		1 17 06
1 quilt, red and blew, &c.	(—)	1 06 00
$54\frac{3}{4}$ plate, at $4\frac{1}{2}$s. per dwt. or (oz.)	( )	12 06 04
1 silver girdle and silke jacket,		1 00 00
1 trunle 4s. an iron pot and hooks 8s.		0 12 00
		26 01 10

The other part,	26 01 10
500 acres of land at Woburn,	50 00 00
The house, garden &c.	120 06 00
$\frac{1}{2}$ the further mil,	100 00 00

5 cowe commons,	10 00 00
23 hay lots,	41 00 00
85 acres of land by mil,	63 10 00
A warming pan and copper frying pan, 4 cows 20l. new mill,	110 00 00
Half Colo. Rainsborough debt,	75 13 00
A copper furnace,	1 10 00
130 acres land at eelpond,	22 00 00
	L.620 00 10

The corte consented that these indentures sh'd be recorded and kept among the private records of this courte.

This indenture made the 20th of the 10th mo. 1647, between John Winthrope of Boston in New England, Esq. and Martha Coytemore the relict of Thom: Coytemore, late of Charles towne in New England afores'd, on the one party, and Increase Nowell of Charlestown afores'd, gent. William Ting of Boston afores'd, marchant, Joseph Hills and Wm. Stitson of Charlestowne also on the other party witnesseth, that whereas by the good providence of God there is a marriage intended shortly between the s'd John Winthropp and Martha Coytemore; and whereas the s'd John having disposed of his estate among his children, and such persons as he was engaged unto, so as he hath not to endowe the s'd Martha, and therefore out of the love he beares to her is careful to have her owne estate so secured to her as that by the blessing of the Lord it may be preserved and remaine to her and her children, after the death of the s'd John Winthropp: It is hereby covenanted, granted, concluded and agreed, by and between the s'd parties, in manner and forme following, videl: that the s'd John and Martha presently upon their intermarriage and during the coverture shall and will stand seized and possess'd of all such houses, mills, lands, tenements, and hereditaments, goods and chattels, whatsoever being the proper estate of the s'd Martha, by and according to the last will and testament of her s'd late husband, and particulerly mention'd and express'd in a certain scedule hereunto annex'd to the use of the s'd Increase Nowell, Wm. Ting, Joseph Hill, and Wm. Stitson, and of the survivers or surviver of them, for the intent and purposes in this present indenture express'd and to no other use, intent or purpose, viz: that they the s'd John Winthropp and Martha shall and may receive and take all the rents, incomes, profits, and benefits of the same during the coverture, without rendring any account—or of any part thereof, and if the said Martha shall have any issue of her body begotten by the s'd John Winthropp, or shall depart this natural life during the [by use destroyed]—it shall be lawful for the said Martha, by her last will and testamt. in writing to bequeath and dispose of all or any part of her s'd estate both reall and personall to and among her children or otherwise according to her will and best discretion, but neither the s'd John, nor Martha, nor both of them, nor any other person shall have any interest or power in the s'd estate, or any part thereof or in any of the rent, revenue, profit or benefit thereof, other then is in this present indenture express'd and intended; except upon such reasonable and fit occasion, as the s'd trustees or the major part of them, or the survivers of them shall under their hands in writing given consent unto, or by the allowance and authority of the general corte, and it is the humble request of all the s'd parties, that this present indenture, and every part thereof may be confirmed by the authority of the s'd general corte and entered among the private records of the same. Witness whereof the parties abovenamed to these presents interchangably have put their hands and seals the day and yeare above written.

A particular of the goods and chattels apportion'd to Mrs. Martha Coytemore—*Inprimis.*

A parcell of books 7. 8. 8d. a feather bed and boulster 3l. together	10	08	08
A bed steed trundle bed with roapes and mats,	1	10	00
2 pr. of striped curtens, windor curtens and valance, and green rug,	2	10	00
1 feather bed, boulster, flock boulster pillow, blankets, red rug and trundle bed,	1	15	00
A pr. brass hollow andirons, fire shovell tongs and creepers,	1	15	00
A Ciprus chest, 2l. 10s. 7 pr. Holland sheets, 10l.	12	10	00
3 diaper table cloathes $3\frac{1}{2}$ duss. napkins, 2 col'd clothes, and a damask napkin,	7	10	00
4 pr. Holland pillow bears, 3 col'd cloths, 1 duss. napkins, 2 towels,	3	05	00
7 pr. course sheets, 3l. 9 towels, 5s. 17 table clothes, 2l.	5	05	00
$3\frac{1}{4}$ dussen napkins, 1.12.6d. 2 pr. sheets and 1 pr. pillow beers 1l. 6s.	2	18	06
1 pr. striped silke curtens and valence, 5 windo curtens, 2 windo cloths, 1 col'd cloth and chimney do.	5	00	00
1 green cloth carpet, 1 col'rd do. 1 chimney do. and a little table cloth,	3	10	00
1 silk red and green quilt, 2, 10s. a little turkey carpet 1l. 6s.	3	16	00
A suite of red tabie 3l. $54\frac{3}{4}$ oz. of plate at 4s. 6d, being half,—whole 12.6.4,	15	06	04
A parcel of cheny plates and saucers 1l. 1 trunk, 2 flaskets, 4 cases, 12s.	1	12	00
A meridian compas and another compas 12s. a pr. scales 5s. a case knives, a screw for almonds, 17s.	1	14	00

An ould coverlet tent and blanket 14s. 26½ lbs. powder at 20d. pr. lb. 2.4.2,	2 18 02
2 brasse skellets 2 spits, 1 jack, 1 stew pan, 2l. 6, halfe the farther mill 100l. and purtenances,	102 06 00
Land beside all apportion'd to ye child 12l. 10s. a tapestry coverlet 1l. 6s.	13 16 00
12 leather chayres 1l. 10s. 2 ould coverlets 5s. 6 blankets 36s. 1 pr. andirons 1,	4 11 00
1 bed boulster, 2 pillows, 2 pr. pillow beers, 1 sealeskin trunk,	4 10 00
1 wicker chaire 3s. 11 quishions 18s. a hamacho 20s.	2 01 00
2 pr. stuffe breeches, 1 coate, 1 jacket, 30s. a spruce chest 10s. andirons and creepers,	2 05 00
135 lbs. of pewter at 12d. pr. lb. 6l. 15s. a parcel tin ware, 10s. a smoothing iron, pestle and mortar,	7 10 00
3 iron pots, 1 [unknown] and 2 kettles 2l. 5s. 1 pr. andirons, 2 iron dripping pans, 1 pr. pot hooks, 2 iron bars 1l. ould iron and a fowling peece 2l. 15, a copper kettle,	7 10 00
A striped carpet 6s. a clock 1l. in ould lumber 5l.	6 06 00
4 cowes 20l. an eighth of the new mill 90l.	110 00 00
Divers small things above the mill, above	6 09 00
Major Gibons 140l. Colonel Rainsborow and his brother,	215 14 00
Other debts, things sould and things not herein mention'd particularly,	54 10 00
Total	*L*.620 10 08

M. Page 245.

To the Honoured General Court.

The oath I took this yeare att my enterance upon the place of assistante was to this effect: That I would truly endeavour the advancement of the gospell and the good of the people of this plantation, (to the best of my skill,) dispencing justice equally and impartially (according to the laws of God and this land) in all cases wherein I act by virtue of my place. I conceive myselfe called by virtue of my place to act (according to this oath) in the case concerning the Negers taken by captain Smith and Mr. Keser; wherein it is apparent, that Mr. Keser upon a sabboth day gave chace to certaine Negers ; and upon the same day tooke divers of them ; and at another time killed others; and burned one of their townes. Omitting several misdemeinours which accompanied these acts abovementioned, I conceive the acts themselves to bee directly contrary to these following laws (all which are capitall by the word of God ; and 2 of them by the lawes of this jurisdiction.)

The act (or acts) of murder (whether by force or fraude) are expressly contrary both to the law of God, and the law of this country.

The act of stealing Negers, or of taking them by force, (whether it be considered as theft, or robbery) is (as I conceive) expressly contrary both to the law of God, and the law of this country.

The act of chaceing the Negers (as aforesayde) upon the sabboth day (beeing a servile worke and such as cannot be considered under any other heade) is expressly capitall by the law of God.

These acts and outrages beeing committed where there was noe civill goverment which might call them to accompt, and the persons by whome they were committed beeing of our jurisdiction, I conceive this court to bee the Ministers of God in this case ; and therfore my humble request is that the severall offenders may be imprisoned by the order of this court, and brought unto their deserved censure in convenient time ; and this I humbly crave, that soe the sinn they have committed may be upon their owne heads, and not upon ourselves (as otherwise it will).

Yrs in all christean observance,

RICHARD SALTONSTALL.

The house of deputs thinke meete that this peticon shall be graunted, and desire our honnored magists. concurrance heerein.

EDWARD RAWSON.

N. Page 246.

Sir,

I WITH your son were at Uncus fort where I dressed seventeen men and left plasters to dresse seventeen more who were wounded in Uncas brother's wigwam before we came. Two Captains and one common soldier were buried, and since we came thence two Captains and one common man more are dead also, most of which were wounded with bullets. Uncas and his brother told me, the Narragansetts had thirty guns which won them the day, else [they] would not care a rush for them. They drew Uncus forces out by a wile, of forty appearing only, but one thousand in ambush, who pursued Uncus men into their own land, where the battle was fought vario marte, till God put fresh spirit into the Moheagues, and so drave the Narragansets back again. 'Twould pity your hearts to see them lie like so many new circumcised Sechemites in their blood. Sir, whatever information you have, I dare boldly say, the Narragansets first brake the contract they made with English last year, for I helped to cure one Tantiquieson, a Moheague captain, who first fingered Miantinomio. Some cunning squaws of Narraganset led two of them to Tantiquieson's wigwam, where in the night they struck him on the breast through the coat with an hatchet, and had he not fenced it with his arm, no hope could be had of his life. Uncus hath been shy to meddle, but still enquires of us what to do, though daily provoked with death of this and that other man, till lately four of Uncus men went into Narraganset and slew two of some other parts. Sir, if the Bay (for all the association which seems *nomen not res*) will not help Uncus against these proud Narragansets, we must do it of necessity to preserve our own life, for we know the number of the Narragansets and their thoughts towards us, and their slighting us, as you, behind your back. They have drawn newly a party from Long Island and labour to engage all the rest to their side, and have laboured to withdraw Uncus his Pequits from him by tender of wampom. (Haud ignota loquor.) The Lord pardon our neglect of Uncus, and charge not the blood on our faces which our fore-slowings had shed; and create more unanimous proceedings twixt Bay and us, else Old England's divisions will soon be with us and end sadly. My zeal to all the Englishes welfare in these parts makes me thus bold. If I err, tis error amoris. But if we be not all of that heap which we find in Josh. 3. tot. I fear we shall be in flames ere we are aware. Expedition and unanimity must never sunder, if any great work follow on here. Excuse my plainness. Sir, I am

Totus tuus

THO. PETERS.

To the worshipful his much honoured friend
JOHN WINTHROP, *Esquire, at his house,*
in Boston, these be presented.

[This letter was written about the spring of 1645. See Haz. II. 48.]

O Page 259.

IN the case between ourselves of this jurisdiction and the French our neighbors, it is granted on all hands:

1st. That Monsieur Delatore (as also Monsieur Dony) living to the eastward of us, each of them in a strong sufficient fort, have from time to time traded great store of pieces, powder and shot to all sorts of Indians (far and near our plantations) enabling them thereby to put in execution any treacherous attempt upon our towns and habitations, which we cannot free from their invasion (as is not unknown to the French.)

2dly. That Monsieur Delatore was a papist, when he first came amongst us (attended with friars, papists, and other such like persons.)

3dly. That Delatore craving of our then Governor the aid of men and ships against Monsieur Dony, the Governor gave allowance for the hiring of several ships, and beating up of drums for volunteers, using arguments in writing to persuade some who were unwilling to engage themselves in this design, doubting the lawfulness thereof.

4thly. In this expedition, admitting so many deep and doubtful consequences, there was no consultation with the General Court, nor with the Council of the Commonwealth, who could not orderly assemble but by warrant from the Governor, and therefore could not interpose, as otherwise they would have done.

5thly. The true state of the case between Latore and Dony was unknown to us, for we may not rest upon the information of a party in the absence of his opposite, and (in this particular) we had nothing else to lead us. We were then ignorant (as we are at this present) which of the two aforesaid might be first or most in fault.

6thly. The case between Latore and Dony did not concern us, (themselves being papists, and subjects of the King of France,) nor were we bound by any rule of scripture to aid Latore, (as the case then stood,) for we did not know that he was in danger of Monsieur Dony, (as himself then pretended,) nor had we any reason to rely upon his own report, especially in so great a case, considering his religion, as also that he had a very able warlike ship, well furnished, and at his own command, beside other vessels and frigates at his fort or elsewhere, which forces (being compared with Monsieur Dony's at that time) might have made it a just question, whether Dony had not more cause to stand in fear of him, than he had of Dony. We had no reason to conceive ourselves bound to act in this case, (as the Samaritan in the Gospel,) for we could not duly and rationally conclude Monsieur Delatore to be as that man who fell among thieves; in which case two things were evident, namely, the distress of the party, and the integrity of his cause, both which, as they then concerned Latore, were very dark and doubtful. But, on the contrary, the scripture speaking against Jehosaphat's confederacy with Ahaz an idolater, speaks expressly to the case in hand, and that with some advantage in such respects as might be mentioned, and are apparent in the text unto such as are considerate.

7thly. Our men and ships hired (as aforesaid) being upon the expedition, and not far from Dony's fort, he sent respectively to Captain Hawkins, signifying the many wrongs and injuries that he had sustained by Delatore; notwithstanding which letter and the declaration therein contained, our men, being landed, killed some of Dony's men, burnt his mill, killed his cattle, great and small, as many as they met with, took his pinnace loaden with beaver and other peltry, in the taking of which pinnace they sorely wounded one of his men, and that without cause, as is confessed by some who were then and there present. This beaver and peltry being brought to Boston was sold by an outcry and divided among the soldiers.

8thly. Our men and ships (as may appear by sufficient proof) might have brought Latore in safety to his fort (which was and is pretended to have been their only aim) without any opposition from or act of hostility against Monsieur Dony.

9thly. Our men upon their return were very ready to own and ascribe unto themselves the killing of Dony's men, reporting they had killed nine, eleven, or more; which argues they transgressed no commands or direction given to the contrary by such as did especially persuade and prevail with them to undertake the service. It much concerned those, by whom the General Court and Council of the Commonwealth were restrained from acting in this case, to have taken good caution for preventing of such wicked and mischievous effects; and if that were done, it is meet it should appear for their own indemnity.

The Lord hath seemed very much to threaten us in many passages pointing at this case, all which (as we conceive) do call us to account for our slowness and backwardness in searching out the same; which (being of so great concernment unto all our confederates) we commend it to the consideration of this honorable Court of Commissioners, desiring their advice and helpfulness for our further proceeding, to the end that guilt (where any is) may be removed, all offences may be cleared, and such demands as have been made by Dony may be both speedily and justly satisfied, that the name of God and our profession may no longer be blasphemed.

RICHARD SALTONSTALL.
WM. HATHORNE.

[The whole is Saltonstall's writing, except H.'s signature, and is endorsed by Gov. Winthrop "delivered to the Commissioners of the United Colonies, 16 (6) 1645." The proceedings of the Commissioners of the United Colonies upon the foregoing which was prepared under authority of the General Court of Massachusetts, may be seen in Haz. II. 50, where they fill nearly four pages.]

P. Page 326.

Springfield this 5 of the 5 mo. 1648.

Sir,

I RECEIVED a letter from you with the hands of four magistrates more to it, to assist two Indians of Quabaug with men &c. for the apprehending of three murtherers at Naucotak, which is about fifteen miles from our town up the river.

These Indians of Quabaug have dealt subtilly in getting Cutshamoquin to get Mr. Eliot to be their mediator to you for the help. The principal argument which Mr. Eliot doth use to move you is, that the murthered are your subjects, and thereupon the warrant from the court runs, that the said Indians may charge either Indians or English to assist them to apprehend them at Naucotak, 1, because the murthered are your subjects, and 2dly, because the murtherers are within your jurisdiction.

But if things be well examined, I apprehend that neither the murthered are your subjects, nor yet the murtherers within your jurisdiction.

I grant they are all within the line of the patent, but yet you cannot say, that therefore they are your subjects, nor yet within your jurisdiction, until they have fully subjected themselves to your government (which I know they have not) and until you have bought their land; until this be done, they must be esteemed as an independent free people, and so they of Naucotak do all account themselves. I doubt lest when ours go with strength of men to disturb their peace at Naucotak, they will take it for no other than a hostile action; witness their deadly feud which they have and do bear to the Monaheganicks ever since they took Sowoquasse from them the last year, which I doubt will be the ground of a further dangerous war, for I hear that Pacoutick will pursue the quarrel and join with the Indians of the Dutch river against them. But the Naxicauset must begin the war, and as I hear either yesterday or this day is like to be the day of fight between them and the Naxicauset; though this river Indians will delay their time till the time that corn begins to be ripe. But now they are making of a very large and a strong fort.

But to return to the case of the murthered. The first three that were murthered the last year lived about six or seven miles on this side Quabaug nearer us, and the murtherers of them are known as they affirm; and there are several small factions of Quabaug, and in all near places there are other small factions. No one faction doth rule all; and one of these petty factions hath made friendship with Cutshamoquin, and that makes Cutshamoquin call them his subjects; but I believe they will stick no longer to him than the sun shines upon him.

The last five that were killed this spring (with one more that escaped) lived in the midway between Quabaug and Nashaway, and yet not properly belonging to either place, but living as neuters, and yet because they were somewhat near neighbours to both places, therefore both places do desire their help against the murtherers. The murtherers of these five are not known; but because the murtherers of the first three are known, therefore they suppose they are the same men. But the man that is escaped saith, that if he can see their faces, he doth know their faces, though he knows not their names.

Mr. Eliot also writ a letter to me to stir me up to assist the said Indians that came from you. 1st. He urgeth me with a command of God to make inquisition for blood, and 2dly with a promise, They shall hear and fear &c. and hence he concludes that there is no fear of a war to proceed from this dealing.

If the first positions can be made good, namely, that the murthered were your subjects, and 2dly that the murtherers were within your jurisdiction, then Mr. Eliot's exhortation to me had been seasonable, or else not.

But yet notwithstanding I have not declined the business, but have bethought myself how to get it effected in the best manner; and therefore advised the Quabaug Indians to stay until Nippunsit returned from Sowoquasse's house, which I expected within two days, but he came not till the third day. Then we had a private conference, and I ordered my speech thus to him, that I had received letters from you, that whereas Chickwallop desired Cutshamoquin to appoint a meeting at Quabaug, it was your desire that the meeting might be at Boston, that you might understand the business as well as the Indian sachems, and that you would take it kindly, if he would talk with the Naucotak sachems to apprehend the three murtherers, and that they would send some to the meeting at Boston.

Thereupon Quacunquasit, one of the sachems of Quabaug, and Nippunsit and others discoursed a long time how to effect this matter, and who to apprehend in the first place. But neither I nor my son for want of language could understand their discourse, but in conclusion they explained unto us what they had concluded on, namely to take two of the four that were at Naucotak; but they thought it best not to meddle with Wottowon and Reskesconeage, because they were of Pamshad's kindred, who is a Maqua sachem, but Nippunsit said he would tell him that they should live hoping he would further them in the taking of the rest; and all the Indians consented to this motion as the most feasible and likely way to attain their end in the rest. The other two, namely Wawhelam and his brother, Nippunsit hath undertaken by some wile or other to bring them to my house in a private way, and then he will leave them to me to apprehend them, and so to send them to you. And this they thought might be effected about ten or twelve days after this conclusion was made, which was made two days before the date of this letter.

And thus by these means they will engage the English as the chiefest parties in their business.

But I must confess I look upon this service in sending them to you as a difficult and troublesome service, for 1, I have no prison to keep them safe, and 2dly, it will occasion great resort of Indians to my house to see what I will do with them, and 3dly, we shall want men; and I perceive that the Indians are afraid to meddle with them, unless they can make the English the principal in the business.

If the Lord should let loose the reins to their malice, I mean to their friends and abettors, it may be of ill consequence to the English that intermeddle in their matters by a voluntary rather [than] by a necessary calling, for they and their friends stand upon their innocency, and in that respect they threaten to be avenged on such as lay any hands upon them.

And any place is more obnoxious to their malice than the bay by far; especially the Naucotak Indians are desperate spirits, for they have their dependence on the Mohawks or Maquas who are the terrour of all Indians.

My advice therefore is, that you will as much as may be take the matter from us; which may thus be effected. send three or four men to our plantation with all speed, that may live being here either at the ordinary or at some other house till the said parties be brought to me, if they be not brought before they come. They may improve their time here by doing some work, and if there be not a sufficient number of Indians to go with them to carry them safe, I may appoint more men that the business may not fail for want of a good guard. Let these persons march here [with] a charge to be private and silent in the business till they see it effected. You may send these men away on the second day. If the Indians should make an escape, and not be taken, yet the charge of three or four men in so weighty a business for the fairer carrying of it on, is not to be stood upon. If they be taken, before they come, I will set a guard upon them for two or three days in hope you will send them with as much speed as may be. Indeed there should not be a day's delay after they come to my house. It will prevent the tumult of Indians and prevent their waylaying. If these two be once apprehended and put to death, then they have determined the death of six more near Quabaug, and only the former two to live.

Thus have I as briefly as I can (though abruptly) related the substance of the matter. I entreat you that the men may call to my son Davis for a letter before they come away. They must be active men and light of foot, for the better countenancing of the business. I shall ere long send you further intelligence about this Pacoutuck business with the Monaheganicks. The Lord is able to divert their intentions, though it is to be suspected it is intended for the utter ruin of the Monaheganicks, and the English will, I fear, be embroiled in the war.

Your assured loving brother in the Lord.

W. PYNCHON.

Haste, haste.

For his loving brother, the Deputy Governour, with speed.

On receipt of this letter, the deputy governour, Dudley, sent it with this address:

"To his honoured friend Mr. John Winthrop, governour, at his house in Boston, deliver it with all speed."

Governour Winthrop writes upon it:

Sir,

I pray acquaint Mr. Eliot with this letter, and let me have your advice about it speedily. So I rest

Your loving brother,

JOHN WINTHROP, Gov'r.

9 (5) 48.

[It was, we may be sure, sent to Dudley from what here follows on the same paper inside.]

Upon reading this letter and conference with Mr. Elyott I give my advice (which you require) for a pause in the business, before we proceed any further in it.

1. For that the ground and warrant of our meddling in it is by this letter taken away, it being denied that the murthered were our subjects or the murtherers within our jurisdiction.

2. If the murtherers should be apprehended and brought to us, the party escaping is, for ought we yet know, all the witness against them, he affirming he knows their faces, which yet is doubtful, the murther being done in the night.

3. It is like in Mr. Pinchon's opinion to draw a war upon us, which, if (as he saith) it be provoked by us voluntarily, not necessarily, we shall incur blame at home and with our confederate English, and want the [aid ?] from heaven in it and comfort in prosecuting it.

4. The charge and difficulty which the sending men out in hay and harvest time would be considered.

5. A pause will advantage us in hearing what the Narragansetts will do upon Uncus whom we must defend.

6. And if so, it cannot be wisdom in us to stir up other Indians against us to join with the Narragansetts.

I have forgotten two other reasons while I was setting down these. I think a messenger would be despatched to Mr. Pinchon to let such Indians loose, if any should be apprehended, which I think will not be, they who have promised not being like to do it, or if Mr. Pinchon see cause to do otherwise, to leave it to him.

THO. DUDLEY.

Q.

In book III. of the Magnalia, Mather has given a catalogue of New England ministers, in three classes, first, of those who were in office when they left England; second, of those who having not finished their education at home, came over here to perfect it before our college was come to maturity to bestow its laurels; third of such ministers, as came over after the acts of uniformity. A careful reader will find frequent occasion to mark the inaccuracy of this ecclesiastical historian; and in this part of his work, where his means were most ample, and his desire most excited to show his correctness, we may often lament the want of it.

I have thought it would, however, be useful to take the lists from Mather, and add, where it was in my power, the time and place of the decease of each individual, supplying the names of baptism, where omitted by him, and correcting any other mistake of the author of the Magnalia.

1. Thomas Allen of Charlestown, returned home, died 21 Sept. 1673.
2. John Allen of Dedham, died 26 August 1671.
3. [Joseph] Avery of Marblehead, died 14 August 1635.
4. Adam Blackman of Stratford, died 1665.
5. Richard Blinman of Gloucester, returned home.
6. Brucy of Brainford, returned home.
7. Edmund Browne of Sudbury, died 24 June 1678.
8. Peter Buckley of Concord, died 9 March 1659.
9. Jonathan Burr of Dorchester, died 9 August 1641.
10. Charles Chauncey of Scituate, died 19 February 1672.
11. Thomas Cobbet of Lynn, died 5 November 1685.
12. John Cotton of Boston, died 23 December 1652.
13. Timothy Dalton of Hampton, died 28 December 1661.
14. John Davenport of New Haven, died 15 March 1670.
15. Richard Denton of Stamford, died about 1663.
16. Henry Dunster of Cambridge, died 27 February 1659.
17. Samuel Eaton of New Haven, returned home, died 9 January 1665.

18. John Eliot of Roxbury, died 20 May 1690.
19. John Fisk of Chelmsford, died 14 January 1677.
20. Henry Flint of Braintree, died 27 April 1668.
21. [Robert] Fordham of Southampton, died 1674.
22. [Henry] Green of Reading, died May 1648.
23. John Harvard of Charlestown, died 14 September 1638.
24. Francis Higginson of Salem, died 6 August 1630.
25. William Hook of New Haven, returned home in 1656, was in favour with Oliver, died 21 March 1668, or (acc Math.) 1678.
26. Thomas Hooker of Hartford, died 7 July 1647.
27. Peter Hobart of Hingham, died 20 January 1679.
28. Ephraim Huet of Windsor, died 4 September 1644.
29. Hull of the Isle of Shoals.
30. [Thomas] James of Charlestown, returned home, Hubbard says, and Prince confirms him, but Wood's Long Island, more probably, makes him remain, and die 1696.
31. Jones of Fairfield.
32. Knight of Topsfield.
33. [John] Knowles of Watertown, returned home in 1650, lived long after.
34. [William] Leveridge of Sandwich, moved to Long Island, was there living in 1674.
35. John Lothrop of Barnstable, died 8 November 1653.
36. Richard Mather of Dorchester, died 22 April 1669.
37. [Daniel] Maud of Dover, died 1655.
38. [John] Maverick of Dorchester, died 3 February 1636.
39. John Mayo of Boston, died May 1676.
40. John Miller of Yarmouth, died at Groton, 12 June 1663.
41. [George] Moxon of Springfield, returned home, died 15 September 1687.
42. Samuel Newman of Rehoboth, died 5 July 1663.
43. [Edward] Norris of Salem, died 10 April 1659.
44. John Norton of Boston, died 5 April 1663.
45. James Noyes of Newbury, died 22 October 1656.
46. Thomas Parker of Newbury, died April 1677.
47. Ralph Patridge of Duxbury, died 1657 or 1658.
48. [Robert] Peck of Hingham, returned home.
49. Hugh Peter of Salem, returned home, executed 16 Oct. 1660.
50. Thomas Peter of Saybrook, returned home.
51. George Phillips of Watertown, died 1 July 1644.
52. [Henry] Phillips of Dedham, returned home in 1642.
53. Abraham Pierson of Southampton, removed to New Jersey.
54. Peter Prudden of Milford, died 1656.
55. [John] Reyner of Plymouth, died 20 April 1669.
56. Ezekiel Rogers of Rowley, died 23 January 1661.
57. Nathaniel Rogers of Ispwich, died 3 July 1655.
58. [Giles] Saxton of Scituate, returned home.

59. Thomas Shepard of Cambridge, died 25 August 1649.
60 Zechary Symmes of Charlestown, died 4 February 1671.
61. [Samuel] Skelton of Salem, died 2 August 1634.
62. Ralph Smith of Plymouth.
63. [Henry] Smith of Wethersfield, died 1648.
64. Samuel Stone of Hartford, died 20 July 1663.
65. Nicholas Street of New Haven, died 22 April 1674.
66. William Tompson of Braintree, died 10 December 1666.
67. William Waltham of Marblehead.
68. Nathaniel Ward of Ipswich, returned home, and died 1653.
69. John Ward of Haverhill, died 27 December 1693.
70. John Warham of Windsor, died 1 April 1670.
71. [Thomas] Welde of Roxbury, returned home, died 1661.
72. [John] Wheelwright of Salisbury, died 15 Novenber 1679.
73. Henry Whitfield of Guilford, returned home.
74. Samuel Whiting of Lynn, died 11 December 1679.
75. John Wilson of Boston, died 7 August 1667.
76. [William] Wetherel of Scituate, died 9 April 1684.
77. William Worcester of Salisbury, died 20 October 1662.
78. [John] Young of Southold, died 1672.

Now it seems to me, that in this department of his great work, the author is less excusable for his numerous errours than in other parts; though "little more than two years" elapsed from the commencement of the Magnalia to the unknown date of the introduction. We are told by him, that in 1668 it was computed, that ninety-four ministers had come to us from England, chiefly in the first ten years, of whom thirty-one were then alive, thirty-six dead, and twenty-seven returned home. It is, however, probable, that this enumeration is very loose, and perhaps was designed to include those of his third classis. He adds, indeed, four other names, Hanserd Knollys, of Dover, Mr. Miles of Swanzey, William Blackstone, and Mr. Lenthall of Weymouth, besides one darkly described without sufficient circumstance for us to vindicate his identity, whom he throws into a class of anomalies, however evident it may be that they belong to his first. But the shadows have been thickening on these humble spots of our history more than a century and a quarter since Mather's inquiries; and yet I discover the names following, of whom all are entitled to rank in the first classis as much as Avery, Eaton, Hull, Mayo, Waltham or Young, and none in the Magnalia is by the present age revered above Roger Williams. The extraordinary carelessness, which omitted the baptismal names of James, Knowles, Leveridge, Maverick, Norris, Skelton, Welde, and Wheelwright, should have caused hesitation in trusting to many other details, in which our careful examination detects deficiencies that in those who have deferred implicitly to the Ecclesiastical History of New England may excite astonishment.

Stephen Batchelor of Hampton.
Francis Bright of Salem.
Browne of Portsmouth.
George Burdett of Dover.
Samuel Dudley of Exeter.
Nathaniel Eaton of Harvard College.
Richard Gibson of Portsmouth.
Thomas Jenner of Weymouth.
Thomas Larkham of Dover.
Lenton.
John Lyford of Plymouth.
Marmaduke Matthews of Malden.
Thomas Mayhew of Martha's Vineyard.
James Parker of Portsmouth.
Rogers of Plymouth,
Sargent of Malden.
James Williams of Plymouth.
Roger Williams of Providence, beside Nathaniel Norcross, whom Winthrop calls a university scholar, and probably, Ralph Wheelock of Dedham and Medfield, or Dedham village.

The second classis of the Magnalia follows:

1. Samuel Arnold of Marshfield.
2. John Bishop of Stamford, died 1694.
3. Edward Bulkley of Concord.
4. [Thomas] Carter of Woburn, died 5 September 1684.
5. Francis Dean of Andover.
6. James Fitch of Norwich, died 18 November 1702.
7. [Thomas] Hanford of Norwalk.
8. John Higginson of Salem, died 9 December 1708.
9. [Samuel] Hough of Reading, died 30 March 1662.
10. [Thomas] James of Easthampton. See No. 30 in former classis.
11. Roger Newton of Milford, died 7 June 1683.
12. John Sherman of Watertown, died 8 August 1685.
13. Thomas Thacher of Boston, died 16 October 1678.
14. John Woodbridge of Newbury, died 17 March 1696.

In making this list, to which should be added, probably,

1. Nicholas Baker of Scituate, died 22 August 1678.
2. Thomas Buckingham of Saybrook.
3. Noah Newman of Rehoboth, died 16 April 1678, I suspect some carelessness, as James is probably the same person, mentioned in the first classis, and Carter, Dean, and Sherman certainly do not belong to this. Perhaps the future inquirer may find, that our Charlestown James, whom Hubbard and Prince so confidently place

afterwards in England, was father of James of Easthampton, though it seems not very likely, and thus Calamy's relation may be reconciled. But till some discovery be made, I shall continue of the opinion expressed in note on p. 94 of Vol. I. The missionary to Virginia in 1642 is supposed by me to be the same person who had been here ten years before, and twelve years afterwards was employed as an instructer of the natives of Long Island. Can either be disproved?

The third classis of the Magnalia follows:

1. James Allen of Boston, died 22 September 1710.
2. John Bailey of Watertown, died December 1697.
3. Thomas Bailey of Watertown, died 21 January 1690.
4. Barnet of New London.
5. James Brown of Swanzey.
6. Thomas Gilbert of Topsfield, died October 1673.
7. James Keith of Bridgewater, died 23 July 1719.
8. Samuel Lee of Bristol, returned home, died 1691.
9. Charles Morton of Charlestown, died 11 April 1698.
10. Charles Nicholet of Salem, returned home.
11. John Oxenbridge of Boston, died 28 December 1674.
12. Thomas Thornton of Yarmouth.
13. Thomas Walley of Barnstable, died 24 January 1678.
14. William Woodrop of Lancaster. This name is misprinted for Woodroffe.

Here we might hope to rely on Mather's information without hesitation, for he was engaged at the same time in the same cause with most of the individuals. Yet the omission of the given name of Barnet causes some doubt; and with regard to Keith, we are sure he was wrong. Yet Mather's father had introduced Keith, when he was only twenty years old, and of course could not have been "of such ministers as came over to New England after the reestablishment of the Episcopal church government in England." See 2 Hist. Coll. VII. 162.

R.

Having been requested by a gentleman, whose requests are moderate enough to be received as commands, to annex to my work a list of the ancient Indian names of our modern towns, &c. as far as in my power, with caution to the reader, that spelling is altogether unsettled, and geography rather doubtful, I have spent some time in preparing the following, which with some days' labour might easily be increased:

Accomack, Plimouth.
Acomenticus,
or
Agamenticus, York.
Acquettinck,
or
Aquiday, Rhode Island.
Acushnett, New Bedford.
Agawam, Ipswich.
. . . ., Springfield.
or
Agowaywam, part of Wareham.
Apaum,
or
Umpame, Plimouth.
Ashuelot, Keene and Swansey.
Assanipi, part of Scituate.
Assoowamsoo,
or
Assawomit,
or
Assawampsit, part of Middleborough.
Babboosuck, part of Amherst, N. H.
Capawack, Martha's Vineyard.
Caucumsquissick, North Kingstown.
Cantaugeanteest, part of Plimouth.
Chabanakongkomum, Dudley.
Chappaquonsett, part of Tisbury.
Chequocket, part of Barnstable.
Coatue, part of Nantucket.
Coatuit, part of Barnstable.
Coaxit,
or
Coxit, part of Dartmouth.
Cocheco,
or
Quochecho, Dover.
Cochichawick,
or
Coojetewick,
or
Cochituit, Andover.
Cogingchaug, Durham, Con.
Cohanit, Taunton and Raynham.
Cokesit, Little Compton.
Comassakumkanit, part of Plimouth.
Conconut, part of Salem.
Contoocook, Boscawen.
Coquitt, part of Dartmouth.
Coskaty, part of Nantucket.
Cotuktikut, part of Middleborough.
Cowesit, part of Wareham.
Cufchankamaug, Windsor.
Cummaquid, Barnstable north harbour.
Cupheag, part of Stratford.
Georgeekee, Thomaston.

Hammonasset, Killingworth.
Harraseekit, Freeport.
Hassanamesitt,
or
Hassanamisco, Grafton.
Hockamock, Easton and Raynham.
Hokkanom, part of Yarmouth.
Houseatonick, Stockbridge.
Hyannis, part of Barnstable.
Kamesit, part of Plimouth.
Keekamuit, part of Bristol.
Kitaumet, part of Plimouth.
Kitteaumut, part of Sandwich.
Konickey, part of Tisbury.
Maanexit, part of Woodstock.
Machemoodus, East Haddam.
Magunkaquog, or
Magunkook, Hopkinton.
Manamooskeagin, Abington.
Manamoyik, Chatham,
Manchage, Oxford.
Maneikshun, part of Plimouth.
Manisses, New Shoreham.
Mannamit, part of Sandwich.
Masacsick, Longmeadow.
Mashamoquet, Pomfret.
Mashapoag, Sharon.
Massassoomineuk, part of Sandwich.
Matakeese, part of Yarmouth.
Matapan, Dorchester.
Mattabeeset, Middletown.
Mattakeeset, Duxbury.
Mattakeset, Pembroke.
. . . ., part of Edgartown.
Mattaneaug, Windsor.
Mattapoiset, part of Rochester.
Mattatock, Waterbury.
Meeshawn, Truro.
Menemsha, part of Chilmark.
Menunkatuck, Guildford.
Miacomit, part of Nantucket.
Mishawum, Charlestown.
Misquamicut, Westerly.
Mohootset, part of Carver.
Monchauset, part of Rochester.
Monponset, Halifax.
Moshasuck, Providence.
Muhhekaneew, Stockbridge.
Musketaquid, Concord.
Musqunnipash, part of Rochester.
Mussauco, Simsbury.
Naamskeket, part of Harwich.
Namasket, or
Namasseket, part of Middleborough.
Nameag, New London.
Nanakumas, part of Nantucket.

Nashamoiess, part of Edgartown.
Nashobah, Littleton.
Nashuakemmiuk, Chilmark.
Nashwash,
or
Nashoway, Lancaster.
Naugatuck, Derby.
Naumkeag, Salem.
Nauset, part of Eastham.
Nawbesetuck, Mansfield, Con.
Nehantick,
or
Neanticut, Lyme.
Neponsit, bounds of Dorchester and Milton.
Newichawanock, Berwick,
Nipmuck river, Blackstone's,
Nisitissit, Hollis.
Nobsquassit, part of Yarmouth.
Nonantum, bounds of Watertown and Newtown.
Nonotuck, Northampton.
Nope, Martha's Vineyard.
Nukkehkummees, part of Dartmouth.
Nunketest, Bridgewater.
Nunnepoag, part of Edgartown.
Oggawame, part of Nantucket.
Ohkonkemme, part of Tisbury.
Okommakamesitt, Marlborough.
Oronoake, part of Stratford.
Ouschankamaug, Windsor.
Pakachoog, part of Worcester.
Pakanokick,
or
Pawkunnawkutt, Bristol.
Pakemitt,
or
Punkapaog, Stoughton.
Pamaquassett,
or
Pattaquasset, Saybrook
Pamet, part of Truro.
Pantoosuck, Plainfield and neighbourhood
Pascomuck, Easthampton.
Patackosi, part of Plimouth.
Patuxet, Plimonth.
Paugasset, Derby.
Paukopunnakuk, part of Plimouth.
Pautucket, Providence.
Pautuxet, Cranston.
Pawcatuck, Stonington.
Penacook, Concord, N. H.
Pentucket, Haverhill.
Pequawket, or
Pigwacket, Fryeburgh.
Pequot, New London and neighbourhood.
Pequot river, Thames.
Perpooduck, Cape Elizabeth.
Pettequamscot, South Kingston, R. I.
Piscatacook, Kent.
Pocasset, the part of the river between Tiverton and Portsmouth.
Pochet, part of Orleans.
Pocomtuck, Deerfield.
Podpis, part of Nantucket,
Podunk, Windsor.
Pohtatuck, Newtown, Con.
Pokesset, part of Sandwich.
Pomperaug, Woodbury.
Pompociticut, part of Stow.
Pontoosuck, Pittsfield.
Popponesset, part of Mashpee.
Poquaig, Athol,
Poquannock, part of Windsor.
Potanumaquut, part of Eastham.
Poughkeeste, part of Sandwich.
Presumscot, part of Falmouth, Me.
Pughquonnuck, part of Stratford.
Pumpisset, part of Sandwich,
Punonakanit, Wellfleet.
Pyquag, Weathersfield,
Quaboag, Brookfield.
Quaket, part of Tiverton.
Quampeagan, part of Berwick.
Quansit, part of Wareham.
Quantissit, part of Woodstock.
Quascacunquen, Newbury.
Quayz, part of Nantucket.
Quilipeak, New Haven,
Quinibaug, Plainfield and neighbourhood.
Quinsigamond, Worcestor or Hopkinton.
Quittaquas, part of Middleborough.
Quittaub, part of Middleborough,
Quononoquot,
or
Canonicut, Jamestown.
Rippowance,
or
Rippowams, Stamford.
Suckiaug, Hartford.
Sagus, Lynn.
Sakonett,
or
Sogkonate, Little Compton.
Sanctuit, part of Barnstable.
Sasacacheh, part of Nantucket.
Sasaquash, or
Sauquish, part of Plimouth.

Satucket,
or
Sawkattukett, Brewster.
Saughtuckquett, Bridgewater.
Scatacook, part of Kent.
Scook, part of Plimouth.
Scusset, part of Sandwich.
Seconckqut, part of Chilmark.
Seipican, Rochester.
Senepetuit, part of Rochester.
Sengekontakit, part of Edgartown.
Sesuet, part of Dennis.
Shaomet, Warwick.
Shabbukin, part of Stow.
Shaukimmo, part of Nantucket.
Shaume, Sandwich.
Shawmut, Boston.
Shawshin,
or
Shawshinock, Billerica.
Shequocket, part of Barnstable.
Shimmoah, part of Nantucket.
Siasconsit, part of Nantucket.
Skunkamug, part of Barnstable.
Sokones,
or
Succonusset, part of Falmouth.
Souhegan, Amhert, N. H.
Sowams, or
Sowamset, Bristol or Barrington?
Spurwink, part of Scarborough.
Sqnabette, part of Raynham.
Squakeag, Northfield.
Squam, part of Nantucket.
. . . ., Ipswich Bay.
Squantum, part of Dorchester,
Squatesit, part of Nantucket.
Squipnocket, part of Chilmark.
Squomscutt, Exeter.
Statehook, part of Sheffield.
Suncook, Pembroke, N. H.
Talhanio, part of Chilmark.
Tashmuit, part of Truro.
Tawawog, New London.
Tecticut, Taunton.
Teightaquid,
or
Titicut, part of Bridgwater and Middleborough.
Tetaukimmo, part of Nantucket.
Tionet, part of Plimouth.
Tockiming, Tisbury.
Totoket, Branford.
Tunxis, Farmington and neighbourhood.
Uncataquissit,
or
Unquety, Milton.
Unquowa, Fairfield.
Waahktoohook, part of Stockbridge.
Wabquisset, part of Woodstock.
Wachusett, Princeton.
Waeuntug, Uxbridge.
Wagutuquab, part of Nantucket.
Wamesitt, Tewksbury.
Wammasquid, part of Nantucket.
Waqua, part of Edgartown.
Waquoit, part of Mashpee.
Waranoke, Westfield.
Washqua, part of Edgartown.
Wawayontat, Wareham.
Wawaytick, part of Chilmark.
Weataug, Salisbury, Con.
Weequakut, part of Barnstable.
Weesquobs, part of Sandwich.
Wekapaug, Southerton?
Wenatukset, Plympton.
Wenaumut, part of Sandwich.
Wenimesset, New Braintree.
Wequaset, part of Chatham.
Weshakim, Lancaster.
Wesko, part of Nantucket.
Wessaguscus, Weymouth.
Westgostogua, North Yarmouth.
Wickataquay, part of Edgartown.
Winicowett, Hampton.
Winnaganset, Boothbay.
Winisemet, Chelsea.
Wollomonuppoag, Wrentham.
Wopowage, Milford.
Wyantenock, New Milford.

S.

Magistrates, usually called assistants, including governours and deputy governours, of the Massachusetts colony.

From the Magnalia, Book II. chap. 6. with corrections and additions.

Where the month is not given, in the first column, it was May.

1628 Mathew Cradock, never came over.
1628 Thomas Goffe, never came over.
1628 Sir Richard Saltonstall, lived at Watertown; returned home in 1631.
1628 Isaac Johnson, died at Boston 30 September 1630.
1628 Samuel Aldersey, never came over.
1628 John Venn, never came over.
1628 John Humfrey, lived at Lynn, left the colony in 1641.
1628 Simon Whetcomb, never came over.
1628 John Browne, never served in Massachusetts.
1628 Increase Nowell, died at Charlestown 1 November 1655.
1628 Richard Perry, never came over.
1628 Nathaniel Wright, never came over.
1628 Samuel Vassal, never came over.
1628 Theophilus Eaton, never served in Massachusetts, was governour of New Haven, and there died 7 January 1658, aged 66.
1628 Thomas Adams, never came over.
1628 Thomas Hutchins, never came over.
1628 George Foxcroft, never came over.
1628 William Vassal, returned home in 1630.
1628 William Pyncheon, lived at Springfield, returned home in 1652.
1628 John Endecott, lived at Salem, died at Boston 15 March 1665, aged 76.
1629 John Pocock, never came over.
1629 Christopher Coulson, never came over.
20 Oct. 1629 John Winthrop, died at Boston 26 March 1649, aged 61.
20 Oct. 1629 Thomas Dudley, at Roxbury 31 July 1653, aged 76.
20 Oct. 1629 Thomas Sharp, returned home in 1631.
20 Oct. 1629 Samuel Sharp, never served in Massachusetts, but was a ruling elder at Salem, died 1658.
20 Oct. 1629 Edward Rossiter, died at Dorchester 23 Oct. 1630.
20 Oct. 1629 John Revell, returned home in 1630.
10 Feb'y 1630 Roger Ludlow, lived at Dorchester, left the colony in 1635.
18 March 1630 Sir Brian Janson, never came over.
18 March 1630 William Coddington, lived at Boston, removed in 1638 to Rhode Island, died at Newport 1 Nov. 1678, aged 77.
18 March 1630 *Simon Bradstreet, died at Salem 27 March 1697, aged 94.
1632 John Winthrop, junr. lived at Ipswich, not chosen after 1649; died governour of Connecticut at Boston 5 April 1676, aged 70.
1634 John Haynes, lived at Cambridge, went to Connecticut in 1637, and was there governour, died at Hartford 1654.
1635 Richard Bellingham, died at Boston 7 December 1672, aged 80.
1635 Atherton Hough, died at Boston 11 Sept. 1650.
1635 Richard Dummer, died at Newbury 14 Dec. 1679.
1636 Henry Vane, lived at Boston, returned home 1637, executed 14 June 1662, aged 50.
1636 Roger Harlackenden, died at Cambridge 17 Nov. 1638, aged 30.
1637 Israel Stoughton, lived at Dorchester, went to England to serve in the parliament's army, died 1644.
1637 Richard Saltonstall, lived at Haverhill, died in England 29 April 1694, aged 83.
1642 Thomas Flint, died at Concord 1655.
1643 Samuel Symonds, died at Ipswich October 1678.
1643 William Hibbins, died at Boston, 23 July 1654.
1645 Herbert Pelham, lived at Cambridge, returned home, not chosen after 1649.
1647 Robert Bridges, died at Lynn 1656.

1650 Francis Willoughby, died at Charlestown 4 April 1671.
1650 Thomas Wiggin of Hampton.
1650 Edward Gibbons, died at Boston 9 Dec. 1654.
1652 John Glover, Dorchester, January 1654.
1652 Daniel Gookin, died at Cambridge 19 March 1687, aged 75.
1653 Daniel Denison, Ipswich 20 Sept 1682.
1654 Simon Willard, Groton, 24 April 1676.
1654 Humphrey Atherton, Dorchester, 16 Sept. 1661.
1659 Richard Russell, Charlestown 14 May 1676, aged 65.
1659 *Thomas Danforth, died at Cambridge 5 Nov. 1699, aged 77.
1662 William Hathorne, died at Salem, 1681.
1662 Eleazer Lusher, died at Dedham 13 Nov. 1672.
1665 John Leverett, died at Boston 16 March 1679.
1665 John Pyncheon, Springfield, died 16 June 1702.
1668 Edward Tyng, died at Dunstable 28 Dec. 1681, aged 81.
1671 William Stoughton, died at Dorchester 7 July 1701, aged 70.
1673 Thomas Clark, died at Boston 13 March 1683.
1676 Joseph Dudley, died at Roxbury 2 April 1720, aged 72.
1677 Peter Bulkley, died at Concord July 1688.
1679 *Nathaniel Saltonstall, died at Haverhill 21 May 1707.
1679 Humphrey Davy, probably removed in 1687.
1680 *James Russell, Charlestown, 28 April 1709, aged 68.
1680 Samuel Nowell, son of Increase, went to England.
1680 *Peter Tilton, Hadley.
1680 *John Richards, died at Boston 1694.
1680 John Hull, died at Boston 29 September 1683.
1680 Bartholomew Gidney, Salem, March 1698.
1680 Thomas Savage, died at Boston 14 February 1682, aged 75.
1680 William Browne, died at Salem 20 January 1688, aged 80.
1681 *Samuel Appleton, Ipswich, died early in 1696.
1682 *Robert Pike, died at Salisbury 12 Dec. 1706.
1683 Daniel Fisher, died at Dedham Nov. 1683.
1683 John Woodbridge, died at Newbury 17 March 1695, aged 82.
1684 *Elisha Cook, died at Boston 31 October 1715, aged 78.
1684 *William Johnson, died at Woburn 22 May 1704.
1684 *John Hathorne, died at Salem 10 May 1717, aged 76.
1684 *Elisha Hutchinson, died at Boston 10 December 1717, aged 76.
1684 *Samuel Sewall, died at Boston 1 January 1730, aged 77.
1685 Oliver Purchase, declined to take the oath. He was of Lynn.
1686 *Isaac Addington, died at Boston 19 March 1715, aged 70.
1686 *John Smith, of Hingham, died May 1695.

In this last year all power was taken away from the people, and on the recovery of their liberties by the glorious revolution of 1689, were chosen, in addition to survivors of above, marked thus (*),

1689 Wait Winthrop, Boston, died 7 Nov. 1717, aged 75.
1689 Samuel Shrimpton, Boston, died, probably January 1698.
1689 Jonathan Curwin, Salem, died 9 June 1718, aged 77
1689 John Phillips, Charlestown, died 20 March 1725, aged 93.
1689 Jeremiah Swaine, Reading.
1690 Sir William Phipps, lived at Boston, died in London, Feb. 1695.
1690 Thomas Oakes, lived at Boston, died at Welfleet, 15 July 1719, aged 76.
1691 William Stoughton, rechosen after a period of unpopularity.

In 1692 the royal charter of William and Mary made a change in the number and manner of election of this branch of the government.

ERRATA,

In addition to those seven, noticed in Vol. I.

Page 14 line 3 from bottom, for *descend* read descends.
—— 50 line 7 from bottom, for 1 *Hist. Coll.* 137 read 1 Hist. Coll. III. 137.
—— 115 line 3 from bottom, for *Nantucket* read Newtown, Long Island, and in next line strike out all after New York.
—— 169 line 3 in note 3 for *Trumbull I.* 194 read Trumbull I. 494.
—— 235 note 2 is a reprint of part of note 2 on page 222.
—— 318 last line in text, and page 319 line 4 and 8 for *Perry* read Percy.

Vol. II. page 28 in note 2, Samuel Dalton was, I am informed, son to Philemon, brother of Timothy, who left no descendants. A similar correction is, probably, required in Vol. I. p. 206, where the Hon. George Partridge is represented as a descendant of Rev. Ralph. I have examined the will of the first minister of Duxbury, and as it contains mention of no son's name, we must conclude that George Partridge, who is known to have been there in 1636, was not born of Ralph, though perhaps he was his companion.

Page 77 line 12 in note, for *Northen* read Northern.
—— 161 last line in notes, for 1689 read 1693.
—— 245 note 2, Leveret *was* chosen governour in 1678, and died in office. Hubbard, 612, caused my error.
—— 322 line 2 in notes, for *Jeremiah* read Jerinnah, a daughter.
—— 375 line 8 from bottom for *intending* read in tender.

GENERAL INDEX.

A.

B.

C.

D.

E.

F.

G.

H.

I.

K.

L.

M.

N.

O.

P.

Q.

R.

S.

T.

U.

V.

W.

Y.